Complete
OUTDOORS
Encyclopedia

Complete
OUTDOORS
Encyclopedia

by Vin T. Sparano

OUTDOOR LIFE BOOKS

HARPER & ROW, PUBLISHERS

NEW YORK, SAN FRANCISCO, HAGERSTOWN, LONDON

DEDICATION

To My Wife Betty

Contents

CONTENTS

PART **VI**

Boating

PART **VII**

Archery

PART **VIII**

Hunting Dogs

PART **IX**

First Aid

CONTENTS

First Aid (continued)

PART **X**

Outdoor Information Guide

Preface
to the Second Edition

In the preface to the first edition of this book, published nearly eight years ago, I wrote "this encyclopedia will provide the outdoorsman with a good working knowledge of all phases of outdoor recreation, including hunting, fishing, camping, boating, archery and hunting dogs." The encylopedia was originally compiled and designed as a data and reference book that would provide general guidance as well as quick and clear answers and solutions. Over the years, this book must have been serving pretty well because the first edition sold over 200,000 copies.

Yet since initial publication of this book, the outdoors scene changed so tremendously that an update was needed. I thought I could handle the task rather easily until I began to study all the details. I soon realized that this would be a major project. As work progressed, I found myself darn near writing a new book, and replacing hundreds of photos and drawings. There were brand new developments in gear, for example. Compound

bows had taken bowhunting by storm. Unbelievably seaworthy center-console boats had been designed, and there were now bigger outboard motors. New space-age materials such as Boron, Kevlar, ABS, Gore-Tex, and many others were now being used in tackle, boats, camping gear, and so on.

I concluded that I would need help to sift through hundreds of pounds of literature and more than 1,000 photographs, selecting the most important and informative. So I asked Bob Elman, a good friend and a highly respected outdoors editor, to lend a hand. Over many evenings and weekends, we covered the encyclopedia page by page, reworking page layouts, substituting illustrations, and rewriting text and captions. Frequently, we scrapped huge sections, substituting new, more informative material. For that help, special thanks goes to Bob.

Later, the revisions were in the hands of Outdoor Life Books. Fortunately, the editors allowed me to continue adding information right up to press time. As you see it now, the *Complete Outdoors Encyclopedia* is the most current reference work of its kind.

Special thanks to contributing editors of the first edition. They were Bill Rooney, Dave Vigren, Howard Brant, and Dick Barnett. I'd also like to thank editors at Outdoor Life Books for valuable editorial supervision on both editions. These people have included John Sill, Henry Gross, Norman Hoss, Neil Soderstrom, and Anne Jensen. Thanks too to Jeff Fitschen who handled the complicated art production.

VIN T. SPARANO

PART I | Hunting and Shooting

Rifle Actions

Popular rifle actions used today by sportsmen fall into two broad classifications—the repeating action and the single-shot action. An old but still another action design is the double-barreled rifle. The double rifle is extremely limited in use for a number of reasons which will be discussed in some detail later.

Among the repeaters, the most popular is the bolt-action rifle, which uses a manually operated steel bolt assembly to chamber and seal a cartridge in the breech. Two other repeating rifle mechanisms are the lever and pump, or slide, actions, which are also manually operated to chamber and seal cartridges for firing. Fourth and last of the repeating rifles is the semi-automatic or autoloader, an action that requires only a pull of the trigger to fire a cartridge, eject the spent case, chamber a new cartridge, and cock the rifle for the next shot.

The single-shot rifles come in three designs: The single-shot bolt action, which differs from the repeating bolt action in that it has no magazine or clip. The break action which, in simplest terms, utilizes a thumb lever to break open the rifle and expose the chamber for loading. The falling-block action, an old design that for all practical purposes was considered dead and obsolete only a few years ago. The Sturm, Ruger Company brought the strong falling-block design back to life in 1966 with the introduction of the Ruger No. 1 Single Shot.

These various actions all have advantages and disadvantages. Only by examining each action in detail can hunters and target shooters select the most practical and effective rifle for their particular use.

Bolt Action

Most widely used rifle in the field and on the range is the bolt action, and there are several good reasons for this. The bolt action is strong and simple. It disassembles easily for cleaning, an important factor for the hunter in the field. The bolt on most modern rifles can be easily slipped out of the receiver and wiped clean of dirt, sand, wet snow. With the bolt removed a hunter who has just taken a fall can simply glance through the breech to check for obstructions in the bore.

Because the bolt affords strong hand leverage, this action is also best for the shooter who handloads his own ammunition. The powerful pull of the bolt is an advantage when extracting dirty or stuck cases. Likewise, cases slightly oversize can usually be chambered with a bit more than normal pressure on closing the bolt. Because the bolt locks a cartridge at the head, the cases are not subjected to stretch when fired and only the neck of the cases generally need to be resized during the reloading process.

The bolt gun also has a one-piece stock which makes for better bedding of the action and barrel and produces greater accuracy than nearly all other rifle designs.

Who should use the bolt action? Because of its reliability and simplicity, the bolt-action rifle is the logical choice for hunters who prefer to hunt in remote areas, where gunsmiths and spare parts are scarce. Because of its superior accuracy, and the fact that it is chambered for nearly all flat-shooting, high-velocity cartridges, the bolt gun is a favorite among mountain and prairie hunters who are generally forced to take game at long ranges.

The bolt action also comes into its own as a target and benchrest rifle. The solid-locking action and one piece stock produces accuracy, and the entire rifle is most adaptable to alterations to satisfy the fancy of the serious target shooter.

Not all bolt-action rifles look alike and handle the same, however. Let's take a look at some typical factory models and learn the reasoning behind their design.

The Winchester Model 70 XTR Standard is typical of bolt actions built for hunting. It is chambered for a variety of calibers, including the .243, .270, .308 Winchester, .30/06 Springfield, .222, .22/250, and .25/06 Remington. The .25/06 has a 24-inch barrel. In the other calibers, this rifle comes with a 22-inch barrel. It weighs about 7½ pounds. Also available are magnum models chambered for the .264, .300, and .338 Winchester Magnums, as well as the 7 mm. Remington Magnum and .375 H&H Magnum. This range of calibers fills the bill for all North American and European game and roughly 90 percent of all African and Asian game.

The .460 Weatherby Magnum rifle fires the world's most powerful cartridge. The .460 Weatherby Magnum cartridge,

NOMENCLATURE OF A BOLT-ACTION RIFLE

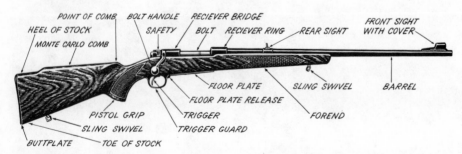

POINT OF COMB · BOLT HANDLE · RECIEVER BRIDGE · FRONT SIGHT WITH COVER · HEEL OF STOCK · SAFETY · BOLT · RECIEVER RING · REAR SIGHT · MONTE CARLO COMB · RECEIVER RING · FLOOR PLATE · SLING SWIVEL · BARREL · FLOOR PLATE RELEASE · PISTOL GRIP · TRIGGER · FOREND · SLING SWIVEL · TRIGGER GUARD · BUTTPLATE · TOE OF STOCK

HOW A BOLT-ACTION RIFLE WORKS

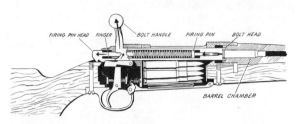

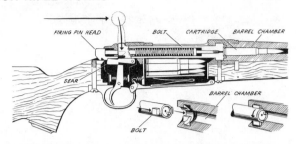

1. Raising the bolt handle unlocks the bolt head from the barrel chamber. At the same time, notch at bottom of the bolt handle catches and pushes up protruding finger of the firing pin head, pushing firing pin to rear.

3. Moving bolt handle forward and turning it downward locks the bolt in the chamber and seals in the cartridge. The sear engages notch on firing pin head, cocking the rifle. (Detail shows how bolt locks into barrel chamber.)

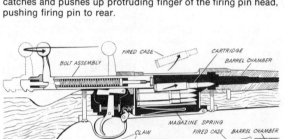

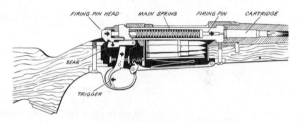

2. Moving bolt assembly back ejects the empty case. A circular spring in the end of the bolt (see detail) exerts pressure on the claw, holding the case tightly. When the mouth of the fired case clears the chamber, the spring-loaded ejector flips the case clear. The pressure of the magazine spring now raises a new cartridge to loading position.

using a 500-grain bullet, produces a muzzle energy of 8,100 foot-pounds. By comparison, the popular .30/06 with a 180-grain bullet has a muzzle energy of 2,910 foot-pounds. Though the .460 Weatherby Magnum is generally limited to the world's largest and most dangerous game, this rifle and caliber combination does point out that the bolt action's strong design can handle the most potent loads.

4. Pulling the trigger disengages sear from the notch on the firing pin head. The main spring forces the firing pin forward, detonating the cartridge.

The Harrington & Richardson Model 301 Ultra is a good example of a bolt-action carbine. Keeping barrel length down improves maneuverability in rough terrain and heavy brush. Built with an 18-inch barrel, it comes in an array of calibers, from .243 to .308 and .30/06. This carbine is full-stocked—a handsome style widely known as Mannlicher-stocked or Mannlicher-style. Several European-made carbines of the same general type—including Mannlicher-Schoenauer and Steyr-Mannlicher models—are imported by American distributors.

Winchester Model 70 XTR

.460 Weatherby Magnum

Remington Model 788

Harrington & Richardson Model 301 Ultra

Weatherby Mark V Varmintmaster

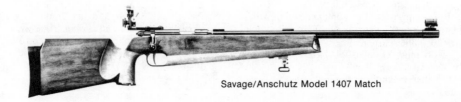

Savage/Anschutz Model 1407 Match

Remington International Match Free Rifle

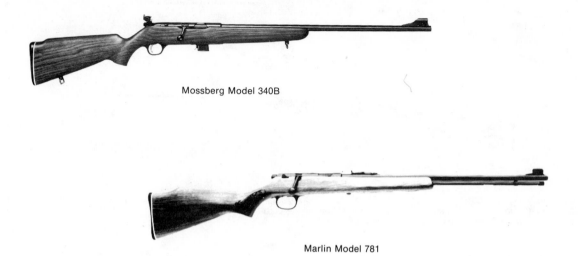

Mossberg Model 340B

Marlin Model 781

One of the more specialized bolt actions is the Winchester Model 70 Varmint, designed for shooting woodchucks, coyotes, foxes and any other varmints at long ranges. Most distinguishing characteristic is the heavyweight barrel, which affords steadier holding and consequently better accuracy. The rifle weighs about 9¾ lb., roughly 3 pounds more than the average bolt action, and has a 24-inch barrel.

The Model 70 XTR Varmint comes without front and rear sights, as do most varminters, since these rifles invariably are mounted with scopes up to 12X or occasionally even higher magnification. Bolt guns designated as varmint models are built for maximum range and precision shooting with high-velocity cartridges. The Winchester version comes in .222 Remington, .22/250 Remington, and .243 Winchester calibers.

For the target shooter, the Anschutz 1407 Match 54 is typical of a finely designed target rifle. It is suitable for all National Rifle Association Matches and meets the requirements of the International Shooting Union. The 1407 Match weighs 10 pounds and has fully adjustable trigger pull. Chambered for .22 Long Rifle only, the rifle's receiver is grooved for micrometer iron sights.

Radical in design is the bolt-action Remington International Match Free Rifle which, as its name indicates, comes under the classification of free-class rifle. Rifles of this type are used in Olympic and World championship shootings. Available in rimfire and centerfire calibers, it has a heavy barrel, adjustable butt plate with hook, and an adjustable palm rest. It is drilled and tapped for receiver sights.

A sportsman looking for a .22 bolt action for informal shooting and small-game hunting will have little trouble finding a model to fill his needs. There are three basic designs for the popular rimfire and the differences deal mainly with cartridge capacity.

The Stevens Model 73, for example, is a single-shot rifle ideal for beginners and youngsters. It is extremely safe. When the bolt is operated, the safety goes on automatically. Closing the bolt cocks it, of course, but the safety must then be moved to the off position before the rifle can be fired.

For those who want more ammunition in their guns, there are rifles such as the Mossberg Model 340B, which has a clip magazine with a capacity of seven cartridges. The bolt is simply operated to eject the spent cartridge and chamber a new round.

Another type of repeating bolt-action .22 employs a tubular magazine. The Remington Model 582 is typical of this design. The tubular magazine holds up to 20 rounds without reloading. Here again the bolt is operated to eject the empty case and chamber a new round.

Repeating rifles, such as the Mossberg and Remington models, are well suited for small game, varmint shooting, and plinking. The single shot, which admittedly has limitations, comes into its own as a youngster's first rifle. All of these .22 rifles have a lot going for them. The rimfire cartridge has almost no recoil or loud muzzle blast to unnerve the shooter, making it easy for beginners to learn proper trigger squeeze and sight picture. Since ammunition is inexpensive, the .22 is also a good investment for anyone who wants a rifle for informal target shooting and plinking.

BOLT-ACTION RIFLES (CENTERFIRES)

Browning Model BBR. Chambered for .25/06 Remington, .270 Winchester, and .30/06 Springfield. A magnum version is chambered for 7 mm. Remington Magnum and .300 Winchester Magnum. Weight is about 8 pounds and the hammer-forged barrel is 24 inches long.

Remington Model 700. Chambered for .17, .222, .22/250, .223, 6 mm. Remington, .243, .25/06, .270, 7 mm. Remington Express, .30/06, .308, 7 mm. Remington Magnum, .300 Winchester Magnum, 8 mm. Remington Magnum, .375 H&H Magnum, and .458 Winchester Magnum. Depending on caliber, barrel is 22, 24, or 26 inches long. Weight is about 9 pounds for the .375 or .458 and 7¼ pounds for all other calibers.

Savage Model 110-C (detachable box magazine). Chambered for .243, .270, 7 mm. Remington Magnum, and .30/06. Also available as Model 110-CL, with a left-handed action and stock (.243 comes in right-handed version only). Weight is approximately 6¾ pounds and barrel length is 24 inches for 7 mm. Remington Magnum, 22 inches for all other calibers.

Ruger Model 77. Chambered for .220 Swift, .22/250, .243, .25/06 6 mm., .270, .30/06, .308, 7 x 57 mm., 7 mm. Remington Magnum, and .300, .338, and .458 Winchester Magnum. Weight of .458 is about 8¾ pounds; the others weigh about 6½ pounds. Barrel length is 22 or 24 inches, depending on caliber, and .220 Swift is available with a heavy 26-inch barrel. Barrel is 22 inches and weight about 6½ pounds. The M77 is also available in .22/250 and .25/06 with heavy 24-inch barrel.

Smith & Wesson Model 1500. Chambered for .243, .270, .30/06, and 7 mm. Remington Magnum. The Magnum has a 24-inch barrel and weighs about 7¾ pounds; the others have 22-inch barrels and weigh about 7½ pounds.

Colt/Sauer Sporting Rifle. Chambered for .22/250, .243, .25/06, .270, 7 mm. Remington Magnum, .308, .30/06, .300 Winchester Magnum, .300 Weatherby Magnum, .375 H&H Magnum, and .458 Winchester Magnum. Barrel length is 24 inches and weight runs from about 7½ pounds to 9¾ pounds, depending on caliber.

Interarms/Mauser Mark X Mannlicher-Style Carbine. Chambered for .243, .270, 7 x 57 mm., .308, and .30/06. Barrel is 20 inches long and weight is 7½ pounds.

BOLT-ACTION RIFLES (RIMFIRES)

Harrington & Richardson Model 865 Plainsman. Chambered for .22 Short, Long, or Long Rifle. Clip magazine holds 5 rounds. Weight about 5 pounds, barrel 22 inches long, overall length 39 inches.

Remington Model 581. Chambered for .22 Short, Long, or Long Rifle. Clip magazine holds 5 rounds. Weight about 5¼ pounds, barrel 24 inches long. This model is also available with left-hand bolt action.

Stevens Model 246. Chambered for .22 Short, Long, or Long Rifle. Tubular magazine holds 15 Long Rifles, 17 Longs, or 22 Shorts. Weight about 5 pounds, barrel 20 inches long.

Mossberg Model 341. Chambered for .22 Short, Long, or Long Rifle. Clip magazine holds 7 rounds. Weight about 6½ pounds, barrel 24 inches long. Magnum version, Model 640K Chuckster, is chambered for .22 WMR and has 5-shot clip.

Marlin Model 783. Chambered for .22 Magnum. Tubular magazine holds 12 rounds. Weight about 6 pounds, barrel 22 inches long. Clip-fed version, Model 782, has 7-shot magazine.

HOW A LEVER-ACTION RIFLE WORKS

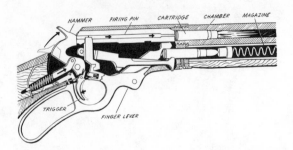

HAMMER   FIRING PIN   CARTRIDGE   CHAMBER   MAGAZINE

SHANK

TRIGGER

FINGER LEVER

1. Beginning with the rifle loaded and cocked, pulling the trigger releases the upper end of the trigger from notch in the hammer, which springs forward and strikes the firing pin, which in turn detonates the cartridge.

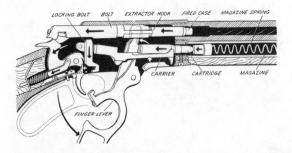

LOCKING BOLT   BOLT   EXTRACTOR HOOK   FIRED CASE   MAGAZINE SPRING

CARRIER   CARTRIDGE   MAGAZINE

FINGER LEVER

2. Moving the finger lever forward moves the locking bolt downward, disengaging it from the bolt, and the finger level tip engages slot in the bolt and moves it rearward. As the bolt slides back, an extractor hook pulls the fired case from the chamber and a spring-loaded ejector on the opposite side of the bolt ejects the case. The magazine spring pushes the cartridge onto the carrier and a cam on the finger lever moves carrier upward toward the barrel chamber.

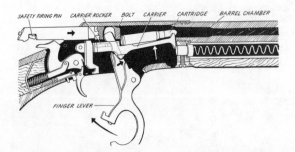

SAFETY FIRING PIN   CARRIER ROCKER   BOLT   CARRIER   CARTRIDGE   BARREL CHAMBER

FINGER LEVER

3. As the finger lever is moved to its forwardmost position and returned slightly, it engages a protruding pin on the carrier rocker and cams the carrier fully upward to the barrel chamber. As the finger lever is returned, its tip, which is engaged in the bolt slot, moves the bolt forward, pushing the cartridge into the chamber. Returning finger lever to the stock raises the locking bolt to matching notch in the bolt and aligns the safety firing pin (see Fig. 1). The gun is now ready for firing.

Lever Action

The lever-action rifle is deeply embedded in American history. Its design produced the first successful repeating rifle in America. It has been labeled "the gun that won the West," and it has become a favorite among deer hunters in the East and Northeast. Today, the smooth and fast lever gun has earned a permanent niche for itself in the hunting clan. Like any rifle design, however, the lever action has advantages and disadvantages. Let's examine the advantages first.

Though the lever gun is not as strong nor as accurate as the bolt-action rifle, it is faster to operate and easier to carry. Its narrow action and smooth lines make it an ideal scabbard gun for western hunters on horseback.

Combine the lever gun's quick handling for snap shots at moving game with the fact that most lever actions are generally chambered for medium-range deer cartridges and it's easy to understand why these rifles have also become a favorite among eastern and northeastern hunters, who get practically all their shots within 50 yards.

Another obvious advantage is that left-handed shooters can operate a lever action just as fast as a right-handed shooter. This is an important factor for the southpaw woods hunter to consider. Though he may have his heart set on a bolt action, he'd be better off with a lever gun, with which he can get off a second or third shot without lowering the rifle from his shoulder.

There are left-hand bolt-action rifles available, but they still cannot be handled from the shoulder as fast as a lever action. The left-handed bolt, however, is a good compromise for the woods hunter who may want to handload his own ammunition and supplement his deer trips with some varmint hunting and target shooting.

There is another advantage, though minor, that should at least be mentioned. The older-type lever actions, such as the Winchester 94 and the Marlin 336, offer an exposed hammer with half-cock safety. The safety is engaged by thumbing the hammer back halfway, where it locks in place. This is a convenient feature for cold-weather hunters who must wear heavy gloves and for left-handed shooters who find other safeties awkward to reach.

To fully cock the gun, the hammer is thumbed back all the way and the rifle is ready to be fired. If a hunter decides to pass up a shot, he simply holds the hammer with his thumb, depresses the trigger, and eases the hammer forward to half-cock safety. The simplicity of the exposed hammer design is a distinct advantage to sportsmen who hunt only a few weeks a year and it's also a safety feature to look for when shopping for a boy's first deer rifle.

The fast lever-action rifle, however, does have shortcomings. Because most lever guns are fitted with two-piece stocks, they are not as accurate as rifles with one-piece stocks. With some exceptions, the older type lever actions are not strong enough to handle the high pressures of some modern cartridges, and they do not have the camming power to chamber and extract dirty or oversized cartridges.

The breech bolts in most lever guns don't lock at the head of the cartridge and the brass cases invariably stretch on firing. This makes lever actions a poor choice for handloaders. While these faults are of little concern to the occasional hunter, they are important factors to the more avid rifleman.

Winchester Big Bore 94 XTR
Lever Action Carbine

Now that both advantages and disadvantages of lever-action rifles have been discussed, let's talk about some of these typical guns presently on the market and how they may vary slightly in design.

The Winchester 94 is the most familiar lever action to hunters. It features top ejection, side loading gate, tubular magazine, and exposed hammer with half-cock safety. In the carbine version, it measures 37¾ inches long and weighs about 6½ pounds. It is chambered for the .30/30 Winchester, a medium-class deer cartridge that can generally be expected to group at about 3½ inches at 100 yards.

The Winchester 94 makes a fine saddle gun where long ranges aren't encountered, and it is a handy lightweight deer gun in the wooded areas of the East and Northeast where most shots are within 100 yards. The .30/30 is adequate for game the size of whitetails.

In 1979, Winchester unveiled the Big Bore 94 XTR, chambered for the new .375 Winchester cartridge. This is the first new chambering in the Model 94 since the .32 Winchester Special was introduced back in 1902. With the new cartridge, a 200-grain bullet develops the same speed that the old .30/30 gets with a 170-grain bullet. To handle the .375 Winchester cartridge safely, the receiver of the Big Bore 94 XTR is beefed up in the rear area of the side panels.

The handy little Model 94 that everyone loves to handle and shoot does have some drawbacks. It is not a long-range weapon and is not chambered for modern high-velocity flat-shooting cartridges. Since it ejects spent cases from the top of the rifle it is not ideally suited for scope mounting, though scopes can be mounted offset and special scopes with long eye relief can be used. Since cases tend to stretch in the action, it is not a good choice for a hunter who plans

to handload his own ammunition. All these factors should be taken into consideration when making a selection.

Another popular lever action is the Marlin 336C. It is chambered for the .30/30 Winchester and .35 Remington, both good brush cartridges that do their work well at medium ranges. In weight, length, and features, the Marlin 336C is similar to the Winchester Model 94. There is, however, one difference. The Marlin has a solid top receiver and ejects its empty cases from the side. This feature permits low scope mounting over the receiver.

The Marlin 336C has roughly the same drawbacks as the Winchester 94. While it is an ideal saddle rifle and deer gun for brush hunters who get most shots at medium-size big game at short ranges, it is not a good choice for the hunter who may want to use his rifle for long shots in prairie and mountain country. Nor is the Marlin 336 chambered for cartridges recommended for big North American game, such as grizzlies, brown bears, moose, and elk.

The Marlin Model 444 should be mentioned here, since it is the world's most powerful lever-action rifle. Using the basic Marlin 336 action design, the rifle is chambered for the .444 Marlin, a shoulderless cartridge which uses a 240-grain bullet and develops a muzzle energy of 3,070 foot-pounds and a muzzle velocity of 2,400 feet per second.

Up to 100–150 yards, the Marlin 444 is deadly on the biggest North American game. At longer ranges, however, both velocity and energy drop rapidly. This comparatively new addition to the Marlin line of lever actions falls into a peculiar position. While it is certainly capable of flattening any vitally hit deer that crosses its path, the awesome cartridge is needlessly powerful for most deer hunters. Because velocity and energy drops off at longer ranges, it does not meet the requirements of a mountain rifle. Perhaps the

Marlin 336C Lever Action Carbine

Savage Model 99-CD with Monte Carlo stock

Marlin 444 is best suitable in such places as Alaska and Canada, where big brown bears, grizzlies, and moose are frequently taken at medium ranges.

The Marlin Model 1894 lever action has been available for several years in .44 Magnum, and in 1979 a carbine version was chambered for the .357 Magnum. While the .357 lacks the power for really big game, it's a perfect companion for the .357 Magnum handgun and is fine for small or medium game at reasonable ranges and for informal target shooting. Much more powerful is the .45/70, for which the Marlin 1895 is chambered. This cartridge, adopted by the Army over a century ago, is a blockbuster in a class with the .444. With handloads especially developed for the Marlin action in the Speer Reloading Manual Number Nine, it is potent enough for heavy game at close to medium range.

Next on the list of popular lever actions is the Savage Model 99, a rifle that is quite different than the Marlin and Winchester lever guns. The Savage 99 uses a rotary magazine and cartridges are loaded from the top, much like a bolt action. In the late 1960's, however, Savage introduced one of its Model 99's with a clip magazine that can be removed from the rifle by pushing a release button on the side of the receiver.

The Model 99 ejects spent cases to the side, which makes the rifle suitable for scope use. While it is a hammerless lever action, the Model 99 has a cocking indicator forward of the tang safety. There is also an indicator on the side of the receiver to show how many rounds are in the magazine.

The Model 99 has a very strong action and it was perhaps the first lever action to be offered in a range of calibers that would push bullets faster and flatter than the typical, round-nosed deer cartridges.

As early as 1914, the Model 99 offered hunters the .250 Savage, which drove an 87-grain bullet 3,000 feet per second, a sensational speed at that time. Today, the 99 in various grades is chambered for six calibers—.22/250 Remington, .205 Savage (also known as .250/3000) and .300 Savage, .243, .308, and .358 Winchester. This array of calibers, compared with those in the Winchester and Marlin lever actions, gives the Savage 99 a slight edge in offering the lever fan a gun that is not necessarily restricted to timber and brush country.

The .243 Winchester and .250 Savage cartridges, for example, can be used on medium game in plains or mountain country where flat trajectory and high velocity are an asset. The .22/250 Remington with a 55-grain bullet and the .243 Winchester with an 80-grain bullet will perform well at long range on woodchucks, coyotes, and so on.

Mossberg's lever action, the Model 479, has also become popular. A traditionally styled carbine with a 20-inch barrel, it has side ejection and offers a choice of straight or pistol-grip stock. Two chamberings are available—.30/30 Winchester and .35 Remington. A unique feature of this lever action is a crossbolt safety. When it's in the safe position, the hammer cannot reach the firing pin.

It is sufficient to say here that there are many good .22 lever-action rifles on the market. While they cannot be considered fine target rifles, the .22 lever guns are enjoyable to use for small-game hunting, plinking, and informal target shooting. Choice is largely a matter of personal preference and the price tag.

Mossberg Model 479 Lever Action Carbine

LEVER-ACTION RIFLES

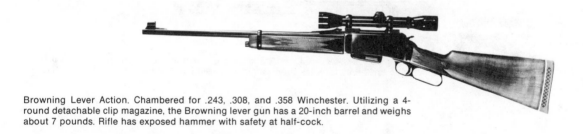

Browning Lever Action. Chambered for .243, .308, and .358 Winchester. Utilizing a 4-round detachable clip magazine, the Browning lever gun has a 20-inch barrel and weighs about 7 pounds. Rifle has exposed hammer with safety at half-cock.

Savage Model 99C. Chambered for .22/250, .243, and .308 Winchester. Weight averages 6¾ pounds and barrel measures 22 inches. Detachable clip magazine holds 4 rounds.

Marlin 1894. Chambered for .44 Magnum. Tubular magazine holds 10 rounds. This carbine weighs about 6 pounds with a 20-inch barrel. Also available in a .357 Magnum version.

Marlin Model 444. Chambered for .444 Marlin. Tubular magazine holds 4 rounds. Weight is about 7½ pounds, barrel 22 inches long.

Winchester Model 9422 XTR. Chambered for .22 Short, Long, and Long Rifle. Tubular magazine holds up to 21 rounds. Also available in .22 Magnum version, with 11-shot magazine. Weight about 6¼ pounds, barrel 20½ inches long. This .22 looks almost exactly like the famous centerfire Model 94.

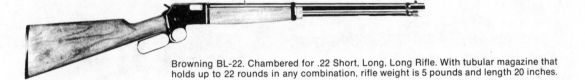

Browning BL-22. Chambered for .22 Short, Long, Long Rifle. With tubular magazine that holds up to 22 rounds in any combination, rifle weight is 5 pounds and length 20 inches.

Marlin Golden 39M. Chambered for .22 Short, Long, and Long Rifle. Tubular magazine holds up to 21 rounds. Weight about 6 pounds, barrel 20 inches long. Another version, Model 39A, has pistol-grip stock, rounded finger lever, 24-inch barrel, and a magazine that holds 19 Long Rifle cartridges, 21 Longs, or 26 Shorts.

Slide, or Pump, Action

Stated simply, the slide, or pump, action is operated by a quick backward and forward movement of the fore-end. This action ejects the spent case, rechambers a fresh cartridge, and cocks the rifle for the next shot.

The pump's obvious advantages are that it can be reloaded manually from the shoulder and it is faster than a lever action. It is a handy brush and timber rifle. The hunter accustomed to pump shotguns will also find this type of rifle a natural to use.

The pump has drawbacks, however. It has a two-piece stock and is therefore not as accurate as a bolt action. In addition, the pump's mechanism is not strong enough to chamber and eject handloaded ammunition whose cases have not been resized to original tolerances. The pump is not a good choice for the hunter looking for maximum accuracy and a rifle that will readily take all handloads.

This pump is a good choice, though, for the deer hunter who puts a great deal of faith in getting off a fast second shot in heavy cover, does not use handloaded ammunition, and uses a pump shotgun on gamebirds and small game.

Remington is one manufacturer that turns out a pump-action rifle in a variety of calibers. Remington labels its pump the Model 760 Gamemaster and chambers it for the 6 mm. Remington, .243, 270, and .308 Winchester, and the .30/06 Springfield. With these calibers, there are pumps suitable for game ranging from coyotes to moose.

The Model 760 has a detachable clip magazine and weighs about 7½ pounds. It has solid top and ejects cases from the side, two features which make the Model 760 good for scope mounting. It is a reliable hunting rifle for men who feel strongly about firepower.

In the .22 class, the pump action has definitely made a place for itself among small-game hunters and plinkers. While it is definitely outclassed on the target range by bolt actions, the little .22 pump and its firepower has taken more than its share of cottontails, squirrels, pests, and other small game. Nearly all of the modern .22 pumps have tubular magazines, side ejection, and are grooved for tip-off scope mounting. These pumps are an excellent choice for hunters who want to add an all-purpose .22 to their gun racks.

HOW A PUMP-ACTION RIFLE WORKS

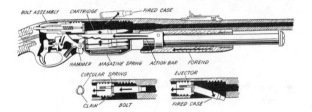

1. Moving the fore-end rearward pushes back the action bar and the bolt assembly, which in turn moves the hammer downward and ejects the empty case. Ejection is accomplished by a circular spring in the end of the bolt (see detail, showing top view) with a claw which hooks under rim of the cartridge and pulls it out of the chamber. When the case clears the chamber, the ejector spring in the bolt flips the case out. Then the magazine spring moves a new cartridge upward.

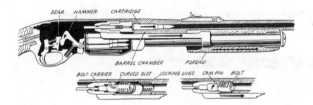

2. Moving the fore-end forward locks the cartridge in the barrel chamber. The notch in the sear holds the hammer so that the rifle is cocked. As the bolt carrier is moved forward, the threads on the bolt contact the locking lugs (see detail). Continued movement of the bolt carrier causes the cam pin on the carrier to engage a curved slot in the bolt, turning the bolt and threading it into locking lugs.

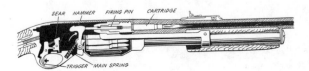

3. Pulling the trigger disengages the sear from notch on the hammer. The main spring forces the hammer against the firing pin, detonating the cartridge. The safety lock and a disconnecting device, which prevents the rifle from going off until the action is closed, is not shown to allow maximum clarity.

Remington Model 760 Gamemaster Pump

PUMP-ACTION RIFLES

Savage Model 170. Chambered for .30/30 and .35 Remington. Designed as a deer rifle, it has short pump stroke of 3¾ inches. Weight is 6¾ pounds and overall length 41½ inches.

Interarms/Rossi Model 62-SA. Chambered for .22 Short, Long, and Long Rifle. Tubular magazine holds up to 20 rounds. This rimfire pump has exposed hammer, 23-inch barrel, and weighs about 5½ pounds.

Remington Model 572 BDL. Chambered for .22 Short, Long, Long Rifle. Tubular magazine has capacity to 20 rounds. Overall length of 42 inches and weight of 5½ pounds.

Semi-Automatic or Autoloading Rifle

The basic requirements of a good hunting rifle are accuracy, reliability, and safety. The semi-automatic or autoloading rifles do not meet these requirements as well as other rifle actions available to sportsmen.

In discussing the semi-automatics and autoloaders, we shall simply refer to them as automatics, since this is what they are most often called by sportsmen. It should be made clear, however, that semi-automatics and autoloaders are not fully automatic, which means that they do not continue to fire as long as the trigger is held back. Such a rifle would, in effect, be a machine gun. Fully automatic rifles are not on the sporting market today and their possession by unauthorized personnel is prohibited by federal law.

Since no manual operation of any lever, bolt, or slide is required with an automatic after the first shot, the biggest advantage of such a rifle has to be firepower. Those quick second or third shots can sometimes mean meat in the pot for hunters in heavy timber or brushy areas. The automatic's usefulness, however, seems restricted to such conditions.

The advantage of firepower can also be a double-edged sword. A big-game hunter, knowing he has only to squeeze the trigger again to send another bullet on its way, may well present a dangerous situation in the woods. For reasons which we will not analyze here, there is a tendency for some users of automatics to empty their clips at fleeing big game after missing that first important shot. This, obviously, is dangerous in thickly wooded areas where other hunters are around. Several states, in fact, prohibit the use of automatics for big-game hunting.

The automatic falls short on other counts. It is not as accurate as the bolt action. It is a poor choice for hunters who may have to take big game or varmints at long range. The automatic design is also tough on cases and tosses them far from the shooter, so it is also a poor choice for the handloader. The gas-operated automatic is not a simple mechanism and is more likely to have malfunctions than other types of rifle actions. The hunter heading into a remote area for an extended hunt would be better off with a bolt action.

While there are some variations to the design of the automatic, these rifles still rely on one of two sources of power for their operation—recoil or gas. Both systems will be explained here very briefly. Readers interested in a detailed treatment of automatic-rifle design can find this information in any specialized gun book.

The recoil system, or blow-back, utilizes a breechblock that is held against the head of the case by a spring. When a cartridge is fired, the breechblock moves to the rear, against spring tension, and ejects the fired case. As the spring moves the breechblock forward, it cocks the rifle and picks up and chambers a fresh round.

Two examples of modern rifles that use this recoil, or blow-back, mechanism are the Browning BAR-22, a full-sized .22 that holds 15 Long Rifle cartridges in a tubular magazine under the barrel; and the Mossberg Model 377 Plinkster, a small-game and plinking rifle that features a thumbhole stock made of structural foam plastic. A tubular magazine runs through the buttstock and it, too, holds 15 Long Rifle cartridges. Both rifles are effective field guns in the hands of those familiar with firearms. An automatic is not recommended as a boy's first gun. It is not for beginners.

HOW AN AUTOLOADING RIFLE WORKS

(Remington Model 742)

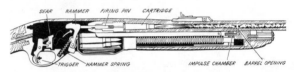

1. Beginning with rifle loaded and cocked, pulling the trigger disengages the sear from notch on the hammer. The hammer spring forces the hammer against the firing pin, exploding the cartridge. After the bullet passes the port, residual gases are metered downward through the barrel opening into the impulse chamber in the fore-end.

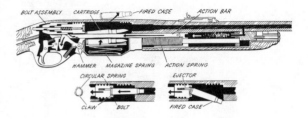

2. Gases force the action bar and bolt-assembly rearward, compressing the action spring, pushing down the hammer and ejecting the empty case. Further rearward travel of the bolt permits the next cartridge to raise into the path of the returning bolt. The ejection mechanism (see detail, showing top view) is the same as in the pump action.

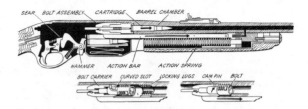

3. Compressed action spring moves the action bar and bolt-assembly forward, causing multiple lugs to lock the bolt into place (see detail also), sealing the cartridge tightly in the barrel chamber. The notch in the sear holds the hammer in cocked position. Pulling the trigger sets the weapon in motion as in the first diagram. The safety lock and a disconnecting device, which prevents the rifle from going off until the action is closed, is not shown to allow maximum clarity.

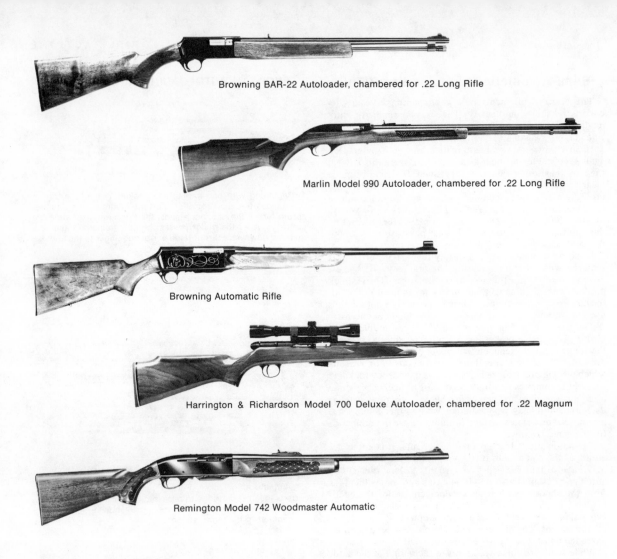

Browning BAR-22 Autoloader, chambered for .22 Long Rifle

Marlin Model 990 Autoloader, chambered for .22 Long Rifle

Browning Automatic Rifle

Harrington & Richardson Model 700 Deluxe Autoloader, chambered for .22 Magnum

Remington Model 742 Woodmaster Automatic

Since the recoil, or blow-back, system used in these and nearly all other .22 automatics does not have a locking breechblock, the design is somewhat limited to rimfire and centerfire cartridges that develop low pressures. There are some modified blow-back designs, such as retarded blow-back, short recoil, and long recoil systems. It is sufficient to say here, however, that they all rely on the same basic principle of recoil for their operation.

Automatics that depend on expanding gas, not recoil, for their operation are quite different in design. In these gas-operated rifles, a hole is drilled through the barrel to channel off gas from the first shot to provide power to work the action. Here is how it works. After that first bullet passes over the hole in the barrel, gases enter the hole and go into a piston chamber in the fore-end. The piston forces a rod that unlocks the breechbolt and pushes it to the rear to eject the spent case and recock the rifle. At this point, a recoil spring takes over. The spring drives breechbolt, rod, and piston forward. On this forward movement, a new cartridge is picked up and chambered for the next shot.

Because these gas-operated automatics have a breechbolt

with lugs that lock at the head of the case, these rifles can handle cartridges that develop very high pressures. One example is the magnum version of the Browning Auto Rifle, which is chambered for the 7 mm. Remington and .300 Winchester Magnum cartridges. The standard version of this rifle, called the High-Power Auto, is available in .243, .270, and .308 Winchester, as well as .30/06 Springfield.

Remington's Model 742 Woodsmaster is another example of an autoloader designed for high-pressure big-game cartridges. It is chambered for the 6 mm. and .280 Remington, the .243 and .308 Winchester, and the old standard .30/06. Like the Browning, it features a detachable box magazine. The Remington is available in a standard and deluxe grade.

If you choose an automatic rifle for big game, after weighing all the advantages and disadvantages, you can't go wrong by selecting one of the rifles covered in this section. All are as reliable and accurate as an automatic can be. Among the various models, you'll also find a range of calibers from flat-shooting high-velocity loads to the big magnums.

AUTOLOADING RIFLES

Ruger Model 44 Autoloading Carbine. Chambered for the .44 Magnum cartridge, this gas-operated model weighs 6 lb. and has a 18½-inch barrel. Tubular magazine holds four rounds in addition to one round in chamber.

Universal Model 1000 Carbine. Chambered for the .30 Caliber M-1 cartridge and gas operated, this carbine weighs 5½ pounds and has a 18-inch barrel. Clip magazine holds five rounds. Also available chambered for the .256 cartridge.

Colt AR-15 Sporter. Chambered for .223 and gas operated, this Colt model has clip magazine blocked to five rounds. Weight is 6¾ pounds and barrel measures 21 inches.

Mossberg Model 377 Plinkster. Chambered for .22 Long Rifle, this autoloader has 15-shot tubular magazine in its buttstock. Thumbhold stock with Monte Carlo comb and roll-over cheekpiece is molded polystyrene; it's very durable, weatherproof, and looks like wood. Weight is about 6¼ pounds (scoped) and barrel length is 20 inches.

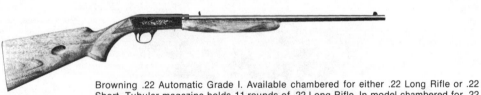

Browning .22 Automatic Grade I. Available chambered for either .22 Long Rifle or .22 Short. Tubular magazine holds 11 rounds of .22 Long Rifle. In model chambered for .22 Short, magazine takes 16 rounds. Weight is about 4½ pounds. In .22 Long Rifle model, barrel is 19¼ inches. In .22 Short model, barrel measures 22¼ inches.

Savage Model 80 Autoloader. Chambered for .22 Long Rifle, this auto has a tubular magazine that holds 15 rounds. Weight is about 6 pounds, barrel is 20 inches long.

Weatherby Mark XXII. Chambered for .22 Long Rifle, this autoloader has clip magazine and 24-inch barrel. Rifle weighs about 6 pounds. Magazines available with 5 or 10 round capacity.

Remington Nylon 66-AB Autoloader. Chambered for .22 Long Rifle, it employs a 14-shot tubular magazine. It has a 19½-inch barrel and weighs only 4 pounds. Stock is nylon with "Apache Black" finish and white diamond inlay; barrel and receiver are chrome-plated. Other versions feature traditional colors for both stock and metal.

Charter Arms AR-7 Explorer. Chambered for .22 Long Rifle. Clip fed with 8-round magazine, this survival-type carbine disassembles with all metal parts (action, barrel, clip) having storage compartments in the moulded fiberglass stock. Metal finish is black anodized aluminum to resist rust. Weight is 2¾ pounds and length when disassembled is 16½ inches.

Single Shots

The single shot fills many outdoor needs and it is disappointing to see that so little attention is given to these firearms in the typical gun book. True, the single shot may never find a place among most hunters of deer and bigger game, but this type of rifle has many uses—and it should be remembered that such activities as one-shot antelope hunts have gained well-deserved prestige and popularity in recent years.

Most, but not all, single shot-rifles are either .22 rimfire bolt actions or break actions. These .22's come into their own as a beginner's gun, a utility gun, a plinking gun, a trapper's and farmer's gun, or, where the laws allow, a part of a camper's gear. Because they are not specialized guns, they fill a variety of needs. Moreover, they are inexpensive. The exceptions to those last two statements are the very specialized and usually expensive .22 single-shot bolt actions used for international target competition—chiefly, free-rifle matches. (The word "free" here refers to a lack of restrictions on sophisticated features such as adjustable buttstock, palm rest, barrel weights, light trigger pull, and so on.)

Of more interest to average American sportsmen are the ordinary, inexpensive single shots, some with full-size stocks for adults and others in scaled-down versions for youngsters. Some of these rifles cock when a round is chambered; others must be cocked manually after the action is closed, and some have automatic safeties. The Savage-Stevens Model 73 and Mossberg Model 321 bolt-action single shots both feature a safety that goes on automatically when the bolt is operated.

Remington's Model 581 might be called a repeater/single shot. This .22 rimfire bolt action is a repeater with a six-shot clip. It comes with a single-shot adapter. With the adapter in place, only one cartridge can be loaded, making it ideal for the novice. After experience has been gained, the 581 can be converted into a repeater by removing the adapter.

A .22 single shot that must be cocked manually after the action is closed is the ultimate in safety as a youngster's first rifle. The Stevens Model 72 Crackshot and Stevens Model 89 are of this type. The 89 is a lever action with the appearance of a "Western" carbine, and the 72 is a revival of the falling-block type that enjoyed great popularity in the early 1900's. Both have exposed hammers that must be manually cocked after loading and closing the action. The beginner—and the instructor—can see at a glance if the rifle is ready to fire. Like the other single shots, these rifles encourage a beginner to aim carefully and practice trigger control. After all, loading rounds singly is slow and the first shot has to count.

Another type of single shot manufactured in the United States is the break action, or top-breaking action. Few single shots of this sort are available today. One is the Harrington & Richardson Model 058 Combination Gun, which features interchangeable smoothbore and rifle barrels—a 20-gauge shotgun barrel and a choice of .22 Hornet or .30/30 Winchester rifle barrel. These rifle calibers provide more power and longer range than the rimfires, of course, so the Model 058 fares well as a versatile, inexpensive gun for a variety of game—birds with the smoothbore, small game, chucks, and such with the .22 Hornet, or deer with the .30/30. Harrington & Richardson also offers the top-breaking .22 Hornet Model 157 and .30/30 Model 158—long known as the Topper Models—without a second, interchangeable barrel.

Depending on caliber, a single shot can take small

Mossberg Model 321K .22 Single Shot

Stevens Model 72 Crackshot, a .22 single shot with falling-block action

Wicliffe '76 Single Shot. This rifle employs a modern action based on the old falling-block Stevens Model 44½. It's available in 11 calibers. Weight is about 6¾ to 8½ pounds and barrel is 22 or 26 inches long, depending on caliber. Shown is Deluxe Grade with custom engraving and inlays on receiver.

game, pronghorns, deer, sheep, black bears—in fact, quite a few species of game, large and small. The demand for good single shots in a wide choice of calibers was recognized by the Sturm, Ruger Company back in 1966, when Bill Ruger introduced the No. 1 Single Shot Rifle. Inspired by the fine old Farquharson action, the Ruger No. 1 has an underlever that operates a falling-block action. It is chambered for calibers ranging from .22/250 to .458 Winchester Magnum.

In the early 1970's, Ruger added another single shot, the No. 3, a carbine chambered for the .22 Hornet, .30/40 Krag, and .45/70. In 1978, the Krag chambering was replaced by the .223 Remington cartridge, and in 1979 the new .375 Winchester was added. This rifle has a 22-inch barrel and weighs only 6 pounds. With a square-comb stock and a rather military appearance, it is reminiscent of carbines of the Civil War era.

Another recently introduced single shot, called the Wickliffe '76, is offered by the Triple-S Development Company. It has a modern action based on the old falling-block Stevens Model 44½. Modern steels and design improvements make it possible to chamber the Wickliffe for cartridges ranging from the .22 Hornet all the way up to the powerful .300 Winchester Magnum.

Models like the Ruger and Wickliffe are rugged, accurate rifles. Mounted with carefully selected scope sights, such arms are more than adequate for big game, as well as the so-called varmint species. Traditionally, sheep hunters favor bolt-action repeaters, but some sportsmen have found these single shots to be very handy for mountain hunting. With game such as sheep, it's almost always the first shot that counts.

Doubles and Combination Guns

The double rifle, in simplest terms, is a double-barreled shotgun action with a strengthened frame, two rifle barrels, and iron sights. It can and has been chambered for a wide range of calibers, from .22 to .470. Because it has no long receiver, the double is short, handy, and fast. In fact, it is the fastest two-shot high-power rifle made.

These features would appear to make the double a dream gun for North American big game taken at medium ranges, but such is not the case. It is extremely unlikely that a double-barreled rifle will ever be manufactured in the United States. Even in England, where most doubles are made, they are generally available only on special order. And in Africa and India, where the double rifle earned a reputation for stopping dangerous game, it has been on the wane for some time. It is being replaced by strong bolt actions, such as the

Winchester Model 70 African and Remington Model 700 BDL, both chambered for the .458 Winchester Magnum, and the Weatherby Mark V in .460 Magnum. Only among muzzle-loaders (which will be described separately) is it at all likely that double rifles may become slightly more common in the near future; muzzle loading is slow, and some black-powder shooters feel that the advantage of a follow-up shot offsets the drawbacks—weight and cost—of a second barrel.

The biggest reason for the decrease in the double rifle is its high cost of manufacture. Getting both barrels aligned so that they place their bullets at the same point of aim, usually 80 or 100 yards, is a tedious and expensive task. It is done by repeated shooting and regulating of a wedge between the barrels until the bullets from both barrels have the same point of impact. The double is also two rifles with two sets of locks and two triggers. What all this means to the hunter is that a good double-barreled rifle may have a price tag ranging anywhere from $1,000 to $5,000.

In addition to high cost, the double has other drawbacks. The ejectors frequently lack the power to pull or toss out stretched or dirty cases. And once a double is sighted for one particular load, other loads cannot be effectively used. As for accuracy, the doubles cannot compete with the comparatively new strong bolt-action repeaters built today. The double rifle has a romantic background, but it cannot be considered a practical firearm for the American hunter.

Combination guns are an interesting breed of rifle and shotgun. Longtime favorites in Europe, they are slowly becoming more popular in the United States. In areas where hunting seasons overlap and laws permit, the combination gun can be a good choice. It can also fill in as an off-season gun for plinking, chuck hunting, crow shooting, and so on.

Basically, there are eight types of combination guns: a rifle barrel under two shotgun barrels, an over-and-under shotgun and rifle combination, a shotgun barrel and two rifle barrels below and to the side, a four-barreled model with two shotgun barrels side by side and two rifle barrels underneath, a double-barreled rifle with a shotgun barrel underneath, an over-and-under shotgun with a rifle barrel to the side, a side by side double-barreled shotgun with rifle barrel on top, and a side by side shotgun and rifle combination.

Several of these combination guns are of uncommon design and rarely seen today. They are generally of European origin, most being built in Germany. It is interesting to note, however, that such a variety of combinations have been conceived by gun builders.

Unfortunately, nearly all European combination guns and

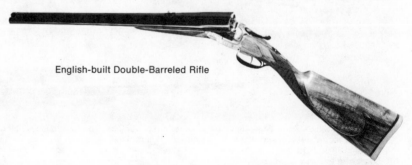

English-built Double-Barreled Rifle

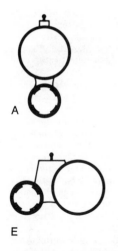
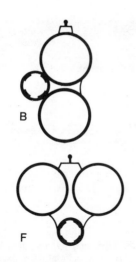
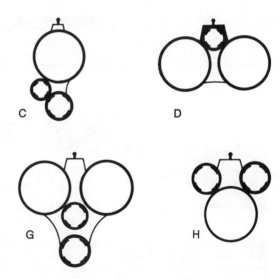

A   B   C   D

E   F   G   H

VARIOUS COMBINATION GUN DESIGNS

A. Over-and-under, shotgun on top, rifle under.
B. Over-and-under shotgun with rifle at side.
C. Shotgun on top with rifles under and at side.
D. Side-by-side shotgun with rifle on top.

E. Side-by-side rifle and shotgun.
F. Side-by-side shotgun with rifle under.
G. Side-by-side shotgun with two rifles under.
H. Side-by-side double rifle with shotgun under.

drillings (any three-barreled combination) are quite expensive. Ferlach, for example, manufactures an over-and-under offering a choice of three shotgun gauges in the top barrel and more than seven rifle calibers in the bottom barrel. This particular Ferlach, labeled Turkey Gun, can be ordered with 12-gauge barrels on top and a .30/06 barrel underneath. Such a rifle could be quite useful to the deer hunter who may also want to take a grouse or two on the same hunt. Or the shotgun barrel could be loaded with buckshot for the big buck that often bursts out of the brush and offers only a fast snapshot. The chief drawback is that imported combination guns like the Ferlach cost about four times as much as an average American hunter pays for a rifle or shotgun. Ferlach and a few other European firms also build typical drillings—three-barreled combinations, usually with two smoothbores side-by-side and a rifle barrel underneath. The drillings, too, are very expensive. With 12-gauge barrels, a Ferlach drilling offers a wide range of rifle calibers—.222, .243, .257 Roberts, 6.5 × 55, 7 × 57, and others. It has 25-inch barrels and weighs about 7½ pounds.

There are several other European firms offering such combination guns. Hege, a German manufacturer, makes a boxlock over-and-under and the purchaser can choose between 12 and 20 gauge for the top barrel and .222 or .30/06 for the bottom barrel. Voere makes a combination gun with a single 20 gauge barrel on top and .222, .222 Magnum, or .223 for the bottom barrel. Krieghoff produces a model with side-by-side 12-gauge barrels over a rifle barrel that can be had in .30/06 or 7 mm. Magnum.

At one time, drillings were made in the United States, but the manufacture of combination guns in this country has always been limited to very few companies. Savage Arms is the only major American firm that has continued to build and improve an over-and-under rifle-shotgun combination. Its early models wore a .22 barrel over a .410. Today, Savage has a series of these guns, the Model 24's, with the rifle barrel chambered for .22 rimfire, .22 rimfire Magnum, .222 and .223 Remington, .30/30 Winchester, and .357 Magnum. The lower, smoothbore, barrel is made in .410 and 20 gauge.

A break-action design, the Savage combination is grooved for scope mounts. The older Model 24's have a barrel-selector button on the side of the receiver. Today's 24's have a spur on the hammer for barrel selection. Prices depend on grade and specifications, but all of the 24's are priced far below the European combination guns.

Scope mounted, the Savage 24 makes an ideal turkey and varmint gun. It's fine for plinking and a good gun for camp, one that would earn its keep by providing small game and birds for the pot. For the farmer, it will keep pests under

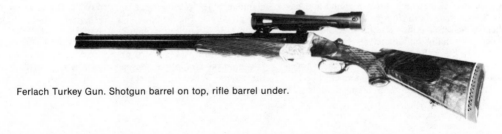

Ferlach Turkey Gun. Shotgun barrel on top, rifle barrel under.

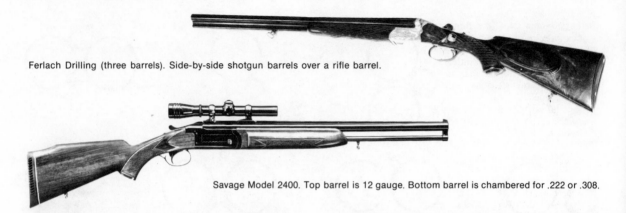

Ferlach Drilling (three barrels). Side-by-side shotgun barrels over a rifle barrel.

Savage Model 2400. Top barrel is 12 gauge. Bottom barrel is chambered for .222 or .308.

control. And, should the occasion arise, the Savage 24 could fill in as an ideal survival weapon. It provides the shooter with a choice of a bullet or shot to take his game. When not in use, the Savage 24 takes down and stows easily.

Muzzle-Loading Rifle

Muzzle-loaders were pushed into obsolescence by breech-loaders long before the end of the nineteenth century, yet the old "front loaders" were never quite buried by progress. Their revival began in the 1930's, gained staggering momentum in the 1960's, and is still growing at a phenomenal rate. One reason is the interest of many Americans in the ways of our forefathers. Another is the challenge of using "primitive" firearms. Probably most important of all is a kind of sporting contagion—word-of-mouth promotion by people who have discovered the fun of shooting muzzle-loaders.

These shooters have their own organization, the National Muzzle Loading Rifle Association, with several hundred affiliated clubs. National and inter-club competitions include offhand shooting, shooting from a rest, flintlock matches, even precision shooting with the big benchrest muzzle-loading rifles like those of the late 1800's. In addition to rifle matches, there are events for muskets, shotguns, and handguns. Most colorful of all are the primitive matches, in which competitors dress in frontier clothing of a bygone era and test not only their shooting ability but other skills such as tomahawk throwing and firebuilding with flint and steel.

Muzzle-loading target competition has become international. American shooters participated in matches held in Switzerland in 1977 and Spain in 1978, for instance. And in both years they came away with the lion's share of medals and trophies.

Another form of competition is promoted by the North/South Skirmish Association, which holds regional and national matches. Teams from both sides of the Mason-Dixon Line name themselves after military units that fought the Civil War. There are individual matches, but the most colorful and interesting are the team events. At the bigger shoots, hundreds of participants all fire at the same time, working against the clock to hit a specified number of breakable targets. Cannon competition is a bonus that leaves

spectators gaping. The din and smoke are unforgettable.

Hunting with muzzle-loaders has also gained immense popularity. More than half the states have special deer seasons for muzzle-loaders, and other states permit their use during the regular deer season. Many other kinds of game are also hunted with these old-fashioned guns. The muzzle-loaders now available are capable of taking all North American game. However, the smaller calibers (.30 to .45) should be limited to small game. Bores from .50 up are best for deer and heavier game such as bears, elk, and moose. Many states stipulate a minimum bore size for deer or big game.

In accuracy, a good muzzle-loading rifle is the equal of a cartridge rifle at moderate range, but trajectory is a problem. A typical muzzle-loader for deer hunting has a muzzle velocity of about 2,000 feet per second when a .50-caliber ball is seated over 110 grains of black powder. With the rifle sighted in to zero at 50 years, this ball will be about four inches low at 100 yards. Sighted to hit two inches high at 50 yards, it will be a close two inches low at 100.

Two basic types of muzzle-loading rifles are in general use: the flintlock and the caplock, or percussion system, which began to replace the flintlock in the early 1800's. To load a flintlock, the proper charge of black powder is first poured down the bore. The shooter then seats a pre-cut, lubricated patch and ball over the muzzle. Using a starter—typically a short dowel with a round handle—the patched ball is moved down into the barrel. With a ramrod, it is pushed the rest of the way until it is seated firmly against the powder. A small amount of very fine black powder (usually the granulation designated as FFFFg) is dropped into the pan; this is the primer. The pan cover, or frizzen, is closed. Instead of the more modern hammer, this action employs a flint held in a cock. When the cock is pulled all the way back, it is ready to fire. At the pull of the trigger, the cock is released and the flint strikes the frizzen a glancing blow, producing a shower of sparks to ignite the fine powder in the flashpan. The flash goes through a small touch hole to ignite the main charge and fire the piece.

With a caplock gun, the percussion cap performs the same function as a modern primer in a cartridge. The cap is seated on a nipple at the end of a little tube leading into the barrel. When the hammer falls, it ignites the priming compound in the cap, driving sparks down the tube to the powder charge. The loading process is the same with a percussion gun as with a flintlock, except that the cap replaces the loose priming charge and flashpan—and the hammer replaces the cock and flint. Caplock rifles are more popular for hunting than flintlocks. The caps are faster and more convenient to use than loose priming powder; there is no need to replace flints; and ignition is faster and surer with a caplock.

A couple of decades ago, most of the muzzle-loaders in use were originals, reconditioned and tested for safety and functional reliability. But antique arms are often too valuable to be taken into the field, and the supply of shootable originals dwindled as muzzle-loading gained unprecedented popularity. During the 1960's, a few imported replicas became available, and in the United States custom and semi-custom makers were busy filling orders for new muzzle-loaders. By the early 1970's, muzzle-loaders were being mass-produced both here and abroad. Today the array is staggering. Moreover, many of the guns are available either finished or in kit form for budget-minded do-it-yourselfers. And the custom makers are still producing finely crafted muzzle-loaders—both replicas and new but authentically traditional designs.

Among the mass-produced models, the Hawken, made by Thompson/Center Arms, is probably most popular. A very well-made half-stock percussion rifle, it is certainly not a true replica of the famous Hawken for which it's named, but it *is* certainly a rugged, dependable firearm. It's available in .45 or .50 caliber and features a 28-inch octagonal barrel that measures $^{15}/_{16}$-inch across the flats. It weighs about 8½ pounds.

Thompson/Center also manufactures a lighter—6-pound—half-stock percussion model called the Seneca, which is available in .36 or .45. A third T/C caplock is the .54-caliber Renegade. It weighs about 8 pounds and, like the others, is an octagonal-barreled half-stock rifle. All of these have adjustable trigger mechanisms that function either as double set or single-stage triggers. Their prices are comparable to those of good, American-made cartridge rifles.

Another popular maker is CVA—Connecticut Valley Arms—which started with imports but now builds its own. CVA's biggest seller is the Mountain Rifle, a half-stock model that resembles an early plains rifle though it is not a true replica. It's available in two basic versions. One has a 32-inch octagonal barrel, $^{15}/_{16}$-inch across the flats, in .45 or .50 caliber. It was first offered only in caplock form, but in 1978 a flintlock Mountain Rifle was added, and both can be bought finished or in a kit.

FIRING MECHANISM OF A FLINTLOCK

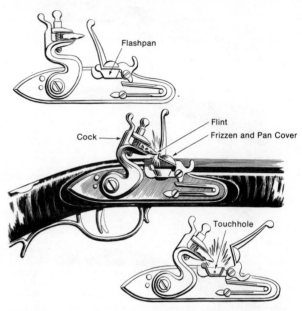

When trigger is pulled, the cock, holding the flint, snaps down and hits the frizzen. The result is a shower of sparks reaching the flashpan and touch hole, which ignites black powder charge in the barrel.

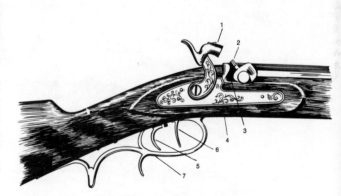

PERCUSSION (CAPLOCK) RIFLE

1. Hammer
2. Nipple
3. Water drain (or snail)
4. Lockplate
5. Set trigger
6. Hair trigger
7. Trigger guard

Connecticut Valley Arms Mountain Rifle in flintlock form, showing close view of double set triggers, which can be used set or unset. This model also comes as a caplock. In either version, it can be bought finished or as a kit.

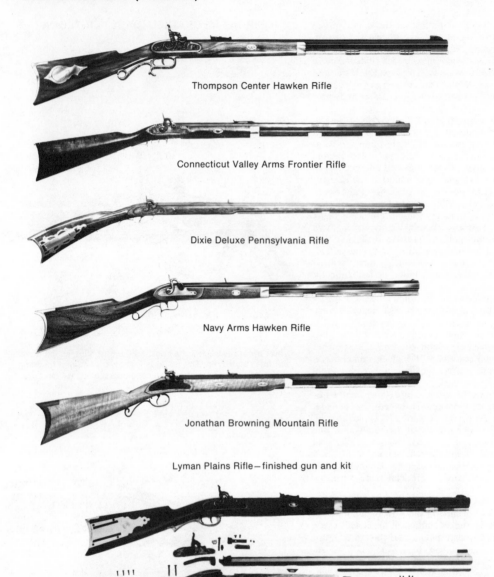

Thompson Center Hawken Rifle

Connecticut Valley Arms Frontier Rifle

Dixie Deluxe Pennsylvania Rifle

Navy Arms Hawken Rifle

Jonathan Browning Mountain Rifle

Lyman Plains Rifle—finished gun and kit

The company also offers a Big Bore Mountain Rifle, a percussion model whose octagonal barrel is bored either .54 or .58 caliber and measures a full inch across the flats. Weights are comparable to those of the Hawkens. These rifles, too, have double set triggers that can be used set or unset. This type of trigger is used even in the CVA Frontier Rifle, a lighter (7-pound) and plainer, budget-priced version of the Mountain Rifle in .45 and .50 caliber. Besides all these, CVA offers a .45 Kentucky Rifle—full-stocked, of course—

in kit or finished form, with percussion or flintlock ignition.

Dixie Gun Works can be called a pioneer in this field. The company started importing muzzle-loaders in the 1950's. Today, the big Dixie catalog—over 500 pages—is crammed with everything a muzzle-loading enthusiast would ever need, including accessories, parts, kits, and finished guns. Dixie's Tennessee Mountain Rifle is a full-stock model patterned after the long rifles of the late flint and early percussion era. Its .50-caliber octagonal barrel is 41½ inches long and ⁷/₈-inch across the flats. Like the originals of this distinctive type, it has browned-iron hardware. You can choose flint or percussion. The Dixie line covers just about everything—from Brown Bess muskets, for example, to swivel-breech rifles (with double barrels and double flint-locks that rotate for the second shot).

Navy Arms is another firm that long ago began importing black-powder guns. Navy still imports a vast assortment and also manufactures its own .50 Hawken rifle—using original Hawken work drawings, no less!

Lyman, a company that offers a vast assortment of shooting products, is in this muzzle-loading business, too. Lyman's Great Plains Rifle, though not billed as a Hawken replica, is a percussion half-stock that's quite representative of the guns once used by the men engaged in the Western fur trade. It has browned-steel hardware and comes in .50 or .54. Lyman imports a number of other muzzle-loaders, both flintlocks and caplocks. The caplocks, like those marketed by Navy Arms, include Civil War replicas.

Browning is also on the muzzle-loading bandwagon. This company's Jonathan Browning Mountain Rifle is named after the father of the famous firearms inventor, John M. Browning. It's not a replica of any single gun but it has features developed by Jonathan Browning when he was a frontier gunsmith. This is a heavy rifle—9½ pounds or so—very traditional in construction and appearance. The calibers are .45, .50, and .54, and there's a choice of polished brass or dull iron hardware.

The muzzle-loading rifles described here are only a sampling of currently popular models. Companies that make or import muzzle-loaders also include The Armoury, Century Arms, Markwell Arms, Hawes, Jana, Shiloh Products, Richland, Trail Guns Armory (which offers a .50 or .58 percussion double rifle called the Kodiak, plus interchangeable 12-gauge shotgun barrels for it), Interarms, Harrington & Richardson, Numrich, Tingle, and many more.

Muzzle-Loading Precautions. Safety is a paramount concern when using any firearm, and extra precautions are mandatory with muzzle-loaders. If the shooter wishes to use an old muzzle-loader rather than a new one, it should not be fired until it has been inspected for safety—and serviced, if necessary—by a gunsmith who is familiar with black-powder guns. Otherwise, such a gun may be unsafe.

In addition to possibly dangerous defects, an old gun is often encountered with a load left in the barrel. This has even been known to happen with modern muzzle-loaders. *Because the load is unknown, it should never be fired.* The bullet or ball should be pulled and the charge removed.

A common practice with percussion guns is to fire a cap, without any powder or ball, to clear the nipple of excess oil; but this should be done only after the barrel is cleared to the breech.

Powder for Muzzle-Loaders. Another precaution concerns the proper powder. Nothing but black powder or Pyrodex should be used in a muzzle-loader. The term "black powder" in this context does not refer to color in the usual sense, because most gun powder is black or gray. The modern powders used in cartridges can be extremely dangerous in a muzzle-loader. The kind to use is the powder that comes in cans labeled "Black Powder" by the manufacturer.

The one exception is Pyrodex, a propellent recently developed for use in black-powder guns. Its burning rate and pressure curve closely follow the characteristics of black powder, but Pryodex is safer to ship and store, and it has become more readily available through retail outlets. Its only disadvantage is that it doesn't ignite well in flintlocks.

Black powder comes in various granulations. The letters Fg identify the coarsest black powder available. The granulations most commonly used in muzzle-loaders are FFg and FFFg. The finest granulation, FFFFg, ignites rapidly and is therefore used to prime the pan of a flintlock.

Accessories. Since a cartridge is literally assembled in a muzzle-loader for each shot, a shooter must carry tools and equipment. A small tool box or tackle box can hold what's needed on a rifle range. Its contents should include:

Rifle balls or other suitable projectiles
Percussion caps or flints
Patches or patch material
Patch (or Maxi-Ball) lubricant
Black powder of suitable granulation or Pyrodex
Priming powder for a flintlock
Extra nipples for a caplock
Adjustable powder measure
Knife for trimming patches
Short starter
Ramrod (extra-long for range use)
"Worm" for pulling lost patches from bore
Ball or bullet puller
Cleaning patches
Cleaning solvent
Rust-preventive oil
Pliers
Screwdrivers
Brass or copper drift for sight adjustments
Light hammer
Nipple wrench for a caplock

The muzzle-loading hunter seldom carries all those items. He wants to travel light, and he's better off carrying his equipment in a shoulder pouch, called a "possibles bag." What it contains is up to the hunter, but only real necessities should be carried. These include enough balls or other projectiles for the day's hunt, a few caps in a capper for a percussion gun, an extra flint or two for a flintlock, patching for both ball and cleaning, a patch knife, and a short starter. In addition, the hunter wants a powder measure and a small powder horn or flask.

With a caplock, a nipple wrench should be added to this list. It's possible (though hardly smart) to forget to put in the powder charge before loading a ball. If this happens, you can remove the nipple and sift in enough powder to blow the "dead ball" out of the barrel.

Muzzle-Loading Information. Finally, any newcomer to the muzzle-loading clan should seek reliable advice and read the loading data available from manufacturers and in black-powder handbooks. There are numerous muzzle-loading publications, including periodicals. An excellent source of information about muzzle-loading skills, products, competitions, hunting news, and so on is the National Muzzle Loading Rifle Association, Box 67, Friendship, Indiana 47021. Members of this organization receive a monthly magazine, *Muzzle Blasts.*

Rifle Stocks

The purpose of a well-designed rifle stock is to put the shooter's eye quickly in line with the sights, enable him to hold the rifle as steady as possible in any position, and to keep the effect of recoil to a minimum. The results are all achieved when the various parts of a rifle stock work in conjunction with one another, and when the shooter feels the stock fits him comfortably.

How can a shooter select a stock that fits him? First, it is sufficient to say here that most factory stocks are well-designed for shooters of average build, and tall men and short men can easily compensate for a stock that does not "feel" exactly right. Most shooters, therefore, are satisfied with a mass-produced stock right from the factory.

Sportsmen who are more concerned about stock fit can make a selection by following the recommended stock measurements and tolerances which will be discussed later in this chapter. There are also the problems of specialized stocks for target shooters and bench-rest shooters. But first let's look at the typical rifle stock and explain the function of each part.

Basically, four parts of the rifle stock determine fit and feel to the shooter. These are the comb, cheekpiece, pistol grip, and fore-end. All four parts come in direct contact with shooter's face and hands.

The comb should be of a height and thickness to insure that the pressure of the cheek against it steadies the shooter's hold and quickly puts his eye in line with the sights. But a comb that is too high and too thick will force a shooter to squeeze his cheek down on the comb to get his eye in line with the sights, and the result is an unnecessary whack on the cheek from the recoil.

Mention should also be made here of the Monte Carlo comb, which is designed to raise and support the shooter's cheek and eye to bring the latter in line with telescope sights, which are a bit higher than open sights. A Monte Carlo comb may run level toward the butt then drop rather sharply near the heel of the stock, or it may slope upward toward the butt. The Monte Carlo that slopes slightly upward from front to rear is a good design, because the comb will recoil away from the face.

A good Monte Carlo will help the shooter who uses telescope sights. On rifles used exclusively with open sights, the Monte Carlo is of little value.

The slope of a comb also determines the drop at heel, which is the distance measured from an imaginary line from the line of sights down to the heel of the stock. In simple words, the greater the drop at heel the more the recoil will be felt. Likewise, the less the drop at heel the less recoil will be felt. A straight stock, with little or no drop at heel, will bring recoil straight back against the shoulder, minimizing the kick. Excessive drop at heel will cause the stock to thrust upward upon firing and bruise or hit the shooter's cheek.

In terms of actual measurements, the drop at heel for an average man using open sights should be 2½ to 2¾ inches. When drop at heel is 3 inches or more on big-bore rifles, the recoil will be uncomfortable. A rifle used with scope sights should have a straighter stock and comb, with less "slope" and less drop at heel—about 2 to 2½ inches is good for the average shooter.

The cheekpiece is an additional aid in supporting the face. Cheekpieces come in all sizes and shapes, but a well-designed and functional cheekpiece is simple and has clean lines. The bottom of the cheekpiece should not extend more than ½ to ⅝ inches from the stock. The forward portion should flow or merge smoothly into a well-rounded comb. It should be flat, giving support to a good portion of the face.

Next of the important parts of a stock is the pistol grip, which should be shaped to enable the shooter to brace the butt against his shoulder while leaving the trigger finger free to squeeze off the shot. It should be curved so that the shooter has no stress or strain on trigger. One rule of thumb in determining a properly curved grip is that the point of the comb should be directly and vertically over the center of the pistol-grip cap.

The circumference of the pistol grip should afford a firm and comfortable hold, without cramping the fingers. For the average shooter, a pistol grip should be round and about 4½ inches in circumference. Men with large hands may prefer a grip closer to 5 inches, but anything over 5 inches is too much wood for comfortable and steady shooting.

NOMENCLATURE OF A RIFLE STOCK

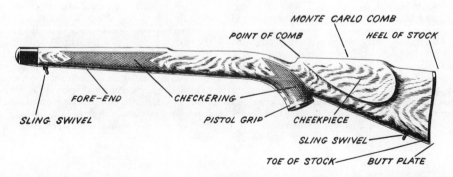

MONTE CARLO COMB
POINT OF COMB
HEEL OF STOCK
FORE-END
CHECKERING
SLING SWIVEL
PISTOL GRIP
CHEEKPIECE
SLING SWIVEL
TOE OF STOCK
BUTT PLATE

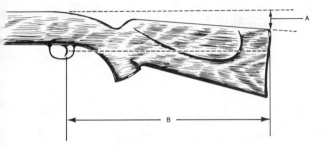

How to measure drop at heel (A) and length of pull (B).

Poor cheekpiece design. Cheekpiece has forward edge to strike shooter's cheek. View from butt also shows it is excessively rounded into comb, not giving full support to face.

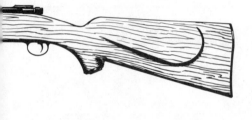 

Good cheekpiece design. Note forward portion blends into comb, leaving no edge to hit cheek. Butt view also shows it is flat, which gives maximum support to face.

The butt of the stock should be wide and flat, to distribute recoil over a large area of the shoulder. The curved narrow butts, frequently seen on muzzle-loaders and early breech-loaders, can make the recoil of big-bore rifles quite painful.

The fore-end of a rifle stock has two purposes 1) control over the rifle 2) keep fingers away from a hot barrel. To accomplish these two objectives, the fore-end should be rounded to fit the contour of the cupped hand and full to keep fingers from making contact with the barrel.

When the palm and fingers of the hand are turned inward, as if to grip a baseball bat or tennis racket, they naturally form a circle or oval—this shape, therefore, is undoubtedly the best for a fore-end. The fore-end can be held fully, the shooter has maximum control, and there are no gaps between the wood and hand. Fore-ends that are triangular in cross-section, have squared jutting "jaws," or slab sides are not only unappealing to the eye, but are awkward to hold.

Length of pull, the measurement between the trigger and butt, is another very important factor in stock design since it determines how quickly and comfortably a shooter will be able to shoulder his rifle firmly and reach the trigger with his finger. Because all men and women are not the same size with same length arms, the length of pull varies. It should be emphasized here, however, that factory stocks generally have a length of pull of 13½ inches, which is a good compromise for average shooters for all-round use. With the exception of very big men with long arms or very short men, a pull of 13½ inches should prove adequate.

For the more serious shooter who may want to alter his factory rifle or is planning to invest in a custom-built rifle, the following chart will be helpful:

SIZE	RECOMMENDED LENGTH OF PULL
Tall men (6'1" to 6'3")	13¾" to 14"
Average men (5'8" to 6')	13¼" to 13½"
Short men, average women	13" to 13¼"
Short women, boys	12¾"

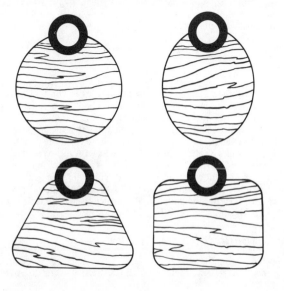 

Round or oval-shaped fore-ends are best for hunting rifles. Either type fill hand, give good control, and keep fingers from barrel.

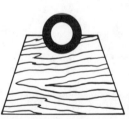

Triangular-shaped or square slab-sided fore-ends are poor for hunting rifles, though their flat bottoms may prove of some use in benchrest shooting.

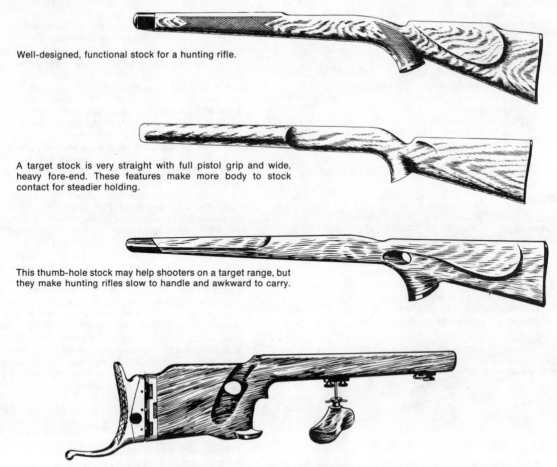

Well-designed, functional stock for a hunting rifle.

A target stock is very straight with full pistol grip and wide, heavy fore-end. These features make more body to stock contact for steadier holding.

This thumb-hole stock may help shooters on a target range, but they make hunting rifles slow to handle and awkward to carry.

Designed for International Match Shooting, this specialized stock has no place in the field but excells on the target range. It has a thumbhole, thumb-rest, and hand-rest which adjusts in height. Bottom of fore-end has an inlaid rail which is the base for the sling swivel, hand-stop, and palm rest. These accessories can be moved along the stock to suit the individual shooter. The buttplate can be adjusted for both height and length. Such specialized stocks usually come fitted with two buttplates—one for standing and the other one for use when in the kneeling and prone shooting positions.

Checkering on a rifle stock definitely has a function, in addition to making a stock attractive. For the hunter, checkering means a non-slip grip on his rifle in wet weather or while wearing gloves. It keeps both hands from sliding or moving on the pistol grip and fore-end, making for a more rigid hold.

Unfortunately, most modern factory stocks now come with checkering that is not really checkering at all. It is merely a design impressed into the wood by machine. This is a step down from the earlier factory stocks which had true checkering, even though most of the work was carelessly done. In those days, most factory stocks were checkered from 14 to 18 lines to the inch.

Custom rifle builders of today still do all their checkering by hand. It is long tedious work, which is one reason for the high cost of custom firearms. These men, who use good hard wood, checker about 24 to 26 lines to the inch. Precision checkering with sharp diamonds is one indication that the stock-maker is a master of his trade.

The features of a rifle stock mentioned thus far pertain to a sporter or hunting rifle. There are exceptions, such as target stocks, thumbhole stocks, stocks with roll-over cheekpieces, and so on. Some of these exceptions are legitimate and aid the shooter, but most just make the rifle awkward to handle. Any hunter who sticks to the functional stock design described in this chapter is sure to find himself with a comfortable and good-handling field rifle.

Woods for Rifle Stocks

The strength and "eye-appeal" of a finished stock depends on several factors. A stock that has considerable figure or "burl" generally comes from a piece of wood cut from where roots and limbs branch out from the trunk of a tree. While this wood may look attractive, it is not necessarily the best for a rifle stock, particularly a one-piece stock. Because there is considerable figure in the wood, it is prone to warping with climatic changes and such warping in the fore-end of a rifle can throw off accuracy under hunting conditions. Such wood is better for shotgun stocks.

The one-piece rifle stock should be straight grained, with the grain running parallel to the direction of the grip and the grain in the fore-end slightly diagonal to the barrel. This keeps warping in the fore-end to a minimum. The grip should never be cut cross-grain, since this would dangerously weaken the stock at a critical point.

It is sufficient to say here that a good stock should have a drying out period of about four or five years, that is from the time it is cut from the tree until it is finally turned into a finished gun stock. The drying period, naturally, allows the wood to lose all its moisture, keeping warping to a minimum in the finished product.

The most common wood used for factory gunstocks is American walnut. Though it generally lacks the fancy figure of other woods, it is a good stock wood. It is most often straight-grained, but occasionally a factory stock of American walnut will show up with attractive burl figure. The configuration depends from which part of the tree the stock blank is cut. If cut from crotch of limbs or roots, the finished stock will nearly always have a fancy figure. American walnut, though not as hard a stock material as European walnut, holds checkering well.

There are many other woods used to make gunstocks. Some are soft, some hard. Some have good figure, others straight grained.

Although wood is the traditional material for the making of gunstocks, some synthetics have also been used. For example, Charter's AR-7 rifle has a stock constructed of a plastic called Cycolac. Back in 1959, Remington brought out its Model 66 rifle, which has a stock of structural nylon. These stocks can be made in any color, and checkering is molded right in. Nylon and similar synthetics are light, extremely strong, and will never warp. But these materials lack the beauty and feel of a good piece of wood. Synthetics are practical on some rugged, inexpensive rimfire models like the Charter and Remington but would meet sales resistance on higher-grade rifles.

Finishing the Gunstock

The best finish for a rifle stock is a straight oil finish, nearly always with boiled linseed oil. It is a durable finish and one that can be easily maintained by simply hand-rubbing on another coat of oil. And it does not crack or peel, which can and does happen with factory stocks finished with varnish or lacquer.

Sanding is the first step to putting a good oil finish on a bare stock. Before any oil is applied, the wood must be made as smooth as possible. After an initial sanding with No. 180-grit sandpaper, wet the wood with a cloth. The moisture will cause the grain to raise and become rough. After the wood has dried, use No. 180 sandpaper again and sand the stock as smooth as possible. Follow this same procedure, using No. 180 sandpaper, one more time.

The next step is to progress to a finer sandpaper, such as No. 240 grit. Once again, wet the stock, allow the grain to raise and the wood to dry, then sand as smooth as possible with the No. 240 paper. When this is done, follow the same procedure again, only this time use No. 320-grit paper. Continue to wet and sand with the No. 320 paper until the grain will no longer raise when wet.

When sanding is completed, the actual oil finish can be applied. If the wood appears quite porous, however, a filler should be used before the oil is rubbed on. Commercial fillers are available, but an excellent filler can be concocted by mixing equal parts of white shellac and alcohol. This should be applied with a brush or cloth, allowed to dry, then sanded off. Depending on the wood, several coats of filler may be necessary. Remember to always allow the filler to dry thoroughly and sand between coats. The stock is now ready for the oil.

There are several commercial oil finishes on the market and any one of them will do a good job if directions are followed carefully. Some of the finishing kits available also provide shortcuts for the refinisher. One method is to add a bit of spar varnish to the oil to bring a fast sheen to the wood. Lacquer and plastic finishes are also available for a fast finishing job.

Let's assume here, however, that a straight boiled linseed oil finish is desired. Properly done, a pure oil finish is extremely durable and, most important, easily maintained. The first step is to apply a fairly heavy coat of linseed oil to the wood and set the stock aside for a day or two, allowing the wood to absorb the oil and dry thoroughly. When this is done, rub the stock down with fine steel wool. You'll note that the wood is already taking on a light satin sheen.

Now comes the hard part. Start to apply thin coats of the oil and rub them well into the wood. The harder the oil is rubbed into the stock the better. After each thin coat of oil is rubbed into the wood, wipe off the excess oil and allow the remaining oil to dry thoroughly. If this is not done, the coats of oil that are not dry will begin to build up gummy deposits on the wood. If this happens, the only alternative is to sand the stock down to bare wood and start the job all over again. It is, therefore, *very* important for a coat of oil to dry thoroughly before another is applied. There is no set number of coats of oil to be rubbed into a stock. The process is simply repeated until the desired finish is obtained. The idea is to build up many thin coats of oil on the wood until the stock takes on a rich satin finish that will resist rain, snow, heat, and so on.

One of the biggest advantages to a good oil finish is that if the stock is lightly scratched in the field or marred in any way, another coat of oil, applied as described here, will bring the finish back to its original condition.

Naturally, the above method is for a stock of bare wood with no finish at all. If it is a factory stock that is to be refinished, the old factory finish, usually varnish or lacquer, must first be removed and the bare wood made as smooth as possible. This is done simply by brushing the stock with commercial varnish remover and waiting for the stock to blister and peel. The old finish can then be scraped off with a knife or razor blade. This is a messy but necessary job and it is not uncommon to use more than one coat of varnish remover to get all of the old finish off the wood. Once this is done, start with the sanding process described above to get a new oil finish.

Getting a good oil finish on a gunstock is not a difficult job, but it is a long and tedious project. The results, however, make the effort worthwhile.

Rifle Barrels

The modern rifle barrel has come a long way since the time of the twist or Damascus barrels of the 19th century. During those early years, barrels were made by twisting and welding strips of iron around a mandrel to form a hollow tube. Such barrels were fine during the black-powder era when pressures were comparatively low and lead bullets were used.

But then came smokeless powder and with it higher temperatures and higher pressures than the black-powder barrels could handle. The high-velocity smokeless-powder cartridges also used metal-jacketed bullets which caused too much abrasion in barrels made of iron or mild steel, a low carbon alloy.

Progress by steel makers and a great deal of experimenting by gun companies resulted in the steel rifle barrel of today. The modern rifle barrel is tough, but it can still be machined easily. It can resist erosion and withstand the stresses and strains created by high pressures. The steel is tough enough so that rifling holds up under the abrasion of metal-jacketed bullets.

The majority of barrels for high-power rifles are made of chrome molybdenum steel. Some barrels are made of stainless steel, which meets all the requirements of a good barrel material and has the additional virtue of being rustproof. One reason stainless steel is not used for all barrels is that it is difficult to machine.

Gun manufacturers get their barrels in the form of long steel bars, which are cut to desired lengths. The bar is then ready for drilling and reaming. Drilling is done by a deep hole drill, a long rod with a V-cut running its entire length. One edge of this V does all the cutting. The barrel rotates at high speed while the deep-hole drill, which remains stationary and does not spin, bores a hole from breech to muzzle.

Once the initial hole is cut, a series of reamers, usually three or more, are used to ream the hole to the desired bore diameter. These reamers make the bore as smooth as possible and ready the barrel for rifling.

Rifling

Rifling, put simply, is a system of spiral grooves cut into the bore to make the bullet spin and stabilize it on its way to the target.

Before going into a discussion of the various forms of rifling, let's first learn the meaning of bore diameter, groove diameter, and lands. These terms will make rifling and rifling methods easier to understand.

Grooves are the spiral cuts running the length of the barrel. The distance from the bottom of one groove to the bottom of the oppposite groove is called *groove diameter*. *Lands* refers to the portion of the bore left between the rifling grooves. The measurement between lands is called *bore diameter*.

There are various forms of rifling, but the type most commonly used today has square-cut lands and grooves.

These grooves, which spiral to the right and are always cut opposite one another, usually number four or six in most factory guns. One exception is Marlin's Micro-Groove barrel, which has 16 shallow grooves cut into the bore. The theory behind many shallow grooves is that it minimizes bullet distortion and increases accuracy.

There are several other forms of rifling, but none, to this writer's knowledge, are used today. One type of rifling, called either segmental or Metford, has lands and grooves with rounded-off edges. It was used in Europe for black-powder guns because it made barrels easier to keep clean. The black powder was not apt to foul the barrel quickly since there were no sharp edges in the rifling to catch particles.

Another form of rifling is the oval bore, which, as its name implies, has an out-of-round bore. The oval actually turns as it moves down the length of the barrel and spins the bullet. At one time, oval-bore rifling was used both in England and the United States.

Still another type of rifling is the parabolic pattern, which gives a pinwheel appearance when looking down the barrel. The type of rifling was used in some rifles around 1920.

Methods of putting rifling into a barrel vary, and this has been particularly true within the past 20 years. At one time, all manufacturers cut rifling into a barrel by the same process, and that was cutting one groove at a time. The cutter bit made one complete pass through the barrel, while at the same time the barrel rotated at a predetermined speed to give the rifling the desired amount of twist. Then, if the barrel was to have four-groove rifling, the barrel was given a quarter turn and another groove cut. These steps continued until all grooves were cut. It is important to note here that the bit could not cut a groove to its proper depth on a single pass, so a number of shallow cuts had to be made until the groove reached correct depth.

Cutting one groove at a time was obviously slow, and this brought about the use of broaches. A broach is a steel tool with several cutting edges. When the tool is pushed or pulled through the bore, each cutting edge removes slightly more steel than the one preceding it. All the rifle grooves are cut in a single operation. Though these broaching tools are expensive and costly to repair, this method is certainly much faster than cutting one groove at a time.

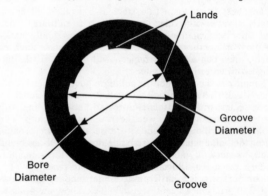

Most common type of rifling has square-cut lands and grooves.

Lands

Groove Diameter

Bore Diameter

Groove

Segmental or Metford Rifling

Oval Bore Rifling

Parabolic Rifling

Still another method of putting rifling in a barrel, called cold forming, was developed during World War II. This procedure involves placing the barrel over a mandrel or carbide die that has the reverse impression of rifling on it. Barrel and mandrel are then placed in a forging machine which pounds the outside of the barrel until the rifling is formed inside the barrel.

Another rifling process involves the use of a carbide rifling button to form the rifling in a bore. The torpedo-like carbide button has reverse spiral grooves machined into it. When pushed or pulled through a bore, the button compresses and forms rifling rather than cutting it. The operation is done by one pass through the barrel and production goes faster. Most manufacturers now use this button rifling method. But most important to the shooter is the fact that button-rifled barrels tend to be more accurate than those rifled by other methods.

Twist

The purpose of rifling in a barrel is to start the bullet spinning and stabilize it in flight after it leaves the muzzle. The rate at which the rifling grooves turn inside the barrel is called twist, and it is always stated as one full turn in a given number of inches. For example, a 1-16 twist means the rifling grooves make one complete revolution in 16 inches of barrel. Likewise, a 1-12 twist means one full turn in 12 inches.

What's the best amount of twist for a bullet? This depends on the bullet's size and velocity, but it is a generally accepted fact that the longer the bullet the faster the rate of twist needed to stabilize its flight. Short, fat bullets need less twist.

Some of our early cartridges, for example, used bullets that were comparatively short and heavy. The .45/70 falls into this category and requires a 1-20 twist to stabilize its bullet. But our later cartridges with longer bullets and higher velocities need a faster twist to spin the bullet properly in flight. The .30/06, the .270 Winchester, the .30/30, and the .308 Winchester have generally been found to perform best with a 1-10 twist.

Unless a sportsman is an avid gun-nut who dabbles in custom-built rifles, he need not concern himself too much with twist, other than understanding how it works and why it is necessary.

Firearms manufacturers have generally determined what amount of twist is best for modern cartridges and factory barrels are built accordingly. The following list, from a major firearms manufacturer, shows the amount of twist they build into their barrels for some popular calibers.

CALIBER	TWIST
17 Remington	1-9
.22/250 Remington	1-14
.222 Remington	1-14
.25/06 Remington	1-10
.243 Winchester	1-9
.270 Winchester	1-10
.30/06	1-10
.308 Winchester	1-10
7 mm. Remington Magnum	1-9
.264 Winchester Magnum	1-9
.350 Remington Magnum	1-16
.300 Winchester Magnum	1-10
.375 H. & H. Magnum	1-12
.458 Winchester Magnum	1-14

Chamber

The oversize portion at the breech end of the barrel is called the chamber of the rifle. It is designed to hold the cartridge that is to be fired. The chamber must be slightly bigger than the cartridge to allow the brass case to expand slightly from the pressure of the exploding powder and contract sufficiently for ejection of the spent case from the chamber.

The throat or neck of the chamber, which encircles the case neck, should likewise be oversize to allow the case neck to expand enough to release the bullet for its flight through the barrel.

Headspace

Any definition or description of a chamber automatically leads into the subject of headspace. To make headspace easier to understand, let's first define a couple of terms: (1) *Headspace* is the distance between the head of a cartridge case and the face of a closed and locked bolt. (2) *Headspace Measurement* is the distance between the face of a closed bolt and the point of contact on the cartridge case that controls the distance the case will go into the chamber. Consequently, headspace measurement determines headspace.

Headspace measurement would be simple if all cartridges chambered the same way, but there are four types of cartridges (rimmed, rimless, belted, rimless pistol), and headspace is measured differently for each type. The accompanying drawings clearly illustrate the headspace measurement for each class or type of cartridge. The drawings also illustrate how each type of cartridge fits in the chamber, showing the contact points between the case and chamber that hold the cartridge in place.

Obviously, since all chambers and cartridges cannot be made exactly alike, there is always some space between the bolt face and the head of the cartridge. In modern high-power rifles, the acceptable tolerance between the bolt face and head of a maximum gauge used to determine headspace is 6/1,000 inches.

If there is too much space between the cartridge head and bolt face, a condition known as *excessive headspace* exists. If there is not enough space between the cartridge head and bolt face, the problem of *insufficient headspace* exists. Either of these conditions in a rifle handling high-

powered cartridges can be dangerous if they go unchecked.

How does a shooter determine whether his rifle has excessive or insufficient headspace? There are several symptoms to look for: When a shooter has difficulty chambering a cartridge or getting the bolt to close or lock, his rifle may have insufficient headspace. Another indication is shiny score marks on the head of the case, which may be the result of the bolt closing too tightly on the cartridge and creating friction between the head of the case and the bolt face. Any of these signs may indicate insufficient headspace. This means pressures may run abnormally high when the rifle is fired.

A shooter who recognizes these signs should not automatically assume his rifle has an insufficient headspace problem. The chamber may be normal and the problem may lie with the cartridges being used, particularly reloaded ammunition. As mentioned above, it is almost impossible for all cartridges of one caliber to have exactly the same dimensions.

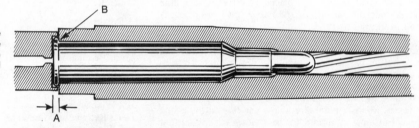

Rimmed Cartridge. Headspace (**A**) is measured from bolt face to front edge of rim. Rim (**B**) holds cartridge in place and stops the travel of the case into the chamber.

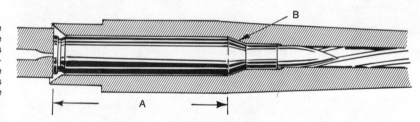

Rimless Cartridge. Headspace (**A**), the distance between the bolt face and case head, is determined by the case shoulder. On rimless cartridges, the shoulder of the case (**B**) stops travel of the cartridge into the chamber.

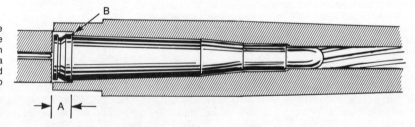

Belted Cartridge. Headspace (**A**) is measured from bolt face to front edge of belt. The belt on the case (**B**) seats against a shoulder in the chamber and stops travel of the cartridge into the chamber.

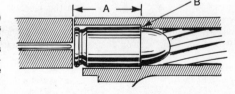

Rimless Pistol. Headspace (**A**) for rimless pistol cartridges is measured from bolt face to edge of case mouth (**B**), which seats against shoulder in the chamber and stops travel of the cartridge into the chamber.

If insufficient headspace is suspected, it is best to take the rifle to a gunsmith and have it checked with headspace gauges. If the problem does exist, it can often be corrected by reaming out the chamber to an acceptable tolerance.

In rifles with excessive headspace, there is too much room between the head of the cartridge and the bolt face. When such a rifle is fired, the head of the cartridge face comes back against the bolt face and the case expands beyond normal limits. The case may stretch or crack near the head or pull itself apart completely.

Determining the possibility of excessive headspace in a rifle is done by examining the spent cases for the following telltale signs:

1. A partial crack or rupture near the head of the case.
2. A stretched ring mark on the brass near the head of the case. This can be considered a warning of possible complete separation of the head from the case.

3. When firing reduced loads in a rimless case, a protruding primer is an indication of excessive headspace.
4. In rimfire cartridges, excessive headspace will produce a bulge near the rim.
5. Total case separation. In this extreme situation, the cartridge pulls apart completely, usually near the head, and only the rear section of the case ejects.

Here again, signs of excessive headspace may not necessarily mean a chamber problem. The symptoms may be the result of the ammunition being used, particularly reloads. A full-length resizing die, for example, may shorten a case and create excessive headspace in a normal chamber. Best bet is to take both rifle and ammunition to a gunsmith and have him check the firearm with headspace and case gauges. Sometimes the problem can be corrected by a change in ammunition or resizing method.

Cartridges

Let's get off to a good start by calling a cartridge by its right name. It's a "cartridge," and calling it anything else is wrong. It's not a bullet, a slug, a shell, nor anything else that does not adequately describe a cartridge. A cartridge is not a single item or unit, but a combination of various components, which include a bullet, case, powder, and primer. Put these four basic components together and you have a "cartridge."

It's not all that simple, however, since cartridges are broken down into types. Among metallic rifle cartridges, there are two basic categories — the rimfires and the centerfires.

The common rimfire cartridge has its primer sealed in and around the entire rim. The firing pin striking the rim anywhere around the edge of the cartridge will ignite the charge. Examples of rimfire cartridges are the .22 Short, the .22 Long, the .22 Long Rifle, the .22 Magnum, and the 5mm. Remington Rimfire Magnum.

The centerfire cartridges have a primer in the center of the base of the cartridge case. The firing pin striking the primer ignites the primer and sets off the powder charge via a flash hole in the brass case. The centerfires make up the bulk of modern sporting ammunition.

THE CENTERFIRE CARTRIDGE

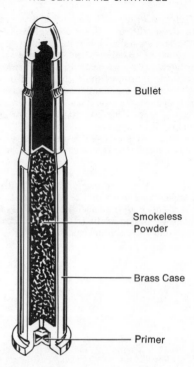

- Bullet
- Smokeless Powder
- Brass Case
- Primer

TYPICAL CENTERFIRE CARTRIDGE CASE

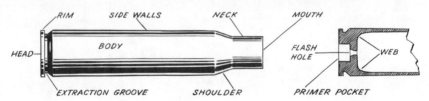

Cartridge Case

Just about all modern rifle cartridge cases are made of brass, which is most suitable for reloading. There are still some plated steel cases in use around, but brass is still the first choice. The cartridge case has a number of important jobs. It houses the powder charge, and it holds the primer and bullet firmly in place. Upon firing a cartridge, the case also seals off gases from escaping from the breech.

There are various parts of a cartridge case and the accompanying sketch covers them all.

Cartridge cases fall into five categories or types: rimmed, semi-rimmed, rebated case, rimless, and the belted case.

The rimmed cases are an old design and are still very much in use today. The .30/30 Winchester, for example, uses a rimmed cartridge case. The rim of the cartridge is the contact point which keeps the cartridge from entering the chamber.

TYPES OF CARTRIDGE CASES

A. Rimmed Case
B. Semi-Rimmed Case
C. Rimless Case
D. Rebated Case
E. Belted Case

A semi-rimmed case is one that has a rim a bit bigger in diameter than the body of the case, and the extraction groove is cut under the rim. The semi-rimmed cases are not too common today and the .225 Winchester may be the only current cartridge using this type of case.

The rebated cartridge case is one of the easiest to spot. The rim is smaller in diameter than the base of the case body. The extraction groove is cut under the rim. An old design, it was apparently revived in the .284 Winchester cartridge.

The rimless case is the design most widely used today. The rim diameter and the diameter of the case body are nearly identical and the extraction groove is cut into the head of the case. The classic .30/06 utilizes the rimless case.

The belted case has become synonymous with the magnum calibers. The design makes it possible to build the strongest case. The belt acts as a reinforcing band and the extraction groove is cut into the belt.

PARTS OF A TYPICAL BULLET

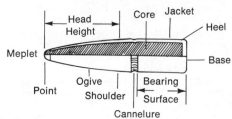

The Bullet

A bullet is simply a component of a cartridge and a non-spherical projectile that is fired through a rifle barrel. But there the simplicity ends. Bullet design differs, depending on whether the bullet is to be used for long-range varmint shooting, brush hunting for whitetails, bear hunting, or hunting thick-skinned dangerous game.

MODERN BULLET DESIGNS

Full-jacketed or non-expanding solid bullet. Only opening in jacket is at base of bullet.

Expanding bullet with round nose and soft point. Large area of lead exposed at tip with one-piece jacket covering sides and base of bullet. Cannelure aids in crimping cartridge case neck into the bullet.

Expanding bullet with round nose and soft point. One-piece jacket has slits in forward portion to weaken nose and bring on quick-controlled expansion.

Hollow-point expanding bullet. Jacket encloses sides and base but is weakened by knurling near tip to promote quick expansion.

Nosler Partition bullet has metal jacket open at both ends to expose lead. Partition strengthens base of bullet and jacket decreases in thickness toward tip. One of the best expanding bullet designs.

Boattail bullet is tapered at base to reduce air drag. A top bullet design for long-range shooting.

Winchester Silvertip has copper jacket that covers side and base of bullet. Tip is covered with soft aluminum case that extends back and under copper jacket. The Silvertip has good "expanding" qualities.

Remington Bronze-Point has a bronze wedge in tip that produces good expansion when it is driven to the rear of the bullet on impact.

Remington Core-Lokt is a soft-point, round-nose bullet. Forward edge of jacket has scalloped edge to insure uniform mushrooming. Bullet is strengthened by increased jacket thickness near base.

Hornady pointed soft-point expanding bullet has lead core exposed at the tip. One-piece jacket covers base and side of bullet. Note pronounced thinning of jacket in nose section.

RWS H-Mantle bullet is a semi-fragmenting bullet design. Outer jacket is steel, covered with cupro-nickle alloy. Tip cap enclosing internal cavity is copper. Jacket is indented at halfway point to separate frangible forward section from base.

Remington hollow-point Core-Lokt has shallow tip cavity to lessen quick expansion. Jacket is purposely thin at nose to weaken it.

For example, bullets designed for varmint shooting, generally in the .17- to .24-caliber class, are constructed with soft lead cores, thin metal jackets, and can be either soft or hollow pointed. They are usually sharp pointed to enable them to retain velocity better, which means a flatter trajectory. This design, however, causes them to expand quickly and disintegrate when they hit.

Such varmint bullets are fine for long-range shooting where there are no obstructions, but they rank a poor second on bigger game, because they are easily deflected by the smallest twig in their path and they go to pieces before good penetration occurs. While it is true that varmint cartridges have taken numerous heads of big game, the fact remains that these bullets are not suitable for big game.

On thin-skinned big game, ranging from deer to moose, bullets are larger in diameter, heavier in weight, and made with soft lead cores and thin jackets. They differ from varmint bullets in that plenty of lead is exposed at the point to give good even expansion or "mushrooming" and reliable penetration. Bullets in this category may also use methods other than exposed lead at the tip to control expansion. Remington, for example, uses a bronze wedgelike point which is driven to the rear on impact and "mushrooms" the bullet. Another Remington design features a scalloped jacket to insure uniform expansion. Winchester covers its lead point with soft aluminum which extends back and under the jacket cover. Whatever the design, the ultimate goal is dependable penetration and controlled expansion.

Finally, there are the bullets built for thick-skinned dangerous game. These bullets are invariably full-jacketed with no lead exposed. Their purpose is to penetrate thick hide and smash bone. No appreciable mushrooming is expected of them. These "solid" bullets are best jacketed in steel and have round or flattened points. Such bullets are for massive African game, such as Cape buffalo and elephants, where a hunter may need fast and deep penetration to stop a charge. They are not practical for any North American big game animals.

A bullet designed with a point at both ends would be best aerodynamically, since it would reduce wind resistance and air drag, but such a bullet, for obvious reasons, is not feasible. The closest we can come to it, however, is the boattail bullet, which tapers slightly at the rear. This is the best choice for long-range shooting. Combine the boattail design with a spire point or spitzer point, and the result is a bullet with top-flight characteristics.

Such pointed bullets, however, have disadvantages. First, they cannot be safely used in rifles with tubular magazines, because recoil may drive the sharp nose of such a bullet into the primer of the cartridge in front of it. Secondly, sharp-pointed bullets have less shocking power on big game than round-nosed bullets, because tissue, like air, offers less resistance to the sharp-pointed bullets. For this reason, the sharp-pointed bullets designed for hunting will nearly always have soft or hollow points.

A term that is mentioned when the subject of bullets comes up is "sectional density," which is the ratio of a bullet's diameter to its weight. The sectional density of a bullet is figured by dividing the bullet's weight in pounds by the square of the diameter. Unless a shooter is good at math, he'll have trouble with the formula. It is important to remember, however, that bullets with a low sectional density are short and fat and velocity is lower than bullets with a high sectional density. Bullets with high sectional density are long, slim and retain velocities well over long ranges.

What does this mean to the average hunter? In simple terms, a bullet with a high sectional density, such as a 130-grain .270, would be fine for game taken at long ranges. For the brush-hunter, however, a chunky .35 caliber deer-class bullet with a low sectional density, would be O.K. in wooded areas where ranges are not extreme.

Still another term that frequently gets tossed around is "ballistic coefficient," which is a complicated principle that relates a bullet's sectional density to the bullet's shape and measures its ability to overcome air resistance.

Unless a shooter plans to get involved in handloading his own ammunition for hunting, there is really no need for him to learn the aerodynamic principles and formulas of bullet design and weight. Firearms manufacturers have gone into extensive research to produce the best bullets for various hunting conditions. Check the chart on page 37 before buying ammunition for a hunting trip.

The Primer

The primer of a cartridge is frequently referred to as the sparkplug of the cartridge, and one would be hard put to find a better description. The primer contains a highly explosive compound which, when struck by the firing pin, ignites the cartridge's powder charge via a flash hole in the brass case.

Thanks to modern manufacturing techniques, the chances of primer malfunction are rather remote. When a malfunction does occur it is generally because of a weak firing pin or because oil, grease, or water has worked its way into the primer. If you're a handloader, keep the primer dry and clean and don't handle it if your fingers have even a trace of lubricant.

The typical American primer for a centerfire cartridge is actually an assembly of several components, including an anvil, a cup, paper, and the priming mixture. The paper lies between the mixture and the anvil. The primer ignites when the firing pin crushes the explosive mixture against the anvil. Just about all primers made in America use chemicals which are noncorrosive and nonmercuric.

There are basically two types of primers in use today: the Boxer and Berdan. The Boxer primer has a built in anvil, which means it can be punched out of a spent case with a decapping pin. This is a great advantage to handloaders.

The Berdan primer does not have a built-in anvil. Instead, the anvil is an integral part of the cartridge case. This makes removal of the primer difficult, which accounts for the increased usage of the Boxer primer throughout the world. To a limited degree, the Berdan primer is still used in Europe.

The difference in reliability between the Boxer and Berdan primer is almost nonexistent—both are dependable. Cartridge cases using the Boxer primer utilize one large flash hole in the primer pocket, while the Berdan primer ignites the powder charge through several small holes around the built-in anvil in the case. The Boxer primer is most widely used because it is a boon to handloaders.

Boxer primers are made in two different sizes and six types, as the following list shows:

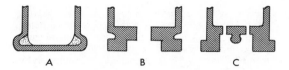

Cutaway of cartridge case heads show three basic designs for primers: A. Rimfire has priming compound completely around rim. Firing pin striking rim anywhere ignites cartridge. B. Boxer primer fits in primer pocket. Firing pin striking primer ignites mixtures and sets off cartridge via flash hole. C. Case for Berdan primer has built-in anvil. When firing pin strikes primer, cartridge is set off via flash holes around anvil.

Primer	Diameter (inches)
Large rifle	.210
Large rifle magnum	.210
Large pistol	.210
Large pistol magnum	.210
Small rifle	.175
Small rifle magnum	.175
Small pistol	.175
Small pistol magnum	.175

The large rifle primers are used with cartridges such as the .270, .308, .30/06, and similar calibers. The large pistol primers are used in such calibers as the .45 Auto, the .44 Special, and so on.

The small rifle primers are used in the .22 Hornet, the .222 Remington, and similar cartridges. The small pistol primers are used in the .32 Smith & Wesson, the .38 Special, and similar cartridges.

The magnum primers, as the above list indicates, are the same in diameter as the other primers. The difference lies in their chemical structure. These magnum primers are built to provide long sustained heat to insure complete ignition when large quantities of powder are used.

There are at least eight manufacturers producing dependable primers for handloaders. If you're going to try your hand at handloading, you'll find that all handloading manuals will list the correct primer size for your cartridge.

Rimfire cartridges, such as the .22's, use a much different priming design. The priming mixture in these small cartridges is distributed completely around the rim of the case. The firing pin, striking anywhere around the rim, will ignite the priming mixture and fire the cartridge.

The Powder

When was the first time a gunpowder was used in a firearm? That's a tough, if not impossible, question to answer. It's generally accepted that the Chinese developed black powder (a mixture of sulphur, charcoal, and potassium nitrate) for use in fireworks and a man named Roger Bacon adapted it to firearms around 1265.

During the pioneer era, before the advent of smokeless powder, black powder was used in muzzle-loading rifles and cap and ball pistols. Black powder is not an ideal propellant and no factory cartridges today are loaded with it. Small batches are still produced, however, for the growing number of gun nuts who enjoy playing with muzzle-loaders.

Black powder has more than a few disadvantages, which we should explain before discussing the development of smokeless powder. First, black powder is explosive and consequently presents a potential danger to the user. If a spark or hot ash should hit a pound of black powder on your reloading bench it could result in a serious explosion. And in spite of the fact that it is an explosive, it burns at a constant rate and it takes a great deal of it to produce enough gas to get a bullet up to acceptable velocity. This was one reason the old muzzle-loaders had long barrels; they were needed to give the black powder enough time to burn and build up pressure. Black powder also gives off great clouds of smoke from the muzzle of an old front-loading gun and fouls a barrel badly. To maintain any kind of accuracy, muzzle-loaders had to be cleaned frequently.

So, unless you're a muzzle-loading enthusiast, forget black powder. It was used at a time when there was nothing else to do the job. Now we have smokeless powder, which is far superior in all respects.

Our modern smokeless powders stem from the discovery of nitroglycerin and guncotton. Nitroglycerin is a liquid which results from the action of nitric and sulphuric acids on glycerin. Guncotton is formed by the action of the same acids on various kinds of cellulose and cotton. Perhaps the single most important fact about smokeless powder is that the rate of burning can be controlled so that its use can be boosted to maximum efficiency in various types of firearms.

It is difficult to categorize smokeless powders because they come in almost endless varieties and shapes, but there are basically two groups—double-base powders and single-base powders.

A double base powder is made when guncotton and nitroglycerin are mixed. Cordite, for example, is a well-known double-base powder. Double-base powder burns quite hot, but gives high velocity with low pressure.

Single-base powders contain no nitroglycerin and are formed by dissolving guncotton in a mixture of alcohol and ether.

As mentioned above, the burning rate of smokeless powder can be controlled and this is done by one of two methods—size of granulation of the powder and coating the grains with a retardant substance. Either of these two methods produces "progressive burning powder."

To put it simply, the smaller the grains of powder the faster the burning rate; the bigger the grains the slower the burning rate. When a retardant coating is used, this coating must first be burned off before the powder burns. The purpose is to get the powder to start burning slowly then increase the rate of burning as the bullet starts its trip through the barrel. The result is a continuous accelerating thrust pushing the bullet.

How can we apply this "progressive burning" principle to cartridges? A few examples should make it clear. Light bullets require less gas pressure to start moving in a barrel than heavier bullets. Using the .308 as an example, a fast burning powder can be used with the 110-grain bullet but a slow-burning powder with the heavier 200-grain bullet.

Let's carry this a step further and take a look at rifle and handgun ammunition. A rifle may have a barrel up to 22 or 24 inches, which means more time is available for a powder to build up pressure, so one of the slower burning powders can be used. In a handgun, however, where peak velocity must be reached quickly because of the short barrel, a very fast powder must be used.

If you're a handloader, the importance of correct powder selection cannot be overemphasized, since it will have a direct bearing on velocity. You'll be confronted with powder in various forms, including circular flakes, small cylinders, and small spheres. A good handloading manual, however, will recommend what kind of powder to use and what velocity you can expect with various bullet weights.

If you're not a handloader but an average hunter, there's no need to worry about the gunpowder in the factory ammunition you buy at your favorite gunshop. If it's from a reputable manufacturer, you can be sure you're getting the right powder behind your bullets.

RECOMMENDED CALIBERS AND BULLET WEIGHTS FOR GAME

FOR VARMINTS

Cartridge	Bullet Weight (grs.)	Muzzle Velocity (f.p.s.)
.17 Remington	25	4020
.5 mm. Remington Magnum	38	2100
.22 Long Rifle	40	1145
.22 Long Rifle	40	1335
.22 Long Rifle H. P.	37	1365
.22 W.R.F. (.22 Rem. Spl.)	45	1450
.22 Win. Automatic	45	1055
.22 Win. Mag. Rimfire	40	2000
.218 Bee	46	2860
.22 Hornet	45	2690
.22 Hornet	46	2690
.222 Remington	50	3200
.222 Remington Mag.	55	3300
.22-250 Remington	55	3810
.223 Remington	55	3300
.224 Weatherby	50	3750
.240 Weatherby	70	3850
.257 Weatherby	87	3825
.220 Swift	48	4110
.225 Winchester	55	3650
.243 Winchester	80	3500
.25-06 Remington	90	3500
.25-06 Remington	100	3300
.6 mm. Remington	80	3544
.25-20 H.V.	60	2250
.256 Win. Mag. (rifle)	60	2800
.250 Savage	87	3030
.257 Roberts	87	3200
.264 Win. Mag.	100	3700
.270 Weatherby	100	3760
.270 Winchester	100	3480
.284 Winchester	125	3200
.308 Winchester	110	3340
.30-06 Springfield	110	3370

FOR BIG GAME

Cartridge	Bullet Weight (grs.)	Muzzle Energy (ft.-lbs.)
†.243 Winchester	100	2090
.250 Savage	100	1760
†6 mm. Remington	100	2260
†.25-06 Remington	120	2590
.25-35 Winchester	117	1370
†6.5 mm. Remington Magnum	120	2780
†.240 Weatherby	100	2554
.257 Roberts	117	1820
†.264 Winchester Magnum	140	3180
†*.270 Weatherby	150	3501
†*.270 Winchester	150	2800
†*.280 Remington	165	2910
†*.284 Winchester	150	2800
*7 mm. Mauser	175	2410

Cartridge	Bullet Weight (grs.)	Muzzle Energy (ft.-lbs.)
7 mm. Remington Express	150	2970
†*7 mm. Remington Magnum	175	3660
†*7 mm. Weatherby	154	3406
.30-30 Winchester	170	1860
.30 Remington	170	1700
*.30-40 Krag	180	2440
*.30-40 Krag	220	2360
*.300 Savage	180	2240
†*.30-06 Springfield	180	2910
*.30-06 Springfield	220	2830
†*.300 Winchester Magnum	180	3770
†*.300 Weatherby	180	4201
.303 Savage	190	1650
*.303 British	180	2580
†*.308 Winchester	180	2720
*.308 Winchester	200	2670
.32 Winchester Special	170	1960
.32 Remington	170	1700
*8 mm. Mauser (8 x 57; or 7.9)	170	2490
8 mm. Remington Magnum	185	3896
†*.338 Winchester Magnum	200	4000
*.338 Winchester Magnum	300	4000
†*.340 Weatherby	200	4566
*.348 Winchester	200	2840
.35 Remington	200	1950
.351 Winchester Self Loading	180	1370
*.358 Winchester	200	2840
*.358 Winchester	250	2810
.375 Winchester	200	2150
*.375 Holland & Holland	270	4500
*.375 Holland & Holland	300	4330
.44 Magnum	240	1630
*.444 Marlin	240	3070
.45-70 Government	405	1570

*Suitable for heavy game, such as elk or moose, as well as for lighter species such as deer.

†For long-range plains or mountain hunting where flat trajectory is important (e.g. sheep, goat).

FOR DANGEROUS GAME

Cartridge	Bullet Weight (grs.)	Muzzle Energy (ft.-lbs.)
*7 mm. Remington Magnum	175	3660
*.30-06 Springfield	220	2830
*.300 Holland & Holland	180	3400
**.300 Holland & Holland	220	3350
*.300 Winchester Magnum	180	3770
**.300 Weatherby	220	4123
8 mm. Remington Magnum	220	3912
*.338 Winchester Magnum	250	4050
**.338 Winchester Magnum	300	4000
**.340 Weatherby	200	4566
*.350 Remington Magnum	250	3220
*.358 Winchester	250	2810
*.375 Holland & Holland	270	4500
**.375 Holland & Holland	300	4330
†.375 Holland & Holland	300 Solid	4330
†.378 Weatherby	300 Solid	5700
†.444 Marlin	240	3070
**.458 Winchester Magnum	510	5140
‡.458 Winchester Magnum	500 Solid	5040
‡.460 Weatherby	500 Solid	8095

*Only for such North American species as Alaskan bear and moose.

**Not for elephants or rhino, but suitable for large Asiatic and African cats.

†Adequate for elephant, rhino, and buffalo.

‡Recommended for toughest, most dangerous game.

Cartridge Selection and Ballistics

It is just about impossible to talk about cartridge selection without also covering the subject of ballistics (velocity, trajectory, and energy), since a shooter must obviously know how a particular cartridge will perform before he makes his choice.

Let's first start out with a basic premise. Game is killed by a good combination of rifle, cartridge, and shooter. The most important is the shooter. The most efficient rifle and cartridge is nearly worthless unless the hunter can comfortably handle his gun and confidently place his bullet in a vital area. If a hunter can't kill a deer with a .30/30, there is no reason to believe he will do much better with a .338 Winchester Magnum.

When a hunter using a deer-class cartridge finds himself wounding and missing game with any amount of frequency, the problem is usually with the man behind the gun . . . not the gun. The solution to such a problem is more time on the range, where a shooter can find where his bullets are going and make the necessary sights adjustments. He should also put in as much practice as possible to develop a steady hold and good smooth trigger squeeze.

Deer Hunting in Brush

Basically, however, there are some guidelines a hunter can follow in selecting a cartridge for his brand of hunting. If he's a typical deer hunter who takes his game in wooded country where ranges are not extreme, he'd be wise to pick a caliber between .30 and .35 handling bullets weighing from 170 to 200 grains. This would give him a fairly heavy bullet pushed along at a not-too-fast velocity that would give it good brush-bucking qualities. Such a bullet would also be less apt to be deflected by brush and, if properly constructed, would not disintegrate on impact. A bullet that goes to pieces when it strikes is all right for varminters, but not for big-game hunters who need bullets that will provide good penetration.

Another fact to keep in mind is that the typical deer hunter, unless he plans to hunt moose or bear as well, should not overpower himself with the mighty magnums, such as the .300 and .338 Winchester cartridges. These big belching berthas can be a definite handicap. Because of their uncomfortable recoil and muzzle blast, these rifles are not fired as often as a hunting rifle should be and the result is that the shooter does not become familiar with his rifle and may also develop a flinch or become "afraid" of his rifle—something that is sure to mean missed or wounded game.

So if you're a deer hunter in brush country, stick to the calibers you can handle comfortably and confidently. A well-placed shot with a .30/30 will kill cleaner than a sloppy shot with one of the big magnums. As mentioned earlier, the deer-class cartridges between .30 and .35 calibers are good choices. A few excellent cartridges for brush hunting are the old-time .30/30, the .308 Winchester, the

.35 Remington, .30/06, .300 Savage, .358 Winchester, .32 Special, and .375 Winchester. Another cartridge worth mentioning is the revived .45/70. Its heavy, slow-moving 405-grain bullet is an excellent brush-cutter for deer up to 150 or even 200 yards.

Western Deer Hunting

The deer hunter in the West has a different problem. He needs a cartridge that will produce high velocity and flat trajectory for the long 200-yard-plus shots he will encounter in mountain and prairie country. He also needs a quick-expanding bullet that is fairly light.

Generally, the Western hunter chooses from the .25- to .30-caliber range of cartridges. Because of the long shooting distances involved, bullet weights are more important here since they will affect trajectory and bullet drop. The proven cartridges for Western hunting include the .270 with the 150-grain bullet, the .243 with the 100-grain bullet, the .25/06 with the 120-grain bullet, the .264 Winchester Magnum with the 140-grain bullet, the 7 mm. Remington Express with the 150-grain bullet, the 7 mm. Remington Magnum with the 175-grain bullet, the .280 Remington with the 165-grain bullet, and the .30/06 with the 180-grain bullet.

It certainly is not unusual for Western sportsmen to include such game as antelope, sheep, and goats in some of their hunts. These medium-size game animals all have one thing in common—they are generally taken at long range. Any of the cartridges and bullet weights listed above for the Western hunter will do the job on these animals.

Big Game/Varmint Cartridges

We've covered cartridges for deer-size game in the West and East, but how about hunters looking for a big-game cartridge that can also be used during the off-season for varmints? If this is the case, any selection will have to be a compromise. The ideal deer cartridge can never be a top-flight woodchuck or varmint load. The best solution is to favor the lighter, high-velocity cartridges that will reach out for chucks but also be adequate for deer. Such compromise cartridges include the .243 Winchester with the 80-grain bullet for varmints and the 100-grain bullet for deer, the .25/06 Remington with the 90-grain bullet for varmints and the 120-grain bullet for deer, and the .250/3000 with the 87-grain bullet for varmints and the 100-grain bullet for deer. Similar combinations include the .257 Roberts, the .270, and the 6 mm. Remington. In a pinch, the .308 and .30/06 with light bullets can also prove adequate for long-range woodchuck shooting.

We're assuming, of course, that a sportsman following these recommendations is shopping for a rifle that will work on both deer and varmints. If a hunter, however, already owns a .270 or .30/06, it would be poor economics for him to unload it and buy another rifle that would be closer to a deer-and-varmint combination gun. It would be much wiser to simply use lighter bullets on varmints and heavier bullets on deer-size game. The .30/06, for example, offers a range of bullet weights from 110 to 220 grains. The .308 offers nearly the same range of bullet weights.

Perhaps another point to keep in mind before possibly swapping your rifle is that most hunters who suddenly become addicted to varmint shooting will invariably end up with one of the specialized high-velocity flat-shooting varmint cartridges, such as the .222 Remington or the .22/250 Remington.

One of the most perplexing yet most interesting problems is the search for the all-round cartridge, one that can fill in during the summer months for chucks, take deer on those annual hunts, and also be put to use on occasional trips for such big game as elk, moose, caribou, and brown and grizzly bears.

Such an all-round cartridge has to be a compromise. No single cartridge does the job well on all game, from chucks to moose. If you choose a powerful cartridge, you must cope with heavy recoil, muzzle blast, and noise, even if you just want to bang away at chucks on a Saturday afternoon. If you choose a lighter cartridge, it may fall slightly short of acceptable power for game such as elk or moose.

But if a hunter can afford just one gun for all game, the old .30/06 is most often recommended. With a 110-grain bullet, it produces a velocity of 3,370 f.p.s. (feet per second), which makes it a more than adequate varmint load. The deer or sheep hunter can use the 180-grain bullet, which leaves the muzzle at 2,700 f.p.s. For bigger game, the 220-grain bullet leaves the muzzle at 2,410 f.p.s. and packs 2,830 foot pounds of energy.

The .30/06 has become more versatile than ever with the introduction of the Remington Accelerator cartridge, which is designed to make a .30/06 or .30/30 rifle into a passable varmint rig. It employs a .224 bullet encased in a .30-caliber plastic vehicle called a sabot. On leaving the muzzle, the sabot and the bullet separate. When fired from a .30/06, the small .224 bullet is then traveling at over 4,000 f.p.s. The same bullet and sabot loaded in a .30/30 case will be moving at 3,400 f.p.s. Accuracy is as good as the rifle from which the Accelerator is fired. If your .30/06 produces one-inch groups at 100 yards with a standard 165-grain load, the Accelerator will probably do likewise. But if your rifle delivers four-inch groups, it will probably continue to do so with the Accelerators.

Most .30/30's are lever actions and not noted for pinpoint accuracy, so the value of the Accelerators in this caliber may be questionable. However, you may be lucky enough to own one of the Remington Model 788 bolt actions that were once chambered for this round. The Accelerators would make it an outstanding combination for deer and varmint shooting.

If the .30/06 is the best all-round load, it isn't the only one. The .308 Winchester is available with bullets weighing 110, 180, and 200 grains. Bullets for the .270 Winchester come in 100, 130, and 150 grains. The .280 Remington and 7 mm. Mauser can also do far more than one job—as can the 7 mm. Remington Magnum for a hunter who can take recoil. All these cartridges have a good variety of bullet weights and good retention of velocity and energy.

Cartridges for Dangerous Game

For heavy and dangerous game, the choice of a cartridge is not difficult because there are not that many American-made cartridges available for such animals. For Alaskan bear, Cape buffalo, and the big Asian and African cats, a hunter can use such cartridges as the .300 Holland & Holland, the .338 Winchester Magnum, the .300 and .340 Weatherby

Magnums, or the .375 Holland & Holland. For the toughest game, such as elephant and rhino, a hunter should use solid bullets in such cartridges as the .378 Weatherby Magnum, the .375 Holland & Holland, the .458 Winchester Magnum, or the .460 Weatherby Magnum.

The listing of recommended calibers and bullet weights for game on page 40 will prove valuable to sportsmen looking for the all-round cartridge or the hunter who wants to add another rifle to his battery, whether it be for woodchucks or Alaska brown bears. Note that muzzle velocity is listed for varmint cartridges, since a flat trajectory is important for this type of long-range shooting. For big game, however, muzzle energy is listed, since knockdown power is needed for the bigger animals.

Ballistics

Ballistics, which is a study of what happens to a bullet in flight when it leaves the muzzle of a rifle, is an extremely valuable aid to a shooter in selecting and comparing the pros and cons of various cartridges. Without getting too technical, ballistics covers trajectory, velocity, and muzzle energy of a cartridge. Before going any further, we should know what these terms mean.

Trajectory is the curved path the bullet takes from muzzle to target. No bullet will travel a flat path to the target—even if velocity were pushed to more than 4,000 feet per second and the range was only 10 yards. A bullet, because of gravitational pull begins to drop the instant it leaves the barrel. It is the degree of the trajectory curve that is of key importance to the shooter, and this is determined by initial muzzle velocity and bullet shape.

The faster a bullet leaves the muzzle the shallower the trajectory curve or, in other words, the "flatter" the path of the bullet. As mentioned above, bullet shape also has an effect on the trajectory curve. Long sharp-pointed bullets handle wind resistance better, retain velocity longer than chunky round-nosed bullets and will produce a flatter bullet path.

Velocity is simply the speed at which a bullet travels, and this is usually measured in feet per second. Generally, the abbreviation "f.p.s." is used after the digits. On nearly all published ballistic charts, figures on velocity are given at the muzzle and at ranges of 100, 200, and 300 yards. The purpose is to tell how well or how poorly a particular cartridge retains its speed. Such figures, as we shall see, are valuable in cartridge and bullet weight selection.

Muzzle energy is a measurement expressed in foot pounds of the impact by a bullet as it leaves the muzzle of a rifle. Ballistic charts nearly always give energy figures for bullets at the muzzle and at ranges of 100, 200, and 300 yards. These figures are useful in determining how rapidly various loads and bullets lose impact power in flight.

What does trajectory, velocity, and energy mean to a hunter or target shooter? The answer is the difference between missing and hitting. Trajectory figures will tell you which cartridges shoot "flatter" than others, though there is really no such thing as a flat-shooting cartridge. The trajectory curve (flight path of a bullet) has often been compared with a baseball player throwing a ball. The farther he must toss a ball, the higher he must throw it to make it reach its target. The same applies to a bullet. The farther the

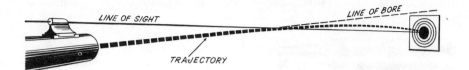

Trajectory, or path of the bullet, never rises above line of bore, but crosses line of sight. To compensate for bullet drop, the bore must be pointed upward and this is done by adjusting rear sight so it is higher than front sight.

target, the higher the muzzle of a rifle must be raised, by adjusting the rear sight upward, to make the bullet travel a greater distance.

The accompanying sketch clearly shows trajectory in relation to line of sight and line of bore. Since the bullet never goes above the line of bore and begins to drop the instant it leaves the muzzle, the rear sight must be adjusted to compensate for the bullet drop.

Published ballistic tables also almost always show trajectory figures, which indicate a bullet's flight path from muzzle to target. The figures, given in inches, indicate the rise or drop of a bullet from the line of sight. Let's take, for example, the .30/06 with a 180-grain bullet. Sighted in at 200 yards, the bullet will hit 2.4 inches high at 100 yards and 9 inches low at 300 yards. Obviously the mid-range figures are valuable when trying to figure out the best range to sight in your hunting rifle, and they also tell you where to hold at ranges closer or farther than the distance for which

your rifle is sighted.

Beginning on page 50 is a compilation of ballistic figures from various ammunition makers. Studying these charts will give you a good insight on how various cartridges perform and how they compare with one another. Use these tables when trying to pick a varmint load that shoots the flattest, or when trying to find the load that offers the widest range of bullet weights for all-round hunting. And if someone says their .270 packs more energy at 100 yards than your .308, you will find that answer here, too.

In order to make this ballistic section as complete as possible, figures on handgun cartridges have also been included, although a description of handguns themselves is covered in a separate chapter.

In addition, so shooters can compare and learn the various sizes of cartridges, starting on this page are photos of the most popular American and European cartridges.

RIFLE CARTRIDGES

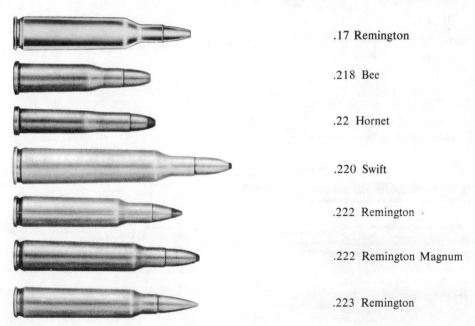

.17 Remington

.218 Bee

.22 Hornet

.220 Swift

.222 Remington

.222 Remington Magnum

.223 Remington

RIFLE CARTRIDGES (Continued)

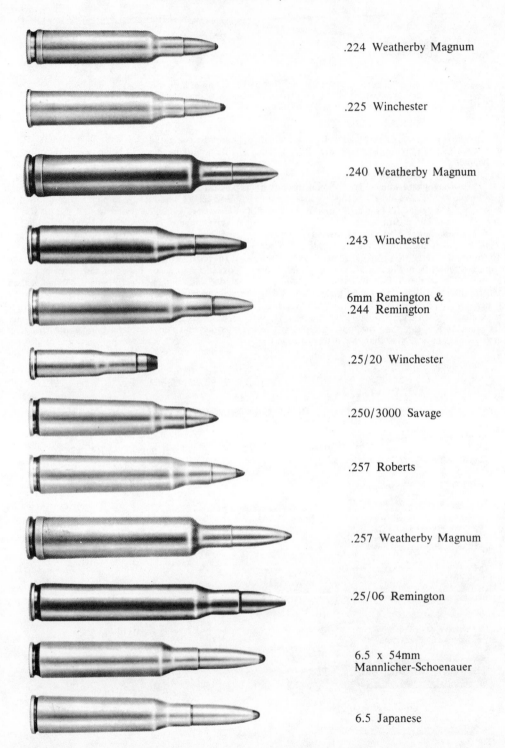

.224 Weatherby Magnum

.225 Winchester

.240 Weatherby Magnum

.243 Winchester

6mm Remington &
.244 Remington

.25/20 Winchester

.250/3000 Savage

.257 Roberts

.257 Weatherby Magnum

.25/06 Remington

6.5 x 54mm
Mannlicher-Schoenauer

6.5 Japanese

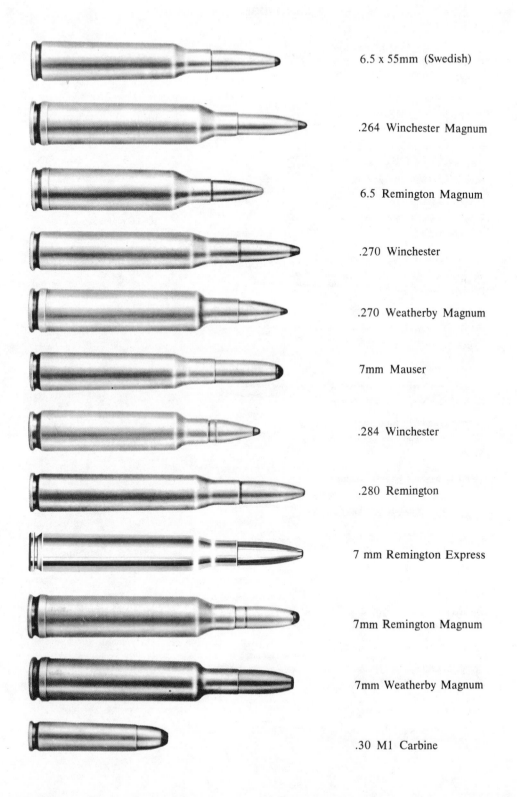

6.5 x 55mm (Swedish)

.264 Winchester Magnum

6.5 Remington Magnum

.270 Winchester

.270 Weatherby Magnum

7mm Mauser

.284 Winchester

.280 Remington

7 mm Remington Express

7mm Remington Magnum

7mm Weatherby Magnum

.30 M1 Carbine

RIFLE CARTRIDGES (Continued)

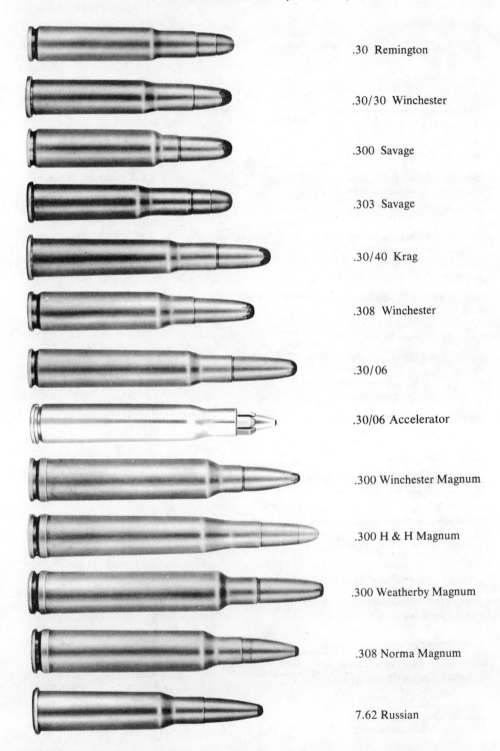

.30 Remington

.30/30 Winchester

.300 Savage

.303 Savage

.30/40 Krag

.308 Winchester

.30/06

.30/06 Accelerator

.300 Winchester Magnum

.300 H & H Magnum

.300 Weatherby Magnum

.308 Norma Magnum

7.62 Russian

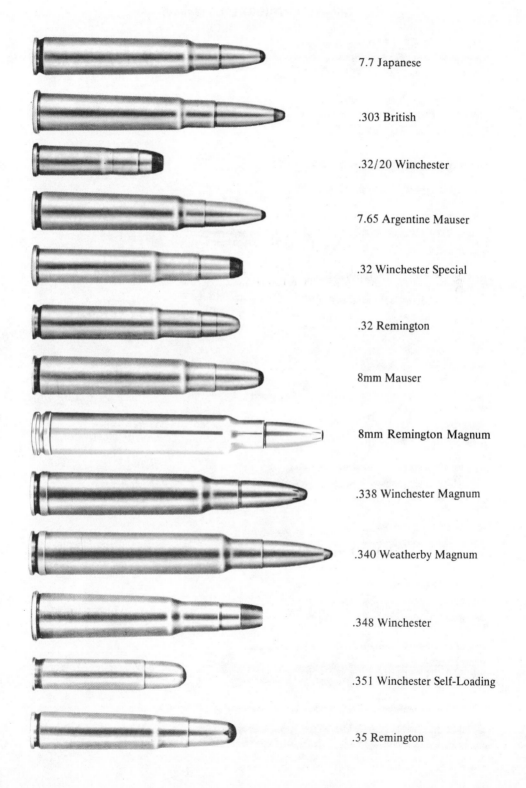

7.7 Japanese

.303 British

.32/20 Winchester

7.65 Argentine Mauser

.32 Winchester Special

.32 Remington

8mm Mauser

8mm Remington Magnum

.338 Winchester Magnum

.340 Weatherby Magnum

.348 Winchester

.351 Winchester Self-Loading

.35 Remington

RIFLE CARTRIDGES (Continued)

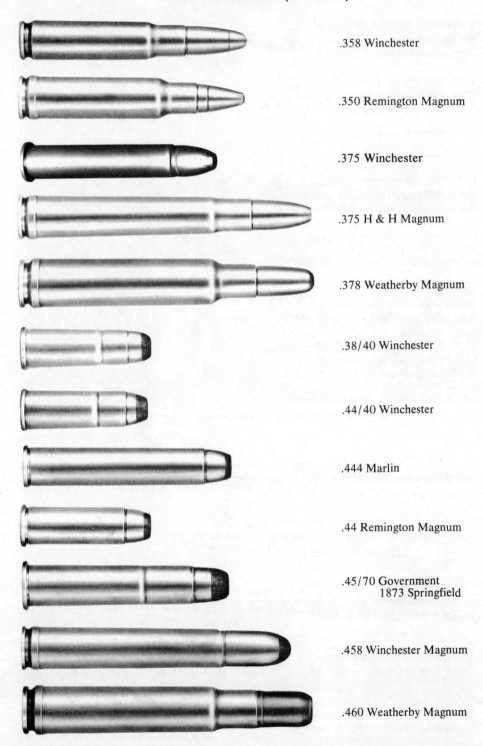

.358 Winchester

.350 Remington Magnum

.375 Winchester

.375 H & H Magnum

.378 Weatherby Magnum

.38/40 Winchester

.44/40 Winchester

.444 Marlin

.44 Remington Magnum

.45/70 Government
1873 Springfield

.458 Winchester Magnum

.460 Weatherby Magnum

PISTOL CARTRIDGES

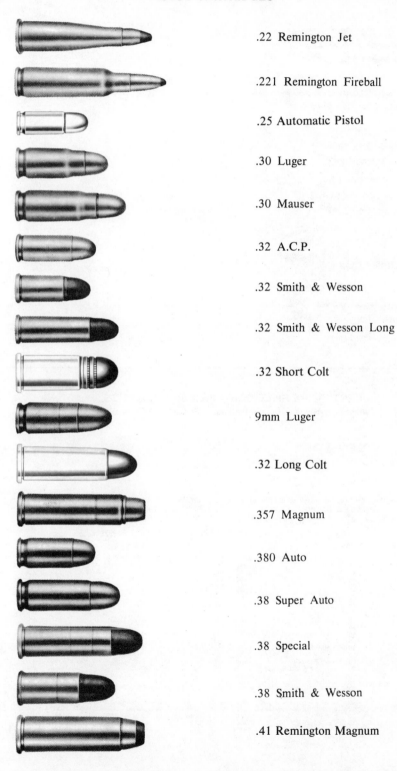

.22 Remington Jet

.221 Remington Fireball

.25 Automatic Pistol

.30 Luger

.30 Mauser

.32 A.C.P.

.32 Smith & Wesson

.32 Smith & Wesson Long

.32 Short Colt

9mm Luger

.32 Long Colt

.357 Magnum

.380 Auto

.38 Super Auto

.38 Special

.38 Smith & Wesson

.41 Remington Magnum

PISTOL CARTRIDGES (Continued)

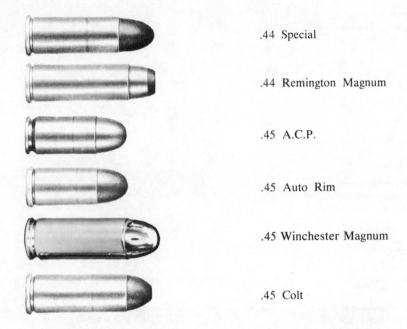

.44 Special

.44 Remington Magnum

.45 A.C.P.

.45 Auto Rim

.45 Winchester Magnum

.45 Colt

CENTERFIRE RIFLE CARTRIDGES—BALLISTICS
Winchester-Western, Remington-Peters, Federal and Speer-DWM

Chart from 1980 *Gun Digest* © 1979 DBI Books, Inc.
Used with permission.

Most of these centerfire loads are available from Winchester-Western and Remington-Peters. Loads available from only one source are marked by a letter, thus: Winchester (a); Western (b); Remington (c); Peters (d); Federal

Cartridge	Bullet Wt. Grs.	Bullet Type	Velocity (fps) Muzzle	100 yds.	200 yds.	300 yds.	Energy (ft. lbs.) Muzzle	100 yds.	200 yds.	300 yds.	Mid-Range Trajectory 100 yds.	200 yds.	300 yds.
17 Remington	25	HP, PL	4020	3290	2630	2060	900	600	380	230	—	1.5	7.3
218 Bee	46	HP	2860	2160	1610	1200	835	475	265	145	0.7	3.8	11.5
22 Hornet	45	PSP	2690	2030	1510	1150	720	410	230	130	0.8	4.3	13.0
22 Hornet (c, d)	45	HP	2690	2030	1510	1150	720	410	230	130	0.8	4.3	13.0
22 Hornet	46	HP	2690	2030	1510	1150	740	420	235	135	0.8	4.3	13.0
222 Remington (a, e)	50	PSP, MC, PL†	3200	2660	2170	1750	1140	785	520	340	0.5	2.5	7.0
222 Remington Magnum (c, d)	55	SP, PL†	3300	2800	2340	1930	1330	955	670	455	0.5	2.3	6.1
222 Remington Magnum (c, d)	55	HP, PL†	3300	2830	2400	2010	1330	975	700	490	0.5	2.3	6.1
223 Remington (a, c, d, e)	55	SP, PL†, PSP	3300	2800	2340	1930	1330	955	670	455	0.5	2.1	5.4
223 Remington (e)	55	MCBT	3240	2880	2540	2230	1280	1010	790	610	0.7	1.9	9.9
22-250 Remington (e)	55	PSP	3810	3270	2770	2320	1770	1300	935	655	0.3	1.6	4.4
22-250 Remington (c, d)	55	HP, PL†	3810	3330	2890	2490	1770	1360	1020	760	0.4	1.7	4.3
225 Winchester (a, b)	55	PSP	3650	3140	2680	2270	1630	1200	870	630	0.4	1.8	4.8
243 Winchester (e)	80	PSP, PL†	3420	3020	2620	2310	2080	1620	1220	950	0.4	1.8	4.7
243 Winchester (c, d)	80	HP, PL†	3450	3050	2675	2330	2115	1650	1270	965	0.4	1.9	4.9
243 Winchester (e)	100	PP, CL, PSP	2960	2700	2450	2220	2090	1730	1430	1190	0.5	2.2	5.5
6mm Remington (a, c, d)	80	PSP, HP, PL†	3450	3130	2750	2400	2220	1740	1340	1018	0.4	1.8	4.7
6mm Remington (a, c, d)	100	PCL, PSP	3190	2920	2660	2420	2260	1890	1570	1300	0.5	2.1	5.1
6mm Remington (e)	80	SP	3450	3130	2756	2400	2220	1740	1340	1018	—	—	—
6mm Remington (e)	100	SP	3190	2920	2660	2420	2260	1890	1570	1300	—	—	—
25-06 Remington (c, d)	87	HP	3500	3070	2680	2310	2370	1820	1390	1030	0.4	2.0	5.1
25-06 Remington (e)	90	HP	3440	3040	2680	2340	2360	1850	1440	1100	0.6	1.7	8.8
25-06 Remington (e)	117	SP	3060	2790	2530	2280	2430	2020	1660	1360	0.8	2.0	10.3
25-06 Remington (c, d)	120	PSP, CL	3120	2850	2600	2360	2590	2160	1800	1480	0.5	2.2	5.6
25-20 Winchester	86	L, Lu	1460	1180	1030	940	405	265	200	170	2.6	12.5	32.0
25-20 Winchester (c)	86	SP	1460	1180	1030	940	405	265	200	170	2.6	12.5	32.0

CENTERFIRE RIFLE CARTRIDGES — BALLISTICS (continued)

Cartridge	Wt. Grs.	Type	Velocity (fps) Muzzle	100 yds.	200 yds.	300 yds.	Energy (ft. lbs.) Muzzle	100 yds.	200 yds.	300 yds.	Mid-Range Trajectory 100 yds.	200 yds.	300 yds.
25-35 Winchester	117	SP, CL	2300	1910	1600	1340	1370	945	665	465	1.0	4.6	12.5
250 Savage (a, b)	87	PSP, SP	3030	2660	2330	2060	1770	1370	1050	820	0.6	2.5	6.4
250 Savage	100	ST, CL, PSP	2820	2460	2140	1870	1760	1340	1020	775	0.6	2.9	7.4
256 Winchester Magnum (b)	60	HP	2800	2070	1570	1220	1040	570	330	200	0.8	4.0	12.0
257 Roberts (a, b)	87	PSP	3200	2840	2500	2190	1980	1560	1210	925	0.5	2.2	5.7
257 Roberts (a, b)	100	ST, CL	2900	2540	2210	1920	1870	1430	1080	820	0.6	2.7	7.0
257 Roberts	117	PP, CL	2650	2280	1950	1690	1820	1350	985	740	0.7	3.4	8.8
6.5mm Remington Magnum (c)	120	PSP, CL	3030	2750	2480	2230	2450	2010	1640	1330	0.5	2.3	5.7
264 Winchester Magnum	100	PSP, CL	3700	3260	2880	2550	3040	2360	1840	1440	0.4	1.6	4.2
264 Winchester Magnum	140	PP, CL	3200	2940	2700	2480	3180	2690	2270	1910	0.5	2.0	4.9
270 Winchester	100	PSP	3480	3070	2690	2340	2690	2090	1600	1215	0.4	1.8	4.8
270 Winchester (e)	130	PP, PSP	3110	2850	2600	2400	2850	2390	2000	1660	0.5	2.1	5.3
270 Winchester	130	ST, CL, BP, PP	3140	2850	2580	2320	2840	2340	1920	1550	0.5	2.1	5.3
270 Winchester (c, d)	150	CL	2800	2440	2140	1870	2610	1980	1520	1160	0.6	2.9	7.6
270 Winchester (a, b, e)	150	PP, SP	2900	2550	2230	1930	2800	2290	1890	1550	0.6	2.5	6.3
280 Remington (c, d)	150	PCL	2900	2670	2450	2220	2800	2370	2000	1640	0.6	2.5	6.1
280 Remington (c, d)	165	CL	2820	2510	2220	1970	2910	2310	1810	1420	0.6	2.8	7.2
7mm Exp. Rem. (c)	150	PSP, CL	2970	2699	2444	2203	2937	2426	1989	1616	1.9	0.0	7.8
284 Winchester (a, b)	125	PP	3200	2880	2590	2310	2840	2300	1860	1480	0.5	2.1	5.3
284 Winchester (a, b)	150	PP	2900	2630	2380	2160	2800	2300	1890	1550	0.6	2.5	6.3
7mm Mauser (e)	139	SP	2660	2400	2150	1910	2280	1850	1490	1190	0.7	3.0	7.8
7mm Mauser	175	SP	2470	2170	1880	1630	2410	1830	1400	1100	0.8	3.7	9.5
7mm Remington Magnum	125	CL	3430	3080	2750	2450	3260	2630	2100	1660	0.6	1.8	4.7
7mm Remington Magnum	150	PP, CL, SP	3110	2830	2570	2320	3260	2940	2430	1990	0.4	2.0	4.9
7mm Remington Magnum	175	SP	2860	2650	2440	2220	3660	2870	2240	1750	0.5	2.4	6.1
7mm Remington Magnum (c, d)	175	PCL	3070	2860	2660	2460	3170	2740	2350	2350	0.5	2.1	5.2
30 Carbine	110	HSP, SP	1990	1570	1240	1040	950	575	370	260	1.4	7.5	21.7
30 Carbine (e)	110	MC	1990	1600	1280	1070	970	620	400	280	0.0	13.0	47.4
30-30 Winchester (e)	125	HP	2570	2090	1660	1320	1830	1210	770	480	0.0	7.3	28.1
30-30 Winchester (c, d)	150	CL	2410	1960	1620	1360	1930	1280	875	616	0.9	4.5	12.5
30-30 Winchester	150	SP	2390	2020	1700	1430	1930	1360	960	680	0.9	4.2	11.0
30-30 Winchester (a, b)	150	PP, ST, OPE	2410	2020	1700	1430	1930	1360	960	680	0.9	4.2	11.0
30-30 Winchester	170	SP, HP, CL, ST, MC	2220	1890	1630	1410	1860	1350	1000	750	1.2	4.6	12.5
30-30 Accelerator (c)	55	PSP	3400	2693	2085	1569	1412	885	531	301	2.0	0.0	10.2
30 Remington	170	ST, CL	2120	1820	1560	1350	1700	1250	920	690	1.1	5.3	14.0
30-06 Accelerator (c)	55	PSP	4080	3485	2965	2502	2033	1483	1074	764	1.0	0.0	5.0
30-06 Springfield (a, b)	110	PSP	3370	2830	2350	1920	2770	1960	1350	900	0.5	2.2	6.0
30-06 Springfield (e)	125	PSP	3140	2780	2450	2140	2190	1710	1710	1340	0.5	2.2	5.6
30-06 Springfield (c, d)	150	BP	2970	2710	2470	2240	2930	2440	2030	1670	0.5	2.4	6.0
30-06 Springfield (e)	150	SP	2910	2620	2340	2080	2930	2280	1760	1340	0.6	2.5	6.5
30-06 Springfield (c,e)	150	ST, PCL, PSP	2970	2670	2400	2130	2930	2370	1920	1510	0.6	2.4	6.1
30-06 Springfield	165	PSP, CL	2800	2534	2283	2047	2872	2352	1909	1534	2.3	0.0	9.0
30-06 Springfield	180	PP, CL, PSP	2700	2330	2010	1740	2910	2170	1610	1210	0.7	3.1	8.3
30-06 Springfield	180	ST, BP, PCL, SP	2700	2470	2250	2040	2910	2440	2020	1660	0.7	2.9	7.0
30-06 Springfield (e)	200	SPBT	2550	2400	2260	2120	2890	2560	2270	2000	0.0	6.0	18.8
30-06 Springfield	220	PP, CL	2410	2120	1870	1670	2830	2190	1710	1360	0.8	3.9	9.8
30-06 Springfield (a, b)	220	ST	2410	2180	1980	1790	2830	2320	1910	1560	0.8	3.7	9.2
30-40 Krag	180	PP, CL	2470	2120	1830	1590	2440	1790	1340	1010	0.8	3.8	9.9
30-40 Krag	180	ST, PCL	2470	2250	2040	1850	2440	2020	1660	1370	0.8	3.5	8.5
300 Winchester Magnum (a, c, e)	150	PP, PCL	3400	3050	2730	2430	3850	3100	2480	1970	0.4	1.9	4.8
300 Winchester Magnum (a, c, e)	180	PP, PCL	3070	2850	2640	2440	3770	3250	2790	2380	0.5	2.1	5.3
300 Winchester Magnum (a, b)	220	ST	2720	2490	2270	2060	3620	3030	2520	2070	0.6	2.9	6.9
300 H&H Magnum	150	ST	3190	2870	2580	2300	3390	2740	2220	1760	0.5	2.1	5.2
300 H&H Magnum	180	ST, PCL	2920	2670	2440	2220	3400	2850	2380	1970	0.6	2.4	5.8
300 H&H Magnum	220	ST, CL	2620	2370	2150	1940	3350	2740	2260	1840	0.7	3.1	7.7
300 Savage	150	SP	2630	2350	2100	1850	2370	1840	1410	1080	0.7	3.2	8.0
300 Savage	150	ST, PCL	2670	2390	2130	1890	2370	1900	1510	1190	0.7	3.0	7.6
300 Savage	150	CL	2670	2270	1930	1660	2370	1710	1240	916	0.7	3.3	9.3
300 Savage (e)	180	SP, CL	2350	2140	1940	1720	2210	1660	1240	920	0.9	4.1	10.5
300 Savage	180	ST, PCL	2370	2160	1960	1770	2240	1860	1530	1250	0.9	3.7	9.2
303 Savage (c, d)	180	CL	2140	1810	1550	1340	1830	1310	960	715	1.1	5.4	14.0
303 Savage (a, b)	190	ST	1980	1680	1440	1250	1650	1190	875	660	1.3	6.2	15.5
303 British (e)	180	PP, CL	2540	2300	2090	1900	2580	2120	1750	1440	0.7	3.3	8.2
303 British (c, d)	215	SP	2180	1900	1660	1460	2270	1720	1310	1020	1.1	4.9	12.5
308 Winchester (a, b)	110	PSP	3340	2810	2340	1920	2730	1930	1340	900	0.5	2.2	6.0
308 Winchester (a, b)	125	PSP	3100	2740	2430	2160	2670	2080	1640	1300	0.5	2.3	5.9
308 Winchester (e)	150	SP	2820	2530	2260	2010	2730	2120	1630	1240	0.6	2.7	7.0
308 Winchester	150	ST, PCL	2860	2570	2300	2050	2730	2200	1760	1400	0.6	2.6	6.5
308 Winchester (e)	180	PP, CL	2610	2250	1940	1680	2720	2020	1500	1130	0.7	3.4	8.9
308 Winchester	180	ST, PCL	2610	2390	2170	1970	2720	2280	1870	1540	0.8	3.1	7.4
308 Winchester (a, b)	200	ST	2450	2210	1980	1770	2770	2170	1750	1400	0.8	3.6	9.0
32 Winchester Special (c, d, e)	170	HP, CL, SP	2250	1920	1630	1370	1960	1390	1000	750	1.0	4.8	12.5
32 Winchester Special	170	PP, ST	2280	1870	1560	1330	1960	1320	920	665	1.0	4.8	13.0
32-20 Winchester	100	SP	1290	1060	940	840	370	250	195	155	3.3	15.5	38.0
32-20 Winchester	100	SP, L, Lu	1290	1060	940	840	370	250	195	155	3.3	15.5	38.0
8mm Mauser	170	PP, CL	2510	2110	1740	1430	2380	1670	1140	770	0.8	7.0	25.7
8mm Remington Magnum	185	PSP	3080	2761	2464	2186	3896	3132	2494	1963	1.8	0.0	7.6
8mm Remington Magnum	220	PSP	2830	2581	2346	2123	3912	3255	2688	2201	2.2	0.0	8.5
338 Winchester Magnum (a, b)	260	PP	3000	2690	2410	2170	4000	3210	2580	2090	0.5	2.4	6.0
338 Winchester Magnum (a, b)	250	ST	2700	2430	2180	1940	4050	3280	2640	2090	0.7	3.0	7.4
35 Remington (c, d)	150	CL	2400	1960	1580	1280	1920	1280	835	545	0.9	4.6	13.0
35 Remington (c, d)	200	PP, ST, CL	2080	1700	1380	1140	1920	1280	860	605	1.2	6.0	16.5
350 Remington Magnum (c, d)	200	PCL	2710	2410	2130	1870	3260	2570	2000	1550	0.7	3.0	7.7
351 Winchester Self-Loading	180	SP	1850	1560	1310	1140	1370	975	685	520	1.5	7.8	21.5
358 Winchester (a, b)	200	ST	2530	2210	1910	1640	2840	2160	1610	1190	0.8	3.6	9.4
375 Big Bore (a)	200	FNPP	2200	1841	1526	—	2150	1506	1034	—	1.1	5.2	—
375 Big Bore (a)	250	FNPP	1900	1647	1424	—	2005	1506	1126	—	1.4	6.4	—
375 H&H Magnum	270	PP, SP	2740	2460	2210	1990	4500	3620	2920	2370	0.7	2.9	7.1
375 H&H Magnum	300	ST	2550	2280	2040	1830	4330	3460	2770	2230	0.7	3.3	8.3
375 H&H Magnum	300	MC	2550	2180	1860	1590	4330	3160	2300	1680	0.7	3.6	9.3
38-40 Winchester	180	SP	1330	1070	960	850	705	455	370	290	3.2	15.0	36.5
44 Magnum (c, d)	240	SP	1750	1360	1110	980	1630	985	655	510	1.6	8.4	—
44 Magnum (b, e)	240	HSP	1760	1360	1090	950	630	970	635	480	1.8	9.4	26.0
444 Marlin (c)	240	SP	2400	1845	1410	1125	3070	1815	1060	675	1.0	5.6	14.5
44-40 Winchester	200	SP	1310	1050	940	830	760	490	390	305	3.3	15.0	36.5
45-70 Government (e)	300	HSP	1810	1410	1120	970	2180	1320	840	630	2.5	22.0	69.0
45-70 Government	405	SP	1320	1160	1050	990	1570	1210	990	880	2.9	13.0	32.5
458 Winchester Magnum	500	MC	2130	1910	1700	1520	5040	4050	3210	2570	1.1	4.8	12.0
458 Winchester Magnum	510	SP	2130	1840	1600	1400	5140	3830	2900	2220	1.1	5.1	13.5

Hollow Point SP—Soft Point PSP—Pointed Soft Point PP—Power Point L—Lead Lu—Lubaloy ST—Silvertip HSP—Hollow Soft Point MC—Metal Case BT—Boat Tail MAT—Match BP—Bronze Point CL—Core Lokt PCL—Pointed Core Lokt OPE—Open Point Expanding FN—Flat Nose †PL—Power-Lokt (slightly higher price).

WEATHERBY MAGNUM CARTRIDGES — BALLISTICS

Cartridge	Bullet Wt. Grs.	Type	Velocity (fps) Muzzle	100 yds.	200 yds.	300 yds.	Energy (ft. lbs.) Muzzle	100	200	300	Mid-Range Trajectory 100 yds.	200 yds.	300 yds.
224 Weatherby Magnum	50	PE	3750	3263	2814	2402	1562	1182	879	640	0.3	1.6	4.3
224 Weatherby Magnum	55	PE	3650	3214	2808	2433	1627	1262	963	723	0.3	1.7	4.4
240 Weatherby Magnum	70	PE	3850	3424	3025	2654	2305	1823	1423	1095	0.3	1.4	3.8
240 Weatherby Magnum	85	Nosler	3500	3106	2739	2398	2313	1821	1416	1085	0.4	1.8	4.6
240 Weatherby Magnum	87	PE	3500	3165	2848	2550	2367	1935	1567	1256	0.3	1.7	4.4
240 Weatherby Magnum	100	PE	3395	3115	2848	2594	2560	2155	1802	1495	0.4	1.8	4.4
240 Weatherby Magnum	100	Nosler	3395	3068	2758	2468	2560	2090	1690	1353	0.4	1.8	4.6
257 Weatherby Magnum	87	PE	3825	3470	3135	2818	2827	2327	1900	1535	0.3	1.4	3.6
257 Weatherby Magnum	100	PE	3555	3256	2971	2700	2807	2355	1960	1619	0.3	1.6	4.0
257 Weatherby Magnum	100	Nosler	3555	3242	2945	2663	2807	2335	1926	1575	0.4	1.6	4.1
257 Weatherby Magnum	117	SPE	3300	2853	2443	2074	2830	2115	1551	1118	0.4	2.1	5.7
257 Weatherby Magnum	117	Nosler	3300	3027	2767	2520	2830	2381	1990	1650	0.4	1.9	4.7
270 Weatherby Magnum	100	PE	3760	3341	2949	2585	3140	2479	1932	1484	0.3	1.5	4.0
270 Weatherby Magnum	130	PE	3375	3110	2856	2615	3289	2793	2355	1974	0.4	1.8	4.4
270 Weatherby Magnum	130	Nosler	3375	3113	2862	2622	3289	2798	2365	1988	0.4	1.8	4.4
270 Weatherby Magnum	150	PE	3245	3012	2789	2575	3508	3022	2592	2209	0.4	1.9	4.7
270 Weatherby Magnum	150	Nosler	3245	3022	2809	2604	3508	3043	2629	2259	0.4	1.9	4.6
7mm Weatherby Magnum	139	PE	3300	3037	2786	2546	3362	2848	2396	2001	0.4	1.8	4.6
7mm Weatherby Magnum	140	Nosler	3300	3047	2806	2575	3386	2887	2448	2062	0.4	1.8	4.6
7mm Weatherby Magnum	154	PE	3160	2928	2706	2494	3415	2932	2504	2127	0.4	2.0	4.9
7mm Weatherby Magnum	160	Nosler	3150	2935	2727	2528	3526	3061	2643	2271	0.5	2.0	4.9
7mm Weatherby Magnum	175	RN	3070	2714	2383	2082	3663	2863	2207	1685	0.5	2.4	6.0
7mm Weatherby Magnum	175	Nosler	3070	2845	2630	2425	3663	3146	2689	2286	0.5	2.1	5.2
300 Weatherby Magnum	110	PE	3900	3465	3057	2677	3716	2933	2283	1750	0.3	1.4	3.7
300 Weatherby Magnum	150	PE	3545	3248	2965	2696	4187	3509	2929	2422	0.3	1.6	4.0
300 Weatherby Magnum	150	Nosler	3545	3191	2857	2544	4187	3392	2719	2156	0.4	1.7	4.3
300 Weatherby Magnum	180	PE	3245	3010	2785	2569	4210	3622	3100	2639	0.4	1.9	4.6
300 Weatherby Magnum	180	Nosler	3245	2964	2696	2444	4210	3512	2906	2388	0.5	2.0	5.0
300 Weatherby Magnum	200	Nosler	3000	2740	2494	2262	3998	3335	2763	2273	0.5	2.3	5.7
300 Weatherby Magnum	220	SPE	2905	2578	2276	2000	4123	3248	2531	1955	0.5	2.6	6.7
340 Weatherby Magnum	200	PE	3210	2947	2696	2458	4577	3857	3228	2683	0.4	2.0	4.9
340 Weatherby Magnum	210	Nosler	3180	2927	2686	2457	4717	3996	3365	2816	0.5	2.0	5.0
340 Weatherby Magnum	250	SPE	2850	2516	2209	1929	4510	3515	2710	2066	0.6	2.7	7.1
340 Weatherby Magnum	250	Nosler	2850	2563	2296	2049	4510	3648	2927	2331	0.6	2.6	6.7
378 Weatherby Magnum	270	SPE	3180	2796	2440	2117	6064	4688	3570	2688	0.5	2.2	5.8
378 Weatherby Magnum	270	Nosler	3180	2840	2515	2220	6064	4837	3793	2955	0.5	2.2	5.5
378 Weatherby Magnum	300	SPE	2925	2564	2234	1935	5700	4380	3325	2495	0.6	2.7	6.9
378 Weatherby Magnum	300	Nosler	2925	2620	2340	2080	5700	4574	3649	2883	0.6	2.5	6.4
460 Weatherby Magnum	500	RN	2700	2395	2115	1858	8095	6370	4968	3834	0.7	3.0	7.8
460 Weatherby Magnum	500	FMJ	2700	2416	2154	1912	8095	6482	5153	4060	0.7	3.0	7.6

Trajectory is given from scope height. Velocities chronographed using 26" bbls. Available with Nosler bullets.
SPE—Semi-Pointed Expanding   RN—Round Nose   PE—Pointed Expanding   FMJ—Full Metal Jacket.

RIMFIRE CARTRIDGES — BALLISTICS

Remington-Peters, Winchester-Western, Federal & Omark/CCI

All loads available from all manufacturers except as indicated: R-P (a); W-W (b); Fed. (c); CCI (d).

CARTRIDGE	WT. GRS.	BULLET TYPE	VELOCITY FT. PER SEC. MUZZLE	100 YDS.	ENERGY FT. LBS. MUZZLE	100 YDS.	MID-RANGE TRAJECTORY 100 YDS.	HANDGUN BARREL LENGTH	BALLISTICS M.V. F.P.S.	M.E. F.P.
22 Short T22 (a, b)	29	C. L*	1045	810	70	42	5.6	6"	865	48
22 Short Hi-Vel. (c)	29	C. L	1125	920	81	54	4.3	6"	1035	69
22 Short HP Hi-Vel. (a, b, c)	27	C.L	1155	920	80	51	4.2	—	—	—
22 Short Std. Vel. (a, b, c)	29	L*	1045	870	70	49	8.7	—	1045	870
22 Short (a)	15	D	1710	—	97	—	—	—	—	—
22 Stinger	32	C. HP	1686	1047	202	78	2.6i	—	—	—
22 Xpediter	29	HP	1680	—	182	—	2.5	—	—	—
22 Long Rifle Yellow Jacket	33	HVTCHP	1500	1075	165	85	2.8	—	1500	165
22 Long Hi-Vel. (c)	29	C. L	1045	870	70	49	8.7	—	1045	70
22 Long Rifle T22 (a, b)†¹	40	L*	1145	975	116	84	4.0	6"	950	80
22 Long Rifle (b)†²	40	L*	1120	950	111	80	4.2	—	—	—
22 Long Rifle (b)†³	40	L*	—	—	—	—	—	6¾"	1060	100
22 Long Rifle (d)†⁴	40	—	—	—	—	—	—	—	—	—
22 Long Rifle Hi-Vel.	40	C	1165	980	121	84	4.0	—	—	—
22 Long Rifle Hi-Vel.	40	C.L	1285	1025	147	93	3.4	6"	1125	112
22 Long Rifle HP Hi-Vel. (b, d)	37	C.L	131	1020	142	85	3.4	—	1255	140
22 Long Rifle HP Hi-Vel. (a, c)	38	C. HP	1280	1020	138	88	6.1	—	1280	138
22 Long Rifle (b, c)	No.	12 Shot	—	—	—	—	—	—	—	—
22 WRF (Rem. Spl.) (a, b)	45	C.L	1450	1110	210	123	—	—	—	—
22 WRF Mag. (b)	40	JHP	2000	1390	355	170	1.6	6½"	1550	213
22 WRF Mag. (b)	40	MC	2000	1390	355	170	1.6	6½"	1550	213
22 Win. Auto Inside lub. (a)	45	C.L	1055	930	111	86	—	—	—	—
5mm Rem. RFM (a)	38	PLHP	2100	1605	372	217	—	Not Available		

†—Target loads of these ballistics available in: (1) Rem. Match: (2) W-W. Super Match Mark III: (3) Super Match Mark IV Pistol Match: (4) CCI Mini-Group.
C—Copper plated   L—Lead (Wax Coated)   L*—Lead, lubricated   D—Disintegrating   MC—Metal Case   HP—Hollow Point   JHP—Jacket Hollow Point
PLHP—Power-Lokt Hollow Point

Chart from 1980 *Gun Digest* © 1979 DBI Books, Inc.
Used with permission.

CENTERFIRE HANDGUN CARTRIDGES — BALLISTICS

Winchester-Western, Remington-Peters, Norma and Federal

Most loads are available from W-W and R-P. All available Norma loads are listed. Federal cartridges are marked with an asterisk. Other loads supplied by only one source are indicated by a letter, thus: Norma (a); R-P (b); W-W

Cartridge	Bullet Gr.	Bullet Style	Muzzle Velocity	Muzzle Energy	Barrel Inches
22 Jet (b)	40	SP	2100	390	8⅜
221 Fireball (b)	50	SP	2650	780	10½
25 (6.35mm) Auto*	50	MC	810	73	2
256 Winchester Magnum (c)	60	HP	2350	735	8½
30 (7.65mm) Luger Auto	93	MC	1220	307	4½
32 S&W Blank (b,c)	No bullet		—	—	—
32 S&W Blank, BP (c)	No bullet		—	—	—
32 Short Colt	80	Lead	745	100	4
32 Long Colt IL (c)	82	Lub.	755	104	4
32 (7.65mm) Auto*	71	MC	905	129	4
32 (7.65mm) Auto Pistol (a)	77	MC	900	162	4
32 S&W	88	Lead	680	90	3
32 S&W Long	98	Lead	705	115	4
32-20 Winchester	100	Lead	1030	271	6
32-20 Winchester	100	SP	1030	271	6
357 Magnum*	110	JHP	1295	410	4
357 Magnum	110	SJHP	1295	410	4
357 Magnum*	125	JHP	1450	583	4
357 Magnum*	158	SWC	1235	535	4
357 Magnum (b)*	158	JSP	1550	845	8⅜
357 Magnum	158	MP	1410	695	8⅜
357 Magnum	158	Lead	1410	696	8⅜
357 Magnum	158	JHP	1450	735	8⅜
9mm Luger (c)	95	JSP	1355	387	4
9mm Luger (c)	100	JHP	1320	387	4
9mm Luger (c)	115	FMC	1155	341	4
9mm Luger (c)	115	STHP	1255	383	4
9mm Luger*	115	JHP	1165	349	4
9mm Luger*	123	MC	1120	345	4
9mm Winchester Magnum (c)	115	FMC	1475	556	5
38 S&W Blank	No bullet		—	—	—
38 Smith & Wesson	146	Lead	685	150	4
38 S&W (c)	146	Lead	730	172	4
38 Special Blank	No bullet		—	—	—
38 Special, IL +P (c)	150	Lub.	1060	375	6
38 Special IL +P (c)	150	MP	1060	375	6
38 Special	158	Lead	855	256	6
38 Special	200	Lead	730	236	6
38 Special	158	MP	855	256	6
38 Special (b)	125	SJHP	Not available		
38 Special	158	SJHP	Not available		
38 Special WC (b)	148	Lead	770	195	6
38 Special Match, IL (c)	148	Lead	770	195	6
38 Special Match, IL (b, c)	158	Lead	855	256	6
38 Special (a)	158	RN	900	320	6
38 Special*	158	SWC	755	200	4
38 Special Match*	148	WC	710	166	4
38 Special +P (b)	110	SJHP	1020	254	4
38 Special +P	125	JSP	945	248	4
38 Special +P	158	LRN	915	294	4
38 Special +P (b)	158	LHP	915	294	4
38 Special +P*	158	SWC	915	294	4
38 Special +P*	158	SWCHP	915	294	4
38 Special +P*	110	JHP	1020	254	4
38 Special +P*	125	JHP	945	248	4
38 Short Colt	125	Lead	730	150	6
38 Short Colt, Greased (c)	130	Lub.	730	155	6
38 Long Colt	150	Lead	730	175	6
38 Super Auto +P (b)	130	MC	1280	475	5
38 Super Auto +P (b)	115	JHP	1300	431	5
38 Auto, for Colt 38 Super (c)	125	JHP	1280	475	5
38 Auto	130	MC	1040	312	4½
38 Auto +P	130	FMC	1280	475	5
380 Auto*	95	MC	955	192	3¾
380 Auto (b)	88	JHP	990	191	4
380 Auto*	90	JHP	1000	200	3¾
38-40 Winchester	180	SP	975	380	5
41 Remington Magnum	210	Lead	1050	515	8¾
41 Remington Magnum	210	SP	1500	1050	8¾
44 S&W Special	246	Lead	755	311	6½
44 Remington Magnum*	180	JHP	1610	1045	4
44 Remington Magnum (b)	240	SP	1470	1150	6½
44 Remington Magnum	240	Lead	1470	1150	6½
44 Remington Magnum	240	SJHP	1180	741	4
44-40 Winchester	200	SP	975	420	7½
45 Colt*	225	SWCHP	900	405	5½
45 Colt	250	Lead	860	410	5½
45 Colt, IL (c)	255	Lub., L	860	410	5½
45 Auto (c)	185	STHP	1000	411	5
45 Auto	230	MC	850	369	5
45 ACP	230	JHP	850	370	5
45 Auto WC*	185	MC	775	245	5
45 Auto*	185	JHP	950	370	5
45 Auto MC (b)	230	MC	850	369	5
45 Auto Match (c)	185	MC	775	247	5
45 Auto Match*	230	MC	850	370	5
45 Winchester Magnum (c)	230	FMC	1400	1001	5
45 Auto Rim (b)	230	Lead	810	335	5½

IL—Inside Lub. JSP—Jacketed Soft Point WC—Wad Cutter
RN—Round Nose HP—Hollow Point Lub—Lubricated
MC—Metal Case SP—Soft Point MP—Metal Point
LGC—Lead, Gas Check JHP—Jacketed Hollow Point
SWC—Semi Wad Cutter SJHP—Semi Jacketed Hollow Point

SHOTSHELL LOADS

Winchester-Western, Remington-Peters, Federal

In certain loadings one manufacturer may offer fewer or more shot sizes than another, but in general all makers offer equivalent loadings. Sources are indicated by letters, thus: W-W (a); R-P (b); Fed.

GAUGE	Length Shell Ins.	Powder Equiv. Drams	Shot Ozs.	Shot Size
MAGNUM LOADS				
10 (a', b)	3½	Max	2	2
12 (a, b, c)	3	4	1⅞	BB, 2, 4
12 (a', b)	3	4¼	1⅝	2, 4, 6
12 (a)	3	Max	1⅜	2
12 (a', b)	2¾	Max	1½	2, 4, 5, 6
16 (a, b, c)	2¾	3¼	1¼	2, 4, 6
20 (a, b, c)	3	3	1¼	2, 4, 6, 7½
20 (a')	3	Max	1⅛	4, 6, 7½
20 (a', b, c)	2¾	2¾	1⅛	4, 6, 7½
LONG RANGE LOADS				
10 (a, b)	2⅞	Max	1⅝	4
12 (a', b, c)	2¾	3¾	1¼	BB, 2, 4, 5, 6, 7½, 8, 9
16 (a, b, c)	2¾	3¼	1⅛	4, 5, 6, 7½, 9
20 (a', b, c)	2¾	2¾	1	4, 5, 6, 7½, 8, 9
28 (a, b)	2¾	Max	¾	6, 7½
28 (c)	2¾	2¼	⅞	4, 6, 7½, 9
410 (b)	2½	Max	½	6, 7½
410 (b)	3	Max	¹¹⁄₁₆	4, 5, 6, 7½, 8
FIELD LOADS				
12 (a, b, c)	2¾	3¼	1¼	7½, 8, 9
12 (a, b, c)	2¾	3¼	1⅛	4, 5, 6, 7½, 8, 9
12 (a, b, c)	2¾	3	1	4, 5, 6, 8
16 (a, b, c)	2¾	2¾	1⅛	4, 5, 6, 7½, 8
16 (a, b, c)	2¾	2½	1	6, 8
20 (a, b, c)	2¾	2½	1	4, 5, 6, 7½, 8, 9
20 (a, b, c)	2¾	2½	⅞	6, 8
SCATTER LOADS				
12 (b)	2¾	3	1⅛	8
TARGET LOADS				
12 (a, b, c)	2¾	3	1⅛	7½, 8, 9
12 (a, b, c)	2¾	2¾	1⅛	7½, 8, 9
16 (a, b, c)	2¾	2¾	1⅛	8
20 (a, b, c)	2¾	2½	⅞	9
28 (a, c)	2¾	2	¾	9
410 (a, b, c)	2½	Max	½	9
SKEET & TRAP				
12 (a, b, c)	2¾	3	1⅛	7½, 8, 9
12 (a, b, c)	2¾	2¾	1⅛	7½, 8, 9
16 (a, b)	2¾	2½	1	9
16 (c)	2¾	2¾	1⅛	8
20 (a, b, c)	2¾	2½	⅞	9
BUCKSHOT				
10 (c)	3½	Sup. Mag.	—	4 Buck—54 pellets
12 (a, b, c)	3 Mag.	4½	—	00 Buck—15 pellets
12 (a, b, c)	3 Mag.	4½	—	4 Buck—41 pellets
12 (b)	2¾ Mag.	4	—	1 Buck—20 pellets
12 (a, b, c)	2¾ Mag.	4	—	00 Buck—12 pellets
12 (a, b, c)	2¾	Max	—	00 Buck— 9 pellets
12 (a, b, c)	2¾	3¾	—	0 Buck—12 pellets
12 (a, b, c)	2¾	Max	—	1 Buck—16 pellets
12 (a, b, c)	2¾	Max	—	4 Buck—27 pellets
16 (a, b, c)	2¾	3	—	1 Buck—12 pellets
20 (a, b, c)	2¾	Max	—	3 Buck—20 pellets
RIFLED SLUGS				
12 (a, b, c)	2¾	3¾	⅞	Slug 5-pack
16 (a, b, c)	2¾	3	⅘	Slug
20 (a, b, c)	2¾	Max	⅝	Slug
410 (a, b, c)	2½	Max	⅕	Slug
STEEL SHOT LOADS				
12 (c)	3	Max	1⅜	BB, 1, 2, 4
12 (c)	2¾	3¾	1⅛	1, 2, 4
12 (a, c)	2¾	Max	1¼	1, 2, 4
12 (a)	3	Max	1½	1, 2, 4
12 (b)	3	Max	1¼	1, 2, 4
12 (b)	2¾	Max	1⅛	1, 2, 4

W-W 410, 28 and 10-ga. Magnum shells available in paper cases only, as are their scatter and target loads; their skeet and trap loads come in both plastic and paper.

R-P shells are all of plastic with Power Piston wads except: 12 ga. scatter loads have Post Wad: all 10 ga., 410-3" and rifled slug loads have standard wad columns.

Federal magnum range, buckshot, slug and all 410 loads are made in plastic only. Field loads are available in both paper and plastic.

– These loads available from W-W with Lubaloy shot at higher price.

Chart from 1980 *Gun Digest* © 1979 DBI Books, Inc.
Used with permission.

CIL Ballistics

BALLISTICS

KKSP—'Kling-Kor' Soft Point
PSP—Pointed Soft Point
SP—Soft Point
CPE—Copper Point Expanding

MC—Metal Cased (Hard Point)
PNEU—Pneumatic
HP—Hollow Point
ST—'Sabretip'

DESCRIPTION	Bullet Wt. Grains	Type	Velocity in Feet per Second Muzzle	100 Yds.	200 Yds.	300 Yds.	400 Yds.	500 Yds.	Energy in Foot Pounds Muzzle	100 Yds.	200 Yds.	300 Yds.	400 Yds.	500 Yds.
22 HORNET	45	PSP	2690	2030	1510	1150	—	—	720	410	230	130	—	—
22 SAVAGE	70	PSP	2800	2440	2110	1840	—	—	1220	925	690	525	—	—
222 REMINGTON	50	PSP	3200	2600	2170	1750	—	—	1140	785	520	340	—	—
243 WINCHESTER	75	PSP	3500	3070	2660	2290	1960	1670	2040	1570	1180	875	640	465
243 WINCHESTER	100	PSP	3070	2790	2540	2320	2120	1940	2090	1730	1430	1190	995	835
244 REMINGTON	75	PSP	3500	3070	2660	2290	1960	1670	2040	1570	1180	875	640	465
6.5 x 53 MM MAN.-SCH.	160	SP	2160	1950	1750	1570	—	—	1660	1350	1090	875	—	—
6.5 x 55 MM	160	SP	2420	2190	1960	1760	1580	1420	2080	1700	1360	1110	885	715
25-20 WINCHESTER	86	SP	1460	1180	1030	940	—	—	405	265	200	170	—	—
25-35 WINCHESTER	117	SP	2300	1910	1600	1340	—	—	1370	945	665	465	—	—
250 SAVAGE	100	PSP	2820	2460	2140	1870	—	—	1760	1340	1020	775	—	—
257 ROBERTS	117	PSP	2650	2280	1950	1690	—	—	1820	1350	985	740	—	—
270 WINCHESTER	100	PSP	3480	3070	2690	2340	2010	1700	2690	2090	1600	1215	890	640
270 WINCHESTER	130	PSP	3140	2850	2580	2320	2090	1860	2840	2340	1920	1550	1260	1000
270 WINCHESTER	160	KKSP	2800	2530	2280	2050	1840	—	2790	2270	1850	1490	1200	—
7 x 57 MM MAUSER	139	PSP	2800	2500	2240	1990	1770	1580	2420	1930	1550	1220	965	770
7 x 57 MM MAUSER	160	KKSP	2650	2330	2040	1780	1550	1350	2500	1930	1480	1130	855	645
7 MM REMINGTON MAGNUM	175	SP	3070	2720	2400	2120	1870	1640	3660	2870	2240	1750	1360	1040
30-30 WINCHESTER	150	PNEU	2410	2020	1700	1430	—	—	1930	1360	960	680	—	—
30-30 WINCHESTER	170	KKSP	2220	1890	1630	1410	—	—	1860	1350	1000	750	—	—
30-30 WINCHESTER	170	ST	2220	1890	1630	1410	—	—	1860	1350	1000	750	—	—
30-30 WINCHESTER	170	MC	2220	1890	1630	1410	—	—	1860	1350	1000	750	—	—
30-30 WINCHESTER	150	ST	2410	2020	1700	1430	—	—	1930	1360	960	680	—	—
30 REMINGTON	170	KKSP	2120	1820	1560	1350	—	—	1700	1250	920	690	—	—
30-40 KRAG	180	KKSP	2470	2120	1830	1590	1400	—	2440	1790	1340	1010	785	—
30-06 SPRINGFIELD	130	HP	3150	2730	2470	2170	1920	1690	2870	2160	1770	1360	1060	820
30-06 SPRINGFIELD	150	PSP	2970	2670	2400	2130	1890	1670	2930	2370	1920	1510	1190	930
30-06 SPRINGFIELD	150	ST	2970	2670	2400	2130	1890	1670	2930	2370	1920	1510	1190	930
30-06 SPRINGFIELD	180	KKSP	2700	2330	2010	1740	1520	—	2910	2170	1610	1210	920	—
30-06 SPRINGFIELD	180	CPE	2700	2480	2280	2080	1900	1730	2910	2460	2080	1730	1440	1190
30-06 SPRINGFIELD	180	ST	2700	2470	2250	2040	1850	1670	2910	2440	2020	1660	1370	1110
30-06 SPRINGFIELD	220	KKSP	2410	2120	1870	1670	1480	—	2830	2190	1710	1360	1070	—
300 WINCHESTER-MAGNUM	180	ST	3070	2850	2640	2440	2250	2060	3770	3250	2790	2380	2020	1700
300 HOLLAND & HOLLAND MAGNUM	180	PSP	2920	2670	2440	2220	2020	1830	3400	2850	2380	1970	1630	1340
300 SAVAGE	150	PSP	2670	2390	2130	1890	1660	—	2370	1900	1510	1190	915	—
300 SAVAGE	150	ST	2670	2390	2130	1890	1660	—	2370	1900	1510	1190	915	—
300 SAVAGE	180	KKSP	2370	2040	1760	1520	1340	—	2240	1660	1240	920	715	—
300 SAVAGE	180	ST	2370	2160	1960	1770	1600	—	2240	1860	1530	1250	1020	—
303 SAVAGE	190	KKSP	1980	1680	1440	1250	—	—	1650	1190	875	660	—	—
303 BRITISH	150	PSP	2720	2420	2150	1900	1670	1470	2460	1950	1540	1200	930	720
303 BRITISH	150	ST	2720	2420	2150	1900	1670	1470	2460	1950	1540	1200	930	720
303 BRITISH	180	KKSP	2540	2180	1860	1590	1360	—	2580	1900	1380	1010	740	—
303 BRITISH	180	CPE	2540	2330	2130	1940	1760	1600	2580	2170	1810	1500	1240	1020
303 BRITISH	180	ST	2540	2300	2090	1900	1730	1580	2580	2120	1750	1440	1200	1000
303 BRITISH	215	KKSP	2180	1900	1660	1460	1250	—	2270	1720	1310	1020	750	—
308 WINCHESTER	130	HP	2930	2590	2290	2010	1770	1560	2480	1940	1520	1170	905	700
308 WINCHESTER	150	PSP	2860	2570	2300	2050	1810	1590	2730	2200	1760	1400	1090	840
308 WINCHESTER	150	ST	2860	2570	2300	2050	1810	1590	2730	2200	1760	1400	1090	840
308 WINCHESTER	180	KKSP	2610	2240	1920	1640	1400	—	2720	2010	1470	1070	785	—
308 WINCHESTER	180	ST	2610	2390	2170	1970	1780	1600	2720	2280	1870	1540	1260	1010
308 WINCHESTER	200	KKSP	2450	2210	1980	1770	1580	1410	2670	2170	1750	1400	1110	875
8 MM MAUSER	170	PSP	2570	2300	2040	1810	1600	—	2490	2000	1570	1240	965	—
32-20 WINCHESTER	115	SP	1480	1220	1050	940	—	—	560	380	280	225	—	—
32 WINCHESTER SPECIAL	170	KKSP	2280	1920	1630	1410	—	—	1960	1390	1000	750	—	—
32 WINCHESTER SPECIAL	170	ST	2280	1920	1630	1410	—	—	1960	1390	1000	750	—	—
32 REMINGTON	170	KKSP	2120	1800	1540	1340	—	—	1700	1220	895	680	—	—
32-40 WINCHESTER	170	KKSP	1540	1340	1170	1050	—	—	895	680	515	415	—	—
35 REMINGTON	200	SP	2100	1710	1390	1160	—	—	1950	1300	865	605	—	—
351 WINCHESTER SELF-LOADING	180	SP	1850	1560	1310	1140	—	—	1370	975	685	520	—	—
358 (8.8 MM) WINCHESTER	200	KKSP	2530	2210	1910	1640	1400	—	2840	2160	1610	1190	870	—
38-40 WINCHESTER	180	SP	1330	1070	960	850	—	—	705	455	370	290	—	—
38-55 WINCHESTER	255	SP	1600	1410	1240	1110	—	—	1450	1130	880	700	—	—
43 (11 MM) MAUSER	385	LEAD	1360	1150	1030	940	—	—	1580	1130	910	750	—	—
44-40 WINCHESTER	200	SP	1310	1050	940	830	—	—	760	490	390	305	—	—
44 REMINGTON MAGNUM	240	SP	1850	1450	1150	980	—	—	1820	1120	710	510	—	—

Short Range Sighting-in—It is preferable to sight-in a rifle at the "recommended sighting" range. However, it is sometimes necessary to sight-in a rifle at a distance shorter than the "recommended sighting" range because you don't have the necessary yardage available. To do this, find from the range table at what distance the bullet will first cross the line of sight. Put up a target at this distance and from a firm rest fire

and Range Table

RANGE TABLE—Values shown in this table are based on a sight height 1½″ above line of bore. RECOMMENDED SIGHTING: ⊕ Indicates the most favourable sighting range in order to minimize the sighting problem at shorter and longer ranges. + Indicates inches high; − Indicates inches low.

First Crosses Line of Sight App. Yds.	50 Yds.	75 Yds.	100 Yds.	125 Yds.	150 Yds.	200 Yds.	250 Yds.	300 Yds.	400 Yds.	500 Yds.	Bullet Wt. Grains	Bullet Type	DESCRIPTION
29.0	—	+1.5	—	—	⊕	-4.0	—	—	—	—	45	PSP	22 HORNET
25.0	—	—	+2.0	—	—	⊕	-4.5	—	—	—	70	PSP	22 SAVAGE
30.0	—	—	+2.0	—	—	⊕	-3.5	—	—	—	50	PSP	222 REMINGTON
30.0	—	—	—	+2.5	—	—	⊕	-3.0	-15.5	-36.5	75	PSP	243 WINCHESTER
27.5	—	—	—	+3.0	—	—	⊕	-3.5	-16.5	-35.5	100	PSP	243 WINCHESTER
30.0	—	—	—	+2.5	—	—	⊕	-3.0	-15.5	-36.5	75	PSP	244 REMINGTON
25.5	—	+1.5	—	—	⊕	-4.0	—	—	—	—	160	SP	6.5 x 53 MM MAN.-SCH.
21.0	—	—	+3.5	—	—	—	-5.0	-13.0	-39.0	—	160	SP	6.5 x 55 MM
16.0	+2.0	—	⊕	-4.0	—	—	—	—	—	—	86	SP	25-20 WINCHESTER
23.0	—	+1.5	—	—	⊕	-4.5	—	—	—	—	117	SP	25-35 WINCHESTER
27.5	—	—	+2.0	—	—	⊕	-3.5	—	—	—	100	PSP	250 SAVAGE
24.0	—	—	+2.5	—	—	⊕	-4.5	—	—	—	117	PSP	257 ROBERTS
31.5	—	—	—	+2.5	—	—	⊕	-3.5	-14.5	-33.5	100	PSP	270 WINCHESTER
27.5	—	—	—	+3.0	—	—	⊕	-4.0	-16.0	-35.5	130	PSP	270 WINCHESTER
28.5	—	—	+2.0	—	—	⊕	-4.0	—	-25.0	—	160	KKSP	270 WINCHESTER
27.0	—	—	—	+4.0	—	—	⊕	-4.5	-18.5	-41.0	139	PSP	7 x 57 MM MAUSER
29.0	—	—	+2.5	—	—	⊕	-4.0	—	-28.5	—	160	KKSP	7 x 57 MM MAUSER
25.0	—	—	—	+3.5	—	—	⊕	-4.0	-18.0	-43.0	175	SP	7 MM REMINGTON MAGNUM
27.0	—	+1.5	—	—	⊕	-4.0	—	—	—	—	150	PNEU	30-30 WINCHESTER
23.0	—	+1.5	—	—	⊕	-4.5	—	—	—	—	170	KKSP	30-30 WINCHESTER
23.0	—	+1.5	—	—	⊕	-4.5	—	—	—	—	170	ST	30-30 WINCHESTER
23.0	—	+1.5	—	—	⊕	-4.5	—	—	—	—	170	MC	30-30 WINCHESTER
27.0	—	+1.5	—	—	⊕	-4.0	—	—	—	—	150	ST	30-30 WINCHESTER
20.0	—	+2.0	—	—	⊕	-5.0	—	—	—	—	170	KKSP	30 REMINGTON
21.0	—	—	+3.0	—	—	⊕	-5.5	—	-41.0	—	180	KKSP	30-30 KRAG
27.0	—	—	—	+3.0	—	—	⊕	-4.0	-19.5	-47.0	130	HP	30-06 SPRINGFIELD
25.0	—	—	—	+3.5	—	—	⊕	-4.0	-17.5	-41.0	150	PSP	30-06 SPRINGFIELD
25.0	—	—	—	+3.5	—	—	⊕	-4.0	-17.5	-41.0	150	ST	30-06 SPRINGFIELD
24.0	—	—	+2.5	—	—	⊕	-4.0	—	-32.5	—	180	KKSP	30-06 SPRINGFIELD
21.0	—	—	—	+4.0	—	—	⊕	-4.5	-20.5	-46.0	180	CPE	30-06 SPRINGFIELD
20.0	—	—	—	+4.0	—	—	⊕	-4.5	-21.0	-48.5	180	ST	30-06 SPRINGFIELD
21.0	—	—	+3.0	—	—	⊕	-5.5	—	-41.0	—	220	KKSP	30-06 SPRINGFIELD
27.5	—	—	—	+3.0	—	—	⊕	-3.5	-14.5	-32.5	180	ST	300 WINCHESTER-MAGNUM
25.0	—	—	—	+3.5	—	—	⊕	-4.0	-17.5	-39.0	180	PSP	300 HOLLAND & HOLLAND MAGNUM
26.0	—	—	+2.5	—	—	⊕	-3.5	—	-29.0	—	150	PSP	300 SAVAGE
26.0	—	—	+2.5	—	—	⊕	-3.5	—	-29.0	—	150	ST	300 SAVAGE
20.0	—	—	+3.5	—	—	⊕	-5.5	—	-43.0	—	180	KKSP	300 SAVAGE
21.5	—	—	+3.0	—	—	⊕	-5.5	—	-35.0	—	180	ST	300 SAVAGE
17.5	—	—	+3.0	—	—	⊕	-5.5	—	—	—	190	KKSP	303 SAVAGE
22.0	—	—	—	+4.5	—	—	⊕	-5.0	-23.0	-53.5	150	PSP	303 BRITISH
22.0	—	—	—	+4.5	—	—	⊕	-5.0	-23.0	-53.5	150	ST	303 BRITISH
23.0	—	—	+3.0	—	—	⊕	-5.0	—	-41.0	—	180	KKSP	303 BRITISH
19.0	—	—	—	+4.5	—	—	⊕	-5.0	-23.0	-52.5	180	CPE	303 BRITISH
17.5	—	—	—	+5.0	—	—	⊕	-5.5	-26.5	-71.0	180	ST	303 BRITISH
16.0	—	—	+4.5	—	—	⊕	-7.0	—	-54.0	—	215	KKSP	303 BRITISH
23.5	—	—	—	+3.5	—	—	⊕	-4.5	-23.5	-59.0	130	HP	308 WINCHESTER
25.0	—	—	—	+3.5	—	—	⊕	-4.5	-20.0	-47.5	150	PSP	308 WINCHESTER
25.0	—	—	—	+3.5	—	—	⊕	-4.5	-20.0	-47.5	150	ST	308 WINCHESTER
23.0	—	—	+3.0	—	—	⊕	-5.5	—	-38.0	—	180	KKSP	308 WINCHESTER
22.0	—	—	—	+4.5	—	—	⊕	-5.0	-21.5	-51.5	180	ST	308 WINCHESTER
22.0	—	—	+3.0	—	—	⊕	-5.0	-12.0	-35.0	-48.5	200	KKSP	308 WINCHESTER
22.5	—	—	+3.5	—	—	⊕	-5.5	—	-33.5	—	170	PSP	8 MM MAUSER
16.5	+2.0	—	⊕	-3.5	—	—	—	—	—	—	115	SP	32-20 WINCHESTER
23.0	—	+2.0	—	—	⊕	-4.5	—	—	—	—	170	KKSP	32 WINCHESTER SPECIAL
23.0	—	+2.0	—	—	⊕	-4.5	—	—	—	—	170	ST	32 WINCHESTER SPECIAL
20.0	—	+2.0	—	—	⊕	-5.0	—	—	—	—	170	KKSP	32 REMINGTON
21.0	+1.0	—	⊕	-2.5	—	—	—	—	—	—	170	KKSP	32-40 WINCHESTER
19.5	—	+2.5	—	—	⊕	-6.0	—	—	—	—	200	SP	35 REMINGTON
16.0	—	+3.0	—	—	⊕	-7.5	—	—	—	—	180	SP	351 WINCHESTER SELF-LOADING
20.5	—	—	+3.0	—	—	⊕	-5.0	—	-38.5	—	200	KKSP	358 (8.8 MM) WINCHESTER
14.5	+2.5	—	⊕	-4.0	—	—	—	—	—	—	180	SP	38-40 WINCHESTER
13.5	—	+4.0	—	—	⊕	-8.5	—	—	—	—	255	SP	38-55 WINCHESTER
16.0	+2.0	—	⊕	-3.5	—	—	—	—	—	—	385	LEAD	43 (11 MM) MAUSER
12.5	+3.0	—	⊕	-4.5	—	—	—	—	—	—	200	SP	44-40 WINCHESTER
13.0	—	+4.5	—	—	⊕	-8.0	—	—	—	—	240	SP	44 REMINGTON MAGNUM

a three-shot group. The centre point of the group is the "centre of impact"—the average spot where the bullets strike. Adjust sights to bring the centre of impact to the centre of the target then fire another group. If the centre of impact is on target the rifle will be sighted in at the range recommended in the range table. It is, however, desirable to fire a target at that range as soon as possible as a double check.

NORMA C.F. RIFLE CARTRIDGES — BALLISTICS

Norma ammunition loaded to standard velocity and pressure is now available with Nosler bullets in the following loads: 270 Win., 130-, 150-gr.; Super 7x61 (S&H), 160-gr.; 308 Win., 180-gr.; 30-06, 150-, 180-gr., All ballistic figures are computed from a line of sight one inch above center of bore at muzzle.

Cartridge	Bullet Wt. Grs.	Type	Velocity, feet per sec.				Energy, foot pounds				Max. height of trajectory, Inches		
			V Muzzle	V 100 yds.	V 200 yds.	V 300 yds.	E Muzzle	E 100 yds.	E 200 yds.	E 300 yds.	Tr. 100 yds.	Tr. 200 yds.	Tr. 300 yds.
220 Swift	50	SP	4111	3611	3133	2681	1877	1448	1090	799	.2	.9	3.0
222 Remington	50	SPSP, FMJ	3200	2660	2170	1750	1137	786	523	340	.0	2.0	6.2
	53	SpPSP	3117	2670	2267	1901	1142	838	604	425	.0	3.5	14.0
22-250 Remington	53	SpPSP (Match Spitzer)	3710	—	—	—	—	—	—	—	—	—	—
22 Savage Hi-Power (5.6x52R)	71	SP, FMJ	2788	2296	1886	1558	1226	831	651	383	.0	4.8	18.06
243 Winchester	100	SP, FMJ	3070	2790	2540	2320	2093	1729	1433	1195	.1	1.8	5.0
6.5 Carcano	139	PPDC	2576	2379	2192	2012	2046	1745	1481	1249	.0	4.7	16.6
	156	SPRN	2000	1810	1640	1485	1386	1135	932	764		Not Available	
6.5 Japanese	139	SPSPBT	2428	2280	2130	1990	1820	1605	1401	1223	.3	2.8	7.7
	156	SPRN	2067	1871	1692	1529	1481	1213	992	810	.6	4.4	11.9
6.5x55	77	SPSP	2725	2362	2030	1811	1271	956	706	562	.0	4.8	18.1
	139	PPDC	2789	2630	2470	2320	2402	2136	1883	1662	.1	2.0	5.6
	156	SPSP	2493	2271	2062	1867	2153	1787	1473	1208	.3	2.9	7.9
270 Winchester	130	SPSPBT	3140	2884	2639	2404	2847	2401	2011	1669	.0	1.6	4.7
	150	SPSPBT	2802	2616	2436	2262	2616	2280	1977	1705	.1	2.0	5.7
7.5x55 Schmidt Rubin (7.5 Swiss)	180	SPSBT	2650	2450	2260	2060	2792	2350	1990	1665		Not Available	
7x57	150	SPSPBT	2756	2539	2331	2133	2530	2148	1810	1516	.1	4.2	6.2
7x57R	150	SPSPBT, FJPBT	2690	2476	2270	2077	2411	2042	1717	1437	.0	5.2	15.2
7mm Remington Magnum	150	SPSBT	3260	2970	2700	2450	3540	2945	2435	1990	.4	2.0	4.9
7x64	150	SPSPBT	2890	2598	2329	2113	2779	2449	1807	1487	.0	3.3	12.5
280 Remington	150	SPSP	2900	2683	2475	2277	2802	2398	2041	1727	.0	3.4	12.4
30 U.S. Carbine	110	SPRN	1970	1595	1300	1090	948	622	413	290	.8	6.4	19.0
308 Winchester	130	SPSPBT	2900	2590	2300	2030	2428	1937	1527	1190	.1	2.1	6.2
	150	SPSPBT	2860	2570	2300	2050	2725	2200	1762	1400	.1	2.0	5.9
	180	PPDC	2610	2400	2210	2020	2725	2303	1952	1631	.2	2.5	6.6
7.62 Russian	180	SPSBT	2624	2415	2222	2030	2749	2326	1970	1644	.2	2.5	6.6
308 Norma Magnum	180	PPDC	3100	2881	2668	2464	3842	3318	2846	2427	.0	1.6	4.6
30-06	130	SPSBT	3281	2951	2636	2338	3108	2514	2006	1578	.1	1.5	4.6
	150	SPSBT	2972	2680	2402	2141	2943	2393	1922	1527	.0	1.9	5.7
	180	SPRN	2700	2494	2296	2109	2914	2487	2107	1778	.1	2.3	6.4
	180	PPDC	2700	2494	2296	2109	2914	2487	2107	1778		Not Available	
30-30	150	SPFP	2410	2075	1790	1550	1934	1433	1066	799	.0	7.0	26.1
	170	SPFP	2220	1890	1630	1410	1860	1350	1000	750	.0	8.1	29.2
7.65 Argentine	150	SPSP	2920	2630	2355	2105	2841	2304	1848	1476	.1	2.0	5.8
303 British	150	SPSP	2720	2440	2170	1930	2465	1983	1596	1241	.1	2.2	6.5
	180	SPSPBT	2540	2340	2147	1965	2579	2189	1843	1544	.2	2.7	7.3
7.7 Japanese	130	SPSP	2950	2635	2340	2065	2513	2004	1581	1231	.1	2.0	5.9
	180	SPSPBT	2493	2292	2101	1922	2484	2100	1765	1477	.3	2.8	7.7
8x57J (.318 in.)	196	SPRN	2526	2195	1894	1627	2778	2077	1562	1152	.0	5.8	21.4
8mm Mauser (.323 in.)	196	SP	2526	2195	1894	1627	2778	2097	1562	1152		Not Available	
358 Norma Magnum	250	SPSP	2790	2493	2231	2001	4322	3451	2764	2223	.2	2.4	6.6
9.3x57	286	PPDC	2067	1818	1595	1404	2714	2099	1616	1252	.0	9.1	32.0
9.3x62	286	PPDC	2362	2088	1815	1592	3544	2769	2092	1700	.0	6.5	23.5

P—Pointed SP—Soft Point HP—Hollow Point FP—Flat Point RN—Round Nose BT—Boat Tail MC—Metal Case DC—Dual Core SPSP—Soft Point Semi Point SPSBT—Soft Point Semi Pointed Boat Tail FJPBT—Full Jacket Pointed Boat Tail SpPSP—Spire point Soft Point PP—Plastic Point NA—Not announced

Chart from 1980 *Gun Digest* © 1979 DBI Books, Inc.
Used with permission.

SPEER-DWM C.F. RIFLE CARTRIDGES—BALLISTICS

These DWM metric calibers are imported by Speer, Inc. Metric cases and bullets for calibers listed may be special-ordered from Speer.

| Caliber | Bullet | | Velocity | | | | Energy | | | | Mid-Range Trajectory | | |
	Wt. Grs.	Type	Muzzle	100 yds.	200 yds.	300 yds.	Muzzle	100 yds.	200 yds.	300 yds.	100 yds.	200 yds.	300 yds.
5.6 x 35R Vierling	46	SP	2030	1500	1140		418	224	130		1.2	7.5	
5.6 x 50R (Rimmed) Mag.	50	PSP					Not Available						
5.6 x 52R (Savage H.P.)	71	PSP	2850	2460	2320	2200	1280	947	846	766	.3	2.3	6.5
5.6 x 61 SE	77	PSP	3700	3360	3060	2790	2350	1920	1605	1345	.1	1.1	3.4
5.6 x 61R	77	PSP	3480	3140	2840	2560	2070	1690	1370	1120	.1	1.3	4.0
6.5 x 54 MS	159	SP	2170	1925	1705	1485	1660	1300	1025	810	.5	4.1	11.5
6.5 x 57 Mauser	93	PSP	3350	2930	2570	2260	2300	1760	1350	1040	.1	1.7	4.8
6.5 x 57 R	93	PSP	3350	2930	2570	2260	2300	1760	1350	1040	.1	1.7	4.8
7 x 57 Mauser	103	PSP	3330	2865	2450	2060	2550	1890	1380	977	.1	1.7	5.2
	162	TIG	2785	2480	2250	2060	2780	2200	1820	1520	.3	2.4	6.7
7 x 57 R	103	PSP	3260	2810	2390	2000	2430	1820	1320	920	.1	1.8	5.3
	139	SP	2550	2240	1960	1720	2000	1540	1190	910	.3	2.9	8.6
	162	TIG	2710	2420	2210	2020	2640	2120	1750	1460	.3	2.4	6.9
7 x 64	103	PSP	3572	3110	2685	2283	2930	2230	1670	1190	.1	1.4	4.4
	139	SP	3000	2570	2260	1980	2780	2040	1570	1200	.2	2.2	6.4
	162	TIG	2960	2603	2375	2200	3150	2440	2030	1740	.2	2.0	6.0
	177	TIG	2880	2665	2490	2325	3270	2820	2440	2130	.2	2.0	5.6
7 x 65 R	103	PSP	3480	3010	2590	2200	2770	2100	1540	1120	.1	1.5	4.7
	139	SP	3000	2570	2260	1980	2780	2040	1570	1200	.2	2.2	6.4
	162	TIG	2887	2540	2320	2140	3000	2320	1930	1650	.2	2.2	6.3
	177	TIG	2820	2600	2420	2255	3120	2660	2300	2000	.2	2.1	5.9
7mm SE	169	ToSto	3300	3045	2825	2620	4090	3480	3010	2600	.1	1.4	3.9
7 x 75 R SE	169	ToSto	3070	2840	2630	2430	3550	3050	2620	2240	.1	1.6	4.5
30-06	180	TUG	2854	2562	2306	2077	3261	2632	2133	1726	.2	2.2	6.3
8 x 57 JS	123	SP	2968	2339	1805	1318	2415	1497	897	477	.2	2.7	8.8
	198	TIG	2732	2415	2181	1985	3276	2560	2083	1736	.3	2.5	7.1
8 x 57 JR	196	SP	2391	1991	1742	1565	2488	1736	1316	1056	.5	3.9	11.2
8 x 57 JRS	123	SP	2970	2340	1805	1318	2415	1497	897	477	.2	2.7	8.8
	196	SP	2480	2140	1870	1640	2680	2000	1510	1165	.4	3.3	9.4
	198	TIG	2600	2320	2105	1930	2970	2350	1950	1620	.3	2.7	7.6
8 x 60 S	196	SP	2585	2162	1890	1690	2905	2030	1560	1245	.4	3.2	9.2
	198	TIG	2780	2450	2205	2010	3390	2625	2130	1770	.3	2.4	6.9
9.3 x 62	293	TUG	2515	2310	2150	2020	4110	3480	3010	2634	.3	2.8	7.5
9.3 x 64	293	TUG	2640	2450	2290	2145	4550	3900	3410	3000	.3	2.4	6.6
9.3 x 72 R	193	FP	1925	1600	1400	1245	1590	1090	835	666	.5	5.7	16.6
9.3 x 74 R	293	TUG	2360	2160	1998	1870	3580	3000	2560	2250	.3	3.1	8.7

FP—Flat Point SP—Soft Point PSP—Pointed Soft Point TIG—Brenneke Torpedo Ideal TUG—Brenneke Torpedo Universal ToSto—vom Hofe Torpedo Stopring

Ballistic Data of RWS Rimfire Cartridges

No.	Cartridge	Bullet		Max. permissible breech pressure lbs./sq. in.	Barrel length inches	Velocity ft. per sec.			Energy ft.lbs.		
		Type	Weight grains			Muzzle	50 yds.	100 yds.	Muzzle	50 yds.	100 yds.
15400	.22 l.r. Standard	lead bullet lubricated	39	18500	25,5	1080	980	900	101	83	71
15404	.22 l.r. R50										
15402	.22 l.r. HV Solid	lead bullet copper-plated	39	18500	25,5	1310	1105	985	149	106	84
15403	.22 l.r. HV Hollow Point	hollow point lead bullet copper-plated	35	18500	25,5	1340	1115	975	140	97	74
15420	.22 short	lead bullet lubricated	28	11400	25,5	920	845	775	52	44	37
15435	.22 short automatic	lead bullet lubricated	28	11400	25,5	970	885	815	59	49	41
15411	Z .22 long Specially reduced charge	lead bullet lubricated	28	5000	25,5	720	635		32	25	

Symbol	Cartridge	Bullet		Max. permissible breech pressure lbs./sq.in.	Barrel-length inches	Velocity ft. per sec.			
		Type	Weight grs.			Muzzle	100 yds.	150 yds.	300 yds.
15470	.22 Magnum	H.P.	40	28 460	22	2020	1460	1260	—
15471	.22 Magnum	F.M.C.	40	28 460	22	2020	1460	1260	—

Ballistic Data of RWS Rimfire Cartridges (continued)

Path of bullet above (+) or below (−) line of sight in inches							
iron sights based on a sight height of 0,8″ above line of bore				telescopic sights based on a sight height of 2″ above line of bore			
25 yds.	50 yds.	75 yds.	100 yds.	25 yds.	50 yds.	75 yds.	100 yds.
+0,6	⊕	−2,9	−7,8	−0,1	⊕	−2,3	−6,6
+1,5	+1,9	⊕	−4,0	+0,7	+1,5	⊕	−3,6
+2,5	+3,9	+3,0	⊕	+1,6	+3,3	+2,7	⊕
+0,3	⊕	−1,9	−6,1	−0,3	⊕	−1,3	−4,9
+0,9	+1,3	⊕	−3,6	+0,1	+0,9	⊕	−3,2
+1,8	+3,1	+2,7	⊕	+0,9	+2,5	+2,4	⊕
+0,4	⊕	−1,9	−6,0	−0,2	⊕	−1,3	−4,8
+1,0	+1,3	⊕	−3,5	+0,2	+0,9	⊕	−3,1
+1,9	+3,0	+2,6	⊕	+1,0	+2,4	+2,3	⊕
+1,1	⊕	−4,2	−12,1				
+2,5	+2,7	⊕	− 6,5				
+0,6	⊕	−3,1	−9,7				
+1,6	+2,1	⊕	−5,5				

Energy ft. lbs.				Time of flight sec.			Mid-Range Trajectory with telescopic sights 2″ above line of bore		
Muzzle	100 yds.	150 yds.	300 yds.	100 yds.	150 yds.	300 yds.	100 yds.	150 yds.	300 yds.
360	190	140	—	0,17	—	—	+ 0,8	+ 2,8	—
360	190	140	—	0,17	—	—	+ 0,8	+ 2,8	—

Exterior Ballistic Data for British Centerfire Rifle Cartridges

Cartridge	Case length inches	Bullet weight (grs.)	Powder weight (grs.)	Velocity (ft./sec.)			Energy (ft./lb.)			Drop (in.)†	
				Muzzle	100 yd.	200 yd.	Muzzle	100 yd.	200 yd.	100 yd.	200 yd.
*297/230 (Morris) Short	9/16	37L	1¾ RN	875	720		63	43		15.0	
*297/230 (Morris) Long	¾	37L	2¾ CN	1200	920	760	120	70	48	15.0	71.0
*p240 H&H Apex Flanged	2½	100CP	38½ NC	2800	2570	2355	1740	1470	1230	2.3	10.0
240 Belted Rimless	2½	100CP	40½ NC	2900	2665	2445	1870	1580	1330	2.2	9.2
*242 Rimless Nitro Exp.	2⅜	100CP	42 NC	3000	2740	2490	1970	1635	1355	2.0	8.6
244 H&H Magnum (Belted)	2¾	100CP		3500	3230	2970	2725	2320	1980	1.6	5.1
297/250 Rook Rifle	13/16	56L	3 CN	1150	940	805	165	110	80	15.5	70.0
256 (6.5mm) Mannlicher	2⅛	160SN	36 NC	2350	2045	1765	1960	1490	1110	3.4	15.5
6.5mm Mann.-Schon.	2⅛	160SN	36 NC	2300	2000	1725	1880	1420	1060	3.6	16.0
275 H&H Magnum (Belted)	2½	160CP	52 NC	2700	2505	2320	2600	2230	1920	2.5	10.5
275 High Velocity (7mm)	2¼	140CP	48 NC	2900	2705	2515	2620	2280	1970	2.2	9.0
276 (7mm) Mauser	2¼	173SN	38 NC	2300	2015	1765	2040	1560	1200	3.9	16.0
p7mm H&H Magnum Flanged	2½	140CP		2650	2450		2184	1867			
*280 Flanged Nitro Exp.	2⅝	140CP	52 NC	2800	2570	2355	2440	2060	1730	2.3	10.0
*280 Flanged Nitro Exp.	2⅝	160HP	52 NC	2600	2300	2020	2400	1880	1450	2.8	12.0
280 Ross Rimless Nitro	2⅝	140CP	54 NC	2900	2665	2445	2620	2210	1860	2.2	9.0
280 Ross Rimless Nitro		160HP	54 NC	2700	2395	2110	2600	2040	1580	2.6	11.5
*280 Jeffery Rimless	2½	140CP	57 NC	3000	2870	2735	2800	2555	2390	2.1	10.0
300 (.295) Rook Rifle	1⅛	80L	4½ CN	1100	915	785	215	150	110	16.5	75.0
300 Sherwood	1½	140L	8½ CN	1400	1195	1060	610	445	350	9.9	44.0
300 H&H Maggum Belted	2¾	150SN	58 C	3000	2660	2350	3000	2360	1835	2.2	9.8
or (30 Super Magnum)		180SN	55 C	2750	2430	2130	3020	2360	1815	2.8	12.5
or (30 Super Magnum)		220SN	49 C	2300	2045	1810	2115	1675	1305	3.9	17.0
p30 Super Flanged H&H	2¾	150SN	55 C	2875	2581		2755	2225			
p30 Super Flanged H&H		180SN	50 C	2575	2309		2653	2131			
p30 Super Flanged H&H		220SN	46 C	2250	2045		2475	2045			
*30 Purdey Flanged Nitro	2⅜	150SN		2700	2385	2090	2430	1900	1460	2.6	11.5
303 British (Mark 6)	2¼	215S	31 C	2050	1855	1670	2010	1650	1330	4.4	19.0
303 British (Mark 7)	2¼	174S	37 C	2450	2250	2055	2320	1960	1640	3.0	13.0
303 British	2¼	150CP	38 C	2700	2465	2240	2440	2030	1680	2.5	11.0
303 British	2¼	174SN	41 NC	2450	2195	1955	2315	1870	1480	3.1	13.5
303 British	2¼	215SN	31 C	2050	1790	1555	2010	1530	1160	4.6	20.0
310 Cadet	1⅛	120L	6 CN	1200	1010	890	385	270	210	14.0	62.0
318 Rimless Nitro Exp.	2⅜	180CP	55 NC	2700	2395	2110	2920	2300	1780	2.6	11.5
318 Rimless Nitro Exp.		250SN	52 NC	2400	2040	1715	3200	2320	1640	3.3	15.0
333 Rimless Nitro Exp.	2⅜	300SN	65 NC	2200	1950	1720	3230	2540	1980	3.9	17.0
*400/350 Nitro Exp.	2¾	310SN	43 NC	2000	1795	1610	2760	2220	1790	4.7	20.0
350 Rigby Magnum Rimless	2¾	225SN	65 NC	2625	2307		3440	2657			
350 No. 2 Rigby Flanged	2¾	225SN		2600			3400				
*360 Nitro Exp. Flanged	2¼	300SN	30 C	1650	1490	1355	1820	1480	1210	6.9	29.0
*360 Nitro for Black Powd.	2¼	190CT	22 C	1650	1285	1070	1150	700	485	7.6	36.0
o400/360 Purdey Flanged	2¾	300SN	40 C	1950	1776		2537	2102			
o400/360 Westley Richards	2¾	314SN	41 C	1900	1724		2520	2072			
o360 No. 2 Nitro Exp.	3	320SN	55 C	2200	1999		3442	2845			
o369 Purdey Nitro Exp.	2⅝	270SN	64½ NC	2500	2135	1800	3760	2740	1950	3.1	14.0
375 Flanged Nitro Exp.	2½	270SN	40 C	2000	1735	1405	2400	1810	1190	4.9	22.0
o375 Rimless W.R. Nitro	2¼	270SN	43 C	2100	1870		2640	2100			
375 Flanged Magnum Nitro	2⅞	270SN	59 C	2600	2280	1980	4060	3120	2360	2.8	12.5
375 Flanged Magnum Nitro		300SN	56 C	2400	2105	1825	3850	2960	2220	3.3	14.5
375 Belted H&H Magnum	2⅞	235CP	62 C	2800	2495	2215	4100	3260	2560	2.4	10.5
375 Belted H&H Magnum		270SN	61 C	2650	2325	2020	4220	3250	2450	2.9	12.0
375 Belted H&H Magnum		300SN	58 C	2500	2200	1915	4170	3230	2450	3.0	13.5
450/400 Nitro Exp.	3	400SN	60 C	2100	1845	1610	3920	3030	2310	4.3	19.0
450/400 Magnum Nitro Exp.	3¼	400SN	60 C	2150	1890	1650	4110	3180	2420	4.1	18.0
404 Jeffery Rimless	2⅞	400SN	60 C	2125	1885	1670	4020	3160	2480	4.2	18.0
p416 Rigby Magnum	2⅞	410SN	71 C	2371	2110		5100				
p425 Westley Richards	2⅝	410SN		2350			5010				
o450 Nitro Exp.	3¼	480SN	70 C	2150	1900	1665	4930	3860	2960	4.1	18.0
*500/450 Magnum Nitro Exp.	3¼	480SN	75 C	2175	1987		5050	4220			
o450 No. 2 Nitro Exp.	3½	480SN	80 C	2175	1904		5050	3900			
o450 Black Powder Exp.	3¼	310L	120Blk	1800	1510		2240	1570			
o450 Nitro for B.P. Exp.	3¼	365CT	52 C	2100	1809		3578	2655			
577/450 Martini-Henry	2¼	480L	38½ C	1350	1210	1110	1950	1560	1320	10.0	44.0
577/450 Martini-Henry B.P.	2¼	480L	85 Blk	1350	1210	1110	1950	1560	1320	10.0	44.0
465 H&H Nitro Exp.	3¼	480SN	73 C	2150	1830	1620	4930	3580	2800	4.1	18.5
470 Nitro Exp.	3¼	500SN	75 C	2150	1890	1650	5140	3980	3030	4.1	18.0
*475 Nitro Exp.	3¼	480SN	75 C	2175	2000	1830	5040	4260	3580	4.2	18.0
r475 No. 2 Nitro Exp.	3½	480SN	85 C	2200	1925	1680	5170	3960	3020	3.9	17.0
o475 No. 2 Jeffery	3½	500SN	85 C	2150	1880	1635	5140	3930	2970	4.1	18.0
o476 Nitro Exp.	3	520SN	75 C	2100	1925	1760	5085	4295	3585	4.6	20.0
500 Nitro Exp.	3	570SN	80 C	2150	1890	1650	5850	4530	3450	4.1	18.0

Exterior Ballistic Data for British Centerfire Rifle Cartridges (continued)

Cartridge	Case length inches	Bullet weight (grs.)	Powder weight (grs.)	Velocity (ft./sec.)			Energy (ft./lb.)			Drop (in.)†	
				Muzzle	100 yd.	200 yd.	Muzzle	100 yd.	200 yd.	100 yd.	200 yd.
*500 Nitro for B.P. Exp.	3	440CT	55 C	1900	1570	1290	3530	2410	1630	5.5	25.0
o500 Black Powder Exp.	3	340CT	136 Blk	1925	1585		2800	1900			
p500 Jeffery Rimless		535SN	95 C	2400			6800				
p505 Gibbs Rimless Magnum		525SN	90 C	2300			6180				
577 Solid Snider	1⅜	480L	70 Blk	1250	1055	940	1670	1190	940	13.0	57.0
r577 Nitro Exp.	3	750SN	100 C	2050	1795	1570	7010	5380	4110	4.5	20.0
o600 Nitro Exp.	3	900S	110 C	1950	1650	1390	7600	5450	3870	5.1	23.0

ABBREVIATIONS

*Discontinued

BP or Blk— Black Powder
C— Cordite
NC— Nitro-Cellulose
CN— Cadet Neonite
RN— Revolver Neonite

SN— Soft Nose
CP— Copper Point
CT— Copper Tube
L— Lead
HP— Hollow Point
S— Solid (Jacketed)

†— Drop is computed from horizontal line of departure for the bullet.
*— Available while stocks last; will then become obsolete.
o— Obsolete; no longer available.
r— Re-introduced and again available.
p— Proprietary Cartridge; available only from specific maker.

INTERCHANGEABILITY CHART

Cartridges in groups shown below will interchange

RIM FIRE
22 W.R.F.
22 Remington Special
22 Win. M/1890
in a 22 Win. Magnum Rim Fire
but not conversely

CENTER FIRE
25-20 Remington
25-20 W.C.F.
25-20 Win.
25-20 Win. Hi-Speed
25-20 Marlin
25 W.C.F.

6 mm Rem. (80 & 90 grain)
244 Rem.

25 Automatic
25 Automatic Colt Pistol (ACP)
25 (6.35 mm) Automatic Pistol
6.35 mm Browning

30-30 Sav.
30-30 Win.
30-30 Marlin
30-30 Win. Hi-Speed
30 W.C.F.

32 Colt Automatic
32 Automatic Colt Pistol (ACP)
32 (7.65 mm) Automatic Pistol
7.65 mm Automatic Pistol

7.65 mm Browning (not interchangeable with 7.65 mm Luger)

32 Short Colt in
32 Long Colt but not conversely
SEE NOTE A

32 S. & W. in
32 S. & W. Long but not conversely

32 S. & W. Long
32 Colt New Police
32 Colt Police Positive

32 W.C.F.★
32 Win.★
32-20 Win. Hi-Speed★
32-20 Colt L.M.R.★
32-20 W.C.F.★
32-20 Win. and Marlin★
SEE NOTE E

38 S. & W.
38 Colt New Police
380 Webley

38 Colt Special
38 S. & W. Special
38 Targetmaster
38 S. & W. Special Mid-Range
38 Special Hi-Speed (•)
   SEE NOTE B
38-44 Special (•)
38 Special
38 Special Flat Point

38 Short Colt in
38 Long Colt but not conversely
   Both can be used in 38 Special

38 Marlin★
38 Win.★
38 Remington★
38-40 Win.★
38 W.C.F.★

38 Automatic in
38 Super but not conversely

380 Automatic
9 mm Browning Short (Corto, Kurz)

9 mm Luger
9 mm Parabellum
SEE NOTE C

44 S. & W.Special but not conversely
SEE NOTE D

44 Marlin
44 Win.
44 Remington
44-40 Win.★
44 W.C.F.

45-70 Government
45-70 Marlin, Win.
45-70-405

NOTE: ★Hi-Speed Cartridges must not be used in Revolvers. They should be used only in rifles made especially for them. Exceptions: items marked (•) are designed especially for the 38-44 S. & W. Revolver and the 38 Colt Shooting Master. Check with the manufacturer of light frame guns prior to use of Hi-Speed ammunition to determine their suitability.

NOTE A: Not for use in revolvers chambered for 32 S. & W. or 32 S. & W. Long.

NOTE B: All 38 Special cartridges can be used in 357 Magnum revolvers but not conversely.

NOTE C: 9mm sub-machine gun cartridge should not be used in hand guns.

NOTE D: 44 Russian and 44 S. & W. Special can be used in 44 Remington Magnum Revolvers but not conversely.

NOTE E: Not to be used in Win. M/66 and M/73.

UNSAFE ARMS-AND-AMMUNITION COMBINATIONS

Although certain cartridges can be used interchangeably in certain firearms—as shown in the chart above—an attempt to fire the wrong cartridge in a given gun can be extremely dangerous. If in doubt, the rule is never to take a chance. Nearly every firearm, no matter where it was produced, is marked in some manner to indicate the proper cartridge for it; that is the *only* load to use unless it is positively known that another cartridge can safely be substituted. In other words, a firearm should be used only with the ammunition for which it is intended. The dimensional difference between a wrong and right cartridge may be so slight that a load will fire in a gun not chambered for it. This usually ruptures the cartridge case, releasing products of combustion that are likely to damage the firearm severely. It may cause very serious injury to the shooter or bystanders. Or it may leave a bullet in the bore, forming an obstruction. The following list of dangerous arms-and-ammunition combinations is provided through the courtesy of the Sporting Arms and Ammunition Manufacturers' Institute. It does not cover all possible unsafe combinations but does enumerate dangerous errors that have been made.

HANDGUNS

In a handgun chambered for	Do not use
32 S&W	32 Auto, 32 Short Colt, 32 Long Colt
38 Auto	38 Super Auto +P**
38 S&W	38 Auto, 38 Short Colt, 38 Long Colt, 38 Special
38 Special	380 Auto, 357 Magnum*, 38 Special High Velocity +P**
45 Colt	44 S&W Special, 44 Remington Magnum
45 Auto	44 Special, 44 Remington Magnum
32-20 Winchester	32-20 High Velocity
38-40 Winchester	38-40 High Velocity
44-40 Winchester	44-40 High Velocity

* Some handguns only.

** As indicated by the +P marking on the case headstamp, this ammunition is loaded to a higher pressure to achieve higher velocity. Use only in firearms especially designed for this type of cartridge and so recommended by the gun manufacturer.

RIMFIRE RIFLES

In a rifle chambered for	Do not use
22 W.R.F.	22 B.B., 22 C.B., 22 Short, 22 Long, 22 L.R., 22 L.R. Shot
22 W.M.R.F.	22 B.B., 22 C.B., 22 Short, 22 Long, 22 L.R., 22 L.R. Shot
22 Winchester Auto	22 B.B., 22 C.B., 22 Short, 22 Long, 22 L.R., 22 L.R. Shot
5 mm. Remington R.F. Magnum	22 B.B., 22 C.B., 22 Short, 22 Long, 22 L.R., 22 L.R. Shot, 22 Winchester Auto
25 Stevens Long	5 mm. Remington R.F. Magnum

CENTERFIRE RIFLES

In a rifle chambered for	Do not use
6 mm. Remington (244 Rem.)	250 Savage
6.5 mm. Remington Magnum	300 Savage
7 mm. Mauser (7 x 57)	300 Savage
7 mm. Remington Magnum	7 mm. Weatherby Magnum, 270 Winchester, 280 Remington, 35 Remington, 350 Remington Magnum
8 mm. Mauser (8 x 57)	35 Remington, 7 mm. Mauser (7 x 57)
8 mm. Remington Magnum	350 Remington Magnum, 338 Winchester Magnum, 358 Norma Magnum
17 Remington	221 Remington Fireball, 30 Carbine
17/223 Remington	17 Remington, 221 Remington Fireball, 30 Carbine
223 Remington	222 Remington
243 Winchester	250 Savage, 225 Winchester
257 Roberts	250 Savage
264 Winchester Magnum	270 Winchester, 284 Winchester, 308 Winchester, 303 British, 350 Remington Magnum
270 Winchester	30 Remington, 30-30 Winchester, 300 Savage, 32 Remington, 308 Winchester, 7 mm. Mauser (7 × 57)
280 Remington	270 Winchester, 30 Remington, 30-30 Winchester, 300 Savage, 32 Remington, 308 Winchester, 7 mm. Mauser (7 × 57)
284 Winchester	300 Savage, 7 mm. Mauser (7 x 57)
30-40 Krag	303 Savage, 303 British, 32 Winchester Special
30-06 Springfield	8 mm. Mauser (8 x 57), 32 Remington, 35 Remington
300 Holland & Holland Magnum	30-06 Springfield, 8 mm. Mauser (8 x 57), 30-40 Krag
300 Weatherby Magnum	338 Winchester Magnum
300 Winchester Magnum	8 mm. Mauser Round-Nose Bullet, 303 British, 350 Remington Magnum, 38-55 Winchester
303 British	32 Winchester Special
303 Savage	32 Winchester Special, 32-40 Winchester
308 Winchester	300 Savage
348 Winchester	35 Remington

SHOTGUNS

(Errors involving wrong shotshells or rifle cartridges)

When the crimp of a shotshell opens upon firing, the shell extends farther than an unfired shell. Shotgun chambers are so designed that when a shell of proper size is fired, it will not extend too far into the forcing cone—the tapered area between chamber and bore. The use of long shells in short chambers (such as 3-inch magnum loads in 2¾-inch chambers) can result in excessive pressures and other hazardous conditions. Do not use shells with a longer designated length than that of the chamber unless their use is specifically recommended by the gun manufacturer.

In addition, typically dangerous errors may involve wrong gauges or the use of rifle cartridges in a .410 bore. Never use a shell of smaller gauge than the gun's designated gauge. For example, never try to fire a 12-gauge shell in a 10-gauge gun, a 16-gauge shell in a 12-gauge gun, or a 20-gauge shell in a 16-gauge gun. Typical—and extremely dangerous—errors with a .410 bore include the following.

In a shotgun chambered for	Do not use
410 Bore	219 Zipper, 30-30 Winchester, 303 British, 32 Winchester Special, 32-40 Winchester, 35 Winchester, 38 Winchester, 38-40 Winchester, 44 Smith & Wesson Special, 44 Remington Magnum, 44-40 Winchester

Rifle Sights

Iron Sights

Mass-produced rifles usually come with a plain open rear sight and bead-type front sight. Few hunters are satisfied with these sights, which really are suitable only for auxiliary use in case a scope becomes inoperative. However, many manufacturers have improved the sights they install. In former years, a low semi-buckhorn rear sight came on almost all rifles, even if the stock had a high Monte Carlo comb for use with a scope. Today, most factory rifles with high combs have appropriately higher open sights, and many of these sights also feature adjustments that permit more precise alignment. The improvements are welcome, but for most purposes open sights still can't match a telescopic sight or an aperture (peep) sight. These rifles are drilled and tapped for scope mounting, and big-game models are rarely seen afield without a scope.

There are two basic types of open sights—the V or U notch and the patridge, which has a square notch used in conjunction with a square blade front sight.

In the first category, there is some controversy about the shape and size of the V or U notch, which may take the form of a shallow V, a deep V, or a V with "ears" and called the buckhorn.

The worst of the lot is the buckhorn with its "ears" that blot out more than half of the target when the sights are lined up. Fortunately, very few guns now come through equipped with buckhorn sights, but there are still enough around to cause problems. One can replace it, of course, but the sight can be partly fixed or improved by filing down the ears to the top of the V.

The deep V is a big improvement over the buckhorn sight, but it also has a drawback. A hunter will most likely sight in his rifle by carefully placing the front bead down into the V notch, which is the correct way to do it. This works well on the range where the shooter has plenty of time to zero in, but problems come up in the field. Shooting at game during the poor light of dusk or dawn or taking snap shots at spooked whitetails, a hunter may not seat the front bead as deep or as carefully in the V as he did on the range. This means he will shoot high and miss his target.

The shallow V is the best compromise for an open rear sight. The absence of any kind of ears means at least half of the target can be seen. The shooter has more light to work with, and the shallow V-notch literally doesn't leave much room for error in seating the bead. Some manufacturers place a white diamond or triangle at the bottom of the V, and this certainly helps to quickly center the bead. If an open sight must be used, the shallow V is the best choice.

Front bead sights for the above, incidentally, come in a variety of colors, including gold, ivory, red plastic. Some show up better than others under certain lighting conditions, but the gold bead has been proven the best for all conditions.

Assuming you're a target shooter and not a hunter, the patridge sight with its square-cut notch rear sight and square blade front sight is actually more accurate and a better choice than the sights utilizing a bead front sight. With this sight, the front blade is centered in the square notch of the rear sight and a 6 o'clock hold is taken. That is, the front blade is placed at the bottom edge of the bullseye. The sight picture should look like an apple sitting on a fence post. This sight combination is surprisingly accurate for target work, but a difficult one to use on game.

The biggest problem with open sights is adjustment, or we should say lack of dependable adjustment. If bullets consistently hit left, the rear sight in its dovetail mount must be tapped to the right—not a very precise technique. If bullets consistently hit high or low, the rear sight must be moved accordingly on the notched bar, to a lower notch to lower the point of impact and to a higher notch to raise it. Sometimes a rifle will shoot high with the sight in its lowest notch. This leaves us with two choices: file down the notch or look for a better sight.

Another problem with open sights is that they require the shooter to focus on three things at once: the rear sight, the front bead, and the target. This is not a simple trick even for the best pair of eyes. A shooter trying to keep everything in focus at the same time will find himself shifting focus back and forth between rear and front sights and his target, and such an arrangement will mean misses.

Shallow-V   **Buckhorn**   **Peep, or Aperture**   **Patridge**

Basic types of iron sights. The buckhorn is the worst of the lot since it covers too much of the animal. The shallow-V is an improvement as it allows a hunter to see more of the game he's shooting at. The aperture or peep sight is the best choice for hunting because it's fast, lets in plenty of light and landscape, and hunter simply puts bead where he wants to hit and squeezes off. The patridge sight is actually the most accurate, but it's a difficult one to use on game and should be used only for target shooting.

The Lyman 57 Universal Receiver Sight is fairly typical of high-quality aperture sights for hunting rifles. Its mount hugs the receiver. (Another version, the 66, is made for autos, pumps, and lever actions with flat receivers.) Elevation and windage are adjustable, with audible 1/4-minute clicks. Release button permits quick removal of the slide assembly so rifle can be used with scope or open sights.

The Williams Foolproof Receiver Sight can be bought with target knobs (as shown) or without them. Protruding adjustment knobs are excellent for target work, but on a hunting rifle they tend to get in the way and snag twigs. Model pictured fits a number of Mossberg, Remington, and Winchester bolt actions. Other Foolproof models are made for most rifles as well as some handguns.

Aperture or Peep Sight

The peep sight is far superior to the best open sight ever designed. The peep is mounted on the receiver of the rifle, only a few inches from the eye, and the shooter looks through it, not at it. The peep sight works on the principle that the eye will automatically center the front bead in the hole. Many hunters and shooters find this hard to believe, but there is no doubt that it works.

It's important to remember not to try to focus on the aperture itself. It's supposed to look slightly blurred. Simply look through the hole and pick up the front bead. Your eye will automatically center it in the hole and all you have to do is put the bead on your target.

The peep sight also offers the important feature of positive adjustment. The aperture can be adjusted for both windage and elevation by means of screws that provide corrections of 1/4 to 1/2 inch at 100 yards.

All peep sights come with insert discs for target shooting. The hole through these discs is generally very small, and they're fine for shooting at paper on the range. Hunters, however, should take this disc and throw it away. It's not needed and only decreases the size of your sight picture.

The peep sight is the fastest of all iron sights for hunting. It lets you see plenty of light, landscape, and nearly all of a game animal when shooting. It may be hard to believe, but a hunter can pick up a running whitetail faster through a peep sight than an open sight . . . then it's just a matter of putting the bead on the animal and squeezing off.

Telescope Sights

Most hunting rifles today have telescope sights mounted on them. Hunters and shooters have come to realize that these rifle scopes are not the fragile optical instruments they were in the 1920's. The modern scope is a rigid dependable sight that under almost all conditions is far superior to any other sight. Its advantages are many; its disadvantages few.

Hunters who are getting on in years and beginning to have difficulty with iron sights when trying to focus rear sight, front sight, and target at the same time, can eliminate this problem with a scope. With a scope the image of the target or game is placed right on the crosshairs, and when the hunter focuses on the crosshairs he will find his target is also automatically in focus. Elderly hunters with failing eyesight can often stretch their hunting years by using a scope.

Another advantage is that game that may ordinarily go unnoticed in protective cover can often be picked up in the magnification of a rifle scope. Scopes also add a margin of safety to hunting. What may look like a deer with the naked eye may well turn out to be another hunter through a 4-power scope. A scope will also lengthen your hunting day by enabling a hunter to see well enough to shoot in the poor light of dawn and dusk.

Disadvantages of a scope are few. A scope will add weight to a rifle, anywhere from 6 ounces to maybe more than a pound. A scope also adds bulk, which sometimes creates a minor problem when carrying the rifle. Rain or snow can also put a scope temporarily out of commission, unless it is equipped with scope caps of some sort. A scope can also be a handicap for short-range snap-shooting at game in thick cover. But all these problems can be solved to a degree.

Scopes are perhaps best classified by type: (1) hunting scopes; (2) scopes for .22 rifles; (3) target and varmint scopes.

Hunting Scopes

Hunting scopes are available with fixed powers from 1.5X to 12X and with variable powers offering magnifications of 1.5X–5X, 2X–7X, 3X–9X, 4X–12X, and 6X–18X. In buy-

Palma Metallic Target Sight

International Small-Bore Front

International Big-Bore Front

Olympic Front

No. 60 Series Globe Fronts

Redfield's Palma Metallic Target Receiver Sight is popular for several types of competitive shooting at paper targets as well as metallic game-silhouette matches. It's shown with a full complement of fronts, which accept a wide variety of sight inserts. An optional adjustable disc permits changes in aperture size.

ing a scope, the shooter has to decide what power to choose and whether to spend extra money for a variable model. The answers depend on the hunting to be done. The highest-powered scopes listed above may be wanted for varminting but are not really suitable for most hunting.

High magnification can actually be a drawback. The greater the magnification, the smaller is the field of view (the width of area visible through the scope). Moreover, high power increases the apparent tremors in the sight picture. With a smaller field of view plus the problem of hold-steady, lining up on moving game can be difficult. Sometimes a shooter can't even find the game in his scope before it disappears into thick cover.

Although fixed-power scopes have by no means become obsolete, variables have been so greatly improved in recent years that they are now more popular among big-game hunters. If your hunting is mostly in woods and brush, your best bet is a variable in the 1.5X–5X class. Many of the newer scopes, including variable models, feature an extra-wide field of view. With a wide-field 1.5X–5X scope cranked down to the lowest setting, the field of view is about 70 feet at 100 yards. At the top setting, it's about 27 feet. A wide-field 2½X fixed-power scope has a field of view of more than 50 feet at 100 yards. But the variable has just as wide

a field at a comparable setting, so it's ideal for hunting white-tails in brushy country.

Among fixed-power scopes, the most popular magnification is 4X. But for all-round hunting, a 2X–7X variable is probably best. Although the 3X–9X is extremely popular, its slightly increased magnification isn't really worth the extra bulk and weight if the scope is to be used for a wide variety of hunting. If you use just one rifle and your hunting ranges from Eastern whitetails to Colorado mule deer, either a fixed-power 4X or a 2X–7X variable would be your best choice. If your hunting is strictly Eastern, you want a wide field of view and you don't need as much power, so the choice is between a 1.5X–5X variable and a 2½X or 3X fixed-power scope. The variable has the edge, though it costs more.

The famous drawbacks of the variable models no longer apply. By comparison with fixed-power scopes, they used to be longer, heavier, and less sturdy than they should have been, and they offered a smaller field of view. But now they've been trimmed, strengthened, and so improved optically that they provide just as wide a field—wider at the lowest settings. A bonus is that they can do special jobs at the high settings, such as spotting holes in a target or picking a trophy head out of a herd.

Weaver V7-W, a wide-view variable-power scope with settings from 2.5X to 7X. For all-round hunting use, variables with this range of magnification are highly recommended.

These Lyman scopes are, from left, 6X, 8X, and 10X SL models, designed for metallic-silhouette competition, and a 20X L.W.B.R. model, used for benchrest competition and other matches.

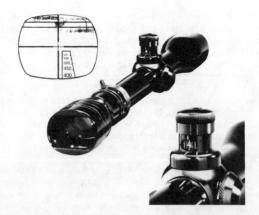

Most popular fixed power for hunting is 4X. This example is Bushnell Scopechief VI, with a Multi-X Reticle (dual-thickness crosswire) and BDC (Bullet Drop Compensator). When such a scope is zeroed-in, you needn't estimate bullet drop. Just estimate distance to a game target and turn the range knob on adjustment turret to the corresponding figure. You then aim dead-on instead of holding over the target.

Redfield 3X-9X Accu-Trac Variable features wide view, dual-thickness 4-Plex crosswires, range-finding reticle scale, and adjustment knob to allow for bullet drop. After reading the range, you turn Accu-Trac knob to the corresponding setting and hold right on target.

Bushnell 2½X Magnum Phantom scope features extremely long eye relief so it can be mounted forward of receiver on top-ejecting lever actions like the Winchester Model 94. Special Phantom mount attaches securely without drilling and tapping the barrel, so there's no safety problem. Scopes with long eye relief are used on handguns as well as on hunting rifles that won't accommodate standard scopes.

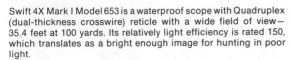

Swift 4X Mark I Model 653 is a waterproof scope with Quadruplex (dual-thickness crosswire) reticle with a wide field of view—35.4 feet at 100 yards. Its relatively light efficiency is rated 150, which translates as a bright enough image for hunting in poor light.

Williams 4X Twilight scope, installed on .44 Ruger carbine with Streamline top mount. Like most good-quality models, Twilight scopes are shockproof, nitrogen-filled and sealed, and have coated lenses. They provide sharp resolution even when light is less than ideal.

Scopes for .22's

Most .22 rifles are used for plinking and hunting small game and it's hard to imagine such a rimfire gun without a scope. The bulk of the .22's available today come equipped with cheap iron sights that can rarely be adjusted for accurate shooting. A receiver or peep sight is certainly an improvement, but a scope will turn most .22's into accurate firearms.

Cost should not be a critical factor here, since scopes for .22 rifles generally run $10 to $20 and they are a good investment. The low cost of these scopes is due mainly to their construction. First, their optics are not as highly corrected as the scopes for big-game rifles. Secondly, they

are usually not constructed strong enough to take the recoil of the big centerfire cartridges.

It's wise here to mention that under no circumstances should one of these scopes be mounted on a high-powered rifle, since it could result in a serious eye injury. These inexpensive scopes for .22's have an eye relief (distance between eye and ocular lens that gives shooter maximum field of view) of about 2 inches. A .22 has just about no recoil, so the eye being this close to the ocular lens presents no problems. Put the same scope on a high-powered rifle with heavy recoil, however, and the scope tube could be driven into the shooter's eye.

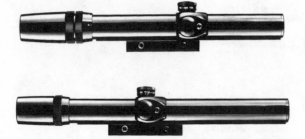

Bushnell Custom .22 Riflescopes with Bullet Drop Compensator —3X-7X variable (upper scope) and 4X model.

Redfield RM 6400 Target & Varmint Model (upper scope) is available in 16X, 20X, or 24X. It's only 17 inches long, weighs only 18 ounces, and mounts entirely on rifle's receiver, eliminating vibrations between receiver and barrel. Redfield 3200 Target Scope is available in 12X, 16X, 20X, or 24X. Old-fashioned target scopes employed adjustments in the mounts. The 3200 was the first sealed target scope with internal adjustments— now the standard construction.

THE LENS SYSTEMS IN WILLIAMS GUIDE LINE SCOPES

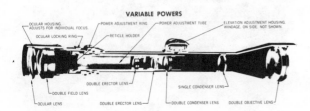

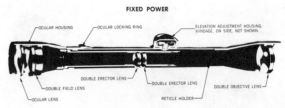

Best power for a scope to be used on a .22 is not as important as it is with big-game rifles. For general use, a 4X scope is fine. For target and squirrel hunting, a 6X would be better. If you can't make up your mind, pick one of the variables with a range of 3X to 6 or 7X. You can't go wrong putting one of these inexpensive scopes on a .22 rifle, especially since cost of mounting the scope is nonexistent. Just about all .22 rifles are grooved for tip-off mounts and the price of the scope usually includes the tip-off mount.

Target and Varmint Scopes

Scopes for long-range varmint shooting and for benchrest and other serious target competition are a special breed. Until a few years ago, the necessary accuracy was obtained only with scopes over two feet long that had fragile adjustments in the mounts. Now, with very few exceptions, powerful and precise target scopes employ internal adjustments, and they measure no more than about 18 inches long. The very long, slender, externally adjusted target/varmint scope is a dying breed. A famous old standard, Lyman's Super-Targetspot, is no longer catalogued. But Lyman and others —Redfield, Leupold, and Weaver, among the best known— offer rugged, precise, internally adjusted target scopes that look like hunting models.

The field of view is smaller than the field in a lower-powered hunting scope, but this doesn't matter in a scope to be used strictly for varminting or target work. Serious varmint shooters generally use scopes with 10X to 15X magnification, though some of them favor even greater power. For target shooting, 15X and 20X scopes are preferred, and benchresters use 20X and even 25X scopes.

A relatively new type of target competition requires the shooter to knock down metallic game silhouettes at various ranges. Accuracy and power are essential, but the rules call for a scoped rifle weighing no more than 10 pounds 2 ounces. For this competition, both fixed-power and variable scopes are used. The favorites are in the 8X-to-12X range. A good silhouette scope is essentially a very precise hunting-type scope. The adjustments are internal but the knobs are not enclosed in protective caps. They must be quick and convenient to use, easy to grasp and read.

An advantage of these scopes is "zero repeatability"— a feature they share with other fine, relatively expensive target scopes. Ordinary scopes may have a bit of slack in the threads of the adjustment screws. To sight in such a scope very precisely, you must take up the slack by turning the adjustment a trifle too far and then turning it back against the load of the reticle cell. A scope with zero repeatability has no slack. Move an adjustment dial four ¼-inch clicks, and you move the point of impact *precisely* 1 inch at 100 yards. What you read on the adjustment dial is what you get. Silhouette-target scopes are currently marketed by Lyman, Redfield, and Weaver.

The Scope Reticle

A scope reticle is simply a fixed or suspended device in a scope tube which marks the aiming point. Reticles come in many sizes and shapes, and they can be confusing to a hunter who is worried about laying out considerable cash for a scope and then discovering the reticle is wrong for him.

The accompanying drawings show some common reticle types, including the traditional plain crosshair, post and crosshair, dot, range-finding gadgets, and dual-thickness (heavy and thin) crosswire. Most reticles are wire, though some makers have used animal hairs, etched glass, or spider silk—the webs of black-widow spiders.

The simpler the reticle, the easier it is to aim with. A sight picture cluttered with multiple crosshairs or other range-finding devices can sometimes be more trouble than it's worth. As with scope power, the best type of reticle depends on the hunting for which it's most often used.

Technology developed during World War II resulted in a blossoming of new designs and optical systems. For years, however, the most popular reticle remained the standard crosshair, sometimes tapered toward the center but usually of uniform thickness. This type was and still is offered with fine wire for target or varmint shooting or heavier wire for big game.

For aiming at moving game in woods and brush, a good variation is the post and crosswire. The vertical post is usually tapered and flat-topped. In variable-power scopes, it generally comes up exactly to the horizontal crosswire. In fixed-power scopes, it generally extends a trifle above the horizontal wire. In either case, its top is the aiming point. The crosswire is merely a horizontal reference line to help the hunter keep from canting his rifle. Such a reticle works well for relatively fast shooting in poor light, because the thick-bottomed post is so easy to see.

But at long range, a post covers too much of the target—as do the coarse crosshairs that have been traditional in many big-game scopes. One solution is the use of fine crosshairs, and another is the combination of a center dot and fine or tapered crosshairs. Many target and varmint shooters like the dot and fine crosshair. For big game in open country, a suspended dot (without crosshair) was at one time quite popular. It's fast to use. This type of dot isn't good for target work, as it covers the bullseye. Even in hunting, the size of the dot is important. A 2-minute dot, for example, covers 2 inches at 100 yards, a 4-minute dot covers 4 inches, and so on. Choose one that won't cover too much of the target in your type of hunting, and remember that knowing its size will help you estimate range. A varmint hunter with a 6X or 8X scope wouldn't want more than a 1-minute dot, but a big-game hunter in open country might want a 2- or even 4-minute dot.

The standard crosshair, post, and dot reticles are no longer as popular as they once were, because a relatively new type has gained eminence for many shooting purposes. This is the dual-thickness crosswire. Leupold introduced it in the late 1960's and called it the Duplex. Now, many makers offer it under different names: the Leupold Duplex, Bushnell Multi-X, Lyman Center Range, Redfield 4-Plex, Weaver Dual X. and Burris Plex.

This type of reticle employs rather heavy vertical and horizontal crosswires that abruptly become fine near the center. Even in poor light, the shooter's eye quickly picks up the coarse wires, and the fine center wires allow precise aiming—even at a small target. If there's one all-round hunting reticle, this is it.

With a bit of practice, such a reticle also permits fast range estimation. Let's say, for instance, that you're hunt-deer with a wide-view Weaver scope, either 4X or 1.5X–4.5X variable at the high setting. In either case, the space between the points of the heavy outer wires at 100 yards is 22 inches. A mature deer's body is only about 18 inches deep, from the top of the back to the belly (a fact that seems to surprise many hunters). If the deer's body, from top to bottom, fills the vertical space between the wires, the deer is about 80 yards away. If it fills half the space, it's 160 yards away. To get the knack of judging range with your reticle, just practice on stationary targets of known size at known distances.

The dual-thickness reticle is so practical and popular that it has replaced the ordinary crosshair as the "standard" type. If you order a scope without specifying the reticle, chances are you'll get the dual design.

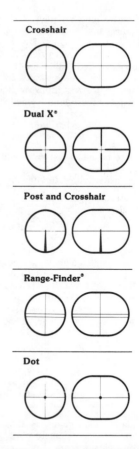

Crosshair

Dual X°

Post and Crosshair

Range-Finder°

Dot

These Weaver reticles represent the most popular types available from most scope manufacturers today. Each type is shown both in standard form and as a wide-view model.

Scope Adjustment

This is simple and easy to understand, but still bears brief explanation. All scopes are adjustable for windage and elevation by two dials on the scope tube. The only exception is with externally adjustable scopes, in which case the windage and elevation dials are a part of the mount. Scopes are adjustable in graduation of $\frac{1}{4}$, $\frac{1}{2}$, or 1-minute clicks, which means one click will move the point of impact $\frac{1}{4}$, $\frac{1}{2}$, or 1 inch at 100 yards respectively.

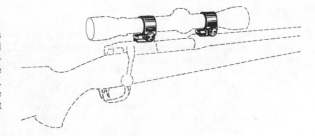

Scope mounted with typical bridge or top mount.

Mounting the Scope

There are several factors to consider before mounting a scope. By discussing the various types of mounts, it will become evident which is the best scope mount for your gun and use.

Bridge or top mount. The bridge mount is chiefly for a hunter who plans to stick a scope on his rifle and leave it there. It's a sturdy mount, suitable for saddle-scabbard carrying and other jolting treatment. One major disadvantage is that the mounting blocks are screwed into the top of the receiver so that, with many rifles, the iron sights can't be used if the scope is damaged and has to be removed. The mount bases hide the open sights. However, this is no longer a problem on many modern rifles that have higher-than-normal factory-installed sights for use with a high-combed stock. Also, some mounts—such as Weaver's top bases—are grooved to allow sighting with the scope removed. With or without these improvements, a sturdy top mount is a good choice for target shooting or the types of hunting in which a scope is just as important as an accurate rifle.

See-through bridge mount. The see-through mount is an old but yet a recently revived idea. This is essentially a bridge mount with a peep hole through the bases so the shooter can also use his iron sights in a pinch. The see-through mount should be particularly appealing to the brush hunter who is never quite sure whether he'll need a scope for a long shot or iron shots for a close quick shot. The basic idea is good and the mount satisfies many hunters. It does have disadvantages, however. For one thing, the scope must necessarily be mounted high, which means the shooter will have to crane his neck upward to get a good sight picture through the tube. This is a good case for only putting these mounts on rifles with Monte Carlo combs or fairly high roll-over cheekpieces. Also, because the scope is mounted high, it makes a bulky package and the sight is more accident prone.

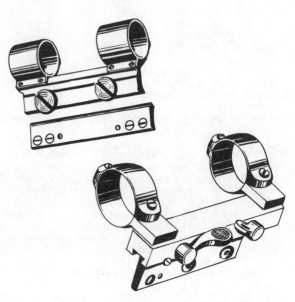

Typical side mount (*top*) and quick-detachable side mount (*bottom*).

All factors considered, the see-through mount is a fair compromise for the hunter who wants instant choice of scope or iron sights. But he will have to accept the fact that the scope will not be mounted in the best possible position, which is as low as possible and directly over the receiver.

Side-bracket mount. This mount is the best and only choice for a hunter who occasionally wants to remove his scope and use iron sights, or who wants to use his scope in conjunction with a receiver or peep sight. The base portion of this mount is generally screwed and pinned to the side of the receiver, so that when the scope and ring portion of the

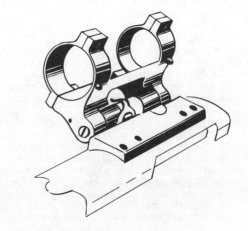

Basic design of swing or pivot mount.

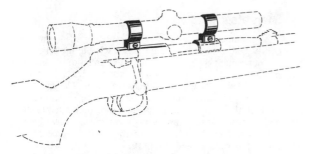

This scope is mounted to a .22 rifle with typical tip-off mount. Note bases of rings are fastened to grooved receiver of rifle.

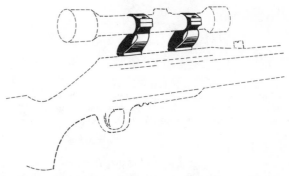

Basic design of a see-through scope mount. Scope is high enough for hunter to use iron sights through openings in mount.

mount is removed, there are no obstructions along the top of the barrel and iron sights can be used.

As mentioned above, the side-bracket mount can also be effectively used in conjunction with a receiver or peep sight that has a removable slide. The scope can quickly be removed and the slide of the receiver sight slipped in. This makes it a fine choice for the hunter heading into a remote area. If the scope should get accidentally knocked out of commission, he can remove it and have a reliable receiver sight to fall back on.

Two excellent side mounts are the Griffin & Howe and the Jaeger. Both mounts will keep the scope on zero, regardless of how many times the scope is taken off and put back on the base mount. Either of the side mounts are a good bet for the brush hunter who wants both scope and iron sights at his disposal. On stand at dawn and dusk, he can use the scope. Stillhunting during the day, he can remove the scope and use open sights or a receiver sights.

Swing or pivot mount. Still another version of the side mount is the swing mount, which is basically a hinged bracket screwed to the side or top of the receiver. With this arrangement, a hunter confronted with a quick shot at close range has only to swing the scope out of the way and use the iron sights. Reputable companies, including Weaver and Pachmayr, make these swing-type mounts and all claim a scope will maintain its zero when swung back and forth.

Offset mount. This mount, which is literally off-set to the side of the receiver, has only one practical application—and that's for rifles that eject fired cases from the top of the receiver, such as the Winchester 94. It is somewhat awkward to use, since the shooter must cock his head over the comb to see through the scope. But if a hunter has a top-ejection rifle and wants to put a scope on it, he doesn't have much choice and he must consider the off-set mount. It does, however, also offer the instant choice of iron or scope sights.

Another alternative for top-ejection rifles are the special scopes with long eye relief—from 10 to 24 inches. These scopes are mounted forward of the top ejection port in the traditional over-the-bore position. While a scope mounted in such a manner looks a bit awkward, the rig is apparently satisfactory.

Tip-off mount. The tip-off mount, because it is not designed as rigidly as other mounts, is relegated to the .22 rifles. The tip-off mount should not be cut short, however. It works fine, is inexpensive, and can be clamped on a .22 rifle in minutes by someone who knows almost nothing about guns.

Whereas most modern high-power rifles come factory drilled and tapped for scope bases, the .22's have the male portion of a dovetail machined into the top of the receivers. The female portion of the tip-off mount, which holds the scope, is simply fastened in place on the receiver with coin-slotted screws.

Generally, the cost of putting a scope on a .22 is non-existent, since nearly all new .22's have grooved receivers and the inexpensive .22 scopes come equipped with the complete tip-off mount.

Williams Guide open sight, Lo-Sight-Thru Mount, and 2X–6X Guide Line Scope mounted on Remington Model 700 bolt action. With this type of installation, you can use scope or see through the mount base to use open sights.

Rifle Accessories

When a hunter finally feels he has put together a winning combination of cartridge, rifle, and sights, he'll find there are a few extra items he'll need to round out his rig. Here we'll cover the most important in detail.

Slings

Anyone who has ever hunted with a rifle knows the value of a sling, whether it's a simple carrying sling or the military-type target sling. A sling means a rifle can be carried on the shoulder or across the back, leaving both hands free for climbing, dragging out game, and so on. And, of course, the sling is used to help steady your hold for a shot.

Three types of slings are available to the hunter—the military sling, the Whelen-type sling, and the carrying sling.

The military sling is fine for match shooting, but it is generally too heavy and wide (1¼ inches) for most hunting rifles. If you're turned on by the military sling, however, there are some manufactured that are lighter and narrower.

A better choice for a hunting rifle is the one-piece Whelen sling, which has a single claw hook to lengthen or shorten it. This sling is about 50 to 55 inches long and measures ¾ to 1 inches wide, just about right for a hunting rifle.

The Whelen sling can also be adjusted to a comfortable carrying length that will also work out well if the hunter wants to use the "hasty sling" position to steady his rifle.

Most hunting rifles wear a simple carrying sling, or strap. There are two basic versions—a straight strap and the increasingly popular "cobra" sling which widens at the fore-end, like a cobra's hood, so that it won't dig into the shoulder. A lining patch of suede, sheepskin, or rough leather prevents it from slipping. Some straight slings have a sliding pad that works as the cobra design does, to distribute the load and prevent the strap from slipping off the shoulder. Fastenings on both straight and cobra slings include claws, leather thongs, buckles, and even Velcro hook-and-pile closures. The cobra type is excellent for general use on a hunting rifle, and a plain one works just as well as an expensive one with decorative tooling.

Swivels

Swivels come in two basic types—those that mount permanently to the rifle and the quick-detachable models.

The permanent types are fine if you're going to put a sling on a rifle and leave it there. But for a few extra dollars, the quick-detachable swivels are a better bargain. The bases of the swivels are mounted on the rifle and the sling-holding portion of the swivel has a spring catch that quickly detaches from the base. This means a hunter can have bases installed on several rifles and use the same sling on all of them. Another advantage is that the brush hunter who finds his sling getting in the way in thick cover can remove the sling and carry it in his pocket. When he's walking out on a woods road, he can snap it back on.

Recoil Pads

Nearly all factory rifles in magnum calibers come equipped with rubber recoil pads to cushion the jolt of the gun's recoil. Most other high-power rifles, however, come with steel, aluminum, or plastic buttplates. These are fine, but do nothing to soften recoil. The hunter who uses his rifle during cold-weather hunting seasons when he's wearing heavy clothing does not need a rubber recoil pad, but a sportsman who uses his rifle year-round would be well-advised to have one installed on his rifle. Recoil can easily bruise a shoulder while target shooting or varmint hunting during the summer months while wearing only a light shirt.

Recoil pads also serve another purpose. They can shorten or lengthen a stock by as much as an inch or so. If you're a six-footer with long arms, have the pad installed without the stock being cut. This will lengthen the stock an inch or more than the standard 13½-inch length of pull on most factory rifles. If you're a short man with short arms and the butt catches under your arm when mounting the gun, have the stock cut and a recoil pad installed for a length of pull from 12 to 12½ inches.

There are three types of recoil pads and selection is mostly a matter of personal preference. All three types serve the same function—absorb recoil.

The side-vented pad, which is generally found on more shotguns than rifles, is good and perhaps a preferred choice if stock is to be lengthened. The solid rubber pad is usually factory installed on guns of magnum recoil.

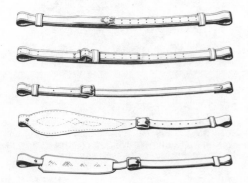

Basic sling designs. From top, military sling, Whelen sling, plain carrying strap, cobra sling, and straight strap with sliding shoulder pad.

Two types of sling swivels. Permanent swivels, left, are fine if sling is rarely taken off rifle. The quick-detachable swivels, right, are a better choice for hunting rifles, since sling can be removed easily and used on several different rifles.

The slip-on pad can be put on and taken off a rifle butt in seconds. It's a good bet for a youngster who is beginning to outgrow his youth's model rifle. The slip-on pad will lengthen the stock and he can get a few more years use out of the gun.

Gun Cases and Saddle Scabbards

It's poor economics to put a $400 rifle and scope rig in a cheap plastic case and expect it to survive unscathed the bumps and jolts of a rough trip. The better protected a rifle and sights, the more likely the sights will remain zeroed in. The rifle itself will also be saved from unnecessary scratches and gouges.

The type of case depends on the hunting done. The average hunter who almost always uses his car to get to his hunting grounds can get by with a good grade gun case made of canvas, vinyl, or leather. Pick a case that has a heavy rubber tip protector at the muzzle end and one that's lined with flannel or fleece. Leather is the best protector in this type of case, but also the most expensive. A good compromise is a lined heavy-duty vinyl case that has a zipper at least one-third the way down from the butt end. If it has a compartment for a cleaning rod, all the better.

If a hunter travels to far-off places, he should pick one of the hard plastic or aluminum gun cases lined with polyurethane foam. The rifle and scope is held firmly in place while it bumps its way through airline and train depots. Here again, cost is a factor. The best cases of this type are expensive. Generally however, one can get a good multi-ribbed hard plastic case with foam lining for about $30. And remember that these same cases can also be used for fishing tackle during the off-season.

Hunters who seek their game from the back of a horse need saddle scabbards. Always made of a good-grade thick leather because of the rugged use they get on mountain trails, these scabbards also make good cases for transporting guns in cars, buses, trains, and so on. Since scabbards are expensive, select one carefully.

A good scabbard should cover the rifle completely, but still leave enough of the rifle butt exposed so that it can be quickly hauled out for a quick dismount and shot. It should also have a boot that can be buckled on during transportation and bad weather, yet can be easily removed during the hunt. The two straps that hold it to the saddle should be 40 to 45 inches long and strong.

One excellent example of a rifle scabbard is manufactured by the George Lawrence Company. Originally de-

O'Connor designed rifle scabbard has buckle-fastened boot cover and is made of thick stiff leather. It affords full protection in bad weather.

signed by the late Jack O'Connor, well-known shooting editor of *Outdoor Life,* the scabbard has a removable boot and adjustable saddle straps.

The Rifle Cleaning Kit

Cost of a cleaning kit is minimal when compared with the price of a good rifle, yet such a kit could keep rifle from rusting and perhaps from becoming inoperable.

The basic cleaning kit should have the following:
A cleaning rod of proper size to fit bore diameter.
A bristle brush, either brass or hard nylon
Cloth cleaning patches
Gun solvent
Gun oil
Linseed oil

Any centerfire rifle using jacketed bullets should be cleaned after each shooting session. First run the bristle brush, soaked with solvent, through the bore. Follow with about two dry cleaning patches, then one clean patch coated with oil. It doesn't take long, but it will keep your bore in top shape.

If you're shooting a .22 rimfire with waxed or grease-coated bullets, such as Remington's Kleanbore ammunition, there's no need to clean the rifle. The bullet's coating is actually a rust preventative and the rifle can be fired indefinitely without cleaning.

Once the bore is taken care of, wipe all metal parts with an oily rag or a silicone-treated gun cloth. This will keep rust from forming on exposed parts.

A lightly oiled rag can also be used on the stock to remove fingerprints or smudges, since such stocks are generally varnished or lacquered. If the stock is deeply scratched, however, rub the wood with linseed oil. The oil will help coat the scratch. This is the next best thing to refinishing the entire stock.

Three recoil pad designs. Vented pad, left, is preferred when stock is to be lengthened. Slip-on pad, middle, has detachable as well as recoil absorbing feature. Solid pad, right, is preferred for rifles with magnum recoil.

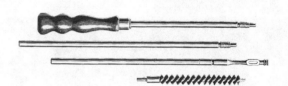

Cleaning rod with attachments for holding a cloth patch and for a wire brush.

Competition Shooting

Competition shooting knows no boundaries. It pits man against man, state against state, and nation against nation. It is a world-wide activity. Matches are governed by the rules and regulations of such organizations as the National Rifle Association and the International Shooting Union. The variety of events in these matches are many and diversified, but most include shooting from the basic positions of standing, prone, kneeling, and sitting.

The following photos from the National Rifle Association illustrate in detail the technique of getting into and shooting from the accepted positions for official match shooting.

Although this information generally applies to competition shooting, the hunter would do well to study each position carefully and adapt his shooting style to them. The human body is a shaky shooting platform at best and these positions have been internationally proven to be the steadiest.

THE PRONE POSITION

1. Before taking the prone position, the shooter faces approximately half right. Feet are apart with body leaning forward slightly and knees flexed. Right hand grasps heel of the buttstock. Left hand is in shooting position with sling adjusted. Shooter's eyes are on his target.

2. In rapid-fire the shooter remains in standing position until the target appears. He then drops forward on his knees. Leg muscles are tensed somewhat to delay movement slightly and avoid knee injury from hard or rough firing point.

3. On reaching kneeling position, body is thrown well forward with toe of rifle butt used to break the fall.

4. With rifle butt on ground left elbow is shoved well forward before coming to rest in final position. Note that shooter's eyes have never left his target.

5. Body is then rolled to left slightly so that rifle butt can be set in shoulder pocket.

6. With rifle butt in place right elbow is brought down to complete the standing-to-prone movement.

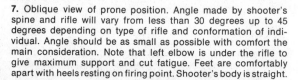

7. Oblique view of prone position. Angle made by shooter's spine and rifle will vary from less than 30 degrees up to 45 degrees depending on type of rifle and conformation of individual. Angle should be as small as possible with comfort the main consideration. Note that left elbow is under the rifle to give maximum support and cut fatigue. Feet are comfortably apart with heels resting on firing point. Shooter's body is straight.

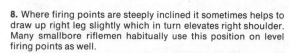

8. Where firing points are steeply inclined it sometimes helps to draw up right leg slightly which in turn elevates right shoulder. Many smallbore riflemen habitually use this position on level firing points as well.

THE STANDING POSITION

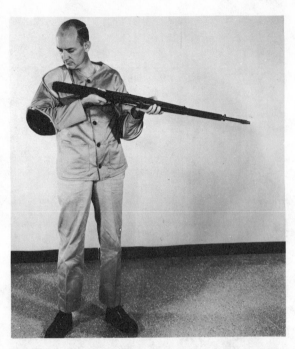

1. To take the Standing position, the shooter faces about 85 degrees with the line of aim. Feet are spread ten to 15 inches apart. Left hand grasps forearm of rifle in shooting position. Toe of rifle butt is placed in shoulder pocket.

2. With toe of butt in place, right arm is elevated and rifle rotated until elbow is as high as possible compatible with comfort. Left elbow is directly under piece. Spine is straight with body weight resting equally on both feet. Left arm does not touch or rest against the body. Sling is in taut or parade position.

3. Same position showing use of hasty sling and shooting glove. Sling can be used only when authorized in program or in matches specifying NRA Standing position.

4. Optional NRA Standing position. Left arm rests against body. Thumb of left hand supports rifle just in rear of balance.

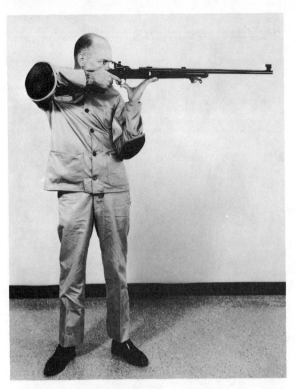

5. Optional NRA Standing position. Left arm and elbow rest against hip. Weight of rifle is supported by fingertips of left hand with thumb under trigger guard and rest of fingers contacting the bottom of the stock.

6. Optional NRA Standing position showing use of Schuetzen-type buttplate and palm rest when such are permitted by match program. Left elbow rests against the hip.

7. Optional NRA Standing position (also qualifies under Rule 5.11 Standing position). Left arm does not touch or rest against the body. Left hand grasps rifle just forward of the balance.

8. Front view of typical Standing position to show placement of left elbow directly under rifle. Right elbow is in high position. This is particularly desirable when shooting high power rifle since it insures maximum contact of butt with shoulder to better absorb recoil. Body weight is borne equally by both feet.

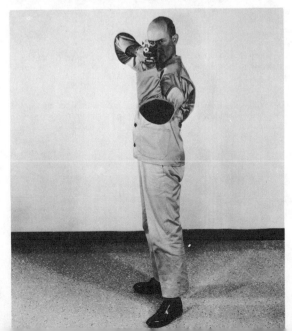

1. Before taking the normal sitting position the shooter faces slightly to right of line of fire. Feet are spread comfortable distance apart. Right hand grasps heel of buttstock. Left hand is in shooting position with sling adjusted. Eyes are on target.

THE SITTING POSITION

2. In rapid-fire the shooter remains in standing position until the target appears. He then sits down, breaking fall with right hand. As right hand contacts firing point the buttocks are shifted to rear until undersides of knees are approximately eight to ten inches from firing point.

3. Right hand is brushed against side of leg to wipe off sand and then grips buttstock.

4. Shooter bends forward from the waist and at same time positions buttstock in pocket of right shoulder with right hand. Left upper arm is positioned on left shinbone.

6. Front view, normal sitting position. Feet are farther apart than knees. Left elbow is under rifle. Weight of body is relaxed well forward into the sling. This position is 'legal' under NRA High Power Rifle Rules; NRA Smallbore Rifle Rules.

5. With buttstock in place, right elbow is positioned against inside of right knee. Right hand grasps stock in firing position.

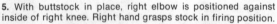

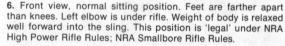

7. Optional NRA Sitting position. Similar to normal sitting position except that body is farther forward, with elbows resting near midpoint of shinbones. Knees may be in contact with arm pits or nearly so. This position is 'legal' under NRA Smallbore Rifle Rules; NRA High Power Rifle Rules.

8. Before taking cross-legged sitting position, shooter faces little more than half right to line of fire. Knees are flexed and feet are crossed. Right hand grasps heel of buttstock. Left hand is in shooting position with sling adjusted. Eyes are on target.

9. On firing command or appearance of target shooter sits down. Right hand is on heel of buttstock.

10. Shooter bends forward from the waist and at same time positions buttstock in pocket of right shoulder with right hand. Feet are drawn up under body.

11. With buttstock in place right elbow is positioned against right shinbone, left elbow against thigh or shinbone. Right hand grasps small of stock in firing position. Feet are drawn up close to the body so that the outer calf of each leg rests on inside of opposite foot. Weight of body is relaxed forward into the sling. This position is 'legal' under NRA High Power Rifle Rules; NRA Smallbore Rifle Rules.

12. Cross-ankled sitting position is assumed in same initial fashion as cross-legged position. The legs are extended well away from the body upon assumption of sitting position. Left elbow rests against the shinbone or inside thigh above knee. Right elbow rests against the shinbone. Same rules provisions as cross-legged position.

THE KNEELING POSITION

1. Before taking the kneeling position the shooter faces to the right of the line of fire and then moves the left foot about 18 inches forward and to the left so that the left foot is aligned approximately on the target.

2. Shooter then drops to the kneeling position with the right buttock resting on the right heel. Angle formed by rifle and right leg should be approximately 90°. Left elbow is positioned so that it will be approximately on or just inside the knee. Right hand positions rifle butt in shoulder pocket.

3. Right hand then grasps small of stock in firing position. Body weight is shifted well forward. Right arm is relaxed. Note that heel of left foot is to rear of knee.

4. Rear view of kneeling position. Right buttock rests against right heel. Body weight is well forward with torso muscles as relaxed as possible.

5. Optional kneeling position showing different placement of right foot. Right buttock contacts right heel with toes pointed to the rear away from the body.

6. Optional kneeling position with shooter sitting on inside of right foot. Left leg is extended. Left foot is forward of knee.

7. Optional kneeling position with shooter sitting on inside of right foot. Left leg is extended with left foot positioned to right opposite right knee. Side of the left foot and ankle is in contact with the firing point.

8. NRA kneeling position showing use of kneeling pad under instep authorized under NRA Smallbore Rifle Rules, NRA High Power Rifle Rules. Both toes and knee of right leg must contact firing point and maximum dimensions of pad are prescribed. Upper left arm contacts knee just above elbow with left heel in rear of knee.

9. Front view of NRA kneeling position showing correct placement of instep pad with both toes and knee of right leg in contact with firing point.

10. Optional NRA kneeling position showing different positioning of left arm in relation to knee. Armpit may actually come into contact with the knee.

Shotgun Actions

The modern shotgun of today falls into one of four basic designs—the break action, which includes the single shot, the side-by-side double and over-and-under double; the pump action; the autoloader, which includes gas and recoil-operated models; and the bolt action.

Selection of a shotgun differs slightly from that of a rifle in that personal preference and cost play a more important role. But there are still some guidelines to follow when choosing one of these smoothbore scatterguns for your game.

Break-Action Single Shot

The single-shot break action is the cheapest and simplest shotgun available today. But, like a good ax or knife, it can do many jobs. Made with or without exposed hammer and in all popular gauges and chokes, this single shot has taken game from squirrels with No. 6 shot to black bear with rifled slugs.

While not the ideal scattergun for hunting, it makes a fine boy's first shotgun. Safe and simple to use, a youngster can use it to break his first clay pigeon, bag his first cottontail, and even accompany dad with it on his first deer hunt.

There are some factors to consider, however. This single shot is a light weapon and has a fair amount of recoil in the bigger gauges. If the gun is for a boy, pick a 20 gauge with a 26-inch modified choke barrel. The recoil of a 12 gauge may be too much for some boys to handle. The 20 gauge also gets the nod over the .410 as a hunting load. With a bit of practice, a young lad can knock over rabbits consistently with a 20 gauge. But with a .410 it generally takes a good shot, particularly on winged game.

It seems to be a popular idea to buy a .410 for a boy's first shotgun, but I wonder how many fathers would want to take out after pheasants and grouse with a .410? So why harness a boy with such a gauge? The .410 shotgun can be an effective hunting arm, but only in the hands of an exceptionally skilled shot. The 20 gauge is a better choice and if the gun is fitted with a recoil pad the recoil can generally be handled by boys of average build.

The single-shot break action also makes a good camper's gun and is a long-time favorite of the farmer. The camper can use the gun for clay-bird shooting or taking a rabbit for the pot, if he's camping during small-game season. The break-action has a quick take-down feature, which means the gun can be stored conveniently in a camper.

For the farmer, such a gun becomes more of a tool than a sporting arm. He uses it to knock off marauding crows and hawks or a fox or two raiding his chicken house. The farmer is better off with a 12 gauge, since he can also use it come deer season. The camper, however, would do well to stick to a 20 gauge, so the entire family can comfortably shoot the gun.

As for safety, the break action can't be beat. Simply break it open and you can carry it around with no fear of an accidental discharge.

Another type of single-shot break action which we will mention briefly is the specially designed trap guns. These guns are fitted with ventilated ribs and are precision bored. They are very expensive and should only be considered by the serious trapshooter.

Typical of inexpensive but well-made single-shot scatterguns are Harrington & Richardson Model 176 Magnums, which come in 10, 12, 16, and 20 gauge. All have long, full-choke barrels. Every bore size is available with a 32-inch barrel, and the two largest can also be had with a 36-inch barrel. All but 16 gauge are chambered for long magnum shells.

Stevens Model 9478 is a new variation on the break-action Model 94-C, which has been popular for over half a century. This latest edition of the single-shot design employs a bottom lever—convenient for either right- or left-handers—to open the action. Gun is made in .410, 20, 12, and 10 gauge. A scaled-down Youth Model is available in .410 or 20 gauge.

Side-by-Side and Over-and-Under Double

These side-by-side and over-and-under doubles are so similar in basic design that they should be discussed together. The side-by-side, as its name indicates, wears its barrels next to each other. The over-and-under has its two barrels stacked vertically, one on top of the other.

As a good, safe, and dependable hunting arm, the doubles are near the top of the list. The traditional doubles have two triggers, one for each barrel, or a non-selective single trigger. On the single nonselective trigger models, the barrel with the more open choke always fires first. On a double choked modified and full, for example, the trigger will always fire the modified barrel first. These doubles, not too expensive, also have a matted rib and extractors, which means the fired shell must be removed manually.

Actual selection of a double depends a great deal on your budget. The better doubles with the more desirable features cost more. There are some basic guidelines to follow, however. If you're an average hunter who gets out about a half dozen times a year and who sticks mainly to rabbits and pheasants, one of the cheaper doubles should fill the bill. If choice of barrel chokes to be fired first is important to you, get a double-trigger model. Otherwise a single nonselective trigger will work just as well.

Some hunters claim the single nonselective trigger is a handicap, since you have no choice of which barrel to shoot first. But, looking at the problem realistically, 9 times out of 10 a hunter will want to shoot the open-choke barrel first anyway, since small game and birds are likely to be close when he gets that first shot.

The double-trigger model does have one edge over the single nonselective trigger, and that's for the hunter who occasionally shoots trap with the tighter choked barrel.

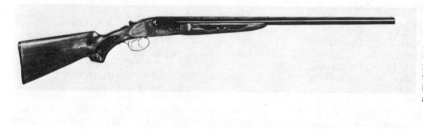

This Savage-Fox Model B is typical of the traditional double-trigger side-by-side shotgun. It's turned out in 12, 16, and 20 gauges and .410 bore. Barrel lengths, depending on gauge, are 26, 28, and 30 inches. Choke combinations include Improved Cylinder and Modified, Modified and Full, and Full and Full.

Winchester's Model 101 is a good example of a modern over-and-under double. It has a single selective trigger and ventilated rib, and comes in various models for hunting, trap, or skeet shooting. The model 101 is available in so many gauges, barrel, and choke combinations that they are too numerous to list here.

The better and more expensive doubles have single selective triggers, which means the hunter can choose the barrel he wants to fire first. These doubles are generally equipped with automatic ejectors and frequently with ventilated ribs, particularly on the over-and-unders.

As we mentioned above, the double is a traditional hunting arm and a top choice for small game, upland game, and waterfowl. Its advantages are many. First, it is the safest hunting gun. To tell if it is loaded, simply break it and take a glance. When hunting in wet and sloppy weather you can also tell at a glance if the bores are obstructed in any way. If you have to jump a small creek or cross a fence, just break the action and the gun will not fire. You also have the choice of two chokes to control shot pattern. And another factor to keep in mind is that for the same barrel length, the overall length of the double is a few inches shorter than autoloaders and pumps. It also balances better because there is more weight between the hands.

If you can afford the extra cash, you can avoid making the above decision of getting a double with a single selective trigger. Then, by manipulating a button near the tang safety, you have a quick choice of which barrel to shoot first—open or tight choke. If you do a great deal of small game hunting, from cottontails to waterfowl, with some trap and skeet tossed in, it would be worth the extra money to pick a scattergun with a selective trigger.

Should your gun be a side-by side or an over-and-under? Here again, it's largely a matter of personal preference. Some shooters like the single sighting plane of the over-and-under. If you have spent a great deal of time shooting a rifle or pump shotgun, you may prefer the over-and-under. Other hunters like the traditional quick-handling feel of a side-by-side. Best bet is to handle both types and let "feel" be the judge.

PARTS OF A TYPICAL PUMP-ACTION SHOTGUN

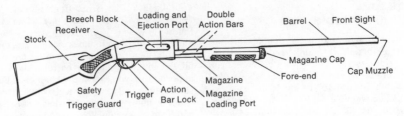

The Pump Shotgun

The pump gun is likely the most most popular scattergun for hunting, though with the past decade it has been getting some stiff competition from the increasing number of doubles introduced to the shooting public.

This manually operated repeater, however, has some distinct advantages. Since it is cheaper to manufacture, the pump can be sold at a lower price—usually less than a good double. Some hunters, particularly waterfowlers, like the magazine capacity of three or more shells. It's also fast and offers a single sighting plane. Fit a pump with a variable choke, and it becomes a good all-round gun. And if you don't like choke device on your muzzle, you can always get a pump that will take interchangeable barrels. A pump with a couple of interchangeable barrels makes a dandy combination. For example, there isn't much that a shotgun hunter can't handle if he has one 28-inch Full-Choke barrel and one 26-inch Improved Cylinder barrel. By simply switching barrels, he'll do well on the trap range with the tight choke and do equally well with the open choke on upland game.

Those who prefer the doubles will point out that pumps are too long, muzzle heavy, and don't have the slim feel and handling qualities of a fine double. This is all true to a degree, but it actually all boils down to the fact that you can get an extremely well-made pump shotgun for the price of a fair double.

The Autoloader

The autoloading, or automatic, shotgun works on one of two principles—recoil or gas. The accompanying sketches show step-by-step how each type of mechanism works. Both types work well and both are equally acceptable in the field. Remington uses gas-operation in its Model 1100, while Browning's well-known automatic is recoil-operated.

The autoloading shotgun has all the advantages and disadvantages of the pump. The only difference is that manual operation after each shot is eliminated with the autoloader, which means faster firepower.

HOW A PUMP-ACTION SHOTGUN WORKS

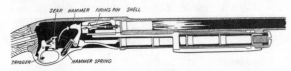

1. Starting with the gun loaded and cocked, pulling the trigger trips the sear, releasing the hammer to strike the firing pin and fire the shell.

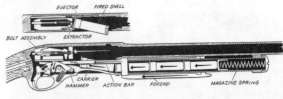

2. Pulling the fore-end rearward moves the action bar and bolt assembly toward the rear, ejecting the fired shell (see also top-view detail of ejection), pressing the hammer down into cocked position, and moving the new shell onto the carrier.

3. Detail of the carrier mechanism (left) shows how the bolt assembly at its rearmost position engages the carrier dog. As the bolt assembly moves forward (right), it moves the carrier dog downward, pivoting the carrier and new shell up into loading position. At the same time the shell latch moves to the right to hold the remaining shells in the magazine.

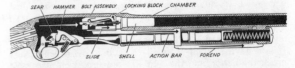

4. As the fore-end action bar and bolt assembly continue to move forward, the new shell is pushed into the chamber, and the sear engages the hammer, locking it. At the final movement of the fore-end, the slide continues forward. pushing the locking block up to lock the action for firing.

PARTS OF A TYPICAL AUTOLOADING SHOTGUN

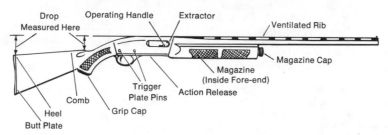

Drop
Measured Here

Operating Handle

Extractor

Ventilated Rib

Magazine Cap

Magazine
(Inside Fore-end)

Action Release

Trigger
Plate Pins

Grip Cap

Comb

Heel

Butt Plate

HOW A GAS-OPERATED SHOTGUN WORKS

HAMMER

FIRING PIN

1. Starting with the gun cocked and loaded, squeezing the trigger releases the hammer, which strikes the firing pin and fires the shell.

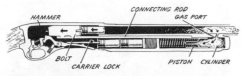

HAMMER

CONNECTING ROD
GAS PORT

BOLT

CARRIER LOCK

PISTON CYLINDER

2. The gas generated by the fired shell is metered down through the gas port in the barrel into the cylinder. The pressure of the gas in the cylinder pushes the piston and connecting rod rearward, moving the bolt from the chamber. As the bolt travels rearward it recocks the hammer and opens the carrier lock.

FIRED SHELL

SHELL MAGAZINE SPRING

CARRIER

3. Further rearward travel of the bolt ejects the spent shell through the side opening, and the magazine spring pushes a fresh shell onto the carrier.

BOLT

PISTON SPRING

CARRIER

PISTON PORT

4. The piston spring starts the piston forward, moving the bolt forward, and pivoting the carrier to bring the new shell into loading position. As bolt moves all the way forward, it loads the new shell into the chamber. Spent gas escapes through the port.

HOW A RECOIL-OPERATED SHOTGUN WORKS

HAMMER

FIRING PIN

1. Starting with the gun cocked and loaded, squeezing the trigger causes the hammer to hit the firing pin and fire the shell.

BOLT CHAMBER

INERTIA
ROD

INERTIA
ROD PIN

2. Backward force of the recoil moves the chamber and bolt $\frac{1}{10}$ inch, kicking the inertia rod pin so that the rod travels rearward. As it travels backward the inertia rod recocks the hammer.

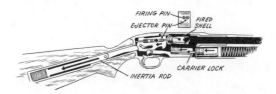

FIRING PIN

EJECTOR PIN

FIRED
SHELL

CARRIER LOCK

INERTIA ROD

3. Full rearward travel of the inertia rod pulls back the bolt, and the ejector pin throws out the spent shell through the side opening. Carrier lock pivots, admitting new shell onto carrier.

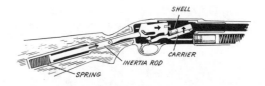

SHELL

CARRIER

INERTIA ROD

SPRING

4. The spring at the base of the inertia rod starts the rod returning, moving the bolt forward. As the bolt begins to move, it pivots the carrier, which lifts the new shell into loading position. Full forward movement of bolt carries new shell into chamber.

When is this fast firepower really needed? It's difficult to say. The average small-game hunter can get by without an automatic and, actually, he's better off with a gun that requires some manual manipulation between shots for safety sake. The rabbit and pheasant hunter rarely gets the chance to cut loose with more than two shots and the speed with which he gets off those two shots is not as critical as some hunters believe.

The autoloader, however, may be preferred for waterfowlers and skeet shooters. Duck hunters often have the chance to get off extra shots and they want to fire those second and third shots fast when a mallard discovers he's been had and retreats like a turpentined cat. And the skeet shooter who is having trouble dusting doubles will appre-

ciate the autoloader since all he has to do is squeeze the trigger to get off a second shot.

The Bolt Action

As far as fast-handling qualities on small game and birds, bolt actions are bottom on the list. Their most important features are that they are cheap and strong. They work out best where fast shooting isn't involved. Hunters in states where rifles are not allowed for deer hunting, for example, may find one of these inexpensive bolt actions a good choice. It's an effective combination when fitted with iron sights and used with shotgun slugs. It's also a more than adequate choice for farmers who want an inexpensive shotgun to protect crops and stock from predators and pests.

Savage-Stevens Model 58 is a bolt-action shotgun with clip magazine. It's chambered for 12, 16, and 20 gauge and .410 bore. With recoil pad and full-choke barrel, it's a good utility gun for shooters of all ages.

Mossberg's Model 395K is a 12-gauge bolt-action shotgun, chambered to accept 2¾- and 3-inch shells. It holds one round in the chamber and two more in the detachable box magazine. You can switch the choke to whatever constriction you want by rotating C-Lect-Choke device on the front of the barrel. A 20-gauge version, Model 385K, has the same features.

Marlin's Goose Gun wears a 36-inch full-choke barrel in front of its bolt action. Capacity is three rounds. Chambered for the 12-gauge 3-inch magnum shell, it will do fine for the budget-minded waterfowler. Marlin also offers a SuperGoose 10, which has a 34-inch full-choke barrel and accommodates 3½-inch, 10-gauge magnum shells.

SIDE-BY-SIDE DOUBLES

Winchester Model 21 Pigeon Grade. A fine double built on special order to fit buyer's personal measurements. Available in all gauges, barrel lengths, and chokes.

Line-up of Beretta doubles. From top, the GR-4, the GR-3, and the GR-2. The GR-4 has automatic ejectors, single selective trigger, and ventilated rib. The GR-3, single selective trigger and ventilated rib. The GR-2 has double triggers. The GR-2 and GR-3 are available in 12 and 20 gauge, the GR-4 in 12 gauge only.

Savage-Stevens Model 311 has double triggers and matted rib. It is chambered for 12, 16, and 20 gauge and .410 bore. Barrel lengths are 26, 28, and 30 inches. Choke combinations include Improved Cylinder and Modified, Modified and Full, Full and Full.

Browning's 12- and 20-gauge B-SS shotguns are side-by-side doubles, chambered for 3-inch shells and available with 26- or 28-inch barrels. B-SS Standard has a full pistol grip and full beavertail forearm. B-SS Sporter, shown here, has a straight-grip stock with longer trigger-guard tang, slimmer forearm, and "satin" oil finish, giving it a more classic appearance.

OVER-AND-UNDER DOUBLES

Savage Model 333, available in 12 and 20 gauge, is an over-and-under with single selective trigger, wide ventilated rib, automatic ejectors, and cocking indicators. Barrel lengths run from 26 to 30 inches. Choke combinations include Skeet and Skeet, Improved Cylinder and Modified, Modified and Full, and Improved Modified and Full.

Interarms/Manufrance Falcor is a 12-gauge over-and-under with 26-, 28-, or 30-inch chromed bores, a single selective trigger, automatic ejectors, and a mono-block action machined from a one-piece forging of nickel-chrome steel.

Browning Citori shotguns come in several grades and two versions—Standard Model, with full pistol grip and beavertail forearm; and Sporter, with straight grip and Schnabel forearm.

Ithaca/Perazzi 12-gauge MT-6 is a semi-custom over-and-under with stock dimensions to meet the customer's specifications. It comes with fitted hard case and features five screw-in choke tubes—Extra Full, Full, Improved Modified, Modified, and Improved Cylinder.

Harrington & Richardson Model 1212 Field Gun is a 12 gauge with 28-inch barrels choked Improved Cylinder and Improved Modified. It also comes as a Waterfowl Model, chambered for 3-inch 12-gauge magnums and with 30-inch barrels choked Modified and Full.

Weatherby Regency is chambered for 12-gauge shells or 20-gauge 3-inch magnums. Its 28-inch barrels are choked Skeet and Skeet, Improved Cylinder and Modified, or Modified and Full. It has selective automatic ejectors and a single selective trigger. Barrel selector is located inside the trigger guard.

PUMP-ACTION SHOTGUNS

Marlin Model 120 Magnum is a pump gun chambered for 12-gauge 3-inch shells. Its tubular magazine holds 5 standard loads or 4 long magnums; 3-shot plug is furnished to conform with migratory-bird regulations. There's a choice of six interchangeable barrels, including a slug barrel with rifle-type sights. Marlin also offers a Field Grade 120 with 28-inch plain barrel (no rib) and modified choke.

Stevens Model 67 pump comes in .410, 20, or 12 gauge. Smallest bore size has a 26-inch full-choke barrel; in 12 or 20 gauge, the 67 has a 28-inch barrel, choked modified or full.

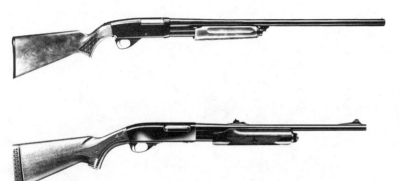

Remington Model 870, like most good pumps, comes in a rifled-slug version for deer hunting. Available in 12 or 20 gauge, it has rifle-type sights, and the barrel is 20 inches long and choked Improved Cylinder. Other 870's come in all gauges, several barrel lengths, and all conventional chokes.

PUMP-ACTION SHOTGUNS (continued)

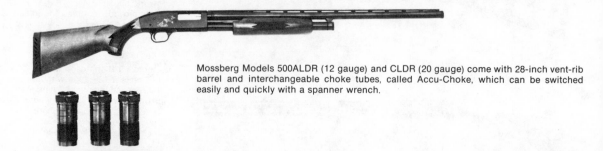

Mossberg Models 500ALDR (12 gauge) and CLDR (20 gauge) come with 28-inch vent-rib barrel and interchangeable choke tubes, called Accu-Choke, which can be switched easily and quickly with a spanner wrench.

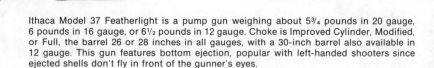

Ithaca Model 37 Featherlight is a pump gun weighing about $5\frac{3}{4}$ pounds in 20 gauge, 6 pounds in 16 gauge, or $6\frac{1}{2}$ pounds in 12 gauge. Choke is Improved Cylinder, Modified, or Full, the barrel 26 or 28 inches in all gauges, with a 30-inch barrel also available in 12 gauge. This gun features bottom ejection, popular with left-handed shooters since ejected shells don't fly in front of the gunner's eyes.

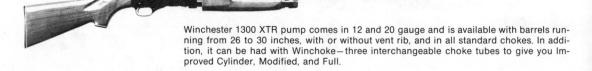

Winchester 1300 XTR pump comes in 12 and 20 gauge and is available with barrels running from 26 to 30 inches, with or without vent rib, and in all standard chokes. In addition, it can be had with Winchoke—three interchangeable choke tubes to give you Improved Cylinder, Modified, and Full.

AUTOLOADING SHOTGUNS

Remington Model 1100 autoloading shotgun with vent rib. Available in 12, 16, 20, 28 gauge and .410 bore. The 12- and 20-gauge versions are chambered for 3-inch shells. Field gun is shown; trap and skeet models are also made.

Remington Model 1100 Deer Gun in 12 and 20 gauge. The 22-inch barrel is bored Improved Cylinder and has adjustable rifle sights.

Winchester Model 1500 XTR field gun in 12 or 20 gauge. Available with vent rib or plain barrel. Also available with Winchoke screw-in chokes to provide a quick choice of muzzle constrictions—Full. Modified, or Improved Cylinder.

Ithaca Model 51 Standard autoloader in 12 or 20 gauge. Available with or without vent rib. Barrel lengths run from 26 to 30 inches, and chokes include Skeet, Improved Cylinder, Modified, and Full. Interchangeable barrels can be ordered.

Ithaca Mag-10 is an autoloading waterfowl gun chambered for 3½-inch 10-gauge Magnums. It's gas-operated and incorporates a "Countercoil" device to absorb the punch of powerful loads. Full-choked barrel is 32 inches long.

Browning B-2000 in 12 or 20 gauge. Available with plain barrel or vent rib. Has 5-shot capacity in standard versions, 4 in versions chambered for 3-inch shells. Standard B-2000 can be bought with an interchangeable magnum barrel for 3-inch shells. Gas system requires no adjustment when switching to these heavier loads.

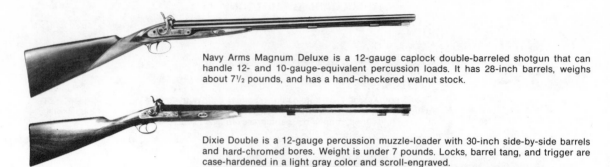

Navy Arms Magnum Deluxe is a 12-gauge caplock double-barreled shotgun that can handle 12- and 10-gauge-equivalent percussion loads. It has 28-inch barrels, weighs about 7½ pounds, and has a hand-checkered walnut stock.

Dixie Double is a 12-gauge percussion muzzle-loader with 30-inch side-by-side barrels and hard-chromed bores. Weight is under 7 pounds. Locks, barrel tang, and trigger are case-hardened in a light gray color and scroll-engraved.

Kodiak, from Trail Guns Armory, can be bought as a .50 or .58 double rifle, 12-gauge double shotgun, .50-caliber/12-gauge rifle-shotgun combination—or, if all interchangeable barrels are ordered, it can be all of those in one gun. It employs percussion locks with a half-cock safety.

Muzzle-Loading Shotgun

Muzzle-loading shotguns, though not as popular as muzzle-loading rifles and handguns, have claimed a growing number of enthusiasts in recent years. Quite a few sportsmen hunt with them—though such guns are slow to load—and quite a few compete in muzzle-loading trap and skeet matches. The supply of shootable antiques began to dwindle quite some time ago, and most of the muzzle-loading smoothbores in use today are new, factory-made guns. Now and then you may see a flintlock, but caplocks are the general rule, and they're designed after the good English, French, and American ones made in the 19th century.

A few are single-barreled, which means they're single shots, of course, but most are side-by-side doubles. Quality varies widely, and it's true that you get what you pay for. Some of the surprisingly inexpensive, low-grade ones are unreliable or even of questionable safety. Good ones, mostly imported, cost no more (sometimes less) than breechloading shotguns of comparable quality, and are available from The Armoury, Dixie, Hawes, Tingle, Navy, Euroarms, Interarms, Trial Guns Armory, and a few other companies.

Navy Arms imports several good ones, including a Magnum Deluxe Model reminiscent of fine English and French doubles of the 1840's. It has 12-gauge barrels, 28 inches long. Euroarms of America offers a quality single shot, also of English heritage. Called the Magnum Cape Gun, it has a 32-inch 12-gauge barrel. Tingle makes one, simply called the Tingle Percussion Single Barrel Shotgun, with a 30-inch 12-gauge barrel. Dixie has, from time to time, imported flintlock shotguns, but these are becoming difficult to buy from that company or any other source because the demand is so limited. Dixie's percussion doubles include a light-weight (6¾-pound) 12-gauge Italian import with 28-inch blued barrels, case-hardened locks, and a European walnut stock with a checkered wrist. Shop around and you should find what you want. Most but not all of the muzzle-loaders are 12 gauge.

Before loading such a shotgun, all oil should be removed with a dry patch, and the nipple—or nipples if it's a double—should be cleared by firing several caps to remove any residual oil from the breech area. Then, you pour the powder charge down the barrel. If you're using a 12 gauge for upland hunting, this would be a 3-dram charge of FFg black powder or a bulk charge of Pyrodex from the same measure setting. Most shotgunning is done with loads measured in drams but, in case you're wondering, 82 grains is the same as 3 drams. The traditional wad column consists of an over-powder card, a couple of filler wads, the load of shot, and an over-shot wad. In this upland load, 1 to 1¼ ounces of shot will work well.

Some shooters use one-piece plastic wads, but you'll get better results with the traditional wad column or a combination of the traditional and contemporary. If you choose the latter, use the over-powder wad and fillers for a cushion but top these with a plastic shot pouch. This will tighten your pattern. After pouring in the shot, you still use an over-powder wad, of course, to hold the load in. Then, with the nipples capped, just cock the gun and fire away.

To obtain information about muzzle-loading trap and skeet shoots, as well as many details about hunting and competitive shooting, contact the National Muzzle Loading Rifle Association, Box 67, Friendship, IN 47021.

Gauge and Shot Size

The system of referring to shotguns by gauges was started many years ago. The inside diameter of a shotgun's bore was designated by the number of lead balls that would fit the bore and would make up one pound. For example, a round lead ball that would fit the bore of a 12 gauge should weigh one-twelfth of a pound, and 12 of these balls would weigh one pound. A 20-gauge would take 20 lead balls that would weigh one pound, and so on. The .410 is the only departure from this system. The .410 is not a gauge at all, but the actual measurement in inches of the diameter of the bore.

The accompanying chart shows in actual size the diameters of shotgun bores in the common gauges. Gauge is also converted into measurement in inches.

BORE DIAMETERS OF SHOTGUN GAUGES

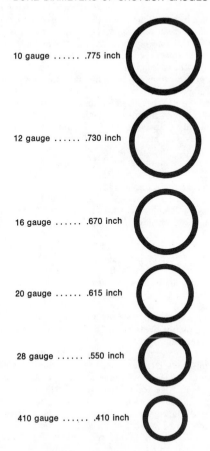

10 gauge . . . . . . .775 inch

12 gauge . . . . . . .730 inch

16 gauge . . . . . . .670 inch

20 gauge . . . . . . .615 inch

28 gauge . . . . . . .550 inch

410 gauge . . . . . . .410 inch

The 12, an All-round Gauge

The typical hunter looks for one shotgun that he can shoot well and use on all game from squirrels to deer. There is no doubt that such an all-round shotgun has to be a 12 gauge. In the very early 1900's the 10-gauge with 1¼ ounces of shot was a hot item and considered a good choice for an all-round gauge. But modern shotshells have changed the scene. Today the 12 gauge can do anything the 10 gauge did, and sometimes do it better.

Gunning for small game and upland birds, a hunter can get by very well with the standard 2¾-inch 12-gauge shotshell loaded with 1¼ ounces of shot. The waterfowl hunter who takes his birds at greater range should use the 12 gauge 2¾-inch Magnum load with 1½ ounces of shot or the 3-inch Magnum load with 1⅜ to 1⅞ ounces of shot. If it's deer you're after, use the 2¾-inch Magnums loaded with 12 pellets of 00 Buckshot, or the 3-inch Magnum with 15 pellets of 00 Buckshot.

The 12-gauge, then, is a good choice for the one-gun man who hunts small game, birds, and deer. He merely varies shotshell loads to do the different jobs.

A typical 12-gauge shotgun, however, is heavier and bulkier than guns in the smaller gauges. The ammunition is also bigger and heavier to carry. This may not mean much to the duck hunter sitting in a blind, but the upland gunner who carries his scattergun all day may find the smaller gauges more suitable.

The 16 Gauge

The 16 gauge simply refuses to die, even though the 12 gauge has it beat as an all-round gauge and the 20 gauge comes off a better choice for a light, quick-handling scattergun for small game and birds. Some hunters claim the 16 gauge is a good compromise between the 12 and 20 gauges, but this is a tough argument to prove.

The standard 16 gauge load carries 1⅛ ounces of shot, exactly the same as the 20 gauge 2¾-inch Magnum load, and ⅛ ounce less than the standard 12-gauge load. The 2¾-inch 16-gauge Magnum shell has 1¼ ounces of shot, the same as the standard 12-gauge field load and the 20-gauge 3-inch Magnum.

True, the 16-gauge gun is a bit lighter than a 12, but it's not as light as a 20. What does all this mean? If you have a 16 gauge, keep it and you will be happy with it. But if you're buying a new shotgun, you're better off narrowing your selection down to the 12 or 20 gauge.

The 20 Gauge

The 20 gauge makes the grade as a top choice for all-round upland gunning and waterfowl shooting over decoys. It's lighter and slimmer than the 12 gauge, which makes it a faster handling gun and a more comfortable one to carry in pheasant fields and through briar patches. The ammunition is also lighter to carry.

And it's a fact that most upland game is shot at under 30 yards, so the 20 has more than adequate killing range. The standard 20-gauge load carries 1 ounce of shot, which is enough for just about all upland hunting. If a hunter expects to take birds under tougher conditions, he can use the 20 gauge 2¾-inch Magnum load with 1⅛ ounces of shot.

For ducks over decoys, the 20-gauge 3-inch Magnum is the ticket. In fact, the 3-inch Magnum load will also do the job at pass-shooting.

Hunters who have both 12- and 20-gauge guns in their racks admit that most often they will pick the 20 when heading for favorite rabbit patches and woodcock covers.

The 28 and .410 Gauge

The 28-gauge seems to fall in some sort of a limbo. For the average upland gunner, the 28-gauge just isn't big enough. The skilled shooter, however, should take a closer look. The 28 is available in a load with ⁷/₈ ounces of shot, which makes it adequate for woodcock, quail, doves, and similar birds. But it takes a top wingshot to knock down these birds with a 28 gauge.

The .410 is another load that has limited use. It's fine for the smaller species that can be taken at close range, but it's not recommended for anything else. True, at one time or another, we've all seen a hunter knock down pheasants with a .410 — but these men are generally skilled shotgunners. The average hunter would be far better off with a 12 or 20 gauge. The same reasoning can be used to discourage a father from buying his son a .410. A wiser choice for a youngster would be a light 20 gauge.

Gauges for Trap and Skeet

When it comes to shooting clay birds, whether on official trap and skeet ranges or in a wooded area with a buddy tossing the birds out with a hand trap, almost any shotgun can be pressed into service for fun and practice. But the serious trap and skeet shooters stick to proven combinations.

On the trap range, for example, nearly all shooting is done with a 12-gauge gun. The barrel is 30 inches long, bored Full Choke, and wears a ventilated rib.

The skeet shooter goes to the opposite extreme. He generally starts with a 12-gauge gun, the most popular for the beginner at skeet. But he can vary his gauges, since regulated skeet matches are broken down into four events: the 12 gauge, the 20 gauge, the 28 gauge small-bore, and the .410 sub-small bore. As the skeet shooter improves at the game, he feels obliged to go to the smaller gauges.

The preferred skeet gun has a 26-inch barrel that is bored "Skeet," which is a choke that falls between Improved Cylinder and Cylinder.

Selecting Shot Size — Lead Shot

Shot (the pellets in a shotshell) is normally made of lead, a relatively cheap metal and one that's soft enough so it won't score gun barrels or damage choke construction. Being heavy, it has good ballistic qualities. It's an ideal metal for the pellets used in most types of shotgunning. Everyone agrees about that, but the subject of the best shot size for a given type of game often starts arguments. Some grouse hunters, for example, prefer shot as large as No. 7½ or even No. 6, claiming the larger sizes plow through foliage well. Others prefer shot as small as No. 9 since a lot more No. 9's go into a shell, and a dense pattern of shot is more likely to put some pellets into the mark.

An accompanying chart, The Shotshell Selector, offers advice formulated by experts. Another chart shows the comparative shot sizes, plus the average number of pellets per ounce.

Selecting Shot Size — Steel Shot

Lead shot has one serious drawback. The fired pellets fall into marshes and fields, where they are picked up as grit by feeding waterfowl. The ingested lead is poisonous. Retained in the gizzards of the birds, it kills large numbers of ducks and geese. In some areas, the problem is insignificant. The diet of the birds is one factor. The hardness of the marsh bottom is another, since lead sinks into soft mud and the birds cannot get it. All the same, widespread poisoning of waterfowl by lead shot has mandated the use of a substitute material in shotshells for duck and goose shooting. No truly ideal non-toxic substitute has yet been found, but steel shot — the subject of research and development programs at ammunition companies for a number of years — has been significantly improved and is now supplied by the major manufacturers in waterfowl loads.

Since steel is only about 70 percent as heavy as lead, it requires more space in a shell than an equal weight of lead. Whereas an average of 135 No. 4 lead pellets make an ounce, you need about 192 steel pellets of the same size to make an ounce. A 1¼-ounce load of steel shot takes up so much more space in a shotshell that the makers have developed new powders that take less space, as well as a special plastic wad that merely acts as a gas seal and shot cup. There is no cushion section, and the shot cup is long enough to cover the entire length of the shot column. This protects the walls of the gun barrel from the hard steel pellets as they travel through the bore.

Because steel is lighter than lead, it is less efficient ballistically. To offset the loss of retained velocity and energy, larger shot must be used. The manufacturers have developed roughly equivalent steel loads in which there is only a small sacrifice in the number of pellets. In an ounce of No. 4 lead shot, for instance, there are 135 pellets; in an ounce of No. 2 steel shot there are 125. A 2¾-inch 12-gauge shell has an average of 169 pellets in a 1¼-ounce No. 4 lead load, 156 pellets in a 1¼-ounce No. 2 steel load. Laboratory and field tests by Remington, Winchester, and Federal have shown that appropriate steel loads (No. 2 steel as a substitute for No. 4 lead, for instance) lose more velocity and energy than lead shot at 40 and 50 yards, but the difference isn't drastic. Three-inch magnum 12-gauge shells with steel shot have become available, but you need not switch to long magnum steel loads in a situation that would call for 2¾-inch lead-shot loads. Assuming you have a gun chambered for 3-inch shells, you use such steel-shot loads only where you would use 3-inch magnum loads of lead shot. Where standard lead-shot loads are used, standard steel-shot loads have power enough.

However, the appropriate shot size obviously differs with steel. From tests by the manufacturers, rules of size have been formulated for switching to steel shot. Essentially, you go up one size for a given use. Shells are commonly available with four sizes of steel shot — No. 4, 2, 1, and BB. In addition, Remington has developed a load of B shot — midway in size between BB and No. 1. The three smallest sizes — No. 4, 2, and 1 — are most often used. Generally speaking, the B and BB sizes are used only by expert gunners for ultra-long-range pass shooting at geese. That makes the guidelines easy: Where you would use No. 5 or 6 lead shot, use No. 4 steel; where you would use No. 4 lead shot, use No. 2 steel; where you would use No. 2 lead shot, use No. 1 steel. To put it another way, use No. 4 steel for ducks over decoys; No. 2 steel for close-range shooting at geese over decoys and for longer-range pass shooting at ducks; and No. 1 steel for pass shooting at geese, or the B or BB size at extremely long range.

Although steel is ballistically inferior to lead, it has one advantage. Because the pellets are so hard, they suffer very little deformation as they pass through a gun's bore. Therefore, they produce slightly tighter patterns than lead. Some hunters have found that they get better results with steel by switching from full choke to modified for pass shooting, except when the range is quite long. As for the power of steel shot at waterfowling ranges, field tests have proved that it will bring down ducks and geese at 50 yards or so just as well as lead if the pattern is properly centered on the target. The average shotgunner shouldn't be trying for ducks or geese at ranges much beyond 50 yards.

A drawback of steel shot is that hunters cannot reload their shells with it. In the future, perhaps, handloading manuals may include loading data for steel shot, but so far they have not. Nor are the proper components available — special hulls, wads, steel shot in bulk, and, most important, the right powders. For the present, at least, waterfowlers will have to buy factory ammunition, and it's expensive because steel shot is much more costly to manufacture than lead shot.

A more widely publicized drawback is the supposed harm that steel shot will do to a shotgun barrel. It is true that double-barreled guns and even some of the older repeaters with relatively thin or soft steel barrels can suffer minor damage — either barrel rings or bulges in the choke area. While these effects aren't hazardous, such guns should be reserved for other kinds of hunting. Most modern guns will not be harmed by steel shot. If in doubt, consult the manufacturer of your shotgun.

THE SHOTSHELL SELECTOR

Lead Shot Unless Indicated "Steel"

	Type of Shell	Size
DUCKS	Magnum or high power	4, 5, 6
		Steel 2, 4
GEESE	Magnum or high power	BB, 2, 4
		Steel BB, 1, 2
PHEASANTS	Field load or high power	5, 6, 7½
QUAIL	High power or field load	7½, 8, 9
RUFFED GROUSE & CHUKARS	High power or field load	5, 6, 7½, 8
DOVES & PIGEONS	High power or field load	6, 7½, 8, 9
RABBITS	High power or field load	4, 5, 6, 7½
WOODCOCK, SNIPE, RAIL	Field load	7½, 8, 9
SQUIRRELS	High power or field load	4, 5, 6
WILD TURKEY	Magnum or high power	BB, 2, 4, 5, 6
CROWS	High power or field load	5, 6, 7½
FOX	Magnum or high power	BB, 2, 4

Courtesy of Federal Cartridge

No.	9	8½	8	7½	6	5	4	2	1	BB
SHOT SIZES Diameter in inches	.08	.085	.09	.095	.11	.12	.13	.15	.16	.18

BUCKSHOT Diameter in inches	No. 4 .24	No. 3 .25	No. 2 .27	No. 1 .30	No. 0 .32	No. 00 .33

SHOT PELLETS PER OUNCE (Approximate)

LEAD				STEEL	
Size	Pellets	Size	Pellets	Size	Pellets
BB	50	6	225	BB	72
2	87	7½	350	1	103
4	135	8	410	2	125
5	170	9	585	4	192

Courtesy of Federal Cartridge

Shotgun Barrel and Choke

The Barrel

Not too long ago the most popular shotgun wore a 30-inch Full Choke barrel. Today, because of modern shotshells with plastic shot collars and protectors which give tighter patterns, the No. 1 choice is a 28-inch barrel with Modified Choke. And upland gunners are even swinging to 24- and 26-inch barrels with Improved Cylinder choke. All this makes sense. A shorter barrel means a lighter gun that is easier to carry and faster to shoot in thick upland cover.

Many years ago, a great number of shotgunners believed that barrels 36 inches and longer shot harder and farther than shorter barrels. This was true in the black-powder days when long barrels were required for full velocity to develop before the shot reached the muzzle. Now, with our modern smokeless powder, full velocity is reached in 24- to 26-inch barrels. In fact, velocity in a 36-inch barrel is slowed down a bit because once the powder is burned and full velocity is reached within 26 inches, friction takes over between shot charge and bore, which decreases velocity.

If some hunters are still convinced they can knock down more game with long barrels, it is only because such barrels give a longer sighting plane and afford better balance and steadiness of swing. This is one reason for the popularity of 30- and 32-inch barrels on the trap range. Velocity has nothing to do with it.

As a general rule, a hunter is better off using as short a barrel as possible without sacrificing balance. Manufacturers know this and build their guns accordingly. Below are recommended barrel lengths for various types of shooting:

TYPES OF SHOOTING	BARREL LENGTH
Long-range duck, goose	30″ or 32″
Waterfowl over decoys	28″ or 30″
Pheasant, grouse	26″ or 28″
Rabbits, squirrels	26″, 28″, or 30″
Quail, doves, woodcock	26″ or 28″
Turkey	28″ or 30″
Deer	26″ to 30″
Trap shooting	30″ to 32″
Skeet shooting	26″ or 28″
All-round shooting	28″

The Choke

The choke on a shotgun is the amount of constriction in the bore of the barrel that is used to control the spread of the shot charge. The greater the constriction, which starts about 3 inches from the muzzle, the tighter the concentration of pellets during flight. Likewise, the lesser the constriction, the greater or wider the spread of pellets in flight.

The choke principle is easily understood by comparing it with a garden hose. Tighten the garden-hose nozzle and you'll get a narrow, heavy stream of water. Open it up and you'll get a wide spray. The choke and the garden-hose nozzle work on basically the same principle.

Chokes on today's shotgun barrels range from Full Choke, which has the most constriction and consequently throws the tightest concentration of shot, to Cylinder, which means no choke at all—that is, no constriction at any point in the bore. Listing them by their common names, the popular range of chokes include Full Choke, Improved Modified, Improved Cylinder, Skeet, and Cylinder.

The constriction in the bore is generally accomplished by reaming or swaging, but much more important than the method is the amount of constriction and its effect on shot spread and pattern. Choke is the difference between bore diameter and muzzle diameter measured in one-thousandths of an inch. This measurement is also referred to as points. For example, the bore of a 12-gauge barrel will measure .730 inches and a constriction of .035 near the muzzle will make it a Full Choke barrel. We can also say the barrel has a 35 point constriction.

Unfortunately, bore diameters and constriction diameters often vary from manufacturer to manufacturer. For example, two 20-gauge guns, both stamped Modified Choke but turned out by two different gun makers, may have a constriction difference of as much as .025 or 25 points. The result is, of course, that not all guns of the same choke will shoot identical patterns. One manufacturer's Full Choke may throw a Modified pattern and vice versa. The only foolproof way of determining the choke of a shotgun is to pattern it.

Before patterning a shotgun, we should know that the choke of a shotgun is determined by the percentage of pellets from the particular shotshell load that fall within a 30-inch circle at 40 yards. The following figures are generally accepted as standard guidelines in determining a barrel's choke:

CHOKE	PERCENTAGE OF SHOT IN 30-INCH CIRCLE AT 40 YD.
Full Choke	70–80 percent
Improved Modified	65–70 percent
Modified	55–65 percent
Quarter Choke	50–55 percent
Improved Cylinder	45–50 percent
Skeet No. 2	50–60 percent
Skeet No. 1 (Cylinder)	35–40 percent

So if you're having trouble with your shotgun, either missing birds with it or getting more than your share of cripples, it would be wise to pattern your gun and see exactly what choke you have and whether your pattern is too dense or sparse for the ranges you're shooting at.

To pattern a shotgun, simply tack up a piece of paper 40 inches by 40 inches. Draw a small bullseye in the center of the paper, then inscribe a 30-inch circle around it. Now check the shotshell load you normally use and compute the number of pellets in it (see charts in previous section). Take a shot at 40 yards at the bullseye, count the pellet holes within the circle, and figure out the percentage that landed in the circle. Check this figure with the above listings and you'll be able to determine the true choke of your shotgun, regardless of the size hole in the barrel or what is stamped on the barrel. Patterning your shotgun and knowing exactly what pattern it throws can be just as important as sighting in a rifle, and there aren't many deer hunters who would go afield without sighting in their rifle.

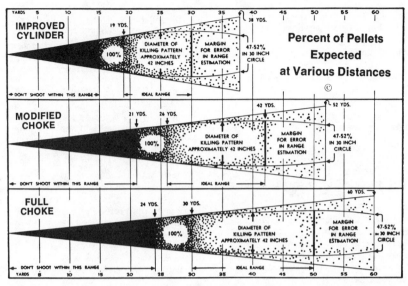

Courtesy of Winchester-Western

It's important to note that these patterns are taken at 40 yards and that most game is taken at considerably closer ranges. In fact, the majority of small game and upland birds are shot at 30 yards or less. So that Full Choke spread that looks great on paper at 40 yards would actually be much smaller and the pellets much more concentrated at, say, 25 yards. To the grouse hunter who rarely shoots his birds at more than 25 yards, this would mean two things: a lot of misses or, if he was an excellent shot, birds shot to pieces. What all this means is that the choke you select depends on the game you're hunting.

The hunter after grouse, rabbits, quail, and woodcock—which are all taken in fairly heavy cover—should use a Modified or Improved Cylinder choke, preferably the latter. If he's a waterfowl gunner, he should use a Modified or Full Choke. Though most duck hunters would feel handicapped with a Modified Choke, this would probably be a better choice. For game such as turkey, usually taken at greater ranges, a Full Choke is the top choice. For all-round small game and bird hunting, the Modified Choke comes off the best compromise.

Solving Shotgun Problems

Knowing the right barrel length and choke for your hunting is fine if you're in the process of buying a new gun. But what about the chap who already has a gun and is dissatisfied because the barrel is too long or the pattern it throws is too dense or too sparse. Suppose his favorite grouse gun has a 26-inch barrel with Improved Cylinder choke and he suddenly decides he wants to take up duck hunting. How does he get a tighter pattern out of it? Or suppose he wants to take his Full-Choke duck gun grouse hunting and wants a wider pattern, but is unwilling to have the shotgun bored out to Improved Cylinder. All these problems can be solved one way or another. Let's take them one by one.

First, let's talk about the fellow who was told that a 30-inch barrel and Full Choke was the greatest combination going. But now he discovers that his barrel is hanging up on limbs and brush in heavy cover while hunting rabbits and grouse and that he's either missing his target or shooting it to pieces. He knows he needs a shorter barrel and a more open choke. There are a few ways he can solve his problem. One way that would involve no expense is to use brush loads (also called scatter loads), a special shot shell that has dividers separating the shot charge. Almost all ammunition makers produce brush loads. Such a shotshell would open his choke one step. That means his Full Choke could be turned into a Modified choke by simply changing ammunition. But, unfortunately, brush loads are usually available in one shot size, generally No. 8. And our hunter still has the problem of the long barrel.

A better alternative would be to have his barrel cut down to 28 inches and bored Improved Cylinder or Modified. Generally, taking 2 inches off a barrel will still leave enough constriction to enable a gunsmith to open the choke. If the hunter wants to cut his 30-inch barrel down to 26 inches, he has a bigger problem. Taking 4 inches off a barrel will remove all constriction and he'll have a Cylinder bore, which may or not be too open for his kind of hunting. We should mention here that some hunters who have chopped 4 inches off their shotguns have found them to be deadly on upland game, probably because they were consistently shooting their game a lot closer than they realized. But if a hunter finds a complete loss of choke in his gun is a handicap he has no choice but to install a variable-choke device, which we'll discuss later on.

As for the grouse hunter who has a 26-inch barrel with an Improved Cylinder choke and wants to start duck hunting, he has no choice but to install a variable-choke device. The same applies to the duck hunter with a Full Choke gun who want a more open choke for upland game but still wants to be able to fall back on a Full Choke for ducks. He can switch to brush loads, but a better solution is a variable choke.

The only exception to the above cases are the shotguns produced to accept interchangeable barrels. With these, a hunter can buy a variety of barrels to suit his needs until his money runs out.

Variable-Choke Selectors

A variable-choke is a mechanical device fitted to the muzzle of a shotgun that enables the shooter quickly and simply to change the choke from Full to Cylinder, with a variety of settings in between. They are available in two basic designs—the interchangeable tube type and the collet type.

The Cutts Compensator is a typical example of the interchangeable tube type choke device. The main body of the device, which also serves as a muzzle brake and reduces recoil, is fitted to the muzzle. A hunter who wants to change his choke merely screws in tubes of various degrees of constriction to give different patterns.

The collet-type variable choke uses an adjustable nozzle-like affair on the muzzle to change choke setting. The hunter simply turns a knurled ring to increase or decrease the constriction at the muzzle to change his choke and pattern. The Poly Choke and LymanCHOKE are good examples of this design.

If you think these variable choke devices are a good deal, you're right. Hunters who can't make up their minds about the best choke for their gun, or who are determined to use one gun for all game, will find a variable choke a good deal. With a variable choke, they can use the same gun for pass shooting at waterfowl at 50 yards and quail gunning at 20 yards.

These variable chokes offer another advantage. They give the hunter the option of having his barrel cut down to as much as 24 or 26 inches. This is a definite asset, since there is no reason for a pump or autoloader to have a barrel longer than 26 inches. And a 24-inch barrel is fast and deadly on game such as quail and woodcock.

Even though these variable choke devices have the settings clearly indicated on them, it's still a good idea to check the pattern at each setting to make sure it's doing the job it's supposed to do.

Cutts Compensator with variety of tubes to change choke. Comes with wrench to screw tubes into muzzle brake, which also reduces recoil as much as 35 percent with 12-gauge high-velocity loads.

LymanCHOKE is a collet-type choke. Different degrees of constriction are made by turning knurled sleeve. Available with recoil chamber (top photo) or plain (bottom photo).

680 Long Range No. 2

690 Long Range No. 3

705 Full Choke

725 Modified Choke

755 Tube

Spreader

Shotgun Stocks

The shotgunner, unlike the rifleman who generally has plenty of time to snug up comfortably to his stock and squeeze off a careful shot, has a different set of problems to cope with. His game is almost always moving—running on the ground or taking to the air in a burst of wingbeats. He rarely has time to mount his gun carefully and shoot slowly. He is forced to focus on his target, snap the shotgun to his shoulder, start his swing, determine lead, and slap the trigger. Human reaction time, from the point of mounting the gun to pulling the trigger, has been clocked at .25 seconds. For the average gunner, that's fast shooting.

What all this means is that the stock fit of a shotgun is very important, perhaps more so than with a rifle. It seems strange then that many hunters will go to great lengths to get a rifle stock that fits their physical frame, yet will grab any scattergun out of the rack and take it out for a day of grouse shooting.

Shotgunners should take the fit of their smoothbores more seriously. We should first understand that a skilled wing-shot actually "points" with the position of his feet and head before he even brings the shotgun to his shoulder. If the stock fits his frame, the gun will almost automatically be on target when he mounts it. If it's a poor fit, he'll likely shoot over, under, in front of, or behind the bird.

If you're a wealthy sportsman who can afford to have shotguns custom built and the stocks shaped to exacting dimensions by means of a complicated "try gun," your problem is simple. The custom gun-builder will see that your stock fits properly.

But the majority of hunters have to solve their own problems of shotgun stock fit and the first step is a basic understanding of various measurements and how they will affect shooting in the field.

Length of Pull

Length of pull is the distance between the butt and trigger. If this measurement is too long, the shooter will catch the heel of the stock on his clothes or under his arm pit. If length of pull is too short, the shooter will find that he will be smacking his nose with the thumb of his right hand when he pulls the trigger and the gun recoils. The proper length of pull, then, is one that will enable a shooter to mount the gun easily, clearing his clothes and keeping the thumb a safe distance from his nose.

The typical factory shotgun comes off the line with a length of pull of about 14 inches, which is usually all right for men 5 feet 8 inches to 5 feet 10 inches tall. A man over 6 feet tall will generally do better with a length of pull of 14¼ to 14½ inches. A boy, woman, or short man about 5½ feet tall, should look for a length of pull of about 13½ inches. The important factor is that the shooter should be able to mount his gun quickly and comfortably.

Drop at Comb

Drop at comb is the distance from the top of the forward edge of the comb and the line of sight. This is an important measurement since the comb, in a sense, is the rear sight of a shotgun because it positions and lines up the eye with the front bead sight. If the comb is too high, it will raise the eye of the shooter. This means he will see more barrel and point the barrel up. When this happens, the shot charge will go higher and he'll likely shoot over his birds.

If the drop at comb is too low, the reverse happens—the gunner will shoot under his birds.

The typical factory-made shotgun has a drop at comb of 1½ inches, which is suitable for a man 5 feet 7 inches to 5 feet 11 inches tall. A 6-footer, however, needs less drop at comb. Thickness of the comb is also a factor. A thick comb will position the eye higher than a low comb.

This business of comb height is perhaps the most common reason for misses. If a hunter sees too much barrel when he quickly mounts his gun and feels he is getting more than his share of misses, it's a good bet that he's overshooting his target. If a hunter feels he must raise his check a bit to get a clear view of the front bead, chances are the comb is too low and he'll shoot under some of his birds.

The one exception to this is the trapshooter, who consistently shoots at a fast rising target and wants to keep the clay bird in sight at all times. He uses a special trap stock with a drop at comb of about 1⅜ inches. This will give him a high comb, which means his shot charge will fly higher. In effect, he has a built-in lead when he shoots directly at a clay bird tossed straightaway.

The hunter, however, gets most of his shots at 20 to 25 yards and frequently prefers to blot out his game at closer ranges. If his gun has a high comb, like the trapshooter's, he'll shoot over the bird.

Firearm manufacturers have accounted for these differences and turn out shotguns labeled field models and trap models. The difference lies mainly in stock dimensions.

Parts and Basic Measurements of a Shotgun Stock.

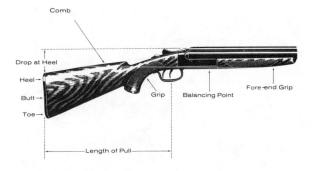

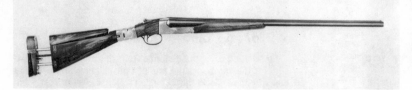

This is a typical "try gun," used by gun makers to build custom stocks that fit their clients exactly. Such try guns are adjustable for drop at comb, drop at heel, length of pull, and pitch.

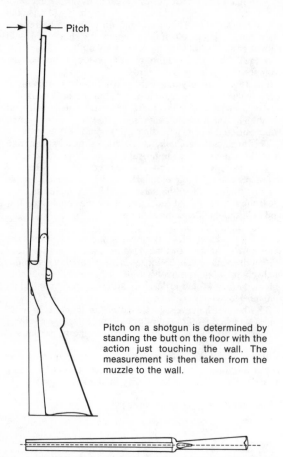

Pitch on a shotgun is determined by standing the butt on the floor with the action just touching the wall. The measurement is then taken from the muzzle to the wall.

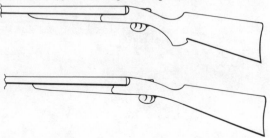

This drawing shows proper cast-off on a double-barreled shotgun for a right-handed shooter. Note butt angles to the right of line of sight. Cast-off is rarely seen on American-made guns.

Here are the two basic stock designs for shotguns—the pistol-grip stock (top) and the English straight stock.

Drop at Heel

Drop at heel is the distance between the heel of the stock and the line of sight. Here again, this measurement depends on the shooter's physical frame. The typical factory shotgun has a drop at heel of 2½ inches, which is fine for all-round use. A squarely built man, however, might prefer less drop at heel—which means a straighter stock. A round-shouldered and bull-necked shooter would be better off with a greater drop at heel.

It's a generally accepted fact that the less the drop at heel—the straighter the stock—the easier the gun will be to mount and shoot. Recoil is also felt less with a straight stock, since the gun will recoil more directly into the shoulder.

Pitch

Pitch is the angle of the buttplate on the butt and is measured from the muzzle. To determine pitch, a shotgun is stood on its butt with the action touching a wall. The measurement is then taken from the muzzle to the wall. The accompanying drawing illustrates it clearly.

Pitch is important in shotguns, since the point of impact can be raised or lowered by changing the angle of the butt. Its major function is to keep the butt solidly against the shooter's shoulder. With too little downward pitch, the butt may slip down and point the gun up, which will make the shot charge fly high. With too much downward pitch, the stock may ride up the shoulder and the shot charge will fly low. A pitch of about 2 to 3 inches is about right for a shotgun with 28-inch barrels.

Cast-Off

Hunters who stick to American-made guns need not be concerned with "cast-off," since guns made in this country rarely have this feature. Cast-off means that, for a right-handed shooter, the butt is angled slightly to the right of the line of sight. Or slightly to the left for a left-handed shooter. Cast-off is supposed to make the gun easier to mount and swing. It is common on British-made shotguns.

Stock Style

Shotgun stocks come in two basic designs—pistol-grip stock and English straight stock. While the English straight stock looks neater and has a trimmer appearance, it's a difficult design to get accustomed to. The wrist is forced into a slightly cramped position, and the shooter has less control over his gun. This straight stock design is popular in Europe, but has never caught on in America.

The modern American shotgun has a pistol grip, which puts the wrist in a comfortable position and affords better control when swinging the gun and shooting.

Shotshell and Ballistics

The changes in shotshell construction within the past decade or so have been phenomenal. Most hunters over 30 years old can probably remember when just about all shotshells were made of paper impregnated with wax. A look inside these shells was often bewildering. They generally had about 10 to 12 components, including brass cup, primer, paper case, base wad, shot, over-powder wad, fillers wads, over-shot wads, and so on.

In those days, ammunition makers ran those components through a complicated process before turning out the finished shell. These shells had several drawbacks. They could not be reloaded more than several times, water would eventually get into the paper body and the case would slowly deteriorate, and the shot charge would frequently deform when it came into contact with the bore.

Things started to change around 1960, when Remington introduced the plastic shell, which was waterproof and offered longer case life for those shooters who handloaded their own shot shells. Then came the plastic shot sleeve or collar, which surrounded and protected the pellets from becoming deformed as the shot charge traveled through the barrel. Many plastic shot sleeves now also form the over-powder wad. Winchester made shotshell construction even simpler when it designed its plastic shells in such a way that made even base wads unnecessary. The over-shot wad was eliminated when the star-crimp came into standard use. The star-crimp utilizes the shell case itself to seal off the top of the completed shotshell. This type of crimp also made reloading easier and less expensive.

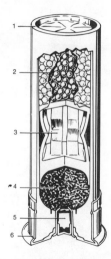

Parts of a modern shotshell: (1) One-piece body includes top crimp and base wad, (2) Shot charge, (3) One piece wad to protect shot and provide sealed gas chamber over powder, (4) Ball powder, (5) Primer, (6) Brass Head.

Perhaps the ultimate in simplified shotshell construction was reached in early 1972 when Remington introduced its RXP shotshell. The RXP shotshell has unibody construction, which means the shell body and base wad are one integral unit. Such construction produces a tough reloadable shell. Inside the shell, Remington's Power Piston is a one-piece combination plastic wad and shotshell protector. The complete shell has about six components . . . a far cry from the old shells with 10 to 12 components.

The shotshells of today are more durable, more uniform, produce denser patterns, and can be reloaded many more times at less cost than the shotshells of a decade or so ago.

The parts of a typical shotshell produced in the 1950's: (1) Shot charge; (2, 3) Felt filler wads; (4) Over-powder wad; (5) Powder; (6) Base wad; (7) Primer cup; (8) Priming mixture; (9) Paper disk; (10) Anvil; (11) Battery cup; (12) Brass shell head; (13) Paper body; (14) Paper seal.

High-speed photography shows shot collar separating from shot charge after it has protected pellets from deforming while travelling through barrel.

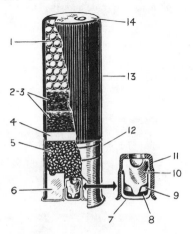

Courtesy Winchester-Western.

Remington-Peters "RXP" shotshell. Note one-piece body and one-piece wad. It would be tough to build a shotshell with fewer components.

Standard Shells

American-made shotguns are chambered for the standard 2¾-inch shotshell. We should mention here, however, that the shell labeled "2¾ inches" is not 2¾ inches long, but about ¼ inch shorter. The 2¾-inch measurement is taken when the case is open, before crimping. The chamber of the shotgun, on the other hand, *is* 2¾ inches. This difference in measurements is to allow enough room to the gun's chamber for the crimp to unfold completely.

The difference in shell length and chamber length should make it obvious that hunters should not attempt to shoot the 3-inch Magnum shotshells in guns chambered for the 2¾-inch standard loads, in spite of what some shotgunners claim. It's all right to shoot a shell that is shorter than the gun is chambered for, but it is dangerous to shoot long shells in guns chambered for shorter shells. The chamber does not allow enough room for the crimp to unfold completely and excessive pressure can build up when the shot charge forces its way through a not-completely-open crimp.

The Magnums

Magnum shotshells are available in both 2¾ and 3-inch size. Just about all shotguns chambered for the 2¾-inch standard shells will take the 2¾-inch Magnum shells. The 3-inch Magnum shell, however, needs guns chambered to handle the longer shells.

Magnum shotshells have more powder and shot than standard field loads, but do not expect them to perform miracles. The extra powder and shot will increase effective range on game because of the extra number of pellets, but the muzzle velocity of a magnum shell is nearly the same as that of a standard high-velocity load.

Magnums, however, do give the hunter an extra edge when gunning for deer and tough game, such as turkeys and geese.

Brush Loads

Brush loads, also called scatter or spreaders loads, are shotshells that have a divider of sorts separating the shot charge into three or four separate sections. When the shell is fired, these partitions spread the shot charge into a more open pattern, in spite of the gun's designated choke. Generally, a brush load will, in effect, open the choke of a gun one setting. Fired in a Full Choke gun, for example, a brush load will throw a Modified pattern. Used in a Modified Choke barrel, a brush load will produce an Improved Cylinder pattern, and so on.

Even though these brush loads are available in one or two shot sizes, generally No. 8, it's surprising they aren't used more by hunters after the smaller gamebirds in thick cover, such as woodcock and quail. A hunter with a double-barreled shotgun choked Full and Modified, for example, can get Modified and Improved Cylinder patterns out of his scatterguns by simply changing loads. And the man with a Modified Choked pump gun would fare much better with brush loads when gunning for quail.

These brush loads are available from all major ammunition makers in 12, 16, and 20 gauge.

Rifled Slugs

The rifled slug is a single projectile fired from a shotgun. It has a hollow base which is spread by the force of the powder gases to fill the bore. It is a deadly shotgun load for deer and bear at short ranges. In a pinch, the rifled slug has even brought down moose. It is a fine brush-bucking load at distances up to 100 yards. Beyond 100 yards, a slug's velocity and energy drops off rapidly and accuracy suffers.

Rifled slugs are at their best and most accurate in guns choked Cylinder—without any constriction at all. Slugs, however, can be shot in any shotgun, regardless of choke, without damaging the bore or choke constriction.

Slugs are also heavy projectiles. A 12-gauge slug weighs 415 grains, a 16-gauge 350 grains, a 20 gauge 282 grains, a .410 bore 93 grains. The 12-gauge slug is best for deer and bear, the 16 and 20 gauge are also adequate. The .410 slug, however, doesn't make the grade and should not be used for deer.

The Brenneke slug, specially designed for shotgun hunting of big game. The slug and wad are joined to form one long projectile, which increases ballistic performance and accuracy. Key-holing is eliminated.

Firearms manufacturers have long recognized the effectiveness of rifled slugs and they produce specially designed shotguns for them. These guns generally have Cylinder choke barrels that measure 20 or 22 inches. The most important feature of these special guns is that the barrels are fitted with adjustable rifle sights, which makes them acceptably accurate deer guns for short-range shooting and brush hunting.

Powder

The designation "drams equivalent" on a box of shotshells still confuses some shooters. The term is actually a throwback to the old black powder days, when the standard load had a powder charge of about 3 drams. Today, of course, shotshells are loaded with modern smokeless powder.

The drams equivalent label, however, is still used. When you pick up a box of shotshells and see it stamped "3¼ drams equivalent," this means that the amount of smokeless powder in the loads will produce the same amount of pressure and velocity as the designated drams of black powder. It's worth noting here that a charge of smokeless powder may weigh half or less than the dram equivalent.

Rifle shooters, evidently realizing the importance of velocity, energy, and trajectory, take a great interest in ballistics, but most shotgunners pay little attention to how hard a shot charge moves once it leaves the barrel. Such information provides a better understanding of how a gun and ammunition will perform at typical or long ranges and on various kinds of game.

With regard to steel shot for waterfowling, published figures have been controversial—even contradictory in some cases—as the manufacturers have continually sought to improve the relatively new powders and other components used with steel pellets. As explained in the section on gauge and shot size, steel No. 2's are the correct substitute for lead No. 4's. A 12-gauge load of 1¼ ounces of No. 4 lead shot retains a velocity of more than 800 feet per second at 40 yards. In a comparison test conducted by ballisticians for one manufacturer, equivalent steel loads—1¼ ounces of No. 2's—retained a 40-yard velocity of well over 700 f.p.s. But evidently those were experimental loads. Currently

manufactured steel-shot loads of the same type, again tested by qualified ballisticians, slow down to less than 700 f.p.s. at 40 yards.

For the waterfowler, exact figures on steel shot are less important than the knowledge that steel does slow down at a considerably greater rate than lead, and it packs less energy at equal range. Although very skillful gunners can kill geese at more than 60 yards even with steel, the average hunter should not attempt shots at ranges much beyond 50 yards. Even at that distance—and here's an important fact that seems to have eluded many hunters—it's necessary to swing the gun farther ahead of a duck or goose when using steel shot than when using lead, in order to compensate for the relatively slow travel of the shot string.

Slug shooters seem to devote more time to studying the performance of their loads than do other shotgunners, but they too would do well to pay more attention to ballistics. The following tables provide data for rifled slugs as well as standard lead-shot loads.

SHOTGUN SHELL BALLISTICS

Gauge	Type load	Shot size	MV fps[1]	Pellet ME fp[2]	Vel. (60 yds.)
10	High Vel.	4	1330	12.7	685
12	Std. Vel.	6	1255	6.8	610
12	High Vel.	6	1330	7.6	630
12	HV 3" Mag.	6	1315	7.4	625
16	Std. Vel.	6	1185	6.0	595
16	High Vel.	6	1295	7.2	620
20	Std. Vel.	6	1165	5.8	590
20	High Vel.	6	1220	6.4	605
20	HB 3" Mag.	6	1315	7.4	625
28	High Vel.	6	1300	7.3	620
410	HV 3"	6	1260	6.8	612

Above ballistics are average. There is some variation between brands and different sizes and weights of shot. The heavier the pellet the greater the remaining energy and velocity at 60 yards.

[1]Muzzle velocity in feet per second.

[2]Muzzle energy, in foot pounds, of one pellet.

Copyright © by Frank C. Barnes and Digest Books, Inc.

RIFLED SLUG BALLISTICS

Gauge	Federal Load Number	Muzzle	Velocity In Feet Per Second 50 yds.	100 yds.	Energy—In Foot/Lbs. Muzzle	50 yds.	100 yds.	Drop—In Inches 50 yds.	100 yds.	Barrel Length*
12	F127	1600	1175	950	2485	1340	875	2.1	10.4	30
16	F164	1600	1175	950	1990	1070	700	2.1	10.4	28
20	F203	1600	1175	950	1555	840	550	2.1	10.4	26
410	F412	1830	1335	1025	650	345	205	1.6	8.2	26

* All calculations based on full choke barrels of this length.

Courtesy of Federal Cartridge

RANGE—Waterfowl hunting usually involves the longest distances for shotgun shooting. The practical range for taking ducks and geese is 35 to 50 yards. Individual pellets, however, may travel great distances. For safety when hunting, consider these possible extreme ranges.

00 Buck	610 yds.
No. 2 Shot	337 yds.
No. 6 Shot	275 yds.
No. 9 Shot	225 yds.

Courtesy of Federal Cartridge

Trap Shooting

A trap field consists of a trap situated in a trap house and five shooting positions spaced 3 yards apart. All five positions are 16 yards from the trap. Five shots are taken by each shooter at each of the five positions. This makes a total of twenty-five shots and this is referred to as a round of trap. Each shooter takes his turn in shooting and upon completion of his five shots moves to the next position. Each time the shooter on the fifth position completes his five shots he goes to the first position, and so on.

Targets are thrown from the trap and must go a minimum of 48 yards and not over 52 yards. The targets must be thrown between 8 to 12 feet high at 10 yards in front of the trap. Each of these traps moves automatically to a position unknown to the shooter; therefore, the shooter never knows where the target will be thrown. In singles shooting, the trap shall be so adjusted that within the normal distribution of angles as thrown by the trap, the right angle shall not be less than straightaway from position one.

There are three different events held in trap shooting. The first type is known as the "16-yard event." This event is held in classes and each shooter is placed in a class according to his ability.

The second event, probably the most popular, is known as "handicap shooting." Each shooter is given a shooting position at a certain distance from the trap. These distances are from 18 to 27 yards, depending on the shooter's ability. The intent of this handicapping is to make the shooters compete on an equal basis. There are no classes in these events and all shooters are competing against each other.

The third type of shooting is known as "doubles." This is a most difficult event as two targets are thrown simultaneously. Unlike 16-yard and handicap shooting, the flight of these targets is fixed, and the left and right targets follow the path of the extreme left and right 16-yard targets.

Almost all shooting is done with the 12-gauge gun. There are no minimum restrictions but the maximum is no more than 1$\frac{1}{8}$ ounces shot and no more than 3 drams of powder. No shot larger than 7$\frac{1}{2}$'s nor any gun larger than a 12 gauge may be used.

All traps must throw unknown angles. Some do this by mechanical means and are powered by electrical motors. The most modern traps load the targets and reset the angles automatically.

Clay pigeons are all of a standard size. They are basically black with a yellow, orange, or white trim. Some are made all black. These color variations are used depending on which has the best visibility. This varies at different gun clubs based on the background of each field.

An area of 1,000 feet deep by 1,000 feet wide is sufficient for safety purposes for a trap field.

Techniques of Trap Shooting

To be a fine trap shot you must point the shotgun. Some persons believe that because of the pattern the shot throws that this should be fairly simple. Once he has tried it he will discover there is a lot of room around the moving target.

Targets are thrown at varying angles; consequently, the shooter must be prepared to shoot anywhere within that given area. The first thing a shooter does when he prepares to shoot is to plant his feet properly. He must be able to turn to the right or left with ease in order to hit targets flying in different directions. A shooter shooting at the first station will get no more than a straightaway target for his extreme right. He can also get an extremely wide angle to the left. Knowing this he should face halfway in between both extremes. Obviously, a shooter should face in the center of both extreme right and left targets on all five stations. If for some reason or another he faces too far in one direction, he will find his body winding up like a spring when he tries to move in the opposite direction. This causes him to slow down or even stop his swing, and he misses or barely hits the target.

The next step in shooting is for the shooter to start his gun in the proper place. The gun should be started halfway between the two extreme angles of the targets. At station one the gun should be pointed on the left corner of the trap house, at station two halfway between the left corner and the center of the trap house, on station three the center of the trap house, on station four halfway between the center and the right corner, and on station five on the right corner of the trap house. Under certain conditions it is advisable to start the gun higher because of wind conditions. A target will sometimes climb considerably even though it is thrown from the trap at the legal height. The amount the gun should be raised should be determined by the shooter based on the amount of climb of the target. There are many shooters who normally start higher simply because they have to move the gun less to get to the target and it is easier for them to shoot in this manner.

Most new shooters are more concerned with the recoil of the gun than anything else. Their first thought is to get the gun on their shoulder comfortably so it won't kick. They place the gun on their shoulder, then try to bring their head down on the stock of the gun. This tends to stretch the neck muscles and pulls the head off the stock. The proper way is to bring the gun up to the face and line up the gun with the eye. Then the shoulder is raised to the gun. With constant practice this becomes a natural act.

When the shooter has accomplished the foregoing, he calls for the target. As he does not know in which direction the target will fly, he must let it get a sufficient distance from the trap house before starting to move the gun. He must never try to guess where the target is going.

Once the direction of the target is determined the next step is to visualize where you want to point the gun in order to break the target. The gun should be held firmly but not tightly by the hand on the grip. The other hand should grip the fore-end lightly, and the arms should be relaxed. Too tight a grip causes a jerky swing on the target. Trap targets take very little lead and the amount of this lead can only be determined by the shooter through his experience. Of course, the targets flying straightaway from the shooter take no lead at all. I have known some very fast shooters who claim they do not lead any target.

Never try to hold a certain lead on the target. The instant you have the gun pointed where you want it, pull the trigger. If you stay with the target, it will drop away from you and you will shoot over it. Try to swing the gun smoothly up to the target.

Eventually you will develop a sense of timing and you will shoot at your targets with a fairly consistent rate of speed. This varies with each person depending on how well co-ordinated he may be. Most beginning shooters shoot too slow; but by shooting with faster shots, they will eventually increase their speed. Unlike upland game birds, trap targets are moving at their fastest rate of speed when they leave the trap house. This does not leave much time to think about a shot. Game birds start slowly and increase their speed as they go giving the shooter more time.

One of the most common errors is to raise one's head off the gun stock. Sometimes this is caused by shooters wanting to get a better look at the target and sometimes by not bringing the gun tight enough into the face. In either case it causes the shooter to shoot over the target.

Handicap trap is the same as 16 yards except the ranges are greater—depending on the shooter's ability. Everything that applies to 16-yard shooting applies to handicap. The gun is moved to a lesser degree but you have to point finer on the targets. You can be a little sloppy in your 16-yard shooting and still get some fair hits but that same sloppiness will cost you targets when shooting at the longer ranges. The more your skill increases the farther back you will shoot. The wind, if it is a strong one, can even blow the target away from where you may have pointed before the shot even gets there. Most good handicap shooters who shoot from 23 to 27 yards are fast shooters. Their speed

gives them better chances at these long ranges. As you increase your range yard by yard in handicap, you have to learn to make slight changes in your shooting. Your mental attitude becomes a problem just because you know it's tougher to shoot from there than it was a yard closer. Handicap shooting takes a lot of practice and most regular trap shooters realize this and do most of their practicing there.

Shooting doubles is the most challenging phase of trap shooting. First of all, you must face in a direction equally distant from both targets. You have the advantage of knowing where both of these targets are going so you are able to do this without any difficulty. Because you know where the first target will be, you can start your gun much higher, which will give you a very short swing. This enables you to move to your second target much faster than you would if you started your gun where you would when shooting singles on that particular station. All of the top doubles shooters are fast shooters. Remember, you are shooting at two targets both going away from you, and the more time you take in shooting, the farther away they will be. Most doubles shooters widen their stance and point their toes farther apart. This prevents their knees from locking the body and preventing their swing to either side.

SHOOTING AT EACH STATION

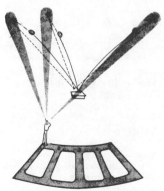

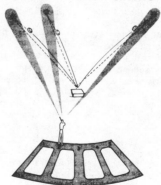

At station one, your feet should be placed as indicated with the left foot pointed toward the left corner of the trap house. Your gun should point at the left corner of the trap house, indicated in the drawing by a black dot. Solid lines indicate the flight angles of three typical targets you may encounter; dotted lines indicate the swing and follow-through of your gun as well as the target breaking point.

At station two, your feet should be placed as indicated with the left foot pointed one quarter of the way in from the left corner of the trap house. Point gun halfway between left corner and center of the trap house.

At station three your feet should be placed with the left foot pointed slightly to the left of the center of the trap house. Your gun should be pointed toward center of trap house.

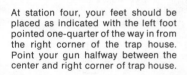

At station four, your feet should be placed as indicated with the left foot pointed one-quarter of the way in from the right corner of the trap house. Point your gun halfway between the center and right corner of trap house.

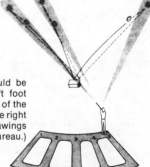

At station five, your feet should be placed as shown with the left foot pointed toward the right corner of the trap house. Point your gun at the right corner of the trap house. (All drawings courtesy of Winchester News Bureau.)

Skeet Shooting

Skeet fields were originally full semicircle, but it was necessary to make some changes for the safety of the shooters. The fields are now altered slightly and the targets are thrown at a slight angle from each trap house. A target must travel a minimum of 55 yards.

There are two trap houses. One is known as the high house and is located immediately behind station one. The targets emerge from this trap house at a height of 10 feet. The other trap house is known as the low house and the target emerges from a height of 3½ feet.

There are eight stations marked out on the field. Seven are an equal distance apart (26 feet, 8 inches) and are placed on the semicircle. The eighth station is in the center of the field midway between the two trap houses. Each shooting station is 3 feet square. Any part of both of the shooter's feet must touch the station.

A single shot is taken at targets from both houses on all eight stations. A target from the high house is always shot first. After finishing the single shots, doubles are fired. At stations one, two, six and seven, two targets are thrown simultaneously and the going away target is fired upon with the first shot and the incoming target with the second shot. This makes a total of twenty-four shots. The twenty-fifth shot is taken immediately following the first target missed and the identical shot must be made. If no misses occur, the shot is taken from low eight.

Shooting is conducted with groups of five persons or less. Each group is known as a squad. Each shooter takes his turn on each station in the order in which they are signed up and continue in that order.

Each group of twenty-five shots is known as a round and is also the amount of shells in each box.

For safety reasons it is considered necessary to have an area 1,000 feet deep and 2,000 feet long for a skeet field. No No. 9 shot can travel this far and this amount of room is more than ample.

There are two types of traps available. One type is hand loaded and the other is automatically loaded. Most targets used are black with a yellow, orange, or white band.

Techniques of Skeet Shooting

Skeet offers a greater variety of shots than any other shotgun game. You know where each target is going; but, in spite of that advantage, you still have to hit them. The beginner has to learn he cannot break targets by shooting at them. After he learns to break a few he gets the general idea that you must shoot in front of each target in order to break it. Lead is the common term for this. The next step is to learn just how much lead for each shot. This will come from practice and from help of other shooters. It is best to try to learn to master one shot at a time, but this is possible only if you can get a skeet field to yourself.

It is reasonable to assume that a target flying at a given rate of speed and a load of shot fired from a shotgun at a given range will meet *if* the proper amount of lead is given.

The confusing thing to many new shooters is what amount of lead is necessary for each shot. Years ago shooters' reaction time was checked by one of the universities and they found that it took approximately two-fifths of a second from the time the mind registered that that was the proper time to pull the trigger to the time the shot left the end of the shotgun barrel. Obviously a fast-swinging shooter is going to move that gun barrel farther in that period of time than a slow-swinging shooter. Because of this we get different answers from different shooters on just how much a target must be led.

Although getting the proper lead on each target is the ultimate objective, attention must be paid to stance and proper gun mounting. Position the feet correctly for each shot by facing the general area where you expect to break the target. The next step is to place the gun at a position in front of the trap house. Many new shooters will place the gun directly even with the trap house. This results in the shooter having to move the gun too fast in order to catch up with the target and he ends up with very poor control of the shotgun. As a rule of thumb a spot approximately one-third of the distance from the trap house to eight post would be about right. Some youngsters with very fast reactions can come in a little closer to the trap house, whereas some of us who are considerably older and find our reactions are slowing down must do just the opposite. The height of the gun should be approximately a couple of feet below the path of the target. This will allow ample room to see a target go downward if the wind happens to push it below its regular flight. Going up with a target that rises presents no problem; but if the target gets below the gun, we lose sight of it entirely.

After we get our feet placed right for the shot we are making and the gun started in the right place in relation to the trap house, the last thing that comes into our mind is to get the correct lead for the shot we are about to make. These three steps are the basic steps for each shot.

Next we must call for the target; the word "pull" is used by most shooters. Do not start the gun moving until the target appears. Bring the gun up to the shoulder at the same time you are moving the gun after the target. It is best to try to keep the gun moving with the target and continue moving out to the correct lead. The instant this lead is reached pull the trigger. Never try to hold a lead in order to break a target at a certain spot on the field. Pull that trigger the instant that lead is reached. One of the two most common faults of experienced shooters is to stop swinging their gun after the lead is reached. You are not apt to make this mistake if you do not try to hold the lead. It is always best to "follow through" with your swing just like the golfers, tennis players, and baseball players do. Beware of the shooter who advises you that the shot you just missed was the result of shooting behind the target. This leads you to believe you did not have enough lead when in reality you stopped swinging your gun.

The other common fault of the experienced shooter is that sometimes he does not "get his head down on the stock." This means he is looking above his barrel instead of down the barrel. This results in shooting over the top of the target.

It is impossible to learn all of these steps at one time. If you try to, you will only confuse yourself. Learn them one at a time. These are the basic steps of becoming a good shooter. Try to memorize the leads for each shot and in time you will automatically remember them. This will also help tremendously with your field shooting. Every shot you make at skeet with the exception of those at eight post are identical to shots you will make in upland bird shooting. It will surprise you how much your field shooting will improve after a few rounds of skeet.

The following illustrations show the shooter's position, aiming point, and suggested lead for each station on a skeet field. The aiming point is indicated by a black dot, the path of the gun's swing by a dotted line, and the point at which the target is broken by a star. (All drawings courtesy of Winchester News Bureau.)

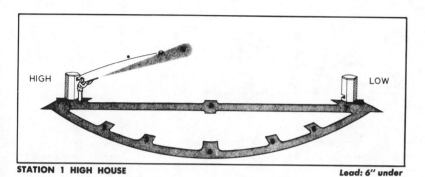

STATION 1 HIGH HOUSE　　　　　　　　　　　　*Lead: 6″ under*

STATION 1 LOW HOUSE　　　　　　　　　　　　*Lead: 1′*

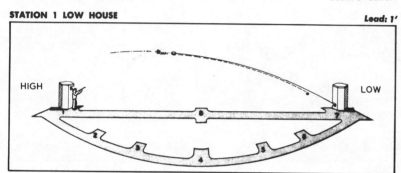

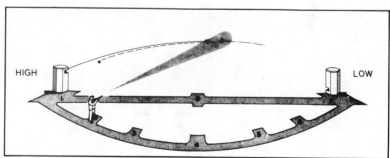

STATION 2 HIGH HOUSE　　　　　　　　　　　　*Lead: 1′*

STATION 2 LOW HOUSE　　　　　　　　　　　　*Lead: 1½′*

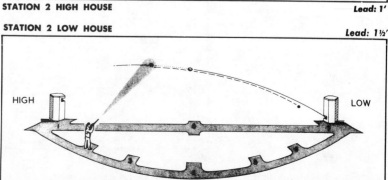

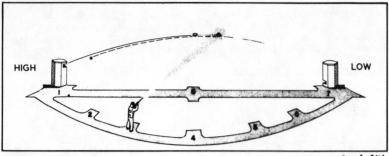

STATION 3 HIGH HOUSE   *Lead: 1½'*

STATION 3 LOW HOUSE   *Lead: 3'*

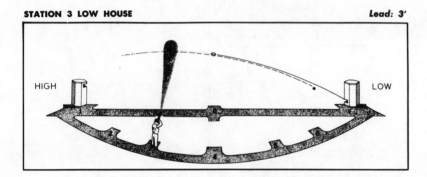

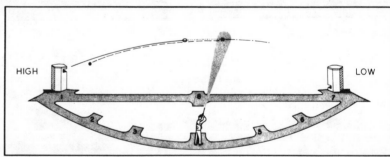

STATION 4 HIGH HOUSE   *Lead: 2½'*

STATION 4 LOW HOUSE   *Lead: 2½'*

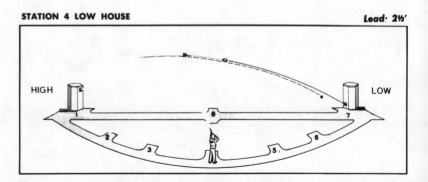

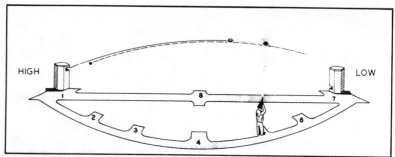

STATION 5 HIGH HOUSE

Lead: 3½'

STATION 5 LOW HOUSE

Lead: 1½'

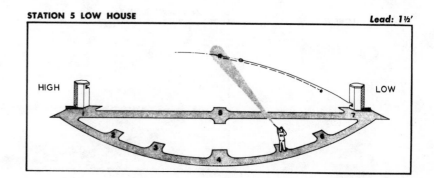

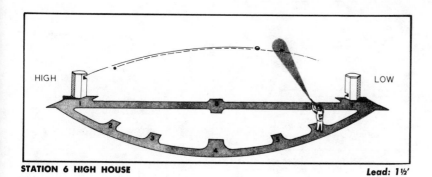

STATION 6 HIGH HOUSE

Lead: 1½'

STATION 6 LOW HOUSE

Lead: 1'

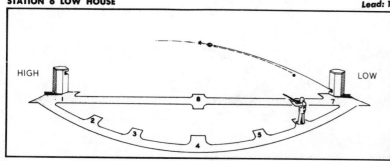

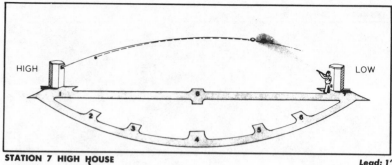

STATION 7 HIGH HOUSE

Lead: 1'

STATION 7 LOW HOUSE

Lead: Point Blank

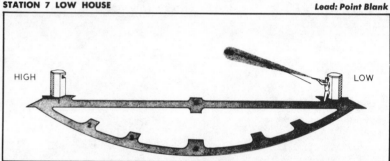

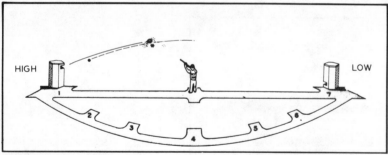

STATION 8 HIGH HOUSE

Lead: Blot out target with muzzle and slap trigger at same time

STATION 8 LOW HOUSE

Lead: Blot out target with muzzle and slap trigger at same time

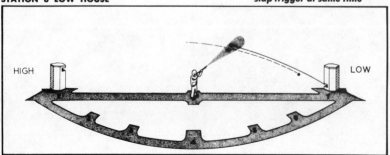

STATION 1 DOUBLES

*Break High House
Target First*

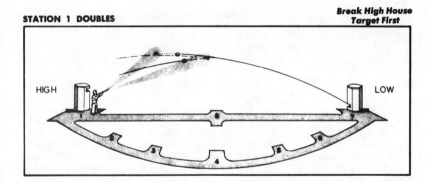

HIGH

LOW

*Break High House
Target First*

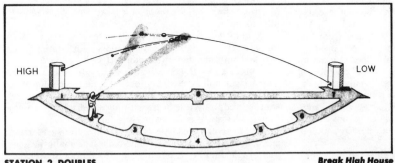

HIGH

LOW

STATION 2 DOUBLES

STATION 6 DOUBLES

*Break Low House
Target First*

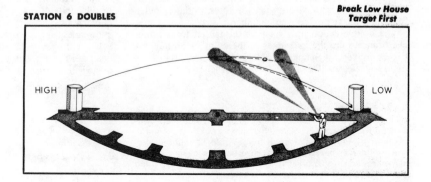

HIGH

LOW

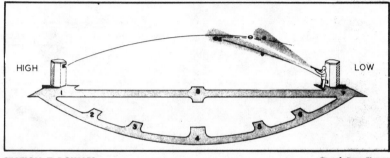

HIGH

LOW

STATION 7 DOUBLES

*Break Low House
Target First*

Handgun Actions

Mechanisms

Before discussing the various sporting uses of the handgun, let's talk about the different types of actions. Apart from a few single-shot models, there are only two basic designs—the semi-automatic and the revolver. The semi-automatic comes in two versions, the blow-back and breech-block design, which are similar to the mechanisms used in semi-automatic rifles. A detailed explanation of these designs is included in the section on "Rifle Actions."

Briefly, the semi-automatic uses gas pressure from the powder to operate the mechanism. The first step in firing an automatic is to pull the slide back and then release it. As the slide moves forward, it will pick up and chamber a cartridge from the magazine, as well as cocking the handgun. When the trigger is pulled and that first round is fired, the energy from the explosion drives the slide backward, ejecting the empty case. As the slide automatically moves forward again, it picks up and chambers the next round and the gun is ready to fire again.

The revolver also comes in two versions—the single action and double action. The single action, put simply, means the hammer must be pulled back for every shot. In effect, it must be cocked manually each time. While cocking the single action, a spur also engages a notch in the cylinder, rotating it to the next loaded chamber.

The double action only requires the trigger to be pulled each time to fire the cartridges in the cylinder. Pulling the trigger moves the hammer back to full cock, rotates the cylinder, releases the sear and fires another round.

Revolver or Semi-Automatic?

Revolver and semi-automatic handguns seem to have an equal number of fans. Ask the owner of a revolver what kind of handgun to buy and he'll tell you a revolver. And the owner of a semi-automatic pistol will swear by his type of gun. There are some basic comparisons between the two designs, however, that hold true.

The revolver is inherently safer because more manual operation is required between shots. But the semi-automatics, which we'll call automatics from here on, will fire more rapidly. The automatics have a larger magazine capacity and are more compact than the typical revolver of the same caliber, but revolvers will handle some ammunition interchangeably. The .357 Magnum, for example, will accept the .38 Special, but not conversely. The automatic may be faster to reload, but the revolver is more rugged and requires little maintenance.

Examining these comparisons, it does become apparent that the revolver makes a better handgun for hunting, plinking, and informal target shooting. It is dependable, needs little care, and has some built-in safety features. A fairly hard trigger pull is needed to cock, rotate the cylinder, and fire additional rounds. With an automatic, once the first shot is fired, only a light trigger pull will discharge another round. The revolver is obviously safer.

The revolver is also easier for the novice to understand and learn how to shoot. Granted, the automatic provides more rapid firepower, but there is no outdoor sport where such firepower is needed. For hunting and plinking, then, the revolver gets the nod.

The automatic does have its fans, however. Roughly half of all handgun matches are won with automatics and the military forces of this country, and most others, use the automatic. This is probably so for a number of reasons. When it comes to target shooting, the automatic is a better balanced firearm, since most of the weight of the gun and the loaded magazine is concentrated in the hand. A target

Schematic drawing shows parts of High Standard's Crusader, an innovative double-action design employing side-plate construction, segmented gears, and hammer travel on an eccentric, permitting a light double-action trigger pull. No rebound system or transfer bar is used because none is needed. When hammer is down, it rests safely on frame and cannot touch firing pin, so accidental discharge is prevented.

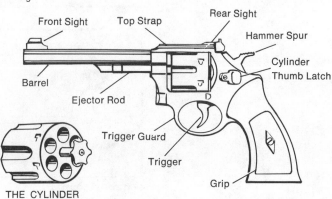

PARTS OF A TYPICAL DOUBLE-ACTION REVOLVER

Front Sight · Top Strap · Rear Sight · Hammer Spur · Cylinder Thumb Latch · Barrel · Ejector Rod · Trigger Guard · Trigger · Grip

THE CYLINDER

PARTS OF A TYPICAL AUTOMATIC

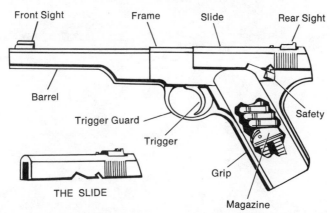

Front Sight — Frame — Slide — Rear Sight — Barrel — Trigger Guard — Trigger — Grip — Safety — Magazine

THE SLIDE

shooter who competes in rapid-fire matches will find he can get his shots off quicker and more smoothly with an automatic. As for the military, its main concern is defense, and rapid firepower is an important consideration. The outdoorsman, on the other hand, is generally not concerned with defense in the field and almost never will he need rapid firepower.

This is all boiled down to a few basic conclusions. For hunting and plinking, the revolver is the best choice. The serious target shooter, who gets involved in official matches, should look to the automatic. If a shooter is involved in all three—hunting, plinking, target shooting—the choice will have to be one of personal preference. Select the handgun that you feel safe and comfortable with.

FIRING PIN — TRANSFER-BAR — LOADING GATE — LOADING GATE HUB — TRIGGER RETURN SPRING — MAINSPRING — CYLINDER LATCH — GATE DETENT SPRING

Cutaway vie.vs show Ruger New Model, the most modern single-action design. Hammer has only two positions—fully forward and fully cocked. There's no "loading" notch or "safety" notch, as none is needed. When loading gate is opened, gate hub depresses a detent spring, lowering cylinder latch so cylinder can be turned. When hammer is forward (Figure 1) it rests on frame. In this position, transfer bar, pivoted at its lower end to the trigger, is lowered, removing any possible connection between hammer and firing pin. Hammer surrounds but cannot touch firing pin, and the revolver can be carried safely with all six chambers loaded. When hammer is cocked and trigger pulled (Figure 2) transfer bar is raised so that its tip is between hammer and firing pin, and it transfers hammer's energy to firing pin, igniting the cartridge. Prior to this Ruger design, transfer bars were usually found only in double-action revolvers.

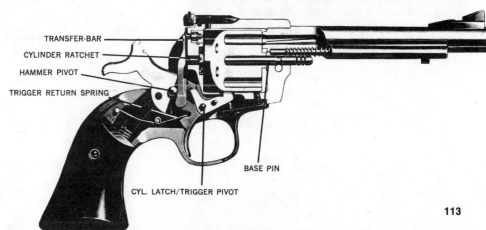

TRANSFER-BAR — CYLINDER RATCHET — HAMMER PIVOT — TRIGGER RETURN SPRING — BASE PIN — CYL. LATCH/TRIGGER PIVOT

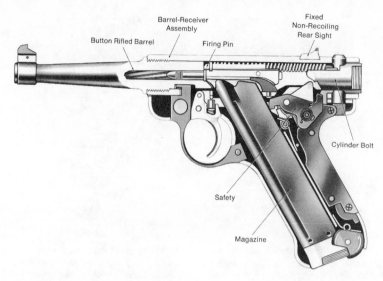

Barrel-Receiver Assembly

Button Rifled Barrel

Firing Pin

Fixed Non-Recoiling Rear Sight

Cylinder Bolt

Safety

Magazine

Cutaway view shows internal mechanism of a modern .22 semi-automatic.

Correct way to hold and load most single-action revolvers. Hammer is in half-cock position so cylinder will rotate. Hinged loading gate is down, and thumb rotates cylinder as cartridges are placed in chambers. This does not apply to New Model Rugers. With these, hammer is lowered rather than half-cocked, and gate will not open unless hammer is down. Opening gate locks hammer, trigger, and transfer bar in position, while a gate hub depresses a spring to allow cylinder rotation.

Correct and safe way to hold and load a double-action revolver. Place fingers through frame and around cylinder as cartridges are loaded into chambers. If you should be required to leave Your revolver unattended at a shooting range, always leave it with cylinder swung out. It will be in its safest position.

Selecting the Handgun

Now that we know the basic mechanics of revolvers and semi-automatic handguns, the question of sights, barrel length, and caliber arises. A shooter may have decided on a revolver, for example, but now he must select a caliber, sights, and so on. If he wants to hunt squirrels, he certainly wouldn't choose a .357 Magnum. And if target shooting is his primary interest, he'll obviously steer clear of fixed sights.

The best way to handle this problem of selection is to choose the gun to fit the sport. Let's discuss them one by one.

Hunting

It takes a skilled marksman to master the handgun, so anyone who decides to hunt with a sidearm needs all the help he can get. One of the important differences between a handgun for hunting and a precision target pistol is weight. The hunter's gun should be lighter, simply because he has to carry it around with him.

Weight, however, helps any shooter to maintain a steadier hold, so the problem is a bit of a double-edged sword. A good rule is to pick a hunting handgun that is not in the featherweight class but is not excessively heavy either. For a .22 handgun, one that weighs from 25 to 35 ounces is about right. For the heavier calibers, such as the .357, .41, and .44 magnums, a handgun should weigh between 40 and 45 ounces.

Sights, as indicated earlier, should be the best available and always with a rear sight that is adjustable for windage and elevation. Micrometer sights usually found on quality target pistols work fine in the game fields. A handgun hunter, like the rifleman, must sight in his firearm and know the point of impact at various ranges. This is only possible with adjustable sights. Fixed sights, such as those generally found on service revolvers, have no place in the field.

The handgun hunter does have another choice when it comes to sights. He can mount a scope on the gun. In addition to magnification, a scope on a handgun serves a very important function. It puts the crosshairs and target in one optical plane so that both are in sharp focus. Without the scope, it is impossible for shooters to bring both sights and target into sharp focus, and this problem gets more acute as handgunners get on in years. Handgun scopes solve this frustrating problem. These special scopes have a long eye relief, generally 10 to 24 inches. Magnification is usually 1.3X or 2.5X.

Barrel length is still another factor to consider. The handgun used for hunting should have a long barrel, and one from 6 to 10 inches is a good handling length. There are several reasons for avoiding the short-barreled models. First, and most important, is that they do not give a long enough sight radius for good accuracy. It's an accepted fact that the longer the distance between the front and rear sights the greater the accuracy potential. In the magnum calibers, the short

barrels also give off greater muzzle flash and noise, both of which could bring on a case of flinches.

With short-barreled handguns in the big calibers there is also the problem of loss of velocity. A .41 Magnum cartridge, for example, will leave the muzzle of a 8⅜-inch barrel at 1,500 feet per second, but only 1,250 f.p.s. from the muzzle of a 4-inch barrel. A short barrel is simply not long enough for full thrust to take place behind the bullet. This situation is particularly important if the shooter handloads his ammunition to maximum charges.

Picking the right caliber depends on the size of the game being hunted. For small game, such as rabbits, squirrels, sitting grouse, and the smaller varmints, a handgun chambered for the .22 Long Rifle is adequate. It's accurate and ammunition is inexpensive (which means plenty of practice shooting at low cost). Revolvers are also available chambered for the .22 Winchester Magnum, which is nothing more than a souped-up .22. The .22 Magnum gives an edge to the hunter after slightly larger small game, such as raccoons, bobcats, possibly fox. The one drawback is that the .22 Magnum is not interchangeable with the .22 Long Rifle. Buying a handgun chambered for the .22 Magnum means ammunition will be more expensive and the gun will likely not be used often for extended shooting sessions and practice. But if the idea of a .22 Magnum appeals to you, there is a solution. Ruger's Single Six Convertible is equipped with two interchangeable cylinders, one chambered for the standard .22, the other for the .22 Magnum. The shooter uses the .22 Magnum cylinder for hunting and switches to the standard .22 cylinder for target practice and plinking.

In recent years, the "convertible" idea has also been adopted by other companies—including Harrington & Richardson and High Standard—so there's a choice of several models for the shooter who wants interchangeable .22 and .22 Magnum cylinders. The Ruger is a single action, the others are double actions.

Another interesting development in recent years has been the revival of single-shot pistols. They've become particularly popular for varminting at longer ranges than the usual handgunning distances, so their owners often scope them. A famous gun of this sort is Remington's XP-100, a bolt-action pistol chambered for the .221 Fireball, a good varminting cartridge. The other single shots are generally break actions. Best known is the Thompson/Center Contender, which comes in a wide variety of calibers, from .22 rimfire, both standard and magnum, to powerful centerfire calibers suitable for big game. Included are a number of good varminting cartridges such as .218 Bee, .22 Hornet, .221 and .222 Remington, and so on. Another break action, the Merrill Sportsman's Single Shot, comes in a similar if not quite as extensive range of calibers. A few big-game hunters use single shots, but most of them prefer repeaters. Revolvers are the favorites, at least partly because they come in very popular calibers.

For big game, the centerfire magnums take the lead, though other calibers will do in a pinch. The .45 Auto, the .44 Special, and the .45 Colt will work on deer-size animals if range is not excessive, say 100 feet or so. Beyond that range, you're pushing your luck and it's best to rely on the magnums.

The big four magnums are the .357, .41, .44, and .45. The .357 Magnum, the smallest of the big four with its

158-grain bullet, develops a muzzle energy of 845 foot-pounds and a muzzle velocity of 1,550 feet per second. Recoil is heavy, but not enough to shake up the average shooter. The .357 is fine for deer, mountain lion, coyotes, and bobcat. It also makes a dandy rig for varmints. The .357 has taken bigger game, such as bear, but using it on animals over 200 pounds is stretching the cartridge beyond its limits.

One very big advantage in selecting a .357 Magnum is that the handgun will also accept the .38 Special, a popular target load. (*Caution:* The .38 Special can be fired in guns chambered for the .357 Magnum—but the .357 Magnum *cannot* be fired in a gun chambered for the .38 Special.) The .357 Magnum, then, is a good combination rig for hunting. The magnum loads are adequate for deer and smaller game. Switch to the .38 Special cartridge and the gun can be used for target shooting and plinking. This is a particularly good combination for the reloader, since the .38 Special is an inexpensive round to turn out.

Next in size is the .41 Magnum, which would probably be considered an excellent load for big-game if the .44 Magnum wasn't around. The .41 Magnum was designed to fill the gap between the .357 and .44 magnums, but it hasn't quite turned out that way. The .41 offers slightly less velocity and energy than the .44, but recoil is still considerable.

The .44 Remington Magnum and .45 Winchester Magnum take top honors for big-game hunting. Their big bullets don't travel quite as fast as the .357 Magnum, but both have a muzzle velocity in excess of 1,450 f.p.s., and they develop nearly double the foot pounds of energy of the .357. Out to 100 yards, a skilled shooter can take big game with either cartridge. Both are ideal for deer and black bears. For that matter, either of them would be good insurance when traveling in grizzly country.

However, neither of these very hefty magnums is for an inexperienced or weak-handed shooter. They're the most powerful factory-loaded handgun cartridges made, and they produce the recoil and muzzle blast that must be expected from such cartridges.

Target Shooting

The man who wants to take up target shooting with a handgun should definitely start out with a .22 rimfire. Because recoil is almost nonexistent with a .22, the shooter can concentrate on developing good shooting habits, such as proper trigger squeeze, grip, stance, and so on. Theoretically, after a training period with a .22 rimfire, a shooter should be able to progress to larger calibers without letting heavier recoil and muzzle blast affect his shooting style.

As mentioned earlier, the revolver is simpler and safer to use. But since the safety factor is not as critical on a supervised target range as it is in the field, a shooter can select either a revolver or automatic. Both are accurate handguns and, under target-range conditions, both are equally reliable. Barrel length for a target pistol should not be less than 6 inches. The only exceptions to this barrel-length rule are the few specially designed target pistols, such as the .45-caliber Colt Gold Cup National Match, which has a 5-inch barrel. But because there aren't many handguns of this quality around, it's best to stick to barrels that fall between 6 and 9 inches for serious target shooting.

Target guns should be heavier than sidearms used for hunting. Target shooters do not have to carry their guns great distances, so weight is not a burden. A heavier gun means a steadier hold on the range and this is important in competition. Generally, a target handgun should weigh between 38 and 48 ounces, depending on caliber. A .22 target pistol can weigh 38 ounces, but a handgun chambered for the .38 Special or .45 Auto usually weighs a bit more.

When a shooter moves from the .22 rimfire to the bigger calibers, he'll have to choose between a revolver and automatic. The two most popular centerfire target cartridges are the .38 Special and the .45 Auto. One factor to keep in mind is that you'll have a wider selection of handguns to choose from with the .38 Special. The .38 Special also kicks less than the .45 Auto.

And if you want to get involved in both hunting and target shooting, the .38 Special is by far a better choice since it can also be fired in .357 Magnum revolvers. A good combination, then, would be a match-grade .357 Magnum, such as the Colt Python. The .357 Magnum cartridges can be used for both hunting and target work. If you find the .357 too much gun for the target range, simply switch to the .38 Special loads and use the same gun.

Needless to say, all target handguns must have the best sight available, and this is generally the Micrometer sight with solid adjustments for windage and elevation.

In addition to these conventional target handguns, there are much more specialized types that are useful only for specific—and very sophisticated—target events. There are .22 Long Rifle free pistols (single shots called "free" in reference to the lack of restrictions on weight, sight radius, trigger pull, type of grips, and so on). There are .22 Long Rifle automatics with adjustable grips, weights, and other features for "standard" international matches. For rapid-fire international matches, there are special automatics chambered for the .22 Short. And there are specially modified revolvers for Police Course matches as well as revolvers and automatics for other combat-style target competitions.

A relatively new target event calls for knocking over metallic game silhouettes at 50, 100, 150, and 200 meters with a handgun or at 200, 300, 385, and 500 meters with a rifle. The handgunning version is divided into two classes, Production and Unlimited. The production guns are what you might expect—the S&W Model 29 and Ruger Super Blackhawk in .44 Remington Magnum, the Thompson/Center Contender with a 10-inch barrel, not only in .44 Magnum and .45 Magnum but also in less familiar handgun calibers like .30/30, .357 Herrett, and .35 Remington. The guns may have production-line actions and contours, but special barrels and wildcat calibers are common. In the Unlimited Class, the guns are even more specialized. You see bolt-action pistols like the Remington XP-100 chambered for cartridges like the .308 and .358 Winchester. Weatherby has a version of the Vanguard bolt action made up as a handgun for this. The Thompson/Center Super 14 Contender—with a 14-inch bull barrel—is really a production gun but is fired in the Unlimited Class. And there are numerous custom and semi-custom guns that are popular for this competition.

Among rifles, too, there are specialized models for sophisticated matches—game-silhouette rifles, free rifles, highly tuned sporters for running-game targets, and so on.

A good source of information on competitive shooting with both handguns and rifles is the National Rifle Association of America, 1600 Rhode Island Ave., N.W., Washington, D.C. 20036.

Plinking

Plinking means shooting at tin cans, paper targets, stationary clay birds, or any other safe target. Plinking has also turned beginners into skilled marksmen. In short, it's an ideal and informal way of learning how to safely handle and shoot guns.

The ideal handgun for plinking is the .22 rimfire, since ammunition is cheap and plinking usually involves a lot of shooting. The .22's recoil is also nil, which means the entire family can get involved. A revolver is the best bet for this type of informal shooting, since it is the safest to handle.

Adjustable sights are advisable even on guns for plinking, though fixed sights are sometimes adequate for busting tin cans.

Theoretically, any gun you happen to have in your hand at the moment can be used for plinking. If you can stand the cost of the more expensive centerfire ammunition, that's fine. But the .22 rimfire is the ideal plinker and also a good choice for the camper who can legally take a handgun along on his trips.

A complete listing of rimfire and centerfire handgun cartridges, as well as data on bullet weights, velocity, and energy, is included in the section on rifle cartridge ballistics.

Hawes/Sauer Marshal Series. Caliber: .357 Magnum, .44 Magnum, and .45 Long Colt. Barrel: 6 inches. Sights: Fixed or adjustable. Action: Single. Class: Hunting.

Ruger New Model Super Blackhawk. Caliber: .44 Magnum or .44 Special interchangeably. Barrel: 7½ inches. Sights: Adjustable. Action: Single. Class: Hunting.

Colt Single Action Army. Caliber: .357 Magnum, .44 Special, and .45 Colt. Barrel: 4¾, 5½, or 7½ inches. Sights: Fixed. Action: Single. Class: Hunting.

Smith & Wesson Model 53. Caliber: .22 Magnum. Barrel: 4, 6, or 8⅜ inches. Sights: Adjustable. Action: Double. Class: Hunting, target.

Harrington & Richardson Model 999 Sportsman. Caliber: .22. Barrel: 6 inches, vent rib. Sights: Adjustable. Action: Double. (Top-breaking.) Class: Hunting, plinking.

Interarms/Astra 357. Caliber: .357 Magnum. Barrel: 3, 4, 6, or 8½ inches. Sights: Adjustable. Action: Double. Class: Hunting.

Dan Wesson Model 15-2H. Caliber: .357 Magnum. Barrel: 2½, 4, 6, 8, 10, 12, or 15 inches. (Interchangeable barrels and grips.) Sights: Adjustable. Action: Double. Class: Target and hunting.

Thompson/Center Super 14 Contender. Caliber: .30 Herrett, .30/30 Winchester, .357 Herrett, .35 Remington, .41 Magnum, and .44 Magnum. Barrel: 14 inches. Sights: Adjustable. Action: Single shot (break-action). Class: Target and hunting.

Colt Python. Caliber: .357 Magnum. Barrel: 2½, 4, or 6 inches. Sights: Adjustable. Action: Double. Class: Target, hunting.

High Standard Crusader. Caliber: .357 Magnum, .44 Magnum, and .45 Colt. Barrel: 4¼, 6½, or 8⅜ inches. Sights: Adjustable. Action: Double. Class: Target and hunting.

Colt Gold Cup National Match. Caliber: .45 Auto. Barrel: 5 inches. Sights: Adjustable. Action: Automatic. Class: Target.

Ruger Mark I Target Pistol. Caliber: .22. Barrel: 6⅞ inches. Sights: Adjustable. Action: Automatic. Class: Target, hunting, plinking.

Smith & Wesson K-22 Masterpiece. Caliber: .22 Long Rif e. Barrel: 6 or 8⅜ inches. Sights: Adjustable. Action: Double. Class: Target, hunting, plinking.

High Standard Supermatic Citation. Caliber: .22 Long Rifle. Barrel: 5½ inches (bull barrel) or 7¼ inches (fluted). Sights: Adjustable. Action: Automatic. Class: Target and hunting.

Browning Challenger II. Caliber: .22 Long Rifle. Barrel: 6¾ inches. Sights: Adjustable. Action: Automatic. Class: Plinking and hunting.

Ruger Standard Automatic. Caliber: .22. Barrel: 4¾ inches. Sights: Fixed. Action: Automatic. Class: Plinking.

Smith & Wesson Model 52. Caliber: .38 S&W Special for Mid-Range Wad Cutter only. Barrel: 5 inches. Sights: Adjustable. Action: Automatic. Class: Target.

High Standard Double Nine Convertible. Caliber: .22 or, with interchangeable cylinder, .22 Magnum. Barrel: 5½ inches. Sights: Adjustable. Action: Double. Class: Plinking and hunting.

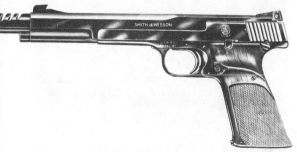

Smith & Wesson Model 41. Caliber: .22 Long Rifle. Barrel: 5 or 7⅜ inches. Sights: Adjustable. Action: Automatic. Class: Target, hunting.

Muzzle-Loading Handgun

Among muzzle-loading handguns, there are replica and non-replica revolvers, replica and non-replica single shots. Of the replica revolvers, copies of the old Colts exceed all others in number. Most of them are used for plinking or informal target shooting. A few sportsmen also use such guns for hunting. For competitive target shooting, the solid-frame replicas such as the Remington Model 1858 and the Rogers & Spencer are a better choice. These are customized for competition by adding adjustable target sights and improved grips, and the actions are smoothed and adjusted. Many of these replicas are imported by the same companies listed in the section on muzzle-loading rifles.

The outstanding non-replica muzzle-loading revolver is the Ruger Old Army Model. The top competitors use this gun. It features adjustable target sights and is available blued or in stainless steel.

For shooters who want truly authentic Colts of the colorful 1850–1870 era, they're now available from the original maker—Colt. These revolvers aren't replicas in the usual sense, but actually a continuation of the production that was halted over a century ago. The 1860 Army, the Dragoons, and the 1851 Navy are among currently available models.

The revolvers are all percussion guns, of course. Single shots come in flintlock as well as percussion versions. The flintlocks are less popular, but they're available from Navy, Dixie, Connecticut Valley Arms, and a few other companies. These pistols are replicas or near-replicas of late 18th and early 19th century guns. They're mostly used for plinking, although flintlock target matches are sometimes conducted. Some models are available in kit form as well as finished.

Some of the same single-shot pistols, or guns very much like them, are available in caplock versions from the same makers or importers, as well as from most of the other companies engaged in the muzzle-loading business. A few of the one-shot caplocks, such as the Tingle .44 Single Shot Percussion Target Pistol and the Thompson/Center .45 Patriot, are popular among serious muzzle-loading target shooters. The Tingle isn't a replica of anything; it's simply a modern percussion target pistol. The T/C Patriot isn't a true replica but is modeled after the very fine dueling pistols of the percussion era.

A flintlock pistol is loaded in the same manner as a flint-lock rifle (see the section on muzzle-loading rifles) except that a pistol charge is considerably lighter than the charge for a rifle of the same caliber. The charge for a percussion pistol is also much lighter than for a rifle of the same caliber, and the loading procedure requires a few words of advice here.

First, clean all the oil from the bore—and from the cylinder if the gun is a revolver. Then fire a couple of caps to clear the nipple (or each nipple of a revolver) to clear out any residual oil. From this point on, the procedures differ for the single shot and the revolver. Let's take the single shot first.

Place the hammer at half-cock and pour the correct measure of powder down the barrel. If the gun is a .45, a suitable charge is 30 grains of FFFg black powder or Pyrodex. Follow it with a patched ball, in this case a .440 ball of pure lead. Good patch material is tightly woven cotton, .015-inch thick. You'll have to give the starter a good bump with the heel of your hand, but a tight-fitting ball is vital for accuracy. After starting it, use the ramrod to push it all the way to the powder. Seat it firmly but don't pound on it. Now, when you seat a percussion cap over the nipple, the gun is ready to fire.

Loading a cap-and-ball revolver begins in the same way—by cleaning out the oil and clearing the nipples. Next, move the hammer to half-cock. The cylinder can then be turned by hand. From a powder measure, drop a proper charge into one chamber and place an unpatched ball over the powder at the mouth of the chamber. If the gun is the Ruger Old Army .44 or another gun of that caliber, a good charge is 25 grains of FFFg black powder, and a .457 round ball is recommended. Cap-and-ball revolvers have built-in ramming systems, and you now turn the cylinder until the loaded chamber is under the rammer. Lower the ramming level to seat the ball against the powder. Repeat these operations until all the chambers are loaded, and then fill the mouth of each chamber with grease. Lubricants are available for this, but ordinary vegetable shortening works well, and so does automotive water-pump grease. Plugging the chamber mouths with grease is insurance against a multiple discharge, and it also softens fouling. Having done this, just cap the nipples and the gun is ready to fire.

Black-powder guns require a thorough cleaning after a firing session and, for best results, quick cleanings during a session. With a single shot, just use a damp patch followed by a dry one after each shot and your score will improve. With a revolver, use the same treatment after firing the full cylinder.

As with muzzle-loading long guns, the National Muzzle Loading Rifle Association provides members with news and information regarding matches, gun shows, and other activities, as well as products. The address of the NMLRA is Box 67, Friendship, IN 47021.

Muzzle-Loading Handguns

Lyman Squareback Navy .36, made from assembly kit

Thompson/Center Patriot .45

Navy Arms Remington 1858 Army .44, stainless-steel version

Richland Arms Pennsylvania Pistol, made from kit

Ruger Old Army Model .44

Connecticut Valley Arms Mountain Pistol, made from kit

Shooting the Handgun

Of all sporting arms, the handgun is the most difficult to master. An outstretched arm, with a couple of pounds of gun at the end, becomes a shaky mass of nerves and muscle. And the short sight radius of the handgun doesn't help matters.

Perhaps the most common mistake made by novice handgunners is that they try too hard to steady their aim. They squeeze the grip harder, which only results in a worse case of the trembles and makes matters worse. The handgun should be held firmly, but not tightly. Don't fight the wandering front sight; let it move back and forth across the target. The secret is trigger squeeze. First take a deep breath, let out half of it, then aim. When the sights cross the bulls-eye, start the trigger squeeze. When it wanders past the bulls-eye, stop the squeeze but maintain pressure on the trigger. Continue the squeeze when the sights cross the target again. Continue to do this and, eventually, the gun will fire at a point when the sights are on target. You should not be aware of when the gun will go off. Just concentrate on a slow, determined trigger squeeze.

In all likelihood, your handgun will have the common patridge sight, which has a square notch rear sight and a square post front sight. The correct way to use this sight is to center the post of the front sight in the square notch of the rear sight. The top of the front post should be level with the top of the rear notch. The accompanying drawing shows the correct sight picture with the patridge sight. The bulls-eye should look like an apple sitting on a fence post.

Novice handgunners also make the mistake of trying to keep both sights and target in focus at the same time, which is impossible. When shooting a handgun, keep the sights in focus. The target should and will be slightly blurred.

The serious target shooter will stick to his one-hand hold, because it is traditional among paper-target shooters and also because regulated competition matches may require it. But the hunter is not shooting at paper. He is shooting at game and a poor shot may well mean a wounded animal or a miss. The handgun hunter needs all the help he can get to steady his hold. In the field, he should always use a two-hand hold, and steady his sights even more by using a rest whenever possible. The steadiest position is prone, with perhaps a rolled-up jacket for a gun rest. If the grass is too high, use the sitting position with your back against a tree. In certain situations, use your knee as a rest.

For the handgun hunter, it all boils down to this: Always use a two-hand hold, and always utilize any rest available to steady your sight picture.

The accompanying photographs illustrate the various handgun grips and shooting positions that have proven the steadiest under most conditions.

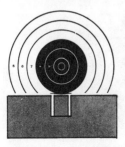

This is how your sight picture should look when using the Patridge sight, the most common and best iron sight for a handgun. While the drawing shows both sight and target in focus, this is impossible to do with the human eye. Keep the sights in focus. The target will and should be slightly blurred.

The correct one-hand hold for a heavy single-action revolver with factory grips. Note the pinky is curled and braced under the grip. Though this looks awkward, it provides additional support.

The correct one-hand hold for a double-action revolver. Hold the grip firmly, but not tightly.

The correct two-hand hold for revolvers. This is the hold hunters should learn well, since it's foolish to use the less-steady one-hand hold when shooting at live game.

OFFHAND. Feet are comfortably spaced, arm is extended straight at target, and body is angled slightly toward direction of fire. Free hand should be at rest in pocket, rather than dangling freely at the side. This position is for target shooting at paper only. Under controlled range conditions a shooter can fire amazing off-hand groups. The hunter, however, has no business shooting at game from this position. He should always use a two-handed hold and a rest whenever possible.

KNEELING. Use this position when grass or brush is too high for the steadier sitting position. Both heels are in line with target and buttock rests on heel. Elbow is bent slightly and rested on knee. Right hand, right elbow, and right knee should be on same vertical plane.

SITTING. The sitting position is good for shooting in high grass when no rest is available. Sit down facing the target, lean body forward, and rest elbows on both knees. Keep both arms as straight as possible, though a slight bend in the arms is O.K. The most important factor is getting both elbows comfortably supported on knees.

SITTING WITH BACK REST. Assume this position whenever there is a tree or a large rock available. Sit down facing target and rest back against the tree or rock so that forearms can be supported by knees and arms can be fully extended. This is an excellent position for hunters on a deer stand in wooded areas.

PRONE. This is the steadiest of all handgun positions. Simply lay flat on the ground, feet comfortably spaced, arms fully extended, and elbows resting on the ground. The line of sight should run directly down the center of shooter's back. A handgun hunter should use this position whenever possible.

Handloading

Rifle Cartridges

If you are considering reloading, it is safe to assume that you have already had considerable shooting experience. Certainly, you have purchased, and fired, a good many rounds of factory loaded ammunition. Hence you are equipped with a working knowledge of the various caliber designations and cartridge shapes, and you have learned to recognize the correct cartridge for your particular rifle. Probably many readers will have an overall understanding of shooting that extends beyond these simple basics. However, for the benefit of the uninitiated, we'll begin at this point.

Each factory loaded cartridge that we purchase and fire, represents extensive thought and care on the part of its manufacturer. If we are to reload a fired cartridge, and duplicate, if possible, the original factory loading, we must first learn to appreciate some of the intricacies of ammunition design. For instance, the fired cartridge case is the most important reloading component. The function of the case, how it is constructed, and its condition after firing, are important considerations to reloaders.

The Cartridge Case

The chief function of a cartridge case is to seal off the breech at the time of firing. To accomplish this, the case walls must expand freely so that they are tight against the sides of the chamber. This sealing action prevents the hot powder gases from leaking back around the cartridge and out through the action. Along with this, the cartridge case must withstand the chamber pressure that is built up during firing. To achieve this, the case requires a structural strength of its own—plus the additional supporting strength supplied by the bolt face and chamber walls. In essence, the case functions as an intrinsic part of the rifle. A rifle is no stronger than the case that is used in it—nor is the case stronger than the rifle.

Cartridge brass is carefully tempered in its final manufacture. The head of the case is thick and tough which gives it the strength and rigidity necessary to resist the force of the chamber pressure. The forward section of the case (neck, shoulder and body) is considerably thinner than the head section. In manufacture, these portions are given an anneal which leaves them soft and ductile. The obvious advantage is that the case walls and neck will now expand freely to release the bullet and seal the chamber while the cartridge is fired.

As shooters, we may have been rather casual in our regard for empty brass cases, but as reloaders we soon come to think differently. Without a quantity of strong and serviceable cases, we would not get far in reloading ammunition for old Betsy. The most usual way for a reloader to obtain serviceable cases is to purchase factory loaded ammunition. After this "store bought" ammo has been fired,

the empty cases are retained for future reloading. The reloader may also purchase new cases from his component dealer.

To make sure your cases are in prime condition, we recommend you start with either new or once-fired cases. Never use brass of unknown origin such as that found on a shooting range.

Each firing and resizing has an influence on the serviceability of the case. The battering of chamber pressure, and the forces applied by the resizing die eventually work-harden the forward portion of the case and destroy its usefulness. When cases have deteriorated due to excessive reloading, they are referred to as "fatigued brass" and must be discarded. To make sure the cases are in good condition, inspect them before each reloading.

Carefully inspect your cases before each reloading. If your cases are new, or once fired, they will not reveal fatigue at the first reloading. However, fatigue signs will show up in subsequent loading, so you must learn to look for them. Check your cases for splits or cracks in the neck, shoulder or body. Reject all cases that show signs of defects, but before discarding them flatten them with a pair of pliers to prevent their reuse.

CONDITION "A" CASE FATIGUE

The condition pictured above illustrates case fatigue. Note how the cracks run lengthwise. Sometimes only pinhole cracks are noticeable, but such cases must also be discarded.

CONDITION "B" EXCESSIVE HEAD SPACE

The condition pictured in this example is quite different from case fatigue. This crack runs around the circumference of the case and indicates an excessive headspace condition. Never use any rifle which shows signs of excessive headspace.

We suggest that you separate your cartridge cases into lots and keep a record of their history. For example, if you purchase two boxes of factory loaded cartridges on a given date, keep all forty rounds together and load them as one lot. Maintaining a record of the brand name, date of purchase, and the number of times you loaded the cases will be helpful in determining your case life, and you will benefit later on when trimming is required.

Trimming is necessary when your cases have lengthened after numerous firings.

All photos and text furnished by Lyman Reloading Products, Middlefield, Conn.

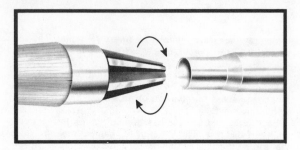

When chamfering turn the reamer lightly, removing very little case material.

When loading new or once-fired cases, it is necessary to remove the sharp inside edges of the case mouth. This operation is called chamfering and its purpose is to ease the insertion of the new bullet. Chamfering is required only for the first reloading of a new or once-fired case. An inexpensive hand reamer chamfers a case easily and with uniformity. Hold the case in one hand, while you lightly turn the reamer in the case mouth with the other hand. Remove very little material and do not cut a sharp knife edge on the case.

Choosing a Load

To select the proper components, study a reloading handbook that lists your specific cartridge. Make a note of the bullet diameter and primer size required for this cartridge. This information will be needed when you purchase components. For example, if your cartridge were a .218 BEE, you would look under the specifications for that cartridge and take note of the following information:

EXAMPLE (.218 BEE)

CARTRIDGE SPECIFICATIONS:
Bullet Dia. Jacketed and Cast .... .224''
Maximum Case Length .... 1.345''
Trim-to Length .... 1.335''
Maximum Overall Length (w/Bullet) .... 1.680''
Primer Size................................... Small Rifle
Lyman Shell Holder Number 10

Now, you must also decide on a bullet weight and a type of powder. For the time being, we suggest that you select a jacketed bullet of a weight with which you are familiar, and that you restrict yourself to the **"starting load"** shown for this bullet weight. Let's suppose you are still using the .218 BEE cartridge and that you have decided to use a **50 grain jacketed bullet with IMR 4198 powder.** You would make note of your load as shown below and then be able to purchase the proper components from your dealer.

EXAMPLE (.218 BEE)

50 Grain Jacketed

Powder	Sug. Starting Grains	Velocity F.P.S.	Max. Grains	Velocity F.P.S.
2400	10.0	2331		
IMR 4227	11.0	2331		
IMR 4198	12.0	2105		

Basic Mechanics

Before getting into the actual loading of a cartridge case, it may be wise to show the reloading procedure in a simplified graphic form. Picturing reloading in this manner will enable you to quickly grasp the fundamentals and to understand why each operation is necessary.

Actually, there are only SIX basic mechanical operations required to reload a cartridge. FOUR of them are performed by the reloading dies. As you read through the text and take note of the illustrations, you will see how a set of only two reloading dies can accomplish all four of these operations. Later on in reloading, you will hear of three and even four die sets. The difference is that two and three die sets combine some of the operations, whereas, a four die set accomplishes each operation separately.

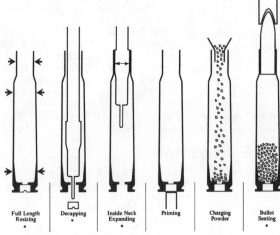

Full Length Resizing • | Decapping • | Inside Neck Expanding • | Priming | Charging Powder • | Bullet Seating •

* Operations 1,2,3, and 6 are performed by reloading dies.

1. FULL LENGTH RESIZING: When a cartridge is fired, the neck, shoulder and body of the case expand to seal the chamber and release the bullet. These portions of the case remain pretty much at their expanded size and do not snap back to their original dimension. Since all chambers are not identical, cases fired in one rifle may not chamber in another unless their walls are reduced to a standard diameter that is acceptable to all rifles. This operation is called resizing.

2. DECAPPING: This operation consists of simply removing the old or fired primer.

3. INSIDE NECK EXPANDING: After a case has been resized, the inside diameter of its neck will be too small to accept the new bullet. Inside neck expanding enlarges the diameter of the neck to a size that will receive and hold the bullet securely.

4. PRIMING: This operation consists of inserting a new primer into the primer pocket.

5. CHARGING POWDER: This operation consists of carefully weighing out and pouring the appropriate powder charge into the case.

STEP 1

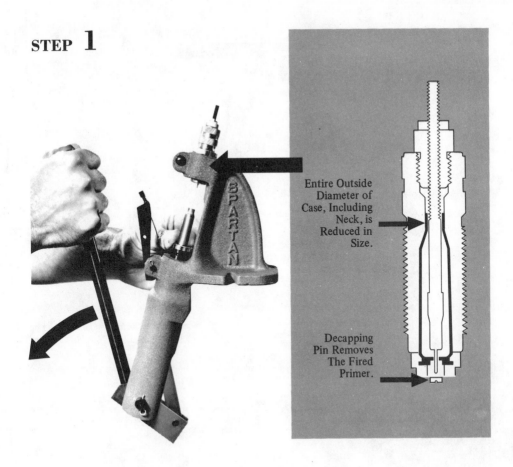

Entire Outside Diameter of Case, Including Neck, is Reduced in Size.

Decapping Pin Removes The Fired Primer.

6. BULLET SEATING: The last operation in the reloading process is the seating of a bullet into the case.

Making Cartridges

Now, if your cases have been properly inspected and you've selected a load, and purchased the necessary components (primers, powder and bullets), you are ready to begin. Your reloading press should be assembled and mounted according to the instructions supplied with the tool. Many reloading presses may be assembled to function either on the up, or on the down-stroke of the handle. The press pictured in our illustrations is operating on the down-stroke. First, lubricate your cases by wiping them with a cloth sparingly greased with a case lubricant. Use care for too much lubricant will trap air in the die and cause "lube dents." Cases dented in this manner may be used for re-loading, for the dents will be ironed out in firing. It is not considered good reloading practice, however, and care should be exercised.

Screw the Full-Length Resizing Die into the head of your press and adjust it according to the instructions supplied with the die.

1. Full-Length Resizing and Decapping

Slide the head of your cartridge case into the shell holder, as pictured in the illustration, and pull the press handle down all the way. If the die is adjusted properly, the entire cartridge case will enter the die flush to the shell holder. Note, in the cutaway drawing how two of the original six reloading operations (full-length resizing and decapping) are accomplished by this step.

2. Inside Neck Expanding and Priming

As your case is withdrawn from the resizing die, two further operations are accomplished. The expanding button will automatically enlarge the neck, as shown in the cutaway drawing, and the priming punch will seat the new primer. As the expanding action of the button is automatic, you need not be concerned with it. You must, however,

STEP 2

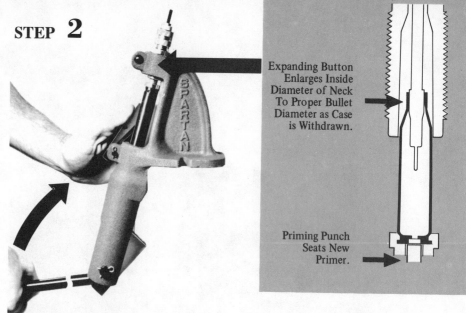

Expanding Button Enlarges Inside Diameter of Neck To Proper Bullet Diameter as Case is Withdrawn.

Priming Punch Seats New Primer.

Seating Primers: Primers are seated mainly by feel. The bottom of the anvil *must bottom* in the primer pocket. Use care and do not crush the primer. Crushed primers give erratic ignition, or fail to fire.

STEP 3

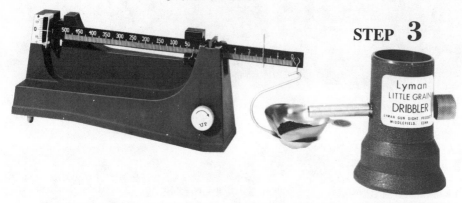

The reloading accessory pictured with the scale is a Lyman Powder Trickler. With a Trickler you can add a few granules at a time, and carefully bring the scale into balance.

Each Graduation On This Side Is Equal To 5 FULL GRAINS

Each Graduation On This Side Is Equal To 1/10 GRAIN

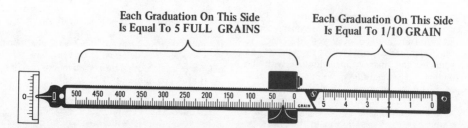

This illustration shows the beam of a modern reloading scale. Note how it is graduated on both sides of the pivot point. The scale is set by moving the two weights (poise) to the proper graduations. The large poise (*on the left*) is used to obtain multiples of FIVE GRAINS, while the small poise (*on the right*) is used for 1/10 FRACTIONS of a grain, or SINGLE grains from one to five.

EXAMPLE: The illustration shows a setting of 27.0 grains. If you wanted to decrease this 1/10 grain, you would simply move the small poise one notch to the right.

place the new primer (cup side up) into the priming punch sleeve. Push the priming arm forward (toward the press) and pull up on the press handle. As the ram is lowered, the priming arm will enter the slot in the side of the ram and seat the primer.

3. Charging Powder

For the weighing of powder, you will require an accurate powder scale. The data section in a reloading handbook specifies the powders that are appropriate for your particular cartridge. It also lists a suggested weight of the powder charge in grains and in fractions of grains. For example, 9.5 grains would be read as NINE and FIVE TENTHS grains. 10.0 grains would be read as TEN grains. We recommend that the novice restrict himself to the suggested starting load. Carefully level the powder scale as explained in the scale instructions and set it to weigh your required charge. The illustration on page 127 explains how to adjust the scale.

Slowly sprinkle small amounts of powder into the scale pan until the beam comes into balance. The beam is in balance when the pointed end (extreme left) is exactly on the zero mark.

Carefully remove the pan and pour its contents into the cartridge case. Use a powder funnel to make sure all the powder enters the case. To avoid the possibility of accidentally "Double Charging" a cartridge, you should develop a foolproof system of loading. A suggested method is to place all the uncharged cases on your left. As you pick up each case for charging, turn it up-side-down and shake it. This will insure that the case is empty. Turn the case right-side-up, charge it and place it carefully on your right. Take care when removing or replacing the scale pan that the poise are not accidentally moved.

4. Bullet Seating

The last step in reloading a cartridge is seating the new bullet. Make certain that the overall length of the finished round is not longer than the MAXIMUM OVERALL LENGTH specified for the particular cartridge. Adhering to this measurement will insure that the cartridge will function through the magazine of your rifle. Also, a bullet that is not seated to the proper depth can engage the rifling and build up pressure upon firing.

This illustration shows how a bullet is seated. Screw the bullet seating die into the head of the press and adjust it according to the instructions supplied with the die. Place a primed, charged cartridge case in the shell holder and a bullet on the mouth of the case. Hold the bullet in place as you pull the press handle all the way down. As the case enters the die, the bullet will be pushed firmly into the neck of the case. Adjusting the seating screw controls the depth to which the bullet is seated. Adjusting the die body controls the crimp.

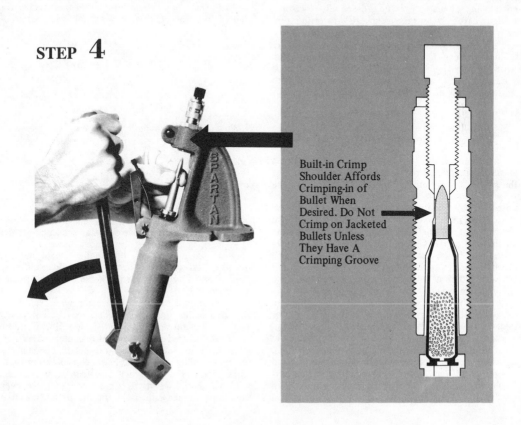

STEP 4

Built-in Crimp Shoulder Affords Crimping-in of Bullet When Desired. Do Not Crimp on Jacketed Bullets Unless They Have A Crimping Groove

Crimping

Crimping is a matter of choice and the seating die may be adjusted to crimp, or not to crimp as you desire. If you are loading hunting loads that will see hard usage in the magazine, it is wise to crimp-in the bullet. This prevents the bullets from unseating when the rifle is under recoil. Best accuracy, however, is usually obtained by not crimping-in the bullet. Target, or varmint loads, are best left uncrimped.

CAUTION: AFTER RELOADING AND BEFORE FIRING, WIPE YOUR CASES TO REMOVE ALL SIZING LUBRICANT. THE PRESENCE OF OIL OR GREASE ON A CARTRIDGE MAY DANGEROUSLY INCREASE THRUST ON THE BOLT FACE.

Pistol Cartridges

In the Rifle Section, we stated that the empty cartridge case is our most important reloading component. This statement applies to handgun cartridges as well. The fired case must be strong and in good condition in order to function properly, and to fulfill its task of sealing the chamber and withstanding chamber pressure. Generally speaking, most handgun cases do not take as severe a battering from chamber pressure and from resizing as do most rifle cases. The wear they do experience, however, will eventually destroy their usefulness. Case life is a relative thing which varies with the pressure of the load. Heavy magnum loads destroy cases rapidly, while the same cases loaded with light mid-range loads may last almost indefinitely.

The Case as a Component

The reloader soon learns to think of his cartridge case as an intrinsic and functional part of the firearm itself. After all, if the case is to rely on the supporting strength of the chamber walls and bolt face, then its dimensions must remain closely to those of the gun chamber. In other words, the cartridge case must be designed and manufactured with the same care and skill as the firearm. In as much as the safety of the load depends on both the strength of the firearm and the case, one is no stronger than the other. To be sure your cases are in good condition, we recommend that you start with either new or once-fired cases. Never use brass of unknown origin such as that found on shooting ranges. Inspect your cases for signs of case fatigue before each reloading. If, as suggested, the cases are new, or once-fired, they will not show fatigue at this first loading. However, fatigue signs are bound to reveal themselves in subsequent loading, so you should learn to watch for them.

It is a wise practice to separate your cases into lots and to keep a record of their history. For example, if you purchase two boxes of factory loaded cartridges on a certain date, keep all one hundred rounds together and load them as one lot. Record the brand name, the date of purchase, and the number of times you loaded these cases. Maintaining a record will be helpful in determining your case life, and you will benefit later on when trimming is required.

Trimming is necessary when the cases have been lengthened after numerous firings.

After you have inspected your cases and culled out the rejects, you are ready to go on to the next step. Before you dispose of the defective cases, however, it is a good idea to flatten them with a pair of pliers to prevent their reuse.

When loading new or once-fired cases, it is necessary to remove the sharp edges inside the case mouth. This operation is called chamfering and its purpose is to ease the insertion of the new bullet. Chamfering is needed only for the first reloading of a new or once-fired case. An inexpensive hand reamer chamfers a case easily and with uniformity. Hold the case in one hand, while you lightly turn the reamer in the case mouth with the other hand. Remove very little material and do not cut a sharp knife edge on the case.

Choosing a Load

To select the proper components, refer to the data pages of a reloading handbook that lists your cartridge. Make a note of the bullet diameter and primer size specified for this cartridge. This information will be needed when you purchase components. For example, if your cartridge was a .38 Special, you would look under the specifications for that cartridge and take note of the following data:

EXAMPLE (.38 SPECIAL)

SPECIFICATIONS:
Bullet Dia. Jacketed & Cast .... .354" to .360"*
Maximum Case Length .... 1.155"
Trim-to Length .... 1.149"
Maximum Overall Length (w/Bullet) .... 1.550"
Primer Size .... Small Pistol
Lyman Shell Holder Number 1

*The correct bullet diameter is related to the groove diameter of your particular handgun. With handguns, this dimension can vary from one handgun to another. The only way to be certain of your exact groove diameter is to slug the barrel.

Now, you must decide on a bullet weight and a type of powder. You will note, in most pistol calibers, that a selection of bullet types (Cast, Jacketed and Half-Jacketed) is available.

If you should decide to use either a Jacketed or a Half-Jacketed bullet, then these bullets may be purchased from your component dealer. Jacketed, or Half-Jacketed bullets are manufactured to a standard diameter which may vary from the groove diameter of your pistol. The starting loads for these bullet types take into consideration these possible variations, and they will be safe to use in your handgun.

If you should decide to use a cast bullet, however, then you must purchase a mold for the bullet specified. The loads shown for cast bullets are quite specific and the correct bullet number and alloy must be used. These bullets should be sized to the groove diameter of your handgun for which a sizing die is available.

EXAMPLE (.38 Special)
158 Grain Jacketed

Powder	Sug. Starting Grains	Velocity F.P.S.	Max. Grains	Velocity F.P.S.
Unique	4.6	688		
2400	9.5	785		

141 Grain Cast
BULLET #358495 (#2 ALLOY)

Powder	Sug. Starting Grains	Velocity F.P.S.	Max. Grains	Velocity F.P.S.
Bullseye	2.0	568		
Unique	3.5	739		
2400	8.0	794		
SR 7625	3.1	550		
SR 4756	4.0	562		
IMR 4227	7.0	550		

Basic Mechanics

Reloading a pistol cartridge requires a series of SIX basic mechanical operations. So that you will understand the fundamentals of each operation, we will first treat them graphically and then explain why each operation is necessary. Four out of the six operations are performed by the reloading dies.

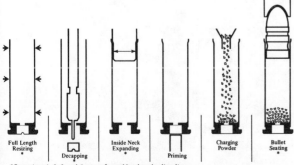

Full Length Resizing *   Decapping *   Inside Neck Expanding *   Priming *   Charging Powder   Bullet Seating *

*Operations 1, 2, 3, and 6 are performed by the reloading dies.

1. FULL LENGTH RESIZING: When a cartridge is fired, the side walls of the case expand to the chamber size of the handgun. This is necessary for the case to function properly and seal the chamber. These walls remain pretty much at their expanded size and do not snap back to original dimensions. Since all pistol chambers are not identical, cases fired in one pistol may not chamber in another. Even the chambers of a revolver cylinder will, in fact, vary from one to another. For this reason, it is necessary to compress the walls of the case to a standard diameter that is acceptable to all handguns. This operation is called resizing.

2. DECAPPING: This operation consists of simply removing the old or fired primer.

3. INSIDE NECK EXPANDING: After the case has been resized, the inside diameter of the neck will be too small to accept the bullet. Inside neck expanding enlarges the inside diameter of the neck to a size which will receive and hold the bullet securely. For pistol cases, a two-step expanding plug is used to open up the inside of the case neck. The first step on this plug is slightly smaller than bullet diameter, while the second step is a few thousandths larger. The idea behind this is to allow the bullet to enter the case freely without shaving lead. The actual difference between the two steps is not visually apparent. The illustrations have been exaggerated for purposes of clarification.

4. PRIMING: This operation consists of inserting a new primer into the primer pocket.

5. CHARGING POWDER: This operation consists of carefully weighing out and pouring the appropriate powder charge into the case.

6. BULLET SEATING: The last operation in the reloading process is seating a new bullet into the case.

In the preceding text we covered reloading graphically and have given the reader a general idea of what is required. Now by employing photographs we will explain the actual reloading of a cartridge. You will note that we are using a set of three reloading dies to perform four of the six operations. Further along in reloading you will hear of two-die sets and even four-die sets. The difference is that two and three die sets combine some of the operations, while a four die set performs each operation separately. Due to their shape, most pistol cartridges require the use of a three die set.

Making Cartridges

We now assume that your cases have been properly inspected, that you have selected a load, and purchased the necessary components. Your reloading press should be assembled and mounted according to the instructions supplied with it. Many reloading presses may be assembled to func-

STEP 1

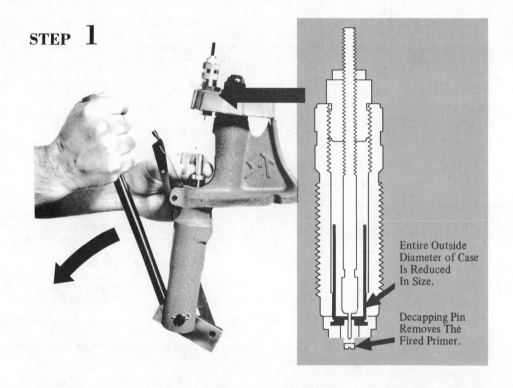

Entire Outside
Diameter of Case
Is Reduced
In Size.

Decapping Pin
Removes The
Fired Primer.

STEP 2

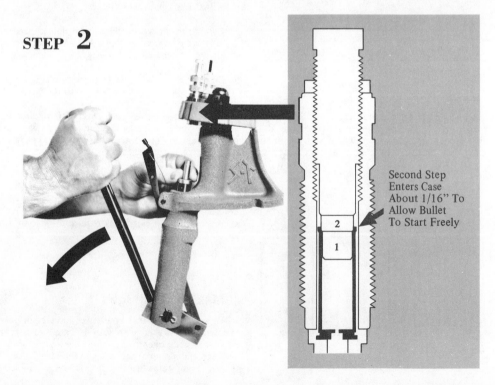

Second Step
Enters Case
About 1/16" To
Allow Bullet
To Start Freely

2

1

tion on either the up, or down-stroke of the handle. The press illustrated here is operating on the down-stroke. First, lubricate your cases by wiping them with a cloth sparingly greased with a case lubricant. This special lubricant will cut friction to a minimum and ease the sizing operation. Apply a very thin coat, for too much grease will trap air in the die and cause "lube dents." Although cases dented in this manner may be used for reloading, as the dents are ironed out in firing, it is not considered good reloading practice. Screw your Full Length Resizing Die into the head of the press, adjust it according to the instructions furnished, and you are ready to commence loading.

1. Full-Length Resizing and Decapping

Slide the head of your cartridge case into the Shell Holder as illustrated, and pull your press handle down all the way. If the die is adjusted properly, the entire cartridge case will enter the die flush to the shell holder. Note, in the cutaway drawing, how two of the original six reloading operations (full-length resizing and decapping) are accomplished by this

step. Pull up on the press handle to remove the case from the die.

2. Inside Neck Expanding

Screw the Neck Expanding Die into the turret head and adjust it according to the instructions supplied with the die. Place the resized cartridge case into the shell holder and pull down on the press handle. Note, in the drawing, how the two-step plug enters and expands the case neck. Actually, there is only a few thousandths difference in diameter between the first and second steps on the plug. This difference is so slight that it is not visually apparent. The illustration has been exaggerated for clarification.

3. Priming

The priming operation takes place as your case is withdrawn from the Neck Expanding Die. Place the new primer (cup side up) into the priming punch sleeve. Push the primer arm forward (toward the press) and pull up on the press handle. As the ram is lowered, the priming arm will enter the slot in the side of the ram and seat the primer.

Setting Primers: Primers are seated mainly by feel. The bottom of the anvil *must bottom* in the primer pocket. Depending on the brand of case and primer being used, this usually works out so that the primer is fully seated when the top of the primer is flush with the head of the case, or a few thousandths below the head. Under no circumstances should primers protrude from the head of the case. Use care not to crush the primer. Crushed primers give erratic ignition, or fail to fire.

STEP 3

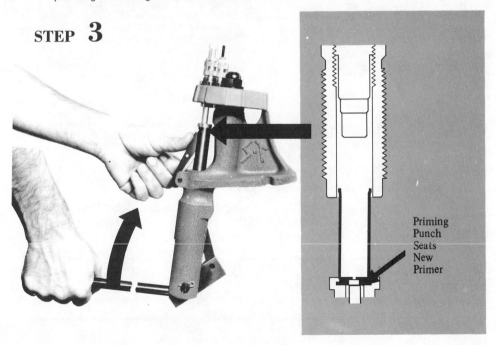

Priming
Punch
Seats
New
Primer

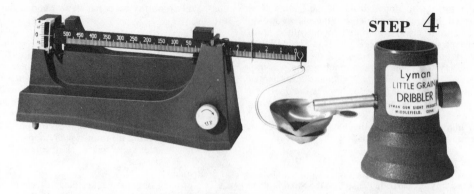

STEP **4**

The reloading accessory shown with the scale is a Lyman Powder Trickler which enables you to add a few granules of powder at a time, and carefully bring the scale into balance.

4. Charging Powder

For the weighing of powder, you require an accurate powder scale. The data section in a handbook specifies the powders appropriate for your particular cartridge. It also lists a suggested weight of the charge in grains and in fractions of grains. For example, 2.2 would be read as TWO and TWO TENTHS grains. 3.0 would be read as THREE grains. We recommend that the novice restrict himself, at least temporarily, to the suggested starting load. Carefully level the powder scale as explained in the instructions and set it to weigh your required charge. The illustration below explains how to adjust the scale.

Slowly trickle small amounts of powder into the scale pan until the beam comes into balance. The beam is in balance when the pointed end (extreme left) is exactly on the zero mark.

Carefully remove the pan and pour its contents into the cartridge case. Use a powder funnel to make sure all the powder enters the case. Because pistol powders are comparatively fast burning, most normal charges take up very little room in the cartridge case. In other words, it is possible to accidentally double charge, or even triple charge many pistol cases. This, of course, would prove extremely dangerous and a foolproof system of loading must be developed. A suggested method is to place all the uncharged cartridge cases on your left. As you pick up each case for charging, turn it up-side-down and shake it. This will insure that the case is empty. Turn the case right-side-up, charge it and place it carefully on your right. Take care, when removing or replacing the scale pan that the poise are not accidentally moved.

The illustration shows the beam of a modern reloading scale. Note how it is graduated on both sides of the pivot point. The scale is set by moving the two weights (poise) to the proper graduations. The large poise (on the left) is used to obtain multiples of FIVE GRAINS, while the small poise (on the right) is used for FRACTIONS of a grain or SINGLE grains from one to five.
EXAMPLE: The illustration shows a setting of 3.0 grains. If you wish to increase this to 8.0 grains, simply move the large poise one notch to the left.

Each Graduation On This Side
Is Equal To 5 FULL GRAINS

Each Graduation On This Side
Is Equal To 1/10 GRAIN

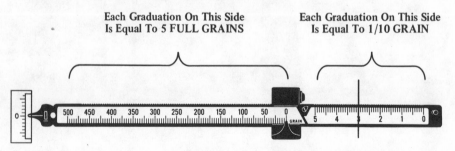

5. Bullet Seating

The last operation in reloading a cartridge case is seating the new bullet. Be sure the overall length of the finished round is not longer than the MAXIMUM OVERALL LENGTH specified for the particular cartridge. Adhering to this measurement will make certain that the finished round will function properly in your magazine or cylinder. Also, a bullet not seated to the proper depth can engage the rifling in an auto loading pistol, and build up pressure upon firing.

This illustration shows how a bullet is seated. Screw the bullet seating die into the head of the press and adjust it according to the instructions supplied. Place a primed, charged cartridge case in the shell holder and start a bullet in the mouth of the case. Pull your press handle all the way down, so when the case enters the die, the bullet will be pushed firmly into the neck of the case. Adjusting the seat-ing screw controls the depth to which the bullet is seated. Adjusting the die body controls the crimp.

Letter "A" indicates headspace in first example below. If case of this type is crimped, it can shorten the overall length of the case and create an excessive headspace condition. Rimmed cases of the "B" type may be crimped if desired. Magnum cartridges, due to their heavy recoil, require the use of a crimp to hold the bullet securely.

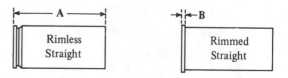

Rimless Straight

Rimmed Straight

STEP 5

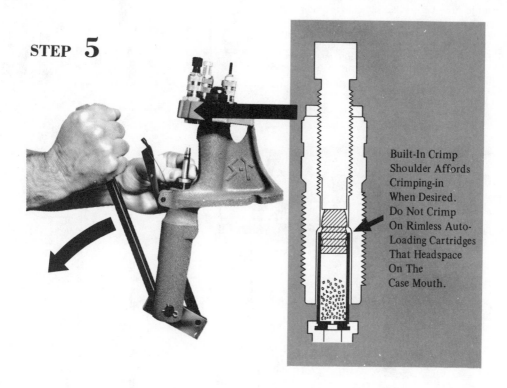

Built-In Crimp Shoulder Affords Crimping-in When Desired. Do Not Crimp On Rimless Auto-Loading Cartridges That Headspace On The Case Mouth.

CAUTION: AFTER RELOADING AND BEFORE FIRING, WIPE YOUR CASES TO REMOVE ALL SIZING LUBRICANT. THE PRESENCE OF OIL OR GREASE ON A CARTRIDGE MAY DANGEROUSLY INCREASE THRUST ON THE BOLT FACE.

Shotshells

Case Inspection

Repeated firing and reloading will eventually wear out your cases so develop the habit of inspecting them carefully before each reloading, and be fussy with them. Check each case for defects in the inner base wad.

At one time we recommended that a small dowel be used as a depth gauge to check the inside of each case. However, this does not always work, because sometimes only small portions of the base wad are blown away, and the dowel method of checking is not exact enough to pick up such small defects.

Discard cases that have torn, split, or blown-away mouths. Such cases will not crimp properly. Check the case walls for pin hole burns. Also, twist the case head slightly in your fingers to see if it has loosened from the case body.

While the foregoing pre-loading inspection is adequate to make sure your cases are in good condition, you should also keep alert to case defects that show up in loading. For instance, if a spent primer decaps too easily, or a new primer seats too easily, then it is an indication that the primer pocket has stretched due to fatigue. This condition can sometimes be picked up in your pre-loading inspection by looking for dark smudges around the primer. Such cases should also be thrown away.

Basic Mechanics

To the novice who has never reloaded his own ammunition, the mechanical procedure of shotshell reloading may at first appear to be somewhat difficult. Actually, it is so amazingly simple that all of the eight basic operations can be learned in a matter of minutes. Let's run through them briefly and see what they consist of.

Loading Shotshells

If you are to accomplish the eight mechanical steps described in the preceding text, you will require a shotshell reloading tool equipped with dies to accommodate your gauge. The basic tool will supply the leverage, while the dies will perform the varied operations required to reload a shotshell.

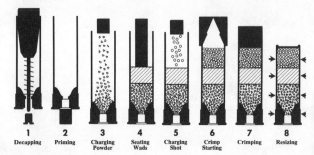

1	2	3	4	5	6	7	8
Decapping	Priming	Charging Powder	Seating Wads	Charging Shot	Crimp Starting	Crimping	Resizing

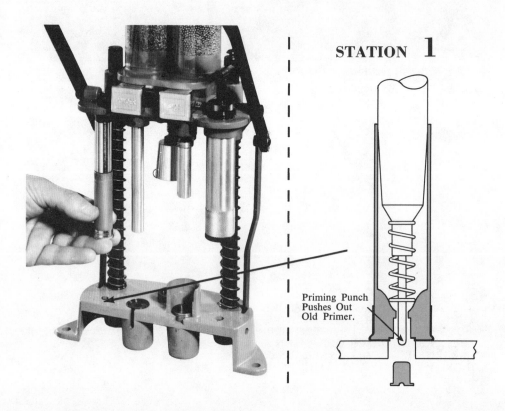

STATION 1

Priming Punch Pushes Out Old Primer.

STATION 1. (Decapping)

The very first operation is to push out the old or fired primer. Select a fired casing and slip the case up over the decapping punch as illustrated. Hold the case in position with your hand as you pull down on the press handle. The punch will move downward and carry the case along with it. Added pressure on the handle at the bottom of the stroke will pop out the spent primer. Raise the handle and remove the casing. It is now ready for the next station.

STATION 2. (Priming and Charging Powder)

On this station we complete two of the eight operations by putting a new primer and a measured powder charge into the case. The new primer is placed (flange down) into the priming base as illustrated. Now, place the head of the shotshell in the circular recess over the primer. As you pull down lightly on the press handle, you will notice that the powder drop tube will enter the case and force it down over the primer. The pressure applied to the handle should be only hard enough to seat the new primer, and no more. Hold the handle in the down position as you operate the powder slide. Pull the slide out and push it in smoothly with a single stroke in each direction. Your shell is now primed and charged with powder. Raise the press handle and remove the case. It is ready for station three.

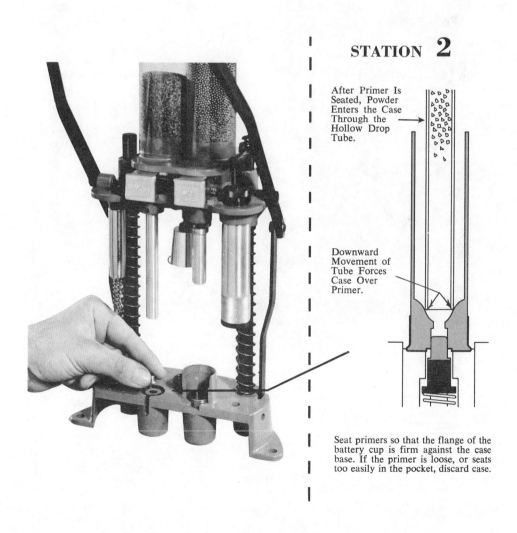

STATION 2

After Primer Is Seated, Powder Enters the Case Through the Hollow Drop Tube.

Downward Movement of Tube Forces Case Over Primer.

Seat primers so that the flange of the battery cup is firm against the case base. If the primer is loose, or seats too easily in the pocket, discard case.

STATION 3. (Seating Wads and Charging Shot)

Once the case has been primed and charged with powder, it advances to station three where we insert the wads and drop in a charge of shot. Here again we perform two loading operations at a single station. In order that the wads may enter the case easily, the case is first inserted into a wad chamber, as shown in the illustration. Start the wads into the chamber by hand and then set the wad chamber (with the case still inside) into base collar over pressure gauge.

Pull down on the press handle and the wad will seat firmly against the powder. A glance at the pressure gauge will tell you how much wad pressure you are applying. Hold the handle down as you operate the shot slide. Pull the slide out and push it in smoothly with a single stroke in each direction.

Raise the press handle and remove your case from the wad chamber. It is now ready for crimping.

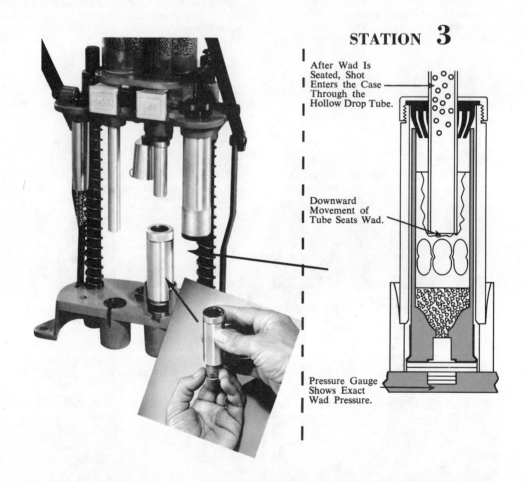

STATION 3

After Wad Is Seated, Shot Enters the Case Through the Hollow Drop Tube.

Downward Movement of Tube Seats Wad.

Pressure Gauge Shows Exact Wad Pressure.

STATION 4. (Starting the Crimp)

The plastic used in today's shotshell cases is a tough material that will not bend into a crimp form as readily as the paper cases. Therefore, it is necessary to complete the crimp in two stages. The first stage is called crimp starting.

Depending on brand and style, cases vary in the number of folds or pleats, which are used to close the crimp. Some cases require eight folds, others six. Make sure that your crimp starter is equipped with the appropriate head for the case you are loading.

To use the crimp starter, simply place your charged case in the alignment base under the starter as shown in the illustration and pull down the handle. The self-aligning arm will pivot the starter head so that it meshes exactly to the existing folds in the case mouth.

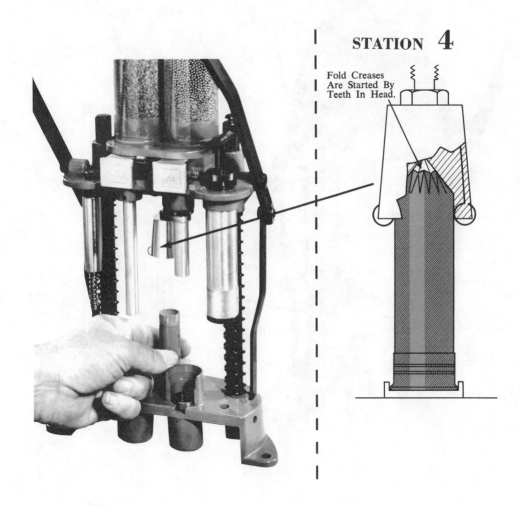

STATION 4

Fold Creases Are Started By Teeth In Head.

STATION 5. (Crimping and Sizing)

This is the final operation in loading a shotshell. At this station we close the mouth of the case with a good firm crimp and resize the walls so that the case will chamber freely.

Slip your shotshell up into the crimping and sizing die as shown in the illustration, and pull the press handle all the way down. Allow the handle to rise slowly. Now, firmly force the press handle up so that the ejector rod contacts the ejector stop. This action will automatically free your finished reload from the die.

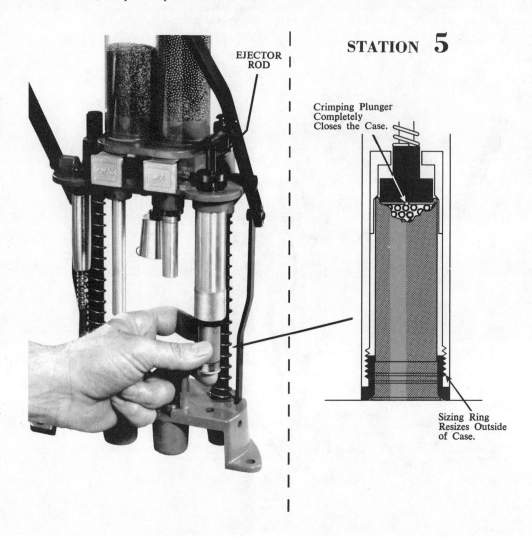

EJECTOR ROD

STATION 5

Crimping Plunger Completely Closes the Case.

Sizing Ring Resizes Outside of Case.

How to Field Dress Your Deer
by Leonard Lee Rue III

1. Start by cutting close circle around the anus and the connecting alimentary canal. Make the cut as deep as knife's reach.

2. Open the belly as shown, being careful not to cut intestines. Fork the incision to pass on either side of the sex organs.

3. Make careful cuts to loosen scrotum and penis. Then pull the detached anus and alimentary canal through pelvic arch.

4. Break the membrane over the chest cavity and reach far up to cut the windpipe loose. Pull out all the organs and entrails.

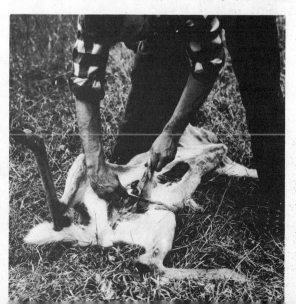

5. One way to handle heart and liver is to put them in a blood-proof plastic bag that keeps meat and your own clothes clean.

6. Tip the carcass as shown and drain out blood collected inside. Wipe body cavity dry with cloth or dead grass.

7. Prop the body cavity open with a stick to let in cooling air. Hang the carcass unless you plan to pack it out immediately.

8. To protect your clothes, sew up the deer before backpacking it out of the woods. Body cavity is spread open again when you get deer to car or camp.

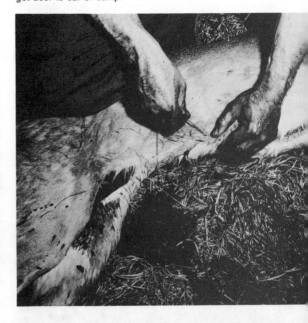

9. Cut off the hair-tufted glands on the hind legs. Some say they taint the meat.

10. At home or at base camp, hang the deer by the neck or the antlers for easier skinning.

11. With a saw or a knife, cut off all four legs at the center joints. Lower legs are waste.

12. Slit skin on the inside of each of the four legs down to the belly cut that you have re-opened.

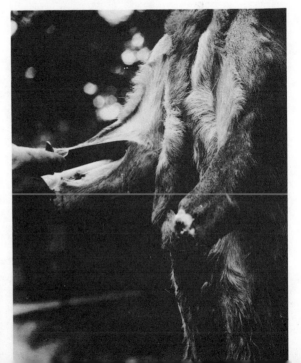

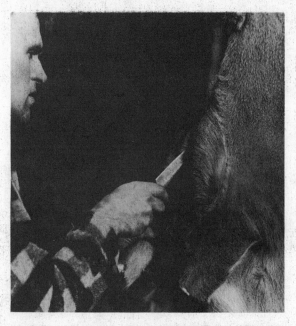

13. Extend belly cut up to the brisket and throat, splitting the breastbone in the process.

14. Cut around the neck. If the head is to be mounted, cut lower than shown so more hide is intact for Taxidermist.

15. Pull the skin on down, using the knife as needed to work the hide loose from the carcass.

16. Hide will pull off like a stubborn banana peel. Knife is used only in the tight spots.

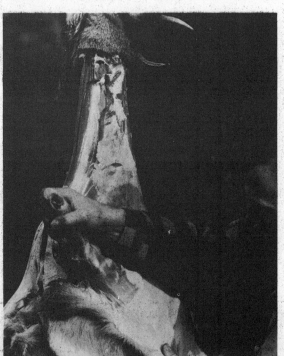

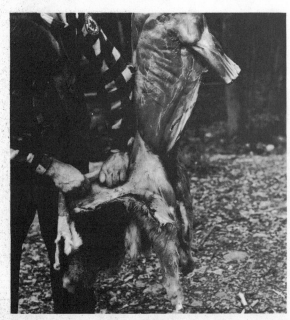

How to Butcher Your Deer

1. The tools for cutting up skinned carcass: cleaver, sharpening steel, knife, and meat saw.

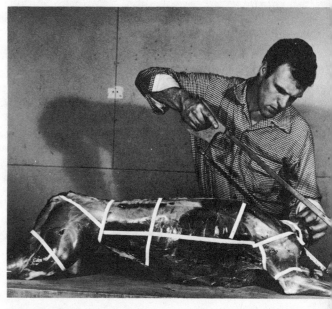

2. Tape on skinned deer shows 11 major cuts to divide each side of the carcass. Start with neck cut.

3. Toughest cut is long one down backbone. Assistant is helpful at this point to steady carcass.

4. After flank has been cut off to be chopped up for deerburger, loin is lopped off.

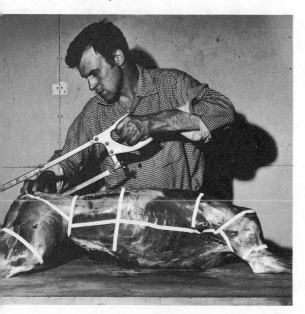

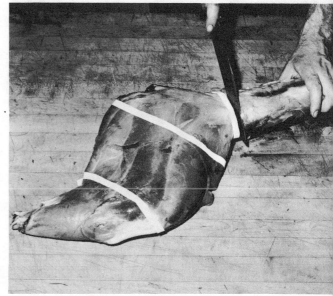

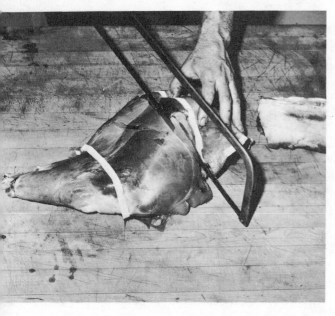

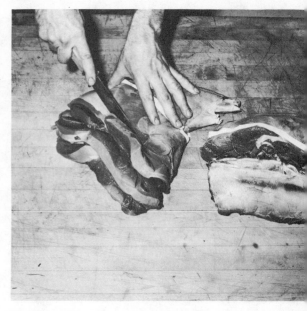

5. Sharp knife cuts to bone, which is severed with saw Hand holds rump roast.

6. Divide round-steak portion in even one-inch thick slices. Saw cuts center bone.

7. Left hand holds the rib chop section. Use the cleaver to lop off the lower ribs.

8. Knife divides rib chops. Cleaver will clip the bone portion. Intact piece makes rib roast.

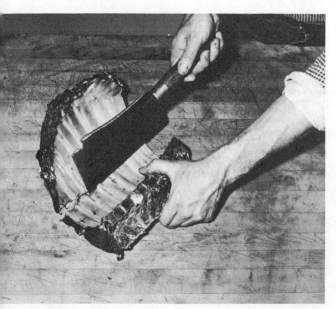

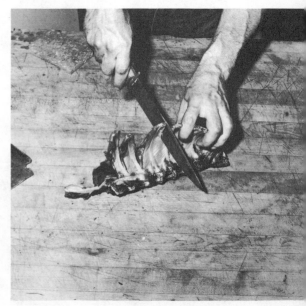

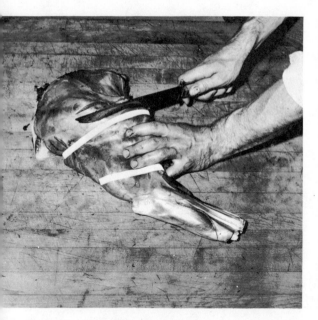

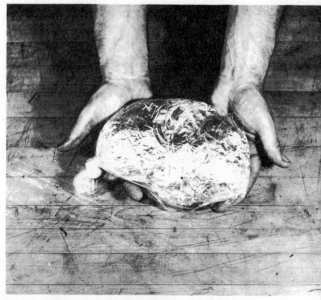

9. On fore shoulder, two tape-marked cuts at top make roasts. Cut up shank for deerburger.

10. Cover foil-wrapped venison with airtight plastic bags tied securely. Frozen, meat keeps indefinitely.

PART II / Game Animals and Birds

Big-Game Animals

Grizzly Bear
Ursus arctos

RANGE: Mostly in inland Alaska, though there are small herds of grizzlies in the Rocky Mountains. A variety of the grizzly, the Alaska brown bear, once considered to be a separate species, inhabits the Alaska Peninsula to its southernmost point. Limited sections of British Columbia, the Yukon Territory, and nearby islands are also inhabited by the brown bear.

IDENTIFICATION: The grizzly bear has a compact, powerful frame, with long thick hair ranging from dark brown through shades of tan to almost yellow. The tips of the hairs are grizzled; hence the bear's name. The grizzly has sharply curved claws, $3^3/_4$ inches long, which it uses for fighting and digging. The grizzly has a prominent shoulder hump, a feature which distinguishes it from the black and polar bears.

SIZE: The typical grizzly is 6 to 8 feet long; the distance from its foot to the top of its hump is about $3^1/_2$ feet. Average weight is 800 pounds, though some grizzlies have gone as high as 1,100.

The world-record grizzly, whose skull was picked up in Bella Coola Valley, British Columbia, in 1970, scored $27^2/_{16}$ points in the Boone and Crockett competition. The record skull measured $17^6/_{16}$ inches long and $9^{12}/_{16}$ inches wide.

The brown bear, largest of the carnivorous, land-based mammals, reaches 8 to 10 feet in length and stands $4^1/_2$ feet at the top of its shoulder. The average male weighs 1,000 pounds, the female rarely more than 800. Some browns on record have weighed over 1,500 pounds.

The world-record Alaskan brown bear, killed by Roy Lindsley on Kodiak Island in 1952, scored $30^{12}/_{16}$ points in the Boone and Crockett Club competition. The record male's skull measured $17^{15}/_{16}$ inches long and $12^{13}/_{16}$ inches wide.

FOOD: The grizzly is classified as a carnivore, but because grasses, sedges, roots, and tubers of plants are readily available the grizzly has omnivorous tendencies. Salmon, mice, snakes, and frogs also supplement this bear's diet.

EDIBILITY: Indians and outdoorsmen used to eat the flesh in early times, but the grizzly bear is primarily a trophy animal today.

Black Bear
Ursus americanus

RANGE: Every Canadian province and Alaska are populated with black bears, as are substantial portions of the United States from Montana south through Arizona and New Mexico. Sections of the Northeastern, Northwestern, and Gulf Coast States are inhabited by the species, along with northern Mexico and northeastern Arkansas.

IDENTIFICATION: Shiny black hair covers a major part of the body, but turns lighter about the eyes and muzzle. A blaze of white adorning the chest is a distinguishing characteristic, as is the absence of the conspicuous shoulder hump of the Alaska brown bear and the grizzly bear.

SIZE: A prime male averages between 300 and 400 pounds; a female far less. Some black bears on record have scaled more than 600 pounds. The average animal stands 3 feet high at the shoulder and measures $5^1/_2$ feet in length.

The world-record bear, killed by Rex W. Peterson and Richard S. Hardy in San Pete County, Utah, in 1970, scored $22^6/_{16}$ points in the Boone and Crockett competition. The skull measured $13^{11}/_{16}$ inches long and $8^{11}/_{16}$ inches wide.

FOOD: The black bear tends to be omnivorous, eating

GRIZZLY BEAR

BLACK BEAR

grasses, fruits, berries, buds, fish, rodents, and sedges. Dead bears, ants, and bees are also on its menu.

EDIBILITY: The meat is dark and tends to be coarse. But it is very good when handled and prepared properly.

Polar Bear
Ursus maritimus

RANGE: Polar bears are found predominantly in regions of the arctic coast, ranging from Labrador west to Alaska's Seward Peninsula, and south along the Hudson Bay and James Bay shore.

IDENTIFICATION: The polar bear's body is almost completely covered by long, thick, yellow-white fur during the entire year. Only the lips, eyes, nose, and toenails are black. The head is small and tapering, the neck long and muscular, and the body somewhat pear-shaped.

POLAR BEAR

SIZE: Though the male averages 1,000 pounds, some have been reported as heavy as 1,600 pounds. A prime male stands 4 feet high at the shoulder, usually measuring 8 feet in length. Females tend to be smaller.

The world-record polar bear was taken by Shelby Longoria in 1963 off Kotzebue, Alaska. The male had a Boone and Crockett Club score of $29^{15}/_{16}$ points, with a skull measuring $18^{8}/_{16}$ inches in length and $11^{7}/_{16}$ inches in width. The polar bear is currently ineligible, until further notice, for the North American Big Game competition.

FOOD: The most-carnivorous bear of all, the polar bear dines on seals, foxes, mollusks, lemmings, birds, caribou, and dead or helpless whales. Often, however, this species eats seaweed, grasses, and roots.

EDIBILITY: The meat is a main staple in the diet of the Eskimos, but the liver can be poisonous due to excessive amounts of Vitamin A within.

Whitetail Deer
Odocoileus virginianus

RANGE: The whitetail deer inhabits a vast section of North America, from southern Canada down through the southern border of the United States. Only a few dry regions of western North America are devoid of whitetails.

IDENTIFICATION: In spring the whitetail sports a bright brownish-red coat made up of thin hair. With the coming of winter a new coat grows, colored with shades of long, kinky hair varying from brownish-gray to blue. The nose is pure black with two white bands behind it. The face is brown and the eyes are circled with white. The darkest part of the body is the middle of the back. Though gradually lighter on other parts of the body, the coloring turns an abrupt white at the stomach. The antlers consist of two main beams that grow outward, backward, and then sweep forward.

SIZE: A typical whitetail is slightly taller than 3 feet at the shoulder, measures 5 to 6 feet in length, and weighs about 150 pounds. The largest whitetail ever recorded, however, weighed 425 pounds.

The world-record whitetail deer, according to the Boone and Crockett Club ratings, scored $206^{5}/_{8}$ points. Though the hunter and the year the trophy was taken are unknown, it is probable that the vicinity of the kill was Sandstone, Minnesota. Both right and left main beams measure 30 inches long and sport 5 points each. The rack's inside spread is $20^{1}/_{8}$ inches.

FOOD: Most types of vegetation are included in the whitetail's diet, which changes with both the season and the area of the country inhabited. Tops on the menu are white cedar, white acorns, witchhazel, pine, red maple, apples, dogwood,

WHITETAIL DEER

oak, sweetfern, sumac, wintergreen, bearberry, oregon-grape, hemlock, willow, greenbriar, snowberry, and arborvitae. Among the cultivated crops it seeks out are soybeans, trefoil, rye, alfalfa, corn, rape, cabbage, clover, and lespedeza.

EDIBILITY: Whitetail venison, if treated like good beef, will taste delicious. Prompt and proper field dressing insures fine meat.

Mule Deer
Odocoileus hemionus

RANGE: The overall area encompassed by the mule deer extends from southeastern Alaska to Mexico, east to west Texas, Minnesota, and Hudson Bay. Those muleys inhabiting the coastal area from Alaska to mid-California are properly termed blacktail deer.

IDENTIFICATION: The mule deer's basic coloring in summer is a brownish-red, changing to a brownish-gray come winter. The nose and the band around the muzzle are black, the face and a section about the eyes are white. Its throat has two white patches separated by a dark bar, its belly and the insides of its legs are whitish, and its hoofs are jet black. The tail is round and white but becomes black about 2 inches from its tip. The ears often reach 11 inches in total length. A buck's antlers, very large and heavy, .ivide into two main beams. Each beam forks into two ćines.

Though closely related to the mule deer, the blacktail does have some distinctions. The ears measure 6½ inches and are narrower, and the tail is dark on top with a white underside. But like the muley the blacktail's coloring is brownish-red in summer and brownish-gray in winter.

SIZE: This species stands about 3½ feet high at the shoulder, measures close to 6½ feet in length, and averages be-tween 175 and 200 pounds in weight. The blacktail is slightly smaller on the average. One mule deer that was recorded weighed 480 pounds.

The world-record mule deer, according to the Boone and Crockett Club record book, was killed in Hoback Canyon, Wyoming. The hunter and the year the deer was killed are unknown. Scoring 217 points, the rack's right main beam, sporting 6 points, measures 28⁴/₈ inches, its left, also sporting a half-dozen points, measures 28²/₈ inches. The rack's inside spread is 26⁶/₈ inches.

The world-record blacktail deer, according to the Boone and Crockett Club record book, scored 170⁶/₈ points. It was taken by Clark D. Griffith, Elk City, Oregon, in 1962. The right beam measures 23¹/₈ inches, the left 24 inches. Both have 5 points. The rack's inside spread is 21⁴/₈ inches.

FOOD: In summer grasses play an important role in the mule deer's diet: rice grass, needlegrass, grama grass, wheat grass, bluegrass, fescue grass, and bromegrass. In winter, when grasses are scarce, browse takes over: mountain mahogany, cliffrose, sagebrush, poplar, bitterbrush, jack pine, sunflower, cedar, oak, snowberry, bearberry, fir, and serviceberry. Although the deer eats almost any vegetation, they prefer fungus, nuts, cactus fruit, acorns, wildflowers, ferns, and berries.

Rating high on the blacktail's menu are wild oats, manzanita, ceanothus, chamise, buckthorn, buttercup, bromegrass, and fescue grass. Cactus fruit, nuts, wildflowers, acorns, fungus, berries, and acorns are also preferred foods.

EDIBILITY: Deer venison, though drier than beef, is delicious.

Elk
Cervus canadensis

RANGE: The bulk of the elk population is in the Rocky Mountains, ranging from British Columbia to New Mexico and Arizona. Herds are also found in some mid-Western and Eastern States. Alberta, Saskatchewan, and Manitoba also have fair-sized elk populations.

IDENTIFICATION: The elk's normal winter coat is brown-gray with long chestnut-brown hair on its head and neck. Legs are dark and belly nearly black. The rump patch and short tail are yellow-white. Cow elk are lighter than bulls. In summer the elk's coat turns reddish.

SIZE: Bull elk range in weight from 600 to as much as 1,000 pounds. Cows are smaller, averaging about 600 pounds. A good-size bull may stand 5 feet at the shoulder and measure 10 feet in length. Antlers of a prime bull will grow up to 5 feet above its head, with each antler sporting from 5 to 7 points and measuring 60 inches or more along the beam.

The world-record head, taken in 1899 in Dark Canyon, Colorado, by John Plute, had a Boone and Crockett Club score of 442³/₈ points. The beams measured 55⁵/₈ and 59⁵/₈ inches long. Right beam had 8 points, the left 7 points. Inside spread measured 45½ inches.

FOOD: The diet consists mainly of grasses and browse.

MULE DEER

ELK

The world-record Alaska-Yukon moose scored 251 points in the Boone and Crockett Club competition. Killed by Bert Klineburger in 1961 at Mt. Susitna, Alaska, the trophy's greatest spread measures 77⁴/₈ inches. Its right palm is 46³/₈ inches long, its left 51 inches long.

The world-record Canada moose, according to the Boone and Crockett Club rating system, scored 238⁵/₈ points. Killed by Silas H. Witherbee in 1914 near Bear Lake, Quebec, the trophy has a right palm measuring 44⁶/₈ inches long with 18 points and a left palm measuring 43¹/₈ inches long with 19 points. The greatest spread is 65⁵/₈ inches.

The world-record Wyoming moose, killed by John M. Oakley at Green River Lake, Wyoming, in 1952, scored 205⁴/₈ points in the Boone and Crockett Club competition. Its greatest spread is 53 inches, its right palm 38⁶/₈ inches long, and its left palm 38⁵/₈ inches long. Both palms sport 15 points.

MOOSE

Some of the prime foods are pinegrass, bluegrass, bluebunch grass, sweet vernal grass, and wheatgrass. Elk eat nearly all the conifers, aspen, and willows. Their diet may also include alder, maple, blackberry, and serviceberry.

EDIBILITY: The meat is dark and much like beef in taste and texture. Elk is considered very good eating.

Moose
Alces alces

RANGE: The Alaska-Yukon moose is found in the Alaskan and Yukon peninsulas; the Canada moose is found in every Canadian province and in sections of northern Minnesota, Wisconsin, and Maine; the Wyoming, or Shiras, moose inhabits the area from the Rocky Mountain region of northern Colorado and Utah northward to the border between Canada and the United States.

IDENTIFICATION: The moose is a large, antlered, ungraceful-looking creature. The primary color is black, though shades of dark brown and russet have been spotted. The nostrils, circles about the eyes, inner parts of the ear, and lower portions of the legs are whitish-gray. The hindquarters are much more tapered than the forequarters, and together they hold the moose's belly approximately 40 inches from the ground. The immense antlers weigh in the area of 90 pounds and often reach 6 feet in length. The tail is 3 inches long and stublike. The ears are large, and the long face finishes up in a wide, down-turned muzzle.

SIZE: A typical large bull is from 6¹/₂ to 7¹/₂ feet tall at the shoulder, measures 8¹/₂ to 10¹/₂ feet in length, and scales between 1,300 and 1,400 pounds. Several recorded bulls have weighed in at as high as 1,800 pounds.

FOOD: A favorite food is dwarf willow, as are white birch, aspen, and balsam fir in forested sections. Come summer the moose seeks shelter from the heat and insects at lakes, where it dines on eelgrass, sedges, pondweeds, and water lilies. Redosier, alder, honeysuckle, chokecherry, striped maple, spiraea, snowberry, dwarf birch, current, elder, cranberry, mountain ash, and cottonwood are also preferred items.

EDIBILITY: Though a bit darker and drier than beef, moose meat is very similar to it in taste.

Bighorn Sheep
Ovis canadensis

RANGE: The Rocky Mountain bighorn is found in remote areas from central British Columbia down through the northern Rocky Mountains. The desert bighorn inhabits a good portion of the southeastern United States and northern Mexico.

IDENTIFICATION: The bighorn has a well-muscled, finely proportioned body set atop stout, strong legs. The head and heavy majestic horns are supported by a rather sturdy neck. The horns, dark brown in color, have conspicuous growth rings and may weigh over 20 pounds. The Rocky Mountain bighorn is dark brown, the desert bighorn pale buff, but the tail is black. White is the color of the animal's muzzle, a patch around the eye, a rump patch, and an edging running along the back of each leg. The ears, though small, are alert.

SIZE: An average ram stands 3 to 3½ feet tall at the shoulder, measuring 5 to 6 feet in length. The ram weighs about 200 pounds. Some on record have surpassed 300 pounds. Ewes are usually a bit less than three-quarters the size of rams.

The world-record Rocky Mountain bighorn sheep, according to the Boone and Crockett Club, was taken by Fred Weiller in Blind Canyon, Alberta, in 1911. The trophy scored 208⅛ points, the right horn being 44⅞ inches long and the left horn being 45 inches long.

The world-record desert bighorn scored 205⅛ points in the Boone and Crockett Club competition. Taken by an Indian in Lower California, Mexico, in 1940, the trophy's right horn measured 43⅝ inches and the left measured 43⅝ inches. The greatest spread came to 25⅝ inches.

FOOD: Grasses comprise the bulk of the bighorn's diet. They include fescue, wheatgrass, sedges, rushes, horsetail, little ricegrass, pentstemon, June grass, and vetch. When the grasses are snow-covered come winter, browse—sagebrush, willow, alder, chokeberry, bitterbrush, rabbitbrush, greasebrush, and mountain mahogany—takes a prominent place on the menu.

EDIBILITY: Many big-game hunters rate bighorn sheep as the finest of all wild-game meat.

Dall Sheep
Ovis dalli

RANGE: This species inhabits the mountainous regions of northern Alaska, east to the western Mackenzie Mountain range.

IDENTIFICATION: Dall rams and ewes are practically snow white except for a few black hairs in their tails. The horns, a bit lighter than those of the Stone ram, have a conspicuous flare that keeps them away from the ram's eyes. Also, the light-yellow horns show well-defined yearly growth marks that depict the animal's age. Ewes have horns that usually resemble thin spikes and rarely grow beyond 15 inches in length. In winter the waxy hair covering the body

BIGHORN SHEEP

DALL SHEEP

reaches 3 inches in length, but this is shed before summer and replaced by a shorter coat.

SIZE: A typical Dall ram weighs between 180 and 200 pounds, stands slightly above 3 feet high at the shoulders, and measures approximately 6 feet in length.

The world-record Dall sheep, killed by Harry L. Swank Jr. in Alaska's Wrangell Mountains in 1961, polled 189⁶/₈ points in the Boone and Crockett Club competition. The right and left horns measure 48⁵/₈ inches and 47⁷/₈ inches respectively. The greatest spread is 34³/₈ inches.

FOOD: Forbes and grasses make up the bulk of the Dall sheep's diet, though it will eat browse, especially the dwarf willow.

EDIBILITY: Most hunters rate the meat far better than that of the domestic sheep. In fact, they consider it the finest in the world.

Stone Sheep
Ovis dalli stonei

RANGE: This subspecies of the Dall is found in northern British Columbia.

IDENTIFICATION: Stone sheep have colorings varying from gray-blue to blue-black to black. Stones do, however, have a light belly, a white rump patch, and a white edging down the rear of each leg. There is also a sort of whitish blotch on the face, which tends to enlarge with age. The horns of the Stone ram are a bit heavier than those of the Dall ram. The coat covering the body measures 3 inches, but it is shed when summer approaches and is replaced by a shorter coat.

SIZE: An average Stone ram scales between 180 and 200 pounds, measures 6 feet in length, and stands just above 3 feet tall at the shoulders.

The world-record Stone sheep, killed by L. S. Chadwick on the Muskwa River of British Columbia in 1936, scored 196⁶/₈ points in the Boone and Crockett Club competition. The right horn is 50¹/₈ inches long and the left is 51⁵/₈ inches long. The greatest spread is 31 inches.

FOOD: Grasses and forbes comprise the major portion of the Stone sheep's diet. It does dine on browse, however, especially the dwarf willow.

EDIBILITY: The meat of the domestic sheep can't compare with that of this fine specimen. Hunters rate its meat as the finest in the world.

Rocky Mountain Goat
Oreamnos americanus

RANGE: The species inhabits the steep slopes of the western mountains from Washington and Idaho up through central Yukon and southern Alaska.

IDENTIFICATION: The mountain goat's body is a short,

blunt, box-like structure, and except for the bottom 8 inches of each leg, it is covered by an abundance of hair. The shoulders are humped and the head is long and narrow. Its lengthy hair is pure white save for a yellow tint, but pure black is the color of its horns, nose, eyes, and hoofs. The horns, rising from the rear of the head, are slender and curve backward. Both the billy and the nanny sport horns and beards. In the billy the horns average 12 inches; in the nanny 9 inches.

SIZE: A typical mountain goat stands just over 3 feet high at the shoulder and measures 5 to 6 feet in length. Though the species averages between 150 and 300 pounds, the heaviest on record weighed just over 500 pounds.

ROCKY MOUNTAIN GOAT

The world-record mountain goat, killed by E. C. Haase in 1949 in British Columbia's Babine Mountains, scored 56⁶/₈ points in the Boone and Crockett Club competition. Both the male's horns measure 12 inches long; the greatest spread between them is 9²/₈ inches.

FOOD: In summer the goat's diet consists of grasses, browse, and forbes; specifically bluegrasses, wheatgrass, purple milk vetch, green lily, strawberry, alpine sorrel, and alpine equisetum. In winter goats switch to aspen, red osier, bearberry juniper, willow, dwarf birch, and balsam fir. Lichens and mosses are year-round favorites.

EDIBILITY: The meat of a trophy billy is usually rather tough as the animal is getting on in years. The meat of the younger animals, though, is used for food.

Caribou
Rangifer tarandus

RANGE: There are four varieties of caribou, formerly classified as subspecies but now considered to be of the same species, for which *Rangifer tarandus* is the accepted scientific name. The mountain caribou inhabits the tundra and coniferous forests of Canada and Alaska; the Barren Ground caribou summers from Canada and northern Alaska to the far north, until the land runs out. In winter, it migrates to the south as far as Saskatchewan and northern Manitoba. The woodland caribou is found in forested areas between northern Idaho and Great Slave Lake and from Newfoundland to the Alaska-Yukon border.

CARIBOU

IDENTIFICATION: The caribou has a dark neck and a long mane running under the neck from chin to chest. In the summer the fur is dark brown, but becomes brown-gray in winter. The belly, rump patch, feet and short tail vary in color from pale gray to yellow-white throughout the year. A wide muzzle circled with white hairs, long fur, and a main beam that sweeps backward, upward, and outward, finishing in a flat palm, typify the species. The mountain caribou is the largest and darkest of the four types. The Barren Ground is the smallest and palest; its neck is a very bright white. Both the male and female of the species have antlers, the male shedding his in December or January, the female during the fawning period in May and June.

SIZE: An average mountain caribou bull measures 7½ to 8 feet in length, close to 4 feet from foot to shoulders, and scales between 500 and 600 pounds. Some recorded mountain caribou have weighed in the vicinity of 700 pounds.

Females are smaller and lighter. The world-record mountain caribou, killed by Garry Beaubien in 1976, scored 462 points in the Boone and Crockett Club competition. The

right beam has 22 points, and measures $43^2/_8$ inches; the left has 19 points and measures $46^2/_8$ inches. The greatest inside spread measures $31^4/_8$ inches.

A typical Barren Ground bull is 6½ feet long, 3½ feet high from toe to shoulders, and averages 375 pounds. Females are smaller and weigh less. The world-record Barren Ground caribou, killed by Ray Loesche in Ugashik Lake, Alaska, in 1967, scored $463^6/_8$ points in the Boone and Crockett Club competition. The right beam measures $51^2/_8$ inches and has 22 points, the left measures $51^5/_8$ inches and has 23 points. The greatest inside spread between beams is $46^7/_8$ inches.

A typical woodland caribou bull is about 8 feet long, measures 4 feet from foot to shoulders, and weighs approximately 400 pounds. Females tend to be smaller in both total weight and size. The world-record woodland caribou was killed sometime prior to 1910 in Newfoundland, scoring $419^5/_8$ points in the Boone and Crockett Club competition. The left beam measures $47^3/_8$ inches and has 18 points, the right $50^1/_8$ inches and has 19 points. The greatest inside spread is $43^2/_8$ inches between beams.

FOOD: Caribou favor lichens as their main food, but also eat grasses, twigs, shrubs, flowers, moss, and practically any other plant matter available.

EDIBILITY: Caribou meat is rated excellent.

Pronghorn Antelope
Antilocapra americana

RANGE: The pronghorn is located in the region from southern Saskatchewan south through the western United States to the Mexican plains.

IDENTIFICATION: The pronghorn is similar to a small deer in body structure and coloring. Both male and female have similar markings—two black horns (both of which are longer than the ears), a bright tannish-red hue on the upper body and the outside of legs. The inside of the legs and underparts are a strong white, as is the rump patch. The necks of both sexes are streaked by two thick brown

PRONGHORN ANTELOPE

bands. The buck, however, has a wide black band that extends from the nose to just below the eyes.

SIZE: A full-grown male may reach 3½ feet in height at the shoulder, and 5 feet in length, with an average weight of between 100 and 140 pounds. Does usually peak at 80 pounds. The world-record head, taken in Antelope Valley, Arizona, in 1878, polled 101⁶/₈ points in the Boone and Crockett Club competition. Both horns measured 19⁴/₈ inches each; the inside spread 14⁷/₈ inches.

FOOD: Diet consists chiefly of vegetable substances such as saltbrush, onion, western juniper, sagebrush, and bitterbrush.

EDIBILITY: Outdoorsmen rate the meat very good.

Bison
Bison bison

RANGE: The wild bison no longer exists in the United States, and those of the species that remain are located in national parks, wildlife refuges, and private ranches in North America. Yellowstone and South Dakota's Wind Cave National Parks, Montana's National Bison Range, and Oklahoma's Wichita Wildlife Refuge have bison, as do Big Delta, Alaska and northern Alberta's Wood Buffalo Park.

IDENTIFICATION: The bison has a humped back, and is the largest wild animal on the North American continent. Lengthy hair, reaching 8 inches in winter and 4 inches in summer, covers its head, neck, shoulders, and forequarters. The hair on the rear section of the bison usually measures one-half the size of the hair on the front section. Hair color ranges from dark brown to black, but the sun often bleaches it to a dark tan. Both male and female have two thick horns, each of which is sharply upturned.

SIZE: A large bull may measure 11½ to 12 feet in length and stands 6 feet high from his foot to the apex of his hump. Bulls usually weigh about 2,000 pounds, while cows are much smaller, scaling 800 to 900 pounds. Records indicate

BISON

that some bison have reached weights of nearly 3,000 pounds.

The world-record bison, killed by S. Woodring in Yellowstone National Park, Wyoming, in 1925, scored 136⁴/₈ points in the Boone and Crockett Club competition. Its right horn measured 21²/₈ inches, its left 23²/₈ inches. The greatest spread between the record's horns is 35³/₈ inches.

FOOD: As the bison hasn't any teeth in the front of its upper jaw its diet consists of grasses such as tumbleweed, gramagrass, dropseed grass, and buffalo grass. Using its tongue and lower incisors, the bison snips off the grasses.

EDIBILITY: When bison weren't as scarce, people raved about the fine flavor of the meat. The bison's tongue and hump meat were considered delicacies. Some bison meat is available today from specimens killed on private ranches.

MOUNTAIN LION

Mountain Lion
Felis concolor

RANGE: This species, which is also known as the cougar, puma, painter, panther, catamount, and American lion, is distributed throughout western North America, from northern British Columbia south to Mexico, east to the Rocky Mountains and Saskatchewan, and along the Gulf States to Mississippi. Southern Florida also features the mountain lion.

IDENTIFICATION: The body color is practically uniform, though it may vary from russet to a near-gray. The fur measures a uniform 1 inch all over the body, dark near the eyes and upper muzzle, and off-white at the forepart of the mouth, lower flanks, and belly. The eyes are frequently yellow, the ears pronounced but well-rounded. Its prominent whiskers tend to be white. The tail, measuring from 2 to 3 feet, has a dark tip. The rounded head appears small in comparison to the body.

SIZE: The mountain lion is the largest North American un-spotted cat. A mature adult measures 7 to 9½ feet in length, stands 26 to 31 inches at the shoulder, and scales up to 275 pounds. Most lions are far lighter, and females are usually two-thirds the weight of males. The heaviest cat weighed over 300 pounds before evisceration.

The world-record cougar, according to the Boone and Crockett Club records, was taken by Garth Roberts in Garfield County, Utah, in 1964. Scoring 16 points, the skull measured $9^4/_{16}$ inches long and $6^{12}/_{16}$ inches wide.

FOOD: Mule deer in particular are the staple of the mountain lion's diet, though he prefers all species of deer. Horses and steers are also preyed upon, colts being a favorite. Chickens, pigs, goats, turkeys, and sheep also have their places on the menu.

EDIBILITY: The meat is reminiscent of lamb or veal in flavor, texture, and taste. The relative lack of fat, however, makes it somewhat dry.

Jaguar
Felis onca hernandesii

RANGE: Quite rare in the United States, the jaguar is located from Mexico southward to Central and South America.

IDENTIFICATION: The body, compact and enormously muscled, is coated with spots. This coat, basically yellow shading to tawny, features small spots around the head, large spots on the legs, and an intermixing of the two across the chest. The spots are actually rosettes, square in shape. The back and sides are covered with large, black rosettes with yellow middles and a black spot in the center. The tail measures just 30 inches long, shorter than the cougar's. The predominantly white feet have tiny black spots. The head is round, the ears short and finely rounded, and the whiskers long, white, and highly prominent.

SIZE: The jaguar is the Western Hemisphere's largest cat, usually measuring 6 to 9 feet in overall length, 2⅓ feet high at the shoulder, and scaling from 200 to 250 pounds. Some specimens have been reported at over 350 pounds.

The world-record skull scored $18^7/_{16}$ points in the Boone and Crockett Club competition. Taken by C. J. McElroy in 1965 in Sinaloa, Mexico, the jaguar's skull measured $10^{15}/_{16}$ inches in length and $7^8/_{16}$ inches in width.

FOOD: Monkeys, parrots, coatis, and turkeys form a part of the jaguar's diet, as do peccaries, cattle, sea turtles, and man himself.

Collared Peccary
Tayassu tajacu

RANGE: The peccary resides in arid, brushy regions and scrub oak forests along the border between the United States and Mexico, extending from eastern Texas west to Arizona.

IDENTIFICATION: The collared peccary resembles a pig

JAGUAR

COLLARED PECCARY

in that it has a lengthy snout with a tough disc at its tip, along with a very short neck, short but stout legs, and a somewhat arched back. Also, its ears are small, erect, and pointed. Though the eyelids have long lashes, the eyes themselves are small. The body is covered with 2-inch-long, bristly, salt-and-pepper gray hair. A thin, white band begins under the animal's throat and joins on its back. Eight inches above its short tail, on the center of its back, is a gaping musk gland.

SIZE: A typical member of this species is 2½ to 3 feet in length, measures 22 inches high at the shoulder, and averages between 40 and 65 pounds in total weight.

FOOD: Prickly pears—fruit and spines—are the javelina's favorite food. It eats roots, tubers, acorns, nuts, fruits, and berries. Being omnivorous the species also dines on insects, the young and eggs of ground-nesting birds, amphibians, and reptiles. Snake meat is a special treat.

EDIBILITY: Peccary meat, dry in texture and light in color, is considered tasty by some people; others tend to disagree.

European Wild Hog
Sus scrofa

RANGE: The species is far from numerous in the United States, and hunters must go to the areas of the initial releases (e.g. Tennessee's Great Smoky Mountains and North Carolina's Hooper's Bald) to find them.

IDENTIFICATION: Thin and muscular (unlike its domesticated relative), the wild boar has tusks measuring up to 9 inches in length. Its snout is long and saucer-like, its eyes rather small, and its always-erect ears about 5 inches long. The wild boar is usually pure black, but, on occasion, its bristly guard hairs may be white. The species' long legs give it nearly the swiftness of a deer.

SIZE: A typical adult measures 30 inches in height at the shoulder and is 4 to 5 feet long. In North America a big boar may weigh from 300 to 350 pounds. Some European

EUROPEAN WILD HOG

wild boars, however, have been recorded at close to 600 pounds.

FOOD: During the warmer months wild boars feed on roots, tubers, fruits, berries, and grasses. The menu also ranges from fawns to nuts, including rabbits, mice, frogs, beechnuts, and even rattlesnakes (to whose poison the wild hog appears to be immune).

EDIBILITY: The wild boar is hunted chiefly for sport and trophies, as its meat is reputed to be tough.

Small-Game Animals

Cottontail Rabbit
Sylvilagus

RANGE: Combined, the four species of the cottontail, which include the Eastern cottontail (*Sylvilagus floridanus*), mountain cottontail (*S. nuttali*), desert cottontail (*S. auduboni*), and New England cottontail (*S. transitionalis*), inhabit much of the United States, except for some sections of the Far West.

IDENTIFICATION: The body pigment is basically brown with the possibility of a reddish or buff cast. Guard hairs with black tips are scattered about, but the belly, chin, and undersides of the legs are white. The underside of the tail is also white, resembling a cotton ball when the rabbit is scampering about—hence, its name. A majority of cottontails have a white spot on the forehead between the eyes. The whiskers, though long, are light and relatively inconspicuous. The ears, 2½ to 3 inches long, are bare on the inside but lightly furred on the outside.

SIZE: The cottontail is from 14 to 19 inches long and stands 6 to 7 inches at the shoulder. Females tend to be a bit larger than males. Weights vary from 2½ to 3½ pounds, the latter being the top weight ever recorded.

FOOD: The diet of the cottontail consists of crabgrass, bluegrass, and other grasses, all kinds of fruits and berries; such cultivated crops as clover, alfalfa, lettuce, beans, wheat, soybeans, and cabbage; weeds such as yarrow and goldenrod; sheep shorrel, wild cherry, and wild shrubs. Sumac is a favorite food come winter.

EDIBILITY: The meat, lightly colored and finely textured, is delicious.

Varying Hare
Lepus americanus

RANGE: The varying hare inhabits the tree limits of Alaska and Canada, south through New England and the Appalachians, to Tennessee in the east, in the Rockies to northern New Mexico, and to mid-California.

IDENTIFICATION: The hare's coat acts as an excellent camouflage costume. Though brown in summer, the coat is shed come winter for a white one. A dark line runs down the center of its back, ending in a dark rump and tail top. The chin, belly, and the undersides of the tail are white, but the throat is a brownish-red. The feet are huge and hairy.

SIZE: A typical member of this species stands 8 to 9 inches at the shoulder and measures 21 inches in length. Though weights vary from 3 to 4½ pounds, the heaviest varying hare ever recorded scaled 5¼ pounds.

FOOD: Almost any vegetation appeals to the hare, but he has his preferences—succulent grasses and the tender tips of woody plants in summer, and dead grasses, buds, and bark in winter. White cedar is a favorite.

EDIBILITY: As the varying hare usually lacks any fat, the meat is dry.

COTTONTAIL RABBIT

VARYING HARE

JACKRABBIT

Jackrabbit
Lepus

RANGE: The whitetail jackrabbit (*Lepus townsendii*) inhabits the sagebrush regions and grasslands from northern New Mexico north to southern Alberta, and from Lake Michigan west to the Sierras.

IDENTIFICATION: The whitetailed jackrabbit's tail is white on both top and bottom. Its conspicuous ears measure 5 to 6 inches in length. In summer, the coat is a light grayish-brown over the sides and back, but the belly is lighter. The ear tips are black. When winter arrives, the coat is completely white or, on occasion, a buff-white. The blacktail's rump is black, as is the top of its tail. Its ears are longer than the white tail's by an inch or so. The underside of the tail is white, as is the belly. The ears are white outside, brown inside, and black-tipped. Though the whitetail sheds twice annually, the color change is relatively insignificant.

SIZE: A typical whitetailed jackrabbit measures between 22 and 26 inches long and weighs from 6 to 10 pounds. The average blacktailed jackrabbit is 18 to 24 inches long and scales between 4 and 7½ pounds.

The heaviest jackrabbit on record was a whitetail which tipped the scales at 13 pounds.

The blacktail jackrabbit (*Lepus californicus*) lives in the deserts and open grassland of the western United States from mid-Arkansas to the Pacific Coast, north to southeastern Washington in the west, and to mid-South Dakota in the east.

FOOD: Though jackrabbits eat practically all kinds of vegetation in their diets, shrubs, weedy plants, and grasses make up the bulk of it. Main food items include spiderling, snakeweed, mesquite, gramagrass, rabbit brush, sagebrush, greasewood, filaree, prickly pear, eriogonum, and saltbrush.

EDIBILITY: Whitetail meat is said to be far preferable to the meat of the blacktail. Younger jackrabbits are more palatable than their elders.

Arctic Hare
Lepus arcticus

RANGE: The Arctic hare is found in the tundra region of northern Canada, from Newfoundland to the Mackenzie River. The Alaskan hare (*Lepus othus*) inhabits the area west of the Mackenzie Delta along the coast of Alaska to the Alaskan Peninsula.

IDENTIFICATION: The hare's fur is pure white in winter, except for the black-tipped ears. In summer the hare's coat becomes brown. There is no lag in the transition from white to brown of the coat in relation to the land. For example, when patches of white and brown are mixed on the coat, the ground is still covered with snow patches.

SIZE: The largest of the North American hares, the Arctic hare measures up to 28 inches long, stands close to 1 foot high at the shoulder, and weighs from 6 to 12 or more pounds.

FOOD: The basic food of the Arctic hare is the dwarf willow —its buds, leaves, catkins, bark, and even roots. Berries, mosses, herbs, and grasses are also eaten.

EDIBILITY: All those who have eaten the meat regard it highly.

European Rabbit
Oryctolagus cuniculus

RANGE: Sometimes called the San Juan rabbit after the islands off the coast of Washington where it still runs wild, the European hare is more commonly found in captivity today. As a game animal it has been a failure.

IDENTIFICATION: Somewhat similar to the cottontail in pigmentation, the European rabbit's hair is a light brown, intermingled with black. The nape of this rabbit's neck is buff, however, while our cottontail has a reddish nape. The tail, belly, and insides of the legs are white, but the tips of the 3½-inch ears are black.

SIZE: Larger than the cottontail, this species can reach some 18 inches in length and scale a top of 5 pounds in weight.

FOOD: The preferred foods are herbs and grasses, but the European hare won't turn away from coarse vegetation when its favorites are scarce.

EDIBILITY: The meat, light in color, is quite tasty

Gray Squirrel
Sciurus

RANGE: The eastern gray *(Sciurus carolinensis)* is located in hardwood forests from eastern Texas and eastern Saskatchewan to the Atlantic Coast, and from the Gulf of Mexico to southern Canada. The Arizona gray *(Sciurus arizonensis)* inhabits pine and oak forests in southeastern and central Arizona. The western gray *(Sciurus griseus)* is also found in oak and pine forests, but in the region from southern California north to Washington.

IDENTIFICATION: The gray squirrel's coloring is a salt-and-pepper gray. The body's underfur is solid gray with guard hairs that go from gray at the base to buff-brown to

GRAY SQUIRREL

black, and finish off in a white tip. The small hairs of the face, muzzle, and ears are a yellow-tan, while those under the throat, its underparts, and the insides of its legs are a rich white.

SIZE: A large adult measures between 17 and 20 inches depending upon its range, the tail taking up approximately 8 to 8½ inches of that length. Males and females tend to weigh the same—slightly over 1 pound. The heaviest gray squirrel recorded scaled 1½ pounds.

FOOD: Nuts are a staple in the squirrel's diet and are cached for later use. They also feed on buds, berries, tree blossoms, fruit, fungi, and field corn, as well as eggs and baby birds.

EDIBILITY: The quality and flavor of squirrel meat are excellent.

Fox Squirrel
Sciurus

RANGE: The eastern fox squirrel *(Sciurus niger)* inhabits the open woods from the Canadian border to the Gulf of Mexico, and from the Atlantic Coast to eastern Colorado. New England is free of the species. The Apache fox squirrel *(Sciurus apache)* resides in southeastern Arizona's Chiricahua Mountains, and in Mexico.

IDENTIFICATION: Northeastern squirrels are frequently gray, and resemble oversized gray squirrels except for the rusty flank markings. In the West, bright rust is the dominant color, and black is the main pigment in the South. The hair tips of the tail are an orange color. The ears are round and large, the whiskers long and conspicuous. The plane from the ear to the nose is straighter than that of the gray squirrel.

SIZE: The typical fox squirrel weighs from 1½ to 3 pounds, the latter being exceptional for the species. Females tend to weigh a bit more than males. The total length is usually 28 inches (1 foot of which is a plumed tail), and the height at the shoulder is between 3½ and 4 inches.

FOOD: Like the gray squirrel, the fox squirrel rates nuts—especially acorns—an important item in its diet. The most important are the nuts of the white oak, black oak, and red oak. Hickory nuts, beechnuts, hazelnuts, black walnuts, butternuts, and pecans are runners-up. Osage oranges are a wintertime treat, and blossoms, the fruit of maples, domesticated and wild fruits and berries, and fungi are favorites during other seasons. The fox squirrel also has a penchant for field corn.

EDIBILITY: The meat of the fox squirrel is highly palatable.

FOX SQUIRREL

Raccoon
Procyon lotor

RANGE: The raccoon inhabits nearly all of the United States, parts of Mexico, and extreme southern Canada, northward along the border between Saskatchewan and Alberta.

IDENTIFICATION: Though this species varies in size and color depending on its location, two conspicuous features distinguish it—(1) the black mask across the eyes and (2) the ringed tail. The latter is usually 10 inches long. The dense underfur is a brownish-red. Guard hairs are tipped with white but come in shades of black, red, yellow, and gray. The white face and ears offer sharp contrast to the

RACCOON

black nose and mask. The soles of the feet are jet black, the topsides light.

SIZE: An average male measures 34 inches in length and stands from 9 inches to a foot high at the shoulder. A typical adult weighs from 12 to 16 pounds, but some males exceed 25 pounds. The heaviest coon ever recorded tipped the scales at 62 pounds, 6 ounces and measured 55 inches from tail tip to nose tip.

FOOD: Wild raccoons eat snakes, eggs, baby birds, baby mice, baby rabbits, mussels, fish, frogs, grapes, berries, apples, and acorns, Crayfish is a delicacy to the raccoon, and both sweet corn and field corn are very important in the diet.

EDIBILITY: Sportsmen have long considered raccoon meat a delicacy.

Woodchuck, Groundhog
Marmota monax

RANGE: Five-hundred-million woodchucks are said to inhabit North America, ranging from eastern Alaska to Labrador, south in the central and eastern United States to Arkansas and Alabama respectively, and to northern Idaho in the West.

IDENTIFICATION: The round, barrel-like body is supported by short, though powerful, legs. Brown is the basic body color, but shades of red to near-black are fairly common. The guard hairs are silver-tipped, giving the animal a grizzled look. The ears are short and round, and the black eyes stick out above its flattened skull.

SIZE: A large male may measure up to 26 inches in length (5 or 6 inches of which is its tail), often stands 6 to 7 inches high at the shoulder, and averages 10 pounds in weight. Females tend to be a bit smaller. The heaviest recorded chuck scaled $15\frac{3}{4}$ pounds.

FOOD: Woodchucks are 99-percent vegetarian, feeding on soy beans, corn, alfalfa, beans, peas, clover, and lettuce among the cultivated crops. Bark, twigs, and buds of low-growing bushes like the sumac and wild cherry are also part of the diet. Fruits and berries, all types, are frequently consumed.

EDIBILITY: Woodchuck meat, particularly that of the young, makes very good eating.

WOODCHUCK, GROUNDHOG

Prairie Dog
Cynomys

RANGE: The whitetailed species (*Cynomys gunnisoni, C. leucurus,* and *C. parvidens*) are found in mountainous valleys from central Arizona and New Mexico to southern Montana. The blacktailed prairie dog (*Cynomys ludovicianus*), though once found in the high plains from southern Alberta and Saskatchewan to the Mexican border, and from the eastern Rocky Mountains to eastern Kansas and Nebraska, is relatively extinct. A small number of them, however, are located in national parks and monuments.

IDENTIFICATION: Unlike its name, the prairie dog is a rodent rather than a dog. The tag comes from its yapping bark. The head comes to a flat surface, and the whiskers are prominent. The ears are short and rounded, and the black eyes are encircled in white. The body hair tends to be short, ranging in color from dark brownish-red to light gray. The animal's underparts are light. The slender tail differentiates between the blacktailed and whitetailed prairie dogs. In the former, the tail has a black terminal tip and measures about 3½ inches in length. The latter's tail is a bit shorter (perhaps 2½ inches long), with a white tip.

SIZE: An adult measures some 15 inches in length, stands 5 inches high at the shoulder, and scales between 1½ and 3 pounds.

FOOD: Vegetation is readily available to the prairie dog, and he takes advantage of it. The blacktail favors gramagrass, wheatgrass, fescue grass, Russian thistle, bromegrass, and bluegrass. The whitetail also dines on Russian thistle and wheatgrass, but adds saltbush, sagebrush, wild onion, dandelion, and nightshade to the menu. Insects, especially grasshoppers, whet the prairie dog's appetite. They eat meat (e.g. ground-nesting birds) once in a while.

EDIBILITY: Though the Indians enjoyed the meat, today's sportsmen dislike the "earthy" flavor.

PRAIRIE DOG

Opossum
Didelphis marsupialis

RANGE: The opossum is found in woods and agricultural regions from Ontario west to eastern Colorado, and east to Florida. Many inhabit the Pacific Coast stretch from Canada through California.

IDENTIFICATION: This species is the only marsupial (pouched animal) in North America, housing its somewhat underdeveloped young in a pouch where they are nourished through the mother's nipples until they can seek out their own food. The animal's ears are black, though often white-rimmed, as are the eyes, legs, and feet. The face and toes are white, while the nose is pink. Because of the silver-tipped guard hairs, the opossum's fur appears salt-and-

OPOSSUM

pepper gray, but the underfur is cotton-white. A white-yellow stain is apparent on the throat due to a gland secretion. The lengthy, whitish tail tends to be practically bare of hair.

SIZE: A typical opossum may measure up to 3 feet in length, 12 to 15 inches of which is the animal's tail. Though this marsupial generally weighs 5 or 6 pounds, one recorded male scaled 14 pounds.

FOOD: Persimmons are one of the opossum's favorite treats, but its diet ranges from mice, ground-nesting birds, moles, shrews, and rabbits to dead and crippled game to fruits and green vegetation. Earthworms, grains, reptiles, and amphibians round out the menu.

EDIBILITY: Those sportsmen who have eaten opossum meat claim it is tasty.

Predators

North American Wolf
Canis

RANGE: The gray wolf (*canis lupus*) is located in the tundra and forests in a major portion of Canada from the United States border north to the Arctic and Alaska, and also in the northern sections of Michigan, Minnesota, and Wisconsin. Parts of northeastern Wyoming, southwestern Colorado, southeastern Arizona, mid-Oregon, and southeastern Utah also feature the gray wolf. The red wolf (*canis niger*) exists solely in western Louisiana and eastern Texas.

IDENTIFICATION: The wolf is large and doglike in appearance, so much so that its head somewhat resembles that of a German shepherd. There is an immense color range that may run the gamut from practically pure white to coal black. The legs and underparts are lighter than the remainder of the body. A scent gland is found at the base of its tail above the anus.

SIZE: A mature male stands up to 38 inches high at the shoulder, measures 6 feet in length, and weighs 100 pounds or more. The heaviest recorded male tipped the scales at 175 pounds. Females tend to be lighter than males.

FOOD: The wolf preys on large game such as caribou, mountain sheep, moose, and deer, as well as marmots, varying hares, grouse, ptarmigan, small birds, eggs, mice, ducks, and geese among the small game. During the salmon runs, the wolf may be found in the vicinity.

NORTH AMERICAN WOLF

COYOTE

Coyote
Canis latrans

RANGE: This species is located throughout western North America from the Arctic Ocean to Mexico, east to James Bay, southern Quebec, and Vermont, and south to the Mississippi River. Other Eastern States either have the coyote naturally or through introduction.

IDENTIFICATION: The face of the coyote is sharp, reminiscent of a wild dog with a shaggy coat and erect ears. Its nose pad is black, but the upper face, the top of the head, and the outer portion of the ears are a sandy grayish-red with black hairs intermingled. The area about the mouth and throat, and the inside of the ears is white. The eyes are yellow, the pupils black. Basically the body color varies from gray to dull yellow. The rough-textured pelage is dark on the back, but gets whiter on the belly. The tail is 2 inches in length and 1/4 inch in width, ending in a dark tip.

SIZE: An average male weighs between 18 and 30 pounds, stands approximately 2 feet tall at the shoulder, and measures 44 to 54 inches in length (of which 12 to 16 inches is its tail). Females tend to be four-fifths the weight and size of males. The heaviest coyotes recorded scaled as much as 75 pounds.

FOOD: The coyote preys on rabbits, antelope, ground squirrels, mice, rats, prairie dogs, livestock, and poultry. Rating second to the initial list are fruits, berries, and melons, both domesticated and wild.

EDIBILITY: Though the Indians ate coyote meat, it is rarely considered table fare nowadays.

Bobcat
Lynx rufus

RANGE: Bobcats are found from the Maritime Provinces westward across southern Canada to southern British Columbia, and southward from the latter to Mexico and the Gulf of Mexico. Except for the area along the Mississippi and Ohio rivers and in the Appalachian Mountains, the cat, which is also called the wildcat, catamount, tiger cat, bay lynx, lynx cat and red lynx, is absent from a considerable portion of the eastern and central United States.

IDENTIFICATION: The bobcat varies color-wise, depending upon its location: the cats in the southwestern desert regions are the palest, while those in the northern, forested region are the darkest. The nose is a pinkish-red, and the base color of the face, back, and sides is yellowish, gray, or brownish-red. A checkering of black or a darker color than that of the base accompanies the face and the body. White is the color under the chin, throat, belly, and tail, and also around the eyes. The 4 to 7 inch tail, however, has a black spot over the tip. The fur, although brittle, is quite long and luxurious. This predator's face seems wide due to its face ruff, and slight tufts of hair stand up from the tips of its ears. The eyes are yellow, the pupils black. In comparison to its body size, the bobcat's legs are long, their large paws well-furred.

SIZE: A typical bobcat measures approximately 50 inches in length, stands 22 inches high at the shoulder, and weighs between 18 and 25 pounds. Female cats tend to be a bit smaller and lighter than their male counterparts. Bobcats in the North are larger than those in the South. Though there are many cases of these predators weighing in the 40- to 45-pound class, one of 76 pounds and another of 69 pounds have been recorded.

FOOD: The main staples in the diet of this species are the rabbit and the hare. The animal also preys readily on squirrels, rats, mice, porcupines, and chipmunks. Ruffed grouse is its favorite among the ground-nesting birds, though all types are eligible for its menu. Deer and wild turkey at times make this list.

EDIBILITY: The meat is eaten very frequently, and its taste is reminiscent of veal.

BOBCAT

LYNX

Lynx
Lynx lynx

RANGE: The lynx is distributed from Newfoundland west to the Arctic Ocean in Alaska, south to northern United States in Minnesota, Wisconsin, Michigan, and New England, and in the Rocky Mountain areas of Wyoming and Utah. It resides as far south as mid-Washington and Oregon and in western Montana. *Lynx subsolanus*, another subspecies, is found solely on the island of Newfoundland.

IDENTIFICATION: This predator's main features are its large, padded feet and its 2-inch-long, black ear tufts. A smoky gray is the lynx's basic color, often intermixed with a tan shading. The large face ruff is white with black barring, and the sharp tips practically meet under its chin. White also appears around the animal's muzzle, inside its ears, beneath its eyes, and on the insides of its legs. The body, though compact, is supported by unusually long legs, and is spotted or barred with a black coloring. The tail, often 4 inches long, is light in color and has a jet-black tip. The lynx is also known as the Canadian lynx, lucivee, wildcat, catamount, and loup-cervier.

SIZE: A typical adult lynx measures between 3 and 3⅓ feet in length, stands from 1½ to 2 feet high at the shoulders, and tips the scales at from 12 to 25 pounds. The heaviest lynx on record weighed 40 pounds.

FOOD: The varying hare is at the top of this predator's mealtime menu, with squirrels, mice, voles, lemmings, beavers, and both spruce and ruffed grouse taking relatively minor roles. The lynx's predatory link with the varying hare is so intense that the former's population level is uncannily proportional to that of the latter. Records prove this out.

EDIBILITY: Lynx meat is light in color and is said to have a flavor similar to chicken.

Gray Fox
Urocyon cinereoargenteus

RANGE: This species inhabits the open forests and brush country across the southern United States, northward in the West to the state of Washington and northern Colorado, and to southern Canada in eastern and central North America. *Urocyon littoralis*, a second species, is found on a couple of the channel islands off the coast of southern California.

IDENTIFICATION: The top of the animal's head and back is a salt-and-pepper gray, but the flanks, the ears, and the

GRAY FOX

area just below them are a rust-red color. Belly, chest, throat, and the inner sides of the legs are whitish. The 12- to 15-inch tail is gray with a prominent black mane running to the black tip. A 4½-inch musk gland is visible on the top of the tail.

SIZE: A typical adult stands 15 inches high at the shoulder, is up to 45 inches from nose tip to tail tip, and scales between 8 and 11 pounds. The heaviest recorded gray fox weighed 19 pounds.

FOOD: Gray foxes prey heavily upon rabbits and ruffed grouse. And, depending on the abundance of the prey animal, fish, snakes, rats, mice, and insects. Dead and crippled animals are easy game for the wary gray fox.

Red Fox
Vulpes vulpes

RANGE: The red fox is distributed from Alaska and northern Canada south to the Gulf of Mexico (except under the fall line of the southeastern states). Though it is found southward to the border of Mexico in places in the West, it is absent in the high plains from Mexico to central Alberta.

IDENTIFICATION: The red fox is slightly built, and resembles a domesticated dog. There are considerable color variations. This species ranges from a dark russet-red to a light yellowish-blond. The nose pad and the outside of the ear tips are black, the upper face rusty, the throat and cheeks white. The bushy tail, somewhat cylindrical in shape, is usually colored the same as the back (the darkest part of the animal), and has a light underside and a huge white tip. The belly tends to be white.

SIZE: A mature red fox is 3 to 3 ½ feet long (13 to 15 inches of which is tail), stands 16 inches high at the shoulder, and weighs from 6 to 15 pounds. The latter is the top weight recorded.

FOOD: Ranking at the top of the list is the meadow mouse, a plentiful and nutritious animal. The red fox also favors rabbits, ruffed grouse, quail, pheasants, muskrats, squirrels, hares, chipmunks, and groundhogs. Preying on poultry yards is frequent. Add weasels, snakes, shrews, beetles, moles, crickets, and grasshoppers to this fox's menu, along with corn, melons, berries, and fruits.

RED FOX

Northwestern Crow
Corvus caurinus

RANGE: Found along the coasts and islands from Kodiak Island to western Washington, the Northwestern crow wanders inland in Washington and Oregon.

IDENTIFICATION: The Northwestern crow tends to be a small replica of the common crow, also having predominantly black body with a purple gloss. Its nostrils are barely visible due to the bristlelike feathers that rise from its forehead. It has large, strong feet, a sturdy bill, and long, thick feet. All are black.

SIZE: This predator rarely grows longer than 16 or 17 inches.

FOOD: The diet consists of shellfish, other invertebrates, insects, offal, seashore carrion, plus some seeds and berries.

FLIGHT SPEED: The norm here is from 20 to 30 mph, but crows have reached speeds of 40 to 45 mph.

Common Crow
Corvus brachyrhynchos

RANGE: Breeding takes place from northern British Columbia, northern Saskatchewan, northern Manitoba, northern Ontario, central Quebec, and southern Newfoundland south to northern Baja California, central Arizona, central New Mexico, Colorado, central Texas, the Gulf Coast, and southern Florida.

IDENTIFICATION: The common crow is a large, predominantly black bird with a purple gloss. The sturdy bill, the long, thick legs, and the large, strong feet are also black. This bird's nostrils are hidden by bristlelike feathers that rise from its forehead. The tail is gently rounded but has a somewhat square tip.

SIZE: This predator measures from 17 to 21 inches in length.

FOOD: Over 650 different items have been discovered in the diet, 70 percent of which is vegetable matter—large amounts of corn and other cultivated crops, as well as wild fruits and seeds. The remainder consists of insects, spiders, reptiles, amphibians, snails, birds and their eggs, carrion, crustaceans, and small mammals.

FLIGHT SPEED: Though the crow usually averages between 20 and 30 mph in flight, he has been known to attain speeds of from 40 to 45 mph.

Fish Crow
Corvus ossifragus

RANGE: The locale for this bird is from the coast of Rhode Island to the coast of southern Florida, west along the Gulf Coast to southeast Texas, and inland along the major waterways.

IDENTIFICATION: The fish crow highly resembles the common crow in that it is also mostly black with a purple gloss, has feathers rising from its forehead that tend to hide its nostrils, and has a sturdy bill, long, thick legs, and large, strong feet, all of which are black. The fish crow, however, is smaller and slimmer than the common crow, and its wings are broader at the base and more pointed at the tips. The tail is gently rounded.

SIZE: This predator averages between 16 and 20 inches in length.

FOOD: Being omnivorous, the fish crow's diet ranges from primarily marine invertebrates, offal, bird's eggs, seashore carrion, and insects to seeds, fruit, and berries.

FLIGHT SPEED: Though the crow can reach speeds of from 40 to 45 mph in flight, its usual speed ranges from 20 to 30 mph.

Upland Gamebirds

Ruffed Grouse
Bonasa umbellus

RANGE: Locale for this bird includes the Yukon and Porcupine River valleys of Alaska and the Yukon. In addition, they are found throughout Canada and the U. S. Pacific Northwest, northern Rocky Mountain states and the Middle Atlantic region.

IDENTIFICATION: The ruffed grouse has a large, square, reddish-brown or gray tail with thin, dark barring, followed by narrow, light barring, followed by a broader black band, and terminating in a light band. A ruff composed of blackish feathers appears on both sides of the bird's neck. The upperparts range in color from gray to brown, mottled with darker

RUFFED GROUSE

colors. The undersides tend to be lighter, on occasion buffy, and are barred with black and dark browns. The head is crested; and a small, bare, red patch appears above each eye. The West Coast members of this species are reddish, those of the Rocky Mountains grayish. Eastern ruffed grouse are brownish. Females and young are duller colored, with less-prominent ruffs.

SIZE: This gamebird measures from 16 to 19 inches in length.

FOOD: About 90 percent of the diet consists of leaves, buds, fruits, seeds, and nuts. The remaining 10 percent is made up of insects.

Blue Grouse
Dendragapus obscurus

RANGE: This gamebird is found from southeastern Alaska down through western Canada and California to northwest New Mexico.

IDENTIFICATION: This gamebird has distinctive large feet, short legs, and a short, stout bill. Its plumage tends to be dusky or grayish-blue in color, and its tail is square-tipped and black. However, some members of the species have a wide terminal band of light color on their tails, while others have a narrow band or no band at all. The male has whitish

BLUE GROUSE

feathers under its tail and on its throat. Above the eyes is a small bare patch of orange or yellow skin. The female is black with brown bars and mottling and sports a dark though light-tipped tail.

The male has smallish inflatable air sacs at the sides of his throat to assist in vocalization.

SIZE: The dusky grouse measures from 15½ to 21 inches in length.

FOOD: A major portion (approximately 90 percent) of the diet is composed of leaves, seeds, and berries. The remainder consists of animal matter such as insects and spiders.

Spruce Grouse
Canachites canadensis

RANGE: This bird, also called Franklin's grouse, is found in Alaska, Canada, and along the entire U. S.-Canadian border, from Washington to Maine.

IDENTIFICATION: In the male, this gamebird's throat, undersides, and tail are black. The upperparts are brown, barred with darker brown, and marked with white at the flanks and the sides of the throat. A small, bright-red patch of bare skin is found just above the eyes of the male. The female lacks this red spot, and the black coloring of the male is replaced by browns in the female.

SIZE: The Spruce grouse averages between 15 and 17 inches in length.

FOOD: Its diet consists of buds and needles of the spruce and other evergreens, along with berries and other vegetable matter. Some insects are also included.

SPRUCE GROUSE

Greater Prairie Chicken
Tympanuchus cupido

RANGE: Western Canada and southern United States are the two areas where this gamebird may be found.

IDENTIFICATION: In general, the prairie chicken, or pinnated grouse, is brown, buff, and barred dark brown above, and a lighter brown and whitish below. On each side of the bird's throat is a cluster of slender black pinnate feathers. In the vicinity of this cluster in the male are large orange air sacs that are inflatable. The tail is short, rounded, and very dark.

SIZE: This grouse measures from 16½ to 18 inches in length.

FOOD: Eighty-five percent of the diet consists of all forms of vegetable matter. Insects, particularly grasshoppers, comprise the remainder.

Sage Grouse
Centrocercus urophasianus

RANGE: This species is found in parts of the western United States and minute sections of southeastern Alberta and southwestern Saskatchewan.

IDENTIFICATION: This gamebird is the only grouse that has a black belly. Its tail feathers are long and pointed, its throat black with a tiny white necklace. The white breast features prominent feathers, and the remainder of the plumage is mottled or barred with white, black, dark brown, and light brown. Yellow is the color of the small, bare-skinned patch above the eye. The hen is mottled and barred in black, browns, and white over most of its body, but, as in the male, the belly is black, flanked by white.

SIZE: The sage grouse is the largest of all grouse, measuring 22 to 30 inches in length. The average female is 22 inches, the average male 28 inches.

FOOD: Its diet consists of tender, succulent vegetation and some insects. Adults eat the leaves of the sage, but their gizzards and stomachs are not constructed to accept harsh foods.

Sharp-Tailed Grouse
Pedioecetes phasianellus

RANGE: This species is located in vast sections of southern Canada, and in several parts of the northern United States south through Nevada, Utah, and Colorado.

IDENTIFICATION: This gamebird has a long, pointed tail, and its body is barred light brown with dark brown and black above. Below, it is whitish. The breast is scaled with brown and the flank is barred with brown and black. The wings are grayish on top, spotted with white. The long central tail feathers are the same color as the bird's back; the remainder of the tail is white. An air sac and a small crest appear on the throat, but the side of the neck is devoid of long feathers.

SIZE: The sharp-tailed grouse measures from 15 to 20 inches in length. Though the same size as the ruffed grouse, it is a bit slimmer.

FOOD: Ninety percent of the menu consists of leaves, grass, fruits, and seeds. Grasshoppers and other insects comprise the rest.

CHUKAR PARTRIDGE

Chukar Partridge
Alectoris graeca

RANGE: The semiarid mountain regions of the western United States, specifically parts of Washington, Idaho, Nevada, Wyoming, Colorado, and California, are this bird's haunts.

IDENTIFICATION: The chukar partridge has a short tail which is brownish-gray above. The wings are the same color. Two black lines that begin at the forehead, run through the eyes and then turn downward, form a "V" on the upper breast which fully encloses the yellow throat and cheeks. The lower breast is gray; the rest of the undersides (the dark-barred flanks inclusive) is yellowish. Red or pink is the color of the legs, bill, and feet. Immature birds are usually duller in color.

SIZE: This gamebird, on the average, measures 13 inches in length.

FOOD: Fruit, seeds, and leaves comprise 60 percent of the diet, the rest being insects and spiders.

Hungarian Partridge
Perdix perdix

RANGE: This gamebird breeds in large sections of southern Alberta and southern Saskatchewan, plus small sections of Manitoba and Ontario. Practically every northern U.S. state has border representatives of this species, down through the northern portions of California, Nevada, Utah, Iowa, Illinois, and Indiana.

IDENTIFICATION: The Hungarian partridge has a gray nape and breast, and a brownish-red face and throat. Its cape, wings, and tail are black. The back, also black, is barred with a brownish-red. The wings have white spots. Undersides are buffy; flanks buffy-gray, barred with a reddish-brown. In the center of the breast a dark brown spot is conspicuous. Gray is the color of the bill, feet, and legs.

SIZE: This species measures between 12 and 14 inches in length.

FOOD: Leaves and shoots of grasses and clover, seeds, berries, grain, spiders, and insects all are part of this gamebird's diet.

Ring-Necked Pheasant
Phasianus colchicus

RANGE: The ring-necked pheasant ranges from southern Canada down through Baja California and northern Mexico, and can be found in parts of Texas, Oklahoma, Kansas, Missouri, Illinois, Indiana, Ohio, and Maryland.

IDENTIFICATION: The cock is more colorful than the hen. It has a head and neck which are a dark metallic green, separated from the rest of the body by a white ring. A bright red patch of bare skin is conspicuous about the eye and on the cheek. The lengthy feathers above the eye form a double crest. The plumage of the underparts, upper back, and shoulders is a rich, bronzy red-brown with dark-brown, black, and white markings. The feathers of the rump and up the lower back are grayish-green; the flank feathers are a light golden brown with dark-brown streaks. The slender, pointed feathers of the tail are dull bronze barred with dark brown, and cover over one-half the length of the body. Legs and feet are gray, the bill is yellowish. The hen is brownish and much paler below, marked with darker browns and black above. Darker brown and whitish bars streak the lengthy yellow-brown tail.

SIZE: This gamebird measures between 21 and 36 inches in length, depending upon sex. The cock tends to be about 10 inches longer than the hen.

FLIGHT SPEED: This bird flies between 35 and 40 mph.

FOOD: Twenty-five percent of the diet consists of insects, the remainder being shoots, nuts, and fruit.

RING-NECKED PHEASANT

Bobwhite Quail
Colinus virginianus

RANGE: This species is sparse out West, located only in parts of southern British Columbia, Washington, Oregon, Idaho, Arizona, and Mexico. But moving eastward, this bird is far more abundant and is found from southeast Wyoming, eastern Colorado, and eastern New Mexico all the way to the Atlantic, save for the New England States.

IDENTIFICATION: The bobwhite quail is a chicken-like bird with strong, lengthy legs; a stout bill; and a short, dark strong tail. Its color tends to vary depending upon its range, but in general the bird is brownish—barred with white and lighter below. Above, it has brown marked with darker brown; frequently, these dark browns have random whitish spots. The dark brown head is slightly crested, featuring white eye stripes. Many—but not all—members of the species have a white throat as well. The female tends to be dull yellow or buff in color.

SIZE: Measuring 8½ to 10½ inches in length, this gamebird is smaller than the average quail.

FLIGHT SPEED: Over short distances, the bobwhite's flight is strong and rapid, often reaching speeds of 40 to 45 miles per hour.

FOOD: Eighty-five percent of its diet consists of all types of plant life; the remainder is primarily insects.

BOBWHITE QUAIL

Harlequin Quail
Cyrtonyx montezumae

RANGE: This gamebird, also known as Mearn's quail, inhabits the far Southwestern United States, ranging from Arizona, New Mexico, and Texas down through the less arid and more mountainous areas of southern Mexico.

IDENTIFICATION: The breast and undersides of the harlequin quail are reddish-brown; the flanks and sides of the neck are gray with conspicuous round, white spots. Long buff feathers comprise the crest at the back of the head, accentuating the head's large appearance. The stocky bird's head is white, and is separated from the breast by a black ring at the neck. Mustaches, earmarks, and a black throat patch are additional features. The wings, tail, and back are variegated designs of black, white, and brown. On the distaff side, the browns are duller, and the female is more lightly colored below and on the throat and head. In addition, there are dark markings behind the eye and at the lower edge of the throat.

SIZE: Measuring 8 to 9½ inches in length, the harlequin is similar in size to the bobwhite quail.

FLIGHT SPEED: The quail clocks 40 to 45 miles an hour, but can sustain this speed only over rather short distances.

FOOD: Acorns, piñon nuts, other seeds and grasses and leaves comprise the harlequin's diet. Insects are rarely eaten.

Gambel's Quail
Lophortyx gambelii

RANGE: The arid Southwest is this bird's haunt, from New Mexico, Colorado, Utah and Nevada through northeastern Baja California.

IDENTIFICATION: The males of the species feature a black forehead that lacks the white spots of the California quail. They also have a buff-colored belly with a big, centrally located black spot. The flank feathers are reddish-brown with white streaks and slashes. The hens are similar to the males in that they also have a buff-colored belly and white streaks across their reddish-brown flanks.

SIZE: The Gambel's quail reaches lengths of from 10 to 11½ inches in length.

FLIGHT SPEED: Forty to 45 miles an hour is the speed of this quail. Though strong and rapid, its flight is usually over short distances.

FOOD: A mere two percent of the diet consists of insects; the major portion consists of leaves, seeds, plant shoots, fruit, and grain.

Mountain Quail
Oreortyx pictus

RANGE: This upland bird resides on the Coast ranges from southern Vancouver Island in British Columbia down to northern Baja California, and in the Sierra Nevada and other ranges of eastern Nevada and California. Introductions into the Western states of Washington, Idaho, Oregon and Nevada have been successful.

IDENTIFICATION: The mountain quail's head, shoulders, lower breast, and crest are a grayish blue. A long, pointed, stiff plume rises from its head. The upper breast and throat are reddish-brown. The neck, also a grayish blue, is separated from the upper breast by a white line. There is also some white around the eyes and about much of the face. The flanks are colored reddish-brown with an upper edging of white, and a series of wide, rounded bars (also white) cover the bottom part of the back. Wings and tail are a neutral brown.

SIZE: This gamebird measures 10½ to 11½ inches in length.

FLIGHT SPEED: Though it has a strong, rapid 40-to-45-mile-an-hour speed, the quail usually flies but short distances.

FOOD: Buds, seeds, fruit, flowers, leaves, and plant shoots comprise most of the diet. An insignificant number of insects is also consumed.

Scaled Quail
Callipepla squamata

RANGE: This bird is found only in Texas north to Colorado, west to Arizona and south to Mexico.

IDENTIFICATION: Dark-edged gray-and-white scales appear to coat the breast, neck, and shoulders of this species. A white topknot caps the gray head. A medium brownish-gray colors the back, wings, and tail; the feet and legs are a blue gray. Both sexes are alike in coloration.

SIZE: This species measures 10 to 12 inches in length, being somewhat bigger than the bobwhite quail.

SCALED QUAIL

FLIGHT SPEED: The quail moves rapidly and strongly over short distances, hitting speeds of from 40 to 45 miles an hour.

FOOD: Insects comprise approximately 30 percent of the diet, with buds, seeds, leaves, and other plant material making up the rest.

California Quail
Lophortyx californicus

RANGE: This quail ranges from southwestern British Columbia to the southern tip of Baja California, and inland from the Pacific to western Nevada. In recent years the species has been introduced in parts of Utah, Nevada, Idaho, Oregon, and Washington.

IDENTIFICATION: The adult male of this species has a long, large-tipped black plume that curves forward from the forepart of its dark reddish-brown cap. The forehead, as well as a line that extends from it to the back of the head above the eye, is white. The necklace beginning behind the eye and bordering the black throat and face is also white. The breast is grayish-blue, as is the back of the neck, the nape of which is spotted with white. The belly feathers are white with black edging, save for the middle of the abdomen —there, they're reddish-brown. The back and tail are medium brown; so, too, are the flanks, which feature white slashes. The hen does not have the reddish-brown patches and the white-and-black patterned head. Her plume tends to be browner and her face whitish with dull brown marks and spots. Otherwise, she highly resembles the male.

SIZE: At from 9½ to 11 inches in length, the California quail is just a bit larger than the bobwhite.

FLIGHT SPEED: Though frequently attaining speeds of 40 to 45 miles per hour, the quail frequently travels only very short distances.

FOOD: Leaves, grain, fruit, seeds, and grass make up about 95 percent of the diet, with insects and other animal matter comprising the remainder.

Wild Turkey
Meleagris gallopavo

RANGE: The wild turkey is common along the Eastern seaboard, across the Gulf and South Central states and in parts of the Rockies.

IDENTIFICATION: The wild version of the turkey is slimmer and has longer legs than the domestic variety. Its wattles, neck, and head are reddish, grading to a blue. The attractive plumage is an iridescent bronze with black bars; the tail tips are buff. The male has a long hank, consisting of hairlike feathers hanging from its breast; the hen usually lacks this "beard." The wings are round and short; the feet and legs are large and strong. The large, sturdy bill appears to be hooked.

WILD TURKEY

SIZE: This gamebird measures from 36 to 48 inches long, with the hen usually averaging some 10 inches shorter than the cock. The average weight of these gobblers is between 15 and 20 pounds.

FLIGHT SPEED: Though the species cannot fly long distances, it can attain speeds of 30 to 35 miles per hour when it does take flight.

FOOD: Twigs, fruit, seeds, and nuts take up 85 percent of the wild turkey's menu; the rest is insects.

EDIBILITY: Turkey meat, traditionally served at the Thanksgiving table, is rich in protein and the B vitamins. Though it's usually fattier than chicken, turkey meat has less fat than that of the duck.

Band-Tailed Pigeon
Columba fasciata

RANGE: The band-tailed pigeon breeds from southwest British Columbia to the mountains of Baja California and northern Nicaragua. It winters from California, Arizona, and New Mexico southward.

IDENTIFICATION: The band-tailed pigeon's head, foreneck, and complete breast are a pinkish-gray. A conspicuous narrow white bar separates the head from the cape. The latter is a metallic, black-bordered grayish-yellow that fades into a greenish-gray back. Rump and wings are gray and flight feathers are almost totally black. The gray-green tail is centrally barred with dark gray. Undertail plumage and belly are white, while the legs, feet, and bill (which ends in a black tip) are yellow. The red-rimmed eyes are also yellow.

SIZE: This gamebird averages between 14 and 15½ inches in length.

FOOD: This species favors nuts, especially acorns. But berries, flowers, fruit, grain, and other seeds and vegetables also make their way into its diet.

Willow Ptarmigan
Lagopus lagopus

RANGE: Large groups are found in the wide-open areas of Canada and Alaska, though some have wandered down into the northern United States east of the Rocky Mountains.

IDENTIFICATION: In summer, the male's belly, feet, legs, and wings are white. Its rather small tail and its bill are black, and the remainder of its plumage is a reddish-brown, including the throat. A "comb," or tiny patch of bare skin located above the eye, is a strong scarlet. The hen, on the other hand, is mottled a buff-brown, and is white above. Her feet, legs, and belly are whitish; the rest of the undersides are wavy-barred with whitish, buff, and brown colorings. In winter, however, both male and female are totally white save for the tail and bill, which remain black.

SIZE: The willow ptarmigan measures from 15 to 17 inches in length.

FOOD: Fruit, buds, leaves, and insects are consumed through the warmer months; in winter, the twigs of shrubs and trees are added to the diet.

EDIBILITY: Ptarmigan flesh is dry in winter, but turns tender and develops an aromatic flavor with the advent of summer.

WILLOW PTARMIGAN

MOURNING DOVE

Mourning Dove
Zenaidura macroura

RANGE: The species breeds throughout North America and southern Canada, and winters from the Great Lakes south to Panama.

IDENTIFICATION: The mourning dove has a smallish black spot behind and below its dark eyes. The tail is wedge-shaped and slender, the feathers being white-tipped except for the longer central ones. The plumage is buff-brown with a metallic purplish sheen at the side of the neck. The wings are gray with a purple tinge to them, though the flight feathers are somewhat darker. Occasionally, the back will be sparsely covered with very dark brown spots.

SIZE: The uplander averages between 11 and 13 inches in length.

FLIGHT SPEED: The mourning dove has been clocked at between 60 to 65 miles per hour.

FOOD: Seeds (mainly those of weeds) practically make up this bird's entire menu. Minute amounts of other vegetable matter are eaten.

White-Winged Dove
Zenaidura asiatica

RANGE: Though this bird is found mainly in the Southwest, there are members of the species throughout the continental U.S. and parts of southern Canada.

IDENTIFICATION: The plumage is predominantly brown-buff, with some purplish tinges (particularly around the head). A conspicuous white patch is visible on the wing. The flight feathers are practically black, and white patches are evident on the partly rounded tail. The orange eye features a minute black spot behind and below it. The feet and legs are red, the bill black.

SIZE: The white-winged dove measures from 11 to 12½ inches in length.

FOOD: Shrubs and cacti, the fruit of trees, grain, and other vegetable matter comprise this gamebird's diet.

American Woodcock
Philohela minor

RANGE: In warmer weather, this bird is found from southeastern Manitoba down through the eastern tip of Texas, and through the entire eastern United States. In winter, it is concentrated in the southeastern United States, spreading a bit farther into Texas, Oklahoma, Arkansas, Alabama, Georgia, and Florida.

IDENTIFICATION: The American woodcock has a straight bill that is twice the size of its head. Its neck is rather short, as is its tail. Above the coloring is a variegated pattern of black, grays, and browns; below, it is rufous. There is a trio of wide, black bands separated both from one another and from the gray forehead by thin, rufous bands. The legs, feet, and bill are a dark flesh color.

SIZE: This species measures 10 to 12 inches in length.

FOOD: Earthworms make up the bulk of the diet, but occa seeds, berries, and insect larvae are significant meals.

WOODCOCK

Waterfowl

Barnacle Goose
Branta leucopsis

RANGE: This species is located along the coastal regions of North America from Labrador down to North Carolina, as well as inland as far as Ohio.

IDENTIFICATION: The barnacle goose's head, bill, and chest are black; in contrast, its face, cheeks, and upper throat are white. The remainder of the bird's upperparts is dark-slate or brownish. Underparts are white. The bird's neck, also black, is rather long.

SIZE: Medium-sized for a goose, this bird averages between 24 and 27 inches in length.

FLIGHT SPEED: Though geese usually fly at speeds of 55 to 60 miles an hour, they are capable of reaching 65 to 70 mph.

FOOD: Grass is the primary dish on the menu.

BLUE GOOSE

Blue Goose
Chen caerulescens

RANGE: The Gulf Coast of eastern Texas and Louisiana is the habitat of this bird.

IDENTIFICATION: The blue goose features a white head, upper neck, and throat. Its back and a major portion of its body are a dark brown-gray. The flight feathers on the wing are black; the tail and the feathers below the wing are white. Though the edge of the bill is black, the rest of the bill and the legs are pinkish. Immature blue geese have dark bills and lack the white heads of their parents.

SIZE: This species is medium-sized, measuring from 25 to 30 inches long.

FLIGHT SPEED: Geese can attain speeds of 65 to 70 miles per hour, but they'll average between 55 and 60 mph.

FOOD: The menu consists of sedges, grain, grasses, and waterweeds.

CANADA GOOSE

Common Canada Goose
Branta canadensis

RANGE: The breeding range is from northern Canada down to central California. There are a couple of colonies south of this line. In the winter, the species travels down to the southern United States and even into northeastern Mexico.

IDENTIFICATION: The body is brownish while the head, tail, neck, feet, and bill are black. Several white patches are apparent on the cheek. The throat and underrump are also white.

SIZE: This species varies widely in size, measuring from 22 to 40 inches in length.

FLIGHT SPEED: Fifty-five to 60 miles per hour is the norm for geese, but they can fly as fast as 65 to 70 mph.

FOOD: The common Canada goose feasts on aquatic vegetation, grain, and grass.

Emperor Goose
Philacte canagica

RANGE: Winters are spent primarily in the Aleutian Islands, but Hawaii and California also feature the species. On rare occasions, some will be found in Oregon.

IDENTIFICATION: The main body coloring is a grayish-blue, but the bird's head and rear portion of its neck are white. The throat is black. The wings and the body feathers are dark-edged, giving this species a scaly appearance. The very young birds have a grayish-blue coloring spotted with white on their heads and necks.

SIZE: Medium-sized for a goose, this bird is from 26 to 28 inches in length.

FLIGHT SPEED: The norm for the goose is from 55 to 60 miles an hour, but full speed nears the 70-mph mark.

FOOD: Shellfish and seaweeds comprise the bulk of the diet. In tundra regions, however, berries and grasses are eaten.

Snow Goose
Chen hyperborea

RANGE: The most abundant of all North American geese, this species inhabits northern Baja California, Mexico, the Gulf Coast, and the Atlantic Coast from New Jersey down through the Carolinas.

IDENTIFICATION: Though predominantly white, the snow goose has black flight feathers. The black-edged bill and the legs of the species are pink. Immature snow geese are gray above, with blackish bills.

SIZE: The snow goose is medium-sized, measuring 25 to 38 inches long.

FLIGHT SPEED: Fifty-five to 60 miles an hour is the usual speed for geese, but they have been known to reach 65 to 70 mph.

FOOD: Waterweeds, sedges, grain, and grasses rank high on the menu.

SNOW GOOSE

Ross' Goose
Chen rossii

RANGE: Though it breeds in a tiny section of the coastal tundra in northwestern Keewatin and northeastern Mackenzie, it relocates in winter in California's Central Valley.

IDENTIFICATION: The Ross' goose resembles the snow goose in that it is white and has black flight feathers on the wings. It differs, however, in that its pink bill is not black-edged. The legs are pink. The bill is relatively rough, and has warts at its base.

SIZE: At 20 to 26 inches in length, this is the smallest American goose.

FLIGHT SPEED: Sixty-five to 70 miles an hour is full speed for the goose, but it cruises at 55 to 60 mph.

FOOD: The menu consists of grasses, sedge, grain, and waterweeds.

White-Fronted Goose
Anser albifrons

RANGE: The western United States breeds most of these birds. They are also found occasionally along the Atlantic Coast.

IDENTIFICATION: Body coloring is a grayish-brown. The feet tend to be either orange or yellow, the forward section of the face white. Young white-fronted geese do not have white faces, although they do have light-colored bills.

SIZE: Ranging from medium to large among geese, this species measures between 26 and 34 inches long.

FLIGHT SPEED: Though geese have topped 65 miles per hour, their usual speed is 55 to 60 mph.

FOOD: The bulk of the diet is composed of berries, nuts, leaves, grain, and grasses. On occasion, aquatic insects are consumed.

Brant
Branta bernicla

RANGE: The brant usually spends its winters along the Pacific Coast from Baja California north to British Columbia, and along the Atlantic Coast from North Carolina up through Massachusetts. However, this far-ranging species is often found farther north or south of these haunts.

IDENTIFICATION: The brant's short neck is black, as is its head, bill, and chest. On the upper neck of the adult there appears a partial white necklace. The remainder of the species' upperparts are brownish or a dark-slate color. The American subspecies has small, light-gray markings on the front section of its white underparts.

175

BRANT

IDENTIFICATION: Both sexes appear similar, having very dark brown bodies with paler cheeks and throat. The black-bordered speculum is purple. The yellow-to-greenish bill has a black knob at its tip. The legs are red or dusky. The underparts appear nearly black when the duck is in flight.

SIZE: The black duck measures from 21 to 26 inches in length.

FLIGHT SPEED: Though it can get up to speeds of 65 to 70 miles an hour, the duck's norm is 55 to 60 mph.

FOOD: Three-quarters of the black duck's diet is vegetable matter, mainly grasses and aquatic plants. The remainder consists of animal matter—specifically crustaceans, insects, mollusks, and small fish.

SIZE: Twenty to 24 inches in length, the brant is smallish to medium-sized among geese.

FLIGHT SPEED: Geese travel at speeds of 55 to 60 miles an hour, but can attain 70 mph if necessary.

FOOD: Sea lettuce and eelgrass are the main foods. Small insects are also occasionally consumed.

Black Brant
Branta nigricans

RANGE: Breeding area includes the coasts of the Canadian Arctic east to longitude 110° W. Winters are spent on the Pacific Coast south to Baja California and inland to Nevada.

IDENTIFICATION: The black brant has a black breast that extends into a blackish belly. Unlike the brant, this species has a complete, rather than partial, white collar around its neck. The forepart of the undersides is also much darker, making the bird appear blacker.

SIZE: A typical member of this species is about 24 inches long.

FLIGHT SPEED: Geese can attain speeds of 65 to 70 miles per hour, though the norm is 55 to 60 mph.

FOOD: Like the brant, this species primarily eats eelgrass, but also dines on sea lettuce.

Black Duck
Anas rubripes

RANGE: Breeding range includes central Canada east to northern Labrador and Newfoundland, and down to the Great Lakes region and eastern North Carolina. In winter, the bird ranges from the southern edge of the breeding area to the Gulf Coast and southern Florida. Its distribution is rather spotty.

BLACK DUCK

Black-Bellied Tree Duck
Dendrocygna autumnalis

RANGE: Though native to southern Texas, this bird has strayed into Arizona and California.

IDENTIFICATION: The bill of this species is a bright pink, the legs a pale pink. The breast is brownish, as are the upperparts. The black-bellied tree duck, as its name indicates, has a black belly. The throat and cheeks are gray, the wings mantled dark.

SIZE: The black-bellied tree duck reaches from 20 to 22 inches in length.

FLIGHT SPEED: The norm for ducks is 55 to 60 miles an hour. They can attain speeds of 65 to 70 mph.

Bufflehead

Bucephala albeola

RANGE: The bufflehead breeds across much of Canada and Alaska. It winters in Mexico and along the Gulf Coast.

IDENTIFICATION: The male has a large, blackish head that is overlayed with a purplish-green iridescence. Above and behind the eye, a white quarter-circle patch is conspicuous. The tail and back are black; the rest of the plumage is white, including a prominent upper-wing patch that is very noticeable when the duck is swimming. The female features a grayish-brown back and head, and lighter-colored flanks that are whitish below. On the lower rear quarter of the head a tiny white spot can be seen.

SIZE: The smallest of the diving ducks, the bufflehead measures 12 to 16 inches long.

FLIGHT SPEED: The duck's normal speed is 55 to 60 miles per hour, but it can reach 65 to 70 mph at times.

FOOD: Eighty percent of the menu is fish, mollusks, insects, and crustaceans. Aquatic plants make up the remainder.

AMERICAN COOTS

Canvasback

Aythya valisineria

RANGE: This species winters in British Columbia, Montana, Colorado, the eastern Great Lakes, and eastern Massachusetts down to central Mexico, the Gulf States, and northern Florida. Breeding takes place from central Alaska to Manitoba and south through California, Utah, Colorado, Nebraska, and Minnesota.

IDENTIFICATION: The back and flanks of the male are whitish, and the head and bill appear longer than those of the Redhead. Where the head and bill merge, there is a slight concave curvature. The female has a brownish breast and head, a whitish belly and flanks, and a light gray back.

SIZE: The canvasback averages between 19 and 24 inches in length.

FLIGHT SPEED: This bird has been clocked at 72 miles an hour.

FOOD: Eighty percent of the diet is composed of vegetable matter—primarily aquatic plants and wild celery of the genus *Vallisneria*. Fish, insects, and mollusks are sometimes eaten.

American Coot

Fulica americana

RANGE: The main breeding area extends in Canada from New Brunswick to British Columbia. In addition, there are colonies in Florida, along the Gulf Coast, and in Panama, Nicaragua, and Baja California. In winter, the bird relocates in southern British Columbia, the American Southwest, the Ohio River Valley, and Maryland down to Panama, the Greater Antilles, and the Bahamas.

IDENTIFICATION: The plumage of the American coot is a darkish gray that becomes a bit lighter below. Beneath the short tail, a patch of white is visible. The eye is red; the feet and legs are a shade of green. The bill, on the stout side and conical, is the color of white china. The downy young are blackish and feature an orange bill; in addition, the feathers about the shoulders, neck, and head are either orange or orange-tipped.

SIZE: Similar in size to a small chicken, this species is 13 to 16 inches long.

FLIGHT SPEED: Though they usually fly at speeds of from 55 to 60 miles an hour, ducks can at times attain 65 to 70 mph.

FOOD: Being omnivorous, the American coot dines on all classes of vegetable matter, as well as crustaceans, worms, snails, tadpoles, and fish.

European Coot

Fulica atra

RANGE: Breeding occurs throughout Europe, save for the northernmost areas. Some stragglers have been sighted in Greenland, Labrador, and Newfoundland.

IDENTIFICATION: The European coot is almost an exact replica of the American coot, except for the fact that the feathers located below the tail are slate gray instead of white.

SIZE: Similar in size to the American coot, this species is from 14 to 16 inches long.

FLIGHT SPEED: Ducks travel at an average pace of 55 to 60 miles an hour. However, speeds of 65 to 70 mph are attainable.

FOOD: This species feeds on plant food and tiny animals. In shallow-water regions, the coot dives for water plants, which it picks clean of snails and other small aquatic animals.

Common Eider
Somateria dresseri

RANGE: The Aleutian Islands, southwestern Alaska, most of Canada and Maine comprise this species' breeding range. Winters are spent at the southern tip of the ice pack and southward to British Columbia, Washington, and the Middle Atlantic states.

IDENTIFICATION: There is a conspicuous amount of white on the back and wings of the male. The white head features a black cap and a pair of pale green patches at the rear. The flight feathers of the wings, the rump, the tail, and the undersides are black; the breast is pinkish. The feet are greenish-gray. The bill tends to be either orange or yellow. The female's bill, however, is grayish, and her body is a light brown with black and dark-brown barrings.

SIZE: The largest of the eiders, the common eider measures 21 to 27 inches in length.

FLIGHT SPEED: Speeds of 65 to 70 miles per hour are attainable, but the norm is 55 to 60 mph.

FOOD: Mollusks make up 80 percent of the American eider's diet. Tiny crustaceans, fish, echinoderms (sea urchins and starfish), and small amounts of plant food are also eaten.

King Eider
Somateria spectabilis

RANGE: The species breeds on the islands and Arctic coasts from northwestern Alaska to Hudson and James Bays and northern Labrador. In winter, this eider is located in the Aleutian Islands, southern Alaska, California, the Great Lakes, New Jersey, and Newfoundland.

IDENTIFICATION: From a distance, the forward half of the male king eider seems white, the rear half black. The crown is gray, the breast pinkish. Traces of pale green are visible on the face, and there is a tiny black crescent beneath each eye. A prominent white patch can be seen on the wing and also on the bottom part of the rump. A black-edged frontal knob at the tip of the orange bill flares out over the forehead. The hen is a browner red than the American eider hen.

SIZE: The king eider is 18 to 24 inches long.

FLIGHT SPEED: Ducks can reach 65 to 70 miles per hour, but normally their pace is 55 to 60 mph.

FOOD: The menu includes mollusks (predominantly mussels), starfish, sea urchins, crustaceans, and insects. A small percentage of the diet is composed of seaweeds and eelgrass.

Spectacled Eider
Lampronetta fischeri

RANGE: The principle breeding region is the Aleutians, but some members of the species are found on rare occasions on Kodiak Island.

IDENTIFICATION: The male spectacled eider's neck, throat, and upperparts are white; its underparts are black. The head is a pale green, and a large white area edged with black — the spectacles — appears around the eyes. The female has brownish plumage and lighter-brown "spectacles."

SIZE: This species is from 20 to 23 inches long.

FLIGHT SPEED: Ducks average 55 to 60 miles an hour, but can reach a top of 70 mph when necessary.

FOOD: This diving duck feasts on crowberries, sedges, pondweeds, and algae (seaweeds).

EDIBILITY: The meat of this duck is reputed to be one of the favorite foods of the Aleutians.

Steller's Eider
Polysticta stelleri

RANGE: Breeding area includes the Arctic coasts and islands of Alaska. A number of these eiders are also found in Maine and Quebec.

IDENTIFICATION: This bird has a thick body and a rather short neck. The drake features a white head with a tiny gray crest at the back. The throat is black, as is the eye-ring. The back, tail, feathers beneath the tail, and neck-ring are black. The breast and the remainder of the under-sides are reddish-brown. The flank, as well as a major portion of the wing feathering visible from the sides, are white. The feet and bills of both sexes are blackish. The female has a whitish and dark-brown eye-ring and a white-bordered blue wing speculum.

SIZE: At from 17 to 19 inches in length, the Steller's eider is small for a diving duck.

FLIGHT SPEED: Ducks reach a top speed of 70 miles an hour, but the norm is 55 to 60 mph.

FOOD: A major portion of the diet consists of fish, worms, insects, mollusks, and crustaceans. The remaining percentage is made up of plant food — algae and pondweeds.

Fulvous Tree Duck

Dendrocygna bicolor

RANGE: This duck resides in California, New Mexico, Texas, and southern Louisiana. Some strays have been sighted around the Great Lakes as far north as Nova Scotia.

IDENTIFICATION: This species has a grayish bill and grayish feet; its head, breast, and underparts are tawny brown, or fulvous, in color. The back and the rear of the neck are a dark brown. The throat features a buffy patch and a series of white slashes that are underlined with dark brown at the side.

SIZE: The smallest of the tree ducks, the fulvous tree duck measures 18 to 21 inches in length.

FLIGHT SPEED: Top speed for the duck is 70 miles per hour, but the normal pace is 55 to 60 mph.

FOOD: The diet consists primarily of grasses, seeds, and weeds. But on several occasions, this duck has been sighted gleaning cornfields.

Gadwall

Anas strepera

RANGE: Breeding occurs in most of western North America and in some of the Middle Atlantic states. Winters are usually passed in Southern Mexico and Florida.

IDENTIFICATION: The breeding plumage of the male is gray; the neck and head are brownish. Black feathers are apparent above and below the gray tail. The prominent white speculum is bordered with black. At the bend of the wing, there is a chestnut-brown patch. The belly is white, the feet yellowish, and the bill dark. The female's body is almost completely dull brown save for the whitish upperparts and white speculum.

SIZE: The gadwall is from 19 to 23 inches long.

FLIGHT SPEED: Speeds of 55 to 60 miles an hour are normal for the duck, but 70 mph is its peak.

FOOD: Approximately 90 percent of the diet consists of aquatic plants, grasses, grains, nuts, and acorns. The remaining 10 percent is animal matter, primarily insects and crustaceans.

Common Golden-Eye

Bucephala clangula

RANGE: This duck breeds in the northern coniferous forest, from the treeline down, in southern Alaska and along the entire U. S.-Canadian border. The bird winters from the bottom edge of the breeding region to the southern United States.

GADWALL

COMMON GOLDENEYE

IDENTIFICATION: The drake features a glossy dark green head with a circular white patch just before, and slightly under, its golden eyes. The breast, neck, flanks, and underside are white. The dark gray back is broadly hatched with white at the sides. The young and the females have red-brown heads, and their neck, breast, and undersides are white. The flanks and a bar across the top of the breast are gray, as is the back. The white on the wing of the drake is more prominent than on the wing of the hen.

SIZE: The American golden-eye measures 15 to 21 inches in length.

FLIGHT SPEED: Ducks average between 55 and 60 miles an hour, but can attain a top speed of 70 mph.

FOOD: Predominantly animal matter comprises this duck's diet—mollusks, insects, fish, and crustaceans. During the breeding seasons, plants are also consumed.

Barrow's Golden-Eye
Bucephala islandica

RANGE: The breeding area in western North America is shaped like an inverted "V," beginning in southeastern Alaska and northwestern British Columbia; one arm extends south to California's High Sierras, the other southeast to the Colorado mountains. Some breeding also takes place in northern Quebec. Winters are spent on the Pacific shores from southern Alaska to central California, and on the Atlantic from Long Island, New York, to the mouth of the St. Lawrence River.

IDENTIFICATION: The Barrow's golden-eye is remarkably similar to the American golden-eye, except for the fact that the female has a shorter bill. The head of the drake is glossed with purple, and there is a white crescent between the bill and the eye.

SIZE: This species is 16 to 20 inches in length.

FLIGHT SPEED: The norm for ducks is 55 to 60 miles an hour; the top speed is 70 mph.

FOOD: Seventy-five percent of the diet is animal matter, principally mollusks. This species consumes more insects than the American golden-eye.

Harlequin Duck
Histrionicus histrionicus

RANGE: Breeding area extends from south-central and southern Alaska (including the Aleutian Islands) south and southeast to British Columbia, the mountains of California, and Colorado. Some breeding takes place in Quebec and Labrador, as well as in Maryland.

IDENTIFICATION: The body of the drake is medium blue-gray except for the reddish-brown flanks. A patch of white is conspicuous in front of the eyes. Behind the eyes, there is a tiny circular spot and a vertical white line. There are also a pair of white slashes radiating from the back onto the breast. A heavy white bar followed by smaller white bars is visible on the wing when the bird is at rest. There is also a reddish-brown streak on the crown. Both male and female have legs, feet, and bills that are grayish-blue. The female's body is medium brown save for the lighter belly and a trio of white spots on the head—two in front, one behind.

SIZE: The Harlequin duck's length range is from 14½ to 21 inches.

FLIGHT SPEED: The typical cruising speed for ducks is 55 to 60 miles an hour, with spurts of up to 70 mph.

FOOD: Animal matter—insects, crustaceans, fish, mollusks, and sea urchins—comprises 97 percent of the diet. The rest is vegetation.

Red-Breasted Merganser
Mergus serrator

RANGE: Breeding occurs near the tree line in Canada, Alaska, and along the U. S.-Canadian border. In winter, this merganser stays in the coastal regions from southeastern Alaska to Baja California, as well as along the Atlantic coast.

IDENTIFICATION: Both sexes have ragged crests, with eyes, bills, legs, and feet that are red. The drake features a metallic green head. The forward and lateral sections of the neck are white, as are the undersides and breast. The breast is crossed by a wide, dark-buff band that is haphazardly streaked with dark brown. The back and parts of the wings are black, the speculum white. There are some white patches on the wings which, like the tail, are shaded dark gray. The flanks and the feathers above and below the tail are finely barred with black.

SIZE: The red-breasted merganser is 19 to 26 inches long; it is smaller than the common merganser.

FLIGHT SPEED: The mergansers can attain speeds of 100 miles an hour.

FOOD: Their diet consists of fish, crustaceans, mollusks, and aquatic insects.

Common Merganser
Mergus merganser

RANGE: Breeding occurs in southern Alaska, across Canada, in the mountains of central California, Arizona, and New Mexico, and east to the Great Lakes region and northern New England, Wintering spots are southerly to New Mexico, the western Gulf Coast, northern Georgia, and South Carolina.

IDENTIFICATION: The drake lacks a crest; its neck and head are dark metallic green. Its bill is a bright red, its back black, its tail gray, its feet orange, and its breast white. The undersides and the flanks usually have a bright pink tinge to them. The female, on the other hand, has a rough crest at the back of its reddish-brown head. The neck is the same color as the head, while the throat is white. The tail and back are medium gray, the flanks light gray. The black and gray wings feature a white speculum. The undersides tend to be whitish.

SIZE: Relatively large for a duck, the American merganser measures 21 to 27 inches in length.

FLIGHT SPEED: Mergansers have been clocked at speeds as fast as 100 miles an hour.

FOOD: A major section of the diet consists of fish, but tiny mollusks, insects, aquatic plants, and crustaceans are also eaten.

Hooded Merganser

Lophodytes cucullatus

RANGE: This species breeds from southeastern Alaska and southern Canada down through the whole of the United States save the southwestern quarter. Winters are passed in the region encompassed by southern British Columbia and Massachusetts south through mid-Mexico, the Gulf Coast, and Florida.

IDENTIFICATION: The drake features a large crest; its head, neck, back, and tail are black. A white quarter-circle is very conspicuous just below and to the rear of the eye. The breast and underparts are white, and a pair of black fingers stretches from the back over to the breast. The feet are a dusk-yellow, the bill blackish, and the eyes yellow. The female has a smaller crest. Her back, tail, and wings are dark gray; in addition, each wing is patched with white. The flanks and upper breast are medium-gray; the remainder of the upperparts is whitish. The face is a dusky grayish-red that fades to a dusky brownish-red at the crest and at the back of the head. The female's bill and feet are a dusk-yellow and her eyes are yellow.

SIZE: The smallest and slimmest of the mergansers, the hooded merganser measures 16 to 20 inches long.

FLIGHT SPEED: Mergansers can attain speeds of approximately 100 miles an hour.

FOOD: The hooded merganser primarily eats animal matter —fish, insects, crustaceans, and amphibians. Small amounts of grasses, pondweeds, grain, and other vegetable foods make up the rest of the menu.

Green-Winged Teal

Anas carolinensis

RANGE: This bird's breeding area is enclosed in a triangular region of North America from west-central Alaska and northwestern Mackenzie south to lower California and east to Newfoundland. Winters are spent in southern British Columbia and through most of the United States.

IDENTIFICATION: Both male and female feature bright, glossy green speculums. The male's head is a bright reddish-brown with a wide, bright green band beginning around the eyes and continuing to the back of the head. The buffy breast is spotted with black. The feathers below the tail are buffy and edged with black. The belly is white; the remainder of the plumage is grayish. The female is grayish-brown, though lighter below. Her feet and bill are grayish.

SIZE: This teal measures 12 to 16 inches in length.

FOOD: Plants (chiefly the aquatic type, but including grasses) comprise 80 percent of the diet. Insects, mollusks, and maggots dining on rotting fish are also consumed.

Blue-Winged Teal

Anas discors

RANGE: Breeding occurs throughout most of Canada and the U. S. southwest and middle Atlantic states.

IDENTIFICATION: Many of the tiny feathers atop the wing are a very pale blue. Both sexes feature lengthy, bright green speculums. The drake has a large white face crescent that can be at times indistinct. His bill is blue-black, his head blue-purple. The breast, flanks, and underparts are dullish brown; the back is a darker brown. Feathers above and below the tail are black, and just forward of the tail is a white patch. The female is brownish; her dusky bill is edged with pink. Her legs are yellowish.

SIZE: This teal measures 14 to 17 inches long.

FOOD: Though primarily a mix of aquatic plants, rice, corn, and grasses, the diet does include about 30 percent animal matter—mollusks, crustaceans, and insects.

Cinnamon Teal

Anas cyanoptera

RANGE: Breeding range is from southwestern Canada and Wyoming south to northern Mexico. In winter, this teal is found from the southwestern United States through Central America and northwestern South America. Some members of this species are occasionally found in the eastern United States.

IDENTIFICATION: The hens and drakes are so similar in appearance that they are nearly impossible to tell apart. Practically all of the plumage is a rich cinnamon brown hue. Back and wings lack such coloring, and instead resemble those of the blue-winged teal.

SIZE: This duck measures 16 inches in length.

FOOD: Eighty percent of the diet consists of grasses, weeds, and aquatic plants; the remainder is insects and mollusks.

Common Teal

Anas crecca

RANGE: Found mainly in Africa and Eurasia, the common teal is also found along the eastern coast of North America as far south as South Carolina.

IDENTIFICATION: The male common teal resembles its green-winged counterpart in almost every way. There are two main differences: the common drake has a horizontal white stripe on its back above the folded wings, and it does not have the vertical white crescent behind the breast. The female is indistinguishable from the female green-winged teal.

SIZE: This species measures 13 to 16 inches in length.

FOOD: About 80 percent of the diet is plant matter—mainly aquatic, but some grasses. This teal also eats insects, mollusks, and the maggots that dine on rotting fish.

American Widgeon
Mareca americana

RANGE: Breeding occurs in Alaska, western Canada and the American Northwest. Wintering spots reach from southern Alaska, the central United States, and New England south to Costa Rica and the West Indies.

IDENTIFICATION: The male of the species features a gray head with a glaring white cap and a metallic green band that extends from just in front of each eye to the rear of the head.

AMERICAN WIDGEON

The breast is pink, while the flanks and back are a tannish-red. The belly tends to be whitish, the wings dark. Each wing has a bright green speculum and a conspicuous white patch on top. The gray tail has black feathers both above and below. Preceding these feathers is a white mark that extends up from the belly. The female baldpate is recognized by her grayish head, brownish back, and tannish-red flanks and breast. The white patch on the male wing is, in the female, light gray. The feet and bills of both sexes are blue-gray.

SIZE: Somewhat larger than the European widgeon, the American widgeon measures 18 to 23 inches long.

FLIGHT SPEED: Ducks average between 55 and 60 miles an hour, but can reach 65 to 70 mph.

FOOD: Over 90 percent of the diet consists of vegetable matter, the remainder being insects and mollusks.

Wood Duck
Aix spousa

RANGE: Breeding ranges stretch from central British Columbia to central California, and are also located in such disparate areas as the Great Lakes, New England, Northeast Canada, the Gulf Coast and Cuba. Winters are spent in the United States and as far south as mid-Mexico.

IDENTIFICATION: This species is considered one of the most beautiful of all native American ducks. It has a big crest and a chunky body. The drake's head is a mix of iridescent green and blackish-purple. On each side of the head, there is a pair of thin white lines—one curving over the eye from the bill to the terminal point of the crest, and the other running parallel to it, but beginning behind the eye. The throat is white, with one finger stretching to just beneath the eyes and the other to the back of the head. Red, black, and white colorings comprise the variegated bill. The neck and breast are a bright reddish-brown. The back is of a dark iridescence, and the flanks are a creamy buff with black and white vertical lines separating them from the breast. The upperparts are whitish. The female of the species has a grayish head that features a whitish ring around the eye. Her throat is white and her back is a moderate brown-gray. The breast and flanks are brownish.

SIZE: The wood duck is 17 to 21 inches long.

FOOD: Mainly a vegetarian, this species dines on shrub and tree seeds, grasses, and aquatic plants. Some insects and tiny spiders are also consumed.

WOOD DUCK

Masked Duck
Oxyura dominica

RANGE: This species is found in Vermont, Massachusetts, Maryland, Louisiana, Wisconsin, Florida, and Texas.

IDENTIFICATION: The drake has a reddish-brown head and a black mask about the entire face. The upperparts are buffy and there are dark spots on the flanks. The wings and tail are dark, and the wings feature a large, white speculum. The black back has red-brown spots. The hen is dark-buff in color, with dark-brown spots and scales. She sports a cap as well as a pair of streaks below it. Her wings and tail are the same color as the male's.

SIZE: The masked duck measures 9 to 11 inches long.

FLIGHT SPEED: The peak among ducks is 65 to 70 miles per hour, the norm 55 to 60 mph.

Mottled Duck
Anas fulvigula

RANGE: This species inhabits the Gulf Coast from Texas to Mississippi, as well as the Florida peninsula.

IDENTIFICATION: This duck is pale brown, mottled with black, in coloring, and its speculum is a bluish-green.

SIZE: The mottled duck, also called the dusky duck, is about 20 inches in length.

FOOD: Though the majority of the diet consists of acorns, berries, grains, grasses, sedges, and aquatic vegetables, tiny amounts of insect material and mollusks are consumed.

Oldsquaw
Clangula hyemalis

RANGE: Breeding takes place in the Arctic tundra from western Alaska through northern Canada. Winters are spent along the coasts from the breeding places to California in the West and North Carolina in the East. An additional wintering area is the Great Lakes.

IDENTIFICATION: The drake alternates between a pair of distinct, rich plumages every year. The hen also has differing summer and winter plumages. In summer, the male's head, neck, breast, and tail are a dull-glossed black; in addition, there is a large, pale-gray patch above the eyes. The dark feathers of the back are bordered with a light brown. The upperparts and huge areas of the wing are white, the feet a grayish-blue. The pinkish bill has a dark tip, a white edge, and a blue patch in the vicinity of its base. Come winter, the upper breast, neck, and head become white, with a black patch under and to the back of the eye. A grayish area is visible about the eye. The forecrown is a buffy-yellow. The rest of the tail, breast, and most of the back, as well as several wing feathers, are black. The remainder of the under-sides and the wings are white. All plumages feature distinctively long tail feathers.

In summer, the hen's back and legs resemble the male's, but the head and neck are a grayish-blue, and the eye-ring is white. A white streak, beginning in back of the eye, runs down the neck, widening near the brown breast. The flanks are a brownish gray, the underparts a light gray. In winter, the female's head and neck turn whitish, as do the flanks and undersides. A gray patch is visible to the back of, and below, the eye, and gray stretches from the cap down the rear of the neck. The bill tends to be grayish despite the season.

SIZE: The oldsquaw measures 14 to 23 inches in length, approximately one-third of which is its tail.

FOOD: Mostly mollusks, crustaceans, insects, and fish are consumed, along with tiny amounts of pondweeds and grasses.

Mallard
Anas platyrhynchos

RANGE: This surface-feeding species is located throughout a major portion of the temperate Northern Hemisphere (save for northeastern Canada).

IDENTIFICATION: The adult male features a metallic-green head and neck that are separated from its bright chestnut breast by a thin, white ring. The underparts are a light gray, the upperparts a dark gray. The tail is both black-and-white, with conspicuously curled feathers on top.

MALLARD

The dark wings have a band of rich iridescent blue; the band is edged on each side first by a thin, black band and then a thin, white band. These bands, called speculums, are partly visible when the bird is at rest. The female also has a speculum, but it is predominantly dark or mottled brown and bordered by white. She has a tiny dark cap and an eye stripe, and lacks the curled tail feathers of the male. The male's bill is yellow, the female's orange. Orange feet are common to both sexes.

SIZE: The mallard ranges from 16 to 27 inches in length.

FOOD: Aquatic vegetables, acorns, berries, sedges, grains, and grasses are consumed, as well as small amounts of mollusks and insects.

Ring-Necked Duck
Aythya collaris

RANGE: Breeding takes place from southern British Columbia to the Maritime Provinces and in the northern parts of the U. S. Winters are spent along the coasts to Massachusetts and southwestern British Columbia.

IDENTIFICATION: The ring-necked duck features a glossy purple head, a black breast, a dark, greenish-glossed back, gray flanks, and white upperparts. The grayish bill has a black tip; the two colors are separated by a thin, white ring. The breast and neck are separated by a brown ring. The female is brownish and has a white ring above the eye and a slender, white line leading from this ring to the back of the head. Male and female both have a conspicuous pale blue patch on the wing.

SIZE: This species measures 14 to 18½ inches in length.

FOOD: Four-fifths of the diet revolves around vegetable matter—mainly sedges, grasses, and aquatic plants. The remainder consists of mollusks and insects.

Ruddy Duck
Oxyura jamaicensis

RANGE: Breeding extends from central British Columbia and the Canadian Prairie Provinces down to Guatemala and the Bahamas. In winter, they relocate to southern British Columbia, the south-central United States, Pennsylvania, and Massachusetts.

IDENTIFICATION: In summer, the drake has a reddish-brown back, neck, and flanks. His cheeks are white, but his cap, spike-like tail, and the flight feathers on the wings are blackish. The bill is a rich blue; the upperparts are whitish and barred lightly with browns. Come winter, the drake is similar to the female, but he retains the white cheeks. The hen features a dark brownish-gray cap, neck, upper breast, back, wings, and tail. Horizontal brown streaks run through her whitish cheeks. The feet, legs, and bill are gray, the undersides whitish, and the flank and lower breast excessively barred with black.

SIZE: The ruddy duck is from 14 to 17 inches long.

FOOD: Approximately 75 percent of the diet consists of wild celery, sedges, pondweeds, and grasses; the remainder includes such animal matter as insects and tiny shellfish.

Pintail
Anas acuta

RANGE: This bird breeds in western and north-central North America, New England and eastern Canada. Winters are spent northerly to southeastern Alaska, along the Gulf Coast and in Massachusetts.

IDENTIFICATION: The male features a rather long, pointed tail which, when in full plumage, accounts for his large size range. The lengthy, slender tail and neck are quite distinctive. His back and flanks are grayish, but he is blackish beneath the tail and on the wing. The head and throat are a bright purple-brown; this color also proceeds down the rear of the neck. The forward part of the neck and the undersides are white, as well as a finger that extends from the

PINTAIL

throat first into the brown area of the head and then to behind the eye. A patch at the rear of the flanks is also white. The feet and the bill are bluish-gray.

SIZE: As mentioned above, the pintail's length varies extensively, depending on tail size. Adults average between 20 and 29 inches in length.

FOOD: The menu reads as follows: aquatic plants, weeds, small mollusks, grasses, crustaceans, grains, and insects.

REDHEAD

Redhead
Aythya americana

RANGE: The breeding range encompasses a triangular area from eastern British Columbia south to lower California, and from there east to the Great Lakes. Come winter, the redhead resides from southwestern British Columbia east to Maryland, and south to lower Baja California, central Mexico, the Gulf Coast, an Florida.

IDENTIFICATION: The male's back, wings, flanks, and tail are gray; the breast is blackish; the head is reddish-brown. The bill and legs of both sexes are grayish-blue. The bill's black tip is separated from the remainder of the bill by a thin, whitish line. The male breast is white. The female is buffy brown and also has a white breast.

SIZE: The redhead is 18 to 22 inches in length.

FOOD: Ninety percent of the diet is aquatic plants; the remainder is mollusks and insects.

Greater Scaup
Aythya marila

RANGE: The scaup breeds in central and south-central Alaska through the Yukon into western Mackenzie. In winter, it relocates from southeastern Alaska down to southern California, and from the eastern Great Lakes and the Canadian Maritime Provinces south to Florida and the Gulf Coast.

IDENTIFICATION: The greater scaup is quite similar to the redhead in appearance except for the fact that the male

of this species features a metallic green head with a purplish cast, and the female greater scaup has a dark brown head with a conspicuous white feather patch. Also, at the bottom of the blue-hued bill the whiteness extends farther into the wing as a gradually thinning, blurry line. The "nail" at the bill's tip is much larger in the greater scaup than in the lesser scaup.

SIZE: This species measures from 15 to 21 inches in length.

FOOD: The menu is an omnivorous one, being 50 percent vegetable (aquatic plants and grasses) and 50 percent animal (crustaceans, insects, and mollusks).

Lesser Scaup
Aythya affinis

RANGE: This scaup breeds from central Alaska and the tree limits of Mackenzie and Keewatin southerly, east of the Coast Ranges to central British Columbia and Idaho, and east of the Rocky Mountains to Colorado, Nebraska, and Iowa; and a bit farther east. In winter, it is found northerly along the coasts to British Columbia and Connecticut, and in the interior to southern Arizona, southern New Mexico, central Texas, Missouri, and the southern Great Lakes area.

IDENTIFICATION: This species has less white in the wing than does the greater scaup, and a smaller dark-colored "nail" at the tip of the bill. The head is often glossy purple rather than green, giving the scaup the appearance of having a slight crest.

SIZE: The lesser scaup measures 14 to 19 inches in length.

FOOD: Being more of a vegetarian than the greater scaup, this species favors aquatic plants and grasses. It does, however, also consume crustaceans, insects, and mollusks.

Common Scoter
Oidemia nigra

RANGE: Breeding areas include western and southern Alaska and the Aleutian Islands. In winter, the species relocates to the Great Lakes, and along the Atlantic from Newfoundland to South Carolina.

IDENTIFICATION: The common scoter's entire plumage is slightly glossy and blackish. The bright orange bill features a grayish "lip." The feet and legs are gray-green. The female is dark brown, but has whitish cheeks and a whitish throat; her bill is a gray blue. The immature scoter looks like the female, but is lighter below. The eyes of this species are dark.

SIZE: Moderate-sized for a diving duck, this scoter measures 17 to 21 inches long.

FOOD: Mollusks are the preferred dish, with crustaceans, fish, and insects the runners-up. About 10 percent of the diet is made up of plant matter.

SURF SCOTERS

Surf Scoter
Melanitta perspicillata

RANGE: Breeding occurs from northeastern Alaska to the western half of Mackenzie and on islands in James Bay. Some have also been seen in central Labrador. Come winter, this scoter resides along the Pacific Coast from the eastern Aleutians to Baja California and on the Atlantic Seaboard from Nova Scotia to North Carolina.

IDENTIFICATION: The male's plumage is black but there is one white patch at the back of the head and another at the forehead. The large, swollen bill consists of white, red, bluish-gray, and yellow colorings in a variegated pattern. The eyes are white. Both sexes have dusky-yellow feet and no trace of white at all on the wings. The female is dark brown, and has white patches on the head not unlike those of the white-winged scoter. But the surf scoter has an additional white patch at the back of the head.

SIZE: Medium-sized among diving ducks, this scoter measures between 17 and 21 inches.

FOOD: Sixty percent of this bird's diet consists of mollusks, and another 10 percent is vegetable matter. Scallops and oysters are also consumed.

White-Winged Scoter
Melanitta deglandi

RANGE: This species breeds in west-central Alaska, northwestern Mackenzie and along the Rocky Mountains. In summer, the bird ranges from eastern Canada, south to Massachusetts. In winter, it moves on to the Great Lakes and along the temperate Atlantic and Pacific coasts.

IDENTIFICATION: This scoter features a glossy purplish plumage that is punctuated by a white speculum and a tiny patch of white about the eyes. The bill is orange, lightening to yellow at the tip. There is a black knob at the base of the bill. The female's body is dark brown, her upperparts white. A pair of white spots are located beneath the eyes, one is forward, the other at the back. Her bill is gray-blue. The feet of both sexes are a dusky-pink, the eyes white. Immature scoters resemble the female.

SIZE: A medium-sized diving duck, this scoter measures between 19 and 23 inches in length.

FOOD: Approximately 75 percent of the diet is composed of mollusks, mussels, clams, and oysters. The remainder is crustaceans, a small amount of plant matter, and insects.

Shoveler
Spatula clypeata

RANGE: The breeding area encompasses Alaska, central and southeastern Canada, both coasts and the Great Lakes area. In winter, the species spreads eastward.

IDENTIFICATION: This species has a wide spatulate bill that is quite distinct among North American birds; this bill is longer than the bird's head. The drake's breeding plumage consists of a metallic green head and neck. The breast, upperparts, tail, and the forepart of the back are white. A wide, red-brown band stretches across the belly from flank to flank. The remainder of the back and the feathers above and below the tail are blackish-green or black. The female is reminiscent of the female cinnamon teal, even to the horizontal, pale blue line above the wing. The eye of the hen is dull brown, that of the drake a rich yellow.

SIZE: The shoveler averages some 20 inches in length.

FOOD: Primarily grasses and aquatic plants. In addition, large amounts of vegetable debris which are strained from the ooze at marsh and pond bottoms. Small amounts of mollusks, aquatic insects, and fish are also eaten.

SHOVELER

Shorebirds

Purple Gallinule
Porphyrula martinica

RANGE: Mainly inhabiting coastal lowlands and large river basins in the triangle formed by Tennessee, Louisiana, and South Carolina, this shorebird has also found its way throughout most of the United States and into southeastern Canada.

IDENTIFICATION: The purple gallinule sports extremely flamboyant colors. A deep, rich purple coats the head, neck, and undersides, while the back, wings, and upper tail feathers are dark greenish with a bronzelike sheen. The feathers below the short tail are white, while the feet and legs are a prominent yellowish-green. The bill is bright red at the base and bright yellow at the tip. A tough, fleshy casque begins at the bottom of the upper bill and flares out to the middle of the head. Immature gallinules are light gray and white below, dark gray above. Their casques and bills are a dull gray. The chicks are glossy black with white bristles on their cap, cheeks, chin, and forehead.

SIZE: Medium-sized for a rail, the purple gallinule measures 13 inches in length (the same size as the Florida gallinule).

FOOD: The menu consists of rice, grain, seeds, insects, small mollusks, and amphibians.

Common Gallinule
Gallinula chloropus

RANGE: This bird is found in southern Canada, throughout much of the United States and in such South American countries as Peru, Argentina, and Brazil.

IDENTIFICATION: The common gallinule resembles the purple gallinule in general appearance, but it is dark gray instead of purple. The yellow-tipped bill and the casque are bright red, and the legs and feet are greenish-yellow. The top edge of flank is white, and it appears as a white streak down the side when the bird is swimming. The central feathers of the undertail are dark gray. The downy young are glossy black, and the skin at the bottom of the black-tipped, reddish bill is a bright red. The chin feathers are curled and stiff, the forehead white.

SIZE: Like the purple gallinule, this shorebird is about 13 inches in length.

FOOD: Though consisting primarily of underwater plants, the diet also features herbs, grasses, seeds, and berries. This gallinule also eats insects, snails, and worms.

Carolina Rail
Porzana carolina

RANGE: The Carolina rail breeds throughout lower Canada. In the U.S., it can be found in the Saskatchewan, Manitoba, Southwest, Plains States and the Midwest.

IDENTIFICATION: Typically, this rail has a body that is compressed laterally. Its cap, nape, tail, back, and wings are brown. In addition, the back and wings are spotted and marked with black and buff coloring. There is irregular barring below that is composed of thin, white lines on medium gray. The rest of the head and breast are a warmish gray, but the face and bib are black. The short, yellowish bill features a blackish tip; the feet and legs are a greenish-yellow. The adult's eye is vermilion, but the eye is yellow in the duller, browner immature sora. The downy young are a glossy black with curled, stiff chin feathers of a rich orange. Their yellow bills are enlarged and reddish at the base.

SIZE: A smallish rail, this bird—also called the sora—is only 8 to 10 inches long.

FOOD: The sora eats more vegetation than is the norm for a rail. The diet consists primarily of aquatic plants, but the consumption of small mollusks, insects, and worms is also high, particularly in the spring.

Virginia Rail
Rallus limicola

RANGE: This shorebird breeds from Guatemala north to southern Canada.

IDENTIFICATION: The Virginia rail has a long bill and very gray cheeks. On its underparts, there are wide, black lines that alternate with thin, wavy white lines. The feet, legs, and bill are pink. The young are nearly black.

SIZE: A medium-sized rail, this bird measures from $8^{1}/_{2}$ to $10^{1}/_{2}$ inches in length.

FOOD: The diet consists of worms, mollusks, aquatic insects, amphibians, and small fish. On occasion, seeds are included.

Greater Yellowlegs
Totanus melanoleucus

RANGE: The breeding grounds are from central Alaska east to Labrador and Newfoundland; the wintering areas are from southwestern British Columbia through the West Indies and Latin America.

IDENTIFICATION: The greater yellowlegs has a slender but sturdy, slightly upturned, blackish bill that is approximately 50 percent longer than the head. The upperparts are dark brown, the outer flight feathers black. The tail (lightly barred) and the back are also black. The bill of this species

GREATER YELLOWLEGS

Wilson's Snipe
Gallinago delicata

RANGE: Though this shorebird breeds in the Arctic tundra down to New York and the mountains of California, it winters from the Gulf States southward to Brazil and Columbia.

IDENTIFICATION: The upperparts of this, the only North American species of snipe, are blackish with buff mottlings. A pair of conspicuous buff stripes are located along the back, and another down the center of the crown. The body is whitish below, but brown-spotted on the throat and tail. The latter is black with a red tip.

SIZE: The Wilson's snipe measures some 11 inches in length, 3 inches of which is its tail.

FOOD: Its menu consists of worms, snails, and insects.

EDIBILITY: The flavor of the flesh is, as the bird's scientific name implies, delicate.

is proportionately longer and stockier than the bill of the lesser yellowlegs.

SIZE: This shorebird is 12½ to 15 inches long.

FOOD: This bird's menu consists of small fish, insects (primarily aquatic), worms, small mollusks, and crustaceans.

LESSER YELLOWLEGS

Lesser Yellowlegs
Totanus flavipes

RANGE: The species breeds from north-central Alaska east to Quebec. Winters are spent along the coastal lowlands from Mexico, the Gulf Coast and South Carolina down through Central America and the West Indies.

IDENTIFICATION: The lesser yellowlegs is practically identical to the greater yellowlegs, except for the fact that the bill of this species is much more slender and, lacking the upturn, much straighter.

SIZE: This shorebird is smaller than the greater yellowlegs, measuring 9½ to 11 inches in length.

FOOD: Like the greater yellowlegs, the lesser yellowlegs consumes insects, small fish, mollusks, and crustaceans.

PART III / Fishing

Spinning

Spinning is a relatively new method of fishing, having become popular in America in the late 1940's. It is unique because the reel is mounted on the underside of the rod rather than on top, as in other methods, and because the reel spool remains stationary (does not revolve) when the angler is casting and retrieving.

In operation, the weight and momentum of the lure being cast uncoils line (usually monofilament) from the reel spool. Unlike conventional revolving-spool reels, in which the momentum of the turning spool can cause backlashes, the spinning-reel user has no such problem, for the line stops uncoiling at the end of the cast. The beginner can learn to use spinning gear much faster than he can master conventional tackle. Still another advantage of spinning gear is that it permits the use of much smaller, lighter lures than can be cast with conventional equipment.

The Reel

On a standard open-face spinning reel, the pickup mechanism is usually of a type called the bail—a metal arm extending across the spool's face. To cast a lure or bait, the angler opens the bail by swinging it out and down. This frees the line which, as a rule, he momentarily controls with his index finger. He casts and then cranks the reel handle—not a full turn but just a small fraction of a turn. This snaps the bail closed, engaging the line.

In place of a manually opened bail, an open-faced reel can be designed with an automatic pickup and a lever, or trigger, control. This is uncommon, but an example is the Berkley Castamatic spinning reel. When you begin the cast with this reel, instead of working the bail you pull a long trigger with your casting hand, then cast in the normal manner and simply release the trigger to stop the line automatically. A smoothly functioning pickup mechanism—whether it employs a conventional bail or a lever control—is an extremely important part of the spinning reel.

Other devices on a spinning reel include the drag and the anti-reverse lock. The drag, an adjustable mechanism usually consisting of a series of discs and friction washers, is fitted on the outer (forward) face of the spool in most reels. The drag permits a hooked fish to take out line without breaking off, while the reel handle remains stationary. The anti-reverse lock, usually a lever mounted on the gear-housing cover, prevents the reel handle from turning in reverse at such times as when a hooked fish is running out or when you are trolling.

Spinning reels are designed for all types of fishing. How does the beginner select the right one for his particular needs? A reel's weight and line capacity are the major determining factors.

For ultralight fishing with tiny lures ($1/16$ to $5/16$ ounce), a reel weighing 6 to 10 ounces and holding 100 yards of $1 3/4$- to 3-pound-test line is the ticket. Reels for light freshwater use weigh 10 to 12 ounces and hold up to 200 yards of 6- or 8-pound-test line. Reels for general freshwater and light saltwater use weigh 12 to 18 ounces and hold up to 250 yards of 8- to 15-pound-test line. Heavy surf-spinning reels weigh upwards of 18 ounces and hold a minimum of 250 yards of 15-pound-test line.

In addition to the open-face spinning reel, there is a closed-face design. This type, too, is mounted under the rod. Its spool and working parts are enclosed in a hood, with the line running through an opening at the front. The pickup mechanism is normally an internal pin, and there's no need for a bail since line control is accomplished by other means. In some of these reels, which were fairly common at one time, line was disengaged from the pickup by backing the handle a half-turn. In others, it was accomplished by pushing a button, working a lever or disc, or pressing the front reel plate. Closed-face reels are no longer common. Zebco, however, makes one called the Omega which is operated with a lever—pretty much like the open-face Berkley Castamatic.

Besides eliminating the bail, closed-face reels give the spool and other parts some protection from the elements and help to keep out sand, dirt, and such. Some fishermen, however, dislike the fact that the line is choked through the constriction at the point of the cone, feeling that this arrange-

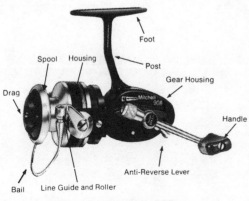

OPEN-FACE SPINNING REEL

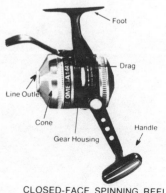

CLOSED-FACE SPINNING REEL

HOW TO MATCH UP SPINNING TACKLE

This chart is meant only as a general guide aimed at helping the fisherman put together, in proper balance, the basic elements of a spinning outfit tailored for fish of a particular weight category. Specific conditions—and the angler's ability and personal preferences—must also be considered when buying a fishing outfit of any kind.

SPECIES OF FISH	REEL	ROD ACTION, LENGTH (Ft.)	LINE (Lb. test)	LURES (Oz.)
Trout, small bass, grayling, panfish	Ultra-light	Ultralight 4 to 6	2, 3	$1/16$ to $5/16$
Smallmouth, large-mouth, and white bass; pickerel, trout, grayling	Light	Light $5^1/2$ to $6^1/2$	4 to 8	$1/4$ to $3/8$
Large bass and trout, walleye pickerel, pike, snook, landlocked salmon	Medium	Medium 6 to $7^1/2$	6 to 10	$3/8$ to $5/8$
Salmon, lake trout, muskellunge, pike, bonefish, tarpon, striped bass, bluefish	Heavy	Heavy 7 to $8^1/2$	10 to 15	$1/2$ to $1^1/2$
General saltwater use (surf and boat)	Extra-heavy	Extra-heavy 9 to 13	12 and up	1 and up

ment somewhat limits casting range and accuracy. Another drawback is that the hood enclosing the spool hides the line from the angler's view, preventing him from seeing line tangles, whether the line is uncoiling smoothly, and such.

Mainly because of the simplicity of spinning reels, there has been little gadgeteering by manufacturers. However, some unusual wrinkles have appeared in recent years. These include bails that open automatically, self-centering (self-positioning) bails, and skirted spools, which prevent line from getting behind the spool—a problem that crops up occasionally and is particularly vexing.

The Rod

There are spinning rods designed for every conceivable kind of sport fishing. They come in lengths of from 4 to 13 feet and weigh from 2 to about 30 ounces. Most are constructed of fiberglass and graphite, though a few are made of bamboo. Construction is one, two, or three-piece; however, spinning rods designed for backpackers may have as many as a half-dozen or more sections.

Spinning rods fall into five general categories: ultralight, light, medium, heavy, and extra-heavy. They are further broken down according to type of reel seat and design of hand grip.

THREE TYPES OF SPINNING RODS

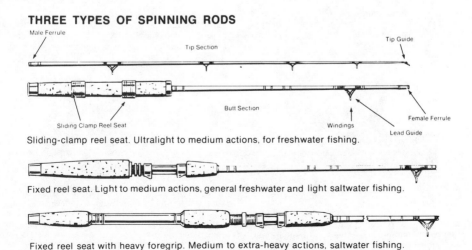

Sliding-clamp reel seat. Ultralight to medium actions, for freshwater fishing.

Fixed reel seat. Light to medium actions, general freshwater and light saltwater fishing.

Fixed reel seat with heavy foregrip. Medium to extra-heavy actions, saltwater fishing.

Shakespeare 2411 is a general-purpose, skirted-spool spinning reel that gives fishermen a choice of automatic or manual return of the bail to retrieve position. It weighs 14.6 ounces, holds 310 yards of 8-pound-test mono, and has gear ratio of 4.6 to 1.

Daiwa Silver Series open-face spinning reels feature skirted spool, manual/automatic bail closure, folding handle, and left- or right-handed retrieve. Models range from ultra-light fresh-water reel (7.8 ounces, 5.4 to 1 gear ratio) to heavy saltwater reel (24.5 ounces, 4.4 to 1 ratio).

Shimano LP-7 is a hefty spinning reel recommended for surf fishing. It has a hardwood grip, skirted spool, retrieve ratio of 3.2 to 1, and a line capacity of 400 yards of 17-pound-test mono.

Zebco Omega 840L features selective top-mounted anti-reverse, self-lubricating drag and bearings, stainless-steel bail springs and self-locking bail screws. Gear ratio is 4.1 to 1. Parallel-wind gear system assures even winding of line.

Berkley Castamatic is an automatic open-face spinning reel. No need to finger the bail. Using your casting hand to operate it, you pull the trigger at the beginning of the cast, then cast in the normal manner, releasing trigger as you do so. Comes spooled with 275 yards of 8-pound mono.

Penn 750SS is a heavy-duty spinning reel with skirted spool, hard-chromed stainless-steel line roller and ball, 3 stainless-steel ball bearings, right- or left-handed retrieve, and 4.6 to 1 gear ratio. Capacity is 250 yards of 20-pound monofilament.

Garcia Ambassadeur 55 features stainless-steel ball bearings, multi-disc stern drag, left- or right-handed retrieve, heavy-duty stainless-steel ball with rotating line roller, and helical gears providing retrieve ratio of 5.1 to 1.

Ryobi Model 3000 has stationary but oscillating spool so that when a fish runs the bail turns rather than the spool, thus avoiding line twist. Other features include skirted snap-off spool, manual/automatic bail, and ceramic line roller to reduce line wear. Gear ratio is 4.2 to 1, weight is 12.5 ounces, and line capacity is 240 yards of 10-pound mono.

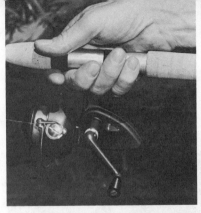

SPINNING: HOW TO CAST
by Joe Brooks

The grip. Proper grip for open-face spinning reel (*left*) puts two fingers on each side of reel's supporting shank. With closed-face reel (*right*), proper grip is ahead of the reel seat. Expert demonstrating grips and other moves in photos that follow is Gordon Dean, an authority on light tackle.

Line control, bail. First step in preparing for a cast with an open-face spinning reel is to catch line where it leaves reel spool with the crooked first finger of right hand (*left*). Then left hand flips line-holding bail to one side, leaving line free to curl off the reel spool when crooked finger lets it go. Caster's finger holds line (*right*) until rod is whipped through casting arc and aimed toward target. Then crooked finger releases the line to let it curl off the reel spool and flow through rod guides for distance cast. The spool of a spinning reel doesn't turn during cast.

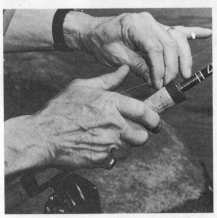

Line control, closed face. Closed-face reel needs different line-holding system to control line prior to cast. Line is run from reel over the back of the rod-holding hand and pressed against cork rod grip with thumb of rod-holding hand. With line held firmly in place with right hand, left hand is used to push reel handle into position that unlocks line-holding bail inside the reel. Thumb will release the line for cast.

To stop lure. Two methods of stopping forward flight of lure after the cast. With closed-face reel (*left*), turn reel handle forward to engage line with hidden reel bail. Using an open-face reel (*right*), control cast distance by fingering line as it curls off reel spool. Turning the handle of open-face reel will also close bail, engage line.

Straightaway cast. Three steps in making straight-ahead cast where there are no special problems or obstructions. The photo at left shows starting position, thumb holding line as the rod points forward and up at about 45°. Then rod is swung back smoothly to the position shown at center, all done with smoother and faster motion than stop-action photos suggest. Then rod is powered forward to position seen at right and held at that angle while lure sails to target. Thumb holding the line to rod grip will be lifted to shoot line through the guides as rod springs forward to aim above the distant target. This is closed-face reel, but line is released at same point in forward sweep with open-face spinning reel. The casting motion is the same with either type of reel—a smooth and rhythmic sweep back and then forward.

Wind conditions. How to cope with the wind is shown in these photos. With wind at his back (*left*) he lets line shoot forward with rod tip high, so wind can take lure for added distance. Casting into wind (*right*), rod is swept forward and down to minimize wind drift as lure shoots low over water.

Sidearm. The sidearm cast is a good wind-bucker and useful when overhead foliage makes a conventional forward cast difficult. Cast starts with rod low and angled forward (*left*). Then comes a backswing and forward sweep that ends with rod pointing toward target (*right*). Line is released just before rod points toward the caster's target. Rod's follow-through motion curves the bait or lure to the mark angler's aiming for. Sidearm casts are particularly useful when wading narrow, tree-bordered streams or in boats holding two or more fishermen. There's plenty of room for casts with sidearm motion.

Underhand lob. This underhand cast is made much like routine sidearm cast, except that rod tip is lower on backswing and higher on forward sweep. A lure given underhand lob will sail in a high, soft arc, hit water gently. This makes good cast for the clear and shallow runs where a splashy cast would scare fish. Underhand lob is also useful when there's foliage blocking overhead casts.

Flip cast. This short-range, cramped-quarters cast depends on upward flip of the rod to toss the lure. Start flip cast by dipping rod tip sharply (*left*). After that quick downswing bends tip of rod, add to rod spring with sharp lifting motion—the move just starting in center photo. If the cast is to be short, release line as the upsweeping rod nears horizontal position. For a longer flip cast, bring rod up to position shown in third photo before releasing the line.

Backhand lob. If overhanging limbs block area over angler's head and to his right, the backhand lob will throw the lure for fair distance. To make the cast, swing rod to position shown at left and then power rod tip up and toward target. High arc drops lure with minimum of splash—a good approach for clear, shallow water.

Bow and arrow. This is a trick fishermen walking banks can use to shoot a lure through holes in streamside brush. Photos show same cast in different positions. The technique is the same: Grasp bend of the lowest hook on lure so that it will clear hand smoothly and safely. Then shoot lure like an arrow, releasing line at rod grip as lure shoots forward.

Grasshopper. Here's the spinning cast that gets a lure into the pockets of water that are screened from routine casts by bushes drooping low over the water. The grasshopper cast puts the lure in the fishy-looking pocket by skipping it off the surface like a flat stone, the lure plunking into the target pool after its first bounce. To execute this cast, Gordon Dean crouches, then swings rod into low backsweep and whips it forward low and level with unusual power. Lure skips into pocket

Retrieve. Proper stance for routine retrieve is shown in photo at left. Rod is high enough that its bend will absorb shock of hard strike by big fish. Position is good for hook-setting, as shown in center photo. Note that angler holds left hand on reel handle to keep line under constant control. Rod butt is braced against his body. Third photo shows how to gain clearance when playing fish in very shallow, snag-filled water.

Fly Fishing

The art of fly fishing dates back to at least the third century A.D. and so is one of the oldest forms of sport fishing. Its adherents—and they are legion—say that it is also the most artistic form of the sport.

Fly fishing is unique in two basic ways: In all other forms of fishing, the weight of the lure or bait is what enables the angler to cast; in fly fishing, the weight of the line itself is cast. In spinning, spincasting, and baitcasting, for the most part, a natural bait or a lure or plug imitating a natural bait is offered to the fish; the fly fisherman's offering is a near-weightless bit of feathers and hair that imitates some insect in one of its forms of life (though some flies—streamers and bucktails—imitate baitfish).

The Reel

It is generally agreed that the reel is the least important item of fly-fishing tackle, and yet without it the angler would find himself amid a tangle of line and leader. The fly reel is mounted below the rod grip and close to the butt end of the rod. In most kinds of fishing the reel's main function is to store line that is not being used. In handling large fish, however, the workings of the fly reel come into play.

There are two basic types of fly reels, the single-action and the automatic.

The single-action reel, which is best when the quarry is either small or quite heavy fish, is so named because the spool makes one complete turn for each turn of the handle. The spool is deep and narrow. The beginner should make sure that the reel has a strong click mechanism to prevent the line from overrunning, and if he'll be tangling with sizable strong-running fish such as striped bass or salmon, he should get a reel with an adjustable drag.

The standard (trout size) single-action fly reel weighs 3 to $5\frac{1}{2}$ ounces and has a spool diameter of 3 to $3\frac{1}{2}$ inches. The spool should be filled with enough line (the fly line itself, usually 30 yards, plus sufficient "backing" line) to reach within about $\frac{3}{8}$-inch of the reel's cross braces. Many fly fishermen like 15-pound-test braided nylon or monofilament as backing.

Chief advantages of the single-action fly reels are that they weigh considerably less than the automatics and that they can hold much more line (backing)—an important factor in handling large fish.

The automatic fly reel has a spring-operated spool that retrieves line automatically when the angler activates the spool-release lever. The spring is wound up as line is pulled from the reel, but line may be stripped from the reel at any time, even when the spring is tightly wound.

Though heavier than the single-action (weight range is 5 to 10 ounces), the automatic greatly facilitates line control. Instead of having to shift the rod from the right to the left hand (assuming the user is right-handed) to reel in line, as the user of the single-action reel must do, the automatic user simply touches the release lever with the little finger of his right hand.

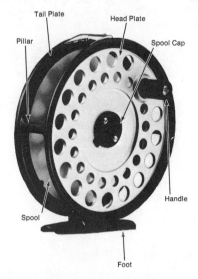

SINGLE-ACTION FLY REEL

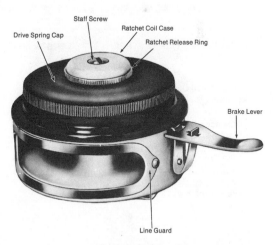

AUTOMATIC FLY REEL

The Rod

The rod is of paramount importance to the fly caster. It must be suited to the kind of fishing he does (dry fly, wet fly, bass bugging, and so on), and it must be matched with the proper fly line.

Fly rods are made of either fiberglass, graphite, or bamboo. Graphite is a comparatively new development. Though expensive, graphite fly rods are faster and more sensitive than fiberglass rods. And, ounce for ounce, graphite is twice as strong as glass. What length rod should the beginner select? A good all-purpose length, according to the recommendations of casting instructors and tackle manufacturers, is 8 to 8½ feet with a weight of about 5 ounces. Such a rod should have medium action.

Action, briefly, is a measure of a rod's flexibility, and it determines the use for which the rod is suited. In fast-action rods, best suited for dry-fly fishing, most of the flex (or bend) is at the tip. Medium-action rods, often used for wet-fly and nymph fishing, bend down to about the middle. Slow-action rods, designed for fishing streamers, bass bugs, and the like, bend well down to and even into the butt.

Good fly rods have a screw-lock reel seat, which holds the reel securely. Line guides are usually made of stainless steel, except that the tip guide and sometimes the stripper guide (the one nearest the reel) may be chrome or highly durable carboloy steel. The largest fly rods, those designed for taking tarpon and other large salt-water fish, have an extension butt, which gives the angler more leverage in fighting the big ones.

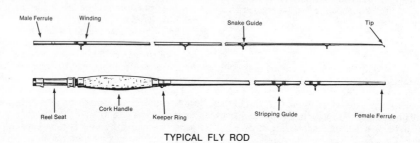

TYPICAL FLY ROD

HOW TO MATCH UP FLY TACKLE

This chart is meant only as a general guide aimed at helping the fisherman put together, in proper balance, the basic elements of a fly-fishing outfit tailored for fish of a particular weight category. Specific conditions—and the angler's ability and personal preference —must also be considered when buying a fishing outfit of any kind.

SPECIES OF FISH	REEL	ROD LENGTH (Ft.)	LINES		
			Level	Double-Taper	Weight-Forward
Trout, small bass, grayling, panfish	Single-action, auto	6½ to 7½	L4 or L5	DT4F or DT5F; DT6S	————
Smallmouth, large-mouth, and white bass; pickerel; trout; grayling	Single-action, auto	7½ to 8½	L6 or L7	DT6F or DT7F; DT8S	WF6F; WF8S
Large bass and trout, landlocked salmon, walleye, pickerel, pike	Single-action	8½ to 9	L8 or L9	DT8F or DT9F; DT9S	WF9F; WF10S
Salmon, lake trout, muskellunge, pike, bonefish, tarpon, striped bass, bluefish	Single-action	9½	L10	DT10F or DT11F	WF10F; WF10S to WF13F; WF13S

KEY TO LINE DESIGNATIONS: L-Level   DT-Double-Taper   WF-Weight-Forward   F-Floating   S-Sinking

NOTE: The line sizes above are given in the letter-and-number system of the American Fishing Tackle Manufacturers Association. These line sizes are meant only as a general guide, and the newcomer to fishing should note that there are a wide range of conditions and circumstances that determine the correct line weight for a given rod.

Pflueger Medalist Model 1498, single-action, with adjustable drag. Weight: 6⅞ ounces. Medium-heavy duty.

Scientific Anglers Single-Action System, with adjustable click-type drag. Comes in sizes designed for line weights 4 to 11.

Berkley 1056 single-action fly reel weighs only 3½ ounces, features lever-bar drag system, and comes with tool kit. Spool presses out for easy line replacement.

Martin Model 49, automatic, with drag. Weight: 9¼ ounces. Line capacity: 35 yards of WF-8-F line or 40 yards of weight-8 level line.

Garcia Mitchell 710 is an automatic fly reel with deeply knurled sideplate for easy winding of the spring with cold or wet hands. Position of line-guide ring is adjustable, and a friction clutch prevents overwinding.

Shakespeare's Model 7593 ultra-light single-action fly reel weighs 4½ ounces and holds up to a No. 6 level fly line Spool diameter is 2³⁄₁₆ inches.

Martin Model 67-A is a 5½-ounce single-action reel with adjustable click drag and push-button-release spool. Converts easily to left-handed use.

HOW TO FLY CAST
by Joe Brooks

Grip the rod properly. There are several ways to grip a fly rod, but it's my opinion that only two of them give the wrist freedom you need for good fly casting.

The grips that I like are shown in the first two photos above. The main difference is that in the first position the thumb is extended along the top of the cork, whereas in the second it is curved around the cork. I find this last hand position, with the thumb curved over to meet my forefinger, a bit more free and easy than the extended-thumb grip. It also gets more power into a conventional overhead cast because it places the back of the hand in a position to exert more force on the rod.

The third photo shows how lightly the rod is held as it pivots in the hand during casting motion. The grip should be comfortable, natural. Just pick the rod up between thumb and first finger and let it settle gently into place.

Switching out line. Before any cast can be made, a working length of line must be switched out through the rod guides. Start by grasping the fly at the hook bend (*left*) and pulling a little more than a rod's length of line and leader through the guides. Letting that line dangle from the rod tip, pull more line off the reel (*center*) and switch the rod forward and back to pull the slack through the guides. Continue pulling off line and false casting until you have enough line working back and forth through the air for a forward cast. Drive the rod forward with extra power when you're ready to deliver the fly.

Wrist position. Wrist of casting arm should never bend back farther than position shown above when making normal overhead backcast. Many beginners handicap themselves by breaking wrist backward, which allows rod and line to fall so low behind them that a good forward toss is almost impossible. An extreme backward bend of the wrist will let the line and rod tip bog down in the water behind you. You'll sometimes see tournament casters tip their rods way back, but that's an expert's stunt. The average angler should stop the rod at 1 or 2 o'clock, as shown.

How to pick up line and fly. Beginners often scare fish by yanking a great length of floating line and leader off the water when they're ready to start a new cast. Avoid that commotion by lifting the rod slightly and gently stripping in line with left hand. Photo shows proper rod grip and position for this maneuver—wrist at shoulder height and above the rod grip. This position allows the angler to strike if a fish hits the fly at the last second. Slowly strip in all but 30 or 35 feet of line and leader, then flip the rod up and back to the 1 or 2 o'clock position. That starts the backcast that precedes the new forward throw.

Where's your elbow on backcast? Expert Joe Brooks advocates high elbow position for backcast. Elbow is lowered smoothly as he powers the rod forward. Elbow remains at chest height while line snakes out to drop fly on target.

The wrist, which is held stiff during the backcast, is flexed forward and down when backcast line straightens behind the angler. The forward motion of wrist and forearm is much like the slow, powerful swing you'd use to hammer a nail into a wall at shoulder height. The rod should go forward to about the 10 o'clock position, then hold steady there as fly, leader, and line fall to the water. Left hand controls slack line.

Get above the parallel. Important thing to remember in making the forward throw is not to aim the cast directly at the point where you want the fly to hit. Aim a few feet above that point, so the fly will stop above the target and fall gently to the surface. If the cast is aimed too low it will drive line and leader down into the water. This shortens the cast, sometimes tangles the leader.

Don't break wrist on backcast. In these two photos Brooks is deliberately tipping his wrist in backcast to show how that common fault can get fly casters in trouble. Rod tips so low that line curls down into the water, where it either bogs down completely or drags enough to ruin the forward cast. Line falling very low behind the angler adds extra weight to the rod and upsets the correct balance of rod power and line weight that's required for good fly casting. To make backcast properly, stop rod at 1 or 2 o'clock position with firm wrist. That keeps line high and roughly parallel with the water—in ideal position for forward cast.

Right way to retrieve. For all-around efficiency, Brooks recommends the strip method of retrieving line. As shown in photo at right, Joe does this by extending thumb and finger of his rod hand to form an extra guide for the incoming line as he strips it in with his left hand. Guiding thumb and finger of rod hand can be clamped on line instantly if fish strikes, giving angler positive control of the line while he retrieves it. He is also ready to pick up line for new cast at any moment. Rod should be pointed at the fly, but with tip slightly elevated. In this position, the tip will offer shock-absorbing spring if a fish is hooked.

The roll cast. The easily learned roll cast pays off heavily when the fisherman has some barrier behind him that prevents a normal backcast. In fact, the roll is a quick way to make a new cast under almost any circumstances. To execute this cast, bring the line in until only 25 feet of line and leader remain on the water (*left*). Then move the rod back to the 2 o'clock position and drive it sharply forward and down (*center*). The line rolls up from the surface and curls forward to drop fly and leader as neatly as a conventional forward cast. Photo at right shows rear view of the roll cast just as Brooks is starting to power the rod forward. Note the smooth forward "roll" of rod tip and line. With a weight-forward tapered fly line, it's possible to shoot out as much as 25 feet of slack line in final phase of roll cast, adding that much distance to cast.

Roll cast pickup. First three photos below show how Brooks uses roll to pick up line as it drifts down after an upstream cast. He merely lifts rod to vertical position as line floats near him, then drives rod forward. He can either let the line roll on out for a short upstream cast or—if more distance is needed—the forward-rolling line can be whipped into a backcast just as it straightens, then shot upstream in a routine forward cast.

Last photo shows how swift current can sweep line down to angler faster than he can strip it in, leaving him in awkward position that would be serious handicap in starting a new cast or striking at a fish. This contorted posture can be avoided by making a quick roll cast to pick up the line.

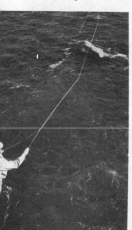

Overhead roll. Cast above is for those small, brush-rimmed pools where a routine roll cast started on the surface would frighten the fish. It's also useful when a strong tail wind defeats a regular backcast. Just pull leader and several feet of line from rod tip and false cast into air with ordinary roll-cast motion, but rotate your wrist to keep airborne line rolling while you strip more line off the reel and feed it through the guides. With 25 or 30 feet of line rolling like a hoop to your right, make the forward cast and follow through, driving the rod well down. This variation of the basic roll is ideal for high wind or tight quarters because the line starts in the air close to you and stays there until you're ready to deliver the fly.

Backhand roll cast. Backhand version of ordinary roll cast (photo at right) is useful when angler's wading along a shoreline that has trees or brush crowding his right arm. This position gives unobstructed casting room over water.

The horizontal cast. Horizontal cast is another brush-dodger, one that's particularly useful when angler is wading a stream that has trees leaning low over the water from both banks. Fish in such streams often feed close to shore, under the low roof of tree limbs. The angler's problem is to get a backcast beneath the overhanging foliage behind him and then drive his forward cast under the foliage that forms a canopy over the rising fish. Horizontal cast, made by holding the rod low and parallel with the water, will get a fly under such obstacles. Line speed is the main trick in this cast. Considerable velocity is needed to keep the low-flying line from sagging into the water. Otherwise the cast is much the same as an overhead throw.

High bank roll cast. Many times the angler finds himself on a high bank with trees close behind him blocking the backcast. This calls for a variation of the roll cast.

Holding the rod out over the high bank, switch out a working length of line and start a routine roll cast by bringing the rod back to 2 o'clock and then driving it forward. The high-bank variation comes as the rod goes forward. Rod tip must be driven farther down than usual to straighten line.

The double haul. This strategy was originated by tournament casters who used it to set new distance records. It's the system that makes long tosses easy. Key to the double haul is that it adds the power of the left hand to the force exerted by the rod hand. Start by grabbing line near rod grip with left hand and pulling down sharply (*left*) as line is picked up for backcast. As line sails back (*center*) left hand is raised to head level to let several feet of line feed into the backcast. Then left hand pulls line forcefully (*right*) as forward cast is started. As forward cast straightens, left hand releases line to let slack shoot through guides and add distance to the forward cast.

Casting over obstruction. You'll often get in a situation where a log or a slab of partially submerged rock separates you from a good fish rising in a pool beyond. Just toss a regular forward cast over the obstruction, aiming a bit high to let the fly fall gently. Line will drape smoothly over the obstruction as shown in photo at left. When fish hits (*right*) strike with rod high. That tightens line, lifts slack off the obstruction. While playing fish, steer him around the obstacle.

The "S" cast. This cast drops the line on moving water in curves that will straighten slowly. That gives the fly a long, natural float, whereas a straighter line on the surface would quickly transmit the motion of the current to the fly, dragging it over the water in a way that spooks fish. There are two good ways to make the "S" cast. One is to shoot the forward cast a bit harder than needed, then stop it abruptly when it's above the target. Other is to wiggle the rod tip from side to side as the line shoots forward.

Baitcasting

Baitcasting is a method of fishing distinguished by the use of a revolving-spool reel. Originally intended by its 19th-century creators as a means of casting live baitfish, baitcasting tackle today is used to present all sorts of offerings — from worms and minnows to spoons and huge jointed plugs — to gamefish in both fresh and salt water. This method is also known as plugcasting.

Before the advent of spinning gear, baitcasting was the universally accepted tackle for presenting bait or lure. Even today many anglers, especially those who grew up with a baitcasting outfit in their hands, prefer this method, even though the revolving-spool reel is more difficult to use than fixed-spool spinning and spincasting reels.

The confirmed baitcaster feels that his gear gives him more sensitive contact with what is going on at the end of his line. He feels that he can manipulate a lure better on baitcasting gear and have better control over a hooked fish. Most fishermen agree that when the quarry is big, strong fish such as muskies, northern pike, and the tackle-straining largemouth bass found in the southern states, a baitcasting outfit gets the nod over spinning or spincasting tackle.

Baitcasting tackle is often preferred for trolling, too, for the revolving-spool reel makes it easy to pay out line behind the moving boat, and the rod has enough backbone to handle the big water-resistant lures used in many forms of trolling.

The Reel

The reel is by far the most important part of a baitcasting outfit, and the budding baitcaster would do well to buy the best reel he can afford.

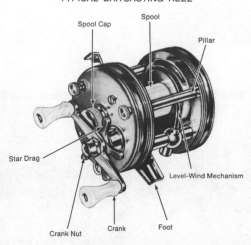

TYPICAL BAITCASTING REEL

Spool Cap
Spool
Pillar
Star Drag
Level-Wind Mechanism
Crank Nut
Crank
Foot

The main distinguishing feature of baitcasting reels is that the spool revolves when line is cast out or reeled in, while in spinning and spincasting reels the spool remains stationary.

Baitcasting reels have a relatively wide, shallow spool, and most have multiplying gears that cause the spool to revolve several times (usually four) for each complete turn of the reel handle. There is also some kind of drag mechanism, which is helpful in fighting big fish. These range from a simple click mechanism to a screw-down nut to a star drag. Some reels have what is called a cub drag, which is adjusted by turning six screws on the base of the handle.

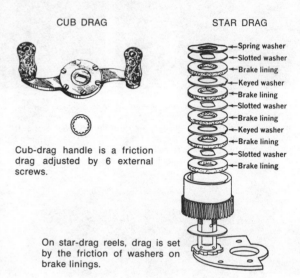

CUB DRAG

STAR DRAG

← Spring washer
← Slotted washer
← Brake lining
← Keyed washer
← Brake lining
← Slotted washer
← Brake lining
← Keyed washer
← Brake lining
← Slotted washer
← Brake lining

Cub-drag handle is a friction drag adjusted by 6 external screws.

On star-drag reels, drag is set by the friction of washers on brake linings.

Almost all of today's good baitcasting reels have an important device called a level-wind. It usually takes the form of a U-shaped loop of heavy wire attached to a base that travels from one side of the spool to the other by means of a wormlike gear. The device permits line to be wound evenly on the spool and thus is a big help in preventing backlashes, which are often caused by line "lumping up" on the spool. A backlash occurs when the speed of the revolving spool is faster than that of the outgoing line, resulting in a "bird's nest," or a tangle of line on the spool.

More and more baitcasting reels are being made with anti-backlash devices. These employ either centrifugal force or pressure on the spool axle or flange to slow down the spool during a cast. However, though antibacklash devices are helpful, the user of a baitcasting reel must still learn to apply thumb pressure to the spool if he is to prevent backlashes under all conditions. Only experience can teach him how much thumb pressure is needed under any given set of circumstances.

A modern development in baitcasting is the free-spool reel. Without this feature, the cast lure not only pulls out line and turns the spool but also turns the gears, the level-wind, and the reel handle. All those moving parts tend to shorten the cast. But in the free-spool reel, most of the gearing is disconnected from the spool before a cast is made, and only the spool (and sometimes the level-wind) turns.

That makes it easier to start and stop the turning of the spool and so permits the use of lighter lures than can be cast with a standard bait-casting reel. Longer casts are also possible. A turn of the handle re-engages the gears of the free-spool reel so that the retrieve can be made.

Until recently, free-spool reels usually were heavier than standard models and required more skill and thumb control to cast without backlashes. Now, however, free-spool reels are available in light, easy-handling models as well.

Lew Childre BB-1 Speed Spool (*right*) has spherical counter-balance weights to improve cast control, maintaining smooth acceleration and thus reducing overruns and backlash. BB-2 is larger version with twice the line capacity (250 yards of 17-pound test) and double counterbalance system; it's designed for steelhead, salmon, muskies, tarpon, and other powerful gamefish.

Daiwa Procaster SM-2 has narrow, high-speed spool, star drag, level-wind guide shielded by sideplate to prevent pinching the hand during retrieve, oversized crank knobs, advanced spool brake to minimize backlashes, and very fast retrieve ratio—5.2 to 1.

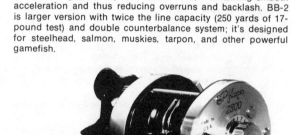

Pflueger 2800 features Hydro-Thumb anti-backlash control, power handle, free spool, star drag, stainless-steel pawl and shaft, anodized aluminum frame, and centrifugal drag adjustment to accommodate a wide range of lure weights. It holds 280 yards of 19-pound-test, 200 yards of 15-pound, or 135 yards of 20-pound line.

Shakespeare President II features free spool, star drag, 5 to 1 gear ratio, and two cast controls. Centrifugal braking system prevents backlash during beginning of the cast, when spool rotates fastest, and Hydro-Film control system slows spool near the end of the cast. Level wind operates both during cast and retrieve.

Ryobi AD-6000, compact and contoured for a palming retrieve, has oversized power knobs, retrieve ratio of 4.6 to 1, and single-piece die-cast frame for close tolerances and light weight. Reel weighs 8½ ounces, holds 250 yards of 12-pound mono or 140 yards of 20-pound mono, and has star drag and free spool.

Garcia Ambassadeur 5600CA has a palming sideplate so that reel can be cradled in hand for greater casting control and hook-setting power. Also features ThumBar free-spool control, star drag, silent level wind, anti-backlash brakes, 4.7 to 1 gear ratio, and takedown without tools.

The Rod

Most baitcasting rods are now made of fiberglass, or graphite, or a composite material called Kevlar, or a very light metallic filament called boron—or a combination of these substances. Such materials—especially graphite, Kevlar, and boron—boast light weight, strength, and sensitivity in desirable proportions, though arguments persist as to which is best for most fishing (or for a given kind of fishing). For example, boron is more sensitive than graphite to such impulses as the tug of a biting fish, but pure boron is said to be impractical so Browning's Silaflex boron rods blend this filament with graphite. Rods containing the blend are claimed to be 120 percent more sensitive than comparable fiberglass rods, 19 percent more sensitive than graphite, and over 20 percent stronger than either.

Rod lengths range from about 4 to more than 7 feet. Some, obviously, are most suitable for specific purposes. The most popular length—because it works well for many kinds of fishing—is 5½ feet. Manufacturers generally classify their rods according to their action, which refers to the lure weights that a rod handles efficiently. Generally, Extra-Light rods can handle lures weighing ¼ ounce or less. Light rods can handle ¼ to ½ ounce. Medium rods are better at handling ⅝ to ¾ ounce, and heavy rods are for ¾ ounce and more.

Baitcasting rods have either a straight handle or an offset handle. The offset-handle type has a depressed reel seat and is recommended for beginners because it places the reel at an above-the-rod level that is most comfortable for thumbing the spool. There is also a double-offset handle, in which the reel seat is depressed and the butt grip is canted downward. This type makes accurate casts almost as simple as pointing your finger.

Other features of baitcasting rods are a finger hook on the underside of the reel seat and various reel-holding devices, including a spring-loaded locking mechanism and a screw-lock.

Baitcasting rods are of one- or two-piece construction. Some have ferrules about midway up the rod, while others have only a detachable handle.

In heavier baitcasting rods, there are two types—the popping rod and the muskie rod. Popping rods have a straight handle, unusually long butt section, a foregrip usually made of cork, and a rubber butt cap. Well suited for heavy freshwater and light saltwater use, popping rods can handle an extensive range of lure weights for various species of fish.

Muskie rods generally have an offset or double-offset handle, cork foregrip, long butt section, and the backbone needed to handle that toothy terror of the North, the muskellunge. The most popular lengths are 5 and 5½ feet, and they can handle lures ranging in weight from ¾ ounce to 3 ounces, with a few of these rods capable of handling monster plugs up to 6 ounces.

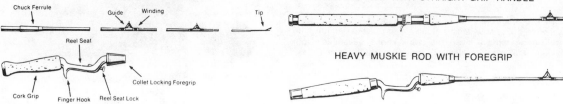

TYPICAL BAITCASTING ROD

Chuck Ferrule · Guide · Winding · Tip · Reel Seat · Collet Locking Foregrip · Cork Grip · Finger Hook · Reel Seat Lock

POPPING ROD WITH STRAIGHT-GRIP HANDLE

HEAVY MUSKIE ROD WITH FOREGRIP

HOW TO MATCH UP BAITCASTING TACKLE

This chart is meant only as a general guide aimed at helping the fisherman put together, in proper balance, the basic elements of a baitcasting outfit. Specific conditions—and the angler's ability and personal preferences—must also be considered when buying a fishing outfit of any kind.

SPECIES OF FISH	REEL	ROD LENGTH (Ft.)	LINES (Lb. Test)	LURE WEIGHTS (Ounces)
Panfish; small bass, pickerel, trout	Multiplying-gear with level-wind	6 to 6½ (Extra-light action)	6 to 8	⅛ to ¼
Bass, pickerel, walleye, small pike, trout	Multiplying-gear with level-wind	5½ to 6½ (Light action)	6 to 12	¼ to ½
Large bass, walleyes, pike, lake trout, muskie, striped bass	Multiplying-gear with stardrag	5 to 6 (Medium action)	10 to 20	⅝ to ¾
Muskie, steelheads, lake trout, salmon, striped bass, bluefish, tarpon, snook	Multiplying-gear with star drag	4½ to 7 (Heavy action)	18 to 25	¾ and up

HOW TO PLUG CAST
by Joe Brooks

The grip. Expert Charlie Fox advocates a relaxed and natural grip. Thumb on the reel spool controls the line. The reel is tipped so that spool is almost vertical with the handles up. This cuts down spool friction.

Basic forward cast. With thumb holding reel spool to prevent premature turning, sight toward target, swing rod up and back with smooth, forceful motion.

Alternate spincast reel. The fixed-spool or spincasting reel will do about same job as revolving-spool bait reels. Mechanically, this reel is much like a spinning reel, except that it has push-button line control. Spincast reels are very good when used with monofilament line to cast light lures. They're easier to master than revolving-spool bait reels. Many beginners like them.

Never taking his eyes off the target, Fox lets rod tip whip down to horizontal position behind him, then starts to drive it forward with speed, power.

Thumb pressure that has been used to hold the reel spool is released as rod points toward the target. Very light thumbing will control the lure's flight.

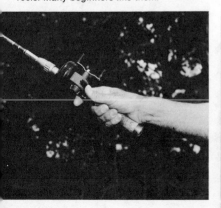

Retrieve. Proper moves in retrieve are shown in photo at left, where lure has just hit water, and three photos below. After lure hits, Fox quickly moves rod to left hand, fingers of his left hand gripping line ahead of reel to clean and control line better as he reels it back onto spool with right hand. Note that he raises rod to about 45° and then he presses butt against body as he reels in. This keeps outfit steady and ready for quick strike.

Cast into the wind. Even with a heavy lure, it takes extra power to cast into a strong wind. Fox makes his backswing with rod angled off to his right, which will keep the rod tip lower than usual throughout casting motion. On forward motion, he releases the reel spool to let line go out when rod is parallel with water, follows through until rod tip is almost in water.

Backhand cast. The backhand cast is used to get out lure when some obstacle behind angler blocks a routine backswing. Fox starts the cast as shown in photo at left. Strong snap of wrist brings rod forward. Note that reel is always in handle-up position as line is released. Reel spool spins better that way.

Sidearm cast. The sidearm cast shown in three photos above is a powerful toss that is good for long-range work and casts into wind. It saves the day when overhead foliage prevents a vertical backswing for conventional forward cast. The casting motions follow the one, two, three pattern: sight at target, swing rod back, whip it forward. The casting arm remains straight and points at the target until the lure is well on its way.

Silent-dive cast. Main purpose of the silent-dive cast is to drop the lure with a light splat, rather than a heavy splash. Small splat like minnow surfacing may attract fish that would be spooked by loud splash. Forward cast is halted in air above target by reel thumbing and haul-back on rod. Braked lure hits softly.

Flip cast. Ever find yourself in a spot where there seems to be no room for any kind of cast? Flip cast shown above can be made where angler's brushed in on both sides and has branches above him. Rod tip is dipped sharply toward angler's feet, snapped up to aim at target as thumb releases reel spool.

Underhand lob. This cast is a short-range toss with a dual purpose: it will work where there's little room for a backcast, and it drops lure gently. The rod tip is kept below parallel during backswing. Forward swing is aimed upward to loft lure. Soft, underpowered lob is good for small pockets of water.

Spincasting

Spincasting is a method of fishing that, in effect, combines a "pushbutton"-type spinning reel with a baitcasting-type rod. This tackle efficiently handles lures and baits of average weight—say, ¼-ounce to ¾-ounce. With lighter or heavier lures, its efficiency falls off sharply. Spincasting is ideal for newcomers to fishing, for it is the easiest casting method to learn and is the ticket for lots of trouble-free sport.

The Reel

Spincasting reels, like spinning reels, operate on the fixed-spool principle—that is, the weight of the lure or bait being cast uncoils line from the stationary spool. Most spincasting reels are of the closed-face type, the spool and gearing being enclosed in a cone-shaped hood.

The major factor distinguishing the spincasting reel from the spinning reel is that spincasting action is controlled by a thumb-activated "trigger" (a pushbutton or a lever) mounted either on the reel or on the butt of the rod. In operation, the spincaster holds his thumb down on the trig-ger until the rod is about halfway through the forward-cast motion. He then releases thumb pressure on the trigger, which frees the line and feeds it through a small hole in the center of the cone, sending the lure on its way.

Spincasting reels have various kinds of adjustable drag mechanisms. In one kind, the drag is set by rotating the cone that surrounds the spool. Other reels have star drags such as those found on baitcasting reels. The drag in still other reels is activated by turning the reel handle.

There are two kinds of spincasting reels, those mounted atop the rod and those mounted below it.

Most spincasting reels are of the top-mounted type and are designed for rods having an offset reel seat. They can be mounted on straight-grip rods, but this combination is uncomfortable to use since the caster must reach up with his thumb to activate the reel trigger.

Below-the-rod spincasting reels are a quite recent development. They look much like the standard semiclosed-face (also called semi-open-face) spinning reels. However, instead of the spinning reel's internal line-pickup pin, these spincasting reels (actually sold as rod-and-reel combinations) have a line-controlling pushbutton built into the rod butt.

Spincast reels are ideal for night fishing because of their trouble-free operation. However, besides the fact that they can handle a rather limited range of lure weights, if very light line is used on these reels the line has a tendency to foul in the housing.

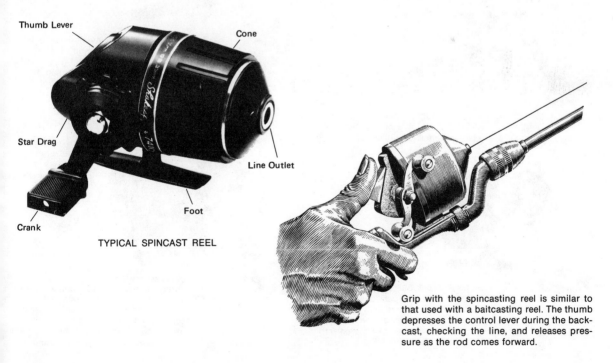

Thumb Lever

Cone

Star Drag

Line Outlet

Crank

Foot

TYPICAL SPINCAST REEL

Grip with the spincasting reel is similar to that used with a baitcasting reel. The thumb depresses the control lever during the backcast, checking the line, and releases pressure as the rod comes forward.

Johnson Sprite 200 weighs only 4 ounces, comes spooled with 395 feet of 4-pound-test mono, and has 5.16 to 1 gear ratio, taking in over 20 inches of line with every crank turn. Other features include fall-away ceramic pick-up pin, ceramic line guide, and multiple-disc drag.

Daiwa Silvercast Series includes medium-light, medium, and medium-heavy spincasting reels for freshwater. All have 4.1 to 1 gear ratio, anti-reverse, right- or left-handed retrieve, and calibrated dial-drag. Medium-heavy model, shown here, weighs 9.2 ounces and holds 160 yards of 8-pound mono.

Martin 220 has star drag, anti-reverse click, stationary spool to prevent line twist, and multi-point pick-up. Comes with 80 yards of 6-pound monofilament. Weight is 6 ounces.

Garcia GK-100 Minireel weighs 4.3 ounces, has retrieve ratio of 4.2 to 1, and features dial-control drag and helical gears. Comes spooled with 100 yards of 4-pound-test monofilament.

Berkley Model 305 spincasting reel has star drag, die-cast gear system, and aluminum shroud with hardened ring. Weight is 8 ounces, retrieve ratio is 3 to 1, and reel comes spooled with 125 yards of 8-pound mono.

Shakespeare Model 7400 has star drag, chrome line guide, high-impact housing, aluminum frame, permanent anti-reverse, and 3 to 1 gear ratio. Comes spooled with 100 yards of 8-pound-test mono. Designed to handle 1/8- to 3/8-ounce lures, it weighs 6.7 ounces.

Martin Model 500 has star drag, dimple brake to eliminate line squeeze, 8-point pick-up, takedown without tools, and Monocon contoured stationary spool to prevent twist and make line peel off smoothly on long casts. Comes with 100 yards of 8-pound mono. Weighs 9 ounces.

Daiwa Goldcast II employs calibrated-dial drag and oscillating spool that cross-wraps line to facilitate longer casts with fewer line jams. Revolving line-guide pin reduces line twist. Gear ratio is 4.1 to 1, and crank converts for right- or left-handed retrieve.

The Rod

Spincasting rods are basically the same as those designed for baitcasting, but there are a few differences. In general, spincasting rods average a bit longer (most popular lengths are 6 and 6½ feet) than baitcasting rods. They have flexible, more-responsive tips, and the guides are usually of the larger spinning-rod type. They may have both a detachable handle and a ferrule-jointed upper section.

TYPICAL SPINCAST ROD

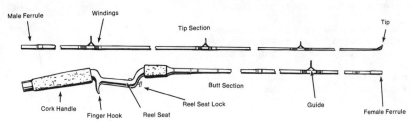

HOW TO MATCH UP SPINCASTING TACKLE

This chart is meant only as a general guide aimed at helping the fisherman put together, in proper balance, the basic elements of a spincasting outfit tailored for fish of a particular weight category. Specific conditions—and the angler's ability and personal preferences—must also be considered when buying a fishing outfit of any kind.

SPECIES OF FISH	REEL	ROD LENGTH (Ft.)	LINES (Lb. Test)	LURE WEIGHTS (Ounces)
Panfish, small trout and bass, pickerel	Light-weight	6½ to 7 (Light action)	4 to 8	⅛ to ⅜
Trout, bass, pickerel, pike, landlocks, walleye	Medium weight	6 to 7 (Medium action)	6 to 12	⅜ to ⅝
Pike, lake trout, steelhead, muskie, salmon, striped bass, snook, bonefish	Heavy, with star drag	6 to 6½ (Medium-heavy action)	10 to 15	½ to ¾

Conventional Tackle for Saltwater Trolling and Casting

A host of saltwater gamefish—from half-pound snapper bluefish to 40-pound yellowtails to bluefin tuna weighing nearly half a ton—draw millions of fishermen to the briny each year. They stand in crashing surf and on jetties and piers, and they sail for deeper water aboard boats of almost every description.

Because of the great difference in weights of saltwater fish, it is important for the fisherman to be armed with balanced tackle that is suited for the particular quarry he is after. Just as the freshwater muskie angler wouldn't use bluegill tackle, the man who's trolling for, say, blue marlin wouldn't use a jetty outfit designed for striped bass.

Balanced tackle—in which rod, reel, line, and other items are all in reasonable proportion to one another—is important for a number of reasons.

For one, a properly balanced outfit—for example, a 9-foot surf rod with squidding reel and 25-pound-test line—is a joy to use. Conversely, if you substituted a 5-foot boat rod for the 9-footer in the above outfit and tried to cast, you would soon be turning the air blue. Hooking and playing a fish is also easier and more effective with properly balanced gear.

There is still another reason for using balanced tackle. Every fisherman, beginner and expert alike, who tosses or trolls lures or bait in the salt has a chance to sink a hook into a record-size gamefish. The rules of the International Game Fish Association, keeper of the official records of marine gamefish, require that any fish submitted for a record be caught on tackle that is "in reasonable proportion . . . to the line size."

Let's take a detailed look at the various kinds of conventional salt-water gear and how to match up the component parts.

Trolling Reels

Trolling is the method of fishing in which a lure or bait is pulled along behind a moving boat. It is also a method in which the reel is of paramount importance.

Saltwater trolling reels are designated by a simple and yet not completely reliable numbering system. This system employs a number followed by a diagonal (/) and then the letter "O", which merely stands for "ocean." The numbers run from 1 to 16, with each one representing the line capacity of the reel. The higher the number, the larger the reel's line capacity.

It should be noted, however, that these numbers are not standardized—that is, one manufacturer's 4/0 trolling reel may have a smaller capacity than another maker's 4/0. A prospective reel buyer would do well to check manufacturer's catalogs to make sure of a reel's line capacity.

Trolling reels are the heavyweights among saltwater reels. Weighing from 18 ounces (for the 1/0 size) up to nearly 11 pounds (for the 16/0), they are designed primarily for handling the largest of gamefish (sailfish, marlin, bluefin tuna, swordfish) but are also effective for bluefish, stripers, channel bass, albacore, dolphin, and the like.

These reels have no casting features (such as antibacklash devices), since their sole function is trolling. Spools are smooth-running, usually operating on ball bearings. The reels are ruggedly built and, of course, corrosion resistant. Unique features include lugs on the upper part of the side plate for attachment of a big-game fishing harness worn by the fisherman, a U-shaped clamp for more secure union of rod and reel, and, in the largest reels, a lug-and-brace arrangement for extra rigidity.

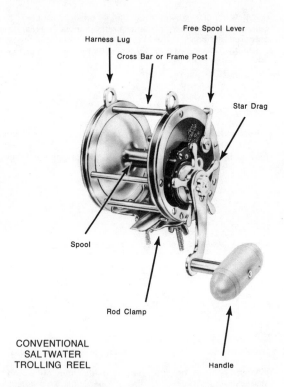

Harness Lug
Cross Bar or Frame Post
Free Spool Lever
Star Drag
Spool
Rod Clamp
Handle

CONVENTIONAL
SALTWATER
TROLLING REEL

By far the most important feature on a trolling reel is the drag. If a reel is to handle the sizzling runs and line-testing leaps of fish weighing hundreds of pounds, its drag must operate smoothly at all times. And the drag must not overheat or it may bind, causing the line to break.

In most reels the drag is of the star type and consists of a series of alternating metal and composition (or leather) washers. In more expensive trolling reels the drag is an asbestos-composition disc that applies pressure directly to the reel spool.

Some quite expensive trolling reels have not one but two drag controls. One is a knob-operated device that lets you preset drag tension to a point below the breaking strength of the line being used. The other is a lever, mounted on the sideplate, that has a number of positions and permits a wide range of drag settings, from very light up to the safe maximum for the line in use. This lever, when backed off all the way, throws the reel into free-spool.

Trolling-reel spools are made of metal, usually either machined bronze or anodized aluminum, and range in width from $1^5/_8$ inches (for the 1/0 size) to 5 inches (for the 16/0).

Some trolling reels are designed especially for wire and lead-core lines. They have narrow but deep spools and extra-strong gearing.

Other features of trolling reels include free-spool lever mounted on the sideplate, a single oversize handle grip, and gear ratios ranging from 1.6:1 to $3^1/_2$:1.

TROLLING REELS AND LINE CAPACITIES (In Yards)

REELS	LINES	1/0	2/0	3/0	4/0	6/0	9/0	10/0	12/0	14/0	16/0
20-lb. mono-filament		350	425								
30-lb. mono-filament		200	275	375							
36-lb. mono-filament					350	600					
45-lb. mono-filament					275	500					
54-lb. mono-filament					200	400					
72-lb. mono-filament						350	500	850			
90-lb. mono-filament							400	600	800	1100	1400
108-lb. mono-filament							300	500	600	1000	1200
20-lb. Dacron		225									
30-lb. Dacron		200	275	350	450						
50-lb. Dacron				200	250	400					
80-lb. Dacron					150	250	400	650	800	1050	1250
130-lb. Dacron							300	450	550	850	1000

Trolling Rods

Big-game trolling rods have the strength and fittings to withstand the power runs and magnificent leaps of such heavyweights as marlin, sailfish, and giant tuna. The great majority of these rods are of fiberglass and graphite construction, though a few bamboo models are still being used.

Almost all blue-water rods have a butt section and a tip section—that is, they seldom have ferrules fitted midway along the "working length" of the rod. In most rods the tip section is about 5 feet long, while butt lengths vary from 14 to 27 inches, depending on the weight of the tip. Tip sections are usually designated by weight, ranging from about 3 ounces to as heavy as 40 ounces, depending on the line being used and the fish being sought.

Trolling rods are rated according to the line-strength classes of the International Game Fish Association. The eight I.G.F.A. classes are: 6-pound line, 12-pound (line testing, when wet, up to and including 12 pounds), 20-pound (line testing, when wet, more than 12 pounds and up to and including 20 pounds), 30-pound (line testing, when wet,

more than 20 pounds and up to and including 30 pounds); 50-pound, 80-pound, 130-pound, and 180-pound.

No rod used in catching a fish submitted for an I.G.F.A. record can have a tip length of less than 5 feet. In the 12, 20, and 30-pound classes, a rod's butt length can be no more than 18 inches. In the 50- and 80-pound classes, butt length can be no more than 22 inches. In the 130 and 180-pound classes, butt length can be no more than 27 inches.

For complete I.G.F.A. rules and regulations, see the section on Fishing for the Record Books.

The fittings on trolling rods include strong, high-quality guides. The first guide above the reel (called the stripping guide) and the tip guide are of the roller type (either single-roller or double-roller). The middle guides, usually numbering four or five, are of the ring type and are made either of heavily chromed stainless steel or of tungsten carbide (carboloy), which is the most durable material. In some rods all of the guides are rollers. Most roller guides have self-lubricating bearings that can be disassembled for cleaning.

Other features of trolling rods include extra-strong, locking reel seats, and gimbal fittings in the end of the butt that enable the rod to be fitted into a socket on a boat's fighting chair or into a belt harness worn by the fisherman.

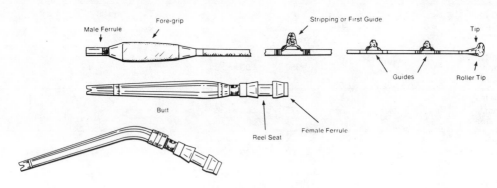

Male Ferrule · Fore-grip · Stripping or First Guide · Tip · Guides · Roller Tip · Butt · Reel Seat · Female Ferrule

SALTWATER TROLLING ROD

HOW TO MATCH UP OFFSHORE TROLLING TACKLE

This chart is meant only as a general guide aimed at helping the fisherman put together, in proper balance, the basic elements of a blue-water trolling outfit tailored for fish of a particular weight category. Specific conditions—and the angler's ability and personal preferences—must also be considered when buying a fishing outfit of any kind.

SPECIES OF FISH	REEL	ROD (Tip-Section Weight, in oz.)	LINE (Lb. Test)
Striped bass, dolphin, wahoo, yellowtail, kingfish, salmon, barracuda, tarpon, school tuna	1/0 to 3/0	3 to 9	12 to 30
Atlantic sailfish, Pacific sailfish, white marlin	3/0 to 6/0	6 to 18	30 to 50
Striped marlin	4/0 to 9/0	6 to 20	30 to 80
Black marlin, blue marlin, swordfish	6/0 to 14/0	9 to 30	30 to 130
Giant bluefin tuna	9/0 to 16/0	16 to 30	50 to 130

Casting and Boat Reels

Conventional (revolving-spool) reels in this category are widely used by saltwater fishermen who cast lures and baits from piers, bridges, jetties, and in the surf, and by sinker-bouncers (bottom fishermen) in boats. Actually an outgrowth and refinement of freshwater baitcasting reels, these reels fill the gap between those freshwater models and big-game trolling reels.

Many surf and jetty casters, especially those who are after big fish, prefer a conventional reel (and rod) over a spinning outfit because the conventional rig is better able to handle heavy lures and sinkers. And a vast majority of bottom fishermen lean toward the revolving-spool reel.

Conventional reels designed for casting, often called squidding reels, have wide, light spools (a heavy spool makes casting difficult) of either metal or plastic (metal is preferred for most uses), and gear ratios ranging from 2:1 to 4½:1. Weights range from about 12 to 22 ounces. In most models the drag is of the star type and there is a free-spool lever mounted on the side plate. Some of these reels have level-wind mechanisms.

Line capacities range from about 250 yards of 12-pound-test monofilament to 350 yards of 36-pound-test mono. For most surf, jetty, and pier situations, 250 yards of line is sufficient.

A few of these reels have a mechanical brake or a thumbing device to help prevent the spool from overrunning during a cast and causing a backlash. In most models, however, as in freshwater baitcasting reels, thumb pressure against the spool is required to control the cast.

Conventional reels designed for deep-sea bottom fishing are quite similar to the casting models but are somewhat heavier and have narrower, deeper spools. They also have larger line capacities and can take heavier lines.

SALTWATER CASTING
(SQUIDDING) REEL

LIGHT SALTWATER
CASTING REELS

Casting and Boat Rods

In choosing a conventional casting rod, more so than with boat (bottom-fishing) rods, the type of fishing to be done and the fish being sought are critical factors. For casting in the surf, for example, the rod must be long enough so that the fisherman can make lengthy casts and hold the line above the breakers. A rod for jetty use, on the other hand, need not be so long. And if you'll be fishing mainly from piers and bridges, you'll need a rod with enough backbone to lift hefty fish from the water and up over the rail.

However, the beginning fisherman can get a casting rod that will handle most of the situations he'll be facing. A good choice would be one that is 8½ to 9 feet in overall length, of tubular fiberglass (rather than solid fiberglass), and has a rather stiff tip. The stiff tip of a conventional rod lets the angler use a wide range of lure weights and enables him to have more control over big fish.

Conventional casting rods are available in lengths from about 8 to 11½ feet and even longer. A few split-bamboo models are still kicking around the beaches, but most are

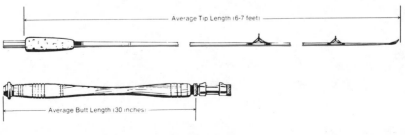

SURFCASTING ROD

now made of fiberglass, graphite, Kevlar, or a combination thereof. Recent developments in graphite show that rods of this material can carry an exceptional wide range of lure weights. In tests, weights of 18 ounces were cast with graphite rods. A majority of these rods are of two-piece construction, breaking either at the upper part of the butt or about midway up the working length of the rod.

These rods are distinguished by the number and arrangement of their guides. In most models, there are only three or four guides, including the tip guide, and all are located in the upper half of the tip section. Why this arrangement? Because these rods are stiffer than most others, fewer guides are required to distribute the strain along the length of the rod. The guides are bunched near the tip because that's where most of the bend occurs when a fish is being played.

Conventional casting rods have sturdy salt-resistant reel seats, usually of anodized aluminum, and butts made of hickory, other sturdy woods, or cork.

Boat, or bottom-fishing, rods, as their name implies, are designed for noncasting use aboard boats—party boats, charter craft, and private boats. They are also used on piers and bridges, in situations in which lure or bait is simply dropped down to the water.

Boat rods are considerably shorter than casting rods, running from about 4½ to 6½ feet in overall length, with a good average length being about 5½ feet. Their shortness makes them highly maneuverable, a factor of more than a little importance aboard a crowded party boat, and makes it easier to handle, say, a 30-pound cod while trying to remain upright on a pitching deck.

As with most other modern rods, boat rods are mostly of fiberglass construction with a growing number of graphite models available. Most are two-piece, with tip section and detachable butt. The number of guides on a boat rod depends on length, but there are seldom more than five. Some of these rods, designed for large fish, have a roller tip. Other boat-rod features are similar to those of casting rods.

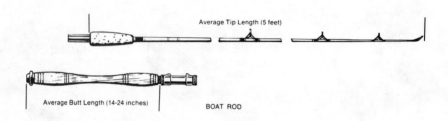

Average Tip Length (5 feet)

Average Butt Length (14-24 inches)

BOAT ROD

HOW TO MATCH UP CONVENTIONAL SALTWATER CASTING TACKLE

This chart is meant only as a general guide aimed at helping the fisherman put together, in proper balance, the basic elements of a salt water casting outfit tailored for fish of a particular weight category. Specific conditions—and the angler's ability and personal preferences—must also be considered when buying a fishing outfit of any kind.

SPECIES OF FISH	REEL	ROD TYPE & LENGTH (In Feet)	LINES (Lb. Test)	LURE WEIGHTS (Ounces)
Small stripers, bluefish, weakfish, snook, bonefish, redfish, salmon, pompano, jacks	Light (with star drag)	Popping 6 to 7	8 to 15	½ to 1
Stripers, big bluefish, school tuna, albacore, bonito, salmon, dolphin, wahoo	Medium	Medium-action 6½ to 8	12 to 30	¾ to 3
Channel bass, black drum, tarpon, dolphin, big kingfish, sharks	Heavy	Heavy-action 7 to 8½	18 to 50	1½ to 5
Surf species (bluefish, stripers, drum, channel bass, etc.)	Squidding (Surf-casting)	Surf 8 to 11½	18 to 45	1½ to 6

Garcia Mitchell 624 Trolling Reel employs indexed star drag, oversized bronze main gear and bushings, and heavily chromed reinforcing rings on sideplates. Capacity is 500 yards of 20-pound mono. Also suitable for wire-line trolling.

Penn International 80-10/0 has lever-action drag control and strike set stop to permit instant setting of drag at proper strike position. Drag system utilizes full-floating disc design. Also features rugged harness lugs and one-piece solid brass rod clamps.

Penn Master Mariner 349HC, trolling (narrow spool for wire or lead-core line), with star drag, narrow spool, and two-lever control. Weight: 37 ounces. Line capacities: 350 yards of 30-pound-test Dacron, 200 yards of 50-pound-test Dacron.

Daiwa Sealine Series includes two wide-spool casting and jigging offshore reels (Models 350H and 450H) plus two with stainless-steel spools (300HW and 400HW for wire-line trolling.) All feature oversized gears, six-element disc drag, and dual-range handle adjustable to two lengths for best leverage in different types of fishing.

Garcia Ambassadeur 10,000CA is a light-tackle big-game reel for boat and surf fishing. Gear ratio is 4.2 to 1, and it automatically shifts to lower gear—2.5 to 1—when extra power is needed. Has centrifugal anti-backlash brake and spool-tension control. Holds 275 yards of 30-pound-test monofilament.

Ryobi Adventure 101 is a 6/0 reel with level wind, anti-backlash, one-piece frame and posts, star drag, major components of stainless steel, two ball bearings, and gear ratio of 2.3 to 1. Holds 550 yards of 30-pound-test Dacron line.

HOW TO SURF CAST
by Joe Brooks

Casting Reel

Fit of rod and reel. Expert Hal Lyman shows how the butt of a surf rod should just reach the caster's armpit when held with thumb on reel spool. A shorter butt section will lack leverage to handle the long rod, while too-long butt adds needless weight. Proper butt length allows the comfortable and powerful two-handed grip shown in second photo at left. Thumb must be in easy reach of the reel spool for casts with this type of reel, for it's thumb pressure on spool that regulates outgoing line.

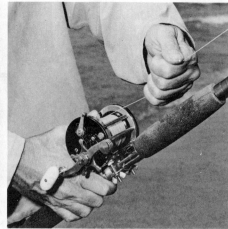

Advance adjustments. Time to set star drag properly is before cast is made (*left*). That way drag is right if fish hits the lure the instant it touches the water. Lyman tests the drag adjustment by pulling line from the reel (*right*). Drag should be tight enough to set the hook in a striking fish but at the same time loose enough to feed out line to a big fish making a determined run. There's no set rule on good drag adjustment. Use your judgment.

Flip to free spool. Once drag is set, caster holds reel spool with one thumb and uses other to flip free-spool lever, which will let spool spin freely during cast. Some levers move forward, some back. It depends on the design of reel you use. This is last mechanical adjustment needed. See top of the next page for proper grip.

Thumbing the spool. Angler's thumb is placed on the reel spool with firm pressure at start of cast to hold spool during back sweep of the casting motion. As rod is powered forward, thumb is lifted to let the weight of lure or sinker take out line. Very light thumbing as line goes out will prevent backlash. Most common thumbing position is shown in the photo at left. A good alternate position is seen in center photo, where thumb is pressed against the side of the reel spool instead of on the line-covered spool core. Photo at right shows how sudden thumb pressure can stop lure's flight. Note how line jumps.

Starting the cast. Since hooks on heavy lure can be dangerous, first move should always be a look behind you to be sure backswing won't hook another angler. Then start cast from stance Lyman demonstrates in left photo. Note that the handle of the reel is down, the dangling lure just above sand as rod is held parallel to beach. Photo at right shows details of grip and reel position as surf caster prepares to sail his bait or lure far out over the ocean breakers.

The casting motion. Panel of photos starting at far left below shows smooth, powerful cast from beginning to end. With his feet set in wide stance for balance, Lyman pulls rod butt powerfully with left hand, pushes at grip behind reel with his right hand. Handle of reel remains down until rod tip is overhead. Reel spool is locked by pressure of thumb until rod tip snaps forward. Then a very light touch of thumb on reel spool prevents line snarl as the outgoing line spins reel spool. Thumb brakes spool again at end of cast. Next steps on next page.

"Fishing" the cast. When the lure hits the water, the angler as quickly as possible gets his gear set to handle a fish. Rod butt is lowered at once and held steady between fisherman's legs, as shown in photo at upper left. With thumb holding reel spool, angler quickly flips the free-spool lever of reel to engage the reel's mechanical drag. Lever is flipped with left hand (*upper right*). The left hand is then moved to the grip ahead of reel (*lower left*). Left hand then holds rod at about 45° while the right hand reels in the lure or plays a hooked fish (*center*). If the lure comes in close to the angler without being hit by a fish, rod is gradually angled to the right. This is to allow rod spring and a safe striking position if fish hits in final feet of retrieve. The danger in striking at fish close in with rod in front of you is that the lure may jerk loose and sail straight back into your face. The typical surf lure is heavy enough to do considerable damage with its sharp hooks. With rod held to one side, a missed strike with a short line will only send the lure flying harmlessly back on the beach behind you. Photo at lower right shows Lyman completing a retrieve properly. He reels in until lure is dangling right for next cast.

Spinning Reel

Proper grip. Spinning reel on surf rod is gripped with two fingers of right hand on each side of the metal shank that supports the reel. Left hand may be farther down rod butt than shown when cast is started. The second photo shows how forefinger of right hand is extended to hold line running between spool and guides. Reel shown here has line-pickup bail removed, a modification some surf spinners make for slight reduction of weight and working parts of spinning reel. They leave knob of pickup arm and put line on it manually when ready to reel in. This isn't quite so convenient as an automatic pickup bail, but it's a foolproof system many surfmen go for.

Casting motions. The actual cast with surf-size spinning tackle, as demonstrated by expert Frank Woolner, is very similar to rod work with a reel that has a revolving spool. The main difference is that the line from the fixed-spool spinning reel is held by angler's crooked forefinger until the rod tip snaps forward toward the target. Then the line is allowed to slip off the finger-tip and coil off the reel spool as the lure drives out over the water. In four photos above, Woolner cocks rod, powers it forward with pull on butt and push on grip at reel seat, aims at distant target as the rod tip starts to pass over his head. His finger releases the line when rod is at about 45° angle in front of him. He can catch the line again with his finger if he wants to stop cast before lure travels maximum distance. Monofilament line is first choice of surf spinners.

Retrieving the lure. Spinning line is hooked on reel's pickup knob as soon as lure hits the water. Then, as shown at right, the caster steadies butt of the rod between his legs and reels in. Most spinning reels are designed for reeling with left hand, while revolving-spool surf reels generally are set up for right-handed reeling. Woolner will angle rod to his right as lure he's retrieving enters shallows. This allows a safe jerk at late-striking fish and also puts rod in position for a new cast.

Ice Fishing

Ice fishing differs greatly from open-water fishing. And it is a demanding sport. It demands an understanding of and an ability to cope with winter weather, it demands a knowledge of the cold-weather habits of the fish, and it demands the use of an unusual assortment of gear, most of it unique to ice fishing.

There are two basic ice-fishing methods: tip-up fishing and jigging. In general, tip-ups are usually used on larger fish—pike, pickerel, walleyes, trout, and such—that prefer bait and require that the angler play the waiting game. Jigging is usually preferred for smaller fish that tend to school up—bluegills, perch, crappies, and the like.

But it should be remembered that those are merely generalizations, not hard and fast rules. For example, jigging (sometimes called chugging) is often productive on lake trout and salmon in the Great Lakes.

Tip-ups

Also called tilts, these come in various styles, but they all perform two basic functions: they hold a baited line leading from a revolving-type reel spool, and they signal the bite of a fish. The most common type of tip-up consists of three strips of wood, each about 18 inches long. Two are crosspieces that form an X as they span the ice hole. The third piece is an upright; at its bottom end is attached a simple line-holding spool, while the upper end holds the signalling device. The signal is usually a piece of very flexible spring steel with a red (some ice anglers prefer black) flag on the end. After the hook is baited and lowered to the desired depth, the steel arm is "cocked"—bent over and down and hooked onto a "trigger." When a fish strikes, an arm on the revolving spool releases the steel arm and it flies erect.

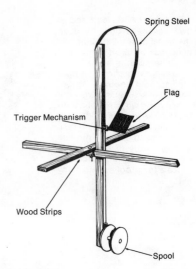

Typical ice fishing tip-up. Shown in cocked position, this model places reel underwater.

In this tip-up the reel is positioned underwater. In other variations the reel is positioned above the ice. Each type has its advantages. The above-the-ice reel can be more sensitively adjusted for light-biting fish, but the line tends to freeze on the reel once it gets wet. The underwater reel largely eliminates the problem of line freeze-up, but the fisherman must remove the tip-up from the hole before he can grab the line.

Baits for tip-up fishing are usually of the live variety. In general, it pays to match the size of the bait to the size of the fish you're after. Baits range from tiny maggots (often called mousies) and grubs for panfish, to worms and small minnows for walleyes, and up to 6-inch baitfish for northern pike.

Snowmobiles, insulated clothing, and modern tents have increased the fun and reduced the rigors of ice fishing for those who would rather not rough it.

A good safety implement is a pair of "ice claws." Commercial ice claws are available, or they can be made from awls or large stove bolts. The sharp ends can be shielded by corks, and holes can be drilled through the handle ends so that they can be strung on a lanyard or cord.

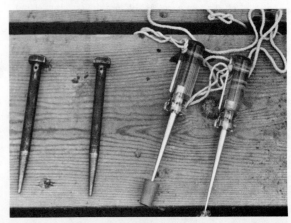

Jigging Rods

As done by ice fishermen, jigging is simply a method of imparting an up-and-down movement to a lure and/or bait. Jigging can be—and is—done with any sort of line-holding rod or stick.

Some jigging rods—more appropriately called sticks—are simply pieces of wood 18 inches or so long, with U-shaped notches in each end. The line—10-pound monofilament is very popular—is wound lengthwise onto the stick around the U-shaped notches and is paid out as needed. There are other types of jigging sticks of varying design, and many ice anglers use standard spinning or spin-cast rods or the butt half of a fly rod.

Rods made specially for ice jigging are simple affairs consisting of a fiberglass tip section 2 or 3 feet long seated in a short butt. The butt may have a simple revolving-spool reel or merely a pair of heavy-wire projections around which the line is wound. The tip section may have 2 to 4 guides including the tip guide. The shortness of such a rod lets the user fish up close to the hole and have better control over the lure or bait at the end of his line.

What sort of enticements does a jigger lower into those frigid depths?

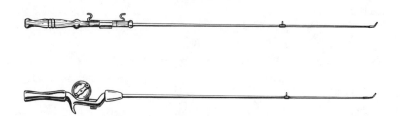

Two types of ice-fishing jigging rods. The rod at top utilizes two wire hooks on handle to hold the line. The model below uses an inexpensive reel on a short, baitcasting-type rod.

Jigging Lures and Baits

These are many and varied, but flashiness is built into most of them. Others produce best when "sweetened" with bait. Two popular jigging lures are: 1) an ungainly looking critter with a heavy body shaped and painted to resemble a baitfish, a hook at each end and a treble hook in the middle of its underside, and a line-tie ring in the middle of its upper surface; and 2) a long, slim, three or four-sided, silvery model with a treble hook at one end and a line-tie ring at the other.

Jigging methods vary with the fisherman and with the fish being sought. However, a productive way to fish many jigging lures, especially flasher types, is to twitch the lure slightly and then jerk it suddenly upward with a quick upward movement of the arm. The proper interval between jerks is learned with experience.

Favorite jigging baits include a single perch eye (either impaled on a small hook or used to sweeten a tiny hair or rubber-bodied ice fly), worms, grubs, maggots, insect larvae, minnows, and cut bait (pieces of skin or flesh cut from the tail or body of such fish as smelt and perch).

Jiggers tend to move about more than tip-up fishermen, boring holes in different areas until they find a productive spot.

METAL JIGGING LURES

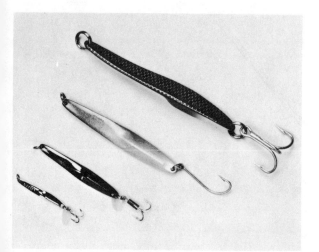

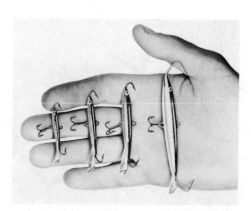

Other Equipment

Like most other forms of fishing, ice angling requires some auxiliary equipment. Most ice anglers prefer to keep such gear to a minimum, for they have to haul it with them wherever they go on the ice.

If you're going to fish through holes in the ice, you need something to make those holes. The ice auger is a popular tool for this job. Augers come in different designs. One has a long handle with a U-shaped bend at the top, and a rounded cutting blade at the bottom. The handle is turned much like that of a manual drill, and the blade cuts a round hole through the ice. Another type looks like a giant screw with sharp widely spaced threads. It is used in the same way.

Then there's the ice spud or chisel. This is a heavy metal handle with a large chisel-type blade at the bottom. The spud's weight helps the angler punch down through the ice, but the user must shape the hole once he has broken through.

An indispensable item of accessory gear is the ice skimmer, a ladle-type device that is used to keep the hole clear of ice chips and chunks and skim ice.

Many ice anglers like to use an ice sounder, which consists of a lead weight and an attached spring clip. It is attached to the fishing line and used to determine the water depth—an important factor because in winter most gamefish are found on or near bottom. A heavy sinker will serve the same purpose.

Ice conditions and thickness are of vital importance to all ice anglers. You should never venture out onto a frozen lake or river until you know the thickness of the ice and what sort of ice it is. Clear blue lake ice, for example, will support much more weight than will slush ice, such as is often found in early winter, and the black ice of late winter. As another example, clear solid river ice is 15 percent weaker than clear blue lake ice. And river and stream ice tends to be considerably thinner in midstream than near the banks.

The following table, prepared by the Lumbermen's Safety Association, gives a general outline of ice thicknesses and the weight loads that they can safely support. It should be remembered that these figures apply to clear blue lake ice that has not been traveled heavily. For early-winter slush ice, the thicknesses should be doubled.

ICE THICKNESS (in inches)	MAXIMUM SAFE LOAD
2	1 person on foot
3	Group in single-file
7½	Car (2 tons gross weight), Snowmobiles
8	Light truck (2½ tons)
10	Medium truck (3½ tons)
12	Heavy truck (8 tons)
15	10 tons
20	25 tons
25	45 tons
30	70 tons
36	110 tons

ICE-FISHING ACCESSORIES

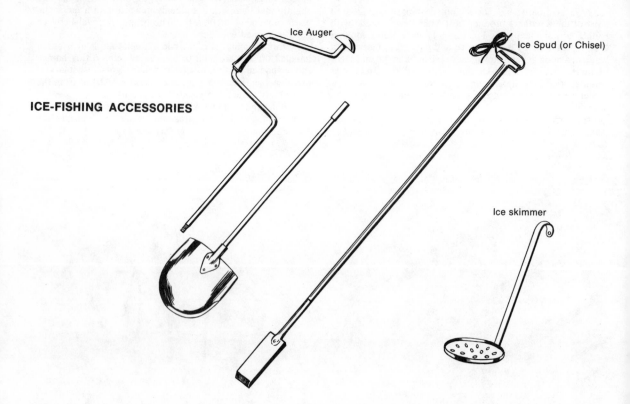

Ice Auger

Ice Spud (or Chisel)

Ice skimmer

Lines and Leaders

No fisherman is stronger than the line that connects him and his quarry. Fishing lines are made of a wide variety of natural and synthetic materials and as a result differ widely in their characteristics and the uses to which they can be put. No two types of lines, for example, have the same degree of elasticity, abrasion resistance, water absorption, weight, and diameter.

Let's take a look at the physical characteristics of the various lines and the uses for which they are best suited.

Monofilament (single-strand nylon). By far the most widely used fishing line today. It is suitable for everything from blue-water trolling to surf casting to fresh-water spinning, and it is the universal material for leaders in both fresh water and salt because of its near-invisibility in water. It is extremely strong and light for its diameter, and it absorbs very little water (3 to 12 percent of its own weight). About the only drawback of monofilament is its relatively high rate of stretch (15 to 30 percent when dry, 20 to 35 percent when wet). For that reason it is not the best choice for such uses as deep-water bottom fishing, in which large fish must be reeled up from considerable depths.

Dacron. A DuPont trademark for a synthetic fiber that is made into a braided line. It is nearly as strong as monofilament but does not stretch so much (about 10 percent). It has virtually the same characteristics whether dry or wet. Its visibility in water is greater than that of monofilament. Dacron's widest use is as trolling line.

Linen. A braided line made from natural fibers and rated according to the number of threads, with each thread having a breaking strength of 3 pounds (6-thread linen has a breaking strength of 18 pounds, 15-thread tests 45 pounds, and so on). This material absorbs considerable water and is stronger when wet. Linen line is subject to deterioration and is heavy and bulky. Very little linen fishing line is made or used today, but because of its negligible stretch and good abrasion resistance it is still preferred by some big-game fishermen.

Cuttyhunk. A braided linen line originally created in the 1860's for the Cuttyhunk Fishing Club on Cuttyhunk Island, Massachusetts. The word Cuttyhunk is often used to denote any linen line.

Silk. Before World War II fly-fishing lines were made of silk and had an oily coating to make them water resistant. Modern materials have made the silk line obsolete, and very few are in use today.

Braided Nylon. Extensively used on revolving-spool reels in fresh and salt water, and sometimes used on spinning reels. Braided nylon's main advantage over monofilament is that it is extremely limp and so is less likely to backlash on conventional reels. It is often preferred over monofilament for fishing with surface lures. But it is less durable than monofilament, has less abrasion resistance, absorbs more water, and is more visible in water.

Lead-Core. This type of line is made by sheathing a flexible lead core in a tightly braded nylon sleeve. It's suitable for deep trolling in both fresh and salt water, and is especially useful for quickly getting a bait or lure down deep without bulky, heavy sinkers or planers. It's color-coded in 10-yard segments for precise depth control.

Wire. These lines, too, are designed for deep trolling in both fresh and salt water. They're made of stainless steel, Monel (nickel alloy), bronze, or copper. Wire is popular for downrigger fishing, but because it's heavy enough to sink on its own, it's also used without downriggers and in many cases eliminates the need for a cumbersome drail weight or planer. Since it has no stretch, the angler can jig the rod and give movement to a bait or lure. However, wire is somewhat tricky until a fisherman gets used to it. Kinks can develop, causing weak spots or possibly cutting an unwary angler's hand. Wire line is generally available in a wider range of test weights than lead-core line.

Wire leaders, usually sleeved in plastic, are widely used to prevent line-cutting when fishing for such toothy battlers as pike, muskellunge, and many salt-water species.

Fly Lines

Ever since the time of Izaak Walton, anglers have been using special lines designed to present insect imitations to trout, salmon, and other fish. The earliest fly lines were made of braided horsehair. Then came oiled silk lines, which were standard until the late 1940's.

Today's fly lines are basically a synthetic coating over a braided core. They are made in various shapes and weights. Some are constructed so that they float (primarily for dry-fly fishing), and others are made to sink (for wet-fly and nymph fishing). A fairly recent development is the floating-sinking, or intermediate, line, the first 10 to 30 feet of which sinks while the rest floats.

The accompanying illustration shows the basic types of fly lines and explains how to select the proper one.

It is impossible to overemphasize the importance to the fly fisherman of balanced tackle. And the most vital element in a fly-fishing outfit is the line. It must "fit" the rod if casting is to be accurate and efficient.

A line that is too heavy for the rod causes sloppy casts, poor presentation of the fly, and lack of accuracy, and it makes it difficult to manipulate the fly once it is on the water. An angler who uses a line that's too light for his rod must flail the rod back and forth during repeated backcasts in order to get out enough line to make his cast, and even then his forward cast might not "turn over" and the line may fall onto the water in a jumbled mass of coils.

Before 1961, fly lines were identified by a system of letters — A to I — with each letter representing a line diameter. For example, an "A" line measured .060-inch in diameter, an "I" line .020-inch.

But when modern fly lines replaced silk after World War II, weight, rather than diameter, became the critical factor in matching a fly line with a rod. So, in 1961 the AFTMA (American Fishing Tackle Manufacturers Association) adopted a universally accepted fly-line identification code. Its three elements give a complete description of a fly line.

The first part of the code describes the line type: L stands for level, DT means double-taper, and WF means weight-forward. The second element, a number, denotes the weight (in grains) of the line's first 30 feet. The third element tells whether the line is floating (F), sinking (S), or floating/sinking (F/S). Therefore, a DT-6-F, for example, is a double-taper, weight-6, floating line.

DIAGRAMS OF TYPICAL FLY LINES*

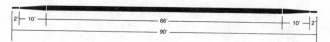

DOUBLE TAPER
Uniform diameter belly section tapered to smaller diameter at each end for gentle delivery of the fly. This "all-purpose" line is reversible—two lines in one.

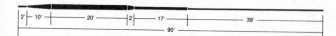

WEIGHT FORWARD
Consists of a front taper, heavy belly section, short rear taper and long length of small diameter "shooting" line. Permits longer casts than level or double taper.

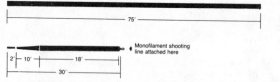

LEVEL
Uniform diameter end to end. Economical.

SHOOTING TAPER
Thirty feet long. Corresponds to the front taper and belly of a *weight forward* fly line. Attaches to monofilament shooting line. A "must" for extremely long distance casts.

*Note   Every fly line has a taper especially designed for that weight and type of line. The dimensions shown above are representative only.

BASS BUG AND SALTWATER TAPERS
Variations of a standard *weight forward* fly line designed expressly for the purposes described.

Double Taper, weight forward and level fly lines are available as floaters, sinkers and intermediates. Floating fly lines are the most widely used. They are ideal for fishing dry flies, bass bugs, panfish bugs, wet flies and nymphs on or near the water surface. Sinking fly lines, although less frequently used, are essential for fishing wet flies, nymphs, streamers and bucktails at considerable depths.

Intermediate, Floating/Sinking and other special fly lines are of limited use. They offer advantages for specific types of fishing.

AFTMA WEIGHT STANDARDS FOR FLY LINES

Code	*Weight	+ Range	Code	*Weight	+ Range	Code	*Weight	+ Range
1	60	54-66	5	140	134-146	9	240	230-250
2	80	74-86	6	160	152-168	10	280	270-290
3	100	94-106	7	185	177-193	11	330	318-342
4	120	114-126	8	210	202-218	12	380	368-392

*WEIGHT IN GRAINS   + ALLOWABLE TOLERANCES

RANGE OF AVAILABLE FLY LINES

AFTMA-CODE DESIGNATION	OLD LETTER DESIGNATION
L-3-F	F
L-4-F	F or E
L-5-S	F
L-5-F	E
L-6-S	E
L-6-F	D
L-7-S	D
L-7-F	C
L-8-S	D or C
L-8-F	C or B
L-9-S	C or B
L-9-F	B or A
L-10-S	B or A
L-10-F	A
DT-4-F	HEH
DT-5-S	HEH
DT-5-F	HDH
DT-6-S	HEH
DT-6-F	HDH
DT-7-S	HDH
DT-7-F	HCH
DT-8-S	HCH
DT-8-F	GBG
DT-9-S	GBG
DT-9-F	GBG
DT-10-S	GAG
DT-10-F	GAAG
WF-5-F	HDG
WF-6-F	HCF
WF-7-F	GBF
WF-7-S	HDG
WF-8-F	GAF
WF-8-S	HCF
WF-9-S	GBF
WF-9-F	GAAF
WF-10-S	GAF
WF-10-F	GAAF
WF-11-F	GAAAF
WF-11-S	GAAF
WF-12-F	—
WF-12-S	—
WF-13-F	—
WF-13-S	—

Key to AFTMA designations: L—Level DT—Double-Taper
WF—Weight-Forward
F—Floating S—Sinking

NOTE: Because the old letter system was based on line diameter and the new AFTMA code is based on line weight, some lines produced under the old system may not match up with the new-system designations shown in the above table. For example, one manufacturer's "E" line might be a weight-5 line under the new system, while another company's "E" may be a weight-4.

Many fly-rod manufacturers today are eliminating the angler's problem of proper line choice by imprinting on the rod itself, usually just above the butt, the proper line size for that particular rod.

However, there are other, general, ways to pick the right fly line. Rod length is one determining factor. These general recommendations may help:

ROD LENGTH	PROPER LINE
7½	DT-4-F
8	DT-5-F
8½	DT-6-F or WF-6-F
9 and 9½	WF-8-F to WF-11-F

Another determining factor is the type of water the angler will be fishing. Here's how to select a line on that basis:

TYPE OF WATER	SUITABLE LINE WEIGHTS (AFTMA Code)
Very small streams	4 and 5
Small and medium streams	5 to 8
Large streams	7 to 11
Lakes (light outfits)	5 to 7
Lakes (heavy outfits)	8 to 11
Salt water	10 to 12

Leaders

There are two basic leader materials, wire and monofilament (single-strand nylon).

Wire leaders—either piano wire (high-carbon or stainless steel) or braided wire—are used generally to protect the line from sharp underwater obstacles and from the teeth, gill plates, and other sharp appendages of both fresh-water and salt-water fish.

Some wire leaders, particularly the braided type, are enclosed in a "sleeve" of nylon, which prevents the wire strands from fraying and eliminates kinking.

Some monofilament leaders perform a similar function. Called shock tippets, they are short lengths (6 feet or shorter in most cases) of strong mono testing up to about 100 pounds, depending on the size of the fish being sought. Shock tippets protect the line from sharp objects and sharp teeth, but they are also able to withstand the sledgehammer strikes of large fish. Shock tippets are especially important to tarpon fishermen.

The main purpose of most monofilament leaders, however, is to provide an all-but-invisible link between the end of the line and the lure, bait, or fly. In spinning and spincasting, a leader is seldom necessary, for the line itself is monofilament. But in baitcasting, in which highly visible braided line is normally used, a monofilament leader at least 6 feet long is a big advantage.

Fly fishing is perhaps the form of the sport in which the leader is most critical. Today's trout, salmon, and other fly-caught fish—both stocked and wild—are far more wise to the ways of the angler than they once were. A sloppy cast, a too-short leader, or an improperly presented fly seldom brings a strike.

Though some fly fishermen feel they can get by with a level leader (one whose diameter is the same throughout its length), a tapered leader makes casting far more pleasant and efficient and brings far more strikes.

A tapered leader must be designed so as to transmit the energy of the cast from the line right down to the fly. But because the fly fisherman's offerings range from dry flies to wet flies to streamers and bucktails to bass bugs, tapered leaders differ too. The proper leader is also determined by water conditions and the size of the fish.

The makeup of a tapered leader starts with the butt section, which is tied to the end of the fly line and the diameter of which should be approximately one-half to two-thirds the diameter of the end of the line. The leader then progresses through progressively lighter (and thinner) lengths down to the tippet, to the end of which the fly is tied.

Most popular leader lengths are 7½ and 9 feet, but under some conditions—such as when casting to trout in low, clear water—leaders of 12, 15, or more feet may be necessary.

You can buy tapered leaders, either knotless or with the various sections knotted together. Each time you change flies, however, you must snip off a bit of the tippet, so it pays to carry small spools of leader material in various strengths so that you can tie on a new tippet when necessary. You can also tie your own tapered leaders.

Leader material is classified according to "X" designations (1X, 2X, 3X, and so on), with the number representing the diameter of the line. Tapered leaders are classified the same way, with the number representing the diameter of the tippet.

SPECIFICATIONS: 7½ FT. TAPERED TROUT LEADERS

0X	1X	2X
24″—.019″	24″—.019″	24″—.019″
16″—.017″	16″—.017″	16″—.017″
14″—.015″	14″—.015″	14″—.015″
9″—.013″	9″—.013″	9″—.013″
9″—.012″	9″—.011″	9″—.011″
18″—.011″	18″—.010″	18″—.009″

3X	4X
24″—.019″	24″—.019″
16″—.017″	16″—.017″
14″—.015″	14″—.015″
6″—.013″	6″—.013″
6″—.011″	6″—.011″
6″—.009″	6″—.009″
18″—.008″	18″—.007″

9 FT. TAPERED TROUT LEADERS

0X	1X	2X
36″—.021″	36″—.021″	36″—.021″
16″—.019″	16″—.019″	16″—.019″
12″—.017″	12″—.017″	12″—.017″
8″—.015″	8″—.015″	8″—.015″
8″—.013″	8″—.013″	8″—.013″
8″—.012″	8″—.012″	8″—.011″
20″—.011″	20″—.010″	20″—.009″

3X	4X	5X
36″—.021″	36″—.021″	28″—.021″
16″—.019″	16″—.019″	14″—.019″
12″—.017″	12″—.017″	12″—.017″
6″—.015″	6″—.015″	10″—.015″
6″—.013″	6″—.013″	6″—.013″
6″—.011″	6″—.011″	6″—.011″
6″—.009″	6″—.009″	6″—.009″
20″—.008″	20″—.007″	6″—.007″
		20″—.006″

12 FT. TAPERED TROUT LEADERS

4X	5X	6X
36″—.021″	36″—.021″	36″—.021″
24″—.019″	24″—.019″	24″—.019″
16″—.017″	16″—.017″	16″—.017″
12″—.015″	12″—.015″	12″—.015″
7″—.013″	7″—.013″	7″—.013″
7″—.011″	7″—.011″	7″—.011″
7″—.009″	7″—.009″	7″—.009″
7″—.008″	7″—.008″	7″—.007″
28″—.007″	28″—.006″	28″—.005″

7½ FT. SALMON, STEELHEAD, BASS BUG LEADERS

EXTRA LIGHT	LIGHT	MEDIUM
.021—.011	.021—.013	.021—.015
18″—.021″	26″—.021″	26″—.021″
16″—.019″	22″—.019″	23″—.019″
14″—.017″	12″—.017″	21″—.017″
12″—.015″	10″—.015″	20″—.015″
10″—.013″	20″—.013″	
20″—.011″		

HEAVY	EXTRA HEAVY
.021—.017	.023—.019
36 —.021″	36″—.023″
34 —.019″	34″—.021″
20 —.017″	20″—.019″

MATCHING TIPPET AND FLY

TIPPET SIZE	FLY SIZE	TIPPET SIZE	FLY SIZE
0X	2 to 1/0	4X	12, 14, 16
1X	4, 6, 8	5X	14, 16, 18
2X	6, 8, 10	6X	16, 18, 20, 22
3X	10, 12, 14	7X	18, 20, 22, 28

BREAKING STRENGTH OF LEADER TIPPETS

"X" CLASS	APPROX. DIAMETER (in inches)	MINIMUM POUND-TEST
6X	.0047	1.2
5X	.0061	3.3
4X	.0071	4.3
3X	.0080	5.2
2X	.0090	6.3
1X	.0098	7.2
0X	.0110	9.0
8/5	.0126	10.0
7/5	.0138	11.8
6/5	.0150	14.3
4/5	.0169	17.0
2/5	.0185	19.8

RECOMMENDED TIPPET STRENGTH FOR VARIOUS SPECIES

FRESH WATER

Bream, Sunnies, other small fish	3-pound test
Smallmouth Black Bass	4- to 6-pound test
Largemouth Black Bass	6- to 8-pound test
Brown Trout,	3-pound test
Brown Trout, using Streamers	5-pound test
Sea run Brown Trout	10-pound test
Brook Trout	3-pound test
Brook Trout, using Streamers	5-pound test
Sea run Brook Trout	6-pound test
Cutthroat Trout	3-pound test
Sea Run Cutthroat, called Bluebacks,	
Harvest Trout	4-pound test
Grayling	3-pound test
Rainbow Trout	4-pound test
Steelhead (sea run Rainbow Trout)	10-pound test
Winter Steelhead	12-pound test

SALT WATER

Mangrove or Gray Snapper	8-pound test
Bonefish	6- or 8-pound test
Tarpon, baby (under 20 pounds)	8-pound test
Tarpon, big (over 20 pounds)	12-pound test
Channel Bass (Redfish)	10-pound test
Striped Bass (to 10 pounds)	8-pound test
Striped Bass (over 10 pounds)	12-pound test
Jack Crevalle	10-pound test
Horse-Eye Jack	10-pound test
Ladyfish	8-pound test
Snook	12-pound test
Spotted Seatrout	10-pound test
Barracuda	12-pound test

**SALTWATER FISH IN DEEP WATER,
BY CHUMMING OR SIGHTING**

Dolphin	10-pound test
Mackerel	10-pound test
False Albacore	10-pound test
Bonito	10-pound test
Grouper	10-pound test
Yellowtail	10-pound test
Bermuda Chub	10-pound test

SPECIAL LEADERS FOR FISH THAT MIGHT BITE OR FRAY THROUGH LEADER TIPPET

Bluefish 10-pound test with 12 inches #4 wire leader added
Sailfish 12-pound test with 12 inches 80-pound-test nylon added
Marlin 12-pound test with 12 inches 100-pound-test nylon added
Tarpon 12-pound test with 12 inches 100-pound-test nylon added
Tuna 12-pound test with 12 inches 100-pound-test nylon added
Barracuda 12-pound test with 12 inches #5 wire leader added
Sharks 12-pound test with 12 inches #5 or #7 heavier wire
   leader added

Fishhooks

Modern hook design and manufacture has come a long way since the first Stone Age bone hooks found by archeologists and dating back to more than 5,000 B.C. Today's fishhooks come in hundreds of sizes, shapes, special designs. They're made from carbon steel, stainless steel, or some rustless alloy. They're hardened and tempered, then plated or bronzed to meet special specifications. Some are thin steel wire for use in tying artificial flies; others are thick steel for big-game fish that prowl offshore waters.

There is no such thing as an all-purpose hook. Fishermen must carry a variety of patterns and sizes to match both tackle and size of fish being hunted. Let's start from the beginning by learning the basic nomenclature of a typical fishhook, illustrated in the accompanying drawing.

Even the various parts of a typical fishhook may vary in design to meet certain requirements. There are sliced shanks to better hold bait on the hook, forged shanks for greater strength in marine hooks, tapered eyes to reduce weight of hooks used in tying dry flies, and so on.

Hook Wire Size

The letter X and the designations "Fine" or "Stout" are used to indicate the weight or diameter of a hook. For example, a 2X Stout means the hook is made of the standard diameter for a hook two sizes larger, and a 3X Stout is made of the standard diameter for a hook three sizes larger.

When we go to lightweight hooks, the designations are reversed. For example, a 2X Fine means the hook is made of the standard diameter for a hook two sizes smaller, and so on.

Obviously, the angler seeking big fish should lean toward the stout hooks, which are not apt to bend or spring when striking the bigger fish that swim our waters, particularly salt water.

Fishermen who use live bait will want the fine-wire hooks, which will not weigh down the bait. The use of flies, particularly dry flies, also requires fine-wire hooks, since their light weight will enable a fly to float more easily.

Shank Length

The letter X and the designations "Long" or "Short" are used to specify shank length of a hook. The formula for determining shank length is similar to that used for wire sizes. A 2X Long means the shank of the hook is the standard length for a hook two sizes larger, and a 4X Long for a hook four sizes larger. A 2X Short is a hook that has a shank as short as the standard length of a hook two sizes smaller, and 4X Short for a hook four sizes smaller, and so on.

Picking a hook with the correct shank length depends on the type of fishing you plan to undertake. A short-shank hook is preferred for bait fishing, since it can be hidden in the bait more easily. The long shank hook is at its best when used for fish with sharp teeth. A bluefish, for example, would have a tough time getting past the long shank and cutting into the leader. Long-shank hooks are also used in tying streamers and bucktails.

Hook Size

Attempts have been made to standardize hook sizes, but none have been very successful. The problem has been that a hook actually has two measurements—the gap and the length of the shank, both of which vary from pattern to pattern.

Only by studying the various patterns and sizes in the accompanying charts (hooks are shown actual size) can an angler become sufficiently familiar with hook patterns to pick the right hook for the job.

As a guide, refer to Natural Saltwater Baits, and note the hook sizes recommended for various species of fish. Match those recommendations with the hook sizes on these pages and compare the differences. With this information, it is not difficult to choose the correct size hook for your type of fishing.

PARTS
OF A
FISHHOOK

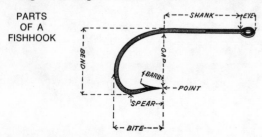

TYPES
AND STYLES
OF HOOK PARTS

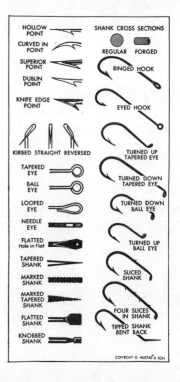

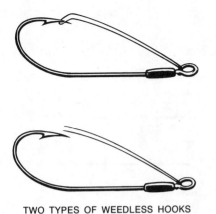

TWO TYPES OF WEEDLESS HOOKS

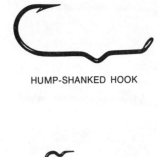

HUMP-SHANKED HOOK

BARBLESS HOOK

Hook Characteristics

In addition to size and shank length, there are other characteristics of hooks to consider when selecting a hook for a specific purpose. The barb, obviously, is a critical part of the hook. A short barb is quick to set in the mouth of a fish, but it also gives a jumping fish a greater chance of dislodging it. A long barb, on the other hand, is more difficult to set but it also makes it a lot tougher for a fish to shake it loose.

So what guidelines should an angler follow? Let's list some basic recommendations. The all-round saltwater fisherman can't go wrong by using the O'Shaughnessy, Kirby, Sproat, or Siwash patterns. And if you happen to have some Salmon hooks, they're perfectly all right to use with a wire leader for barracuda and other toothy fish.

If you're a flounder fisherman, you'll find that the Chestertown and Carlisle patterns are your best bet. The long-shanked Chestertown makes it especially easy to unhook flounders, which may well be a primary reason for using them when fishing for these flatfish.

If you're a bait fisherman, use the sliced shanked Mustad-Beak or Eagle Claw patterns. Those extra barbs on the shanks do a good job keeping natural baits secured to the hook.

Fishermen can also become confused when they see hooks with straight-ringed eyes, turned-up eyes, and turned-down eyes. This should not present a problem. If you're replacing hooks on lures or attaching hooks to spinners, use a straight-ringed eye. If you're tying short-shanked artificial flies, pick the turned-up eye, which will provide more space for the hook point to bite into the fish. The turned-down eye is the best bet for standard flies and for bait fishing, since it brings the point of the hook closest to a straight line of penetration when striking a fish.

Curved shanks also lead to some confusion. Without getting into specific details, let's say simply that a curved shank, curved right or left, has its place in baitfishing. The offset point has a better chance of hitting flesh when a strike is made.

When casting or trolling with artificial lures or spinners, however, the straight-shanked hook is a better choice, since it does not have a tendency to spin or twist, which is often the case with curved-shanked hooks.

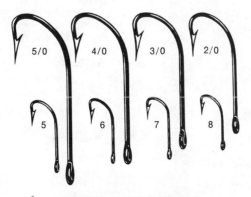

SUPERIOR MUSTAD-LIMERICK

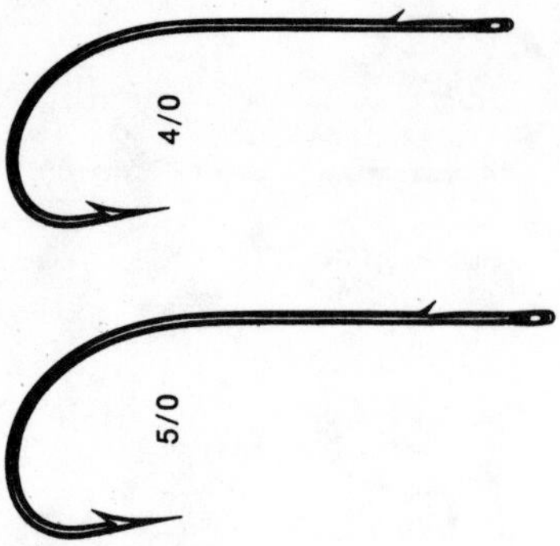

HOLLOW POINT
MUSTAD-SPROAT WORM HOOK

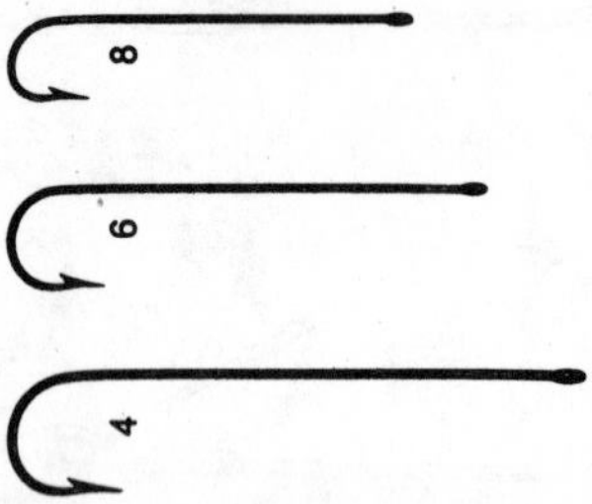

4/0

5/0

SUPERIOR MUSTAD-ABERDEEN
CRICKET HOOK

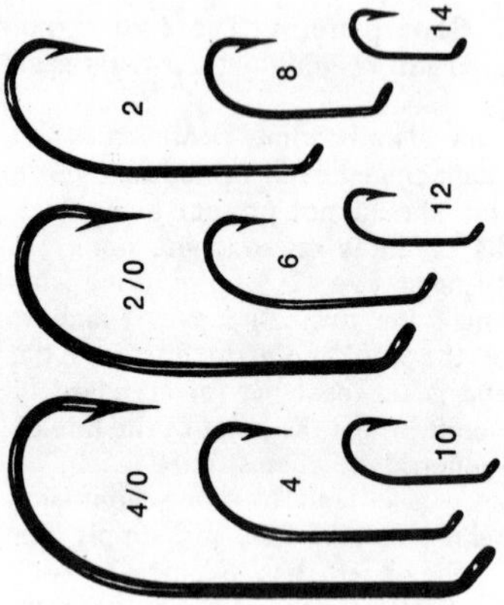

8

6

4

SUPERIOR MUSTAD-SPROAT
FLY HOOK, TURNED DOWN BALL EYE

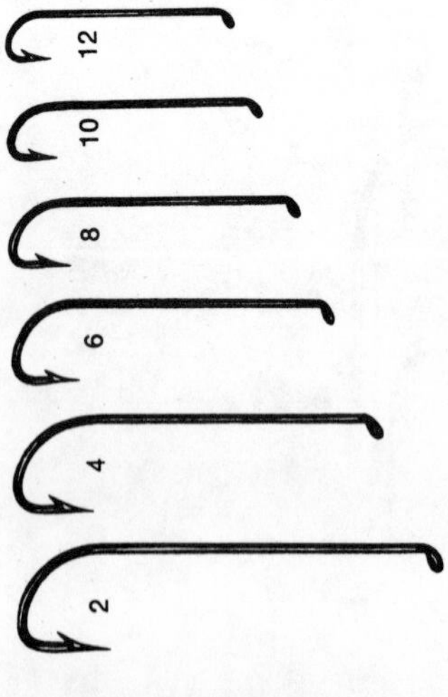

4/0   2/0   2

4   6   8

10   12   14

HOLLOW POINT MUSTAD-LIMERICK
FLY HOOK, TURNED DOWN TAPERED EYE

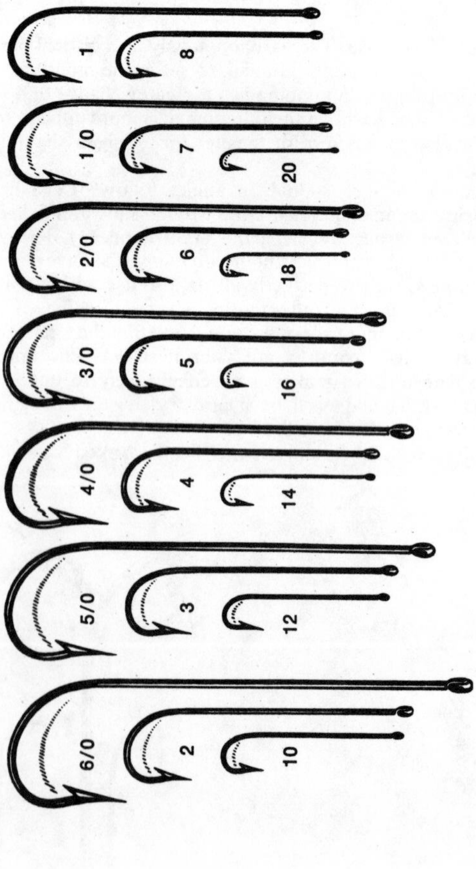

12

10

8

6

4

2

SUPERIOR MUSTAD-CARLISLE

6/0   5/0   4/0   3/0   2/0   1/0   1

2   3   4   5   6   7   8

10   12   14   16   18   20

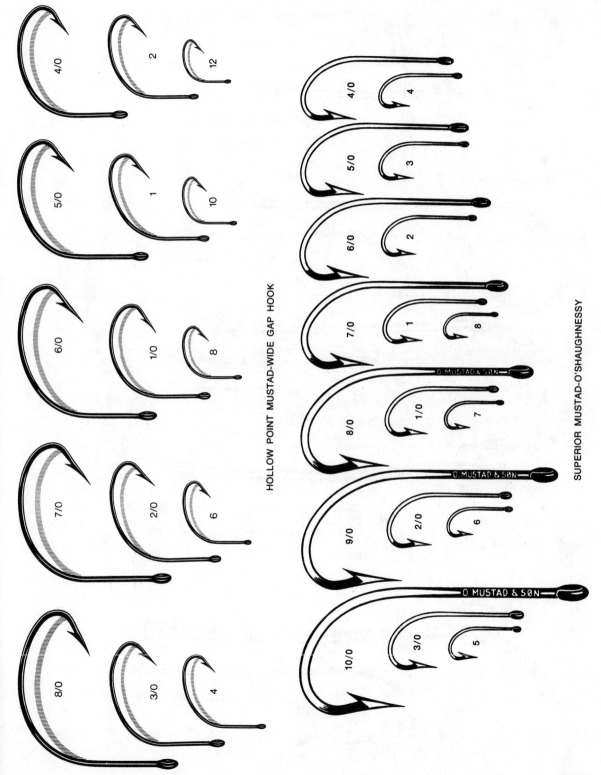

4/0

2

12

5/0

1

10

6/0

1/0

8

7/0

2/0

6

8/0

3/0

4

HOLLOW POINT MUSTAD-WIDE GAP HOOK

4/0

4

5/0

3

6/0

2

7/0

1

8

O. MUSTAD & SON

8/0

1/0

7

O. MUSTAD & SON

9/0

2/0

6

O MUSTAD & SON

10/0

3/0

5

SUPERIOR MUSTAD-O'SHAUGHNESSY

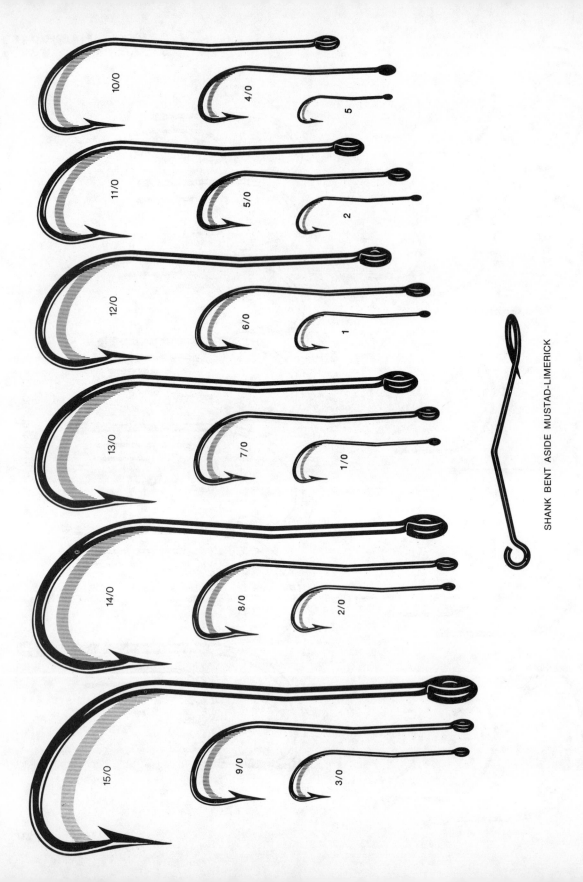

SHANK BENT ASIDE MUSTAD-LIMERICK

10/0
4/0
5

11/0
5/0
2

12/0
6/0
1

13/0
7/0
1/0

14/0
8/0
2/0

15/0
9/0
3/0

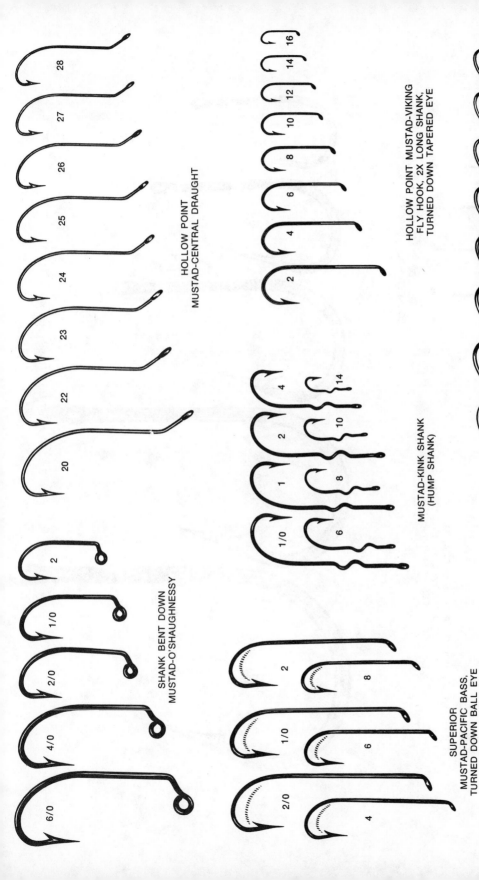

HOLLOW POINT
MUSTAD-CENTRAL DRAUGHT

HOLLOW POINT MUSTAD-VIKING
FLY HOOK, 2X LONG SHANK,
TURNED DOWN TAPERED EYE

MUSTAD-KINK SHANK
(HUMP SHANK)

HOLLOW POINT MUSTAD-BEAK, TURNED DOWN TAPERED EYE

SHANK BENT DOWN
MUSTAD-O'SHAUGHNESSY

SUPERIOR
MUSTAD-PACIFIC BASS,
TURNED DOWN BALL EYE

HOLLOW POINT MUSTAD-VIKING
FLY HOOK, 5X SHORT SHANK,
TURNED DOWN TAPERED EYE

HOLLOW POINT MUSTAD-BEAK,
TURNED DOWN TAPERED EYE,
TWO SLICES IN SHANK

HOLLOW POINT MUSTAD-BEAK
FLOUNDER HOOK, SPECIAL LONG SHANK

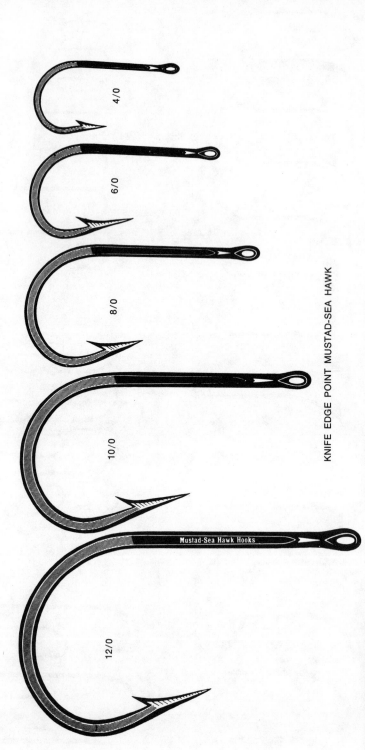

KNIFE EDGE POINT MUSTAD-SEA HAWK

Mustad-Sea Hawk Hooks

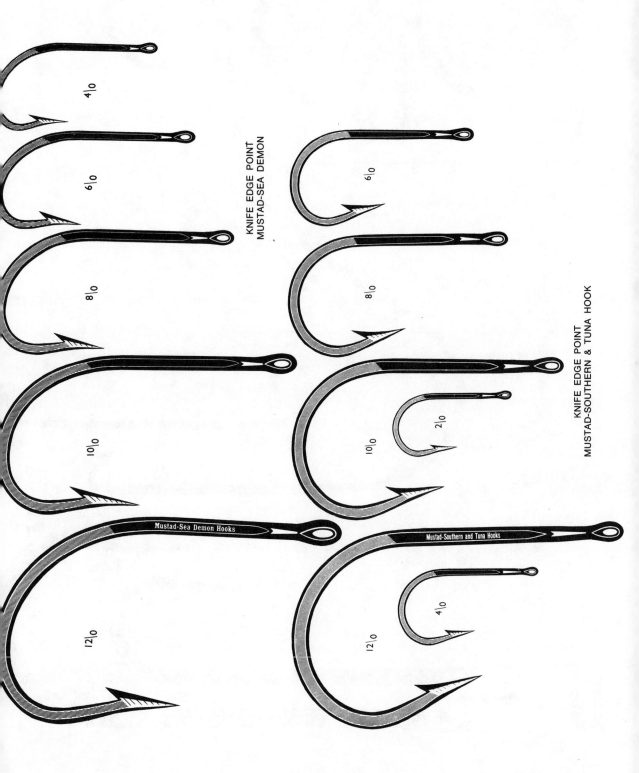

4|0

6|0

8|0

10|0

Mustad-Sea Demon Hooks

12|0

KNIFE EDGE POINT
MUSTAD-SEA DEMON

6|0

8|0

10|0

2|0

Mustad-Southern and Tuna Hooks

12|0

4|0

KNIFE EDGE POINT
MUSTAD-SOUTHERN & TUNA HOOK

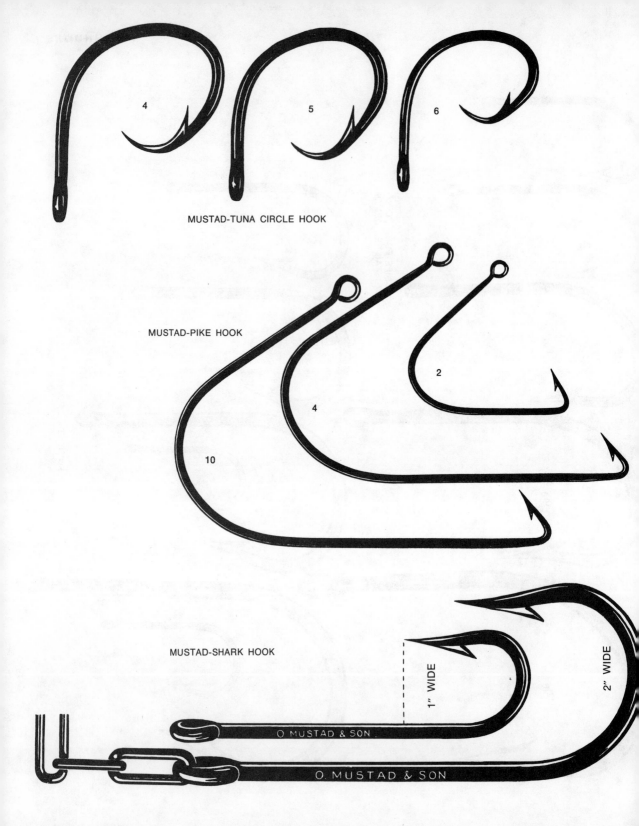

MUSTAD-TUNA CIRCLE HOOK

MUSTAD-PIKE HOOK

MUSTAD-SHARK HOOK

1" WIDE

2" WIDE

O. MUSTAD & SON

O. MUSTAD & SON

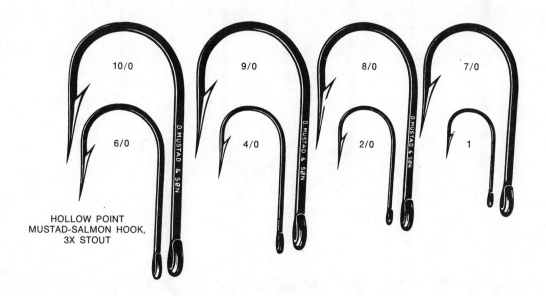

10/0 9/0 8/0 7/0

6/0 4/0 2/0 1

HOLLOW POINT
MUSTAD-SALMON HOOK,
3X STOUT

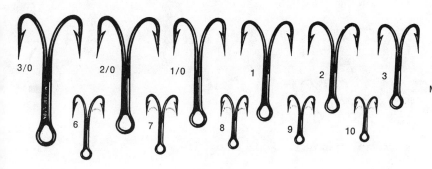

3/0 2/0 1/0 1 2 3

6 7 8 9 10

SUPERIOR
MUSTAD-DOUBLE HOOK,
BRAZED SHANK

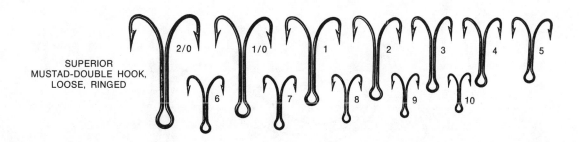

SUPERIOR
MUSTAD-DOUBLE HOOK,
LOOSE, RINGED

2/0 1/0 1 2 3 4 5

6 7 8 9 10

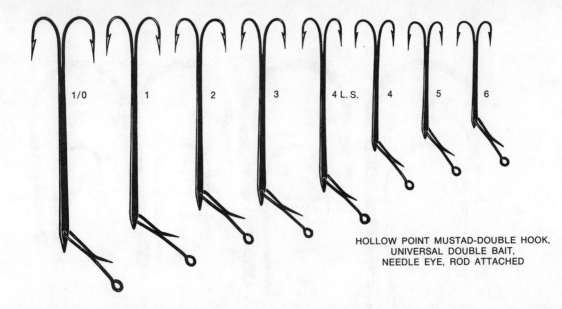

HOLLOW POINT MUSTAD-DOUBLE HOOK,
UNIVERSAL DOUBLE BAIT,
NEEDLE EYE, ROD ATTACHED

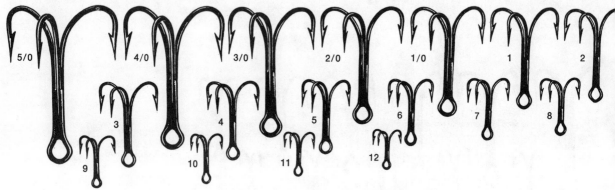

SUPERIOR MUSTAD-TREBLE HOOK, SPROAT BEND

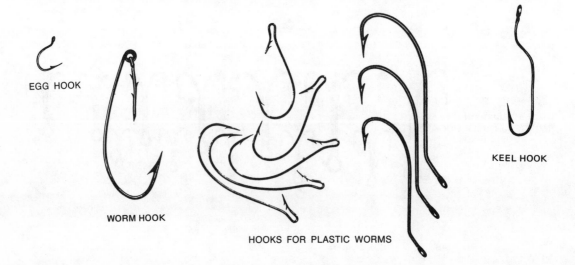

EGG HOOK

WORM HOOK

HOOKS FOR PLASTIC WORMS

KEEL HOOK

Artificial Lures

Fishing with bait is enjoyable, certainly, but there's something about fooling a fish with an artificial that gives most anglers a special charge.

A neophyte fisherman who visits a well-stocked sporting-goods store or tackle shop is confronted with a bewildering array of plugs, spoons, spinners, jigs, flies, bugs, and others. Some artificials look like nothing that ever swam, crawled, or flew, and yet they catch fish.

Let's look at each type of artificial and see how and why it works and how it should be fished.

Plugs

Plugs are lures designed to imitate small fish for the most part, though some plugs simulate mice, frogs, eels, and other food on which gamefish feed. Plug action—meaning the way it moves when retrieved by the angler—is important and is something on which manufacturers expend much money and time.

The type, size, and weight of the plug you select is determined by the fish you are after and the kind of fishing outfit you are using. The charts, found elsewhere in this book, on how to match up various kinds of fishing tackle will help the beginner choose the right weight plugs.

There are five basic types of plugs: popping, surface, floating-diving, sinking (deep-running), and deep-diving.

POPPING PLUGS

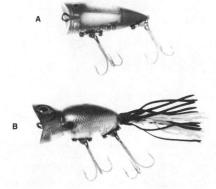

(A) **Chuggar Spook.** Resting on surface at an angle, this plug makes splashing and popping sound when jerked. At its best when worked along shoreline at dawn and dusk for bass, though the plug will take nearly any freshwater species feeding on the surface.

(B) **Hula Popper.** Hollow or cupped face imparts popping and surface commotion when retrieved in short jerks. An effective surface plug for bass, particularly at night when fished close to shore.

POPPING PLUGS (SALT WATER)

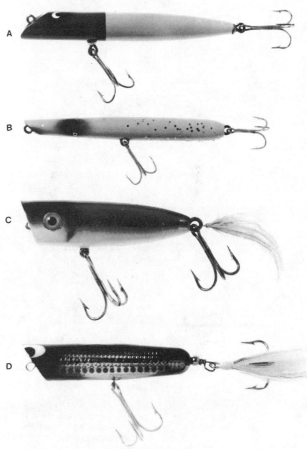

(A) **Eppinger School Striper.** An effective plug on coastal waters, bays, and rivers. Will bring strikes from striped bass, bluefish, snook, tarpon, and similar inshore species.

(B) **Pencil Popper.** Good casting plug because of its heavier tail section, this lure floats at an angle and should be retrieved in short jerks. A favorite in northeastern coastal waters for school stripers and bluefish.

(C) **Trouble Maker.** Top producer of striped bass, bluefish, tarpon, snook and similar species. Big enough to be fished from the surf and jettyies, yet a good lure for coastal bays and rivers. Most productive in calm water.

(D) **Phillips "77".** Top-water popper that will produce both in northeastern coastal waters and on the big flats of Florida. Retrieved with sharp jerks, the "77" will draw strikes from any species that decides to feed on the surface.

SURFACE PLUGS

(A) Sputterbug. Spinner at head of plug churns surface as it is retrieved fast. A slow retrieve produces a paddling noise. A good producer of bass, muskies, pickerel. Fish it along the edge of reed beds and near lily pads.

(B) Crazy Crawler. A top bass lure for dawn, dusk, and night-time fishing. Retrieve it just fast enough for the two metal arms to paddle water. Stop it occasionally, pause, twitch it once or twice, then resume retrieve. Designed to simulate a swimming animal.

(C) Dylite Spinning Frog. Basically a fly-rod lure weighted and designed for spinning, this imitation frog should be cast close to shore, or on bank and lilly pad, then twitched or hopped into the water. Weedless hook makes it a good bet for lily pads and weed patches. The twitch and pause retrieve is recommended.

(D) Jitterbug. Swimming animal lure with side-by-side crawling action. Has gurgling sounds and leaves V-wake of bubbles on surface. An effective lure for bass, pike, muskies, pickerel.

(E) Mirrolure (Floater Model). Rests on top, but dips below surface when jerked. Action must be imparted by rod tip, but plug is productive on bass, pike, muskies, pickerel, and small saltwater species.

(F) LeBoeuf Creeper. A big frog lure with paddling, crawling action. Large size makes it particularly effective in northern waters for pike, muskies. Also a good lure for bass, pickerel.

(G) Tiny Torpedo. Rests on surface, but tail propeller creates noisy bubbling action when lure is jerked. Designed to imitate a wounded minnow, the plug will take bass, pickerel, muskies, pike.

(H) Zara Spook. A torpedo-type lure that darts, dives, bobs when jerked. While good for bass, pike, muskies, and pickerel, it has proven particularly productive in Florida's mangrove waters for snook and tarpon.

Popping. These plugs float on the surface and have con- cave, hollowed-out faces. The angler retrieves a popping plug by jerking the rod tip back so that the plug's face digs into the water, making a small splash, bubbles, and a popping sound. Some make a louder sound than others. This sound is especially attractive to largemouth bass, pike, muskies, and some inshore saltwater species, such as striped bass. Most popping plugs (and most other plugs, for that matter) have two sets of treble hooks. Popping plugs are most productive when the water surface is calm or nearly so. They should usually be fished very slowly.

Surface. These plugs float on the surface, but they can be fished with various kinds of retrieves and create a dif- ferent kind of surface disturbance than poppers do. Designed with an elongated, or bullet-shaped, head, they create surface disturbance by various means, including propellers (at the head or at both head and tail), a wide metal lip at the head, and hinged metal "wings" just behind the head. They can be

twitched so that they barely nod, retrieved steadily so that they chug across the water, or skimmed across the top as fast as the angler can turn his reel handle. The proper retrieve depends on the lure's design and, of course, on the mood of the fish. It's best to try different retrieves until you find one that produces.

Floating-Diving. These plugs are designed to float when at rest and dive when retrieved. Some float horizontally while others float with the tail hanging down beneath the surface. They are made to dive by an extended lip at the head, either a part of the plug body itself or an attached metal piece. The speed of the retrieve determines the depth of the dive. The faster the retrieve, the deeper the dive. Most of these plugs have a side-to-side wobbling action. An erratic retrieve — dive, surface, dive, surface — is often productive, and these plugs are also effective when made to swim just above a submerged weed bed, rock pile, and so on.

FLOATING-DIVING PLUGS

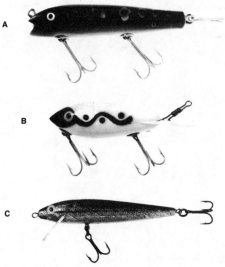

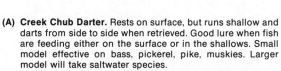

(A) Creek Chub Darter. Rests on surface, but runs shallow and darts from side to side when retrieved. Good lure when fish are feeding either on the surface or in the shallows. Small model effective on bass, pickerel, pike, muskies. Larger model will take saltwater species.

(B) Bomber. A deep-working plug that can be cast or trolled. Works well during midday when bass, pickerel, and pike seek deep cool water. The faster the retrieve or trolling speed, the deeper the plug will run.

(C) Rebel Shiner. Floats at rest, but dives and has side-to-side wobbling action when retrieved. Cast or trolled, this plug will take all fresh-water species from bass to salmon. Large model has proven it's worth in coastal and offshore waters.

(D) Thinfin Silver Shad. A floater-diver that has wobbling and darting action when retrieved or trolled. Good for bass, pickerel, pike, muskies, as well as some saltwater species.

(E) Creek Chub Pikie. Old-time favorite that dives and wobbles side to side. Good for most freshwater species, but has be- come a standby for pike and muskie fishermen. It can be cast or trolled, and depth is determined by adjustable metal lip.

(F) Flatfish. Dives and swims with rapid side-to-side wobble. The faster the retrieve or trolling speed, the deeper the plug will run. Available in variety of sizes to cover species from panfish to muskies and salmon.

Sinking (deep-running). These plugs sink as soon as they hit the water and are designed for deep work. Some sink slower than others and can be fished at various depths, depending on how long the angler waits before starting his retrieve. Most of these plugs have some sort of wobbling action, and some fairly vibrate when retrieved. Some have propellers fore and aft.

These plugs are excellent fish-finders: the fisherman can start by bouncing them along bottom, and if that doesn't work, he can work them at progressively shallower depths until he finds at what depth the fish are feeding. It should be remembered that deep-running plugs don't have to be fished in deep water; for example, in small sizes they're tops for river smallmouths.

Deep-Diving. These plugs may float or sink, but all are designed with long and/or broad lips of metal or plastic that cause the plugs to dive to depths of 30 feet or more as the angler reels in. As with other diving plugs, the faster the retrieve, the deeper the dive. Most of these lures have some sort of wobbling action. They are ideally suited for casting or trolling in deep lakes and at the edges of dropoffs, and they work best in most waters when the fish are holding in deep holes, as they do during midday in July and August.

DIVING PLUGS (SALT WATER)

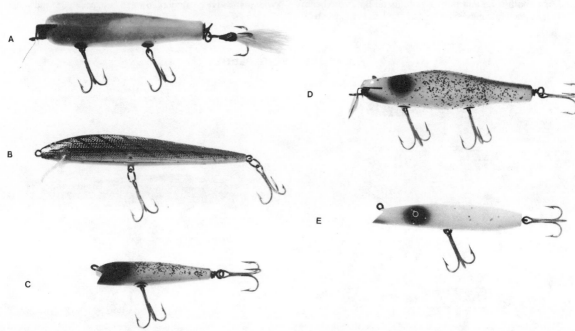

(A) Atom Plug. Cast or trolled, this plug can be worked deep or shallow, depending on angle of adjustable metal lip. Productive lure for inshore species, such as striped bass, bluefish, tarpon, snook. A favorite among northeastern surf and jetty fishermen.

(B) Rebel. A lure that has gained a reputation in both fresh and salt water, the big Rebel can be cast or trolled for nearly all salt-water species that prowl coastal waters, including striped bass, bluefish, permit, snook, tarpon, barracuda, and similar fish.

(C) Creek Chub Darter. Floats at rest and darts side-to-side when retrieved. A good lure species in coastal bays and flats.

(D) Creek Chub Surfster. A favorite of surf fishermen, this cucumber-size plug can easily be cast beyond the breakers for striped bass and bluefish. Most effective when worked close to jetties at dawn, dusk, and night time.

(E) Stan Gibbs Darter. Heavy tail section makes this plug easy to cast far out. It floats at rest, but darts side-to-side when retrieved. From beach, boat, or jetty, this plug will get strikes from nearly all saltwater inshore species. It's a favorite of the striped-bass fisherman.

DEEP DIVERS AND SINKING PLUGS

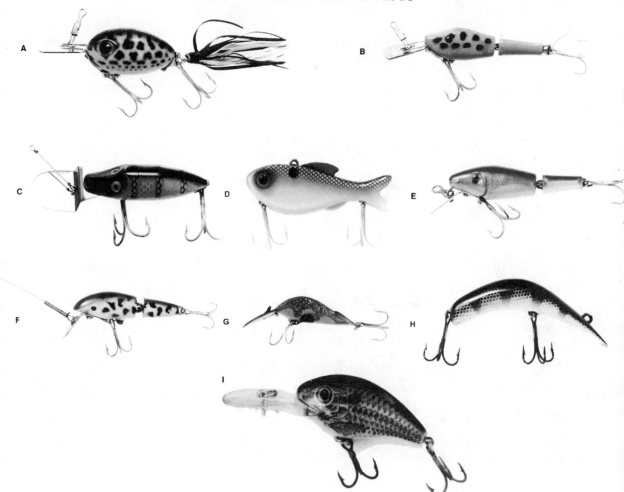

(A) Arbogaster. Long and wide metal lip puts this lure down deep with a fast wiggle. Basically a bass plug, it will also take pike, muskies, pickerel.

(B) Hula Pikie. Sinks slowly and dives deep on retrieve. Can be cast or trolled. The faster the speed, the deeper plug will run. Good midday lure for bass, walleyes, pike, and pickerel.

(C) River Runt. Sinks slowly and dives deeper with side-to-side action when retrieved. Faster the retrieve, deeper plug will run. Effective on bass, pickerel, pike, walleyes, muskies.

(D) Tru-Shad. A sinking plug, this lure vibrates with fast wiggle on retrieve. Models vary from medium depth to deep running. Good for bass, pickerel, walleyes, pike.

(E) Mirrolure. This plug sinks when it hits surface and dives deeper on retrieve. Can be cast or trolled and comes in variety of sizes for fish ranging from crappies to bass and pike.

(F) Cisco Kid. A fast sinking plug that dives deeper on retrieve. Effective when trolling over or casting into deep holes for bass, walleyes, pickerel, pike.

(G) Spoonplug. A wobbling lure designed to run deep enough to bump the bottom. Especially effective on soft bottoms, where this all-metal lure creates small puffs of mud as it digs along. Good for sulking bass during hot weather.

(H) Lazy Ike. Banana-shaped plug that has rapid-side-to-side wobble when retrieved or trolled. Variety of sizes make this a good choice for panfish on up to salmon.

(I) "Naturalized" Rebel. A deep-diving plug, this has a relatively new type of finish, accomplished by photo-transfer process, to give lures an ultra-realistic appearance of live baitfish.

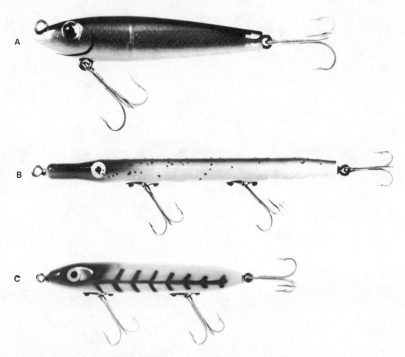

(A) Mirrolure (Sinking Model). A big weighted lure that casts easy and sinks fast. Has little, if any, built-in action. Lure must be worked with a jerk-and-crank retrieve. Lack of built-in action is no handicap, however. This shiny-sided plug draws strikes from striped bass, bluefish, tarpon, snook, barracuda, and similar inshore species.

(B) Boone Needlefish. In bay waters, from the surf, and off jetties, this sinking plug has taken its share of striped bass, bluefish, weakfish. Has no built-in action. Lure must be retrieved with jerks.

(C) Boone T.D. Special. A sinking plug that can be worked at any depth. Equally effective on New Jersey striped bass and Florida's tarpon and snook.

Spoons

Spoons are among the oldest of the artificials. If you cut the handle off a teaspoon, you'd have the basic shape of this lure.

Spoons are designed to imitate small baitfish of one kind or another, so flash is an important feature in many of these lures. Most spoons have a wobbling side-to-side action when retrieved.

Many spoons have a silver or gold finish, while others are painted in various colors and combinations of colors. Most have a single free-swinging treble hook at the tail; others have a single fixed hook. Weedless arrangements are becoming more and more popular on both types.

In general, the smaller spoons are better in streams and ponds, while the larger ones are a good choice for lakes. However, the angler must remember that with two spoons of equal weight but different size, the smaller one will cast easier in wind and sink faster, while the larger will sink slower and swim at shallower depths.

What's the best retrieve for a spoon? Again, that depends on weather and water conditions and other circumstances, including the mood of the fish. But generally an erratic retrieve, with twitches and jerks of the rod tip, is better than a steady retrieve because it makes the spoon look like an injured baitfish. Attaching a strip of pork rind to a spoon often adds to its fish appeal.

TYPICAL SPOONS

(A) **Cop-E-Cat.** A larger version of the well-known Dardevle, this spoon can be cast or trolled for pike, muskies, salmon, steelhead.

(B) **ABU-Toby.** Fins give this spoon a darting action. Good casting lure for pike, muskies, pickerel, trout.

(C) **ABU-Kostar.** Heavier than most freshwater spoons, this lure is used frequently by trollers. It's productive on salmon, lake trout, pike, muskies.

(D) **Red Eye Wiggler.** A wobbler that imparts good action at any speed of retrieve. Cast or trolled, an effective lure for pike, muskies, pickerel, lake trout.

(E) **Johnson's Silver Minnow.** An old favorite wobbling spoon. With a strip of pork rind on its weedless hook, it can be fished in weed and brush-infested waters. Excellent for pickerel, pike, muskies, trout, coho salmon.

(F) **Mr. Champ.** A wobbling spoon that won't spin or twist line. Serves well for casting, jigging, trolling. Will take most species, such as bass, panfish, trout, pickerel, pike.

(G) **Limper.** A darting spoon that can be used for jigging as well as casting and trolling. Good for pickerel, pike, muskies, bass, trout. Available with single hook for coho salmon.

(H) **Al's Goldfish.** An effective wobbler that can be cast or trolled for trout and salmon. Works equally well for bass, pickerel, pike.

(I) **Tony Accetta Pet.** Also available with weedless hook, this wobbling spoon is best fished with a strip of pork rind. Can be cast or trolled for trout, salmon, bass, pickerel, pike.

(J) **Sidewinder.** This spoon has a side-to-side action in addition to its wobble. A good fast-water lure for trout and salmon, as well as a good choice for most warm-water species.

(K) **Phantom Wobbler.** A slab of pearl-like material is added to this wobbling spoon. Fine choice trout and salmon, and should prove equally effective on bass, pike, and pickerel.

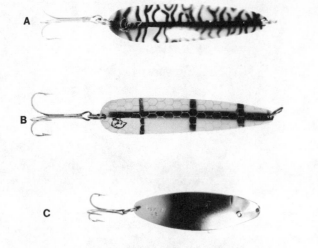

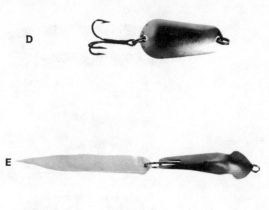

(A) Eppinger Cop-E-Cat. Big mackerel-finish spoon has action similar to the well-known Dardevle, except it is designed for casting and trolling in coastal waters. Trolled deep on wire line it will take bluefish; cast from surf or boat it will take stripers.

(B) Eppinger Seadevle. Similar to the Cop-E-Cat, except slimmer, this spoon is built for salt-water casting and trolling. Large sizes will get strikes from stripers, bluefish, yellowtails. Small models will catch mackerel, pollack.

(C) Reed R.T. Flash. Well-designed spoon that can be cast, trolled, even jigged. Good lure in coastal waters for tinker mackerel, snappers, weakfish, kingfish. Trolled off shore with wire line or trolling lead, it will take most bigger inshore species.

(D) Wob-L-Rite. A heavy brass spoon that is easy to cast great distances. Will wobble on a steady retrieve or can be jigged. Good choice for deep jigging reef species or surf and boat casting.

(E) Tony Accetta Spoon. Available in various sizes, this spoon has proven itself in coastal waters. Usually rigged with pork rind strip, as shown here, it is an effective trolling and casting lure for nearly all inshore game fish.

Spinners

Spinners, like spoons, are designed to imitate baitfish, and they attract gamefish by flash and vibration. A spinner is simply a metal blade mounted on a shaft by means of a revolving arm or ring called a clevis. Unlike a spoon, which has a wobbling action, a spinner blade rotates around the shaft when retrieved.

Other parts of a simple spinner include a locking device to accommodate a hook at one end of the shaft, a metal loop to which the line is tied at the other end of the shaft, and a series of metal or plastic beads that separate the blade from —and keep it from jamming against—the locking device and loop. In some spinners, notably the Colorado, the blade is mounted on a series of swivels instead of on a shaft.

Most spinners have either one or two blades. However, in some forms of fishing, particularly deep-water trolling for lake trout, eight or more spinner blades are mounted in tandem on a length of wire.

Most spinner blades have either a silver or a gold finish. Some, however, are painted in various colors, including black, yellow, and white, while others are striped and still others are made of simulated pearl. In general, the brighter finishes are best in shaded or discolored water and on overcast days, while the darker finishes are better in very clear water under bright skies.

Spinner blades have various shapes and other physical characteristics. Both shape and thickness determine how the blade reacts when retrieved. To illustrate this point, let's take a look at a few types of simple spinners, often used with bait, that have proven their worth over the years.

FOUR BASIC TYPES OF SPINNERS

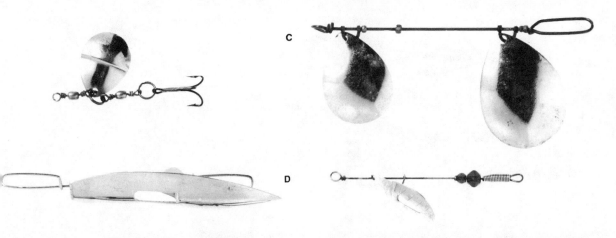

(A) Colorado Spinner. Old favorite that fills a variety of needs. Can be cast or trolled, with or without natural bait on tail treble hook. Small sizes can be effectively used with a fly rod in streams for trout. A worm or salmon egg on the tail hook frequently makes spinner extra attractive to fish. Good for just about all fresh-water species.

(B) Willow Leaf Spinner. A single or double-hook rig can be attached to this spinner to make it a good trolling lure. Used with worms or minnows, it takes fish in both fresh and salt water. Particularly effective when trolling blood or sand-worms for striped bass.

(C) Indiana Double-Blade. A multi-purpose spinner rig, this can be cast or trolled with a single or double-hook fixed to its shaft. Can be used as attractors when trolling for pike, pickerel, muskies, and similar freshwater species. This Indiana spinner has even been used on party boats by fisherman drifting cut bait along the bottom for fluke and flounder.

(D) June Bug Spinner. One of the most versatile spinners, it is available with one or two blades, with weighted or un-weighted shaft. As with other spinner rigs, it can be used with a single or double hook. The June Bug is especially effective when trolled with a nightcrawler or baitfish for pike, pickerel, walleyes, perch, muskies, and bass.

Colorado. Has a wide, nearly round blade that rotates well out from the shaft. Because it has considerable water resistance and spins relatively slowly, it is best suited for use in lakes and in streams with slow currents. A Colorado spinner used with a worm is a proven taker of trout, walleyes, and other fish.

Willow Leaf. Has a long, narrow blade that spins fast and close to the shaft. Having minimum water resistance, it is well suited for use in fast-flowing water. A willow-leaf spinner is often used with a worm, minnow, and other natural baits.

June Bug. Unusual in that the blade is attached directly to the shaft (there is no clevis), has a sort of "leg" that braces the blade against the shaft, and has a hole in the middle. A June Bug spinner with its hook sweetened by a nightcrawler

is a potent combination for trout, walleyes, and many other gamefish. The June Bug comes in various designs.

Spinner-blade sizes are usually classified by numbers. But the numbers vary with the manufacturers and are not a reliable guide for the buyer. It's easy enough to simply look over a selection of spinners and select the size that seems right for your particular purpose.

Many spinner-type lures are produced today and are extremely popular, especially among freshwater fishermen. In all of them, the basic attracting element is a revolving spinner blade. Most have some sort of weight built in along the shaft and a treble hook at the tail. In many, the treble hook is hidden or at least disguised with bucktail, feathers, or a skirt of rubber or plastic strands. Weedless hooks are becoming increasingly popular on these lures.

Crank Baits

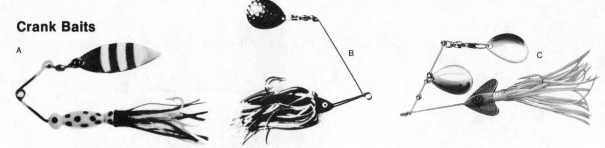

Typical safety-pin-type spinner baits include **(A)** Busy Body, **(B)** Heddon Climax, and **(C)** Tournament Hawaiian Wiggler

TYPICAL WEIGHTED SPINNERS

(A) Mepps Black Fury

(B) Mepps Aglia Plain

(C) Mepps Aglia with squirrel tail

(D) ABU Reflex

(E) Mepps Aglia Comet with plastic minnow

WEEDLESS SPINNER-TYPE LURES

(A) Sputterfuss

(B) Shimmy Wiggler

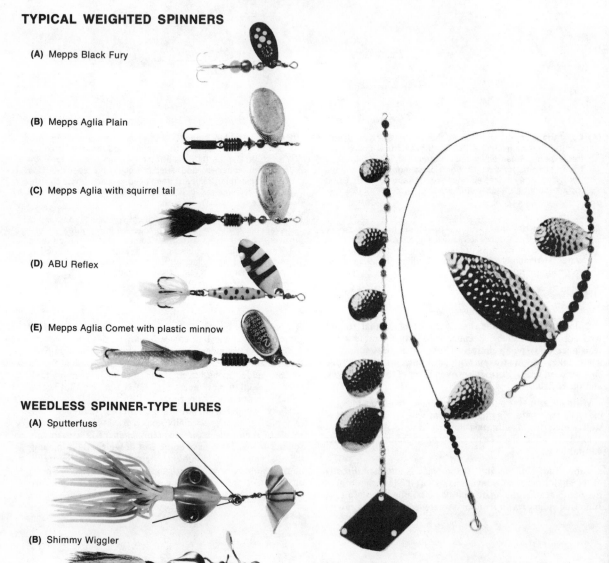

Typical trolling rigs for lake trout and other deep-running fish are **(A)** the Webertroll and **(B)** the Dave Davis Spinner.

Jigs

Generally speaking, a jig is any lure with a weighted head (usually lead), a fixed hook, and a tail of bucktail, feathers, nylon, or similar material. Jigs are made in sizes of 1/16-ounce to 6 ounces and even heavier, and they will take just about any fish that swims in fresh water and salt. Jigs imitate baitfish, crustaceans, and other gamefish forage. In some jigs, the hook rides with the point up, to minimize the chance of snagging.

Jigs, and related lures, take many forms, Here's a look at the most popular types.

Feathered Jig. Often called Japanese feathers, this jig is commonly used in saltwater trolling and casting. It consists of a heavy metal head with eyes. Through the head runs a wire leader, to the end of which the hook is attached. Running from the head down to the hook is a long tail, usually of feathers. A plastic sleeve covers the feathers for about half their length.

Bonito Jig. Similar to the feathered jig but smaller and having a fixed hook embedded in the metal head. Line is tied to ring on head. Used for salt-water trolling and casting.

Bucktail Jig. Consists of a lead head, embedded hook, and trailing tail of bucktail. Head has ring to which line is attached. Head is painted, with the most popular colors being white, red, yellow, and combinations of those colors. The most popular member of the jig family, bucktail jigs are used on a wide variety of freshwater and saltwater gamefish, especially largemouth and smallmouth bass, walleyes, pike, striped bass, bluefish, and many other bottom-feeders.

SALTWATER JIGS

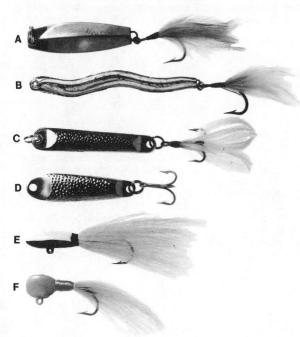

(A) Metal (Block-Tin) Squid with single free-swinging feathered hook.

(B) Metal (Block-Tin) Sand Eel with single free-swinging feathered hook.

(C) Spermullet hammered steel jig with treble feathered hook.

(D) Hopkins Shorty hammered steel jig.

(E) Bullet or Torpedo bucktail jig with single fixed hook.

(F) Upperman bucktail jig with single fixed hook.

JIGS AND JIG-AND-EEL RIGS

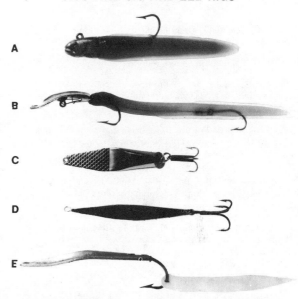

(A) **Alou Bait Tail.** Lead head, single hook, and plastic body, this rig comes in a variety of sizes for both fresh and salt water. It can be cast, trolled, or jigged.

(B) **Alou Shoestring.** A rigged artificial eel with weighted head and double hooks. In smaller sizes it can be effectively cast or trolled. In larger sizes, it will take big stripers, bluefish.

(C) **Garcia Egon Lure.** A typical jig with free-swinging treble hook. Cast or jigged, it can be fished effectively from surf, jetty, or boat. Should even work well through the ice for big trout.

(D) **Diamond Jig.** The mainstay of East Coast deep jiggers. Simple in design, it takes stripers, blues, mackerel, cod, pollock, and similar species. Frequently used in conjunction with one or more surgical tube teasers attached one foot or so above the jig.

(E) **Block-Tin Squid.** An old favorite, shown here with a pork rind strip, has proven itself a good casting and trolling rig for stripers, bluefish, and other inshore species.

SALTWATER TROLLING LURES

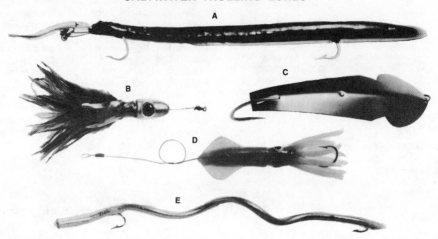

(A) **Alou Cow Killer.** An artificial eel with lead head and double hooks. Weighing six ounces and measuring 18 inches, it's the heaviest artificial eel made. Excellent for big striped bass and other large salt-water game fish.

(B) **Barracuda Jig.** A rig more commonly known as Japanese feathers, it is basically a trolling lure for offshore work on billfish, tuna, albacore, and bluefish.

(C) **Tony Accetta Pet Spoon.** Big with a single fixed hook, this type of lure is more commonly known as a bunker spoon. It

can be trolled with large strip of pork rind or an eel. One of the most effective lures for striped bass.

(D) **Leisure Lures' Plastic Squid.** With long wire leader running through body and attached to single hook, this rig is designed for offshore trolling for billfish, tuna, albacore, bluefish, and similar species.

(E) **Alou Custom Cure Trolling Tube.** A good offshore and inshore trolling lure, this double-hook tube can be twisted or formed to regulate shape and action to suit a variety of conditions.

Bullet Bucktail Jig. Same as standard bucktail jig except that head is bullet-shaped, coming to a blunt point.

Shad Dart. Small jig (usually weighing about ¼ ounce) with relatively long, narrow head, flat face, and short tail of bucktail or similar material. Usually painted in two colors, with most popular combinations being red and white, yellow and white, and red and yellow. An extremely popular lure for American (white) shad in East Coast rivers.

Metal (Block-Tin) Squids. Falling under the general category of jigs are these lures, which are used mostly in salt water for striped bass, bluefish, and the like. Made to resemble baitfish, they have a long, narrow body of block tin, stainless steel, chrome, or nickel-plated lead and either a single fixed hook or a free-swinging treble hook, with or without a tail of bucktail. Most metal squids range in length from 3 to 6 inches. All have bright finishes, usually silvery; in some the finish is smooth, while others have a hammered finish that gives a scalelike appearance. Among the most popular metal squids are types such as the Hopkins (which has a hammered finish; a long, narrow, flat body; and a free-swinging treble hook), the diamong jig (four-sided body, treble hook), and the sand eel (long, round, undulating body). A strip of pork rind often adds to the effectiveness of metal squids.

Jig and Eel. Consists of a small metal squid onto which is rigged a common eel, either the real McCoy (usually dead

and preserved) or a plastic artificial. These rigged eels range in length from about 6 inches up to a foot or longer. The jig and eel is a deadly combination for striped bass, big snook, redfish, and sea trout. Best retrieve depends on various conditions, but usually a slow, slightly erratic swimming motion is best.

How do you fish a jig? Most jigs—except the jig-and-eel combination and those designed for trolling—should be retrieved with sharp upward jerks of the rod tip so that they look like fleeing darting bait. Most jigs have little action of their own (though some are designed to wiggle when retrieved), so the angler must impart fish-attracting motion.

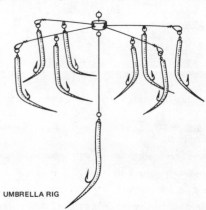

UMBRELLA RIG

Plastic Lures

Hundreds of years from now the history books may refer to our era as the Age of Plastic. And fishermen haven't escaped the gaze of the plastics manufacturers.

On the market today are soft-plastic lures that imitate just about anything any fish will eat. There are plastic worms, eels, snakes, crickets, crawfish, minnows, shrimp, hellgrammites, mullet, flies, beetles, grasshoppers, frogs, and many, many more. Even salmon eggs!

Surprisingly, a good many of these synthetic creations catch fish. A prime example is the plastic worm, which came into its own in the mid and late 1960's. It has accounted for some eye-popping stringers of largemouth bass, especially in big Southern lakes. A plastic worm threaded on a weedless hook and slithered through lily pads or an underwater weed bed is a real killer. Some plastic worms come with a weighted jig-type head and/or a spinner at the front.

PLASTIC LURES AND BAITS

(A) **Creme Shimmy Gal.** Use with weedless weighted or unweighted hook at head. Worked slowly along bottom, it's a good bass lure.

(B) **Bass Buster Jig Worm.** Combination lead-head jig and plastic worm. Stiff tuft of hair makes it weed resistant. Good bottom lure for bass.

(C) **Creme Eel.** Tops for big bass. Use with weighted or unweighted hook at head. Retrieve slow along bottom.

(D) **Creme Coho Herring Cut Bait.** Designed for coho salmon fishing, this plastic bait is most often used when drift fishing.

(E) **Creme Shrimp A-Go-Go.** Made with lead head, single fixed hook, and plastic body. Designed to imitate a shrimp, this jig works equally well in fresh or salt water.

(F) **Creme Salmon Egg Cluster.** Good steelhead lure.

(G) **Lisk Grub Jig.** A plastic fly rod lure that takes bass, panfish.

(H) **Lisk Weedless Jig.** Used with fly rod or ultralight spinning tackle, this inch worm imitation will catch bass, panfish, trout.

(I) **Creme Willow Fly.** An effective plastic lure for trout.

(J) **Creme Green Frog.** Use with fly rod or light spinning tackle. Good bass lure.

(K) **Creme Yellow Grasshopper.** A plastic lure for light spinning, it will take bass and trout.

(L) **Creme Black Cricket.** On a fly rod, this plastic insect will work on bass, trout, panfish.

(M) **Creme Hellgrammite.** On a fly rod, the hellgrammite, a trout's natural food, can be deadly.

Pork Rind

Pork rind, as used by fishermen, is the skin from the back of a hog. It is sold in jars containing a liquid preservative to prevent spoilage and to retain the rind's flexibility.

It used to be that pork rind was used only as an addition to a spoon or other lure. For example, a single-hook spoon with a 2- or 3-inch strip of pork rind was—and still is—a popular combination for pickerel, pike, and the like.

Pork rind is still widely used that way today. It is sold in many shapes and sizes, from tiny half-inch V-strips for panfish up to 6-inch strips for muskies and saltwater gamefish. Most of it is white.

But in recent years a number of all-pork-rind lures have appeared. They take such forms as spring lizards, worms, and jointed eels. These rind lures, many of them black, can be extremely effective, for they seem to give off an aroma or taste that fish like.

SOME PORK RIND DESIGNS

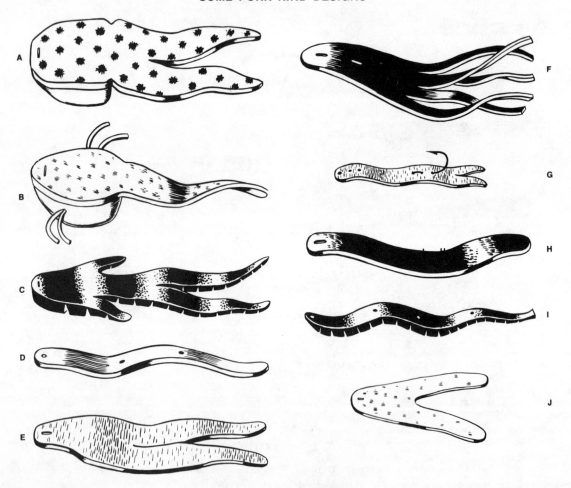

(A) Frog (Pork Chunk)
(B) Polly Woggler
(C) Spring Lizard
(D) Jig Strip
(E) Spinning Strip

(F) Pork Skirt
(G) Hook Strip
(H) Fly Strip
(I) Eel
(J) V-Strip

Flies

An artificial fly is a combination of feathers, hair, floss, tinsel, and other materials tied to a hook in such a way as to imitate a natural insect (dry and wet flies, including nymphs) or a baitfish (streamer flies and bucktails). Flies are used to take many gamefish but are designed principally for trout and salmon. There are four basic kinds of artificial flies: dry, wet (including nymph), streamer, and bucktail.

Dry Flies

The dry fly, designed to imitate a floating insect, is tied so that the fibers of the hackles (feathers) used stick out at approximately right angles to the shank of the hook. A properly tied dry fly sits high and lightly on the tips of its hackles, riding the surface of the water.

There are countless dry-fly patterns, but almost all of them fall into one of nine basic types. Here is a brief description of each type:

Downwing (or Sedge). Has a built-up body, hackle, and wings lying flat along the shank of the hook. It floats with hook underwater.

Divided Wing. The standard dry-fly type. Has two erect, separated wings of feather fibers, hackle, tapered body, and stiff, slender tail. It floats with hook above or partly underwater.

Hairwing. Has upright wings made of deer hair, as well as hackle, tapered body, and stiff tail. Floats with hook above or partly underwater.

Fanwing. Has large, flat, erect wings; hackle, body, and a stiff tail. Floats with hook above or partly underwater. The large wings make this fly readily visible to the angler.

Bivisible. Has no wings. White hackle is wound on body at the fly's head, and hackle of another color (brown, gray, and black are most popular) covers most of the remainder of body. The tail is stiff. Floats high, with hook above water, and is highly visible to angler.

Spentwing. Has slender wings that stick out horizontally from a tapered body, hackle, and stiff tail. Floats on wings and body with bend of the hook underwater.

Spider. Has no wings. The hackle is extra long and stiff. There is no body in the smaller sizes, a tinsel or herl body in the larger sizes. Stiff, extra long tail. Floats on hackle tips and tail with hook well out of the water.

Variant. Has upright divided wings, extra long and stiff hackle, very light body (or none at all), and stiff, extra long tail. Floats on hackle tips and tail with hook well out of water.

Hair Body. Has upright divided wings, hackle, body of clipped deer hair or similar material, and a stiff tail. Floats with hook partly underwater.

Keel Fly. Shank of the hook is weighted, causing the fly to ride upright in the water. The keel principle also has been applied to wet flies and streamers.

The budding fly fisherman who walks into a fishing-tackle store is sure to be overwhelmed by the display of artificial flies. Which patterns are best for his particular needs? Only experience can answer that question. However, here are ten basic dry-fly patterns—and the most productive sizes—that should be found in every trouter's fly box:

Light Cahill, Size 16
Gray Midge Hackle, Size 20
Black Flying Ant, Size 20
Red Variant, Size 14
Black Gnat, Size 12
Gray Wulff, Size 10
Blue Dun, Size 16
Adams, Size 12
Quill Gordon, Size 14
Jassid, Size 20

TYPICAL FLY
AND NOMENCLATURE

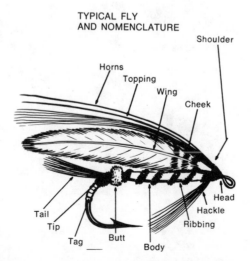

Shoulder
Horns
Topping
Wing
Cheek
Head
Hackle
Ribbing
Tail
Tip
Tag
Butt
Body

BASIC TYPES OF DRY FLIES

SPIDER

DOWNWING

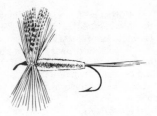

DIVIDED WING

VARIANT

HACKLE

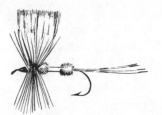

FANWING

HAIRBODY

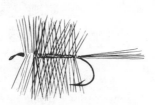

BIVISIBLE

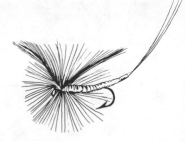

SPENTWING

GAUZE WING

KEEL FLY

PARACHUTE FLY

Wet Flies

Wet flies are tied to imitate submerged insects, either those that have fallen to the surface and drowned or those that are rising from the stream or lake bottom to the surface to hatch. Nymphs, which are classified as wet flies, are imitations of the larval or nymphal stages of underwater insects that rise to the surface before hatching.

As with dry flies, there is a bewildering number of wet-fly patterns. However, most of them fall into one of four basic types. Here's a brief description of each type:

Divided Wing. Two prominent separated wings tied at about a 30° angle from the shank of the hook. A wisp of hackle, body, stiff tail.

Hairwing. Wing of deer hair extending over shank of hook, wisp of hackle, body, tail.

Featherwing. Swept-back wing of feather fibers, soft hackle, tapered body, sparse tail.

Hackle. Soft hackle tied on at head and extending back over built-up body all around fly. Sparse tail.

Here are ten wet-fly patterns that should produce well for the trout fisherman:

Gray Hackle, Yellow Body, Size 10
Brown Hackle, Size 10
Coachman, Size 12
Royal Coachman, Size 12
Black Gnat, Size 14
Quill Gordon, Size 14
Blue Dun, Size 16
Light Cahill, Size 16
March Brown, Size 12
Ginger Quill, Size 16

Nymphs

It is impossible to break down the various nymph patterns into broad classifications. However, most nymphs have the

BASIC TYPES OF WET FLIES

DIVIDED WING HAIRWING

FEATHERWING HACKLE

following basic characteristics: no wings; wisps of soft hackle at head; tapered body, usually of dubbed fur; sparse tail of a few feather fibers.

Here are ten nymph patterns that no trout fisherman should be without:

March Brown, Size 12
Ginger Quill, Size 14
Yellow May, Size 12
Fresh Water Shrimp, Size 8
Light Mossback, Size 6
Large Stone Fly, 2X Long-Shank Size 8
Large May Fly, 2X Long-Shank Size 10
Caddis, 2X Long-Shank, Size 10
Dark Olive, 2X Long-Shank, Size 12
Montana, Size 4

OTHER TYPES OF WET FLIES

WOOLY WORM GAUZE WING KEEL FLY

SPIDER BASS FLY PANFISH TEASER

Streamers and Bucktails

Streamer flies and bucktails are tied to imitate a minnow or other baitfish on which gamefish feed. They are widely used in both fresh water and salt. Many saltwater streamers and bucktails, and some used in fresh water, have two hooks—the main hook, on which the dressings are tied, and a trailer hook. Streamers and bucktails are well-known for producing big fish.

Streamers are tied with long wings of feathers. Bucktails are similar—but more durable—flies tied with wings of hair, usually deer hair. Most streamers and bucktails are tied on Size 8 and 10 long-shank hooks. Some have bodies, but in others the bare shank of the hook shows.

Here is a list of ten of the most productive streamer patterns and ten top bucktail patterns (best hook sizes are 6 to 12, unless otherwise noted):

STREAMERS	BUCKTAILS
Black Ghost	Black Prince
Gray Ghost	Brown and White
Supervisor	Black and White
Mickey Finn	Red and White
Black-Nosed Dace	Mickey Finn
Red and Yellow	Platinum Blonde, Size 1/0
Colonel Fuller	Strawberry Blonde, Size 1/0
Red and White Multi-wing, Size 1	Brown Muddler Minnow, Sizes 1/0 to 10
Black Marabou	White Muddler Minnow, Sizes 1/0 to 10
White Marabou	White Marabou Muddler, Sizes 1/0 to 6

BASIC TYPES OF STREAMERS

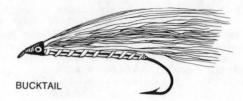

BUCKTAIL

FEATHER STREAMER

MARIBOU

MUDDLER MINNOW

TYPES OF NYMPHS

DARK HENDRICKSON

STONEFLY CREEPER

MAYFLY NYMPH

STONEFLY NYMPH

MARCH BROWN

TYPES OF TERRESTRIALS

ANT

BEETLE

GRASSHOPPER

HORNBERG

INCH WORM

JASSID

Terrestrials

A class of artificial flies that is unique and deserves special mention is the terrestrials—a group of flies, both wet and dry, that are tied to imitate insects that are born on land and then fly, jump, fall, crawl, or are blown into the water and become food for trout and other fish. Such insects include ants, grasshoppers, inchworms, beetles, houseflies, and others.

Among the most popular and productive terrestrial patterns are the Inchworm, the Black Ant (especially in very small sizes), and the Jassid. The Jassid is a relatively new fly that was developed in Pennsylvania and is particularly effective in limestone streams. It is tied on tiny hooks, with best sizes being 18, 20, and 22.

Choosing the Right Fly

Selecting the correct fly to use at any given time is a problem that has both delighted and dumfounded anglers since the dawn of this sport. Dry fly or wet? What color? What size?

The answers to those questions can often be found in the water at your feet. Study it carefully, both at the surface and underneath. If insects are flying from the surface, you are in the middle of a hatch, and you should select a dry fly that imitates as closely as possible the color and size of the natural insects. If you see subsurface insects, choose a wet fly or nymph of similar size and color.

However, spotting and identifying the natural may be difficult, due to water conditions, the minute size of the insects, and the sparseness of the hatch (a "hatch" occurs when aquatic insects rise from the stream or lake bottom and change from the larval stage to winged adult flies). Also, the fisherman may not have the right size and color of artificials in his fly box.

The following table will aid the angler in solving the problem of fly choice. It gives the approximate date on which each insect can be expected to emerge, or hatch, from the water and the general localities in which these hatches occur.

TROUT STREAM INSECT EMERGENCE TABLES

COMMON NAME	SCIENTIFIC NAME	HABITAT	EMERGENCE DATE
Little Black Stonefly (3)	Taeniopteryx maura	Pa., W. Va., Tenn., Mass., N. Y., Minn., Mo., Md., Kan.	Apr. 15
Red Quill (1)	Ephemerella subvaria	N.Y., Pa., N. J., Ont., Quebec	Apr. 16
	Epeorus pleuralis, iron fraudator		Apr. 17
Little Black Caddis (2)	Chimarra aterrima	Pa., Can., N. Y., N. J., Del., Ind., Ga., Fla., Washington	May 1
Red Legged March Fly (5)	Bibio femoratus	Pa., N. Y., N. J.	May 1
Smokey Alderfly (5)	Sialis infumata	Que., N. S., N. Y., New England, N. J., Pa., Wash., Mich., Ill., Minn., Calif.	May to Sept.
Black Midge (5)	Glyptotendipes lobiferus	Pa., N. Y., N. J., Ont.	May 1
Light Stonefly (3)	Isoperla signata	Pa., N. Y., N. S.	May 8 to May 25
Penns Creek Caddisfly (2)	Brachycentrus numerosus	Well distributed through the northern hem.	May 15
Black Quill (1)	Leptophlebia cupida	Pa., Ohio, N. S., Nfld., Ill., Can., N. Y., N. H., N. C., R. I., N. J., Ont., Quebec, Mass.	May 16
Early Brown Spinner (1)	Leptophlebia cupidus	Same as above	May 15
Yellow Spider (4)	Antocha saxicola	Well distributed throughout the northern hem.	May 15
Stonefly (3)	Neophasganophora capitata	Pa., N. Y., Md., Mass., Minn., Quebec, N. S., Ind., Ill., Mich., Kan., Tenn., N. C.	May 16
Spotted Sedge (2)	Hydropsyche slossonae	Pa., N. Y., N. H., Ill.	May 20
Pale Evening Dun (1)	Ephemerella dorothea and rotunda	Pa., N. Y., Can.	May 20
March Brown (1)	Stenonema vicarium	Pa., N. Y., N. B., N. H., Quebec, Tenn.	May 21
Great Red Spinner (1)	Stenonema vicarium	Same as above	May 21
Green Caddis (2)	Rhyacophila lobifera	Pa., N. Y., Ill.	May 21
Dark Green Drake (1)	Hexagenia recurvata	Pa., N. Y., Mass., Me., W. Va., Mich.	May 23
Brown Drake (1)	Hexagenia recurvata	Same as above	May 24
Ginger Quill Dun (2)	Stenonema fuscum	Pa., N. Y., Ont., Que., New Brunswick	May 25
Pale Evening Spinner (1)	Ephemerella dorothea and rotunda	Same as Pale Evening Dun	May 26
Ginger Quill Spinner (1)	Stenonema fuscum	Same as Ginger Quill Dun	May 26
Fish Fly (5)	Chauliodes sericornis	Pa., N. Y., Md., Ga., Ohio, Minn.	May 26
Green Drake (1)	Ephemera guttulata	Pa., N. Y., Tenn., Ont., Quebec	May 28
Black Drake (1)	Ephemera guttulata	Same as Green Drake	May 28
Gray Drake (1)	Ephemera guttulata	Same as Green Drake	May 28
Iron Blue Dun (1)	Leptophlebia johnsoni	Pa., N. Y., N. H., Que., Ontario	May 28
Grannon (5)	Brachycentrus fuliginosus	Pa., N. Y., Wash., Ontario	May 29
Jenny Spinner (1)	Leptophlebia johnsoni	Same as Iron Blue Dun	
Brown Quill (1)	Siphlonurus quebecensis	Pa., N. Y., N. C., Ont., Quebec	June 1
Green bottle or			Variable
Blue bottle fly (5)	Lucilia casear	Commonly distr.	
Whirling Cranefly (4)	Tipula bella	Pa., N. Y., N. J.	June 1
Orange Cranefly (4)	Tipula bicornis	Same as above	June 1
Golden Eyed Gauze Wing (5)	Chrysopa occulata	Commonly distr.	Variable
White Mayfly (1)	Stenonema rubromaculatum	Pa., N. Y., Mass., Ill., Ont., Quebec, N. B., N. S.	June 2
White Gloved Howdy (1)	Isonychia albomanicata	Pa., N. Y., Ont., N. C.	June 27
Yellow Sally (3)	Isoperla spp.	Commonly distr.	June 28
Golden Spinner (1)	Potomanthus distinctus	Pa., N. Y., W. Va., Ohio	June 28
Willow or Needle Stonefly (3)	Leuctra grandis	Pa., N. Y., N. J., North Carolina	June 28
Stonefly Nymph (3)	Acroneuria lycorias	Pa., N. H., N. Y., Mass., Me., W. Va., Mich., Wisc., Que.	
Brown Silverhorns (2)	Athripsodes wetzeli	Pa., N. Y. Similar species in Wisc. and Ontario	June 29
Big Orange Sedge (2)	Neuronia postica	Pa., Ga., Mass., Wisc., Newfoundland and Washington, D. C.	June 30 July 1
Yellow Drake (1)	Ephemera varia	Pa., N. Y., Mich., N. H., Ont.	July 1
White Caddis (2)	Leptocella exquisita, leptocella albida, leptocella spp.	Florida to Canada	July 1
Deer Fly (5)	Chrysops vittatus	Eastern and Northern States	Variable
Green Midge (5)	Chironomus modestus	Pa., N. Y., N. J., Ontario	July 4

NOTE. The number in parentheses following the common name of the insect indicates the following: 1. Mayfly; 2. Caddisfly; 3. Stonefly; 4. Cranefly; 5. Miscellaneous.

Compiled by Chas. M. Wetzel.

Bass Bugs

If any form of fly fishing approaches the thrill of taking a wary trout on a dry fly, it is having a belligerent largemouth or smallmouth bass burst through the surface and engulf an enticingly twitched bass bug.

Bass bugs are fly-rod lures created to imitate such bass morsels as frogs, bees, dragonflies, and mice. Because of the size of a bass's mouth, these surface lures are tied on large hooks—No. 4 to 2/0 in most cases. However, smaller versions of these bugs are made for panfish.

Most bass bugs fall into one of two categories: those with solid bodies (usually of cork, plastic, or balsa wood) and those with bodies of deer hair.

Many cork or balsa bugs have some hackle or bucktail at the tail to partly disguise the hook. Some have a perpendicular hollowed-out face so that when the angler jerks the rod tip the bug makes a popping sound that often brings a bass charging out of his lair. These bugs are called poppers. Others have a more streamlined body and are designed to be twitched slowly rather than jerked.

Deer-hair bugs are, as you might expect, made of deer hair wound onto a hook and clipped to form the body shape of a mouse, large insect, and such. These bugs are best fished very slowly.

Weedless arrangements, usually stiff monofilament or light wire, are becoming more and more popular on bass bugs today.

SOLID-BODY BUGS

DEER-HAIR BUGS

(A) **Fly Rod Popper.** Hollowed-out face makes popping sound when jerked. Good dawn and dusk lure for smallmouth and largemouth bass and other warm-water fish.

(B) **Firebug.** Torpedo-head bug with phosphorescent plastic body and tail strip. Effective night-time lure for bass.

(C) **Dylite Popping Frog.** Hollowed-out face with bucktail "legs," this popping bug takes bass along shore and near lily pads.

(D) **Dylite Nitwit.** A slim, rubber-legged bug for panfish.

(E) **Dylite Slim Bug.** Small popper effective for both bass and panfish.

(A) **Hair Bug.** Made of carefully trimmed deer hair, this bug is at its best when twitched in glass-smooth water. Tied especially for bass.

(B) **Henshall Lure.** Trimmed deer-hair bug with hair dyed for special effect. Tops for bass.

(C) **Hair Mouse.** Tied with deer hair and trimmed to imitate a mouse, this bug will work on bass, pickerel, and pike.

(D) **Mountain Hopper.** A good deer-hair bug for bass, trout, and panfish.

Tying Flies and Bugs

There are few pleasures in the sport of fishing that can match that of taking a trout, salmon, or other fish on a fly of your own creation. And there are other reasons for taking up this ancient art. On winter evenings, with the snow piled high outside and a bitter wind rattling the shutters, you can sit at the tying bench, reliving past fishing experiences and putting together the ingredients for future ones. And once you get the hang of it, you can tie respectable flies for a fraction of what you would pay for them in a store.

Tools

The fly-tyer needs only a few inexpensive tools. Let's take a look at each one and its use:

Vise. The most important device in the fly-tyer's workshop, the vise is used to hold a hook securely and in the best position for the tyer to work around it. Most popular vise is the lever-and-cam type.

Hackle Pliers. Used to hold the tips of hackle feathers so that the tyer can wind the feathers onto the hook. Squeezing the sides of the pliers opens the jaws. There are two types: rubber-cushioned and English style. Both work well. A surgeon's artery forceps also makes an adequate hackle pliers.

Scissors. Best type is a pair of sharp fine-point scissors with either straight or curved blades. Larger scissors are helpful for making hair bugs. Scissors are used to cut thread and other dressing materials and perform other auxiliary duties.

Bobbin. A device that holds the spool of tying thread and hangs down from the hook, providing necessary tension on the thread, while the tyer is at work. Most bobbins have a tube through which the thread is fed. Bobbin saves thread, and it is especially useful to tyers who have rough hands that tend to fray the thread.

Dubbing Needle. A large, fairly heavy, sharp steel needle set in handle of wood or plastic. It performs many duties, including picking out fur bodies to make them fuzzier, picking out wound-under hackle, dividing wings, separating strands of floss and the like, applying head lacquer, and making the whip finish.

Other helpful fly-tying tools and auxiliaries include tweezers, hackle gauge, magnifying glass, hackle cutter, hackle clip, hackle guards, whip finisher, head lacquer, and thread wax.

How to Tie Flies

The following information from well-known fisherman and fly-tyer Tom McNally, and the accompanying drawings, show the simple step-by-step procedure involved in tying the basic flies—streamers, nymphs, dry flies, wet flies.

BASIC FLY TYING TOOLS

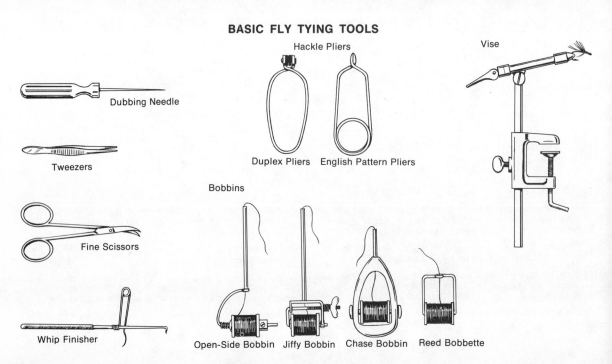

Dubbing Needle

Tweezers

Fine Scissors

Whip Finisher

Hackle Pliers

Duplex Pliers   English Pattern Pliers

Bobbins

Open-Side Bobbin   Jiffy Bobbin   Chase Bobbin   Reed Bobbette

Vise

Writing of fly tying, a friend of mine described this ancient art as "the technique of fastening various materials on a hook to suggest real or fancied insects or food for the purpose of deceiving fish." I like that definition. It clears fly tying of the mysticism with which many would like to bury it. Actually, it's not difficult to turn out handsome, fish-catching flies. Anyone with a yen to learn can become a reasonably accomplished fly-tyer. Persons with special aptitude learn how to do it almost overnight.

Many years ago I taught my wife to tie flies after three evening sessions at my worktable. Today, she shows me a trick or two. Some years ago I taught my mother—who was looking for a hobby—to make shad flies and popping bugs. Those she produced were sold in tackle stores. I don't know how many friends I've introduced to fly tying, and none failed eventually to turn out flies that were both attractive and fishable.

Fly tying was going on in Macedonia 2,000 years ago. A wasplike insect called hippuras was imitated by dressing a hook with purplish yarn and creamy hackles. The flies were floated, dry-fly fashion, on the Astraeus River. Ever since then, anglers have been using artificial flies—many of them tying their own. Judging from the growing interest in fly tying, fishermen will continue dressing their own hooks so long as there's fishing to be done. One doesn't have to be a watchmaker, a surgeon, or an engineer to tie flies. All that's needed is a little common sense—and practice.

To become a professional or recognized fly-tyer, of course, takes experience. And the intricacies of producing masterful flies would require a book-length treatise. But any beginner who absorbs the details here and studies the illustrations, should be able to tie the simpler flies. Once big streamers and wet flies are mastered, and once you get the "feel" of the materials, the smaller and more complicated dry flies and nymphs can be attempted. The techniques are basically the same.

Why is fly tying growing in popularity? Because tyers save money? No, it's because fly tying is fun. Fishermen get more personal satisfaction out of gilling a bonefish or netting a trout with a hook they themselves stuck into a vise and dolled up with feathers, tinsel, and fur.

Dollars can be saved by home-tying, of course. A fly that would cost 85¢ at the tackle shop can be self-made for about 5¢. You can get a start in the fly-tying game for about $15. A well-rounded outfit of tools and materials, sufficient to produce hundreds of flies, can be had for $25 to $30. Your hunting, or that of friends, will add duck, goose, turkey, pheasant, and grouse feathers to your stock of materials, as well as rabbit, fox, squirrel, and skunk fur. Deer, moose, elk, and bear skins are useful. The hair or feathers from almost any wildlife can be utilized by the fly-tyer.

The tyer's mainstay, however, is the common barnyard chicken. Its hackles are used in nearly every fly. The great bulk of fly-tying materials comes from material houses, but even direct purchase is inexpensive. If you wind up like most tyers, thoroughly wrapped up in the hobby, you'll take on enough materials in a few years to open your own supply house. But like other fly-tyers, you wouldn't part with a hair of your motley assortment.

To begin, you'll need a few basic tools: vise, hackle pliers, scissors, razor blade. In the early days, flies were tied by holding the hook between one's fingers, but in 1897 D. H.

Thompson ended this by producing a lever-and-cam type vise—the style most widely used and copied today. The vise is your most important single piece of equipment, and a good one (about $10) should be purchased. Fine-pointed scissors will run a dollar or two, the hackle pliers about $1.50. You may want a bobbin to hold your spool of tying thread. It's inexpensive, frequently replaces hackle pliers, saves thread, and generally makes fly tying easier.

A beginner's basic materials should include thread (size 00 nylon), lacquer or head cement, hooks, hackles (neck, back, and breast feathers from roosters or gamecocks), duck wing quills, mallard breast feathers, golden-pheasant tippets, assortments of silk floss and chenille (a kind of tufted cord), tinsel, and peacock herl from the "eyed" tail feathers of peacocks, as well as mylar, a shiny metallic material that comes in narrow strips and in tube form. These materials, and more, usually are stocked by better sports and hobby stores. Some firms that deal in fly-tying material supply catalogs, generally with photographs, that describe and price materials. The hook is the most important single factor in fishing, so tie your flies with the best.

Streamers

Although you may have no use for large streamer flies, they are easy-to-tie jobs that are ideal for your first lessons in fly tying. Stick to streamers until you get the knack of handling the tools and materials. It won't be necessary to follow a standard pattern in tying one of these big streamers, so the need for specific materials is lessened.

Always prepare your working area, tools, and materials, before starting a fly. Rig a bright lamp on your desk, and place a large sheet of white cardboard or white paper under your vise to provide a white background while you work on the fly. That makes the fly easier to see, materials simpler to locate. You'll need a short length of chenille, floss, or wool for the body of your streamer. Preferred colors are black, white, yellow, or red. About six hackles three to four inches long will make the wing, and they can be one of the colors mentioned, mixed colors, or natural brown or barred-grizzly feathers from Plymouth Rock chickens. Two or three extra hackles, colored differently than ones used in the wing, also will be needed.

Mount your vise at a comfortable height and clamp a No. 2 hook in it. The tying thread must be started on the hook. Most tyers first wax the thread since this waterproofs it, helps it hold to the hook, generally produces a stronger fly. However, waxing takes time, and I doubt that it's vital to the durability of a fly. I haven't waxed thread for years, yet my flies stay together. I apply a generous portion of fly-tying cement to the hook shank, then wind the tying thread from the hook eye to the bend. The cement waterproofs the thread and locks it to the hook.

When you've reached the hook bend with your thread, (see drawing No. 1) cut off any excess, then tie in one end of the chenille (floss or wool) by looping the tying thread over it tightly (drawing 2). Wind the thread back to the hook eye, and let the bobbin hang or attach hackle pliers to the thread to keep it taut. The body material can be wound to within $1/16$ inch of the hook eye (drawing 4), and tied off with the thread (drawing 5). The thread is looped in tight turns over the material to keep it in place. Be careful not to

TYING A STREAMER FLY

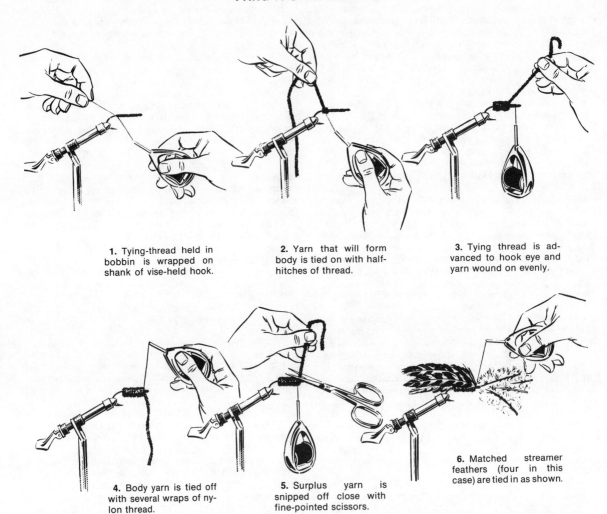

1. Tying-thread held in bobbin is wrapped on shank of vise-held hook.

2. Yarn that will form body is tied on with half-hitches of thread.

3. Tying thread is advanced to hook eye and yarn wound on evenly.

4. Body yarn is tied off with several wraps of nylon thread.

5. Surplus yarn is snipped off close with fine-pointed scissors.

6. Matched streamer feathers (four in this case) are tied in as shown.

bring body material all the way out to the hook eye or you'll have no room to tie off other materials or to form the fly's head. Excess body material is clipped off. Now comes the most difficult part of fly tying—attaching wings. Whether the fly is a streamer, nymph, wet, or dry, beginners usually have most trouble with wings.

Choose from four to six hackles and use your fingernails to clean some of the fuzzy fibers from the stems at the butt ends of the feathers. Now group the feathers in streamer-wing fashion and—holding them securely between two fingers of the left hand—place them in position on top of the hook, with the webby butts extending beyond the eye. They're tied in with tight loops of thread (drawing 6). Be sure to hold them tightly while tying. Otherwise the hackles will turn on the hook and go in cockeyed. After making several tight turns over the butts, you can clip off the surplus (drawing 7).

Final step is hackling the head of the fly. The hackle feather (two or more may be needed to make a bushy fly) is wound around the hook so that the separate fibers flare outward like bristling hairs. This is the technique used in putting hackles on wet and dry flies. Good hackles are especially important on a dry fly because they make it float. Strip the web from the hackle feather, place it against the head of the fly at an angle (drawing 8), and secure with a few tight loops of thread. The hackle, gripped at the loose end by hackle pliers, should be turned around the fly two or three times. Then the thread can be wound over them once or twice, and the hackle tips cut off (drawing 10). Now the fly head is finished with several turns of tying thread (drawing 11), and the thread knotted off with a series of half-hitches. Cement the head of the fly (drawing 12) to waterproof it and keep knots secure. The whip-finish knot—identical to the one rod-makers use in attaching guides—is better than half-hitches,

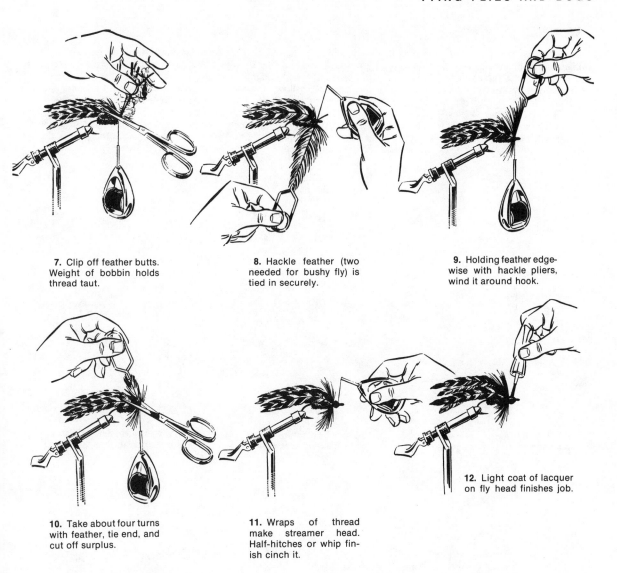

7. Clip off feather butts. Weight of bobbin holds thread taut.

8. Hackle feather (two needed for bushy fly) is tied in securely.

9. Holding feather edge-wise with hackle pliers, wind it around hook.

10. Take about four turns with feather, tie end, and cut off surplus.

11. Wraps of thread make streamer head. Half-hitches or whip finish cinch it.

12. Light coat of lacquer on fly head finishes job.

but it's a little beyond the beginning stage. Actually half-hitches, properly knotted and cemented, will keep a fly together indefinitely. The whip finish can be executed either manually or with the aid of a device called a whip finisher. For a look at both methods, see end of this section.

The streamer is now finished, unless you'd like to paint "eyes" on it. This is easy to do with red, yellow, white, or black lacquer. You can buy small bottles of lacquer that have tiny brushes fixed to the caps. Most fly-tyers paint their fly heads black. Lacquer dries in a few minutes. The fly's "eyes" are put on over the black base by dipping the blunt end of a finishing nail or wood match in light-color lacquer and touching it to the head of the fly. Soon as that dries, a dark "pupil" is added. It's my opinion that such dolling up adds nothing to a fly's fish-appeal, but it makes a fly more attractive to fishermen.

When you can tie one of these large streamers so it's proportioned correctly and won't come apart if you tug at a feather, you've mastered the fundamentals of fly tying. Methods you've learned in making this fly apply to any other pattern, including wets, nymphs, and dries.

The better streamers have tails, tinsel bodies, tinsel over chenille, wool or floss, perhaps colorful "cheeks" and "topping." The tying in of all these extras can be learned by following an advanced book on fly tying or watching some experienced tyer.

Large streamers can be made with marabou feathers, bucktail hair, or saddle hackles. Either way, they're good for large trout, black bass, pike, walleyes, and salt-water species such as bonefish, striped bass, snook, and tarpon.

Wet Flies

A wet fly, whether bass or trout-size, is tied much like a streamer, except that wing material usually is cut from duck-wing quills or large turkey quills. Turkey quills are used in the typical wet fly shown in the accompanying illustrations. Other materials in this fly are red duck quill, silver tinsel, black silk floss, and red hackles.

Start your tying thread the same as to tie a streamer, only continue wrapping it around the hook to build up a tapered body (see wet-fly drawing No. 1). Cut a small section from the red duck quill and bind it down at the bend of the hook (drawing 2) with a few turns of thread. Be sure the tail is tied in tightly and is centered on top of the hook. Drawing 3 shows the finished tail, with excess cut off. Next tie in a length of silver tinsel and several strands of black floss. The tying thread should be brought to the eye of the hook, floss wrapped over the body, followed by the tinsel (drawing 4). Floss and tinsel are secured by thread at the head of the fly, and the surplus is trimmed off (drawing 5).

TYING A BASS WET FLY

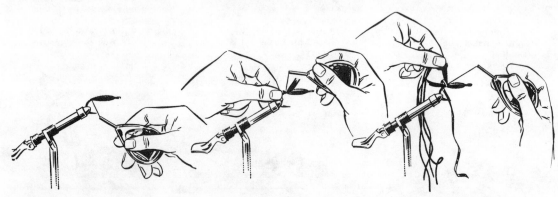

1. Start fly by building up rounded body with tying thread.

2. Tail of fly is cut from duck's wing feather and tied as shown.

3. Body material: one strand tinsel, three threads black floss.

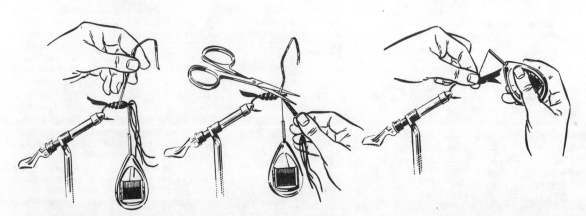

4. Floss goes on first and is held by thread loop while tinsel is wound.

5. Tie down floss and thread near hook eye. Snip off surplus.

6. Cut two matched sections from turkey wing feather for fly wings.

Attaching the wing is next. Select a pair of turkey quills and cut sections, one from each side of a feather, approximately half an inch wide. Place the two wing sections together, tips matched, curved sides facing. Grasp them firmly between thumb and forefinger and place them on the shank behind the eye, as in drawing 6. (Pinching the wings firmly during the tying-on can't be over-emphasized. When wings are poorly done, it's usually because they were not held firmly while being tied.) Bring the tying thread over the wings and down on the opposite side sliding it slightly back between the fingers. Pinching the wings tightly, pull the thread down, following with several turns over the butts. Now the wing should appear as in drawing 7 with butts ready to be trimmed. Final step is tying soft red hackle behind the fly head, just as was done with the big streamer. Drawings 9 through 11 show this step. Tying thread should be half-hitched (drawing 12) and lacquered (drawing 13).

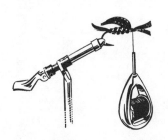

7. Use several wraps of thread to cinch the fly wings securely.

8. Snip off butt fragments of wings close to hook shank.

9. Dark hackle feather is tied at head and wound on edgewise.

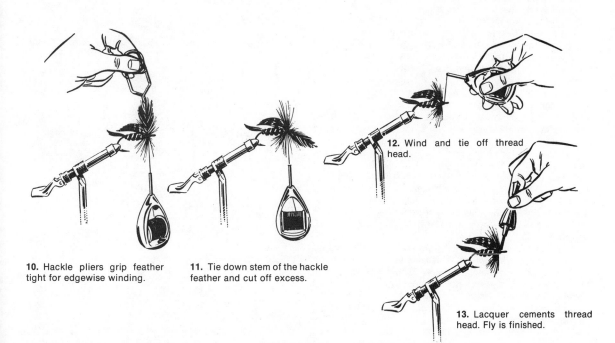

10. Hackle pliers grip feather tight for edgewise winding.

11. Tie down stem of the hackle feather and cut off excess.

12. Wind and tie off thread head.

13. Lacquer cements thread head. Fly is finished.

Nymphs

Nymphs are the trout-catchingest flies made, good also for smallmouth bass and panfish. One of the simplest to make is the "attractor" type—which doesn't imitate any particular live nymph but suggests several kinds of real nymphs.

Begin the nymph by tying in a "tail" (see typical-nymph drawing 1). Tail material can be fibers from a feather, sections of peacock herl, deer, or boar hairs. Pig bristle makes an excellent tail because it isn't broken easily by fish. A narrow section cut from a turkey feather, or olive or black duck quill, will serve to make the nymph's back or wing case. Tie it in just above the tail (drawing 2). A short length of tinsel and some wool yarn, chenille, or floss (drab colors) are put on next (drawing 3). Wind the tying thread back and forth over the shank, making a tapered body form, then wind on the body material and tinsel (drawing 4), tying them off near the hook eye. The quill section is brought forward, covering the top half of the nymph's body, tied down at the hook eye with a few tight turns of thread (drawing 5), and surplus is trimmed. Spin a small, webby hackle around the head, tie off, and trim so fibers extend only from the underside of the nymph to simulate legs. I usually lacquer a nymph's head, but some tyers lacquer the body too.

Dry Flies

The bivisible—invented by the late Edward R. Hewitt—is the easiest dry fly to build. The bivisible is made by winding stiff, dry-fly-quality rooster neck hackles along the shank of a hook. Usually two or three hackles are needed to give a bivisible bulk enough to float well. Simplest way to start a bivisible is by tying in the tip sections of a couple of hackles at the bend of a hook allowing the tips to extend backward to form a tail. The tying thread is then brought forward to the hook eye, the hackles turned around the hook tightly and finally tied down at the hook eye. That's all there is to this all-hackle dry fly. You'll find that it's a fish-catcher, too.

Excluding salmon flies, dry flies with upright wings are the most difficult flies to tie. Don't attempt them until you've had experience at tying the other types, and then start by making simple patterns. If you concentrate on large dries, no smaller than hook size 6 or size 8, the work will come to you faster.

The materials used for dry flies are selected for flotation, for resistance to water absorption. Chenille, for example, becomes heavy with water, so it's never used in a good dry fly. The hackles and tail are what float a fly, so the finest quality gamecock or rooster neck hackles should be used. Common dry-fly body materials include floss, raffia (fiber from the raffia palm), deer or moose hair, quill, peacock herl, and muskrat fur.

To make a Black Gnat dry fly (see typical dry-fly illustrations) start the tying thread as usual. Cut a narrow section from each side of a matched, slate-colored, duck wing quill. Place the wing sections together, curved sides out. Grasping them firmly between thumb and forefinger, place them on the hook over the eye (drawing 1) and bring the thread over the sections and down, taking several tight turns. Still holding the sections firmly between the fingers, raise them erect, bring the tying thread in front of them, and make enough turns against the wing bases to keep them upright, as shown

TYING A TYPICAL NYMPH

1. Tie in three strands of peacock herl for the tail.

2. Piece of turkey feather represents folded wing.

3. Dark wool yarn and silver tinsel are body materials.

4. Wind on tinsel last to get rib effect shown.

5. Tie down wing, add wisp of hackle and make thread head.

TYING A DRY FLY (Black Gnat Patte

1. Wrap hook shank with thread and tie on wings.

2. Turns of thread anchor wings. Now tie on tail.

3. Tie in black yarn and wind it forward to wings.

4. Tie on hackle feather and wind it on edgewise.

5. Trim off surplus and tie and lacquer fly head.

in drawing 2. Spread the wings apart, and wrap thread between them to the opposite side of the hook, reversing to describe a figure 8 between the sections. Tie in a few stiff black hairs or some suitable hackle fibers for a tail (drawing 2). Cut off the excess tail fibers, then tie in black silk floss (drawing 3) and bring the tying thread forward to front of wings. A glossy-black hackle feather (two may be needed) is tied in front of the wings as shown in drawing 4. Secure the hackle feather with several turns of thread. Then use hackle pliers to grasp the tip of the hackle and take a turn or two in front of the wings and two or three turns in back. Catch the hackle tip with tying thread and bind it down. Cut off the surplus end of the hackle feather. Finish the fly with a small, neat head made with the tying thread. Lacquer the head. That's all. Your first winged dry fly is finished. Your second dry fly will be easier than the first, the third easier still, and so on.

Cork Bug

You can buy cork bodies in many different shapes and sizes, or you can shape and size your own from a large piece of cork, using a razor blade and an emery board or small file. Be sure to sand the body smooth so that you get a good finish when you paint it.

Here are the basic steps in making a cork-bodied bug:

Place a hump-shanked hook (available at most tackle-supply outlets) in the vise, coat the shank with liquid cement, and wrap the part that is to be covered by the cork body with tying thread. With a razor blade make a slit in the cork body, fill the slit with cement, and press the cork into position on the hook shank (Drawing No. 1).

Give the cork body two coats of liquid cement, clear enamel, or wood sealer, and let dry.

Tie to the shank of the hook, behind the cork body, four or six neck hackles (badger is a good choice) so that they flare out well and thus give a lifelike action when on the water (Drawing No. 2).

Wind on two or three soft hackle feathers to form the collar, tie them off, and cement the windings. Paint cork body with enamel of whatever color suits you, and paint on eyes (Drawing No. 3).

TYING A TYPICAL CORK BUG

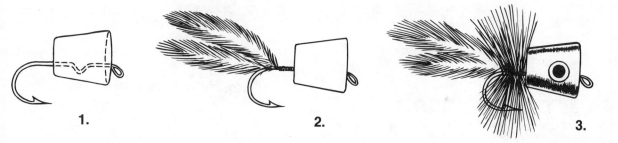

1.　　　　　　　　**2.**　　　　　　　　**3.**

Tying the Whip Finish

Budding fly-tyers who are confronted with drawings of how to tie the whip finish may be inclined to switch to golf. But though this knot looks complicated, it can be mastered in about ten minutes of practice, once the basic steps have been learned. The whip finish is undoubtedly the neatest way to finish off a fly. It is practically invisible, even on tiny dry flies.

There are two ways to make the whip finish—manually (that is, with the fingers alone) and with the aid of an ingenious little device called the whip finisher.

Here's how to do it manually (for purposes of clarity, the sketches show the knot itself, without the finger manipulations, which are impossible to show in detail and which the tyer will pick up with a bit of practice):

Grasp thread (which is hanging down from hook) with the last three fingers of the left hand, about six inches below the hook. Position the right hand so that its back is facing the tyer, and grasp the thread two inches down from the hook with the first two fingers and thumb. Twist the right hand to the right and forward so that the palm is facing upward. There is now a loop in the thread, as shown in Drawing No. 1.

With the left thumb and forefinger (which are free), grasp the left-hand side of the loop, and begin to wind it around both the hook and the return portion of the loop (Drawing No. 2). Use the right hand to help the left in making one complete turn around the hook (Drawing No. 3).

Make about six complete turns around the hook and the return part of the loop, making the first half of each turn with the left hand and the last half with the right hand.

After the last turn is completed, hold the loop vertically taut with the left hand, and with the right hand insert into the loop, parallel with the hook, a dubbing needle (or a toothpick). Raise the dubbing needle until the loop is held taut by it (Drawing No. 4).

HOW TO MAKE THE WHIP FINISH WITHOUT A TOOL

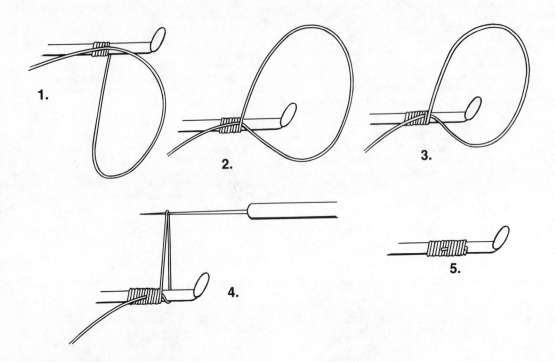

HOW TO USE WHIP FINISH TOOL

Then, with the left hand, pull on the free end of the thread, contracting the loop until the needle rests on the head of the fly. Remove the needle, pull the thread tight, and clip it off close (Drawing No. 5). The whip finish is now complete. Winding should be coated with head cement.

The whip-finisher ties the same exact knot but eliminates the somewhat complicated finger manipulations. Here is how to use it:

Take the tool in the right hand, and place it near the hook and parallel with the hook shank. Run the thread from the hook around the spring retainer at Point A (Drawing No. 1).

Bring the end of the thread back near the fly, and with the tool's nose hook pick up the thread between the fly and Point A (Drawing No. 2).

Now, keeping the thread taut with the left hand and in line with the fly, position the nose of the tool as close to the fly hook as possible — in fact, the fly hook can rest in the curve at the base of the tool's nose hook.

Rotate the tool clockwise around the hook shank, causing the thread to wind around both the hook and itself. Try to keep the windings tight up against one another. Make about six such turns (Drawing No. 3).

Keeping the thread taut, remove the thread from the tool's nose hook, and pull the thread with the left hand until the spring retainer is drawn up to the hook. Remove the retainer, pull the thread tight, and trim it off close to the windings. Apply head cement.

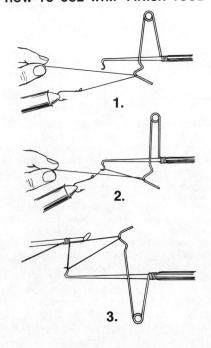

Natural Freshwater Baits

Natural baits undoubtedly account for more fish than all the artificials combined. It stands to reason that a fish is more apt to tumble to the real McCoy than to an imitation, and there are many times when natural baits are just about the only way to catch fish.

Early spring, when the water is high, roily, and discolored, is a top time for naturals, as are the dog days of summer, when most freshwater gamefish are sulking in deep holes. Some fish—notably catfish and carp—almost never take an artificial and are caught exclusively on bait.

The way you attach a bait to the business end of your tackle is an important factor. It may well determine whether or not you hook that gamefish that mouths your minnow, whacks your worm, and so on.

How you rig a natural bait depends to a large degree on how you are going to fish it. For that reason, the sketches show more than one way to rig some of the popular baits. For example, minnows are shown rigged in seven different ways: the simple once-through-with-the-hook methods are best for still-fishing, since they avoid killing the bait and allow it to swim freely. The other methods are best for trolling.

NATURAL BAITS AND WHAT THEY CATCH

Minnows	Largemouth and smallmouth bass, trout, pickerel, pike, walleyes, perch, crappies, rock bass
Earthworms	Trout, white bass, rock bass, perch, crappies, catfish, sunfish, whitefish
Nightcrawlers	Largemouth and smallmouth bass, trout, pickerel, pike, walleyes, muskies, catfish, sturgeon
Crickets	Trout, crappies, perch, rock bass, sunfish
Grubs	Trout, crappies, perch, rock bass, sunfish
Caterpillars	Trout, largemouth and smallmouth bass, crappies, perch, rock bass, sunfish
Crayfish	Smallmouth bass, walleyes, trout, catfish
Hellgrammites	Trout, largemouth and smallmouth bass, walleyes, catfish, rock bass
Nymphs (mayfly, caddisfly, stonefly, and others)	Trout, landlocked salmon, perch, crappies, sunfish
Grasshoppers	Trout, largemouth and smallmouth bass, perch, crappies
Newts and salamanders	Largemouth and smallmouth bass, trout, pickerel, rock bass, walleyes, catfish
Frogs	Largemouth and smallmouth bass, pickerel, pike, muskies, walleyes
Wasp larvae	Perch, crappies, sunfish, rock bass
Suckers	Pike, muskies, smallmouth and largemouth bass
Mice	Largemouth and smallmouth bass, pike, muskies
Freshwater shrimp (scud)	Trout, smallmouth and largemouth bass, perch, crappies, rock bass, sunfish
Dragonflies	Largemouth and smallmouth bass, crappies, white bass, rock bass
Darters	Trout, smallmouth and largemouth bass, walleyes, pickerel, crappies, rock bass
Sculpins	Largemouth and smallmouth bass, walleyes, pickerel, rock bass
Salmon eggs	Trout, salmon
Cut bait (perch belly, etc.)	Pickerel, pike, muskies, largemouth and smallmouth bass, walleyes
Doughballs	Carp, catfish

SOME NATURAL FRESHWATER BAITS

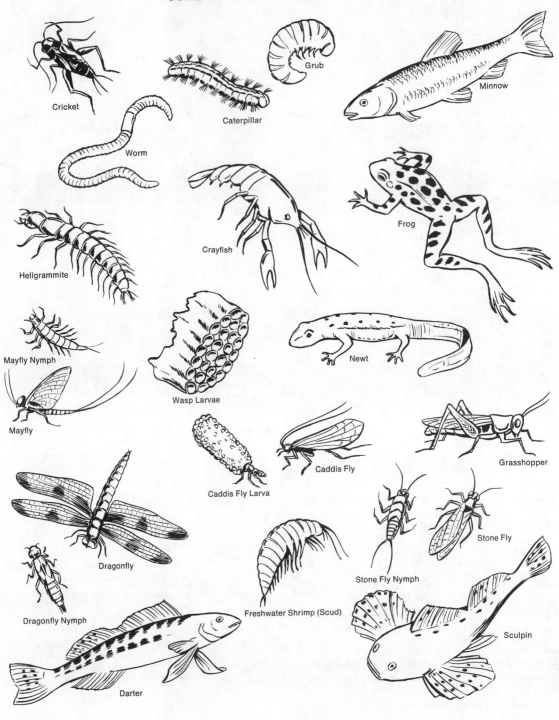

Cricket

Caterpillar

Grub

Minnow

Worm

Crayfish

Frog

Hellgrammite

Mayfly Nymph

Wasp Larvae

Newt

Mayfly

Caddis Fly Larva

Caddis Fly

Grasshopper

Dragonfly

Stone Fly

Stone Fly Nymph

Dragonfly Nymph

Freshwater Shrimp (Scud)

Sculpin

Darter

HOW TO RIG FRESHWATER BAITS

SINGLE WORM RIG

TRAILING WORM RIG
FOR LARGE FISH

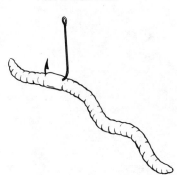

GRASSHOPPER
IN HARNESS

SIMPLE GRASSHOPPER RIG

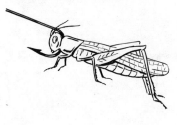

TAIL-HOOK RIG
FOR CRAYFISH

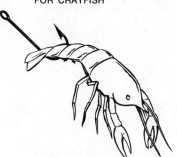

FROG IN HARNESS

LIP-HOOK RIG FOR FROGS

TWO METHODS OF
HOOKING MINNOW

HOW TO RIG FRESHWATER BAITS (continued)

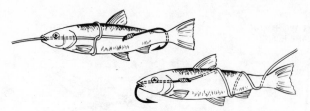

TWO METHODS OF
SEWING ON MINNOWS

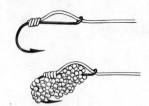

SALMON EGG CLUSTER HELD
TO HOOK VIA LEADER LOOP

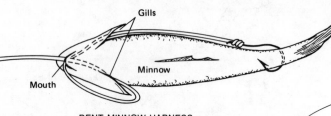

BENT-MINNOW HARNESS

Pass hook and leader through bait's mouth and out gill on one
side, then through mouth again and out gill on other side. Pull
leader fairly taut and hook near tail. This will bend minnow,
imparting a crippled swimming motion.

DRIFT-FISHING RIG FOR STEELHEADS

SKITTERING RIG
(USING PERCH BELLY)

SPINNER-AND-WORM
RIG FOR PERCH

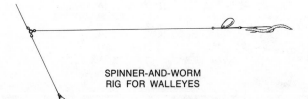

SPINNER-AND-WORM
RIG FOR WALLEYES

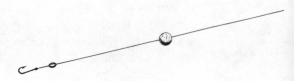

PANFISH RIG

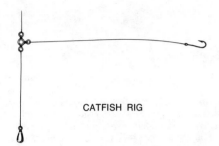

CATFISH RIG

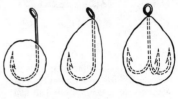

DOUGHBALL HOOKING RIGS
FOR CARP

SUCKER-IN-HARNESS
RIG FOR MUSKELLUNGE

A   Tie double strand
    knot on hook.

B   Tie knot
    on top of nose.

C   Tie knot behind back
    of lower fin.

D   Wrap around body
    and tie on top of neck.

HOOK THROUGH COLLAR
OF HELLGRAMMITE

THREE-HOOK NIGHTCRAWLER RIG

Natural Saltwater Baits

Natural baits are no less important in salt water than they are in fresh water. That fact is well known to anyone who has seen a school of ravenous bluefish slash viciously into a horde of spearing, mossbunkers, or the like.

What natural saltwater baits should you use and when? Those are questions that only time and experience can help you answer accurately. Generally, it pays to use any bait that is prevalent when and where you are fishing. A few discreet questions at a bait shop in the fishing area will go a long way toward helping you choose a productive bait.

How you rig a saltwater bait can be a vital factor. The primary consideration in rigging most baits is to make them appear as lifelike as possible, whether they are to be trolled, cast out and retrieved, or bounced on the bottom. The following sketches show proven ways to prepare and rig the most popular baits used in saltwater.

NATURAL BAITS FOR SALTWATER FISH

SPECIES OF FISH	NATURAL BAITS AND LURES	RECOMMENDED METHODS	HOOKS
Albacore	Feather lures	Trolling	7/0
Amberjack	Strip baits, feathers, spoons, plugs	Trolling, casting	6/0 to 9/0
Barracuda	Bait fish, plugs, feathers, spoons	Trolling, casting	1/0 to 8/0
Bass, California kelp	Sardines, anchovies, clams, mussels, sea worms, shrimp	Trolling, casting, still-fishing	1 to 1/0
Bass, channel	Mullet, mossbunker, crab, clam, spoons, plugs	Casting, still-fishing, trolling	6/0 to 10/0
Bass, giant sea	Cut bait, mullet, mackerel, sardines	Still-fishing, trolling	12/0 to 14/0
Bass, sea	Squid, clam, sea worm, crab, killie	Drifting, still-fishing	1/0 to 5/0
Bass, striped	Sea worm, clam, eel, metal squids, plugs, jigs, live mackerel	Casting, trolling, drifting, still-fishing	2/0 to 8/0
Billfish (sailfish, marlin, swordfish)	Balao, mackerel, squid, bonito, strip baits, feathered jigs	Trolling	4/0 to 12/0
Bluefish	Rigged eel, cut bait, butterfish, plugs, spoons, feathers	Trolling, casting, drifting, still-fishing	3/0 to 8/0
Bonefish	Cut bait (mainly sardine and conch), flies, plugs, spoons	Casting, drifting, still-fishing	1/0 to 4/0
Bonito	Feather lures, spoons	Trolling	4/0 to 6/0
Codfish	Clam, crab, cut bait	Still-fishing, drifting	7/0 to 9/0
Croaker	Sand bugs, mussels, clam, sardine, sea worm	Still-fishing, casting,	1/0 to 6/0
Dolphin	Bait fish, feather lures, spoons, plugs, streamer flies	Trolling, casting	2/0 to 6/0
Eel	Killie, clam, crab, sea worm, spearing	Still-fishing, drifting, casting	6 to 1/0
Flounder, summer	Squid, spearing, sea worm, clam, killie, smelt	Drifting, casting, still-fishing	4/0 to 6/0
Flounder, winter	Sea worm, mussel, clam	Still-fishing	6 to 12 (long-shank)
Grouper	Squid, mullet, sardine, balao, shrimp, crab, plugs	Still-fishing, casting	4/0 to 12/0
Grunt	Shrimp, crab, sea worm	Still-fishing	2 to 1/0
Haddock	Clam, conch, crab, cut bait	Still-fishing	1/0 to 4/0
Hake	Clam, conch, crab, cut bait	Still-fishing	2/0 to 6/0
Halibut	Squid, crab, sea worm, killie, shrimp	Still-fishing	3/0 to 10/0

NATURAL BAITS FOR SALTWATER FISH

SPECIES OF FISH	NATURAL BAITS AND LURES	RECOMMENDED METHODS	HOOKS
Jack Crevallé	Bait fish, cut bait, feathers, metal squid, spoons, plugs	Trolling, still-fishing, casting, drifting	1/0 to 5/0
Jewfish	Mullet, other bait fish	Still-fishing	10/0 to 12/0
Ladyfish	Killie, shrimp, flies, spoons, plugs	Trolling, casting, still-fishing, drifting	1/0 to 5/0
Ling	Clam, crab, cut bait	Still-fishing	4 to 2/0
Mackerel	Bait fish, tube lures, jigs, spinners, streamer flies	Trolling, still-fishing, casting drifting	3 to 6
Perch, white	Sea worm, shrimp, spearing, flies, spoons	Still-fishing, casting	2 to 6
Pollack	Squid strip, clam, feather lures	Still-fishing, trolling	6/0 to 9/0
Pompano	Sand bugs, jigs, plugs, flies	Trolling, casting, drifting, still-fishing	1 to 4
Porgy	Clam, squid, sea worm, crab, mussel, shrimp	Still-fishing	4 to 1/0
Rockfish, Pacific	Herring, sardine, mussel, squid, clam, shrimp	Still-fishing, drifting	1/0 to 8/0
Snapper, mangrove	Cut bait, shrimp	Trolling, still-fishing, drifting	1/0 to 6/0
Snapper, red	Shrimp, mullet, crab	Trolling, still-fishing, drifting	6/0 to 10/0
Snapper, yellowtail	Shrimp, mullet, crab	Trolling, still-fishing	4 to 1/0
Snook	Crab, shrimp, bait fish, plugs, spoons, spinners, feathers	Casting, drifting, still-fishing	2/0 to 4/0
Sole	Clam, sea worm	Still-fishing	4 to 6
Spot	Crab, shrimp, bait fish, sea worm	Still-fishing	8 to 10
Tarpon	Cut bait, bait fish, plugs, spoons, feathers	Trolling, casting, drifting, still-fishing	4/0 to 10/0
Tautog (blackfish)	Clam, sea worm, crab, shrimp	Still-fishing	6 to 2/0
Tomcod	Clam, mussel, shrimp	Still-fishing	6 to 1/0
Tuna, bluefin	Mackerel, flying fish, bonito, squid, dolphin, herring, cut bait, feathered jigs	Trolling	6/0 to 14/0
Wahoo	Bait fish, feather jigs, spoons, plugs	Trolling, casting	4/0 to 8/0
Weakfish	Shrimp, squid, sea worm	Still-fishing, casting, drifting, trolling	1 to 4/0
Whiting, northern	Sea worm, clam	Still-fishing, drifting, casting	4 to 1/0
Yellowtail	Herring, sardine, smelt, spoons, metal squids, feather lures	Trolling, casting, still-fishing	4/0 to 6/0

HOW TO RIG SALTWATER BAITS

PREPARING AND USING MENHADEN AS CUT BAIT

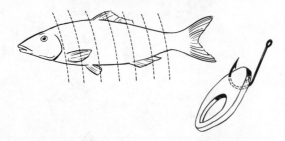

RIGGING A MULLET OR GRUNT FOR BOTTOM FISHING

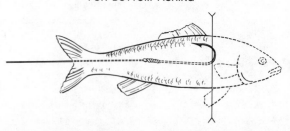

Front part of fish is discarded. Hook with wire leader is threaded through body, and the hook is embedded at the front with its point exposed.

RIGGING A MULLET FOR TROLLING

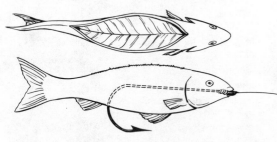

Fish is split down the back, and the backbone and entrails are removed and discarded. Hook is run through body and out vent, eye of hook and fish's mouth are sewn together, and the back is sewn up.

PLUG-CUT BAITFISH

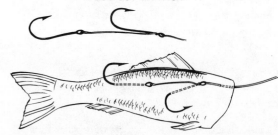

Can be cast out and retrieved like a plug. Especially productive for big snook and tarpon.

HERRING FOR TROLLING

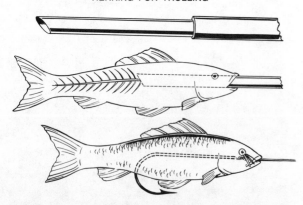

Fish is first deboned by running a hollow metal tube, its tip sharpened and cut at an angle, through mouth and over backbone. Deboning makes herring more flexible and lifelike. Hook as shown.

RIGGING A DEAD SOFT-SHELL CRAB

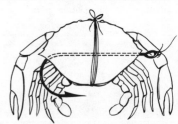

HOOKING A SAND SHRIMP

RIGGING TWO SHRIMP ON SINGLE HOOK

RIGGING A SINGLE SHRIMP

HOOKING A WHOLE CRAB

HOOKING HALF A CRAB

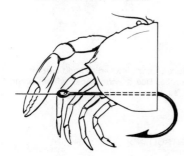

HOOKING A SQUID HEAD

HOOKING WHOLE SQUID FOR BOTTOM FISHING

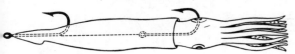

THREE-HOOK SQUID RIG

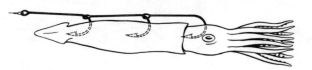

SQUID AND LEADHEAD JIG

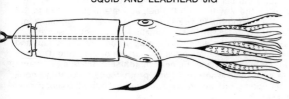

HOOKING A SANDWORM OR BLOODWORM

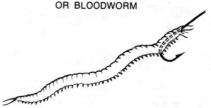

TWO WAYS TO HOOK A LIVE EEL

BAIT-AND-PLUG RIG FOR TROLLING

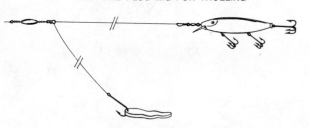

FISH-FINDER RIGS

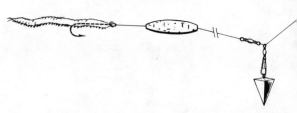

The small piece of cork is used to keep bait off the bottom and away from crabs. Use a wire leader when fishing for sharp-toothed fish, such as bluefish.

TWO WAYS TO RIG BALAO FOR BIG-GAME TROLLING

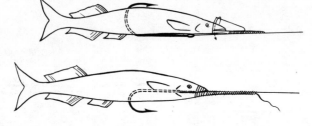

RIGGING A WHOLE EEL
WITH TIN SQUID
FOR TROLLING AND CASTING

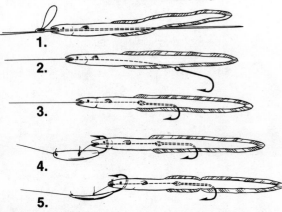

1.

2.

3.

4.

5.

To rig an eel this way, you'll need a long needle with an eye. Form a loop in some relatively heavy line (about 36-pound-test), and run the loop through the needle's eye. Run the needle through the eel from mouth to vent (Drawing No. 1). Pull the loop all the way through the eel, and attach to it a 6/0 to 8/0 hook (Drawing No. 2). Draw protruding line and hook shank into eel (Drawing No. 3). Take a small block-tin squid, and run its hook through the eel's head (or lips) from bottom to top, and tie the line to the eye on the flat surface of the squid (Drawing No. 4). With light line, tie eel's mouth shut, make a tie around the eel's head where the hook protrudes to prevent the hook from ripping out, and make a similar tie around the vent (Drawing No. 5).

RIGGING A WHOLE UNWEIGHTED EEL

Hooks are attached to light chain, heavy monofilament, or linen line.

RIGGING AN EELSKIN WITH METAL SQUID

To a Montauk or Belmar-type metal squid is attached a ring onto which the eelskin is tied.

RIGGING AN EELSKIN WITH PLUG

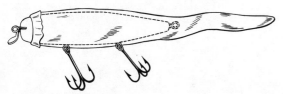

Eelskin is slipped over the plug, whose tail treble hook has been removed. Bottom treble hooks protrude as shown, and skin is tied on at the plug's head.

TWO-HOOK BAITFISH RIG FOR SHORT-STRIKING FISH

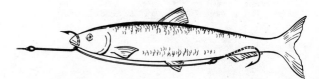

HIGH-LOW CODFISH RIG

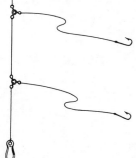

TYPICAL BOTTOM-FISHING RIG

SPREADER RIG FOR BOTTOM FISHING

MOOCHING RIG WITH KEEL SINKER

Mooching is a system of drift-fishing with bait. The keel sinker prevents the line from twisting, but the swivel at its terminal end permits the bait to spin.

SPINNER-AND-SEAWORM
RIG FOR TROLLING

TWO WAYS TO HOOK LIVE BAITFISH

HOOKING DEAD HERRING AND SIMILAR
BAITFISH FOR TROLLING OR CASTING

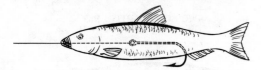

HOOKING HALF A BAITFISH

COMBINATION SURF RIG

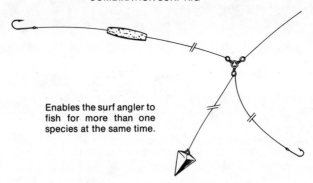

Enables the surf angler to
fish for more than one
species at the same time.

Terminal-Rig Accessories

The items of fishing gear covered in this chapter are various components of the rigs shown in previous chapters. These accessories are as important as links in a chain, so buy the best you can afford. A well-constructed snap swivel of the correct size, for example, won't literally come apart at the seams under the surge of a good muskie, as has happened to this writer.

Swivels come in many forms and sizes, but basically a swivel consists of two or three round metal eyes connected in such a way that each eye can rotate freely and independently of the others. Swivels perform such functions as preventing or reducing line twist, enabling the angler to attach more than one component (sinker and bait, for example) to his line, and facilitating lure changes.

Sinkers, like swivels, come in many shapes and weights. Usually made of lead, they are used to get a bait (or lure) down to the desired depth.

Floats are lighter-than-water devices that are attached to the line. They keep a bait at a predetermined distance above the bottom and signal the strike of a fish. Floats are usually made of cork or plastic and come in many forms.

BARREL SWIVEL

Used to join line and leader.

LOCK SNAP SWIVEL

End of wire snap hooks around itself, and spring tension keeps the snap locked. Preferred over standard snap swivel for sizable fish.

CONNECTING LINK

Used to attach sinker to a terminal rig and can also be used as a component in a fishfinder rig.

THREE-WAY SWIVEL

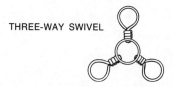

SNAP SWIVEL

Used to join line and lure.

INTERLOCK SNAP SWIVEL

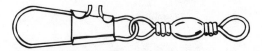

Stronger than standard swivel.

BALL-BEARING SWIVEL

Less apt to bind than standard swivel.

CROSS-LINE SWIVEL

TERMINAL-RIG ACCESSORIES

BIG-GAME SWIVEL

For heavy-duty use. Also comes with locking snap.

CLINCHER SINKER

Line is inserted in slot, and "wing" on each end is pressed down and over the line.

DIAMOND SINKER, TROLLING

PYRAMID SINKER

Sharp edges dig into sand and mud, resisting pressures of tidal currents and wave action and helping the angler "hold bottom."

KEEL SWIVEL SINKER

Used for trolling; eliminates line twist.

SPLIT-SHOT SINKER

Line is inserted in slot, and split shot is pinched on. Split-shot sizes range from BB to OO. Split shot find their widest use in fresh-water fishing.

EGG SINKER

Line goes through hole drilled through core. Can be used as basis of a fish-finder rig since line slides freely through hole.

DIPSEY SINKER

BANK SINKER

Preferred for fishing when and where tide and waves are no problem. Also good for fishing from rocks and jetties, for its rounded edges are apt to slide over rock crevices rather than hang up in them.

TROLLING LEAD

TROLLING DRAIL

Eliminates line twist; gets bait or lure down into the depths.

DOWNRIGGER – TERMINAL RIG WITH CABLE, CANNON BALL, AND MULTI-BEAD RELEASE

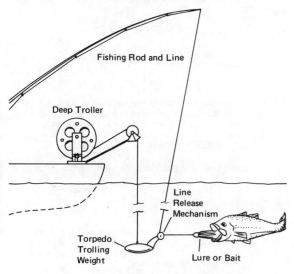

Fishing Rod and Line

Deep Troller

Line Release Mechanism

Torpedo Trolling Weight

Lure or Bait

PLASTIC BALL FLOAT

Spring-loaded top section, when depressed, exposes small U-shaped "hook" at bottom into which line is placed. Releasing the top section reseats the "hook," holding the line fast.

PENCIL FLOAT

Line is attached at both ends. A strike causes one end to lift from the surface.

CARO-LINE FLOAT

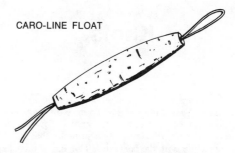

This cork float comes with a doubled length of line running through it lengthwise. The fishing line is run through the loop, and then the loop is pulled through the cork body, seating the line. Generally used in surf fishing to keep a bait off the bottom and away from crabs.

TROLLING PLANER

A heavily weighted device with metal "wings" that permits trolling at considerable depth.

CORK BALL FLOAT

TEETER FLOAT

Floats with slender section perpendicular to water; is highly sensitive to the strike of a fish.

PLASTIC PORCUPINE FLOAT

Light and highly sensitive to strike of a fish.

Knots

Anyone who aspires to competence as a fisherman must have at least a basic knowledge of knots. Most anglers know and use no more than half a dozen knots. However, if you fish a lot, you are sure to run into a situation that cannot be solved efficiently with the basic ties. The aim of this chapter is to familiarize the angler with knots that will help him handle any line-tying situation he is likely to encounter.

All knots reduce—to a greater or lesser degree, depending upon the particular knot—the breaking strength of the line. Loose or poorly tied knots reduce line strength even more. For that reason, and to avoid wasting valuable fishing time,

it is best to practice tying the knots at home. In most cases, it's better to practice with cord or rope; the heavier material makes it easier to follow the tying procedures.

It is important to form and tighten knots correctly. They should be tightened slowly and steadily for best results. In most knots requiring the tyer to make turns around the standing part of the line, at least five such turns should be made.

Now let's take a look at the range of fishing knots. Included are tying instructions, the uses for which each knot is suited, and other information.

BLOOD KNOT

Used to connect two lines of relatively similar diameter. Especially popular for joining sections of monofilament in making tapered fly leaders.

1. Wrap one strand around the other at least four times, and run the end into the fork thus formed.

2. Make the same number of turns, in the opposite direction, with the second strand, and run its end through the opening in the middle of the knot, in the direction opposite that of the first strand.

3. Hold the two ends so they do not slip (some fishermen use their teeth). Pull the standing part of both strands in opposite directions, tightening the knot.

4. Tighten securely, clip off the ends, and the knot is complete. If you want to tie on a dropper fly, leave one of these ends about 6 to 8 inches long.

STU APTE IMPROVED BLOOD KNOT

Excellent for joining two lines of greatly different diameter, such as a heavy monofilament shock leader and a light leader tippet.

1. Double a sufficient length of the ligher line, wrap it around the standing part of the heavier line at least five times, and run the end of the doubled line into the "fork" thus formed.

2. Wrap the heavier line around the standing part of the doubled lighter line three times, in the opposite direction, and run the end of the heavier line into the opening, in the direction opposite that of the end of the doubled line.

3. Holding the two ends to keep them from slipping, pull the standing parts of the two lines in opposite directions. Tighten the knot completely, using your fingernails to push the loops together if necessary, and clip off the ends.

DOUBLE SURGEON'S KNOT

Used to join two strands of greatly unequal diameter.

1. Place the two lines parallel, with the ends pointing in opposite directions. Using the two lines as a single strand, make a simple overhand knot, pulling the two strands all the way through the loop, and then make another overhand knot.

2. Holding both strands at each end, pull the knot tight and clip off the ends.

IMPROVED CLINCH KNOT

Use to tie flies, bass bugs, lures, and bait hooks to line or leader. This knot reduces line strength only slightly.

1. Run the end of the line through the eye of the lure, fly, or hook, and then make at least five turns around the standing part of the line. Run the end through the opening between the eye and the beginning of the twists, and then run it through the large loop formed by the previous step.

2. Pull slowly on the standing part of the line, being careful that the end doesn't slip back through the large loop and that the knot snugs right up against the eye, and clip off the end.

DOUBLE-LOOP CLINCH KNOT

Same as Improved Clinch Knot except that line is run through eye twice at the beginning of the tie.

DOUBLE IMPROVED CLINCH KNOT

Same as Improved Clinch Knot except that line is used doubled throughout entire tie.

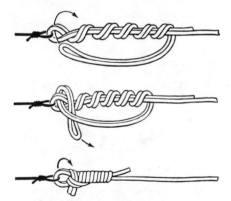

SHOCKER KNOT
Used to join two lines of unequal diameters.

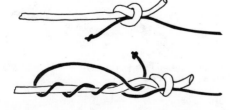

PALOMAR KNOT

1. Pass line or leader through the eye of the hook and back again to form 3- or 5-inch loop.

2. Hold the line and hook at the eye. With the other hand, bring the loop up and under the double line and tie an overhand knot but do not tighten it yet.

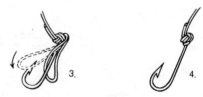

3. Hold the overhand knot. With the other hand, bring the loop over the hook.

4. Pull the line to draw the knot to the top of the eye. Pull both tag end and running line to tighten. Clip tag end off about 1/8 inch from knot.

PERFECTION LOOP KNOT

Used to make a loop in the end of line or leader. Make one turn around the line and hold the crossing point with thumb and forefinger (Figure 1). Make a second turn around the crossing point, and bring the end around and between loops A and B (Figure 2). Run loop B through loop A (Figure 3). Pull upward on loop B (Figure 4), tightening the knot (Figure 5).

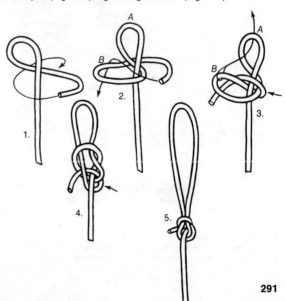

TURLE KNOT

Used to tie a dry or wet fly to a leader tippet. Not as strong as the Improved Clinch Knot, but it allows a dry fly's hackle points to sit high and jauntily on the surface of the water.

1. Run end of leader through eye of hook toward the bend, and tie a simple overhand knot around the standing part of the line, forming a loop.

2. Open the loop enough to allow it to pass around the fly, and place the loop around the neck of the fly, just forward of the eye.

3. Pull on the end of the leader, drawing the loop up tight around the neck of the fly.

4. Tighten the knot completely by pulling on the main part of the leader.

DROPPER LOOP KNOT

This knot is frequently used by fishermen for putting a loop in the middle of a strand of monofilament.

1. Make a loop in the line and wrap one end overhand several times around the other part of the line. Pinch a small loop at point marked X and thrust it between the turns as shown by the arrow.

2. Place your finger through the loop to keep it from pulling out again, and pull on both ends of the line.

3. The knot will draw up like this.

4. Finished loop knot.

NAIL KNOT

This is the best knot for joining the end of a fly line with the butt end of a fly leader. The knot is smooth, streamlined, and will run freely through the guides of the fly rod. *Caution:* This knot is designed for use with the modern synthetic fly lines; do not use it with an old silk fly line, for the knot will cut the line.

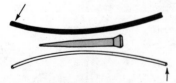

1. Place the end of the fly line and the butt end of the leader—pointing in opposite directions—along the length of a tapered nail. Allow sufficient overlap.

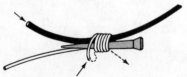

2. Wrap leader five or six times around itself, the nail, and the fly line, keeping windings up against one another. Run butt end of leader back along the nail, inside the wraps.

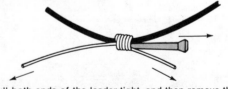

3. Pull both ends of the leader tight, and then remove the nail and tighten again by pulling on both ends of the leader.

4. Pull on both line and leader to test the knot, and clip off ends, completing the knot.

NAIL KNOT (Alternate)

Tying procedures are the same as for the standard Nail Knot, except that in place of the nail, use an air-inflation needle of the type used to inflate basketballs and footballs. The tip of the needle must be cut or filed off so that the tube is open at both ends. A large hypodermic needle with its point snipped off also works well. In tying step No. 3, the butt end of the leader—after having been wrapped five or six times around the fly line, leader, and tube—is simply run back through the tube (needle). Then the knot is tightened, the tube removed, and the final tightening is done.

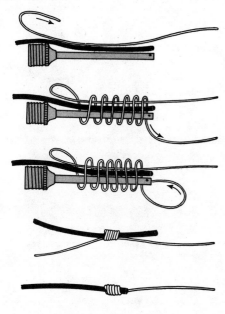

DOUBLE NAIL KNOT

Used to join leader sections of the same or slightly different diameters. It is especially useful in saltwater fly fishing and in making heavy salmon leaders.

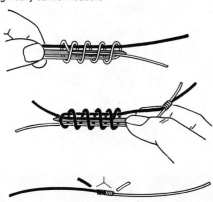

Tying procedure involves making two Nail Knots, one around each of the two leader sections. As each knot is formed, it is tightened only enough to prevent it from unraveling. When both are formed, each leader is pulled slowly so that the knots come together and are tightened securely.

OFFSHORE SWIVEL KNOT

1. Slip loop of double-line leader through the eye of the swivel. Rotate loop 1/2 turn to put a single twist between loop and swivel eye.

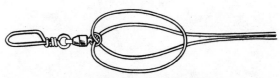

2. Pass the loop with the twist over the swivel. Hold the loop end, together with both strands of double-line leader, with one hand. Let swivel slide to the other end of the double loops now formed.

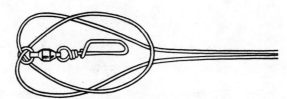

3. Still holding loop and lines, use the other hand to rotate swivel through center of both loops. Repeat at least five times.

4. Continue holding strands of double-line leader tightly but release the end of the loop. Pull on swivel and loops of line will begin to gather.

5. To draw knot tight, grip the swivel with pliers and push the loops toward eye with fingers, still keeping strands of leader pulled tight.

UNI-KNOT SYSTEM

The Uni-Knot System consists of variations on one basic knot that can be used for most needs in fresh- and saltwater fishing. The system was developed by Vic Dunaway, editor of *Florida Sportsman* magazine and author of numerous books. Here's how each variation is tied, step by step.

1. TYING TO TERMINAL TACKLE

A. Run line through eye of hook, swivel, or lure at least 6 inches and fold it back to form two parallel lines. Bring the end of the line back in a circle toward the eye.

B. Turn the tag end six times around the double line and through circle. Hold double line at eye and pull tag end to snug up turns.

C. Pull running line to slide the knot up against eye.

D. Continue pulling until knot is tight. Trim tag end flush with last coil of the knot. This basic Uni-Knot will not slip.

2. LOOP CONNECTION

Tie the same basic Uni-Knot as shown above—up to the point where coils are snugged up against the running line. Then slide knot toward eye only until the desired loop size is reached. Pull tag end with pliers to tighten. This gives a lure or fly free, natural movement in the water. When fish is hooked, knot slides tight against eye.

3. JOINING LINES

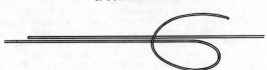

A. With two lines of about the same diameter, overlap ends for about 6 inches. With one end, form Uni-Knot circle and cross the two lines at about the middle of the overlap.

B. Tie the basic Uni-Knot, making six turns around the two lines.

C. Pull tag end to snug the knot.

D. Use loose end of the overlapped line to tie second Uni-Knot and snug it up in the same manner.

E. Pull the two lines in opposite directions to slide the two knots together. Pull tight and snip tag ends close to outermost coils.

4. JOINING LEADER TO LINE

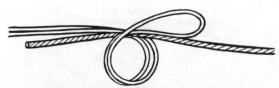

A. Using leader no more than four times the pound-test of the line, double the end of line and overlap with leader for about 6 inches. Make Uni-Knot circle with the doubled line.

B. Tie a Uni-Knot around leader with the doubled line, but use only three turns. Snug up.

UNI-KNOT SYSTEM (continued)

C. Now tie a Uni-Knot with the leader around doubled line, again using only three turns.

D. Pull knots together tightly. Trim tag ends and loop.

5. JOINING SHOCK LEADER TO LINE

A. Using leader of more than four times the pound-test of the line, double the ends of both leader and line back about 6 inches. Slip line loop through leader loop far enough to permit tying Uni-Knot around both strands of leader.

B. With doubled line, tie a Uni-Knot around doubled leader, using only four turns.

C. Put finger through loop of line and grasp both tag end and running line to pull knot snug around leader loop.

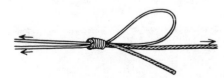

D. With one hand, pull long end of leader (not both strands). With the other hand, pull both strands of line (as arrows indicate). Pull slowly until knot slides to end of leader loop and slippage is stopped.

6. DOUBLE-LINE SHOCK LEADER

A. As a replacement for Bimini Twist or Spider Hitch, first clip off amount of line needed for desired length of loop. Tie the two ends together with an overhand knot.

B. Double the end of the running line and overlap it 6 inches with knotted end of the loop piece. Tie a Uni-Knot with the tied loop around the double running line, using four turns.

C. Now tie a Uni-Knot with the doubled running line around the loop piece, again using four turns.

D. Hold both strands of double line in one hand, both strands of loop in the other. Pull to bring knots together until they barely touch.

E. Tighten by pulling both strands of loop piece (as two arrows indicate) but only main strand of running line (as single arrow indicates). Trim off both loop tag ends, eliminating overhand knot.

7. SNELLING A HOOK

A. Thread line through the hook eye for about 6 inches. Hold line against hook shank and form Uni-Knot circle. Make as many turns as desired through loop and around line and shank. Close knot by pulling on tag end.

B. Tighten by pulling running line in one direction and hook in the other. Trim off tag end.

LOOP KNOT

Tie overhand knot in line, leaving loop loose and a sufficient length of line below the loop to tie the rest of the knot. Run end through hook eye and back through loop in line, and then tie another overhand knot around standing part of line. Pull tight.

DAVE HAWK'S DROP LOOP KNOT

Used to attach lure to line or leader via a nonslip loop that will permit freer lure action than would a knot snugged right up to the eye of the lure.

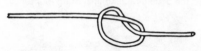

1. Tie overhand knot about 5 inches from end of line, pull tight, and run end through the lure eye.

2. Bring end back parallel with standing part of line, bend end back toward lure, and make two turns around parallel strands.

3. Slowly draw the knot tight, and then pull on the lure so that the jam knot slides down to the overhand knot.

END LOOP

Used to form a loop in the end of a line.

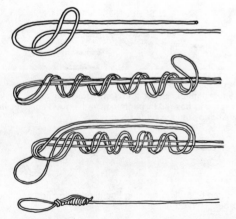

BUFFER LOOP

Used to attach lure to line or leader via a nonslip loop.

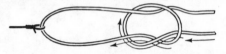

1. Tie simple overhand knot in line, leaving loop loose and leaving end long enough to complete the knot, and then run end through eye of lure.

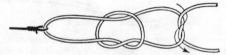

2. Run end back through loose loop, and make another overhand knot, using end and standing part of line.

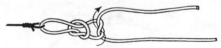

3. Tighten overhand knot nearest to lure eye, and then tighten second overhand knot, which, in effect, forms a half-hitch against first knot.

4. Finished knot.

KNOTTING BACKING LINE TO FLY LINE

1. Double the end of the backing line, make one wrap around the fly line, and pull all of the backing line through the loop at its doubled end so that the lines appear as in drawing.

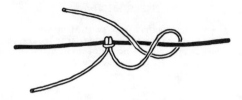

2. With end of the backing line, make a half-hitch around the fly line, and pull it tight against the original knot.

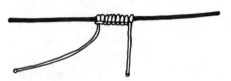

3. Continue making such half-hitches (8 or 10 should be enough) until the tie appears as in drawing.

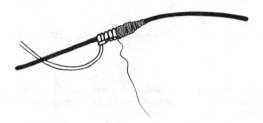

4. Wrap the entire tie with nylon thread, including part of the end of the backing line. This step is simplified by placing the fly line in a fly-tying vise.

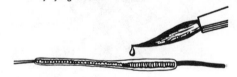

5. Give the entire tie a good coat of lacquer.

FLY-LINE SPLICE

Used to join two fly lines.

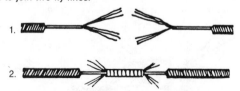

Remove the coating from 2¼ inches of the end of each line, and fray about 1 inch (Figure 1). Enmesh the frayed ends of one line with those of the other, and wrap most of this joint with nylon thread (Figure 2). Then make another series of wrappings over the entire splice (Figure 3). Finish the job with coats of varnish.

ALBRIGHT KNOT (MONO TO MONO)

Used to join lines of dissimilar diameter, such as fly line to leader and heavy shock leader to finer leader tippet.

Double the end of the heavier line, forming a long U. Bring the lighter line up into the U, and make about 10 wraps—in the direction of the bottom of the U—around the U and the standing part of the lighter line, bringing the end of the lighter line out the bottom of the U (Figure 1). Pull slowly and evenly until the knot is tight (Figure 2).

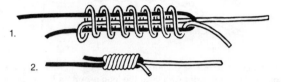

ALBRIGHT KNOT (MONO TO WIRE)

Used when short length of wire leader is needed below mono-filament leader tippet to prevent sharp-toothed fish from biting through the leader. The fly is attached to the wire leader with a brass crimping sleeve. Also used to tie mono leader to wire or lead-core line so that knot will pass through guides and tip tops smoothly. Eliminates need for swivel.

Bend end of wire leader into a U or open-end loop. Run end of monofilament into the tip of the U, make about 7 wraps around the doubled wire, and run the end of the monofilament back out through the tip of the U (Figure 1). Hold both leaders to prevent the knot from slipping, and slowly draw the wraps of monofilament tight (Figure 2). Clip off ends, and the knot is finished (Figure 3).

HAYWIRE TWIST

Used to tie wire to hook, lure, or swivel, or make loop in end of wire.

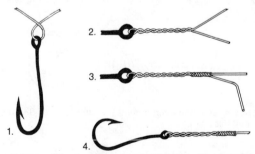

Run about 4 inches of the end of the leader wire through the eye of the hook, lure, or swivel, and then bend end across standing part of wire as in Figure 1. Holding the two parts of the wire at their crossing point, bend the wire around itself, using hard, even, twisting motions. Both wire parts should be twisted equally (Figure 2). Then, using the end of the wire, make about 10 tight wraps around the standing part of the wire (Figure 3). Break off or clip end of wire close to the last wrap so that there is no sharp end, and job is complete (Figure 4).

BIMINI TWIST

Used to create a loop or double line without appreciably weakening the breaking strength of the line. Especially popular in bluewater fishing for large saltwater fish. Learning this knot requires practice.

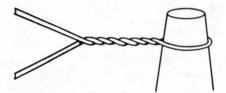

1. Double the end of the line to form a loop, leaving yourself plenty of line to work with. Run the loop around a fixed object such as a cleat or the butt end of a rod, or have a partner hold the loop and keep it open. Make 20 twists in the line, keeping the turns tight and the line taut.

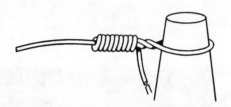

2. Keeping the twists tight, wrap the end of the line back over the twists until you reach the V of the loop, making the wraps tight and snug up against one another.

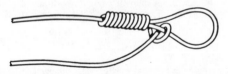

3. Make a half-hitch around one side of the loop, and pull it tight.

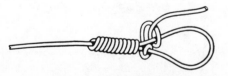

4. Then make a half-hitch around the other side of the loop, and pull this one tight.

5. Now make a half-hitch around the base of the loop, tighten it, clip off excess line at the end, and the Bimini Twist is complete.

SPIDER HITCH

Serves same function as the Bimini Twist. Many fishermen prefer the Spider Hitch, as it's easier and faster to tie—especially with cold hands—and requires no partner to help, nor any fixed object to keep loop open. It's equally strong.

1. Make a long loop in the line. Hold the ends between thumb and forefinger, with first joint of thumb extending beyond finger. Then use other hand to twist a smaller reverse loop in the doubled line.

2. Slide the fingers up line to grasp small reverse loop, together with long loop. Most of small loop should extend beyond the thumb tip.

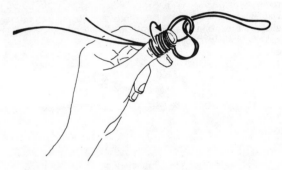

3. Wind the doubled line from right to left around both thumb and small loop, taking five turns. Then pass remainder of doubled line (large loop) through the small loop.

4. Pull the large loop to make the five turns unwind off thumb, using a fast, steady pull—not a quick jerk.

5. Pull the turns around the base of the loop tight and trim off tag end.

Care and Repair
of Fishing Tackle

There's more than a germ of truth in the old saying, "A fisherman is no better than his tackle." Of course, that has also been said of quarterbacks!

Seriously, though, it pays in more ways than one to keep your gear in good working order. For one thing, proper maintenance can add a good many years to the working life of rods, reels, and other tackle on which hard-earned money has been spent. And legions of fishermen have discovered, to their chagrin, that unoiled reels can "freeze up," neglected rods can snap, and rusty lure hooks can give out—just when that lunker comes along.

The following tackle-care tips should help to prevent such problems.

Care of Rods

Today's rods are designed for long life, but they still require some basic maintenance. The steps recommended below should keep any rod in good working order. How often they should be applied depends upon how often the rods are used and whether they are used in fresh or salt water. It should be remembered that saltwater rods—in fact, all saltwater gear—requires much more care than freshwater rods. Even the best of tackle cannot withstand the corrosive action of salt.

1. Wash the rod, including the guides, thoroughly with soap and fresh water, rinse it with hot water, and let it dry completely. If the rod is used in salt water, this step should be taken after each use.
2. Clean the ferrules well, and give them a very light coating of grease to help prevent oxidation of the metal.
3. Apply a light coating of wax (automobile wax does a good job) to the entire rod—excluding cork handle, if the rod has one, and guides.
4. At least once each season, varnish the rod. Two thin coats are better than one heavy coat. To avoid creating bubbles in the varnish, apply it with a finger or a pipe cleaner.
5. Put the rod into its container, and store it in a dry, safe place. If the rod is bamboo, it must be placed so that it lays flat; if stored on end, it may develop a "set" or permanent bend. Caution: never store in a rod case a cork-handled rod whose handle is wet, or mildew will form on the cork.

Care of Lines

Check each line for cracking, aging, wear, and rot. If the entire line is no longer serviceable, discard it. If one end has taken all the use, reverse the line. Fly lines tend to crack at the business end after considerable use. If the cracking is confined to the last foot or so, clip off the damaged section

or, if the line is a double-taper, reverse it. If the damage is more widespread, replace the line.

Check particularly for nicks and other weak spots in monofilament, and test its breaking strength. If it's weak, replace it.

With braided line, check for dark spots, signifying rot, and test the breaking strength. Replace if weak.

Care of Reels

Reels are the most important item of fishing gear and must be cared for properly. The following check list should be followed:

1. Rinse reel thoroughly with hot fresh water. If used in salt water, do this after each trip.
2. Oil sparingly.
3. Release drag tension to eliminate spring fatigue.
4. Check reel's operation. Replace worn or missing parts, and send reel to manufacturer for repair if necessary.
5. Cover reel with very light coating of grease, and store in a safe, dry place, preferably in a cloth bag (cloth permits air to enter and escape). Leather cases lock out air.

Care of Tackle Accessories

Accessory equipment deserves equal time from the fisherman. Saltwater lures, for example, are expensive, so take a few minutes to rinse them off with hot fresh water after each use so that they don't corrode. The same goes for swivels, hooks, and other salt-water accessories.

The following check list covers a general overhaul of a tackle box and its contents:

1. Remove the contents of the box, and place the items in some kind of order on a table rather than simply dumping them in a pile.
2. Use a vacuum cleaner to remove dust and dirt and other loose particles. If the box is metal, wipe the inside with an oily rag, and lubricate the hinges. If it is plastic, wash it with soap and water.
3. Examine the hooks and lures, and discard rusty hooks and all lures that are beyond repair. Make a list of those lures you'll need to restock the box while they are fresh in your mind.
4. Repair salvageable lures. A soft-wire soap pad can be a great help in sprucing up dingy plug bodies and restoring the finish on spinner blades and spoons. Check for broken, rusty, or dull lure hooks, replacing the hooks if necessary or sharpening them with a small whetstone.
5. Sharpen all hooks, and give them a light coating of oil to prevent rust.
6. Wash the bag of your landing net with a mild detergent.
7. Patch all holes and weak spots in hip boots and waders, and store them in a dark, cool spot. Best way to store boots is to hang them upside down by the boot feet. A sturdy heavy-wire coat hanger, cut in the middle of the bottom section and bent judiciously, makes an excellent and inexpensive boot-hanger.

Rod-Wrapping Tricks of the Trade

Guides and Tension: Guides should be purchased in matched sets to assure uniformity. Feet of guides should be dressed with a file to a fine taper. Next sight your rod; you will note a slight bend, or offset. Apply guides opposite the bend; this will bring it into a straight position. Guides should be affixed with snug wrapping tension, so that you may sight after wrapping and make slight guide adjustments before applying color preserver. Do not wrap guides to absolute breaking point of thread. Remember, 10 or 20 wraps of thread exert very heavy pressure on feet of guides. It is possible to damage a blank by wrapping too tight.

Threads: Sizes 2/0 to E are most commonly used. Size 2/0 or A for fly, casting, or spinning rods. Size E for the heavier fresh-water spinning or salt-water rods. Naturally the finer size 2/0 thread will make a neater job, but, being lighter, it is not quite as durable.

Trim: You may trim the basic color of your wrap with 5 to 10 turns of another color thread. This is done just as outlined in instructions for basic wrap.

Color Preserver and Rod Varnish. Good color preserver has plastic in it, and should be quite thin in order to penetrate the wrappings. Good-grade varnish is essential to durability of finish. A brush may be used to apply both the color preserver and rod varnish, however air bubbles are usually present when a brush is used. To maintain a smooth finish, make certain these bubbles are out. A very satisfactory method of minimizing air bubbles is to apply both the color preserver and rod varnish with your index finger. Usually color preserver can be worked in with index finger. This will prevent any shading of the wrapping color.

Courtesy of Reed Tackle

HOW TO WRAP GUIDES

1. Start by wrapping over the end of the thread toward the guide so thread end is held down by the wrapping. Using the tension from whatever type tension device you are using to hold the wrapping tight, continue to turn the rod so that each thread lies as close as possible to the preceding turn.

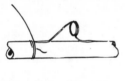

2. About 5 to 8 turns from the finish of the wrap, insert the loop of tie-off thread. (This can be 6″ of heavier thread or a fine piece of nylon leader material.) Finish the wrap over this tie-off loop.

3. Holding the wrap tightly, cut the wrapping thread about 4″ from your rod. Insert this cut end through the tie-off loop. Still holding onto the wrapping thread, pull cut off thread under the wraps with tie-off loop.

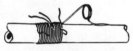

4. With a razor blade, trim cut off end as close as possible to the wrap. With the back of a knife or your finger nail, push wrapping up tight so that it appears solid, and none of the rod or guide shows through.

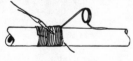

SUGGESTED GUIDE SPACING CHART

ALL MEASUREMENTS ARE FROM TIP OF ROD DOWN
FIGURES INDICATE MEASUREMENTS AT THE GUIDE RIM

	ROD LENGTH & TYPE	LURE-WEIGHT RANGE
SPINCASTING, BAITCASTING	5½-ft.	⅛ to ⅓ oz.
	6-ft.	⅛ to ⅜ oz.
	6-ft.	¼ to ¾ oz.
	6-ft.	⅜ to 1¼ oz.
	6-ft. 4-in.	1/16 to ¼ oz.
	6-ft. 4-in.	⅜ oz.
	6-ft. 4-in.	⅛ to ½ oz.
	6-ft.	⅜ to ⅝ oz.
	6-ft. 4-in.	¼ to ⅝ oz.
FLY RODS	5-ft. 5-in.	
	6-ft.	
	7½-ft.	
	7-ft. 8-in.	
	8-ft.	
	8-ft.	
	8-ft.	
	8½-ft.	
	8½-ft.	
	8½-ft.	
	9-ft.	
	9-ft.	
	10-ft.	
SPINNING RODS	6-ft.	up to ¼ oz.
	6-ft.	up to ⅜ oz.
	6½-ft.	1/16 to ¼ oz.
	6½-ft.	⅛ to 1 oz.
	6½-ft.	⅛ to ⅜ oz.
	7-ft. combination Spin & Fly Rod	1/16 to ⅜ oz.
	7-ft.	1/16 to ⅜ oz.
	6½ ft.	¼ to ⅝ oz.
	7-ft.	up to 1½ oz.

FLY-LINE WEIGHTS	1st	2nd	3rd	4th	5th	6th	7th	8th
	4½"	12"	23"	36"				
	4	10	18	28	40			
	4	8¼	13	18	24½	32⅛	42	
	3½	7½	12	17⅜	23⅝	31⅞	42½	
	4	10	18½	28½	41			
	4	10	18½	28½	41			
	4	10	18½	28½	41			
	4	10	18	28	40			
	4	10	18½	28½	41			
5 Floating, 6 Sinking	5	13	25	40				
5 Floating, 6 Sinking	3	7½	12	17¾	25	33	42½	
6 Floating, 7 Sinking	6	13	21	30	41½	60		
6 or 7 Floating, 7 Sinking	6	13	21	30	43	62		
6 or 7 Floating, 7 Sinking	6	13	21	30	41	52	66	
7 Floating, 7 Sinking	6	13	21	30	40	53	66	
7 or 8 Floating, 7 or 8 Sinking	6	13	21	30	41	53	66	
7 or 8 Floating, 7 or 8 Sinking	6	13	21	30	40	56	73	
7 Floating, 7 Sinking	6	13	21	30	40	56	73	
8 or 9 Floating, 8 or 9 Sinking	6	13	21	30	40	56	73	
7 or 8 Floating, 7 or 8 Sinking	5	11	18	26	35	45	58½	73
8 or 9 Floating, 8 or 9 Sinking	5	11	18	26	35	45	58½	73
9 or 10 Floating, 9 or 10 Sinking	6	13	22	32	43	54½	66½	80½
	5½	15½	27½	40½				
	3½	10	19	29¼	41½			
	3½	8½	15	23	33	46		
	5	10⅜	16⅜	23⅜	31⅞	44		
	3½	8½	15	23	33	46		
5 or 6 Floating, 6 Sinking	4	10	18	27½	38½	52½		
	4	10	18	27½	38½	52½		
	3½	8½	15	23	33	46		
	4	10	18	27½	38	51		

Spacing of Rod Guides

Whether you are building a fishing rod from scratch (that is, taking a fiberglass blank and adding butt, reel seat, and guides) or refinishing an old favorite, you must pay close attention to the placement of the guides along the working length of the rod.

Putting too many or too few guides on a rod, or placing them improperly, may detract from proper rod action and put undue strain on the line and the rod.

The preceding chart gives the correct number of guides—and exact spacing measurements—for most popular spinning, bait-casting, spin-casting, and fly rods.

Selecting the Tip Top and Other Guides

The rod-builder, like just about everyone else, gets what he pays for. It doesn't pay to skimp on rod guides, especially if the rod is to be used in salt water or for heavy freshwater fish such as pike, muskies, and salmon.

Guides are made of various metals, including hardened stainless steel, chrome (or chrome-plated Monel), agate, and tungsten-carbide, with the carbide types being the most durable. Roller guides for heavy saltwater fishing are usually made of stainless steel, Monel, or nickel alloy.

The rod-builder should note that guides are available in sets tailored to particular rod types and lengths.

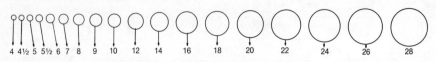

ACTUAL SIZES OF TIP GUIDES IN 1/64"

TYPES OF ROD GUIDES

SNAKE (FLY ROD)

LOOP OR FOULPROOF (Spinning)

RING (Baitcasting and Spincasting)

ROLLER (Big Game)

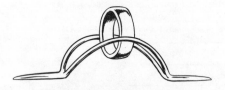

BRIDGE (Baitcasting Spincasting)

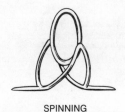

SPINNING

ROLLER (Big Game)

The tip top must fit snugly over the end of the rod, and so its selection is sometimes a problem. The chart below will help the rod-builder overcome this problem. It shows the actual sizes, in 64ths of an inch, of the inside diameters of a wide range of tip-top guides. To determine what size tip top you need, simply place the end of the rod tip over the circles until you find the correct size.

Selecting Rod Ferrules

Ferrules are jointlike devices inserted along the working length of a fishing rod that enable the rod to be dismantled into two or more sections. Ferrules are generally made of metal (nickel, brass, or aluminum), fiberglass, graphite, or a synthetic.

A ferrule set consists of two parts, the male ferrule and the female ferrule. The male section should fit snugly into the female section.

What size ferrule do you need for your rod? The chart below will help you find out. It shows the actual sizes, in 64ths of an inch, of the inside diameters of a wide range of ferrules. To determine the correct ferrule for your rod, simply place the upper end of the butt section (if it is a two-piece rod) over the circles until you find the right fit.

TYPES OF ROD TIPS

RING WITH SUPPORT
(Spinning, Baitcasting, Spincasting)

FLY ROD

FOULPROOF (Spinning)

ROLLER (Big Game)

INSIDE DIAMETER OF FERRULES

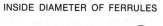

11/64   12/64   13/64   14/64   15/64

16/64   17/64   18/64   19/64   20/64

21/64   22/64   23/64   24/64   25/64

26/64   27/64   28/64   29/64   30/64

Fishing for the Record Book

Where was the record largemouth bass caught? What's the weight of the biggest striped marlin ever taken? Where does a fisherman enter his catch for consideration as a possible record?

Answers to these questions and just about any other on fish records can be found in the following lists of records compiled and kept by the International Game Fish Association, 3000 E. Las Olas Boulevard, Fort Lauderdale, Florida 33316.

The International Game Fish Association, keeper of marine game fish world records for sportfishermen and women since 1939, assumed responsibility for maintaining records for saltwater fly fishing and freshwater angling in 1978.

The Association, long known for its development of ethical marine angling practices and promotion of the wise use of fishery resources, entered the freshwater arena when *Field & Stream* magazine transferred its 68 years of records to IGFA in March 1978. Following this lead, the Saltwater Flyrodders of America, International, designated IGFA as the official keeper of world saltwater fly fishing records,

and the International Spin Fishing Association entrusted IGFA with their historical record files.

"IGFA's goal is to bring all sportfishing records and gamefishing data under one roof, forming a central information center for anglers, scientists, and other fishing interests throughout the world," says IGFA.

Current record programs include all-tackle records for both freshwater and saltwater fishing, as well as saltwater line class records and tippet class records for saltwater fly fishing.

While record-keeping is an important aspect of IGFA's activities, it is a relatively small part of this nonprofit organization's programs in behalf of recreational fishermen. Financed by its membership, the association also works toward fair oceanic legislation and wise fishery management. It also maintains an international library of fish and fishing. It is developing and maintaining a history of angling. It supports scientific data collection programs on game fish resources. And it generally works to preserve the quality of sport fishing.

IGFA Freshwater All-Tackle World Records

All-tackle records are kept for the heaviest freshwater fish of each species caught by an angler in any line class category up to 60 kg (130 lb). Following are the all-tackle records granted as of January 1, 1979.

SPECIES	SCIENTIFIC NAME	WEIGHT	PLACE	DATE	ANGLER
Bass, largemouth	*Micropterus salmoides*	10.09 kg 22 lb 4 oz	Montgomery Lake Georgia, USA	June 2, 1932	George W. Perry
Bass, redeye	*Micropterus coosae*	3.71 kg 8 lb 3 oz	Flint River Georgia, USA	Oct. 23, 1977	David A. Hubbard
Bass, rock	*Ambloplites rupestris*	1.36 kg 3 lb	York River Ontario, Canada	Aug. 1, 1974	Peter Gulgin
Bass, smallmouth	*Micropterus dolomieui*	5.41 kg 11 lb 15 oz	Dale Hollow Lake Kentucky, USA	July 9, 1955	David L. Hayes
Bass, spotted	*Micropterus punctulatus*	3.92 kg 8 lb 10 oz	Smith Lake Alabama, USA	Feb. 25, 1972	Billy Henderson
Bass, white	*Morone chrysops*	2.40 kg 5 lb 5 oz	Ferguson Lake California, USA	March 8, 1972	Norman W. Mize
Bass, whiterock	White X striped	9.07 kg 20 lb	Savannah River Georgia, USA	May 5, 1977	Ron Raley
Bass, yellow	*Morone mississippiensis*	1.02 kg 2 lb 4 oz	Lake Monroe Indiana, USA	March 27, 1977	Donald L. Stalker
Bluegill	*Lepomis macrochirus*	2.15 kg 4 lb 12 oz	Ketona Lake Alabama, USA	April 9, 1950	T.S. Hudson
Bowfin	*Amia calva*	8.95 kg 19 lb 12 oz	Lake Marion South Carolina, USA	Nov. 5, 1972	M.R. Webster

IGFA FRESHWATER ALL-TACKLE WORLD RECORDS

Buffalo, bigmouth	*Ictiobus cyprinellus*	25.40 kg 56 lb	Lock Loma Lake Missouri, USA	Aug. 19, 1976	W.J. Long
Buffalo, smallmouth	*Icitiobus bubalus*	14.74 kg 32 lb 8 oz	Sardis Reservoir Mississippi, USA	Oct. 22, 1977	Eddie O'Daniel
Bullhead, black	*Ictalurus melas*	3.62 kg 8 lb	Lake Waccabuc New York, USA	Aug. 1, 1951	Kani Evans
Carp	*Cyprinus carpio*	25.08 kg 55 lb 5 oz	Clearwater Lake Minnesota, USA	July 10, 1952	Frank J. Ledwein
Catfish, blue	*Ictalurus furcatus*	43.99 kg 97 lb	Missouri River South Dakota, USA	Sept. 16, 1959	Edward B. Elliott
Catfish, channel	*Ictalurus punctatus*	26.30 kg 58 lb	Santee-Cooper Res. South Carolina, USA	July 7, 1964	W.B. Whaley
Catfish, flathead	*Pylodictis olivaris*	36.06 kg 79 lb 8 oz	White River Indiana, USA	Aug. 13, 1966	Glenn T. Simpson
Catfish, white	*Ictalurus catus*	4.67 kg 10 lb 5 oz	Raritan River New Jersey, USA	June 23, 1976	Lewis W. Lomerson
Char, Arctic	*Salvelinus alpinus*	13.46 kg 29 lb 11 oz	Arctic River N.W. Terr., Canada	Aug. 21, 1968	Jeanne P. Branson
Crappie, black	*Pomoxis nigromaculatus*	2.26 kg 5 lb	Santee-Cooper Res. South Carolina, USA	March 15, 1957	Paul E. Foust
Crappie, white	*Pomoxis annularis*	2.35 kg 5 lb 3 oz	Enid Dam Mississippi, USA	July 31, 1957	Fred L. Bright
Dolly Varden	*Salvelinus malma*	14.51 kg 32 lb	Lake Pend Oreille Idaho, USA	Oct. 27, 1949	N.L. Higgins
Drum, freshwater	*Aplodinotus grunniens*	24.72 kg 54 lb 8 oz	Nickajack Lake Tennessee, USA	April 20, 1972	Benny E. Hull
Gar, alligator	*Lepisosteus spatula*	126.55 kg 279 lb	Rio Grande River Texas, USA	Dec. 2, 1951	Bill Valverde
Gar, longnose	*Lepisosteus osseus*	22.82 kg 50 lb 5 oz	Trinity River Texas, USA	July 30, 1954	Townsend Miller
Grayling, Arctic	*Thymallus arcticus*	2.69 kg 5 lb 15 oz	Katseyedie River N.W. Terr., Canada	Aug. 16, 1967	Jeanne P. Branson
Kokanee	*Oncorhynchus nerka*	2.99 kg 6 lb 9 oz	Priest Lake Idaho, USA	June 9, 1975	Jerry Verge
Muskellunge	*Esox masquinongy*	31.72 kg 69 lb 15 oz	St. Lawrence River New York, USA	Sept. 22, 1957	Arthur Lawton
Perch, white	*Morone americana*	2.15 kg 4 lb 12 oz	Messalonskee Lake Maine, USA	June 4, 1949	Mrs. Earl Small
Perch, yellow	*Perca flavescens*	1.91 kg 4 lb 3 oz	Bordentown New Jersey, USA	May, 1865	Dr. C.C. Abbot
Pickerel, chain	*Esox niger*	4.25 kg 9 lb 6 oz	Homerville Georgia, USA	Feb. 17, 1961	Baxley McQuaig, Jr.
Pike, northern	*Esox lucius*	20.92 kg 46 lb 2 oz	Sacandaga Reservoir New York, USA	Sept. 15, 1940	Peter Dubuc
Redhorse, silver	*Moxostoma anisurum*	1.87 kg 4 lb 2 oz	Gasconade River Missouri, USA	Oct. 5, 1974	C. Larry McKinney
Salmon, Atlantic	*Salmo salar*	35.89 kg 79 lb 2 oz	Tana River Norway	1928	Henrik Henriksen
Salmon, chinook	*Oncorhynchus tshawytscha*	42.18 kg 93 lb	Kelp Bay Alaska, USA	June 24, 1977	Howard C. Rider
Salmon, chum	*Oncorhynchus keta*	12.33 kg 27 lb 3 oz	Raymond Cove Alaska, USA	June 11, 1977	Robert A. Jahnke
Salmon, landlocked	*Salmo salar*	10.20 kg 22 lb 8 oz	Sebago Lake Maine, USA	Aug. 1, 1907	Edward Blakely
Salmon, coho	*Oncorhynchus kisutch*	14.06 kg 31 lb	Cowichan Bay B.C., Canada	Oct. 11, 1947	Mrs. Lee Hallberg
Sauger	*Stizostedion canadense*	3.96 kg 8 lb 12 oz	Lake Sakakawea North Dakota, USA	Oct. 6, 1971	Mike Fischer

IGFA FRESHWATER ALL-TACKLE WORLD RECORDS

Shad, American	*Alosa sapidissima*	4.13 kg 9 lb 2 oz	Enfield Connecticut, USA	April 28, 1973	Edward P. Nelson
Sturgeon, white	*Acipenser transmontanus*	163.29 kg 360 lb	Snake River Idaho, USA	April 24, 1956	Willard Cravens
Sunfish, green	*Lepomis cyanellus*	0.96 kg 2 lb 2 oz	Stockton Lake Missouri, USA	June 18, 1971	Paul M. Dilley
Sunfish, redbreast	*Lepomis auritus*	0.69 kg 1 lb 8 oz	Suwannee River Florida, USA	April 30, 1977	Tommy D. Cason, Jr.
Sunfish, redear	*Lepomis microlophus*	2.04 kg 4 lb 8 oz	Chase City, Virginia, USA	June 19, 1970	Maurice E. Ball
Trout, brook	*Salvelinus fontinalis*	6.57 kg 14 lb 8 oz	Nipigon River Ontario, Canada	July, 1916	Dr. W.J. Cook
Trout, brown	*Salmo trutta*	16.30 kg 35 lb 15 oz	Nahuel Huapi Argentina	Dec. 16, 1952	Eugenio Cavaglia
Trout, cutthroat	*Salmo clarki*	18.59 kg 41 lb	Pyramid Lake Nevada, USA	Dec., 1925	John Skimmerhorn
Trout, golden	*Salmo aguabonita*	4.98 kg 11 lb	Cook's Lake Wyoming, USA	Aug. 5, 1948	Chas. S. Reed
Trout, lake	*Salvelinus namaycush*	29.48 kg 65 lb	Great Bear Lake N.W. Terr., Canada	Aug. 8, 1970	Larry Daunis
Trout (rainbow, steelhead, or kamloops)	*Salmo gairdneri*	19.10 kg 42 lb 2 oz	Bell Island Alaska, USA	June 22, 1970	David Robert White
Trout, sunapee	*Salvelinus aureolus*	5.21 kg 11 lb 8 oz	Lake Sunapee New Hampshire, USA	Aug. 1, 1954	Ernest Theoharis
Trout, tiger	Brown X brook	7.71 kg 17 lb	Lake Michigan Wisconsin, USA	Aug. 2, 1977	Edward Rudnicki
Walleye	*Stizostedion vitreum vitreum*	11.34 kg 25 lb	Old Hickory Lake Tennessee, USA	Aug. 1, 1960	Mabry Harper
Warmouth	*Lepomis gulosus*	0.90 kg 2 lb	Sylvania Georgia, USA	May 4, 1974	Carlton Robbins
Whitefish, lake	*Coregonus clupeaformis*	5.89 kg 13 lb	Great Bear Lake N.W. Terr., Canada	July 14, 1974	Robert L. Stintsman
Whitefish, mountain	*Prosopium williamsoni*	2.26 kg 5 lb	Athabasca River Alberta, Canada	June 3, 1963	Orville Welch

IGFA Saltwater All-Tackle World Records

All-tackle records are kept for the heaviest saltwater fish of each species caught by an angler in any line class category up to 60 kg (130 lb). Following are the all-tackle records granted as of January 1, 1979.

SPECIES	SCIENTIFIC NAME	WEIGHT	PLACE	DATE	ANGLER
Albacore	*Thunnus alalunga*	40.00 kg 88 lb 2 oz	Mogan Port, Gran Canaria, Canary I.	Nov. 19, 1977	Siegfried Dickemann
Amberjack, greater	*Seriola dumerili*	67.58 kg 149 lb	Bermuda	June 21, 1964	Peter Simons
Barracuda, great	*Sphyraena barracuda*	37.64 kg 83 lb	Lagos Nigeria	Jan. 13, 1952	K. J. W. Hackett
Bass, black sea	*Centropristis striata*	3.62 kg 8 lb	Nantucket Massachusetts, USA	May 13, 1951	H. R. Rider
Bass, giant sea	*Stereolepis gigas*	255.60 kg 563 lb 8 oz	Anacapa Island California, USA	Aug. 20, 1968	James D. McAdam, Jr.
Bass, striped	*Morone saxatilis*	32.65 kg 72 lb	Cuttyhunk Massachusetts, USA	Oct. 10, 1969	Edward J. Kirker
Bluefish	*Pomatomus saltatrix*	14.40 kg 31 lb 12 oz	Hatteras North Carolina, USA	Jan. 30, 1972	James M. Hussey
Bonefish	*Albula vulpes*	8.61 kg 19 lb	Zululand South Africa	May 26, 1962	Brian W. Batchelor
Bonito, Atlantic	*Sarda sarda*	4.64 kg 10 lb 4 oz	Block Island Rhode Island, USA	Oct. 21, 1978	Daniel Vaccaro
Bonito, Pacific	*Sarda spp.*	10.65 kg 23 lb 8 oz	Victoria, Mahe Seychelles	Feb. 19, 1975	Mrs. Anne Cochain
Cobia	*Rachycentron canadum*	50.03 kg 110 lb 5 oz	Mombasa Kenya	Sept. 8, 1964	Eric Tinworth
Cod	*Gadus morhua*	44.79 kg 98 lb 12 oz	Isle of Shoals New Hampshire, USA	June 8, 1969	Alphonse J. Bielevich
Dolphin	*Coryphaena hippurus*	39.46 kg 87 lb	Papagallo Gulf Costa Rica	Sept. 25, 1976	Manuel Salazar
Drum, black	*Pogonias cromis*	51.28 kg 113 lb 1 oz	Lewes Delaware, USA	Sept. 15, 1975	Gerald M. Townsend
Drum, red	*Sciaenops ocellata*	40.82 kg 90 lb	Rodanthe North Carolina, USA	Nov. 7, 1973	Elvin Hooper
Flounder, summer	*Paralichthys dentatus*	10.17 kg 22 lb 7 oz	Montauk New York, USA	Sept. 15, 1975	Charles Nappi
Jack, crevalle	*Caranx hippos*	23.13 kg 51 lb	Lake Worth Florida, USA	June 20, 1978	Stephen V. Schwenk
Jewfish	*Epinephelus itajara*	308.44 kg 680 lb	Fernandina Beach Florida, USA	May 20, 1961	Lynn Joyner
Kawakawa	*Euthynnus affinis*	9.52 kg 21 lb	Kilauea, Kauai Hawaii, USA	Aug. 21, 1975	E. John O'Dell
Mackerel, king	*Scomberomorus cavalla*	40.82 kg 90 lb	Key West Florida, USA	Feb. 16, 1976	Norton I. Thomton
Marlin, black	*Makaira indica*	707.61 kg 1560 lb	Cabo Blanco Peru	Aug. 4, 1953	Alfred C. Glassell, Jr.
Marlin, blue (Atl.)	*Makaira nigricans*	581.51 kg 1282 lb	St. Thomas Virgin Islands	Aug. 6, 1977	Larry Martin
Marlin blue (Pac.)	*Makaira nigricans*	522.99 kg 1153 lb	Ritidian Point Guam	Aug. 21, 1969	Greg D. Perez
Marlin, striped	*Tetrapturus audax*	189.37 kg 417 lb 8 oz	Cavalli Islands New Zealand	Jan. 14, 1977	Phillip Bryers
Marlin, white	*Tetrapturus albidus*	79.00 kg 174 lb 3 oz	Vitoria Brazil	Nov. 1, 1975	Otavio Cunha Reboucas
Permit	*Trachinotus falcatus*	23.35 kg 51 lb 8 oz	Lake Worth Florida, USA	Apr. 28, 1978	William M. Kenney
Pollock	*Pollachius virens*	21.06 kg 46 lb 7 oz	Brielle New Jersey, USA	May 26, 1975	John Tomes Holton

Pompano, African	*Alectis ciliaris*	15.30 kg 33 lb 12 oz	Islamorada Florida, USA	Feb. 11, 1978	Joseph M. Nowdomski
Roosterfish	*Nematistius pectoralis*	51.71 kg 114 lb	La Paz Baja, Mexico	June 1, 1960	Abe Sackheim
Runner, rainbow	*Elagatis bipinnulata*	15.25 kg 33 lb 10 oz	Clarion Island Mexico	Mar. 14, 1976	Ralph A. Mikkelsen
Sailfish (Atlantic)	*Istiophorus platypterus*	58.10 kg 128 lb 1 oz	Luanda Angola	Mar. 27, 1974	Harm Steyn
Sailfish (Pacific)	*Istiophorus platypterus*	100.24 kg 221 lb	Santa Cruz Island Ecuador	Feb. 12, 1947	C. W. Stewart
Seabass, white	*Cynoscion nobilis*	37.98 kg 83 lb 12 oz	San Felipe Mexico	Mar. 31, 1953	L. C. Baumgardner
Seatrout, spotted	*Cynoscion nebulosus*	7.25 kg 16 lb	Mason's Beach Virginia, USA	May 28, 1977	William Katko
Shark, blue	*Prionace glauca*	198.22 kg 437 lb	Catherine Bay N.S.W., Australia	Oct. 2, 1976	Peter Hyde
Shark, hammerhead	*Sphyrna spp.*	318.87 kg 703 lb	Jacksonville Beach Florida, USA	July 5, 1975	H. B. "Blackie" Reasor
Shark, porbeagle	*Lamna nasus*	210.92 kg 465 lb	Padstow, Cornwall England, U.K.	July 23, 1976	Jorge Potier
Shark, shortfin mako	*Isurus oxyrinchus*	481.26 kg 1061 lb	Mayor Island New Zealand	Feb. 17, 1970	James B. Penwarden
Shark, thresher	*Alopias spp.*	335.20 kg 739 lb	Tutukaka New Zealand	Feb. 17, 1975	Brian Galvin
Shark, tiger	*Galeocerdo cuvieri*	807.40 kg 1780 lb	Cherry Grove S. Carolina, USA	June 14, 1964	Walter Maxwell
Shark, white	*Carcharodon carcharias*	1208.38 kg 2664 lb	Ceduna South Australia	Apr. 21, 1959	Alfred Dean
Skipjack, black	*Euthynnus lineatus*	6.57 kg 14 lb 8 oz	Cabo San Lucas Baja, Mexico	May 24, 1977	Lorraine Carlton
Snook	*Centropomus undecimalis*	24.32 kg 53 lb 10 oz	Rio de Parasmina Costa Rica	Oct. 18, 1978	Gilbert Ponzi
Spearfish	*Tetrapturus spp.*	30.50 kg 67 lb 4 oz	Manteo North Carolina, USA	Oct. 6, 1978	Jerry Dean Leonard
Swordfish	*Xiphias gladius*	536.15 kg 1182 lb	Iquique Chile	May 7, 1953	L. Marron
Tanguigue	*Scomberomorus commerson*	38.75 kg 85 lb 6 oz	Rottnest Island West Australia	May 5, 1978	Barry Wrightson
Tarpon	*Megalops atlantica*	128.36 kg 283 lb	Lake Maracaibo Venezuela	Mar. 19, 1956	M. Salazar
Tautog	*Tautoga onitis*	9.69 kg 21 lb 6 oz	Cape May New Jersey, USA	June 12, 1954	R. N. Sheafer
Trevally, giant	*Caranx sexfasciatus*	52.61 kg 116 lb	Pago Pago American Samoa	Feb. 20, 1978	William G. Foster
Tuna, bigeye (Atl.)	*Thunnus obesus*	170.32 kg 375 lb 8 oz	Ocean City Maryland, USA	Aug. 26, 1977	Cecil Browne
Tuna, bigeye (Pac.)	*Thunnus obesus*	197.31 kg 435 lb	Cabo Blanco Peru	Apr. 17, 1957	Dr. Russel V. A. Lee
Tuna, blackfin	*Thunnus atlanticus*	19.05 kg 42 lb	Bermuda	June 2, 1978	Alan J. Card
Tuna, bluefin	*Thunnus thynnus*	560.19 kg 1235 lb	North Lake P.E.I., Canada	Oct. 17, 1978	Michael Mac Donald
Tuna, dogtooth	*Gymnosarda unicolor*	69.62 kg 153 lb 8 oz	Cooktown Qld., Australia	Sept. 25, 1975	William E. Chapman
Tuna, longtail	*Thunnus tonggol*	29.50 kg 65 lb	Port Stephens N.S.W., Australia	Apr. 20, 1978	Michael James
Tuna, skipjack	*Katsuwonus pelamis*	18.11 kg 39 lb 15 oz	Walker Cay Bahamas	Jan. 21, 1952	F. Drowley

IGFA SALTWATER ALL-TACKLE WORLD RECORDS

TIE	*Euthynnus pelamis*	18.14 kg 40 lb	Baie du Tambeau Mauritius	Apr. 19, 1971	Joseph R. P. Caboche, Jr.
Tuna, south. bluefin	*Thunnus maccoyii*	100.00 kg 220 lb 7 oz	Tasman Island Tasmania, Australia	June 10, 1978	Stanley Gibbon
Tuna, yellowfin	*Thunnus albacares*	176.35 kg 388 lb 12 oz	San Benedicto I. Mexico	Apr. 1, 1977	Curt Wiesenhutter
Tunny, little	*Euthynnus alletteratus*	12.24 kg 27 lb	Key Largo Florida, USA	Apr. 20, 1976	William E. Allison
Wahoo	*Acanthocybium solandri*	67.58 kg 149 lb	Cat Cay Bahamas	June 15, 1962	John Pirovano
Weakfish	*Cynoscion regalis*	8.84 kg 19 lb 8 oz	Trinidad West Indies	Apr. 13, 1962	Dennis B. Hall
Yellowtail, California	*Seriola lalandi dorsalis*	22.67 kg 50 lb	Alijos Rocks Mexico	June 5, 1978	Jerry Reid
Yellowtail, southern	*Seriola lalandi lalandi*	50.34 kg 111 lb	Bay of Islands New Zealand	June 11, 1961	A. F. Plim

IGFA Saltwater Line Class World Records

Following are all men's and women's world saltwater fish records granted in IGFA line class categories as of January 1, 1979. Records are listed alphabetically according to common names of species.
M = Men's records; W = Women's records

ALBACORE
Thunnus alalunga

LINE CLASS	WEIGHT	PLACE	DATE	ANGLER
M-3 kg (6 lb)	13.83 kg (30 lb, 8 oz)	San Diego, California, USA	Oct. 14, 1978	Gerald A. Garrett
W-3 kg (6 lb)	11.79 kg (26 lb)	San Diego, California, USA	Sept. 12, 1976	Lorraine Carlton
M-6 kg (12 lb)	17.91 kg (39 lb, 8 oz)	Balboa, California, USA	July 23, 1958	Dr. R. S. Rubaum
W-6 kg (12 lb)	13.38 kg (29 lb, 8 oz)	San Diego, California, USA	Oct. 5, 1963	Jane Holland
M-10 kg (20 lb)	28.00 kg (61 lb, 11 oz)	Arguineguin, Gran Canaria, Canary I.	Nov. 15, 1977	Charles Chtivelman
W-10 kg (20 lb)	23.25 kg (51 lb, 4 oz)	Arguineguin, Gran Canaria, Canary I.	Nov. 26, 1977	Mrs. Charles Chtivelman
M-15 kg (30 lb)	31.75 kg (70 lb)	Cape Point, South Africa	Aug. 25, 1974	Geoff. Sonnenberg
W-15 kg (30 lb)	26.98 kg (59 lb, 8 oz)	Montauk, New York, USA	Aug. 14, 1971	Eileen B. Merten
M-24 kg (50 lb)	32.25 kg (71 lb, 1 oz)	S. Miguel, Azores	Nov. 17, 1973	Eduardo do R. Melo
W-24 kg (50 lb)	23.50 kg (51 lb, 12 oz)	Arguineguin, Gran Canaria, Canary I.	Nov. 18, 1977	Mrs. Charles Chtivelman
M-36 kg (80 lb)	40.00 kg (88 lb, 2 oz)	Mogan Port, Gran Canaria, Canary I.	Nov. 19, 1977	Siegfried Dickemann
W-36 kg (80 lb)	29.00 kg (63 lb, 14 oz)	Arguineguin, Gran Canaria, Canary I.	Oct. 11, 1977	Mrs. Genevieve Margoulies
Tie W-6 kg	13.38 kg (29 lb, 8 oz)	Morro Bay, California, USA	Sept. 3, 1973	Barbara Louise McKinney

AMBERJACK, greater
Seriola dumerili

LINE CLASS	WEIGHT	PLACE	DATE	ANGLER
M-3 kg (6 lb)	30.39 kg (67 lb)	Fort Pierce, Florida, USA	Jan. 15, 1976	Dave Chermanski
W-3 kg (6 lb)	14.06 kg (31 lb)	Jupiter, Florida, USA	Apr. 21, 1978	Cynthia Boomhower
M-6 kg (12 lb)	36.96 kg (81 lb, 8 oz)	Key Largo, Florida, USA	Feb. 6, 1977	Jimmy Lewis
W-6 kg (12 lb)	11.73 kg (92 lb)	Bimini, Bahamas	Jan. 30, 1978	Bess Greenberg
M-10 kg (20 lb)	46.04 kg (101 lb, 8 oz)	Palm Beach, Florida, USA	Feb. 26, 1964	Robert R. Boomhower
W-10 kg (20 lb)	45.13 kg (99 lb, 8 oz)	Palm Beach, Florida, USA	May 17, 1978	Katie Adamson
M-15 kg (30 lb)	67.58 kg (149 lb)	Bermuda	June 21, 1964	Peter Simons
W-15 kg (30 lb)	45.81 kg (101 lb)	Palm Beach, Florida, USA	Mar. 31, 1970	Mrs. Cynthia Boomhower
M-24 kg (50 lb)	59.87 kg (132 lb)	La Paz, Baja, Mexico	July 21, 1964	Howard H. Hahn
W-24 kg (50 lb)	48.98 kg (108 lb)	Palm Beach, Florida, USA	Dec. 30, 1967	Peggy Kester Mumford
M-36 kg (80 lb)	64.80 kg (142 lb, 14 oz)	Bermuda	Aug. 7, 1969	Nelson Chesterfield Simons
W-36 kg (80 lb)	48.30 kg (106 lb, 8 oz)	Pinas Bay, Panama	July 9, 1960	Helen Robinson
M-60 kg (130 lb)	60.32 kg (133 lb)	Islamorada, Florida, USA	Apr. 6, 1968	Louis E. Woster
W-60 kg (130 lb)	38.55 kg (85 lb)	Palm Beach, Florida, USA	Apr. 29, 1971	Mrs. Cynthia Boomhower

BARRACUDA, great
Sphyraena barracuda

LINE CLASS	WEIGHT	PLACE	DATE	ANGLER
M-3 kg (6 lb)	22.42 kg (49 lb, 7 oz)	Cairns, Qld., Australia	Sept. 25, 1974	Robert Oliver
W-3 kg (6 lb)	14.06 kg (31 lb)	Fort Pierce, Florida, USA	Feb. 3, 1976	Gloria J. Applegate
M-6 kg (12 lb)	22.33 kg (49 lb, 4 oz)	Margarita, Venezuela	Jan. 9, 1960	Gerardo Sanson
W-6 kg (12 lb)	20.07 kg (44 lb, 4 oz)	Key West, Florida, USA	July 4, 1975	Caroline Whittaker
M-10 kg (20 lb)	28.00 kg (61 lb, 11 oz)	Maracaibo, Venezuela	June 11, 1978	David L. Bohorquez
W-10 kg (20 lb)	22.45 kg (49 lb, 8 oz)	Cairns, Qld., Australia	Sept. 6, 1976	Mrs. Barbara Boxer
M-15 kg (30 lb)	34.47 kg (76 lb)	Seychelles	Oct. 14, 1976	Amhand Moosa
W-15 kg (30 lb)	19.50 kg (43 lb)	Key Largo, Florida, USA	Dec. 9, 1956	Mrs. Robert M. Scully
M-24 kg (50 lb)	37.64 kg (83 lb)	Lagos, Nigeria	Jan. 13, 1952	K.J.W. Hackett
W-24 kg (50 lb)	21.43 kg (47 lb, 4 oz)	Pemba Channel, Kenya	July 27, 1973	Mrs. Ingrid Papworth
M-36 kg (80 lb)	30.39 kg (67 lb)	Islamorada, Florida, USA	Jan. 29, 1949	Harold K. Goodstone
W-36 kg (80 lb)	30.05 kg (66 lb, 4 oz)	Cape Lopez, Gabon Republic	July 17, 1955	Mme. M. Halley
Tie W-6 kg	20.07 kg (44 lb, 4 oz)	Cairns, Qld., Australia	Aug. 22, 1976	Mrs. Jill Hooper

IGFA SALTWATER FLY ROD WORLD RECORDS

BASS, black sea
Centropristis striata

LINE CLASS	WEIGHT	PLACE	DATE	ANGLER
M-3 kg (6 lb)	2.35 kg (5 lb, 3 oz)	Virginia Beach, Virginia, USA	May 1, 1974	Harry L. Hall, Jr.
W-3 kg (6 lb)	1.89 kg (4 lb, 3 oz)	Virginia Beach, Virginia, USA	Apr. 7, 1974	Mrs. Charlotte J. Wright
M-6 kg (12 lb)	2.55 kg (5 lb, 10 oz)	Great South Bay, New York, USA	May 14, 1974	Michael Harrington
W-6 kg (12 lb)	1.92 kg (4 lb, 4 oz)	Virginia Beach, Virginia, USA	May 21, 1972	Mrs. Michael E. Hayes
M-10 kg (20 lb)	3.06 kg (6 lb, 12 oz)	Freeport, New York, USA	Nov. 3, 1975	James Lanzarotta
W-10 kg (20 lb)	2.32 kg (5 lb, 2 oz)	Virginia Beach, Virginia, USA	May 17, 1971	Mrs. Charlotte J. Wright
M-15 kg (30 lb)	3.43 kg (7 lb, 9 oz)	Virginia Beach, Virginia, USA	Dec. 17, 1977	James J. Robinson
W-15 kg (30 lb)	2.66 kg (5 lb, 14 oz)	Cape Henry, Virginia, USA	Oct. 2, 1972	Mary Lou Penny Durney

BASS, giant sea
Stereolepis gigas

LINE CLASS	WEIGHT	PLACE	DATE	ANGLER
M-3 kg (6 lb)	Vacant—Minimum Acceptance Weight—25.36 kg (56 lb)			
W-3 kg (6 lb)	Vacant—Minimum Acceptance Weight—25.36 kg (56 lb)			
M-6 kg (12 lb)	51.02 kg (112 lb, 8 oz)	San Francisco Island, Mexico	June 12, 1957	D.B. Rosenthal
W-6 kg (12 lb)	Vacant—Minimum Acceptance Weight—40.82 kg (90 lb)			
M-10 kg (20 lb)	192.77 kg (425 lb)	Point Mugu, California, USA	Oct. 1, 1960	C.C. Joiner
W-10 kg (20 lb)	54.43 kg (120 lb)	Malibu, California, USA	Jan. 6, 1957	Jane D. Hill
M-15 kg (30 lb)	203.21 kg (448 lb)	Coronado Islands, Mexico	Apr. 13, 1975	R.H. Gautier
W-15 kg (30 lb)	49.21 kg (108 lb, 8 oz)	San Pablo, Mexico	Dec. 29, 1963	Frances Enfinger
M-24 kg (50 lb)	252.73 kg (557 lb, 3 oz)	Catalina Island, California, USA	July 1, 1962	Richard M. Lane
W-24 kg (50 lb)	190.05 kg (419 lb)	Coronado Islands, Mexico	Oct. 8, 1960	Bettie Sears
M-36 kg (80 lb)	255.60 kg (563 lb, 8 oz)	Anacapa Island, California, USA	Aug. 20, 1968	James D. McAdam, Jr.
W-36 kg (80 lb)	205.02 kg (452 lb)	Coronado Islands, Mexico	Oct. 8, 1960	Lorene Wheeler
M-60 kg (130 lb)	233.14 kg (514 lb)	San Clemente, California, USA	Aug. 29, 1955	J. Patterson
W-60 kg (130 lb)	Vacant—Minimum Acceptance Weight—192.52 kg (425 lb)			
Tie M-60 kg	233.14 kg (514 lb)	San Clemente, California, USA	Nov. 15, 1961	Joe M. Arve

BASS, striped
Morone saxatilis

LINE CLASS	WEIGHT	PLACE	DATE	ANGLER
M-3 kg (6 lb)	17.23 kg (38 lb)	Atlantic City, New Jersey, USA	Nov. 5, 1973	Charles P. Bliss
W-3 kg (6 lb)	14.51 kg (32 lb)	Cape Cod Bay, Massachusetts, USA	July 3, 1975	Mae B. Foster
M-6 kg (12 lb)	27.95 kg (61 lb, 10 oz)	Block Island, Rhode Island, USA	July 5, 1956	L.A. Garceau
W-6 kg (12 lb)	21.31 kg (47 lb)	Umpqua River, Oregon, USA	Aug. 21, 1958	Mrs. Margaret Hulen
M-10 kg (20 lb)	30.39 kg (67 lb)	Block Island, Rhode Island, USA	May 31, 1963	Jack Ryan
W-10 kg (20 lb)	26.08 kg (57 lb, 8 oz)	Block Island Sound, New York, USA	Aug. 28, 1959	Mary R. Aubry
M-15 kg (30 lb)	28.80 kg (63 lb, 8 oz)	Jones Beach, New York, USA	Aug. 17, 1973	William E. King, Jr.
W-15 kg (30 lb)	29.25 kg (64 lb, 8 oz)	North Truro, Massachusetts, USA	Aug. 14, 1960	Rosa O. Webb
M-24 kg (50 lb)	32.65 kg (72 lb)	Cuttyhunk, Massachusetts, USA	Oct. 10, 1969	Edward J. Kirker
W-24 kg (50 lb)	29.03 kg (64 lb)	Sea Bright, New Jersey, USA	June 27, 1971	Mrs. Asie Espenak
M-36 kg (80 lb)	Vacant—Minimum Acceptance Weight—24.46 kg (54 lb)			
W-36 kg (80 lb)	25.40 kg (56 lb)	Sandy Hook, New Jersey, USA	June 7, 1955	Mrs. H.J. Sarnoski
Tie M-10 kg	30.39 kg (67 lb)	Greenhill, Rhode Island, USA	Oct. 3, 1965	Wilfred Fontaine

IGFA SALTWATER LINE CLASS WORLD RECORDS

BLUEFISH

Pomatomus saltatrix

LINE CLASS	WEIGHT	PLACE	DATE	ANGLER
M-3 kg (6 lb)	9.10 kg (20 lb, 1 oz)	Montauk, New York, USA	Nov. 13, 1977	Jeff Schneider
W-3 kg (6 lb)	6.88 kg (15 lb, 3 oz)	Nantucket, Massachusetts, USA	Sept. 30, 1977	Dorothy B. Clarke
M-6 kg (12 lb)	10.97 kg (24 lb, 3 oz)	San Miguel, Azores	Aug. 27, 1953	M.A. da Silva Veloso
W-6 kg (12 lb)	7.54 kg (16 lb, 10 oz)	Montauk, New York, USA	June 24, 1961	Gloria Better
M-10 kg (20 lb)	10.77 kg (23 lb, 12 oz)	Cape May, New Jersey, USA	Oct. 9, 1971	William Di Santo
W-10 kg (20 lb)	11.11 kg (24 lb, 8 oz)	Nags Head, N. Carolina, USA	Nov. 12, 1971	Mrs. Rita Mazelle
M-15 kg (30 lb)	9.97 kg (22 lb)	Avon, N. Carolina, USA	Nov. 27, 1969	Michael E. Hayes
W-15 kg (30 lb)	9.75 kg (21 lb, 8 oz)	Truro, Massachusetts, USA	Oct. 10, 1970	Ruth M. Anderson
M-24 kg (50 lb)	14.40 kg (31 lb, 12 oz)	Hatteras, N. Carolina, USA	Jan. 30, 1972	James M. Hussey
W-24 kg (50 lb)	10.85 kg (23 lb, 15 oz)	Nags Head, N. Carolina, USA	Nov. 19, 1970	Mrs. Joyce Payne Bell

BONEFISH

Albula vulpes

LINE CLASS	WEIGHT	PLACE	DATE	ANGLER
M-3 kg (6 lb)	6.32 kg (13 lb, 15 oz)	Islamorada, Florida, USA	Apr. 9, 1978	Dick Moeller
W-3 kg (6 lb)	5.95 kg (13 lb, 2 oz)	Islamorada, Florida, USA	Apr. 5, 1973	Charlotte Rowland
M-6 kg (12 lb)	7.25 kg (16 lb)	Bimini, Bahamas	Feb. 25, 1971	Jerry Lavenstein
W-6 kg (12 lb)	6.80 kg (15 lb)	Bimini, Bahamas	Mar. 20, 1961	Andrea Tose
M-10 kg (20 lb)	7.71 kg (17 lb)	Mabibi, Zululand, S. Africa	May 24, 1976	Peter F. Mason
W-10 kg (20 lb)	6.23 kg (13 lb, 12 oz)	Exuma, Bahamas	Jan. 3, 1956	Mrs. B.A. Garson
M-15 kg (30 lb)	8.61 kg (19 lb)	Zululand, South Africa	May 26, 1962	Brian W. Batchelor
W-15 kg (30 lb)	Vacant—Minimum Acceptance Weight—6.34 kg (14 lb)			

BONITO, Atlantic

Sarda sarda

LINE CLASS	WEIGHT	PLACE	DATE	ANGLER
M-3 kg (6 lb)	3.85 kg (8 lb, 8 oz)	Woods Hole, Massachusetts, USA	Sept. 7, 1976	Dennis Kowal
W-3 kg (6 lb)	Vacant—Minimum Acceptance Weight—2.71 kg (6 lb)			
M-6 kg (12 lb)	3.43 kg (7 lb, 9 oz)	Martha's Vineyard, Massachusetts, USA	Oct. 16, 1978	Bradley Poehler
W-6 kg (12 lb)	Vacant—Minimum Acceptance Weight—2.71 kg (6 lb)			
M-10 kg (20 lb)	4.33 kg (9 lb, 9 oz)	Brielle, New Jersey, USA	Nov. 7, 1978	Barry Goldman
W-10 kg (20 lb)	Vacant—Minimum Acceptance Weight—2.71 kg (6 lb)			
M-15 kg (30 lb)	4.53 kg (10 lb)	Block Island, Rhode Island, USA	Oct. 23, 1978	Larry S. Williams
W-15 kg (30 lb)	Vacant—Minimum Acceptance Weight—2.71 kg (6 lb)			

BONITO, Pacific

Sarda spp.

LINE CLASS	WEIGHT	PLACE	DATE	ANGLER
M-3 kg (6 lb)	5.10 kg (11 lb, 3 oz)	Montague Island, N.S.W., Australia	Mar. 27, 1978	Bill Jenkins
W-3 kg (6 lb)	2.72 kg (6 lb)	Golfito, Costa Rica	Feb. 13, 1976	Jean A. Lovetang
M-6 kg (12 lb)	4.53 kg (10 lb)	Bahia Potrero, Guanacaste, Costa Rica	Aug. 15, 1978	William A. Amos
W-6 kg (12 lb)	3.17 kg (7 lb)	Salinas, Ecuador	Aug. 29, 1976	Isabel Maria Maspons
M-10 kg (20 lb)	10.07 kg (21 lb, 3 oz)	Malibu, California, USA	July 30, 1978	Gino M. Picciolo
W-10 kg (20 lb)	3.85 kg (8 lb, 8 oz)	Salinas, Ecuador	Aug. 17, 1976	Mrs. Maureen Murphy
M-15 kg (30 lb)	9.40 kg (20 lb, 11 oz)	Montague Island, N.S.W., Australia	Apr. 1, 1978	Bruce Conley
W-15 kg (30 lb)	7.00 kg (15 lb, 6 oz)	Greenwell Point, N.S.W., Australia	Mar. 25, 1978	Betty Solomon

COBIA

Rachycentron canadum

LINE CLASS	WEIGHT	PLACE	DATE	ANGLER
M-3 kg (6 lb)	26.98 kg (59 lb, 8 oz)	Key West, Florida, USA	Mar. 25, 1978	Joseph Ferrigno
W-3 kg (6 lb)	24.94 kg (55 lb)	Key West, Florida, USA	Mar. 8, 1976	Mrs. William B. DuVal
M-6 kg (12 lb)	31.75 kg (70 lb)	Gulf of Mexico, Texas, USA	May 13, 1955	H.A. Norris, Jr.
W-6 kg (12 lb)	25.51 kg (56 lb, 4 oz)	Key West, Florida, USA	Mar. 8, 1976	Mrs. William B. DuVal
M-10 kg (20 lb)	41.27 kg (91 lb)	Crystal Beach, Florida, USA	Apr. 25, 1962	Roy English
W-10 kg (20 lb)	30.39 kg (67 lb)	Cape Charles, Virginia, USA	July 5, 1968	Judith Anne Gingell
M-15 kg (30 lb)	45.35 kg (100 lb)	Point Lookout, Qld., Australia	Oct. 4, 1962	Peter R. Bristow
W-15 kg (30 lb)	31.07 kg (68 lb, 8 oz)	Onancock, Virginia, USA	June 6, 1968	Mrs. Frances M. Roberts
M-24 kg (50 lb)	50.03 kg (110 lb, 5 oz)	Mombasa, Kenya	Sept. 8, 1964	Eric Tinworth
W-24 kg (50 lb)	38.55 kg (85 lb)	Point Lookout, Qld., Australia	Aug. 15, 1964	Margaret Keid
M-36 kg (80 lb)	40.82 kg (90 lb)	Ocean City, Maryland, USA	Aug. 31, 1949	Charles J. Stine
W-36 kg (80 lb)	43.99 kg (97 lb)	Oregon Inlet, N. Carolina, USA	June 4, 1952	Mary W. Black
Tie M-6 kg	31.80 kg (70 lb, 2 oz)	Key West, Florida, USA	Jan. 27, 1973	Alan H. Walton

COD

Gadus morhua

LINE CLASS	WEIGHT	PLACE	DATE	ANGLER
M-3 kg (6 lb)	9.20 kg (20 lb, 4 oz)	Oresund, Denmark	Feb. 23, 1977	Jan Warrer Olesen
W-3 kg (6 lb)	7.96 kg (17 lb, 9 oz)	Freeport, New York, USA	Jan. 7, 1976	Mrs. Ronnie DeLuca
M-6 kg (12 lb)	24.94 kg (55 lb)	Plum Island, Massachusetts, USA	July 6, 1958	W.C. Dunn
W-6 kg (12 lb)	10.31 kg (22 lb, 12 oz)	Montauk, New York, USA	May 20, 1978	Mary A. Risteen
M-10 kg (20 lb)	44.79 kg (98 lb, 12 oz)	Isle of Shoals, New Hampshire, USA	June 8, 1969	Alphonse J. Bielevich
W-10 kg (20 lb)	32.43 kg (71 lb, 8 oz)	Cape Cod, Massachusetts, USA	Aug. 2, 1964	Muriel Betts
M-15 kg (30 lb)	36.74 kg (81 lb)	Brielle, New Jersey, USA	Mar. 15, 1967	Joseph Chesla
W-15 kg (30 lb)	16.61 kg (36 lb, 10 oz)	Fire Island, New York, USA	May 1, 1977	Lucienne Jessen
M-24 kg (50 lb)	36.54 kg (80 lb, 9 oz)	Boston, Massachusetts, USA	May 14, 1972	William Bright
W-24 kg (50 lb)	24.55 kg (54 lb, 2 oz)	Nantucket, Massachusetts, USA	Sept. 28, 1970	Gail A. Mosher
M-36 kg (80 lb)	Vacant—Minimum Acceptance Weight—33.97 kg (75 lb)			
W-36 kg (80 lb)	37.08 kg (81 lb, 12 oz)	Middlebank, Massachusetts, USA	Sept. 24, 1970	Mrs. Sophie Karwa

DOLPHIN

Coryphaena hippurus

LINE CLASS	WEIGHT	PLACE	DATE	ANGLER
M-3 kg (6 lb)	21.00 kg (46 lb, 5 oz)	Pt. Venus, Tahiti, Fr. Polynesia	Feb. 10, 1973	Alban Ellacott
W-3 kg (6 lb)	19.95 kg (44 lb)	Tavernier, Florida, USA	Apr. 28, 1977	Ruth C. Stoky
M-6 kg (12 lb)	27.30 kg (60 lb, 2 oz)	Rio de Janeiro, Brazil	July 15, 1978	Fernando Gomes Pedrosa
W-6 kg (12 lb)	25.00 kg (55 lb, 2 oz)	Mazatlan, Mexico	Oct. 18, 1964	Marguerite H. Barry
M-10 kg (20 lb)	29.37 kg (64 lb, 12 oz)	Islamorada, Florida, USA	June 7, 1970	Donald H. Jackson
W-10 kg (20 lb)	37.81 kg (83 lb, 6 oz)	Mazatlan, Mexico	Apr. 24, 1972	Mrs. Eugene W. Wooten
M-15 kg (30 lb)	31.75 kg (70 lb)	Boca de Yuma, Dominican Republic	Apr. 15, 1978	Eduardo Read
W-15 kg (30 lb)	33.42 kg (73 lb, 11 oz)	Cabo San Lucas, Baja, Mexico	July 12, 1962	Barbara Kibbee Jayne
M-24 kg (50 lb)	39.46 kg (87 lb)	Papagallo Gulf, Costa Rica	Sept. 25, 1976	Manuel Salazar
W-24 kg (50 lb)	30.39 kg (67 lb)	Miami Beach, Florida, USA	Jan. 2, 1968	Janet Shepro
M-36 kg (80 lb)	34.92 kg (77 lb)	Nags Head, N. Carolina, USA	July 3, 1973	Louis Van Miller
W-36 kg (80 lb)	30.39 kg (67 lb)	Chub Cay, Bahamas	Mar. 13, 1966	Ruth Stanley
Tie M-10 kg	29.42 kg (64 lb, 14 oz)	Bimini, Bahamas	Feb. 27, 1977	Dr. Ron Harris

IGFA SALTWATER LINE CLASS WORLD RECORDS

DRUM, black   *Pogonias cromis*

LINE CLASS	WEIGHT	PLACE	DATE	ANGLER
M-3 kg (6 lb)	29.93 kg (66 lb)	Cape Charles, Virginia, USA	Apr. 28, 1976	Joe Fielder
W-3 kg (6 lb)	25.00 kg (55 lb, 2 oz)	Villas, New Jersey, USA	May 27, 1977	Ruth B. Verity
M-6 kg (12 lb)	40.37 kg (89 lb)	Delaware Bay, New Jersey, USA	May 14, 1971	John K. Osborne, Jr.
W-6 kg (12 lb)	26.64 kg (58 lb, 12 oz)	Atlantic Beach, N. Carolina, USA	May 8, 1959	Juel W. Duke
M-10 kg (20 lb)	40.82 kg (90 lb)	Onancock, Virginia, USA	Sept. 10, 1975	George C. Phillips, Jr.
W-10 kg (20 lb)	36.51 kg (80 lb)	Cape Charles, Virginia, USA	April 27, 1974	Louise M. Gaskill
M-15 kg (30 lb)	48.53 kg (107 lb)	Cape Charles, Virginia, USA	April 29, 1974	Everette M. Masten, Jr.
W-15 kg (30 lb)	36.28 kg (80 lb)	Cape Charles, Virginia, USA	May 24, 1975	Diane Dattoli
M-24 kg (50 lb)	51.28 kg (113 lb, 1 oz)	Lewes, Delaware, USA	Sept. 15, 1975	Gerald M. Townsend
W-24 kg (50 lb)	42.18 kg (93 lb)	Fernandina Beach, Florida, USA	Mar. 28, 1957	Mrs. Stella Moore
M-36 kg (80 lb)	50.34 kg (111 lb)	Cape Charles, Virginia, USA	May 3, 1974	G.L. Hopkins
W-36 kg (80 lb)	50.34 kg (111 lb)	Cape Charles, Virginia, USA	May 20, 1973	Betty D. Hall

DRUM, red   *Sciaenops ocellata*

LINE CLASS	WEIGHT	PLACE	DATE	ANGLER
M-3 kg (6 lb)	16.21 kg (35 lb, 12 oz)	Avon, N. Carolina, USA	Nov. 16, 1977	Harry Thoburn
W-3 kg (6 lb)	13.72 kg (30 lb, 4 oz)	Empire, Louisiana, USA	Apr. 5, 1973	Priscilla Jordan
M-6 kg (12 lb)	31.38 kg (69 lb, 3 oz)	Gwynns Island, Virginia, USA	July 10, 1975	John Oscar Everett
W-6 kg (12 lb)	23.36 kg (51 lb, 8 oz)	Cape Hatteras, N. Carolina, USA	Nov. 19, 1958	Joan S. Dull
M-10 kg (20 lb)	32.85 kg (72 lb, 7 oz)	Hatteras Island, N. Carolina, USA	Nov. 27, 1973	Wayne Plageman
W-10 kg (20 lb)	28.57 kg (63 lb)	Hatteras Inlet, N. Carolina, USA	Apr. 8, 1978	Shelby J. Harrison
M-15 kg (30 lb)	40.82 kg (90 lb)	Rodanthe, N. Carolina, USA	Nov. 7, 1973	Elvin Hooper
W-15 kg (30 lb)	31.52 kg (69 lb, 8 oz)	Cape Hatteras, N. Carolina, USA	Nov. 16, 1958	Jean Browning
M-24 kg (50 lb)	37.64 kg (83 lb)	Cape Charles, Virginia, USA	Aug. 5, 1949	Zack Waters, Jr.
W-24 kg (50 lb)	24.95 kg (55 lb)	Smith Island, Virginia, USA	Oct. 9, 1966	Margaret M. Hutson
M-36 kg (80 lb)	Vacant–Minimum Acceptance Weight–30.80 kg (68 lb)			
W-36 kg (80 lb)	Vacant–Minimum Acceptance Weight–30.80 kg (68 lb)			

FLOUNDER, summer   *Paralichthys dentatus*

LINE CLASS	WEIGHT	PLACE	DATE	ANGLER
M-3 kg (6 lb)	8.24 kg (18 lb, 3 oz)	Fire Island, New York, USA	Dec. 11, 1974	Dr. Einar F. Grell
W-3 kg (6 lb)	3.85 kg (8 lb, 8 oz)	Montauk Point, New York, USA	Sept. 25, 1976	Ronnie DeLuca
M-6 kg (12 lb)	9.07 kg (20 lb)	Topsail Island, N. Carolina, USA	Oct. 26, 1972	Chris A. Bowen
W-6 kg (12 lb)	5.49 kg (12 lb, 2 oz)	Avalon, New Jersey, USA	Sept. 8, 1957	Mrs. Alfred Bernstein
M-10 kg (20 lb)	9.07 kg (20 lb)	Oak Beach, L.I., New York, USA	Sept. 7, 1948	F. Howard Kessel
W-10 kg (20 lb)	8.58 kg (18 lb, 15 oz)	Jones Beach, New York, USA	Sept. 7, 1977	Mabel M. Andretta
M-15 kg (30 lb)	9.12 kg (20 lb, 2 oz)	Montauk, New York, USA	Sept. 20, 1958	Gay F. Schwinzer
W-15 kg (30 lb)	6.20 kg (13 lb, 11 oz)	Long Branch, New Jersey, USA	Aug. 20, 1953	Mrs. Leslie H. Taylor

HALIBUT, Atlantic

Hippoglossus hippoglossus

LINE CLASS	WEIGHT	PLACE	DATE	ANGLER
M-3 kg (6 lb)	Vacant—No Minimum Weight			
W-3 kg (6 lb)	Vacant—No Minimum Weight			
M-6 kg (12 lb)	Vacant—No Minimum Weight			
W-6 kg (12 lb)	Vacant—No Minimum Weight			
M-10 kg (20 lb)	Vacant—No Minimum Weight			
W-10 kg (20 lb)	Vacant—No Minimum Weight			
M-15 kg (30 lb)	Vacant—No Minimum Weight			
W-15 kg (30 lb)	Vacant—No Minimum Weight			
M-24 kg (50 lb)	Vacant—No Minimum Weight			
W-24 kg (50 lb)	Vacant—No Minimum Weight			
M-36 kg (80 lb)	Vacant—No Minimum Weight			
W-36 kg (80 lb)	Vacant—No Minimum Weight			
M-60 kg (130 lb)	Vacant—No Minimum Weight			
W-60 kg (130 lb)	Vacant—No Minimum Weight			

HALIBUT, California

Paralichthys californicus

LINE CLASS	WEIGHT	PLACE	DATE	ANGLER
M-3 kg (6 lb)	Vacant—No Minimum Weight			
W-3 kg (6 lb)	Vacant—No Minimum Weight			
M-6 kg (12 lb)	Vacant—No Minimum Weight			
W-6 kg (12 lb)	Vacant—No Minimum Weight			
M-10 kg (20 lb)	12.24 kg (27 lb)	San Pedro, California, USA	June 10, 1978	Richard Tunnicliff Covington
W-10 kg (20 lb)	Vacant—No Minimum Weight			
M-15 kg (30 lb)	Vacant—No Minimum Weight			
W-15 kg (30 lb)	Vacant—No Minimum Weight			
M-24 kg (50 lb)	Vacant—No Minimum Weight			
W-24 kg (50 lb)	Vacant—No Minimum Weight			
M-36 kg (80 lb)	Vacant—No Minimum Weight			
W-36 kg (80 lb)	Vacant—No Minimum Weight			

HALIBUT, Pacific

Hippoglossus stenolepis

LINE CLASS	WEIGHT	PLACE	DATE	ANGLER
M-3 kg (6 lb)	Vacant—No Minimum Weight			
W-3 kg (6 lb)	Vacant—No Minimum Weight			
M-6 kg (12 lb)	Vacant—No Minimum Weight			
W-6 kg (12 lb)	Vacant—No Minimum Weight			
M-10 kg (20 lb)	Vacant—No Minimum Weight			
W-10 kg (20 lb)	Vacant—No Minimum Weight			
M-15 kg (30 lb)	Vacant—No Minimum Weight			
W-15 kg (30 lb)	Vacant—No Minimum Weight			
M-24 kg (50 lb)	Vacant—No Minimum Weight			
W-24 kg (50 lb)	Vacant—No Minimum Weight			
M-36 kg (80 lb)	Vacant—No Minimum Weight			
W-36 kg (80 lb)	Vacant—No Minimum Weight			
M-60 kg (130 lb)	Vacant—No Minimum Weight			
W-60 kg (130 lb)	Vacant—No Minimum Weight			

JACK, crevalle

Caranx hippos

LINE CLASS	WEIGHT	PLACE	DATE	ANGLER
M-3 kg (6 lb)	4.47 kg (9 lb, 14 oz)	Miami, Florida, USA	Jan. 12, 1978	Jay Wright, Jr.
W-3 kg (6 lb)	3.18 kg (7 lb)	Empire, Louisiana, USA	May 20, 1978	Gayl I. Henze
M-6 kg (12 lb)	11.79 kg (26 lb)	Charleston, S. Carolina, USA	July 29, 1978	Martin James Wisse, Jr.
W-6 kg (12 lb)	16.21 kg (35 lb, 12 oz)	Jupiter, Florida, USA	Apr. 10, 1978	Cynthia Boomhower
M-10 kg (20 lb)	19.84 kg (43 lb, 12 oz)	Lower Matecumbe Key, Florida, USA	Oct. 28, 1978	Kenneth H. Stephens
W-10 kg (20 lb)	15.42 kg (34 lb)	Key West, Florida USA	July 23, 1978	Jacqueline M. Leader
M-15 kg (30 lb)	23.13 kg (51 lb)	Lake Worth, Florida, USA	June 20, 1978	Stephen V. Schwenk
W-15 kg (30 lb)	Vacant—Minimum Acceptance Weight—13.60 kg (30 lb)			
M-24 kg (50 lb)	22.45 kg (49 lb, 8 oz)	Palm Beach, Florida, USA	May 7, 1978	Ralph O. Cannon, Jr.
W-24 kg (50 lb)	Vacant—Minimum Acceptance Weight—22.67 kg (50 lb)			

JACK, horse-eye

Caranx latus

LINE CLASS	WEIGHT	PLACE	DATE	ANGLER
M-3 kg (6 lb)	Vacant—No Minimum Weight			
W-3 kg (6 lb)	Vacant—No Minimum Weight			
M-6 kg (12 lb)	Vacant—No Minimum Weight			
W-6 kg (12 lb)	Vacant—No Minimum Weight			
M-10 kg (20 lb)	Vacant—No Minimum Weight			
W-10 kg (20 lb)	Vacant—No Minimum Weight			
M-15 kg (30 lb)	Vacant—No Minimum Weight			
W-15 kg (30 lb)	Vacant—No Minimum Weight			
M-24 kg (50 lb)	7.71 kg (17 lb)	Palm Beach, Florida, USA	Sept. 25, 1978	Ralph O. Cannon, Jr.
W-24 kg (50 lb)	Vacant—No Minimum Weight			

JEWFISH

Epinephelus itajara

LINE CLASS	WEIGHT	PLACE	DATE	ANGLER
M-3 kg (6 lb)	140.38 kg (309 lb, 8 oz)	Flamingo, Florida, USA	Jan. 15, 1977	Kenny Bittner
W-3 kg (6 lb)	Vacant—Minimum Acceptance Weight—18.12 kg (40 lb)			
M-6 kg (12 lb)	165.78 kg (365 lb, 8 oz)	Flamingo, Florida, USA	Mar. 31, 1975	Kenny Bittner
W-6 kg (12 lb)	49.89 kg (110 lb)	Islamorada, Florida, USA	Aug. 2, 1961	Mrs. Gar Wood, Jr.
M-10 kg (20 lb)	156.37 kg (344 lb, 12 oz)	Flamingo, Florida, USA	Jan. 11, 1976	Al Polofsky
W-10 kg (20 lb)	19.27 kg (42 lb, 8 oz)	Florida Bay, Florida, USA	Nov. 7, 1969	Helen Robinson
M-15 kg (30 lb)	195.04 kg (430 lb)	Ft. Lauderdale, Florida, USA	Apr. 25, 1967	Curt Johnson
W-15 kg (30 lb)	144.24 kg (318 lb)	Dry Tortugas, Florida, USA	Mar. 14, 1966	Dottie Hall
M-24 kg (50 lb)	167.37 kg (369 lb)	Marathon, Florida, USA	Apr. 25, 1956	C.F. Mann
W-24 kg (50 lb)	131.54 kg (290 lb)	Marathon, Florida, USA	May 5, 1967	Mrs. Leslie Lear
M-36 kg (80 lb)	308.44 kg (680 lb)	Fernandina Beach, Florida, USA	May 20, 1961	Lynn Joyner
W-36 kg (80 lb)	166.01 kg (366 lb)	Guayabo, Panama	Feb. 8, 1965	Betsy B. Walker
M-60 kg (130 lb)	187.67 kg (413 lb, 12 oz)	Key West, Florida, USA	Feb. 22, 1976	Mick Herndon
W-60 kg (130 lb)	148.32 kg (327 lb)	Flamingo, Florida, USA	June 24, 1969	Helen Robinson

KAWAKAWA

Euthynnus affinis

LINE CLASS	WEIGHT	PLACE	DATE	ANGLER
M-3 kg (6 lb)	8.84 kg (19 lb, 8 oz)	Port Stephens, N.S.W., Australia	Aug. 3, 1975	Jonathan M. Rowley
W-3 kg (6 lb)	7.71 kg (17 lb)	Cairns, Qld., Australia	Oct. 31, 1977	Jill Hooper
M-6 kg (12 lb)	6.50 kg (14 lb, 5 oz)	Dunk Island, Qld., Australia	July 19, 1978	George Pallos
W-6 kg (12 lb)	6.80 kg (15 lb)	Gold Coast, Qld., Australia	Apr. 25, 1976	Judy Gay
M-10 kg (20 lb)	9.50 kg (20 lb, 15 oz)	Tweed Heads, N.S.W., Australia	Dec. 4, 1977	Paul Hague
W-10 kg (20 lb)	6.75 kg (14 lb, 14 oz)	Praslin Island, Seychelles	Oct. 31, 1978	Dot Jensen
M-15 kg (30 lb)	7.76 kg (17 lb, 2 oz)	Cairns, Qld., Australia	Oct. 10, 1977	Dick Mulholland
W-15 kg (30 lb)	Vacant—Minimum Acceptance Weight—4.07 kg (9 lb)			
Tie M-15 kg	7.76 kg (17 lb, 2 oz)	Bermagui, N.S.W., Australia	June 6, 1978	James L. Blackie

MACKEREL, king

Scomberomorus cavalla

LINE CLASS	WEIGHT	PLACE	DATE	ANGLER
M-3 kg (6 lb)	24.72 kg (54 lb, 8 oz)	Empire, Louisiana, USA	Apr. 8, 1978	Maumus F. Claverie, Jr.
W-3 kg (6 lb)	19.73 kg (43 lb, 8 oz)	Stuart, Florida, USA	Dec. 31, 1976	Janey Franklin
M-6 kg (12 lb)	27.18 kg (59 lb, 15 oz)	Key West, Florida, USA	Jan. 23, 1978	Pete Peacock
W-6 kg (12 lb)	22.73 kg (50 lb, 2 oz)	Empire, Louisiana, USA	Dec. 6, 1975	Priscilla Jordan Claverie
M-10 kg (20 lb)	34.92 kg (77 lb)	Bimini, Bahamas	May 13, 1957	Clinton Olney Potts
W-10 kg (20 lb)	29.71 kg (65 lb, 8 oz)	Palm Beach, Flordia, USA	Feb. 14, 1965	Patricia E. Church
M-15 kg (30 lb)	34.01 kg (75 lb)	Walker Cay, Bahamas	May 22, 1966	Thomas J. Sims, Jr.
W-15 kg (30 lb)	29.03 kg (64 lb)	Palm Beach, Florida, USA	Dec. 23, 1973	Barbara Hinkle
M-24 kg (50 lb)	35.72 kg (78 lb, 12 oz)	La Romana, Dominican Republic	Nov. 26, 1971	Fernando Viyella
W-24 kg (50 lb)	35.38 kg (78 lb)	Guayanilla, Puerto Rico	May 25, 1963	Ruth M. Coon
M-36 kg (80 lb)	40.82 kg (90 lb)	Key West, Florida, USA	Feb. 16, 1976	Norton I. Thomton
W-36 kg (80 lb)	30.39 kg (67 lb)	Pompano Beach, Florida, USA	Apr. 14, 1972	Fran S. Colyer

MARLIN, black

Makaira indica

LINE CLASS	WEIGHT	PLACE	DATE	ANGLER
M-3 kg (6 lb)	110.67 kg (244 lb)	Pinas Bay, Panama	Jan. 26, 1976	Edwin D. Kennedy
W-3 kg (6 lb)	18.37 kg (40 lb, 8 oz)	Dunk I., Qld., Australia	July 26, 1977	Jill Hooper
M-6 kg (12 lb)	167.00 kg (368 lb, 2 oz)	Lizard Island, Qld., Australia	Sept. 26, 1975	Terry Russell
W-6 kg (12 lb)	160.11 kg (353 lb)	Pinas Bay, Panama	Mar. 6, 1968	Evelyn M. Anderson
M-10 kg (20 lb)	476.73 kg (1051 lb)	Cairns, Qld, Australia	Oct. 7, 1976	Peter W. Mahood
W-10 kg (20 lb)	189.60 kg (418 lb)	Pinas Bay, Panama	Jan. 11, 1968	Mrs. Carl Dann III
M-15 kg (30 lb)	390.99 kg (862 lb)	Lizard Island, Qld., Australia	Nov. 10, 1978	Stephen Sloan
W-15 kg (30 lb)	250.38 kg (552 lb)	La Plata Island, Ecuador	July 3, 1953	Mrs. W.G. Krieger
M-24 kg (50 lb)	509.84 kg (1124 lb)	Cairns, Qld., Australia	Oct. 31, 1969	Edward Seay
W-24 kg (50 lb)	396.44 kg (874 lb)	Cairns, Qld., Australia	Oct. 16, 1976	Kay Mulholland
M-36 kg (80 lb)	564.49 kg (1244 lb, 8 oz)	Cairns, Qld., Australia	Oct. 31, 1977	David Packman
W-36 kg (80 lb)	600.10 kg (1323 lb)	Cairns, Qld., Australia	Nov. 8, 1977	Georgette Douwma
M-60 kg (130 lb)	707.61 kg (1560 lb)	Cabo Blanco, Peru	Aug. 4, 1953	Alfred C. Glassell, Jr.
W-60 kg (130 lb)	691.73 kg (1525 lb)	Cabo Blanco, Peru	Apr. 22, 1954	Mrs. Charles E. Hughes

MARLIN, blue (Atlantic)

Makaira nigricans

LINE CLASS	WEIGHT	PLACE	DATE	ANGLER
M-3 kg (6 lb)	Vacant—Minimum Acceptance Weight—18.12 kg (40 lb)			
W-3 kg (6 lb)	Vacant—Minimum Acceptance Weight—18.12 kg (40 lb)			
M-6 kg (12 lb)	203.21 kg (448 lb)	St. Thomas, Virgin Islands	Sept. 6, 1971	Frank L. Miller
W-6 kg (12 lb)	101.18 kg (223 lb, 1 oz)	Bimini, Bahamas	Apr. 9, 1960	Suzanne H. Higgs
M-10 kg (20 lb)	195.04 kg (430 lb)	St. Thomas, Virgin Islands	Aug. 31, 1970	Charles R. Senf
W-10 kg (20 lb)	181.89 kg (401 lb)	San Juan, Puerto Rico	Nov. 16, 1975	Carmina Miller
M-15 kg (30 lb)	239.80 kg (528 lb, 10 oz)	Vitoria, Brazil	Jan. 6, 1976	Luiz M. de Britto Pereira
W-15 kg (30 lb)	246.07 kg (542 lb, 8 oz)	Walker Cay, Bahamas	May 2, 1974	Mrs. Almeta Schafer
M-24 kg (50 lb)	364.00 kg (802 lb, 7 oz)	Playa Grande, Venezuela	Dec. 4, 1976	Ruben Jaen C., M.D.
W-24 kg (50 lb)	287.35 kg (633 lb, 8 oz)	Bimini, Bahamas	Mar. 27, 1970	Mrs. Audrey Grady
M-36 kg (80 lb)	511.65 kg (1128 lb)	Hatteras, N. Carolina, USA	June 5, 1975	Fulton H. Katz, M.D.
W-36 kg (80 lb)	365.00 kg (804 lb, 11 oz)	Abidjan, Ivory Coast	Dec. 19, 1976	Josiane Feuillet
M-60 kg (130 lb)	581.51 kg (1282 lb)	St. Thomas, Virgin Islands	Aug. 6, 1977	Larry Martin
W-60 kg (130 lb)	461.98 kg (1018 lb, 8 oz)	South Pass, Louisiana, USA	July 23, 1977	Linda Koerner

IGFA SALTWATER LINE CLASS WORLD RECORDS

MARLIN, blue (Pacific)   *Makaira nigricans*

LINE CLASS	WEIGHT	PLACE	DATE	ANGLER
M-3 kg (6 lb)	Vacant—Minimum Acceptance Weight—18.12 kg (40 lb)			
W-3 kg (6 lb)	Vacant—Minimum Acceptance Weight—18.12 kg (40 lb)			
M-6 kg (12 lb)	112.60 kg (248 lb, 4 oz)	Keahole Pt., Hawaii, USA	Aug. 12, 1975	Stephen Zuckerman
W-6 kg (12 lb)	Vacant—Minimum Acceptance Weight—34.01 kg (75 lb)			
M-10 kg (20 lb)	125.87 kg (277 lb, 8 oz)	Keahole Pt., Hawaii, USA	Aug. 12, 1976	Stephen Zuckerman
W-10 kg (20 lb)	184.16 kg (406 lb)	Mazatlan, Mexico	May 18, 1972	Marguerite H. Barry
M-15 kg (30 lb)	198.67 kg (438 lb)	Bay of Islands, New Zealand	Dec. 2, 1972	William W. Hall
W-15 kg (30 lb)	201.62 kg (444 lb, 8 oz)	Milolii, Isle of Hawaii, USA	Aug. 25, 1978	Georgette Douwma
M-24 kg (50 lb)	364.00 kg (802 lb, 8 oz)	Cape Cook Pt., Kona, Hawaii, USA	Aug. 21, 1978	B.G. Nation
W-24 kg (50 lb)	288.26 kg (635 lb, 8 oz)	Kailua, Kona, Hawaii, USA	Sept. 20, 1976	June Stukey
M-36 kg (80 lb)	415.49 kg (916 lb)	Kailua, Kona, Hawaii, USA	Aug. 28, 1973	Eric Tixier
W-36 kg (80 lb)	305.72 kg (674 lb)	Waikiki, Oahu, Hawaii, USA	Apr. 15, 1978	Charlotte E. Ferreira
M-60 kg (130 lb)	498.95 kg (1100 lb)	Le Morne, Mauritius	Feb. 20, 1966	Andre D'Hotman de Villiers
W-60 kg (130 lb)	303.45 kg (669 lb)	Kailua, Kona, Hawaii, USA	Aug. 27, 1973	Mrs. Doris H. Jones

MARLIN, striped   *Tetrapturus audax*

LINE CLASS	WEIGHT	PLACE	DATE	ANGLER
M-3 kg (6 lb)	92.98 kg (205 lb)	Cabo San Lucas, Baja, Mexico	Apr. 3, 1972	W. Matt Parr
W-3 kg (6 lb)	85.27 kg (188 lb)	Cabo San Lucas, Baja, Mexico	June 8, 1974	Kathryn McGinnis
M-6 kg (12 lb)	113.39 kg (250 lb)	Palmilla, Baja, Mexico	Apr. 16, 1965	R.M. Anderson
W-6 kg (12 lb)	95.25 kg (210 lb)	Las Cruces, Baja, Mexico	June 20, 1959	Lynn F. Lee
M-10 kg (20 lb)	153.31 kg (338 lb)	Sydney, N.S.W. Australia	Oct. 20, 1968	H. John McIntyre
W-10 kg (20 lb)	154.22 kg (340 lb)	Bay of Islands, New Zealand	Jan. 21, 1977	Robyn Hall
M-15 kg (30 lb)	161.93 kg (357 lb)	Botany Bay, Sydney, N.S.W. Australia	Oct. 24, 1976	Don Patterson
W-15 kg (30 lb)	131.08 kg (289 lb)	Iquique, Chile	May 18, 1954	Mrs. L. Marron
M-24 kg (50 lb)	166.69 kg (367 lb, 7 oz)	Tutukaka, New Zealand	Mar. 17, 1978	Osbald Ferrall
W-24 kg (50 lb)	181.89 kg (401 lb)	Cavalli Islands, New Zealand	Feb. 24, 1970	Mrs. Margaret Williams
M-36 kg (80 lb)	189.37 kg (417 lb, 8 oz)	Cavalli Islands, New Zealand	Jan. 14, 1977	Phillip Bryers
W-36 kg (80 lb)	151.04 kg (333 lb)	Ruahine Reef, New Zealand	Apr. 20, 1971	Jennifer Amos
M-60 kg (130 lb)	180.53 kg (398 lb)	Mayor Island, New Zealand	Dec. 30, 1974	John Kenneth Boyle
W-60 kg (130 lb)	Vacant—Minimum Acceptance Weight—141.33 kg (312 lb)			

MARLIN, white   *Tetrapturus albidus*

LINE CLASS	WEIGHT	PLACE	DATE	ANGLER
M-3 kg (6 lb)	36.74 kg (81 lb)	Montauk, New York, USA	July 19, 1975	Stephen Sloan
W-3 kg (6 lb)	30.39 kg (67 lb)	La Guaira, Venezuela	Sept. 20, 1972	Kathryn McGinnis
M-6 kg (12 lb)	46.94 kg (103 lb, 8 oz)	Bimini, Bahamas	Apr. 8, 1952	G.A. Bass
W-6 kg (12 lb)	55.33 kg (122 lb)	Bimini, Bahamas	Mar. 30, 1953	Dorothy A. Curtice
M-10 kg (20 lb)	58.28 kg (128 lb, 8 oz)	Bimini, Bahamas	Mar. 9, 1960	James F. Baldwin
W-10 kg (20 lb)	58.62 kg (129 lb, 4 oz)	Bimini, Bahamas	Apr. 11, 1963	Mrs. J.M. Watters
M-15 kg (30 lb)	69.40 kg (153 lb)	Rio de Janeiro, Brazil	Nov. 19, 1977	Antonio Rocha Soares
W-15 kg (30 lb)	54.71 kg (120 lb, 10 oz)	Bimini, Bahamas	Mar. 29, 1956	Mrs. M. Meyer, Jr.
M-24 kg (50 lb)	79.00 kg (174 lb, 3 oz)	Vitoria, Brazil	Nov. 1, 1975	Otavio Cunha Reboucas
W-24 kg (50 lb)	58.96 kg (130 lb)	Montauk, New York, USA	Aug. 13, 1951	Mrs. P. Dater
M-36 kg (80 lb)	64.86 kg (143 lb)	Miami Beach, Florida, USA	Apr. 17, 1977	Dr. Doug Valentine
W-36 kg (80 lb)	64.41 kg (142 lb)	Ft. Lauderdale, Florida, USA	Mar. 14, 1959	Marie Beneventi
M-60 kg (130 lb)	Vacant—Minimum Acceptance Weight—54.36 kg (120 lb)			
W-60 kg (130 lb)	Vacant—Minimum Acceptance Weight—54.36 kg (120 lb)			
Tie M-36 Kg	65.00 kg (143 lb, 4 oz)	Puerto Rico, Gran Canaria, Canary I.	July 26, 1977	Alan James Roscoe

IGFA SALTWATER LINE CLASS WORLD RECORDS

PERMIT
Trachinotus falcatus

LINE CLASS	WEIGHT	PLACE	DATE	ANGLER
M-3 kg (6 lb)	17.23 kg (38 lb)	Key West, Florida, USA	Mar. 19, 1972	Stuart C. Apte
W-3 kg (6 lb)	14.74 kg (32 lb, 8 oz)	Key West, Florida, USA	Mar. 1, 1976	Mrs. Ted Bartz
M-6 kg (12 lb)	22.67 kg (50 lb)	Miami, Florida, USA	Mar. 27, 1965	Robert F. Miller
W-6 kg (12 lb)	17.91 kg (39 lb, 8 oz)	Key Largo, Florida, USA	Mar. 16, 1977	Mary Archer Willis
M-10 kg (20 lb)	22.90 kg (50 lb, 8 oz)	Key West, Florida, USA	Mar. 15, 1971	Marshall E. Earnest
W-10 kg (20 lb)	17.23 kg (38 lb)	Islamorada, Florida, USA	Mar. 21, 1954	Mrs. W.K. Edmunds
M-15 kg (30 lb)	23.35 kg (51 lb, 8 oz)	Lake Worth, Florida, USA	Apr. 28, 1978	William M. Kenney
W-15 kg (30 lb)	17.23 kg (38 lb)	Key West, Florida, USA	Apr. 9, 1963	Helen Robinson
M-24 kg (50 lb)	22.56 kg (49 lb, 12 oz)	Stuart, Florida, USA	Dec. 7, 1976	Mark R. Arnold
W-24 kg (50 lb)	17.69 kg (39 lb)	Islamorada, Florida, USA	Apr. 2, 1966	Shelagh B. Richards
Tie W-10 kg	17.23 kg (38 lb)	Islamorada, Florida, USA	June 11, 1961	Louise Meulenberg

POLLACK
Pollachius pollachius

LINE CLASS	WEIGHT	PLACE	DATE	ANGLER
M-3 kg (6 lb)	7.28 kg (16 lb, 1 oz)	Plymouth, England, U.K.	Aug. 13, 1978	Peter J. Peck
W-3 kg (6 lb)	Vacant—No Minimum Weight			
M-6 kg (12 lb)	Vacant—No Minimum Weight			
W-6 kg (12 lb)	Vacant—No Minimum Weight			
M-10 kg (20 lb)	Vacant—No Minimum Weight			
W-10 kg (20 lb)	Vacant—No Minimum Weight			
M-15 kg (30 lb)	Vacant—No Minimum Weight			
W-15 kg (30 lb)	Vacant—No Minimum Weight			
M-24 kg (50 lb)	Vacant—No Minimum Weight			
W-24 kg (50 lb)	Vacant—No Minimum Weight			

POLLOCK
Pollachius virens

LINE CLASS	WEIGHT	PLACE	DATE	ANGLER
M-3 kg (6 lb)	12.02 kg (26 lb, 8 oz)	Montauk, New York, USA	May 18, 1977	Raymond Ruddock
W-3 kg (6 lb)	6.87 kg (15 lb, 2 oz)	Plymouth, England, U.K.	Mar. 10, 1973	Mrs. Rita Barrett
M-6 kg (12 lb)	16.32 kg (36 lb)	Hunts Pt., Nova Scotia, Canada	Aug. 10, 1965	Perry MacNeal
W-6 kg (12 lb)	7.00 kg (15 lb, 7 oz)	Nova Scotia, Canada	July 9, 1963	Janet D. Wallach
M-10 kg (20 lb)	17.06 kg (36 lb, 10 oz)	Fire Island, New York, USA	Nov. 1, 1974	Charles Fischett
W-10 kg (20 lb)	17.23 kg (38 lb)	Westport, Nova Scotia, Canada	Aug. 20, 1971	Ruth G. Verber
M-15 kg (30 lb)	18.14 kg (40 lb)	Brielle, New Jersey, USA	Oct. 22, 1973	Tom Wier
W-15 kg (30 lb)	15.90 kg (35 lb, 1 oz)	Fire Island, New York, USA	Aug. 23, 1975	Patty Ishkanian
M-24 kg (50 lb)	21.06 kg (46 lb, 7 oz)	Brielle, New Jersey, USA	May 26, 1975	John Tomes Holton
W-24 kg (50 lb)	13.15 kg (29 lb)	Manasquan, New Jersey, USA	Nov. 3, 1958	Ann Durik

POMPANO, African
Alectis ciliaris

LINE CLASS	WEIGHT	PLACE	DATE	ANGLER
M-3 kg (6 lb)	Vacant—No Minimum Weight			
W-3 kg (6 lb)	11.67 kg (25 lb, 12 oz)	Jupiter, Florida, USA	May 3, 1978	Cynthia Boomhower
M-6 kg (12 lb)	15.30 kg (33 lb, 12 oz)	Islamorada, Florida, USA	Feb. 11, 1978	Joseph M. Nowdomski
W-6 kg (12 lb)	11.33 kg (25 lb)	Duck Key, Florida, USA	Jan. 1, 1978	Ilai Lichtenstein
M-10 kg (20 lb)	13.26 kg (29 lb, 4 oz)	Key West, Florida, USA	Jan. 16, 1978	Joe Machiorlatti
W-10 kg (20 lb)	Vacant—No Minimum Weight			
M-15 kg (30 lb)	Vacant—No Minimum Weight			
W-15 kg (30 lb)	Vacant—No Minimum Weight			
M-24 kg (50 lb)	Vacant—No Minimum Weight			
W-24 kg (50 lb)	Vacant—No Minimum Weight			

ROOSTERFISH

Nematistius pectoralis

LINE CLASS	WEIGHT	PLACE	DATE	ANGLER
M-3 kg (6 lb)	18.00 kg (39 lb, 10 oz)	Buena Vista, Baja, Mexico	July 10, 1977	Herbert R. Kameon
W-3 kg (6 lb)	19.73 kg (43 lb, 8 oz)	Punta Colorado, Baja, Mexico	July 11, 1977	Pat Snyder
M-6 kg (12 lb)	24.94 kg (55 lb)	Buena Vista, Baja, Mexico	July 13, 1978	Herbert R. Kameon
W-6 kg (12 lb)	20.41 kg (45 lb)	San Jose del Cabo, Baja, Mexico	June 11, 1951	Mrs. W.G. Krieger
M-10 kg (20 lb)	38.92 kg (85 lb, 13 oz)	La Paz, Baja, Mexico	June 15, 1966	Willard E. Hanson
W-10 kg (20 lb)	26.60 kg (58 lb, 10 oz)	Buena Vista, Baja, Mexico	June 23, 1977	Cindy De La Mare
M-15 kg (30 lb)	51.71 kg (114 lb)	La Paz, Baja, Mexico	June 1, 1960	Abe Sackheim
W-15 kg (30 lb)	44.90 kg (99 lb)	La Paz, Baja, Mexico	Nov. 30, 1964	Lily Call
M-24 kg (50 lb)	36.28 kg (80 lb)	Cabo Blanco, Peru	June 13, 1954	Clyoce J. Tippett
W-24 kg (50 lb)	38.61 kg (85 lb, 2 oz)	La Paz, Baja, Mexico	Nov. 24, 1956	Mrs. Esther Carle
M-36 kg (80 lb)	40.82 kg (90 lb)	Loreto, Baja, Mexico	Dec. 22, 1960	Clement Caditz
W-36 kg (80 lb)	29.93 kg (66 lb)	La Paz, Baja, Mexico	Dec. 1, 1964	Lily Call
M-60 kg (130 lb)	45.35 kg (100 lb)	Cabo Blanco, Peru	Jan. 12, 1954	Miguel Barrenechea
W-60 kg (130 lb)	Vacant—Minimum Acceptance Weight—38.50 kg (85 lb)			

RUNNER, rainbow

Elagatis bipinnulata

LINE CLASS	WEIGHT	PLACE	DATE	ANGLER
M-3 kg (6 lb)	7.99 kg (17 lb, 10 oz)	Isla Coiba, Panama	Dec. 4, 1974	Stuart C. Apte
W-3 kg (6 lb)	5.66 kg (12 lb, 8 oz)	Pinas Bay, Panama	Dec. 10, 1975	Mary Wallace Josepho
M-6 kg (12 lb)	9.63 kg (21 lb, 4 oz)	Isla Coiba, Panama	Apr. 4, 1977	Philip Tyler
W-6 kg (12 lb)	6.40 kg (14 lb, 2 oz)	Isla Coiba, Panama	Feb. 27, 1978	Jo-Ann Egly
M-10 kg (20 lb)	11.33 kg (25 lb)	Pinas Bay, Panama	May 9, 1965	Donald J.S. Merten
W-10 kg (20 lb)	6.60 kg (14 lb, 9 oz)	Isla Coiba, Panama	Feb. 2, 1978	Ms. Mike Hoopes
M-15 kg (30 lb)	11.68 kg (25 lb, 12 oz)	Oahu, Hawaii, USA	Nov. 26, 1967	Richard Y. Sakimoto, MD
W-15 kg (30 lb)	8.37 kg (18 lb, 7 oz)	San Benedicto Island, Mexico	Dec. 6. 1977	Mary Helen Jones
M-24 kg (50 lb)	15.25 kg (33 lb, 10 oz)	Clarion Island, Mexico	Mar. 14, 1976	Ralph A. Mikkelsen
W-24 kg (50 lb)	10.43 kg (23 lb)	Oahu, Hawaii, USA	May 9, 1961	Lila M. Neuenfelt
Tie W-10 kg	6.69 kg (14 lb, 12 oz)	Challenger Bank, Bermuda	July 17, 1978	Dorry Lusher

SAILFISH (Atlantic)

Istiophorus platypterus

LINE CLASS	WEIGHT	PLACE	DATE	ANGLER
M-3 kg (6 lb)	39.00 kg (85 lb, 15 oz)	Luanda, Angola	Feb. 14, 1974	A. de Jesus Gaspar dos Santos
W-3 kg (6 lb)	31.75 kg (70 lb)	Tavernier, Florida, USA	Feb. 12, 1977	Ruth C. Stoky
M-6 kg (12 lb)	45.30 kg (99 lb, 13 oz)	Luanda, Angola	March 27, 1974	A. de Jesus Gaspar dos Santos
W-6 kg (12 lb)	37.64 kg (83 lb)	Key Largo, Florida, USA	Apr. 4, 1965	Helen K. Grant
M-10 kg (20 lb)	58.00 kg (126 lb, 13 oz)	Luanda, Angola	Mar. 30, 1975	Mario Rui Alves Da Silva
W-10 kg (20 lb)	48.30 kg (106 lb, 8 oz)	Luanda, Angola	Mar. 15, 1975	Mrs. Pamela Jean Durkin
M-15 kg (30 lb)	52.75 kg (116 lb, 5 oz)	Luanda, Angola	Mar. 22, 1972	Jose Eduardo Gaioso Vaz
W-15 kg (30 lb)	43.54 kg (96 lb)	Key Largo, Florida, USA	Feb. 4, 1976	Jennifer W. Hutto
M-24 kg (50 lb)	58.10 kg (128 lb, 1 oz)	Luanda, Angola	March 27, 1974	Harm Steyn
W-24 kg (50 lb)	49.10 kg (108 lb, 4 oz)	Luanda, Angola	Mar. 30, 1971	Mrs. Ellen Botha
M-36 kg (80 lb)	Vacant—Minimum Acceptance Weight—43.48 kg (96 lb)			
W-36 kg (80 lb)	Vacant—Minimum Acceptance Weight—43.48 kg (96 lb)			

SAILFISH (Pacific)

Istiophorus platypterus

LINE CLASS	WEIGHT	PLACE	DATE	ANGLER
M-3 kg (6 lb)	76.20 kg (168 lb)	Salinas, Ecuador	Sept. 7, 1974	Santiago Maspons
W-3 kg (6 lb)	52.73 kg (116 lb, 4 oz)	Pinas Bay, Panama	July 19, 1975	Lovern K. Scott (Bulauca)
M-6 kg (12 lb)	77.79 kg (171 lb, 8 oz)	Pinas Bay, Panama	Jan. 9, 1976	Felipe Estrada E.
W-6 kg (12 lb)	66.45 kg (146 lb, 8 oz)	Palmilla, Baja, Mexico	Nov. 14, 1962	Evelyn M. Anderson
M-10 kg (20 lb)	87.54 kg (193 lb)	Acapulco, Mexico	Jan. 8, 1978	Anthony T. Russo
W-10 kg (20 lb)	71.21 kg (157 lb)	La Plata I., Ecuador	Sept. 14, 1961	Jeannette Alford
M-15 kg (30 lb)	89.81 kg (198 lb)	La Paz, Baja, Mexico	Aug. 23, 1957	Charles Kelly
W-15 kg (30 lb)	80.74 kg (178 lb)	Santa Cruz I., Ecuador	Feb. 27, 1955	Martha A. Hall
M-24 kg (50 lb)	87.28 kg (192 lb, 7 oz)	Acapulco, Mexico	Oct. 4, 1961	W.W. Rowland
W-24 kg (50 lb)	87.09 kg (192 lb)	La Paz, Baja, Mexico	Sept. 6, 1950	Gay Thomas
M-36 kg (80 lb)	89.81 kg (198 lb)	Mazatlan, Mexico	Nov. 10, 1954	George N. Anglen
W-36 kg (80 lb)	90.26 kg (199 lb)	Pinas Bay, Panama	Jan. 17, 1968	Carolyn B. Brinkman
M-60 kg (130 lb)	100.24 kg (221 lb)	Santa Cruz I., Ecuador	Feb. 12, 1947	C.W. Stewart
W-60 kg (130 lb)	85.72 kg (189 lb)	Yanuca, Fiji	Dec. 7, 1967	Mrs. C.L. Foster

SEABASS, white

Cynoscion nobilis

LINE CLASS	WEIGHT	PLACE	DATE	ANGLER
M-3 kg (6 lb)	Vacant—Minimum Acceptance Weight—9.07 kg (20 lb)			
W-3 kg (6 lb)	Vacant—Minimum Acceptance Weight—9.07 kg (20 lb)			
M-6 kg (12 lb)	29.48 kg (65 lb)	Ensenada, Baja, Mexico	July 8, 1955	C.J. Aronis
W-6 kg (12 lb)	23.75 kg (52 lb, 6 oz)	Newport Beach, California, USA	June 3, 1959	Ruth Jayred
M-10 kg (20 lb)	32.65 kg (72 lb)	Catalina, California, USA	Aug. 13, 1958	Dr. Charles Dorshkind
W-10 kg (20 lb)	28.12 kg (62 lb)	Malibu, California, USA	Dec. 6, 1951	Mrs. D.W. Jackson
M-15 kg (30 lb)	37.98 kg (83 lb, 12 oz)	San Felipe, Mexico	Mar. 31, 1953	L.C. Baumgardner
W-15 kg (30 lb)	26.98 kg (59 lb, 8 oz)	Catalina Island, California, USA	May 2, 1968	Janice Jackson
M-24 kg (50 lb)	35.04 kg (77 lb, 4 oz)	San Diego, California, USA	Apr. 8, 1950	H.P. Bledsoe
W-24 kg (50 lb)	20.04 kg (44 lb, 3 oz)	Catalina Island, California, USA	May 2, 1968	Gail Cruz
M-36 kg (80 lb)	33.56 kg (74 lb)	Catalina Island, California, USA	May 11, 1968	Allan D. Tromblay
W-36 kg (80 lb)	Vacant—Minimum Acceptance Weight—28.53 kg (63 lb)			

SEATROUT, spotted

Cynoscion nebulosus

LINE CLASS	WEIGHT	PLACE	DATE	ANGLER
M-3 kg (6 lb)	5.27 kg (11 lb, 10 oz)	Piankatank River, Virginia, USA	May 13, 1977	Virgil Pendleton Hughes
W-3 kg (6 lb)	3.65 kg (8 lb, 1 oz)	Pensacola Sound, Florida, USA	Apr. 24, 1973	Rose Marie Bonifay
M-6 kg (12 lb)	6.35 kg (14 lb)	Ponce de Leon Inlet, Florida, USA	Aug. 10, 1972	Allen Kent Gibbens
W-6 kg (12 lb)	4.64 kg (10 lb, 4 oz)	Jupiter, Florida, USA	June 1, 1958	Nancy Dukes
M-10 kg (20 lb)	7.25 kg (16 lb)	Mason's Beach, Virginia, USA	May 28, 1977	William G. Katko
W-10 kg (20 lb)	4.53 kg (10 lb)	Pellicer Creek, Florida, USA	Feb. 25, 1950	Mrs. Bertram Lee
M-15 kg (30 lb)	6.97 kg (15 lb, 6 oz)	Jensen Beach, Florida, USA	May 4, 1969	Michael J. Foremny
W-15 kg (30 lb)	6.35 kg (14 lb)	Stuart, Florida, USA	Apr. 25, 1970	Marilyn C. Albright
Tie M-6 kg	6.43 kg (14 lb, 3 oz)	Jensen Beach, Florida, USA	Feb. 21, 1974	Les Mowery

SHARK, blue

Prionace glauca

LINE CLASS	WEIGHT	PLACE	DATE	ANGLER
M-3 kg (6 lb)	110.00 kg (242 lb, 8 oz)	Cronulla, N.S.W., Australia	Oct. 2, 1977	Paul Edward Caughlan
W-3 kg (6 lb)	87.54 kg (193 lb)	Botany, N.S.W., Australia	Dec. 15, 1974	Mrs. Dulcie Chee
M-6 kg (12 lb)	141.52 kg (312 lb)	Montauk, New York, USA	Oct. 28, 1963	John S. Walton
W-6 kg (12 lb)	82.10 kg (181 lb)	Challenger Bank, Bermuda	June 4, 1978	Rosalind E. Dunmore
M-10 kg (20 lb)	134.97 kg (297 lb, 9 oz)	Port Hacking, N.S.W., Australia	Oct. 2, 1977	Mark Dent
W-10 kg (20 lb)	132.90 kg (293 lb)	Montauk, New York, USA	July 21, 1963	Lucette Rinfret
M-15 kg (30 lb)	198.22 kg (437 lb)	Catherine Bay, N.S.W., Australia	Oct. 2, 1976	Peter Hyde
W-15 kg (30 lb)	129.04 kg (284 lb, 8 oz)	Montauk, New York, USA	Aug. 11, 1959	Jacqueline Mittleman
M-24 kg (50 lb)	168.51 kg (371 lb, 8 oz)	Montauk, New York, USA	Sept. 27, 1969	Jack Bellock
W-24 kg (50 lb)	135.17 kg (298 lb)	Montauk, New York, USA	Oct. 5, 1959	Valerie Wuestefeld
M-36 kg (80 lb)	185.97 kg (410 lb)	Rockport, Massachusetts, USA	Sept. 1, 1960	Richard C. Webster
W-36 kg (80 lb)	185.97 kg (410 lb)	Rockport, Massachusetts, USA	Aug. 17, 1967	Martha C. Webster
M-60 kg (130 lb)	181.43 kg (400 lb)	Le Morne, Mauritius	Oct. 17, 1976	Philip Fleming
W-60 kg (130 lb)	151.50 kg (334 lb)	Rockport, Massachusetts, USA	Sept. 4, 1964	Cassandra Webster

SHARK, hammerhead

Sphyrna spp.

LINE CLASS	WEIGHT	PLACE	DATE	ANGLER
M-3 kg (6 lb)	46.20 kg (101 lb, 13 oz)	Luanda, Angola	Dec. 29, 1974	M. Quintela Maia de Loureiro
W-3 kg (6 lb)	Vacant—Minimum Acceptance Weight—34.42 kg (76 lb)			
M-6 kg (12 lb)	151.95 kg (335 lb)	Miami, Florida, USA	Mar. 19, 1977	Bill Peacock
W-6 kg (12 lb)	54.99 kg (121 lb, 4 oz)	Luanda, Angola	Nov. 3, 1974	Luisa Maria Picarra Baptista
M-10 kg (20 lb)	170.00 kg (374 lb, 12 oz)	Marley, N.S.W., Australia	Dec. 4, 1977	David M. Vader
W-10 kg (20 lb)	86.18 kg (190 lb)	Bay of Islands, New Zealand	April 13, 1974	Robyn Hall
M-15 kg (30 lb)	196.00 kg (432 lb, 1 oz)	Port Stephens, N.S.W., Australia	March 4, 1978	Monty Bull
W-15 kg (30 lb)	128.36 kg (283 lb)	Bay of Islands, New Zealand	Jan. 4, 1976	Mrs. Robyn Hall
M-24 kg (50 lb)	191.87 kg (423 lb)	Bermagui, N.S.W., Australia	Feb. 14, 1976	Terry McCallum
W-24 kg (50 lb)	208.65 kg (460 lb)	Sydney, N.S.W., Australia	Dec. 29, 1974	Pamela Hudspeth
M-36 kg (80 lb)	281.23 kg (620 lb)	Freeport, Texas, USA	Aug. 15, 1976	Dan Wright
W-36 kg (80 lb)	202.75 kg (447 lb)	Hobe Sound, Florida, USA	May 26, 1975	E.R. (Betsy) Browning
M-60 kg (130 lb)	318.87 kg (703 lb)	Jacksonville Beach, Florida, USA	July 5, 1975	H.B. "Blackie" Reasor
W-60 kg (130 lb)	184.16 kg (406 lb)	Lottin Point, New Zealand	Feb. 26, 1974	Mrs. H.M. Wood

SHARK, porbeagle

Lamna nasus

LINE CLASS	WEIGHT	PLACE	DATE	ANGLER
M-3 kg (6 lb)	Vacant—Minimum Acceptance Weight—13.59 kg (30 lb)			
W-3 kg (6 lb)	Vacant—Minimum Acceptance Weight—13.59 kg (30 lb)			
M-6 kg (12 lb)	29.93 kg (66 lb)	Montauk, New York, USA	June 8, 1958	M.H. Merrill
W-6 kg (12 lb)	Vacant—Minimum Acceptance Weight—23.10 kg (51 lb)			
M-10 kg (20 lb)	81.64 kg (180 lb)	Block Island, Rhode Island, USA	Aug. 9, 1960	Frank K. Smith
W-10 kg (20 lb)	Vacant—Minimum Acceptance Weight—61.15 kg (135 lb)			
M-15 kg (30 lb)	86.86 kg (191 lb, 8 oz)	Montauk, New York, USA	May 28, 1964	Carl Monaco
W-15 kg (30 lb)	100.92 kg (222 lb, 8 oz)	Isle of Wight, England, U.K.	Aug. 14, 1969	Mrs. Paula Everington
M-24 kg (50 lb)	175.99 kg (388 lb)	Montauk Point, New York, USA	Oct. 28, 1961	John S. Walton
W-24 kg (50 lb)	108.18 kg (238 lb, 8 oz)	Montauk, New York, USA	May 17, 1966	Bea Harry
M-36 kg (80 lb)	207.74 kg (458 lb)	Padstow, Cornwall, England, U.K.	May 15, 1977	William (Derrick) John Runnalls
W-36 kg (80 lb)	104.32 kg (230 lb)	Montauk, New York, USA	May 17, 1965	Bea Harry
M-60 kg (130 lb)	210.92 kg (465 lb)	Padstow, Cornwall, England, U.K.	July 23, 1976	Jorge Potier
W-60 kg (130 lb)	167.37 kg (369 lb)	Looe, Cornwall, England, U.K.	July 20, 1970	Mrs. Patricia Winifred Smith

IGFA SALTWATER LINE CLASS WORLD RECORDS

SHARK, shortfin mako

Isurus oxyrinchus

LINE CLASS	WEIGHT	PLACE	DATE	ANGLER
M-3 kg (6 lb)	155.13 kg (342 lb)	Port Hacking, N.S.W., Australia	Sept. 22, 1974	Norman Richard Smith
W-3 kg (6 lb)	52.16 kg (115 lb)	Botany Bay, N.S.W., Australia	Oct. 27, 1974	Mrs. Dulcie Chee
M-6 kg (12 lb)	118.70 kg (261 lb, 11 oz)	Montauk, New York, USA	Oct. 1, 1953	C.R. Meyer
W-6 kg (12 lb)	83.00 kg (183 lb)	Sydney, N.S.W., Australia	Aug. 1, 1971	Mrs. Pamela Hudspeth
M-10 kg (20 lb)	266 kg (586 lb, 6 oz)	Catherine Hill Bay, N.S.W., Australia	Oct. 9, 1977	Peter William Thompson
W-10 kg (20 lb)	143.33 kg (316 lb)	Bimini, Bahamas	May 25, 1961	Dorothea L. Dean
M-15 kg (30 lb)	387.37 kg (854 lb)	Port Stephens, N.S.W., Australia	May 9, 1971	John Howard Barclay
W-15 kg (30 lb)	170.55 kg (376 lb)	Sydney, N.S.W., Australia	Sept. 7, 1969	Helen Gillis
M-24 kg (50 lb)	349.04 kg (769 lb, 8 oz)	Sydney, N.S.W., Australia	Dec. 7, 1975	John Richard Farrell
W-24 kg (50 lb)	216.81 kg (478 lb)	Broughton Island, Australia	May 17, 1957	Mrs. Ron Duncan
M-36 kg (80 lb)	428.10 kg (943 lb, 12 oz)	Sydney, N.S.W., Australia	Nov. 28, 1976	Joe Remetean
W-36 kg (80 lb)	399.16 kg (880 lb)	Bimini, Bahamas	Aug. 3, 1964	Florence Lotierzo
M-60 kg (130 lb)	481.26 kg (1061 lb)	Mayor Island, New Zealand	Feb. 17, 1970	James B. Penwarden
W-60 kg (130 lb)	413.56 kg (911 lb, 12 oz)	Palm Beach, Florida, USA	Apr. 9, 1962	Audrey Cohen

SHARK, thresher

Alopias spp.

LINE CLASS	WEIGHT	PLACE	DATE	ANGLER
M-3 kg (6 lb)	41.50 kg (91 lb, 8 oz)	Santa Monica Bay, California, USA	May 14, 1977	James D. Olson
W-3 kg (6 lb)	15.42 kg (34 lb)	Santa Monica Bay, California, USA	June 8, 1977	Ruth Kameon
M-6 kg (12 lb)	66.67 kg (147 lb)	Santa Monica Bay, California, USA	June 18, 1977	James D. Olson
W-6 kg (12 lb)	62.59 kg (138 lb)	Santa Monica Bay, California, USA	May 15, 1977	Sylvia A. Naibert
M-10 kg (20 lb)	93.89 kg (207 lb)	Catalina Channel, California, USA	Sept. 6, 1975	Leo Dee
W-10 kg (20 lb)	79.15 kg (174 lb, 8 oz)	Santa Monica Bay, California, USA	May 28, 1977	Sylvia A. Naibert
M-15 kg (30 lb)	149.23 kg (329 lb)	Newport Beach, California, USA	June 4, 1978	Micheal Welt
W-15 kg (30 lb)	136.07 kg (300 lb)	Bay of Islands, New Zealand	June 23, 1972	Mrs. Anne Clark
M-24 kg (50 lb)	198.00 kg (436 lb, 8 oz)	Lottin Point, New Zealand	Feb. 22, 1978	A.G. Eastgate
W-24 kg (50 lb)	166.01 kg (366 lb)	Bay of Islands, New Zealand	May 6, 1972	Mrs. Avril Semmens
M-36 kg (80 lb)	335.20 kg (739 lb)	Tutukaka, New Zealand	Feb. 17, 1975	Brian Galvin
W-36 kg (80 lb)	187.33 kg (413 lb)	Bay of Islands, New Zealand	June 28, 1960	Mrs. E.R. Simons
M-60 kg (130 lb)	306.62 kg (676 lb)	Mayor Island, New Zealand	Feb. 23, 1978	Robert Charles Faulkner
W-60 kg (130 lb)	330.67 kg (729 lb)	Mayor Island, New Zealand	June 3, 1959	Mrs. V. Brown

SHARK, tiger

Galeocerdo cuvieri

LINE CLASS	WEIGHT	PLACE	DATE	ANGLER
M-3 kg (6 lb)	Vacant—Minimum Acceptance Weight—22.65 kg (50 lb)			
W-3 kg (6 lb)	Vacant—Minimum Acceptance Weight—22.65 kg (50 lb)			
M-6 kg (12 lb)	Vacant—Minimum Acceptance Weight—45.30 kg (100 lb)			
W-6 kg (12 lb)	71.44 kg (157 lb, 8 oz)	Botany, N.S.W., Australia	Jan. 12, 1975	Mrs. Dulcie Chee
M-10 kg (20 lb)	171.00 kg (377 lb)	Swansea, N.S.W., Australia	Nov. 30, 1975	Frank Spruce
W-10 kg (20 lb)	133.58 kg (294 lb, 8 oz)	Sydney, N.S.W., Australia	Feb. 24, 1973	Pamela Hudspeth
M-15 kg (30 lb)	448.15 kg (988 lb)	Port Stephens, N.S.W., Australia	Apr. 25, 1977	Paul James Besoff
W-15 kg (30 lb)	449.50 kg (990 lb, 15 oz)	Botany Bay, N.S.W., Australia	Jan. 29, 1977	Mrs. Dulcie Chee
M-24 kg (50 lb)	461.76 kg (1018 lb)	Cape Moreton, Qld., Australia	June 12, 1957	Bob Dyer
W-24 kg (50 lb)	207.74 kg (458 lb)	Cape Moreton, Qld., Australia	July 3, 1957	Mrs. Bob Dyer
M-36 kg (80 lb)	591.94 kg (1305 lb)	Sydney, N.S.W., Australia	May 17, 1959	Samuel Jamieson
W-36 kg (80 lb)	532.06 kg (1173 lb)	Cronulla, N.S.W., Australia	Mar. 24, 1963	June Irene Butcher
M-60 kg (130 lb)	807.40 kg (1780 lb)	Cherry Grove, S. Carolina, USA	June 14, 1964	Walter Maxwell
W-60 kg (130 lb)	596.02 kg (1314 lb)	Cape Moreton, Qld., Australia	July 27, 1953	Mrs. Bob Dyer

IGFA SALTWATER LINE CLASS WORLD RECORDS

SHARK, white

Carcharodon carcharias

LINE CLASS	WEIGHT	PLACE	DATE	ANGLER
M-3 kg (6 lb)	Vacant—Minimum Acceptance Weight—18.12 kg (40 lb)			
W-3 kg (6 lb)	Vacant—Minimum Acceptance Weight—18.12 kg (40 lb)			
M-6 kg (12 lb)	43.82 kg (96 lb, 10 oz)	Mazatlan, Mexico	Apr. 30, 1964	Ray O. Acord
W-6 kg (12 lb)	Vacant—Minimum Acceptance Weight—32.61 kg (72 lb)			
M-10 kg (20 lb)	484.44 kg (1068 lb)	Cape Moreton, Qld., Australia	June 18, 1957	Bob Dyer
W-10 kg (20 lb)	167.37 kg (369 lb)	Cape Moreton, Qld., Australia	July 6, 1957	Mrs. Bob Dyer
M-15 kg (30 lb)	477.63 kg (1053 lb)	Cape Moreton, Qld., Australia	June 13, 1957	Bob Dyer
W-15 kg (30 lb)	364.23 kg (803 lb)	Cape Moreton, Qld., Australia	July 5, 1957	Mrs. Bob Dyer
M-24 kg (50 lb)	850.94 kg (1876 lb)	Cape Moreton, Qld., Australia	Aug. 6, 1955	Bob Dyer
W-24 kg (50 lb)	363.33 kg (801 lb)	Cape Moreton, Qld., Australia	June 11, 1957	Mrs. Bob Dyer
M-36 kg (80 lb)	1063.23 kg (2344 lb)	Streaky Bay, S. Australia	Nov. 6, 1960	Alfred Dean
W-36 kg (80 lb)	413.68 kg (912 lb)	Cape Moreton, Qld., Australia	Aug. 29, 1954	Mrs. Bob Dyer
M-60 kg (130 lb)	1208.38 kg (2664 lb)	Ceduna, S. Australia	Apr. 21, 1959	Alfred Dean
W-60 kg (130 lb)	477.18 kg (1052 lb)	Cape Moreton, Qld., Australia	June 27, 1954	Mrs. Bob Dyer

SKIPJACK, black

Euthynnus lineatus

LINE CLASS	WEIGHT	PLACE	DATE	ANGLER
M-3 kg (6 lb)	3.54 kg (7 lb, 13 oz)	Cabo San Lucas, Baja, Mexico	May 24, 1977	Allan J. Carlton, Jr.
W-3 kg (6 lb)	6,57 kg (14 lb, 8 oz)	Cabo San Lucas, Baja, Mexico	May 24, 1977	Lorraine Carlton
M-6 kg (12 lb)	5.78 kg (12 lb, 12 oz)	Alijos Rocks, Baja, Mexico	Sept. 25, 1978	Fred Christopherson
W-6 kg (12 lb)	3.85 kg (8 lb, 8 oz)	Cabo San Lucas, Baja, Mexico	May 24, 1977	Lorraine Carlton
M-10 kg (20 lb)	4.64 kg (10 lb, 4 oz)	Cabo San Lucas, Baja, Mexico	May 24, 1977	Allan J. Carlton, Jr.
W-10 kg (20 lb)	5.95 kg (13 lb, 2 oz)	Thietus Bank, Baja, Mexico	Sept. 27, 1976	Barbara McKinney
M-15 kg (30 lb)	4.96 kg (10 lb, 15 oz)	Cabo San Lucas, Baja, Mexico	May 24, 1977	Allan J. Carlton, Jr.
W-15 kg (30 lb)	Vacant—Minimum Acceptance Weight—2.71 kg (6 lb)			

SNOOK

Centropomus undecimalis

LINE CLASS	WEIGHT	PLACE	DATE	ANGLER
M-3 kg (6 lb)	15.87 kg (35 lb)	Miami, Florida, USA	Apr. 16, 1977	Gerald Hernandez
W-3 kg (6 lb)	9.12 kg (20 lb, 2 oz)	Captiva, Florida, USA	Aug. 2, 1972	Wilma Bell Brantner
M-6 kg (12 lb)	19.73 kg (43 lb, 8 oz)	Parasmina, Costa Rica	Oct. 11, 1976	James Snyder
W-6 kg (12 lb)	14.74 kg (32 lb, 8 oz)	Jupiter, Florida, USA	Aug. 2. 1957	Mrs. Nancy Neville
M-10 kg (20 lb)	24.32 kg (53 lb, 10 oz)	Rio de Parasmina, Costa Rica	Oct. 18, 1978	Gilbert Ponzi
W-10 kg (20 lb)	18.82 kg (41 lb, 8 oz)	Fort Pierce, Florida, USA	Jan. 15, 1978	Barbara Hodges
M-15 kg (30 lb)	19.50 kg (43 lb)	Lake Worth, Florida, USA	May 18, 1952	Lee K. Spencer
W-15 kg (30 lb)	15.30 kg (33 lb, 12 oz)	Ft. Lauderdale, Florida, USA	July 29, 1951	Mrs. Cecile G. Pollard
M-24 kg (50 lb)	18.14 kg (40 lb)	West Palm Beach, Florida, USA	Apr. 8, 1972	Ralph R. Boynton
W-24 kg (50 lb)	14.28 kg (31 lb, 8 oz)	Stuart, Florida, USA	July 17, 1951	Mrs. B.N. Fox
Tie W-6 kg	14.74 kg (32 lb, 8 oz)	Ft. Lauderdale, Florida, USA	July 24, 1966	Rosemary Schafer

SPEARFISH

Tetrapturus spp.

LINE CLASS	WEIGHT	PLACE	DATE	ANGLER
M-3 kg (6 lb)	Vacant—No Minimum Weight			
W-3 kg (6 lb)	Vacant—No Minimum Weight			
M-6 kg (12 lb)	Vacant—No Minimum Weight			
W-6 kg (12 lb)	Vacant—No Minimum Weight			
M-10 kg (20 lb)	Vacant—No Minimum Weight			
W-10 kg (20 lb)	Vacant—No Minimum Weight			
M-15 kg (30 lb)	30.50 kg (67 lb, 4 oz)	Manteo, North Carolina, USA	Oct. 6, 1978	Jerry Dean Leonard
W-15 kg (30 lb)	6.57 kg (14 lb, 8 oz)	Pine Trees, Kona, Hawaii, USA	March 23, 1978	Mary Wallace Josepho
M-24 kg (50 lb)	25.17 kg (55 lb, 8 oz)	Keahole Point, Hawaii, USA	Jan. 3, 1978	Haakon Nordaas
W-24 kg (50 lb)	Vacant—No Minimum Weight			
M-36 kg (80 lb)	12.13 kg (26 lb, 12 oz)	South Pass, Louisiana, USA	June 16, 1978	Gregory R. Gutgsell
W-36 kg (80 lb)	17.69 kg (39 lb)	Keahole, Hawaii, USA	June 11, 1978	Joyce Jordan

SWORDFISH

Xiphias gladius

LINE CLASS	WEIGHT	PLACE	DATE	ANGLER
M-3 kg (6 lb)	48.30 kg (106 lb, 8 oz)	Cabo San Lucas, Baja, Mexico	June 11, 1972	James Perry
W-3 kg (6 lb)	Vacant—Minimum Acceptance Weight—34.42 kg (76 lb)			
M-6 kg (12 lb)	54.43 kg (120 lb)	Palmilla, Baja, Mexico	June 1, 1968	Russell M. Anderson
W-6 kg (12 lb)	Vacant—Minimum Acceptance Weight—40.77 kg (90 lb)			
M-10 kg (20 lb)	88.90 kg (196 lb)	Miami, Florida, USA	May 21, 1978	Mark Houghtaling
W-10 kg (20 lb)	90.60 kg (199 lb, 12 oz)	Key West, Florida, USA	June 30, 1978	Olga N. West
M-15 kg (30 lb)	177.81 kg (392 lb)	Nantucket, Massachusetts, USA	Aug. 3, 1976	John F. Willits
W-15 kg (30 lb)	Vacant—Minimum Acceptance Weight—106.45 kg (235 lb)			
M-24 kg (50 lb)	205.47 kg (453 lb)	Miami Beach, Florida, USA	July 15, 1976	Bob Trowbridge
W-24 kg (50 lb)	223.28 kg (492 lb, 4 oz)	Montauk Point, New York, USA	July 4, 1959	Dorothea Cassullo
M-36 kg (80 lb)	277.93 kg (612 lb, 12 oz)	Key Largo, Florida, USA	May 7, 1978	Stephen Stanford
W-36 kg (80 lb)	350.17 kg (772 lb)	Iquique, Chile	June 7, 1954	Mrs. L. Marron
M-60 kg (130 lb)	536.15 kg (1182 lb)	Iquique, Chile	May 7, 1953	L. Marron
W-60 kg (130 lb)	344.28 kg (759 lb)	Iquique, Chile	June 30, 1952	Mrs. D.A. Allison

TANGUIGUE

Scomberomorus commerson

LINE CLASS	WEIGHT	PLACE	DATE	ANGLER
M-3 kg (6 lb)	24.50 kg (54 lb)	Peron Islands, N. Terr., Australia	Mar. 24, 1978	Graeme Copley
W-3 kg (6 lb)	14.54 kg (32 lb)	Bathurst I., N. Terr., Australia	Sept. 11, 1977	Judy Jenkins
M-6 kg (12 lb)	26.42 kg (58 lb, 4 oz)	Cairns, Qld., Australia	Aug. 24, 1976	Peter Toohey
W-6 kg (12 lb)	30.84 kg (68 lb)	Cairns, Qld., Australia	Aug. 25, 1976	Mrs. Wilma Childs
M-10 kg (20 lb)	35.38 kg (78 lb)	Flinders Reefs, Qld., Australia	May 16, 1970	Edward J. French
W-10 kg (20 lb)	Vacant—Minimum Acceptance Weight—26.72 kg (59 lb)			
M-15 kg (30 lb)	34.47 kg (76 lb)	Innisfail, Qld., Australia	Mar. 28, 1975	Alan Fitzmaurice
W-15 kg (30 lb)	30.84 kg (68 lb)	Hayman I., Qld., Australia	May 14, 1969	Lady Joan Ansett
M-24 kg (50 lb)	38.75 kg (85 lb, 6 oz)	Rottnest I., West Australia	May 5, 1978	Barry Wrightson
W-24 kg (50 lb)	28.80 kg (63 lb, 8 oz)	Cairns, Qld., Australia	Jan. 8, 1976	Mrs. Lynne Waddington
M-36 kg (80 lb.)	36.74 kg (81 lb)	Karachi, Pakistan	Aug. 27, 1960	George E. Rusinak
W-36 kg (80 lb)	29.03 kg (64 lb)	Bazaruto I., Mozambique	Sept. 12, 1959	Mrs. A.C. Lee
Tie M-6 kg	26.53 kg (58 lb, 8 oz)	Lizard Island, Qld., Australia	Aug. 28, 1976	Des Schumann

IGFA SALTWATER LINE CLASS WORLD RECORDS

TARPON
Megalops atlantica

LINE CLASS	WEIGHT	PLACE	DATE	ANGLER
M-3 kg (6 lb)	57.49 kg (126 lb, 12 oz)	Flamingo, Florida, USA	Apr. 13, 1978	James Falowski
W-3 kg (6 lb)	42.09 kg (92 lb, 13 oz)	Key West, Florida, USA	Mar. 16, 1976	Mrs. Charles O. Frasch
M-6 kg (12 lb)	77.33 kg (170 lb, 8 oz)	Big Pine Key, Florida, USA	Mar. 10, 1963	Russell C. Ball
W-6 kg (12 lb)	67.58 kg (149 lb)	Key West, Florida, USA	Apr. 18, 1976	Mrs. Charles O. Frasch
M-10 kg (20 lb)	110.22 kg (243 lb)	Key West, Florida, USA	Feb. 17, 1975	Gus Bell
W-10 kg (20 lb)	68.94 kg (152 lb)	Florida Bay, Florida, USA	Apr. 23, 1977	Dana S. Murphy
M-15 kg (30 lb)	128.36 kg (283 lb)	Lake Maracaibo, Venezuela	Mar. 19, 1956	M. Salazar
W-15 kg (30 lb)	77.56 kg (171 lb)	Marathon, Florida, USA	May 21, 1968	Mrs. Henry Sage
M-24 kg (50 lb)	109.88 kg (242 lb, 4 oz)	Cienaga Ayapel, Colombia	Jan. 7, 1955	A. Salazar
W-24 kg (50 lb)	86.41 kg (190 lb, 8 oz)	Boca Grande, Florida, USA	May 27, 1970	Patricia J. Mang
M-36 kg (80 lb)	98.88 kg (218 lb)	Tampa Bay, Florida, USA	May 6, 1973	Rick Wotring
W-36 kg (80 lb)	92.08 kg (203 lb)	Marathon, Florida, USA	May 19, 1961	June Jordan
M-60 kg (130 lb)	95.25 kg (210 lb)	Port Isabel, Texas, USA	Nov. 13, 1973	Thomas F. Gibson, Jr.
W-60 kg (130 lb)	Vacant—Minimum Acceptance Weight—81.54 kg (180 lb)			

TAUTOG
Tautoga onitis

LINE CLASS	WEIGHT	PLACE	DATE	ANGLER
M-3 kg (6 lb)	6.52 kg (14 lb, 6 oz)	Virginia Beach, Virginia, USA	May 17, 1972	Linwood A. Martens
W-3 kg (6 lb)	4.08 kg (9 lb)	Bayville, New York, USA	July 20, 1975	Deborah Kuno
M-6 kg (12 lb)	5.99 kg (13 lb, 3 oz)	Virginia Beach, Virginia, USA	Apr. 20, 1975	Nicholas J. Durney, Sr.
W-6 kg (12 lb)	4.76 kg (10 lb, 8 oz)	Montauk, New York, USA	June 2, 1973	Mrs. Joseph M. Rinaldi
M-10 kg (20 lb)	9.52 kg (21 lb)	Jamestown I., Rhode Island, USA	Nov. 6, 1954	C.W. Sundquist
W-10 kg (20 lb)	4.87 kg (10 lb, 12 oz)	Asharoken Beach, New York, USA	May 7, 1962	Trudy H. King
M-15 kg (30 lb)	9.69 kg (21 lb, 6 oz)	Cape May, New Jersey, USA	June 12, 1954	R.N. Sheafer
W-15 kg (30 lb)	5.07 kg (11 lb, 3 oz)	Virginia Beach, Virginia, USA	May 17, 1971	Mrs. Charlotte J. Wright

TREVALLY, giant
Caranx sexfasciatus

LINE CLASS	WEIGHT	PLACE	DATE	ANGLER
M-3 kg (6 lb)	8.50 kg (18 lb, 11 oz)	Darwin, N. Terr., Australia	June 3, 1978	Sid Jenkins
W-3 kg (6 lb)	Vacant—No Minimum Weight			
M-6 kg (12 lb)	7.60 kg (16 lb, 12 oz)	New Ireland I., Papua New Guinea	Jan. 8, 1978	Stephen Chow
W-6 kg (12 lb)	Vacant—No Minimum Weight			
M-10 kg (20 lb)	Vacant—No Minimum Weight			
W-10 kg (20 lb)	6.10 kg (13 lb, 7 oz)	Dunk Island, Qld., Australia	July 21, 1978	Roslyn Peel
M-15 kg (30 lb)	35.60 kg (78 lb, 7 oz)	Mtwapa Creek, Kenya	Feb. 10, 1978	Hans Sochen Ross
W-15 kg (30 lb)	Vacant—No Minimum Weight			
M-24 kg (50 lb)	Vacant—No Minimum Weight			
W-24 kg (50 lb)	Vacant—No Minimum Weight			
M-36 kg (80 lb)	31.20 kg (68 lb, 12 oz)	Mombasa, Kenya	Jan. 7, 1978	John De Villiers
W-36 kg (80 lb)	Vacant—No Minimum Weight			
M-60 kg (130 lb)	52.61 kg (116 lb)	Pago Pago, American Samoa	Feb. 20, 1978	William G. Foster
W-60 kg (130 lb)	Vacant—No Minimum Weight			

IGFA SALTWATER LINE CLASS WORLD RECORDS

TUNA, bigeye (Atlantic)

Thunnus obesus

LINE CLASS	WEIGHT	PLACE	DATE	ANGLER
M-3 kg (6 lb)	Vacant—Minimum Acceptance Weight—4.53 kg (10 lb)			
W-3 kg (6 lb)	Vacant—Minimum Acceptance Weight—4.53 kg (10 lb)			
M-6 kg (12 lb)	Vacant—Minimum Acceptance Weight—9.06 kg (20 lb)			
W-6 kg (12 lb)	Vacant—Minimum Acceptance Weight—9.06 kg (20 lb)			
M-10 kg (20 lb)	67.13 kg (148 lb)	Atlantic City, New Jersey, USA	July 22, 1978	Ron Jones
W-10 kg (20 lb)	20.86 kg (46 lb)	Key Largo, Florida, USA	Jan. 17, 1959	Dorothea L. Dean
M-15 kg (30 lb)	110.90 kg (244 lb, 8 oz)	Ocean City, New Jersey, USA	Aug. 27, 1978	Patrick Wall
W-15 kg (30 lb)	41.00 kg (90 lb, 6 oz)	Arguineguin, Canary Islands	Mar. 28, 1977	Mrs. Joyce Chtivelman
M-24 kg (50 lb)	170.32 kg (375 lb, 8 oz)	Ocean City, Maryland, USA	Aug. 26, 1977	Cecil Browne
W-24 kg (50 lb)	Vacant—Minimum Acceptance Weight—45.30 kg (100 lb)			
M-36 kg (80 lb)	160.00 kg (352 lb, 11 oz)	Arguineguin, Canary Islands	Sept. 8, 1976	Dr. Michel Margoulies
W-36 kg (80 lb)	144.13 kg (317 lb, 12 oz)	Hudson Canyon, New Jersey, USA	July 23, 1978	Charlene Sanford
M-60 kg (130 lb)	164.00 kg (361 lb, 8 oz)	Mogan Port, Gran Canaria, Canary I.	June 15, 1977	Horst Domider
W-60 kg (130 lb)	151.00 kg (332 lb, 14 oz)	Mogan Port, Gran Canaria, Canary I.	June 16, 1977	Mrs. Waltraud Lehmann

TUNA, bigeye (Pacific)

Thunnus obesus

LINE CLASS	WEIGHT	PLACE	DATE	ANGLER
M-3 kg (6 lb)	13.38 kg (29 lb, 8 oz)	Salinas, Ecuador	May 31, 1975	Luis Alberto Flores A.
W-3 kg (6 lb)	Vacant—Minimum Acceptance Weight—9.96 kg (22 lb)			
M-6 kg (12 lb)	16.78 kg (37 lb)	Salinas, Ecuador	May 28, 1975	Knud Holst
W-6 kg (12 lb)	12.27 kg (27 lb, 1 oz)	Salinas, Ecuador	Jan. 29, 1970	Mrs. Marilyn Schamroth
M-10 kg (20 lb)	48.98 kg (108 lb)	San Diego, California, USA	Aug. 10, 1968	John E. Muckenthaler
W-10 kg (20 lb)	12.24 kg (27 lb)	Cabo Blanco, Peru	Aug. 13, 1955	Mrs. O. Owinas
M-15 kg (30 lb)	73.93 kg (163 lb)	San Diego, California, USA	Aug. 15, 1970	Forrest N. Shumway
W-15 kg (30 lb)	60.32 kg (133 lb)	Coronados Islands, Mexico	Oct. 7, 1970	Mrs. Sally Johnson
M-24 kg (50 lb)	127.00 kg (280 lb)	Salinas, Ecuador	Jan. 21, 1967	Luis Alberto Flores A.
W-24 kg (50 lb)	108.86 kg (240 lb)	Salinas, Ecuador	Jan. 11, 1969	Helen C. King
M-36 kg (80 lb)	150.59 kg (332 lb)	Cabo Blanco, Peru	Jan. 26, 1953	Emil Wm. Steffens
W-36 kg (80 lb)	151.95 kg (335 lb)	Cabo Blanco, Peru	Mar. 25, 1953	Mrs. Wendell Anderson, Jr.
M-60 kg (130 lb)	197.31 kg (435 lb)	Cabo Blanco, Peru	Apr. 17, 1957	Dr. Russell V.A. Lee
W-60 kg (130 lb)	152.40 kg (336 lb)	Cabo Blanco, Peru	Jan. 16, 1957	Mrs. Seymour Knox III

TUNA, blackfin

Thunnus atlanticus

LINE CLASS	WEIGHT	PLACE	DATE	ANGLER
M-3 kg (6 lb)	13.15 kg (29 lb)	Challenger Bank, Bermuda	Aug. 6, 1972	Keith R. Winter
W-3 kg (6 lb)	12.70 kg (28 lb)	Islamorada, Florida, USA	Mar. 26, 1978	Ruth C. Stoky
M-6 kg (12 lb)	15.98 kg (35 lb, 4 oz)	Key West, Florida, USA	May 8, 1976	Barry Dorf
W-6 kg (12 lb)	12.13 kg (26 lb, 12 oz)	Bermuda	Oct. 18, 1957	Mrs. L. Edna Perinchief
M-10 kg (20 lb)	16.83 kg (37 lb, 2 oz)	Challenger Bank, Bermuda	July 25, 1977	Richard (Rip) Simons
W-10 kg (20 lb)	14.57 kg (32 lb, 2 oz)	Bermuda	Oct. 23, 1968	Mrs. Herbert N. Arnold
M-15 kg (30 lb)	17.23 kg (38 lb)	Bermuda	June 26, 1970	Archie L. Dickens
W-15 kg (30 lb)	17.23 kg (38 lb)	Islamorada, Florida, USA	May 22, 1973	Elizabeth Jean Wade
M-24 kg (50 lb)	19.05 kg (42 lb)	Bermuda	June 2, 1978	Alan J. Card
W-24 kg (50 lb)	14.06 kg (31 lb)	Bermuda	Aug. 30, 1967	Mrs. Glenn Sipe

IGFA SALTWATER LINE CLASS WORLD RECORDS

TUNA, bluefin   *Thunnus thynnus*

LINE CLASS	WEIGHT	PLACE	DATE	ANGLER
M-3 kg (6 lb)	9.97 kg (22 lb)	Montauk, New York, USA	Aug. 21, 1978	Stephen Sloan
W-3 kg (6 lb)	18.82 kg (41 lb, 8 oz)	Virginia Beach, Virginia, USA	July 3, 1977	Mrs. William B. DuVal
M-6 kg (12 lb)	19.27 kg (42 lb, 8 oz)	Rudee Inlet, Virginia, USA	June 30, 1977	Joe Fielder
W-6 kg (12 lb)	15.39 kg (33 lb, 15 oz)	Guadalupe Island, Mexico	Dec. 20, 1962	Mrs. Rae Pasquale
M-10 kg (20 lb)	51.93 kg (114 lb, 8 oz)	Montauk, New York, USA	July 25, 1959	Mundy I. Peale
W-10 kg (20 lb)	42.18 kg (93 lb)	Provincetown, Massachusetts, USA	Sept. 14, 1958	Willia H. Mather
M-15 kg (30 lb)	97.97 kg (216 lb)	Ocean City, Maryland, USA	Aug. 6, 1977	Byron Phillips
W-15 kg (30 lb)	53.29 kg (117 lb, 8 oz)	San Diego, California, USA	Sept. 10, 1968	Gladys A. Chambers
M-24 kg (50 lb)	407.00 kg (897 lb, 4 oz)	Arguineguin, Canary Islands	Mar. 25, 1977	Charles Chtivelman
W-24 kg (50 lb)	234.96 kg (518 lb)	Bimini, Bahamas	May 13, 1950	Mrs. William Myers
M-36 kg (80 lb)	478.53 kg (1055 lb)	North Lake, P.E.I., Canada	Oct. 6, 1978	Carl Mickelsen
W-36 kg (80 lb)	400.97 kg (884 lb)	North Lake, P.E.I., Canada	Sept. 25, 1977	Patricia M. Kuhnle
M-60 kg (130 lb)	560.19 kg (1235 lb)	North Lake, P.E.I., Canada	Oct. 17, 1978	Michael Mac Donald
W-60 kg (130 lb)	530.71 kg (1170 lb)	North Lake, P.E.I., Canada	Oct. 2, 1978	Colette Perras, M.D.

TUNA, dogtooth   *Gymnosarda unicolor*

LINE CLASS	WEIGHT	PLACE	DATE	ANGLER
M-3 kg (6 lb)	9.00 kg (19 lb, 13 oz)	Tubai I., Tahiti, Fr. Polynesia	Jan. 2, 1976	Alban Ellacott
W-3 kg (6 lb)	Vacant–Minimum Acceptance Weight–2.71 kg (6 lb)			
M-6 kg (12 lb)	35.25 kg (77 lb, 11 oz)	Lizard Island, Qld., Australia	Oct. 1, 1975	John Pelton
W-6 kg (12 lb)	17.23 kg (38 lb)	Denis Island, Seychelles	Mar. 27, 1976	Georgette Douwma
M-10 kg (20 lb)	45.58 kg (100 lb, 8 oz)	Denis Island, Seychelles	Apr. 12, 1977	Pierre Burkhardt
W-10 kg (20 lb)	29.93 kg (66 lb)	Denis Island, Seychelles	Apr. 7, 1977	Georgette Douwma
M-15 kg (30 lb)	64.49 kg (142 lb, 3 oz)	Lizard Island, Qld., Australia	Aug. 29, 1975	John C. Johnston
W-15 kg (30 lb)	32.88 kg (72 lb, 8 oz)	Denis Island, Seychelles	Mar. 30, 1977	Georgette Douwma
M-24 kg (50 lb)	31.07 kg (68 lb, 8 oz)	Denis Island, Seychelles	Mar. 24, 1976	Robert Douwma
W-24 kg (50 lb)	43.20 kg (95 lb, 4 oz)	Cairns, Qld., Australia	Oct. 5, 1974	Eleanor D. Inscho
M-36 kg (80 lb)	55.45 kg (122 lb, 4 oz)	Cairns, Qld., Australia	Oct. 10, 1974	Colin L. (Bill) Hinchen
W-36 kg (80 lb)	47.40 kg (104 lb, 8 oz)	Cairns, Qld., Australia	Sept. 11, 1974	Gloria J. Applegate
M-60 kg (130 lb)	69.62 kg (153 lb, 8 oz)	Cooktown, Qld., Australia	Sept. 25, 1975	William E. Chapman
W-60 kg (130 lb)	Vacant–Minimum Acceptance Weight–41.67 kg (92 lb)			

TUNA, longtail   *Thunnus tonggol*

LINE CLASS	WEIGHT	PLACE	DATE	ANGLER
M-3 kg (6 lb)	14.00 kg (30 lb, 13 oz)	Moreton Island, Qld., Australia	Apr. 18, 1977	Lawrie Munro
W-3 kg (6 lb)	Vacant–Minimum Acceptance Weight–9.51 kg (21 lb)			
M-6 kg (12 lb)	29.50 kg (65 lb)	Port Stephens, N.S.W., Australia	Apr. 20, 1978	Michael James
W-6 kg (12 lb)	17.00 kg (37 lb, 8 oz)	Moreton Bay, Qld., Australia	Apr. 5, 1975	Christine Stoddard
M-10 kg (20 lb)	23.50 kg (51 lb, 13 oz)	Tangalooma, Qld., Australia	Mar. 20, 1976	Peter Bielz
W-10 kg (20 lb)	20.00 kg (44 lb)	Moreton Bay, Qld., Australia	Apr. 5, 1976	Mrs. Kim Carolan
M-15 kg (30 lb)	27.18 kg (59 lb, 15 oz)	Bermagui, N.S.W., Australia	Apr. 27, 1976	J.H. Allen
W-15 kg (30 lb)	Vacant–Minimum Acceptance Weight–14.49 kg (32 lb)			
M-24 kg (50 lb)	27.21 kg (60 lb)	Bermagui, N.S.W., Australia	Mar. 17, 1975	N. Noel Webster
W-24 kg (50 lb)	Vacant–Minimum Acceptance Weight–20.38 kg (45 lb)			
M-36 kg (80 lb)	Vacant–Minimum Acceptance Weight–20.38 kg (45 lb)			
W-36 kg (80 lb)	Vacant–Minimum Acceptance Weight–20.38 kg (45 lb)			

IGFA SALTWATER LINE CLASS WORLD RECORDS

TUNA, skipjack

Katsuwonus pelamis

LINE CLASS	WEIGHT	PLACE	DATE	ANGLER
M-3 kg (6 lb)	9.52 kg (21 lb)	Keahole, Hawaii, USA	July 19, 1972	Rufus Spalding, Jr.
W-3 kg (6 lb)	6.57 kg (14 lb, 8 oz)	San Diego, California, USA	Sept. 3, 1976	Joanne Birtcher
M-6 kg (12 lb)	12.47 kg (27 lb, 8 oz)	San Juan, Puerto Rico	Oct. 20, 1974	Miguel E. Correa
W-6 kg (12 lb)	11.05 kg (24 lb, 6 oz)	Walker Cay, Bahamas	Mar. 26, 1965	Patricia E. Church
M-10 kg (20 lb)	17.80 kg (39 lb, 4 oz)	Challenger Bank, Bermuda	July 13, 1978	Keith R. Winter
W-10 kg (20 lb)	12.70 kg (28 lb)	St. Thomas, Virgin Islands	July 16, 1977	Gloria J. Applegate
M-15 kg (30 lb)	15.08 kg (33 lb, 4 oz)	San Juan, Puerto Rico	July 14, 1966	Jose L. Campos
W-15 kg (30 lb)	13.60 kg (30 lb)	Mayaguez, Puerto Rico	Sept. 25, 1977	Martha Ann Baco
M-24 kg (50 lb)	18.11 kg (39 lb, 15 oz)	Walker Cay, Bahamas	Jan. 21, 1952	F. Drowley
W-24 kg (50 lb)	14.06 kg (31 lb)	San Juan, Puerto Rico	Dec. 26, 1954	Gloria G. de Marques
Tie M-24 kg	18.14 kg (40 lb)	Baie du Tambeau, Mauritius	Apr. 19, 1971	Joseph R.P. Caboche, Jr.

TUNA, southern bluefin

Thunnus maccoyii

LINE CLASS	WEIGHT	PLACE	DATE	ANGLER
M-3 kg (6 lb)	14.27 kg (31 lb, 7 oz)	St. Helens, Tasmania, Australia	June 10, 1977	Barry Charlton
W-3 kg (6 lb)	5.44 kg (12 lb)	Montague I., N.S.W., Australia	Mar. 12, 1976	Miss Julie McDonald
M-6 kg (12 lb)	25.40 kg (56 lb)	S. Neptune Island, S. Australia	April 12, 1965	Eldred H.V. Riggs
W-6 kg (12 lb)	17.91 kg (39 lb, 8 oz)	Tasmania, Australia	May 27, 1963	Mrs. Bob Dyer
M-10 kg (20 lb)	58.96 kg (130 lb)	Hippolytes, Tasmania, Australia	Mar. 2, 1976	Anthony John Little
W-10 kg (20 lb)	22.22 kg (49 lb)	Fiordland, New Zealand	Apr. 17, 1977	Miss Schonda Vincent
M-15 kg (30 lb)	100.00 kg (220 lb, 7 oz)	Tasman I., Tasmania, Australia	June 10, 1978	Stanley Gibbon
W-15 kg (30 lb)	Vacant—Minimum Acceptance Weight—22.65 kg (50 lb)			
M-24 kg (50 lb)	97.00 kg (213 lb, 13 oz)	Mon. Lanterns, Tasmania, Australia	May 31, 1977	Gerald Harvey
W-24 kg (50 lb)	Vacant—Minimum Acceptance Weight—33.97 kg (75 lb)			
M-36 kg (80 lb)	80.00 kg (176 lb, 5 oz)	Hippolytes, Tasmania, Australia	Apr. 15, 1978	David John Hallam
W-36 kg (80 lb)	Vacant—Minimum Acceptance Weight—45.30 kg (100 lb)			
M-60 kg (130 lb)	Vacant—Minimum Acceptance Weight—45.30 kg (100 lb)			
W-60 kg (130 lb)	Vacant—Minimum Acceptance Weight—45.30 kg (100 lb)			

TUNA, yellowfin

Thunnus albacares

LINE CLASS	WEIGHT	PLACE	DATE	ANGLER
M-3 kg (6 lb)	28.91 kg (63 lb, 12 oz)	Moriches, New York, USA	Aug. 26, 1978	Tred Barta
W-3 kg (6 lb)	17.23 kg (38 lb)	Challenger Bank, Bermuda	June 12, 1977	Donna De Silva
M-6 kg (12 lb)	65.77 kg (145 lb)	Port Stephens, N.S.W., Australia	Aug. 23, 1970	Don McElwaine
W-6 kg (12 lb)	34.47 kg (76 lb)	St. Thomas, Virgin Islands	May 10, 1969	Gloria J. Applegate
M-10 kg (20 lb)	80.62 kg (177 lb, 12 oz)	St. George's, Grenada	Apr. 9, 1976	Michael Robert Grimes
W-10 kg (20 lb)	62.59 kg (138 lb)	St. George's, Grenada	Apr. 10, 1976	Sue Gillibrand
M-15 kg (30 lb)	108.86 kg (240 lb)	Keahole Point, Kona, Hawaii, USA	July 7, 1978	J.I. (Dick) de Villiers
W-15 kg (30 lb)	111.13 kg (245 lb)	Kaiwi Pt., Kona, Hawaii, USA	July 28, 1978	Ann Blumenfeld
M-24 kg (50 lb)	131.25 kg (289 lb, 6 oz)	Clarion Island, Mexico	Mar. 10, 1978	Joseph M. Semunovich
W-24 kg (50 lb)	112.26 kg (247 lb, 8 oz)	Waianae, Oahu, Hawaii, USA	July 12, 1977	Patricia Haunani Rego
M-36 kg (80 lb)	176.35 kg (388 lb, 12 oz)	San Benedicto Island, Mexico	April 1, 1977	Curt Wiesenhutter
W-36 kg (80 lb)	118.61 kg (261 lb, 8 oz)	Kailua, Kona, Hawaii, USA	July 4, 1978	Evangeline Komo
M-60 kg (130 lb)	139.70 kg (308 lb)	San Benedicto Island, Mexico	Jan. 18, 1973	Harold J. Tolson
W-60 kg (130 lb)	115.21 kg (254 lb)	Kona, Hawaii, USA	Aug. 19, 1954	Jean Carlisle
Tie W-6 kg	34.47 kg (76 lb)	Sydney, N.S.W., Australia	July 31, 1976	Pamela Hudspeth
Tie M-15 kg	109.20 kg (240 lb, 12 oz)	Keahole Point, Kona, Hawaii, USA	Aug. 4, 1978	Stephen Zuckerman

TUNNY, little
Euthynnus alletteratus

LINE CLASS	WEIGHT	PLACE	DATE	ANGLER
M-3 kg (6 lb)	9.29 kg (20 lb, 8 oz)	Key West, Florida, USA	Apr. 22, 1978	David L. Vatter
W-3 kg (6 lb)	7.37 kg (16 lb, 4 oz)	Juno, Florida, USA	May 27, 1976	Cynthia Boomhower
M-6 kg (12 lb)	11.31 kg (24 lb, 15 oz)	Sea Bright, New Jersey, USA	Oct. 2, 1977	Mark Anthony Niemczyk
W-6 kg (12 lb)	7.59 kg (16 lb, 12 oz)	Juno, Florida, USA	May 26, 1976	Cynthia Boomhower
M-10 kg (20 lb)	9.52 kg (21 lb)	Kitchen Shoals, Bermuda	Jan. 19, 1978	Willard G. Kelly, Esq.
W-10 kg (20 lb)	9.63 kg (21 lb, 4 oz)	Palm Beach, Florida, USA	Aug. 19, 1978	Mrs. Joan Zeitlin
M-15 kg (30 lb)	12.24 kg (27 lb)	Key Largo, Florida, USA	Apr. 20, 1976	William E. Allison
W-15 kg (30 lb)	6.91 kg (15 lb, 4 oz)	Marathon, Florida, USA	July 4, 1976	Jane E. Spruance
Tie M-10 kg	9.66 kg (21 lb, 5 oz)	Sugarloaf Key, Florida, USA	July 2, 1978	Jose I. Lopez

WAHOO
Acanthocybium solandri

LINE CLASS	WEIGHT	PLACE	DATE	ANGLER
M-3 kg (6 lb)	23.13 kg (51 lb)	Mayaguez, Puerto Rico	Mar. 4, 1978	Leroy V. Battistini
W-3 kg (6 lb)	12.81 kg (28 lb, 4 oz)	Isla de la Plata, Ecuador	Nov. 3, 1975	Maria Isabel Maspons
M-6 kg (12 lb)	33.56 kg (74 lb)	Isla de Coiba, Panama	June 26, 1973	George A. Bernstein
W-6 kg (12 lb)	32.14 kg (70 lb, 14 oz)	Bermuda	Aug. 13, 1978	Mrs. Margaret De Silva
M-10 kg (20 lb)	52.16 kg (115 lb)	Bermuda	July 2, 1961	Leo Barboza
W-10 kg (20 lb)	37.64 kg (83 lb)	St. Thomas, Virgin Islands	Mar. 5, 1968	Gloria J. Applegate
M-15 kg (30 lb)	48.53 kg (107 lb)	Miami, Florida, USA	Apr. 8, 1978	Ted Parker
W-15 kg (30 lb)	49.24 kg (108 lb, 9 oz)	Cape May, New Jersey, USA	July 17, 1977	Charlene Mascuch
M-24 kg (50 lb)	56.24 kg (124 lb)	St. Thomas, Virgin Islands	Mar. 29, 1967	Joseph H.C. Wenk
W-24 kg (50 lb)	51.25 kg (113 lb)	Yanuca, Fiji	June 30, 1967	Jan K. Bates
M-36 kg (80 lb)	63.04 kg (139 lb)	Marathon, Florida, USA	May 18, 1960	George Von Hoffman
W-36 kg (80 lb)	47.40 kg (104 lb, 8 oz)	Walker Cay, Bahamas	May 2, 1965	Mrs. Lloyd Dalzell
M-60 kg (130 lb)	67.58 kg (149 lb)	Cat Cay, Bahamas	June 15, 1962	John Pirovano
W-60 kg (130 lb)	50.29 kg (110 lb, 14 oz)	Port Eads, Louisiana, USA	May 8, 1976	Erin M. Burks

WEAKFISH
Cynoscion regalis

LINE CLASS	WEIGHT	PLACE	DATE	ANGLER
M-3 kg (6 lb)	7.93 kg (17 lb, 8 oz)	Fire Island, New.York, USA	Aug. 25, 1976	Joseph Giallanzo
W-3 kg (6 lb)	5.10 kg (11 lb, 4 oz)	Peconic Bay, New Suffolk, N.Y., USA	May 18, 1978	Kay M. Robinson
M-6 kg (12 lb)	7.00 kg (15 lb, 7 oz)	Cape May, New Jersey, USA	May 28, 1978	James E. Collins
W-6 kg (12 lb)	6.12 kg (13 lb, 8 oz)	Jones Inlet, L.I., New York, USA	May 20, 1978	Sandra Brendel
M-10 kg (20 lb)	7.22 kg (15 lb, 15 oz)	Virginia Beach, Virginia, USA	May 9, 1976	William C. Reid
W-10 kg (20 lb)	6.49 kg (14 lb, 5 oz)	Fire Island, New York, USA	Aug. 23, 1978	Michelle Mescall
M-15 kg (30 lb)	6.91 kg (15 lb, 4 oz)	Delaware Bay, New Jersey, USA	April 30, 1977	David T. Myers
W-15 kg (30 lb)	6.46 kg (14 lb, 4 oz)	Chesapeake Bay, Virginia, USA	Aug. 9, 1978	Mrs. Joan M. Albright
Tie M-10 kg	7.25 kg (16 lb)	Ocean City, Maryland, USA	Sept. 11, 1976	Donald M. Cannon

YELLOWTAIL, California

Seriola lalandi dorsalis

LINE CLASS	WEIGHT	PLACE	DATE	ANGLER
M-3 kg (6 lb)	6.46 kg (14 lb, 4 oz)	San Diego, California, USA	June 2, 1978	J.D. (Dou) McAdam
W-3 kg (6 lb)	Vacant—No Minimum Weight			
M-6 kg (12 lb)	7.76 kg (17 lb, 2 oz)	San Clemente I., California, USA	June 2, 1978	Mark A. Davis
W-6 kg (12 lb)	Vacant—No Minimum Weight			
M-10 kg (20 lb)	Vacant—No Minimum Weight			
W-10 kg (20 lb)	Vacant—No Minimum Weight			
M-15 kg (30 lb)	19.56 kg (43 lb, 2 oz)	Alijos Rocks, Mexico	June 6, 1978	Jim Stout
W-15 kg (30 lb)	9.12 kg (20 lb, 2 oz)	Coronado Islands, Mexico	June 15, 1978	Jean S. Hinckley
M-24 kg (50 lb)	22.67 kg (50 lb)	Alijos Rocks, Mexico	June 5, 1978	Jerry Reid
W-24 kg (50 lb)	Vacant—No Minimum Weight			
M-36 kg (80 lb)	Vacant—No Minimum Weight			
W-36 kg (80 lb)	Vacant—No Minimum Weight			

YELLOWTAIL, southern

Seriola lalandi lalandi

LINE CLASS	WEIGHT	PLACE	DATE	ANGLER
M-3 kg (6 lb)	17.23 kg (38 lb)	Bangitoto Channel, New Zealand	Dec. 17, 1972	Dr. Gabriel D. Tetro
W-3 kg (6 lb)	7.25 kg (16 lb)	Sydney, N.S.W., Australia	Sept. 24, 1972	Pamela Hudspeth
M-6 kg (12 lb)	29.71 kg (65 lb, 8 oz)	Cavalli Islands, New Zealand	July 13, 1972	J. Farrell
W-6 kg (12 lb)	27.66 kg (61 lb)	Cavalli Islands, New Zealand	June 14, 1976	Mrs. Barbara Brittain
M-10 kg (20 lb)	34.01 kg (75 lb)	Whakatane, New Zealand	Feb. 23, 1976	M. Maxwell
W-10 kg (20 lb)	30.16 kg (66 lb, 8 oz)	Cape Brett, New Zealand	July 12, 1970	Margaret Niven
M-15 kg (30 lb)	39.91 kg (88 lb)	Cape Brett, New Zealand	June 25, 1963	J.R. Chibnall
W-15 kg (30 lb)	34.20 kg (75 lb, 6 oz)	Sir Joseph Young Banks, Australia	Sept. 18, 1977	Mrs. Betty Solomon
M-24 kg (50 lb)	50.34 kg (111 lb)	Bay of Islands, New Zealand	June 11, 1961	A.F. Plim
W-24 kg (50 lb)	37.19 kg (82 lb)	Three Kings I., New Zealand	Oct. 1, 1975	Mrs. Francine Swales
M-36 kg (80 lb)	48.98 kg (108 lb)	Cape Brett, New Zealand	Jan. 15, 1962	Robin O'Connor
W-36 kg (80 lb)	36.74 kg (81 lb)	Cape Brett, New Zealand	May 18, 1960	Kura Beale
M-60 kg (130 lb)	43.09 kg (95 lb)	White Island, New Zealand	Apr. 11, 1975	James Victor Bayliss
W-60 kg (130 lb)	36.74 kg (81 lb)	Mayor Island, New Zealand	Apr. 8, 1966	Patricia E. Jack

IGFA Saltwater Fly Rod World Records

Following are all saltwater fly rod world records granted in tippet classes as of January 1, 1979.
Records are listed alphabetically according to common names of species.

ALBACORE / *Thunnus alalunga*

TIPPET CLASS	WEIGHT	PLACE	DATE	ANGLER
6 lb	Vacant—No Minimum Weight			
10 lb	11.85 kg (26 lb 2 oz)	San Diego, California, USA	July 15, 1972	Les Eichhorn
12 lb	11.45 kg (25 lb 4 oz)	Todos Santos, Mexico	Aug. 7, 1966	Harry Bonner
15 lb	12.47 kg (27 lb 8 oz)	San Diego, California, USA	Aug. 15, 1970	Charles Davis

AMBERJACK, greater / *Seriola dumerili*

TIPPET CLASS	WEIGHT	PLACE	DATE	ANGLER
6 lb	13.46 kg (29 lb 11 oz)	Sebastian Inlet, Florida, USA	Sept. 15, 1972	Dave Chermanski
10 lb	33.79 kg (74 lb 8 oz)	Key West, Florida, USA	Jan. 25, 1975	Frank Inscho
12 lb	36.28 kg (80 lb)	Fort Pierce, Florida, USA	Jan. 15, 1976	Dave Chermanski
15 lb	47.06 kg (103 lb 12 oz)	Key West, Florida, USA	Jan. 28, 1977	Dr. William J. Munro

BARRACUDA, great / *Sphyraena barracuda*

TIPPET CLASS	WEIGHT	PLACE	DATE	ANGLER
6 lb	6.86 kg (15 lb 2 oz)	West Palm Beach, Florida, USA	July 16, 1972	Dave Chermanski
10 lb	13.38 kg (29 lb 8 oz)	Key West, Florida, USA	Jan. 2, 1971	Mike Leverone
12 lb	15.19 kg (33 lb 8 oz)	Key West, Florida, USA	Sept. 6, 1976	Robert Trosset, Jr.
15 lb	16.89 kg (37 lb 4 oz)	Key West, Florida, USA	Dec. 16, 1975	Roy Terrell

BASS, black sea / *Centropristis striata*

TIPPET CLASS	WEIGHT	PLACE	DATE	ANGLER
6 lb	Vacant—No Minimum Weight			
10 lb	Vacant—No Minimum Weight			
12 lb	Vacant—No Minimum Weight			
15 lb	Vacant—No Minimum Weight			

BASS, giant sea / *Stereolepis gigas*

TIPPET CLASS	WEIGHT	PLACE	DATE	ANGLER
6 lb	Vacant—No Minimum Weight			
10 lb	Vacant—No Minimum Weight			
12 lb	Vacant—No Minimum Weight			
15 lb	Vacant—No Minimum Weight			

BASS, striped / *Morone saxatilis*

TIPPET CLASS	WEIGHT	PLACE	DATE	ANGLER
6 lb	11.22 kg (24 lb 12 oz)	American River, California, USA	Dec. 2, 1973	Alfred Perryman
10 lb	29.25 kg (64 lb 8 oz)	Smith River, Oregon, USA	July 28, 1973	Beryl E. Bliss
12 lb	18.25 kg (40 lb 4 oz)	Umpqua River, Oregon, USA	July 13, 1970	R. M. Wadsworth
15 lb	23.36 kg (51 lb 8 oz)	Smith River, Oregon, USA	May 18, 1974	Gary L. Dyer

BLUEFISH / *Pomatomus saltatrix*

TIPPET CLASS	WEIGHT	PLACE	DATE	ANGLER
6 lb	6.60 kg (14 lb 9 oz)	Chesapeake Bay, Virginia, USA	June 24, 1977	Mev Van Doren
10 lb	6.69 kg (14 lb 12 oz)	Salisbury, Massachusetts, USA	Aug. 18, 1973	Arnold Korenblum
12 lb	7.90 kg (17 lb 7 oz)	Virginia Beach, Virginia, USA	Nov. 16, 1968	Jeff Dane
15 lb	7.48 kg (16 lb 8 oz)	Virginia Beach, Virginia, USA	Nov. 16, 1968	W. A. Thigpen

BONEFISH / *Albula vulpes*

TIPPET CLASS	WEIGHT	PLACE	DATE	ANGLER
6 lb	6.01 kg (13 lb 4 oz)	Islamorada, Florida, USA	Nov. 6, 1973	Jim López
10 lb	5.95 kg (13 lb 2 oz)	Islamorada, Florida, USA	Oct. 9, 1976	Dick Pope, Jr.
12 lb	5.89 kg (13 lb)	Islamorada, Florida, USA	Oct. 30, 1969	Bart Foth
15 lb	5.81 kg (12 lb 13 oz)	Islamorada, Florida, USA	Feb. 21, 1974	Ron Wagner

IGFA SALTWATER FLY ROD WORLD RECORDS

BONITO, Atlantic / *Sarda sarda*

TIPPET CLASS	WEIGHT	PLACE	DATE	ANGLER
6 lb	3.06 kg (6 lb 12 oz)	Bermuda	June 28, 1972	Lefty Kreh
10 lb	3.34 kg (7 lb 6 oz)	Montauk, New York, USA	Sept. 28, 1971	Robert Popovics
12 lb	Record being reviewed			
15 lb	6.06 kg (13 lb 6 oz)	Key West, Florida, USA	Nov. 30, 1975	Al Polofsky

BONITO, Pacific / *Sarda spp.*

TIPPET CLASS	WEIGHT	PLACE	DATE	ANGLER
6 lb	Vacant—No Minimum Weight			
10 lb	7.03 kg (15 lb 8 oz)	Monterey Bay, California, USA	Sept. 15, 1972	Bob Edgley
12 lb	Vacant—No Minimum Weight			
15 lb	Vacant—No Minimum Weight			

COBIA / *Rachycentron canadum*

TIPPET CLASS	WEIGHT	PLACE	DATE	ANGLER
6 lb	17.91 kg (39 lb 8 oz)	Key West, Florida, USA	March 15, 1972	Roy Terrell
10 lb	31.29 kg (69 lb)	Florida Bay, Florida, USA	Dec. 9, 1967	Ralph Delph
12 lb	27.21 kg (60 lb)	Flamingo, Florida, USA	Jan. 22, 1975	Richard W. Moore
15 lb	23.58 kg (52 lb)	Key West, Florida, USA	March 16, 1971	Jim López

COD / *Gadus morhua*

TIPPET CLASS	WEIGHT	PLACE	DATE	ANGLER
6 lb	2.66 kg (5 lb 14 oz)	Port Maitland, N.S., Canada	June 22, 1973	Lou Truppi
10 lb	4.02 kg (8 lb 14 oz)	Port Maitland, N.S., Canada	June 22, 1973	Lou Truppi
12 lb	Vacant—No Minimum Weight			
15 lb	Vacant—No Minimum Weight			

DOLPHIN / *Coryphaena hippurus*

TIPPET CLASS	WEIGHT	PLACE	DATE	ANGLER
6 lb	10.43 kg (23 lb)	Tongue of Ocean, Bahamas	March 6, 1975	Harold Siebens
10 lb	16.32 kg (36 lb)	Tongue of Ocean, Bahamas	April 29, 1977	Harold Siebens
12 lb	26.30 kg (58 lb)	Piñas Bay, Panama	Dec. 6, 1964	Stu Apte
15 lb	20.41 kg (45 lb)	Tongue of Ocean, Bahamas	Dec. 17, 1971	Harold Siebens

DRUM, black / *Pogonias cromis*

TIPPET CLASS	WEIGHT	PLACE	DATE	ANGLER
6 lb	Vacant—No Minimum Weight			
10 lb	Vacant—No Minimum Weight			
12 lb	21.77 kg (48 lb)	Indian River, Florida, USA	April 4, 1977	Dave Chermanski
15 lb	Vacant—No Minimum Weight			

DRUM, red / *Sciaenops ocellata*

TIPPET CLASS	WEIGHT	PLACE	DATE	ANGLER
6 lb	6.26 kg (13 lb 13 oz)	Banana River, Florida, USA	May 30, 1972	Dave Chermanski
10 lb	4.84 kg (10 lb 11 oz)	Islamorada, Florida, USA	Aug. 2, 1973	William W. Pate, Jr.
12 lb	17.57 kg (38 lb 12 oz)	Chesapeake Bay, Virginia, USA	Aug. 8, 1967	Ree Ellis
15 lb	Record being reviewed			

FLOUNDER, summer / *Paralichthys dentatus*

TIPPET CLASS	WEIGHT	PLACE	DATE	ANGLER
6 lb	Vacant—No Minimum Weight			
10 lb	Vacant—No Minimum Weight			
12 lb	Vacant—No Minimum Weight			
15 lb	Vacant—No Minimum Weight			

IGFA SALTWATER FLY ROD WORLD RECORDS

HALIBUT, Atlantic / *Hippoglossus hippoglossus*

TIPPET CLASS	WEIGHT	PLACE	DATE	ANGLER
6 lb	Vacant—No Minimum Weight			
10 lb	Vacant—No Minimum Weight			
12 lb	Vacant—No Minimum Weight			
15 lb	Vacant—No Minimum Weight			

HALIBUT, California / *Paralichthys californicus*

TIPPET CLASS	WEIGHT	PLACE	DATE	ANGLER
6 lb	Vacant—No Minimum Weight			
10 lb	Vacant—No Minimum Weight			
12 lb	Record being reviewed			
15 lb	Vacant—No Minimum Weight			

HALIBUT, Pacific / *Hippoglossus stenolepis*

TIPPET CLASS	WEIGHT	PLACE	DATE	ANGLER
6 lb	Vacant—No Minimum Weight			
10 lb	16.32 kg (36 lb)	Whidbey Island, Washington, USA	July 31, 1969	John Smart
12 lb	10.48 kg (23 lb 2 oz)	San Francisco, California, USA	April 29, 1973	Ronald Dong
15 lb	Vacant—No Minimum Weight			

JACK, crevalle / *Caranx hippos*

TIPPET CLASS	WEIGHT	PLACE	DATE	ANGLER
6 lb	8.67 kg (19 lb 2 oz)	Key West, Florida, USA	Feb. 14, 1970	Lefty Kreh
10 lb	15.30 kg (33 lb 12 oz)	Sebastian Inlet, Florida, USA	Nov. 19, 1972	Dave Chermanski
12 lb	13.83 kg (30 lb 8 oz)	Sebastian Inlet, Florida, USA	Nov. 19, 1972	Dave Chermanski
15 lb	8.78 kg (19 lb 6 oz)	Pez Maya, Mexico	Aug. 16, 1972	William W. Pate, Jr.

JACK, horse-eye / *Caranx latus*

TIPPET CLASS	WEIGHT	PLACE	DATE	ANGLER
6 lb	Vacant—No Minimum Weight			
10 lb	Vacant—No Minimum Weight			
12 lb	Vacant—No Minimum Weight			
15 lb	Vacant—No Minimum Weight			

JEWFISH / *Epinephelus itajara*

TIPPET CLASS	WEIGHT	PLACE	DATE	ANGLER
6 lb	Vacant—No Minimum Weight			
10 lb	Vacant—No Minimum Weight			
12 lb	161.48 kg (356 lb)	Islamorada, Florida, USA	March 15, 1967	Bart Foth
15 lb	Vacant—No Minimum Weight			

KAWAKAWA / *Euthynnus affinis*

TIPPET CLASS	WEIGHT	PLACE	DATE	ANGLER
6 lb	Vacant—No Minimum Weight			
10 lb	6.35 kg (14 lb)	Mozambique	June 15, 1958	Joseph W. Brooks
12 lb	Vacant—No Minimum Weight			
15 lb	Vacant—No Minimum Weight			

MACKEREL, king / *Scomberomorus cavalla*

TIPPET CLASS	WEIGHT	PLACE	DATE	ANGLER
6 lb	3.13 kg (6 lb 14 oz)	Islamorada, Florida, USA	Feb. 9, 1978	Saul Greenspan
10 lb	10.88 kg (24 lb)	Port Canaveral, Florida, USA	Nov. 5, 1973	John F. Meyer
12 lb	17.23 kg (38 lb)	Key West, Florida, USA	Jan. 12, 1971	Jim López
15 lb	19.27 kg (42 lb 8 oz)	Key West, Florida, USA	Jan. 12, 1971	Jim López

IGFA SALTWATER FLY ROD WORLD RECORDS

MARLIN, black / *Makaira indica*

TIPPET CLASS	WEIGHT	PLACE	DATE	ANGLER
6 lb	20.97 kg (46 lb 4 oz)	Cairns, Qld., Australia	Sept. 14, 1972	William W. Pate, Jr.
10 lb	17.23 kg (38 lb)	Cairns, Qld., Australia	Sept. 14, 1972	Laura E. Pate
12 lb	17.52 kg (38 lb 10 oz)	Cairns, Qld., Australia	Sept. 10, 1972	William W. Pate, Jr.
15 lb	19.22 kg (42 lb 6 oz)	Cairns, Qld., Australia	Sept. 8, 1972	William W. Pate, Jr.

MARLIN, blue (Atlantic) / *Makaira nigricans*

TIPPET CLASS	WEIGHT	PLACE	DATE	ANGLER
6 lb	Vacant—No Minimum Weight			
10 lb	Vacant—No Minimum Weight			
12 lb	Vacant—No Minimum Weight			
15 lb	43.54 kg (96 lb)	Havana, Cuba	Aug. 21, 1978	William W. Pate, Jr.

MARLIN, blue (Pacific) / *Makaira nigricans*

TIPPET CLASS	WEIGHT	PLACE	DATE	ANGLER
6 lb	Vacant—No Minimum Weight			
10 lb	Vacant—No Minimum Weight			
12 lb	Vacant—No Minimum Weight			
15 lb	Vacant—No Minimum Weight			

MARLIN, striped / *Tetrapturus audax*

TIPPET CLASS	WEIGHT	PLACE	DATE	ANGLER
6 lb	Vacant—No Minimum Weight			
10 lb	Vacant—No Minimum Weight			
12 lb	67.13 kg (148 lbs)	Salinas, Ecuador	May 1967	Lee Wulff
15 lb	66.22 kg (146 lbs)	Salinas, Ecuador	Feb. 10, 1970	William W. Pate, Jr.

MARLIN, white / *Tetrapturus albidus*

TIPPET CLASS	WEIGHT	PLACE	DATE	ANGLER
6 lb	Vacant—No Minimum Weight			
10 lb	30.84 kg (68 lb)	Fort Pierce, Florida, USA	Dec. 23, 1972	Dave Chermanski
12 lb	26.53 kg (58 lb 8 oz)	Caracas, Venezuela	Sept. 30, 1976	Judge W. O. Mehrtens
15 lb	36.28 kg (80 lb)	La Guaira, Venezuela	Sept. 17, 1975	William W. Pate, Jr.

PERMIT / *Trachinotus falcatus*

TIPPET CLASS	WEIGHT	PLACE	DATE	ANGLER
6 lb	8.84 kg (19 lb 8 oz)	Isle of Pines, Cuba	May 16, 1957	Joseph W. Brooks
10 lb	13.60 kg (30 lb)	Marathon, Florida, USA	May 12, 1972	Greg Costa, Jr.
12 lb	13.66 kg (30 lb 2 oz)	Key West, Florida, USA	May 3, 1970	C. W. Walton
15 lb	13.15 kg (29 lb)	Key West, Florida, USA	June 2, 1975	Gene Anderegg II

POLLACK / *Pollachius pollachius*

TIPPET CLASS	WEIGHT	PLACE	DATE	ANGLER
6 lb	Vacant—No Minimum Weight			
10 lb	Vacant—No Minimum Weight			
12 lb	Vacant—No Minimum Weight			
15 lb	Vacant—No Minimum Weight			

POLLOCK / *Pollachius virens*

TIPPET CLASS	WEIGHT	PLACE	DATE	ANGLER
6 lb	4.02 kg (8 lb 14 oz)	Port Maitland, N.S., Canada	June 22, 1973	Lou Truppi
10 lb	4.87 kg (10 lb 12 oz)	Newport, Rhode Island, USA	Nov. 24, 1968	R. H. Smith
12 lb	3.85 kg (8 lb 8 oz)	Trinity Ledge, N.S., Canada	June 21, 1972	Lou Truppi
15 lb	8.39 kg (18 lb 8 oz)	Port Maitland, N.S., Canada	June 22, 1973	Lou Truppi

IGFA SALTWATER FLY ROD WORLD RECORDS

POMPANO, african / *Alectis ciliaris*

TIPPET CLASS	WEIGHT	PLACE	DATE	ANGLER
6 lb	Vacant—No Minimum Weight			
10 lb	Vacant—No Minimum Weight			
12 lb	15.19 kg (33 lb 8 oz)	Palm Beach, Florida, USA	Dec. 21, 1969	Gil Drake, Jr.
15 lb	6.57 kg (14 lb 8 oz)	Key Largo, Florida, USA	May 28, 1973	Jim Thomas

ROOSTERFISH / *Nematistius pectoralis*

TIPPET CLASS	WEIGHT	PLACE	DATE	ANGLER
6 lb	2.12 kg (4 lb 11 oz)	Buena Vista, Baja, Mexico	Nov. 26, 1976	Denton Hill
10 lb	4.39 kg (9 lb 11 oz)	Buena Vista, Baja, Mexico	Nov. 27, 1975	Denton Hill
12 lb	Vacant—No Minimum Weight			
15 lb	11.56 kg (25 lb 8 oz)	Mulege, Baja Calif., Mexico	May 17, 1974	Harold Winkle

RUNNER, rainbow / *Elagatis bipinnulata*

TIPPET CLASS	WEIGHT	PLACE	DATE	ANGLER
6 lb	2.72 kg (6 lb)	Bermuda	June 29, 1972	Lefty Kreh
10 lb	1.92 kg (4 lb 4 oz)	Tongue of Ocean, Bahamas	April 17, 1975	Harold Siebens
12 lb	Vacant—No Minimum Weight			
15 lb	2.79 kg (6 lb 2 oz)	Tongue of Ocean, Bahamas	Nov. 18, 1974	Harold Siebens

SAILFISH, Atlantic / *Istiophorus platypterus*

TIPPET CLASS	WEIGHT	PLACE	DATE	ANGLER
6 lb	Vacant—No Minimum Weight			
10 lb	22.45 kg (49 lb 8 oz)	Isla de Cozumel, Mexico	April 13, 1975	C. A. Peacock, Jr.
12 lb	25.17 kg (55 lb 8 oz)	Isla de Cozumel, Mexico	April 17, 1977	John Emery
15 lb	34.02 kg (75 lb)	La Guaira, Venezuela	Sept. 18, 1975	William W. Pate, Jr.

SAILFISH, Pacific / *Istiophorus platypterus*

TIPPET CLASS	WEIGHT	PLACE	DATE	ANGLER
6 lb	Vacant—No Minimum Weight			
10 lb	46.60 kg (102 lb 12 oz)	Costa Rica	Aug. 11, 1973	Flip Pallot
12 lb	61.68 kg (136 lb)	Piñas Bay, Panama	June 25, 1965	Stu Apte
15 lb	52.16 kg (115 lb)	El Coco, Costa Rica	July 25, 1967	Gil Drake
Tie 10 lb	46.60 kg (102 lb 12 oz)	Costa Rica	July 14, 1976	Stu Apte

SEABASS, white / *Cynoscion nobilis*

TIPPET CLASS	WEIGHT	PLACE	DATE	ANGLER
6 lb	Vacant—No Minimum Weight			
10 lb	Vacant—No Minimum Weight			
12 lb	Vacant—No Minimum Weight			
15 lb	Vacant—No Minimum Weight			

SEATROUT, spotted / *Cynoscion nebulosus*

TIPPET CLASS	WEIGHT	PLACE	DATE	ANGLER
6 lb	3.96 kg (8 lb 12 oz)	Banana River, Florida, USA	Dec. 5, 1974	Dave Chermanski
10 lb	2.80 kg (6 lb 3 oz)	Sebastian Inlet, Florida, USA	Sept. 9, 1972	John Meyer
12 lb	4.08 kg (9 lb)	Jensen Beach, Florida, USA	Jan. 2, 1972	Elwood Colvin
15 lb	5.27 kg (11 lb 10 oz)	Jensen Beach, Florida, USA	March 31, 1971	Clarence Snook

SHARK, blue / *Prionace glauca*

TIPPET CLASS	WEIGHT	PLACE	DATE	ANGLER
6 lb	12.24 kg (27 lb)	Dana Point, California, USA	Sept. 24, 1975	Lawrence J. Summers
10 lb	Vacant—No Minimum Weight			
12 lb	Vacant—No Minimum Weight			
15 lb	43.09 kg (95 lb)	Dana Point, California, USA	Sept. 24, 1975	Bob Edgley

IGFA SALTWATER FLY ROD WORLD RECORDS

SHARK, hammerhead / *Sphyrna spp.*

TIPPET CLASS	WEIGHT	PLACE	DATE	ANGLER
6 lb	Vacant—No Minimum Weight			
10 lb	Vacant—No Minimum Weight			
12 lb	Vacant—No Minimum Weight			
15 lb	Vacant—No Minimum Weight			

SHARK, porbeagle / *Lamna nasus*

TIPPET CLASS	WEIGHT	PLACE	DATE	ANGLER
6 lb	Vacant—No Minimum Weight			
10 lb	Vacant—No Minimum Weight			
12 lb	Vacant—No Minimum Weight			
15 lb	Vacant—No Minimum Weight			

SHARK, shortfin mako / *Isurus oxyrinchus*

TIPPET CLASS	WEIGHT	PLACE	DATE	ANGLER
6 lb	Vacant—No Minimum Weight			
10 lb	Vacant—No Minimum Weight			
12 lb	Vacant—No Minimum Weight			
15 lb	Vacant—No Minimum Weight			

SHARK, thresher / *Alopias spp.*

TIPPET CLASS	WEIGHT	PLACE	DATE	ANGLER
6 lb	Vacant—No Minimum Weight			
10 lb	Vacant—No Minimum Weight			
12 lb	Vacant—No Minimum Weight			
15 lb	Vacant—No Minimum Weight			

SHARK, tiger / *Galeocerdo cuvieri*

TIPPET CLASS	WEIGHT	PLACE	DATE	ANGLER
6 lb	Vacant—No Minimum Weight			
10 lb	Vacant—No Minimum Weight			
12 lb	Vacant—No Minimum Weight			
15 lb	Vacant—No Minimum Weight			

SHARK, white / *Carcharodon carcharias*

TIPPET CLASS	WEIGHT	PLACE	DATE	ANGLER
6 lb	Vacant—No Minimum Weight			
10 lb	Vacant—No Minimum Weight			
12 lb	Vacant—No Minimum Weight			
15 lb	Vacant—No Minimum Weight			

SKIPJACK, black / *Euthynnus lineatus*

TIPPET CLASS	WEIGHT	PLACE	DATE	ANGLER
6 lb	Vacant—No Minimum Weight			
10 lb	Vacant—No Minimum Weight			
12 lb	Vacant—No Minimum Weight			
15 lb	Vacant—No Minimum Weight			

SNOOK / *Centropomus undecimalis*

TIPPET CLASS	WEIGHT	PLACE	DATE	ANGLER
6 lb	10.06 kg (22 lb 3 oz)	Sebastian River, Florida, USA	July 24, 1971	Dave Chermanski
10 lb	12.92 kg (28 lb 8 oz)	Stuart, Florida, USA	July 10, 1972	Martin Gottschalk
12 lb	Record being reviewed			
15 lb	11.56 kg (25 lb 8 oz)	Punta Gorda, Florida, USA	June 5, 1974	Leslie M. Ager

IGFA SALTWATER FLY ROD WORLD RECORDS

SPEARFISH / *Tetrapturus spp.*

TIPPET CLASS	WEIGHT	PLACE	DATE	ANGLER
6 lb	Vacant—No Minimum Weight			
10 lb	Vacant—No Minimum Weight			
12 lb	Vacant—No Minimum Weight			
15 lb	Vacant—No Minimum Weight			

SWORDFISH / *Xiphias gladius*

TIPPET CLASS	WEIGHT	PLACE	DATE	ANGLER
6 lb	Vacant—No Minimum Weight			
10 lb	Vacant—No Minimum Weight			
12 lb	Vacant—No Minimum Weight			
15 lb	Vacant—No Minimum Weight			

TANGUIGUE / *Scomberomorus commerson*

TIPPET CLASS	WEIGHT	PLACE	DATE	ANGLER
6 lb	Vacant—No Minimum Weight			
10 lb	15.87 kg (35 lb)	Carnarvon, Qld., Australia	April 15, 1972	Max Garth
12 lb	Vacant—No Minimum Weight			
15 lb	Vacant—No Minimum Weight			

TARPON / *Megalops atlantica*

TIPPET CLASS	WEIGHT	PLACE	DATE	ANGLER
6 lb	37.42 kg (82 lb 8 oz)	Flamingo, Florida, USA	June 25, 1977	Stu Apte
10 lb	47.62 kg (105 lb)	Islamorada, Florida, USA	May 19, 1975	William W. Pate, Jr.
12 lb	69.85 kg (154 lb)	Key West, Florida, USA	April 10, 1971	Stu Apte
15 lb	81.64 kg (180 lb)	Homosassa Springs, Florida, USA	May 23, 1978	Joe Robinson

TAUTOG / *Tautoga onitis*

TIPPET CLASS	WEIGHT	PLACE	DATE	ANGLER
6 lb	Vacant—No Minimum Weight			
10 lb	Vacant—No Minimum Weight			
12 lb	0.79 kg (1 lb 12 oz)	Warwick, Rhode Island, USA	May 19, 1972	Dr. A. Chatowsky
15 lb	2.55 kg (5 lb 10 oz)	Lloyds Neck, New York, USA	June 22, 1978	Albert Apmann

TREVALLY, giant / *Caranx sexfasciatus*

TIPPET CLASS	WEIGHT	PLACE	DATE	ANGLER
6 lb	Vacant—No Minimum Weight			
10 lb	Vacant—No Minimum Weight			
12 lb	Vacant—No Minimum Weight			
15 lb	Vacant—No Minimum Weight			

TUNA, bigeye (Atlantic) / *Thunnus obesus*

TIPPET CLASS	WEIGHT	PLACE	DATE	ANGLER
6 lb	Vacant—No Minimum Weight			
10 lb	Vacant—No Minimum Weight			
12 lb	Vacant—No Minimum Weight			
15 lb	Vacant—No Minimum Weight			

TUNA, bigeye (Pacific) / *Thunnus obesus*

TIPPET CLASS	WEIGHT	PLACE	DATE	ANGLER
6 lb	Vacant—No Minimum Weight			
10 lb	Vacant—No Minimum Weight			
12 lb	Vacant—No Minimum Weight			
15 lb	Vacant—No Minimum Weight			

IGFA SALTWATER FLY ROD WORLD RECORDS

TUNA, blackfin / *Thunnus atlanticus*

TIPPET CLASS	WEIGHT	PLACE	DATE	ANGLER
6 lb	Vacant—No Minimum Weight			
10 lb	10.88 kg (24 lb)	Bermuda	June 30, 1973	Jim López
12 lb	12.70 kg (28 lb)	Bermuda	July 6, 1972	Jim López
15 lb	15.50 kg (34 lb 3 oz)	Islamorada, Florida, USA	Dec. 17, 1977	Rip Cunningham

TUNA, bluefin / *Thunnus thynnus*

TIPPET CLASS	WEIGHT	PLACE	DATE	ANGLER
6 lb	Vacant—No Minimum Weight			
10 lb	Vacant—No Minimum Weight			
12 lb	Vacant—No Minimum Weight			
15 lb	4.30 kg (9 lb 8 oz)	Montauk, New York, USA	Aug. 14, 1966	Stephen Sloan

TUNA, dogtooth / *Gymnosarda unicolor*

TIPPET CLASS	WEIGHT	PLACE	DATE	ANGLER
6 lb	Vacant—No Minimum Weight			
10 lb	Vacant—No Minimum Weight			
12 lb	Vacant—No Minimum Weight			
15 lb	Vacant—No Minimum Weight			

TUNA, longtail / *Thunnus tonggol*

TIPPET CLASS	WEIGHT	PLACE	DATE	ANGLER
6 lb	Vacant—No Minimum Weight			
10 lb	9.07 kg (20 lb)	Carnarvon, Qld., Australia	Oct. 1, 1972	Max Garth
12 lb	7.93 kg (17 lb 8 oz)	Carnarvon, Qld., Australia	Sept. 30, 1972	Max Garth
15 lb	Vacant—No Minimum Weight			

TUNA, skipjack / *Katsuwonus pelamis*

TIPPET CLASS	WEIGHT	PLACE	DATE	ANGLER
6 lb	6.69 kg (14 lb 12 oz)	Santa Barbara, California, USA	Dec. 7, 1975	Patt Wardlaw
10 lb	Vacant—No Minimum Weight			
12 lb	6.80 kg (15 lb)	Santa Barbara, California, USA	Dec. 15, 1975	Patt Wardlaw
15 lb	4.96 kg (10 lb 15 oz)	Santa Barbara, California, USA	Dec. 7, 1975	Patt Wardlaw

TUNA, southern bluefin / *Thunnus maccoyii*

TIPPET CLASS	WEIGHT	PLACE	DATE	ANGLER
6 lb	Vacant—No Minimum Weight			
10 lb	Vacant—No Minimum Weight			
12 lb	Vacant—No Minimum Weight			
15 lb	Vacant—No Minimum Weight			

TUNA, yellowfin / *Thunnus albacares*

TIPPET CLASS	WEIGHT	PLACE	DATE	ANGLER
6 lb	Vacant—No Minimum Weight			
10 lb	7.25 kg (16 lb)	Los Coronados, Mexico	Oct. 11, 1967	Harry Bonner
12 lb	30.61 kg (67 lb 8 oz)	Bermuda	July 7, 1973	Jim López
15 lb	36.74 kg (81 lb)	Bermuda	July 10, 1971	Jim López

TUNNY, little / *Euthynnus alletteratus*

TIPPET CLASS	WEIGHT	PLACE	DATE	ANGLER
6 lb	8.27 kg (18 lb 4 oz)	Cape Canaveral, Florida, USA	July 24, 1972	Dave Chermanski
10 lb	Vacant—No Minimum Weight			
12 lb	5.89 kg (13 lb)	Long Branch, New Jersey, USA	Oct. 12, 1967	Jas. Hawthorn
15 lb	8.07 kg (17 lb 13 oz)	Canaveral, Florida, USA	July 17, 1971	Skip MacKay

WAHOO / *Acanthocybium solandri*

TIPPET CLASS	WEIGHT	PLACE	DATE	ANGLER
6 lb	7.99 kg (17 lb 10 oz)	Isla Coiba, Panama	Oct. 12, 1975	Stu Apte
10 lb	7.48 kg (16 lb 8 oz)	Isla Coiba, Panama	Oct. 12, 1975	Stu Apte
12 lb	6.91 kg (15 lb 4 oz)	Isla Coiba, Panama	Oct. 12, 1975	Stu Apte
15 lb	9.12 kg (20 lb 2 oz)	Isla Coiba, Panama	Oct. 12, 1975	Stu Apte

WEAKFISH / *Cynoscion regalis*

TIPPET CLASS	WEIGHT	PLACE	DATE	ANGLER
6 lb	4.05 kg (8 lb 15 oz)	Delaware Bay, New Jersey, USA	May 19, 1975	Ronald D. Conner
10 lb	3.26 kg (7 lb 3 oz)	Barnegat Inlet, New Jesey, USA	Aug. 10, 1975	Robert E. Priel
12 lb	4.76 kg (10 lb 8 oz)	Lloyds Neck, New York, USA	June 18, 1978	Ralph Votta
15 lb	1.92 kg (4 lb 4 oz)	Delaware Bay, New Jersey, USA	May 18, 1973	Richard C. Mitchell
Tie 15 lb	1.98 kg (4 lb 6 oz)	Brandywine Shoal, N.J., USA	June 28, 1973	Ronald D. Conner

YELLOWTAIL, California / *Seriola lalandi dorsalis*

TIPPET CLASS	WEIGHT	PLACE	DATE	ANGLER
6 lb	6.88 kg (15 lb 3 oz)	Loreto, Baja Calif., Mexico	Jan. 30, 1973	Harry Kime
10 lb	14.74 kg (32 lb 8 oz)	Loreto, Baja Calif., Mexico	March 14, 1972	Christy Blough
12 lb	13.26 kg (29 lb 4 oz)	Loreto, Baja Calif., Mexico	March 7, 1973	Norman Le Gore
15 lb	14.51 kg (32 lb)	Loreto, Baja Calif., Mexico	March 27, 1973	Timothy Jewell

YELLOWTAIL, southern / *Seriola lalandi lalandi*

TIPPET CLASS	WEIGHT	PLACE	DATE	ANGLER
6 lb	Vacant—No Minimum Weight			
10 lb	Vacant—No Minimum Weight			
12 lb	Vacant—No Minimum Weight			
15 lb	Vacant—No Minimum Weight			

International Angling Rules (Excerpts from official *Rule Book*)

The following angling rules have been formulated by the International Game Fish Association to promote ethical and sporting angling practices, to establish uniform regulations for the compilation of world game fish records, and to provide basic angling guidelines for use in fishing tournaments and any other group angling activities.

The word "angling" is defined as catching or attempting to catch fish with a rod, reel, line, and hook as outlined in the international angling rules. There are some aspects of angling that cannot be controlled through rulemaking, however. Angling regulations cannot insure an outstanding performance from each fish and world records cannot indicate the amount of difficulty in catching the fish. Captures in which the fish has not fought or has not had a chance to fight do not reflect credit on the fisherman, and only the angler can properly evaluate the degree of achievement in establishing the record.

Only fish caught in accordance with IGFA international angling rules, and within the intent of these rules, will be considered for world records.

Editor's note: Following are the rules for freshwater and saltwater fishing (combined). There is a separate set of rules for saltwater fly rod fishing, which is available from the IGFA, 3000 East Las Olas Blvd., Ft. Lauderdale, FL 33316

RULES FOR FISHING IN FRESH AND SALT WATER

Equipment Regulations

A. LINE
1. Monofilament, multifilament, and lead core multifilament lines may be used.
2. Wire lines are prohibited.

For line classes, see "World Record Requirements" in Rule Book.

B. DOUBLE LINE
The use of a double line is not required. If one is used, it must meet the following specifications:

1. A double line must consist of the actual line used to catch the fish.
2. The double line on all weights of tackle up to and including the 24 kg (50 lb) line class shall be limited to 15 feet (4.6 meters). For heavier tackle, the line shall not be doubled for more than 30 feet (9.2 meters). Double lines are measured from the start of the knot, braid, roll or splice making the double, to the farthermost end of the knot, splice, snap, swivel, or other device used for securing the trace, leader, lure or hook to the double line.
3. The double line must not be lengthened beyond the stated limitations to compensate for a leader shorter than the maximum length allowed.
4. The double line must be connected to the leader, if one is used, with a knot, splice, snap, swivel, or other device.

C. LEADER
The use of a leader is not required. If one is used, it must meet the following specifications:

1. The leader on all weights of tackle up to and including the 24 kg (50 lb) line class shall be limited to 15 feet (4.6 meters). For heavier tackle the leader shall not exceed 30 feet (9.2 meters). There are no minimum lengths. The length of the leader is the overall length including any lure, hook arrangement or other device.
2. The leader may not be lengthened beyond the stated limitations to compensate for a double line shorter than the maximum length allowed.
3. The leader must be connected to the line with a knot, splice, snap, swivel, or other device.
4. There are no regulations regarding the material or strength of the leader.

D. ROD
1. Rods must comply with sporting ethics and customs. Considerable latitude is allowed in the choice of a rod, but rods giving the angler an unfair advantage will be disqualified. This rule is intended to eliminate the use of unconventional rods.

2. The rod tip must be a minimum of 50 inches (130 cm) in length. The rod butt cannot exceed 27 inches (70 cm) in length. These measurements must be made from a point directly beneath the center of the reel. A curved butt is measured in a straight line. (The above measurements do not apply to surf casting rods.)

E. REEL
1. Reels must comply with sporting ethics and customs.
2. Power driven reels of any kind are prohibited. This includes motor, hydraulic, or electrically driven reels, and any device which gives the angler an unfair advantage.
3. Ratchet handle reels are prohibited.
4. Reels designed to be cranked with both hands at the same time are prohibited.

F. HOOKS FOR BAIT FISHING
1. For live or dead bait fishing no more than two single hooks may be used. Both must be firmly imbedded in or securely attached to the bait. The eyes of the hooks must be no less than a hook's length (the length of the largest hook used) apart and no more than 18 inches (45 cm) apart. The only exception is that the point of one hook may be passed through the eye of the other hook.
2. The use of a dangling or swinging hook is prohibited.
3. A two-hook rig for bottom fishing is acceptable if it consists of two single hooks on separate leaders or drops. Both hooks must be imbedded in the respective baits and separated sufficiently so that a fish caught on one hook cannot be foul-hooked by the other.
4. All record applications made for fish caught on two-hook tackle must be accompanied by a photograph or sketch of the hook arrangement.

G. HOOKS AND LURES
1. When using an artificial lure with a skirt or trailing material, no more than two single hooks may be attached to the line, leader, or trace. The hooks need not be attached separately. The eyes of the hooks must be no less than an overall hook's length (the overall length of the largest hook used) apart and no further than 12 inches (30 cm) apart. The only exception is that the point of one hook may be passed through the eye of the other hook. The trailing hook may not extend more than a hook's length beyond the skirt of the lure. A photograph or sketch showing the hook arrangement must accompany a record application.

2. Gang hooks are permitted when attached to plugs and other artificial lures that are specifically designed for this use. Gang hooks shall be limited to a maximum of two hooks (either single, double, or treble, or a combination of any two). These hooks must be permanently and directly attached to the lure and must be free swinging. A photograph or sketch of the plug or lure must be submitted with record applications. If not satisfactory, the plug or lure itself may be requested.

H. OTHER EQUIPMENT

1. *Fighting chairs* may not have any mechanically propelled devices which aid the angler in fighting a fish.

2. *Gimbals* must be free swinging, which includes gimbals that swing in a vertical plane only. Any gimbal that allows the angler to reduce strain or to rest while fighting the fish is prohibited.

3. *Gaffs and nets* used to boat or land a fish must not exceed 8 feet (2.5 meters) in overall length. (When fishing from a bridge, pier, or other high platform or structure, this length limitation does not apply.) In using a flying or detachable gaff, the rope may not exceed 30 feet (9.2 meters). The gaff rope must be measured from the point where it is secured to the detachable head to the other end. Only the effective length will be considered. If a fixed head gaff is used, the same limitations shall apply and the gaff rope shall be measured from the same location on the gaff hook. Only a single hook is permitted on any gaff. Harpoon or lance attachments are prohibited.

4. *Floats* are prohibited with the exception of any small flotation device attached to the line or leader for the sole purpose of regulating the depth of the bait. The flotation device must not in any way hamper the fighting ability of the fish.

5. *Entangling devices*, either with or without a hook, are prohibited and may not be used for any purpose including baiting, hooking, fighting, or landing the fish.

6. *Outriggers, downriggers, and kites* are permitted to be used provided that the actual fishing line is attached to the snap or other release device, either directly or with some other material. The leader or double line may not be connected to the release mechanism either directly or with the use of a connecting device.

7. *A safety line* may be attached to the rod provided that it does not in any way assist the angler in fighting the fish.

Angling Regulations

1. From the time that a fish strikes or takes a bait or lure, the angler must hook, fight, and bring the fish to gaff without the aid of any other person, except as provided in these regulations.

2. If a rod holder is used and a fish strikes or takes the bait or lure, the angler must remove the rod from the holder as quickly as possible. The intent of this rule is that the angler shall strike and hook the fish.

3. In the event of a multiple strike on separate lines being fished by a single angler, only the first fish fought by the angler will be considered for a world record.

4. A harness may be attached to the reel or rod, but not to the fighting chair. The harness may be replaced or adjusted by a person other than the angler.

5. Use of rod belt or waist gimbal is permitted.

6. When angling from a boat, once the leader is brought within the grasp of the mate, or the end of the leader is wound to the rod tip, more than one person is permitted to hold the leader.

7. One or more gaffers may be used in addition to persons holding the leader. The gaff handle must be in hand when the fish is gaffed.

The following acts will disqualify a catch:

1. Failure to comply with equipment or angling regulations.

2. The act of persons other than the angler in touching any part of the rod, reel, or line (including the double line) either bodily or with any device during the playing of the fish, or in giving any aid other than that allowed in the rules and regulations. If an obstacle to the passage of the line through the rod guides has to be removed from the line, then the obstacle (whether chum, floatline, rubber band, or other material) shall be held and cut free. Under no circumstances should the line be held or touched by anyone other than the angler during this process.

3. Resting the rod in a rod holder, on the gunwale of the boat, or on any other object while playing the fish.

4. Handlining or using a handline or rope attached in any manner to the angler's line or leader for the purpose of holding or lifting the fish.

5. Shooting, harpooning, or lancing the fish being played (including sharks) during any stage of the catch.

6. Chumming with or using as bait the flesh, blood, skin, or any part of mammals other than hair or pork rind used in lures designed for trolling or casting.

7. Beaching or driving into shallow water any fish hooked from a boat in order to deprive the fish of its normal ability to swim.

8. Changing the rod or reel while the fish is being played.

9. Splicing, removing, or adding to the line while the fish is being played.

10. Intentionally foul-hooking a fish.

11. Catching a fish in a manner that the double line never leaves the rod tip.

The following situations will disqualify a catch:

1. When a rod breaks in a manner that reduces the length of the tip below minimum dimensions or severely impairs its angling characteristics.

2. Mutilations to the fish caused by sharks, other fish, mammals, or propellers that remove or penetrate the flesh. (Injuries caused by leader or line, scratches, old healed scars or regeneration deformities are not considered to be disqualifying injuries.) Any mutilation on the fish must be fully explained in a separate report accompanying the record application.

3. When a fish is hooked on more than one line.

Regulations Governing Record Catches

GENERAL INFORMATION

1. Protested applications or disputed existing records will be referred to the IGFA Executive Committee for review. Its decisions will be final. IGFA reserves the sole right to either grant or reject any record applications. All IGFA decisions will be based upon the intent of the regulations.

2. In case of a disputed species identification, photographs of the catch will be submitted to two qualified ichthyologists for their decisions. When a question of identification arises, the angler will be notified and given ample opportunity to submit further evidence of identification.

3. In some instances, an IGFA officer or member of the International Committee or a deputy from a local IGFA member club may be asked to recheck information supplied on a claim. Such action is not to be regarded as doubt of the formal affidavit, but rather as evidence of the extreme care with which IGFA investigates and maintains its records.

WITNESSES TO CATCH

Saltwater fly rod catches must be witnessed to qualify for a world record. It is important that the witness can attest to compliance of the international fly fishing rules and regulations.

On all other record claims, witnesses to the catch are highly desirable if at all possible.

WEIGHTS NEEDED TO DEFEAT OR TIE EXISTING RECORDS

1. To replace a record for a fish weighing less than 20 pounds (9.07 kg), the replacement must weigh at least 4 ounces (113.39 gm) more than the existing record.

2. To replace a record for a fish weighing 20 pounds (9.07 kg) up to 100 pounds (45.35 kg), the replacement must weigh at least 8 ounces (226.7 gm) more than the existing record.

3. To replace a record for a fish weighing 100 pounds (45.35 kg) or more, the replacement must weigh at least one half of 1 percent (.005%) more than the existing record weight. Examples: At 200 pounds (90.71 kg) the additional weight required would be 1 pound (.45 kg); at 400 pounds (181.43 kg) the additional weight required would be 2 pounds (.90 kg).

4. Any catch which matches the weight of an existing record or exceeds the weight by less than the amount required to defeat the record will be considered a tie. In case of a tie claim involving more than two catches, weight must be compared with the original record (first fish to be caught). Nothing weighing less than the original record will be considered.

5. Estimated weights will not be accepted. (See *Weighing Requirements.*)

TIME LIMIT ON CLAIMS

Claims for record fish caught in U.S. continental waters must be received by IGFA within 60 days of the date of catch. Claims for record fish caught in other waters must be received by IGFA within three months of the date of catch.

If an incomplete record claim is submitted, it must be accompanied by an explanation of why certain portions are incomplete. An incomplete claim will be considered for a record if the following conditions are met:

1. The incomplete claim with explanations of why portions are incomplete must be received by IGFA within the time limits specified above.

2. Missing data must be due to circumstances beyond the control of the angler making the record claim.

3. All missing data must be supplied within a period of time considered to be reasonable in view of the particular circumstances.

Final decisions on incomplete claims will be made by IGFA's Executive Committee.

WEIGHING REQUIREMENTS FOR RECORD FISH

The fish must be weighed by an official weighmaster (if one is available) or by an IGFA official or by a recognized local person familiar with the scale. Disinterested witnesses to the weight should be used whenever possible.

The weight of the sling, platform, or rope (if one is used to secure the fish on the scales) must be determined and deducted from the total weight.

At the time of weighing, the actual tackle used by the angler to catch the fish must be exhibited to the weighmaster and weight witness.

No estimated weights will be accepted. Fish weighed only at sea or on other bodies of water will not be accepted.

All record fish should be weighed on scales that have been checked and certified for accuracy by government agencies or other qualified and accredited organizations. All scales must be regularly checked for accuracy and certified in accordance with applicable government regulations at least once every twelve months.

If at the time of weighing the fish, the scale has not been properly certified within twelve months, it should be checked and certified for accuracy as quickly as possible, and an official report stating the findings of the inspection prior to any adjustments of the scale must be included with the record application.

If there is no official government inspector or accredited commercial scales representative available in the area where the fish is weighed, the scales must be checked by weighing objects of recognized and proven weight. Objects weighed must be at least equal to the weight of the fish. Substantiation of the correct weight of these objects must be submitted to IGFA along with the names and complete addresses of accredited witnesses to the entire procedure.

IGFA reserves the right to have any scale recertified for accuracy if there are any indications that the scale might not have weighed correctly.

SPECIES IDENTIFICATION

If there is the slightest doubt that the fish cannot be properly identified from the photographs and other data submitted, the fish should be examined by a qualified scientist or retained in a preserved or frozen condition until a qualified authority can verify the species or until notified by IGFA that the fish need no longer be retained.

Preparation of Record Claims

To apply for a world record, the angler must submit a completed IGFA application form, the mandatory length of line or fly leader used to catch the fish, and acceptable photographs of the fish, the tackle used to catch the fish, the scale used to weigh the fish, and the angler with the fish.

APPLICATION FORM

The official IGFA world record application form must be used for record claims. This form may be reproduced as long as all items are included.

The angler must fill in the application personally.

IGFA also recommends that the angler personally mail the application, line sample or fly leader, and photographs.

When making any record claim, the angler must indicate the specified strength of the line or tippet used to catch the fish. In the cases of line class and tippet class records, this will place the claim in an IGFA line or tippet class category. If the line or tippet overtests its particular category, the application will be considered in the next highest category; if it undertests into a lower line or tippet class category, the application will not be considered for the lower line class. The heaviest line strength permissible for both freshwater and saltwater records is 60 kg (130 lb) class. The heaviest tippet strength permissible is 7 kg (15 lb). If the line or tippet overtests these maximum strengths, the claim will be disallowed.

Extreme care should be exercised in measuring the fish as the measurements are often important for weight verification and scientific studies. See the measurement diagram on the record application to be sure you have measured correctly.

The angler is responsible for seeing that the necessary signatures and correct addresses of the boat captain, weighmaster, and witnesses are on the application. If an IGFA officer or representative, or an officer or member of an IGFA club is available, he or she should be asked to witness the claim. The name of a boatman, guide, or weighmaster repeated as witness is not acceptable.

The angler must appear in person to have his application notarized. In territories where notarization is not possible or customary, the signature of a government commissioner or resident, a member of an embassy, legation or consular staff, or an IGFA officer or International Committee member may replace notarization.

Any deliberate falsification of an application will disqualify the applicant for any future IGFA world record, and any existing records will be nullified.

LINE OR TIPPET SAMPLE

All applications for saltwater fly rod records must be accompanied by the lure, the entire tippet, and the leader along with one inch of the fly line beyond the attachment to the leader. These components must be intact and connected. The lure will be returned to the angler on request.

All applications for freshwater and saltwater all-tackle records must be accompanied by 80 feet (25 meters), including the entire double, of the actual line used in making the catch.

All applications for saltwater records in line classes from 3 kg (6 lb) through 15 kg (30 lb) must be accompanied by 50 feet (15 meters), including the entire double, of the actual line used in making the catch.

All applications for saltwater records in line classes from 24 kg (50 lb) through 60 kg (130 lb) must be accompanied by 80 feet (25 meters), including the entire double, of the actual line used in making the catch.

Backing: For all-tackle and line class records, a catch made using two lines of different strengths that are spliced, tied, or joined together shall be classified under the heavier of the two lines. Samples of both lines must be submitted. Backing not connected to the fishing line is acceptable. No sample of such backing need be submitted.

Each line sample must be in one piece. It must be submitted in a manner that it can be easily unwound without damage to the line. A recommended method is to take a rectangular piece of stiff cardboard and cut notches in two opposite ends. Secure one end of the line to the cardboard and wind the line around the cardboard through the notched areas. Secure the other end, and write your name and the specified strength of the line on the cardboard. Do not submit the line in a hank.

PHOTOGRAPHS

Photographs showing the full length of the fish, the rod and reel used to make the catch, and the scale used to weigh the fish must accompany each record application. A photograph of the angler with the fish is also required.

So that there can be no question of species identification, the clearest possible photos should be submitted. This is especially important in the cases of marlin, bass, salmon, trout, shark, tuna and other fishes that may be confused with similar species. Shark applications should also include a photograph of the shark's head and the front teeth.

Photographs should be taken of the fish in a hanging position and also lying on a flat surface on its side. In both types of photographs no part of the fish should be obscured.

When hanging, the fish should be broadside to the camera with the fins fully extended and with the tip of the jaw and sword or spear clearly shown. Do not hold the tip of any fin. Do not stand in front of the fish. Do not hold the fish in your hands. A sky background for the fish is most desirable. Backgrounds cluttered with objects and people many times complicate identification and detract from the photograph.

When photographing a fish lying on its side, the surface beneath the fish should be smooth and a ruler or marked tape placed beside the fish if possible. Photographs from various angles are most helpful.

An additional photograph of the fish on the scale with actual weight visible helps to expedite the application.

Photos taken by daylight are highly recommended if at all possible.

Note: Now that IGFA has a bimonthly newsletter to keep anglers up to date on world record catches, it is more important than ever that we have clear, publishable photographs of the fish and the angler. If you have action shots of the catch, we would like to see them also.

Editor's note: This is a miniature facsimile of the official application, which should be obtained from IGFA.

Field Care and Filleting of Fish

What you do with keeper fish during the first couple of hours after catching them will largely determine how palatable they will be once they reach the table. It hardly makes sense to spend hard-earned money and precious free time to catch fish and then to let the fish spoil through neglect.

If you're fishing from a boat, don't just toss the fish on the floor or deck to spoil in the sun. Be sure to have a fish box or ice chest aboard, and keep it well stocked with ice. Ice cubes or ice flakes are better than block ice, for they allow the fish to be surrounded by ice.

If the boat is a rowboat or other small craft, bring along a fish stringer, preferably one with a series of safety-pin-type clips. A stringer lets you keep the fish in the water and alive until you reach shore and head home. However, if the fish has been hooked deeply or is in otherwise poor condition, don't put him on the stringer. Kill him instantly, and try to keep him as cool as possible. A fish that is killed as soon as it is caught will be in better condition than one that dies slowly.

If you are fishing in a stream, keep the fish you catch in a creel, not in a pocket of a fishing vest or jacket. Best creels are those made of wicker, which permits air to circulate freely inside. To keep the fish as fresh as possible, line the creel with moss, clean green leaves, or newspapers, and keep the lining at least damp by immersing the creel in the water periodically.

Whichever method you use to keep fish fresh in the field, be sure to clean them as soon as possible after they are caught—preferably at once. If the entrails are left in a dead fish for any length of time, chances are they will spoil the meat.

It takes only half a minute or so to efficiently gut most any fish, if you use the following method:

Take a sharp knife, and insert it in the anal opening on the underside of the fish. Slit the skin forward from there to the point of the V-shaped area where the forward part of the belly is attached to the gills. Put your finger into the gills and around that V-shaped area, and pull sharply to the rear. You will thus remove the gills and all or most of the entrails. Then, with the fish upside down, put your thumb into the body cavity at the anal opening, and press the thumbnail up against the backbone. Keeping the nail tight against the bone, run your thumb forward to the head, thereby removing the dark blood from the sac along the backbone.

That completes the cleaning process—unless you want to remove the fins. This is easily done with the knife but is even easier with a small pair of wire clippers or scissors.

One more tip. More good fish meat is probably ruined during the drive home than during any other point in its trip from the water to the plate. Take the time to ice the fish properly for the drive home. Here's how:

Don't pack the fish in direct contact with the ice. The ice is sure to melt, and the fish, lying in the water, might well deteriorate, becoming soft and mushy. It's far better to put the fish in plastic bags, seal the bags so that they are watertight, and then pack the bags in the ice. The fish will stay cool—and dry—until you get home.

When you get the fish home, scale or skin them. If they are fresh-water fish, wash them thoroughly, inside and out, in cool tap water. If they are salt-water fish, prepare a heavy brine solution, and brush them thoroughly (a pastry-type brush works well) with the brine until they are clean.

Separate the fish into lots, each of which will make a meal for yourself or your family, and wrap each lot in good freezer paper, sealing tightly to prevent freezer burn. Freeze the fish as quickly as possible.

Some fishermen prefer not to field dress their fish, but to fillet and skin them. This method, which appears difficult but is actually quite simple, has a number of advantages. First, gutting the fish is not necessary since entrails are left intact and never touched with a knife. Second, messy scaling is also an eliminated step because the fillet is skinned and the skin discarded, scales and all. Finally, and perhaps most important, the fillets are literally bone free.

Filleting fish is also a good idea for fishermen on extended trips, where sizable quantities of fish are to be packed out or transported home. Head, entrails, fins, and skin are left behind and only clean and meaty fillets are brought home.

The accompanying photographs show how to quickly and easily fillet a fish from start to finish.

Too many fish in the pickerel family are being wasted because anglers do not know how to cope with the Y-bones. *Bone-free* fillets of pickerel, pike and muskellunge are delicious. Give it a try!

To bake the fish whole, first, scale the fish; then follow steps 1 through 4, but leave fillets *attached* to skin. Then skewer or sew skin together to form a pocket for stuffing.

Pan frying or baking: No need to scale it, just wet scales and work scaleside down on dry newspapers. No slipping. Follow steps 1 through 4; then with thin, flexible knife, press blade flat against skin and with sawing motion, slide knife along freeing fillets from the skin. Your efforts should result in 4 bone-free fillets ready for the frying pan or for dusting with prepared baking mix before placing them in the oven.

The narrow strips along each side of the back can be rolled up pinwheel-fashion and held together with an hors d'oeuvre toothpick run through flatwise. If you like this system, strip the flank flesh and make pinwheels of all of it. The pinwheels come out with a handle for easy eating or dipping in sauces.

Caution: Cuts at (2) and (4) are only made down *to* the tough skin, not through it.

Notes on the Y-bone cuts (4): Until you have dressed a few, run the tip of an index finger along the fish to locate the line of the butts of the Y-bones. Ease the knife through the flesh on these cuts, slightly twisting the blade edge away from the bones. The knife is pushed through, as opposed to regular cutting action. It will follow the bone-line easily. If it catches a bone, back up, increase the angle and continue. The Y-bone strip and the back-bone will rip out in single strips if pinched between the thumb and index finger next to the skin to lift the head end from the skin. Grasp the lifted portion and rip out toward the tail.

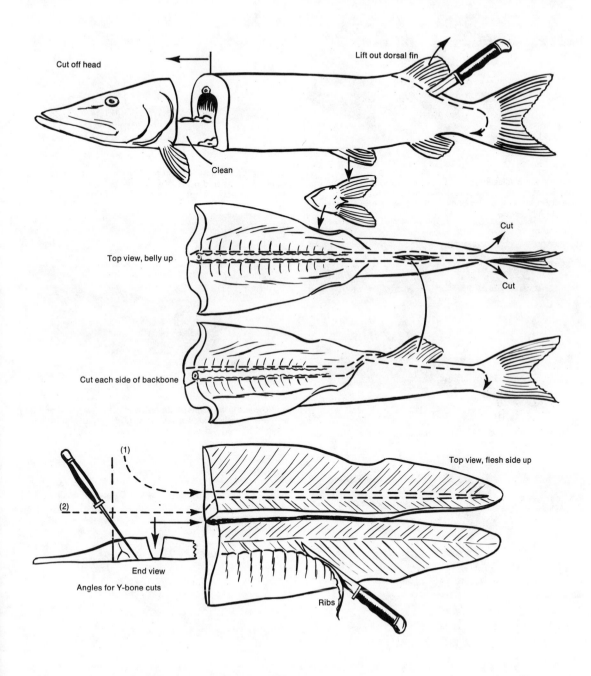

Cut off head

Lift out dorsal fin

Clean

Top view, belly up

Cut

Cut

Cut each side of backbone

(1)

(2)

End view

Angles for Y-bone cuts

Top view, flesh side up

Ribs

Courtesy Vermont Fish and Game Department

HOW TO FILLET A FISH

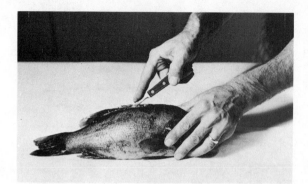

1. Using sharp fillet knife, hold fish upright and make a cut as close as possible to the dorsal fin. The cut should run lengthwise from base of tail to back of fish's head and as deep as backbone or spine.

2. Turn fish over and made an identical cut on the other side.

3. For purposes of illustration, fish here is held upright to show the two initial cuts.

4. Next lay the fish flat and make another cut as shown, diagonally from behind head down to just behind entrail sac, which holds stomach and other organs. Take care not to break sac.

5. Now work the knife blade down into the two cuts and begin to carefully slice fillet away from body. Hold knife blade flat against rib cage to avoid wasting meat.

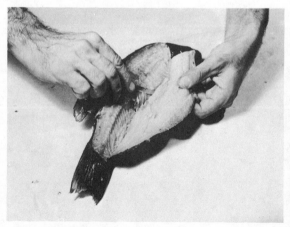

6. Still holding blade flat, slice through the underside skin and free fillet from the fish.

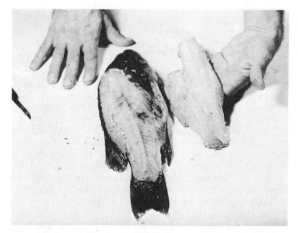

7. This is how the fillet should look when cut from the side of fish. Note fillet was cut as close as possible to the rib cage, keeping waste to a bare minimum. The entrail sac is also intact. There are no broken organs, digestive juices, nor blood to taint the fillet.

8. Turn the fish over and remove fillet from the other side of the fish exactly the same way.

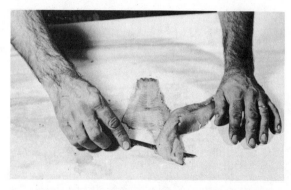

10. With a sawing motion, holding blade flat and down against skin, cut meat free of skin. The fillets and skins will separate surprisingly easy.

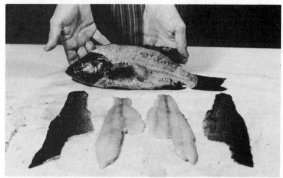

11. Here's what you should now have: The fish with entrail sac and skeleton, along with skins, ready for the trash can. In center of the photograph are the two neatly cut fillets. Obviously, with this method, there is no need to scale the fish.

9. Next step is skinning the fillets. Place them, flesh side up, flat on table. Work knife blade between meat and skin, holding skin down firmly with fingers. If skin is too slippery to be held effectively with fingers, try using tines of ordinary kitchen fork.

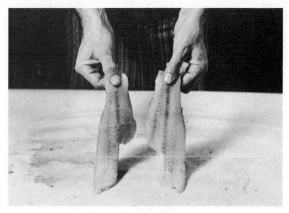

12. The finished product: two boneless smallmouth bass fillets ready for the pan. Note entire operation only slightly soiled table. With little practice, this filleting method takes less than five minutes per fish.

Water Temperature and Fish

There is no doubt left in anglers' minds of the importance of water temperature and its direct bearing on the activities of fish. Water temperature will tell you where fish gather and where they feed at various times of the year.

It is a scientifically proven fact that every species of fish has a preferred temperature zone or range and it will stay and generally feed in this zone. Smallmouth bass, for example, prefer water 65 to 70 degrees. During spring, this temperature range may be in shallow water, and in hot mid-summer weather this range may be in depths of 30 feet or more. In other words, locate the depth that reads 65 to 70 degrees and you're sure to find smallmouths.

Taking temperature readings of water is not difficult, whether you use a sophisticated electronic thermometer or an inexpensive water thermometer lowered into the water on a fishing line. One electronic thermometer on the market has a probe attached to a cable that is marked at regular intervals, so depth and temperature can be read simultaneously.

The inexpensive water thermometers can also do the job, and many also indicate depth by inserting a water pressure gauge in the thermometer tube. With these thermometers, allow at least 30 seconds to one minute for a reading. Also, the fishing line attached to it should be marked off in regular intervals, say 5 feet, so you can determine just how deep you are lowering the thermometer in the water.

The accompanying chart shows popular fresh and salt-water fish and their preferred temperature zones. Look up the fish you are seeking and the water temperature it prefers. Then begin taking temperature readings from the surface on down, at 5 foot intervals, until you locate the correct zone and depth. Concentrate your efforts at that depth and you'll soon discover how important this water temperature business is.

PREFERRED FEEDING TEMPERATURE ZONES FOR FRESH AND SALT WATER FISH

SPECIES	TEMPERATURE (F)	SPECIES	TEMPERATURE (F)
Albacore	60-65	Mackinaw	47
Amberjack	65	Muskellunge	60-75
Barracuda	65-70	Pike	60-75
Big Eye Jack	58	Permit	72
Billfish	57-81	Pollack	45
Bluefish	68	Rainbow Trout	50-68
Bluegill	65-75	Red Snapper	55-60
Blue Marlin	74	Sauger	58
Bonita	64	Shark	70+
Brook Trout	50-65	Skipjack	73
Brown Trout	50-65	Smallmouth Bass	60-70
Calico Bass	63-67	Smelt	50
Chain Pickerel	50-70	Splake	49
Channel Catfish	70-75	Sockeye (Washington)	52
Chinook Salmon	54	Steelhead	47
Cod	45	Striped Bass	55-65
Coho (Michigan)	52-54	Sturgeon (River)	66
Crappie	65-75	Tuna	73
Cutthroat Trout	47	Walleye	55-70
Dolphin	75	White Bass	65-75
Flounder	67	White Marlin	68
Kelp Bass	63-67	White Perch	55-70
Kokanee	50	White Sea Bass	65-70
Lake Trout	40-55	Yellowfin Tuna	72
Largemouth Bass	65-75	Yellow Perch	60-75
Landlocked Salmon	45-55	Yellow Tail	65

NOTE: Where temperature range is not indicated, use plus-and-minus two degrees to determine range.
Compiled by Vexilar, Inc.

PART *IV*/*Game Fish*

Species of Freshwater Fish

Atlantic Salmon

SCIENTIFIC NAME: *Salmo salar*

DESCRIPTION: Atlantic salmon are anadromous fish, meaning that they are spawned in freshwater rivers and then migrate to the ocean to spend most of their lives before returning to fresh water to spawn themselves. When fresh from the sea, Atlantics are steel blue on top and silvery on sides and belly, and have dark spots on their sides. As their stay in fresh water lengthens, the colors become darker, with the sides taking on a pinkish hue as spawning time arrives. Very young salmon are called parrs. Parrs have distinctive dark vertical bars called parr markings. Unlike Pacific salmon, all of which die after spawning, about 15 percent of Atlantic salmon survive the spawning act and return to sea.

RANGE: The highly prized Atlantic salmon once ranged from Delaware north through Quebec and the Canadian Maritime provinces to Greenland, and in the western Atlantic Ocean in the British Isles and parts of Scandinavia. But today, because of "progress"—meaning dams, pollution, and urban and suburban sprawl—the range of the Atlantic salmon in the U.S. is restricted to a handful of rivers in Maine, though efforts are being made to restore this fine gamefish to the Connecticut and other northeastern rivers.

HABITAT: In fresh water, the Atlantic salmon must have clean, flowing, cold water. In upstream spawning areas, shallow water over a gravel bottom is a must so that the fish can create "redds," or spawning beds. When in the ocean, these salmon range over vast areas but tend to concentrate on feeding grounds, which are only recently being discovered.

SIZE: Mature Atlantic salmon weigh from 9 to about 75 pounds, with the average being about 12. Their size depends on how many years they have spent in the sea, where their growth is fast. Salmon that return to fresh water after only one or two years at sea are called grilse and weigh up to about 6 or 8 pounds.

FOOD: These fish feed on small baitfish and such when in the ocean, but upon entering fresh water they stop feeding almost completely. And yet they can be induced to strike an artificial lure, particularly dry and wet flies.

Landlocked Salmon

COMMON NAMES: Landlocked salmon, landlock, ouananiche, Sebago salmon.

SCIENTIFIC NAME: *Salmo salar sebago*.

DESCRIPTION: The landlocked salmon is very similar in coloration and general appearance to the Atlantic salmon, of which the landlock is a subspecies. It is assumed that the subspecies descended from Atlantic salmon trapped in freshwater lakes thousands of years ago. As their name suggests, landlocks do not spawn in the sea. They either spawn in their home lakes or descend outlet streams to spawn.

RANGE: Landlocks range over much of New England (they are most numerous in Maine), in Quebec and other parts of eastern Canada, and north to Labrador. They have been introduced in New York and other eastern states and in South America.

HABITAT: The landlock survives best in deep, cold lakes that have a high oxygen content.

SIZE: Most landlocks average 2 to 3 pounds, but a six-pounder is not unusual, and an occasional 10-pounder is caught. Maximum weight is about 30 pounds.

FOOD: Landlocks feed mostly on small baitfish, particularly smelt.

Chinook Salmon

COMMON NAMES: Chinook salmon, king salmon, tyee salmon, blackmouth (immature stage).

SCIENTIFIC NAME: *Oncorhynchus tshawytscha*.

DESCRIPTION: The chinook, like all other Pacific salmon, is anadromous and seems to prefer the largest of Pacific Coast rivers for spawning. Chinooks have a dark-blue back that shades to silver on the sides and to white on the belly. Small dark spots, barely noticeable in fish fresh from the sea, mark the upper part of the body.

RANGE: Chinook salmon range from southern California to northern Alaska, being more numerous in the northern part of that area. They often travel enormous distances upriver to spawn; in the Yukon River, for example, chinooks have been seen 2,000 miles from the sea.

HABITAT: Chinooks prefer large, clean, cold rivers, but often enter small tributary streams to spawn in shallow water over gravel bottom.

SIZE: The chinook is the largest of the Pacific salmon, reaching weights of over 100 pounds. Rarely, however, does a sport fisherman catch one of more than 60 pounds, and the average size is about 18 pounds.

FOOD: Chinooks eat ocean baitfish (herring, sardines, candlefish, anchovies), freshwater baitfish, and fish roe.

Dog Salmon

COMMON NAMES: Dog salmon, chum salmon

SCIENTIFIC NAME: *Oncorhynchus keta*

DESCRIPTION: The dog salmon closely resembles the chinook salmon but has black-edged fins and lacks the chinook's dark spots on back, dorsal fin, and tail. During spawning, the male dog salmon often exhibits red or green blotches on its sides. The dog salmon is rarely taken by sport fishermen.

Dog Salmon

RANGE: One of the five species of Pacific salmon, the dog salmon is found from central California north to Alaska, but is far more numerous in Alaska than farther south. In their sea migrations, dog salmon travel as far as the Aleutians, Korea, and Japan.

HABITAT: Like all other salmon, the dog spawns in gravel in fresh-water rivers, usually spawning in the lower reaches of the parent streams but occasionally found far upstream.

SIZE: Dog salmon reach weights of 30 pounds or a bit more but average 6 to 18 pounds.

FOOD: The diet of dog salmon consists mainly of baitfish and crustaceans.

Sockeye Salmon

COMMON NAMES: Sockeye salmon, red salmon, blueback salmon.

SCIENTIFIC NAME: *Oncorhynchus nerka.*

Sockeye Salmon

DESCRIPTION: The sockeye is similar to the chinook but has a small number of gillrakers and has tiny spots along the back. When spawning, sockeye males turn a dark red, with the forward parts of the body being greenish. Females range in color from olive to light red. Sockeyes are more often caught by sport fishermen than are dog salmon, and they will take artificial flies and are good fighters.

RANGE: Sockeyes are found from California to Japan but few are encountered south of the Columbia River. A landlocked strain of the sockeye (see Kokanee Salmon), originally found from British Columbia south to Oregon and Idaho, is being stocked in freshwater lakes in various areas of the U.S.

HABITAT: Spawns over gravel in freshwater lakes, especially those fed by springs.

SIZE: Sockeyes reach a maximum weight of about 15 pounds, but the average is 4 to 9 pounds.

FOOD: Sockeyes feed mainly on crustaceans but also eat small baitfish.

Humpback Salmon

COMMON NAMES: Humpback salmon, pink salmon.

SCIENTIFIC NAME: *Oncorhynchus gorbuscha.*

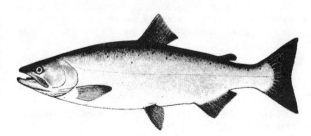

Humpback Salmon

DESCRIPTION: Similar to the other salmons but smaller, the humpback has small scales, and its caudal fin (tail) has large, oval, black spots. At maturity, or at spawning time, the males develop a large, distinctive hump on their backs. The humpback is among the most commercially valuable of the Pacific salmons and is becoming more popular with sport fishermen.

RANGE: The humpback is found from California to Alaska and as far away as Korea and Japan.

HABITAT: Spawns over gravel in freshwater rivers, usually near the sea.

SIZE: Smallest of the Pacific salmons, the humpback averages 3 to 6 pounds, attaining a maximum weight of about 10 pounds.

FOOD: Humpbacks subsist largely on a diet of crustaceans, baitfish, and squid.

Coho Salmon

COMMON NAMES: Coho salmon, silver salmon, hooknose

SCIENTIFIC NAME: *Oncorhynchus kisutch*

DESCRIPTION: The coho is generally silvery with a bluish back and has small dark spots along the upper part of the sides and tail. When the spawning urge takes hold, the males assume a reddish coloration, but when they enter fresh water they become almost black. The coho is highly prized as a sport fish, striking artificials readily and leaping breathtakingly when hooked.

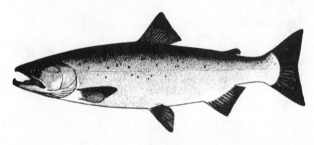

Coho Salmon

RANGE: The coho is found from California to Alaska and as far from the U.S. west coast as Japan. It has also been transplanted with unprecedented success to the Great Lakes, and at present attempts are being made to establish the coho in large freshwater lakes in many other parts of the U.S.

HABITAT: Spawns in gravel in freshwater rivers, either near the sea or far upstream.

SIZE: Cohoes reach weights approaching 30 pounds but average 6 to 12 pounds.

FOOD: A coho's diet is mainly baitfish, squid, crustaceans, and crab larvae.

Kokanee Salmon

COMMON NAMES: Kokanee, silver trout, blueback, little redfish, Kennerly's salmon, landlocked sockeye, redfish, silversides.

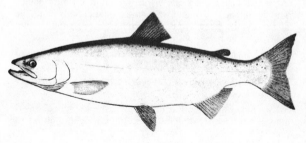

Kokanee Salmon

SCIENTIFIC NAME: *Oncorhynchus nerka kennerlyi*

DESCRIPTION: The kokanee is a landlocked strain of the anadromous sockeye salmon. Biologically identical with the true sockeye (though much smaller), the kokanee is silvery on sides and belly, but during spawning the males have reddish sides and the females slate-gray sides. Kokanees resemble some trout but differ from all trout in that they have more than 12 rays in the anal fin. The kokanee is the only Pacific salmon that matures in fresh water. Much prized by sport fishermen.

RANGE: The kokanee's original range extended from Idaho and Oregon north to Alaska, but it has been introduced in recent years in lakes as far south as New Mexico and as far east as New England.

HABITAT: Spawns in gravel, both in lakes and in tributary streams, and ranges throughout lakes at other times.

SIZE: Much smaller than the true sockeye salmon, the kokanee reaches a maximum weight of about 4 pounds. Average length varies greatly, depending upon water and food conditions. In some places they never exceed 10 inches, while in other places — California's Donner Lake, for example — their average length is over 18 inches.

FOOD: Kokanees feed almost exclusively on tiny forage, including minute crustaceans and other plankton.

Arctic Char

COMMON NAMES: Arctic char, arctic trout, alpine trout, Quebec red trout.

SCIENTIFIC NAME: *Salvelinus alpinus*

Arctic Char

DESCRIPTION: The arctic char is a far-north salmonid whose colors vary greatly. Sea-run char are quite silvery as they enter fresh-water rivers, but their fresh-water colors soon predominate, turning the char into a stunning fish, with sides ranging in color from pale to very bright orange and red. Char are usually spotted in red, pink, or cream and have the white-edged fins of the brook trout. But they lack the brook trout's vermiculations (wormlike markings) on the back. There are both anadromous and landlocked strains of arctic char.

RANGE: Arctic char are found in northern Canada, Alaska, Iceland, Greenland, Scandinavia, England, Ireland, Scotland, parts of Europe, and the Soviet Union.

Sunapee Trout

HABITAT: As its range indicates, the char thrives in very cold clean water, preferring fast shallow river water near the mouths of tributary streams. Relatively little is known about the nomadic movements of anadromous char, but they apparently spend the summer near the mouths of rivers, where they feed heavily before moving inland.

SIZE: Arctic char reach weights of nearly 30 pounds, but the average weight is 2 to 8 pounds.

FOOD: Char feed on a species of smelt called capelin and on sand eels, various baitfish, some crustaceans, and occasionally on insects.

Brook Trout

COMMON NAMES: Brook trout, speckled trout, speck, squaretail.

SCIENTIFIC NAME: *Salvelinus fontinalis*

DESCRIPTION: This best-loved of American native fish is not a true trout but actually a member of the char family. It is a beautiful fish, having a dark back with distinctive wormlike markings (vermiculations), sides marked with yellow spots and with red spots encircled in blue, a light-colored belly (bright orange during spawning), and pink or red lower fins edged in white. Wherever they are found, brook trout willingly take the offerings of fly, bait, and lure fishermen alike, a fact that has contributed to their decrease in many areas, though pollution has done far more to decimate populations of native brookies.

RANGE: Originally native only to northeastern North America from Georgia to the Arctic, the brook trout is now found in suitable waters throughout the U.S., Canada, South America, and Europe. Stocking maintains brook trout in many waters, but true native brookies are becoming rare.

HABITAT: Brook trout must have clean cold water, seldom being found in water warmer than 65°. They spawn both in lakes and in streams, preferring small spring-fed brooks.

SIZE: Though the rod-and-reel record for brook trout is 14½ pounds, fish half that size are a rarity today. In fact, a 5-pounder is an exceptional brook trout, and fish of that size are seldom found anywhere but in Labrador, northern Quebec and Manitoba, and Argentina. Native brook trout caught in streams average 6 to 12 inches in length.

FOOD: Brook trout eat worms, insects, crustaceans, and various kinds of baitfish.

Sunapee Trout

COMMON NAMES: Sunapee trout, Sunapee golden trout.

SCIENTIFIC NAME: *Salvelinus aureolus*

DESCRIPTION: This attractive fish—which may be a member of the char family or a distinct species of trout (there is some disagreement on the subject)—has a dark-bluish back that lacks the wormlike markings of the brook trout. Its sides have spots of pinking white, yellow, or red, and the yellowish or orange fins are white-edged.

RANGE: Originating in New Hampshire, principally in Sunapee Lake, the Sunapee trout is exceedingly rare, being found only in Sunapee Lake and in a few lakes and ponds in northern New England. The introduction of lake trout in Sunapee and other lakes has had a deteriorating effect on populations of Sunapee trout.

HABITAT: Little is known about the wanderings of this fish, but it is known that in Sunapee Lake these trout move into the shallows in spring and fall, while in summer they are found in the deepest parts of the lake—60 to 100 feet, where the water is quite cold.

SIZE: Many years ago 10 and 12-pound Sunapees were taken in the lake from which they derive their name, but today the fisherman is lucky to catch a 15-incher.

FOOD: Smelt makes up the majority of the Sunapee trout's diet.

Dolly Varden Trout

COMMON NAMES: Dolly Varden trout, Dolly, western char, bull trout, salmon trout, red-spotted trout.

SCIENTIFIC NAME: *Salvelinus malma*

DESCRIPTION: This member of the char family somewhat resembles the brook trout but lacks the brookie's wormlike back markings and is usually more slender. It has red and yellow side spots and the white-edged fins typical of all chars. In salt water the Dolly is quite silvery. The Dolly, said to have been named after a Charles Dickens character, is not so popular in some parts of its range as are the other trout species, possibly because it is not as strong a fighter.

RANGE: Occurring from northern California to Alaska and as far from the U.S. as Japan, the Dolly is found in both fresh water and, in the northern part of its range, in salt water.

HABITAT: Dolly Vardens spawn in gravel in streams. At other times of year, stream fish are likely to be found in places similar to those preferred by brook trout, such as under rocks, logs, and other debris and lying in deep holes. In lakes they are likely to be found near the bottom near reefs and dropoffs. They are seldom found near the surface.

SIZE: Dolly Vardens reach weights of upwards of 30 pounds. Average size is 8 to 18 inches in some places (usually streams), 3 to 6 pounds in other spots (usually lakes).

FOOD: These are primarily bottom feeders, though in streams they feed heavily on insects and may be taken on flies. Large fish feed heavily on baitfish, including the young of trout and salmon. It has been said that these trout will eat anything, and that may be true, considering that in some areas fishermen shoot ground squirrels, remove the legs and skin them, and use the legs for Dolly Varden bait!

Lake Trout

COMMON NAMES: Lake trout, togue, mackinaw, gray trout, salmon trout, forktail, laker.

SCIENTIFIC NAME: *Salvelinus namaycush.*

DESCRIPTION: More somberly hued than most other trout, the laker is usually a fairly uniform gray or blue-gray, though in some areas he is a bronze-green. He has irregular pale spots over head, back, and sides and also has the white-edged fins that mark him as a char.

RANGE: The lake trout is distributed throughout Canada and in the northern U.S., principally in New England, New York's Finger Lakes, the Great Lakes, and many large western lakes. Stockings have widened the laker's range considerably and have restored the species to portions of the Great Lakes where an incursion of lamprey eels decimated the laker populations in the 1950's and early 60's.

HABITAT: Lake trout are fish of deep, cold, clear lakes, though in the northern part of their range they are found in large streams. Lakers prefer water temperatures of about 45° and are rarely found where water rises above 70°. In the southern part of their range they are usually found only in lakes that have an adequate oxygen supply in the deeper spots.

SIZE: The lake trout is the largest of our trout species, reaching weights of more than 100 pounds. Their average size often depends on the size, depth, and water quality of a given lake.

FOOD: Though the young feed on insects and crustaceans, adult lake trout eat primarily fish such as smelt, small kokanee salmon, ciscoes, whitefish, and sculpin.

Rainbow Trout

COMMON NAMES: Rainbow trout, steelhead, Kamloops rainbow, Kamloops trout, redsides.

SCIENTIFIC NAME: *Salmo gairdneri.*

DESCRIPTION: This native American trout takes three basic forms: the nonmigratory rainbow, which lives its entire life in streams and/or lakes; the steelhead, which is spawned in freshwater rivers, migrates to the sea, and returns to the rivers to spawn (large rainbows that live in the Great Lakes and elsewhere in the Eastern U.S. also are called steelheads but are not true members of the steelhead clan); and the Kamloops rainbow, a large subspecies found mostly in interior British Columbia. Though the rainbow's colors vary greatly, depending upon where he is found, the fish generally has an olive or lighter-green back shading to silvery or white on lower sides and belly. There are numerous black spots on the upper body from head to tail and a distinctive red stripe along the middle of each side. Sea-run and lake-run rainbows are usually quite silvery, with a faint or nonexistent red stripe and few spots. The rainbow is an extremely important sport fish and will take flies, lures, and bait willingly. It usually strikes hard and is noted for its wild leaps.

RANGE: The natural range of the rainbow trout is from northern Mexico to Alaska and the Aleutian Islands, but stocking programs have greatly widened that range so that it now includes most of Canada, all the northern and central states, and some of the colder waters in such southern states as Georgia, Tennessee, Arkansas, and Texas.

HABITAT: The rainbow, like all trout, must have cold, clean water, though it does fairly well under marginal conditions. It is found in shallow lakes and deep lakes, in small streams and large ones. It may be found at the surface one day, feeding on the bottom the next. The rainbow's universality is due partly to the fact that it can do well in a wide variety of environments.

SIZE: The average nonmigratory stream rainbow runs from 6 to 18 inches in length, though some much larger specimens are occasionally taken. Nonmigratory lake fish tend to run considerably larger—up to 50 pounds and more. An average migratory steelhead runs from 8 to 12 pounds, but this strain reaches 35 pounds or so.

FOOD: Rainbows feed heavily on insect life but also eat baitfish, crustaceans, worms, and the roe of salmon and trout. The diet of the Kamloops rainbow is mainly Kokanee salmon.

Cutthroat Trout

COMMON NAMES: Cutthroat trout, cut, native trout, mountain trout, Rocky Mountain trout, black-spotted trout, harvest trout, Montana black-spotted trout, Tahoe cutthroat, Yellowstone cutthroat.

SCIENTIFIC NAME: *Salmo clarki.*

Cutthroat Trout

DESCRIPTION: Occurring in both nonmigratory and anadromous forms, the cutthroat trout gets its common name from the two slashes of crimson on the underside of its lower jaw. Its scientific name honors William Clark of the famed Lewis and Clark expedition. The cutthroat is often mistaken for the rainbow, but it lacks the rainbow's bright-red side stripe, and its entire body is usually black-spotted, while the rainbow's spots are usually limited to the upper half of the body. The cutthroat usually has a greenish back, colorful gill plates, sides of yellow or pink, and a white belly. Coastal cutthroats are greenish-blue with a silvery sheen on the sides and heavy black spots. The cutthroat is a fine sport fish, taking flies—particularly wet flies—readily and showing an inordinate liking for flashy spoons.

RANGE: The cutthroat is found from northern California north to Prince William Sound, Alaska, and inland throughout the western U.S. and Canada.

HABITAT: A fish of clean, cold water, the cutthroat frequents places like those preferred by the brook trout—undercut banks, deep holes, logs and other debris. They prefer quiet water, generally, in streams. Unlike other trout that go to sea, anadromous cutthroats do not range widely in the ocean depths. Instead, they remain in bays at the mouths of their home streams or along the nearby ocean shores.

SIZE: Though cutthroats of up to 41 pounds have been caught by anglers, they seldom exceed 5 pounds and average 2 to 3 pounds. Four pounds is large for a sea-run cutthroat.

FOOD: Young cutthroats feed mainly on insect life, while adults eat insects, baitfish, crayfish, and worms.

Golden Trout

COMMON NAMES: Golden trout, Volcano trout, Sierra trout.

SCIENTIFIC NAME: *Salmo aguabonita.*

DESCRIPTION: This rare jewel of the western high country is the most beautiful of all trout. The golden trout has an olive back, crimson gill covers and side stripes, while the remainder of the body ranges from orange-yellow to gold. The dorsal fin is orange-tipped, and the anal and ventral fins are white-edged. Each side contains about 10 black parr markings. The coloring differs from lake to lake. The golden is a rarely caught but highly prized sport fish.

Golden Trout

RANGE: Originally found only in the headwaters of California's Kern River, the golden is now present in high-mountain lakes in many western states, including California, Wyoming, Idaho, Washington. Modern fish-breeding and stocking techniques have extended the range of the golden—or, rather, a golden-rainbow trout cross—to the Eastern states, including West Virginia and New Jersey.

HABITAT: The true golden trout is found in small, high lakes and their tributary streams at elevations of 9,000 to 12,000 feet. The water in these lakes is extremely cold, and weed growth is minimal or nonexistent. Because of the golden's spartan habitat, he can be extremely moody and difficult to catch.

SIZE: Golden trout are not large, a two-pounder being a very good one, though some lakes hold fair numbers of fish up to 5 pounds. Maximum size is 11 pounds.

FOOD: Golden trout feed almost exclusively on minute insects, including terrestrial (land) insects, but also eat tiny crustaceans and are sometimes caught by bait-fishermen using worms, salmon eggs, and grubs.

Brown Trout

COMMON NAMES: Brown trout, German brown trout, Loch Leven trout.

SCIENTIFIC NAME: *Salmo trutta.*

DESCRIPTION: Introduced in North America in the 1880's, the brown trout is a topnotch dry-fly fish, and yet its daytime wariness and whimsy can drive fishermen to the nearest bar. The brown trout is generally brownish to olive-brown, shading from dark brown on the back to dusky yellow or creamy white on the belly. Sides, back, and dorsal fin have prominent black or brown spots, usually surrounded by faint halos of gray or white. Some haloed red or orange spots are also present. Sea-run browns and those in large lakes are often silvery and resemble landlocked salmon.

RANGE: The brown is the native trout of Europe and is also found in New Zealand, parts of Asia, South America, and Africa. It is found in the U.S. from coast to coast and as far south as New Mexico and Arkansas and Georgia.

HABITAT: The brown trout can tolerate warmer water and other marginal conditions better than the other trout species can. It is found in both streams and lakes, preferring hiding and feeding spots similar to those of brook trout. It often feeds on the bottom in deep holes, coming to the surface at night.

SIZE: Brown trout have been known to exceed 40 pounds, though one of more than 10 pounds is exceptional. Most browns caught by sport fisherman weigh $1/2$ to $1\frac{1}{2}$ pounds.

FOOD: Brown trout feed on aquatic and terrestrial (land) insects as well as worms, crayfish, baitfish, fish roe. Large specimens will eat such tidbits as mice, frogs, and small birds.

Grayling

COMMON NAMES: Grayling, Arctic grayling, Montana grayling.

SCIENTIFIC NAME: *Thymallus arcticus.*

DESCRIPTION: Closely related to the trouts and white-fishes, the grayling's most distinctive feature is its high, wide dorsal fin, which is gray to purple and has rows of blue or lighter dots. Its back is dark blue to gray, and the sides range from gray to brown to silvery, depending upon where the fish lives. The forepart of the body usually has irregularly shaped dark spots. The grayling is a strikingly handsome fish and a fly-fisherman's dream.

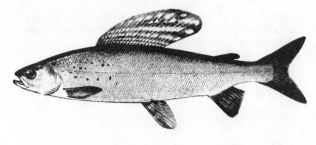

Grayling

RANGE: The grayling is abundant in Alaska throughout northern Canada from northern Saskatchewan westward, and northward through the Northwest Territories. It is less common in the U.S., ranging in high areas of Montana, Wyoming, and Utah. Recently developed grayling-breeding procedures are extending the range of this fish into Idaho, California, Oregon, and other mountain states.

HABITAT: The grayling is found in both lakes and rivers but is particularly at home in high and isolated timberline lakes. In lakes, schools of grayling often cruise near shore. In rivers, the fish are likely to be found anywhere, but they usually favor one type of water in any given stream.

SIZE: Maximum weight of grayling is 20 pounds or a bit heavier, but in most waters, even in the Arctic, a two-pounder is a good fish. In U.S. waters, grayling seldom top 1½ pounds.

FOOD: The grayling's diet is made up almost entirely of nymphs and other insects and aquatic larvae, though this fish will also eat worms and crustaceans.

Rocky Mountain Whitefish

COMMON NAMES: Rocky Mountain whitefish, mountain whitefish, Montana whitefish.

SCIENTIFIC NAME: *Prosopium williamsoni.*

DESCRIPTION: The Rocky Mountain whitefish resembles the lake whitefish, though its body is more cylindrical. Coloration shades from brown on the back to silver on the sides to white on the belly. The dorsal fin is large but not nearly as large as that of the grayling. Where it competes with trout in a stream, the Rocky Mountain whitefish is considered by many anglers as a nuisance, though it fights well and will take dry and wet flies, spinning lures, and bait.

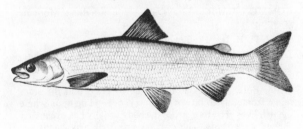

Rocky Mountain Whitefish

RANGE: The Rocky Mountain whitefish is endemic to the western slope of the Rocky Mountains from northern California to southern British Columbia.

HABITAT: Found in cold, swift streams and in clear deep lakes, these whitefish school up in deep pools after spawning in the fall and feed mostly on the bottom. In spring the fish move to the riffles in streams and the shallows in lakes.

SIZE: Rocky Mountain whitefish reach 5 pounds, but a three-pounder is an exceptional one. Average size is 11 to 14 inches and 1 pound.

FOOD: These fish feed almost entirely on such insects as caddis and midge larvae and stonefly nymphs. They also eat fish eggs, their own included.

Lake Whitefish

COMMON NAMES: Lake whitefish, common whitefish, Great Lakes whitefish, Labrador whitefish, Otsego bass.

SCIENTIFIC NAME: *Coregonua clupeaformis.*

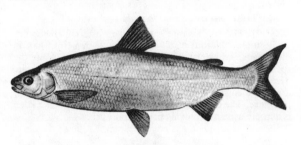

Lake Whitefish

DESCRIPTION: Similar in appearance—though only distantly related—to the Rocky Mountain whitefish, the lake whitefish has bronze or olive shading on the back, with the rest of the body being silvery white. It has rather large scales, small head and mouth, and blunt snout. Large specimens appear humpbacked. Lake whitefish, because they spend much of the year in very deep water, are not important sport fish.

RANGE: Lake whitefish are found from New England west through the Great Lakes area and throughout much of Canada.

HABITAT: These fish inhabit large, deep, cold, clear lakes and are usually found in water from 60 to 100 deep, though they will enter tributary streams in spring and fall. In the northern part of their range, however, lake whitefish are often found foraging in shallow water, and they will feed on the surface when mayflies are hatching.

SIZE: Lake whitefish reach weights of a bit more than 20 pounds, but their average size is something less than 4 pounds.

FOOD: Lake whitefish feed primarily on small crustaceans and aquatic insects but will eat baitfish when available.

Cisco

COMMON NAMES: Cisco, herring, lake herring, common cisco, lake cisco, bluefin, Lake Erie cisco, tullibee, shortjaw chub, grayback.

SCIENTIFIC NAME: *Coregonus artedii* (and others).

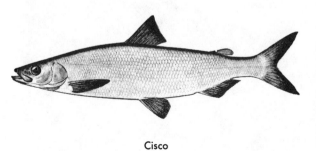

Cisco

DESCRIPTION: Though the cisco superficially resembles members of the herring family, it is not a herring but rather a member of the whitefish family. The cisco has a darker back (usually bluish or greenish) than the true whitefish. The body is silvery with large scales. There are more than 30 species and subspecies of ciscoes in the Great Lakes area alone, and all of them look and act alike. Ciscoes occasionally provide good sport fishing, particularly on dry flies, but they are more important commercially.

RANGE: The various strains of ciscoes occur from New England and New York west through the Great Lakes area and range widely through Canada. Their center of concentration seems to be the Great Lakes area.

HABITAT: Ciscoes prefer large, cold, clear lakes, usually those having considerable depth. Little is known of the wanderings of these fish; some species are found from the surface to several hundred feet down. They spawn in July and August over hard bottom. In summer ciscoes often comes to the surface to feed on hatching insects, usually at sundown.

SIZE: The size of a cisco depends on its species. Some average only a few ounces in weight, while the largest attain a maximum weight of about 7 pounds. Average length is about 6 to 20 inches.

FOOD: Insect life—mainly bottom-dwelling types—is the blueplate special of the cisco, though it sometimes feeds on surface insects and on minute crustaceans and worms.

American Shad

SCIENTIFIC NAME: *Alosa sapidissima.*

DESCRIPTION: The American shad is an anadromous fish—meaning one that ascends coastal rivers to spawn but spends much of its life in salt water. A member of the herring family, the shad has a greenish back, with the remainder of the body being silvery. There are usually a few indistinct markings on the forebody. Shad put up a no-holds-barred battle on hook and line and are important sport and commercial fish, though pollution is putting a dent in their populations in some areas.

RANGE: American shad were originally native only to the Atlantic but were introduced in the Pacific in the 1870's. On the Atlantic coast they are found from Florida to the Gulf of St. Lawrence, while in the Pacific they range from San Diego, California, to southern Alaska. They are also found in Scandinavia, France, Italy, Germany, Russia, and elsewhere.

HABITAT: American shad swarm up large coastal rivers to spawn in the spring—from March to May, depending upon the location of the river. They are particularly susceptible to anglers below dams and in holes and slow runs just upstream of riffles, where they tend to rest before continuing upriver. They generally spawn in the main river.

SIZE: The average weight of an American shad is 3 to 5 pounds, while maximum weight is 12 to 13 pounds. Egg-laden females are usually heavier than males.

FOOD: While in the ocean American shad feed almost exclusively on plankton, so far as is known. After they enter fresh water on the spawning runs, these fish apparently do not feed at all. Curiously, however, they will strike at a small variety of artificial lures, including small, sparsely dressed wet flies and leadhead jigs tied on a gold hook and having a wisp of bucktail at the tail.

Largemouth Bass

COMMON NAMES: Largemouth bass, bigmouth bass, black bass, green trout, Oswego bass, green bass.

SCIENTIFIC NAME: *Micropterus salmoides.*

DESCRIPTION: The largemouth bass is among the most important of this continent's fresh-water gamefish. In physical makeup it is a chunky fish, with coloration ranging from nearly black or dark green on the back, through varying shades of green or brownish-green on the sides, to an off-white belly. The largemouth's most distinctive marking, however, is a horizontal dark band running along the side from head to tail. In large, old bass particularly, the band may be almost invisible. There are two reliable ways to distinguish the largemouth from its close relative and look-alike, the smallmouth bass: 1) the largemouth's upper jaw (maxillary) extends back behind the eye, while the smallmouth's does not; 2) the spiny part of the largemouth's dorsal fin is almost completely separated from the softer rear portion, while in the smallmouth the two fin sections are connected in one continuous fin.

RANGE: The largemouth is native to or stocked in every state in the "lower 48" and is found as far south as Mexico and as far north as southern Canada.

HABITAT: Largemouths are found in slow-moving streams large and small and in nonflowing waters ranging in size from little more than puddles to vast impoundments. It thrives best in shallow, weedy lakes and in river backwaters. It is a warm-water fish, preferring water temperatures of 70 to 75°. Largemouths never venture too far from such areas as weed beds, logs, stumps, and other sunken debris, which provides both cover and food. They are usually found in water no deeper than 20 feet.

SIZE: Largemouth bass grow biggest in the southern U.S., where they reach a maximum weight of a little over 20 pounds and an 8 or 10-pounder is not a rarity. In the north largemouths rarely exceed 10 pounds and a 3-pounder is considered a good catch.

FOOD: The largemouth's diet is as ubiquitous as the fish itself. These bass eat minnows and any other available baitfish, worms, crustaceans, a wide variety of insect life, frogs, mice, ducklings.

Smallmouth Bass

COMMON NAMES: Smallmouth bass, black bass, bronzeback.

SCIENTIFIC NAME: *Micropterus dolomieui.*

DESCRIPTION: A top gamefish and a flashy fighter, the smallmouth bass is brownish, bronze, or greenish-brown in coloration, with the back being darker and the belly being an off-white. The sides are marked with dark, vertical bars, which may be indistinguishable in young fish. (For physical differences between the smallmouth bass and its look-alike relative, the largemouth bass, see Largemouth Bass.) The smallmouth is not as common as, and is a wilder fighter than, the largemouth.

RANGE: The smallmouth's original range was throughout New England, southern Canada, and the Great Lakes area, and in large rivers of Tennessee, Arkansas, and Oklahoma. However, stocking has greatly widened this range so that it now includes states in northern and moderate climates from coast to coast.

HABITAT: Unlike the largemouth bass, the smallmouth is a fish of cold, clear waters (preferring water temperatures of no higher than 65° or so). Large, deep lakes and sizable rivers are the smallmouth's domain, though he is often found in streams that look like good trout water—that is, those with numerous riffles flowing over gravel, boulders, or bedrock. In lakes, smallmouths are likely to be found over gravel bars between submerged weedbeds in water 10 to 20 feet deep, along dropoffs near shale banks, on gravel points running out from shore, and near midlake reefs or shoals. In streams they often hold at the head of a pool where the water fans out, and in pockets having moderate current and nearby cover.

SIZE: Maximum weight attained by smallmouth bass is about 12 pounds. In most waters, however, a 4 or 5-pounder is a very good fish, and average weight is probably 1½ to 3 pounds.

FOOD: Smallmouths eat baitfish and crayfish mainly, though they also feed on hellgrammites and other insect life, worms, small frogs, and leeches.

Redeye Bass

COMMON NAMES: Redeye bass, Coosa bass, shoal bass, Chipola bass.

SCIENTIFIC NAME: *Micropterus coosae.*

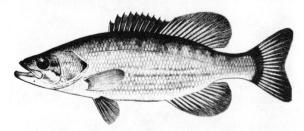

Redeye Bass

DESCRIPTION: Given full status as a distinct species in about 1940, the redeye bass is a relative of the smallmouth. Though this fish is often difficult to identify positively, especially in adult form, the redeye young have dark vertical bars (which become indistinct with age) and brick-red dorsal, anal, and caudal fins. This fin color, and the red of its eyes, are the redeye's most distinctive physical traits. The redeye is a good fighter and is good-eating.

RANGE: An inhabitant of the southeastern states, the redeye bass is found mainly in Alabama, Georgia, and South Carolina. It is also found in the Chipola River system in Florida.

HABITAT: The redeye bass is mainly a stream fish, usually inhabiting upland parts of drainage systems. They often feed at the surface.

SIZE: Maximum weight of the redeye is 6 pounds, but, in Alabama at least, the average weight is about 12 ounces.

FOOD: A large portion of the redeye's diet is insects, but also feeds on worms, crickets, and various baitfish.

Spotted Bass

COMMON NAMES: Spotted bass, Kentucky bass, Kentucky spotted bass.

SCIENTIFIC NAME: *Micropterus punctulatus.*

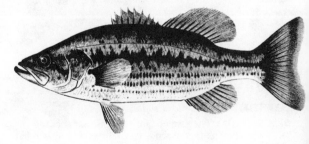

Spotted Bass

DESCRIPTION: The spotted bass, recognized as a distinct species only since 1927, is quite similar in appearance to the largemouth bass and has characteristics of both the largemouth and the smallmouth. The spotted bass is olive green on the back with many dark blotches, most of which are diamond-shaped. A series of short blotches form a horizontal dark band along the sides which is somewhat more irregular than that of the largemouth. Spots below the lateral line distinguish the spotted bass from the largemouth, and that spotting, plus the lack of vertical side bars, distinguishes it from the smallmouth bass.

RANGE: The spotted bass is found in the Ohio-Mississippi drainage from Ohio south to the states bordering the Gulf of Mexico, western Florida, and west to Texas, Oklahoma, and Kansas.

HABITAT: In the northern part of its range, the spotted bass prefers large, deep pools in sluggish waters. Its preferred habitat in the southern part of its range is quite different, consisting of cool streams with gravel bottoms and clear spring-fed lakes. In lakes, spotted bass are sometimes found in water as deep as 100 feet.

SIZE: Maximum weight of spotted bass is 8 pounds, but few specimens top 4 or 5 pounds.

FOOD: Spotted bass, like most other members of the bass family, feed on various baitfish and insects, frogs, worms, crustaceans, grubs, and the like.

Bluegill

COMMON NAMES: Bluegill, bluegill sunfish, bream, sun perch, blue perch, blue sunfish, copperbelly, red-breasted bream, copperhead bream, blue bream.

SCIENTIFIC NAME: *Lepomis macrochirus.*

DESCRIPTION: Many's the fisherman who cut his angling teeth on the bluegill, most widely distributed and most popular of the large sunfish family. The color of the bluegill varies probably more than that of any other sunfish, ranging in basic body color from yellow or orange to dark blue. The shading goes from dark on the back to light on the forward part of the belly. The sides of a bluegill are usually marked by 6 to 8 irregular vertical bars of a dark color. A bluegill's prominent features are a broad black gill flap and long, pointed pectoral fins. Bluegills are excellent fighters, and if they grew to largemouth-bass size, they would break a lot of tackle.

RANGE: The bluegill's range just about blankets the entire 48 contiguous states.

HABITAT: The bluegill prefers habitat very much like that of largemouth bass—that is, quiet, weedy waters, in both lakes and streams, where they can find both cover and food. In daytime, the smaller bluegills are usually close to shore in coves, under overhanging trees, around docks. The larger ones are usually nearby but in deeper water, moving into the shallows early and late in the day.

SIZE: Maximum size of bluegills is about 4½ pounds in weight and 15 inches in length, but average length is 4 to 8 inches.

FOOD: A bluegill's food consists chiefly of insect life and vegetation. Other items on the diet include worms, grubs, small baitfish, crustaceans, small frogs, grasshoppers, and the like.

Redear Sunfish

COMMON NAMES: Redear sunfish, redear, shellcracker, stumpknocker, yellow bream, chinquapin.

SCIENTIFIC NAME: *Lepomis microlophus.*

DESCRIPTION: A large and very popular sunfish in the South, the redear has a small mouth, large and pointed pectoral fins, and a black gill flap with a whitish border (the bluegill lacks the white gill-flap border). The body color is olive with darker-olive spots, and the sides have 5 to 10 dusky vertical bars. The redear is distinguishable from the pumpkinseed—the member of the sunfish family that it most closely resembles—by the lack of spots on the dorsal fin.

RANGE: The redear sunfish ranges from southern Illinois and southern Indiana south to the Florida and the other Gulf states and westward to Texas and New Mexico. Its heaviest concentration is in Florida.

HABITAT: The redear sunfish shows a definite liking for large, quiet waters, congregating around logs, stumps, and roots. It will, however, frequent open waters and seems to require less vegetation than other sunfish.

SIZE: The redear is more likely to run to large size than is most any other sunfish. Three pounds seems to be maximum weight, but 2-pounders are not uncommon.

FOOD: Redears depend mainly on snails for food, but will eat other mollusks, crustaceans, worms, and insects.

White Crappie

COMMON NAMES: White crappie, papermouth, bachelor perch, papermouth perch, strawberry bass, calico, calico bass, sago, grass bass.

SCIENTIFIC NAME: *Pomoxis annularis.*

DESCRIPTION: This popular fresh-water panfish is a cousin to the true sunfish. In coloration, its back is an olive-green and the sides silvery-olive with 7 to 9 dark vertical bands, while the sides of the very similar black crappie (which see) have irregular dark mottlings. Another, more reliable way to tell the white crappie from the black is the number of spines in the dorsal fin: the white has 6 while the black has 7 or 8. The white is more elongated in general shape, while the black, by comparison, has a high, rather arched back.

RANGE: Original range of the white crappie extended from Nebraska east to the Great Lakes, south through the Mississippi and Ohio river systems, and throughout most of the South as far north as North Carolina. Stocking has greatly extended that range, though the white crappie is predominantly a southern species.

HABITAT: The white crappie can live under more-turbid conditions than can the black crappie—in fact, it prefers silty rivers and lakes to clear water and is common in Southern impoundments and cypress bayous, warm and weedy ponds, slow streams. The ideal home for these schooling fish is a pile of sunken brush or a submerged treetop. In summer crappies often seek such a spot in deep holes, moving into the shallows in the evening to feed.

SIZE: White crappies average 6 to 10 inches in length and less than a pound in weight. However, individuals of more than 5 pounds have been caught by sport fishermen, and 2 or 3-pounders are not rare.

FOOD: White crappies eat baitfish for the most part—gizzard shad is their blue-plate special in Southern lakes—but also feed on worms, shrimp, plankton, snails, crayfish, and insects.

Black Crappie

COMMON NAMES: Black crappie, calico, calico bass, papermouth, grass bass.

SCIENTIFIC NAME: *Pomoxis nigromaculatus.*

DESCRIPTION: This near-identical twin of the white crappie is dark-olive or black on the back. Its silvery sides and its dorsal, anal, and caudal fins contain dark and irregular blotches scattered in no special pattern. (For physical differences between black and white crappie, see White Crappie.) Though it is a school fish like the white crappie, the black crappie does not seem to populate a lake or stream so thickly as does the white.

RANGE: The black crappie, though predominately a northern-U.S. fish, is found from southern Manitoba to southern Quebec, and from Nebraska to the East Coast and south to Texas and Florida. However, stocking has widened this range to include such places as British Columbia and California.

HABITAT: The black crappie prefers rather cool, clear, weedy lakes and rivers, though it often shares the same waters with the white crappie. The black is a brush-lover, tending to school up among submerged weed beds and the like. It occasionally feeds at the surface, particularly near nightfall.

SIZE: Same as white crappie.

FOOD: Same as white crappie.

White Bass

COMMON NAMES: White bass, barfish, striped bass, streak.

SCIENTIFIC NAME: *Roccus chrysops.*

DESCRIPTION: This fresh-water member of the ocean-going sea-bass family has boomed in popularity among sport fishermen in recent years, thanks to its schooling habits, eagerness to bite, tastiness of its flesh, and increase in its range. The white bass is a silvery fish tinged with yellow toward the belly. The sides have about 10 narrow dark stripes, the body is moderately compressed, and the mouth is basslike. The white bass may be distinguished from the look-alike yellow bass (which see) by its unbroken side stripes (those of the yellow bass are broken) and by its projecting lower jaw (the upper and lower jaws of the yellow are about even). The white bass is astonishingly prolific.

RANGE: White bass are found in the St. Lawrence River area and throughout the Mississippi and Missouri river systems, west into Texas, and in most of the other southern and southwestern states.

HABITAT: The white bass lives in large lakes and rivers but appears to prefer large lakes containing relatively clear water. The burgeoning number of large, deep reservoirs constructed recently in the South and Southwest are tailor-made for the white bass. These fish like large areas of deep water and need gravel or bottom rubble for spawning. Schools of whites can often be seen feeding voraciously on or near the surface, particularly in the evening.

SIZE: Maximum size of white bass is about 6 pounds, but average size is ½ to 2 pounds. A 3 or 4-pounder is an excellent specimen.

FOOD: Baitfish, particularly gizzard shad, form the main part of the white bass's diet, though it will also eat crustaceans, worms, and insect life.

Yellow Bass

COMMON NAMES: Yellow bass, barfish, brassy bass, stripe, striped bass, streaker.

SCIENTIFIC NAME: *Roccus mississippiensis.*

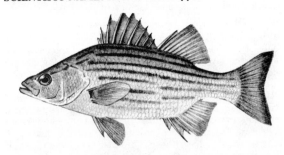

Yellow Bass

DESCRIPTION: Quite similar in appearance to the white bass (for physical differences, see White Bass), the yellow bass has an olive-green back, silvery to golden-yellow sides with 6 or 7 dark, horizontal, broken stripes, and a white belly. Like the white bass, the yellow is a member of the sea-bass family. It is a school fish, but its population levels tend to fluctuate drastically from year to year.

RANGE: The range of the yellow bass is quite restricted, being mainly the Mississippi River drainage from Minnesota to Louisiana and eastern Texas, plus the Tennessee River drainage, plus Iowa. Even within its range, the yellow is found only in scattered lakes and streams.

HABITAT: One of the yellow's primary habitat requirements is wide, shallow, gravelly areas and rocky reefs. This fish prefers large lakes and large rivers, especially those with clear water. Yellow-bass schools tend to roam in deep water in daytime, coming into the shallows to feed late and very early.

SIZE: Most yellow bass caught by sport fishermen range from 8 to 11 inches, or ¼ to ¾ pound. Maximum size is probably about 3 pounds.

FOOD: Yellow bass feed almost exclusively on baitfish, but occasionally take crustaceans and insects.

White Perch

COMMON NAMES: White perch, silver perch, sea perch.

SCIENTIFIC NAME: *Roccus americanus.*

DESCRIPTION: This fish is not a perch but rather a bass. And though it is often found in fresh water, it is not a freshwater bass. It is a member of the sea-bass family and superficially resembles one other member of that family, the saltwater striped bass, though it is much smaller. The white perch is greenish to blackish-green on the back and silvery on the sides, particularly when living in salt water (freshwater individuals are usually darker). Young white perch have indistinct stripes on the sides, but adult fish lack them.

RANGE: In salt water, white perch range along the Atlantic coast from Nova Scotia to North Carolina. They are found inland as far as the Great Lakes and are especially abundant in New York State and New England.

HABITAT: In salt water, white perch are most likely to be found in brackish ponds and backwaters formed by coastal sandbars. Anadromous members of the clan run up rivers to spawn. In inland lakes, these fish lie in deep water over a sand or gravel bottom during the day, sometimes at 50 feet or deeper, but often come into shoreside shallows in evening and at night to feed. At those times, and on dark days, schools of white perch may be seen breaking the surface.

SIZE: White perch seem to run larger in salt and brackish water than in fresh water. Average size, generally, is 8 to 10 inches, though 2-pounders are not rare. They seldom exceed 4 pounds.

FOOD: In salt water, white perch forage on small fish, shrimp, squid, crabs, and the like. In fresh water, their diet includes larval and other insect forms, crustaceans, baitfish, and worms.

Yellow Perch

COMMON NAMES: Yellow perch, ringed perch, striped perch, coon perch, jack perch.

SCIENTIFIC NAME: *Perca flavescens.*

DESCRIPTION: The yellow perch, in no way related to the white perch, is an extremely popular fresh-water panfish. Though its colors may vary, the back is generally olive, shading to golden-yellow on the sides and white on the belly. Six to 8 rather wide, dark, vertical bands run from the back to below the lateral line. Though the body is fairly elongated, the fish has a somewhat humpbacked appearance.

RANGE: The yellow perch is a ubiquitous species, being found in most areas of the U.S. It is most common from southern Canada south through the Dakotas and Great Lakes states into Kansas and Missouri, and in the East from New England to the Carolinas. Stockings have established it in such places as Montana and the Pacific slope.

HABITAT: The yellow perch is predominately a fish of lakes large and small, though it is also found in rivers. It prefers cool, clean water with plenty of sandy or rocky bottom areas, though it does well in a wide variety of conditions. As a very general rule, the best perch lakes are large and have only moderate weed growth. These fish feed at various levels, and the fisherman must experiment until he finds them.

SIZE: The average yellow perch weighs a good deal less than a pound, though 2-pounders aren't uncommon. Maximum weight is about 4½ pounds.

FOOD: Yellow perch eat such tidbits as baitfish (including their own young), worms, large plankton, insects in various forms, crayfish, snails, and small frogs.

Walleye

COMMON NAMES: Walleye, walleyed pike, pike, jack, jackfish, pickerel, yellow pickerel, blue pickerel, dore, pike-perch.

SCIENTIFIC NAME: *Stizostedion vitreum.*

DESCRIPTION: The walleye is not a pike or pickerel, as its nicknames might indicate, but rather the largest member of the perch family. Its most striking physical characteristic is its large, almost opaque eyes, which appear to be made of glass and which reflect light eerily. The walleye's colors range from dark olive or olive-brown on the back to a lighter olive on the sides and to white on the belly. Here's how to tell the walleye from its look-alike relative, the sauger: 1) the lower fork of the walleye's tail has a milky-white tip, absent in the sauger; 2) the walleye's dorsal-fin foresection has irregular blotches or streaks, unlike the definite rows of spots found on the sauger's dorsal. The walleye isn't the best fighter among gamefish, but he makes up for that shortcoming by providing delectable eating.

RANGE: The walleye is found in most of Canada as far north as Great Slave Lake and Labrador. Its original U.S. range was pretty much limited to the northern states, but stocking has greatly widened this range to include all of the East and most of the far-west and southern states.

HABITAT: The walleye loves clear, deep, cold, and large waters, both lakes and rivers, and prefers a sand, gravel, or rock bottom. He is almost always found on or near the bottom, though during evening and night hours he may move into shallow water to feed. Once you find a walleye hole, you should catch fish there consistently, for walleyes are schooling fish and are unlikely to move their places of residence.

SIZE: Top weight of walleyes is about 25 pounds, but a 6 to 8-pounder is a brag fish. Most walleyes that end up on fishermen's stringers weigh 1 to 3 pounds.

FOOD: Walleyes feed primarily on small fish and crayfish. Strangely enough, though they don't often eat worms, nightcrawlers are a real walleye killer, especially when combined with a spinner.

Sauger

COMMON NAMES: Sauger, sand pike, gray pike, river pike, spotfin pike, jack fish.

SCIENTIFIC NAME: *Stizostedion canadense.*

Sauger

DESCRIPTION: The sauger is very much like the walleye in all important respects, except that it is quite a bit smaller. It is olive or olive-gray on back and sides and has a white belly. Its large glassy eyes are very much like those of the walleye. (For physical differences between the sauger and the walleye, see Walleye.)

RANGE: The sauger's range is generally a blueprint of the walleye's. However, sauger are most common in the Great Lakes, other very large lakes in the northern U.S. and southern Canada, and in the large rivers (and their tributaries) such as the Mississippi, Missouri, Ohio, and Tennessee.

HABITAT: In this category, too, the sauger is much like the walleye, though the sauger can tolerate siltier or murkier water than can the walleye and tends to stick to deeper waters. A good place to look for sauger is in tailwaters below dams.

SIZE: The sauger's maximum weight is about 8 pounds, but it seems to reach that size only in the Missouri River system. Average size is 1 to 2 pounds.

FOOD: Same as the walleye.

White Sturgeon

SCIENTIFIC NAME: *Acipenser transmontanus.*

DESCRIPTION: This huge, primitive throwback to geological history is one of 16 species of sturgeon in the world, 7 of which occur in the U.S. It is the largest fish found in this country's inland waters and the only member of the sturgeon family that is considered a gamefish. The white sturgeon does not have scales but rather five rows of bony plates along the body. It has a large, underslung, sucking mouth, and its skeleton is cartilage rather than true bone. Sturgeon roe is better known as caviar. Though relatively few anglers fish for these behemoths, careful regulation of the fishery is necessary to prevent depletion of the white-sturgeon populations.

RANGE: The white sturgeon is found along the Pacific coast from Monterey, California, to Alaska. They are also found inland in the largest of rivers, including the Columbia and Snake.

HABITAT: Some white sturgeon are entirely landlocked, but many spend much of their lives at sea and ascend large west-coast rivers to spawn. In large rivers they lie on the bottom in deep holes.

White Sturgeon

SIZE: The largest white sturgeon reported taken pulled the scales down to 1,800 pounds. Average size is difficult to determine.

FOOD: In freshwater the white sturgeon uses its vacuum-cleaner mouth to inhale crustaceans, mollusks, insect larvae, and other bottom organisms. Bait used by sturgeon anglers includes nightcrawlers, lamprey eels, cut bait, and even dried river moss.

Channel Catfish

COMMON NAMES: Channel catfish, fiddler.

SCIENTIFIC NAME: *Ictalurus punctatus.*

DESCRIPTION: This sizable member of the large catfish family (which includes bullheads) is undoubtedly the most streamlined, gamest, and most agile of the whole clan. In coloration the channel cat is steely-blue on top and shades to white on the belly, though young ones may be silvery even along the back. It is the only spotted catfish (it has dark speckles on the sides, though these spots may be missing in large specimens) with a deeply forked tail.

RANGE: The channel catfish occurs from the Saskatchewan River and entire Great Lakes area southward into Mexico. Stocking has transplanted this fish far west and east of that natural range.

HABITAT: Channel catfish are found in lakes but are more common in rivers, especially large ones. They are likely to be found in faster, cleaner water than other catfish and seem to prefer a bottom composition of sand, gravel, or rock. Like all other catfish, they are bottom feeders and are especially active at night.

SIZE: Channel cats are among the larger members of the catfish family, attaining weights of up to about 60 pounds. Average size is 1 to 5 pounds.

FOOD: The channel cat's varied menu includes just about anything he can get his jaws around—small fish, insects, crustaceans, worms, grubs, frogs, and many other aquatic food forms.

Blue Catfish

SCIENTIFIC NAME: *Ictalurus furcatus.*

Blue Catfish

DESCRIPTION: The blue is the largest member of the catfish clan. It has a deeply forked tail, but lacks the spots of the channel catfish. In color, the blue catfish is pale blue on the back, a lighter silvery blue on the sides, white on the belly. The most reliable way to tell the blue from other catfish is by the number of rays on its straight-edged anal fin (there are 30 to 36).

RANGE: The blue catfish is found mainly in the Mississippi River system but occurs south into Mexico and has been introduced into some rivers on the Atlantic coast.

HABITAT: The blue is a catfish of large rivers and is likely to be found below the dams creating large impoundments, especially in the southern U.S. It prefers less-turbid waters than do most other catfish and seems to do best over bottoms of rock, gravel, or sand. It feeds in rapids or fast chutes.

SIZE: This heavyweight grows to well over 100 pounds. The average size, however, is 2 to 15 pounds.

FOOD: The blue catfish feeds primarily on small fish and crayfish. A favorite bait in some areas is a whole golden shad.

Brown Bullhead

COMMON NAMES: Brown bullhead, horned pout, speckled bullhead.

SCIENTIFIC NAME: *Ictalurus nebulosus.*

DESCRIPTION: Probably the most popular of the catfish—at least, it's the most often caught— the brown bullhead is

a rather slender catfish with typical catfish features: sharp dorsal spine and sensitive barbels (the "feelers" projecting from the mouth area). The brown bullhead's chin barbels are dark brown or black. The tail has almost no fork, and the anal fin has 22 or 23 rays. The back is yellowish brown to light chocolate and has vague dark mottlings, the sides are lighter, and the belly is yellow to milky white.

RANGE: Brown bullheads occur from Maine and the Great Lakes south to Mexico and Florida, but stocking has greatly expanded this range.

HABITAT: Brown bullheads prefer relatively deep, weedy waters in lakes and slow-moving streams. They may be found over sand and gravel bottom and also over mud. They are almost exclusively bottom feeders.

SIZE: The brown bullhead seldom weighs more than 3 pounds, with its average size being 6 to 16 inches.

FOOD: Insect larvae and mollusks form the majority of this fish's menu, but it will eat everything from worms, small fish, and frogs to plant material and even chicken-livers (a favorite catfisherman's bait).

Black Bullhead

COMMON NAMES: Black bullhead, horned pout.

SCIENTIFIC NAME: *Ictalurus melas.*

Black Bullhead

DESCRIPTION: Quite similar in appearance to the brown bullhead, the black bullhead is black to yellow-green on the back, yellowish or whitish on the sides, and bright-yellow, yellow, or milky on the belly. Its chin barbels are dark or spotted, and its pectoral spines have no serrations. The body is chunky.

RANGE: The area in which the black bullhead is most numerous takes in New York, west to the Dakotas, and south to Texas. However, the fish has been introduced into most other areas of the U.S.

HABITAT: The black bullhead is a fish of muddy, sluggish, turbid streams and lakes. It seems to do well, in fact, in any kind of environment except cool, clear, deep water. It is a bottom-grubber.

SIZE: The largest black bullhead taken by sport fishing weighed 8 pounds, but this catfish seldom tops 2 pounds.

FOOD: Same as brown bullhead.

Carp

COMMON NAMES: Carp, common carp.

SCIENTIFIC NAME: *Cyprinus carpio.*

DESCRIPTION: This big, coarse, much maligned rough fish belongs to the minnow family and is related to the goldfish. In color the carp is olive to light brown on the back, golden-yellow on the sides, and yellowish-white on the belly. At the base of each of its large scales is a dark spot. On each side of the upper jaw are a pair of fleshy barbels, and the dorsal fin has a serrated spine. Though the carp is cussed out by most sport fishermen and often poisoned out of lakes and streams, he is taken by rod and line, bow and arrow, spear, ice gig, and set line, and he can put up a whale of a battle.

RANGE: Introduced into the U.S. in 1876, the carp has found its way into just about every area in the nation. He is also widely distributed through Europe and Asia.

HABITAT: The carp can live almost anywhere and under almost any conditions—except cold, clear waters. He is almost always found on the bottom, except during spawning, when schools of carp are often seen slashing about on the surface.

SIZE: Carp reach a maximum size of about 60 pounds, but average weight is 8 to 15 pounds.

FOOD: Carp are mainly vegetarians, feeding on aquatic plant life and plankton, though they also eat insects and are often caught by anglers on doughballs, cornmeal, and such.

Alligator Gar

SCIENTIFIC NAME: *Lepisosteus spatula.*

DESCRIPTION: Exceeded in size in fresh water only by the western sturgeons, the alligator gar is the largest of the ancient gar family. It can be distinguished from its relatives by an examination of the teeth. Young alligator gars have two rows of large teeth on each side of the upper jaw; other gars have only a single row. The alligator gar has a long, cylindrical body that is olive-green or brownish-green along the back and lighter below. The sides and rear fins have mottlings or large dark spots. Gars are of minor importance as sport fish, though they wage a wild no-holds-barred battle when taken on rod and line.

RANGE: The alligator gar is found mainly in the Mississippi and Ohio river systems as far north as Louisville, Kentucky, and St. Louis, Missouri and as far south as northeastern Mexico.

HABITAT: Alligator gars prefer sluggish rivers, lakes, backwaters and such over muddy, weedy bottoms. They often congregate in loose schools, usually near the surface, where they roll about.

SIZE: Largest reported alligator gar was 10 feet long and weighed 302 pounds. Average size is undetermined.

FOOD: Various kinds of fish, notably the freshwater drum (or gaspergou) are the principal food of alligator gars, though

anglers catch them on wire nooses baited with minnows and on bunches of flosslike material that tangle tenaciously in the gar's teeth.

Longnose Gar

SCIENTIFIC NAME: *Lepisosteus osseus.*

DESCRIPTION: The longnose gar is the most common and most widely distributed of the entire gar family. Its name derives from its long, slender beak (nose). Other distinguishing characteristics are its overlapping diamond-shaped scales and the unusual position of its dorsal fin—far back near the tail and almost directly above the anal fin. Coloration is similar to that of the alligator gar (which see).

RANGE: The longnose gar occurs from Quebec's St. Lawrence drainage west to the Great Lakes (excluding Superior) and as far as Montana, south along the Mississippi system and down into Mexico.

HABITAT: The longnose lives in much the same habitat as does the alligator gar, though it is more likely to be found swimming and feeding in flowing water—that is, where there is a moderate current.

SIZE: Smaller by far than the alligator gar, the longnose reaches a length of 4 to 5 feet.

FOOD: The longnose, like the alligator gar, feeds mostly on other fish, though it also eats plankton and insect larvae when young.

Muskellunge

COMMON NAMES: Muskellunge, maskinonge (and a variety of other spellings), muskie, pike, blue pike, great pike, jack, spotted muskellunge, barred muskellunge, tiger muskellunge.

SCIENTIFIC NAME: *Esox masquinongy.*

DESCRIPTION: Moody, voracious, and predacious, the muskellunge, largest member of the pike family, presents one of the greatest challenges of any fresh-water fish. His adherents probably catch fewer fish per hour that do those who fish for any other fresh-water species, and yet muskie fishermen are legion—and growing in number. The muskellunge—whose name means "ugly fish" in Ojibway dialect—is green to brown to gray in overall color, depending upon its geographical location. Side markings are usually vertical bars, though the fish may be blotched or spotted or lack any distinctive markings. The muskie has no scales on the lower part of cheek and gillcovers; other members of the pike family have scales in those areas. There are three subspecies of the muskellunge: the Great Lakes muskie, the Ohio (or Chautauqua) muskie, and the tiger (or northern) muskie.

RANGE: The Great Lakes muskie is generally a fish of the Great Lakes basin area. The Ohio (Chautauqua) muskie occurs in New York's Chautauqua Lake and through the Ohio drainage. The tiger (northern) muskie is common in Wisconsin, Minnesota, and western Michigan. In overall distribution, the muskellunge is found as far north as the James Bay and Hudson Bay drainages in northern Canada, across the northern U.S. from Wisconsin east to New York and Pennsylvania, and south into Tennessee, North Carolina, Georgia, and in much of the northern-Mississippi drainage. Stocking and propagation methods are greatly widening the muskie's range.

HABITAT: Muskies live in rivers, streams, and lakes, usually only in clear waters, though they may inhabit discolored water in the southern part of their range. They prefer cold waters but can tolerate water as warm as 70 to 75°. Favorite hangouts for adult muskies are shoreline weed beds, particularly near deep water, and such items of cover as logs, stumps, and rocks. They are usually found in water shallower than 15 feet, though midsummer may find them as deep as 50 feet.

SIZE: Muskies reach weights of more than 100 pounds. However, the biggest rod-caught specimen weighed just shy of 70 pounds, and the average is 10 to 20 pounds.

FOOD: Muskies feed mainly on fish, including its own young as well as suckers, yellow perch, bass, and panfish. But they also eat crayfish, snakes, muskrats, worms, frogs, ducklings, squirrels, and just about anything else they can sink their ample teeth into.

Northern Pike

COMMON NAMES: Northern pike, pike, northern, snake, great northern, jackfish, jack.

SCIENTIFIC NAME: *Esox lucius.*

DESCRIPTION: This baleful-looking predator of the weed beds is of great importance as a sport fish. In color it is dark-green on the back, shading to lighter green on the sides to whitish on the belly. Its distinctive side markings are bean-shaped light spots, and the fins are dark-spotted. The entire cheek is scaled, but only the upper half of the gill cover contains scales. The dorsal fin, as in all members of its family, is far to the rear of the body, almost directly above the anal fin.

RANGE: The pike is found in northern waters all around the globe. In North America it occurs from Alaska east to Labrador, and south from the Dakotas and the St. Lawrence to Nebraska and Pennsylvania. Stockings have extended this range to such states as Montana, Colorado, North Carolina, and Maryland.

HABITAT: Over its entire range, the pike's preferred living conditions are shallow, weedy lakes (large and small); shallow areas of large, deep lakes; and rivers of moderate current. In summer pike are normally found in about 4 feet of water near cover, in fall along steep stormy shores.

SIZE: In the best Canadian pike lakes, rod-caught pike average 5 to 25 pounds, but in most waters a 10 to 15-pounder is a very good pike. Maximum weight is somewhat over 50 pounds.

FOOD: Pike are almost entirely fish-eaters but are as voracious and predacious as the muskie (which see) and will eat anything that won't eat them first.

Chain Pickerel

COMMON NAMES: Chain pickerel, jack, chainsides.

SCIENTIFIC NAME: *Esox niger.*

DESCRIPTION: This attractive pikelike fish with the chain-link markings is the largest of the true pickerels. Body color ranges from green to bronze, darker on the back and lighter on the belly. Its distinctive dark chainlike side markings and larger size make the chain pickerel hard to confuse with the other, less-common pickerel (mud or grass pickerel and barred or redfin pickerel).

RANGE: The chain pickerel originally was found only east and south of the Alleghenies, but its range now extends from Maine to the Great Lakes in the north and from Texas to Florida in the south.

HABITAT: The pickerel is almost invariably a fish of the weeds. It lurks in or around weed beds and lily pads, waiting to pounce on unsuspecting morsels. It is usually found in water no deeper than 10 feet, though in hot weather it may retreat to depths as much as 25 feet.

SIZE: Chain pickerel attain a maximum weight of about 10 pounds, but one of 4 pounds is bragging size. Average weight is 1 to 2½ pounds.

FOOD: Pickerel eat fish for the most part, though they will also dine on frogs, worms, crayfish, mice, and insects.

Redhorse Sucker

COMMON NAMES: Redhorse sucker, redhorse, northern redhorse, redfin, redfin sucker, bigscale sucker.

SCIENTIFIC NAME: *Maxostoma macrolepidotum.*

DESCRIPTION: Many anglers look on the entire sucker clan—of which the redhorse is probably the best known and most widely fished for—as pests or worse. And yet countless suckers are caught on hooks, netted, trapped, and speared every year, particularly in the spring, when their flesh is firm and most palatable. The redhorse, like all other suckers, has a large-lipped, tubelike, sucking mouth on the underside of its snout. Overall color is silver, with the back somewhat darker. The mouth has no teeth, and the fins lack spines.

RANGE: The redhorse is found east of the Rocky Mountains from the U.S. midsouth north to central and eastern Canada.

HABITAT: Unlike some of its relatives, the redhorse prefers clean, clear waters and is at home in large and medium-size rivers, even swift-flowing ones, and in lakes. These fish seem to prefer sandy shallows in lakes, deep holes in streams. As spawning runs begin in the spring, the redhorse congregates at the mouths of streams.

SIZE: The redhorse's maximum weight is about 12 pounds. Most of those taken by anglers weigh 2 to 4 pounds.

FOOD: This bottom-feeding species eats various small fish, worms, frogs, crayfish, various insects (both aquatic and terrestrial), and insect larvae.

Splake

SCIENTIFIC NAME: (None).

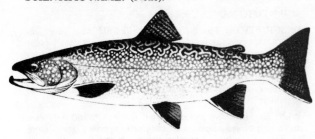

Splake

DESCRIPTION: The splake is a trout hybrid created by crossing lake trout with brook trout. The name is a combination of *sp*eckled (brook) trout and *lake* trout. The first important crossing of these two trout species was done in British Columbia in 1946, and some of the new strain were stocked in lakes in Banff National Park in Alberta. The body shape of splake is midway between that of the brook trout and lake trout—heavier than the laker, slimmer than the brookie. Like the true lake trout, the splake's spots are yellow, but its belly develops the deep orange or red of the true brook trout (see Brook Trout and Lake Trout). Splake mature and grow faster than lake trout. Unlike many other hybrids, the splake is capable of reproducing.

RANGE: The splake's range is quite spotty, including a number of western-Canada lakes, at least one of the Great Lakes, and a few lakes in the northern U.S. Stockings are slowly increasing this range.

HABITAT: Quite similar to that of the true lake trout.

SIZE: As yet undetermined.

FOOD: Similar to that of lake trout.

Tiger Trout

SCIENTIFIC NAME: (None).

DESCRIPTION: This hybrid is a cross between the female brown trout and the male brook trout. The tiger's most prominent physical characteristic is the well-defined vermiculations (wormlike markings) on back and sides. Lower fins have the white edges of the true brook trout. The tiger is an avid surface feeder and is considerably more aggressive than either of its parent species. Under hatchery conditions, only 35 percent of the tiger's offspring develop. The tiger occasionally occurs under natural conditions but does not reproduce.

RANGE: The tiger, being a hybrid, has no natural range, but stockings have introduced it into a few streams in the U.S. At least one state, New Jersey, has stocked this trout in its waters on an experimental basis.

HABITAT: Undetermined, but probably similar to that of the brook trout.

SIZE: Undetermined.

FOOD: Undetermined, but probably similar to that of the brook trout.

Rock Bass

COMMON NAMES: Rock bass, goggle eye, redeye, rock sunfish, black perch, goggle-eye perch.

SCIENTIFIC NAME: *Ambloplites rupestris*

DESCRIPTION: The rock bass isn't a bass—it's one of the sunfishes. And though it isn't much of a fighter, it is fun to catch and is sometimes unbelievably willing to gobble any lure, bait, or fly it can get its jaws around. Basic color of the rock bass is dark olive to greenish-bronze, with the belly lighter. The sides contain brownish or yellowish blotches, and a dark spot at the base of each scale produces broken horizontal streaks. The mouth is much larger than that of most other sunfishes, and the anal fin has 6 spines, while that of most of the other sunfishes has only 3 spines. There is a dark blotch on the gill flap.

RANGE: The rock bass occurs from southern Manitoba east to New England, and south to the Gulf States. Stockings have somewhat widened this range in recent years.

HABITAT: Rock bass prefer large, clear streams and lakes and are often found in the same waters as are smallmouth bass. As their name suggests, the more rocks and stones on the bottom, the better a fisherman's chances of finding rock bass. The species seems to prefer pools or protected waters to fast current or open waters.

SIZE: Top weight of rock bass is a bit more than 2 pounds. Most of those caught by fishermen are 6 to 10 inches long and weigh about ½ pound.

FOOD: A voracious eater, the rock bass eats crawfish, minnows and other baitfish, worms, adult and larval insect life, and the like.

Hickory Shad

SCIENTIFIC NAME: *Alosa mediocris (or Pomolobus mediocris).*

DESCRIPTION: The hickory shad—like its larger relative, the American shad—is a herring. In color it is gray-green above, with silvery sides and underparts. Behind the upper part of the gill cover is a horizontal row of dark spots, usually numbering about 6. Spots on the upper rows of scales form faint horizontal lines. Upper jaw is shallow-notched, and lower jaw projects prominently. The hickory shad is not so important a food or sport fish as is the American shad.

RANGE: The hickory shad is found along the Atlantic Coast from the Bay of Fundy south to Florida.

HABITAT: An anadromous species (living in salt water but ascending fresh-water rivers to spawn), the hickory shad's movements in the ocean are little-known. But in the spring it goes up the rivers, often the same rivers in which American shad spawn, though its runs usually precede those of the American shad.

SIZE: Though 5-pounders have been reported, the hickory shad seldom tops 2½ pounds in weight or 24 inches in length.

FOOD: The hickory shad feeds more on fish than does the American shad, and it is often caught by anglers using artificial flies and small spoons.

Freshwater Drum

COMMON NAMES: Freshwater drum, sheepshead, gray bass, gaspergou, white perch, croaker, crocus, jewelhead, grunter.

SCIENTIFIC NAME: *Aplodinotus grunniens.*

DESCRIPTION: This species is the only freshwater member of the drum (croaker) family, which has about 3 dozen salt-water members. The fresh-water drum has a blunt head, rounded tail, long dorsal fin, and a humped back. Colors are pearl-gray on back and upper sides, silvery on remainder of sides, and milky-white on the belly. A rather faint lateral line runs all the way into the tail. These fish make a weird "drumming" noise which, when they feed near the surface on calm evenings, seems to come from everywhere. It is caused by repeated contractions of an abdominal muscle against the swim bladder. Another oddity: the otoliths, or ear bones, of freshwater drum were used as wampum by Indians, as lucky pieces, and to prevent sicknesses.

RANGE: Freshwater drum are found from Guatemala north through eastern Mexico and the Gulf States to Manitoba, northern Ontario, Quebec, and the Lake Champlain area. East to west, they range from the Atlantic Coast to the Missouri River drainage.

HABITAT: Found principally in large lakes and large, slow rivers, this species prefers modest depths (10 to 40 feet) and silty or muddy bottoms. It is a school fish, often congregating below large dams.

SIZE: Freshwater drum attain a maximum weight of about 60 pounds, but average size is 1 to 5 pounds.

FOOD: Primarily a bottom feeder, this species feeds almost entirely on mollusks—clams, mussels, and snails—which it "shells" with its large, strong teeth. Other foods include crawfish and some baitfish.

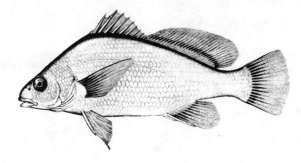

Freshwater Drum

Species of Saltwater Fish

Blue Shark

SCIENTIFIC NAME: *Prionace glauca.*

DESCRIPTION: This large shark species, which has a reputation as a man-eater, is distinguished by its abnormally long pectoral fins and by its bright-cobalt color (the belly is white). It has the long snout of many members of the large shark family, and the dorsal fin is set well back on the back, nearly at the midpoint.

RANGE: Blue sharks are found throughout the tropical and temperate waters of the world.

HABITAT: Though often seen in shallow waters on the U.S. Pacific Coast and on the surface in other northern areas, the blue shark is usually caught in deep water. It often roams in packs, while at other times it is found singly or in pairs.

SIZE: Blue sharks average less than 10 feet in length, but are reported to attain lengths of better than 20 feet. Largest rod-caught blue weighed 410 pounds.

FOOD: Blue sharks eat mainly mackerel, herring, squid, other sharks, flying fish, anchovies, and even such tidbits as seagulls and garbage deep-sixed from ships.

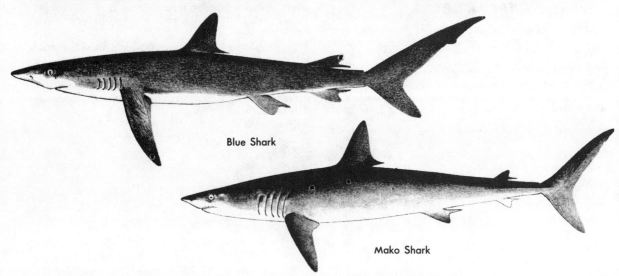

Blue Shark

Mako Shark

Mako Shark

COMMON NAMES: Mako shark, mackerel shark.

SCIENTIFIC NAME: *Isurus oxyrhinchus.*

DESCRIPTION: This huge, dangerous, fast-swimming, and hard-fighting shark is closely related to the white shark. It differs from the white mainly in the dorsal and pectoral fins, the tips of which are rounded in the mako, rather pointed in the white. In color the mako is dark-blue to bluish-gray above, shading to silver on the belly. The mako differs from the porbeagle shark in that its second dorsal fin is positioned a bit forward of the anal fin, while the porbeagle's second dorsal is directly above the anal.

RANGE: The mako is an inhabitant of the tropical oceans and the warmer areas of the Atlantic Ocean. It is not abundant in U.S. waters, though it is found as far north in the U.S. Atlantic as Cape Cod. It seems to be most numerous around New Zealand.

HABITAT: Makos tend to stay near the surface in open-ocean areas.

SIZE: Makos reach lengths of better than 12 feet and weights of over 1,000 pounds

FOOD: Staples of the mako's diet include tuna, mackerel, and herring. For some reason it often attacks, but seldom kills, swordfish.

White Shark

COMMON NAMES: White shark, great white shark, man-eater.

SCIENTIFIC NAME: *Carcharodon carcharias.*

DESCRIPTION: The white shark—enormous, vicious, and incredibly powerful—is one of the largest of all fish. Its usual colors are grayish-brown, slate-blue, or gray, while the belly is an off-white. Large specimens are sometimes a general off-white. The white shark is built blockier than the look-alike mako, having a much deeper body. The white has a pointed snout, triangular serrated teeth, and a crescent-shaped caudal fin.

RANGE: The white shark is found throughout the world in tropical and temperate waters, though it seems to prefer warm-to-temperate regions over tropics. It is not numerous anywhere.

HABITAT: White sharks generally stay well offshore and, as above, seem to prefer relatively cool waters.

SIZE: The white shark is a true behemoth; one specimen 36½ feet long has been captured. The weight of that fish must have been astronomical, considering that one white shark 13 feet long weighed 2,100 pounds! Whites 20 feet long are not uncommon.

FOOD: White sharks eat such things as other sharks 4 to 7 feet long, sea lions, seals, sturgeon, tuna, sea turtles, squid, and refuse.

Porbeagle Shark

COMMON NAMES: Porbeagle shark, mackerel shark.

SCIENTIFIC NAME: *Lamna nasus.*

DESCRIPTION: The porbeagle is a blocky-bodied shark that closely resembles the mako, though it is much less game. Best way to distinguish the porbeagle from both the mako and the white shark is the location of the second dorsal fin—the porbeagle is the only one whose second dorsal is directly above the anal fin. In color the porbeagle shades from black to blue-gray on the back to white on the belly. Its anal fin is white or dusky.

RANGE: The porbeagle is found on both sides of the Atlantic as far south as the Mediterranean and Africa. On the U.S. Atlantic coast is has been taken from South Carolina to the St. Lawrence Gulf. It is also found along most of the Pacific Coast.

HABITAT: The porbeagle is a fish of temperate waters. In warm waters it is found closer to shore and nearer the surface, but when the water cools it may head for depths as great as 80 fathoms.

SIZE: The porbeagle apparently reaches a maximum length of about 12 feet, though the largest definitely recorded stretched 10 feet. Largest rod-caught porbeagle weighed 400 pounds.

FOOD: Porbeagles thrive on school-type fish such as mackerel and herring and on bottom fish including cod, hake, and flounders.

Thresher Shark

SCIENTIFIC NAME: *Alopias vulpinus.*

DESCRIPTION: The thresher shark is nearly as large as the mako and is an excellent fighter, making breathtaking jumps and long runs. The thresher has one unique physical characteristic—its inordinately long upper lobe of the tail, or caudal fin, which is at least as long as the body. The thresher is dark gray, bluish, brown, or black on back and sides, while the belly is white, sometimes with gray mottling.

RANGE: Threshers are found from Nova Scotia to Argentina and from Ireland to the Cape of Good Hope. It occurs throughout the Mediterranean, in the Pacific from Oregon to Chile, and as far from the U.S. as Hawaii, Japan, and Australia.

HABITAT: The thresher is most at home at or near the surface in subtropical to temperate waters.

SIZE: Threshers reach lengths of 20 feet and weights of half a ton.

FOOD: The thresher uses its long tail to herd and injure such schooling fish as mackerel, menhaden, and bluefish.

Tiger Shark

SCIENTIFIC NAME: *Galeocerdo cuvieri.*

DESCRIPTION: One of the so-called requiem sharks, the aptly named tiger is often the culprit in attacks on swimmers. In color, it is usually a general steel-gray or brownish-gray with a white belly, though the young have bars and spots on back and upper sides. Upper lobe of the tail is long and slender, and the snout is short and sharp-pointed.

RANGE: Tiger sharks are found throughout the world's tropical and subtropical regions.

HABITAT: Though sometimes caught offshore, the tiger seems to be largely a coastal fish, and it occasionally comes into quite shallow waters. It stays near the surface.

SIZE: Tigers are reported to reach lengths of 30 feet. Maximum weight is unknown, but 13 to 14-footers tip the scales at 1,000 to about 1,500 pounds.

FOOD: Tiger sharks are omnivorous and cannibalistic. They eat their own kind, as well as fish of most species and crabs, lobsters, and even sea lions and turtles. Examinations of their stomachs have revealed such things as tin cans, parts of crocodiles, and even human remains.

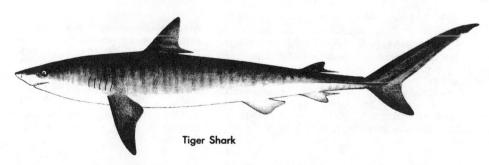

Tiger Shark

Hammerhead Shark

Hammerhead Shark

COMMON NAMES: Hammerhead shark, hammerhead, great hammerhead

SCIENTIFIC NAME: *Sphyrna mokarran.*

DESCRIPTION: There's no mistaking the hammerhead shark. Its small eyes are located at each end of its unique and grotesque head, which looks as if it had been modeled after the head of a huge mallet that had been pounded nearly flat. Gray or sometimes brownish-gray on back and sides, off-white on the underparts, the hammerhead's dorsal fin is less erect than that of any of its Atlantic relatives. Though not officially classified as a gamefish, the hammerhead is a large and powerful adversary. Its hide makes fine leather, and its liver contains a high-grade oil.

RANGE: In the western Atlantic the hammerhead occurs from North Carolina to Argentina. It is found elsewhere in the tropical and subtropical areas of the Atlantic, as well as in the eastern Pacific and the Indo-Pacific.

HABITAT: Hammerheads often travel in schools and may be found both near shore and far offshore.

SIZE: Average size is difficult to determine, but hammerheads apparently reach a maximum length of about 18 feet and a maximum weight of considerably more than 1,600 pounds.

FOOD: Voracious and cannibalistic, the hammerhead eats just about anything unlucky enough to get in its way, including big tuna, tarpon, and other sharks.

Swordfish

COMMON NAMES: Swordfish, broadbill, broadbill swordfish.

SCIENTIFIC NAME: *Xiphias gladius.*

DESCRIPTION: The swordfish is one of the elite of saltwater fish, much sought by both commercial and sport fishermen. It is distinguished from the other billfish (sailfish and marlin) by its much-longer, flat bill (sword) and by its lack of scales and pelvic fins (the other billfish have both). The swordfish's dorsal and anal fins are sickle-shaped. Its color is usually dark-brown or bronze, but variations of black to grayish-blue are common. The belly is usually white, but the dark colors sometimes extend right down to the fish's undersides.

RANGE: Swordfish are migratory and are found worldwide in warm and temperate waters. Their occurrence in U.S. and adjacent waters extends in the Atlantic from Newfoundland to Cuba and in the Pacific from California to Chile.

HABITAT: Swordfish are open-ocean fish, usually feeding in the depths but often seen "sunning" on the surface.

SIZE: Maximum size of swordfish is a matter of some uncertainty, but specimens of nearly 1,200 pounds have been taken on rod and line. Average size is probably 150 to 300 pounds.

FOOD: Swordfish use their greatest weapon, the sword, to stun and capture such food as dolphin, menhaden, mackerel, bonito, bluefish, and squid.

Blue Marlin

SCIENTIFIC NAME: *Makaira nigricans.*

DESCRIPTION: This king of the blue water is probably the most highly prized of big-game fish, mainly because of its mammoth size and spectacular fighting abilities. In general coloration the blue marlin is steel-blue on the back, shading to silvery-white on the belly. In most specimens the sides contain light vertical bars, which are not nearly so prominent as those of the white marlin. The dorsal and anal fins are bluish-purple and sometimes have dark blotches. The blue marlin's distinguishing physical traits include a relatively short dorsal fin and a relatively long anal fin, and a body shape that is considerably rounder than other billfish.

RANGE: Blue marlin are found in warm and temperate seas throughout the world. In U.S. and nearby waters they occur from the Gulf of Maine to Uruguay in the Atlantic, from Mexico to Peru in the Pacific.

HABITAT: Blue marlin are deepwater fish almost exclusively, and they are often seen cruising and feeding on the surface.

SIZE: Maximum size of blue marlin is something over 2,000 pounds, with the average being 200 to 500 pounds. Males seldom exceed 300 pounds, so those monsters often referred to as Big Daddy should really be called Big Mamma. Because the biggest blue marlin are thought to be in the Pacific, the International Game Fish Association separates these fish into two categories—Atlantic and Pacific.

FOOD: Blue marlin eat a broad range of fish life, including bluefish, mackerel, tuna, and bonito, as well as squid and octopus.

Freshwater Fishes

Paintings by Duane Raver. Courtesy North Carolina Wildlife Resources Commission.

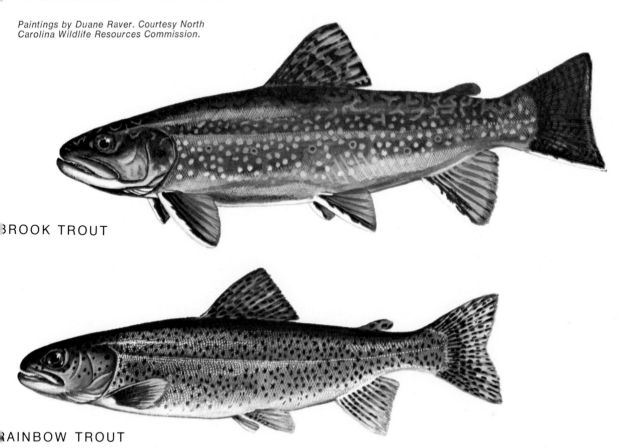

BROOK TROUT

RAINBOW TROUT

BROWN TROUT

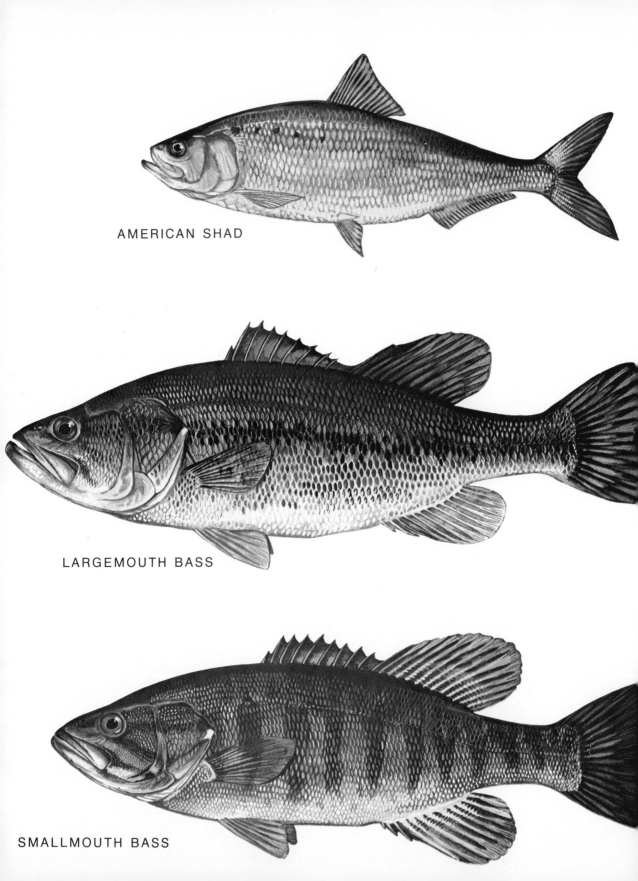

AMERICAN SHAD

LARGEMOUTH BASS

SMALLMOUTH BASS

BLUEGILL

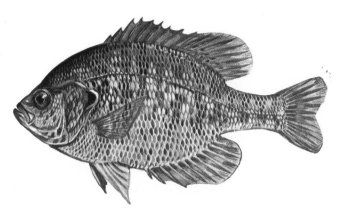

REDEAR SUNFISH

BLACK CRAPPIE

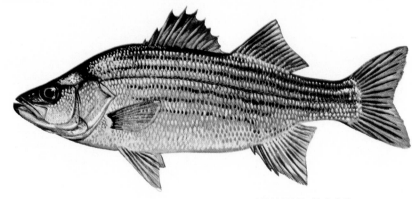

WHITE BASS

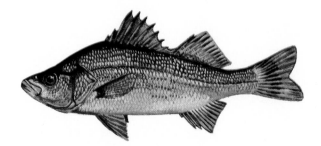

WHITE PERCH

YELLOW PERCH

WALLEYE

CHANNEL CATFISH

BROWN BULLHEAD

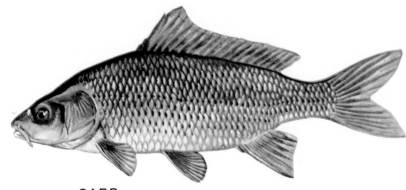

CARP

LONGNOSE GAR

CHAIN PICKEREL

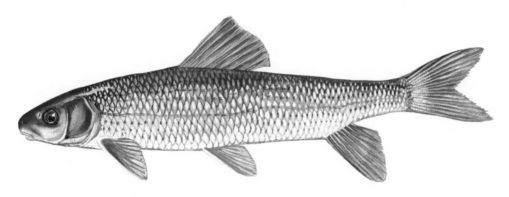

REDHORSE SUCKER

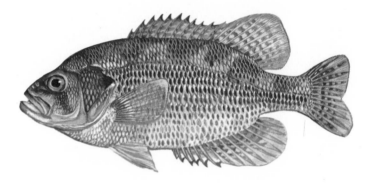

ROCK BASS

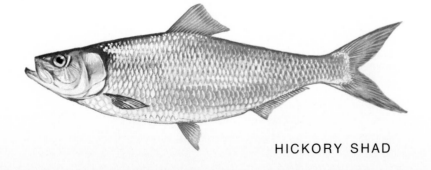

HICKORY SHAD

Saltwater Fishes

*Paintings by Duane Raver. Courtesy Alexandria
Drafting Company, Alexandria, Virginia.*

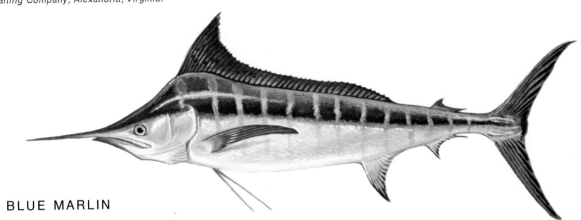

BLUE MARLIN

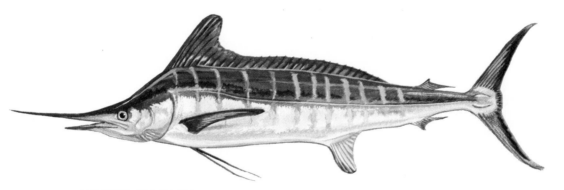

WHITE MARLIN

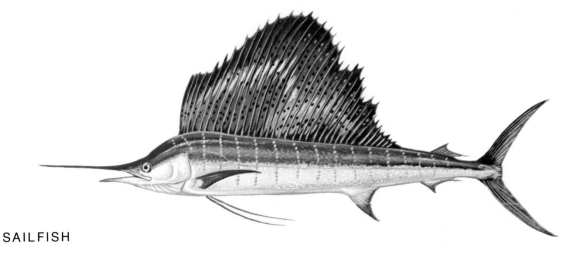

SAILFISH

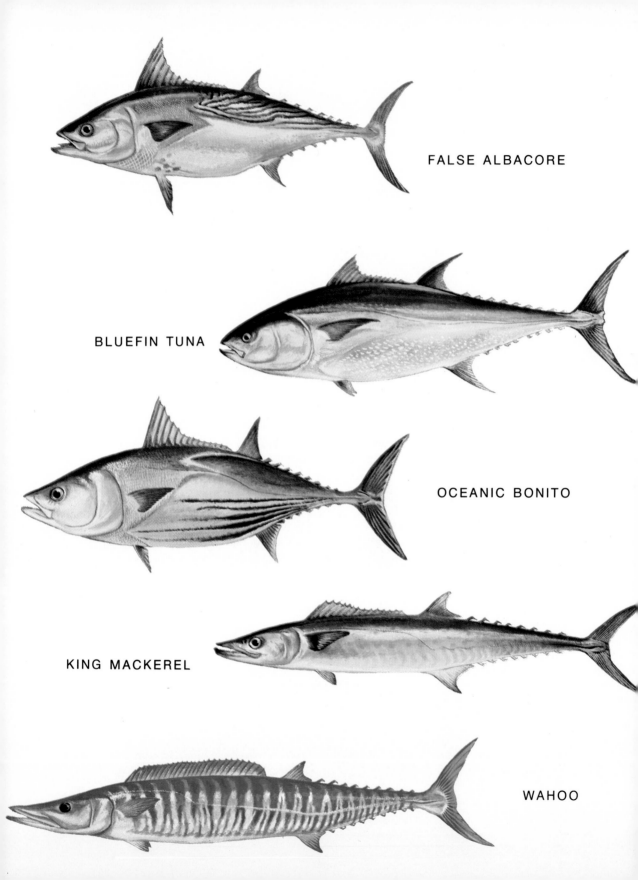

FALSE ALBACORE

BLUEFIN TUNA

OCEANIC BONITO

KING MACKEREL

WAHOO

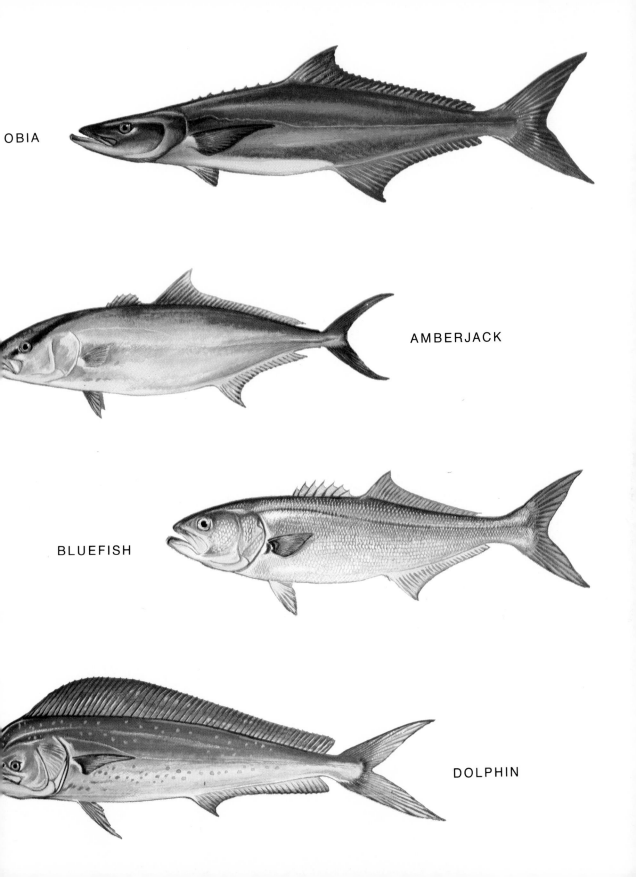

OBIA

AMBERJACK

BLUEFISH

DOLPHIN

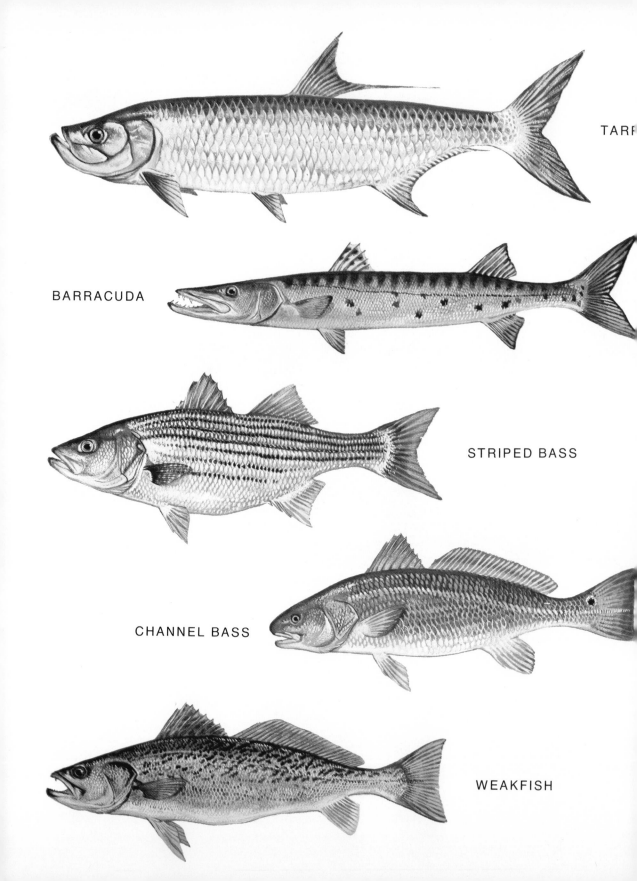

TARP

BARRACUDA

STRIPED BASS

CHANNEL BASS

WEAKFISH

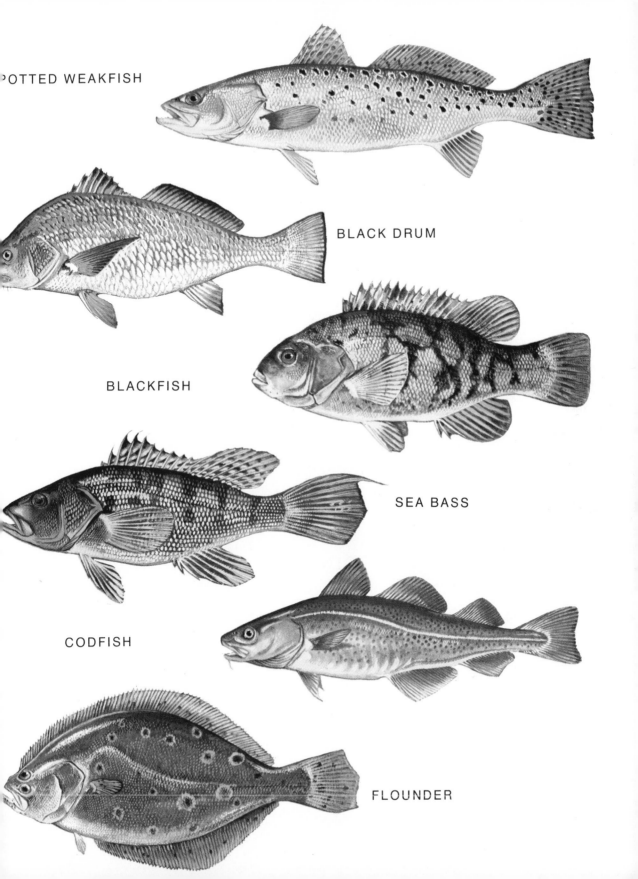

POTTED WEAKFISH

BLACK DRUM

BLACKFISH

SEA BASS

CODFISH

FLOUNDER

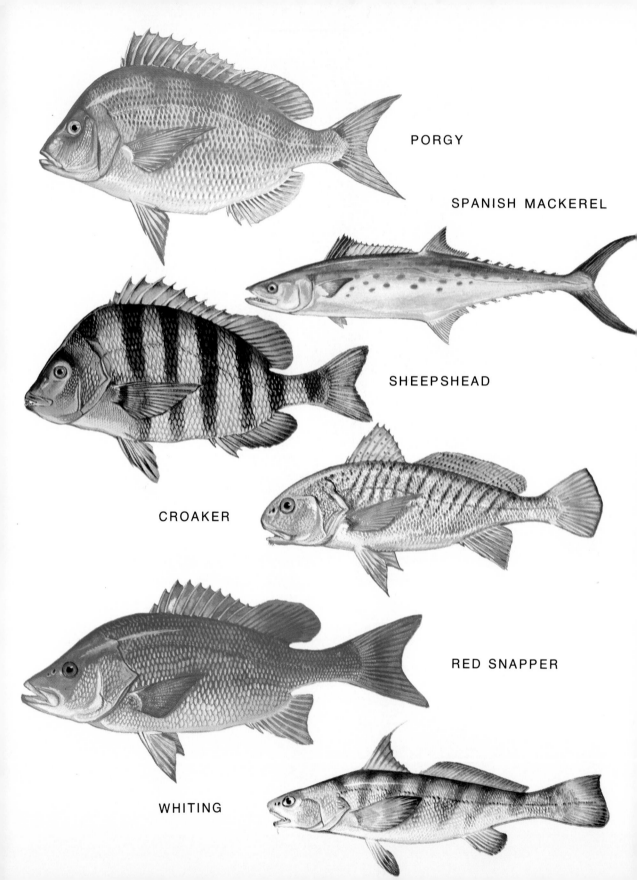

PORGY

SPANISH MACKEREL

SHEEPSHEAD

CROAKER

RED SNAPPER

WHITING

White Marlin

SCIENTIFIC NAME: *Makaira albida (or Tetrapturus albidus).*

DESCRIPTION: The white marlin is considerably smaller and less universal than the blue marlin. Its colors are a brilliant greenish-blue on back and upper sides, changing abruptly to white at the lateral line. The sides have an irregular number of vertical bands of light blue or lavender. A unique feature of the white marlin is the rounded tips of its dorsal and anal fins. The body is slender and relatively flat-sided.

RANGE: The white marlin is limited to the Atlantic, occurring from Nova Scotia to Brazil and from the Azores to St. Helena Island and South Africa. Centers of concentration at differing times of year seem to be off Ocean City, Maryland, and near Venezuela.

HABITAT: Like the blue marlin, the white is a fish of warm and temperate waters and is a migrant.

SIZE: Most whites caught by fishermen weigh 40 to 60 pounds, but the species apparently reaches 160 pounds.

FOOD: The white is mainly a fish eater but will dine on anything it can capture.

Black Marlin

SCIENTIFIC NAME: *Makaira indica (or Istiompax indicus).*

DESCRIPTION: Possibly the largest of the marlins, the black is an ocean giant that is most easily distinguished from other marlins by the fact that its pectoral fins stick out at right angles from the body and are held rigidly in that position. The pelvic fins of the black marlin are shorter than those of other marlins, usually less than 1 foot long. The black marlin is seldom truly black, though its color varies greatly. Most are slate-blue on the back and upper sides, shading to silvery white on the underparts. The sides occasionally exhibit pale blue stripes.

RANGE: Black marlin seem to be found almost exclusively in the Pacific and Indian oceans, being found as far north as southern California and Mexico. One area of abundance seems to be off the coast of Peru.

HABITAT: Little is known of the movements of the black marlin, though it is certainly a fish of the open oceans, and evidence indicates that it migrates only short distances if at all.

SIZE: The record rod-caught black marlin weighed 1,560 pounds, but specimens of up to 2,000 pounds have been taken commercially. Average size is probably 300 to 500 pounds.

FOOD: Various fish species (a tuna of 158 pounds was found in a black marlin's stomach) and squid are the main items in the black's diet.

Striped Marlin

SCIENTIFIC NAME: *Makaira audax (or Tetrapturus audax).*

DESCRIPTION: Smaller than the blue and black marlins, the striped marlin, as its name suggests, is most easily distinguished by the stripes on its sides. These stripes vary both in number and in color, which ranges from pale blue to lavender to white. Body colors are steel-blue on back and upper sides, shading to white on the bottom areas. The striped marlin also has a high, pointed dorsal fin, which is usually taller than the greatest depth of its body. Like all the other marlins, the striped variety puts up a breathtaking battle.

RANGE: Striped marlin are found in the Indian Ocean and in the Pacific from southern California to Chile.

HABITAT: Striped marlin are open-ocean fish. The fairly well defined local populations seem to make short north-to-south migrations. Like all the other marlins, they are often seen feeding on the surface.

SIZE: The average rod-caught striped marlin weighs about 200 to 250 pounds, but the species grows to more than 500 pounds.

FOOD: Striped marlin feed on a wide variety of fish life (anchovies, bonito, mackerel, and many others), and on squid, crustaceans, octopus, and anything else that might get in their way.

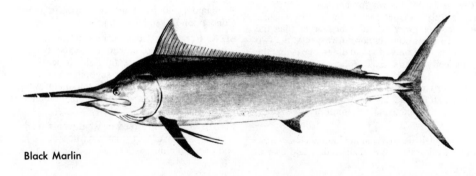

Black Marlin

Atlantic Sailfish

SCIENTIFIC NAME: *Istiophorus albicans.*

DESCRIPTION: The uncommonly beautiful sailfish probably adorn more den and living-room walls than do any other marine gamefish. They are spectacular fighters, hurling themselves high out of the water time and time again. You can't mistake the sailfish for anything else that swims—thanks to its enormous purple (or cobalt-blue) dorsal fin, which it often seems to flaunt at fishermen. Body colors range from striking blue on back and upper sides to silver-white below the well-defined lateral line. Side markings usually consist of a variable number of pale vertical bars or vertical rows of pale spots. The dorsal fin usually is marked with numerous black spots. A sailfish's pelvic fins are longer than those of other billfish.

RANGE: The Atlantic sailfish is commonly found in the Atlantic Ocean from Cape Hatteras to Venezuela, with winter concentrations off the east coast of Florida. This species is also found off England, France, Africa, and in the Mediterranean.

HABITAT: Sailfish are most often seen—and are almost always caught—on or near the surface. However, studies of their preferred diet indicates that they do much of their feeding in middle depths, along reefs, and even on the bottom.

SIZE: Most Atlantic sailfish caught by sport fishermen weigh 30 to 50 pounds. Maximum size is probably a bit larger than the rod-and-reel record of 141 pounds.

FOOD: According to studies made of the feeding habits of Atlantic sailfish in Florida waters, these fish feed mainly on a wide variety of fish life (tuna, mackerel, jacks, balao, needlefish, herring, and a few other species made up 83 percent of the Atlantic sail's diet). They also feed on squid and octopus.

Pacific Sailfish

SCIENTIFIC NAME: *Istiophorus greyi.*

DESCRIPTION: It is not known for certain whether the Pacific sailfish is truly a distinct species from the Atlantic sailfish, though it does grow considerably larger than the Atlantic variety. In most other important respects, the two fish are exactly alike. The only physical difference is that the Pacific sailfish's body colors tend to be somewhat more muted. It should be noted that in sport fishing for sailfish, marlin, and all other large pelagic gamefish, the trend today is toward releasing all fish that are not wanted for food (sailfish are not particularly good to eat) or mounting. (See Atlantic Sailfish.)

RANGE: Pacific sailfish are found in the Pacific Ocean from about Monterey, California, south to Ecuador, and also in the vicinity of the Hawaiian Islands and elsewhere in the South Pacific.

HABITAT: See Atlantic Sailfish.

SIZE: Pacific sailfish put on a good deal more weight than their relatives in the Atlantic. Maximum weight is about 240 pounds, but the average rod-caught Pacific sail weighs from 60 to 100 pounds.

FOOD: See Atlantic Sailfish.

Bluefin Tuna

COMMON NAMES: Bluefin tuna, bluefin, horse mackerel.

SCIENTIFIC NAME: *Thunnus thynnus.*

DESCRIPTION: The bluefin is the king of the tunas, all of which are members of the mackerel family. Bluefins, from those of school size (15 to 100 pounds) to giants of nearly half a ton, have incredible strength and tenacity, and they are much sought by both sport and commercial fishermen. The bluefin has the blocky, robust body of a typical heavyweight. The head is rather small, and the snout is pointed. The bluefin has shorter pectoral fins than any of the other American tunas. It has two dorsal fins—the forward one retractable and the rearward one fixed. Tail is sickle-shaped. In color the bluefin is steel-blue on back and upper sides, shading to light gray or creamy white on lower parts. In small bluefins, the lower sides have vertical white lines.

RANGE: Bluefin tuna are found throughout the world, mostly in temperate and subtropical waters. In the western Atlantic they occur in abundance from the Bahamas north to the Labrador Current. In the Pacific they seem to be less abundant, being found in greatest numbers in the general area of Catalina Island.

HABITAT: The bluefin is generally a fish of the open ocean, though school-size bluefins occasionally come quite close to shore. In summer bluefins show up in large numbers from New Jersey to Nova Scotia, the smaller fish showing up first and closer to shore. Atlantic areas where bluefins tend to congregate and provide good fishing include the New York Bight, Block Island to Rhode Island, Cape Cod Bay, Wedgeport and St. Margaret's Bay in Nova Scotia, and Conception Bay in Newfoundland.

SIZE: For all practical fishing purposes, bluefins can be grouped in two size categories: school fish (those weighing 15 to 100 pounds) and adult fish (those weighing more than 100 pounds). The average schoolie weighs 30 to 50 pounds, while the giant bluefins attain maximum weights estimated to be 1,500 pounds or more. The rod-and-reel record is 1,065 pounds.

FOOD: Bluefin tuna feed on whatever is available, including a wide variety of fish (including herring, sand lance, hake, and even dolphin), as well as squid and crustaceans.

Yellowfin Tuna

COMMON NAMES: Yellowfin tuna, allison tuna.

SCIENTIFIC NAME: *Thunnus albacares.*

DESCRIPTION: Considerably smaller than the bluefin, the yellowfin tuna is a top sport and commercial fish, particularly in the Pacific. In color the yellowfin is steel-blue or nearly black on back and upper sides, silvery-white on lower parts. Characteristics that distinguish it from the bluefin are its much longer pectoral fins and the generous amount of yellow in most of the fins. The yellowfin is difficult to distinguish from some of the other tunas, but in large specimens the second dorsal fin and anal fin are much longer than those of any other tuna. The side markings of the yellowfin include a sometimes indistinct golden-yellow horizontal streak and white spots and vertical stripes on the lower sides.

RANGE: Yellowfins are found worldwide in tropical and subtropical waters. They are most numerous in the Pacific, where they are found widely off the coast of southern California and Baja California. They also range from the Gulf of Mexico north to New Jersey.

HABITAT: Yellowfin tuna are more southerly in general range than are bluefins. They are open-ocean fish, though there is some evidence that they do not make such long-range migrations as bluefins do.

SIZE: Yellowfins are thought to reach a maximum size of some 500 pounds. However, the rod-and-reel record is only 269 pounds, and average size is less than 100 pounds.

FOOD: Same as bluefin tuna.

Big-Eye Tuna

COMMON NAMES: Big-eye tuna, Pacific big-eye tuna, Atlantic big-eye tuna.

SCIENTIFIC NAME: *Thunnus obesus.*

DESCRIPTION: Its eyes are not abnormally large, so it's difficult to determine how the big-eye tuna got its name. Its coloration is similar to that of its big brother, the bluefin, though its pectoral fins are longer. It is often hard to distinguish the big-eye from some of the other tunas. Its dorsal and anal fins are never greatly elongated (as in the large yellowfins), and the finlets running along back and belly from dorsal and anal fins to tail are yellow with black margins. Though Atlantic and Pacific big-eyes are the same species, the International Game Fish Association separates them for record-keeping purposes.

RANGE: Big-eye tuna range throughout the world in tropical and subtropical waters.

HABITAT: Big-eyes are fish of the open oceans and deep water, as witness the fact that many are caught by commercial longline fishermen.

SIZE: Big-eyes probably reach weights of 500 pounds and seem to grow somewhat bigger in the Pacific than in the Atlantic. Average size is about 100 pounds.

FOOD: Same as bluefin tuna.

Blackfin Tuna

SCIENTIFIC NAME: *Thunnus atlanticus.*

DESCRIPTION: Far more restricted in range than any of the other popular tunas, the blackfin is also one of the smallest members of the family. It is darker in color than the other tunas and has fewer gillrakers. The finlets behind the dorsal and anal fins are totally dark — not marked with yellow as are most of the other tunas.

RANGE: Blackfin tuna are found only in the western Atlantic Ocean, ranging from Cape Cod south to Brazil.

HABITAT: Blackfins are open-ocean, deep-water fish, like almost all the other members of the tuna family.

SIZE: The blackfin's top weight is probably not more than 40 pounds. World-record rod-caught fish weighed 36 pounds. Average is probably about 10 pounds.

FOOD: The blackfin's diet is about the same as that of the other tunas, except that its prey is proportionately smaller.

Albacore

COMMON NAMES: Albacore, longfin tuna.

SCIENTIFIC NAME: *Thunnus alalunga.*

DESCRIPTION: The albacore is what you are likely to get when you buy a can of "all-white-meat tuna." It is one of the tunas, and thus a member of the mackerel family. The albacore's most outstanding physical trait is its abnormally long pectoral (side) fins, which extend from behind the gills well past the second dorsal fin, ending about even with the third dorsal finlet. Coloring is an iridescent steel-blue above, shading to silvery-white on the belly. Fins are generally blue and bright yellow.

RANGE: Albacore are found in tropical, subtropical, and temperate waters in most parts of the world. In U.S. and adjacent waters they are primarily a Pacific species, being plentiful from southern British Columbia to southern California and Baja. In the Atlantic quite a few are caught off Florida, and they are occasionally found as far north as Massachusetts.

HABITAT: Albacore almost never come close to shore. They haunt deep, open waters and often feed near or on the surface. When on top, they can be seen smashing wildly into schools of frenzied baitfish.

SIZE: Albacore of up to 90 pounds have been taken in nets, and the record rod-caught fish went 69 pounds. Average weight is 5 to 25 pounds.

FOOD: Albacore feed on a wide variety of fish, as well as squid and crustaceans.

Oceanic Bonito

COMMON NAMES: Oceanic bonito, bonito, skipjack, skipjack tuna, oceanic skipjack, striped tuna.

SCIENTIFIC NAME: *Euthynnus pelamis (or Katsuwonus pelamis).*

DESCRIPTION: The oceanic bonito is the most important member of the bonito group (which also includes the common, or Atlantic, bonito and the striped bonito, among others) and is the only bonito classified as a gamefish by the International Game Fish Association. The oceanic bonito is striking blue above and silvery below, with some shadings of yellow and red. It is unique in having four or more well-defined dark stripes running from the area of the pectoral fin to the tail along the lower part of the body.

RANGE: Oceanic bonito are found in tropical and subtropical waters throughout the world. In U.S. and adjacent waters, it is most common off the southern coasts.

HABITAT: All the bonitos are fish of offshore waters, though they come relatively close to shore if that is where their favorite food is. They are school fish and generally feed on or near the surface.

SIZE: The average weight of oceanic bonito is probably 10 to 18 pounds. Maximum is about 40 pounds.

FOOD: All the bonitos feed on a wide variety of fish, plus squid and crustaceans.

King Mackerel

COMMON NAMES: King mackerel, kingfish, cavalla, cero.

SCIENTIFIC NAME: *Scomberomorus cavalla.*

DESCRIPTION: Fast, strong, and good to eat is the king mackerel, largest member of the Spanish-mackerel family in U.S. waters. Its streamlined body—colored in iridescent bluish-green above and shading to platinum below—seems built for speed, which the fish exhibits both in the water and above it in soaring leaps. The king's meandering lateral line and its lack of other side markings set it apart from most other fish. The lack of black in the rear part of the first dorsal fin distinguishes the king mackerel from other Spanish mackerels in our waters.

RANGE: Generally found from Brazil north to North Carolina and occasionally up to Cape Cod, the king mackerel is most numerous in the Gulf of Mexico and southern Atlantic.

HABITAT: King mackerel range in schools and usually stick to open water, though they sometimes hover near the outer reaches of bays, feeding on baitfish. March is the peak of the king-mackerel season for Florida anglers, while in the Gulf the fishing runs from spring into September.

SIZE: The average rod-caught king mackerel weighs 5 to 15 pounds, but the species apparently reaches a length of 5 feet and a weight of 100 pounds.

FOOD: King mackerel feed almost exclusively on smaller fish.

Wahoo

COMMON NAMES: Wahoo, queenfish, peto, ocean barracuda.

SCIENTIFIC NAME: *Acanthocybium solandri.*

DESCRIPTION: It is probably well that wahoo are neither as numerous as striped bass nor as large as bluefin tuna, for they are one of the wildest things with fins. They smash a trolled lure or bait with incredible force, make blitzing runs, and hurl themselves far out of the water (reports have it that wahoo have leaped over a fishing boat lengthwise!). The wahoo resembles no other fish, though it is shaped generally like the king mackerel. Its iridescent colors include blue or blue-green above, shading through coppery tints to silver below. The sides have narrow, wavy, dark, vertical bars. Older fish may lack the side markings.

RANGE: Wahoo range throughout the world in tropical and subtropical waters. In the Atlantic they stray as far north as the Carolinas but are most often caught off the Florida Keys, Mexico, and the West Indies.

HABITAT: Unlike most other mackerel-like fish, wahoos are loners—that is, they do not range in schools. They live in deep water, often staying near the edges of deep drop-offs or along reefs.

SIZE: The average wahoo caught by anglers weighs 10 to 25 pounds, but the species is reported to hit 150 pounds.

FOOD: Wahoos eat various fish including flying fish, mackerel, mullet, as well as squid.

Cobia

COMMON NAMES: Cobia, crab-eater, ling, lemonfish, coalfish, black salmon, black bonito, cabio, cobio.

SCIENTIFIC NAME: *Rachycentron canadum.*

DESCRIPTION: The cobia is something of a mystery fish. Little is known of its wanderings or life history, and the species has no close relatives. In color the cobia is dark brown on the back and lighter brown on the sides and belly. A wide, black lateral band extends from snout to base of tail. Less-distinct dark bands are found above and below the lateral. The first dorsal fin is actually a series of quite short, stiff, wide spines that look nothing at all like a standard dorsal.

RANGE: The cobia is found in many of the world's tropical and warm-temperate waters. It occurs in the western Atlantic from Massachusetts to Argentina, but its greatest abundance is from Chesapeake Bay southeast to Bermuda and in the Gulf of Mexico.

HABITAT: Young cobia are often caught in inlets and bays, but older fish seem to prefer shallower areas of the open sea. Cobias are almost invariably found around some kind of cover—over rocks, around pilings or bottom debris, and particular under floating objects such as buoys, weeds, and other flotsam.

SIZE: Cobia reach top weights of over 100 pounds. Average size is 5 to 10 pounds in some areas, though in other areas, notably Gulf waters, 25 to 50-pounders are not uncommon.

FOOD: Cobias feed largely on crabs, though they also eat shrimp and small fish of all kinds.

Amberjack

COMMON NAMES: Amberjack, greater amberjack, horse-eye bonito.

SCIENTIFIC NAME: *Seriola dumerili.*

DESCRIPTION: Amberjacks are related to the pompanos and jacks, and more distantly to the tunas and mackerels. The amberjack is a stocky, heavy-bodied fish with a deeply forked tail, the lobes of which are quite slender. Body colors are blue-green or blue on the back, shading to silvery in the underparts. The fins have some yellow in them. A well-defined dark band runs upward from the snout to a point behind the eye. Mostly a solitary wanderer, the amberjack sometimes gathers in small groups in preferred feeding areas.

RANGE: Though occasionally found as far north as New England, the amberjack is primarily a fish of southern Atlantic waters from the Carolinas south to Florida and nearby islands. In the Pacific it is abundant from southern Mexico southward.

HABITAT: Reefs are the favorite habitat of amberjacks, though these fish often cruise for food at moderate depths— approximately 20 to 40 feet.

SIZE: The average rod-caught amberjack probably weighs 12 to 20 pounds, though ambers of up to 50 pounds are far from rare. Maximum size is about 150 pounds.

FOOD: Amberjacks prey on many smaller fish and on crabs, shrimp, crustaceans, and anything else it can handle.

Pacific Yellowtail

COMMON NAMES: Pacific yellowtail, yellowtail, California yellowtail.

SCIENTIFIC NAME: *Seriola dorsalis.*

DESCRIPTION: A member of the amberjack family, the Pacific yellowtail is probably the most popular sport fish on the Pacific Coast. It is not of great commercial value. The yellowtail has a horizontal swath, ranging in color from brassy to rather bright yellow, running from eye to tail. Above the stripe the color is blue-green to green; below it the color is silvery. Fins are dusky yellow except the caudal fin (tail), which is bright yellow. The yellowtail is a tremendously powerful fighter.

RANGE: Yellowtails have been caught from Mazatlan, Mexico, through waters of Baja California, and north to the southern Washington coast. The world-record yellowtail was taken off New Zealand, but it is not known for sure whether it was of the same species as the Pacific yellowtail.

HABITAT: Yellowtails are fish of the mid-depths for the most part and are migratory. A preferred hangout is a kelp bed, and rocks often harbor yellowtails. Concentrations of yellowtails are at the Coronado Islands, around Catalina Island, and off San Clemente, Calif.

SIZE: Yellowtails reach weights of over 100 pounds, but average size is 8 to 25 pounds.

FOOD: Like many other voracious marine species, the yellowtail usually feeds on whatever is available. It seems to prefer sardines, anchovies, mackerel, squid, and crabs.

Jack Crevalle

COMMON NAMES: Jack crevalle, jack, common jack, cavally, cavalla, horse crevalle, toro.

SCIENTIFIC NAME: *Caranx hippos.*

DESCRIPTION: Probably the best-known member of a very large family, the jack crevalle is considered a fine game-fish by some anglers but a pest by others. The crevalle is short, husky, and slab-sided. It is yellow-green on back and upper sides, yellow and silvery on lower areas. There is a dark mark on the rear edge of the gill cover, and the breast is without scales except for a scaled patch just forward of the ventral fins.

RANGE: The jack crevalle is found from Uruguay to Nova Scotia in the western Atlantic, and from Peru to Baja California in the eastern Pacific. It is most numerous from Florida to Texas.

HABITAT: The crevalle seems to prefer shallow flats, though large solitary specimens are often taken in deep offshore waters. It is a schooling species.

SIZE: Jack crevalles of better than 70 pounds have been caught, and 45-pounders are not uncommon in Florida waters. Average size is probably 2 to 8 pounds.

FOOD: Smaller fish are the main course of the jack crevalle, but shrimp and other invertebrates are also on the menu.

Rainbow Runner

COMMON NAMES: Rainbow runner, rainbow yellowtail, runner, skipjack, shoemaker.

SCIENTIFIC NAME: *Elagatis bipinnulatus.*

Rainbow Runner

DESCRIPTION: The rainbow runner, an excellent gamefish, is a member of the jack family but doesn't look like most of the others. It is streamlined, not deep-bodied and chunky, and its coloration is striking. The back is a vivid blue or green-blue, while the lower areas and the tail are yellow. Along the upper sides is a broad dark-blue stripe, and below that are other, less-prominent blue stripes. Fins are greenish-yellow. Finlets at rear ends of dorsal and anal fins distinguish the rainbow runner from the amberjack, which it somewhat resembles.

RANGE: Occurring in tropical waters worldwide, the rainbow runner is found in the Atlantic from Colombia to Massachusetts; in the Pacific it has been recorded from Peru and the Galapagos Islands to Baja California.

HABITAT: The wanderings of this fish, which is nowhere numerous, are little known. Trollers catch rainbow runners off Florida's east coast and in the Gulf of Mexico.

SIZE: Maximum size is about 30 pounds, but most rainbow runners caught go about 15 inches in length.

FOOD: Rainbow runners feed mostly on smaller fish.

Permit

COMMON NAMES: Permit, great pompano, round pompano, palometa.

SCIENTIFIC NAME: *Trachinotus falcatus (or Trachinotus kennedyi).*

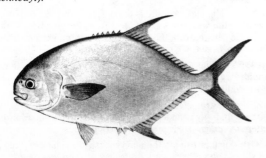

Permit

DESCRIPTION: The shy and wary permit, a much-prized gamefish, is the largest of the pompanos. Blocky and very deep-bodied (sometimes nearly half as deep as total body length), the permit's coloration varies greatly, especially in the young. Adults are generally bluish or gray on back, with the rest of the body being silvery. Very large ones may be almost entirely silvery with a green-blue tinge. Permit are far more numerous than many anglers think, but while they are often seen, they are much less often hooked and boated, for they put up a fight that is much more powerful than that of a bonefish. It usually takes at least a half-hour to tire a big permit.

RANGE: In the Atlantic permit are found from Brazil to Massachusetts, in the West Indies, and in Bermuda. A Pacific variety is found from Ecuador to southern California. It is most abundant off southern Florida.

HABITAT: Permit are found from the surf out to deep water. They tend to stay in channels and deep holes but often come onto shallow tidal flats to feed, at which time their tails and backs can be seen above the surface.

SIZE: Permit reach weights of 50 pounds, but those caught by anglers probably average 15 to 25 pounds.

FOOD: Mainly bottom-feeders, permit prefer crabs and other invertebrates, plus small fish.

Bluefish

COMMON NAMES: Bluefish, chopper, tailor, snapper, jumbo.

SCIENTIFIC NAME: *Pomatomus saltatrix.*

DESCRIPTION: Savage, cannibalistic, delicious, abundant, willing—all those adjectives fit the bluefish, only member of the family Pomatomidae. In coloration, the bluefish is a rather dark blue on the back, shading through blue-gray and gray-silver to silvery on the belly. A fisherman getting his first look at a pack of blues attacking a horde of baitfish finds the sight hard to believe. The water boils white and then turns red and brown with the blood of the frenzied baitfish and the regurgitated stomach contents of the savage blues. Once hooked, the bluefish makes the angler fervently thankful that these fish don't reach the size of tuna, for blues are among the most powerful fighters in the sea.

RANGE: Blues are found in the western Atlantic from Massachusetts to Argentina, off the northwest coast of Africa, the Azores, Portugal, and Spain, and in the Mediterranean and Black seas. They are also found in the eastern Indian Ocean, the Malay Peninsula, Australia, and New Zealand.

HABITAT: Though primarily a deep-water species, particularly the large ones, bluefish often come right into the surf and sometimes go quite a distance up brackish-water rivers. Blues are rather erratic wanderers, though their general migration routes are fairly constant. They usually travel in large schools. In winter they are most numerous in Florida. As the waters warm, they head north to such bluefishing hotspots as the Carolinas, New Jersey, and New England. Tidal rips are top spots to look for blues.

SIZE: Bluefish average 2 to 5 pounds, though 15- to 20-pounders are not uncommon, and there was a 45-pounder taken off the coast of North Africa.

FOOD: Bluefish will eat anything they can handle—and some things that they can't, to which fact many a fisherman who has been bitten by a just-boated blue will attest. Menhaden is a bluefish's blue-plate special, and other preferred foods are mullet, squid, and eels.

Dolphin

COMMON NAMES: Dolphin, bull dolphin, dorado, mahi-mahi.

SCIENTIFIC NAME: *Coryphaena hippurus.*

DESCRIPTION: The dolphin (a cold-blooded species that should not be confused with the warm-blooded dolphin, which is a mammal and a member of the porpoise family) is spectacular in both coloration and fighting ability. Purple and blue on the dorsal surface, iridescent green and yellow on sides and lower body, the dolphin's merging colors are enhanced by scattered blue dots. The head is extremely blunt, being almost vertical in large specimens (called bulls, though they may be either male or female). The dorsal fin extends from head nearly to tail. The dolphin is an explosive battler and an acrobatic leaper.

RANGE: Dolphins range widely in tropical and subtropical seas. In the western Atlantic they are found in relative abundance from North Carolina (particularly in or near the Gulf Stream) south into the Gulf of Mexico as far west as Texas. In the Pacific they range as far north as Oregon but are most numerous off southern California.

HABITAT: Dolphin are usually school fish, though large ones are often loners. They are fish of the open oceans; however, they lie under and cavort near various patches or bits of flotsam—floating grass, pieces of driftwood, and the like.

SIZE: The largest dolphin on record weighed nearly 77 pounds. However, most rod-caught dolphin go 5 to 15 pounds.

FOOD: The food of dolphins includes a wide variety of smaller fish, squid, and crustaceans. In many parts of the dolphin's range, the flying fish forms a large portion of its diet, and it can often be seen soaring far out of the water in pursuit of a flying fish.

Tarpon

COMMON NAMES: Tarpon, silver king, sabalo.

SCIENTIFIC NAME: *Megalops atlantica.*

DESCRIPTION: The tarpon, considered the king of gamefish by the majority of those who have caught him, is a leaper to end all leapers. Tarpon jumps of 8 feet above the surface and 20 feet long have been measured. Tarpon are related to herring and shad and, oddly enough, to smelt and salmon. Usually blue or greenish-black on the back, the tarpon's sides and underparts are a sparkling silver. Scales are very large, and there is a bony plate between the branches of the bottom jaw. The dorsal fin has no spines, but its last (rear) ray is abnormally extended and whiplike. Pectoral fins are quite low on the body. The tarpon's spectacular fighting tactics and hard, bony mouth make him difficult to subdue—one fish boated out of 20 strikes is about average success for a tarpon fisherman. The tarpon's only shortcoming is that he isn't much on the table. Most rod-caught tarpon are released.

RANGE: Tarpon are found on both sides of the Atlantic in tropical and subtropical water. In the western Atlantic they stray as far north as Nova Scotia and range well south in the Gulf of Mexico. Main concentrations seem to be off southern Florida, Texas, and eastern Mexico.

HABITAT: Except in winter, when they apparently retreat to deeper water, tarpon are schooling fish of shallow waters. They frequent such places as mangrove flats, shoals, brackish bayous, cuts, inlets, and the lower reaches of coastal rivers. Sometimes they travel many miles upriver into fresh water. They are seldom far from the shore in summer.

SIZE: Though the rod-and-reel record is 283 pounds, tarpon reportedly attain weights in excess of 300 pounds. The average size of adult tarpon is probably 30 to 100 pounds. Tarpon of well over 100 pounds are subdued each year on fly rods!

FOOD: Tarpon feed on a variety of marine life including pinfish, mullet, needlefish, and other small fish, plus crabs and shrimp.

Bonefish

COMMON NAMES: Bonefish, ratfish, banana.

SCIENTIFIC NAME: *Albula vulpes.*

DESCRIPTION: What the tarpon is to leaping, the bonefish is to running. No one using sporting tackle can stop the blazing initial run of a hooked bonefish, which may tear 150 yards or more of line from a reel. The bonefish's body, built for speed, is torpedo-shaped. Colors are bronze or blue-green on the back, shading through bright silver on the sides to white on the belly. The sides occasionally have some dark mottlings. The bonefish is sometimes confused with the ladyfish, but telling them apart requires only a look at the mouth. The bonefish's upper jaw—a snout, really—is far longer than the lower, giving the fish a suckerlike look. The ladyfish has jaws of about equal length. Bonefish are related to tarpon.

RANGE: Bonefish are found in all tropical marine waters, being caught in such widely separated places as South Africa, Brazil, and Hawaii, where the biggest ones are found. By far the largest concentrations of bonefish in North America are around the Florida Keys and in the Bahamas.

HABITAT: Bonefish are a shallow-water species. They move onto very shallow tidal flats, sometimes in water only 6 inches deep, with the high tide to feed and then drop back into deeper water as the tide ebbs. On the flats is where fishermen, particularly fly fishermen, seek this ultrawary quarry.

SIZE: Bonefish probably reach a maximum weight of about 20 pounds or a bit more, but one of over 8 pounds is worth bragging about. Average size is about 4 to 6 pounds.

FOOD: Bonefish are primarily bottom feeders, preying on crabs (particularly the hermit crab), shrimp, squid, sand fleas, and other crustaceans and mollusks.

Striped Bass

COMMON NAMES: Striped bass, striper, linesides, rock, rockfish, squidhound, greenhead.

SCIENTIFIC NAME: *Roccus saxatilis.*

DESCRIPTION: The striped bass is probably the most popular of coastal gamefish. He is abundant, he fights well, and he "eats well." He is not likely to be mistaken for any other gamefish in his range, primarily because of his general shape, his side stripes (there are 7 or 8 horizontal dark stripes on each side), and the separation between the front and rear dorsal fins. Coloration is dark-green to almost black on the back, silver on the sides, and white on the underparts. The striper is anadromous, living in the sea but ascending rivers to spawn.

RANGE: On the Atlantic Coast the striped bass is found from the Gulf of St. Lawrence south to the St. Johns River in Florida and in the Gulf of Mexico from western Florida to Louisiana. Introduced on the Pacific Coast in the 1880's, the striper is found there from the Columbia River south to Los Angeles, California. Center of the striper's range in the Atlantic is Massachusetts to South Carolina; in the Pacific it is in the San Francisco Bay area. Efforts to establish the striped bass in fresh water have been successful in such spots as the Santee-Cooper impoundment in South Carolina, Kerr Reservoir in North Carolina, some stretches of the Colorado River, and elsewhere.

HABITAT: Striped-bass are almost exclusively coastal fish, seldom ranging more than a few miles offshore. Among the striper's favorite haunts are tidal rips, reefs, rocky headlands, jetties, bays, inlets, channels, canals, and reedy flats in tidal marshes.

SIZE: Most striped bass caught by anglers probably fall between 3 and 15 pounds, but many fish of 40 to 60 pounds are caught each year, most of them by trollers in the Cape Cod to Delaware range. The rod-and-reel record, standing since 1913, is a 73-pounder, but there are reliable records of a 125-pounder having been caught off North Carolina in 1891.

FOOD: The striper is a voracious feeder that preys on a wide variety of fish and invertebrates. The list includes herring, mullet, menhaden, anchovies, flounders, shad, silver hake, eels, lobsters, crabs, shrimp, seaworms, squid, clams, and mussels.

Snook

COMMON NAMES: Snook, robalo.

SCIENTIFIC NAME: *Centropomus undecimalis.*

DESCRIPTION: A fine fighter and excellent table fare, the snook is a much-sought prize of southern waters. In color the snook is brown, green, or brownish-gold on the dorsal surface (back), shading to greenish-silver on sides and becoming lighter on the belly. Distinctive traits include a depressed upper jaw and a jutting lower jaw, a somewhat humped back, and, probably most distinctive of all, a prominent dark lateral line that usually extends to and into the tail. The snook strikes a fishermen's offering with a startling smash but is an unpredictable feeder.

RANGE: Snook are found throughout tropical waters on the Atlantic and Pacific coasts, though they stray as far north as Delaware. They are plentiful along the Florida coasts and along the Gulf Coast in the U.S. and Mexico.

HABITAT: Snook are shallow-water fish that frequent such spots as sandy shores, mangrove banks, tidal bayous and canals, flats, bays, bridges and pilings, sometimes going upstream into fresh water. In cold weather they lay in deep holes.

SIZE: Snook probably average 2 to 5 pounds, but 10-pounders are not rare, and top weight is better than 50 pounds.

FOOD: The voracious snook feeds on many varieties of fish, particularly mullet, but also eats crabs, shrimp, and crustaceans.

Great Barracuda

COMMON NAMES: Great barracuda, barracuda, cuda.

SCIENTIFIC NAME: *Sphyraena barracuda.*

DESCRIPTION: This toothy warrior is the subject of misunderstanding by both anglers and swimmers. Proven records of barracuda attacks on swimmers are relatively rare, though this fish, apparently out of curiosity, often approaches quite close to swimmers. Many fishermen write the 'cuda off as a poor fighter, but he usually puts on a powerful, acrobatic battle when hooked on sporting tackle. Shaped much like the fresh-water pikes, the great barracuda is bluish-gray or greenish-gray on the back, silvery on the sides, whitish on belly. Dark, irregularly shaped blotches mark the sides, particularly toward the rear. Teeth are large and pointed. The 'cuda is a poor food fish and, in fact, may be poisonous.

RANGE: The great barracuda occurs in the American Atlantic from Brazil as far north as the Carolinas, though it occasionally strays north to Massachusetts. Centers of abundance are in Florida waters and in the West Indies.

HABITAT: Though barracuda are found in depths ranging from a couple of feet to 200 feet, they are mainly a shallow-water species. Preferred hangouts are reefs, flats, and around mangrove islands. The largest specimens are usually found near offshore reefs.

SIZE: Known to reach a weight of better than 100 pounds and a length of 6 feet, the great barracuda probably averages 5 to 25 pounds. However, 50-pounders are not uncommon.

FOOD: Voracious in appetite, the barracuda feeds on a wide variety of smaller fishes, preying largely on whatever is most numerous in any given area. A favorite prey is mullet, though it will eat everything from puffers to small tuna.

Channel Bass

COMMON NAMES: Channel bass, red drum, redfish.

SCIENTIFIC NAME: *Sciaenops ocellata.*

DESCRIPTION: The name Channel Bass is actually a misnomer, for this species isn't a bass at all but rather a member of the croaker family. An important East and Gulf Coast gamefish, the channel bass is copper or bronze in overall body coloration. It can be distinguished from the black drum, which it resembles, by its lack of chin barbels and the presence, at the base of the upper part of the tail, of at least one large black spot. Food value of the channel bass varies with size. Small ones—often called puppy drum or rat reds—are fine eating, but large specimens have rather coarse flesh and are only fair eating.

RANGE: Channel bass are found along the Atlantic and Gulf coasts from Massachusetts to Texas.

HABITAT: These coastal fish are found off sandy beaches for the most part, moving shoreward as the tide rises to feed in holes, behind sand bars, and on flats. They are also found in such spots as the lee of mangrove islands, in sloughs, channels, and bayous.

SIZE: Channel bass reach weights of well over 80 pounds, though those of 50 pounds or more are relatively rare.

FOOD: Channel bass are bottom feeders, eating mainly crustaceans, mollusks, and seaworms, though they sometimes prey on smaller fish, particularly mullet and mossbunker.

Weakfish

COMMON NAMES: Weakfish, common weakfish, gray weakfish, squeteague, yellowfin, tiderunner.

SCIENTIFIC NAME: *Cynoscion regalis.*

DESCRIPTION: The weakfish gets its name not from its fighting qualities, which are excellent, but rather from its quite delicate mouth, which is easily torn by a hook. This popular, streamlined gamefish is olive, green, or green-blue on the back and silver or white on the belly. The sides are quite colorful, having tinges of purple, lavender, blue, and green, with a golden sheen. The back and upper sides contain numerous spots of various dark colors. The lower edge of the tail is sometimes yellow, as are the ventral, pectoral, and anal fins. The weakfish is excellent table fare.

RANGE: This weakfish occurs along the U.S. Atlantic Coast from Massachusetts south to the east coast of Florida. Populations center around Chesapeake and Delaware bays, New Jersey, and Long Island.

HABITAT: Basically a school fish (though large ones are often lone wolves), these weakfish are a coastal species, being found in the surf and in inlets, bays, channels, and saltwater creeks. They prefer shallow areas with a sandy bottom. They feed mostly near the surface but may go deep if that is where the food is.

SIZE: The average size of weakfish seems to be declining. Today, most rod-caught fish go 1 to 4 pounds. Those early-

fall "tiderunners" of past decades, fish of up to a dozen pounds, are seldom seen nowadays. Biggest rod-caught weakfish hit 19½ pounds.

FOOD: Weakfish eat sea worms, shrimp, squid, sand lance, crabs, and such small fish as silversides, killies, and butterfish.

Spotted Weakfish

COMMON NAMES: Spotted weakfish, spotted sea trout, speckled trout, trout, speck.

SCIENTIFIC NAME: *Cynoscion nebulosus.*

DESCRIPTION: This species is a southern variety of the common weakfish (see "Weakfish"), which it resembles. As its name might suggest, its markings (many large, dark, round spots found on sides and back and extending onto dorsal fin and tail) are far more prominent than those of the common weakfish. In general body coloration the spotted weakfish is dark gray on back and upper sides, shading to silver below. Like the common weakfish, the spotted variety has a projecting lower jaw and two large canine teeth at the tip of the upper jaw. It is a top food fish.

RANGE: The spotted weakfish occurs throughout the Gulf of Mexico, in Florida waters, and north to Virginia, though it is found as a stray as far north as New York. It is most abundant in the Gulf and in Florida.

HABITAT: Very much like that of the common weakfish.

SIZE: The average size of spotted weakfish is somewhat smaller than that of common weakfish. Most rod-caught spotted weaks fall in the 1 to 3-pound range. Maximum size is about 15 pounds.

FOOD: In many areas spotted weakfish feed almost exclusively on shrimp. They may also eat various smaller fish, particularly mullet, menhaden, and silversides, as well as crabs and seaworms.

California White Sea Bass

COMMON NAMES: California white sea bass, sea bass, white sea bass, croaker, white corvina.

SCIENTIFIC NAME: *Cynoscion nobilis.*

DESCRIPTION: Not a true sea bass, the California white sea bass is a relative of the weakfish of the Atlantic. It is a rather streamlined fish whose front and rear dorsal fins are connected. Body colors are gray to blue on the back, silvery on the sides, and white on the belly. The tail is yellow. The belly is somewhat indented from pelvic fins to vent. There is a dark area at the base of the pectoral fins.

RANGE: The California white sea bass has an extreme range of Alaska to Chile, but it is not often found north of San Francisco. Population center seems to be from Santa Barbara, California, south into Mexico.

HABITAT: The white sea bass seldom strays far offshore and is most often found in or near beds of kelp. Night fishing is often very productive.

SIZE: The white sea bass averages about 15 to possibly 25 pounds, though specimens of over 40 pounds are not uncommon. Maximum weight is a bit more than 80 pounds.

FOOD: White sea bass feed on a variety of small fish, plus squid, crabs, shrimp, and other mollusks and crustaceans.

California Black Sea Bass

COMMON NAMES: California black sea bass, giant black sea bass, giant sea bass.

SCIENTIFIC NAME: *Stereolepis gigas.*

DESCRIPTION: This large, blocky fish is a Pacific version of the Eastern sea bass. It is black or brownish-black in general coloration, lighter on the underparts. Because of its size and color, the California black sea bass cannot be confused with any other species in its somewhat limited range.

RANGE: The California black sea bass is most numerous off Baja California and southern California, though it ranges north to central California.

HABITAT: The California black sea bass is strictly a bottom fish, being found in deep water, usually over rocks, and around reefs.

SIZE: The rod-and-reel-record California black sea bass weighed 557 pounds, which is probably about the maximum for the species. Average size is 100 to 200 pounds.

FOOD: California black sea bass feed on a variety of fish including sheepsheads, and on crabs and other mollusks.

Black Drum

COMMON NAMES: Black drum, drum, sea drum.

SCIENTIFIC NAME: *Pogonias cromis.*

DESCRIPTION: A member of the croaker family, the black drum is not so popular a gamefish as is the red drum. It is most easily distinguished from the red drum (channel bass) by the lack of a prominent dark spot near the base of the tail. Overall color of the black drum ranges from gray to almost silvery, usually with a coppery sheen. Young specimens usually have broad vertical bands of a dark color. Body shape is short and deep, the back is arched, and the undersurface is somewhat flat. There are barbels on the chin.

RANGE: Black drum are an Atlantic species found from southern New England to Argentina, though they are rare north of New York. Centers of abundance include North Carolina, Florida, Louisiana, and Texas.

HABITAT: Usually found in schools, black drum prefer inshore sandy areas such as bays, lagoons, channels, and ocean surfs, and are often found near wharves and bridges.

SIZE: The black drum is known to reach a maximum weight of nearly 150 pounds. However, the average size is 20 to 30 pounds.

FOOD: Black drum are bottom feeders, preferring clams, mussels, crabs, shrimp, and other mollusks.

Giant Sea Bass

COMMON NAMES: Giant sea bass, spotted jewfish, jewfish, spotted grouper, guasa.

SCIENTIFIC NAME: *Epinephelus itajara (or Promicrops itaiara).*

DESCRIPTION: Probably the largest of the groupers, the giant sea bass is not the gamest of fighters, but its weight alone makes up for that shortcoming. Overall color ranges from black to grayish-brown, and back and sides are mottled. The upper sides contain dark spots. The tail is convex along the rear margin. The flesh of the giant sea bass (most often called jewfish) is quite tasty. During World War II it was sold as "imported salt cod."

RANGE: The precise range of the giant sea bass seems uncertain. However, it is found in warmer waters of both the Atlantic and the Pacific and is most abundant in Florida waters and off the Texas Gulf Coast.

HABITAT: Despite its large size, the giant sea bass is most often found in relatively shallow water along the coast. It is at home under ledges and in reefs, in rocky holes, around bridges, and in deep channels.

SIZE: Though the rod-and-reel record is a 680-pounder, giant sea bass reach weights of at least 750 pounds. Average is probably 100 to 250 pounds.

FOOD: Giant sea bass feed on a variety of small reef fish, including sheepsheads, and on crabs and squid.

Blackfish

COMMON NAMES: Blackfish, tautog, oysterfish.

SCIENTIFIC NAME: *Tautoga onitis.*

DESCRIPTION: The blackfish is a member of the wrasse family, most of which are very brightly colored. The blackfish, however, is a drab gray or gray-brown with irregular black mottlings. Body shape is relatively long and quite plump. The snout is blunt, lips are thick, and the jaws hold powerful crushing teeth. Edge of tail is straight. Dorsal fin is quite long and spiny. The blackfish's flesh is very tasty but for some reason is not much utilized. The blackfish is an accomplished bait-stealer.

RANGE: The blackfish is an Atlantic species found from Nova Scotia to South Carolina. It is most numerous from Cape Cod to Delaware Bay.

HABITAT: Blackfish are a coastal bottom species, preferring such lies as mussel beds, rocky areas both inshore and offshore, the outer edges of jetties and piers, and old wrecks. They are seldom found in water deeper than 60 feet.

SIZE: The average rod-caught blackfish weighs about 3 pounds, but 6 to 8-pounders are far from unusual, and the species reaches a maximum weight of about 25 pounds.

FOOD: Blackfish are bottom feeders that eat such items as barnacles, mussels, crabs, snails, sea worms, shrimp, and even lobsters.

Sea Bass

COMMON NAMES: Sea bass, black sea bass, blackfish, humpback, black will.

SCIENTIFIC NAME: *Centropristes striatus.*

DESCRIPTION: The sea bass, though small, is one of the most popular of gamefish in its somewhat restricted range. It has a rather stout body shape, with a high back and a moderately pointed snout. The apex of each gill cover holds a sharp spine. Overall color is gray to brownish-gray to blue-black, lighter on the underparts. Sides are sometimes mottled and at other times appear to have light horizontal stripes formed by rows of dots. Dorsal fin also has rows of spots. Most distinctive trait of the sea bass is the elongated ray on the upper edge of the tail—it sticks out far to the rear of the rest of the tail. Sea bass are fine eating.

RANGE: Sea bass are found from Maine to northern Florida, but are most common from Cape Hatteras to Cape Cod.

HABITAT: Sea bass are bottom dwellers of coastal areas. Preferred depths seem to be 20 to 50 feet, though large sea bass are often found at depths of up to 100 feet, especially in winter. Sea bass like such spots as mussel beds, rocky areas, wrecks, pilings, bridges, offshore reefs and ledges, and rocky heads.

SIZE: Sea bass hit about 8 pounds maximum. Average is 1 to 3 pounds.

FOOD: Sea bass feed on smaller fish but prefer clams, mussels, crabs, shrimp, sea worms, and squid.

Atlantic Codfish

COMMON NAMES: Atlantic codfish, codfish, cod.

SCIENTIFIC NAME: *Gadus morhua.*

DESCRIPTION: This pot-bellied heavyweight of the northern Atlantic is the cause of many a runny nose among sport and commercial fishermen in the cold-weather months. The thick-bodied Atlantic cod seems to have two color phases: red and gray. In the red phase the fish may vary from orange to reddish-brown. The gray phase ranges from black to greenish to brownish-gray. The underparts are lighter, and the sides have many dark spots. The pale lateral line distinguishes the Atlantic cod from the haddock. The cod differs from the look-alike pollock in its longer chin barbel and the fact that its upper jaw projects past the lower (the opposite is true of the pollock). The cod's dorsal fin is in three spineless sections, and the anal fin, also spineless, has two sections—an unusual fin makeup.

RANGE: In the western Atlantic the cod is found from Greenland south to North Carolina. In the eastern Atlantic it ranges throughout the Baltic Sea, from northern Scandinavia east to some parts of Russia, and south to the Bay of Biscay.

HABITAT: Atlantic cod are schooling fish for the most part, bottom feeders, and lovers of cold water. Though the young may be found in shallow water, cod generally prefer depths of 60 feet or more and are sometimes found down to 1,500 feet. Sport fishermen usually catch cod at the 50 to 300-foot levels. Cod migrate north and south to some extent, but most movement is from relatively shallow water, where they are likely to be found in winter, to the deeps, where they go in summer. Cod seem to prefer areas with a rocky or broken bottom and such places as wrecks.

SIZE: The average Atlantic cod taken by sport fishermen probably falls into the 6 to 12-pound category, but the rod-and-reel record is more than 80 pounds, and the species is known to exceed 200 pounds. Cod of up to 60 pounds are not unusual in the New Jersey to southern New England area.

FOOD: Atlantic cod feed on a variety of bottom life including various small fish (notably herring), crabs, clams, squid, mussels, snails, sea worms, and lobsters.

Pollock

COMMON NAMES: Pollock, Boston bluefish, green cod, coalfish.

SCIENTIFIC NAME: *Pollachius virens.*

Pollock

DESCRIPTION: The pollock, in effect, lives under the shadow of its famous relative, the Atlantic cod. A better fighter than the cod (probably because it is generally taken from shallower water), it has a shorter chin barbel than its relative, and its lower jaw projects beyond the upper (the cod's upper jaw projects farther than the lower). The pollock is not spotted, as is the cod, and its tail is more severely forked. Pollock's colors range from dark olive-green to brownish on upper parts, yellowish to gray on the lower sides, to silvery on the belly. Like the cod, its flesh is excellent eating.

RANGE: Pollock range in the western Atlantic from the Gulf of St. Lawrence to Chesapeake Bay and in the eastern Atlantic from Iceland south to the Bay of Biscay.

HABITAT: In general, pollock are found in somewhat shallower water than are cod, and they are often caught at intermediate depths. Occasionally, usually during May at such points as Cape Cod's Race Point Rip, pollock come into shallow water near shore and can be taken on or near the surface.

SIZE: Most pollock caught by sport anglers weigh 4 to about 12 pounds. However, the species has a maximum weight of some 45 pounds.

FOOD: Pollock feed on a variety of fish—including herring and small cod—and on shrimp and some crustaceans and mollusks, as well as sea worms.

Summer Flounder

COMMON NAMES: Summer flounder, fluke, flatfish.

SCIENTIFIC NAME: *Paralichthys dentatus.*

DESCRIPTION: The summer flounder is of one of 500-odd members of the flatfish family, a curious group. They begin life in an upright position and have an eye on each side of the head. As they grow, however, the body begins to "tilt," in some species to the right, in others to the left, and the eye on the downward-facing surface begins to travel to the upward-facing surface. Finally, the transformation is complete, and the fish spends the rest of its life on its side, with both eyes on the same side of the head (above and just to the rear of the point of the jaw). The summer flounder is white on the side that comes in contact with the ocean floor. The color of the upper surface depends on the physical makeup of the ocean floor, but is usually olive, brown, or gray, with prominent dark spots and some mottling. Body is flat and quite deep. Dorsal and anal fins are extremely long.

RANGE: The summer flounder occurs in the U.S. from Maine to South Carolina.

HABITAT: The summer flounder lives on the bottom, often buried in sand or mud. In summer it is found in shallow water, sometimes in depths of only a few feet, while in winter it moves offshore into as much as 50 fathoms of water. It frequents bays and harbors, the mouths of estuaries, and is often found around bottom obstructions such as wrecked ships.

SIZE: Most summer flounders caught by sport fishermen weigh 1 to 4 pounds, but the species' maximum size is probably close to 30 pounds.

FOOD: Summer flounders eat a wide variety of small fish, as well as sea worms, crabs, clams, squid, shrimp.

Winter Flounder

COMMON NAMES: Winter flounder, flatfish, blueback, blackback, black flounder, mud dab.

SCIENTIFIC NAME: *Pseudopleuronectes americanus.*

DESCRIPTION: One of the smaller members of the vast flatfish family, the winter flounder differs from the summer flounder in its smaller size and weight and in the fact that it is "right-eyed" (that is, has both eyes and the skin pigmentation on the right side of its head) while the summer flounder is "left-eyed." The winter flounder is white on the underside (the side on which it lies on the ocean floor), while on the other side the colors range from reddish-brown to slate-gray, usually with some dark spots. The mouth is small, and the lateral line is relatively straight. The winter flounder is widely sought for food by both sport and commercial fishermen.

RANGE: The winter flounder has an extreme range of Labrador south to Georgia, but is most common from the Gulf of St. Lawrence to Chesapeake Bay.

HABITAT: The winter flounder is found mostly in shallow water—as shallow as one foot, in fact—but is occasionally found at depths of up to 400 feet. It lies on the bottom, preferring sand or mud but accepting clay, gravel, and even a hard bottom. In the fall this species tends to move toward the shallows, while in spring the movement is toward deeper water.

SIZE: Winter flounders average from 1/2 to 1 1/2 pounds in weight and 8 to 15 inches in length. Maximum size is about 8 pounds, and such heavyweights are often called snowshoes.

FOOD: Winter flounders eat such items as seaworms, crabs, shrimp, and minute crustaceans, as well as small fish and fish larvae.

Roosterfish

COMMON NAMES: Roosterfish, papagallo, gallo, pez de gallo.

SCIENTIFIC NAME: *Nematistius pectoralis.*

DESCRIPTION: The roosterfish—a relative of the jacks and pompanos, which it resembles at least in body shape—gets its name from the 7 extremely long (far longer than the greatest body depth) spines of the forward dorsal fin, which vaguely resemble a rooster's comb. Body colors are green to gray-blue on upper areas, white to gold below. Two black stripes curve downward and then rearward from the forward dorsal fin, which itself has a white horizontal stripe. The roosterfish is a furious fighter and a fine table fish.

RANGE: Roosterfish are a Pacific species occurring from Peru as far north as southern California. They are particularly abundant in the Gulf of California.

HABITAT: Little is known of the movements and life history of the roosterfish. However, fishermen often catch them in sandy inshore bays and by trolling in open water. The fish are sometimes seen swimming on the surface, their dorsals erect and waving above the surface.

SIZE: Average size of roosterfish is estimated at 5 to 20 pounds. Maximum is probably about 130 pounds.

FOOD: The dietary preferences of the roosterfish aren't known in detail, but these fish certainly feed on most any small fish that are available. They strike artificial lures and plugs willingly.

Porgy

COMMON NAMES: Porgy, northern porgy, scup.

SCIENTIFIC NAME: *Stenotomus chrysops.*

DESCRIPTION: The porgy (most often called scup in some areas in its range) is what might be called a salt-water panfish. It has a somewhat ovate high-backed body with a small mouth and strong teeth. Basic body color ranges from silvery to brown, and there are usually 3 or 4 dark vertical bars on the sides. Dorsal fin is quite spiny. The porgy's flesh is highly palatable, and it is caught by both sport and commercial anglers, though in some areas rod fishermen consider the porgy a nuisance.

RANGE: The porgy (northern porgy) is found from Nova Scotia south to the Atlantic Coast of Florida. In summer and fall it is quite abundant off the coasts of New England, New York, and New Jersey.

HABITAT: Porgies seem to prefer some bottom debris such as mussel beds. They live on or near the bottom in the middle depths of the Continental Shelf.

SIZE: Porgies average ½ to 2 pounds. Maximum size is about 4 pounds, and such individuals are often called humpbacks.

FOOD: Porgies feed mainly on small crustaceans, worms, mollusks, and occasionally on vegetable matter.

Spanish Mackerel

SCIENTIFIC NAME: *Scomberomorus maculatus.*

DESCRIPTION: This beautiful streamlined fish, though of modest size as mackerels go, is a magnificent fighter, making sizzling runs and soaring leaps. Body shape is rather compressed, and colors range from an iridescent steel-blue or occasionally greenish on the dorsal surface to a silvery blue below. Side markings are mustard or bronze spots, quite large. Dorsal fin is in two sections, and there are dorsal and anal finlets. Its side spots, lack of stripes, and absence of scales on the pectoral fins distinguish the Spanish mackerel from the king mackerel and the cero.

RANGE: Spanish mackerel occur from Cape Cod south to Brazil but are never numerous in the northern part of their range. They are most plentiful from the Carolinas into the Gulf of Mexico.

HABITAT: This warm-water species is usually found in open waters, cruising about near the surface and slashing into schools of baitfish. They do, however, make occasional forays into the surf and into bays and channels in search of food.

SIZE: Spanish mackerel average 1½ to 4 pounds but reach a maximum weight of about 20 pounds. A 10-pounder is a very good one.

FOOD: Spanish mackerel feed primarily on a wide variety of small baitfish, and on shrimp. A favorite bait in some areas, particularly Florida waters, is a very small baitfish called a glass minnow.

Sheepshead

COMMON NAMES: Sheepshead, convict fish.
SCIENTIFIC NAME: *Archosargus probatocephalus.*

DESCRIPTION: Similar in shape and general appearance to the porgy, the sheepshead is a high-backed blunt-headed species whose bait-stealing abilities have frustrated countless fishermen. Its small mouth has a formidable set of rock-hard close-coupled teeth that are quite capable of demolishing a crab and biting through a light-wire hook. Basic color is silvery though the dorsal surface's color is closer to gray. Sides have 5 to 7 dark vertical bands, spines of the dorsal fin are quite large and very sharp, and scales are large and coarse. Sheepsheads fight well and are excellent on the table.

RANGE: The sheepshead is found from Nova Scotia south to the northeastern Gulf of Mexico. It is far more numerous in the southern part of its range, particularly in Florida waters.

HABITAT: The sheepshead is a gregarious species that moves with the tides to wherever the food is plentiful. It is an inshore fish, taking up residence in bays and channels and around bridges, piers, pilings, and the like.

SIZE: Sheepsheads average 1 to about 5 pounds but may attain weights in excess of 20 pounds.

FOOD: Its teeth are a dead giveaway to this species' dietary preferences, which include crabs, mollusks, barnacles, and the like, as well as shrimp.

Pompano

COMMON NAMES: Pompano, common pompano, sunfish.
SCIENTIFIC NAME: *Trachinotus carolinus.*

Pompano

DESCRIPTION: This high-strung, slab-sided character is the most abundant and most important member of the pompano family, which includes such fish as the much-prized permit. It has a small mouth, blunt head, and a relatively shallow body (body depth decreases proportionally with growth). Dorsal-surface colors range from gray-silver-blue to blue-green, and sides and underparts are silvery. Ventral surfaces are flecked with yellow. Dorsal fin is bluish, and most of the other fins are yellowish. The pompano is an epicurean's delight.

RANGE: The pompano is found from Brazil north to Massachusetts, and also in the West Indies and in Bermuda waters. It is particularly numerous in Florida and the Gulf of Mexico.

HABITAT: Pompano are inshore school fish, feeding on the bottom in shallow water in the surf, in channels and inlets and bays, and around bridges. They occasionally range well up into rivers with the tide.

SIZE: Pompano average about 2 pounds in weight, and maximum size is thought to be about 8 pounds.

FOOD: Pompano feed mostly on bivalve mollusks and on small crustaceans, notably a small beetlelike crustacean called the sand flea.

California Corbina

COMMON NAMES: California corbina, corbina, corvina, whiting, sea trout.

SCIENTIFIC NAME: *Menticirrhus undulatus.*

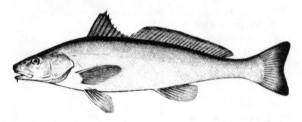

California Corbina

DESCRIPTION: The wary and unpredictable corbina, a member of the whiting group, is among the most popular of fish caught in inshore waters of the Pacific. Basic color is some shade of blue-gray, and identifying characteristics include a blunt snout; a short, high forward dorsal fin and a long, lower rear dorsal fin; and small barbels at the tip of the lower jaw. The corbina is a strong underwater fighter and an excellent food fish.

RANGE: The corbina is found from the Gulf of California north to Point Conception.

HABITAT: Primarily a target of surf fishermen, the corbina is an inshore species found primarily along sandy beaches and in shallow bays, moving into the surf line on the incoming tide.

SIZE: Corbina reach a maximum weight of about 8 pounds. Average size is 2 to 3 pounds.

FOOD: Crabs of various kinds are the favorite food of the corbina, but it also feeds on clams, sea worms, and crabs.

Atlantic Croaker

COMMON NAMES: Atlantic croaker, croaker, hardhead, golden croaker.

SCIENTIFIC NAME: *Micropogon undulatus.*

DESCRIPTION: Most-common and most-prized of the eastern-U.S. members of the huge croaker family, the Atlantic croaker is a strong fighter and delicious eating. The croaker family gets its name from the sound — audible for quite a distance — it makes by repeated contractions of its swim bladder and a unique "drumming muscle." The Atlantic croaker has a small, tapered body; a short, high forward dorsal fin and a long, lower rear dorsal fin; and small barbels on the chin. Colors are brassy-gold and silver, and upper parts of the body contain numerous dark spots that sometimes form slanting bars.

RANGE: The Atlantic croaker is found from Massachusetts south to Florida and west to Texas and eastern Mexico. In recent years, however, its numbers have declined in the northern part of the range. Center of abundance seems to be from the Carolinas to Florida and in the northern Gulf of Mexico.

HABITAT: Atlantic croakers are seldom found far from estuaries, preferring sandy shallows, shallow shell beds, sloughs, lagoons, and weedy flats. However, cold weather often sends the fish into deeper water.

SIZE: Atlantic croakers average $\frac{1}{2}$ to about $2\frac{1}{2}$ pounds and attain a maximum size of about 5 pounds.

FOOD: Predominantly bottom feeders, Atlantic croakers feed on clams, crabs, sea worms, shrimp, snails, mussels, and sand fleas.

Red Snapper

SCIENTIFIC NAME: *Lutjanus blackfordi.*

DESCRIPTION: Most widely known for its eating qualities, the red snapper is among the best known of the more than 200 species of snappers found in the world's warm seas. The red snapper's color pattern (rose-red overall, though paler-red on underparts, with red fins and eyes, and a black spot on each side), long pectoral fin, and more-numerous anal-fin rays distinguish this species from other snappers.

RANGE: The red snapper occurs from the U.S. middle-Atlantic and Gulf coasts southward throughout the tropical American Atlantic.

HABITAT: The red snapper's preference for deep waters — it is sometimes found as deep as 100 fathoms and seems most prevalent at 20 to 60 fathoms — detracts from its importance as a sport fish. It usually is found a few feet above a hard bottom.

SIZE: Most red snappers caught commercially run from 5 to about 30 pounds. Maximum size seems to be about 35 pounds.

FOOD: Red snappers eat baitfish and various deep-water mollusks and crustaceans.

Northern Whiting

COMMON NAMES: Northern whiting, whiting, northern kingfish, kingfish.

SCIENTIFIC NAME: *Menticirrhus saxatilis.*

DESCRIPTION: The northern whiting is one of four whitings (all members of the large croaker family) that inhabit the U.S. Atlantic and Gulf coasts. Basic color is silver-gray or silver-brown, and the upper part of the body contains rather indistinct dark vertical bands. Mouth is small, and there is a single chin barbel. The northern whiting is the only one of the four U.S. whitings in which the third and largest spine of the forward dorsal fin, when laid flat, reaches well past the beginning of the long and soft rear dorsal fin. The northern whiting is an excellent food fish.

RANGE: The northern whiting is found on the U.S. Atlantic coast from Maine to Florida.

HABITAT: Northern whiting are usually found over a sandy bottom in the surf, shallow sloughs and bays, and, as the water cools, in depths as great as 100 feet or more.

SIZE: Averaging about 1 pound, the northern whiting reaches a maximum size of about 3 pounds and 18 inches in length.

FOOD: The northern whiting feeds mainly on small baitfish, sea worms, and small crustaceans.

PART V / Camping

Tents

Tents are manufactured in a variety of shapes and sizes, and whether you're just doing some backyard camping or heading for a couple of weeks in the Rockies, there's a tent made for you and your family.

Wall Tents

Many campers, particularly those who have spent time in the army, are familiar with the traditional wall tent. Its main advantages are that it has ample headspace, can house a wood-burning stove in cold weather, and readily sheds water off its inverted V roof.

A psychological benefit of the wall tent is that it somewhat resembles a small house in design, but upon closer examination, we see it is not quite as comfortable as it looks, nor is it very stable in wind.

There usually are no floors or windows, nor netting at the flap doors. Moreover, the walls tend to be so low that the only walking space is directly below the ridgepole. The large end pole that stands in the center of the doorway is another nuisance.

A wall tent is inexpensive and to erect it you only need two upright poles, a ridgepole, guy ropes, and pegs. Ventilation is poor in rainy weather, the tent offers little resistance to the wind, the door flaps leave myriad openings for insects and, if closed, make the tent's interior quite dark and warm. Auto campers appreciate the heavy wall tent as it can be pitched right next to their cars. But for those who wish to travel light, it is a poor choice.

The wall tent is generally available in sizes ranging from 6½' x 6½' to 16' x 20', although larger sizes are sold in army surplus stores. The side walls run from 2 to 4 feet in height, but 3 feet is standard. Heights at the center are usually 7–7½ feet, adequate for the average adult.

This type of tent with a 7' x 9' floor space will provide sufficient room for two campers with gear. A trio of hunters will require a 9' x 12' wall tent for comfort.

Cottage or Cabin Tents

If you're planning a long stay in an area and need plenty of space, the cottage or cabin tent just might be the answer.

This style of tent features vertical sides that give you more space for your gear than do tents with short side walls. The eaves are high and there are large windows with storm flaps. You've also got walking room to spare and sewn-in floors. Though the number of poles required to pitch it may approach 10, modern cottage tents generally employ light aluminum telescoping poles that are not difficult to handle. Guy lines are not required with most cottage and cabin tents, though the outside edges of the tent floor should be staked down. There is no awning above the door. A large area of level ground is needed to put up the tent. A 8' x 10' tent can sleep four persons; a 9' x 12', five to six.

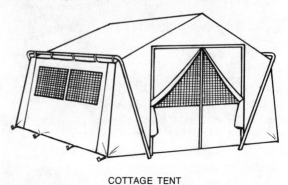

COTTAGE TENT

Umbrella Tents

The umbrella tent is best designed for the motorist who goes touring with his own shelter. A pyramid-shaped roof and straight sides distinguish this unit.

Wind resistance is exceptional and the vertical walls give you plenty of space for storing gear. The ample headroom lets you walk around without stooping, and, save the door awning, there aren't any large, flat surfaces that will hold rain or catch snow. A big door and one or more windows in the sides give good ventilation on warm evenings.

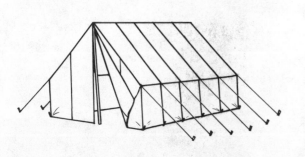

WALL TENT

UMBRELLA TENT

A sewn-in, waterproof floor keeps out drafts, bugs, and surface moisture, while a 4- to 6-inch doorsill strip in some models wards off snakes and small animals. With assembly time ranging from four to five minutes, this is a fine tent to have when a storm is approaching.

One of the main faults of the umbrella tent, however, is its pole arrangement. If it has but one pole (rare nowadays), you will need a small umbrella frame to hold the cloth straight. The center pole takes up entirely too much room inside, and its sole advantages are that you can reach up and slacken the umbrella frame when it rains, rather than having to go outside to loosen the stakes, and that useful shelves can be attached to the pole. Most current umbrella tents feature four aluminum poles, so if you're backpacking or canoeing, ignore this one.

Models come in interior and exterior-pole styles. The former type can cause wear and capillary leaks due to metal rubbing against canvas. The latter is preferable as there is no center pole. Thus, there is more room inside. The exterior-pole setup is somewhat heavier and more expensive, however.

Another drawback is weight—30 to 65 pounds, depending on its size and method of pole support.

A couple can be accommodated by a 7' x 8' or an 8' x 8' model. Four persons would be better off in a 9½' x 9½' or 10' x 10'. Don't get anything bigger as it's unwieldy to pitch. You're better off with two small umbrella tents if the crew is large.

Wedge Tents

Although the Boy Scouts and the U.S. Army have taken a fancy to the wedge tent (also called the pup tent, "A" tent, Hudson Bay tent, or snow tent), it's not recommended if you're thinking of camping in any comfort. The wedge tent has no place to stand upright.

But there are several factors in this tent's favor: It's inexpensive, quite simple to erect, lightweight, sheds rain and snow rather well, and is quite stable (if properly pitched) on a windy day.

Heating this type of tent in cold weather is difficult, as a campfire inside is out of the question and a small heater can lead to asphyxiation if enough fresh air is not allowed into the tent.

A 5' x 7' tent of this style can sleep two people. Weight with stakes and poles approximates 6 pounds.

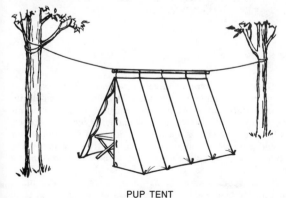

PUP TENT

Pyramid Tents

For shedding rain and snow, the pyramid, or miner, tent is the best designed for the purpose. Also, when well pitched at the base and supported by an outside tripod of poles or a strong centerpole, this tent can brave almost any windstorm.

A 7' x 7' tent of this style is adequate for sleeping and shelter, but buy the zipper-door type rather than the one with tie tapes as there will be less chance of leakage at the door.

Keep the doors open on hot days and use a reflector fire when the weather is brisk; wood stoves are not suitable in these small tents. Another flaw is that they are somewhat cramped, and an alcohol, gas, or oil stove can make the air stuffy.

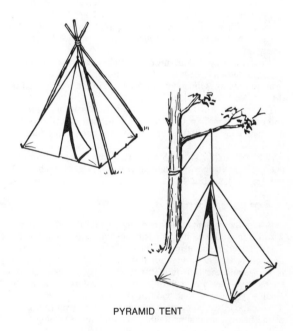

PYRAMID TENT

Baker Tents

Similar to the wall tent except for one wall that is raised to form a front awning, the baker tent is quite roomy and is exceptional as a campfire tent. Temperatures can be far below the freezing point but this tent, provided it has a good fire in front of it, will keep you warm. Green logs or rocks can be stacked up behind the fire to reflect heat into the open tent.

Important: A waterproofing solution with fire-resistant chemicals should be used to treat the baker tent. Also, keep the fire at a reasonable level and the awning pitched high enough so that the two do not meet to create a hazard. As the roof is flat, a tight-woven fabric or a fine waterproofing is essential to help shed rain.

BAKER TENT

If you're looking for privacy, this tent is not for you. As the illustration shows, the front is wide open and, if the porch is dropped down, ventilation is minimal as there are few models with windows. And besides that, in a driving rain the tent may have to be repositioned so as not to get the occupants wet.

Wind can be more harmful to a baker tent than it can to a wedge, pyramid, or wall tent. Therefore, face the tent away from prevailing winds and, if a storm is in the offing, anchor the tent with long stakes.

The open baker tent is poor protection from mosquitoes and other biting flies. Cheesecloth or netting placed over the entrance can be helpful, but bed nets for each individual are more convenient and effective.

A 6' x 8' baker tent will sleep two campers comfortably, and perhaps three with a tight fit. A baker larger than 8' x 10' will render your fire virtually useless.

Forester Tents

When there is a question of light weight and optimum warmth in cold weather, the forester tent is the best choice. The interior is so designed that the heat of a campfire will be well reflected throughout the entire unit. Pitching time is short, and the tent is stable if correctly pitched. It also sheds heavy rain and withstands high winds. The tent is small—typically 6 feet wide at the front and 8 feet deep. The shape of the interior is triangular, narrowing to a point at the back. Two campers will have sufficient sleeping room in this tent, but it is best for a lone camper who will have enough space for food and gear. During seasons when insects are a problem, individual bed nets are recommended for protection.

FORESTER TENT

Lean-to Shelters

This shelter is not only the simplest one, but also the lightest and cheapest. It is merely a square sheet of fabric hemmed at the edges and provided with eyelets or loops through which supporting ropes are placed.

In the dry southwestern section of the United States, outdoor enthusiasts have learned that a tent is rarely necessary from July through September. Thus, the popularity of the lean-to.

An 8' x 10' shelter, preferably waterproofed, can be set up in a variety of ways: draped over a pole to resemble a pup tent, angled higher to create a baker tent type of shelter roof plus an awning, raised as a flat roof, etc.

If the fabric is untreated, it could leak at once—and badly, too. Also, the fabric may wilt or burn if placed too close to a fire. Otherr disadvantages are deterioration from intense sunlight and the tendency of some material to tear.

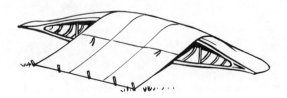

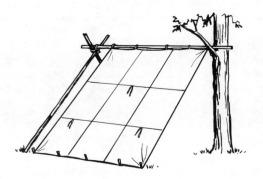

CANVAS LEAN-TO TARP

Pop Tents

The canvas igloo is relatively new on the tent scene, and it can be assembled in a short time. Commercial models are usually waterproof and mildew resistant, with an exterior rib setup to aid in pitching. One model, 7 feet in diameter, will sleep two adults. But if you're a trio, a 9-foot diameter would prove more satisfactory. Not all styles permit you to stand upright, so sweeping out the sewn-in floor could prove a problem.

There appears to be some controversy as to this unit's stability in high winds. Some experts say it can be set up in

POP TENT

Mountain or Backpack Tents

In any weather except a very hot summer's day, the mountain tent (a form of backpacking tent) is a feasible proposition. But wintertime is the season when this tent really shows off its stuff.

A stove—never an open wood fire—placed in the forepart of the tent will keep you warm in the coldest times. The vent at the peak of the tent must be opened before you light your stove, as the fumes can be lethal.

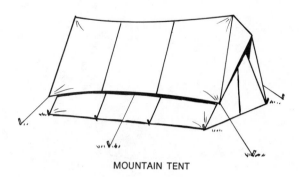

MOUNTAIN TENT

sand without stakes and remain sturdy; others assert that unless the individual or his gear is present inside, the pop tent may blow over.

Zippered storm flaps on some creations will keep out wind and insects, and a window assists in cross-ventilation. A few models also feature an awning.

Explorer Tents

The explorer tent has a number of advantages: it is lightweight, wind-resistant, has adequate floor space, and, when checked thoroughly, bug-free.

This unit features a sewn-in floor as well as a large, netted front door that is shaped somewhat like a huge porthole.

It is advisable with some models to take along one or two telescopic poles if the area you're camping in has no timber. This tent should be anchored to a point a minimum of 5 feet off the ground. Other styles, however, feature an exterior frame, a center pole or guy ropes that attach to pegs. The floor is sewn-in on most models. Front flaps are somewhat standard, and there usually is adequate screening to keep out insects.

Tepee Tents

If you're staying in one spot for a long while, the tepee is a good choice. Unfortunately, marketed models are not as well designed as the original Indian tepees. Some do feature smoke-flaps, but they are smaller than those of the true tepee. The smoke leaves the tent at the point where the poles come together, rather than directly above the fire as in the early tepees. Tepees of old had several advantages. A weathertight seal would be created at the apex of the tent when the smoke-flaps were closed. Contemporary tepees do not feature this.

The floor is oval-shaped, and it is possible to stand upright within 3 feet of the front and 2 feet of the rear. As many as 15 people can be housed in an 18' x 21' tepee, but rather uncomfortably. Wind-resistance is high despite the extensive wall area. The tepee is primarily for permanence, so the heaviness of the total unit (300 pounds including cover, lining, poles, and pegs), plus the extensive time needed for its erection, rule it out if you're constantly on the move.

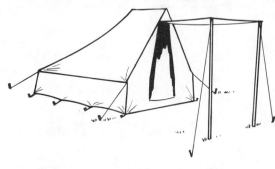

EXPLORER TENT

In Canada and Alaska, mosquitoes can be a problem. For this reason, many outdoorsmen turn to the explorer tent when they're northward bound. Once the netting sleeve is tied shut—after shooing any tiny stragglers—you're in for a comfortable evening. The steep walls are designed to readily shed rain and to provide additional storage space. A 7' x 7' explorer tent sleeps one or two campers, and weighs a mere 10 to 12 pounds.

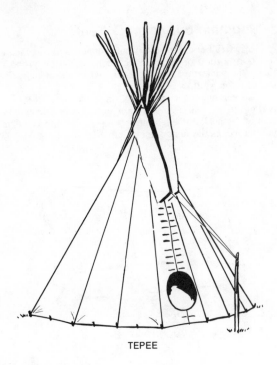

TEPEE

Tent Poles

As most economy-minded campers are do-it-yourselfers, homemade tent poles are a good place to save money. Obtain a 2″ x 2″ board the same height as your tent. With a saw, cut the wood at a sharp angle into two equal pieces. Then affix a metal bracket to the angled end of each piece. The two halves will lock together firmly when necessary.

One commercial model features a metal sleeve that slides to lock the joint. Another factory-made tent pole is the adjustable Safetite aluminum upright that has a metal clamp instead of setscrews or nuts. If this pole is lost, you can substitute a wooden or steel pole in its place. Even a broomstick will work in an emergency. Both styles are available in several sizes to suit your tenting needs.

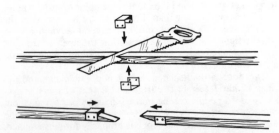

After sawing 2″ x 2″ board in half at a 45-degree angle, screw metal brackets to the ends of each. The two halves will lock together firmly.

Factory tent pole has sliding metal sleeve to lock joint.

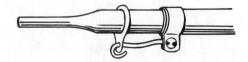

Commercial aluminum upright known as Safetite has no setscrews, no nuts to search for.

Tent Pegs

Just as tent poles can be homemade or purchased over the counter, the same goes for tent pegs, also known as tent stakes.

The array available is large enough to satisfy any camper, as the following list indicates:

1. Aluminum
2. Iron
3. Steel
4. Wood
5. Iron spike
6. Homemade wood
7. Camp-constructed branch

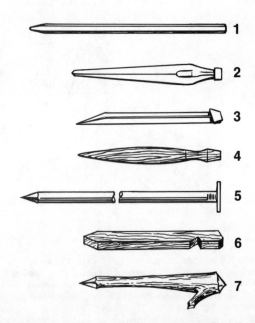

Variety of tent pegs ranges from field-made (wood) to store-bought styles of steel, iron, and lightweight aluminum.

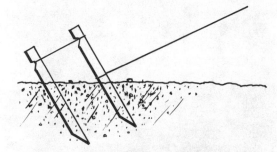

Tent pegs can be anchored in ground in this manner.

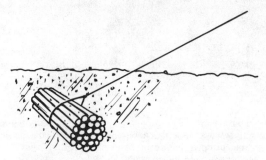

As a substitute for pegs, a number of small sticks can be buried in soft ground to secure tent. This is called the "deadman" technique.

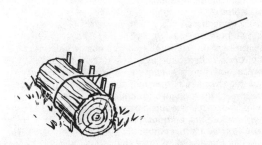

A small bundle of marsh grass or a log may be tied behind a row of short sticks to achieve the same purpose.

The auto-camper can buy iron or aluminum tent pegs as weight makes little difference. The backpacker, on the other hand, must keep pack weight in mind. Therefore, he may resort to cutting his own wooden stakes. The softer the ground, the deeper the stakes must be buried. As a substitute for tent stakes, you can bury a bundle of stiff marsh grass, brush, or sticks in sand or dirt. In winter, blocks of ice or frozen snow will also make for a more rigid tent when you're out of pegs.

Tent Fabrics

Cotton. You may have heard the terms "canvas," "duck," and "balloon silk" mentioned when you were looking for a cotton tent. All three are various forms of cotton used in the

manufacture of tents. Canvas and duck are a bit heavier than balloon silk—a long-fibered, high-quality cotton. Until World War II, practically every tent was made of cotton. Today, nylon, Dacron, and other synthetic fibers which have proven to be very lightweight are replacing cotton in tent manufacture.

Duck and canvas, if properly waterproofed, will shed water well, but are relatively heavy. The heavier the fabric, however, the stronger the tent. Conventional cotton tents are made in grades of 8, 10, and 12 ounces. The 8-ounce type is more fit for a hiking tent while the 12-ouncer would be required for a wall tent and the like. Another advantage is that cotton "breathes" well. Thus, there's no stuffiness.

The disadvantages of a mediocre cotton tent are several: It weighs more than the synthetic tents, and it may leak water and tear readily. Also, this material can only be dry-cleaned, as machine-washing would destroy it.

Nylon. This synthetic has two prime advantages to the camper. It is relatively lightweight and is far less bulky to pack. Its disadvantages are that condensation forms in humid weather and, when the fabric is wet, the seams do not swell. This can lead to a clammy tent. Mountain tents and other styles valuable to the backpacker are often made of nylon.

Some nylon tents are waterproof, and some of the newer ones do breathe, as cotton does, but this material cannot be "breathable" and waterproof at the same time. Most of the nylon tents that breathe therefore come equipped with waterproof overhead flies (a cover suspended over the roof). Some nylon tents have cotton roofs—another solution to the same problem. And some are a blend of nylon and cotton.

Dacron. Like nylon, this synthetic is lightweight. In addition, it can be either dry-cleaned or machine-washed. Unfortunately, it tends to be bulky when rolled up, and also is somewhat water-retentive.

Polyester. The newest tent fabric is spun polyester. This synthetic has nylon's strength, is lightweight, and breathes and repels water pretty much as cotton does. Like the other synthetics, polyester can be blended with cotton to achieve the desirable qualities of both fabrics.

Tents featuring blends of synthetic fibers and cotton are the most excellent of all for camping. They're highly water-repellent, strong, lightweight, and porous enough to provide maximum comfort. Probably the best way to locate these models is to look for the ultra-high price tags.

Flame-Resistant Tents. Regardless of fabric, more and more tents are now treated to be flame-resistant—sometimes called fire-retardant. It should be stressed that this treatment, though it is an excellent safety precaution, does not make the tents fireproof. A flame-resistant tent bears a label whose wording may vary slightly but whose message is clear: "*Warning. Keep all flame and heat sources away from this tent fabric.* This tent is made with flame-resistant fabric. . . . *It is not fireproof.* The fabric will burn if left in continuous contact with any flame source. The application of any foreign substance to the fabric may render the flame-resistant properties ineffective."

Care of Tents

Many tents have been in constant use for over 20 years. Others have been inadvertently destroyed by campers in a matter of days.

White Stag Van Tent is designed for camper vans with sliding side doors but will also work with swing-out doors—or it can be set up without the van. It has front and rear zip-shut doors. waterproof duck walls, heavy-duty waterproof floor, canvas roof, nylon-zipper side windows, aluminum frame, and guy lines and hooks for windy weather.

Wenzel Thunderbird Cabin Tent comes in 10 × 8, 12 × 9, and 14 × 10 foot sizes. It features cotton-drill top, polyester-cotton walls, heavy-duty floor, four-way cross ventilation through big screened windows and door. With spring-button aluminum frame, this tent goes up easily and quickly.

Eureka Catskill Tent comes in two-, three-, and four-person versions. The one shown sleeps two. It's light and sturdy, easy to pack and carry. The walls are made of breathable ripstop nylon; wrap-around floor and fly are waterproof. Aluminum A-frame supports the front, aluminum pole the rear.

Eureka Space Tent comes in two floor sizes—10 × 10 or 11¾ × 11¾ feet. This umbrella-style tent has oversized eaves and is 8 feet high at center. Awning is 7 × 10 or 8 × 12 feet, providing a spacious dining fly. Net-curtain accessory turns awning into a screened dining room. Material is water- and mildew-resistant treated poplin, with floor of waterproof nylon and vinyl splash cloth extending 14 inches up the sides.

Reputed to be sturdy, efficient, and secure, the Draw-Tite retails in sizes from the one-man Alpine up to the six-man Alpine, all from L.L. Bean. The corrosion-proof aluminum framework always keeps the floor and walls taut. Fabric is a durable 6½-ounce combed poplin.

Coleman Classic comes in four sizes, from a 7¾ × 5-foot back-pack model up to the 11 × 10-foot Family Classic which can sleep five. It features Lock-O-Matic telescoping frame poles for getting tent up fast: Twist pole ¼-turn to unlock and slide it to correct length, then twist back to lock it; color-coded pole tips interlock quickly and provide stormproof connection. Top is heat-reflecting white drill, floor is waterproof vinyl-coated nylon, walls are spun polyester. (Backpack version has ripstop nylon fly and coated nylon taffeta walls.)

There is no reason why your tent, often the most expensive item of camping gear you own, cannot live a normal existence if you give it the proper care.

When you buy a tent, it is advisable to condition the canvas by pitching it for several days in the open air, and spraying it lightly with your garden hose to get it used to moisture.

A campfire should be kept safely away from your tent as well as downwind from it, as canvas is far from fireproof.

Canvas is vulnerable to mildew—a parasitic growth which develops in dampness. To prevent mildew from forming, your tent should be as dry as possible before you pack it. If you get caught in a heavy shower and must roll up a wet tent, you had better unroll it within three or four hours for a thorough drying. If you have D-rings on the outside of your pack, lash the tent to these rings and let it hang in a loose pile to dry. Occasionally change the tent's position to obtain as complete a drying as possible. Check seams, edges, reinforcements, and sod cloth for dampness, as the entire tent should be dry.

Needless to say, moisture is but one of the adversaries your tent faces. Trees, particularly in late spring, drop blossoms, along with an assortment of leaves, twigs, and sap. All can be damaging to the tent fabric, the waterproofing, and the dyes. Bombardment by birds is another hazard.

For these reasons, your tent should be kept as clean as possible. When you're finished tenting, spread out the material and brush it well on every side, particularly at wrinkles, seams, and the section of the floor by the door, where the most dirt accumulates. When you wash the tent, use soap and water.

Bird droppings shouldn't be allowed to harden, but if you're too late, you can work them loose and brush them off with a stiff brush. If you use a knife to remove droppings or dried pitch from the canvas, be sure the blade is dull and that you don't cut into the fabric. Any discolorations left behind can be removed with lighter fluid. But if the fabric has undergone wax treatment, forget it. The lighter fluid will not only remove the foreign matter, but the wax as well. The use of brown soap and water is a less effective, but safer, method of treating discolorations.

Poles and stakes should be kept separate from the fabric when packing. Otherwise, you may be in for some damage. Guy ropes, however, can be placed inside the fabric when you're rolling it up, except for one rope. That piece should be used to tie up the completed roll. Rolling is more feasible than folding for your tent as the latter causes the fibers in the cloth to break.

Never dry a tent on the ground or let it hang outside till sundown. Absorbed moisture could cause mildew to begin. Optimum times to take down the tent are late morning or early afternoon, after the sun has done its work.

After a trip is completed and you're home again, pitch the tent and thoroughly hose it down. Then let it dry overnight, loosely packed.

When possible, try to open the tent on a daily basis to permit the air to circulate through it. This will dry up any moisture. If you store your tent, keep it in a dry, cool area, and loosely rolled so as to permit maximum circulation of air.

Avoid bumps and pressures against a pitched tent during rain. Such objects can cause slow leaks to spring in the material.

Temporary repairs on your tent can be made with small patches and patching cement. Adhesive tape can mend small tears for a while, but a sewing machine designed for canvas can do the repair work so it will last for the lifetime of the tent.

Recreational Vehicles

Just over a decade ago, an all-too-common scene along our nation's highways was an automobile or station wagon headed for a camping weekend or vacation trip with its passengers squashed by equipment, and other gear toppling from the vehicle's overburdened roof rack.

That was when the recreational-vehicle industry was in its infancy, and those campers who had either travel trailers, pickup campers, tent trailers, motor homes, or van conversions were among the enviable few.

But today the business has reached maturity. The RVs are in many cases designed with America's economy-oriented society in mind, and statistics indicate that an RV owner no longer need be a man with money to burn, though there are models for this type, too.

Tent Trailers

Tent or camp trailers are collapsible tents on wheels that are towed by a car. The trailer usually opens up to form beds with foam mattresses on opposite sides of a camping or living area a foot or more off the ground. In recent years, erection in some models has been simplified through hydraulic or electric crank-up systems that work by merely pushing a button.

Tent trailers range in body length from 6 to 13 feet, and the standard width is 6½ or 7 feet. The lightweights scale 500 pounds but the heavyweights may register 1,800 pounds or perhaps more when the load is full. Low price is the big draw for this RV.

Depending on how much you would care to spend for a tent trailer, there is a wide array of equipment, both standard and optional. Current styles usually feature huge screened windows to protect campers from insects; built-in refrigerators and kitchens; plastic tops; screen doors rather than zippered flaps; and wardrobes, toilets, and lighting arrangements. Optional gear on many models includes 12-inch wheels rather than 8-inchers, electric brakes, road covers for added protection, and boat or canoe carrying racks. Although camping trailers come equipped with brake lights, directional signals, standard clearance, and leveling jacks (all), use two safety chains rather than one, as this prevents the unit from swaying, or "fishtailing," to a dangerous degree.

It is wise to remember that you'll save by having the optionals put on prior to delivery rather than deciding on them several weeks afterward.

When it comes to advantages and disadvantages, the tent trailer has its share of each.

On the plus side, the rig has a low profile, permitting the driver a rear view through his center-mounted mirror that is very similar to what he would see if he were towing no rig at all. This same low profile lends itself to a reduction in wind resistance, simplifying the tasks of the driver.

The fact that the open rig is shaped like a tent is psychologically satisfying to a number of campers, as they can realistically enjoy the outdoor life under canvas, yet be far enough above the ground so that crawlers, creepers, and dampness aren't too close for comfort.

The light weight of the unit permits it to follow along rather inconspicuously, and it's simpler to park or back into a tight place than are the other RVs. Also, it can be used in numerous far-off and unpaved regions where the motor home, and the travel trailer might not succeed. In addition, higher speeds are attainable and the effect on gasoline mileage is slight.

A recent innovation in some camping trailers is a hinged kitchen unit that can serve inside the rig or be swung around so that it doubles as an outdoor barbecue.

The canvas section of the tent trailer can mildew, leak, tear, or shrink if it's not properly cared for. One manufacturer, however, produces models that contain no canvas at all. The vehicles have folding walls constructed of durable

Coleman Valley Forge is a mid-size, lightweight tent trailer that sleeps up to six. It features an ice-box, work counter, and three-burner range. Road height is 47 inches.

Apache Solid State, from Vesely, has double-paneled folding walls made of thermoplastic and aluminum. It's available in six floor plans and sizes, including one model with shower and hot water.

Interior view of Coleman tent trailer shows roomy arrangement of cabinets, galley, table, and bunks. When folded, it all fits into a box 11 feet long and less than 3 feet deep.

Starcraft Galaxy tent trailer has a swing-out kitchen unit for indoor or outdoor cooking and dining. Tent opens out to a length of 21 feet—135 square feet of living and sleeping room.

Viking's 13-foot Mini-Gasser S is light enough to be towed by a small compact car, yet big enough for comfort. It comes with gas bottle, water tank, ice-box, and two-burner LP range.

ABS thermoplastic, as well as sliding screened windows. The self-storing entrance door, made of aluminum, is an integral part of the front wall. This means it will stay attached every time you fold down the trailer.

Road dust is more apt to filter into tent trailers than into other RVs, but the problem isn't serious.

Pickup Campers

Truck campers fall into three categories. The big seller is the unit that can be installed in and readily removed from the bed of the pickup, leaving the truck free for countless other chores outdoors. The second most popular is the rig that is permanently installed on the chassis of the truck. The third is a basic roof or shell that clamps onto the truck bed. This unit will suffice if you only need one or two bunks and an area to sit down. The shell is adequate for two hunters.

The first model mentioned is slid onto the truck when you're ready to use it. (The tailgate is either lowered or completely removed.) Other times, the camper can rest on tripods or jacks. The interior has standing room; a kitchen with a sink, a stove, and a refrigerator; a dinette that converts to a bed; plus space for storing groceries and clothing. A majority of these units also have an extended area over the cab to serve as sleeping quarters by night and storage space by day. The larger rigs may include a shower and toilet. Optionals include a radio, air-conditioning, a trailer hitch, a step bumper, and an auxiliary gas tank. One model even boasts an expanded rear door plus a ramp so you can ride your ATV or snowmobile right up into the vehicle and tote it with you.

The camper—minus the truck—may weigh from 800 pounds to well over a ton. The length ranges from 6 to 12 feet.

The permanently mounted campers are often wider and longer than the other two styles because the bed of the truck is eliminated, and they're also superior in regard to self-containment. The chassis-mounts vary between 10 and 18 feet and weigh from 1,500 to 2,700 pounds. The legal maximum width is 8 feet, and these beauties often have that expanse. Formerly, most units were 6 feet wide.

The chassis-mounts are said to have better roadability and easier driving over lengthy hauls than the non-permanent campers, but campers as a whole have some advantages over the other RVs.

Since the vehicle is basically a truck—perhaps 4-wheel-drive—it can negotiate roads that a motor home and a travel trailer couldn't begin to navigate. The non-permanent pickup camper leaves the truck for numerous other purposes.

If it's pouring outside, you can merely park the vehicle and proceed to prepare supper or simply relax. No problems with firewood and tent stakes.

Riding in the camper coach is permissible while on the road, so the cab needn't be overcrowded. An intercom can even be installed to aid communication between the rear and the cab.

Now for the disadvantages:

Whenever you want to travel, you must take the entire camp with you. This necessitates securing gear and putting away all utensils and dishes.

Coachmen's truck campers come in six lengths with 10 floor plans and can fit any pickup, even a half-ton. Standard equipment includes stainless-steel sink, three-burner range, water tank with electric pump, gas bottle, and 110V power cord for 30 amp service connection.

Space View Truck camper by Space Age is 11 ft. long, 7½ ft. wide. That's room enough for up to six persons to eat, sleep, cook, and wash, plus ample space for taking along a rowboat, beach chairs, and other gear.

Henco truck caps come in 26-, 28-, and 30-inch-high versions for 8-foot truck beds, and there's a 28-inch-high model for short-bed trucks. Options include panoramic windows and biparting windows for cab access.

Winnebago's insulated truck cap has lights, sliding windows, double-latched swing-up rear, and plenty of space for gear. (Contents in this photo include the author's dog in a travel-kennel.) Optional features include a boat rack.

Coleman Country Squire is a folding pick-up camper that closes down to truck-cap size, opens like a tent trailer to provide over 6-foot head room, and holds storage compartments, sink, two-

burner range, two double beds, two bench seats, cooler, water tank and hookup, LP bottle, and dining table. It fits most half-ton pick-ups. Heater and carpeting are optional.

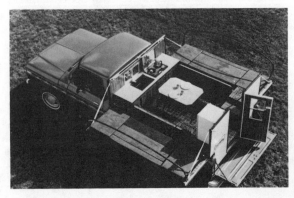

Highway driving can occasionally be frightening. A gusty headwind or strong crosswinds can turn the rig into a huge sail, making the driver's job a difficult one—power steering or no!

When the time comes to store this vehicle, you might be in for some trouble. Several suburban regions prohibit parking on driveways, necessitating the rental of space or the use of your garage. With the unit measuring from 8½ to 10 feet in height when it is high enough on the jacks to be loaded, or on the pickup itself, you'll probably find that the ceiling of your garage isn't quite high enough. Take this into account before buying.

Travel Trailers

The travel trailer is a permanent living area that features one or more rooms, and is mounted on two or four wheels, depending on its weight and size. Travel trailers range in length from 12 to 35 feet, with the 22-footer apparently the most popular according to sales figures. The array of vehicles is extensive, and there is a comparably wide range of prices. The interiors are usually plywood while the exteriors are aluminum. Foam insulation resides between the two, and the entire unit sits on a welded chassis of steel.

A six-footer could stand up easily in the average trailer as the overall distance from floor to roof is 7 to 8 feet. The unit is rarely less than 7 feet wide, and often closer to the maximum of 8 feet.

With the accent on compact and subcompact automobiles in recent years, the trailer industry has followed the trend and produced a large selection of mini-travel trailers.

To be self-contained, a vehicle must be able to supply sewage disposal, water, and power. To do this, it must hold a minimum of 30 gallons of water; a holding tank for wastes; and enough bottled gas to take care of stove, heater, and refrigerator. The average travel trailer is conveniently self-contained, with sleeping space, heater, toilet, and shower. When it comes to optionals, you can have air-conditioning, television, stereo, and even a bathtub. With all of these comforts just behind the towing vehicle, it's easy to see why this RV is so popular.

The travel trailer also holds the upper hand over the pickup camper and the motor home in that you can park it and use the car or truck exclusively. With the other two, you have to drag your kitchen sink along wherever you go.

But there is less of an area where you *can* go if you want to take the trailer. It won't negotiate the same roads a pickup camper will, particularly if the latter is equipped with 4-wheel-drive.

And on the negative side . . .

Unless the trailer can be adjusted to a low silhouette to somewhat resemble a tent trailer, you may have some trouble driving it at first. Sway is a problem, often caused by poor distribution of weight over the axle of the trailer. To prevent it, try to place the bulk of the weight forward of the trailer's wheels. Also decrease front-tire pressure prior to your trip. It can speed up tire wear but may save your life. Use an equalizer hitch if the trailer weighs over a half-ton, to shift more weight to the car's front wheels.

Power steering seems to be the culprit in many trailer accidents as the inexperienced driver tends to oversteer once swaying begins.

Shasta 1600 travel trailer is a compact model that sleeps four— or six with optional beds—and features a water system, marine toilet, shower, and galley with four-burner range. Other Shastas include 15 different lengths and 22 floor plans.

Vesely Apache travel trailer is a lightweight model (about 1,575 pounds standard, 1,850 in the deluxe model shown). Deluxe features include a bed assembly that slides out of rear panel for immediate use. Other features are electric/gas refrigerator, LP bottle and hookup, gas range, dinette, closet, and couch. Sleeps four.

Easy to spot at any gathering of travel trailers is the Airstream, a rig that is aerodynamically designed on the outside to slice into wind resistance. Each model—from the 18- to the 31-footers—has carpeted floor and many standard accoutrements.

Starcraft Travel Star trailers come in 10 models, from 18½ to 26 feet long. All feature trim exteriors, roomy interiors. Model 240 interior, shown here, sleeps four to eight, depending on installation of optional cabinet bunks.

Argosy Minuet is a 22-foot self-contained travel trailer with standard features, but is a very lightweight model designed for towing behind small American compact cars.

Coachmen Cadet is a 23-foot travel trailer featuring a rear bathroom with separate bathtub and shower area plus wardrobe. Equipment includes four-burner range with oven and lighted hood, stainless-steel sink, and refrigerator.

As mentioned earlier in this chapter, you would be smart to have the correct options put on your car during assembly. Such items as oversize radiators, extra-blade fans, heavy-duty springs and shock absorbers, heavy-duty batteries and alternators, fade-resistant brake linings, etc., will cost you far more to put in after you've had the auto for a while.

Trailers can be used in winter, but you may want to store your own. If so, remember to do the following: Drain the complete water system, septic holding tank and the water heater. Also drain traps or pour alcohol into them. Remove the tires to prevent deterioration. If you want to leave the tires on, jack up the trailer to relieve the tires of weight. Also take the hubcaps off as they tend to rust quickly. When snow accumulates to over a few inches on the trailer roof, clear it off—but not with a shovel. A broom will do.

Motor Homes

The motor home is a self-contained home on wheels, and the driver sits near facilities for dining, cooking, sleeping, sanitation, water supply, and usually air-conditioning.

One manufacturer's standard equipment includes wall-to-wall foam padded nylon carpet, storage drawers, a 4-burner stove with automatic oven, a dinette that converts into a bed, tinted windows, two skylight roof vents, a fire extinguisher, a bedroom privacy curtain, a cigarette lighter, four adjustable defroster vents, and many other worthwhile items. Optionals are quite numerous in many models. For the extra cost, you can include an AM-FM radio with four speakers, a trailer hitch, a dash-mounted water-tank gauge, wraparound windshield curtains, head- and arm-rests for driver and co-pilot, plus many other conveniences to make for a safer and more enjoyable excursion in your motor home.

The rigs measure from 17 to 30 feet in length, with the 20- to 24-foot models being the best-sellers.

The interior of the unit is plywood with the outside constructed of molded fiberglass or aluminum. The counter and table tops are made of material that can readily withstand any punishment.

Owing to the vehicle's enormous size and its overhang, you must travel on good roads. Parking also may be a problem, but this is not true in all cases. That same overhang, though, can come in very handy when you're launching a boat. And motor homes are excellent vehicles to trailer such craft behind.

One drawback of the motor home is its shoebox shape, but some new models are being aerodynamically designed so as to cut down on the hazards of wind.

If you store your motor home during the winter, remove water from every pipe in the system and leave valves in the open position. Also make certain that water is drained from the toilet and toilet-holding tank, and follow this up with a thorough cleansing and deodorizing. LP gas-tank valves should be closed securely, as well as all windows and roof vents. The refrigerator should also be cleaned and emptied, and the door left open. Take out all food from the vehicle, as well as such items as fishing tackle which may leave undesirable odors. Give the vehicle a walk-through check on occasion, airing it out when possible. As tires are usually left fully inflated on the motor home, move the unit a couple

Starcraft Starblazer 2203 motor home has an exterior length of just over 22 feet. It houses a tub and shower, lavatory, closet and storage cabinets, range and oven, refrigerator, sink, two tables, and swivel chairs. Sleeps four.

Coons Diamond Micro-Minihome is a 17-footer with bath, table, full galley, holding tank, and fiberglass insulation, mounted on a Ford, Dodge, or Chevy. Sleeps up to six with an optional bunk.

Xplorer 307 Xtrava motor home is 25 feet 7 inches long and has an aerodynamic molded-fiberglass exterior. Body is steel-reinforced fiberglass and urethane foam with steel bracing. This is the Sidebath Model, with bathroom (shower, sink with vanity, and toilet) mounted amidships rather than at rear—where a private "stateroom" has a 54-inch-wide double bed.

Itasca Suncruiser, on a Dodge chassis with a 360-cubic-inch engine, is available in 23- and 26-foot models. Standard in 26-footer are rear twin beds, dinette that converts to bed, lounge area, full galley, full bath, and convertible couch. Instead of twin beds, you can have convertible couch with swivel chairs and fold-out table or vanity.

Coachmen Leprechaun is a 22- or 24-foot mini motor home with refrigerator, four-burner lighted range with oven, double stainless-steel sink, sleeping areas up front, and private bath at rear. Eight models provide a wide range of floor plans and options.

Launching a 17-ft. boat is sometimes a chore, but with a little help from a motor home, the job is accomplished easily. The dual rear wheels give the vehicle excellent traction on soft surfaces, and the long overhang stops those same four wheels from even touching the water.

Holiday Rambler typifies the big, luxury-model motorhomes with spacious living quarters and full array of appliances. This model has rear bathroom, sleeping quarters, full kitchen and lounging area. Its appointments include TV set.

Apache Motor Home is available in 20-, 21-, and 23-foot models on a Dodge or Chevy chassis. The 20-footer, designed for sportsmen, has four-wheel-drive, a built-in gun rack, and other features not found in conventional models.

Shasta 22-foot Mini Model is available with rear bath or "bunkhouse" floor plan. Other models—six in all—include 20- and 25-footers. They're built on Ford, Chevy/GMC, or Dodge chassis.

Left: Motor homes need dual batteries to provide enough juice for your vehicle. In this rig, we found a 220-amp. battery as well as a 70-amp. unit. *Center:* Hot water is an important item aboard any vehicle. Here's the LP-powered heater that's handling the job. *Right:* Near the rear bumper, you'll find a compartment housing an exterior electric hook-up.

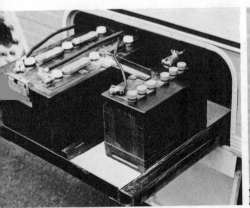

of feet each week or so to avoid continuous stress on one section of the tire due to the total weight of the home being on it and the three to five other tires. Otherwise, jack up each wheel on occasion and slightly rotate it.

Fifth-Wheel Trailers

Fifth-wheel trailers—often just called fifth-wheelers—are the newest type of RV. The fifth wheel is the hitch, a modification of the fifth-wheel hitch used on tractor-trailer rigs. It goes over the axle of a pickup truck and is bolted to the frame, not just to the floor of the truck bed. The trailer itself has a cutout so that it can hang over the pickup's bed by about 7 feet, reducing the combined length of towing vehicle and trailer. A 29-foot fifth-wheeler, for example, extends only about 22 feet from the rear of the truck when it's hitched.

This design has several purposes. Most obviously, it provides extra interior trailer space in proportion to the rig's overall length. The objective is spacious luxury. The type of hitch also reduces trailer sway, helps insure against jack-knifing, and makes for an extremely secure, safe coupling. In addition, hitching is easier. A big king pin hangs down and couples to the hitch in the pickup bed. As you back the truck toward the king pin, you can see it clearly, and this makes the connection easier than positioning a conventional coupler over a ball.

Fifth-wheelers come in a variety of lengths, from compact 18-footers to models as long as 35 feet. Most are in the 26- to 32-foot range. Some of the smaller ones can be towed by a half-ton pickup, but most need a three-quarter or one-ton pickup truck.

Although the construction techniques are pretty much the same as for travel trailers, the insulation tends to be better, the appliances bigger. Many fifth-wheelers are more like motor homes than travel trailers. The master bedroom, built into the overhang, may be big enough for a large double bed or twin beds. Some models have sliding glass patio doors and very spacious, open-looking interiors. And some have "tip-out" alcoves that crank out when parked at a campsite. Small couches or lounges fit to make the main floor less cluttered. Depending on size and interior features, fifth-wheelers sleep from four to eight persons. Like motor homes, they are, of course, expensive.

Van Conversions

Van conversions, also called van campers, have become extremely popular. One reason is that some models cost little more than a full-size station wagon. Another is that they're easier to handle and park than some of the bigger camping rigs, and they can be used for everyday purposes around home, like an ordinary van or station wagon. Thus they combine the advantages of a super station wagon and "pocket" motor home. Many models provide not only sleeping bunks but a galley and even a shower and toilet, making them completely self-contained camping rigs.

The RV manufacturers convert all the standard van models—Chevrolet, Dodge, Ford, and GMC—using vans with both short and long wheelbases. Some RV companies stretch the width or length to provide jumbo interiors.

You can't stand up inside a standard van, so headroom is an important part of conversion. Most often, the roof is cut

Blazon Elite 188 Towlounge forms a matched pair with Elite 375 Center Bath Fifth Wheel Trailer. Towing vehicle seats five, can haul loads like a pick-up, and has over-the-cab sleeper plus a lounge with table, three seats, ice box, and countertop that provides space for 12V TV.

Dodge Custom Sportsman van features extra-large taillamps, deep windows, swing-out rear door, optional vents or sun roof, and a wide variety of trim options.

Coachmen Modelay van camper has two bucket seats, overhead bed, convertible gaucho couch, two-burner gas stove, ice box, and stainless-steel sink. Choice of chassis includes Chevy, Dodge, Ford, or GMC. Four models are available.

off and a raised fiberglass structure is substituted, resulting in more than 6 feet of interior height. However, the added frontal area can cause extra drag, and the increased height may make the vehicle slightly more susceptible to wind sway. Another approach is to increase headroom only in the galley area, by building a dropped floor well. The disadvantage here is that you can stand straight only in that area—when preparing meals. Also, the floor well reduces ground clearance, which can be important on rough roads. A third way is to install an expandable top that lies almost flat (adding only about 4 inches to the van's height while driving) and can be popped up to provide headroom when desired.

A typical interior might have a dinette that can be turned into a double bunk, plus another double bunk over the driver's cockpit. The galley generally contains a sink, range, and refrigerator or cooler. Models with a lavatory contain a chemical toilet, wash basin, and shower.

Snowmobiles

The snowmobile is the only vehicle available for traveling in remote, snow-covered regions. It's steered by ski-type runners up front and is propelled by a continuously running belt or track below the vehicle that grips the surface of the snow and sends the sled flying over it.

Low-priced models are compacts with engines averaging 225 cc, but the big ones are known in the snowmobiler's lingo as "class 5 modifieds." The latter is the largest on the market, featuring a 350-pound toboggan with an 85-hp, 800-cc engine. These machines hit 90 and beyond with little effort.

The track on the typical snowmobile measures 15 inches in width, and permits you to steer the vehicle by shifting your weight. Tracks, however, sometimes reach 30½ inches.

Snowmobiles can get into many areas where a car or an RV wouldn't stand a chance. Before the age of the snowmobile, conservation officers had to don their snowshoes. In times of accident or disaster in snow-bound areas, help can get there quickly with a snowmobile to provide rapid medical assistance and transportation to hospital. For the outdoorsman, the snowmobile offers enjoyment. He can go hunting, ice-fishing, racing, or skijoring (skiing behind a snowmobile) with the rig.

But there have also been numerous complaints about the snowmobile. A common one is excessive noise, and this is a point that ecologists often bring up. Minnesota has a law in the books prohibiting a new machine to be sold unless it is equipped with a muffler limiting engine noise to 86 decibels at 50 feet (auto noise measures 70 decibels). New York State limits noise to 74 decibels.

Also, some people chase deer and other game animals with their snowmobiles. This practice, of course, is against the law.

Though a few snowmobiles on the market feature reverse transmission on an optional basis, most do not have standard reverse, making them somewhat dangerous. Accidents such as fatal or maiming collisions with automobiles, trains, pipes, fences, etc. also show the hazards of driving the vehicle.

Other disadvantages include its heavy weight; its often low, cramped size; and narrow cleats that often don't adhere to the ice and snow.

The heavier snowmobiles cannot negotiate all types of snow, but there are relatively new, lightweight models designed for better flotation on soft snow. Be careful with a heavier one, which may bog down. Also be sure to wear appropriate clothing for safety and warmth. Insulated snowmobile suits are recommended. So are helmets, goggles, and face masks. Some of the snowmobiles themselves have built-in safety features such as padded handle bars and break-away windshields—excellent improvements.

In addition, the noise has been substantially reduced in recent years. Machines built since June 30, 1976, and certified by the Snowmobile Safety and Certification Committee of the International Snowmobile Industry Association emit no more than 73 decibels at 50 feet when traveling 15 miles an hour, and similarly certified machines produced since February 1, 1975, emit no more than 78 decibels at 50 feet when traveling *at full throttle*.

Snowmobiling has become more than a mechanized means of traveling over snow; it has become a sport (and almost a way of life in some regions). Trail systems have been de-

Futura 400 (left) and Mirage are Moto-Ski models. Both have front-mounted, two-cylinder, fan-cooled engines and torque-reaction slide suspension. Electric start is available on the Futura as a factory-installed option.

Galaxy, by Polaris, is a two-passenger snowmobile available with fan-cooled 340cc or 440cc engine. Options on the 440 include electric start and rubber track. This stable trail-riding machine was tested for 1,250 miles in Alaska's western coast and exceeded every reliability rating.

veloped in forest lands to accommodate snowmobilers without interfering with skiers or other winter-sports enthusiasts. Regulations have been established by states—and in some cases by the snowmobilers themselves—to promote safety. Some trails have stop signs, yield signs, and even information kiosks at strategic locations. Perhaps the most important improvements have come from the snowmobiling clubs, which have promoted responsible snowmobiling—not only in terms of safety but in terms of concern for wild animals and forest vegetation. When carried on in such a responsible manner, the sport is harmless to wildlife.

Obviously, the snowmobile season is rather short. Therefore, correct storage of your vehicle is essential.

Store it in a dry place, and block it off the ground to take the weight off the skis and track. Loosen the track tensioner. Drain the fuel tank and pour a quart of SAE 30 into the oil tank. Then roll the machine from side to side so the fuel-tank walls are well lubricated. Drain the carburetor. Take out the spark plug and pour a tablespoon of SAE 30 oil through the spark plug hole. Turn the engine over four times by pulling the starter rope. Then replace the spark plug. Clean the outside of the engine and spread a thin film of oil over any of its exposed surfaces that could corrode.

Camp Bedding

Gerry Super Snug mummy bag is insulated with PolarGuard, has a temperature rating down to 10 below zero, and weighs 5¾ pounds. In regular size, it's 82 inches long, including hood.

Sleeping Bags

Insulation

The warmest and lightest insulation used in today's sleeping bags is down, the breast feathers of a goose or a duck. Besides being quite soft and warm, down holds the heat generated by the body. It does not, fortunately, hold body moisture. This throwing-off process is known as "breathing," and prevents the bag from becoming uncomfortably clammy.

"Loft"—the height of a sleeping bag when fully fluffed and unrolled—is a good indication of the bag's insulating ability. A couple of the newer synthetic fillers, PolarGuard and Hollofil II, exhibit good loft and offer about two-thirds as much insulating efficiency as down per pound. But for certain purposes—canoe- or boat-camping, wet-weather camping, or camping from spring through fall, when the temperature isn't extremely cold—the newer synthetics have several advantages over down.

For one thing, down becomes almost useless as an insulator when it gets wet, and it dries slowly. Polyesters provide warmth even when wet, and they dry quickly. For another thing, down tends to shift around in a bag, making lumps and thin, cold spots unless extensive sewing "quilts" it in place. PolarGuard is batt-like and so doesn't shift and needs quilting. Hollofil II needs almost as much quilting as down. Finally, the synthetics cost less, primarily because the raw materials are cheaper than down.

Even some of the polyester-and-acrylic combination fillers provide some warmth when wet, assuming that outside temperatures aren't extremely cold. And, like down, the newer polyesters retain body heat while allowing body moisture to escape and evaporate. Some synthetic-filled bags are more compressible than down—in spite of their good loft when fluffed out—and this can be another advantage when gear space is limited.

Other filler materials include wool, cotton (poplin), kapok, and Dacron. Except for Dacron, these insulators mat easily and aren't very resilient. Yet they may suffice in relatively thin, warm-weather bags, and such bags are comparatively inexpensive.

The label and/or packaging of a good sleeping bag usually states the weight of the filler and the temperature range or minimum temperature at which the bag will keep you comfortable. Of course, with a bag which doesn't provide much insulation, you can wear extra sleeping clothes to add 20° to 30°F effectiveness to the bag. But it pays to buy a bag of good quality—both for warmth and durability—and to compare weights and comfort ranges before deciding which one to buy. Three pounds of one synthetic filler, for example, may keep you comfortable when the temperature dips to 30 degrees, while you'll need only about 2 pounds of down at that temperature. Consider the kind of camping you'll be doing and the price you can afford—and then shop aggressively.

Liners

Although a majority of sleeping bags on the market have an inner lining made of flannel, it is worthwhile to purchase an additional flannel liner. If you can carry the extra weight, an extra liner helps to regulate warmth during the night. Should it be warm when you fall asleep, you can take out the lining completely or use it folded underneath as a mattress pad. If the temperature drops substantially later on, the liner can be readily shifted so that you sleep between the layers or under the both of them. This separate liner will stop drafts where the sleeper's head protrudes and will provide further insulation near the areas of the zipper and/or snap fasteners, where cold air may enter.

By purchasing a variety of liners, you can adjust your sleeping bag for practically any weather. That's the reason why a four-season camper usually relies on liners.

An advantage of the removable liner is that cleaning will be no problem, and the bag itself will remain unsoiled within. Tie-tabs on your sleeping bag are good for quickly attaching or removing such liners.

Liners are also made of synthetics. One manufacturer claims that its 3-pound liner consisting of 2 pounds of polyester fibers will add approximately 20 degrees to the minimum comfort range. Going a step further, another liner-maker boasts that his product can convert a 3-pound Dacron sleeping bag, rated for 35 degrees, into a 5-pound bag that should keep the sleeper warm in zero temperatures.

In summer, when it may be too hot for a sleeping bag, you can sleep in the liner alone.

Shells for Sleeping Bags

It is important that sleeping bags breathe, letting body moisture escape. Otherwise, you wind up with a sauna effect.

Beware of any bag—especially a cheap one—advertised as waterproof. Such shells may be coated so they won't allow body vapors to pass through. On the other hand, some excellent waterproof shells, such as those made of a nylon and Gore-Tex laminate, do breathe while being impermeable to rain.

Economical "stationwagon" bags often have an inner shell of cotton flannel and an outer shell of heavy cotton.

These bags are practical for warm-weather car-tenting or for use in a rec vehicle. But since they are heavy, bulky, and highly moisture-absorbent in relation to the warmth they provide, they are not suitable for backpacking or canoe camping.

Better bags filled with down or polyesters usually have inner and outer shells made of nylon in ripstop or taffeta weaves. Both fabrics breathe. They also feel good next to the skin, wear well, resist mildew and fading, and are unaffected by machine washing.

There are also bivouac covers, which serve like mini-tents but drape over you and your sleeping bag like a sock—complete with mosquito netting. These covers normally have an airtight and waterproof underside and a waterproof (though breathable)) topside made of materials such as Gore-Tex. Larger bivouac covers can house a couple of sleepers and their gear. Though more restrictive than tents, these covers are lighter and so get the nod from weight-conscious backpackers.

Zippers

Zippers on mummy bags typically run three-quarter length or full-length down one side. A rectangular sleeping bag should be equipped with a heavy-duty zipper that runs completely down one side and across the bottom. This type of zipper permits you to open the bag completely for a thorough airing, and lets you zip together two matching sleeping bags. Two bags zipped together will accommodate two adults or up to four youngsters.

For both mummy and rectangular bags, zippers should have slides at both ends that allow you to ventilate the head and foot ends independently. Both slides should have finger tabs inside and out.

Zippers themselves may be made of metal, nylon, or other synthetics. Metal tends to feel colder in cold weather, work harder in all weather, and frost-up in winter. A sleeping bag zipper should be large, whether it be of the conventional ladder design of most metal zippers or of the toothed-interlock or the continuous coil designs used for synthetic zippers. Large zippers don't catch and abrade shell fabrics

as readily as smaller, toothed zippers do—especially smaller metal-toothed zippers. Of all zippers, the continuous coil is easiest on fabric.

Most sleeping bags have a baffle panel—weatherstripping made of insulated material to prevent air from traveling through the zipper. This strip lies along the inner surface of the zipper, and, in better bags, may be from 1 to 1½ inches thick and from 3 to 4 inches wide. A cheaply made bag, needless to say, would have little or no weatherstripping and/or a short (30- to 36-inch) zipper that may tend to drag when the bag is closed or opened.

Dry-Cleaned Bags

We stress proper airing of the sleeping bag, particularly when it has been dry-cleaned. An oft-told tale that bears repeating now deals with a teen-ager who had slept in a bag that had only recently been dry-cleaned and then left for 1½ days in a car trunk. The boy's parents found him in a coma after the first night. Eleven days later, he was dead. The hospital reports said death was due to the inhaling of perchloroethylene fumes that had been trapped within the insulation. The solvents used in dry-cleaning may leave behind long-lasting lethal fumes. A thorough airing is a must. The mummy bag, to be discussed in more detail further along, can literally turn into a shroud if not properly aired, because often only the sleeper's nose is exposed.

Mattress Pockets and Canopies

If there were ever two items in the camper's sleeping world that might be termed virtually vestigial, they are the mattress pocket and the canopy.

The former is built-in on a goodly number of bags, yet its value is plainly in doubt. The intended purpose of the device is to act as a pocket for an inserted air mattress, but the mattress is extremely difficult to remove in the morning. Inserting the mattress into the bag is not a simple task, either. A better sleeping setup is to place the air mattress on a ground cloth or on smooth ground, the sleeping bag on top.

The canopy serves little purpose. It may act as a protec-

White Stag Superior is a rectangular-cut sleeping bag, 33 by 80 inches. Cover and lining are nylon. Delrin zipper opens from top or bottom. Insulation is a double layer of Hollofil II—a choice of 2½ or 3½ pounds—and bag is washable.

Gerry Winterlite is a down-filled mummy bag—33 ounces of goose down—with cross baffles, ripstop nylon shell, and integral zipper. It weighs about 4 pounds and is rated comfortable down to 10 below.

tive covering for the sleeping bag itself when rolled up or as a cloth panel to hold such items as eyeglasses or a flashlight which might come in handy during the night. But if the bag comes already equipped with a carrying case or stuff bag, the canopy is useless. It may ward off a light drizzle or gentle snow, but should a moderate or worse storm come up, offers no protection at all.

Styles

Sleeping bags come in two basic configurations – the rectangular bag and the mummy bag. A variation, designed for recreational vehicles, is called a station-wagon bag, but this is simply an oversized rectangular bag. The rectangular type is basically a three-season bag but is available in grades from summer-weight to heavy winter-weight. The mummy bag is intended primarily for cold weather; it fits more closely and cinches tight about head and shoulders, impeding exchange of inside and outside air.

Except for a few huge station-wagon bags, the rectangular style is usually offered in a choice of three sizes. The junior (or small-adult) size often measures 33 x 68 inches. Most common is the adult size, 33 x 75 inches or 36 x 80 inches. The third size is extra-large – 39 x 84 inches or 41 x 86 inches – for large adults.

An important thing to remember when purchasing a sleeping bag is that two sizes are listed in the catalogs – the cut size and the finished size. Your best bet is totally to disregard the cut sizes as they indicate the size of the material prior to construction. The finished size is the figure you should concentrate on as it is the actual length and width of the completed bag. The finished size should be your guide. (Previous figures are all finished sizes.) Two sleeping bags may be paired together by opening and completely unzipping both. One should be placed atop the other so that the bottoms of both zippers meet. Then, simply connect each zipper at the point where the two meet. Double bags when used by two persons tend to be warmer than they are when used individually.

Such double bags have the same cover width on top as they do underneath. One manufacturer saw this problem recently and developed what is known as the Four Seasons sleeping bag. The benefit is that the top cover is one foot wider than the bottom. The 50″ x 76″ bag is well insulated, and provides the sleepers with more room to move around because of its style. A junior bag is a waste of money; get an adult bag for your youngster as, with proper care, it will last him or her several years.

Rectangular bags in general are fine for car, canoe, and recreational-vehicle camping. But if you're backpacking, you'll probably have to put your faith in the mummy bag. You won't be making the wrong move, though.

As we've said, weight is an important consideration to the backpacker, and the mummy bag is designed with this in mind. It is widest at the shoulders – usually 33″ – and tapers to about 19″ at the feet. This tapering makes the bag fit like a robe, and that means additional warmth. Some mummy bags can keep the sleeper comfortable at zero and weigh only 3 or 4 pounds, half the weight of comparably warm oblong bags. Mummy bags are usually filled with down and have nylon covers.

Another valuable item for the backpacker is the stuff bag,

into which he actually stuffs his sleeping bag. This method of storage saves wear on the bag through compression fatigue, and also helps to fluff it up when you're extracting it for use. Stuff bags usually are waterproof.

White Stag Cascade mummy bag is insulated with Hollofil II. It comes in regular size or extra-long and has oval foot pocket, double-layer construction, draw-cord hood, elastic roll-up straps, two-way zipper, and draft tube for extra insulation.

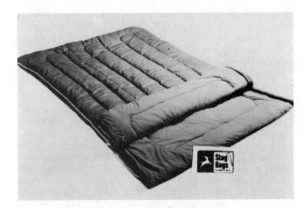

White Stag Wagon-Camper-Trailer Sleeping Bag is the over-sized rectangular "station-wagon" style. It measures 56 by 72 inches, is insulated with 3 pounds of synthetic fill in the bottom and 2 pounds in the top, and has a washable cotton cover with flannel lining.

Air Mattresses

An air mattress is not essential for sleeping in the outdoors, but it does add comfort. Most are made of nylon, which is lightweight enough for backpacking.

The chief drawback is that an air mattress can be used only at temperatures of about 45°F and higher unless you lay some insulation over the mattress. Otherwise, cold air in the mattress will convect body heat away. Another disadvantage is that air mattresses are subject to puncture as well as leakage from seams and valves. So a special patching kit should always accompany you on your travels.

Catalog listings of air mattresses often give both the deflated size and the inflated size. The latter is the one you should pay attention to, as that is what you will be sleeping on.

The average adult can be comfortably accommodated on a mattress measuring between 70 and 74 inches. A six-footer would require the longest standard length—75 inches. A stout camper might need 32 inches of mattress across his back, but most people can fit comfortably on 28- to 30-inchers with adequate elbow room.

There are two designs of air mattresses—the I-beam style and the tufted. The I-beam typically consists of five tubes that resemble steel construction beams when viewed from one end. The tufted design is wafflelike in appearance, and provides the sleeper with full support. It's more comfortable than the I-beam style, but is the more expensive of the two. When buying an air mattress, either I-beam or tufted, choose one with a metal valve, never the rubber or plastic type. The metal valves have screw tops.

If you sleep with a pillow, there's no need for you to do without one outdoors. Many sleeping bags come with built-in air pillows, or else the pillows—either filled with down, synthetic fibers, or air—can be bought separately.

There are many air mattresses made solely of plastic or rubber. Avoid them. Although plastic or rubber air mattresses are lighter than the recommended fabric-rubber combinations, they are delicate and tear easily.

Until recently, there were three ways to inflate an air mattress: with a hand pump, a foot pump, or your own lungs. Now there are also some cleverly designed self-inflating mattresses. If yours doesn't inflate itself, using your own lung power isn't very difficult, but the resulting moist vapor can condense and freeze in cold weather. A hand pump adds weight to your gear. Lightweight plastic foot pumps are popular; although they are bulky, they provide dry air quickly.

When you inflate an air mattress, keep it out of the sun. Otherwise, the heat will cause the air to expand, possibly breaking the mattress. Also, never use a gas-station air-pressure pump to inflate a mattress.

To deflate an air mattress, unscrew the metal cap, leaving the valve completely open. Then put a heavy object on the mattress to force air to escape more quickly. The last step is to slowly roll the mattress, beginning with the end opposite the valve, until all the air has been expelled.

When not in use, an air mattress should be blown up slightly and kept away from heat. Use it only for sleeping; it is not meant to be a surfboard. If the mattress does get wet, though, stand it up in an airy, shady place.

Foam Pads

Sleeping pads are of two basic types: 1) hard, closed-cell foams and 2) soft, open-cell foams. The hard pads contain sealed bubbles that resist compression. The soft pads contain bubbles and a network of passages that allow air to escape when compressed.

Hard-foam pads are sold in thicknesses ranging from $3/8$ to 1 inch and provide almost as much insulating loft as the pad's thickness. Soft-foam pads must be purchased 4 to 5 times as thick as hard foams to provide as much insulating loft when compressed under your body. Though more comfortable, soft-foam pads are bulkier to carry, and they absorb ground and body moisture—adding inconvenience and weight.

Both hard- and soft-foam pads can be purchased in various lengths and widths. To capitalize on the advantages of each type of pad, some manufacturers laminate them together. Here, the top layer is soft foam for comfort, and the bottom layer is the hard foam for insulation and water-tightness. Or you may see a soft-foam pad enclosed in a fabric cover. Better covers have a cotton upper surface, so that body moisture won't be trapped on top, and a lower surface of waterproofing-coated nylon.

Tough, young backpackers use hard foams almost exclusively. But age and desire for comfort, usually lead even the toughest backpackers to combine the use of hard foam with either soft foam or an air mattress.

Canvas Cots

A cot in your tent can waste floor space if you have a sloping-wall tent. Also, it's quite a task to set up alone. Canvas cots also tend to let cold air circulate beneath them, but some six-inch-high models come equipped with down or Dacron batting. This insulation isn't compressed by the camper's weight while he sleeps, so it remains at peak efficiency. On the other hand, cots are comfortable, if weight and bulk are unimportant.

If you decide on a canvas cot, get a model that is about 12 or 14 inches off the ground so it can double as a tent seat.

I-Beam construction of this air mattess renders it less comfortable than the wafflelike pattern—but it is also less expensive.

Air mattresses can range from poor to excellent in durability. One very good type is this tufted version, which boasts pliability and dependability even in temperatures of 20 degrees below zero.

Footgear

Leather Boots

The sturdiest boots are those constructed totally of leather, the best all-round material for four-season wear. Leather boots permit the feet to "breath," giving off moisture that would otherwise tend to make the camper's feet hot and uncomfortable and cause blisters. Some manufacturers have treated boots with waterproofing compounds, but leather so treated seals in body heat and moisture.

The proper height for a boot is about six inches. A higher boot may constrict your leg muscles as well as restrict free circulation. Also, high boots are hot and heavy in summertime. The boot should also be uninsulated, for reasons we'll discuss shortly.

Avoid boots with leather soles and heels; they are not very water resistant. Leather soles wear quickly and slip on smooth rocks, pine needles, dry grass, and the like. Get boots with soles and heels of rubber or one of the tough synthetics. Rubber soles provide a good grip, and are flexible, long-lasting, and tough.

Many campers like boots with a platform, or straight-bottom, sole that has no heel. These soles are not recommended for mountain climbing. A heel permits you to hold back when you're descending a slope. Cleat-like treads (Vibram) are good if you hike on rocky trails.

Be certain that the tops of the boots are made of soft leather so that enough insulation is provided. The air space between the sock and the boot and the area around your foot should permit free, comfortable movement. In winter, a boot should keep cold air out and warm air in; that air space, if sufficient, will help achieve this dual purpose. The toe and heel should be hard, to give your feet the protection they need.

Some styles of leather boots are insulated. If the temperature is below freezing, and dry, such boots may be suitable for casual walking. But for all-round use, they are a poor choice. They become stuffy, heavy, and hot during strenuous activity, and when wet take a long time to dry. In cold weather you are better off with plain .leather boots and several pairs of socks of varied weights which you can change if one pair becomes wet.

Before you try out your new boots on a hike, a thorough breaking-in is in order. Obviously, the spanking-new leather may be rather tough. That's why shoe grease should be applied, but not to any particular excess. Otherwise, your boots will become overly soft and all but worthless. Also, try short hikes at regular intervals with the new boots so that your feet will get accustomed to them. Bend your feet frequently to make each boot more pliable. Old-timers used to break in their boots by standing in a bucket of water till the boots were saturated, then walk around in them until they were dry.

Through proper care, you can add substantial life to your boots. When you're finished for the day and your boots are coated with mud, wash it off thoroughly. Then fill them with wads of newspaper and place them in a warm, dry area (not above 100 degrees F.). When they're dry, rub some shoe grease into the leather to soften and waterproof it.

Another simple way to waterproof leather boots is to treat them with paraffin or a silicone-dressing spray. The method of waterproofing preferred by most outdoorsmen is to use neat's-foot oil. (Keep the oil off rubber heels and soles as it may prove harmful to them.) Prior to application, wash the leather with warm water and mild soap. The purpose of this measure is to open the leather's pores for better absorption of the oil. Be sure the leather is still wet when you rub on the oil. A handy applicator is an old toothbrush as its bristles help get the oil deep into the seams.

For securing the boot to the foot, rawhide laces and eyelets have proved the best, with nylon strings running a close second. Some outdoorsmen prefer the quicker hooks, but they are not quite as reliable as laces. And if you get a cheap set of hooks, they'll break, rust, or bend in no time. Also, hooks often catch on twigs.

Rubber and Leather Boots

Though the all-leather boot is the best all-round boot for hiking, for wet weather many outdoorsmen prefer shoepacs. These boots have a leather top and a rubber bottom and are the perfect choice for hiking in rain, swamplands, and wet snow. The leather tops shed moisture well if they're properly oiled or greased, and are flexible. As these tops aren't as airtight as they would be if they were of rubber composition, they provide good ankle support and a wide, roomy area for the foot. This air space lets you wear two pairs of socks—woolen over thermal—to withstand the cold down to zero degrees F. The rubber bottoms of the shoepac perform the all-important function of keeping the feet dry.

As you've noted, shoepacs are designed for the wet-weather enthusiast. That's why the neat's-foot oil treatment described earlier should be used to waterproof the boots. But be careful not to harm the rubber bottoms when applying the oil.

Manufacturers have developed shoepacs up to 18 inches in height, but a model from 8 to 12 inches should prove adequate. The extra inches will just hinder the circulation in your leg, and will add extra, unnecessary lacing and unlacing time to your chores outdoors.

Rubber Boots—Uninsulated

The camper who fishes on his outings often finds himself pushing boats off beaches, and sloshing in water in his small craft. The top choice in footgear for this man is the uninsulated rubber boot.

The optimum choice is a boot about 12 or 13 inches high with no more than three eyelets at the top. The remainder of the boot is totally enclosed, protecting the feet from water.

In extreme cold, two pairs of socks—heavy woolen ones over thermal or athletic-type socks—are warmer than a single pair of heavy socks, and keep your feet dry and comfortable for quite a while.

When you shop for footgear, take along two pairs of socks to insure getting the proper size. You're better off learning about a too-snug fit in the store than when your feet begin to hurt on a cold day outside.

Rubber Boots—Insulated

Insulated rubber boots are a good choice for ice-fishing or sitting on a deer stand for lengthy periods—both of which are done in bone-chilling temperatures. These boots are much too heavy for conventional hiking, and even a lengthy walk will cause your feet to become clammy and sweaty. Another disadvantage is that if you should snag the outside layer, water may seep into the insulated lining. The proper procedure at this point is to squeeze and roll the moisture toward the area of the punctures until it is completely outside. Then prop open the tear with a twig or toothpick to let the insulation air out. Wait till all the moisture is removed before repairing the tear with a rubber-tube patch.

A final word on the insulated rubber boot: As mentioned, it can become clammy inside. By merely sprinkling talcum in the boot at night, you'll find that the clamminess will disappear, and your feet will slide in easier and not bunch up your socks uncomfortably.

Many outdoorsmen wear boot liners inside waterproof boots. These add to the warmth and reduce clamminess. Liners such as Royal Red Ball's Bama Sokkets have an outer layer of cotton tricot to act as a blotter and an inner layer of insulating, moisture-resistant acrylic fiber. For a comfortable fit with liners, you may need slightly larger boots than you'd otherwise wear. When buying new boots, therefore, it's best to try them on over the liners.

Leather Boots—Insulated

Though not quite as waterproof as the insulated rubber boot, the insulated leather boot has some virtues. It generally gives more comfortable fit and provides better ankle support.

You can't remove the insulation for cleaning and drying, and you can't adjust the boot to rising temperatures. Thus boots tend to become hot, stuffy and heavy in warmer weather.

Most insulated leather boots are quite waterproof, but in wet weather over an extended period some moisture will seep inside. To further waterproof your boots, try the silicone-dressing sprays, paraffin, or the neat's-foot oil method described earlier.

Hip Boots and Waders

The duckhunter and the fisherman find themselves up to their knees—and often higher—in water. Hip boots or waders are an essential part of their equipment.

When the water is no more than knee-deep and a substantial amount of walking is required, hip boots will suffice. For the fisherman or marshland hunter, the uninsulated hip boot is best. It features the standard heavy-rubber foot that is welded to a top of strong fabric—usually a laminated nylon-rubber-nylon sandwich—with a thin inner bond of waterproof rubber. Although some models are manufactured with uppers of rubber-coated fabric, the welded ones are recommended. Though the price is just a bit higher, they're more flexible and far lighter.

The winter steelheader, fall surf fisherman, or duck hunter will find the insulated hip boot to be his best buy. The weather is usually bitter, and the core of insulation built into the shoe and ankle of the hip boot will keep him warm.

If you are a stream fisherman who wades on slick rocks, felt-soled hip boots are required. They provide sure-footed, quiet movement. They wear quickly but can be replaced with special felt-sole kits available in sporting goods stores. These kits also can be used to apply felt soles to rubber-soled boots.

Waders are simply hip boots with waterproof tops that extend to the waist, or even to the chest. Some have stocking feet of thin rubber or a rubberized fabric, over which wading shoes are worn. Others have boot feet with waterproof uppers. The boot-foot style is simpler to put on, carry, and store; it is also less apt to develop leaks.

Snowshoes

When snow depths reach a foot or more, conventional boots are rendered virtually ineffectual. At such times snowshoes must be worn on outdoor treks. The purpose of the snowshoe is to distribute the weight of the body over a greater surface of snow than the shoe sole alone, thereby increasing support.

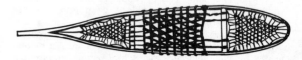

For relatively open country with just traces of brush or timber, the Alaskan snowshoe will suffice.

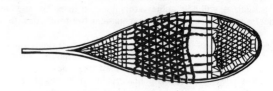

In areas of heavy brush, use the Michigan snowshoe.

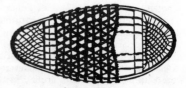

When you need to make frequent turns, such as on hills or mountains, strap on a pair of bearpaws.

Snowshoes come in three basic styles—the Alaskan, the Michigan, and the bearpaw—plus several modifications of each of these styles.

The Alaskan is also known as the Yukon, pickerel, trial, or racing snowshoe. It's good for long-distance walking, even with a heavy load. Long and narrow, it has a conspicuous upward curl at the toe and a tail at the rear—a design suited to open country and powder snow with little timber or brush.

The "classic" style, the one that conforms to most pictures, is the Michigan, also known as the Maine or Algonquin snowshoe. It, too, has a tail, but tends to be wider and shorter than the Alaskan, and with less front curl—usually 2 inches or under—making it suitable for brushy country.

The bearpaw has no tail and little (or occasionally no) front curl. Its shape is more or less oval, but the forepart is often slightly wider than the rear. Shorter than the other types, it's good for hilly, brushy terrain, especially where abrupt turns are common. This is believed to be the most ancient of all snowshoe designs.

One modification, sometimes called the Green Mountain snowshoe, is narrower than the usual bearpaw and almost uniform in width. One advantage is that it's easy to learn to walk on and is very maneuverable. Another is that it's compact. Green Mountain snowshoes and more or less similar models are popular with snowmobilers and, indeed, are sometimes called snowmobile snowshoes.

Another variation, known simply as a modified bearpaw, has a short tail, which helps to prevent twisting. Still another, usually called the cross-country snowshoe, is a narrow, slightly elongated bearpaw (like the Green Mountain) with a tail that helps prevent twisting but isn't long enough to snag. Good for relatively even but somewhat brushy terrain, it's essentially a cross between the bearpaw and the Alaskan.

The relatively new, non-wooden snowshoe frames are mostly of the same basic configuration as the bearpaw or Green Mountain but a bit more rectangular.

Traditionally, snowshoes are composed of frames made of ash—a tough and flexible wood—and rawhide webbing. The webbing must remain taut to perform properly, and freezing weather does the trick. Thus, keep snowshoes far from the campfire and warm cabins. Moisture can dangerously stretch the webbing. Using spar varnish or polyurethane, you can give your webbing a protective, waterproof

coat. Additional wrappings of rawhide near the snowshoe's toe can add to its life. As crusted snow usually affects the toe area first, this precaution should prove useful.

The size of the snowshoe depends on the weight of the snowshoer. The following chart will help you to determine the correct size for your boot.

BODY WEIGHT	MICHIGAN	ALASKAN	BEARPAW
35 to 50 lbs.	9″ x 30″	———	———
50 to 60	10″ x 36″	———	———
60 to 90	11″ x 40″	———	———
100 to 125	12″ x 42″	———	———
125 to 150	12″ x 48″	10″ x 48″	———
150 to 175	13″ x 48″	10″ x 56″	14″ x 30″
175 to 200	14″ x 48″	12″ x 60″	13″ x 33″
200 to 250	14″ x 52″	———	14″ x 36″

Between seasons, remove and replace all broken, weak, or frayed webbing. Clean the entire snowshoe rapidly with soap and water to prevent any unnecessary stretch. Dry the pair a minimum of 36 hours if some or all of the rawhide has been replaced.

In recent years, several new materials for snowshoe frames have come into use, as have two new kinds of webbing. In addition to fine-grain ash, frames are now made of aluminum, magnesium, or synthetics. Frames of metal or plastic are durable, won't warp, and require no maintenance. On the other hand, wood has more esthetic appeal, won't usually crack in extreme cold, and doesn't readily cake with heavy snow. Wood remains the biggest seller.

Instead of naked or varnished rawhide webbing, leading snowshoe makers now offer rawhide coated with polyurethane, which has superior moisture resistance. Most modern of all is nylon-coated neoprene lacing, which is very strong, doesn't stretch or absorb water, doesn't attract gnawing animals, and needs no seasonal varnishing or any other maintenance. With use, however, it does become abraded and hairy-looking, so a great many snowshoers prefer the tradition of rawhide combined with the protection of polyurethane.

As you may suspect, a device is needed to hold the snowshoe to your boot. The harness is a leather or leather-and-nylon strap arrangement which permits the toe to tilt downward and the heel to rise.

Camp Clothing

Warm Weather

Underwear. The underclothing you wear at home or at work will suffice, although cotton boxer-type shorts, which cling less to your skin, are more comfortable than the jockey style. Two pairs of shorts and two T-shirts will last for a hike of less than a week, one set for wearing and one for washing. Drying in the sun ordinarily takes about two hours.

Though underwear can go for two days without a wash, the same *does not* go for your socks. A daily change and washing are necessary to health and comfort. Cotton wash-and-wear socks are recommended; wool may be too warm and scratchy. Light wool sweat socks with low boots are fine only in mountainous areas. In coastal regions that are flat and sandy, you may not need socks but simply sneakers. Prior to a day's hike, cut down on perspiration with a healthy sprinkle of foot powder or baby powder in your boots.

Waffle-weave underwear is intended for cooler temperatures, but the top part worn under a thin cotton shirt will keep you warm in an early-morning chill.

Outerwear. Khaki (cotton) pants are appropriately light and durable. Look for cuffless models that are an inch or so shorter than your regular pants, because cuffs tend to catch mud, water, stones, and twigs. Denims are also sturdy, but most are too snug for the active camper.

Allow extra room between your crotch and the top of your trousers, for bending and taking lengthy steps. Roomy pockets are important, but don't overfill them. Make sure the seams have been reinforced for longer wear.

Bermuda shorts are acceptable in hot areas, but they don't guard against underbrush and sunburn. A short-sleeved cotton shirt during the day is fine, but be careful of too much sun on your forearms. At night when mosquitoes and other insects appear, you will need a long-sleeved cotton shirt. Shirttails which fall well below the waist are advisable. Have a sweater or sweatshirt on hand for the evenings.

As mentioned in another section, waterfowl down is the prime insulating material. But synthetics, such as Dacron 88, are acceptable and less expensive. A lightweight, quilted, insulated jacket that uses a good synthetic will keep the early-morning fisherman comfortably warm and dry all summer.

Headgear. A cotton hat like baseball players wear screens your head from the sun. Though the bill in the front shields your face from rain, you may need the additional protection of a light nylon, hooded jacket to cover your neck in a downpour.

Cool Weather

Underwear. On cool fall days when the temperature hovers around 40 degrees, leave on the warm-weather shorts and T-shirt, but add a one- or two-piece suit of cotton underwear with full sleeves and legs. Thermal-weave or waffle-weave underwear supplies greater warmth and more ventilation than the flat design. The weaving pattern consists of protrusions and hollow pockets close to the skin which trap body heat.

Two-layer underwear—often labeled Duofold—is another reliable insulated model. The smooth cotton layer facing the skin absorbs perspiration and passes it through the insulating air space to the outer layer of cotton, nylon, and wool. Moisture evaporates from the outer layer.

Wool socks are unparalleled for warmth. Make sure they extend a couple of inches over your boot tops. To prevent blisters on your feet, wear a thin pair of cotton socks underneath. The combination keeps your feet comfortable and free of moisture.

Outerwear. A good choice for cool weather is the heavy-duty work khakis simply called "work clothes" by most stores. As with summer outdoor pants, cuffless styles are best. Wear the inseam a few inches shorter than usual and look for reinforced seams. The cut of the pants should be full rather than ivy-league trim to facilitate climbing, bending, etc. An extra inch between crotch and belt is also helpful.

If you prefer wool pants, get a lightweight pair. Twill fabric, which frequently consists of 65 percent Dacron polyester and 35 percent cotton, is a sturdy and less expensive alternative.

Loose-fitting trousers are important. A size larger at the waist may not be flattering, but with a heavy shirt, thicker undergarments, and a sweater to tuck in, it is a wise idea. A belt or suspenders are fine, and deep pockets on the trousers are also convenient.

Fall is a good time for lightweight wool or flannel shirts. These too should allow freedom of movement. Wool is warmer, and with a waffle-weave turtleneck worn underneath, you're ready for real cold. The shirttail should extend several inches below the waist so it doesn't slip out while you're moving. The buttons should be big so they are easy to handle with cold fingers.

A quilted, insulated jacket insures warmth if the insulating agent is down or a good-quality synthetic. The quilting prevents the insulation from bunching up. Excess moisture is absorbed and expelled through the insulation and fabric. Slip the jacket on whenever a shirt alone won't be enough. The jacket should have pockets and a strong, trustworthy zipper.

Down jackets are matchless for warmth and insulation, but prices are high. In cool weather, synthetics such as PolarGuard and Dacron Hollofil II are quite adequate.

Headgear. A billed cap of wool, cotton, or leather is the first choice.

The beret and the Tam O'Shanter are underrated as hats in the United States, but either one supplies a large amount of heat to your head, and body. Both styles can be pulled down to protect your ears, and each is compact, inexpensive, and long-lasting.

The watch cap—the type worn by merchant seamen—or the ski hat is acceptable. If it isn't too cool, they can be worn with the cuff doubled up, and in harsh cold, both can be pulled down to cover the neck, ears, and forehead.

Cold Weather

When temperatures drop to zero and below, your life may depend on the clothing you wear.

Underwear. The T-shirt and boxer shorts you wore in summer and fall should be the first clothes you put on. Follow with the full set of waffle-weave or quilted underwear. The waffle-weave traps body heat and permits moisture to escape at the neck, a more rapid exit point than the underwear itself. The quilted underwear gives warmth by stopping the circulation of air inside your clothing.

Top-grade wool socks provide superior warmth and durability through many hard months and washings. Avoid colored wool, which may cause allergy, infect a blister, or discolor other clothing you may have thrown in your laundry pail.

A properly fitted sock is snug enough not to bunch about the toe or heel, but is not too tight to cause discomfort.

Wool socks reinforced with a strong synthetic such as Dacron or nylon last longer and are less expensive in the long run, but lose some advantage in ventilation, softness, and warmth. Socks made totally of nylon, Dacron, Orlon, or another synthetic are also not on a par with wool when it comes to softness and getting rid of moisture. Cotton socks are comfortable only till they're soaked with water or perspiration.

One large manufacturer features wick-dry socks that boast an inner surface of hydrophobic yarn to carry sweat away from your foot. The outer hydrophilic layer absorbs and holds the moisture. Some manufacturers offer battery-powered electric socks.

The wisest choice, however, is a pair of good-quality, wool hunting socks worn over a pair of cotton socks. Whatever the height of your boots, select socks which are three inches higher. Lap the extra material over the boot.

Outerwear. Cuffless wool pants and a lightweight wool shirt — with large buttons for ease of handling — furnish ample warmth when worn over the proper underwear. The advantage of wool to the camper who also hunts is that it is noiseless. And wool does a fine job of shedding and repelling water.

Take along a quilted jacket insulated with down or one of the better synthetics. The camper who feels too restricted in a quilted jacket might choose a less cumbersome vest insulated with down or a good synthetic. A vest with a good zipper front, a button-down collar, and a flap pocket on either side is a treasure; more so when it is low enough in the rear to cover the kidneys. In extreme cold, the topmost outer garment can also be an oversize wool hunting shirt or jacket.

Heavy wool or leather gloves worn over a pair of cotton work gloves protect the hands. Although mittens may keep you somewhat warmer, they inhibit your ability to grasp triggers, utensils, etc., such that gloves are a better choice.

Headgear. A wool hunting cap with earflaps along with a wool or cotton scarf is suitable. On a deer stand in a windy area, this combo is perfect. Place the scarf around the neck or over your head under the cap. Hoods tend to restrict head movement and muffle sounds coming from the sides and back, but a scarf can be quickly loosened when necessary.

The watch cap and ski hat tend to hamper peripheral vision. They are acceptable substitutes for the wool hunting cap, however, because they pull down completely to protect almost everything from the top of the head to the neck, revealing only the eyes, nose, and mouth.

Rain Gear

There are two styles of rainwear: the rainsuit and the poncho.

The rainsuit is a waterproof jacket and pants, while the poncho is a square of waterproof fabric with a hole for the head. The poncho does little to restrict the arms, but flares enough to protect the legs — when you are standing — and let in cooling air. A poor choice for the shotgunner or the woodchopper, it tends to be clumsy and dangerous.

For sitting in a duck blind or boat most of the day, take a rainsuit. It should have drawstring pants and a hooded zipper jacket with elastic or snap-fastener wrists. These features will also keep out wind.

Though somewhat expensive, Neoprene-coated nylon fabric is a good buy in rainsuits. It's durable, waterproof, and lightweight, and doesn't stiffen so much in cold weather as do the popular and less expensive rubberized cotton suits. The inexpensive vinyl or plastic suits are worthless because they rip. Easily split seams, snagged material, and stiffness in cold weather are further drawbacks.

The backpacker, however, may find the poncho preferable to the rainsuit because of its lighter weight. A poncho with a rear flap will protect the pack as well.

Don't buy a cheap poncho. A good one slips on easily and doubles as a ground tarp, makeshift lean-to, or tent.

For fishing offshore or on lakes, however, the rainsuit is recommended. It keeps your entire body dry whether you are standing or sitting. Most serious sportsmen own both the rainsuit and poncho.

Camp Stoves and Heaters

An open wood fire in a public campground is becoming a rare sight. For too long, careless campers have haphazardly cut down trees for fuel and left their fires unattended, causing costly forest fires which destroyed thousands of acres of woodland every year. As a result, most campgrounds today prohibit open fires. Even if they didn't, the lack of available wood would be a prohibition in itself.

Thus, the modern camper has been compelled to carry a stove on his camping trips, and in some ways has improved his lot. Certainly women are more at home with a stove than a wood fire. A stove does away with blackened cooking utensils, hot sparks, and eye-watering smoke.

Wood Stoves

The Sheepherder's stove is the best known of the wood-burning types. But due to their weight and awkwardness, wood stoves in general are fading from the camping scene. The Sheepherder's stove is constructed of sheet metal and often features a small oven for baking, as well as several sections of piping to carry smoke outside the tent. An asbestos collar around the pipe where it passes through the tent is a necessity. Some models fold flat and have telescoping piping. Nevertheless, the wood stove is impractical for the average camper, particularly because modern tents are not equipped to handle stovepipes.

Gasoline Stoves

With inexpensive white, unleaded gasoline a readily available commodity these days, the gasoline stove has become the leader among camp stoves. It's fine for year-round use as bitter-cold weather has little or no effect on gasoline.

The typical gasoline stove with just one burner weighs 2½ pounds and has a tank capacity of 2 pints of fuel, which should keep it burning approximately 3½ hours. For large families, there are two- and three-burner models that weigh up to 25 pounds.

The two-burner stove is the best choice for general camping. For large families, on a short outing one two-burner and one single-burner stove are better than a bulky three-burner stove. But for cabin or long-term camping, choose the three-burner model. The backpacker can get along with just one burner. Some backpacker models tip the scales at a mere 20 ounces and can fit in a large coat pocket. Hunters and fishermen who just want a quick pot of coffee or hot soup during the day appreciate the lightweight one-burner stoves.

Propane Stoves

Highly popular among warm-weather campers is the stove that runs on propane gas, also known as LP or liquified petroleum. In winter, propane stoves do not work well as

Coleman Peak 1 Backpack Stove is a gasoline model that holds 10 ounces of fuel and will burn at high heat for 1¼ hours or simmer for 3½ hours. A built-in tip cleaner prevents clogging, and a "purge position" on the burner control blows the generator clean.

Optimus SVEA 123R is a gasoline stove with a cover that doubles as cooking pot. It's compact, weighs just over a pound, needs no pumping or priming, and cooks up to 1¾ hours on one filling.

Trailblazer PS-3600 is a propane single-burner that folds flat. It's stable and big enough for an 8-inch pan, yet compact enough for easy backpacking even in a small day pack.

Optimus 731 "Mousetrap" is a butane stove that weighs only 11½ ounces, folds to sandwich size, has a burning time up to four hours, and employs a refillable snap-in cartridge.

416

the cold tends to reduce the temperature of the gas, thereby diminishing the vital heat output.

A five-pound, single-burner stove is typical with the usually disposable 14.1-ounce cylinder of gas. A double burner stove weighs about 12 pounds, often uses a separate cylinder for each burner. For extended stays in camp, many manufacturers make large-capacity, refillable tanks of propane that can be carried aboard a plane, boat, or packhorse.

As with gasoline stoves, we recommend a two-burner stove for general camping, and one single-burner and one double-burner model for larger families.

The advantages of propane gas over white gasoline are the ease with which it lights and its carrying convenience. Also, no pumping, priming, and pouring are necessary because the sealed containers of propane readily attach to the stove.

On the other hand, propane is not as easily available throughout the country as is gasoline. Before leaving home, take into account the length of your trip, whether or not you are carrying an ample supply of propane gas, and the proximity along your route of stores stocking propane. Another problem with propane is that you're never quite sure if you

The flame on this two-burner gasoline stove from Coleman can be regulated by turning knob atop 3½-pint fuel tank. Windscreens at side prevent breezes from flickering or extinguishing flame.

Propane is used to fuel this attractive two-burner stove from Coleman. The burners, spaced on 11-inch centers, produce up to 10,000 BTU's of steady, precisely controllable heat.

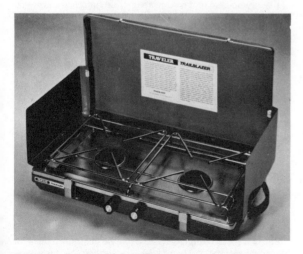

Trailblazer Traveler PS-7200 Deluxe is a two-burner propane camp stove with a heavy chrome drip pan, 3-foot hose, and regulator valve. It folds into a slim carrying case, 20 by 11 by 3½ inches.

Bernzomatic Porta Chef Deluxe camp stove is a two-burner with a 13-by-20-inch cooking surface and easily cleaned drip pan. Operates on 14.1 or 16-ounce propane cylinder and closes into 3-inch-thick carrying case. Flame can be fully regulated.

are running low. Thus it's a good idea to have two cylinders.

Getting down to economics, studies have shown that the average camp meal costs about a few cents to cook with gasoline, but approaches 50 cents when propane is used. With the advantages that propane stoves have in summer, many campers care little about the added expense. Another featherweight gas used in contemporary stoves is butane, also a liquified petroleum.

Canned Heat

Known commercially as Sterno, this is a solid, non-melting fuel that's odorless and safe, and burns clearly and steadily until totally consumed. You can extinguish it as many times as you like by simply replacing the pry-off top. The touch of a match will quickly re-light it. Sterno is sold in two sizes. The 7-ounce can burns for 1½ hours while the 2⅝-ounce can lasts 45 minutes. A pint of water can be brought to a boil with Sterno in just 15 minutes, but canned heat is not intended for much else.

Primus's Picnic Kitchen consists of a highly dependable combo of an extra-large two-burner propane stove plus a bright 100-candlepower propane lantern that sits atop a rugged, refillable steel cylinder. Not for the backpacker, this duo weighs 30 lbs.

Stoves designed specifically for cans of Sterno can be purchased, ranging from stamped metal racks for 50 cents and under to two-burner models for about two dollars.

Reflector Oven

This device is used for baking bread, rolls, pies, muffins, cake, fish, and meat at your campsite. It is a simple, collapsible, lightweight (about three pounds) contraption made of sheet aluminum that reflects the heat of a stove or campfire onto the food. A stainless steel shelf provides the more even heating, but an aluminum shelf will suffice. A good shelf can handle up to 10 pounds of food.

Delectable rolls, muffins, baked bread, and even a roast can be prepared in this Reflector Camp Oven from Eddie Bauer, Expedition Outfitter. Superlight aluminum oven will comfortably accommodate a pair of 8-inch square pans.

Dutch Oven

If you're traveling by auto or horseback, you can haul a Dutch oven to camp. Otherwise, leave it home. Made of cast iron, it can weigh close to 10 pounds.

The Dutch oven is a large pot with a sunken lid. Three stubby legs keep the bottom from coming into contact with the coals. Hot coals are also placed on the lid.

Frying, boiling, and baking are simple chores for this oven although it warms and cools rather slowly. The heat, however, is even and steady.

Box Oven

One major manufacturer markets a collapsible oven—the box oven—which has about the same capacity as the typical Dutch oven, and can be used with a gasoline stove for baking pies, biscuits, etc. This oven may be used on wood fires after some modifications have been made, providing it is always placed over the coals, never over the flame. Otherwise, your food will become smoked.

Camp Heaters

Called catalytic heaters because they use a catalyst—usually platinum—which burns the fuel (gasoline, propane, etc.), these heaters do not produce any flame, odor, or carbon monoxide.

Fairly new as camp gear, the catalytic heater provides an effective heat that can be regulated according to your needs. The heat output is measured in BTUs—British Thermal Units. Because of its safety, the catalytic heater is well ahead of other types on the market.

Trailblazer Traveler CH5000 propane catalytic heater provides 5,000 BTU, features lifetime platinum catalyst, positive-activation control valve, chromed steel grill, and tough, compact (12 × 8 × 15-inch) steel case with storage space for a spare cylinder.

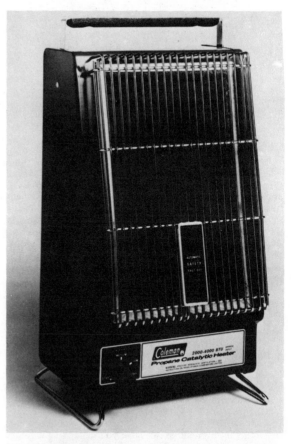

Coleman Model 5445C700 propane catalytic heater is adjustable from 2,000 to 4,000 BTU and features an automatic safety-shutoff valve that stops the fuel flow if the heater should go out. It works like the thermocouple on a home furnace.

Coleman Winter Cat is a gasoline catalytic heater that's adjustable from 5,000 to 8,000 BTU. It has a 6-quart fuel tank and will heat for about 21 hours at highest setting or 29 hours at low setting on one tankful.

Camp Lighting

Gasoline Lanterns

For all-round use, the gasoline lantern is the most practical camp light. The fuel employed is white or unleaded gasoline (readily available throughout the United States), and it is fed from a pressure tank to relatively fragile mantles made of ash. A vapor given off by the gasoline collects in one or two mantles, and is ignited with a match. Should the lantern flare at this point, check for a generator leak. A wise move is to bring along a spare generator—they also tend to clog—and one or two extra mantles. They do add weight to the total unit, but you'll be in the dark without them should something go wrong.

Pumping a built-in tank device before lighting and at intervals during burning should insure adequate candlepower. If the pressure drops and the light seems to dim or pulsate at times, bring this pump into play to correct the pressure.

The typical gasoline lantern is constructed of stainless steel and brass with a porcelain reflector (also called deflector) to provide ventilation and help direct the light in a wide circle or in one particular spot. A globe of clear Pyrex glass encircling the lit mantles is durable enough to withstand heat. The capacity of the fuel tank is normally two pints, enough for ten to twelve hours of intense light. Before bedtime, turn off the fuel valve. The minute amount of vapor remaining in the mantles will give you enough light to get into your sleeping bag. The gasoline lantern is unaffected by wind, rain, and cold. It is a valuable piece of camp equipment, but its weight—often close to ten pounds when you add in fuel—rules it out for the backpacker.

Propane Lanterns

If your camping is usually confined to summer weekends, the propane-gas lantern is for you. There is no generator to clog and replace or liquid fuel to spill and perhaps taint your food. Working off lightweight propane gas that is sold in a 14.1-ounce (usually throwaway) cylinder, this lantern can give you anything from a soft glow to a bright beam. Large-capacity propane lanterns are also sold.

As with gasoline lanterns, one or more mantles are used to catch the gas vapors, but no pumping and priming are required. Porcelain reflectors are also featured to place the light where you want it. One propane cylinder can last from ten to fifteen hours, depending on how intense a light you require.

Since you never know how much gas remains in the cylinder, it is a necessity to take along a pair of cylinders, as well as extra mantles.

Weight is a problem with propane lanterns and backpackers should avoid them. But if you are traveling by auto, propane lanterns are suitable, provided the weather isn't too cold. Otherwise, the pressure in the tank drops and you're lucky if you even get a dim glow.

Battery-Powered Lights

Flashlights are available in all stores stocking camp gear, but get the right kind. There are three- and four-cell models which throw a lot of light, but a two-cell flashlight is adequate. Also, anything larger than two cells means surplus weight. Choose a model with an angle head so that it can be hung on your belt or stood on end, leaving both hands free.

Besides being durable and water-resistant, the flashlight should have a shiny or bright finish—perhaps with a luminous stripe painted on it—so it can be located easily. Some flashlights are colored olive-drab, making them a chore to find. Avoid them. A hang-up ring is also helpful, and a slightly recessed glass lens is close to shatterproof because of the protective lip.

Dry-cell batteries aren't too efficient when the weather turns cold; they'll throw a rather dim light. Your best bet is to warm them in your hands or place them under your sleeping bag at night.

You can even get some use out of dead batteries in an emergency by a crude method of recharging. Slowly warm them by the fire and punch holes in the sides. Add as much water as they'll hold, and return the batteries to the flashlight. Don't expect more than a couple minutes of feeble light, though.

When carrying your flashlight in your pack, tape the switch in the off position. Or else reverse one of the batteries in the tube. This will prevent accidently turning on the flashlight. Also, keep in mind that batteries last longer when they are burned for only short periods of time.

If you prefer a battery-powered lantern over a flashlight, you can get up to 50 hours of intense light if the weather is mild. These lanterns work on six-volt batteries and generally weigh about five pounds. If weight is not important, get the wide-beam rather than the searchlight model.

Candles

Primitive is the word for the candle as a light source, but it's 100 percent reliable and multi-purpose. It can be used to boil a pot of water, start a fire, mend a leaky spot in your tent.

No matter what kind of camper you are—backpacker through RVer—a few handy candles are a worthwhile investment. It must be stressed that the proper kind is the stearic-acid plumber's candle, made of animal fat. Paraffin candles that you may have at home for decorative purposes or maneuvering about when a fuse blows are useless in camp. A short period in a warm pack, and you'll have a melted mass.

Never leave your tent unattended with a burning candle inside, even if it is in a candle lantern—as it should be.

And a final note of caution on the use of candles. Some modern waterproofing mixtures have proven to be flammable. If you are a backpacker and recently have waterproofed your small tent with a commercial product, carefully check the ingredients. Should any one of them be flammable, *do not* use a candle in your tent.

Coleman's double-mantle gasoline lantern has an 8¾-inch ventilator. This device reflects a wide circle of light around, out from, and under its base, yet screens out any up-glare.

Coleman Model 275 is a double-mantle gasoline lantern that operates for 8 hours or more on one filling. Generator tip is automatically cleaned at each lighting.

This dual-beam, single-mantle lantern is a product of Bernz-Omatic. With Propane fuel, there is no pumping or priming necessary, nor is there a generator that could clog. A built-in light reflector illuminates a broad area. The disposable propane cannisters will burn as long as 14 hours, depending on the brightness you need.

Bernzomatic Portalight LT76 works with disposable 14.1- or 16-ounce propane cylinder. This single-mantle unit burns for 10 to 14 hours and gives light equivalent to 100-watt bulb. Double-mantle model is also available.

Trailblazer Traveler PL-3010 is a double-mantle propane lantern that comes packaged with 16.4-ounce disposable cylinder, burns up to 9 hours or more, depending on setting, and measures only 11 by 17 inches.

Coleman Charger is a rechargeable electric lantern with non-glare fluorescent bulb rated up to 1,000 hours. It works from its own sealed-power battery, from 110-volt house current or 12-volt car cigarette lighter, and can be recharged from either current.

Camp Cook Kits

For a party of four campers willing to accept the fact that filet mignon will not be on the menu, the most practical cook kit—in auto-, tent-, or trailer-camping—is the commercial nesting set in which the pots, pans, plates, and cups fit inside one another.

The Boy Scout aluminum cook kit, a nesting set, is fine for a quartet of hungry campers. This model is the most compact package possible. A burlap cover bag is inexpensive and protects against dents and dirt. It consists of:

1 8-quart kettle
1 4-quart stewpot
1 2-quart stewpot
2 frypans with handles
1 spouted pot
4 plates
4 plastic cups

Extra plates and cups can be purchased for a group of more than four. Cups should be plastic rather than aluminum, since aluminum gets too hot to hold or drink from when it contains hot coffee or broth. Aluminum also lets liquids cool too quickly.

If you don't mind some additional weight there are commercial kits made of stainless steel. Much more durable than aluminum and simpler to clean, stainless steel is also heavier and more expensive. Make sure that the plates, frying pans, and cups are not too thin, as they too will become too hot or cold to handle.

Teflon keeps food from sticking and makes cleaning easier. Teflon-coated utensils require special tools to protect the thin coating from scratching, but if the added weight and bulk are no problem, these are excellent items.

In addition to knife-fork-and-spoon sets for each camper, the cook needs a tool kit. Again, use the Boy Scout model as a guide. It includes:

1 carving knife
1 paring knife
1 potato peeler
1 long fork
1 spoon
1 ladle
1 turner
1 bottle/can opener

The tools are encased in a cloth kit that can be hung up, and the total unit weighs just 1½ pounds.

The backpacker who must limit his supplies to a minimum may be inclined toward a more compact unit. The one the Scouts prefer, known as the Scout Mess Kit, features:

1 aluminum frypan
1 stewpot with cover
1 plate
1 plastic cup

The removable handle on the frypan provides a clamp to secure the unit. A canvas cover protects the utensils.

Examine any mess kit before buying it, especially if it's not the Scout model; it is best to discover a missing utensil

Palco's family-size aluminum nesting kit suits most any group of four. It contains a 6-quart bucket with a cover that doubles as a 9¼-inch frypan; a 7⅞-inch fry pan; a 4-quart pot; a 2-quart pot; a coffeepot with cover; plus four plates and four plastic cups.

Five-piece aluminum mess kit is suitable for the individual camper. It includes saucepan, frypan (with handle), pot with cover, and durable plastic cup. Entire set nests inside cover that has an adjustable shoulder strap.

in the store. Avoid gadgets from folding toasters to corn poppers to immersion heaters, advertised to simplify camp meals, until you are certain you need them. Begin with the basics and experiment.

To make cleaning easier, use all-purpose paper (toilet paper, for example) to wipe excess food out of your plate immediately after eating. Beware of slipshod washing, which can produce gastric upsets such as dysentery the next meal around.

A pair of lightweight cotton gloves may save the cook from getting burned, cut, or grimy. And while soap, towels, dishrags, and scouring pads (plastic, steel wool, or copper wire) add ounces to your gear, they also speed up the cleaning and drying process.

Aluminum foil, though not recommended as a cook kit in itself, proves quite useful as a supplementary item. As a pot liner foil keeps foods from gumming up the pot. Wrapped around the bottom of the pot, it stops blackening from the fire. The same result can also be achieved by rubbing the pot's exterior with a bar of soap.

Paper plates and paper cups save time in cleaning up, but the choice is up to the individual camper or family.

The travel kitchen or chuckbox is recommended if you're camping in a motorized vehicle. Available assembled or in kits, these kitchens have five or six compartments to store separately items such as utensil kits, clean-up kits, nonperishable foods, and the like. Because of weight and bulk, the kitchen is inappropriate to horsepacking, canoeing (with portages), and backpacking trips. Many outdoorsmen make wood-box arrangements with their own modifications after several years of camping.

Canteens come in various styles—round, oval, and a flask-shaped model that clips to the belt. All can be filled with practically any liquid and, if you care to, you can freeze the entire contents. Aluminum models are more rugged than plastic ones. Some feature a chained screw cap and most have a shoulder strap. Canvas covers ward off dirt and dents.

The main concern in purchasing a canteen is proper size. Many tenderfoot campers make the mistake of hauling along a canteen with a 4-quart capacity. That's a gallon, and awfully heavy to carry. For most day-long outings, a 1-quart model is sufficient. For weekends, a 2-quart canteen is advisable, particularly if potable water is a rarity in the area you are in. Water-purification tablets are inexpensive and valuable if you're not sure how drinkable the water is.

Camp Tools

Hatchets

Way back when trees were plentiful, many outdoorsmen wielded a full-length ax, relegating the smaller hatchet to novice woodchoppers. Nowadays, when wood is an all-too-precious resource, the hatchet has become the most common woodcutting tool at the campsite.

Invest extra money in a premium-quality hatchet. The one-piece styles are the best, with all-steel construction from the head to the bottom of the handle. A cheap hatchet, which may have loose headwork, might injure a nearby camper or shatter after several sessions of chopping. As perspiration can make a handle slippery, get a hatchet with a handle of rubber, wood, or leather laminations which will provide a secure grip.

Should you prefer a hatchet with a wood handle, make sure the handle is chemically bonded to the head. This process insures that it will rarely, if ever, come loose. Some choppers prefer wood handles because there isn't as much cushioning in them. Though the resultant shocks may be uncomfortable, they signify that you are chopping ineffectively. When the shocks cease, you will know you are handling your hatchet correctly.

Some hatchets feature neither the one-piece construction nor the bonded head. These models frequently use a wedge to secure the head to the handle. As this is far from safe, check this type of hatchet frequently during chopping.

Hatchets—also known as belt axes—come in a number of sizes and weights. The right choice obviously depends on your own needs. For all-round use, however, a hatchet with a 1-pound head and a handle about a foot long is an excellent choice. Slightly larger ones are preferred by some campers, and manufacturers have recently offered much smaller ones, as well. The light, very short-handled models, sometimes called backpackers' axes or hunters' axes, are fine for chopping kindling or the wood for a small campfire, and they can also be used to fashion wooden tent stakes (but then, so can a knife). They're useless for heavier work, though adequate for their intended purpose.

Despite its smaller size when compared to the ax, the hatchet is an important tool which needs special care. Never throw a hatchet. Besides ruining the bit and other important parts, you may injure someone.

Only use a hatchet to hammer metal stakes or nails if it is a half-hatchet, which features a regular hatchet blade at one end of the head and a tempered hammer head on the other end. A conventional hatchet used for such purposes soon becomes worthless.

A durable leather sheath with a sturdy leather buffer strip or rivets facing the cutting edge should be used to carry the hatchet. If you don't have a sheath handy, drive the blade into a stump or a log so it is not dangerously exposed. (Avoid the double-bitted hatchet on the market featuring blades at both ends of the head. It is dangerous except in the hands of a skilled chopper.)

To cut a piece of wood, use the contact method. Place the edge of the hatchet on the stick. Lift the two and then bring both down together hard on the chopping block. To split wood, place the hatchet edge in a crack. Again, lift the two and bring hatchet and stick down hard on the log or stump. Once contact has been made, slightly twist the hatchet hand to separate the pieces.

On a cold day, heat the hatchet slightly before putting it to work so it won't become brittle and crack.

To pass a hatchet to another person, hold it vertically, head down with the blade facing away from the two of you. Give the receiver more than enough room to grasp the top of the hatchet handle. When you are carrying it in camp, hold the hatchet firmly by its head, keeping the cutting edge away from you.

If not inside your pack while hiking, the hatchet should be strapped to the outside and sheathed. When the hike is a short one, sheath the hatchet and carry it on your belt on your right hip. Never strap it near the groin or kidney area.

Axes

Some chopping chores call for an ax. The camping trip, in this case, is usually for a week or more, and the work might include felling a tree or cutting firewood.

Among the many types of axes available, there are four common ones—the Hudson Bay single-bit, the Kentucky single-bit, the Michigan single-bit, and the Michigan double-bit.

Best of the quartet for today's camper is the Hudson Bay single-bit ax. It's heavy enough to wield comfortably—weighing approximately four pounds—with a handle that's the right size, some 26 inches, for the average chopper. A squared end on one side permits this ax to drive nails and stakes without damaging the head. Although the Kentucky and Michigan single-bits are helpful, the Hudson Bay model is most useful.

Double-bit axes, such as the Michigan style, are popular with seasoned axmen. A double-bit ax typically sports a three-foot handle and a three-pound head which speeds up extensive chopping. A cutting edge on either side of the head allows the chopper to grind one blade thin for felling huge trees and hefty logs. The other blade may be thicker, for splitting wood. Also, with a pair of blades sharpening need not be done as often as with a single-bit ax.

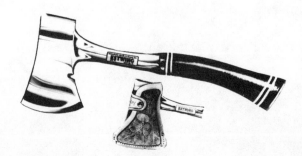

Durable in all climates, this 13½-inch, 24-ounce Sportsman's Ax from Estwing has one-piece steel construction for safe handling. A 12-inch, 18-ounce version is available for youngsters.

Buck Hunters Axe is a short-handled hatchet, or belt ax, with a 2½-inch cutting head. It comes with a sheath. Such small hunting and backpacking hatchets cannot perform heavy camp chores but can chop kindling and take care of heavier jobs than a sheath knife.

To split kindling for a fire, hold a branch on a chopping log and cut thin slivers from the bottom up.

Once a tree has been felled, strip the branches by always cutting with the slant of the branch.

To section a tree trunk, begin by chopping about halfway through one side. Then turn it over and start to chop through the other side.

FOUR TYPES OF AXES

HUDSON BAY SINGLE-BIT

KENTUCKY SINGLE-BIT

MICHIGAN SINGLE-BIT

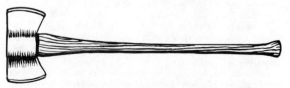

MICHIGAN DOUBLE-BIT

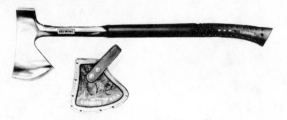

No loose ax heads or broken handles to worry about with Estwing's all-steel Camper's Ax. Nylon-vinyl handgrip on this 26-inch model assures a safe, sure grip. Leather sheath protects the 4-inch cutting edge.

To sharpen a double-bit ax, embed it in a log (*top*) and file one edge, using downward strokes only. File far back from the edge, gradually thinning down the blade till a fanlike pattern appears. Then, take the ax in your hand (*center*) and, with a whetstone, use circular strokes on one side. Sharpen the other side by letting the head twist so the handle points down (*bottom*).

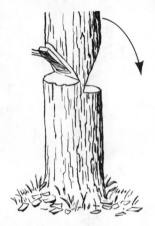

To fell a tree, chop a notch about a third of the way into the side of the tree's natural lean. Then cut a second notch on the opposite side and about two inches above the first. The tree will fall in the direction of the lean.

The double-bit ax has some disadvantages. When an ax of this type is stuck in a low stump or log, that upright, exposed blade can cause a vicious, perhaps fatal, gash. Dual cutting edges also do not provide room for the pounding head, an essential item in campsite work.

Unless you are an adept axman, leave the double-bit model on the store shelf. And, unless you are taking up logging or are planning to build your own cabin, avoid single bits that boast 30-inch handles and 3-pound heads. A scaled-down model such as the Boy Scouts of America favor, with a 26-inch handle and a two-pound head, is best. Lighter to carry and swing, it is also easier to use.

The handle of an ax, no matter what size, should be made of seasoned hardwood with a grain that is both fine and straight. The handle itself should also be straight. Check to see that the "hang" of the ax is proper. Hang is determined by holding the ax in front of you and sighting down as though it were a rifle. Should the center of the handle be in line with the cutting edge of the blade, the hang is correct.

Inspect the point where the handle fits the eye of the steel head, unless you have a one-piece model. If even the slightest gap shows there, look for another ax. An imperfect fit means the handle may work loose soon after continued chopping or pounding.

Several manufacturers use a chemical bond to anchor the ax handle to the head. This holds more securely than the wedges—either wood or steel—which conventionally attach the two parts. Wedges, however, are efficient.

Apply yellow, red, or bright blue paint to the ax head once you buy it. The paint helps locate the ax in weeds or brush if it is lost. The paint also assists in bonding the handle and head together. Last, if the paint cracks over the eye, it is a clear danger signal that the handle is loosening inside and may come off at any time.

Wood sap contains acids and moisture which can rust the blade. Proper care includes using a couple drops of machine oil every once in awhile, to keep the steel free of corrosive rust. The handle which grows coarse from use needs sanding with either fine emery cloth or sandpaper. Rub the raw wood exposed by this sanding with linseed oil for protection. Don't paint the ax handle, as it will chip eventually or become too slick.

The ax should be warmed to a comfortable temperature before use in subfreezing weather. Otherwise, it is too brittle and may crack. A fire works quickly, but a short period under your heavy coat will also warm the blade. Friction will keep the ax warm enough once chopping has begun.

Keep the ax sheathed when carrying it. A strip of thick rubberized hose is a good substitute if you don't have a commercial sheath. Passing the ax requires that the first man hold it near its belly, with its head facing down and out. The second man grasps the end of the handle and says "Thank you," to indicate he has a firm grip on the ax.

To drive nails and stakes, use the butt (poll) end of the head—never the bit.

Keeping your ax as sharp as possible saves time in chopping and guards against damage to the bit. The proper way to sharpen an ax follows:

If you have a preference, or a certain form of work to do, a grindstone—not a dry stone or an emery wheel—must nevertheless be used initially. First, grind the blade to the required thinness on each side. Begin the grind about three inches behind the cutting edge itself and develop a fan-shaped effect. Next, roll off a bevel by grinding just a half-inch away from the edge. The taper should be gradual from the half-inch point down to the edge. Beveling helps toss chips away more quickly and prevents blade breakage.

Use a flat file with a coarse, rapid-cutting edge on one side and a smooth side to finish up. If you are outdoors, drive a peg into the ground and rest the ax blade on it. At home, a vise works better.

Holding the file level with the blade, begin working at the top of the roll, or one-half inch from the edge. File away the flat to a distance about three inches from the edge. Again, produce a fan-shaped effect. Use the coarse side during this work, stroking from the edge back toward the ax head. File in one direction only, lifting the file clear on the return. Never file farther back than three inches, as you will destroy the support of the sides of the ax and cause it to stick stubbornly in the wood.

Now for the bevel, using the smooth side of the file. Begin a half inch from the edge, rolling the bevel down to it. Then— still using that smooth side—remove any rough scratches on the flat of the blade.

Repeat the process on the reverse side or the ax head.

What most axmen don't do is hone their axes with a hard, fine grit stone. This procedure adds much to the lifetime of an ax. It's a simple task which is highly recommended.

With the edge facing away from you, hold the stone over the bit at approximately a 45-degree angle. Rub the stone over that edge from heel to toe, using a revolving motion and letting the stone lean forward a bit. Turn the ax blade and once again use the revolving motion, this time on the other side of the blade. Move from toe to heel.

Honing removes burrs from an ax edge which would otherwise flatten out and slow the cutting process.

Camp Saws

To cut wood neatly into particular sizes, the saw is the proper tool. An ax or a hatchet wastes a lot of wood, can't be too exact, and stands the chance of causing injury with flying chips or the blades themselves. Saws are precise and much faster than either ax or hatchet, a camper can get the knack of using them with just a couple of minutes' instruction.

Lighter saws are suitable for camping, as the heavier models are impractical to carry along. There are three saws used by backpackers and other campers who must limit the bulk and weight of their packs—the bow saw, the folding saw, and the cable saw.

The collapsible bow-type saw, also known as the Swede saw, features a thin, narrow blade of flexible steel. This blade is held taut by a tubelike, jointed metal frame which can be taken apart and slipped into a case up to 1½ feet long. Several models are designed to carry spare blades.

A blade from 20 to 24 inches in length handles wood from 8 to 10 inches in thickness. Larger-diameter logs, however, require the use of a 30- or 36-inch blade.

Bow-saw frames come in U-shapes and L-shapes, but the former is recommended. The L-shaped models, though more compact, diminish the amount of blade that may be applied on the wood.

The pocket-size folding saw is lighter in weight. Measuring approximately 10 inches when closed, this saw will tackle many small sawing jobs and is a good choice for the backpacker who can afford a few extra ounces of equipment.

The outdoorsman who backpacks with the absolute mini-

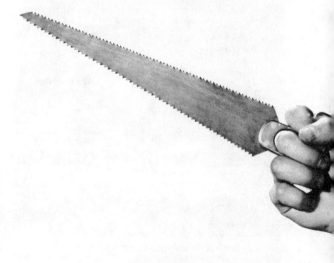

This little 9-ounce belt saw from Eddie Bauer can handle big jobs such as quartering an elk and small tasks such as cutting branches. The 11-inch blade features both coarse and fine teeth, and sure-grip finger hold means proper control. Comes with top-grade cowhide belt that can also house hunting knife.

From Swen Products comes the noted Sven-Saw, a folding model weighing a mere pound. Folded, the saw is only 24 inches long and 1¾ inches wide, stores easily in a packsack.

Bow saw from True Temper takes on this tree branch with ease. Blade is tempered chrome, and safety guard on the tubular-steel handle insures a tight grip.

mum will have a wire cable saw in his pack. This ultralight saw is a barbed steel cable, 18 inches long. At either end there is a steel ring through which your finger or a stick may be placed. The process is slow, but better than nothing.

The camp saw usually has a thicker blade and longer teeth with more *set* than the carpenter's saw. Set means the teeth slant out at a sharp angle to either side. This produces a thicker cut than would the thickness of the saw blade above the teeth. For this reason the blade should not be permitted to be pinched when you're cutting.

To avoid pinching, and the consequent damage to the set, extend the log over the end of a sawhorse so that the weight of the piece being cut widens the opening as the blade moves through it. When the saw isn't in use, its needle-sharp teeth should be sheathed to prevent dulling from rocks or metal. A discarded, split garden hose, a leather sheath, or even a burlap bag will work well.

To keep your saw sharp, hire a professional saw sharpener. But if you're out in the woods with a hopelessly dull saw, carefully use a file to tone up the edges. With slow, careful strokes, you can do an adequate job that will last until you are able to bring the saw to a pro.

Have kerosene on hand to lubricate a saw covered with pitch or sap which can only harm the edges. Before storing your saw, apply some oil. Without it, rust will set in, making the blades drag and the teeth dull.

Knives

On March 6, 1836, James Bowie and other heroic Texans died fighting Santa Anna and his men at the battle for the Alamo. Bowie left behind a huge legend and a huge knife that came to be known as the Bowie knife. The weapons patterned after this knife often sported 16-inch blades and weighed several pounds. They were fine for fighting bears, but useless for general outdoor chores.

The same goes for Arkansas toothpicks and other big, fancy knives on the market. As conversation pieces, they are interesting but they are not designed for the fisherman, the hunter, or the camper.

A multibladed knife—the type sold by the Boy Scouts is suitable—will simplify most camp jobs. The four-bladed model can cut, open cans and bottles, drive screws, and punch holes in belts, pack straps, and other leather materials. The five-bladed style features a metal punch in addition to the previously mentioned blades.

A stainless-steel pocketknife is suggested for fishermen as it wards off rust and tarnish and requires less care. Every camper should carry this kind of knife, whether on a one-day outing or an extended trip. Such jobs as game dressing, fish cleaning, tent-peg whittling, and potato peeling go better with a pocketknife.

Among the sheath knives, there are excellent ones and there are poor ones. The latter are far too long—and in some cases, too thick—for everyday use. The maximum blade size should be five to six inches, and that's only for dressing big game or for a lengthy, rugged camping trip. A four-incher will suffice for small game, and may work well on some of the larger animals. There is no need for a knife larger than a six-incher.

Sheath knives come in a number of patterns, and one should fit your needs. There are several factors to consider when buying one.

Check the blade. It should be reasonably simple and straight along the top with the cutting edge curved slightly upward near the tip to form a sharp point. Beware of blood grooves and notches in the blade for opening bottles. They are totally unnecessary and probably add to the price.

Though a wood handle may not impress you as much as a solid metal one, it's a much better choice. Wood supports a firm grip even if it is soaked with water or blood. Metal and smooth plastic get slick when they are wet and are bitter cold to the touch when temperatures drop.

The sheath for the blade should have a metal lining or large brass rivets to stop the point from jabbing through. Double thickness of leather on the back is added protection.

The advantage of the sheath knife over the pocketknife is that the former is always open and ready for use. It does more heavy-duty work than the pocketknife. But for fine work, the pocketknife is the right choice.

Never throw your knife. It's bad for the blade. Don't use the knife as a screwdriver, pry bar, hammer, or anything else it was not designed for. This will only shorten its life.

Poking the knife into campfires or into the ground also damages the blade.

Clean your knife after each use and keep it dry. When storing the blade, do not sheathe it. Rust-causing moisture may be contained inside the sheath itself.

Fold a pocketknife prior to passing it along. The blade of the sheath knife should be placed flat on the extended hand, with the handle facing the receiver. The receiver will then grasp the handle, turning the edge upward.

Never cut toward yourself. Even in fine cutting, work in your direction only when no other angle is practical.

Wear the knife on your belt, alongside your thigh. This way, it won't interfere with kneeling or sitting. Never wear the knife in front of you.

Keep your knifeblade sharp *at all times*. A dull blade is no

KNIFE STYLES FOR DIFFERENT JOBS

Bowie-style with 6-in. blade and blood groove. Designed for heavy-duty all-round use. Generally too heavy for most sportsmen, with longer blade than needed.

Short 3¼-in. blade design. Fine knife for panfish, small game, birds. Particularly good for the trophy hunter who must carefully skin out a head.

Skinning knife. Has wide 4-in. blade with fine edge. Excellent for skinning big game, its usage is limited in other areas.

Boning knife. For the hunter who butchers his own game, this knife is almost a must. Keep it sharp and just about every bone in a big-game animal can be easily removed.

A standard design, somewhat on the heavy side, with a 5-in. blade. A good choice for the sportsman who wants one knife for all jobs.

Straight 4-in. blade design for fish and small game. It has a fine point. Light, small, and a good choice as an all-round knife that will not be used for heavy-duty work.

A good combination design that has features of a skinning knife but is helpful on small game as well. Blade is usually 4½ in.

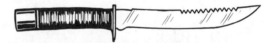

For fishermen only, this knife is usually about 10 in. overall and has a flexible blade for filleting plus a fish scaler.

Lock-open folding utility and hunting knives have become increasingly popular in recent years. This is the Buck Folding Hunter, which has a handle of Macassar ebony wood and solid brass bolsters.

Schrade Old-Timer Model 510T is a lock-open folding knife with 3½-inch blade. The overall size, closed, is 4¾ inches, and it comes in a leather snap-flap belt sheath.

less dangerous than a sharp one. It forces the user to exert more pressure to move the knife. Should the blade slip, it is more difficult to stop because of that additional force. The wound you sustain from a dull blade will most likely be deeper, more torn, and take longer to heal than the neat slice of a sharp blade.

To keep the edge beveled, follow the instructions below. (Never use a grinding machine as it could thin the blade too much.)

1. Wet a small sharpening stone thoroughly with water or place on it a few drops of oil depending on the type of stone.
2. If the blade edges are damaged or badly worn, use the medium-coarse side of the sharpening stone. If the blade simply needs to be rehoned to a keen edge, the fine-grain side should be enough. Raise the rear edge of the blade off the sharpening stone ⅛ inch (20 degrees). Then, as if you are slicing a thin layer from the top of the stone, count off 10 firm-pressure strokes in one direction only.

3. Now, turn the blade over, raising the rear edge up ⅛ inch (20 degrees). Repeat the 10 firm slicing strokes in the opposite direction.
4. Using lighter pressure, alternate one stroke to a side till you count off a total of six strokes.
5. Repeat steps 2, 3, and 4 once again, but this time use the fine-grain side of the sharpening stone.

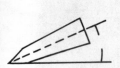
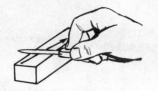

To sharpen your knife, raise the back edge of the blade off the stone about ⅛ in. or 20 degrees (*left*). Stroke with firm pressure in just one direction, 10 times (*center*). Then turn the blade over, regain the 20-degree angle, and stroke 10 times in the other direction (*right*).

Backpacks

Throughout this section on camping, there have been references to the backpacker, the outdoorsman who takes to the open air with all he needs on his back.

The backpacker is a keen weight watcher. He keeps in mind at all times that he should have with him the barest of essentials, and not one ounce more.

There are five basic pack designs. The type the individual sportsman needs depends upon the load he expects to carry as well as the distance he must carry it. The five designs are:

1. Day pack
2. Rucksack
3. Backpack and frame
4. Packbasket
5. Hip or waist pack

The Day Pack

The day pack, known to most campers as the knapsack, is pretty much what its name indicates—a pack which is useful on a daytime outing. It is little more than a rectangular canvas or nylon pack with shoulder straps which may or may not have side pockets, but never a metal frame.

When filling the day pack, place soft items—a poncho, a sweater—against the part of the pack that will press against your back. Also, don't load this pack too heavily as the total weight of the full pack will pull down uncomfortably on your shoulders and against your back.

For pack material, nylon is recommended for the adult camper as it is lightweight and waterproof. However, for youthful campers, who may carelessly toss their packs around, a canvas day pack can take more punishment and is less expensive. Some day packs have waist straps as well as shoulder straps to take some weight off the shoulders.

The Rucksack

The rucksack seems to fall midway between the day pack and the larger packs for carrying big loads on long outings. The backpacker who uses the rucksack is usually out for a full day and must cook a couple of meals in the field.

Unlike the day pack, the rucksack features one or two outside pockets as well as an inside or outside metal frame. This frame prevents the pack from sagging, and puts less

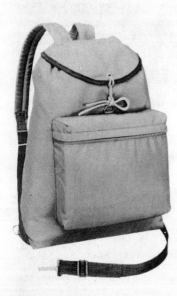

One-day hikes can be handled by the frame-free Dayhiker from Camp Trails. Made of waterproof, rugged Nylon, the backpack is quite spacious inside. The outside pocket has a strong zipper closure. Total weight: 12 ounces.

L.L. Bean's entrant in the day pack field is this packsack primarily designed for deer hunters. Constructed of tough, water-repellent army duck, this model weighs just 13 ounces.

Coleman Peak 1 Model 730 day pack is made of tough Cordura nylon with two compartments and zippered outside pocket. Such packs are popular for hiking, climbing, cycling, and cross-country skiing.

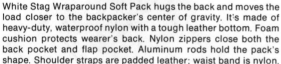

White Stag Wraparound Soft Pack hugs the back and moves the load closer to the backpacker's center of gravity. It's made of heavy-duty, waterproof nylon with a tough leather bottom. Foam cushion protects wearer's back. Nylon zippers close both the back pocket and flap pocket. Aluminum rods hold the pack's shape. Shoulder straps are padded leather; waist band is nylon.

White Stag Teardrop day pack is waterproof nylon with nylon zippers, weather flaps, shoulder straps, waist band, and carrying handle. Main zipper is slanted for quick access and wide opening.

tension on the back. These features make it preferable to the day pack in numerous ways.

A sleeping bag is too bulky to put inside a rucksack, but it can be rolled short and lashed to the top or rolled long into a horseshoe shape and lashed to the top and sides. This pack is ill suited for backpacking canned goods, steel traps, and other hardware that can bite into your back.

The rucksack should have web or leather shoulder straps that are a minimum of 2 inches wide and thick enough so as not to curl into narrow bands from a heavy pack. These bands can cut mercilessly into your shoulders.

Strong buckles, snaps, and rings of bronze, brass, or rust-proof steel are essential. Beware of an overabundance of tricky snaps, zippers, and buckles. They add to the cost, and usually just bring trouble.

Although such synthetics as nylon and Dacron are being used widely for rucksacks, a good choice is heavy canvas. The extra weight will seem inconspicuous, considering the padding to your back that canvas provides. Incidentally, a canvas pack is also simpler to waterproof and keep waterproof than one made of synthetic fibers.

Backpack and Frame

For the serious backpacker whose trips last from one to two weeks, the backpack and frame is the best choice.

The unit consists of a frame constructed of a light metal alloy, and a backpack with both shoulder straps and back supports. The frame is attached to the backpack.

Of all the frames, those made of magnesium are the best. They are lightweight and sturdy, but they are expensive. A practical choice is a frame of an aluminum alloy. It will have shoulder and waist straps, on some models a nylon mesh to keep the load away from the back. This mesh allows air to circulate between pack and back.

As you need roominess for all of your equipment, the

good backpack has five or six outside pockets for smaller, oft-used items. Inside the pack itself are two large compartments for larger items. Below the pack, on the frame, there is room to strap on a sleeping bag. Gear that won't fit inside the pack can be safely lashed to the frame.

Remember that backpack and frame can be removed from one another, permitting the packer to lash such bulky objects as an outboard motor to the frame for easy transportation.

There are certain things to look for in choosing such a backpack, some of which were mentioned earlier. The best choice for lightness would be a waterproof nylon backpack as it will keep the rain off your gear. Look for a top flap on the pack that is long enough to cover the top of the bag when it is full; heavy-duty, corrosion-proof zippers on the exterior side and back pockets that won't jam and will keep out dirt and rain; seams and pockets that can withstand rugged use, and shoulder and waist straps that should be at least 2 inches wide so they won't curl up and cut you. Also, shoulder straps and harnesses for back support should be adjustable to allow for tightening and taking up slack as the load is increased or decreased.

Don't buy a pack just because it fulfills these requirements. Try on various models. The pack and frame should permit the load to be carried vertically with its center of gravity close to your back. In this manner the weight will be transferred to the legs, the most powerful part of the human body.

The backpack should weigh approximately 2 pounds, the pack frame 3 to 4 pounds. That means frame and pack together should weigh close to 5 pounds.

The total amount of gear and food carried depends on the individual. An average man can camp on his own for three days, using a good pack and frame, with carefully selected equipment and freeze-dried food weighing a total of 20 to 25 pounds. That same man can stay in the bush for up to two weeks if he carries a pack with 40 pounds of sustenance.

Coleman Peak 1 backpack frames are of relatively new design and material—one piece, molded from high-impact synthetic called RAM-FLX, which has controlled flexibility to move and bend with wearer's body for greater comfort. Shown here is Model 770, whose top compartment detaches for use as a fanny pack. All the straps feature Lash-Tabs for quick detaching.

White Stag 5 + 5 pack has over 3 cubic feet of space in all its compartments and pockets. Bottom compartment is big enough to hold sleeping bag or tent. On top, two vertical spaces open by top zippers. Beneath, two large compartments open with double-slider zippers running around three sides. Five outer pockets accommodate maps, poncho, and many small items. This model is designed for large or extra-large frame.

Gerry Series 70 pack frames are aluminum alloy, with joints epoxied to form a bond as strong as the metal. Padded waist strap has sliding ring to fit hips of any size and exert continuous pull on frame to prevent sway. Back bands are breathable mesh. Buckle is quick-release type. Neck opening between padded shoulder straps is adjustable.

Gerry Trek Pack comes in small, medium, and large sizes. It features heavy-duty hold-open bar, large main compartment, lower sleeping-bag compartment, big netted drying pocket, covered coil zippers with double sliders, leather accessory-strap patches, and four outside pockets plus map pocket. Fabric is urethane-coated nylon.

There is, of course, a limit to how much a person can comfortably carry over a certain period of time. The following limits (weight includes pack, frame, gear, meals) ought to be observed:

Men—35 to 40 pounds
Women—20 to 25 pounds
Children—15 pounds

Stray from these weight limits and you'll find backpacking a chore rather than a pleasure.

The Pack Basket

The pack basket is an old-time favorite that seems to retain limited popularity because of tradition rather than utility.

Made of thin strips of wood from willow or ash logs, the pack basket is light and rigid. The construction protects the contents from breakage and the packer's back from rough or sharp objects inside. Trappers appreciate the basket for packing tools, axes, and traps. Canoeists favor it for packing odd-size canned goods and gear. Nevertheless, the basket is not recommended for general backpacking.

The Hip or Waist Pack

This pack provides an ideal alternative for the man who doesn't like to carry a pack by means of shoulder straps. As the name implies, the pack rests on the hips and lower back, and easily carries whatever small gear a hunter, fisherman, or camper might bring along on a one-day trip.

Pack basket is the safest way to carry breakable goods. This model, from L.L. Bean, is hand-woven from selected seasoned white ash. Adjustable webbing harness and contour shape let it rest correctly against your back.

There's no strain on the back with this little item, called the Fanny Pack, from Camp Trails. You can wear the unit up front, on either side, or at the fanny, leaving shoulders free.

When the load is just a few basics, and the trip a short one, Camp Trails' Belt Pouch is a good choice. It is made of waterproof nylon to withstand rain, and closes with a full-length zipper.

Ropes and Knots

Ropes for camp use are made of either natural or synthetic materials. The natural fibers come in hemp, available in such types as manila and sisal, and in cotton strands of everyday cotton fiber which has been specially treated.

Synthetic fibers such as Dacron, nylon, and polypropylene often prove from 50 to 100 percent stronger than hemp or cotton rope of equal diameter. These waterproof synthetics do not swell or kink when they are wet. They are likewise unaffected by such hemp maladies as fungus, mildew, and dry rot.

A disadvantage of synthetics is the price. Cotton rope typically costs one-tenth the amount of most synthetic rope of the same diameter. Hemp costs are usually one-third those of synthetics. And knots made in synthetic rope do not hold as well as those in hemp or cotton. In the case of nylon rope, the stretch range may be up to 20 percent of the total length.

The following chart shows the approximate breaking strengths in pounds of dead weight of the various types of ropes:

DIAMETER	SISAL	MANILA	POLY-PROPYLENE	DACRON	NYLON
1/4"	480	600	1,050	1,600	1,800
3/8	1,080	1,350	2,200	3,300	4,000
1/2	2,120	2,650	3,800	5,500	7,100
3/4	4,320	5,400	8,100	11,000	14,200
1	7,200	9,000	14,000	18,500	24,600

The *safe working load* for a brand new rope is one-quarter the breaking strength. If the rope has been through average use, figure one-sixth of the breaking strength. Dropping the load or jerking the rope doubles the strain, and knots and splices diminish its strength, sometimes drastically.

To care for a hemp rope, remember that moisture causes damage. Keep this rope as dry as possible, whether you are storing it or using it. By hanging hemp or cotton rope in a dry, high, cool place, you protect it from harmful rodents. The sweat-salt traces left on a rope by human hands otherwise attract mice and rats with their ever-sharp teeth.

Synthetics need little protection from water but can be substantially weakened by acids, oils, and intense heat.

Now, let's tie some knots.

Whipping. The purpose of a whipping, using several turns of a strong thread, is to prevent the end of a rope from unraveling. Hold the thread taut during the wrapping turns. The section of the thread where the arrow points is given a half-dozen turns once the pull-through loop has been formed. The loop should be pulled snug and the end trimmed. If the rope is synthetic, melt it with a cigarette lighter for a tighter

seal. Hemp and cotton also seal more securely if dipped in a quick-setting glue.

Clove Hitch. To fasten a rope end to a tree, pole, post, or stake, use the clove hitch.

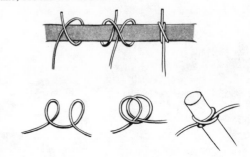

Square Knot. Also known as the reef knot, the square knot attaches two ends of the same rope, or joins two similar-sized ropes or lines. The chances of this knot's slipping are nil.

Bowline. Easy to tie and untie, the bowline is best for such tasks as leading or hitching a horse with a rope around its neck. When you need to tie a loop around an object, the bowline is secure and will not slip.

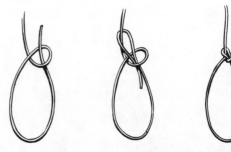

Turns with Half Hitches. To make a simple knot for tying a rope end to a pole or ring, make two turns around the object, followed by a pair of half hitches. For additional strength, use more of each.

Double Sheet Bend. When you are linking up a pair of ropes of varied diameters, try the double sheet bend. Make the simple loop in the thicker of the two ropes, using the thinner one for the turns. The double sheet bend is preferable to the single style because it is safer and takes perhaps a second longer to finish up.

Carrick Bend. The carrick bend will join ropes to tow or support hefty loads. It doesn't jam and can be easily untied.

Guy-line Hitch. The guy-line hitch tightens tent and other guy ropes that need adjustment. Begin with two basic overhand knots, with the rope running through the top one. The bottom overhand knot will slide up or down to give or take slack on the guy line or tent rope. You needn't worry about tearing the tent fabric with this hitch.

Timber Hitch. For towing logs or hitching to a pole or tree a rope that must sustain constant, strong pressure, the proper knot is the timber hitch. It ties in seconds and will not jam.

Horse Hitch. An infallible knot for tying a horse or boatline to a tree, pole, or ring is the horse hitch. The running end of the rope passed through a broad loop at the completion of the hitch will make it more secure.

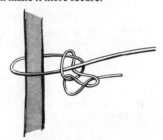

Ring Knot. This knot works best when tied to a ring, such as a swivel end or a metal loop in a lure. If you are using slick monofilament fishing line, do not trim the loose end too closely or it may slip.

Slip Knot. The slip knot is simple and won't untie very quickly. A half hitch or two around the standing part of the rope or line will further bind this knot.

Water Knot. Any outdoorsman who fishes should be familiar with the water knot. Adequate for joining fishing lines, leaders, ropes, or small cords, the water knot begins with an overhand knot made loosely in the end of either line. Put the running end of the other line through it, and secure it using an overhand knot around the first line's standing part.

Next, pull both overhand knots together. Half hitches on either side will tighten the knot. Trim the water knot carefully to prevent it from catching in your rod guides.

Figure-8 Knot. Tie the figure-8 knot just like the overhand knot, but give the loop a half-twist before the running end is passed through. Also an end knot, the figure-8 is slightly less compact than the overhand but significantly stronger.

Taut-Line Hitch. Primarily for tightening tent ropes, the taut-line hitch is actually a running loop that holds under strain.

Form a loop around the anchor. Then with the running end, make a pair of small turns around the standing part, spiralling it in the direction of the inside of the loop. A half hitch tied around the standing part, outside of the big loop, completes the loop knot.

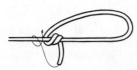

Bowline on a Bight. The bowline mentioned earlier has a variation called bowline on a bight which is especially useful for climbing.

Make an overhand loop and place the bight through it. Pull the bight downward to the end of the big loop formed by the running end. Then, separate the bight, putting the big loop through it. Slide the running-end bight upward so it goes around the standing part. Pull it tight, and the knot is ready.

Spanish Bowline. Different from the bowline on a bight in that its two loops are separated, the Spanish bowline is another variation. It functions as an improvised seat and backrest.

A slip knot about twice the size of either of the completed loops is the first step. Give the loop a half-twist so the standing part crosses in the rear. Keep the running end of the slip knot tight against the standing part where they form parallel lines. At the same time, hold the turn at the back of the knot, and immediately slide the bight next to the running end outward. Stop when it forms a loop equal in size to the original slip knot.

The resulting X pattern should now be slid up the loops until both are rather small. Reach through the pair from the back, taking the bight below the X and pulling it through. You will now have both loops and an X pattern between the two.

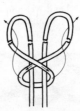

Butterfly Loop. When three persons are climbing, the man in the middle should be held with a fixed or butterfly loop. This loop also makes an excellent harness for dragging weighty loads.

Make a bight as big as you want the loop to be. Twist it one complete turn, forming a loose figure 8. Fold this double loop over the standing part to produce a pair of intertwined loops. Pass the tip of the original bight through the two loops where the overlapping takes place. Pull on the bight to tighten.

Campfires

To start a campfire, clear a site—always on rock or dirt—by removing all ground debris for at least three feet on all sides, this prevents any combustible material such as rubbish and underground roots from igniting and causing a possible forest fire. When using the top of a ledge for your fire, beware of small cracks through which hot coals might tumble into flammable material.

A good fire for cooking, lighting, or heat starts with tinder, thin sticks of kindling, and medium-size sticks of firewood. Stack them loosely or in pyramid fashion in that order. Now stand on the upwind side and light the tinder from there. This directs the flame upward and into the mass of tinder. Lighting from the downwind side leaves you little opportunity to direct the flame.

Once the tinder is well ignited, blow on it or fan the fire gently with your hat. The tinder will light the slim sticks which in turn will set the medium-size sticks ablaze.

Tinder, which forms the bottom layer of the fire, is any small-size fuel that ignites readily. Any scrap of dry paper will do, especially waxed paper and the like.

There are also wood sources of tinder. Birch bark that is stripped and wadded loosely, and dry cedar bark both perform well. Sagebrush bark, dead evergreen twigs still on the tree with brown needles intact, and dry, dead grass or weeds that are crushed into a ball are also effective.

Pitch is a primary burning agent which is found in the decayed trunks and upturned roots of woods such as spruce, pines, and fir. It also works efficiently as tinder when sliced up with the wood still attached. To tell if a wood contains pitch alert yourself to the resinous odor and weighty heft of the wood. Even heavy rains don't change the quality of pitch slabs as excellent tinder.

If you are handy with a knife and adept at whittling, you can make fuzz sticks (also known as fire sticks). Shave lengthy splinters from almost any dry, soft stick, leaving as many splinters attached as possible. When you have what resembles a tiny pine tree, thrust it upright into the ground and place some tinder around it. Set a match to the lower slivers, and you have a fine fire starter.

You can squirt a little kerosene, stove gasoline, or lighter fluid on the kindling as an alternative to gathering tinder. Be sure, however, to use these liquid fuels *prior to* striking your match to prevent an explosion. Kindling, which consists of thin, dry sticks, is ordinarily placed loosely in a teepee shape above the tinder, or criss-crossed on top of it.

The basic firewood is not added until both tinder and kindling are in place. This wood is necessarily heavier than the kindling, usually longer, and from three to four, or possibly even six, inches in thickness. Small logs or thick branches are prime sources of this firewood, which catches from the combustible material beneath to provide a strong and stable fire.

Woods vary in burning qualities. They "catch fire" primarily in relation to their dryness, cut size, and resin content. They give heat and good cooking coals primarily in relation to their density—the denser the wood, the more mass available for combustion.

Any dry (seasoned) wood will be good kindling if cut to finger thickness. Wood of conifers tends to catch fire more easily than that of deciduous trees because its high amounts of resin ignite at lower temperatures than the gases generated from wood fibers alone. But conifers tend to be smokier, and their resin pockets cause more popping and sparks.

If you are forced to burn unseasoned wood, as in a survival predicament, ash is one of the best because of its low moisture content "on the stump." For cooking, if very dry, the densest deciduous woods are best. These include the oaks, hickories, locusts, beech, birches, ashes, and hawthorns. Yet in parts of western states, you may find that conifers are the only woods available. In northwestern Canada and Alaska, birch and alder are about the only abundant, dense deciduous woods.

Hunter's Fire

Among the many possible arrangements of the basic campfire, the hunter's fire is a simple, dual-purpose one that provides hot coals for cooking along with heat and light.

Start your fire as described earlier and wait for a bed of hot coals to form. At that point, place two green logs on either side of the fire to resemble a corridor. If this is done before the coals form, the fire will eventually eat right into the logs. Rocks can also be used to form a corridor. The camper out for a brief time or on a string of one-night stands on a pack trail or canoe route benefits most from this type of fire.

If the fire dies down, place a support under the ends of the logs to let more air in through the sides.

TWO TYPES OF HUNTER'S FIRE

Keyhole Fire

Like the hunter's fire, the keyhole fire supplies heat and light, and a place for cooking chores. Also for short-term use, this campfire consists totally of flat, small rocks arranged in a keyhole-shape. It features a corridor three to six feet long and one foot wide, and a circle adjacent to the rectangle.

KEYHOLE FIRE

Indian Fire

When wood fuel is at a premium and it is necessary to conserve what you have, try the Indian fire. Note that five thick logs radiate outward from the center. Tinder should be placed at this midpoint. As the logs burn, push them gradually into the middle.

INDIAN FIRE

Begin the fire in the center of the corridor, and wait till you see that the surrounding rocks are hot and the trench is lined with a bed of coals. Using a piece of dry firewood, push the blazing wood to one end of the trench. The remainder stays at the other end for cooking. When the cooking coals seem to be losing their vigor, move some of the other coals to the cooking area.

Some outdoorsmen prefer two keyhole fires rather than one, particularly for large groups of campers, so there are always a substantial amount of hot coals to work with.

Reflector Fire

The reflector fire provides heat to a tent or an oven. A small raft of one-inch-thick logs, rocks or sod, or aluminum foil will direct heat to the desired spot. A conventional fire built in front of the reflector safely warms up a baker tent or practically any other type of tent. The reflector oven using this fire lets you bake biscuits and such.

The reflector fire requires flames to project enough heat to a selected spot. Coals alone unfortunately radiate in all directions, making cooking more difficult.

Indian Fireplace

If you have to contend with strong winds, the Indian fireplace is appropriate. Dig a hole that is a bit larger than your kettle, and build a small fire at the bottom. Using a forked shaped stick to support a straight stick with one end secured in the ground, hang the kettle over the hole. If you have enough fuel set the pot in the hole itself, but be sure there is adequate space at the bottom for air to circulate.

The lower end of the stick for hanging the kettle doesn't have to be buried or driven into the ground if a heavy enough rock or log is handy. Just lay this weight on the end of the stick, or wedge the stick under it securely.

INDIAN FIREPLACE

REFLECTOR FIRE

Trench Fire

When stoves and wood are nowhere to be found, and the pots you are using have no bails, set up a trench fire.

Dig a trench as deep as you need, parallel to the direction of the prevailing wind. Leave the upwind end open to provide an effective draft. If the trench is very narrow, its sides may support the pots. Otherwise, use green sticks to hold up your cooking gear.

TRENCH FIRE

Dingle Stick

One of the simplest and most practical campfires utilizes the dingle stick, a device that holds a pot securely over a fire. The illustrations show two arrangements of the dingle stick. Be sure to choose a durable stick for either one.

DINGLE STICKS

Swedish Fire Lay

An efficient fire for heating a single kettle, pot, coffeepot, or frying pan is the Swedish Fire Lay. It's especially convenient in confined spaces. Its foundation is a small fire with the sticks arranged in a star shape, like the basic Indian fire. Around this foundation, three split chunks of log, each

about a foot long, are stood on end. Tilt the split logs in at the top, propping them against one another to form a pyramid. The heat travels up the logs to the top, and eventually they'll begin to burn. But even before they do, the top will be hot, and it serves as a base for the cooking utensil.

SWEDISH FIRE LAY

Rain or Snow

Starting a fire in driving rain or snow is usually possible, and often easy. On rain-soaked ground, you can construct a foundation for the fire using slabs of bark, rocks, or broken limbs. On snow, build the foundation from thick pieces of green or punky and wet downfall. Avoid all fires beneath trees capped with snow, as the rising heat will melt the snow and possibly extinguish your fire.

The optimum wood under these conditions comes from standing dead trees. Most of the wood chopped from their insides will be dry enough to burn. Birch bark, pitch-saturated evergreen, and white ash are excellent choices, even when moist.

When you have gathered tinder, kindling, and firewood, look for a natural overhang—a rock ledge, for example. If none is available, improvise with a flat rock, a slab of bark, or a log propped up at an angle. A poncho, a canvas tarp, or a tent awning is even better.

Prepare the firewood, and search out a dry area to strike a match on. Your match case will probably be dry, and zippers and buttons on the inside of clothing will work in a pinch. Try scraping the match against your thumbnail, or even on the edge of your teeth as a last resort. Then, shield the initial fire until the heavy firewood is securely aflame. At that point, the fire stands little chance of being put out by the elements.

Make certain to carefully douse any fire you build with bucketful after bucketful of water when you are finished with it. Don't stop until every piece of wood is drenched. Then, stir the coals till all sparks and steam are gone. A healthy mound of wet mineral soil guarantees that the fire is completely and safely extinguished.

Camp Foods
and Menus

To plan nutritious camp menus, consider four basic questions: 1) How many meals of each type (breakfast, lunch, etc.) will there be? 2) Where will they be prepared—in a blind, on a mountainside? 3) How will the supplies be transported (backpack, RV, etc.)? 4) How many persons are in the group and what kind of appetites do they have?

Apply the answers to the three main groups of foods—carbohydrates, proteins, and fats—and determine the necessary amount of calories.

Calories supply energy. How many calories you need depend on your weight, your rate of metabolism, and how much work you are doing. Everyday camping chores use up about 3,000 calories per day, while backpacking requires 4,000 calories for the same period. Cold weather and a steep climb call for as many as 5,000 calories. When your intake of calories is less than your output, fat already stored by your body will be burned off. To prevent weight loss, it is necessary to consume a sufficient amount of calories daily.

The protein requirement depends primarily on body weight. A man weighing 130 pounds needs 60 grams of protein per day while a 175-pound man needs 80 grams. Proteins are essential because they build and repair body tissues. Good sources are cheese, meat, milk, eggs, and fish.

The following tables of the caloric and protein contents of a number of basic foods, compiled by Gerry, Division of Outdoor Sports Industries, Inc., is helpful in evaluating foods for camp purposes.

A wide variety of dehydrated or freeze-dried foods are available through sporting-good stores, camp equipment dealers, and even supermarkets. Both processes take as much water out of the food as possible to permit lightweight packing and simple preparation.

Straight dehydration is an air-drying process wherein heat dries the food but leaves it flexible. Once the food is cooked, the water returns. Freeze-drying, on the other hand, removes water by quick-freezing and placement of the food in a vacuum chamber. The pressure drops in the chamber and heat is added. The ice then sublimates slowly, meaning it goes directly from solid to gaseous form with no intermediate liquid state. The resultant food is the same size, slightly paler, and far lighter, Soaking the food from 10 to 30 minutes brings on the flavor. Besides being odor-free, the freeze-drying process leads to finer taste and quality than standard dehydration.

The outdoor cook should stress simplicity, but variety is possible. Have cereal with dried fruit one day and pancakes with syrup the next. Lunches can go from cheese to sausage to peanut butter. Suppers can be more elaborate if you'd like, and precooked items are worthwhile in that respect. By adding water to certain foods, the camp chef can prepare delicious chicken or beef stew. And water is always available if you are near a stream or lake.

Consider prepackaging of such foods as sugar, salt, bacon, and flour. There's no need to lug along a box of salt or a bag of flour if you won't need much more than a quarter of the contents. Premeasure this food. Then pack and label it, specifying for which meal and which day it is intended.

Remember to include supplementary or trail foods. They are not a part of any set meal but may increase flavor (condiments, for example), add flexibility to the menu, or give rapid-fire energy. Supplementary foods are high in protein. Foods like the Space Food Stick, for example, substitute as lunch or emergency food when cooking a full meal is impractical. Often high in calories, fats, and carbohydrates, raisins, nuts, chocolate, bacon bars, and hard candy, for example, provide instant energy and keep the saliva flowing in your mouth so it doesn't become uncomfortably dry.

On the opposite page, thanks to Gerry, Division of Outdoor Sports Industries, Inc., is a three-day sample menu of highly nutritious meals for two backpackers. Most items are available at your supermarket.

CARBOHYDRATES

Foods from this group should account for about 60% of your caloric requirement.

	CALORIES PER OUNCE	GRAMS OF PROTEIN PER OUNCE
Beans, dried	97	6.2
Bread, Dark Rye	66	1.8
French	73	2.3
Whole Wheat	73	2.6
Corn Meal	100	2.3
Farina	100	3.2
Lentils, dried	98	6.9
Macaroni Products	100	3.6
Noodles, egg	107	4.0
Oatmeal	110	4.0
Rice, instant	98	2.1
Soy Flour	78	11.9
Wheat Germ	108	3.6
Whole Wheat, instant	98	3.5
White Flour	100	3.0
Whole Wheat Flour	100	3.6
Apples, dried	87	.4
Apricots, dried	86	1.5
Bananas, dried	89	1.0
Dates	89	.5
Figs	84	1.1
Peaches, dried	83	.8
Pears, dried	84	.6
Prunes	84	.6
Raisins	84	.6
Beets, dried	83	1.6
Cabbage, dried	91	2.4
Carrots, dried	94	1.4
Celery, dried	79	2.5
Onions, dried	95	1.5
Potato, instant	100	1.2
Tomato Powder	96	2.3
Caramels	120	.5
Hard Candies	111	0
Honey	89	0
Milk Chocolate	152	1.6
Sweet Chocolate	144	.5
Sugar, granulated	111	0
Breakfast Cocoa, dry unsweetened	92	2.5

PROTEIN

Foods from this group should account for almost all of your protein requirement and about 20% of your caloric requirement.

	CALORIES PER OUNCE	GRAMS OF PROTEIN PER OUNCE
Cheese, Natural Cheddar	110	6.7
Process Cheddar	105	6.2
Grated American	110	8.7
Grated Parmesan	130	12.6
Dry Skim Milk	100	9.9
Dry Whole Milk	139	7.2
Cashews	170	5.4
Peanuts	168	7.5
Peanut Butter	173	7.3
Hard Salami	114	9.7
Chicken, canned boned	49	6.1
Lunch Meat, canned	76	4.2
Hamburger, freeze, dried	155	17
Steaks, freeze-dried	162	18
Pork Chops, freeze-dried	164	19
Corned Beef, canned	65	6.8
Dried Beef	55	9.6
Eggs, dried whole	166	13.5
Ham, smoked	107	4.7
Tuna, canned	71	6.7

FATS

Food from this group should account for about 20% of your caloric requirement.

	CALORIES PER OUNCE	GRAMS OF PROTEIN PER OUNCE
Butter or Margarine	205	.2
Cashews	170	5.4
Peanuts	168	7.5
Peanut Butter	173	7.3
Bacon, medium fat	175	2.5
Lard or Cooking Fat	250	0
Egg, dried whole	166	13.5

Should you be traveling by RV, you may want these foods in heavier packages to accommodate those aboard. For an extended trip or travel with a larger group, multiply the meals on this menu accordingly. The longer the trip, the greater the chance for variety. Once you get the hang of it, it's simple to develop your own nutritional menu.

Keep in mind that fresh food is fine the first day out, but thereafter stick to foods that will not spoil quickly, if at all, on what might be a humid trail.

THREE BREAKFASTS

#1	#2	#3
4 oz. Pancake Mix (water only needed)	4 oz. Dried Egg with Baco-Bits	2 packets Instant Pre-cooked Oatmeal or Cream of Wheat
1½ oz. Syrup Crystals (or brown sugar)	3 oz. Applesauce Flakes	3 oz. Raisins or Apricots
3 oz. Tang or other Orange Juice Crystals	2 Packets Hot Chocolate	3 oz. Grapefruit or Grape Powder
2 Packets Instant Coffee		2 Tea Bags
2 Packets Sugar		2 Packets Sugar
2 Packets Pream, etc.		

THREE LUNCHEONS

#1	#2	#3
1 Loaf Thin Sliced Party Rye Bread	16 Pillsbury's Space Sticks	5 oz. Triscuit or Swedish Rye
¼ lb. Natural Cheese	6 oz Landjaeger Sausage or Hard Salami or Pepperoni	1 Can Meat Spread
1 qt. size Wyler's Lemonade	1 qt. Wyler's Grapefruit Drink	1 qt. Tang Orange Juice
½ lb. Hard Candy, wrapped	½ lb. Hard Candy, wrapped	½ lb. Hard Candy, wrapped
Butter or Peanut Butter in Squeeze Tube		Butter in Squeeze Tube

THREE DINNERS

#1	#2	#3
1 Package Beef Gravy Mix with Army Ration Meat Bar or Dried Beef with Cream Sauce	1 Can Tomato Puree	5 oz. Cheese Sauce
	1 Can Spam	6 oz. Egg Noodles
6 oz. Mashed Potato Flakes	Dried Peppers	3 oz. dried Apricots
	6 oz. Instant Rice	2 Packets Instant Coffee
1 pkg. Instant Pudding	1 pkg. Jello	2 Packets Sugar
2 Tea Bags	2 pkgs. Hot Chocolate	2 Packets Pream
2 Packets Sugar		

PART VI / Boating

Hull Design

The shape of a boat's hull is the biggest factor in how it will do its job for you. Hull design has always been the most intriguing subject among people who know boats and keep up with new developments, for changes in hull lines, skillfully conceived, have brought about some dramatic developments in how boats perform.

There are really just two types—displacement and planing hulls. But boat hulls in common use today are far from simple. In some, characteristics of the two types have been combined in order to get the best of both. Also, a variety of specific shapes have been designed to do certain things well that another shape cannot do. And there remain several traditional hull shapes that change little in the midst of a marine-design revolution, continuing to do a modest job well, and often at minimum cost.

Displacement Hulls

Displacement hulls push through the water rather than on top of it, and therefore speed is limited. A round-bottomed, full-keeled displacement hull rides comfortably down in the water where wave and wind action has relatively little effect. The Indian canoe, the Viking ship, and the Great Banks fishing dory (a flat-bottomed boat) were all displacement-type hulls. They were narrow-beamed and pointed at both ends—for excellent reasons. They could be moved through the water more easily with only oars or sail for power; could be maneuvered in either direction; following seas had much less effect than on a flat stern; and a pointed trailing end dissipated suction created by the water displacement. Today we have squared-off sterns to provide useful space for motors and deck; but the displacement hull will probably be tapered back from a wide point amidships.

The seakindliness of a displacement hull is due principally to its low center of gravity. It rises with the swells, and a surface chop has little effect. A full-displacement hull with round quarters is less affected by beam seas (waves rolling in from one side or the other), while its full keel gives a good bite in the water, helping you to hold a course through winds and current. Because weight in a displacement hull is much less critical than in a planing hull, it can be sturdily, even heavily, built, to take the worst punishment.

Small displacement hulls are excellent for passing rocky river rapids and surviving the worst chop on a lake. In large boats, cabin space is lower in the water where it is more comfortable and secure-feeling, especially on long cruises. On big water you might be annoyed at first by the constant roll; but the roll period is slower than the chop-chop surface banging of a planing hull on the same water, and never as sharp. What's more, the displacement hull will keep you dry in wave action that would soak you continually in a planing hull.

Just how limited is a displacement hull's speed? There is an actual formula. The square root of the waterline length times 1.5 equals possible speed. An 11-foot lake fishing boat might measure 9 feet at the waterline, for instance: the square root of 9 is 3; multiplied by 1.5, you get 4.5. That boat's probable maximum speed is 4½ mph. Load it deeper so the waterline is extended and you increase the possible top speed slightly. But there's no point in loading it down with a husky outboard, for you won't increase the speed significantly above the formula figure.

How narrow? Designers work on ratios of from 3½:1 up to 5:1, length to width. To some, this describes a "tippy" boat, tender when you step in or lean over.

While a small displacement hull such as a canoe or Maine guideboat can dump you in a sudden, then skitter away high and dry on top of the water while you try to grab it, a bigger displacement hull, say from 18 feet up, is as safe even for novices as anything in the water. And since speed is inherently limited, a small motor is in order. This makes for a safe, economical way to cruise or to fish all day in a limited distance. You just move along at a modest, steady rate, dry and comfortable in big water, though not so comfortable in a small displacement-type boat on calm water, where tippiness is tiresome. You conserve your resources and enjoy the boat's natural action, and the boat is always under control. That's the portrait of boating with a displacement hull.

Modified displacement hulls and semi-planing hulls are made so that the after-third or more of the bottom is flattened. A flat bottom toward the stern rides higher as speed

Silverton Mainship 34 trawler (above) exhibits a typically stable, seaworthy displacement hull. Lowe Line Superior aluminum fishing boats include a 14-footer (right) that makes a good choice for cartopping.

is applied, instead of digging in and pushing the bow up, as will happen in a full displacement hull. The flat section aft also reduces the tendency to roll. These boats have wider transoms, and can use bigger motors and run faster. You'll find modified round-bottom hulls in small aluminum fishing boats as well as in deep-sea fishing boats, with a wide range of particular variations in design.

Round-Bottomed Cartoppers

Small aluminum fishing boats and fiberglass dinghies are often modified hulls that have round-bottom characteristics, yet they can move at high speed. You need a displacement hull for sitting on a choppy lake all day; nothing else will do. Using a motor of up to 25 hp, put the boat in the water and give it full speed. If the bow goes up and the stern digs in until you are depressed in a bowl the prop action makes in the water, reduce speed; it's a displacement hull, and your power is beyond the safe hull speed.

These boats have a rather full bow entry in relation to the beam, and there is a small keel. The middle and aft sections will be distinctly rounded, in contrast to the V-shaped cartop hull. If the sides taper toward the stern you will find it better for rowing.

Canoes

For average canoeing ability in quiet water, the shape with a rather flat bottom is comfortable, stable, and carries a good load. A small keel helps you to hold a straight course. It is harder to paddle, however, than the really round-bottomed shape used by white-water canoeists. This shape has hardly any flat on the centerline, and no keel to hang up on rocks and to slow maneuvers. Raised ends are essential to quick maneuvering.

Punt, Pram, Johnboat

Anyone can build and care for a flat-bottomed boat. This is the least complicated and least costly hull shape, and the amateur can build a large craft on simple lines at low cost. Flat-bottomed hulls pound more than others, but while newcomers dislike their clumsy appearance and strictly functional design, serious sportsmen continue to choose them for hunting and fishing on quiet waters, for they make an excellent platform.

Punt, pram, and johnboat are often indistinguishable except in name. What might be called a pram down East and a punt on England's Thames could be called a johnboat in Missouri. These square-ended, flat-bottomed hulls are the most stable and best load carriers of all little boats. They are rather heavy handling, and are designed for use in quiet water, where their low sides and flat bottoms come into their own.

The true punt is made to be poled. Sides are straight, and both ends are identical, rising flat at about 45 degrees. The bottom slopes up slightly toward the ends. The pram has bowed sides, tapering forward, and the bottom rises toward the bow. The bow end rises at a rather shallow angle, and the stern end is broader. The pram is usually rowed or sailed, but may be powered with a small outboard or electric motor.

The johnboat, popular with outdoorsmen, is made by a number of aluminum-boat manufacturers. The hull figure

Grumman FRP-18 (made of fiberglass-reinforced plastics) is an 18-foot touring canoe with aluminum seats and gunwales. This flat-bottomed canoe has a long waterline ratio for good tracking and a slightly flared bow for a dry ride.

Small Sunset pram has lapstrake molded in plastic material, adding to strength and looks of the boat.

has nearly as many variations within the basic plan as the number of regions in which it has been built and used. For instance, in marshy country a coffin-shaped johnboat was built with stern wide enough only for one person; it tapered toward a slight flare forward, then in again toward a narrow bow. Sometimes the bow was decked over to cover parcels and goods. The bottom sloped up from the flare both fore and aft, easing the push through vegetation and making it easy to maneuver in open water. This version continues to be a useful fishing boat in marshland and bayous.

Modern aluminum johnboats range from 12 to 20 feet long. The bottom slopes up a bit forward from a low point directly in the midsection, and is rockered aft. Sides may be bowed somewhat forward and slope in toward the bottom. Three or four seats, with a wide bow seat, provide reinforcement in a broad-beamed hull that can carry a big load. Aluminum johnboats are rowed, poled, and powered with an outboard.

Alumacraft Model 1562C Jon is a medium-sized johnboat with a rockered bottom forward and some flare in the midsection to keep it dry inside.

Here's a flat-bottomed rowing skiff that has safe proportions.
It's the Grumman 13-foot rowing-camper; weight 130 pounds.

Flat-Bottomed Skiff

Put a pointed bow on the flat-bottomed shape and you have
a hull that gives sharper entry to oncoming waves and reduces
the tendency to pound that is characteristic of the square-
ended johnboat or pram. It also reduces stability, however.

For good rowing qualities a skiff is built with a relatively
narrow stern; sides curve upward both fore and aft so that
the tip of the bow and stern both clear the water slightly.
The "active" bottom is the broad midsection. Such a boat is
relatively easy to control and safe. For outboard power the
stern is built wider and lower. Flat-bottomed skiffs 12 to 14
feet long are common in all parts of the country. In shorter
lengths this hull is unstable, for the bow is too light.

The Dory

This hull is fun to handle and it's also a very competent one.
You can take it through the surf or into fast shallow rivers,
for its two pointed ends and narrow bottom make it easy to
row and control. Flaring, tall sides keep it dry inside, but
this shape is somewhat tender, especially in small sizes. For
use with an outboard the design is modified by squaring off
the stern. This presents a V-shaped transom—far from ideal
for handling an outboard. Modern dory hulls have wider
and lower sterns to improve handling with a motor. Mounting a small inboard engine amidships is the solution to
powering the traditional double-end dory.

Classic dory hull is the 15½-foot Gloucester rowing dory.

Planing dory, built by John Lammers of the Yukon Territory, is
seaworthy in rough weather and responds well to steering.

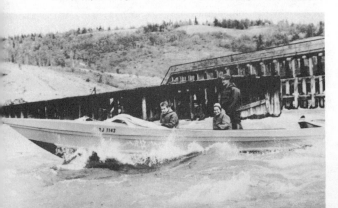

Planing Hulls

They are built for speed. Given enough acceleration
(called planing speed), the hull rises to the water's surface,
levels off, and planes along the top. Design efficiency and
possible power impose the only limits on its speed. The
objective is to reduce wetted surface (friction) and the
weight of the bow wave that a nonplaning hull pushes before
it. To achieve this, a lightweight hull is important; but weight
is related to power. A planing hull can have a wider beam;
length-to-width ratios range from 2.5: to 3.5:1. Wider beam,
especially in the aft sections, makes more space for the
power plant. In relation to power carried, the hull is lightweight.

On plane, this hull is more nimble in handling, since a substantial part of it is airborne and steering action is quicker.
The wider beam and hard chines (where bottom and sides
meet) make for a more stable boat in calm water, though
less so in a big roll.

But advantages in speed and handling bring penalties.
A planing hull is more subject to wind and wave action—
a surface chop can feel like a rock-strewn road at high
speed. Big ocean waves can put you under; it's the tendency
of an unmodified planing hull to cut through waves, rather
than to rise with them. The lack of a useful keel on some
planing hulls makes it hard to hold a course in heavy going.
Aggravating these effects is the tendency of the bow to
lift as more power is applied; the "active" hull on plane is
aft, where the greatest weight is located in the broad beam
and power plant. To overcome this, the designer may locate
tanks in the bows, if there is space there. Power trim may
adjust the planing angle to level. Or trim tabs may be added

at the stern. These are metal wedges, preferably with an adjustable feature, that help to thrust the stern up and bow down at planing speed. When a planing boat holds a horizontal angle at plane, it is easier to steer, gives a drier ride, and rides better.

But it goes without saying that much boating is on quiet water, where the planing hull has few if any serious problems. In any case, not many planing hulls now made are the pure type—flat bottoms or simple Vs. We have adapted planing advantages to practical conditions, and come up with combinations that are safe, fast, comfortable, and still easy to handle.

Cabin Dory

This is one flat-bottomed boat that is still being made in sizes of 20 feet or more. The explanation is that the dory hull's sloping sides and narrow bottom give it some of the features of a deep-V hull in handling rough water. On the Gulf and the Northeast and Northwest coasts you will see cabin boats with dory hulls made locally which have high bows running back to a flat, low stern, which is also wider than the stern of a displacement dory hull. The wide, flat section of bottom aft makes this a planing hull. But even at low speed it draws less water than a V-shaped hull and can be run in rough surf and shoal water where no other boats of the size would be safe.

V-Bottomed Skiff

The first design aimed to combine planing ability with the kinder qualities of the displacement hull was the simple V bottom, with flat planes rising from the keel to hard chines. By now, V-bottomed skiffs under 20 feet have slightly rounded chines to improve turning and reduce the slap of beam waves; the bottom aft is flattened; and the bow is deeper, with a sharp forefoot section. This makes a hull that is comfortable for all-day use on big lakes and bays, and can still plane off for a fast trip there and back. The bow deck line often has a wide flare overhanging the fine pointed bow. As the bow cuts the waves, the flare casts the spray aside, keeping you dry in moderate waves.

Mako 23-footer is a fiberglass boat with a deep-V hull. Employing inboard diesel power, it has a center console.

V-Bottomed Cartopper

Most cartop boats are planing hulls; to be light enough to qualify as a boat you can lift to a rack on top of the car, construction must be light. A planing hull is the logical type. Cartoppers that plane are usually modified-V hulls, though they may look round-bottomed at a glance. The bow is sharp, molding to a flat aft bottom with rounded chines and broad stern. If the shape tapers back to a narrower stern for easy rowing, you pay for it in reduced planing ability when you light up the outboard.

Grumman 3.8m is a stable aluminum V-bottomed skiff with a 54-inch beam. This 12-foot 4-inch boat is suitable for cartopping.

Starcraft Super Sport is a V-bottomed open-bow runabout, made in 16-, 18-, and 22-foot lengths.

Modified deep V on the Aquasport 170 shows a deep bow, sloped forefoot, merging into a flatter section aft for comfortable day-long fishing inshore or offshore.

Bertram 58-foot Convertible is a deep-V craft with a 650-hp diesel engine. Flying bridge can be enclosed and air conditioned. This is a high-performance offshore fishing machine.

Viking 35-foot Sport Fisherman, a modified deep V, is a canyon runner in nearly any sea.

Deep-V Bottom

From a performance standpoint—when big demands are put on a hull—the best combination of displacement and planing hull traits is in the deep V. Invented by designer Ray Hunt, the deep-V bottom extends from a slightly rounded forefoot all the way to the stern. The V shape at the stern works well with inboard/outdrive power, where the lower unit provides rudder action. Twin I/O installations put the propellers on either side of the V point and partially protected by it.

In a well-designed deep-V hull, the rounded, deep forefoot and full keel enable it to perform well in big waters, rising with the seas and rounding off a chop even at high speed. But how does such a hull rise on plane? With the help of longitudinal strakes, or steps in the bottom. As power is poured on, the strakes help the hull step up onto plane, while the V shape and flared bows part the wave tops and keep you reasonably dry. World ocean-racing records have been broken again and again with deep-V hulls.

Fishermen who went to deep-V hulls as a solution to

heavy going when running far offshore in the Great Lakes and on the coasts found, however, that the original hull was anything but a nurse at slow trolling speeds. We often heard complaints of wallowing when the hull was off plane. To overcome hard steering and the elemental effects of a displacement-hull commercial fishing boat, some designs have been slightly flattened astern, with sharper chines for steadiness at slow speed. Others have cut off the point of the V beyond the forefoot in an effect related to the dory hull. Twin I/Os help immensely in handling at trolling speeds on big water.

This 28-foot Luhrs, a typical Jersey sea skiff, shows a dramatically wide V bow and flare.

The Sea Skiff

This boat is often described as round-bottomed, but in fact it is usually a combination of V-hull and displacement-hull design. Forward, a rounded bilge helps it rise with waves and pound less in a chop. The bottom, with rounded chines, slants to a shallow V to form a keel, and flattens aft. The Jersey sea skiff, a remarkably practical and able hull for fishing in bigger waters, will taper to a narrower stern than many planing hulls have. This raises the planing speed, but makes it a safer boat for getting home and running inlets when the following sea may present the most trouble. Sea skiffs are usually planked with lapstrake. The strakes help lift the hull to reach plane when power is applied, and reduce roll in big water. But this also increases the total wetted surface or drag on the hull. Wood lapstrake hulls have great pliability and shock resistance, which admirably suits fishing the coasts.

Multiple Hulls

You've heard them called tri-hulls, cathedral, trihedral, gullwing and more. The basic principle is the catamaran, adding stability to a hull by means of a secondary hull. In the catamaran, the secondary hull is called an outrigger. A trimaran has two outriggers—one on each side of the load-bearing hull.

This idea, applied to modern fiberglass and aluminum boat design, has just about taken over boat manufacture in the 15–20 foot class. First, it has brought unbelievable stability to the small boat, even in rough water. Second, it has made the entire deck usable; you can fight a big fish standing on the gunwales or bows of such a boat without rocking it dangerously. The deck area is actually increased up to 100 percent, since a much wider beam in the same length is possible, with a bow line topside that is more square than pointed. This makes a boat that is useful all over. For families and for fishermen and hunters who tend to concentrate on matters other than boat handling when the fun and action warms up, it has great value.

You can see why the multiple-hull design has brought about a revolution in small boats. Naturally the hulls are unified—built in a single structure, while the Polynesian and east Indian catamaran and trimaran boats had hulls joined with wood poles bound at each hull. Between keel points are sculptured hollow spaces, where air is trapped when the boat is on plane, making a cushion against the chop and providing a lifting effect. In a tri-hull design the middle hull is deepest (often with a deep-V bow and forefoot line), and the side hulls are minor points interrupting the rise of the V toward the waterline, sometimes acting as deep chines.

This hull is slower to plane than the other V hulls, for the multiple points tend to push a bow wave ahead of the boat until planing speed is reached. Also, wetted area is greater, holding the hull off plane until considerable power pushes it up. It's also a heavy hull compared to others of the same length. Obviously it takes more gas to operate. You have to reckon the greatly increased useful deck area and stability against these drawbacks.

A second revolution that has become as big as the muliple-hull takeover is the boom in bass boats with multiple-hull characteristics. These bass boats, made of fiberglass, aluminum, or Kevlar, are mostly 14- and 16-foot boats with two- or three-point molded hulls. The difference is that the beam is quite narrow, requiring less power and making them practical in weedy waters and in the brush-filled shorelines of reservoir lakes. The sledlike hull points of the bottom are only a few inches lower than the flat areas between. This hull is potentially very fast, but that's hardly the purpose in a bass boat.

You can almost see how they built this hull, and what the designer had in mind for the hull shape. It's the bow of the 26-foot Cuttyhunk bass boat, built by Mackenzie.

Chrysler Bass Runner 115 is a luxury bass boat with a gull-wing hull design providing a wide keel and raised prow. It gets up onto plane fast and has plenty of deck space.

Ranger Fish 'n' Play Model 1850 is an I/O (inboard/outdrive) with a winged-V hull. It typifies the "new breed"—now more standard than new—of luxury bass boats.

Boat Construction

The material of which a boat is made and the way that material is used in building a boat has a direct effect on its cost, strength, weight, buoyancy, and durability. Of more than five million motorboats in use, some 27 percent are wood, 36 percent are fiberglass, and 31 percent are aluminum. The division is surprisingly even, although this is bound to change. Commercial builders have turned mostly to fiberglass and aluminum hulls because they are easier to mass-produce. And people are buying them because the man-made materials need less upkeep than wood.

Wood

It's hard to appreciate the work and time needed to keep a wood boat in good shape until you have stripped a hull down to clean, bare board, repaired rot and loose fastenings, filled and sanded it all smooth, then fiberglassed, repainted, and refinished it inside and out.

Wood is a natural material. It feels good, absorbs sound, absorbs shock, and can be worked and repaired by anyone. An important advantage over fiberglass and aluminum is that wood is naturally buoyant. Wood burns, but it's less flammable—especially the hardwoods—than most think. The best buys you'll find in used boats are wood. People love wood boats, and those who build their own usually choose wood.

Generally, round-bottomed, wood displacement hulls are built on temporary molds with ribbands connecting to delineate the shape. Structural members are bent to the molds. Planking is lined up and secured by the structure. V-bottom,

Construction of a wooden Pacemaker offshore boat shows mahogany planking being fastened to steam-bent frames with silicon bronze screws. Stem (big bow timber at right), knee, and keel are solid oak. Planing hulls, with flat bottom section toward stern, are often built inverted, later righted for inside construction and fittings.

Sawn frames are used in construction of modified-V hull of 26-foot MacKenzie Cuttyhunk bass boat. All timbers are seasoned white oak. This is characteristic shape for light, able lapstrake fishing boats like one below.

planing hulls are generally built on sawn frames (sawn lumber firmly joined at angles where the contour changes). Here, the frames make permanent molds to which the planks or plywood is attached.

But wood boats take their characteristics from the way the hull is covered as well as from the hull shape. Structural features, weight, strength, and to an extent water characteristics go hand in hand with the planking method. Some of the methods have been almost abandoned in favor of simpler and cheaper ones, but are described because valuable older hulls made with great skill are still available.

Plywood

The attractions of building with marine-grade plywood are economy, simplicity, and availability of the material. Most amateur boat builders, especially those who build from kit plans, use plywood. There are fewer fastenings, and the tricky work of fitting plank lines into a pleasing boat shape is largely avoided. Of course, plywood serves best in boats with rather simple design, since it won't take compound bends. The dory, with flat bottom and flat-curved sides, is a good example. In bigger boats plywood is used with hard chines and flat bottoms for flat-V designs.

One big-boat builder starts with a frame of white oak ribs, over which sheets of plywood are laid from sheer to sheer

as a tough and tight inner hull. Over the inner hull another of solid mahogany planks is built in carvel fashion.

Don't be alarmed when you see fist-size patches in marine plywood: voids in the core have been filled. When used in exterior hull covering, the seams, which expose the laminations, must be thoroughly treated and sealed, and the surface fiberglassed to protect the end-grain exposed in all plywood. Repair is simpler than in any other wood boat. Maintenance is relatively easy, but must be regular. Delamination of the wood plies can result from spray collecting in the bilges as well as from outside the hull, so many plywood boats are fiberglassed both inside and out.

Plywood is also used in sawn strips for other planking methods.

Carvel

This is a tighter and stronger form of carvel planking. originated thousands of years ago. Planks are laid edge to edge to form a smooth hull. Simple carvel planking is fastened only to ribs or frames, which must be closely spaced and therefore make a boat heavier. Calking is put between planks, the exterior edges of which are grooved slightly to hold the calk. In water, planks swell into the calk for tightness; out of water (and this goes for planks above the waterline) drying tends to open seams. A simple carvel-built boat is not a very dry one, and requires seasonal work to keep ship-shape.

Plywood is now used effectively by amateur boat builders. Glen-L Can Yak, shown here in three stages of construction, can be purchased in kit form. Finished boat is a sleek combination of kayak and canoe.

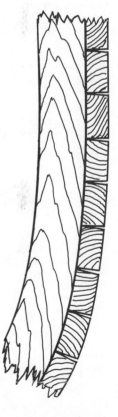

Carvel planking is grooved for caulking, which is driven between planks. In larger boats, screw holes may be counterbored and wood-plugged, keeping the smooth carvel look and keeping the fasteners tightly seated, as well.

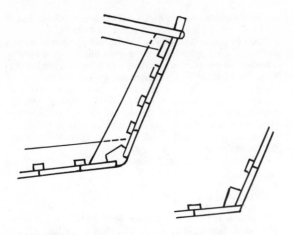

Batten-seam construction: Battens are notched into frames and seal planking seams from inside. At left, construction for bigger boats. Right, simpler construction often seen in homemade rowboats.

Batten-Seam

This is a tighter and stronger form of carvel planking. Staunch battens are notched into the frames, and planks are laid so that seams fall at the centers of battens. This closes the seams from behind, and planks are shaped so that seams are tight when laid, without calking on the exterior. Pliable batten compound is spread on battens and plank edges, and planks are screwed along the edges through the battens into frames.

Lapstrake

A favorite method for building boats that are very light and strong, its other names are clinker-built or clinch, referring

Lapstrake (clinker) planking is an expert's job, and may be as simple or carefully detailed as you bargain for. As you can see, strakes are fitted from the garboard at the keel upward.

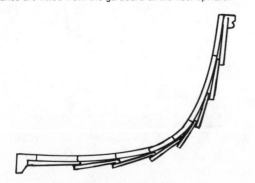

to clinched nails traditionally used in fastening. Planks are overlapped, resembling clapboard on a house. The effect looks "boaty." Relatively thin, wider planks can be used, and are fastened to each other along the overlap and also through frames where they occur. Frames can be wider spaced than in most other construction. Seam compound is applied to the overlap before fastening.

Lapstrake building is an expert's job; planking must be painstakingly lined up with the boat's shape, without stealers (which are cut to fit awkward places in carvel construction, where their use in the flat skin does not destroy appearance). Repairing damage to lapstrake is also an expert's job.

Strip Planking

This is a popular and successful way for amateurs to build wood boats, but it requires too many fastenings to be the choice of professional builders. Narrow strips (about 1¼ inch for a 20-foot boat) are used in planking. Another variation of carvel, it combines light weight with great strength, long life, and minimum maintenance compared to ordinary carvel planking. The narrow planks will not often warp or lift, which happens even with professionally built carvel boats when planking that is too wide and thin has been used.

Tight, strong seams are achieved by shaping the edges, one side concave, the other convex. Edges are covered with marine glue as a plank is laid, the plank is clamped tight in place and edge-nailed through the width of two planks and into a third. Only each third or fourth plank is fastened through frames. Fewer and lighter frames reduce weight and save interior space, as in lapstrake planking. All the fastenings in strip planking make it hard to repair; the job should be turned over to a skilled worker.

Diagonal Planking

Strong, true, and trim boats are produced this way. An amateur can handle it successfully in its simpler forms. For instance, a single layer of ¼-inch diagonal strips can be applied to plywood transverse frames for very small and light boats, such as a shallow duckboat. Strips are laid at 45 degrees to the centerline, glued and fastened to each frame at the crossing point. The edge of each strip is glued before the next is laid, and clamped in place for fastening to frames. In this lightweight construction, fiberglassing the hull both inside and out is imperative for watertightness and strength.

In larger and heavier boats, planks are laid tight in two layers and overlapped. This is an easy way for an amateur to build a dinghy-shaped boat. The keel, sheer, and longitudinal frames make the bones in this construction without transverse framing, except in offshore boats. Double-planking compound, available in marine stores, is laid between layers of planks. An unusually strong, lightweight hull results.

Professionals build double-diagonal hulls. One method is to plank in two layers laid at opposite 45-degree angles. Another is to lay the first layer at the angle, the second straight fore and aft as in strip planking. The first layer is fiberglassed; and you will find older boats whose first layer has been covered with construction canvas and glued before laying the second layer of planking.

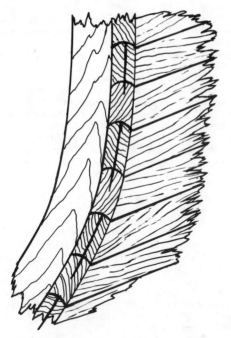

In strip planking, tight, strong seams have concave-convex edges. Edges are glued as planks are clamped in place. Then planks are edge-nailed. Frames are fastened from inside.

A duckboat can be built with thin wood strips laid diagonally at 45 degrees to centerline. Strips are edge glued, fastened to frames where they cross. This planking must be fiberglassed inside and out for watertight and strong result.

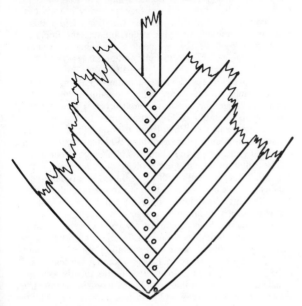

About Wood

Whether you are buying or building a wood boat, characteristics of different woods should be compared to qualities you need in a boat. Things to consider are decay resistance, impact and flex strength, dry weight, and suitability to various parts of the boat and to various sizes of boat. Before buying, read about wood and wood-boat construction in detail. Talk to those who really know about marine woods and construction, such as a local boat builder and a lumber dealer who specializes in boat lumber. To build a wood boat, regardless of size, always start with a set of plans that have been used in building a number of successful boats.

Aluminum

Light weight, low cost, and low maintenance make aluminum a popular and useful material, especially in small boats such as cartoppers. Another important quality often overlooked: it won't burn. These boats can be noisy, and poorly made aluminum hulls will "pong" as panels flex under pressure and temperature change. Some makers use sound-deadening rubber-based paints, asbestos, and other coatings on the inside. In larger hulls, a layer of flotation is sandwiched between two aluminum skins, providing safety and

Diagonal planking methods: *A,* two thin layers of plank overlap, so all seams are covered. *B,* in double-diagonal, layers of plank are reversed, outer layer running at 90 degrees from under layer. *C,* Diagonal planking finished with outer layer of straight fore-and-aft gives smooth, trim appearance of strip planking.

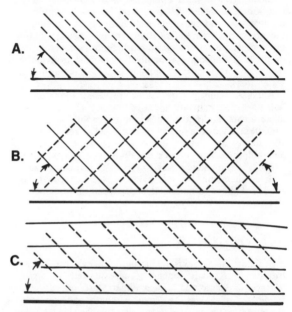

A.

B.

C.

Building Starcraft's Starchief inboard/outboard includes welding as well as riveting of some seams. Careful Amish worker in Goshen, Ind., plant here uses pneumatic riveter on exterior while partner backs it inside. The rocker device for turning hull to working angles is required.

quiet, too. It may surprise you, but an unpainted and uninsulated aluminum boat is not hot, but cool: sun rays are radiated through the metal into the water.

Aluminum boat building came of age with development of the 5000 and 6000 series of marine aluminum, which contain no copper. The 5000 series is alloyed with magnesium and manganese, the 6000 series with magnesium and silicon. Corrosion is not a problem, even in salt water, if the boat is built with marine aluminum. A reputable maker will declare this in a label on the boat.

Electrolysis presents a real danger to aluminum hulls in salt water, however. Copper, steel, nickel, or chromium, for instance, will cause electrolytic decay in aluminum in the presence of an electrical current in salt water. Motor ignitions and electronic gear and lighting systems must be properly grounded by a qualified technician to avoid this danger. For this reason, aluminum boats sell better in freshwater areas.

Aluminum hulls may be welded or riveted, and frequently both fastening methods are used. Stretch-forming presses make almost any hull form possible. Smooth, structurally sound extrusions provide strength needed in keels, stringers and ribbing, transom and gunwales. You will dent an aluminum hull oftener than crack and rip it open, but even at the worst it is surprisingly easy to repair. If you don't like the look of aluminum you can paint it, but then you have a surface that has to be maintained beyond anti-fouling.

Fiberglass

Seamless, impervious to marine parasites, rot, or electrolysis, fiberglass is popular because it needs little maintenance or caution in use in either fresh or salt water. Laminated fiberglass has great strength and versatility. Because it can be molded in any shape, it has aided development of hull shapes that are more useful and popular, such as the cathedral hulls. If made with a good gel coat, the slick surface is faster in the water.

If you are used to wood, however, you will have to get used to a much noisier boat. The nonabsorbent surface will not deaden sound, although sound-deadening materials are often applied by the maker. You should realize that fiberglass itself is heavier than water and will sink like a stone unless flotation is built in or added to the construction. Also, fiberglass will burn—or rather, it will smoke and smolder to destruction unless precautions are taken. Interest is increasing in use of fire-retardant resins such as Hetron, which has been used successfully in lifeboats of the Canadian Navy and Department of Transportation, and by Uniflite, a large U.S. boat builder.

A well-made fiberglass boat will be totally free of leaks, but it's a common misconception that fiberglass *can't* leak and that therefore any fiberglass boat will be securely dry. In careless production, pinhole leaks will occur because resin has been unevenly applied to the glass cloth and mat, resulting in dry patches in the glass where water can enter. These places are also weak.

Fiberglass boats are production boats now, of necessity; the cost and complexity of molds, skills, and technology have made custom or amateur-built boats rather rare. Building methods are by contact or hand layup, matched-metal die molding, and spray-up.

Contact or Hand Layup

Quality construction of larger and more valuable boats is by this method. A male mold is carefully made of wood, the details complete. On this, a female mold is formed of plastic materials. Laminations are laid, outside in. First, the gel coat: This is the outside surface of the boat and is an epoxy or polyester resin in which desired color is mixed, but without fiberglass body. Next comes a layer of fiberglass mat made of random fibers woven together, very porous but a suitable base for the finish just laid. Into this is laid polyester resin with a mohair or nylon roller, binding the fibers and creating a bond to the gel coat. Depending on required strength and weight of the hull, additional layers of fiberglass cloth, woven rovings (cord-twisted fiberglass for strength) are laid, and the reverse order—cloth, mat, and inside gel coat. All layers are rolled or painted with resin to bond them together and to the next layer. The exact composition and number of laminations may be varied to suit design requirements. When layup is complete, the laminate is cured at atmospheric temperature. When the resin hardens, it permanently bonds the fiberglass in a tough sheet.

The roller or brush work with resin is most important. Too much laid on will result in weakness in any lamination because a bulk of resin will be unstructured—without fiberglass. Too little anywhere will result in a dry patch that may become porous, delaminate and leak, as noted above.

Foam planks, balsa wood, or plywood can be laid at the core to add strength and built-in flotation, and these cores also help to reduce noise and vibration. In bigger boats, the core is laid with resin I-beams joining laminations on either side at intervals to give structure to this sandwich construction. Some builders avoid any wood in the construction to dispel fear of rot and parasites. Others swear by the shock-resistance and flex of wood in the core.

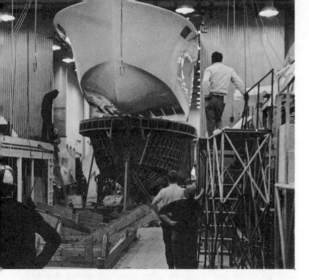

The hull of an Alglas cruiser, just removed from the mold, was made by hand layup of laminations. Its fine gel coat glistens in the light and will make it easier to move in the water. Complex shapes that are possible in fiberglass molding, including molded bottom strakes, are apparent in this photo.

The big advantage of contact or "hand" layup is that the whole hull or deck is visible at one time. Defects such as air bubbles or dry patches can be seen and remedied before proceeding. Sometimes a hull mold is made in halves to aid this; a large wheel is often built into the mold platform to roll the lamination into accessible positions as it proceeds.

Extra layers of lamination needed at chines, keel, stem, and transom are applied according to design needs. Stringers and stiffening of fiberglass or plywood may be bonded in place as the schedule proceeds, and bulkheads and motor mounts in larger craft laid after the glass hull is complete. Even hardware may be fastened and bedded in during glassing.

Matched-Die Molding

This method is used in large-volume production of fiberglass hulls under 20 feet. A fiberglass preform is made on a shaped vacuum screen placed over a metal male mold. The female mold is pressed onto it, heat applied, and the hull (including any core and ribs) is quickly fused into a unit. Voids and flaws cannot be seen during fabrication, but techniques of reputable builders are advanced and there are few rejects.

In some production lines, fiberglass fibers and catalyzed resin are shot with a chopper gun into a female mold and cured at atmosphere.

Other Plastics

Boat building with other plastics and other methods is developing. One new process for molding polyethylene increases rigidity without increasing weight, and also provides inherent flotation. The solid skin and cellular core are molecularly one piece (no laminations) formed in low-pressure injection molding. A number of different plastics can be used in this method.

Ferro Cement

Recent successes in this method have stimulated considerable interest and boat-building activity. Professional building has so far been concentrated in the Pacific Northwest and Florida.

But why build a boat of cement? Costs run from half to three quarters of other materials. And ferro-cement boats seem to last forever. They are practically maintenance-free, without seams and impervious to rot and insects, and of course are fireproof. Resistance to shock and abrasion is said to be excellent. Penetration of a ferro-cement hull by severe impact is practically unknown. Collision and grounding may cause local damage with limited cracks. Leakage is easy to control, and repair is made by hammering out a bulge and sealing cracks with epoxy or patching cement.

It sounds heavy? Not necessarily so: Ferro-cement, wood, fiberglass, and steel boats of 35 to 45 feet all weigh about the same. Above 45 feet, ferro-cement boats are usually lighter; below 35 feet, they're usually heavier than boats of other materials. Under 20 feet, using conventional methods, the weight per foot is prohibitive.

A ferro-cement boat can be built of any shape that steel reinforcing can be formed to. Vertical frames of steel pipe or bar are shaped on plans or plywood forms, then stringers are welded to space and hold the frames rigidly, and vertical bars of smaller size added. Six to eight layers of chicken wire, half on each side of the rod structure, are stapled on to hold firmly when loaded with mortar. Galvanized chicken wire is used conventionally, but good results with square welded mesh have recently been reported. Two layers are used on each side, with stringers of only a quarter inch. This reduces structural bulk, and the finished hull thickness does not exceed half an inch and weighs only eight or nine pounds per square foot. Using this method, boats of less than 20 feet may be entirely practical in ferro-cement.

Type I portland cement, the common building material, is suitable for use in fresh water. In salt water, Type II is needed to withstand sulphate action.

Air-entrained mortar produces the best results. This is mortar made with countless tiny air bubbles from a chemical agent in the mix. It flows on smoother, and when hardened is a safety factor in freezing temperatures. Only sand—no gravel—is used in the mix.

Plastering the hull requires two workers. One on the inside pushes the mortar through the structure while one on the outside smoothes the surface. The quality of the work depends on leaving no voids while filling the mesh, and working rapidly without dry joints (wet on dry concrete). A cement hull can be epoxied to reduce surface drag.

Bulkheads and cabin are usually ferro-cement as well. The reinforcement for these structures may be welded into the hull structure, or brackets which have been welded to the hull structure can be bolted to brackets welded to the inserted structures, which in that case are made separately. Engine mounts may be laid on plates welded into the hull structure. Stress-bearing hardware should be welded to the structure before cementing.

Although most boats made with ferro-cement in the U.S. so far have been sailboats, success with work-boat hulls for military and food-fishing use indicates that hard-working offshore fishing skiffs can be built at low cost. Perhaps there's a lively future here for local boat builders, unable to compete with production fiberglass boat building, when ferro-cement methods have been stabilized.

Fabric

Wood-Canvas

Making a wood-canvas canoe by Old Town, an outstanding maker, is started by shaping white cedar ribs around a canoe form. Red cedar planking is clinch-nailed to these, then mahogany gunwales are attached. Seamless canvas, Dacron, or a reinforced plastic is used for the outside skin. Seats are framed with ash; seat-bottoms are cane. Thwarts are separate, not embodied in the seats. A small keel may extend the entire bottom length for directional stability, or may be omitted on white-water canoes. Coats of waterproof varnish are laid on exposed wood surfaces, and the entire exterior is brushed with a high-gloss enamel to reduce water friction. Such a canvas canoe will stand many years of hard use.

Duckboats, kayaks, and portable canvas-covered rowboats are made by similar methods.

Inflatables

The "rubber" boat is practically a thing of the past. Serviceable inflatables now are made by laminating nylon on both sides with neoprene or Hypalon, which toughen the fabric, resist aging, and withstand petroleum and sun, as well as abrasion. Thick patches reinforce wear and chafing points. The neoprene-nylon ply is tremendously strong for its weight, and a boat made of it can take collision and grounding on rocks better than any other hull.

The secret to the serviceability of a quality inflatable is its low air pressure—only two or three pounds. It inflates quickly, but leaks, if any, are slow—usually very small breaks that are easy to repair. A good inflatable is made with at least three buoyancy chambers, any of which will keep the boat afloat.

Serviceability, almost no maintenance, and portability are the reasons for the popularity of inflatables. The reason more outdoorsmen don't own one is high price, disproportionate to construction time and materials used.

Marine Motors

Naturally your choice of power should be matched to the boat you select. Don't feel limited, however, to what you see already mounted. The great variety of motor designs and horsepower ratings available, and the versatility of these motors, give you options that sportsmen have never had before. You can customize your boat-motor rig precisely to your own preferences—if you inform yourself before you buy.

An offshore fishing boat, for instance, doesn't have to be powered by a 4-cycle inboard engine, though it's traditional. It's common now to see unusually seaworthy deep-V hulls in the 25-foot range heading offshore with either twin outboard engines or a single huge outboard up to 300 horsepower with a dependable V-6 engine.

Similarly, a 14-foot bass boat doesn't necessarily "take" a 10-hp trolling motor; depending on the boat's power rating, you can mount a huskier outboard for covering distance *plus* a small gas or electric troller—or you can do with the troller and a pair of oars. And for that matter, you don't have to paddle your own canoe; a 2-hp gas or electric motor will do it for you handsomely.

The motor to buy is the one that you particularly want and that is safe and sensible for your use. Power your boat adequately, but take care not to overpower it. Check the BIA plate and the maker's specs for recommended and maximum power rating for that boat.

Outboard

The outboard is a self-contained power unit that, happily, does not require through-hull fittings. It is lightweight in relation to horsepower produced and it can be installed or removed quickly and inexpensively.

Mounted outside the boat, its fuel and vapor can be kept safely out of bilges and cabin; deck space is clear of engine or hatches. You have positive steering with outboard power—the whole motor turns, and the propeller thrust is in the direction that will help turn the boat, instead of at an angle to a rudder. The outboard tilts up for shallow running, beaching, or trailering. There are no underhull fittings that have to be protected at all costs.

Since the 2-cycle outboard lacks a separate crankshaft oil reservoir, it is lubricated by mixing oil with the gasoline fuel. If you're a long-time boating buff, modern outboards seem surprisingly quiet—but they're noisier than inboards. A large outboard presents something of an obstacle to fishing lines; and the propeller, out from the hull, can be a hazard to divers and skiers. Mounted on the transom, the outboard is an unbalanced weight that is trimmed by adjusting the position of its thrust relative to the plane on which the boat is moving—but it *can* be trimmed, whereas an inboard-powered boat must have its load trimmed instead. And for the same reasons that an outboard is easy to remove, it's easy to steal.

or the upstream canoer, the 1.7-hp eptune Mighty Mite weighs 17 ounds and has a built-in gas tank.

Suzuki's DT2 is a 2-hp motor that weighs only 22 pounds and is suitable for trolling or for powering a variety of small-displacement craft, including canoes and inflatables.

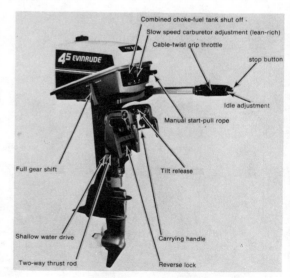

Combined choke-fuel tank shut off
Slow speed carburetor adjustment (lean-rich)
Cable-twist grip throttle
stop button
Idle adjustment
Manual start-pull rope
Full gear shift
Tilt release
Shallow water drive
Carrying handle
Two-way thrust rod
Reverse lock

Evinrude's two-cylinder 4.5-hp motor has features not always found in outboards of this size. It boasts a cable-twist grip throttle, full gear shift, shallow-water drive, carburetor adjustment, and combined choke and gas shut-off. Idle-speed adjustment and stop button are in the throttle handle for easy one-handed operation.

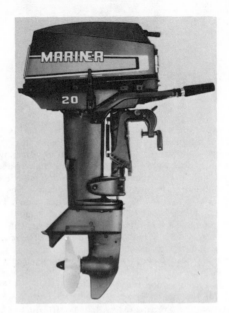

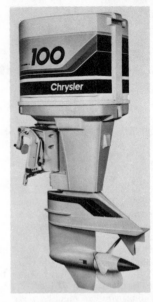

Mercury's 7.5-hp outboard features a 140-degree thermostat to regulate operating temperatures and improve idling. Additional recent modifications have been made to Mercury 7.5- and 9.8-hp motors for excellent performance at low speeds.

Mariner 20 is a two-cylinder 20-hp engine with 6.3-gallon fuel-tank capacity, magneto ignition, and five trim positions. It features saltwater-corrosion protection in prop and drive shafts, clamp screws, and fasteners.

Chrysler's 100-hp outboard has a missile-shaped power-flow drive unit for high-speed performance, cross-scavenged fuel system for quick acceleration, and electronic ignition for trouble-free starts.

Smallest member of Evinrude's V-6 family is this 150-hp motor. Its ignition system has a separate powerpack for each bank of cylinders, and the powerhead has a total displacement of 149.4 cubic inches.

Most powerful outboard is Johnson 235-hp Sea-Horse, made for good-sized offshore outboard fishing hulls. It's lighter than comparable inboard powerplants, so less horsepower is needed to push heavy loads at planing speeds.

Johnson 150-hp Sea-Horse was introduced in mid-1978—the fourth in Johnson's V-6 series of outboards.

Johnson's 12- and 24-volt electric trolling motors feature an offset steering tube, whose bend permits easier steering and retrieval because the motor's weight and thrust are centered and balanced around the pivoting axis. Steering, on-off switch, and speed selector are all on the foot pedal for no-hands operation. Both models deliver 22 pounds of thrust.

OMC (makers of Evinrude and Johnson) took the lead in designing outboards that are increasingly compact, with lower profiles. All major makers further reduce weight in some of their models each year. Effective muffling, breakerless ignition—above all, great reliability have been achieved. Manufacturers have reduced exhaust emissions and rawfuel leaks in outboards, and motors are available with drainless operation—an important advance in protecting water quality. The prospect of owning an outboard has never been more attractive.

The horsepower race among outboard manufacturers continues, with engines up to 300 horsepower available. Surprisingly enough, these big outboards with V-6 engines are more fuel efficient per horsepower than smaller motors. A 300 horsepower outboard, for example, burns less gas at cruising speed than twin 150's.

Electrics

The small, silent electric trolling motor purred along unnoticed by all but the most devoted fishermen and hunters until a few years ago, when it took off. Why? Better designs have made electric trollers more versatile; there are more models to match boats that people buy; and the new permanent-magnet motors are more efficient—that is, they run longer on a battery charge. These motors are also slimmer and they pass through water and weeds with less resistance.

Because models and characteristics are changing rapidly, partly due to the new-found popularity, we'll go into some detail about how they work and what features are important. All electrics are easy to start and operate. Endearing traits include low cost, light weight (the least is six pounds—plus storage battery), and near-silent running. Electric is the ideal power for quiet waters, where silence and small movement are important to the careful fisherman and hunter.

What's the penalty? Slow speed (about 3½ mph with a canoe and one man and gear—2½ mph with a cartopper); and the storage battery, which will give you only about four hours continuous trolling time on one battery charge.

But it's unlikely that you'll ever run an electric continuously for that long. In the careful sport it suits, your electric will be turned off frequently, and with experience you'll learn how to conserve a battery charge. If you are casting or staked out with decoys, it's not hard to get a full day's sport from one battery with full charge. Trolling is another matter; then a second battery and your own battery charger are good investments.

How much current a motor draws, of course, determines how many hours of running time you can get on a battery charge. Several things affect this. The permanent-magnet motor, and quality manufacture of switches and windings, are definite advantages. Speed is a big factor in current draw—electrics are most efficient at low speed settings. If your motor draws six amps to move your boat at 1½ mph, it might draw 16 to 18 amps to go 2½ mph. Also, some motors are designed with a higher speed range than others and will take more from your battery throughout the range.

Several companies now offer electrics with higher thrust than ever before. Minn Kota Model 85 delivers 28 pounds of thrust—as much as a 2-hp gasoline outboard. This motor employs an 11-inch propeller.

Mariner Electric fishing motors produce 23 pounds of thrust. Shown here is the transom-mounted manual-control version. It's also available deck-mounted with either manual or remote control. All versions operate on a single 12-volt battery.

Shakespeare Model 888 is a bow-mounted remote-control electric, powered by a 12-volt battery. It features a chrome-plated adjustable 28-36-inch tube, night light, ball-bearing steering, 54-inch control cable, and foot pedal with three speeds and on-off switch

Most models house the motor in a pod under water, connected to the propeller by direct drive. A sturdy control shaft from 20 to 34 inches long mounts to the boat's gunwale, transom or bow, and controls are located at the top. This motor position eliminates transmission gears, gives quieter operation, and leaves only the control head at the top to get in the way of action. Waterproof shaft seals and tough motor housings take care of the once-important problem of a wet motor resulting from hitting rocks and logs.

For regular use in water that is filled with weeds and obstructions, some sportsmen prefer electrics that have the motor on top of the shaft, with the tiller and controls attached to the motor housing. A flexible-cable drive permits a curved shaft that tends to shed weeds and slip over obstacles, with only the propeller at the end to hang up. A problem in this design is that the drive cable may whip against the sleeve when turning at top rpm. The cable has to be set at exact length to avoid this.

The ultimate convenience is a remote foot-pedal control that's available with many top-of-line models. All remotes give you no-hands steering and on-off motor. Depress the pedal and the motor goes. Roll the ball of your foot over the pedal and three switches can activate a servo motor on the shaft that will give you right, middle, or left "rudder."

A variable speed control, which comes with remote-controlled models, is realized to full advantage only if you can control it from a remote box placed on the seat beside you.

Remote controls radically change the weight and cost features of electrics, however. Weight is increased two or three times, price is increased drastically. Plug-in remotes, which let you detach the controls from the mounted motor unit, keep it a manageable package to tote to the car.

Most electrics can be mounted on the transom, on either side of the boat, or at the bow. Canoes give you an even choice, but most boats handle best with the electric attached to the transom. It's hard to hold a true course when it's attached on a midship gunwale, and at the bow—unless you have a remote control—you have to sit in the most uncomfortable place in the boat in order to run it.

Many experienced hands prefer bow mounting because they can see the direction of steering while looking ahead, and because this gives them more exact steering, since the motor leads the boat.

Other things to look for on electrics: Make sure the shaft length fits the freeboard of your boat, especially at the bow. The prop should be six inches down in the water for its best bite. Brackets and tilt-control hardware must be well designed, so that the unit does not wobble or shift. Also, it should permit you to swing or bring the motor inside the boat readily for moving out fast with your regular outboard power.

Inboard (gasoline)

The typical inboard engine's similarity to an auto engine brought it to popularity and keeps it there. When our cars come to be powered by rotaries and turbines, so will inboard boats. Inboard engine blocks are manufactured by car or truck engine makers, then are converted to marine use. It is always possible to make repairs locally because it's the commonest type of engine we have.

The 4-cycle inboard is heavier than a comparable outboard, requires permanent installation, and keeps fuel and vapor inside the boat. It also occupies a lot of space. But it's lighter on gas and oil, the lubricating oil system puts out less smog and takes less maintenance, and muffling and insulation can control its noise.

A major advantage is the inboard motor's location amidships, where the hull is capacious and weight is best handled. With fixed through-hull propeller shaft and separate rudder, however, an inboard installation presents rather delicate bottom gear that must always be protected. Since the shaft runs at a downward angle to clear the prop action, its thrust is less efficient, pushing at an upward angle.

The V drive helps to beat these drawbacks. This may also permit a lower engine location right against the stern, an advantage on some smaller inboard boats. Penn Yan improved on this design with a tunnel section in the hull to protect the propeller, a design favored by the insurance companies. Another solution is the popular inboard/outdrive.

The first and last word about inboards is to the skipper: Keep critical attention on good ventilation and fuel fixtures, and on the quality and condition of fuel lines.

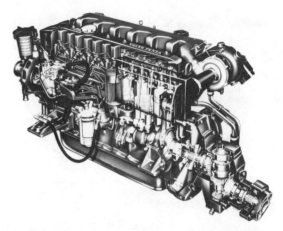

Volvo Penta PRO40 is a low-weight, compact inboard diesel designed for heavy-duty operation. It weighs 970 pounds and has a shaft output of 124 hp at 3600 rpm. An I/O 130-hp version is also available.

Diesel

You'll see diesels now in many sportfishing boats under 50 feet that could not have accommodated this heavy machinery 20 years ago. Compact designs and lighter metals in the high-compression cylinder walls have put them in hearty competition with gasoline engines in some categories.

While the diesel burns only half as much fuel as its gasoline counterpart, and diesel fuel costs less, the diesel doing the same job weighs a third more and initial cost is twice as much. But with a diesel you can increase your cruising range with the same gallonage, or reduce fuel carried to save weight. Because this fuel is less volatile, you have a safer boat. On a still day, however, diesel exhaust odor will mix your joys. This engine makes sense if you use your boat hundreds of hours each year for extended cruising and chasing gamefish.

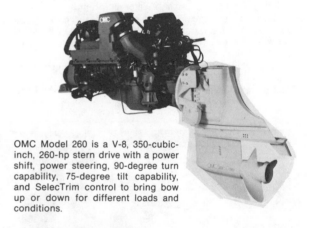

OMC Model 260 is a V-8, 350-cubic-inch, 260-hp stern drive with a power shift, power steering, 90-degree turn capability, 75-degree tilt capability, and SelecTrim control to bring bow up or down for different loads and conditions.

Stern Drive

The stern drive, or inboard/outboard, as you might know, is an inboard 4-cycle engine mounted at the stern with an outboard drive. The propeller of a stern drive drives parallel with the boat, and the lower unit of the outdrive turns, giving positive prop steering as with an outboard motor. There is no separate rudder. Power lift is much favored, as is an automatic kickup release that may save the lower unit when it hits an obstacle.

Stern drives are popular on smaller cruisers and open boats, for it is a compact inboard power arrangement that is feasible even where there is insufficient space for underdeck installation. The stern drive is a heavy machine to be located at the transom on small boats. It is a successful match with fast, deep-V hulls, for the point of the V helps to protect the propeller, and prop steering combines with the keel action of the V bottom to reduce side-slip in turns and maneuvers. It is more expensive than a straight inboard engine, but obviously more versatile.

Mercruiser Model 898 positions the stern drive near the 200-hp median for powering runabouts and small cruisers. This 198-hp model stresses engine efficiency and fuel economy.

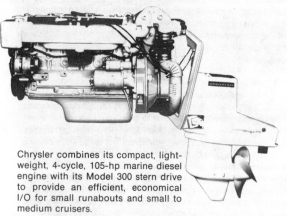

Chrysler combines its compact, light-weight, 4-cycle, 105-hp marine diesel engine with its Model 300 stern drive to provide an efficient, economical I/O for small runabouts and small to medium cruisers.

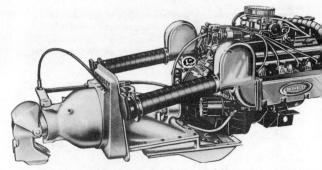

Makers of the Berkeley jet drive advise on the importance of the proper combination of hull design and performance characteristics of the jet drive, which has a sharply ascending efficiency curve at higher speeds.

Jet Drive

Here is another exciting promise that has become a practical buy for the sportsman. Water-jet propulsion is most efficient at high speeds, and having fast acceleration the big market is for water skiers. But some kinds of fishing it means a lot to have nothing below or behind to foul the lines.

Any inboard engine can be used with a jet pump. The engine is linked by direct drive to a high-speed impeller, and a water jet is forced out a nozzle to propel the boat.

With the nozzle gate raised, the jet pushes the boat forward. With gate down, the jet is deflected downward and forward to reverse the boat.

Jet boats used to tend to spin out at high speeds. To improve directional stability, Manufacturers have put a small rudder under the jet nozzle and keels one inch deep on either side of the impeller screen on the boat's bottom.

Any jet intake will be clogged eventually by thick weeds, but the impeller shrugs off sand, and passes small gravel without harm.

These photos of OMC's stern drive show features that make a high-performance stern drive safe and maneuverable even in shallow water. This outdrive permits turns as tight as 90 degrees (photo at left); up-tilting as high as 75 degrees (center) for beaching, trailering, or changing props; and trim control (right) so that the ride can be "fine-tuned."

Makers of Gasoline Inboard Engines

BERKELEY PUMP CO. "Packajet Engine" (415) 843-9400
Box 2007, Berkeley, Cal. 94710

CHRYSLER MARINE DIV. (313) 879-3000
Box 2641, Detroit, Mich. 48288

COMMANDER MARINE (305) 688-6681
4760 N.W. 128th St. Rd., Miami, Fla. 33054

FLAGSHIP MARINE ENGINE CO., INC. (516) 378-7001
159 S. Main St., Freeport, N.Y. 11520

GRAYMARINE CO. (414) 231-4560
339 W. 20th Ave., Oshkosh, Wis. 54903

HARDIN MARINE, INC. (714) 956-9100
1711 S. Claudina Way, Anaheim, Cal. 92805

HARMAN MARINE (213) 748-8661
1110 E. 14th St., Los Angeles, Cal. 90021

KIEKHAEFER AEROMARINE "K.A.M." (414) 921-5330
Box 1458, Fond du Lac, Wis. 54935

MARINE POWER CORP., A CHRIS-CRAFT CO. (305) 946-4000
555 S.W. 12th Ave., Pompano Beach, Fla. 33060

MERCURY MARINE "MerCruiser" (414) 921-8220
1939 Pioneer Rd., Fond du Lac, Wis. 54935

OMC STERN DRIVE, DIV. OUTBOARD MARINE CORP. (312) 689-5700
3145 Central Ave., Waukegan, Ill. 60085

OSCO MOTORS CORP. (215) 855-8268
Souderton, Pa. 18964

PANTHER MARINE PRODUCTS (213) 998-6221
9010 Eton St., Canoga Park, Cal. 91304

PLEASURECRAFT MARINE ENG. CO., "PCM" (614) 837-7172
Box 130, Canal, Winchester, Ohio 43110

SEAMASTER (301) 952-1010
Box 68, Upper Marlboro, Md. 20870

STOKES MARINE SUPPLY (401) 725-5790
740 York Ave., Pawtucket, R.I. 02861

THERMO ELECTRON "Crusader" (313) 264-1200
7100 E. 15 Mile Rd., Sterling Heights, Mich. 48077

Makers of Stern Drive Engines

BMW MARINE PRODUCTS (201) 573-2000
Montvale, N.J. 07645

BAJA BOATS (714) 232-2252
3581 Dalbergia St., San Diego, Cal. 92113

CHRYSLER MARINE DIV. (313) 879-3000
Box 2641, Detroit, Mich. 48288

COMMANDER MARINE (305) 688-6681
4760 N.W. 128th Rd., Miami, Fla. 33054

FLAGSHIP MARINE ENGINE CO., INC. (516) 378-7001
159 S. Main St., Freeport, N.Y. 11520

HARDIN MARINE INC. (714) 956-9100
1711 S. Claudina Way, Anaheim, Cal. 92805

HARMAN MARINE (213) 748-8661
1110 E. 14th St., Los Angeles, Cal. 90021

MARINE POWER CORP., A CHRIS-CRAFT CO. (305) 946-4000
555 S.W. 12th Ave., Pompano Beach, Fla. 33060

MERCURY MARINE "MerCruiser" (414) 921-8220
1939 Pioneer Rd., Fond du Lac, Wis. 54935

OMC STERN DRIVE, DIV. OUTBOARD MARINE CORP. (312) 689-5700
3145 Central Ave., Waukegan, Ill. 60085

OSCO MOTORS CORP. (215) 855-8268
Souderton, Pa. 18964

PANTHER MARINE PRODUCTS (213) 998-6221
9010 Eton St., Canoga Park, Cal. 91304

PLEASURECRAFT MARINE ENGINE CO. (614) 837-7172
Box 130, Canal Winchester, Ohio 43110

RENAULT MARINE DIESEL USA, INC. (305) 524-5511
505 S.E. 27th St., Ft. Lauderdale, Fla. 33335

STEWART & STEVENSON SERVICES, INC., "Dieseldrive" (713) 923-2161
Box 1637, Houston, Texas 77001

STOKES MARINE SUPPLY (401) 725-5790
740 York Ave., Pawtucket, R.I. 02861

VOLVO PENTA OF AMERICA (201) 786-7300
Rockleigh Industrial Park, Rockleigh, N.J. 07647

Makers of Diesel Inboard Engines

AMERICAN LIGURIAN CO., INC. "Amilco" (203) 324-7351
15 Ralsey Rd. S., Stamford, Conn. 06902

BAJA BOATS (714) 232-2252
3581 Dalbergia St., San Diego, Cal. 92113

CATERPILLAR TRACTOR CO., ENGINE DIV. (309) 578-6071
100 N.E. Adams St., Peoria, Ill. 61629

CHRYSLER MARINE DIVISION (313) 879-3000
Box 2641, Detroit, Mich. 48288

CUMMINS ENGINE CO., INC. (812) 379-6870
1000 5th St., Columbus, Ind. 47201

DETROIT DIESEL ALLISON DIV. (313) 592-5000
13400 W. Outer Dr., Detroit, Mich. 48228

FARYMANN DIESEL CORP. (201) 381-6767
1592 Hart St., Rahway, N.J. 07065

HARMAN MARINE (213) 748-8661
1110 E. 14th St., Los Angeles, Cal. 90021

ISUZU DIESEL OF NORTH AMERICA (313) 522-5255
32429 Schoolcraft Rd., Livonia, Mich. 48150

JOHNSON & TOWERS, INC. (609) 234-6990
Rt. 38 & Briggs Rd., Mt. Laurel, N.J. 08054

LEHMAN POWER CORP. (201) 486-5700
800 E. Elizabeth Ave., Linden, N.J. 07036

LISTER DIESELS, INC. (913) 764-3512
555 E. 56 Hwy., Olathe, Kan. 66030

MURPHY DIESEL CO. (414) 645-2255
5317 W. Burnham St., Milwaukee, Wis. 53219

OSCO MOTORS CORP. (215) 855-8268
Souderton, Pa. 18964

PERKINS ENGINES, INC. (216) 489-6000
515 Eleventh St. S.E., Canton, Ohio 44711

PETTERS LTD. "Petter Diesel" (612) 574-5000
1400 73rd Ave. N.E., Minneapolis, Minn. 55432

PEUGEOT CITROEN ENGINES (201) 935-8400
One Peugeot Plaza, Lyndhurst, N.J. 07071

RENAULT MARINE DIESEL USA, INC. (305) 524-5511
505 S.E. 27th St., Ft. Lauderdale, Fla. 33335

STEWART & STEVENSON SERVICES, INC. "Dieseldrive" (713) 923-2161
Box 1367, 4516 Harrisburg Blvd., Houston, Texas 77011

STOKES MARINE SUPPLY (401) 725-5790
740 York Ave., Pawtucket, R.I. 02861

UNIVERSAL MOTOR-MEDALIST "Atomic" (414) 231-4100
Box 2508, 1552 Harrison St., Oshkosh, Wis. 54903

VOLVO PENTA OF AMERICA (201) 786-7300
Rockleigh Industrial Park, Rockleigh, N.J. 07647

J. H. WESTERBEKE CORP. (617) 588-7700
Avon Industrial Park, Avon, Mass. 02322

YANMAR DIESEL ENGINE CO., LTD.
1-1 Yaesu 4-Chome, Chuo-Ku, Tokyo 104, Japan
U.S. DISTRIBUTOR: Mack Boring & Parts Co., 2365 Rt. 22, Union, N.J. 07083

Makers of Gasoline Outboard Motors

RATED HP @ RPM	NO. CYLINDERS	2- OR 4-CYCLE	CU IN DISPLACEMENT	WEIGHT (LBS.)	ELEC. START	SHIFT	START-IN-GEAR PROTECTION?	SHAFT LENGTH (INCHES) STD	LONG
AMERICAN HONDA (213) 321-8680									
100 W. Alondra Blvd., Gardena, Cal. 90247									
7.5 @ 5200	2	4	12.0	75	na	fnr	no	17/22	
9.9 @ 5700	2	4	12.0	75	na	fnr	no	17/22	
AMERICAN LIGURIAN CO., INC. "Amilco" (203) 324-7351									
Box 1005, 15 Ralsey Rd. S., Stamford, Conn. 06902									
Rotary engine									
9.5 @ 4800	1	—	—	77	—	fnr	—	21.85	
								16.93	
AQUABUG INTERNATIONAL, INC. (516) 536-8217									
100 Merrick Rd., Rockville Centre, N.Y. 11570									
1.2 @ 7500	1	2	1.39	13	na	300°	—	14/17	
3.0 @ 6500	1	2	3.05	21	na	360°	—	17	
CHRYSLER MARINE DIV. (313) 879-3000									
Box 2641, Detroit, Mich. 48288									
4 @ 5250	1	2	5.00	35	na	fn	no	15/20	
6 @ 4750	2	2	10.00	52	na	fnr	yes	15/20	
7.5 @ 4750	2	2	10.00	53	na	fnr	yes	15/20	

RATED HP @ RPM	NO. CYLINDERS	2- OR 4-CYCLE	CU IN DISPLACEMENT	WEIGHT (LBS.)	ELEC. START	SHIFT	START-IN-GEAR PROTECTION?	SHAFT LENGTH (INCHES) STD	LONG
CHRYSLER MARINE DIV., continued									
Sailor 180									
7.5 @ 4750	2	2	10.00	60	na	fnr	yes	15/20	
12 @ 4750	2	2	15.41	58	opt	fnr	yes	15/20	
Sailor 280									
12 @ 4750	2	2	15.41	79	std	fnr	yes	15/20	
20 @ 4750	2	2	28.57	113	opt	fnr	yes	15/20	
30 @ 4750	2	2	34.10	113	opt	fnr	yes	15/20	
45 @ 5000	2	2	42.18	127	std	fnr	yes	15/20	
55 @ 5000	2	2	49.90	183	std	fnr	yes	20	
Skier 700									
70 @ 4750	3	2	72.39	224	std	fnr	yes	20	
75 @ 4750	3	2	72.39	224	std	fnr	yes	20	
85 @ 5000	3	2	72.39	224	std	fnr	yes	20	
Charger 85									
85 @ 5000	3	2	72.39	245	std	fnr	yes	20	
100 @ 5000	4	2	96.55	251	std	fnr	yes	20	
115 @ 5000	4	2	99.90	253	std	fnr	yes	20	

RATED HP @ RPM	NO. CYLINDERS	2- OR 4-CYCLE	CU IN DISPLACEMENT	WEIGHT (LBS.)	ELEC. START	SHIFT	START-IN-GEAR PROTECTION?	STD	LONG

CHRYSLER MARINE DIV., continued

Charger 115

115 @ 5000	4	2	99.90	269	std	fnr	yes	20	
140 @ 5250	4	2	103.00	253	std	fnr	yes	20	

Charger 140

140 @ 5250	4	2	103.00	269	std	fnr	yes	20	

CLINTON ENGINES CORP. (319) 652-2411
Clark & Maple Sts., Maquoketa, Iowa 52060

Compacts

2.0 @ 3800	1	2	5.76	25	na	f	no	15	
3.5 @ 4600	1	2	7.20	35	na	f	no	15	
5.5 @ 5600	1	2	8.30	37	na	f	yes	15	
7.5 @ 6000	1	2	9.20	38	na	fn	yes	15	

Deluxe

5.5 @ 5600	1	2	8.30	40	na	fn	yes	15	
7.5 @ 6000	1	2	9.20	49	na	fnr	yes	15	
9.0 @ 6000	1	2	10.14	50	na	fnr	yes	15	

THE ESKA CO. (319) 556-4460
2400 Kerper Blvd., Dubuque, Iowa 52001

1.2 @ 7500	1	2	1.39	13.5	na	f/360°	no	15	
2.5 @ 6000	1	2	3.05	21	na	f/360°	no	15	
3.5 @ 4250	1	2	5.20	33	na	f/360°	no	15	
5.0 @ 5500	1	2	6.00	34	na	f/360°	no	15	
5.0 @ 5500	1	2	6.00	41	na	f/360°	no	15	
7.5 @ 5650	1	2	8.17	37	na	fn/360°	no	15	
7.5 @ 5650	1	2	8.17	44	na	fn/360°	no	15	
9.9 @ 4750	2	2	15.00	61	na	fnr	no	15	
15 @ 5500	2	2	15.00	62	na	fnr	no	15	

EVINRUDE MOTORS (414) 447-5500
4143 North 27th St., Box 663, Milwaukee, Wis. 53201

2 @ 4500	1	2	2.64	24	no	360°	no	15	
4 @ 4500	2	2	5.28	38	no	360°	no	15/20	
6 @ 4500	2	2	8.84	54	no	fnr	yes	15/20	
9.9 @ 5000	2	2	13.20	72	opt	fnr	yes	15/20	
9.9 @ 5000	2	2	13.20	77	opt	fnr	yes	20	
15 @ 6000	2	2	13.20	72	opt	fnr	yes	15/20	
25 @ 5000	2	2	31.80	101	opt	fnr	yes	15/20	
35 @ 5500	2	2	31.80	114	opt	fnr	yes	15/20	
50 @ 5000	2	2	44.99	195	no	fnr	yes	15/20	
55 @ 5500	2	2	44.99	180	std	fnr	yes	15/20	
70 @ 5000	3	2	49.70	230	std	fnr	yes	20	
75 @ 5500	3	2	49.70	198	std	fnr	yes	15/20	
85 @ 5000	4	2	99.60	288	std	fnr	yes	20/25	
100 @ 5000	4	2	99.60	288	std	fnr	yes	20/25	
115 @ 5000	4	2	99.60	288	std	fnr	yes	20/25	
140 @ 5000	4	2	99.60	293	std	fnr	yes	20/25	
150 @ 5000	6	2	149.40	381	std	fnr	yes	20/25	
175 @ 5000	6	2	149.40	381	std	fnr	yes	20/25	
200 @ 5250	6	2	149.40	381	std	fnr	yes	20/25	
235 @ 5250	6	2	149.40	396	std	fnr	yes	20/25	

JOHNSON OUTBOARDS "Sea Horse" (312) 689-5421
200 Sea-Horse Dr., Waukegan, Ill. 60085

2 @ 4500	1	2	2.64	24	na	360°	—	15	
4 @ 4500	2	2	5.30	38	na	360°	—	15/25	
6 @ 4500	2	2	8.80	54	na	fnr	yes	15/20	
9.9 @ 5000	2	2	13.20	72	opt	fnr	yes	15/20	
15 @ 6000	2	2	13.20	72	opt	fnr	yes	15/20	
25 @ 5000	2	2	31.80	101	opt	fnr	yes	15/20	
35 @ 5500	2	2	31.80	114	opt	fnr	yes	15/20	
50 @ 5000	2	2	44.90	195	na	fnr	yes	15/20	
55 @ 5500	2	2	44.90	187	std	fnr	yes	15/20	
70 @ 5000	3	2	49.70	230	std	fnr	yes	20	
75 @ 5500	3	2	49.70	230	std	fnr	yes	15/20	
85 @ 5000	4	2	99.60	288	std	fnr	yes	20/25	
100 @ 5000	4	2	99.60	288	std	fnr	yes	20/25	
115 @ 5000	4	2	99.60	288	std	fnr	yes	20/25	
140 @ 5000	4	2	99.60	296	std	fnr	yes	20/25	
150 @ 5000	6	2	149.40	381	std	fnr	yes	20/25	
175 @ 5000	6	2	149.40	385	std	fnr	yes	20/25	
200 @ 5250	6	2	149.40	385	std	fnr	yes	20/25	
235 @ 5250	6	2	149.40	406	std	fnr	yes	20/25	

KENTERPRISES "Porta Mini" (415) 325-9919
Box 2287, Menlo Park, Cal. 94025

1.2 @ 6500	1	2	1.34	11	na	f/360°	yes	15/20	
2.5 @ 5500	1	2	3.05	18	na	f/360°	yes	15/20	

MARINER OUTBOARDS (414) 923-3200
1939 Pioneer Rd., Fond du Lac, Wis. 54935

2 @ 5000	1	2	2.62	20	na	no	15/20		
3.5 @ 5000	1	2	3.84	42.5	na	fn	no	15/20	
5 @ 5500	1	2	5.61	52	na	fnr	no	15/20	
8 @ 5500	2	2	10.01	58	na	fnr	yes	15/20	
9.9 @ 5500	2	2	15.01	77	opt	fnr	yes	15/20	
15 @ 5500	2	2	15.01	77	opt	fnr	yes	15/20	
15 @ 5500	2	2	15.01	82.5	na	fnr	yes	15/20	
20 @ 5500	2	2	23.92	96	na	fnr	yes	15/20	
28 @ 5500	2	2	26.24	101	opt	fnr	yes	15/20	
40 @ 5500	2	2	36.13	132	opt	fnr	yes	15/20	
48 @ 5500	2	2	46.38	183	opt	fnr	yes	15/20	
60 @ 5800	2	2	46.38	185	std	fnr	yes	15/20	
70 @ 5500	3	2	49.80	190	std	fnr	yes	15/20	
80 @ 5500	4	2	66.60	244	std	fnr	yes	15/20	
90 @ 5000	6	2	99.80	290	std	fnr	yes	20	
115 @ 5500	6	2	99.80	290	std	fnr	yes	20	
140 @ 5800	6	2	99.80	290	std	fnr	yes	20	
175 @ 5800	6	2	121.90	349	std	fnr	yes	20/25	

MERCURY OUTBOARDS (414) 921-8220
1939 Pioneer Rd., Fond du Lac, Wis. 54935

4 @ 4700	2	2	5.50	36	na	fn		15/20	
4.5 @ 5500	1	2	5.50	53	na	fnr		15/20	
7.5 @ 5500	2	2	10.90	64	opt	fnr	yes	15/20	
9.8 @ 5500	2	2	10.90	64	opt	fnr	yes	15/20	
20 @ 5500	2	2	21.90	94	opt	fnr	yes	15/20	
40 @ 5500	2	2	33.30	142	opt	fnr	yes	16/20	
50 @ 5500	4	2	43.80	168	opt	fnr	yes	16/20	
70 @ 5500	3	2	49.80	190	std	fnr	yes	16/20	
80 @ 5500	4	2	66.60	244	std	fnr	yes	15/20	
90 @ 5000	6	2	99.80	290	std	fnr	yes	20	
115 @ 5500	6	2	99.80	290	std	fnr	yes	20/25	
140 @ 5800	6	2	99.80	290	std	fnr	yes	20/25	
150 @ 5500	V-6	2	121.90	349	std	fnr	yes	20/25	
175 @ 5800	V-6	2	121.90	349	std	fnr	yes	20/25	
200 @ 5800	V-6	2	121.90	331	std	fnr	yes	20/25	

MONTGOMERY WARD "Sea King" (312) 467-2678
2 Montgomery Ward Plaza, Chicago, Ill. 60671

2 @ 7000	1	2	5.76	23	na	360°	—	15	
3.5 @ 4600	1	2	5.76	33	na	360°	—	15	
4.0 @ 5250	1	2	5.00	37	na	360°	—	15	
7.5 @ 6000	1	2	8.59	38	na	fn	—	15	
7.5 @ 6000	1	2	8.59	48	na	fn	—	15	
7.5 @ 4750	2	2	10.00	53	na	fnr	—	15	
9 @ 6000	1	2	10.14	49	na	fnr	—	15	
15 @ 5100	2	2	15.41	58	na	fnr	—	15	
35 @ 5000	2	2	35.90	123	na	fnr	—	20	

PENN DEVELOPMENT CORP. "Carniti" (412) 471-4181
3810 Crooked Rd., N. Versailles, Pa. 15137

6 @ 3600	1	4	19.80	147	opt	fnr	—	36	

diesel, air cooled

16 @ 3000	1	4	33.60	264	opt	fnr	—	39	

diesel, air cooled

SEAGULL MOTORS
Fleet Bridge, Poole, Dorset BH 17.7 AG., Great Britain
U.S. Distributors:
Imtra Corp., 151 Mystic Ave., Medford, Mass. 02155 (617) 391-5660
Inland Marine Co., 79 E. Jackson St., Wilkes-Barre, Pa. 18701 (717) 822-7185
Seagull Marine, 1851 McGaw Ave., Irvine, Cal. 92714 (714) 979-6161

2 @ 3600	1	2	3.81	26	na	f	—	14	
3 @ 4200	1	2	3.81	28	na	f	—	16/22	
4.5 @ 4000	1	2	6.10	35	na	f	—	16/22	
5.5 @ 4500	1	2	6.10	38	na	fn	—	16/22	

SEARS ROEBUCK AND CO. "Gamefisher" (312) 875-8317
Sears Tower 40-16, Chicago, ILL. 60684

1.2 @ 6500	1	2	1.39	13.5	na	f	no	15	
3.5 @ 4250	1	2	5.20	32	na	f	no	15	
5.0 @ 5500	1	2	6.00	33	na	f	no	15	
5.0 @ 5550	1	2	6.00	35	na	f	no	20	
7.5 @ 5650	1	2	8.17	35	na	fn/360°	no	15	
7.5 @ 5650	1	2	8.17	37	na	fn/360°	no	15	
7.5 @ 5650	1	2	8.17	39	na	fn/360°	no	15	
9.9 @ 4750	2	2	15.00	61	na	fnr	no	15	
15.0 @ 5500	2	2	15.00	62	na	fnr	no	15	

Electric Outboard Motors

SPIRIT MARINE, DIV. OF ARCTIC ENTERPRISES, INC. (218) 681-1147
Box 635, Thief River Falls, Minn. 56701

RATED HP @ RPM	NO. CYLINDERS	2- OR 4-CYCLE	CU IN DISPLACEMENT	WEIGHT (LBS.)	ELEC. START	SHIFT	START-IN-GEAR PROTECTION?	STD.	LONG
2 @ 4500	1	2	3.10	24	na	360°	no		15
3.5 @ 4500	1	2	4.26	41.8	na	360°	yes	15	20
5 @ 5500	2	2	6.89	50.5	na	fnr	yes	15	20
9.9 @ 5000	2	2	15.70	77	na	fnr	yes	15	20
16 @ 5500	2	2	17.30	77	na	fnr	yes	15	20
20 @ 5500	2	2	24.20	100	opt	fnr	yes	15	20
25 @ 5500	2	2	27.30	100	opt	fnr	yes	15	20
50 @ 5300	2	2	44.00	178	opt	fnr	yes	15	20
65 @ 5500	2	2	48.68	183	std	fnr	yes	15	20
85 @ 5300	3	2	73.02	233	std	fnr	yes	20	

SUZUKI INTERNATIONAL, INC. (213) 921-2423
13767 Freeway Dr., Santa Fe Springs, Cal. 90670

RATED HP @ RPM	NO. CYLINDERS	2- OR 4-CYCLE	CU IN DISPLACEMENT	WEIGHT (LBS.)	ELEC. START	SHIFT	START-IN-GEAR PROTECTION?	STD.	LONG
2 @ 4800	1	2	3	22	na	360°	no	s	
3.5 @ 4800	1	2	4.30	42	na	fn/360°	no	s/l	
5 @ 5800	2	2	6.90	47	na	fnr	no	s/l	
7.5 @ 5800	2	2	10.00	62	na	fnr	no	s/l	
9.9 @ 5500	2	2	15.60	83	na	fnr	yes	s/l	
16 @ 5800	2	2	17.30	83	na	fnr	yes	s/l	
19.8 @ 5700	2	2	24.20	99	opt	fnr	yes	s/l	
25 @ 5700	2	2	27.30	99	opt	fnr	yes	s/l	
50 @ 5500	2	2	44.10	179	std	fnr	yes	s/l	
65 @ 5500	2	2	48.70	179	std	fnr	yes	s/l	
85 @ 5300	3	2	73.50	233	std	fnr	yes	s/l	

VOLVO PENTA OF AMERICA (201) 786-7300
Rockleigh Industrial Park, Rockleigh, N.J. 07647

RATED HP @ RPM	NO. CYLINDERS	2- OR 4-CYCLE	CU IN DISPLACEMENT	WEIGHT (LBS.)	ELEC. START	SHIFT	START-IN-GEAR PROTECTION?	STD.	LONG
3.9 @ 5300	1	2	4.88	31	na	f/360°	no	15	23
6 @ 5200	2	2	8.54	51	na	fnr/360°	no	15	20
9 @ 5700	2	2	8.54	51	opt	fnr/360°	no	15	20
14 @ 5800	2	2	11.97	68	opt	fnr	no	15	20
23 @ 5900	2	2	20.20	88	opt	fnr	no	15	20

Electric Outboard Motors

BYRD INDUSTRIES, INC. (901) 635-9122
South Industrial Park, Ripley, Tenn. 38063

MODEL	SPEEDS	MAX THRUST (LBS.)	MAX AMPS 12V	VOLTAGE(S)	SHAFT LENGTH (INCHES) STD	LONG	WEIGHT (LBS.)
1225	3	18	23	6/12	36	42	17 0
1250	3	18	23	6/12	36	42	31 0
1260	3	18	23	6/12	36	42	18 0
1275	3	18	23	6/12	36	42	24 0
2425	6	24	18	12/24	36	42	18 0
2450	6	24	18	12/24	36	42	30
2460	6	24	18	12/24	36	42	19 0
2475	6	24	18	12/24	36	42	25.0

THE ESKA CO. (319) 556-4460
2400 Kerper Blvd., Dubuque, Iowa 52001

MODEL	SPEEDS	MAX THRUST (LBS.)	MAX AMPS 12V	VOLTAGE(S)	SHAFT LENGTH (INCHES) STD	LONG	WEIGHT (LBS.)
1898	2	7 5	9	6/12	27	—	4
1891	10	9	13	6/12	31.5	—	8
1892	20	12 5	15	6/12	31.5	—	9.5

EVINRUDE MOTORS (414) 447-5500
4143 N. 27th St., Box 663, Milwaukee, Wis. 53201

MODEL	SPEEDS	MAX THRUST (LBS.)	MAX AMPS 12V	VOLTAGE(S)	SHAFT LENGTH (INCHES) STD	LONG	WEIGHT (LBS.)
EB 52A & 82A	var	12	20	12	adj	—	32
EB 54R & 84R	var	22	23	24	adj	—	33

Notice to readers: Apparent discrepancies in thrust/amperage figures may be the result of differing test procedures.

Electric Outboard Motors

JOHNSON OUTBOARDS "Sea Horse" (312) 689-5422
200 Sea-Horse Dr., Waukegan, Ill. 60085

MODEL	SPEEDS	MAX THRUST (LBS.)	MAX AMPS @ 12V	VOLTAGE(S)	SHAFT LENGTH (INCHES) STD	LONG	WEIGHT (LBS.)
E25	var	15	20	12	adj	—	25
E28	var	15	20	12	adj	—	25
E45	6	22	23	24	adj	—	25
E48	6	22	23	24	adj	—	25

MARINER OUTBOARDS (414) 923-3200
1939 Pioneer Rd., Fond du Lac, Wis. 54935

MODEL	SPEEDS	MAX THRUST (LBS.)	MAX AMPS @ 12V	VOLTAGE(S)	SHAFT LENGTH (INCHES) STD	LONG	WEIGHT (LBS.)
ELEC TM	var	18-23	18-23	12	34	—	—
ELEC DM	var	18-23	18-23	12	30	—	—
ELEC RC (remote)	var	18-23	18-23	12	31	—	—

MERCURY OUTBOARDS (414) 921-8220
1939 Pioneer Rd., Fond du Lac, Wis. 54935

MODEL	SPEEDS	MAX THRUST (LBS.)	MAX AMPS @ 12V	VOLTAGE(S)	SHAFT LENGTH (INCHES) STD	LONG	WEIGHT (LBS.)
Thruster (3 mdls.)	var	18-23	18-23	12	adj	—	—

MINN KOTA INC. (218) 233-1316
201 N. 17th St., Moorhead, Minn. 56560

MODEL	SPEEDS	MAX THRUST (LBS.)	MAX AMPS @ 12V	VOLTAGE(S)	SHAFT LENGTH (INCHES) STD	LONG	WEIGHT (LBS.)
10	2	6	8	12	27	—	9
15	3	9	13	12	30	—	11
35	3	12	18	12	30	—	14
55	var	15	19.5	12	30	36	16
65	4	18	23	12	30	36	17
75	3	24	23@24	12/24	30	36	17
85	var	28	28	12	30	36	20
355	var	15	19.5	12	36	—	22
365	4	18	23	12	36	—	22
375	3	24	23@24	12/24	36	—	22
385	var	28	28	12	36	—	25
535	3	12	18	12	36	—	27
555	var	15	19.5	12	36	—	29
565	4	18	23	12	36	—	30
575	3	24	23@24	12/24	36	—	30
585	var	28	28	12	36	—	33
Mag 12 TM	var	15	19.5	12	30	36	18
Mag 18 TM	4	18	23	12	30	36	18
Mag 24 TM	3	24	23@24	12/24	30	36	18
Mag 28 TM	var	28	28	12	30	36	20
Mag 12	var	15	19.5	12	36	40	30
Mag 18	4	18	23	12	36	40	30
Mag 24	3	24	23@24	12/24	36	40	30
Mag 28	var	28	28	12	36	40	33
Mag 12 RM	var	15	19.5	12	36	—	22
Mag 18 RM	4	18	23	12	36	—	22
Mag 24 RM	3	24	23@24	12/24	36	—	22
Mag 28 RM	var	28	28	12	36	25	—

MONTGOMERY WARD "Sea King" (312) 467-2678
2 Montgomery Ward Plaza, Chicago, Ill. 60671

MODEL	SPEEDS	MAX THRUST (LBS.)	MAX AMPS @ 12V	VOLTAGE(S)	SHAFT LENGTH (INCHES) STD	LONG	WEIGHT (LBS.)
50609	3	9	13	12	30	—	14
50612	3	12	18	12	30	—	19
50615	var	15	19.5	12	30	—	13
50620	4	20	23	12	30	—	25
50630	4	30	25	12	30	—	32

MOTOR-GUIDE (601) 323-4345
Box 825, Starkville, Miss. 39759

MODEL	SPEEDS	MAX THRUST (LBS.)	MAX AMPS @ 12V	VOLTAGE(S)	SHAFT LENGTH (INCHES) STD	LONG	WEIGHT (LBS.)
1300	3	16 5	23	12	36	—	25
5100	var	19	21	12	30	36	32
2500	3	16 5	23	12	36	40	28
6400	4	24	23	12	30	40	32
7400	4	33	23@24	12/24	30	40	32
2100	var	19	21	12	36	40	35
2700	4	24	23	12	36	40	35
3400	4	33	23@24	12/24	36	40	36

SEARS ROEBUCK & CO. "Gamefisher" (312) 875-8317
Sears Tower 40-16, Chicago, Ill. 60684

MODEL	SPEEDS	MAX THRUST (LBS.)	MAX AMPS @ 12V	VOLTAGE(S)	SHAFT LENGTH (INCHES) STD	LONG	WEIGHT (LBS.)
59102	2	8 5	10 5	6/12	27	—	5
59008	15	10 5	13	6/12	31 5	—	8
59009	25	13 5	15	6/12	31 5	—	10
59015	3	18	24	6/12	30	—	12
59032 (remote)	3	12	19	12	—	36	22
59033 (remote)	3	18	24	12	—	36	26

Boats for Fishing

You'll catch more fish and enjoy it more if you suit your boat and motor combination to the type of fishing you do. A good rule is: Small boats for sheltered waters; big, beamy boats for big waters. But that is only the beginning. Most of us want a boat that will handle more than one type of fishing sport well, so that what we look for is the best combination of qualities. If you analyze your needs and preferences and decide what is really important, you'll be able to select a boat-motor combination with confidence.

Boats for Sheltered Waters

Trout ponds, little bass lakes and such are not called quiet waters because nothing happens there. They *are* quiet, and the noise you make there will be the loudest heard all day unless it's moose country. Therefore it is sensible to use the quietest boat you can find. If you stay within about 12 feet length, with narrow beam, the size of your shadow will be reduced, and boat action will be in scale with the surroundings. Canvas and inflatable canoes, latex-painted aluminum canoes or skiffs, or an inner-tube rigged with a web seat fit quiet waters perfectly. You can put these into the water soundlessly, with little more than a ripple. If you want to catch fish here, and keep the fishing good, make your outfit as simple as possible. Leave the outboard at home, bring only a paddle or pole, and be proud of your inexpensive rig. You've matched nature, and that is the sportsman's art.

For small rivers and streams the canoe or sportboat are time-honored choices and cannot be beat. Both have a narrow beam and move easily against the current. Add a small outboard and you're in clover. The sportboat is probably more comfortable for two fishermen and gear when casting and moving for long hours, but experience with a canoe will win you by its easy movement, light weight, and silence. A length of 15 feet or more gives enough space for two casting rods and is safer, unless you are an expert.

When you put into lakes only a few miles across, many types of boats suit the action. First, observe the wave action, wind, and depth; then take a good look at the boats commonly used there. They probably suit those conditions remarkably well.

If the surface is usually quiet, consider a boat that will give you platform space with shallow draft, such as the johnboat or pontoon boat. If your sport is fishing bass and crappies out of the brush and weeds, look for a boat with narrow beam that is easy to push and pry loose; the canoe or sportboat does it well.

The most popular boat in America today may well be the bass boat. The phenomenal boom in this new breed, rather long, narrow, and up on sled runners, is well deserved because it fits the sport so well. The hull, developed on southern lakes, is a cross between the johnboat and tri-hull. It is very stable, yet rises quickly to the top of the water and moves fast when you want to cross the lake. With its shallow draft you can get in almost anywhere there is water that holds fish. Seats are designed for all-day fishing, rod-holders are located where you want them—it's all thought out. The narrow beam makes it easy to handle a bass while you stay seated, and helps you push through the weeds. There are only two drawbacks: weight and price, both big. You will need a 25-hp outboard motor, and for this one you will need a boat trailer or your own mooring for the season.

The favorite all-arounder, however, is the aluminum fishing boat. Successful makes are designed to adapt to the widest variety of conditions. With flotation built in they are good in fairly rough water, are lightweight and easy to handle, can be stored anywhere, and certainly cost little for the service they give. You see them on all inland waters, whatever the area and fishing sport. They come from 12 feet up; probably the most serviceable length is 14 feet. A 10-hp outboard is the common power match, but they will take huskier pushers if that's what you need.

For remote waters where the approach is on foot, look at inflatables. You backpack in, then inflate at the water's edge with a CO_2 cartridge or foot pump. Inflatables handle rather badly and tend to kite in the wind, but they are very stable and surprisingly tough, and are a lot of fun. Other candidates are small canoes, kayaks, and canvas boats, but most of these take two men to tote.

Flat-bottomed, round-ended canoe is comfortable and easy to handle, and gives you a silent boat in small, protected waters.

Sturdy, good-sized inflatables can be easily stored, and there are good ones with mounts for outboard motors.

Tough aluminum utility boats like this Alumacraft are a good choice for cruising inland waters.

Square-stern 16- to 18-foot canoes like this Michi-Craft are great for trolling or cruising with a small outboard motor.

Lightweight canoes like this 15-foot Old Town can easily accommodate one or two canoers plus gear and supplies, and they're also fine for fishing calm rivers and lakes.

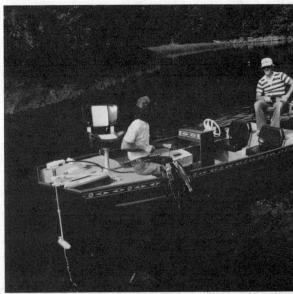

Aluminum bass boats like Lowe Line's 17-foot Hustler Pro feature raised casting decks and adjustable fishing chairs. This model is rated for use with outboards up to 70 hp.

Float-Trip Boats

Several schools of thought about boats for float trips are all cogent and tend to follow regional custom—not for custom's sake, but because water conditions vary considerably. A broad, fairly slow river without rapids will usually see shallow-draft boats that maneuver slowly but offer comfort and convenience in their broad-beamed stability. Johnboats, large inflatables, pontoon boats and river-style houseboats fit these conditions. Such boats have broad front ends that are inefficient in meeting waves or cutting much speed, but those aren't the needs. All you need is enough power to push a heavy bow wave upstream when you return. Knowing your stream, the weight and size of the boat will help you determine how much power you need.

For fast rivers with rapids and white waters, the needs are more demanding. First you need a hull that will withstand a lot of punishment; it must be built strong to survive bumping hard into rocks, logs, and gravel bottoms without damage. Flotation must be positive—sufficient to support the craft, occupants and load if swamped. Maneuverability is very important, as is a bow design that will lift and throw off white water. Light weight is necessary so that portages will be easy. The choice is usually a canoe for rivers where narrow bends and fast water between rocks make maneuverability essential. Expert white-water canoeists prefer craft under 15 feet, with round bottoms and no keel for quicker handling. However, since a canoe of this design won't hold much, the choice for float trips is usually a bigger canoe with high ends.

Inflatables are usually chosen for big, fast rivers. A big inflatable has great stability and is forgiving when you bounce it off banks and obstructions; and it's roomy enough to let you relax when the going is straight. But maneuvering a big inflatable is a real problem. Some experienced float men add a broad, shallow tiller for steering. On some rivers this is essential. Don't plan on powering your boat on fast streams, but arrange for transport at the lower end.

Boats for Open Waters

Big lakes, river estuaries, coastal bays, inlets, and off the beaches: size and seaworthiness are absolutely essential here. The bigger the water, the greater are potential dangers and needs for a capable hull that will bring you safely back through all weather, yet serve you comfortably in routine use and help you to catch more fish. Open waters are not the places for a flat-bottomed 12-foot skiff. Look at what is being used. You will see deep bow points, rounded chines on smaller boats, probably with flat planing surface aft, and enough freeboard to keep dry when the wind comes up. If your waters commonly have a sharp chop, as in many Great Lakes locations, you will need more freeboard, and the hull shape should ride comfortably in those conditions. Too much freeboard can be a curse, however, making fish handling difficult and presenting a big profile to the wind, causing eternal drifting.

Fishermen who run out to the reefs on the Great Lakes to anchor and drop a line for perch want a boat that gives a comfortable seat for hours on end, riding the waves without slapping and shipping water. The man who trolls for lake trout or coho salmon prefers a competent running boat

Lowe Line's Lake Jon aluminum fishing boats, designed for stability and easy handling, are 18 inches deep with a 56-inch beam. They're made in 12-, 14-, and 16-foot lengths.

that also provides a good platform for fighting and landing the fish, with a bow shape that will handle the waves when they rise, and that can move off fast to change locations and make the run home.

Calm days on open waters—and many big lakes a fraction of the size of the Great Lakes fit the case—are deceptive. The water looks as calm as your little bass lake when you start out in the morning. By noon you are occupied with sun-

Starcraft aluminum Mariners are center-console boats—16-, 18-, and 21-footers—featuring modified-V hull and windshield grab-rail for choppy conditions. They're suitable for deep trolling on big waters.

With a powerful gasoline outboard at the stern and remote-control electric outboard at the bow, 19-foot Ranger 198V bass boat can plane across big lakes at high speed or dawdle along for trolling.

Hydra-Sport 21-footer has a deep-V hull built of Kevlar. This center-console model is a big-water boat, suitable for offshore fishing.

burn and poor fishing, so that when the wind and big waves come up at three p.m. you're taken by surprise. Getting back to shore can be dangerous then if you are out in a 12- or 14-footer with a 10-hp motor. Think in terms of 16 feet and more length, with plenty of beam in relation to length. For big inland lakes and coastal bays you will need a motor of 25 hp and up. For trolling the ocean beaches a motor or twin motors from 85 hp up are indicated.

Now you have to plan your boat more carefully for the sport. For trolling in such waters you need a broad, clear stern for handling the lines. For casting, you should consider a boat that provides a good casting platform both fore and aft.

Offshore Boats

Perhaps the most versatile boats we have are the Mako-type boats. Deep bows permit them to handle the seas, but this slopes into a moderately flat mid and stern bottom that permits them to plane easily and ride over the flats without scraping. This design is also very stable for its seaworthiness. These boats are best described as inshore-offshore boats, great for fishing coastal bays and reefs, for running the inlets, and going offshore—but not for great distances or into really big-water country.

But it is increasingly common to see these boats, some of them outboard powered, offshore on calm days. Big twin motors are mounted on a broad transom. This kind of rig, of course, costs only a fraction of the outlay for an all-out sportfishing boat, and is much easier and simpler to handle— at least until the going gets rough. The limited fuel supply that can be carried and the modest size (about 20 feet) impose a limit on how far you can run offshore—possibly ten to twenty miles off the beach at most.

The all-out sportfishing boats, which sail in all kinds of weather and offshore seas, are a breed apart from the others. Until you have handled a boat on the ocean, following the fish on really big water, it's hard to imagine what is required of a boat in these conditions. Not only are these boats bigger (from 25 to 55 feet), with deeper hulls and more beam, but they are built to take tremendous forces. Big power is needed, as well as great reliability and fuel economy, and a frequent choice is twin diesels.

Layout is most important in the offshore sportfisherman in order to handle the boat efficiently when baiting and after hooking a big fish so that it is not broken off or lost due to a slack line, but boated in a minimum of time. (With an inadequate boat or inept skipper, it can take hours to boat a good billfish; in that time, tackle and equipment break down, people have accidents brought about by fatigue, and the boat itself can be endangered.) The steering station should give the captain a clear view of the cockpit and stern as well as forward. The cockpit will be clear of all tackle and equipment except the fighting chairs, with a clean rail from the deckhouse all around the stern. Sportfishing boats are being built now with engine hatches under the cabin floor so that the action is not interrupted by having to do something for the machinery.

Big sportfishing boats made by Chris-Craft and Pacemaker with gas turbine power have created a new experience in the offshore sport. Instead of having to shout above the engine roar, you can communicate in normal tones. This is very important when the action is fast. Giving and getting a command promptly can make all the difference. On turbine-powered boats there is only a whisper of sound from the engine plant, and all vibrations are reduced to a fraction. Being able to hear other sounds on the ocean, too, is a great help in tournament fishing. For day-after-day running out on the blue water, the turbine-powered boat is relaxing and efficient.

Hewes Super Redfisher is a 17½-footer with a 6-foot 4-inch beam, constructed with DuPont Kevlar 49. Hull weight is 750 pounds. With the motor up, draft is only 9 inches, making it an ideal boat for fishing the flats. Photo by Bob Stearns

The Striker 54-foot flybridge sportfisherman has an unusually large bridge. This boat has a cruising speed of 22 knots and a range of 900 miles without refueling.

Sea Ray Weekender is a 25-foot cruiser with deep-V hull. Cruisers of this kind have the capabilities for offshore fishing.

Starcraft 25-foot Starcruiser is a fiberglass stern-drive deep-water fishing boat with 9½-foot beam. Standard equipment includes 72-gallon fuel tank, saltwater hardware, bilge pump and blower, swivel-pedestal helm seats, and interior lights.

Pacemaker Yacht's SF26 Wahoo has a one-piece reinforced fiberglass modified-V hull. Designed for serious fishing, it features padded coamings, bow rails, large fishbox, hawse pipes to prevent tangles, and over 3 feet of freeboard fore and aft.

Mako 25-footer has deep-V hull, 14-inch draft, and 8-foot beam. Equipped with a tuna tower, it's a fine fishing boat. It accommodates twin outboards with power up to 300 hp. Features include big bait well and fishbox plus large console and spacious storage compartments.

Boats for Hunting

Any boat is potentially a hunting boat. If you have a fishing boat, it will probably serve your hunting needs well. Every boat discussed in the last section has been used successfully in hunting, even the big sportfishermen.

If hunting is your sole game, you may want a specialized boat such as a canvas duckboat. There are good reasons, however, for having a boat that will do several things well. If you must travel far on water to reach your hunting ground, you need outboard speed to save time. If you usually hunt in protected waters, you may still want to go to the big lakes or the shore to hunt. You may want to spend the night in your boat on some trips. You may like more than one kind of boat hunting—float hunting for deer, for small game, waterfowling.

If you already own a good-size fishing boat and trailer, a good solution for the all-round hunter is to get an additional, specialized hunting boat. On the water, you can use the big boat to cover distance, then use it as your "lodge," where you make your meals, keep supplies, and bed down overnight. Towing the small hunting boat behind, you can hop in when you're ready to hunt and have a small, maneuverable boat that is quiet and easy to handle, able to get in close and keep a low profile.

Float Hunting

Any of the flat-bottomed, low-sided boats such as the johnboat make practical float hunters. These boats have tremendous load-carrying capacity for their size, so that two hunters and their gear, including camping equipment and tent, are no problem at all. And I have seen two deer laid across the gunwales of a johnboat in addition to everything else, and there was still enough freeboard to move slowly back upstream to the car.

The stability and broad beam of these boats is another reason for their popularity with float hunters. You can stand to shoot with confidence, take a wide stance, and move around easily. Besides, bird dogs like them, while they dislike tippy and confining boats.

The flat bottom is ideal for setting up the frame of a blind, and you can pop up a small aluminum-framed tent there for overnight shelter if you're in marshland. "Waiting hour after hour in cold, cramped quarters" just doesn't describe the experience of hunters in a johnboat. There's plenty of room for sleeping bags plus a heater to ease the wait.

Big inflatables are also popular with float hunters. They are comfortable to lounge around in while floating or waiting it out. But the flexible construction means that you should kneel or sit to shoot. A big plus is the light weight of an inflatable, making portages easy, and you can turn it over on shore for a blind, propping up one side for gunning while you stay in the shadow.

An outboard of 10 to 20 horsepower is suitable for either of these types. You have to be guided by the boat's size, the load you carry, distances you have to motor upstream and the strength of the current, and of course the maximum-hp rating of the boat.

Important: Check out your state's hunting laws before you shoot from a boat. Some states require that you have the outboard tilted up and not operating when you shoot. Others will not permit shooting from a boat equipped with a motor.

Duckboats

These suit any hunting for shy game, especially in a small hunting ground such as island country, where you need something stealthy to succeed. Double enders are most popular: a small duckboat, canoe, or kayak. If you can, leave the motor at home and use paddles or oars; work around your base, and move your base often. If you need a motor to cover distance and reach fallen game before the current takes it, think of a really small outboard. An electric trolling motor is preferred by some hunters because it never breaks the quiet.

Duck Boats Unlimited makes this nicely designed two-man boat. It's fiberglass and features a skid-proof foredeck and swivel seats. Note that it's compact, yet has plenty of room for decoys, gear, and dog.

This aluminum ducker for two hunters has a square transom suitable for an outboard, but the boat is easy to row.

Canoe pontoons available from Grumman hang on arms that fasten to gunwales, leaving space for more gear.

The decked-over double-ender will keep you dry and snug, but the limitation is tight space. There is room for only one hunter and little else. You'll have to return to camp oftener unless you're a Spartan who knows the art of traveling ultralight.

Small hunting canoes afford more space. If you use a canoe, treat yourself to detachable buoyant pontoons. This makes shooting more secure and the whole thing more relaxed. A well-made aluminum canoe with reinforced ends is great for forcing a low lie in the marsh, and also for breaking through the thin sheet of ice in late fall. You would wreck a wooden or canvas canoe doing this unless you cover the ends with aluminum or plastic sheet.

Take the trouble to paint your aluminum canoe before you go hunting. There's nothing like blazoning the horizon with sunrays reflected from a mirror finish to earn you a bird-laugh. Camouflage paint colors should be chosen to suit the seasonal color of your hunting grounds.

Kingfisher II Rowing Skiff, from Trend Plastics, is a 16-foot fiberglass replica of lapstrake mahogany-and-cypress Wisconsin guide boats used at the turn of the century. It has aluminum gunwale and two adjustable fiberglass seats. Stable and easy-handling, it's fine for both hunting and fishing.

Grumman 3.8m aluminum duck boat can accommodate two gunners, plus dog, decoys, and gear. This 12-foot 4-inch boat has lockable under-the-seat storage and is available with dead-grass camouflage paint.

Stalker Hunting Boat is a fiberglass double-ender, suitable for gunning on waters were layout boats or the old Merrymeeting sculls are used. It has a side-mount for small gasoline or electric outboard.

Boats for Camping

Boat camping is a natural way to extend your enjoyment of fishing, hunting, and life in the outdoors. Instead of having to backtrack to your starting point toward the end of the day, just when things are going well, you can put ashore at the first suitable site if you are prepared for camping. If your boat is big enough, you can anchor and camp aboard. Still another version of boat camping is to trailer or cartop a boat to your base camp and extend your range from there by means of the boat.

For those whose primary pleasure is camping, a boat gets you away from crowded metropolis-like campgrounds. Going camping by boat gives you a private preserve in the outdoors, brings you closer to unspoiled nature, and increases your alternatives for camping locations tenfold.

Camping with Small Boats

When you camp with a canoe, cartopper, inflatable, johnboat or other really small boat, you can pack your supplies and tent or sleeping bags in the boat, travel through the wilderness on water, then make your camps ashore. This style suits many lake chains and small rivers. With careful packing, there is room for your supplies and gear, two adults, or a couple and small child in this size of boat.

When you plan your trip, make a list based on roughing it, with the minimum of equipment, only one change of clothing, backpack-style tentage, concentrated and freeze-dried foods, and a streamlined fishing or hunting outfit. There is a distinct pleasure in traveling light, and as the experience progresses, you'll be glad to have discovered a simple way to camp. Portages will be light, and if you get a dunking the damage is not irreparable.

A canoe for camping should be from 16 to 18 feet long and fairly narrow to make paddling easier. If you are going to camp on a lake, use a canoe with a keel. This will help you hold your course easily in a wind. With canoe ends slightly rockered you can adjust course fairly easily even with a heavy load. For canoe camping on a river, avoid a canoe with much of a keel, and stick to the camping length. Loaded with gear, a canoe with a keel will catch rocks and snags too often for comfort. The camping length, as opposed to shorter white-water canoes, will keep handling easy. There is a lot in favor of using a small motor on a canoe for camping. In that case, choose a canoe with full rather than fine ends so the motor will not cause the ends to dig in.

If you find yourself in hostile territory when night falls, with protected land on both sides of you, don't give up. You can make do for one night by wedging the canoe between rocks or submerged logs, heat your stew with a sterno stove, and crawl into your sleeping bags where you are.

A cartop boat will increase your load capacity, and by using an outboard you will extend your range considerably compared to paddling, or drifting. Don't forget that you will have to carry enough gas to make it between refueling points. Determine gas-pump locations in advance, and make sure you can get to them from the water's edge. Cartop fishing boats are ideal for light camping, but avoid flat-bottomed skiffs, which lack stability needed for long water routes with a big load.

Inflatable boats are excellent for drift camping on a large river. Four people can camp with a 16-foot inflatable; this boat can carry big loads, and the relatively wide beam makes it easy to load and stay aboard for long hours without getting cramped. At night you can use an inflatable as a lean-to over your sleeping bags and avoid carrying a large tent.

A full-size johnboat of 16 feet or so is too big and heavy to cartop, but it's a good candidate for trailering or loading in the back of a truck, your gear already packed in the boat. The johnboat design is excellent for boat camping, as it can carry great loads for its size. Small aluminum johnboats do suit cartopping, however, and driving is faster and easier with your boat on the car's roof than trailing behind the vehicle.

White-water canoeists have a nylon cover to keep provisions, tentage, and their lower halves dry. With load spread out they keep the center of gravity low, and the canoe is easier to maneuver in white water.

Square-stern 19-foot canoe can carry more than half a ton—ten times its weight—of people and gear. With small outboard, it is ideal for long canoe trips.

Sawyer Cruiser is a 17-foot 9-inch canoe designed for camping, cruising, and amateur racing. Its light weight—68 pounds in fiberglass or 47 pounds in Kevlar—is an advantage in handling and portaging, yet it has ample room for gear and supplies.

Flat-bottomed, sharp-nosed ample-beamed 18-foot canoes like the Old Town Laker (fiberglass) or Guide (cedar plank) are excellent for long trips. This one is on Marsh Lake, Yukon Territory.

Family Runabouts

When the family with a new runabout gets over its novelty and has learned to water ski, going camping with the boat is an interesting next stage. This is an imaginative and ambitious way to use the family's recreational resources.

Since runabouts have more beam and weight capacity than a fishing boat or canoe of the same length, you are not quite so limited in the amount of gear and supplies aboard. Often there is enough space to do simple cooking aboard and bed down. Runabouts from 16 to 19 feet suit camping best. You can use the runabout to go greater distances at better speeds with its greater horsepower capacity. If the boat is really not big enough to eat and sleep aboard, use its range to reach choice campsites, with more variety.

A family boat of 18 or 19 feet is generally big enough for four people and even a couple of small children in addition

to live aboard, more or less, if they are good organizers. Boats of this size have several advantages: You can travel on large open waters such as the Great Lakes, large river estuaries, and the Inland Waterway, moving in close along shore on weather days or to camp for the night, and also pass through fairly shallow places when you have to. Many families enjoy camping vacations in the Florida Keys aboard larger runabouts. These boats are a size that can be trailered at fair highway speeds so that reaching a distant vacation area is not a big problem.

Many makers offer camper tops as options for family runabouts. These vary considerably in quality of materials, workmanship, and design for prices that are universally high. Shop with your eyes open when buying a runabout if you think you will use it for camping. A good camper top is made of high-grade nylon with double seams, double zippers, tough plastic windows and nylon-mesh screening. Designs

Husky outboard fishing boat can be trailered with tent and gear inside to make efficient family loading.

Coleman RAM-X 13 is molded of impact-resistant, mar-resistant petrochemical material that slides easily over rocks or obstructions, is buoyant, and is color-permeated so it never needs repainting. RAM-X canoes are also available in 15- and 17-foot models.

Riviera Model C-16 deck boat, built on 16-foot aluminum pontoons, is suitable for summertime fishing-camping jaunts. It's also available in 20-foot size.

Starcraft's Stardeck is a 19-foot fiberglass deck boat, designed for I/O or outboard power. It has a 91½-inch beam and features modular instrumentation for easy servicing.

The sweet life: You can nose a pontoon camper ashore almost anywhere, sleep and cook aboard, and its light weight handles easily. Deck is just right for river fishing.

They can carry their small camp along in this broad-beamed 15-footer. It's an easy trailering size, and well designed for either fishing or hunting.

Glastron's Aventura V-210 is a trailerable 21-foot family cruiser that sleeps four comfortably. It has a 96-inch beam, 1500-pound capacity, and 47-gallon fuel tank.

VillaVee 288, by Cruisers Co., is a 28-foot 8-inch wide-cabin family cruiser with a beam measuring 10 feet 8 inches. Access to engines and two aft storage compartments is through flush hatches in the roomy cockpit.

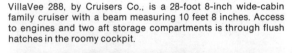

that have at least one large area with stand-up height are most useful. Tight closure all around is usually achieved with plastic rubber chanel which presses together, and strong grommets and double-reinforced eyelets anchor the camper top to the boat. If you cannot get a camper top to suit you with the boat you want to buy, shop around for a good tent maker who will make the top to your specifications.

Optional camper built-ins are a good investment if they are efficiently designed and well made. A fold-up alcohol stove with two-burners stows out of the way in a side storage space under the gunwales. Deluxe double lounge seats with comfortable padding and vinyl covering are made to fold down to make a bed for one person. Removable seats can be lifted out to make more space on deck for sleeping bags.

Houseboats and Cruisers

Whether this should be called camping is decided by your own point of view and how you go about it. If you want to camp, you'll do so, and some families are inveterate campers even in a 50-foot houseboat with automatic laundry and electric stove. The lure of building a campfire ashore, and pup-tenting for the young along the way, is very attractive when you have a boat with shallow draft that can nudge shore when you like. With a small houseboat or pocket cruiser, camping is still a natural extension of what you can do with such a boat. Here planning is more relaxed because you can keep more aboard. People who like camping in a travel trailer or motor home will find this scale to their taste.

Houseboats and small cruisers are used extensively on big rivers, along the shores of the Great Lakes, and on other open waters where you can keep in touch with shore and duck in if the weather blows up. These hulls have fairly shallow draft customarily, so that you have many options in where you go.

One pleasure with a houseboat or small cruiser is to nose up to a river bank or anchor near shore, then have a barbecue ashore, follow the deerpaths, explore islands, and walk the beaches. You can tow a small dinghy or stow it on the cabin roof for fishing and going ashore. Some carry a bicycle to run into towns along the way for groceries, laundry, and mail.

Trip Planning and Information

Boat camping requires some planning that is not covered by usual cruise planning alone. State agencies will suggest waterways that are suitable for boat camping, and can tell you where campsites are maintained along the way that you can use. Camping guidebooks are also useful, for you can join what you know about water routes with what the books can tell you about campsites and facilities. The major oil companies publish cruising guides with useful information about landings, gas docks, and family facilities along the main waterways such as the Great Lakes, Mississippi River, the San Joaquin-Sacramento delta, Inland Waterway, and others.

A directory of some 250 canoe rental locations throughout the country and also a canoe camping guidebook are available free from Grumman Boats, Marathon, N.Y. 13803. Advance reservation is usually necessary in popular vacation times. Some canoe rental stations are well-known outfitters who can help you plan a canoe camping trip with expert information about the area and about methods that the tyro needs.

A West Coast magazine, *Family Houseboating*, has a complete list of the nation's houseboat rental stations. Write: Family Houseboating, Box 2081, Toluca Lake, Calif.

Whenever you are in doubt of camping and beach rights on your prospective camping route, get in touch with state or local authorities. This can spare you disappointment and problems when you get there.

Certainly whatever your style and outdoors preference, boat camping is among the most versatile, pleasurable, and creative pursuits we know.

Buying a New or a Used Boat

New Boats

Before you start shopping for a boat, do some careful reasoning with yourself.

● Where are you going to use the boat? In fresh or salt water, big waters or small, calm waters? It makes an enormous difference in what kind of boat you need. Do you want a boat specially suited to one location and use—or do you want a versatile boat you can use in a number of different locations?

● How big a boat do you need? That depends on the size of the water, the distances you'll go, and how many people will be aboard. Just you and a fishing and hunting partner—or the whole family plus friends now and then? Between choosing a boat that's too small and one that's bigger than minimal needs, it makes sense to buy a bigger boat. But you can buy too much boat—too much for you to handle, and maintain, and too much out of your wallet.

● Where will you keep it? In a marina, on a trailer, or in a public mooring? Learn the terms—you might decide you can live with a smaller or lighter boat.

● Where will you store it in off-season? You're lucky if you can store it at home. Boatyards charge by length and type of boat, so learn the going rates, and what service they will give you.

● Does your choice have a BIA plate—a metal plate attached to the hull that certifies the Boating Industry Association has determined these figures: maximum horsepower rating, number of adult persons or maximum total weight it can carry on calm water, and total net load of persons, motor, and gear properly located aboard.

● Questions to ask about small fishing boats: What kind of flotation does it have? Is flotation impervious to alcohol and petroleum products? Is it located in the gunwales or high enough to keep the boat upright if swamped, or under seats, floor, or in the bow too low, so the boat will turn bottom up. Will the boat stay afloat with a normal load, or support only the hull weight when flooded?

● Is it round-bottomed or V-bottomed? Will it sit comfortably in the water you use it on, hour after hour? Is there enough freeboard (height of sides above the waterline) for your waters? Is the transom dangerously low, or is there a well closed off by a bulkhead to keep the boat dry and safe?

● What is the gauge thickness of an aluminum hull, and how are seams finished—welded, riveted, or both? Are seams reinforced? Can you find cast or stiff extruded aluminum at the bow and keel? Are edges and corners smooth and rounded?

● Is the transom reinforced, with strong corner plates? Is an outboard pad built in, or do you have to add one? Do you know how to do it? Do splash rails really keep water out of the boat? Does the whole hull have fairly stiff integrity when it's lifted, or does it twist and pong too much?

● Want to cartop your boat? Then it has to be light enough to heft up by yourself or with one person helping. A boat of 11 or 12 feet that weighs from 85 to 100 pounds is right for one-man cartopping. Boats that weigh up to 130 pounds really need two to cartop.

● Look for these things in a fiberglass boat: The gel coat (glassy smooth outer surface) should be free of checks, hairline cracks, bubbles, thick and thin places. Study the dark side of the boat, looking toward brighter light: Can you see pin holes of light coming through? Then the layup has been resin-starved. Are there bare, rough spots where the gel coat is absent and unhardened fabric is exposed? Insufficient resin or epoxy will produce delamination and leaks. Too much resin unsupported by fiberglass will produce weak places that can crack and break. The smoother and more even the gel coat, the faster your boat will be in the water, and the less work it will need to clean.

● Inquire in detail about fiberglass construction. Is the boat made by hand layup or by production-line mold pressing? The latter should cost less. Is wood or fiberglass used in the stringer (structural reinforcement) system? Where is the flotation? Is it molded in or added on? Are transom, bow, keel, and deck joints reinforced with extra laminations? Is hardware bolted through the hull with backing plates, or bolt-anchored into structural members? Both are satisfactory. Screwed-on hardware is useless in fiberglass hulls.

● When buying a wood boat, look for planks that are long, with fewer ends that water can find a way into, and that can work loose from fastenings. Joints in hull planks should be butted or joined at a flat angle and blocked inside, not joined on a frame. Butts must be staggered, never in line vertically. Butt blocks should overlap the butt seam at least half an inch, rounded away from the plank to drain well. These details are signs of quality construction, especially important if you are buying from an individual builder.

● Except in canoes and small rowboats, look for relatively thick, narrow planks. Economy building with the opposite dimensions results in magnified swelling with warping at the seams and rapid permeation of the thin walls. This can mean great danger in an aging boat.

● Fastenings in a wood boat should be stainless steel, bronze, or other noncorrosive alloy, for even the best-sealed boat collects moisture inside that will get to the fastenings. Rust and eventual rot of the wood pursue iron or galvanized fittings like an infection.

● Want to trailer your boat? Make sure there's a trailer on the market that fits your boat well; the manufacturer will tell you. Otherwise, you'll have to buy one custom-made

● The bigger the boat, the more you need to know before buying. In boats of 16 to 20 feet you have the widest variety of hull types, carrying capacity, construction value, horsepower capacity, and price. In this range you should definitely know the speed and power you'll need. Should you plan on one motor, or two—say, a big outboard or inboard/outdrive, plus a small trolling motor. Figure this in price.

● Look at through-hull fittings. They must be completely sealed and lipped in a professional manner to avoid delamination, rot, and leaks.

● On any boat, what options and equipment do you need? Find out what is standard in the purchase price, and what you will have to buy besides. This can change the look of the total figure.

● Will your choice depreciate fast or slowly? The value of well-made aluminum or fiberglass boats will depreciate slowly after the first 18 months. And they are easy to keep new-looking for years. The same is not true of many wood boats. This makes a difference if you expect to trade your boat periodically for a better one.

● Finally, do you know how to handle the boat you are buying? If it's your first, by all means enroll in a U.S. Power Squadron course in small-boat piloting and seamanship. You'll get more out of the course if you have just bought your own boat and can practice what you learn.

Used Boats

Many of the points to look for when buying a new boat apply to finding a good buy in a used boat, with the difference that by the time you see them, original faults are more obvious. The trick in buying real value for your money in a used boat is to check out points that are not so obvious.

● Where has the boat been stored? Covered and enclosed storage is best. If stored exposed, look for signs of freezing damage (expanded seams, splits at fastenings, braces, and joints). And look for rust and corrosion, including the power plant.

● Was it used in fresh or salt water? If in salt, look thoroughly for borer damage to wood hulls. Look for electrolysis damage to metal hulls and all exterior metal parts, including fastenings (rivets and screws). Inspect the motor's lower unit and prop for electrolysis and corrosion. The seller is justified in asking from 10 to 30 percent more for a boat used only in fresh water.

● Is the hull hooked? The hook is a dread ailment that can afflict an otherwise sound wood or fiberglass hull. It is an unwanted curve, usually concave, in the bottom centerline of the boat resulting from improper support during storage. Using the wrong trailer can do this. Best to buy a small boat that has been stored bottom up and covered.

● What's the condition of hull fastenings and hardware? They tell a tale. Too many loose rivets and screws indicate the hull has taken too much stress and perhaps abuse, or that maintenance has been slack.

● Inspect the transom carefully. Here's where careless use and original construction weakness are bound to turn up. Are the joints with the sides and bottom sound, or are there signs of cracking, splits, and separation? Can the transom pad be replaced without damaging the boat?

● Take the cover off. Is it clean. Signs of prolonged overheating probably indicate heavy use for waterskiing, hard acceleration, and big overload. Turn it on and watch for thick smoke. Fill the grease port on the lower gear, take the rig for a spin, and look again. If the grease is gone, look out. The gears may be badly worn. A badly knicked propeller indicates hard, careless use.

● Pitted surface on an aluminum hull shows electrolysis. Don't buy that boat. But dents, or just a few broken rivets, mean little. You can knock out the dents and restore a few rivets. Loose rivets all over can't be repaired—the holes are too wide.

● Crazing of the surface on a fiberglass boat's gel coat may only tell its age, with little effect on quality. But cracks are serious. Look for signs of delamination at the transom, bow, and joints on a fiberglass boat. If serious, it's hard to restore and you better look further.

● In wood hulls, beware of signs of rot, borers, and poor original construction that will come to light after several years. Stick an icepick into the transom wood, near joints, and around the keel. Inspect closed underfloor bilge areas, where rot is frequent. Warped or loose boards indicate poor and inexpert maintenance, or economy-type construction. Too many loose fastenings mean a costly overall repair job, and perhaps you'll find rot around the fastenings.

● Look inside the hull, in the point of the bow, at transom corners, and under floorboards for signs of collision damage, just as you'd look at the frame and undersides of a car body. Are repairs well made? Any signs of rot or leaking around them? They should be sounder and tighter than the rest of the hull.

● Don't pass up a used boat just because it has a hole punched in it, unless there are signs of rot that gave way. A simple hole—even a large one—can mean a big bargain to you that might be easily repaired. Aluminum and fiberglass are easier to patch than wood.

● If a used boat costs several thousand dollars, as big ones do, buy only subject to a clean bill from a professional boat surveyor. He can find things that you can't, and advise you on the extent of damage and deterioration.

● Finally, know who you're doing business with. Make sure you can come back, though it's just for information. All you want from him is a fair deal, not a steal.

Anchors, Moorings, and Ropes

An anchor is essential to safe boat operation, yet many boat liveries where small fishing boats are rented put their boats out without either anchor or lines. When you know the importance of having an anchor, you will insist on having an effective one aboard even on a normally calm lake, and enough anchor line to give safe scope. In addition to safety, an anchor is necessary to hold position in a breeze or current when fishing and hunting. For the sportsman, a boat is half useless without a good anchor.

Mushroom anchors depend on weight to a large extent for holding the boat. A well-made mushroom anchor has holes cast in the cup to let water and mud drain; still, it is a job to haul one of these from deep water with mud or marl bottom.

Cadmium-plated folding anchor from Grumman weighs only 2 pounds. Its four flukes lock open and will hold on most bottoms. It's suitable for canoes and small boats.

The major misconception about anchors is that the heavier the anchor, the more it will hold. This is not the case. The key is the meaning of *hold*. An anchor does not function by weighing down but by holding onto the bottom effectively. A concrete block weighing twenty pounds may roll on a sloping bottom and slide on a hard bottom as the breeze tugs at the boat. Finally, with luck, it may come up against a flat-sided rock, where it might hold until the breeze shifts. In the same situation, a Danforth or a kedge anchor weighing only three pounds will probably hold the boat fast after kedging only several feet until its sharp flukes find a grip in the bottom.

Many small boats are equipped with mushroom-type anchors. These have a solid, weighty feel—even the small ones. Regardless of the direction in which they are pulled, the lip of the cup will drag in contact with the bottom and possibly hold. But when they hook a bottom snag or settle in mud, the weight of the cast-iron mushroom plus the weight of the bottom becomes a formidable load to haul up through the water.

Since anchor weight and size suitable to a boat of a given size vary widely according to the anchor design and to local conditions, no guidelines can be given that apply to all anchor types in common use. (Remember that concrete blocks and cans with cast-in concrete are among the commonest of small-boat anchors.) However, guidelines for Danforth and mushroom-type anchors are provided in the accompanying tables.

A mushroom anchor may be adequate on a protected lake with a firm bottom, but on a fast-moving stream this anchor will be ineffective. On a large, open water, a concrete block or another type of simple, heavy anchor can be a

This lightweight Danforth anchor is made in various sizes for boats from 10 feet up. When the anchor line is attached to the sliding ring on the shank, a snagged anchor can be drawn out backwards by backing boat across anchor. This arrangement is perfect for use on snag-filled bottoms.

hazard. When the wind blows, the anchor will roll until the boat is in water deeper than the length of the anchor rope. The anchor then becomes a load on the bow, dipping deeper in the trough of waves than it should.

A number of anchor designs for pleasure boats have been developed which are effective by application rather than weight. One of the best is the Danforth. This anchor will hold on a hard bottom and can be retrieved on a rock-filled bottom. Most have trip features for releasing the anchor when it gets caught on the bottom.

The length of the anchor line is an important factor in effective anchoring. In calm waters, twice the depth of the water is enough line. This assumes you are in the boat and can bring it easily to shore if a sudden storm comes up or your motor gives out. In open waters, your anchor line should be three to five times the depth of the water. For riding overnight or when the boat is unattended, you need seven times the depth. Obviously the reason is holding power. If the length of line plus the anchor design permit the pull to be applied horizontally against the anchor's purchase on the bottom, it will help it to hold. On boats 17 feet and larger, a short length of strong chain next to the anchor will help the anchor hold its bite and reduce chafing of the rope against rocks and the anchor itself.

The best way to free most anchors that are stuck in the bottom is by pulling straight up. If you find you cannot do this, try snubbing the line until it runs vertically down to the snagged anchor. Take a bite around the cleat to hold the line tight, then rock the boat fore and aft, or let wave action do this until the anchor is worked free. The force of the boat's motion is greater than you can apply by hand.

When anchoring on large or windy waters, reckon the directions of wind and wave action before setting anchor. If you have a choice of anchoring on a lee or windward shore, choose the lee. Then your boat won't be blown or washed onto the rocks by morning. In a popular mooring place, set your anchor so that you have several boat lengths between you and other craft. Then if a storm arises, even the worst fury won't cause damage.

Anchoring small boats is made easy and quick for the lone sportsman with a hand-operated winch and bow pulley. This is Worth's Anchormate.

Many fishermen like to drag or tow their anchor when drift fishing in windy, deep waters. This is somewhat of a hazard to the anchor and line, and the anchor must be fully hauled to start the motor again to regain the best position. You might prefer instead to store a sea anchor or two for the purpose. This is a canvas bucket that acts as a drag. It is attached with a halter to a light nylon line that can be hauled in easily.

SUGGESTED DANFORTH ANCHOR SIZES

LENGTH OF BOAT	BEAM		STANDARD SIZES			HI-TENSILE SIZES	
	SAIL	POWER	WORKING	STORM	LUNCH	WORKING	STORM
10 ft.	4 ft.	4 ft.	2½	4	Hook	5	5
15 ft.	5 ft.	5 ft.	4	8	—	5	5
20 ft.	6 ft.	6 ft.	8	13	—	5	12
25 ft.	6½ ft.	7 ft.	8	13	5	12	12
30 ft.	7 ft.	9 ft.	13	22	5	12	18
35 ft.	8 ft.	10 ft.	22	22	5	18	18
40 ft.	9 ft.	11 ft.	22	40	5	18	28
50 ft.	11 ft.	13 ft.	40	65	12	28	60
60 ft.	12 ft.	14 ft.	65	85	12	60	90

MUSHROOM ANCHOR WEIGHTS

LENGTH OF BOAT	POWER:	SAIL: (Racing)	SAIL: (Cruising)
25′	225 lbs.	125 lbs.	175 lbs.
35′	300 lbs.	200 lbs.	250 lbs.
45′	400 lbs.	325 lbs.	400 lbs.
55′	500 lbs.	450 lbs.	550 lbs.

How to Set a Mooring

An anchored mooring is cheaper than a dock, and in many crowded public facilities it is the only choice. The authorities may stipulate the minimum mooring that is acceptable. You may want to improve on this, particularly if you have a valuable boat. In any case, remember that your boat might do damage if it drags its mooring or breaks loose—and the responsibility is yours.

On soft bottoms, heavy iron mushroom-type moorings are often used successfully. Chain is attached from the mooring anchor to a floating buoy, where the boat is tied, usually with a snap hook on a short line from the bow. Even a big mushroom mooring can be pulled through the mud if a really hard storm or hurricane blows, however, and it is against this occasional danger that you must prepare when setting a permanent mooring. A single mooring anchor assumes adequate scope on the line to hold in a blow; but scope of this length is impossible in crowded anchorages. Therefore, three anchors are sometimes used, set in an equilateral triangle with only one boat-length of extra scope

FORE-AND-AFT MOORING
FOR CROWDED ANCHORAGE

THREE-ANCHOR MOORING
WITH DANFORTH ANCHORS

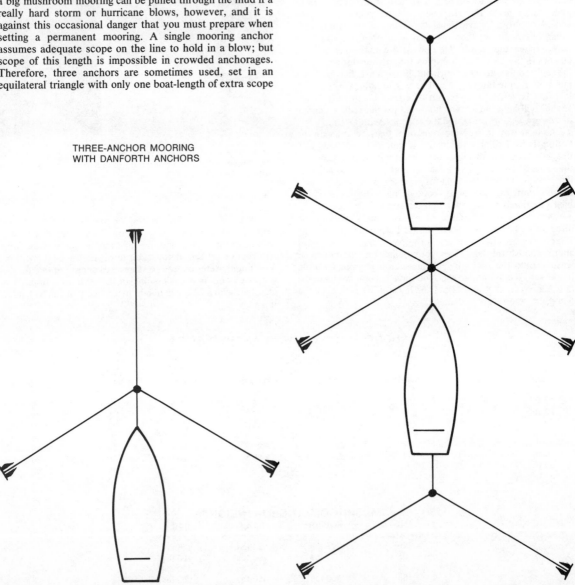

to the buoy (see diagram). An alternative in the most crowded locations is fore-and-aft anchoring, with two anchors to each buoy, and each boat tied to the buoy both fore and aft of it.

Anchor Lines and Strength

Synthetic fibers have produced ropes that are a blessing to boatmen. The new ropes are somewhat more expensive than manila and linen rope, but they are stronger for their size, lighter, more comfortable to handle, do not rot or mildew, and are easy to work. One drawback is that they resist bite in tying; therefore knots must be positive. Granny knots and loose knots are out. Elasticity is always a factor to be considered when using any line for anchoring or tying a boat at a dock. Nylon rope is more than four times as elastic as manila when loaded repeatedly; Dacron is about 50 percent more elastic than manila, but is more sensitive than nylon to abrasion from the side. Here, courtesy of Plymouth Yacht Ropes, are comparative strengths for common boating ropes:

ROPES: COMPARATIVE STRENGTH AND WEIGHT

		MINIMUM TENSILE STRENGTH (LBS.)*			AVERAGE TENSILE STRENGTH (LBS.)			
Circ.	Dia.	Ship Brand Manila	Yacht Manila	Linen Yacht	Nylon and Gold Line	"Dacron"	Poly-ethylene	Poly-propylene
9/16"	3/16"	450	525	600	1100	1050	690	1050
3/4"	1/4"	600	688	1020	1850	1750	1150	1700
1"	5/16"	1000	1190	1520	2850	2650	1730	2450
1-1/8"	3/8"	1350	1590	2090	4000	3600	2400	3400
1-1/4"	7/16"	1750	1930	2700	5500	4800	3260	4300
1-1/2"	1/2"	2650	2920	3500	7100	6100	4050	5300
1-3/4"	9/16"	3450	3800	4350	8350	7400	5000	6400
2"	5/8"	4400	4840	5150	10500	9000	6050	7600
2-1/4"	3/4"	5400	5940	7100	14200	12500	9000	10000
2-3/4"	7/8"	7700	8450	9400	19000	16000	12000	13000
3"	1"	9000	9900	12000	24600	20000	15000	16500
3-1/2"	1-1/8"	12000	13200	——	34000	21500	18500	19500
3-3/4"	1-1/4"	13500	14850	——	38000	24500	21000	22000
4-1/2"	1-1/2"	18500	——	——	55000	36000	29000	31500

For the approximate average tensile strength, add 20% for Ship Brand and Yacht Manila Ropes; 20% for Linen Yacht Rope.

RECOMMENDED ANCHOR LINES FOR POWER CRAFT

	ANCHOR	OVER-ALL LENGTH OF BOAT					
		Under 20'	20'–25'	25'–30'	30'–40'	40'–50'	50'–65'
Length of Anchor Lines	Light	100'	100'	100'	125'	150'	180'
	Heavy		150'	180'	200'	250'	300'
Diameter if Nylon	Light	3/8"	3/8"	1/2"	9/16"	3/4"	7/8"
	Heavy		1/2"	9/16"	3/4"	1"	1-1/8"
Diameter if 1st Class Manila	Light	1/2"	1/2"	5/8"	3/4"	1"	1-1/4"
	Heavy		5/8"	3/4"	1"	1-3/8"	1-1/2"
Diam. if Plymouth Bolt Manila	Light	7/16"	7/16"	9/16"	5/8"	7/8"	1"
	Heavy		9/16"	5/8"	7/8"	1-1/8"	1-1/4"

Knots Used in Anchoring and Mooring

Part of the fun in owning a boat is in learning and using boat knots. Most of the knots commonly used in boating are illustrated in the Camping section of this book. Here are ways to make knots and splices needed for anchoring and mooring your boat.

THE EYE SPLICE

This splice is used in the end of a rope for mooring and anchoring. It is the strongest and most permanent rope loop. After end strands are unlaid, the rope is bent to form an eye of the size required, and end strands are spliced into the strands on the standing rope.

SHORT SPLICE

This is the strongest of splices for joining ends of two pieces of rope, but it cannot be used to run through a pulley due to the bulk of the splice.

1. Lash rope about twelve diameters from each end (A). Unlay the strands up to the lashings. Whip strands to prevent untwisting and put together as in diagram above, alternating the strands from each end. Pull up taut.

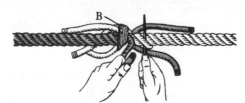

2. Now tie down all the strands temporarily (B). Take off the lashing from one side of the rope and raise one strand on this side, using a fid. Take the middle strand of the opposite side. Tuck it over one strand and under the raised strand. Pull it up taut.

3. Tuck against the twist or "lay" of the rope. What happens is that the tuck goes over one strand, under the second, and out between the second and third.

4. Roll the rope toward you. Pick up the second strand. Repeat the same operation. Then do it again with the third strand. You have now made one full tuck.

To taper the splice, first make one more tuck just like the first one. Then make the third tuck the same way, but first cut off ⅓ of the yarns from the strands. For the fourth tuck, cut off ½ the remaining yarn.

For the untapered short splice, you do not cut the strands. You just make three more tucks, exactly like the first one.

5. Take both lashings (which were applied in No. 1 and No. 2) off the other side of the rope. Repeat above operations.

6. To finish, cut off ends of strands, leaving about one or two inches protruding.

To Splice Nylon Rope — The above procedure applies to splicing of nylon and other synthetic ropes except that one additional full tuck should be used.

LONG SPLICE

Slightly weaker than the short splice, but it allows the rope to run freely through a properly-sized pueely and causes less wear at the point of splicing.

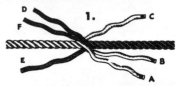

1. Unlay the end of each rope about 15 turns and place the ropes together, alternating the strands from each end, as shown above.

2. Start with any opposite pair, unlay one strand and replace it with strand from the other part. Repeat operation with another pair of strands in the opposite direction as shown above.

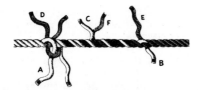

3. Now tie each pair of opposing strands, as B and E above, with an overhand knot, tuck each strand twice (see Figure 4), as in the Short Splice, and then twice more as for the Tapered Splice—see page 30. Or, halve each strand (see A and D), and tie with an overhand knot before tucking. By this latter method a smaller splice results—but at a considerable sacrifice of strength.

4. Roll and pound well before cutting strands off close to rope.

BOWLINE

The bowline is often used for temporary anchor knots. It never jams or slips if properly tied.

THE DOUBLE BOWLINE

To Tie: Make an overhand loop with the end held toward you, exactly as in the ordinary Bowline. The difference being that you pass the end through the loop *twice*—making *two* lower loops, A and B. The end is then passed *behind* the standing part and down through the first loop again as in the ordinary Bowline. Pull tight. Used as a seat sling, the outside loop B goes under the arms—inside loop A forms the seat.

THE BOWLINE IN BIGHT

Here's a useful knot to know when you want to attach tackle to, say, the middle of a line when both ends of it are made fast. To Tie: Grasp the rope where you want the new knot, shape it into a loop in one hand and strike this against the two lines leading to the loop, held in the other hand. Then complete the first bight used in tying a regular Bowline. Now, open the loop after it has passed through the bight and bring the whole knot through it. Pull the loop tight over the standing part.

THE RUNNING BOWLINE

Tie the regular Bowline around a loop of its own standing part. This makes an excellent slip knot, commonly used to retrieve spars, rigging, etc. And with lighter rope or twine, it makes a good knot for tightening at the beginning of tying a package.

CLOVE HITCH

This is the most effective quick way to tie a boat line to a mooring post. It can be tied in the middle or end of a rope, but it is apt to slip if tied at the end. To prevent slipping, make a half-hitch in the end to the standing part.

Preparing for Winter Storage

This work is necessary to keep your boat serviceable and to protect your investment in it. If you live where you can enjoy year-round boating, there are important semi-annual maintenance jobs that you will recognize. If you can store your boat at home the job will be greatly simplified, but if you store it in a boatyard you may have to work within the yard's schedule. In deciding whether to store your boat outside or in a heated garage, for instance, there are two dangers that must be avoided: formation of ice on the boat, and continual dry heat. Small aluminum boats are affected less than wood, fiberglass, or fabric ones. Hard freezing and ice can pop fastenings, open seams, split and check the surface, and cause permanent warp in straight lines. Dry heat for long periods can destroy the resins in woods (including wood stringers and outfittings in other than wood boats) and dry out calking and seam compounds. If you store your boat outdoors in natural humidity conditions, keep it covered so that water cannot collect and form ice. Indoors or out, free ventilation is essential so that condensation can evaporate.

● First, make sure your boat is properly cradled for storage. If you have a trailer that fits your boat you have no problem. Level the trailer on chocks, wheels off the ground. If you own a small aluminum boat, it will store well turned face down, resting on the strongly built gunwales. If you must build a cradle for a larger boat, make accurate templates and cut cradle supports for transom, engine bed, construction center, and stem at least.

● Clean the bottom and outside hull entirely of algae, fungi, and barnacles. This must be done immediately, before they harden and dry fast. At this time you'll get a good look at the condition and know what repairs have to be made before spring launching.

● Scrub down the entire boat inside, starting at the top. Flush and clean out bilges with bilge cleaner. Flush out freshwater tanks, fish and bait boxes, and freshwater lines with disinfectant solution and let them dry. Remove all traces of salt water, polish, clean, and spray on preservative.

● Wash canvas tops, curtains, and rope lines with mild soap and rinse with fresh water. Spray with preservative before storing in a dry place.

● Treat serious rust at once. Clean down to bare metal or remove and replace. Reputty fastenings, spray fixed hardware with clear vinyl, spray moving hardware with light machine oil.

● Make sure every corner of the boat, every fitting and joint, is dry, clean, and free of fungi. Treat inside corners in a wood boat with dry-rot compound. Put dessicants wherever needed. Air the boat by opening all hatches on each dry, bright day.

Follow motor storage procedures given in the owner's manual. Cover these points particularly:

● Flush cooling system with fresh water and rust inhibitor, then drain system well.

● Disconnect fuel lines and run idle until out of fuel.

● Disconnect battery, wipe connectors and terminals clean, then follow maker's battery storage procedures.

● Clean carburetor bowl with automative carburetor cleaner or lacquer thinner. Slosh the cleaner fluid around in a portable gas tank and pour out through the fuel lines and drain it well. This removes gummy substance left by fuel.

● Remove spark plugs with a spark-plug wrench, squirt lubricating oil into each cylinder, then turn crankshaft by hand to distribute the oil. Replace spark plugs.

● Leave motor head and lower unit clean of heavy dirt, rust, and grease deposits. Wipe the head and lower unit with an oily cloth.

● Make sure lower unit grease reservoir is left full.

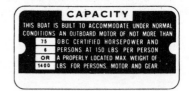

Some boats have a metal capacity plate, usually mounted near the operator's position.

Preparing for Spring Launching

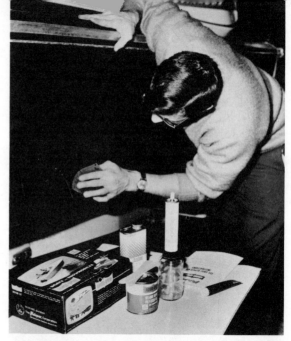

Most owners start too late, missing a month or two of good boating before they are ready to launch. Use the post-holiday winter quiet to do inside work you want to accomplish: Build cabinets, a fish box, circulating bait well, other basement shop jobs. Keep your eye on the old girl throughout the winter if she's stored outside. At the first robin, go down and look her over, head to foot. Make an estimate of nobs, tools, and materials you'll need. First, do the outside hull—everything it needs to give you a safe and trouble-free season. A wood hull should be sanded down to clean, bare wood, whether you are restoring just a place or two where needed or refinishing the complete hull. Peeling and cracking on top indicates trouble underneath. Down to bare wood, you may discover the source. Sand the wood smooth, fill cracks and holes and over fastenings, replace damaged boards, and dust clean before starting to paint.

Marine paints will take ten times the abuse and last three times longer than they did twenty years ago; but they have their price. Proceed carefully until you know what to do. Get paint-maker's recommendations and specifications for your hull. Polyester paints will give you an amazingly tough coat when properly applied, but you will probably do better with an epoxy-based paint over fiberglass. Talk to your dealer and other owners. If you want to paint an originally unpainted aluminum boat, get the boat-maker's specifications; certain paints can't be used.

Before you paint a bare fiberglass hull or cabin, think twice. You will not be able to sand and strip it as you did the wood hull before. To repaint, you have to leave the first paint or risk damaging the gel coat. Most owners for this reason try to bleach out discolorations and stains. Spots can be scoured and buffed. Ask for recommended materials at a marine store. Damaged spots can be patched with fiberglass. Best overall treatment is to wax well with marine-grade wax and sail on. If you must paint it, use steel-wool which will give tooth for the paint, and use paints recommended by manufacturers.

Any surface must be absolutely clean before repainting. On cabin woods, spar varnish is usually used; it's tough and looks boaty. Oiled and waxed cabin wood is serviceable and looks more homey. Whatever your choice, on high-wear places that scuff and go bare quickly, use a good grade of clear plastic vinyl on top, renewed every spring.

If you find mildew or water inside, note how they got in and repair the damage. Next fall you will use more dessicant in some corners, buy a better tarp, or add weatherstripping to your windows. Neutralize foul odors before you launch; it's easy. Try the supermarket.

Flush out all freshwater systems again with disinfectant, fill the tanks, and turn on the pressure. A drip is a leak. Fix it before you sail and you'll have a drier, safer boat. Check all through-hull fittings. If you find any sign of leaking or rot, restore the watertight fit and get the best advice you can to make it permanent.

Scratches, nicks, and color fading on a fiberglass boat can be repaired with an inexpensive kit from Valspar. Kit contains a polyester base material, mix jar for use with power spray, hardening agent, spatulas, dip tube, acetone, sandpaper, and instructions. After wax and high gloss has been removed with #400 sandpaper, acetone wipe-down insures a clean surface. Gouges and deep scratches are filled first, then gel coat is applied with power spray. Large range of colors can be mixed to match boat colors. Kit can be used repeatedly by cleaning utensils with acetone after each use.

Look at your motor-owner's manual and see what it advises for launching make-ready. Make sure these points are covered:

● Check spark plugs; replace if necessary with new plugs correctly gapped to maker's specs.

● Inspect all ignition wiring, wipe clean and use electrical spray. Replace any burned or cracked wiring. Look for trouble points.

● Replace distributor points if pitted. Points and timing must be set to engine-maker's specs using a dwell meter.
  Replace fuel filter. Replace oil filter as well in inboard engine.

● Discard all fuel left from the previous season, clean tanks and lines with anti-sludge liquid. Change inboard's oil. Grease according to owner's manual and maker's specs.

● Fill fuel tanks, start motor, then inspect all fuel lines and cocks for leaks, wear, and malfunction. Discard any part of the fuel system that might give trouble during the season and replace it carefully.

● Clear all vents and breather holes.

PREPARING FOR SPRING LAUNCHING

● Check operation of bilge blower by switching it off after one minute's operation, then sniffing carefully in bilges, under engine hatch, and around gas tanks and lines. Add a second blower if there is any doubt that the blower is effective.

● Install new drive belt on water pump. Check coolant temperature on gauge after warmup. If engine is running hot, flush out cooling system and check water-pump operation.

● Change oil in lower unit. Push new grease through lower-unit reservoir, using lubricants to maker's specs.

● When the engine is warm, check transmission fluid and fill.

● Inspect propeller for heavy nicks. If it should be replaced, do it now. It will be more trouble to do it later.

PAINT REQUIREMENTS FOR DIFFERENT BOATS

TYPE and SIZE		TOPSIDE	BOTTOM	WATERLINE	DECK	VARNISH	INTERIOR	ENGINE
Dinghy	10'	1 Qt.	1 Pt.	—	—	1½ Qts.	—	—
Rowboat	14'	2 Qts.	1 Qt.	—	—	—	—	—
Outboard	14'	2 Qts.	1 Qt.	—	1 Pt.	1½ Qts.	—	½ Pt.
Runabout	18'	2 Qts.	2 Qts.	½ Pt.	1 Qt.	1 Qt.	—	½ Pt. or 16 oz. Spray
Runabout	24'	2 Qts.	3 Qts.	½ Pt.	1½ Qts.	3 Qts.	—	1 Pt. or 16 oz. Spray
Utility	24'	2 Qts.	3 Qts.	½ Pt.	1½ Qts.	1 Qt.	—	1 Pt. or 16 oz. Spray
Cruiser	25'	3 Qts.	3 Qts.	1 Pt.	2 Qts.	2 Qts.	2 Qts.	1 Pt. or 16 oz. Spray
Cruiser	32'	2 Gals.	1½ Gals.	1 Pt.	2 Qts.	3 Qts.	2 Qts.	1 Pt. or 16 oz. Spray
Auxiliary	36'	2 Gals.	2 Gals.	1 Pt.	1 Gal.	1 Gal.	3 Qts.	1 Pt. or 2 16 oz. Spray
Cruiser	40'	2½ Gals.	2 Gals.	1 Pt.	1½ Gals.	1 Gal.	1 Gal.	1 Pt. or 2 16 oz. Spray
Yacht	60'	4 Gals.	5 Gals.	1 Qt.	3½ Gals.	2½ Gals.	3 Gals.	1½ Qt. or 2 16 oz. Spray
Sailboat	20'	2 Qts.	3 Qts.	1 Pt.	1 Gal.	2 Qts.	—	—

The above quantities are for repainting or revarnishing with two coats. For two coats applied to a bare surface, double the above quantities.

Boat Trailers

Trailering a boat on rough roads poses few problems if the tow-car's suspension and clearance are adequate.

What size boat is trailerable? That is really a conundrum. The answer depends on how much you are willing to put into trailering. Each year's new-boat announcements include a large cabin cruiser with the claim, ". . . and it can be trailered!" The fact is that it actually *can* be trailered, but it may be a professional transport job. You will need a heavy-duty custom-built trailer, and should have a heavy-duty truck to make it go. And then it might do the boat no good. It's not a consumer proposition.

Then there are the very small boats you see rattling around on a trailer that weighs twice as much. A newcomer to boating has bought a special bargain offer of a boat and trailer combined, when he should have been advised to car-top his boat or load it in the back of a wagon. Trailering is no sport unless you really need a trailer; then it can be an asset.

Common boat sizes for regular trailering are 14 to 20 feet. It is true that some 12-footers weigh more than 120 or 130 pounds, weight that can be lifted to the top of a car easily by two people. If you buy a heavy 12-footer or a light 14-footer, consider buying a one-man boat loader that will make cartopping practical. On the other end of the range, boats over 20 feet (and some less) commonly have a deep bow, broad beam, and big weight that make all sorts of problems in trailering. For a starter, most state and all federal highways have a width limit of eight feet; beyond that you'll need a special permit and arrangements to travel.

If you are going to buy a boat in the prime size range for trailering, should you get a trailer at the same time? You will probably get a better fit for your boat if you do. The maker can supply information about trailer specifications for current-model hulls, and the dealer will probably carry trailers that suit.

But if you live near the water, why have a trailer? First, you save on mooring fees and winter storage. Second, your boat will be a much bigger asset if you can take it along on vacations, trail it to another water when you want to fish and hunt or camp away from home. Keeping a boat on its trailer in your yard, you can keep bottom fouling cleaned off instead of facing a big job once or twice a year. Make it part of your routine when washing and waxing the car, and you will have a hull that is always in good shape. Keep a tarp over the boat and motor when it's idle on the trailer. When it sits in your own yard you are relieved of worry about vandalism at the mooring.

Choosing a Trailer

The best advice is to get a trailer one size bigger than your present boat requires. This will accommodate the occasional extra-heavy load you will pack in it. If you get a trailer larger than that, your boat will not be properly supported and the trailer will be awkward to tow, bouncing around because the boat is not heavy enough to hold in on the road.

Proper hull support is essential in a trailer. This is where the boat maker's advice is important. Three critical points are: full support at the transom, at the bottom forefoot, and at the construction center, either where greatest weight is built in amidships or under the engine stringers in an inboard boat. You must avoid a trailer mismatch that will, over a period of time, cause the hull to hook or rocker. A well-engineered trailer for a boat of 500 pounds or more will have pairs of strong, securely set rollers on good bearings at frequent intervals for the entire bottom length.

Regardless of size, the trailer must enable you to back down to the water and launch your boat efficiently without getting the trailer-wheel hubs in the water. This may mean that you will need a tilt bed. If so, make sure the tilt operates easily fully loaded, and that the pivots are built to last.

Winch quality is important for heavier boats. Wobbly or ill-fitting crank, wheel, and ratchet won't do. For a boat of 1,500 pounds or more you might consider adding an electric winch. It saves a lot of knuckle busting, and it will be well-made mechanically so that slips won't occur.

Trailer suspension, wheel mounts, and general construction should be spelled out by the trailer maker. Study these and get full information from the dealer about use and maintenance. Leaf springs are good on a heavy trailer; a soft ride is not important, while good support is. If you trail 3,500 pounds or more load, tandem wheels are needed.

You will have to look up state laws on trailers for your region, then equip your trailer and the tow vehicle according to the most exacting of these. Should you have brakes on the trailer the laws specify over what weights trailer brakes are required; but you may decide you want brakes even if yours is below the limit. In that case look into electric brakes that operate in tandem with your car's foot pedal but can be operated independently with a hand control. Quality trailer brakes are practically foolproof, make driving safer and

You can trailer big, heavy boat if you have to, but come prepared for it. The car should be equipped with extra-heavy-duty suspension. It's really a job for a truck.

Hitch stabilizer is important in towing a heavy load at turnpike speeds. Stabilizers for loads of 3,500 pounds and more have heavy-duty torsion bars flanking the tongue.

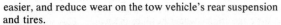

This trailer has "bull's eye" rollers that guide boat to center when loading, but it lacks side rollers needed for a hull of this size. Operator keeps wheel hubs out of water to avoid having to repack wheel bearings.

easier, and reduce wear on the tow vehicle's rear suspension and tires.

Insist on a frame-mounted hitch, even though the salesman may try to give you a shallow hitch bolted to the body pan when you buy that new wagon. As for bumper-mounted hitches, they are dangerous. With a frame-mounted hitch you will be able to step up in weight over a big range without additional expense, and you'll trail your present boat without worry. You will need an umbilical electric hookup to your car's electrical system for trailer lights and brakes or other accessories. Cable, clamps, and plugs come in a package at reasonable price. On your car you'll need "western" type rear-view mirrors—big rectangular ones mounted on arms on each side that let you see around the trailer. For a trailer load of 3,000 pounds or more you should have an equalizing hitch that compensates a big load in normal travel and substantially reduces danger in a crash stop.

Loading Your Boat and Trailer

Most makers recommend loading with five to seven percent more weight ahead of the trailer axle. This prevents fishtailing and gives you good load control. If you are going on an extended trip with camping and sporting gear loaded

inside the boat (you and your family will be happy to get it out of the car), watch the weight distribution, weigh big items as they are loaded, and don't under any circumstances exceed the maker's maximum weight limit. Your trailer will be designed to haul your boat and motor with the correct load in front of the axle. Additional weight inside the boat should maintain this distribution, or the position of the boat on the trailer bed should be adjusted accordingly. A well-made trailer will let you do this.

Trailer Maintenance

Wheel bearings are the critical point. When traveling, stop every few hours to feel for excessive heat at the hubs. If the news is bad, let them cool off, then creep to the nearest service station and have them repack the wheel bearings. Have the bearings inspected before each trip, and have them repacked at the start of each season.

Keep the hitch and mount free of rust, repaint each season with metal paint on clean metal, and grease moving joints on an equalizing hitch only as the maker specifies. You'll find that a well-made boat trailer will last at least as long as the boat if it's well cared for. And you will be delighted when you learn what you can take along trailered in the boat.

Safe Boating

Outdoor sportsmen don't have a clean record when it comes to accidents afloat. Do you know why? It has little to do with the perquisites of fishing and hunting, but much to do with neglecting to control the boat and guard personal safety aboard. A sportsman who has not schooled himself in basic boating safety and safe habits will forget about it when the action gets lively. Here's your chance to start right.

Basic Tool Kit

Every boat must be equipped to get home on its own. The exact selection of tools, spare parts, and supplies necessary must be suited to your boat and motor and to problems you are most likely to encounter.

Ordinary pliers
Vice-grip pliers
Diagonal-cutting pliers
Long-nose electrician's pliers
Screwdrivers
Spark-plug wrench to fit
Combination open-end and box wrenches in sizes 3/8" to 3/4"
Sharp knife

Every boat should carry basic safety, emergency, and handling equipment. On the left is a hand-operated pump, on the right a first-aid kit and boat hook (for taking a line that's thrown). In the first mate's hand is the fire extinguisher.

Spare Parts

Spark plugs of correct specifications
Distributor cap, rotor, condenser, point set
Fuel pump and filter
Oil filter
Water-pump impeller
V-belts to match each size used
Spare fuel lines, cocks, and fittings
Gaskets and hoses
Bailing-pump diaphragm
Fuses and bulbs to double for each used

All-Purpose Kit

50-ft. chalk line
Molly screws and pot menders for small cracks and holes
Nails, screws, bolts and nuts, washers
Hose clamps
Electrical tape
Insulated wire
Cotter pins
Packing
Elastic plastic bandage material
Small blocks of wood that can be carved
Machine oil

Outboard Motor Troubleshooting Checklist

● Check gas supply and tank pressure; squeeze bulb several times.

● Check to be sure propeller is not wrapped in weeds, line, or net. If line is wrapped around prop, try slow reverse to loosen it; then cut off pieces until you can pull the rest free.

● Look for loose ignition wire at battery terminals.

● Remove ignition wire from any spark plug, crank the motor; spark should jump from wire end to engine head; if no spark, check back to ignition switch.

● If you have a hot spark, look into fuel feed; pull gas feed line off from side of outboard; blow through line until you hear bubbles in tank.

● Clean the carburetor bowl and fuel filter.

● Did you remember to add oil to gas tank in right proportion?

Safe Boating Procedures

First, it is important to know your boat. Get familiar with its equipment and discover its limitations. If it's a livery rental, check it over completely before you push off.

Make a habit of checking off safety equipment aboard. First, locate the safety items required by law. Then compare your optional equipment with the Coast Guard's list of recommended equipment in the same section.

Count the life preservers, and make sure that each passenger has one that will keep him afloat in the water.

Warning Display Signals

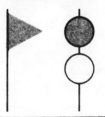

SMALL CRAFT* **DAYTIME:** Red Pennant.

NIGHTTIME: Red Light Over White Light.

Indicates: Forecast winds as high as 33 knots and sea conditions considered dangerous to small-craft operations.

GALE **DAYTIME:** Two Red Pennants.

NIGHTTIME: White Light Over Red Light.

Indicates: Forecast winds in the range 34-47 knots.

STORM **DAYTIME:** Square Red Flag With Black Square Centered.

NIGHTTIME: Two Red Lights.

Indicates: Forecast winds 48 knots and above no matter how high the wind speed. If the winds are associated with a tropical cyclone (hurricane), storm warnings indicate forecast winds of 48-63 knots.

HURRICANE **DAYTIME:** Two Square Red Flags With Black Squares Centered.

NIGHTTIME: White Light Between Two Red Lights.

Indicates: Forecast winds of 64 knots and above, displayed only in connection with a hurricane.

Check the fuel supply, the condition of the tank and feed line. Make sure the spark is strong and regular. Take along at least 1½ times as much fuel as you estimate you will need. If you run into heavy waves, your boat will take more fuel to go the same distance.

Carry a map you can read—a proper chart if the water is a large one—and a compass that is reliable near machinery.

Put tackle, guns, decoys, nets, and other gear where they are secure and won't clutter walkways and footing. There is a bonus for the sportsman who keeps everything in place on board: He always knows where to find it when the action gets hot.

Gasoline vapors are explosive and will settle in the low areas of a boat. Keep doors, hatches, ports, and chests closed during fueling, stoves and pilot lights off, electrical circuits off, and absolutely no smoking! Keep the fill nozzle in firm contact with the fill neck to prevent static spark. Don't spill, for you'll have to dry it up before starting the engine. Do not use gasoline appliances aboard—they're lethal risks. Use alcohol and other less volatile, unpressurized fuels.

After fueling, ventilate thoroughly before pressing the starter. One minute is the minimum safe ventilation time. Big boats should be ventilated longer, with effective blowers operating and all ports opened. Keep your fuel lines in perfect condition and the boat's bilges clean.

Electrical equipment, switches, and wiring are some prime sources of boat fires and explosions. Avoid knife switches or other arcing equipment aboard. Keep batteries clean and ventilated.

Do not overload your boat. Make sure you have safely adequate freeboard before casting off. Look ahead to water conditions and weather changes you might encounter.

Keep an alert lookout. If you have a boat over 20 feet, name your mate and agree he'll keep lookout any time you can't. You have more to watch than other boats and shallow water. Watch for obstructions such as big rocks and floating logs.

Swimmers are hard to see in the water. Running through swimmers or a swimming area is the most sensitive violation a boat can make. If in doubt, give beaches and rafts a wide swing.

Your wake is potent. You can swamp small craft such as a canoe or rowboat, damage shorelines and shore property, disturb sleepers, and ruin fish and wildlife sport for hours by running fast through small passages and shallows.

Learn the Rules of the Road and obey them at all times. Copies are available free from the Coast Guard. Most collisions are caused by those "one-time" violations.

Make sure at least one other person aboard knows how to operate the boat and motor in case you are disabled or fall overboard.

Know a plan of action you will take in emergencies—man overboard, a bad leak, motor won't run, collision, bad storm, or troublesome passenger.

Storm signals and danger signs are often informal. Learn to read the weather, and keep alert to what passing boats are trying to tell you.

Wear your life preserver—or at least make sure children and non-swimmers wear theirs. In any case, don't sit on life preservers.

In a capsizing, remember that your are safer if you stay with the boat, where you can be seen. It will help you stay afloat until help arrives.

Under Coast Guard legislation, it is illegal for anyone to build, sell, or use a craft that does not conform to safety regulations. Check with your dealer, and check with yourself to make sure your boat measures up.

PART *VII* / Archery

Bows

Archery as a sport today is practiced in a variety of ways. There are archers who prefer to shoot at conventional targets; roving bowmen who ramble through woodlands testing their skill on tree stumps and other natural targets; field archers who roam a course shooting at targets that simulate hunting conditions. Then there are bowhunters, some of whom have taken every game animal from the groundhog to the bull elephant with well-placed arrows. An interesting offshoot of bowhunting is bowfishing, in which a harpoon-type rig is used to shoot coarse fish.

Like the hunter who uses various types of guns designed for different species of game, the bowman also uses various types of bows according to his sport. While there are differences among bows—those designed for championship performance on the target range, others for plinking and roving, and still others for hunting big-game animals—foremost to remember when purchasing any bow is its draw or pull weight, that is, the amount of strength required to pull the string back to full draw. "Overbowing" is the cardinal sin of the beginner.

Compound Bows

The acceptance of compound bows—especially for hunting deer and other good-sized game—has been so pronounced in the last few years that some manufacturers make no other type or else make only a few recurve models. This newest concept in archery was invented by H. W. Allen of Billings, Missouri, and most compounds are manufactured under license from Mr. Allen. A compound bow looks a bit strange but is simple in operation. Attached to its relatively short, stout limbs is a small pulley system. A conventional bow string is connected to two strands of cable that run over the wheels—an idler pulley plus an eccentric pulley at each end of the limbs—in the manner of a block and tackle. This device solves bow-weight problems, vastly increases the power and accuracy of an arrow, and eases the draw and release.

To understand some of the reasons, consider how energy is applied in a firearm. A rifle produces greater bullet velocity than a handgun because the rifle's longer barrel applies gas pressure for a longer distance, thus increasing the foot-pounds of energy exerted on the projectile. The eccentric pulleys on a compound's limb tips accomplish the same thing by applying maximum pull weight for a greater number of inches. With an ordinary recurve bow, the pressure decreases steadily from the instant of release as the bow string moves forward. With a compound, the peak pull-weight poundage is about at mid-draw. Thus, as the bow string moves forward, the pressure increases to a peak before decreasing. This substantially raises the foot-pounds of energy applied to the arrow.

Also, with a conventional bow the release pressure must overcome the inertia not only of the arrow but of the bow

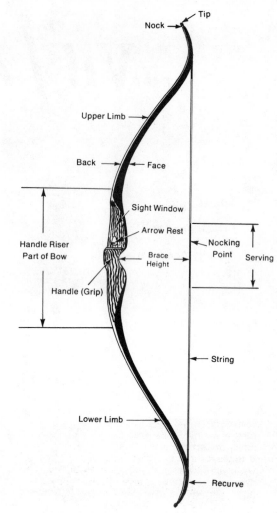

THE PARTS OF A RECURVE BOW

string and the moving part of each limb. In a compound, limb-tip travel is reduced from about 8 inches to 3 and inertia is greatly reduced. In a conventional bow with a 50-pound pull weight, 50 pounds must propel the weight of the limbs 8 inches while also propelling the arrow and center of the string 20 inches to the string-rest position. With the pulleys and three strands (bow string plus two strands of cable), the same pull results in three times the power—150 pounds.

Due to the action of the eccentric pulleys, the pull weight reaches a maximum and then relaxes—eases off—somewhat before full draw is reached. This reduces finger strain and muscle fatigue at full draw, making a compound bow easier to shoot well. The same principle also permits the use of lighter arrows. A compound with a 50-pound peak setting

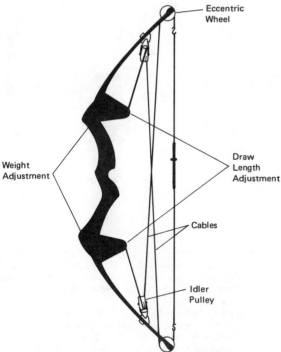

Eccentric Wheel

Weight Adjustment

Draw Length Adjustment

Cables

Idler Pulley

THE PARTS OF A COMPOUND BOW

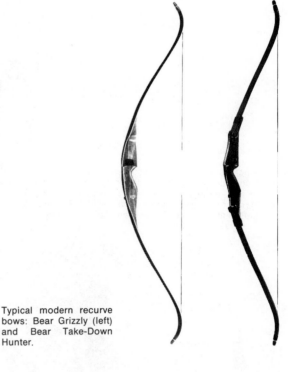

Typical modern recurve bows: Bear Grizzly (left) and Bear Take-Down Hunter.

will hold at full draw at approximately 40 pounds, so an arrow spined for a 40-pound pull is about right. (Manufacturers include arrow-matching instructions with their bows, and these instructions should be followed.) The lighter arrows, released in the compound manner, have a flatter trajectory—a bonus advantage.

In many compound bows, draw lengths can be adjusted somewhat, and peak weight can be adjusted within a 10-pound range. Target compounds are usually 56 to 58 inches long. Hunting models generally range from 48 to 50 inches, and bows to be used for both purposes are about 51 inches long. The weight of the bows ranges from about $3\frac{1}{2}$ to $4\frac{1}{4}$ pounds. They're made in either a one-piece style or in the take-down style. The cables are steel. The handle

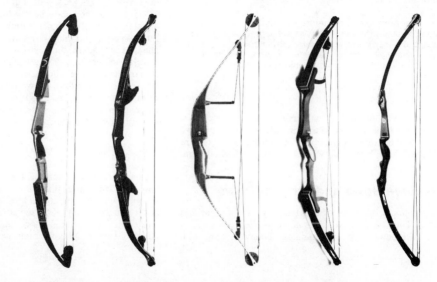

Typical compound bows (from left): Bear Kodiak Special, Bear Magnum, Browning Tracker, Pro-Line Hurricane IV, and York Coronet Hunter.

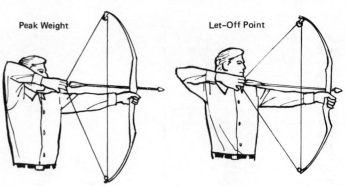

Peak Weight   Let–Off Point

Drawing shows why the compound bow is easy to hold at full draw and release smoothly. Peak draw weight is reached when archer has drawn bow string only partway back. Weight then eases down as string comes back to let-off point, so less strength is needed to pull it back and hold it steady.

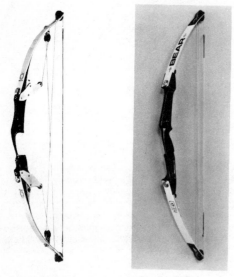

Two of Bear Archery's compounds. Starfire (left) is a six-wheel tournament bow with locking keyways for precise limb alignment and 6½-inch sight window for 80-meter shots. Charger is a two-wheel split-limb tournament bow with laminated hard-rock-maple limbs. Both have adjustable peak weights.

risers may be magnesium or hardwood. In top-quality bows, the limbs are laminated wood and fiberglass. Less expensive models may be solid fiberglass. Even these, however, are more costly than high-quality bows of conventional design.

Recurve Bows and Straight Bows

Conventional bows are of two basic types—straight and recurve. The straight bow, as its name implies, has straight limbs. Such bows were once standard. Today, few are sold,

but there are archers who enjoy the ancient and classic style, and some of these people make their own straight bows. The limbs of a recurve bow curve back and then, near the tips, curve forward. This type has become standard.

The modern recurve bow is popular because it casts an arrow at greater speed with less draw weight than older styles. A relatively short recurve bow has excellent cast and is also maneuverable in brush, so models measuring 50 to 60 inches are popular for hunting. Longer bows—some of them 64 to 70 inches—are more stable, easier to draw, and smoother to release, so long models are used for target shooting. A bow for both purposes will have a compromise length.

Like compounds, conventional recurves are made both in one-piece style and take-down models. A take-down bow can be packed in a suitcase by a traveling hunter, and this type of bow is strong, reliable, and safe.

Wood alone is still used in making some bows—primarily inexpensive models. Lemon and hickory are the most common woods. Hickory withstands cold better than lemon-wood, but neither material produces the best cast. Various metals (especially tubular aluminum) have also been used by bowyers. Aluminum bows are unaffected by temperature changes but, again, the cast is poor. Solid fiberglass is used, too. It's impervious to weather but lacks the shooting qualities of "composite" bows, which are now most common. These are laminations of two or more different materials—metal, wood, fiberglass, and various synthetics. The laminated composite bows produce excellent cast and are, in general, better than any other type.

Draw Weight

For tournament shooting (as well as plinking), select a bow that you can easily bring to full draw and hold for 10 seconds without shaking unduly. A little tremor is all right, but if you are forcing yourself to hold the bow at full draw, it is too heavy for you. An accompanying chart shows recommended draw weights for men, women, and youngsters.

A hunter should use a bow with as much draw weight as he can shoot comfortably. This will give an arrow the speed needed for penetration on game. It will also produce flatter trajectory—hence, more hits on game at unknown distances. Moreover, the faster an arrow arrives, the less chance a game animal has to "jump string" (dodge the arrow). For hunting deer, a recurve bow should have a minimum draw weight of about 50 pounds, even if your state's game laws set a somewhat lower minimum, and a compound bow should have a minimum peak weight of 50 to 55 pounds. With a little practice, an average man can usually shoot a bow 5 or 10 pounds heavier than that with ease.

Of course, a lighter draw weight is adequate for smaller game, and a heavier draw is required for game larger than deer. Recommended weights are listed in the accompanying chart. With a compound bow, the draw weight is the peak weight—the amount you must pull through before the weight decreases at full draw. With a recurve bow, draw weight is the number of pounds it takes to draw the bow string back to 28 inches. For each inch of draw above or below 28 inches, add or subtract 2 pounds to determine the approximate weight of your personal draw length.

Bow Handling

Remember these "don'ts" when handling a bow. A bow at full draw, according to the manufacturer's specifications, is usually considered to be $^8/_{10}$ broken. For example, if you have a bow that is designed for 30-inch arrows and pulls 50 pounds at full draw, at that particular point it is $^8/_{10}$

RECOMMENDED DRAW WEIGHTS FOR TARGET SHOOTING

	20 lb. & under	20 lb.	25 lb.	30 lb.	35 lb.	40 lb.	40 lb. & over
Children 6-12	X	X					
Teen (Girl)		X	X				
Teen (Boy)		X	X	X			
Ladies			X	X	X		
Men				X	X	X	

RECOMMENDED DRAW WEIGHTS FOR HUNTING

Game	Rabbit and Squirrel	Coyote and Fox	Deer and Bear	Elk	Moose
30–40	X				
40–50	X	X			
50–60	X	X	X		
60–70	X	X	X	X	X
70–80	X	X	X	X	X

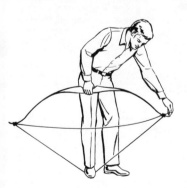

Bow stringer places identical stress on both limbs. Slip leather pockets over bow tips, place foot over center of cord, and pull up. Bowstring will slip into nock.

Lacking a bow stringer, one way to string a bow is to brace the tip against your instep, holding the bow as shown, and flex it by applying opposite pressure with each hand. Then slide the bowstring into the nock.

Third method of stringing bow is to insert right leg between string and bow, hooking tip over shoe, and use thigh as a fulcrum to flex the bow as you slip string into nock.

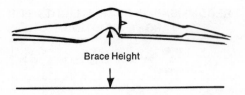

Correct brace height, given with manufacturer's specifications, is measured from bowstring to handle as shown by arrows.

broken. If you drew the bow past the 30-inch mark, you would subject it to serious stress that could cause it to break.

Another way to shatter a bow is to pull to full draw without an arrow and then release the string. Under no circumstance release a bowstring without an arrow in the bow or attempt to overdraw the bow.

Quality bows can also be broken or have limbs twisted by incorrect stringing techniques. String a bow carefully and you'll have it for years. Perhaps the most efficient way to string a bow is with a bow stringer, a device designed to place identical stress on both limbs as in actual shooting. It also eliminates the possibility of the bow accidentally jumping out of your hands and causing injury to yourself or bystanders. The bow stringer is a stout length of nylon cord with leather pockets fitted at both ends which are slipped over the bow tips. By placing your foot over the center of the cord, the bow is readily raised and the limbs bent, permitting the string to be slipped into the nock. To prevent the bowstring from slipping off the opposite nock when stringing, place an elastic band or bow-tip protector over the lower nock and secure the string in place.

Without the assistance of a bow stringer, there are two acceptable ways to string your bow, and they are shown in the accompanying illustrations.

Once the bow has been strung, brace height is an important consideration. Brace height is the distance from the bowstring to the deepest cut in the handle on the face of the bow, below the arrow shelf. Proper brace height for a particular bow is given in the manufacturer's specifications; but this is not a rigid figure, and by altering it slightly some archers find that they shoot better. Brace height can be altered by twisting the bowstring to shorten it or by untwisting it to lengthen it. Care, however, should be used not to twist the string excessively, for this will damage it, and ultimately the bow.

The proper brace height for your bow depends entirely on your shooting style and the conditions under which you are shooting. There is no brace height which will give you maximum performance every time. For example, as your bow "warms up" during a sustained shooting session, the string will have a tendency to stretch. Conversely, after a period of idleness, the string will return to its original length. For this reason it is important that you "tune" your bowstring before and during every shooting session.

Proper brace height for your bow and your individual shooting style will give you the least amount of wrist slap, string noise, and vibration, and an arrow that does not wobble in flight.

Bow Care

When not shooting always keep your bow unstrung and hang it vertically or lay it across pegs supporting both limbs. Keep your bow in a case when transporting it, to protect it from damage. When using a bow during rain or snow, coat it generously with high-grade automobile or furniture wax to protect its finish, and wipe it dry after a day afield in bad weather. Prior to sustained periods of storage, apply a generous coat of wax to protect the bow's finish. In cold weather, "flex" the bow several times to warm it up before shooting.

Another important consideration is the nocking point that is added to the bowstring serving. A nocking point is nothing more than a small piece of tape, attached to the bowstring at right angles to the bow to prevent the arrow from slipping up and down or off the bowstring, to aid in consistent shooting. To locate the nocking point, place an arrow on the bowstring as you would when actually shooting the bow, and add the nocking point above, below, or on both sides of the arrow on the string serving. This is essential for the bowhunter, who hasn't time to position his arrow correctly on the string when he sights game. With a nocking point, he can quickly feel and place his arrow in the exact position every time.

Most bows manufactured today are weighed-in at a given draw length. For example, a bow will be marked 55 pounds at 28 inches. This simply means the manufacturer has weighed the bow when it has been drawn back to 28 inches, the standard length of most arrows. But if the bow is drawn less than 28 inches or more than 28 inches its pull decreases and increases accordingly. If you use a 28-inch arrow and desire a 55-pound bow, than the bow marked 55 pounds at 28 inches is for you. On the other hand, if you draw a 26-inch arrow, a bow measured and weighed for a 28-inch draw will lose 2 pounds per inch. Hence, despite the fact the bow is marked 55 pounds, at your 26-inch draw it will only pull some 51 pounds. Conversely, if you use a 29-inch arrow, the pull will be increased by 2 pounds to 57.

Proper arrow measurement for your individual requirements varies greatly with every archer. Proper arrow measurement techniques are shown in the accompanying illustration.

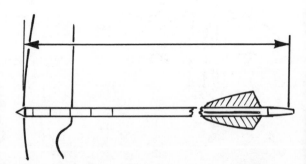

Correct arrow length can be determined by using a measuring arrow marked in inches. At full draw, your correct arrow length is the point at which the arrow stops in relation to the front of the arrow shelf.

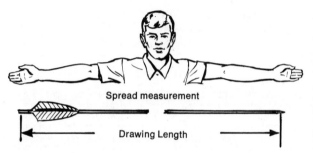

Spread measurement

Drawing Length

Alternate method of determining correct arrow length: Measure your arm spread and choose the correct arrow from the table below.

Spread Measurement	Arrow Length
57″-59″	24″-25″
60-62	25-26
63-65	26-27
66-68	27-28
69-71	28-29
72-74	29-30
75-77	30-31

Arrows

The single most important piece of archer's equipment is the arrow. Any bow of a reputed manufacturer will probably perform well, but not so with an arrow. Purchase a bow within your price range, but under no circumstance should you buy the least expensive arrows.

Matched arrows are a set of one dozen, absolutely straight and of identical length. Each is perfectly round and made of the same material. They are fletched exactly alike, and all balance at the same point. All are of equal weight and have the same spine (stiffness) for your particular bow.

The nomenclature of the arrow, the "archer's messenger," is shown in the accompanying illustration. The arrow is composed of a shaft, nock, fletching, crest, and point. Fiberglass and aluminum arrow shafts are beginning to replace the traditional wood in popularity, but wood shafts in a finely matched set still hold their own.

Wood arrow shafts come in several varieties. The arrow constructed of a single piece of wood is termed the "self" arrow. The "footed" arrow is a self arrow whose forward segment has a section of extreme hard wood carefully spliced to it. This design fortifies the foreshaft against weakening and breakage. The diameter of a wood arrow shaft is usually $9/32$ inch, $5/6$ inch or $11/32$ inch, depending on the draw weight of your bow. Light women's and children's bows ordinarily use the $9/32$-inch shaft. Men's target shafts are $5/16$ inch in diameter. Most hunting arrows constructed of wood are $11/32$ inch in diameter.

The nock is a simple notch in the end of the arrow, or a specially designed plastic contrivance, which holds the arrow on the bowstring. It should be deep enough to keep the arrow on the string and wide enough to permit an easy fit on the string with crowding. In former years, nocks were made of such items as horn and fiber, but today cellulous plastic that is easily die-cast and as tough as nails is common nock material. It is readily fitted to the arrow shaft by means of an 11-degree tapered hole inside the nock itself. The nock end of the shaft is tapered and with cellulous cement it is quickly and efficiently glued to the shaft.

Plastic nocks are available in a wide variety of colors and sizes. To replace them, burn them off with a match. The plastic nock burns quickly without damaging the wood. Many plastic nocks contain a small knob or marker which is aligned with the cock feather to permit a bowman easy reference by feel during rapid shooting. With this marker reference, the bowman simply feels for the eruption on the nock and immediately knows the cock feather is in line.

The fletching of feathers on the arrow keeps it stable in flight. "Fletching" is the old English name for a man who attaches feathers to an arrow, hence arrow feathers are known by that term. Most feathers are added to the arrow shaft somewhere between one-quarter to one-half inch below the nock. The size of the feathers is directly proportional to the arrow head or point used. In target shooting some use a feather of some $2\frac{1}{2}$ inches in length and not over a half-inch in height at any given point. Hunting arrows that contain large and heavy broadhead blades have a fletching of some four to six inches in length.

Standard fletching consists of three individual feathers, spaced 120-degrees apart. The "cock" feather, or odd colored feather, is the one positioned at right angles to the bow. The odd color tells the archer how to place the arrow to the bow. In addition to the cock feather are usually a brace of hen or identically colored feathers. Feathers on one arrow are mainly of turkey right and left wing feathers. It makes no difference which feather is used, right or left, but in constructing a matched set of arrows either all rights or all lefts are used.

Today, many bowhunters prefer all feathers to be the same color. Solid orange, white or yellow are most often

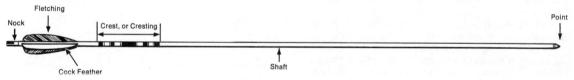

THE PARTS OF AN ARROW

Nock

Fletching

Crest, or Cresting

Point

Cock Feather

Shaft

used because they are more easily detected in flight in the early dawn or twilight hours.

There are many methods of arrow fletching. The feathers can be added to the shaft in a straight line. Most archers prefer to add them to the shaft in a slight spiral, for spiral fletching allows the arrow to rotate in flight, creating more stability. Many bowmen today also prefer four and six fletched arrow shafts, again, for better stability. The basic arrow in wide use today is the three-feather fletched version.

The prime concern with all fletching, however, is uniformity: the feathers must be all right or all left wing, of uniform equal thickness, and carefully fletched to the arrow. Most feathers are not more than a half-inch high at any given point. A feather of greater height retards the flight. On the other hand, an arrow whose feathers are too low will vastly reduce stability and cause wobbling in flight.

In former years swan and goose wing quills were in common use, and today there are some plastic feathers, but turkey feathers still dominate the field. At one time arrow feathers were cut to length and attached to the shaft by tying them with sinew, but today a wide variety of fletching jigs perform this task. The feather is "base-ground" before it is applied to the shaft. Base grinding means that the quill itself is ground until a mere wisp remains to hold the feather to the quill itself. The feathers are glued to the shaft by means of cellulous cement. A feather burner burns the feather to shape once the feather is attached to the arrow.

The arrow crest is a distinguishing mark added to the arrow for quick identification.

Woods used for the construction of arrow shafts over the years consisted of Norway Pine, Douglas fir, birch, and Port Orford cedar.

Port Orford cedar comes from the West Coast forests in the United States and from the mountain region north of Palestine, where it is known as the cedars of Lebanon. Port Orford cedar has an extremely straight grain and provides the finest spine of any wood material.

All woods have a tendency to warp, however. Hence the introduction of other materials in recent years. Aluminum provides a uniformity that wood cannot equal and it is unaffected by wide temperature changes.

Aluminum arrows today are selected by tournament archers for their uniformity and outstanding precision performance. While some bowhunters choose aluminum shafts for hunting, most prefer the fiberglass shaft that appeared after World War II. The development of quality fiberglass arrows followed.

Aluminum tends to be too noisy afield and is invariably rendered useless once it strikes an animal, tree, rock, etc. The fiberglass arrow shaft lacks these drawbacks. It is unaffected by temperature changes, can be produced to exacting specifications, and will not warp or bend out of shape, the most common fault of other materials. The rugged fiberglass arrows are capable of deep penetration in game animals and are thus most widely used by bowhunters throughout the world.

Although fiberglass arrows cost about twice as much as high-grade wooden arrows, their quality and durability make them a good buy for many archers. Their shafts are tubular. The fiberglass is wrapped around a metal mandrel which is removed after construction. These arrows are made in suitable sizes for bow weight and draw length. The sizes are

FIBERGLASS ARROW SHAFT SIZE SELECTION CHART

Target Arrows

BOW WEIGHT AT DRAW LENGTH	DRAW LENGTH								
	23″	24″	25″	26″	27″	28″	29″	30″	31″
20–25	0	0	0	1	2	3	4	5	6
25–30	0	0	1	2	3	4	5	6	7
30–35	0	1	2	3	4	5	6	7	8
35–40	1	2	3	4	5	6	7	8	9
40–45	1	2	3	4	6	7	8	9	10
40–50	2	3	4	5	6	7	8	9	10
50–55		4	5	6	7	8	9	10	11
55–60		5	6	7	8	9	10	11	11
60–65			7	8	9	10	11	11	12
65–70			8	9	10	10	11	12	12
70–75				10	10	11	12	12	12

Hunting and Field Arrows

BOW WEIGHT AT DRAW LENGTH	DRAW LENGTH								
	23″	24″	25″	26″	27″	28″	29″	30″	31″
30–35	1	2	3	4	5	6	7	8	9
35–40	2	2	3	4	5	6	7	8	9
40–45		3	4	5	6	7	8	9	10
45–50		4	5	6	7	8	9	10	11
50–55		5	6	7	8	9	10	11	11
55–60			7	8	9	10	11	11	12
60–65			8	9	10	11	11	12	12
65–70			9	10	11	11	12	12	12
70–75				10	11	12	12	12	12
75–80				11	11	12	12	12	12
80–85				11	12	12	12	12	
85–90					12	12	12		

ALUMINUM SHAFT SIZE SELECTION CHARTS

ACTUAL BOW WEIGHT	ARROW LENGTH									SHAFT WEIGHT (wall thickness)	
	22"	23"	24"	25"	26"	27"	28"	29"	30"		
15-20	1413*	1413*	1413*			1713	1713	1713		EX. LIGHT	(.013)
			1416	1416	1516	1616	1616			LIGHT	(.016)
20-25	1413*	1413*			1713	1713	1813	1813		EX. LIGHT	(.013)
	1416	1416		1516		1616		1716		LIGHT	(.016)
25-30	1413*			1713	1713	1713	1813	1813	1913	EX. LIGHT	(.013)
	1416	1416	1516		1616		1716	1816		LIGHT	(.016)
			1518	1518		1618				MEDIUM	(.018)
30-35				1713	1713	1813	1813	1913	2013	EX. LIGHT	(.013)
		1516		1616		1716	1816	1816	1916	LIGHT	(.016)
			1518		1618		1718		1818	MEDIUM	(.018)

ACTUAL BOW WEIGHT	25"	26"	27"	28"	29"	30"	31"	32"	33"	SHAFT WEIGHT (wall thickness)	
35-40	1713	1813	1813	1913	2013	2013	2114	2213	2213	EX. LIGHT	(.013)
	1616	1716	1816	1816	1916	1916	2016			LIGHT	(.016)
	1618		1718		1818	1918				MEDIUM	(.018)
40-45		1813	1913	2013	2013	2114	2213	2213		EX. LIGHT	(.013)
	1716	1816	1816	1916	1916	2016	2016			LIGHT	(.016)
			1718	1818	1918	1918	2018	2117*		MEDIUM	(.018)
					1820	1920		2020	2020	HEAVY	(.020)
45-50		1913	2013	2013	2114	2213	2213			EX. LIGHT	(.013)
	1716	1816	1916	1916	2016					LIGHT	(.016)
	1718		1818	1918	1918	2018	2018	2117*		MEDIUM	(.018)
				1820	1920	1920	2020	2020	2219	HEAVY	(.020)
50-55			2013	2114	2213	2213				EX. LIGHT	(.013)
		1916	1916	2016	2016					LIGHT	(.016)
	1718	1818	1918	1918	2018	2018	2117*	2117*		MEDIUM	(.018)
			1820	1920	1920	2020	2020	2219	2219	HEAVY	(.020)

Recommended Broadhead Shaft Size and Finished Arrow Weight*

ACTUAL BOW WEIGHT		BROADHEAD ARROW LENGTH†					
		27"	28"	29"	30"	31"	32"
45	SHAFT SIZE	1818	1918	2016	2018	2018	2117
	WEIGHT IN GRAINS	466	504	493	555	550	573
50	SHAFT SIZE	1918	2016	2018	2018	2117	2117
	WEIGHT IN GRAINS	493	483	543	555	561	573
55	SHAFT SIZE	1918	2016	2018	2117 / 2020	2117 / 2219	2117 / 2219
	WEIGHT IN GRAINS	493	483	543	549 / 588	561 / 619	573 / 632
60	SHAFT SIZE	2018	2018	2117 / 2020	2117 / 2219	2117 / 2219	2219
	WEIGHT IN GRAINS	519	531	538 / 576	549 / 605	561 / 619	632
65	SHAFT SIZE	2018	2117 / 2020	2117 / 2210	2117 / 2219	2219	
	WEIGHT IN GRAINS	519	526 / 562	538 / 592	549 / 605	619	
70–80	SHAFT SIZE	2020	2117 / 2020	2117 / 2219	2219		
	WEIGHT IN GRAINS	549	526 / 562	538 / 592	605		

Weight includes: shaft, 125 grain broadhead point, broadhead adapter and fletching.

The shaft sizes suggested are suitable for average hunting use, taken from many years of experience of some of the country's most successful hunters.

"Clean" flight and flattest possible trajectory are important—there is an optimum arrow weight range for every bow weight—bow speed—shooting technique combination. Excessive arrow weight can cause a bow to perform below its design efficiency, therefore decreasing arrow speed, accuracy, and penetration.

numbered from 1 through 12, whereas wooden arrows are lettered from A through K. (Aluminum arrows are also numbered.) Some glass hunting arrows are available with inserts that allow the use of either broadheads or field points on the same shaft.

A matched set of arrows must be carefully adjusted in weight and spine to the individual bow and carefully matched in length to your individual draw length. Spine or "stiffness" of an arrow is of utmost importance. An arrow with too soft a spine tends to shoot to the right of the point of aim. Conversely, too stiff a spine deflects the arrow to the left of the point of aim. The spining of arrows is difficult to comprehend. Formerly bowmen merely flexed arrow shafts in their hands to determine stiffness. Today the vari-

ous arrow shaft manufacturers have developed formulas which quickly and easily determine arrow spine.

When an arrow is released from a bow, the weight of the bowstring and the friction against the bow handle bends the arrow slightly to the right. As the string moves forward, it violently draws the arrow shaft to the left. As the arrow leaves the string the shaft recovers stability by straightening, or by bending toward the right until it has fully corrected itself and assumed a straight course. An arrow must be spined exactly to the individual bow weight if it is to bend uniformly and recover quickly. Too weak a spine will send the arrow to the right; too stiff, and it will shoot to the left.

The weight of individual shafts is important. Although the exact weight of the arrows is not critical, every arrow in a matched set must weigh within a few grains of the others for uniform shooting. The lightest arrows possible are best for tournament shooting, while slightly heavier shafts are more suitable for field and hunting.

The method for determining correct arrow length for individual requirements was discussed in the preceding section. When purchasing arrows you must know your proper arrow length and obtain a complete set that is further matched in weight and spine to your individual bow.

Various types of arrows draw to different lengths. The target arrow with its target point is usually drawn to the end of the pile. Field and broadhead-blade points, however,

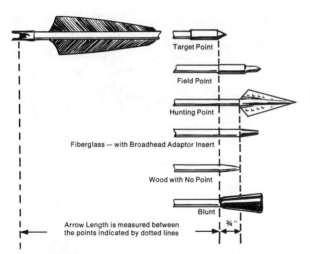

Various arrow points draw to different lengths.

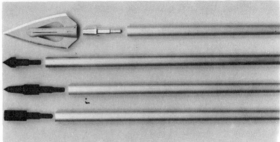

Convertible arrows made by Bear Archery Company have shaft threaded for inserting different points.

Flu-flu arrows with high fletching to retard flight are used for wing-shooting and hunting small game.

can be added to an arrow shaft by increasing the shaft length by three-quarters of an inch. This is usually done to prevent the bowhunter with a razor-sharp broadhead blade from overdrawing.

Most quality wood, aluminum and fiberglass arrows in use today have either tapered ends or some type of insert for the attachment of arrow points. Thus an archer who purchases one set of matched arrows can quickly add field points to his shaft (which should weigh the same as the broadhead you plan to use during the hunting season) for between-season field practice on the target butt. When hunting seasons open, it is simple to remove the field points and add broadhead blades. Many matched field-hunting arrow sets are often fitted with six arrows using field points and six fitted with broadhead blades. Passing the point over an open flame, being careful not to burn the shaft itself, will remove it easily from the shaft.

Among the many arrow types designed for special purposes, there are only a few the archer should be concerned with. These are the target arrow, field or roving arrow, hunting arrow, and flu-flu and fish arrows.

Most high-quality target arrows are now made of lightweight aluminum alloy. They are fletched with small feathers and have light target-points. These arrows are intended for shooting into a straw-type mat or target butt.

The field, roving, and hunting arrows are basically the same. They are usually more ruggedly constructed than the target arrow, though of similar materials to withstand great abuse. They are heavier and contain larger fletching to permit more stability in flight. The roving or field arrow uses a point that should weigh the same as the broadhead blade the hunter anticipates using during the hunting seasons. The field or roving arrow, then, is primarily a practice arrow for the bowhunter since it weighs exactly the same as the hunting arrow. Roving or field arrows become hunting arrows merely by changing the points to broadheads and vice versa.

The flu-flu arrow is used for hunting or wing-shooting where the bowmen is required to shoot his arrows skyward. The flu-flu arrow has abnormally high fletching to retard its flight. The high feathers prevent the arrow from traveling more than 30 to 50 yards. The point is usually a blunt or small-game type and is ideal where small game and especially squirrel hunting are legal with the bow and arrow. flu-flu's are also used by enterprising bird hunters who have the courage to attempt wing-shooting for upland game birds. Blunt points are far superior to all other type points for small-game hunting. Broadhead blades used so efficiently by bowhunters on big-game animals will not stop the small game birds and animals as will the blunt. The blunt point stuns the small bird or animal, allowing the bowmen quick recovery of his quarry.

Another arrow type in wide use today is the fish or harpoon arrow. Bowfishing with the bow and arrow for coarse fish such as carp and suckers is a challenging sport. The fish arrow must be heavy in order to penetrate the waters depths, hence heavy-solid fiberglass arrows are appropriate. The conventional turkey feathers must also be replaced, and today rubber-type arrow fletching appears on most fishing arrows. The fish arrow contains a removable barbed fish point. For further details on this sport, see the chapter on bowfishing.

All arrows require some care in use and storage. Most arrows are best stored in the boxes they came in. Never stack wood arrows haphazardly in an inaccessible corner of the closet, as they will warp. Keeping arrows in a quiver is fine with fiberglass or aluminum, but wood arrows must be stored to avoid warpage.

During sustained periods of storage, watch arrow fletching carefully to prevent moth damage. It is also a good idea to lightly oil field, blunt, broadhead, and fish points. Wood arrow shafts should be waxed with a good grade auto wax before use in the field. Fiberglass and aluminum require no other care. In extremely damp or rainy weather, coat arrow fletching with a silicote-based liquid or spray to keep it from becoming matted to the shaft.

Archer practices with flu-flu arrows in preparation for upland-bird season. Blunt points are most effective on gamebirds.

Bowstrings

One of the least expensive items in the archer's kit, yet one of the most important, is the bowstring. A string that is too long or constructed of fewer strands than required to sustain the pull weight can cause severe damage to a quality bow.

The bowstring is subjected to extreme wear at three points — the nocking position of the arrow and the nock point at the bow tips. A bowstring should be checked carefully prior to each shooting stint for any signs of fraying or excessive wear. At the slightest indication of wear, the string should be immediately replaced.

Through the years bowstrings have been made from a wide variety of materials including rawhide, sinew, linen or flax, hemp, fortisan (a synthetic rayon yarn), Dacron, and Kevlar. Dacron is most universally accepted by modern bowmen. Bowstrings are composed of a number of strands in accord with bow weight.

Inexpensive bowstrings used for children's lightweight target bows are made of hemp and have a single loop. The single loop string has the one advantage of being suited to any bow length, since it can be tied to one nock of the bow at any length desired. However, quality bowstrings are made of top-grade Dacron, with double loops, to exact dimensions.

weight at a particular arrow length as well as its overall length. For example, a bow marked 50 lbs @ 28"–60" simply means that it will draw 50 pounds at a 28-inch draw length and measures 60 inches in overall length. Therefore, when purchasing a bowstring for this bow simply remember its draw weight of 50 pounds and the bow's overall length — 60 inches. Manufacturers invariably build into the bowstring the necessary compensation for overall length, and the bowstring marked 60 inches is actually not 60 inches, but some 3 inches shorter.

A new bowstring has a tendency to stretch and can stretch almost an inch after hard use. Keep this point in mind, for after a day spent shooting with a new string it will have stretched enough to reduce the brace height of your bow.

If you find the string has stretched to a point where your bow's brace height is too low, the bowstring can be shortened by merely twisting it several turns. Be careful, however, not to twist the string excessively or you could cause excessive wear and damage to the string itself. Usually several turns is sufficient to bring the new string back to brace height.

After sustained periods of shooting, the bowstring should be rewaxed. Apply gently an additional layer of wax and briskly rub into the string with a piece of brown wrapping

Quality bowstrings are inexpensive and of prime importance to accurate shooting. The bowman should never venture to the target butt or hunting field without an extra.

RECOMMENDED STRANDS FOR BOWSTRINGS

V-207	TYPE-B-1100 2	V-138
11s-20-30#	8s-20-30#	14s-15-24#
12s-30-40#	10s-25-35#	16s-25-34#
13s-40-50#	12s-35-45#	18s-35-44#
15s-50-58#	14s-45-55#	20s-45-51#
17s-58-65#	16s-55-80#	22s-52-57#
18s-65-75#		24s-58-62#
19s-75-85#	**DACRON SUPER 43**	26s-63-75#
21s-85-100#	**AS ABOVE OR WITH**	28s-75-90#
	FEWER STRANDS	

Although some archers make their own strings to suit their bows, top-grade bowstrings can be purchased so inexpensively today that it is hardly worth the time or effort required to make a string.

The double-loop Dacron bowstring is composed of a varied number of strands for varied pull weights and averages some 3 inches shorter than the bow it was constructed for. Hence the pull and the length of the bow are important numbers to remember when purchasing bowstrings. Most quality bows manufactured today are marked with the draw paper. The paper, quickly moved over the surface of the string, tends to melt the wax and permit it to penetrate into the individual strands.

To prevent excess wear to the string, a serving, consisting of cotton thread, is added to the string at both nocking points and where the arrow is fitted to the string. The serving at the arrow nock position is of such a length to cover the string where the arrow is fitted and where the archer places his fingertips.

String serving, especially at the arrow nock position, takes severe wear. At any sign of fraying, the serving should be renewed with the aid of a string serving tool.

Of prime importance, every bowstring should have an arrow nocking point to permit the arrow to be placed on the bowstring in exactly the same location every time and to prevent the arrow from sliding off, or up and down, the string.

Remember, however, that the nocking point should not be positioned on the bowstring until after the string has been used several times to eliminate all possible stretch. There are numerous commercially produced nocking points in use today, but a suitable nocking point can be quickly made by simply wrapping the nock point location with a piece of tape or several turns of serving thread.

There are several other necessary items that can and should be fitted to the bowstring, especially when in the hunting field. The bowstring should be fitted with brush buttons and string silencers (see Accessories). Brush buttons are fitted to the bowstring at the bow's nock points to prevent brush and leaves from catching between string and bow. String silencers, usually constructed of pieces of rubber and attached to the bowstring at midpoint between the serving and nocking area, are also added to eliminate excessive string noise that can spook game in the field.

In conclusion, remember that bowstrings are cheap insurance and can easily mean the difference between success and failure in the field or on the range. Always carry a few extra strings with you as added insurance whenever you are shooting.

AMO BOWSTRING TENSION CHART

BOW LENGTH	STRING LENGTH	*BOW WEIGHTS					
		+ (8) 20-30 lbs.	+ (10) 25-35 lbs.	+ (12) 35-45 lbs.	+ (14) 45-55 lbs.	+ (16) 55-75 lbs.	+ (18) 75-100 lbs.
72	69	80 lbs.	90 lbs.	110 lbs.	130 lbs.	150 lbs.	170 lbs.
71	68	"	"	"	"	145	165
70	67	75	85	105	125	"	"
69	66	"	"	"	"	"	"
68	65	"	"	"	"	140	160
67	64	70	80	100	120	"	"
66	63	"	"	"	"	"	"
65	62	"	"	"	"	135	"
64	61	65	75	95	115	"	155
63	60	"	"	"	"	"	"
62	59	60	70	90	110	130	"
61	58	"	"	"	"	"	150
60	57	"	"	"	"	"	"
59	56	55	65	85	105	125	"
58	55	"	"	"	"	"	145
57	54	"	"	"	"	"	"
56	53	50	60	80	100	120	"
55	52	"	"	"	"	"	"
54	51	"	"	"	"	"	140
53	50	45	55	75	95	115	"
52	49	"	"	"	"	"	"
51	48	40	50	70	90	"	135
50	47	"	"	"	"	110	"
49	46	"	"	"	"	"	"
48	45	35	45	65	85	"	130

* Bow weight categories are based upon bow weight at 28″ draw length.
+Number in parenthesis is suggested number of strands in type B or V207 dacron or equivalent.

Archery Accessories

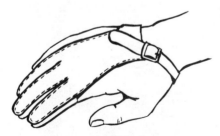

THREE-FINGER ARCHERY GLOVE

Shooting Gloves

To prevent the string from irritating the drawing fingers and to assist in releasing it smoothly and without creep, some sort of leather protection is required. Fitted on the three fingers of the bowman's drawing hand, this protection is available either as a three-finger shooting glove or a tab. Most shooting gloves are of the skeleton type, with leather finger stalls or tips that fit over the three drawing fingers. These are available in either right- or left-handed models, in varied sizes.

THREE-FINGER SHOOTING TABS

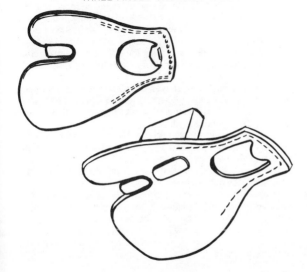

The shooting glove provides ample all-round protection to the bowman's drawing hand and is widely accepted among archers in both the hunting and target fields. However, there is another group of bowmen who prefer the three-finger tab over the glove simply because they have better "feel" of the bowstring when using the tab.

The tab is cheaper than the glove. Constructed of cordovan leather, tabs are available to fit one or two fingers of the shooting hand. They are slotted to permit the arrow nock to pass. The tab affords excellent protection for the balls of the fingers, but not for the inside of the fingers. In recent years tabs have been made with finger separators. In any case, you will require some sort of finger protection for the bowstring drawing hand. The choice is up to the individual.

Arm Guards

The next item of importance so essential for the bowman is some sort of protection for the wrist and lower forearm of the bow arm. When a bowstring is released it may strike the inside of the archer's forearm, and without some sort of protection for this tender portion of the anatomy, the arm can become severely and dangerously bruised.

The arm guard buckles or snaps about the wrist of the bow arm. It is made of cordovan leather, with a few steel stays sewed between the leather and lining for added protection.

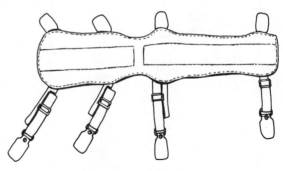

HUNTING ARMGUARD

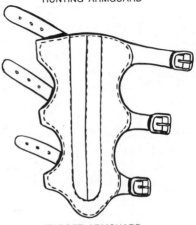

TARGET ARMGUARD

Quivers

Aside from the shooting glove or tab and the arm guard the archer needs something to carry his arrows afield or to the target range—a quiver. Quivers that hold anywhere from a half dozen to a few dozen arrows are available in many styles, each designed for a specific purpose.

The ground quiver, a metal stake with an attached metal ring, is stuck in the ground to hold arrows when shooting from a stationary position on the target field. The ground quiver is popular with the target archer. Center-back and

Bow quiver, which holds arrows at the ready, is widely used in the hunting field. *Courtesy New Jersey Game Dept.*

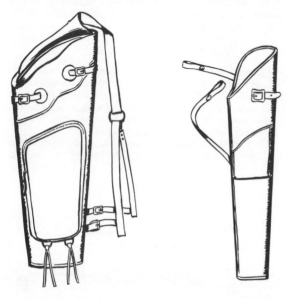

SHOULDER QUIVER   BELT QUIVER

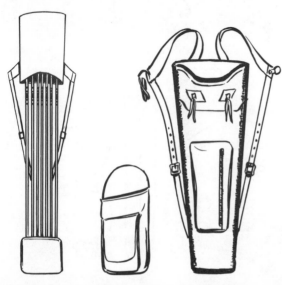

ST. CHARLES   POCKET QUIVER   CENTER-BACK
QUIVER   QUIVER

shoulder quivers are used by bowhunters. Belt and pocket quivers are used by both tournament and field archers. In recent years, bowhunters have adopted the bow quiver, which attaches directly to the bow itself.

The shoulder quiver is the traditional bowhunter's quiver. It is available in either right- or left-hand models, permitting the archer to reach back with his bowstring hand, grasp the nock end of the arrow, and with a forward swing draw the arrow from the quiver. The only drawbacks to the shoulder quiver is that, in the hunting field, the arrows projecting from the quiver tend to catch on tree limbs or rattle freely and spook game.

The center-back quiver was developed to help eliminate the problem of arrows getting caught in brush. The quiver fits the center of the bowman's back, the protruding arrows resting neatly behind his head.

Used widely by target archers, belt and pocket quivers are smaller than back and shoulder models, holding at the most a half-dozen arrows.

The bow quiver, attached directly to the bow, provides the fastest delivery and also ample protection for the arrows. Most quality quivers are equipped with some sort of metal shield to cover the broadhead blades. Without a shield to protect the blades, a bow quiver can be a dangerous piece of equipment with exposed razor-sharp broadheads. Bow quivers are constructed to hold four to six arrows; some as many as eight.

Bow Sights

The bow sight is a relative newcomer to the archery field. The early bowman used no mechanical sighting aids—he aimed "instinctively." The modern archer, however, has a wide variety of bow sights to choose from. Archery tournaments are divided into two divisions, the instinctive and the free style. It is the free style group that uses the bow sight.

Bow sights have become highly sophisticated, and many have micrometer windage and elevation adjustment knobs, prisms, and aperture inserts, as well as a variety of post sighting points for shooting at varied yardages.

It is interesting to note that both schools—free style and instinctive—have turned in equally creditable scores in the hunting field. The bow sight used for hunting is usually made with a number of sighting posts; each post is sighted for a given or known range for a particular bow.

Pro-Line Pro Bo Opti-Site is a battery-powered lighted hunting sidht with three pins adjustable for windage and elevation. Red light locates pins quickly during early morning or evening.

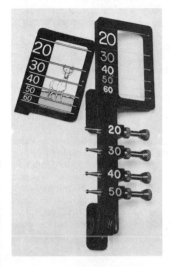

Pro-Line's Pro Bo Model 1200 Deluxe side-mount target sight has 12 extension settings, micro windage adjustment, glass level, and optional apertures.

Hunting and target sight from Bear Archery Co. is calibrated for accurate setting. Numbers have no meaning except as a gauge for setting sight.

Bear Shur-Hit hunting sight bolts to Bear compounds and many other bows. It can also be tape- or screw-mounted. Four sight pins can be finger-tightened and pre-set for various yardages.

Yardage markers on Browning hunting sight allow archer to sight in his bow at various ranges and pick the right one for his shot.

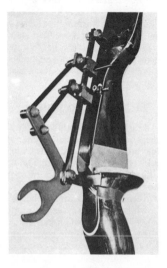

A flick of the wrist adjusts this hunting sight from Sprandel Bowsight Co. to shoot dead-on at 10 to 40 yards.

Torque stabilizer is used in target archery to eliminate vibration and absorb the recoil energy created when the bowstring is released.

Stabilizers

The torque stabilizer is perhaps one of the more recent innovations in the field of tournament or target archery, and is gradually gaining in popularity in the hunting field. The torque stabilizer does exactly what its name implies—it stabilizes the bow when the string is released. Miniature torque stabilizing inserts are fitted into tourney bows, to absorb the forward shock and thrust of the bowstring.

Torque stabilizers are fitted to the bow face just below the bow handle and vary in length according to the bowman's preference. This stabilizing unit quickly dampens vibration. It further provides the tournament archer with additional weight for added stability, permitting a far more steady hold and smoother follow-through after the arrow has been released. But above all the stabilizer absorbs the bow's recoil energy and greatly assists the archer in achieving accuracy.

Other Equipment

Brush buttons. Although not required by the target archer, the bowhunter and field archer should add brush buttons to his bowstring to prevent snagging his bow in brush and undergrowth when afield. The brush button is made of soft rubber and is quickly added to the bowstring at both string nocking points on the bow.

Silencers. Bowstring silencers are also a requisite for the bowhunter. Bowstrings have an uncanny ability to "twang" when released, which can quickly spook game. The string silencers, fitted to the bowstring midway between the string serving and the nocking points, reduce such noise. A simple

pair of string silencers can be easily made simply by attaching a portion of a rubber band to the string. However, quality string silencers are available at a nominal price.

Camouflage. The sheen and sparkle of a highly polished bow can readily startle game. The glitter can be eliminated by the addition of some sort of camouflage, such as a cloth sock slipped over the limbs of the bow. Camouflage tape is also used, but if you use it remember to wax your bow well to prevent damage to the finish when the tape is removed. Many hunting bows are also available with a camouflage finish.

Bow Stringer. The bow stringer is another important piece of equipment. A quality bow that is not strung properly will wear quickly and warp, eventually even break. However, the bow stringer eliminates this problem. Made of a stout length of nylon rope and a pair of leather bow-tip protectors, the stringer quickly, efficiently, and safely strings the archer's bow.

Bowstring Nocking Points. These are added to the bowstring to permit positioning the arrow in the same spot each time and to prevent the arrow from slipping off the string when afield. A number of archery manufacturers produce varied nocking points at a nominal price.

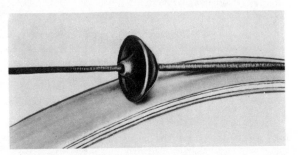

Brush buttons attached to bowstring near each nock prevent bow from snagging on undergrowth.

Bow-tip protectors. Made of soft rubber, the bow tip protector prevents scuffing the bow when stringing, keeps bow tips in good condition, and holds the bow string in place when stringing.

Bow sling. Used primarily by tournament bowmen, the bow sling provides perfect balance and holds the bow in shooting position, giving the archer confidence that his bow cannot fall.

Kisser button. This device is used primarily by target archers to assure consistency of draw. Attached to the bowstring, it touches the bowman's lip when at full draw to signal you are at proper draw.

Archery targets. Available in 24-inch, 36-inch, and 48-inch sizes, archery target matts are often made of Indian cord grass covered with burlap. Conventional "ringed" target faces as well as animal faces are available. Using a proper archery target is essential for the preservation of your arrows. Shooting quality arrows into a rock-studded field can quickly ruin them. On the other hand, broadhead hunting arrows should not be used when shooting at the conventional archery matt since a few well-placed broadheads can quickly reduce this target to a pile of straw.

Bowstring silencers eliminate "twang" in hunting field that spooks game.

Hunting bow should be covered with camouflage material to prevent polished limbs from glaring in the sun and spooking game. This archer is well camouflaged all over.

Various types of nocking points for guiding the arrow onto the bowstring at the same spot each time.

BOW-TIP PROTECTOR

BOW SLING

KISSER BUTTON

How to Shoot

Shooting the modern bow and arrow, as with all other forms of shooting sports, requires patience and endless practice in order that the basic techniques required to strike a target consistently become instinctive. No man can expect to pick up a trap or skeet gun for the first time and break 25 straight targets on the clay-bird layouts. Neither can the neophyte archer expect to place all his arrows in the gold or drop a buck deer as it approaches his stand in the twilight hours without acquiring the fundamentals of shooting: stance, nocking, aiming, release, and follow-through.

Stance

Proper stance is essential in archery. Shooting the bow and arrow differs from other forms of shooting in that considerable strength and effort is required. Hence the shooting stance must not only be comfortable, the feet must be correctly positioned in order that the body be properly braced.

Stand with your feet about 15 inches apart and at right angles to the target. You must be comfortable, and if you can feel more comfortable with a slightly wider stance, take it. But remember not to stand with your feet too close to-gether since such a stance creates strain and invariably results in poor aiming techniques and sloppy shooting.

After finding the best shooting stance for yourself, remember it well and stick to it; do not vary the position. Consistency is the key to success in archery.

Nocking

Nocking simply means placing the arrow on the bowstring. Foremost to remember is that the arrow must be fitted to the bowstring in exactly the same place each time, hence the use of a string "nocking point" which assures the bowman of the correct position.

Before the introduction of center-shot bows and those with built-in arrow rests, the bowman used his hand as an arrow rest, but this made for inconsistent shooting since he could not place his hand exactly in the same position every time. The arrow rest on most modern bows eliminates this age-old problem.

Once you have correctly positioned the string nocking point on the bowstring you are ready to place (nock) the arrow. With the bow firmly, but not tightly, held in the left hand at the left side grasp an arrow in the quiver with the thumb and forefinger of the right hand. (All instructions assume a right-handed archer.)

With one motion, as you remove the arrow from the quiver, bring the bow to waist height in a horizontal position, and place the arrow across the bow. Center the arrow on the bowstring at the predetermined nocking point with the

Correct shooting stance is important in achieving accuracy with the bow and arrow. Stand at right angles to the target with feet spread to assure a firm, yet balanced position.

Arrow should be positioned on the rest and nocked at the same point each time. A nocking point should be added to the bowstring to permit accurate placement of the arrow.

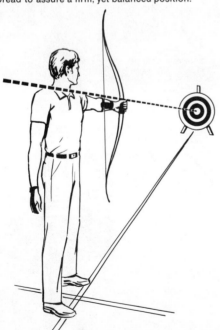

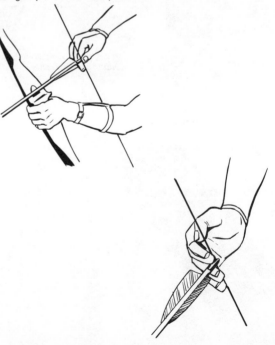

fingers of the right hand, holding the arrow firmly at the bow handle with the forefinger of the left hand. Place the first three fingers of the right hand on the bowstring, one finger above the arrow nock, the second two fingers below. It is not necessary to grasp the arrow nock tightly.

Drawing

Prior to starting the draw, cock your head toward the target, breathe deeply and relax, bringing the bow and fitted arrow into shooting position by extending your left arm forward with the elbow pointing slightly to the left and with the bow vertical or cocked slightly to the right. (The target and tournament archer prefers to keep his bow vertical; the bowhunter tends to cant it to the right.) Be certain that the bow hand, and especially the forearm, is not in the path of the bowstring, otherwise it could be struck as the arrow is released.

Now you are ready to draw back the bowstring to full draw position. It is at this point that the beginner may encounter the problem of the arrow slipping from the arrow rest. This happens when the bowman tries to apply pressure to the bowstring by curling his fingers around it, causing the string to roll to the left and the arrow to slip off the bow handle.

The bowstring should be grasped only with the pads of the three fingers of the drawing hand, with the hand, wrist, and forearm in a straight line. This way, the string will be rolled to the right and keep the arrow on its shelf.

The full draw position. With the three fingers of the drawing hand, and the aid of the back, shoulder, and chest muscles, the bowstring is drawn to an anchor point near the chin or cheek.

As you bring the bow to full draw, keep the elbow of the drawing arm at right angles to the body. Such a position will bring the muscles of the shoulder and upper back into play and make drawing the bow much easier. Remember to push with the left shoulder and pull with the right side of the body. The chest, shoulders, and back will do the work.

Bring the bowstring back to full draw to the position near cheek or chin, being certain the string is "anchored" at the same point each time. Tournament archers invariably use the low anchor point with the bowstring hand resting just below the chin and the string touching the nose. On the other hand, the bowhunter likes to be closer to his line of sight and usually prefers the high anchor point with the second finger of the drawing hand anchored at the corner of the mouth. Some bowhunters anchor just below the eye as well. Again, the exact anchor point depends primarily on your individual preference and shooting style. But remember, once the anchor point has been established, do not vary it.

If you are a right-handed archer and you have established that your shooting eye is the right eye, then shoot with both eyes open. In all kinds of shooting, most top-notch shooters use both eyes. Closing one eye merely limits your vision. However, if your left eye is your shooting eye, learn to shoot left-handed.

Many tournament archers use a small rubber button, called a "kisser," fitted to the bowstring to determine full draw. It is positioned on the string at the correct anchor point for the individual bowman and centered between the lips. With the anchor point under the chin, the bow should be held vertical. The bowhunter, on the other hand, with his higher anchor point, tilts both his head and bow.

The low anchor position (*left*) and the high anchor position (*right*). Choice of position depends on individual preference.

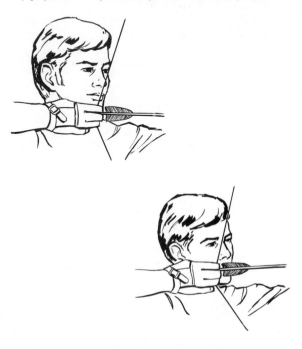

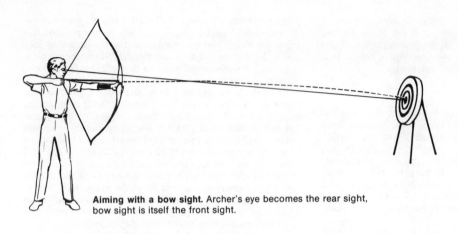

Aiming with a bow sight. Archer's eye becomes the rear sight, bow sight is itself the front sight.

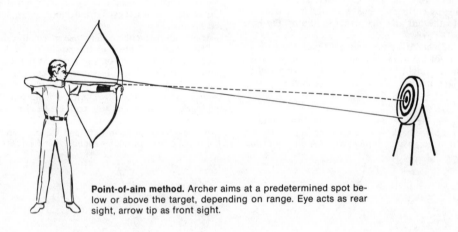

Point-of-aim method. Archer aims at a predetermined spot below or above the target, depending on range. Eye acts as rear sight, arrow tip as front sight.

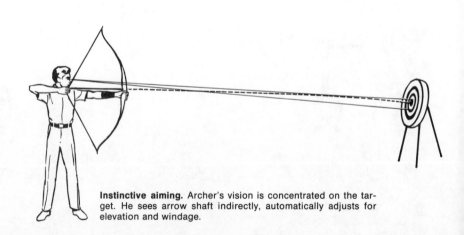

Instinctive aiming. Archer's vision is concentrated on the target. He sees arrow shaft indirectly, automatically adjusts for elevation and windage.

Aiming

You are now at the full-draw position, relaxed, with the bow held firmly and the arrow resting snugly in the anchor position. You are now ready to aim.

There are three basic methods of aiming, each designed for a specific form of shooting: the bow sight method, the point-of-aim, and the instinctive style.

The instinctive style is without doubt the oldest method of aiming a bow and arrow. It is extremely accurate and consistent up to a distance of 40 yards. At ranges of 20 to 25 yards it is deadly, hence it is the method most used by bowhunters.

In instinctive aiming, your foremost attention is directed to the target while you see the arrow shaft indirectly. Concentrating on the target, your indirect vision automatically adjusts and compensates for elevation and windage. Foremost to remember is that everything must be done in exactly the same manner each time you draw, sight, and release an arrow. Your anchor point must be constant; the arrow must be drawn to its exact full length each time and positioned exactly on the bowstring and on the arrow rest. Uniformity is the key. Instinctive shooting comes from practice and more practice, but once you begin using this method you will be surprised at how swiftly you will become proficient.

The second most popular method, commonly used by target archers, is the point-of-aim method. As shown in the diagram, using the point-of-aim system the archer does not aim at the center of his target, but at a predetermined location below or above the target according to its range. Unlike instinctive shooting, the anchor point usually is located directly under the chin with the bowstring touching lips and nose, the bow held in the vertical position.

With the point-of-aim method the eye acts as the rear sight and the point of the arrow acts as the front sight. Through trial and error, the archer determines the exact trajectory of his arrow for the particular bow he is shooting and adjusts his "sights" accordingly. The average target bow of about 40 pounds draw usually shoots dead-on at 80 yards range. At more than 80 yards the archer sights at an object above the point of intended impact; short of 80 yards he would center on a point below the target.

Target archers using the point-of-aim technique usually have a small stake which they push into the ground for a point of aim when the aim is below the target. The point-of-aim method is widely used by target archers, but it is ineffective for bowhunters since the exact range must be known.

The third method of aiming is with a bow sight. When using a bow sight, the archer's eye becomes the rear sight and the bow sight itself becomes the front sight.

The simplest form of sight is nothing more than a pin or marker of sorts attached to the bow just above the handle that is adjusted for windage and elevation by moving it up or down, to the right or left.

The refined bow sight has adjustment knobs for windage and elevation, and is quickly adjusted. Remarkable scores have been compiled by bowmen using such a sight. However, like the point-of-aim method, the bow sight must be adjusted to a given range before it becomes effective.

The Release

Hold the bow at full draw just long enough to be certain your aim is correct, then relax your fingers, permitting the bowstring to slip smoothly away. Any undue movement of the three fingers of the drawing hand will cause "creep," which can greatly effect the accuracy of the release. Another common fault among neophyte archers is what is termed "plucking" the string—pulling or drawing the bow hand away from the string. This is sure to spoil your aim. Again, the exact manner of release rests with the individual archer.

Follow-Through

Your arrow is away, speeding toward its target. At the moment the arrow is released, the tension in your body, created during the draw and sighting, is totally relaxed. At this point you must follow through.

A proper follow-through is just as essential to accuracy as any other step in correct shooting. At the moment of release the shooting hand and right shoulder move backward slightly. The bow should slip loosely in the bow hand, but the bow arm should be kept extended and the shooting hand held firmly at the anchor point. Follow-through is essential to prevent a relaxation of shooting stance just before the release of the arrow.

Proper follow-through is essential for accuracy. Bow arm should remain extended, shooting hand held firmly at the anchor point.

Bowhunting

Within the last decade, bowhunters in North America have taken moose, deer, and the three species of bears. In Africa, bowmen have felled rhino, elephant, Cape buffalo, leopard, and lion. Clearly, bowhunting as a sport has become enormously popular, to the extent that almost every state has set aside a special game season for archers.

Among all our game, deer are still the favorite of the bowhunter—especially whitetails. For it has been said that if a bowman can successfully bag a whitetail deer, he can easily take any other game animal in the world.

Bowhunting requires more patience and perseverance than firearm hunting. The bowhunter must be within relatively close range to be assured a hit in a vital area. And he must be certain that his arrow has a clear path to its target, for the slightest twig or hidden branch can quickly deflect a shaft from its mark.

To be assured a positive hit in the vital area of an animal the size of a deer, the bowhunter would be wise not to shoot at any deer beyond a range of 45 yards. While it's true deer have been bagged with the bow and arrow at far greater distances, it is by its very nature a short-range weapon. Limit your distance before you loose an arrow; your chance of a successful hit and a clean kill will be vastly enhanced.

Trail Watching

The eastern bowhunter after whitetails employs varied hunting methods. Most bowmen prefer "runway" watching —finding a well-worn deer trail and sitting motionless several yards away to wait for a deer to amble by. Others

Arrow deflection presents the greatest challenge to the bowhunter. This buck may be within range, but if the arrow touches a twig or branch the shot will go astray.

like to stillhunt, that is, to walk up a deer. Some bowmen also like to hunt in teams of three or four, and there are others who "drive" deer, emulating the firearm deer hunter in many sections of the East.

Trail watching calls for several pre-season trips to your favorite deer area. Deer are creatures of habit, and when not pushed or spooked prefer to select the easiest route between bedding, watering, and feeding grounds. They move from these areas usually twice a day, at dusk from ridgetop bedding grounds down to feed and water, returning to the high country at dawn along specific runways. Trails used by deer can be easily recognized: they are well-worn and often contain tracks and droppings. By carefully selecting a good vantage point several yards off the main trail, with a clear path to the target area, the bowhunter's opportunity for success is greater than in other methods of hunting.

A good location for the bowmen is near an apple orchard. Whitetails love apples and will travel many miles to find them. If you can find such a spot, especially with fruit-laden trees, you're in luck. Look for well-used trails leading into the orchard and choose a stand that will afford you a good shot as the deer enter the orchard. Better yet, select a good apple tree that will afford a comfortable position and climb into the tree.

Of utmost importance when trail watching is that the archer must remain motionless and be well hidden or camouflaged. This may sound easy, but it's not. Deer are most easily spooked by motion, and a bowhunter who slaps at buzzing insects or squirms restlessly will never see a deer.

One way to avoid detection when trail watching is to use a blind. If a blind is properly constructed with material from the surrounding area, the bowhunter is perfectly concealed and can readily move about without being detected by the deer. The blind can be constructed several yards from a well-used runway at ground level or in a tree.

Bow is a short-range weapon capable of killing every type of game, but it is especially popular for deer.

Trailwatching is a productive method of hunting forest whitetails. Archer conceals himself along a deer runway (*right*) and waits for a deer to come within range.

Tree stand may be uncomfortable but is a good vantage point from which to watch for approaching game.

Mechanical tree stand permits the bowman to climb a tree trunk and provides a steady platform. *Courtesy Baker Mfg. Co.*

Perhaps one of the handiest items for the bowman to carry afield, if he anticipates constructing a blind, is a spool of monofilament fishing line. He can wind several yards of line between two trees, then carefully interweave brush and foliage. Burlap bags are also useful in blind construction. Remember to construct the blind so that it provides good visibility and offers complete freedom of movement when the bow is brought to full draw.

Tree stands include everything from a limb to an elaborately constructed platform. The advocates of the tree stand reason that usually deer do not look up, and if a blind is placed in a tree, often a deer will approach at close range. In fact, tree-stand hunting is considered so effective that in some states it is outlawed.

The most effective time of day for trail watching is at dawn and late twilight when deer move between feeding-watering and bedding grounds. During the day, when deer are not pushed or spooked, they will simply bed down and refuse to move. However, if there are a number of hunters in the woods, deer will be kept moving and the runway method then can be effective throughout the midday hours. But usually trail watching is only productive from daybreak to 9 a.m. and again from 3 p.m. to dark.

Remember to take account of the wind. When you are stationed along a runway, the wind should never be blowing at your back in the direction you expect the deer to come. Your scent will be carried to the deer. Keep the wind in your face, and deer approaching you will not detect your presence.

Stillhunting and Stalking

While not as effective as trail watching, stillhunting and stalking are more thrilling, steeped as they are in the traditions of the longbowmen of yesteryear. The stillhunter prowls silently through the woods, hoping to sight a deer, and then stalk the game to within bow range. This is a good method during the daylight hours when the deer are bedded-down.

Wind direction plays the most important role in stillhunting. Always hunt with the wind in your face. If you sight a deer, only move when the animal's head is down in feeding position. Never attempt to approach a deer when its head is erect and ears are cocked—it will immediately spook. But when the deer brings its head down, you can move toward it, instantly freezing again as it snaps its head upward again. Make use of every bit of cover. Watch for other deer in the general area, too. You can be stalking one animal only to be startled when another snorts a few yards away.

Driving

Another effective way of hunting whitetails is by driving. Here a group of bowhunters band together to bring home their venison. Deer driving is productive during the midday hours. For a drive to be successful, several hunters must work in close agreement with one another and be intimately familiar with the territory they plan to hunt.

In a properly organized deer drive several bowhunters take stands along varied known escape routes of deer in a particular piece of woodlot, while several others move through the woodlands "pushing" any deer that is in the cover to the waiting bowmen. Successful drives have been

Archer who elects to stillhunt for whitetails must take advantage of wind, cover, and terrain. This method is especially productive during midday when deer are bedded down.

managed with only 5 or 6 bowmen; 8 to 10 bowhunters make an ideal group.

In a successful bowhunting deer drive, the elected drivers move toward the standers as silently as possible. In this way even the drivers have an occasional opportunity of getting a shot. Often a wary old buck won't move ahead of the driver, but instead will quarter and cut back through the drive, and the alert driver will then have an opportunity for a shot. When posting standers, remember to place one or two hunters on the flanks, since a wary whitetail will often attempt to slip through or out the flank of a drive. With flanker standers this possibility is eliminated and will usually produce a shot for the hunter.

The successful deer drive should be planned with extreme care. A captain of the hunt should be elected. He is the one who should know the area most intimately. Standers should be spaced sufficiently far apart so that they will not interfere with each other. Drivers should also be placed sufficiently far apart, but in as parallel line as possible to the standers and be extremely cautious and aware of the other hunters in the area. When possible, deer should be driven crosswind.

Driving deer does have one disadvantage. Often a driven deer will come bounding through the forest at top speed, an almost impossible target for the bowhunter. A whitetail deer at top speed is moving at about 40 miles per hour. To hit such a rapidly moving target, the bowman would have to "lead" his target by 12 feet at 10 yards; 24 feet at 20 yards; and 35 feet at 30 yards. Such a running target should not be taken for it is almost impossible to strike the vital area of a running deer under such conditions. Unless you are extremely close to a moving deer do not attempt a shot; invariably the deer will be struck far back and will escape, probably with an arrow wound.

At some point during your bowhunting days, you're going to release an arrow at an animal only to have it "jump the string." How many times have you heard a bowhunter remark that his arrow was flying directly at the deer's chest area, but it jumped aside and the arrow flew harmlessly by?

While we doubt that the deer saw the arrow coming toward it, jumping the string is nothing more than an instinctive reflex action. Compared with a rifle bullet, an arrow is comparatively slow in flight; and the twang of a bowstring, or the whispering of the arrow as it moves in flight, is sufficient to cause a deer to jump.

Small Game

Although bowhunters have hunted the world for trophy big-game animals, small-game and varmint hunting is also popular. It's a year-round sport; during the legal hunting season the bowhunter can seek small game, while the remainder of the year he can devote to varmints.

The woodchuck is the ideal bowhunter's game since it requires the utmost stalking skill to approach the wary animal and considerable shooting finesse to bring it to bag. While most small-game targets should be hunted with field blunt arrows, the woodchuck requires broadheads.

Woodchucks venture from their dens during the early morning and late evening hours, spending the remainder of the day comfortably snoozing in the cooling depths of their dens. Consequently the bowman must be afield during the early morning and late twilight hours. Some hunters prefer

Woodchuck is ideal off-season target for the bowhunter.

to wait motionlessly within a few yards of a den for the 'chuck to appear. Others prefer to stalk the 'chuck, attempting to get as close as possible before loosing an arrow. Both methods are successful, although the hunter who stalks his game will undoubtedly sight more animals.

Woodchucks emerge from their dens in early spring and spend the remainder of the summer stuffing themselves with clover in preparation of their long winter's sleep, giving the hunter several months of the year to stalk his quarry. The successful 'chuck hunter can be assured that come deer season he won't miss too many bucks.

Other small game eagerly sought by bowmen include rabbits and squirrels, quail, ringneck pheasants, turkey, and grouse. While successful wingshooting has been enjoyed by a few professionals, the average hunter would find it difficult to hit birds on the wing.

The flu-flu arrow must be used when hunting squirrels in trees. This is an arrow shaft fletched with sufficient feathers to retard its flight. Such shafts will not travel much beyond 50 yards and can be readily recovered. The broadhead blade, while perfect for big-game animals, does not work as well on small game. The blunt point or field point should be used when hunting small game. There are a number of small-game points currently available, ranging from empty rifle or pistol cartridge cases to special blunts, which produce a great deal of shocking power. A fine commercially manufactured small-game point in wide use today is termed the "rubber blunt."

Since small-game hunting seasons vary from state to state, as well as regulations pertaining to legal weapons, be sure to check your local game laws before venturing afield with the bow and arrow. For example, in most states the prospective bowman must compete with the firearm hunter since there are few states which offer special small-game seasons specifically for archers. But hunting small game with the bow and arrow is a keenly satisfying pastime and in the long run will enhance your skills as a bowman and provide hours of relaxing enjoyment afield before and after the big-game hunting seasons.

Where To Hit Big Game

The most important factor in killing big game quickly and cleanly is arrow (or bullet) placement. You'll minimize the chance of losing wounded game if you take time to study the animals you hunt and learn the location of vital organs, as well as where to aim in order to hit those vital organs when the animal is seen at different angles.

The accompanying drawings show the anatomy of a deer —the most popular game for bowhunters—and the aiming points that are important. Remember that an arrow kills by hemorrhage. A bowhunter should note especially the location of main arteries.

A neck shot should not be attempted except at close range, and even then it's only a fair choice. An arrow in the neck may possibly damage the spinal column and cause the deer to drop quickly, but you don't want to gamble on that. If you hit a big artery such as the carotid, bleeding will be profuse and you may not have to track the deer far. However, your chance of causing major hemorrhaging is better if you can place the arrow *low* in the neck (in the brisket area) or in the chest cavity.

The best shots should really be described in terms of vital areas rather than vital organs. The forward one-third of a deer's body is a vital area since it houses heart, lungs, several major arteries, spine, and shoulder. An arrow penetrating one of the organs will bring down a deer (though not as quickly as a bullet). When possible, try for the heart. If you miss, the arrow has a good chance of hitting one of the other vital organs—particularly the lungs. Even though a lung-shot deer may not drop because of shock (since an arrow produces little shock by comparison with a bullet), the animal will die through hemorrhaging.

In this case, however, the deer may travel a good distance, so tracking is even more important for the bowhunter than for the rifleman. If you're not sure where your arrow struck, the blood may tell you. If you spot blood on brush a few feet off the ground and to the side of the tracks, it's coming from the side of the deer—a good indication of a lung hit. Frothy blood also signifies a lung hit. Bright red blood usually means a heart or lung shot. Brownish-yellow blood, particularly if you see white hair in it, means the deer is gut-shot. This is unfortunate. A gut-shot deer can travel a long way, and you'll just have to stick with the track.

If you're in a tree stand, shooting down as a buck walks below, less of the vital area will be exposed than when you have a broadside shot. The best place to aim then is between the shoulder blades. An arrow there may penetrate heart, lungs, or arteries. A shot at a quartering animal should not be quite the same as a broadside shot, either. When a deer is quartering away, your point of aim should be somewhat farther back on the body. A straight-traveling broadhead will penetrate from that rearward point forward into the vital area.

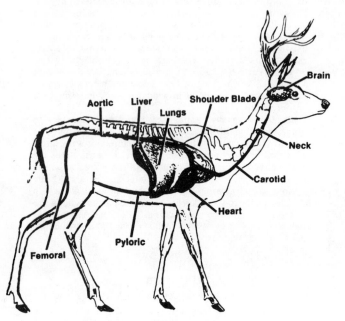

Drawing shows location of deer's vital organs. Also note placement of major arteries, as arrow kills by hemorrhage.

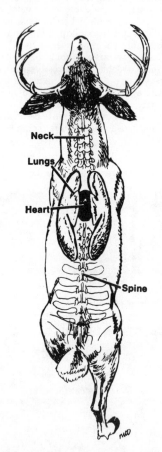

If buck walks beneath tree stand, try for shot between shoulder blades to penetrate vital area.

Bowfishing

Most bowhunters have learned that the hunting seasons are brief and that they must either turn to target archery or to the sport of bowfishing.

In fresh water the most popular species sought by bowmen is the carp, which can attain heavyweight proportions. Other species hunted are suckers, buffalofish, squawfish, dogfish and gar. In salt water, stingrays, skates, barracuda, and sharks all offer sport.

The tackle required to convert to bowfishing consists of a few inexpensive items—a bow reel, some line, and a few bowfishing arrows.

A bow reel is nothing more than a special large spool to which at least 50 feet of stout nylon line is attached. The bow reel itself is easily and quickly fastened to the bow with tape and can be easily removed when the big-game hunting season arrives. Some bow reels manufactured today do not require taping to the bow, but have a bracket which can be instantly attached or removed from the bow. Most bow reels contain a small catch built into the reel spool to keep the line from peeling off when making shots at extreme angles.

For most freshwater fishing, 36-pound-test nylon line can handle most fish the bowman will encounter, but for those enterprising bowmen who take to salt water seeking larger species, then nylon line to 100-pound test is in order. Any bow you use for big-game hunting will suffice for bowfishing.

Arrows must be of solid fiberglass for durability. A fish weighing in excess of several pounds can easily roll on an arrow once it is struck and snap a wood shaft or bend an aluminum one. The solid, glass arrow also has the extra weight required to drive it into the water. From a husky hunting bow a solid fiberglass arrow can often be driven to depths of 10 feet and more.

Conventional feather fletching is out for the bowfisherman since feathers can quickly be ruined in water. The bowfishing arrow is therefore manufactured with rubber fletching, and if you are shooting at extremely close range, even this can be eliminated. However, since most bowfishing arrows are equipped with rubber fletching, the bowfisherman should use them.

The solid fiberglass fishing arrow is equipped with some sort of barbed or harpoon head which is not permanently fastened to the arrow shaft. Instead, the head slips over the end of the arrow and is attached to a line that runs through a small hole in the shaft just above the nock, then down the length of the shaft and is tied to the hole in harpoon head itself.

Once a fish is struck, it is easy to handline it in. However, when seeking large, heavy fish, some bowmen prefer to eliminate the bow reel and attach the line directly to a fishing rod and reel. When using the rod and reel, strip some 20 yards of line through the rod guides and carefully coil it on

Bowfishing gear is simple and inexpensive: a bow reel, line, and a few bowfishing arrows. *Courtesy Bear Archery Co.*

Young lady drawing this compound is about to catch a carp. Popular accessories for both compounds and recurve bows include fishing reels and lines. Arrow is fiberglass with barbed, or harpoon, head.

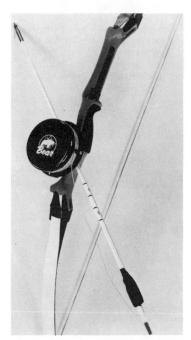

Best way to bowfish is to use a boat and cruise until you spot your quarry.

Saltwater kingdom is wide open to the bowfisherman. Here Fred Bear lands a parrotfish he has just shot off the Florida Keys.

the bottom of the boat or in a small tub or bucket, and attach the forward end of the line to the arrow.

Arrow points or harpoon heads vary widely. For greatest penetration, the single barbed point is best, but the double barbed rig is needed for big fish, especially in salt water.

Foremost to remember when shooting fish underwater is to aim low. Your view underwater is affected by light refraction and when fish are working under the water's surface and viewed at an angle your quarry is always lower than it appears to be. A few shots taken at such targets will quickly show the bowman where he should aim his arrow.

Polaroid sunglasses should be worn when bowfishing to help you see the quarry. The best time is midday, when the sun warms the surface and brings the fish up within easy view. Without polaroid sunglasses the bowfisherman will be at a loss to spot fish.

Carp provide outstanding sport for the bowhunter, especially during early spring and summer when, heavy with roe, they move into the shallows of rivers and lakes to spawn. Many southern bowmen also find action hunting garfish—

the shortnosed gar, which rarely exceeds three feet in length; the longnose gar, which usually attains a length of five feet; and the giant alligator gar, which can attain a length of eight feet and a weight in excess of 300 pounds. Hot summer evenings are best for hunting large gars. Bowhunters paddle slowly through the water searching with a flashlight for these prehistoric giants. They always use a wire leader between the harpoon head and line.

In salt water, the bowfisherman can choose from a wide variety of fish. Fast and furious action can be found by searching the flats in back-bay country for skates and stingrays. Rays are powerful creatures and once harpooned can tow a boat with ease. When seeking large rays, remember to add additional line to the bow reel to allow for their powerful, surging run.

Bowfishing has become so popular in recent years that most states now have special seasons for taking rough fishes. Check local regulations for most states require that a bowman have a regular fishing license.

Archery Organizations

There are numerous archery organizations in the United States whose purpose is to regulate competition and bring together bowmen from all parts of the world.

National Archery Association of the U.S.A.

Undoubtedly the oldest archery association, the N.A.A. was organized in 1879; its first president was the famous bowman Maurice Thompson.

The National Archery Association was formed primarily to provide the necessary rules and regulations for local, state, regional and national archery tourneys. It further conducts qualifying U.S. tryouts for the international F.I.T.A. team selections. A member of the Olympic Association, N.A.A. sponsors interscholastic, collegiate, and other archery programs, and is the United States representative to the international body of archery, the F.I.T.A. Headquarters for the N.A.A. is 1951 Geraldson Drive, Lancaster, PA 17601.

National Field Archery Association

The N.F.A.A. was formed in the late thirties by a group of West Coast archers who were tired of the formal type of shooting promoted by N.A.A. and wanted competition that simulated field or hunting conditions. Thus the first field course was developed with targets at varying ranges. In 1946, the newly organized N.F.A.A. held its initial National Field Tourney in Michigan.

The N.F.A.A. conducts and oversees state, regional, and national field tourneys as well as a host of mail tournaments. Headquarters is Route 2, Box 514, Redlands, California 92373.

Federation Internationale de Tir à l'Arc

This is the international body governing world archery. The organization was founded in 1931 and today comprises 36 nations. It conducts many tourneys to establish world archery records. Since World War II, the F.I.T.A. has conducted international archery tournaments every two years. Their rules are identical to those of the National Archery Association. For information, contact: Via Passione, 420122, Milano, Italy.

Fred Bear Sports Club

The FBSC's main purpose is to help save the sport of hunting from being outlawed. It serves as a national clearinghouse on anti-hunting information and rumors. It provides state or local support, when requested, from a nationally based bowhunting organization. The FBSC also publishes "The Big Sky"—its official publication—and disseminates information regarding unfair and malicious attacks by anti-hunting groups in general, and bowhunting in particular.

The FBSC attempts to educate the general public on the contribution of sportsmen to proper wildlife management and conservation. The FBSC has also devised indoor and field rounds for bowhunters. For more information, contact the club at: Dept. TBS, Rural Route 4, Gainesville, Florida 32601.

Professional Archers Association

The Professional Archers Association is just what the name implies—a group of professionals who shoot for money and who are organized to teach sport.

This organization is strictly for professionals—those who compete in tournaments and who have developed a standardized method of teaching archery.

To become a P.A.A. professional instructor, an applicant must be 18 years of age, must pass a written exam, and must meet the other requirements as set by the P.A.A. Constitution.

The Professional Archers Association headquarters is 4711 S. Brennan Road, Hemlock, MI 48626.

American Indoor Archery Association

The A.I.A.A. comprises members who are interested in the betterment of their sport—indoor shooting both on an individual and league basis. The A.I.A.A. has in recent years developed several indoor rounds designed solely for the indoor archer, plus a score of novelty events. A.I.A.A. headquarters is P.O. Box 174, Grayling, Michigan 49738.

Pope and Young Club

Like its brother, the famed Boone and Crockett Club, the Pope and Young Club was organized to promote conservation, the highest ethics of sportsmanship, and to establish world records for game taken with the bow and arrow.

The Pope and Young Club, organized in 1957, took its name from two world-famous bowmen, Dr. Saxton Pope and Arthur Young. An extremely exclusive club, it limits its membership to 100 regulars and only a handful of associates. To qualify for membership in this elite bowhunting group one must, in fair chase, have bagged three different species of North American big-game animals with the bow and arrow, with one scoring in the trophy class by Pope and Young standards.

Pope and Young further has a number of Official Measurers scattered throughout the country in order to find and score record-class trophies taken by bowhunters. To be listed in the Pope and Young record book an archer does not have to be a member of this organization. If he has a trophy, taken in fair chase and during the legal bow and arrow hunting season, his trophy will be recognized, provided it meets Pope and Young standards for qualification. Pope and Young Club headquarters is Route 1, Box 147, Salmon, Idaho 83467.

Professional Bowhunters' Society

This group was organized to upgrade, promote, and preserve the sport of bowhunting and provide representation on issues at all levels. By-laws promote certain "minimums" of equipment to be used for bowhunting.

PART VIII | Hunting Dogs

Profiles of Breeds

Beagle

HISTORY: While the origin of the Beagle is not definitely known, this small hound was widely bred in England before it was imported into the United States between 1860 and 1870.

There was a great deal of breeding among the various strains of Beagles brought into America to develop a small strong hound capable of hunting small game in all types of cover. Unfortunately, so much of this breeding took place during the late 1800's that problems arose as to what constituted the perfect Beagle. This was finally settled by the founding of the American-English Beagle Club in 1884, an organization that set the standards for the ideal Beagle.

For the most part, these standards are the same as those presently set forth by the National Beagle Club of America. Today, the Beagle is the most popular of all the hound breeds.

DESCRIPTION: The most common color combination of the Beagle is black, white, and tan, though many good Beagles may show up in any hound color.

Here, briefly, are some of the physical characteristics to look for in a purebred Beagle.

The head (skull) should be long and domed toward the rear. Cranium should be broad. Eyes large, set well apart, and brown or hazel in color.

The muzzle should be medium in length and straight, with a square cut at the nose. The nostrils open and large.

Ears should be set low, close to the head, and long enough to reach nearly the end of the dog's nose when drawn out. A good Beagle's ears are also rounded at the tips, with the forward edges of the ears angling slightly toward the cheeks.

The jaws are level and throat free of folds of skin. Shoulders are muscular and slope cleanly. The chest broad and deep. Shoulders and chest should not be overly muscular, which would interfere with freedom of action when working thick cover or chasing cottontails.

The back is muscular and short. The ribs well spread, giving the hound plenty of lung room. Legs are short and straight, with feet round and firm. Pads should be full and hard. Hindquarters should be strong and well muscled, giving the Beagle plenty of propelling power.

The tail is set high with a slight curve, but not so curved as to turn forward over the back. The tail should have a brush and give the appearance of being a bit short for the size of the Beagle. The coat is of medium length with a close hard texture.

SIZE: Beagles generally stand 11 to 15 inches tall at the shoulder. A good Beagle will not exceed 15 inches. Beagles generally fall into two size categories: 13- or 15-inch class, the measurement referring to height at the highest point of the shoulder. Choice of size class is generally a matter of personal preference. Weight, depending on size, ranges from 20 to 40 pounds.

HUNTING ABILITY: There is no doubt that the Beagle is a born hunter and a good gun dog. His specialty is rabbits, and few, if any, breeds can beat him at routing out his quarry. He has a keen nose, and when he "opens up" on a rabbit, his combination bawl and cry is music to the ears of the hunter.

The Beagle is also an enthusiastic and hardy worker and will not hesitate to work through thick briar patches to hunt out small game. He learns his lessons quickly, and generally all the training he needs is exposure to rabbits. When he sees a cottontail he almost instinctively knows what to do and takes up the chase. This makes the Beagle a good choice for the hunter who does not have the time for extensive training sessions with his dog.

Beagle

By no means is the Beagle limited to chasing rabbits. He makes an excellent squirrel dog. When it comes to pheasants, he is second only to the pointing breeds and spaniels. In fact, the Beagle is worth his salt on just about every kind of upland game. A Beagle from good hunting stock may flush, locate, and retrieve downed birds.

For the hunter whose budget cannot carry the expense of a high-priced professionally trained dog, the Beagle is strongly recommended. He does not need much kennel room and is quick to adjust to all climates. The little hound is a faithful companion and topnotch hunter in the field and well worth the low cost of feeding and housing him.

DISPOSITION: In addition to his excellent hunting ability, the friendly little Beagle makes a fine family dog and companion for children. A loyal and merry little hound, the Beagle will usually lick the hand of a child who pulls his tail or twists his ear. His happy and affectionate disposition makes him a favorite choice for a family pet.

Basset

HISTORY: The Basset Hound's history is a long one, dating back to medieval times. Originating in France, the breed's ancestry includes the old French bloodhound and the now-extinct St. Huberts hound.

According to legend, the Basset resulted from attempts to develop a dog that pursued game surely but very slowly, the only pace that the French aristocracy—terribly debauched and badly out of physical shape—could follow. Bassets were brought to England in the late 1860's and later to America, where they were crossed with other Bassets that reached America by way of Russia. From those breedings have come the American Basset Hound.

DESCRIPTION: It's been said that the Basset has the coloring of a foxhound, the head of a bloodhound, the legs of a Dachshund, and the body of a barnyard bull. There's no mistaking this breed, thanks to his inordinately long ears, heavy folds of skin around the entire head, and deep-set, incredibly sad, brown eyes.

A Basset should meet the following physical standards:

Head should be quite large, skull narrow and long, with a characteristic point. Head, in short, should resemble that of a bloodhound. Folds of skin should wrinkle perceptibly when the dog puts his nose to the ground.

Nose should be strong and not snipy. Ears should be long enough so that they can be folded well over the tip of the nose.

Neck should be powerful, shoulders sloping, and forelegs short, extremely strong, and heavy-boned. Rib cage should be well-rounded, chest broad and powerful, hindquarters muscular and heavy-boned.

The coat should resemble that of the Beagle: dense, fairly short, and of medium texture. Any good hound color is permissible, but most Bassets have some version of the tricolor combination (black, tan, and white).

SIZE: Bassets, like Beagles, stand 10 to 15 inches at the highest point of the shoulder, with the average height about 13 inches. Bassets, however, are much heavier than Beagles, some of them weighing as much as 80 pounds. Average weight is probably about 50 pounds. The Basset is heavy-boned and appears to weigh much less than he actually does.

HUNTING ABILITY: The Basset is second only to the Beagle as a rabbit and hare hunter, and his nose is as keen as any other hound's with the exception of the bloodhound. Bassets also will run pheasants and grouse, and some have even been taught to retrieve. They can easily be trained to tree game and so make fine coon, possum, and squirrel dogs.

The Basset runs game much slower and more painstakingly than does a Beagle, and many hunters prefer that kind of a chase. And most Bassets do not give tongue (bark) so readily on a scent trail as do most Beagles. The Basset's voice is much deeper and more resonant than the smaller hound's

If the Basset has a hunting fault, it is that it will often stay quite close to the hunter until it strikes a scent trail. Most Beagles, on the other hand, range well out from the hunter and search widely for scent.

Basset

DISPOSITION: As the Beagle is merry and affectionate, the Basset is sadly dignified and extremely friendly. Though its affectionateness is not so outward as the Beagle's, the breed is hard to beat as a family dog, house pet, and hunting companion.

Black and Tan

HISTORY: The Black and Tan—generally recognized as a coonhound, though it can be trained to run everything from possums to cougars—is the oldest of the coonhound breeds. The history of the Black and Tan (and that of most of the other trail and tree hounds) is cloudy at best, for early breeding records, when they were kept at all, were vague and inaccurate. However, it has been pretty well established that the foundation stock of the modern Black and Tan came from an old Virginia foxhound strain known as the Virgina Black and Tan (or Ferguson-Virginia Black and Tan). As the strain was developed, primarily to run possums and raccoons, records-keeping procedures and breeding practices improved, and the modern Black and Tan came to be recognized as a breed. It is one of six trail-hound breeds recognized by the United Kennel Club and the only one recognized by the American Kennel Club.

DESCRIPTION: In looks, performance, and voice, the Black and Tan is the ideal of what a coon hunter is looking for in a dog. It has a houndlike appearance and yet is built for speed and agility.

The body is relatively short but quite powerful, particularly in hindquarters and in the broad chest. The back is almost level, the stern long and tapering. Legs are straight, strong, and well-boned, and the feet are well-knuckled and heavily padded.

The Black and Tan has probably the most attractive head of any of the trail hounds. It is broad and evenly rounded, the muzzle is deep and squared off, and the dark-brown eyes are large and clear. The ears are quite long (when spread,

Black and Tan

they should measure tip to tip about the same as the dog's shoulder height) and set low on the head. The coat is a little shorter and the hair somewhat finer than that of the other trail hounds. Colors are jet black over the entire body, except for tan areas over the eyes and on chest, feet, and stern. Some white on the chest is permitted.

SIZE: As trail hounds go, the Black and Tan is of medium size. Males stand 24 to 26 inches at the withers, females 22 to 24 inches. Weight should always be proportionate to an animal's bone structure and height. Males should not exceed 60 pounds, females should not weigh more than 40.

HUNTING ABILITY: Born to hunt, the Black and Tan has a full-choke nose, great determination, and durability. It is versatile, too. Though it is most often used to run raccoons and foxes, the Black and Tan is often put on the trail of deer, bear, boar, bobcat, lynx, and mountain lion.

The Black and Tan, particularly those used exclusively on coons, works almost entirely by foot scent (scent secreted by glands in or near the feet of the animal being pursued). He is fast on the trail—an important factor in getting a predator up a tree. He has a magnificent voice and seems to enjoy using it. The Black and Tan's treeing instinct is as strong as that of any hound.

DISPOSITION: The Black and Tan is quite affectionate, though less showily so than the Beagle. It is not quarrelsome with other dogs and takes readily to being run in a pack. It is a rather shy breed and reacts with equal sensitiveness to praise and discipline. And yet it is more than willing to engage in a tooth-and-fang battle with coons, bobcats, and even larger game.

Bluetick

HISTORY: The Bluetick has a relatively short breed history, being recognized as a distinct breed (by the United Kennel Club) only since the 1940's. But its ancestry—though a matter of some conjecture, as with most hounds—is a long one.

Some dog fanciers claim that the Bluetick (and all other coonhound breeds except the Plott hound) branches from Black and Tan stock. Others say it is an offshoot of the English Coonhound. However, many authorities are of the opinion that the Bluetick's progenitor was the French Gascony Bluetick, used widely as a deer and boar hound in France and England as far back as the 13th century. The Gascony hounds were widely acclaimed for their impressive voice, appearance, and performance. The Bluetick is one of the six recognized coonhound breeds.

DESCRIPTION: The Bluetick's name describes his color, which is unique. The highly attractive coat, in most individuals, is almost solidly ticked with black, which appears blue against the white background. The Bluetick usually has a black head, some black spots on the body, and some tan trim. The coat is similar in texture to the Black and Tan's, but is somewhat heavier.

The Bluetick is quite "houndy" in general appearance. Many are quite strong and large, powerfully muscled, with massive head, while others are somewhat smaller and lighter, being bred for speed on the trail.

Often the Bluetick's body is longer, in relation to height, than that of the Black and Tan. Shoulders and chest are broad and powerful, hindquarters are heavily muscled, and legs are straight and substantially boned. Feet are well padded.

Despite its heft and muscle, a Bluetick should move gracefully and effortlessly. A good one can leap a 5-foot-high fence almost without breaking stride.

The Bluetick's head resembles the Black and Tan's but may be a bit heavier and have longer ears.

SIZE: Blueticks exhibit some variance in size. They reach larger maximum sizes than any of the other tree hounds, some of them exceeding 100 pounds, though the official standard limits a Bluetick's weight to between 45 and 80 pounds. Most of those heavyweights are tough old cougar and bear-hunting hounds.

Average height ranges a minimum of from 21 inches at the withers for females to a maximum of 26 inches for males.

Bluetick

HUNTING ABILITY: Like the Black and Tan, the Bluetick has an excellent nose and a clear bawling voice. It is a top cold-trailer (that is, it is capable of picking up and following a scent trail that is many hours old) and has a highly refined treeing instinct.

Also like the Black and Tan, the Bluetick is used to pursue a wide variety of game, including raccoons, foxes, bobcats, bears, and mountain lions. Once he has his quarry up a tree, the Bluetick will hold it there for hours or even days, if necessary, until the hunters reach the scene.

Like most hounds, the Bluetick needs little formal training, learning most of his lessons "on the job."

DISPOSITION: The Bluetick in general has the typical hound personality: friendly, affectionate, even-tempered. Like trail hounds as a whole, however, they can be stand-offish with strangers.

English Coonhound

HISTORY: Anyone who tries to pin down the genealogy of any hound breed or strain has cut himself a mighty big slice of trouble. With no other hound breed is this fact truer than with the English Coonhound. The breed's actual origins are lost in the mists of antiquity. However, it was first recognized as a distinct breed — and formally registered — in 1900. At that time the individual members were dogs with heavy blue or red ticking (spotting or dotting). Today, however, the breed will accept registered Treeing Walkers and Blueticks (the English and the Bluetick share common ancestors), grade (unregistered) dogs of those types, and English-type dogs with blue or red ticking into its registry files. In fact, you may even hear English Coonhounds called redticks. And you may well have to take an owner's word that his hound is an English Coonhound, a Bluetick, or a Treeing Walker. The English is one of the six recognized coonhound breeds.

DESCRIPTION: Because of its melting-pot background and present-day registration confusion, it is difficult to categorize the description of the English Coonhound. Many individual dogs recognized as Blueticks, for example, are nearly identical in conformation to many individuals recognized as English Coonhounds.

In general, however, the English standard today calls for a smaller, lighter dog than the Bluetick standard.

The ideal English is a medium-size dog with typical hound proportions. It has a broad rib cage and chest and generally appears to be built for speed and stamina.

The head is broad across the skull, muzzle is square, and ears are set relatively low and are of medium length. Eyes are large and widely set. The big, flaring nostrils indicate good scenting capabilities.

As for coat color, the English can be any good hound color or combination of colors, including blue ticking, red ticking, black and white, tan and white, and tricolor. Among the members of the breed, those dogs of red ticking and blue ticking are more numerous than English of any other color.

SIZE: English Coonhounds range in height at the shoulders from 21 inches (for the smallest females) to 25 inches (for the tallest males). Weights depend upon height for the most

part; an average English in the 24-inch category would weigh approximately 60 pounds.

HUNTING ABILITY: The English (and all other coon-hounds, for that matter) differs from other trail or predator hounds mainly in his ability to put an animal up a tree. And the English is as good at that as any other coonhound breed.

A hound's working ability is what determines his worth — or lack of it — to a hunter. The English, because of the many different hound types involved in its genealogy and present makeup, may exhibit any of a great number of working characteristics, none of which can be said to be typical of the breed.

For example, some English are good cold-trailers but work slowly on the trail. Some others are wide-working "drifting" types. Because of this great variety in working traits among this breed, it is wise for any prospective buyer to know exactly what he wants and to become thoroughly familiar with the individuals on the dog's pedigree and with the animal's parents.

DISPOSITION: All hounds are good-natured animals, and the English Coonhound is no different. He laps up praise and petting and yet takes discipline well. He is at home either in the house or outside in the roughest of weather.

Redbone

HISTORY: The Redbone — one of six coonhound breeds recognized by raccoon hunters everywhere and by such organizations as the United Kennel Club, American Coon Hunters Association, and American Hound Association — originated back in the 19th century, when breeders of the Redbone strain of foxhounds began to feel that their dogs were too slow and methodical on the trail. As a result, these dogs were switched from running foxes to running raccoons. Their ability at chasing the smaller and slower game was quickly recognized, and the Redbone was recognized as a distinct coonhound breed in about 1900 by the U.K.C.

Since that time the Redbone has increased in favor among raccoon hunters, mainly because of the work of such well-known breeders as Brooks Magill, R. J. Blakesley, and W. B. Frisbee.

DESCRIPTION: The Redbone's most distinctive physical characteristic is its coat, which is a solid deep-red, though some white on the brisket or feet isn't objectionable.

The Redbone's build complements his beautiful coat. The body is large and quite powerful, with long, straight legs, strong hindquarters, and a tail carried smartly. The head is not so typically "houndy" as that of the Bluetick and the Black and Tan. Ears are set somewhat higher on the head, muzzle and skull are a bit lighter. However, some Redbones have extremely long ears and a heavy head — particularly those of R. J. Blakesley's Northern Joe strain.

Not every red-colored hound is a Redbone, but most are.

SIZE: The Redbone's size and weight — though perhaps more uniform — are typical of most trail hounds. Shoulder height ranges from 21 inches for females to a maximum of

26 inches for males. Weights are proportionate to shoulder heights, but maximum is about 90 pounds and average is 45 to 75 pounds.

HUNTING ABILITY: An excellent voice that might even be described as sweet, a good cold nose, tenaciousness, and an acute treeing ability—those traits describe the Redbone as a hunter.

The breed's cold nose (the ability to pick up and follow an old scent trail) has caused some breeders to shy away, reasoning that a dog with a medium nose would waste less time on a bad track. However, the cold-trailing ability is much prized by many breeders and hunters.

Treeing Walker   Redbone

In general, Redbones bark only occasionally while the trail is cold, but their barking picks up in tempo and intensity as the trail gets warmer. This fact, which makes it easy for the listening hunter to determine the freshness of the track, cannot be said of all trail hounds. Some Blueticks and Black and Tans, for example, will give tongue so often, even on a cold track, that they can be accused of babbling, a fault in a hound.

When a Redbone pushes a coon or other quarry up a tree, its voice changes from a bawl to a chop.

The Black and Tans and the Blueticks have sometimes been criticized as being somewhat lacking in fighting ability. Not so the Redbone, which is a real scrapper, though that trait, while important if the dog is chasing bears or big cats, is not so important when the quarry is coons.

DISPOSITION: The Redbone has a kindly demeanor and, like most hounds, makes a fine family pet and companion. Also like most hounds, when he is on the trail his mind and body are totally committed to the chase, so the hunter is wasting lungpower if he attempts to call the dog in. In general, the Redbone lives to hunt, is easily taught, and is tractable.

Treeing Walker

HISTORY: The Treeing Walker, one of the six recognized coonhound breeds, almost certainly is an offshoot of the Walker strain of foxhound, though Bluetick blood may also be present. The Walker foxhound is the result of 50 years of careful breeding from the same stock of hounds by two Kentucky sportsmen and neighbors, George Washington Maupin and John W. Walker. Eventually the Maupin-Walker dogs were outcrossed to the legendary Tennessee Lead (a hound that was said to have been literally stolen from a pack of Tennessee hounds that was in the process of running a deer) and two imports from England—Rifler and Marth. Those three dogs proved to be excellent fox hunters, and their offspring, crossed again with other English imports, eventually came to be known as Walker foxhounds.

It has been theorized that the first Treeing Walkers were working Walker foxhounds that, because of advanced age, lack of speed on trail, and a well-developed treeing instinct, gave up on foxes and took to treeing raccoons.

The Treeing Walker was recognized as a distinct breed in the mid-1940's.

DESCRIPTION: The Treeing Walker looks much like the Walker foxhound. A wide range of coat colors is permissible, but the most popular and predominant combination is a white background with black spots and tan markings. The saddle is often black. Hair is of medium length and texture.

The head is fairly long, and the skull is slightly domed and broad. The brown or hazel eyes are houndlike and set well apart. The ears are set moderately low, and when stretched out they should reach nearly to the tip of the nose.

Neck is of medium length and rises free from muscular shoulders. Throat is free from folds of skin. Chest is deep, ribs well sprung. Back is moderately long, muscular, and strong. Forelegs are straight and well-boned, and pasterns are short and straight.

If there is a notable difference in appearance between the Treeing Walker and the Walker foxhound, it is that the Treeing Walker is a bit "houndier." Of the other coonhound breeds, the one that most closely approaches the Treeing Walker in looks is the English.

SIZE: Weight scales for the Treeing Walker run 50 to 75 pounds for males, 40 to 65 pounds for females. Recommended shoulder height for males is 25 inches, for females 21 inches.

HUNTING ABILITY: Due probably to its foxhound ancestry, the Treeing Walker's hunting traits include good range, speed, and general aggressiveness. Those characteristics—plus his reputation as a "drifter"—set the Treeing Walker apart from most of the other coonhound breeds. A drifter is a dog that doesn't hesitate to range away from the line when the track gets tough, rather than puzzle things out at close quarters. Many hunters don't like this trait in a hound, but there's no quarreling with the fact that it produces game. The opposite of a drifter is a "straddler," a dog that sticks to the track like glue. Black and Tans, Blueticks, and, to a lesser extent, English and Redbones are known to be straddlers. Treeing Walkers are not the best at cold-trailing, but their treeing instinct is highly developed.

DISPOSITION: The Treeing Walker's temperament is much like that of most of the other coonhound breeds: not quite so gentle and affectionate as the Beagle but more so than, say, the Plott Hound. The breed takes discipline well, and training is simply a matter of exposing the animal to the game he is expected to run. Like most hounds of all types, the Treeing Walker is quite healthy and does not demand much in the way of living conditions. It must be remembered, however, that any dog worth his salt in the field merits proper care.

Plott Hound

HISTORY: In 1750 a man named Jonathan Plott brought to the mountains of North Carolina from his native Germany a pack of hounds, offspring of generations of dogs used to hunt the big and tough German wild boars. These dogs proved to be proficient at hunting black bears, numerous then in the Carolina mountains. For 30 years Plott kept the strain pure and free from any outcross, selecting his breeding stock carefully.

In 1780 Henry Plott took over the pack from his father and decided to introduce into the strain some blood from a line of Georgia bear hounds called "leopard" or "spotted-leopard" dogs. Only that one cross took place, and the Plott family descendants—who are still breeding Plott Hounds today—vehemently deny rumors of subsequent crossings of Plotts with Black and Tans, Bloodhounds, and other breeds.

In 1946 the United Kennel Club recognized the Plott Hound as a distinct breed. It is generally recognized as a coonhound breed, though its widest use until recent years had been as a bear and boar hound in the Great Smoky Mountains of Tennessee and North Carolina.

Plott Hound

DESCRIPTION: In color the Plott is brindle (brindle is a mixture of gray and yellowish-brown, with darker streaks) with a black saddle and sometimes white points. The coat is thicker, heavier, and provides more protection from the elements than that of any of the other trail hounds.

The Plott is of medium height. Its head is rather large and blocky, and the jaws are those of a fighter. The body has a wiry but well-balanced appearance, though it is not so heavily muscled or boned as is that of the Bluetick or Black and Tan. The build is something like that of a husky pointer. Ear length tends to vary (see "Hunting Ability").

Agility is one of the Plott Hound's strong points; he moves with the grace of a cat.

The Plott's voice is not the most attractive of the trail hounds. The chop, in particular, is higher in pitch than that of the other trail hounds.

SIZE: This breed's standard calls for males to weigh no more than 60 pounds and females to weigh no less than 40 pounds. Despite the standard, the breed's weight is on the average somewhat less than that of the other trail hounds. Some individuals, on the other hand, reach 90 pounds.

The Plott's height ranges from 21 inches at the shoulder for bitches to 25 inches for males.

HUNTING ABILITY: The Plott is a tough character, as befits a dog bred to battle boars and bears. The breed is also used to hunt wolves, mountain lions, bobcats, coyotes, deer, and various small game including raccoons.

The breed's hunting ability seems to depend upon whether an individual dog is of the long-eared or short-eared "type," both of which were developed by the Plott family. The short-eared type is generally considered to be faster and a more efficient fighter of dangerous game, and so it is usually preferred by bear and boar hunters. The long-eared type is said to have a better voice, to be a better cold-trailer, and to be more "open" on trail. There also seems to be a sort of "happy-medium-type" Plott, which is gaining favor among hunters.

DISPOSITION: Because theirs is a relatively tough life—most of them live in the mountains under rugged conditions and often find themselves within striking distance of an animal that can fight back—the Plott's temperament is less gentle and affectionate than that of most other hounds.

In fact, Plotts may be downright quarrelsome, and owners have learned the folly of keeping several in the same pen, for these dogs have a tendency to fight.

American Foxhound

HISTORY: The Foxhound is the oldest sporting dog in the U.S., dating back to early Colonial times. The year 1650 is the date generally accepted as the Foxhound's introduction into the U.S. In that year a friend of Lord Baltimore's, Robert Brooke, brought to Maryland from England a hound pack used primarily on foxes.

Foxhunting's popularity—and that of the hounds bred for the purpose—spread from Maryland to Virginia, Pennsylvania, New Jersey, New York, New England, and throughout the South in the ensuing 150 years. Among the sport's adherents were George Washington, Thomas Jefferson, Alexander Hamilton, and John Marshall. Washington, in fact, was given seven "staghounds" by the Marquis de Lafayette. Though these large French dogs did not take well to foxhunting, their blood, and to a greater extent the blood of English and Irish hounds imported by foxhunters in the Southeast U.S., went into the development of the Foxhound we know today.

For all intents and purposes, however, the American Foxhound was developed within the past 150 years and is largely the result of the breeding practices of a number of families, most of them in the South. Those practices have brought about the recognition by foxhunters of some 20 or so strains of Foxhounds (foxhunters are prone to regard these strains as breeds, but they are actually strains, a strain being a line of dogs showing similar characteristics as a result of selective breeding).

The Foxhound strains include the Walker, Trigg, and July — by far the most popular — as well as the Brooke, Birdsong, Goodman, Travis, Buckfield, Robinson, Wild Goose, Arkansas Traveler, Avent, Hudspeth, Tucker, Hampton-Watts-Bennett, Shaver, Bywaters, Whitlock Shaggie, Trumbo, Sugar Loaf, Cook, Byron, Gossett, and New England Native.

The history of many of these strains is lost in antiquity, usually because of slipshod or nonexistent records-keeping practices. Among those that are known are the following:

Walker — (See Treeing Walker).

Trigg — Dr. T. Y. Henry, a grandson of Patrick Henry, kept at his Virginia home a pack of hounds that had fine reputations as fox chasers. On a trip south for his health, Henry met Col. George L. F. Birdsong of Georgia. A friendship developed that resulted in Birdsong's acquiring the entire Henry pack when Henry found out that in Florida, his new home, the dogs couldn't resist chasing the deer that were abundant there. Birdsong crossed his dogs with a Maryland hound and then began corresponding with Col. Haiden C. Trigg of Kentucky, who was looking for some new blood with which to put some speed into his pack of slow-moving black-and-tan hounds. Birdsong sent three of his hounds to Trigg, who thereupon began the breeding process that was to give rise to the strain of foxhounds that today bear his name.

July — A Mr. Miles G. Harris of Georgia secured a fine hound named July from a hunter in Maryland. This dog, of Irish derivation and believed to be related to dogs bred by Dr. Henry of Virginia, was crossed on Col. Birdsong's hounds. Hounds tracing back to that breeding and others by Georgia hunters, are today known as Julys (or Georgia Julys).

Buckfield — In about 1858 a Canadian peddler is said to have brought to the town of Buckfield, Maine, a red and blue-mottled bitch that looked like a cross between a foxhound and an Irish Setter. This dog was mated with a black stump-tailed hound owned by another passer-through described as a tramp. Result of this mating was Bose, a compact, red, shaggy bitch and a topnotch foxhunter. She is supposedly the fountainhead of the Buckfield strain.

Robinson — A man named B. F. Robinson of Kentucky developed this strain by breeding Irish hounds to hounds

from some of the established Maryland packs. The strain that resulted bears his name.

Goodman — One W. C. Goodman obtained some of the Robinson dogs and crossed them with some of his own dogs, which were of the Maupin-Walker type. Most individuals of this strain were excellent fox dogs.

Wild Goose — These are Tennessee hounds originally developed in Virginia in the 1830's by John Fuquay and C. S. Lewis and later brought to Tennessee by Lewis.

Arkansas Traveler — Judge C. Floyd Huff of Hot Springs, Arkansas, owned some "Missouri" hounds that were somewhat lacking in size and bone. To build them up, he introduced some blood from English hounds and some from a pack of Kentucky dogs. The results were the Arkansas Traveler strain, dogs that set a fast pace in that state and Louisiana.

American Foxhound

Avent — These dogs were the result of a mixture of Ferguson Virginia Black and Tans, dogs called "Bachelors," and native hounds that had enjoyed much success around Avent's home town of Hickory Valley, Tennessee. The Avent dogs were hunted widely in South Carolina, in the Mississippi Delta (on bears), in the West (for wolves and coyotes), and even in Africa (for lions and other big game).

DESCRIPTION: Speed, endurance, and toughness are a Foxhound's trademarks, and his physical attributes should reflect those trademarks.

Because there are so many strains, it is all but impossible to use specifics in describing the typical Foxhound. But since most Foxhounds, regardless of strain, are related, a general picture of this breed can be painted.

A Foxhound can be expected to be sturdily built overall, but the body should not be so heavy that the dog's speed or endurance is impeded. Legs should be strong and straight, feet catlike, chest and hindquarters powerful, ribs well-sprung.

The head should be proportionate to the rest of the body — that is, not too large or too small — cleanly formed, and must not have loose skin as in the Basset. Ears should be of medium length (when extended outward they should reach nearly to the tip of the nose) and should be set rather low on the head. Eyes are dark brown.

The coat should be of typical hound length and hard-textured. The predominant Foxhound colors are similar to those of Beagles and Bassets, but there is a great variation in colors, which include black and tan, orange and white, solid red, and many others.

SIZE: Because of the great variety in Foxhound types, there is considerable variation in the size of these dogs. In general, however, males should be no taller than 25 inches at the shoulder nor shorter than 22 inches. Females average an inch shorter. Weights range, on the average, from 50 to 65 pounds. Too much weight tends to reduce the dog's speed and stamina.

HUNTING ABILITY: The American Foxhound is unsurpassed in speed, courage, endurance, and tenacity. It is far rangier and a better producer of game than its English ancestors.

In effect, the American Foxhound's hunting ability is measured by the kind of hunting he is asked to do. There are two major forms of fox hunting practiced in the U.S.

In the South the sport of fox hunting is rooted almost entirely in the chase. The foxes, usually hunted at night, are not shot, but rather are highly valued for their ability to lead hound packs on runs that are fast, merry, loud, and usually long. For this kind of sport the hound must be inordinately fast, hard-driving, and capable of following hot scent that may be floating some distance from the actual track. He must be able to range out well in order to hit the scent of a moving fox (these dogs are expected to find their own foxes).

In the North foxes are most often hunted on snow and during the day, and the object is for the hounds to run the fox around to hunters who station themselves at likely crossings. The foxes are usually shot, for their fur value or for bounty. Dogs for this form of the sport must have cold-trailing ability, for they are seldom put down until a track is found by the hunters, and the track may be an old one. Competition is lacking for the most part, for only one or two dogs are usually put on a track — at least until the fox is up and running, at which time other hounds may be released. Speed is less important in these Northern dogs than is a loud and clear voice. Such a voice serves to let the owner know the direction of the chase and also prods the fox.

It should be noted that American Foxhounds are used to run game animals ranging from rabbits to mountain lions.

DISPOSITION: The American Foxhound's appealing and friendly facial expression is a key to his temperament, in most individuals. He is relatively gentle, takes well to training (though little formal training, other than obedience work, is needed) and discipline, and possesses the common-sense sagacity that all hounds seem to have in one degree or another. He is also greatly adaptable, being able to work out different conditions of terrain, weather, and quarry. And yet he can be cantankerously independent.

English Springer Spaniel

HISTORY: The word "spaniel" has its origins in the Roman term for Spain: Hispania. But there is no concrete proof that this type of dog originated in Spain. It is known, though, that spaniels have been in existence for thousands of years. In New York's Metropolitan Museum there is a figure of a spaniel-like dog that dates back to about 3000 B.C.

Starting in about 1800, spaniel-type dogs were classified in three rather loose categories that were based mainly on size. Dogs of under 14 pounds were called lap (or comforter) spaniels, those of 14 to 28 pounds were called cocker spaniels, and those weighing more than 28 pounds were called springer, English, or field spaniels.

The English Springer Spaniel that we know today apparently dates back to about 1812, when the Boughey family

Photo by Robert Elman

English Springer Spaniel

of Shropshire, England, began to keep a relatively pure line of these dogs. The first trials for Springers, run under the auspices of the sporting Spaniel Club, were held in England in 1895. The larger and faster Springers began to dominate the trials, outhunting the cocker, Clumber, and field spaniels, and sportsman esteem for the Springer grew.

The generally agreed-upon date for the introduction of the purebred Springer into America is 1907, but the breed did not take hold until a Manitoba dog fancier, Eudore Chevrier, began to import and train large numbers of these dogs in about 1921.

The English Springer Field Trial Association was formed in 1924, and the first trials were held that same year. A standard for the breed was devised, and the American Kennel Club approved it in 1932.

DESCRIPTION: The English Springer Spaniel is a flushing dog — that is, he hunts the ground ahead of his master — but within shotgun range — and puts gamebirds into flight, rather than points them.

The Springer's coat is flat and somewhat wavy (but not curly), of medium length, and dense enough to provide protection against water, weather, and briary vegetation. There is a fringe of wavy hair on throat, brisket, chest, and bell. Coat colors include liver and white (the most prevalent), liver and tan, black and white, black and tan, tan and white, black and white and tan, and others. Unacceptable color combinations are red and white, and lemon and white.

The ears are long and set on at about eye level. The tail is docked. The feet are webbed for swimming and for work in muddy and swampy areas. Toes are well-arched, and pads are deep and horny. The body is muscular and relatively heavily boned.

In general, the Springer's physical conformation should give him speed, agility, and endurance.

SIZE: The Springer is a medium-size hunting dog. Weights range from 45 to 50 pounds for males and from 42 to 47 pounds for females. Shoulder height ranges from 18 to 22 inches.

HUNTING ABILITY: Being a flushing dog rather than a pointing dog, the Springer must work within range of his master's gun. The breed has a natural tendency to work close and so is easily taught to flush gamebirds.

Many Springers, given the proper training, also make at least passable retrievers and can learn to mark the spots where shot birds fall. They are topnotch bird finders and fetchers in thick cover and in swamps, and they can handle rough weather well.

The Springer will hunt any gamebird, but it is far more popular with hunters who seek birds that tend to run rather than fly (such as pheasants and desert quail) than it is with men who hunt tight-sitting game (bobwhite quail and the like). In fact, the recent upsurge in Springer popularity in America is due mainly to the rise of the pheasant as the top gamebird in the northern U.S. Running birds are right down a Springer's alley, while they tend to corrupt the performance of a pointing dog.

DISPOSITION: The Springer's temperament is gentle, particularly with children, and friendly. The breed adapts well to various maintenance conditions—that is, it is as much at home in the home as in the kennel. It takes well to training and discipline.

Cocker Spaniel

HISTORY: At one time, beginning in the early 19th century, all spaniel-type dogs were classified according to size, with the cockers (14 to 28 pounds) ranking between the lap spaniels (under 14 pounds) and the field spaniels (over 28 pounds). The name "cocker" comes from the woodcock, which the cockers were bred to hunt.

But the Cocker Spaniel as a distinct breed is generally believed to have originated with a dog named Obo, whelped in England in 1879. Obo, 10 inches tall at the shoulder and weighing 22 pounds, led directly to the separate registration of Cockers in the English stud book, beginning in 1893. The first field trial for Cockers was held in 1899.

Cocker Spaniel

Many English Cockers were imported to America, where a separate strain, the American Cocker, was developed. The fountainhead of that strain is said to have been a dog named Braeside Bob.

The first major Cocker trial held in the U.S. was run in 1924 under the auspices of the Cocker Spaniel Field Trial Club of America. Field trials were largely responsible for maintaining the breed's value as hunting dogs, but that value declined markedly, particularly with the onset of World War II, which had the effect of almost entirely eliminating Cocker field trials. Trials were resumed after the war, but by then the breed was largely relegated to bench shows and pet status. Very few Cockers are seen in the game coverts today.

DESCRIPTION: The Cocker, like the Springer Spaniel, is a breed that flushes, rather than points, gamebirds.

The modern Cocker Spaniel is actually two dogs: the American Cocker and the English Cocker. The American Cocker is perhaps the most beautiful of all the spaniels. It has a rounded skull, large and rather prominent eyes, and long ears that are placed at eye level or a bit lower. The leather of the ears reaches to the muzzle when they are outstretched.

The American's body is rather short, with a much broader chest than in other spaniels. The top line slopes from the withers to the croup. Feet are strong and compact, with thick pads.

The American Cocker comes in three varieties, based mainly on color. The three are black, any other solid color (but including black and tan), and parti-colors. The black variety usually has a thicker coat and feathering than the other color types.

The English Cocker's muzzle is slightly longer than the American's, and there is not the excess of hair as in the American black variety. Colors vary, including many self colors (all black, all liver, and all red) and parti-colors, as well as roan colors of blue, red, orange, liver, and lemon. The English Cocker is leggier than the American.

SIZE: The English Cocker is somewhat heavier than the American Cocker, ranging from 28 to 34 pounds for the males, 26 to 32 pounds for the females. The American Cocker should weigh no less than 22 pounds and no more than 28 pounds.

HUNTING ABILITY: As stated above, the Cocker Spaniel today is far more popular as a bench-show animal and house pet than as a hunter of gamebirds. Therein lies the breed's major disadvantage, as far as hunters are concerned — it is difficult to find a good hunting strain of Cocker Spaniel.

If an interested hunter can find a dog whose recent ancestry contains good hunting and field-trial stock, he is on the right track. The man should then try to determine whether the dog has the following desirable characteristics: courage, a well-developed instinct for following bird scent, willingness to work, and tractability. The dog should like the water (particularly if the man wants the dog to do some waterfowl retrieving) and should be willing to charge right in to get a bird even though the water may be cold or rough. And the dog should be willing to work all kinds of cover with enthusiasm and fair speed.

In general, the English Cocker is a better bet than the American as a hunting dog. That is partly due to the fact that in England Cockers are required to prove their worth in a field trial before they can become eligible to qualify as a bench champion, a practice that has prevented the widespread deterioration of the hunting instinct that has plagued the American Cocker.

The Cocker, being the smallest of the spaniels, is not so effective in heavy cover or in water work. The Cocker is not as fast or as effective a hunter as the Springer Spaniel. It is, however, faster than the Clumber or Sussex spaniels and so is generally preferred over those breeds.

DISPOSITION: Good Cockers — especially those that are to be used for hunting — should have a happy, bubbly type of disposition. In recent years, however, many Cockers have been extremely high-strung and nervous, given to urinating on the floor because of excitement and to biting people for little reason. Shyness and hysteria are other character faults, but those, like the others, may well be on the way out, thanks to the efforts of Cocker breeders.

Cockers from good hunting stock are alert and take correction in stride.

American Water Spaniel

HISTORY: The American Water Spaniel is one of only a very few hunting-dog breeds that was developed entirely in the U.S. Though it has been in existence as a recognizable type for almost 100 years, the American Water Spaniel was not recognized officially until 1920, when the United Kennel Club accepted a Wisconsin dog for registration as an American Water Spaniel. The Field Dog Stud Book sanctioned the breed in 1938, and the American Kennel Club followed suit in 1940.

The breed's development was centered in the pheasant belt of the Midwest and in New England. One of the men largely responsible for that development was a Wisconsin

American Water Spaniel

physician and surgeon, Dr. F. J. Pfeifer, whose Curley Pfeifer was the first American Water Spaniel registered with the U.K.C. Dr. Pfeifer's kennels contained as many as 130 of these dogs at one time.

It was Dr. Pfeifer's opinion that the breed was the result of a cross between the English Curly-Coat Retriever and the Field Spaniel. In all probability there was also some Irish Water Spaniel blood. The breed's original purpose was to retrieve ducks shot by hunters in small skiffs.

DESCRIPTION: Once called the American *Brown* Water Spaniel because of its rich liver color, this breed's coat is closely curled or deeply waved, but not kinky. The hair is quite dense, to give protection in water and heavy cover.

The forehead is covered with short smooth hair and lacks the tuft or topknot that is characteristic of the Irish Water Spaniel. The American's tail is covered with hair while the Irish's tail is ratlike.

There apparently are two strains within the American Water Spaniel breed. One type is small, compact, and somewhat benchlegged, while the other is quite a bit larger and longer-legged. The larger strain is preferred by jumpshooters.

SIZE: The American Water Spaniel stands 15 to 18 inches at the shoulder and weighs 25 to 45 pounds. It is compact and built close to the ground.

HUNTING ABILITY: The American Water Spaniel is a natural hunter and over the years has maintained all the "hunt" that was originally bred into him. That is probably due to the fact that this breed has not attracted the attention of dog-show people.

The American is essentially a flushing dog, though it is occasionally classified as a retriever. It can be trained to quarter about in the uplands in front of the hunter, to scent and chase up upland game, to drop to shot, and to retrieve upon command. Its main use in the uplands is on birds that tend to run rather than fly, such as pheasants and various Western quail.

The American is a fair waterfowl retriever but can't compare to the various retriever breeds for that purpose, though it is a tougher water breed than any of the other spaniels.

The American doesn't rank as tops in any facet of hunting-dog work. On the other hand, he is an excellent choice as a multipurpose dog, capable of both flushing game and fetching it and able to perform moderately well in a duck blind. And the American will hunt anything from pheasants, grouse, and woodcock to rabbits and squirrels.

DISPOSITION: The American Water Spaniel is likable, friendly, intelligent, even-tempered, and tractable. He is a natural hunter and a quick learner, and he seldom possesses personality quirks. He takes well to training and discipline and adapts well to varying conditions of terrain and weather. Though he has an appealing way about him, the American, more so than most other spaniels, seems to be distrustful of strangers.

Welsh Springer Spaniel

HISTORY: No one knows exactly when the Welsh Springer Spaniel first came upon the dog scene, though it is known to be an ancient breed indeed. As one might expect, the breed was developed in Wales but found its way into England and Scotland and eventually to America and such far-flung lands as India, Australia, and Siam. The breed standards were drawn up by the Welsh Springer Spaniel Club of England and later adopted by the American Kennel Club.

DESCRIPTION: The Welsh Springer Spaniel—in contrast to the Cocker and English Springer, which may be a wide variety of colors—is red and white only. The coat is flat and thick and silky, and it has a soft understory that provides protection from briary cover and from rugged water and weather conditions.

Ears are quite hairy and set low on the head. Legs are straight and fringed with hair. Tail is plumed.

Welsh Springer Spaniel

SIZE: The Welsh Springer is a bit smaller than the English Springer and a great deal larger than the Cocker Spaniel. The Welsh ranges in weight from 35 to 45 pounds.

HUNTING ABILITY: The Welsh Springer is a flushing-type rather than a pointing dog. Its importance as a hunting breed is limited, however, and very few of these dogs are seen in the game coverts.

Nonetheless, the Welsh Springer can be taught to hunt in front of the gun like other flushing spaniels, though his training, particularly obedience training, may be more difficult and time-consuming than for any of the other spaniels.

If this breed has a strong point, it is probably that it is able to work under temperature extremes, particularly on land (it is not able to stand very cold water, as retrievers can). It is capable of hunting upland game when the weather is quite warm.

The Welsh Springer has an acutely tuned nose and is a willing worker. However, his working pace is somewhat slower than that of the English Springer.

DISPOSITION: The Welsh Springer Spaniel has a pleasant and even temperament. He is kind and gentle with children, is fiercely loyal, and is dependable. His training may take more time than with some other breeds, but he takes discipline well.

Clumber Spaniel

HISTORY: The first mention, in print, of the Clumber Spaniel was an 1807 article that appeared in a British publication, Sporting Magazine. An engraving with the article showed part of a painting in which a number of long, low, heavy-bodied dogs surrounded the gamekeeper of the estate—called Clumber House—of the Duke of Newcastle, Henry Clinton. The spaniel-like dogs, which the magazine article called "springers, or cock-flushers," were said to have been a gift of the Duke of Noailles of France. The gamekeeper, William Mansell, was said to have "studied to increase, unmixed, this peculiar race of flushers."

Clumbers dominated the early field trials held for spaniels, despite the fact that at least one authority—the American dog writer James Watson, thought the breed was of "little use" in the field because of its slowness. But then the Cockers and Springers became faster, and the Clumbers began to lose favor.

Clumbers never became popular in America, mainly because no "specialty" club was ever formed to espouse the breed. No trials are held for Clumbers.

DESCRIPTION: The Clumber might be said to be the Basset Hound of the bird-dog set. Slow-moving, short-legged, and heavy-bodied, it gives the appearance of being very powerful. The head is large and massive, with relatively short ears. Neck is long and thick, and the shoulders are heavily muscled. The back is long, broad, and straight, free from droop or bow. Legs are short but heavy-boned, and the feet are large.

The coat is straight and silky, not too long but very dense, and has long and abundant feather. White predominates in the coat color, which varies from lemon and white to orange

Clumber Spaniel

and white, with the body having almost no lemon or orange. Ears are (or should be) solid lemon or solid orange. Muzzle and legs are ticked.

SIZE: Today's Clumber Spaniel is somewhat larger than the English Springer, standing 17 to 18 inches tall at the shoulder but weighing 55 to 65 pounds for males, 35 to 50 pounds for bitches.

HUNTING ABILITY: Clumbers were bred as "retired gentlemen's shooting dogs" and were used in restricted areas such as turnip patches and truck gardens and in small game preserves with large populations of birds. In such places the slow-moving, close-working Clumber was a major advantage. However, most American conditions of cover, terrain, and game require a dog that works at a much faster pace and covers a good amount of ground. That is the main reason the Clumber has never found wide favor in this country. He is so rare here, in fact, that finding a good one is extremely difficult.

Nonetheless, the Clumber is a topnotch game-flusher and will retrieve well if trained properly. Because of his light coat, he is said to be unparalleled as a hot-weather hunter.

DISPOSITION: One of the Clumber's advantages (perhaps the only advantage, so far as many American hunters are concerned) is that he is about the most easily trained of all the spaniels. He takes training and discipline well, remembers his lessons, and does not have to be retrained. Though some early accounts of the breed's temperament called these dogs "naturally ill-tempered" and said they "would not work for every person," such temperament quirks have apparently been bred out.

Tolling Dog

You won't find the Tolling Dog listed in any of the American breed registries. It is "officially" recognized only by the men who use these dogs—and they are used in a most intriguing way.

In Europe, especially France and England, and in Nova Scotia (the only place in North America where these dogs are known to be used) dogs are used to "toll"—or lure—waterfowl. In Europe the dogs—belonging, apparently, to no specific breed—were trained to run up and down a stream bank at the confluence of the stream with a larger body of water. The antics of one of these dogs would arouse the curiosity of ducks sitting offshore on the larger body of water, and they would swim closer to investigate. Eventually, if things worked out as planned, the birds would wind up trapped inside a funnel-shaped net stretched across the stream's outlet. As the birds would move in, the dog would put on his show farther up the shore, thus drawing the birds in closer and closer to the shore and the net.

In Nova Scotia, the Tolling Dog is used in a similar fashion, except that he draws waterfowl in to a hunter's shotgun. The hunter finds a lake that is harboring a respectable number of ducks. He then builds a blind or uses natural camouflage on the shore, preferably on an outjutting point or on an island. The dog puts on his act on the shore near the blind, occasionally barking sharply. For some reason the ducks cannot overcome their curiosity, and they come within range of the hunter.

The Nova Scotia Tolling Dog is bred more or less true to type and looks like a red fox in size, coat texture, and color. (It is claimed that foxes use similar tactics to lure waterfowl and other birds.) As might be expected, Tolling Dogs are far from numerous.

Labrador Retriever

HISTORY: There is little doubt that the Labrador originated in the Canadian province of the same name, probably from a strain of dog bred in and around St. John's. The breed's greatest development, however, took place in England and began when the Second Earl of Malmesbury imported some of the dogs from Newfoundland (Labrador). The Third

Labrador Retriever

Earl of Malmesbury is given the credit for giving the breed its name and keeping it relatively pure. It is generally agreed, though, that some early English breeders introduced some blood from other retrievers, notably the flat-coat and curly-coat types.

In 1903 the Labrador was recognized as a breed by the English Kennel Club, and in 1906 Labradors were first entered in English field trials.

Labradors first appeared in the U.S. in the late 1920's, and the first licensed Labrador field trial in this country was held in 1931, in Orange County, New York. And Labradors swept the first three placements in the first all-retriever-breed trial, held in 1934 at East Setauket, New York. Since that time the Labrador has outdistanced all other retriever breeds in popularity among hunters and field-trialers. That popularity is due in large measure to such early breeders as J. F. Carlisle and Averell Harriman. About 65 percent of all retriever registrations today are Labradors.

DESCRIPTION: The Labrador's overall appearance is that of a strongly built, close-coupled, and active animal. In comparison with the Flat-Coat and Curly-Coat retrievers, the breeds which the Lab most resembles, he is wider in the head and through the chest, and wider and more powerful in loins and hindquarters. Generally the Lab is shorter of leg than other retrievers and of a solider build.

The Lab's skull is broad and has a slightly pronounced brow, and the head is clean-cut and free from any fleshiness. Jaws are long and powerful, not snipy. Ears hang rather close to the head and well back, are set somewhat low, and should not be large and heavy. Eyes are brown, yellow, or black.

Neck is long and powerful, shoulders long and sloping. Legs are straight from shoulder to ground, and feet are compact, with well-arched toes and well-developed pads.

The tail, almost totally free of feathering but clothed all around with short, thick hair and having a rounded look, is quite thick near the base but tapers gradually toward the tip.

The coat is short, very dense, and without waviness. The coat color is generally all black, though other solid colors—yellow being the most abundant—are permissible, as is a white spot on the chest.

SIZE: The standard for Labrador Retrievers calls for shoulder heights as follows: 22½ to 24½ inches for males, 21½ to 23½ inches for females. Average weights of Labs in working condition are 60 to 75 pounds for males and 55 to 70 pounds for bitches.

HUNTING ABILITY: The Labrador well deserves its position of preeminence among retrievers. It is the No. 1 choice of men who want a dog that will fetch birds on both land and water. The Lab takes naturally to water and to the job of retrieving, at which he is at his best. Properly trained—and this breed takes training very well—the Lab will sit or lie quietly in a boat or blind or walk at heel until ordered to retrieve.

The Lab is probably best known for his waterfowl work. His rugged build and constitution, and his short but protective coat, enable him to withstand extremes of heat or cold. He is second in toughness only to the Chesapeake Bay Retriever.

Though retrieving downed gamebirds is his specialty, the Labrador has phenomenal scenting powers and can also be trained to quarter ahead of the hunter and flush upland game, including pheasants, grouse, quail, woodcock, and the like. When working upland coverts, the Lab is quick, stylish, and aggressive—traits that also endear him to field-trialers. He will also trail wounded and running birds such as pheasants.

And Labradors, because of their tractability and trainability, are often used as seeing-eye dogs.

Finally, Labradors have compiled an enviable record in retriever field trials, topping all other breeds in numbers of dogs entered and in placements won.

DISPOSITION: Even-tempered, likable, friendly—all describe the Labrador. He makes an excellent pet for the hunter's family, though the more aggressive individuals of this breed may be too rough for small children (however, the most aggressive Labs are usually the best hunters). The Lab is very easily trained and quite intelligent, takes discipline without cringing or quitting, and is never mean. Some Labs (like some dogs of any breed) tend to be roamers when left to their own devices.

Golden Retriever

HISTORY: The Golden Retriever is directly descended from a strain of very large light-colored dogs known as Russian Trackers. These animals were part of a circus troupe touring England in 1860. A certain nobleman, Sir Dudley Majoribanks, saw the dogs and was so impressed that he bought the entire group of eight.

Sir Dudley bred the dogs for 10 years without outcrossing. But in 1870, feeling that the dogs—which weighed as much as 100 pounds—were too large and cumbersome to be hunters, he crossed the Russian Trackers with the bloodhound. The outcross reduced the size of the breed, improved its scenting abilities, and gave the coat a somewhat darker color

Golden Retriever

and a finer texture. In 1911 these dogs were recognized as a distinct breed by the English Kennel Club, and at about that same time the Golden Retriever Club of England was formed.

It was about the turn of the century when the first Goldens came to North America, brought to Vancouver Island, British Columbia by British army personnel. The breed spread rapidly on the Pacific Coast, even as far as Alaska. One of the breeders most responsible was Bart Armstrong, of Winnipeg, Manitoba. The Golden was recognized by the Canadian Kennel Club in 1927 and by the American Kennel Club in 1932.

DESCRIPTION: From puppyhood, when he is a round little ball of yellow fluff, through adulthood, the Golden Retriever is a beautiful animal. The gorgeous coat—rich red overall (it must not be too light, like cream, or so dark as, say, the red of an Irish Setter)—and soft, honest facial expression give the Golden an attractiveness few other breeds can match.

Standard for the Golden Retriever calls for a broad skull set on a clean and muscular neck. Muzzle is powerful and wide. Eyes are dark and set well apart, kindly in expression, and have dark rims.

The coat may be either flat or wavy, and it is dense and water resistant, with a good undercoat.

Ears are small and well set on. Feet are round and cat-like, not splayed. Forelegs are well-boned and straight, hind legs strong and muscular. Tail is straight, not curled at the tip or carried over the back.

Body in general is well-balanced, short-coupled, and deep through the chest. Shoulders are well laid back and long in the blade.

SIZE: Ideal weights for Golden Retrievers in top working condition are as follows: 65 to 68 pounds for males, 55 to 60 pounds for bitches. Shoulder heights average 23 to 24 inches for males, 20½ to 22 inches for bitches.

HUNTING ABILITY: The Golden's status as the second most popular retrieving dog in the U.S. attests to the breed's ability as a bird finder and fetcher.

The Golden ranks behind the Chesapeake and the Labrador as a straight retriever of downed waterfowl, particularly under rigorous conditions. Icy water is easily absorbed by the Golden's silky coat, so he does not perform at his best under most waterfowling situations (in warmer climates, however, the Golden makes a fine waterfowl retriever).

The Golden seems to be at his best on dry land. He hunts well in front of the upland gunner, quartering nicely and hunting an area thoroughly and methodically. He marks downed birds well and, of course, is an accomplished fetcher.

The Golden isn't as good as the Labrador in the upland coverts, lacking the Lab's speed, style, and aggressiveness. But he tops the Chesapeake in that department.

The Golden, on the other hand, is about the most reliable of all bird-fetchers when it comes to nonslip retrieving. (A nonslip retriever is a dog that walks at heel or sits quietly at the handler's side until ordered out to retrieve.)

The Golden's coat can be a problem, for it collects burrs in the uplands, mud in the marshes. The coat requires considerable attention.

DISPOSITION: There is no more affectionate breed than the Golden Retriever. He thrives on verbal and physical praise, is wonderfully understanding and gentle with children, and makes the best pet of any of the retriever breeds.

The Golden is exceptionally intelligent and tractable. He is eminently trainable too—provided that the trainer uses patience and a soft hand. Too much two-fisted discipline can turn this otherwise docile and biddable animal into an obstinate sulker that will refuse to learn or work.

Chesapeake Bay Retriever

HISTORY: It is generally agreed that the Chessie, as this breed is affectionately known, descended at least partly from the Newfoundland dog of some 150 years ago. It therefore shares a common heritage with the Labrador.

Chesapeake Bay Retriever

It is said that an English brig was wrecked off the shores of Maryland in 1807. Aboard the vessel—and rescued—were two Newfoundland puppies, a dingy red male and a black female, that became the property of local breeders. These dogs were reported to have extraordinary retrieving ability.

Stories vary on the development of the breed from that point. Some have it that the two Newfoundland dogs were crossed with yellow and tan coonhounds. Another story, amusing but absurd, says that a Chesapeake bitch was mated to an otter! Still another account, possibly the true one, is that the Newfoundland dogs were crossed with English water poodles.

The Chessie's popularity grew rather rapidly, and by 1918, when the American Chesapeake Club was founded, the breed had become the No. 1 duck dog not only in the Chesapeake area but also in such places as Manitoba, Minnesota, and along the Mississippi Flyway. The breed was recognized by the American Kennel Club in 1931.

DESCRIPTION: Beauty, it is said, is in the eyes of the beholder. Under that premise the Chesapeake is the apple of the eye of many a duck and goose hunter. But actually the Chessie is a sort of homely animal. And Chesapeake breeders have resisted efforts to beautify the breed—an attitude that, from the hunter's standpoint, is very fortunate, since a breed's "beautification" is usually accompanied by a drastic decline in its hunting abilities.

The Chessie's most unusual traits are his dense and oily coat (which enables this dog to be oblivious to the coldest water), yellow eyes, rather long tail, and his color, which ranges from a light shade quite reminiscent of dead grass to chocolate brown.

Skull is broad, muzzle is powerful, and the ears are rather small and set well up on the head. The thick and muscular neck appears to be too short for the body. Shoulders are powerful, and chest strong, deep, and wide.

Hindquarters are especially powerful, for swimming. Legs are of medium length, well-boned, and straight. The feet appear abnormally large.

SIZE: Male Chesapeake Bay Retrievers weigh 65 to 75 pounds on the average, females 55 to 65 pounds. Shoulder heights are 23 to 26 inches for males, 21 to 24 inches for females.

HUNTING ABILITY: The Chesapeake is unparalleled as a retriever of ducks and geese in rugged wintry weather. There are a number of reasons for this standing.

For one, the Chessie has an unbounded love for the water, the icier the better. He hits the water with abandon, which can be somewhat disquieting to occupants of a floating blind.

For another, this dog's coat—heavy, woolly, and oily—prevents his skin from ever getting wet and accounts for his ability to withstand bitter cold water. A couple of shakes, and the coat is freed of ice and water.

The Chessie has great strength, stamina, and aggressiveness. These dogs have been known to fetch more than 200 ducks in one day under the most inhuman weather conditions and to swim a mile to retrieve a single bird.

The Chessie is possessed of a fine memory. A well-trained one can mark and recall the falls (locations of downed ducks) of as many as six birds at a time.

If the Chesapeake has a fault in the area of waterfowl retrieving, it is that some individual Chessies tend toward hard-mouth, the practice of clamping the teeth so tightly on a bird being retrieved that the bird's flesh is marked or damaged. Training can overcome that problem.

The Chesapeake does have a place in the uplands, but that place is as a nonslip retriever (a dog that stays at heel until ordered out to fetch) rather than as a flusher of game.

DISPOSITION: The Chesapeake's temperament is a good deal less even than is the Labrador's. The Chessie does not take to strangers well, and he is something of a rugged individualist. He doesn't make as good a pet as most of the other hunting breeds, and he is inclined to fight when put into a kennel with other dogs. His enthusiasm can make him difficult to train. But such enthusiasm, when linked with drive and aggressiveness, is what makes for a topnotch hunting dog.

Irish Water Spaniel

HISTORY: In Ireland in the early part of the 19th century, there existed two distinct strains of water spaniels. The north-of-Ireland strain was small, particolored, and had a wavy coat. In the south of Ireland, around the River Shannon bogs, was a larger dog with a curly coat. This larger dog is thought to be the progenitor of the dog we know today.

The Irish Water Spaniel as it is presently known is directly traceable to one Justin McCarthy, who in 1850 was actively breeding Irish Water Spaniels, using the larger strain with the curly coat. His most famous dog was Boatswain, whose name is found in the pedigree of one of the early dogs registered in the American Stud Book.

Irish Water Spaniel

These dogs apparently first appeared in the U.S. in the 1860's. However, the first official registrations appeared in 1878 in the stud book of the National American Kennel Club, forerunner of the American Kennel Club. The breed is one of the first retrievers to be imported into this country.

The Irish, bred to work the thick cover and cold waters of Ireland's bogs, came into great favor among U.S. market hunters, especially in the Midwest, and its fame spread to both the East and West coasts. The Irish's popularity probably was never greater than in the early 1920's, but that popularity began to fall off as that of the other retriever breeds increased, mostly because the Irish could not hold their own in field trials with the other breeds. Today the Irish is seldom seen in the duck marshes.

DESCRIPTION: The Irish Water Spaniel is the largest of all the spaniels. He is a rather heavy-boned animal whose solid-liver coat is composed of tight, crisp ringlets. The face, however, is smooth and free of any long or curly hair. The leg hair gives the dog the appearance of wearing pantaloons and should not look like the feathering of a setter.

One of the breed's most noticeable physical characteristics is its almost ratlike tail—the reason this breed is sometimes called the rat-tail. Actually, the tail isn't hairless. It is covered with short, smooth hair—except near the root, where the hair is much longer and curly.

Head is cleanly chiseled, skull rather large with a prominent dome, eyes dark hazel and browless. Ears are long, lobular, and set low on the head. Neck is long, shoulders sloping and clean, chest deep but not too wide between the legs. Body overall is of medium length. Feet are large, thick, and well clothed with hair both above and between the toes.

SIZE: Irish Water Spaniels develop slowly, both physically and mentally. They may not reach physical maturity until the age of two years. Generally, males weigh 55 to 65 pounds and stand 22 to 24 inches at the shoulder. Females weigh 45 to 58 pounds and stand 21 to 23 inches at the shoulder.

HUNTING ABILITY: The Irish has a few things going for him. His thick, ropy, oily coat enables him to withstand the rigors of a typical duck-shooting situation: frigid water, wind, sleet, mud, and the like. He is leggy enough to work in heavy marsh cover and such. And he loves the water and is a strong swimmer. If he's properly (and patiently) trained he can become a proficient retriever of waterfowl—particularly in jump-shooting situations in wadable marshes—and nonslip retriever in the uplands. And if you're very lucky, he might develop a knack for flushing game ahead of the upland shooter.

It must be said, on the other hand, that the Labrador, the Golden, and the Chesapeake can be expected to do the job of retrieving better, faster, and easier than the Irish. The Irish is no great shakes in routing out and flushing upland game. And his coat, though it offers him fine protection, is an abomination from the hunter's standpoint, for it seems to form mats and pick up burrs as if by magic. And the comings and goings of an Irish in a duck blind can all but inundate the occupants with water and mud.

To top it off, the Irish is far more difficult to train than is any of the other retriever breeds.

DISPOSITION: The Irish Water Spaniel's temperament is an odd but often engaging melange of clownishness, perversity, stubbornness, desire to please, and even theatricality. The Irish tends to be loyal to a master but suspicious of strangers. He thrives on affection and companionship but will not stand abuse. His training calls for an inordinate amount of patience and the ability to coax rather than force. Once the Irish learns a lesson, though, he learns it well and remembers it.

Flat-Coat Retriever

HISTORY: The Flat-Coat derives from the original water dogs of Newfoundland, probably from a cross between the St. John's and the Labrador strains. It is also likely some blood from the Gordon and Irish Setters and possibly even the Russian Tracker (fountainhead of the Golden Retriever) was used to advantage in the development of the Flat-Coat.

The earliest-known Flat-Coat was an animal displayed at a show in Birmingham, England, in 1860 by a man named Braisford. This dog looked a good deal like a Labrador but was larger and its coat was much heavier and longer-haired. This dog was an excellent water dog and also performed well on upland gamebirds such as pheasants.

The breed was stabilized and developed under the hand of such breeders as Dr. Bond Moore of Wolverhampton, England. Before the Labrador's popularity began to soar, Flat-Coats served as gamekeepers' dogs over much of England. They are still used on estates and moors, mostly as retrievers.

Though recognized by the American Kennel Club, the Flat-Coat has never gained much popularity in the U.S. and is seldom seen in field trials. None has become a field-trial champion.

DESCRIPTION: The Flat-Coat Retriever is possessed of a distinctive coat that is dense, sleek, and fine-haired (the breed was once called the Wavy-Coat Retriever, but as the breed was developed the hair straightened). Color is either

Flat-Coat Retriever

all black or all liver, though a small white spot on the chest is not unusual.

The head is long and nicely molded, while the skull is flat and somewhat broad. The dark-brown or hazel eyes convey an intelligent expression. Ears are relatively small and well set on close to the side of the head.

Neck is long, chest deep and fairly broad, and the back short, square, and well-ribbed, with muscular quarters. Forelegs are perfectly straight and well-boned down to the feet, which are round and strong. The limbs should be well-feathered when the animal is in full coat.

SIZE: The Flat-Coat Retriever stands 21½ to 24 inches at the shoulder and weighs between 60 and 75 pounds.

HUNTING ABILITY: Because the Flat-Coat has never mustered much support in the U.S. and is far from numerous here, its ability to cope with conditions of cover, terrain, and game common in the U.S. has not really been put to the test. It must be said, however, that the Flat-Coat's work in field trials has never measured up to that of the Labrador, Chesapeake, and Golden retrievers.

The Flat-Coat is a fine retriever, particularly of upland gamebirds. He is a strong swimmer and loves water work, including marking, fetching, and delivering.

Because the Flat-Coat's silky hair absorbs water, this breed is not at its best under cold-water conditions. It is also far from the best at hunting for and rousting out birds in front of the gun.

The breed was once notoriously hard-mouthed, but that is no longer true.

DISPOSITION: The Flat-Coat has an even, pleasant disposition; he is unsurpassed as a companion. He is intelligent, tractable, and rugged. Though he may occasionally exhibit a hard-headed or stubborn streak, he takes training and discipline well.

Curly-Coat Retriever

HISTORY: Though the precise origin of this animal is beclouded by time, it is known that the Curly-Coat is the oldest of all breeds that are now called retrievers. It is likely that this breed stemmed from a cross of the St. John's Newfoundland with the Irish (or English) Water Spaniel, despite the fact that the Curly-Coat lacks the Irish's topknot. Some poodle blood was undoubtedly introduced in order to increase the tightness of the curl.

The Curly-Coat has existed as a true breeding strain since 1855. It was first shown on the bench and run in field trials in 1859, in England, and was acknowledged by the international shows in 1864, when it was given a separate classification.

Beginning in about 1890 Curly-Coats were extensively exported to New Zealand and Australia, where they are today a very popular breed. The first Curly-Coats were brought to the U.S. in 1907. The breed is recognized by the A.K.C.

DESCRIPTION: The Curly-Coat Retriever is indeed a handsome animal. He is named for the mass of crisp, tight curls that cover his body from the occipual crest of the head to the point of his tail. The color is either black or dark-liver, with a bit of white on the chest not overly unusual.

The head is long and well-proportioned, skull not too flat. Eyes are black or brown and rather large; ears are rather small and set on low, lying close to the head, and are covered with short curls.

Shoulders are deep and muscular, the chest not too wide but quite deep, and the body rather short, muscular, and well-ribbed. The legs are quite long, the forelegs being straight. Feet are compact. The tail is moderately short and carried fairly straight.

The Curly-Coat has the longest legs and lightest build of all the retriever breeds.

SIZE: Height and weight are not vitally important in the Curly-Coat; in fact, the breed standard gives neither maximum nor minimum figures for height or weight. On the average, however, the Curly-Coat stands 24 inches at the shoulder and weighs 65 to 75 pounds.

HUNTING ABILITY: It is surprising that the Curly-Coat has never found favor among U.S. hunters, for he is a fine water dog and would make any waterfowler happy with his abilities to mark and remember the locations of shot birds, to fetch them unerringly, and to deliver them.

Curly-Coat Retriever

This breed's love for the water is almost a mania, and his thick coat enables him to swim for hours in the bitterest water. The dog will dive for crippled ducks, which often hold onto submerged vegetation with their bills and would die there and otherwise be lost to the hunter.

The Curly-Coat will also do the job in the uplands, though not so capably as in the marshes. In the uplands he is best suited as a nonslip retriever—a dog that stays at his master's side until he is sent out to retrieve. The Curly-Coat is seldom used to hunt out in front of the gun.

That thick coat that provides such good protection in rugged weather is also a shortcoming. For it picks up mud, burrs, and the like and requires considerable care.

The breed once had a reputation for being hard-mouthed, but that is no longer true.

DISPOSITION: Eager to please, steady, and affectionate are three adjectives that fit the Curly-Coat. He is intelligent, has a gentle temperament, and makes a splendid companion. His field traits include eagerness, endurance, and a good nose. He is easy to train and takes discipline in stride.

Pointer

HISTORY: The Pointer (formerly known as the English Pointer) dates back as far as the 14th or 15th century. Its exact origins are not known, though many fanciers of the breed believe that the first Pointers came from Spain. However, equally reliable records indicate that dogs of similar conformation and traits existed at about the same time in France, Belgium, Portugal, and other European countries. The French "Braque"—described as a dog that "stops at scent and hunts with the nose high"—was such an animal.

There can be little doubt, however, that England is the nation must responsible for the breed as we know it today. Among the English nobility whose breeding practices helped the Pointer to soar in popularity were Thomas Webb Edge, John Legh, Lord Combermere, the Earl of Sefton, Thomas Statter, Lord Derby, and George Moore. The fountain-

Pointer

The coat is short, flat, and firm. Coat color ranges from liver and white (the most common) to black and white, lemon and white, or solid white, any of which is highly visible in the field.

SIZE: The Pointer is a medium to fairly large animal, as bird dogs go. Average weight is 50 to 65 pounds, though some small specimens, particularly bitches, may weigh as little as 35 pounds and some large males may hit 80 pounds. Shoulder height is 24 to 25 inches.

HUNTING ABILITY: The Pointer is at present the "top dog" among the pointing breeds, both in the field and in trials, and that stature is well earned. This breed is fast, enduring, and has a great nose and sometimes uncanny bird sense (the ability to recognize and home in on birdy-looking cover and to anticipate what birds are going to do and react to it).

The Pointer's strong suit is quail, particularly bobwhites, on which he has no peer. There are few sights in the hunting world that can match that of a stanch Pointer locked up in a statuesque point over a covey of bobwhites.

But this dog has also proven himself on pheasants, one of the most demanding assignments for any bird-dog breed. He will also work well on any of the Western quail and on woodcock and grouse, though closer-working breeds are usually preferred for the latter two species.

The Pointer has a deeply ingrained and well-defined instinct to hunt and to point. He has a rugged constitution and can withstand long hours in hot weather, a factor that has made him extremely popular in the Southern U.S. Some other breeds, however, are better able to stand bitter-cold weather.

DISPOSITION: The Pointer has a temperament that might best be termed reserved. Though he is not unresponsive to gentle and kind treatment, he cannot truthfully be called affectionate. He is not much for hand-licking. In fact, he sometimes assumes an air of indifference toward people other than his master. That aloofness may be attributed to the fact that the Pointer—most individuals, at any rate—just lives to hunt gamebirds, and unless he's doing that job he's not happy. Of course, in the Pointer, as in any other dog breed, you may find an individual dog that seems to be the rule-proving exception.

The Pointer's rugged disposition is an asset, as far as training is concerned. The breed will tolerate a considerable amount of force by a trainer without becoming balky or allowing itself to be made into a "mechanical" dog lacking style and dash.

heads of the breed in England were such dogs as Brockton's Bounce, Statter's Major, Whitehouse's Hamlet, and Garth's Drake.

The 19th-century Pointer in England was a large, relatively slow, big-boned animal that was ideal for hunting slow-flying, tight-sitting grouse, birds that were raised domestically and freed in rather restricted hunting areas. But such dogs were far from ideal for hunting in the United States, where the birds were wild and scattered.

Since the mid-19th century the breed has undergone a drastic change, thanks to the efforts of such dog fanciers and breeders as T.H. Scott, S.A. Kaye, U.R. Fishel, C.H. Foust, and A.G.C. Sage. Sage's Alabama plantation, called Sedgefields, has long been famous as a trial grounds.

The Pointer today is fast, agile, and wide-ranging, able to seek out birds and pin them. Such qualities were passed down from such famous U.S. Pointers as Mary Montrose, Becky Broomhill, and Ariel, each of which won the National Championship three times.

Most top hunting Pointers are registered with the Field Dog Stud Book, while most show-type Pointers are on the lists of the American Kennel Club.

DESCRIPTION: The Pointer is a beautiful animal, the epitome of what a bird dog should look like. Streamlined, and with a build that bespeaks speed and endurance, he carries his head high.

The Pointer's skull is long and moderately wide, with the forehead rising well at the brows. Muzzle is long, square, straight. Ears are thin and silky, long enough to reach just below the throat when hanging normally. Eyes are soft and dark. Neck is long, clean, and firm.

Shoulders are long and oblique, with the tops of the blades close. Chest is deep, and as wide as the shoulders will permit. Ribs are well-sprung. Back is strong, with a slight rise to the tops of the shoulders. Tail is straight, strong, and tapered, carried level or just above the line of the back.

Quarters are very muscular, legs moderately short but well-boned. Feet are round, deep, and well-padded, with well-arched toes.

English Setter

HISTORY: The English Setter dates back at least as far as the 16th century. Etchings and other illustrations of that time show a pointing dog that looks very much like the English. The breed in all probability originated in Spain, from a cross between a Spanish pointing dog with one or more spaniel-type dogs. The early setters were known as "setting spaniels" because they "set" (pointed) their game. One of the earliest dog writers called the setter "a spaniel improved."

English Setter

Many setter strains were developed in England, among them Featherstone, Lovat, Southesk, Naworth Castle, Seafield, and Laverack. Edward Laverack, the first major breeder of the English Setter, set the breed's type during a period of some 35 years of demanding inbreeding.

In the 1870's or 1880's Laverack and R. Purcell-Llewellin imported some outstanding setters to North America. The Llewellin strain, established from Laverack stock, became very popular in the U.S. (see Llewellin Setter).

During the English Setter's early days in this country, the breed was all but untouchable in field trials. In fact, the Setter's performance was so superior to that of the Pointer (whose ascendancy had not yet begun) that putting the two into head-to-head competition was not considered sporting. The Pointer has since, of course, surpassed his longer-haired rival. The first National Bird Dog Championship, held in 1896, was won by a Setter—Count Gladstone IV. Other famous English Setters include Count Noble (whose name is found in the pedigrees of many of today's Setters), Druid, Sport's Peerless, and Florendale Lou's Beau.

DESCRIPTION: The English Setter is a graceful and handsome animal, alert and agile. In general build he is not so heavily muscled, particularly in the hindquarters, as the Pointer, and his chest is not so broad. Following are the standards for the breed:

The head is long and lean, not so broad and square as that of the Pointer, and the dome tends more toward an oval shape. Muzzle is long and square, but not so square (particularly in trial dogs) as the Pointer's. Ears are set low and well back and are of moderate length, and they are covered with silky hair. Eyes are dark brown and project an intelligent and mild expression.

Neck is long and lean. Shoulder blades stand moderately close at the tops. Chest is deep but not overly wide. Ribs are well-sprung. Back is strong and either straight or sloping upward slightly to shoulders. Legs are strong, straight, well-boned, and muscular. Feet are closely set and strong, with tough pads and well-arched toes that are covered with thick, short hair.

Tail is straight and tapers to a fine point, and its feathering is straight and silky but not bushy.

Field and trial English Setters should not be overly tall and thin, as are many show Setters, for this conformation detracts from the ruggedness needed for field work.

The Setter's coat is long and flat and without curl. Colors vary, but they include white and black; white, black, and tan; white and orange; white and chestnut; blue belton; orange belton; and others. Among the most popular color combinations is white with a mixture of black, tan, lemon, and orange.

SIZE: Similar in size and weight to the Pointer, the English Setter ranges in average weight from 50 to 60 pounds, with some small bitches weighing as little as 35 pounds and large males weighing up to about 75 pounds. Average height at the shoulders is 24 to 25 inches.

HUNTING ABILITY: The English Setter is the only pointing dog that rivals the Pointer in drive, speed, nose, and bird sense. Though the Setter has not even approached the Pointer in field-trial accomplishments, the two are not so far apart in performance for the general hunter.

Though the Pointer is the generally acknowledged king of quail country, meaning the Southern U.S., many quail hunters prefer the English Setter because he tends to work a bit closer to the gun.

Just as the Pointer, because of his short hair, is better able to withstand hot-weather conditions, the Setter, because of his long hair, is unquestionably better than the Pointer under the rigors of winter hunting. The Setter is also better able to cope with briars and other tough cover, again because of his thick and protective coat.

That long hair, on the other hand, can pose a maintenance problem for the Setter owner. Burrs and matted hair may take hours to remove. Some Setter fanciers suggest that this problem can be reduced by trimming the feathering on a dog's underparts, tail, and ears.

English Setters are particularly adept at handling pheasants. A top Setter will even circle ahead of a running pheasant to pin it and prevent it from flushing wild. Too, a Setter is more apt to keep in touch with the hunter than is a Pointer.

In Midwestern and Northern states, the Setter does more than a passable job of water work, hauling pheasants and Hungarian partridge out of potholes and performing similar damp duties.

A prospective dog buyer—and this advice applies not only to English Setters but to all other hunting-dog breeds—should be certain that any dog in which he is interested comes from ancestors that have proven their worth as hunting dogs.

DISPOSITION: The English Setter is not a tough nut, as are many pointers. He literally thrives on attention and affection, and he will dispense those same feelings. The Setter is seldom timid, but he is sensitive, and a trainer would do well to keep that fact in mind. Too much force can cow a Setter or make him a sulker, and the breed cannot take too much punishment.

The Setter takes well to gentle, unhurried training tactics, and he learns his lessons well, being less apt to forget or disregard them than is the Pointer. He is also more likely to become a one-man dog than is a Pointer.

It pays for a hunter to make a companion of an English Setter. The dog is sure to meet the man more than halfway.

Irish Setter

HISTORY: The Irish Setter, a product of the British Isles, was not always the solid-mahogany-red animal that we know today. Most of the original Irish were red and white, though the red predominated.

The development of the Irish Setter rather closely paralleled that of his English cousin (see English Setter). The Irish dogs, a bit more rough and rugged, were much prized by hunters, for they performed many tasks, ranging from seeking out and pointing such upland gamebirds as woodcock, grouse, and quail, to the retrieving of waterfowl from the most frigid of waters.

Irish Setter

The Irish Setter's heyday in the U.S. began, for all intents and purposes, in 1876, when one of the early imports, an Irish named Erin, won an important stake at the Tennessee State Sportsmen's Association field trials, only the third trial series ever held. The Irish won a surprising number of placements in early trials—surprising because of the small number of Irish Setters entered in the competitions.

A dog named Elcho might well be considered the fountainhead of the breed in the U.S. Elcho—imported from Dublin by Charles H. Turner of St. Louis—won fame in bench shows. Most of today's Irish Setters are traceable to Elcho.

The breed's outstanding beauty has led directly to a decline in its field capabilities, and thus to a drop in popularity among hunters. In the early part of the 20th century (and continuing even today) many breeders became interested in

bench shows and so bred into many Irish Setters physical characteristics that improved the breed's already handsome looks but were a handicap in the hunting field. That factor, plus the rapid rise in the popularity of the Pointer and other bird-dog breeds, has shunted the Irish into the background in hunter popularity.

DESCRIPTION: The Irish Setter is generally hailed as the most beautiful of all the sporting breeds. It should be noted, however, that physical characteristics can vary considerably from hunting to show stock.

The physical standards are of interest mainly to dog fanciers who are concerned with show animals and in many instances do not accurately describe Irish Setters from good hunting stock.

In general, the hunting Irish is a dog with a powerful build, being well-boned and quite muscular, particularly in the quarters. Head is good and broad. The coat is rather heavy, flat, and silky. Coat color is a deep mahogany, often with white areas on chest, feet, and face.

Show breeding produces such characteristics as a rather snipy or narrow head, slim hips, weak quarters, long legs, and a lack of roundness in the rib cage, a shortcoming that usually causes a dog to lack endurance.

Basically, the Irish Setter is an English Setter with a red coat.

SIZE: The Irish Setter, being of somewhat slighter build than the English Setter or the Pointer, will weigh a bit less. An average Irish of normal height will weigh about 55 pounds. Shoulder height ranges from 25 to 26 inches.

HUNTING ABILITY: Though field excellence is hard to find in today's Irish Setter breed as a whole, there are still a few breeders who concentrate on hunting ability. If you can find a dog from good hunting stock, you might well find yourself stuck on this breed.

A good hunting Irish has a nose that is the equal of that of any other breed. He is rugged, sturdy, and enduring and can handle bitter weather with the best of them. He has a deeply ingrained pointing instinct, though many field trialers dislike the Irish's tendency to point with a rather low tail, a factor that takes away from the stylishness of a point.

Few Irish Setters display the dash or the wide range of the English Setter or Pointer, but the Irish generally does his job in a businesslike manner, covering the terrain thoroughly. Above all, the Irish almost always keeps in visual touch with the hunter—that is, he hunts for the gun, not for himself.

The coat is a drawback. That dark red of the Irish is more difficult to see in thick cover than is that of the English or the Pointer, both of which have some white.

DISPOSITION: The Irish Setter is an extremely affectionate animal that thrives on attention. Of all the pointing breeds, he is the most likely to become a "one-man dog" and may, in fact, hunt only for his master.

The Irish has long carried a reputation for being stubborn and hard to handle. That may have been true of some of the early imports into this country, but it does not apply to the Irish of today.

However, it is true that patience and kindness, rather than force and abuse, should be the bywords of the trainer of an Irish. The breed is eager to please, a factor that can also be used to a trainer's advantage.

German Shorthaired Pointer

HISTORY: The basic original stock from which the German Shorthair evolved was an early Spanish pointing dog, probably crossed with the Braque, an early French pointing animal. Later a cross with the Bloodhound added to the breed's nose, and still later Foxhound blood was added to improve the speed and endurance (though this infusion may well have detracted from the dog's bird sense).

A strange mixture? It would be for American hunting conditions, but the German breeders, who followed a rigorous selective-breeding program, knew what they wanted—a multipurpose dog suitable for hunting on German shooting preserves. These preserves held many varieties of game, both feathered and furred, and the ideal dog had to have

German Shorthaired Pointer

a good nose and trailing ability for such game as rabbits and foxes, pointing instinct and bird sense for upland gamebirds such as grouse and woodcock, and the size, strength, and courage to handle such big game as wild boar and deer.

The German Shorthair filled the bill as well as any dog in existence.

The German Short-Haired Pointer Club of America, with headquarters in Minneapolis, did much to further the development of the breed in this country. The breed is slowly becoming quite popular in the U.S., probably because it is a jack-of-all-trades.

DESCRIPTION: Good individuals of this breed are extremely attractive animals. In general, they are relatively tall and quite strong, slightly lower in the hips than in the shoulders. The legs are straight, and the overall build is powerful.

The German Shorthair's head is similar in conformation to that of the Pointer, except that it is longer, a bit narrower, and not so squared off at the muzzle. The ears are quite long and often quite houndlike, and they are set lower on the head than are a Pointer's.

Shoulders are muscular and moderately wide, chest deep and wide, ribs well-sprung.

The tail is docked, or cut, to approximately one-third of its original length and is carried almost straight out behind.

Coat is short, flat, and firm. Its texture is somewhat heavier than the Pointer's. Color is all liver or different combinations of liver and white that may involve ticking, spotting, or both.

SIZE: German Shorthair males weigh 55 to 70 pounds, females 45 to 60. Shoulder heights range from 23 to 25 inches in males, 21 to 23 inches for females. However, specimens of this breed tend to be taller and heavier than other pointing breeds. For example, a Shorthair standing 26 inches at the shoulder is not at all uncommon.

HUNTING ABILITY: The German Shorthair as a bird dog has an excellent nose, medium range, and moderate speed. His head is generally carried rather low, and he tends to crouch while on point (actions that are not stylish), and his somewhat bulky build prevents him from being as fast as the Pointer and English Setter.

However, while those factors make the Shorthair a poor choice for pheasants in big fields or for such open-country birds as sharptailed grouse, they make him eminently practical for the man who hunts woodcock, ruffed grouse, and quail in heavy cover. And the Shorthair, despite his relatively thin coat, will retrieve shot waterfowl, even from bitter water.

DISPOSITION: The German Shorthair has a mild and even temperament. He is seldom quarrelsome, though he can certainly hold his own in a fight. This dog is tractable and not overly difficult to train—provided he has the natural instincts to begin with.

The Shorthair does exhibit a tendency to be possessive, and dogs of that type make very good watchdogs. The Germans prize this quality highly, calling it "sharpness," but some hunters consider it a shortcoming.

Gordon Setter

HISTORY: Tradition has it that some two centuries ago the Duke of Gordon heard reports of a dog, owned by a shepherd in the highlands of Scotland, that was an accomplished finder of game. The Duke acquired the dog, a Collie-type bitch named Maddy, and crossed it with the setters that were kept at Gordon Castle. The result was what we know today as the Gordon Setter.

But the Gordon may have had even earlier origins. It is possible that the breed was developed from a "black and fallow setting dog" that was described in print as early as the first half of the 1600's.

In 1842 a man named George Blunt brought Rake and Rachel, both bred at Gordon Castle, to the U.S. Unlike today's Gordons, these animals were white with black-and-tan markings. The two dogs were bred, and a resulting puppy wound up, via Daniel Webster, in the hands of Henry Clay, who apparently had no great love of dogs but who seems to have been won over by the beguiling pup.

In the 1880's a lighter, more streamlined Gordon was brought to the U.S. It proved to be a hunting and show animal.

There was a time—the late 1800's—when the Gordon Setter knew few peers as a bird-finding hunting dog. But the English Setter, Pointer, and, to a lesser degree, Irish Setter—bred for speed and for other qualities needed to handle the decreasing amount of game in this country—soon outstripped the Gordon in popularity.

DESCRIPTION: The Gordon Setter is a bird dog of great beauty. Its body symmetry and proportions are similar to those of other setters, except that the Gordon is a slight bit heavier and often has slightly shorter legs.

Gordon Setter

The Gordon's beauty is rooted in its heavy coat of smooth, silky hair. The color is jet black, except for mahogany markings above the eyes and on chops, ear linings, chest, belly, and feather. The coat should be as free from white hair as possible. Feathering should be generous on legs, underparts, and tail.

The Gordon is wide across the forehead and has a fairly long muzzle. Nose is big and broad. Eyes are dark brown and have a wise look. Chest is deep, and ribs are well sprung. Forelegs are big-boned and straight, hind legs muscular.

Feet have close-knit, well-arched toes, plenty of hair between the toes, and generous pads. The tail is relatively short (should not reach below the hocks) and is carried horizontal or nearly so.

SIZE: The Gordon is a bit heavier than the other setters, ranging in weight from 45 to about 75 pounds. Shoulder height varies from 23 to 27 inches. The official standard for the breed allows considerable range in size, to suit sportsmen in various parts of the U.S.

HUNTING ABILITY: The Gordon Setter is rarely seen today in the hunting fields. His decline in popularity since the late 19th century can be ascribed to a number of factors, chief among them being that few breeders made any effort to widen the breed's range and increase its speed, as was done with the English Setter and the Pointer. Good range and speed are qualities that more and more hunters are demanding, because of the increasing scarcity of gamebirds. Also, the Gordon lacks the dash, determination, and stylishness of the English Setter and Pointer.

The above is not meant to imply that the Gordon is a poor hunter. He has an excellent nose and a good pointing instinct, and his heavy coat enables him to handle the heaviest of cover. (On the other hand, that same coat, because of its black and mahogany coloration, tends to make the dog hard to see in heavy cover.)

Though the Gordon is a slow hunter, he is also a sure hunter and tends to keep in touch with the hunter. Those factors make the Gordon a good choice for the man who hunts ruffed grouse and woodcock.

The Gordon is quite trainable, and is easily broken to retrieving. He makes a good retriever from land or water.

DISPOSITION: The Gordon Setter's most endearing quality is his loyalty. He forms such a strong attachment to his owner or handler that he may not hunt for anyone else. That loyalty, however, should not be allowed to become so pronounced that, for example, the dog finds it impossible to readjust to his owner after spending some time under the whistle of a trainer.

The Gordon is responsive to training, eager to please, and wary of intruders. He jealously guards his human family and is regarded as a "most-pettable" dog.

Llewellin Setter

HISTORY: The Llewellin Setter is not a distinct breed but rather one of the many strains of the English Setter (see English Setter). But it attained such a high degree of popularity that it once was accorded virtual—if not official—breed status among hunters. The Field Dog Stud Book recognizes the Llewellin as a distinct strain of English Setter. The American Kennel Club does not distinguish between the various setter strains.

The Llewellin had its beginnings in England in about 1825, when one Edward Laverack began a rigorous setter-breeding program. Using a bitch from a strain said to have been kept pure for 35 years, he produced some noteworthy hunting animals.

In 1871 another Englishman, R. Purcell Llewellin, while attending a field trial, bought a pair of male setters—Dan and Dick, offspring of parents named Field's Duke and Statter's Rhoebe—and later bred them to Laverack bitches that he already owned. This was the foundation of the Llewellin strain.

Llewellin, aided greatly by his kennel manager, G. Teasdale Buckell, did much to develop and popularize the strain that bears his name.

American sportsmen were greatly impressed with the hunting capabilities of the Llewellin Setters and imported many of the animals to this country. (Oddly, the fountainheads of the Llewellin strain, Field's Duke and Statter's Rhoebe, never amounted to much as field dogs.)

Among the early Llewellin imports to the U.S. was Count Noble, a prepotent dog and a great trial winner. When Noble died, he was mounted, and the mount is now on display at the Carnegie Museum in Pittsburgh.

Another import was Gladstone, whose work in trials and in the field did much to promote setter popularity in the U.S. Gladstone was the loser in a well-publicized two-day quail hunt in which he was worked against a "native" (American-bred) setter named Joe Jr.

The Llewellin Setters took the U.S. by storm. In the strain's heyday the ownership of a true Llewellin was a matter of great prestige. But that heyday was short-lived, and the ascendancy of the Pointer relegated the Llewellin to the status of an also-ran. Today very few true Llewellins are found in the hunting fields.

DESCRIPTION: Same as English Setter, with the following exception:

Some dog fanciers incorrectly assume that any lightly marked blueticked setter is a Llewellin. However, color and physical appearance are invalid criteria. The Field Dog Stud Book recognizes as members of the Llewellin strain only those animals that are traceable back, without outcross, to the Duke-Rhoebe-Laverack origins.

SIZE: Same as English Setter.

HUNTING ABILITY: Same as English Setter.

DISPOSITION: Same as English Setter.

Weimaraner

HISTORY: The Weimaraner, one of the Continental pointing breeds, originated nearly a century and a half ago in Weimar, Germany, where the Grand Duke Charles Augustus held court. The court was a gathering place for the sporting gentry of Germany.

The demands of those hunters were high; they wanted a dog that would trail land game, fetch from water, and point upland birds—and also be a companion. Toward that end they used a number of dog strains, none of which is known for certain. However, the old German bloodhound was probably one. That bloodhound, called the schweisshunde, was a sort of super-bloodhound and a source of most of that country's hunting breeds.

For many years Germans guarded the Weimaraner jealously, treating it almost as a national dog. This careful supervision even extended so far as to cause the passage of a law making it a legal offense for a commoner to own a Weimaraner.

The breed was introduced in the U.S. in 1929, when a man named Howard Knight of Providence, R.I., imported two of the animals. No breed has ever been given such a welcome or so much publicity. Claims of the Weimaraner's

Weimaraner

field prowess and high intelligence included "Smartest Dogs in the World." It was even said that they could perform such feats as answering the telephone and taking care of children.

That publicity, unfortunately, proved to be the breed's undoing. He became greatly popular with the general public, and unsound breeding programs, including programs aimed mainly at producing show stock, resulted. Only recently has the Weimaraner shown signs of overcoming the pressures of its early days in the U.S. The breed was recognized by the American Kennel Club in 1944.

DESCRIPTION: The Weimaraner has been dubbed the "Gray Ghost" because of his distinctive overall gray color, which may vary all the way from a bright or silvery gray, through a yellowish-gray, to a dark or blue-gray. The nickname also accrues from the dog's silent manner of movement. In texture the breed's coat is short, flat, and dense, and it gives a sleek or velvety appearance. The woolly undercoat protects the animal from rough weather.

The Weimaraner's back should be firm and level, not sagging—a fault seen in many individuals of the breed some years ago. The body in general is quite large and extremely muscular, and the build is much like that of the German Shorthaired Pointer.

The tail is docked to about one-third to one-half of its normal length, docked length being about 1½ inches just after birth and about 6 inches at maturity. Docking, incidentally, has a utilitarian purpose—if the tail were left its normal length, it would whip about in heavy cover and be cut by briars.

The Weimaraner's eyes are also rather distinctive, being blue-gray or amber but appearing to change color with varying light conditions.

SIZE: The Weimaraner is a big dog, taller and heavier than the German Shorthair. Shoulder height averages 24 to 26 inches for males, 22 to 25 inches for bitches. Average weights are 65 to 85 pounds for males, 55 to 75 pounds for bitches.

HUNTING ABILITY: The Weimaraner has managed to survive the overpublicity of its first quarter-century in the

U.S., and today serious efforts are being made toward the reestablishment of the breed as a working gun dog.

In general, the Gray Ghost has a well-developed pointing instinct and is fairly stanch. It has good bird sense and a strong penchant for retrieving. It loves the water.

The Weimaraner is not a fast worker in the field. He is more of a stalker and in fact might even be legitimately called a pussy-footer (a trait due probably to his bloodhound origins). This characteristic makes him a good choice for both pheasants and ruffed grouse and for some of the Western and Southwestern gamebirds that like to run rather than fly.

The breed's water work is not outstanding. He will do an acceptable job on short retrieves along waterways, for example, but for ambitious retrieves on open water or mud flats, where he must follow hand signals, the Weimaraner is not the best choice.

It has been said that the Weimaraner tends toward being hard-mouthed (holding retrieved game so tightly in his teeth that he marks or pierces the skin). This tendency, too, may be ascribed to the breed's bloodhound ancestry.

DISPOSITION: The Weimaraner is a garrulous, friendly fellow. He has a good temperament, being tractable and taking well to training. He is also quite intelligent—one individual, Grafmar's Ador, won his obedience degree at the tender age of six months and was at that time the youngest dog ever to accomplish that feat.

The breed learns its lessons not only early but also well. He also adapts well to the home, making an excellent family pet and a topnotch watchdog.

Brittany Spaniel

HISTORY: The distant ancestors of the Brittany Spaniel—and those of all other pointing-dog breeds—lived in Spain, where they were used to "set" (point) upland game. Further development of these breeds took place in France and began more than 1,000 years ago.

Some dog historians believe that the Brittany Spaniel as we know it today is distantly related to the red and white setter, original ancestor of the Irish Setter. Whether or not that is true, the first tailless ancestor of today's Brittany is a pup that resulted from the crossing of a white-and-lemon woodcock-hunting dog brought to France's Brittany area by an Englishman, and a white-and-mahogany bitch owned by a Frenchman. The pup developed into a topnotch hunting dog and was much in demand as a stud.

The breed's early development was mainly the result of the efforts of a French breeder and sportsman, Arthur Enaud. He used an Italian pointer and the French Braque (also a pointing dog) as outcrosses, thereby improving the bloodlines. The use of outcrosses was then discontinued, and Enaud adhered closely to selective breeding practices, firmly establishing the breed's type.

It is thought that the first Brittany Spaniels brought to the U.S. arrived here in 1912. However, it was not until 1934-36 that the first sizable importations were made and efforts were intensified to establish the breed here. A prime mover in those efforts was Louis Thebaud.

Brittany Spaniel

Since that time the Brittany has become well-known in this country and well respected for his abilities in the hunting field.

DESCRIPTION: The Brittany is unique among spaniels—for a number of reasons. For one, he is often called "the spaniel that looks like a setter." For another, he is often born without a tail.

The Brittany's head is much like that of the English Setter, except that it is shorter, a bit wider across the dome, shorter and higher set in the ears, and a little lighter in the muzzle. While most of the other pointing breeds have dark-brown eyes, the Brittany's eyes are a deep amber. They convey an expression of extreme alertness, intelligence, and tractability.

The coat is a good deal like that of the setter, but is heavier and either quite smooth or slightly wavy. The Brittany's coat should not be so heavily feathered or so silky as that of the setters. Coat color in the Brittany is liver and white or orange and white, preferably with roan ticking. The white usually predominates.

Overall, the Brittany is small, closely knit, and strong, with well-fringed thighs, muscular shoulders, deep chest, broad and strong hindquarters. Tail is naturally short, but docking is occasionally needed to keep it to a length of 4 inches.

SIZE: The Brittany is the smallest of all the pointing-dog breeds. The shoulder height ranges from 17 to 19¾ inches, and weight averages 35 to 45 pounds.

HUNTING ABILITY: The Brittany is the only spaniel with a highly developed pointing instinct, and it is almost always considered as a pointing breed. The Britt is also the widest-ranging of all of the spaniels. In fact, its range is only slightly shorter than that of Pointers and Setters. And the Brittany has the ability to adapt his range to the type of terrain he is hunting, staying close to the gun in thick cover and moving well out there in open country. He is at his best, however, in thick stuff and will keep in touch with the hunter. Thanks to his spaniel ancestry, he can easily be trained to fetch.

As a result of that fine admixture of characteristics, the Britt can be used on woodcock and ruffed grouse, on pheasants and other open-country birds such as quail and sharp-tailed grouse, and to retrieve shot game from land or water.

The Brittany has fine bird sense, pointing intensity, and style. He also has good speed. His coat provides fine protection from brambles and other rugged cover, and because of its coloration it is easily seen.

A good indicator of the Brittany's increasing favor among hunters is the fact that more and more Britts are being entered in field trials today.

DISPOSITION: The Brittany is quite friendly, highly intelligent, extremely alert, and very tractable. He makes a fine companion for the one-dog man as well as an excellent family pet. Though not really timid, the Britt is rather sensitive, so rough handling or harsh treatment should be avoided. Gentle coercion is the ticket during training sessions.

Wirehaired Pointing Griffon

HISTORY: In 1874 E.K. Korthals, a young Dutchman living near Haarlem, Holland, became preoccupied with creating a new breed of hunting dog, a dog that would have a keen nose, ability to trail, an instinct to point birds, and the ruggedness to enable it to withstand rigorous conditions. The young man's father, a wealthy banker, apparently became so angered with his quest that the younger Korthals was obliged to leave home.

It was in Germany, and later in France, that much of Korthals' breed development took place (in France the Wirehaired Pointing Griffon is known today as the Korthals Griffon). Korthals—using woolly-haired, rough-coated, and short-haired animals as basic stock—came up with a harsh-coated animal. It is generally believed that the blood of the otterhound, setter, pointer, and probably a large spaniel were used. The result was a useful—and unusual—hunting animal.

Wirehaired Pointing Griffon

DESCRIPTION: The Wirehaired Pointing Griffon's most striking physical characteristic is his unique coat, which, though short-haired, is best described as unkempt. It is made up of harsh bristles, a good deal like those of a wild boar. The bristles form on the dog's head a "moustache" and heavy eyebrows. Coat colors are mixed: steel-gray, gray-white, and chestnut—never black.

The skull is long and narrow, the muzzle square. The large eyes are iris-yellow or light brown. Ears are of medium size, set rather high. Nose is always brown. Neck is rather long, shoulders long and sloping. Ribs are slightly rounded. Forelegs are straight and muscular and have short wiry hair, as do the hind legs, which are well developed. Feet are round, firm, well-formed. Tail is bristly and has no plume, and it is usually docked to one-third of its normal length.

SIZE: The Wirehaired Pointing Griffon has an average shoulder height of 19½ to 23½ inches. Weight averages about 56 pounds.

HUNTING ABILITY: Though the Wirehaired Pointing Griffon has been known in the U.S. since 1901, it has never acquired even a modicum of popularity with American hunters. It is seldom seen here. The reasons are many. For one, the breed is too slow to be suitable for many gamebird-hunting situations in this country. For another, the breed's coat and color fail to appeal to U.S. hunters.

The Griffon is not the best choice if the game to be hunted is such open-country birds as quail and Hungarian partridge. He is much better suited to heavy-cover work on such targets as woodcock and ruffed grouse. He is an excellent retriever on both land and water, being a strong swimmer and having a rough coat that affords excellent protection from frigid water and briary cover.

Despite those strong points, however, the Wirehaired Pointing Griffon is unable to compete on even terms with many of the established pointing breeds.

DISPOSITION: Because so few Wirehaired Pointing Griffons exist in the U.S. today, an accurate rundown on the breed's temperamental and mental makeup is difficult. However, these dogs are known to be quite intelligent. They learn their lessons well and take readily to training. It is safe to say that the breed is highly unlikely to have any behavioral quirks that would make it unsuitable as a hunting companion in the field or as a family pet.

Vizsla

HISTORY: More than 500 years ago, certain Magyar tribes, then the ruling element in Hungary, set about to develop a dog that would hunt all the many varieties of game that abounded in that country. Then (as now in most of Europe) dogs were expected to take game as it came—that is, be capable of trailing hare, wild boar, bear, and deer, as well as pointing and retrieving feathered game.

The result of that development was the Vizsla (properly pronounced "Veesh-lah"), also known as the Magyar Vizsla. Little is known about the early development of this breed, except that a generous amount of hound blood (probably bloodhound) was used. The early Vizsla differed only slightly from the other Continental pointing breeds (Ger-

Vizsla

can a dog be made to handle many varieties of game satisfactorily.

No dog can be expected to excel in all forms of hunting. But the Vizsla will, if brought along patiently, find, point, and retrieve gamebirds. Training procedures should cover one kind of game at a time.

Generally, the Vizsla performs better as a close worker in heavy cover than he does as a wide-ranging animal in open country. Consequently, he is better on ruffed grouse and woodcock than on pheasants and quail. He is most popular in the Midwestern U.S.

Field trials have done much to improve the field work of the Vizsla. The parent organization, the Vizsla Club, holds a national Vizsla trial each year.

DISPOSITION: The Vizsla's temperament is much like that of most of the Continental pointing breeds. He is quietly friendly, intelligent, and alert. He learns his lessons well, but the trainer must be sure that his pupil knows what is expected of him and how he (the dog) should do it. Many Vizslas do not take kindly to strangers, but they are not vicious. The breed makes a good home companion.

man Shorthair, German Wirehair, Brittany Spaniel, and Weimaraner).

Though famed in Hungary and elsewhere in Europe, the Vizsla was little known until after World War I, when fanciers of the breed formed clubs, held trials, and did much to publicize the breed. Col. Jeno Dus of the Hungarian Cavalry, genealogy registrar and breed supervisor, also did much to further the cause of the Vizsla in the U.S.

The Vizsla was recognized by the American Kennel Club in 1960. Many Vizslas are registered with the Field Dog Stud Book.

DESCRIPTION: No conformation standards have been set up for this breed, but in general the Vizsla is an average-size short-haired pointing dog having a neat, sleek appearance.

The Vizsla is often called the Yellow Pointer because of his sedge-colored (rich yellow or yellowish-brown) coat. The coat is smooth and easily cared for. The tail, like that of all the other Continental breeds, is normally docked to one-third of its standard length. This is to prevent it from being cut and torn by briars and other rough cover.

SIZE: The Vizsla is about the same size as other short-haired pointing dogs, standing about 25 inches high at the shoulder and having an average weight of about 70 pounds.

HUNTING ABILITY: The Vizsla—and the other Continental pointing breeds—has enjoyed a considerable increase in popularity among U.S. hunters in recent years. The breed's versatility in the field is the principal reason.

In the good old days—when game was plentiful, limits were generous, and hunting country was abundant—hunters sought rather specialized game dogs: a wide-ranging quail dog, an open-country pheasant dog, a close-working grouse dog. But today game is scarcer, hunting country is more restricted, and limits are lower. It's not practical for today's hunter to limit himself to one kind of game. He wants a dog that will help him get pheasants, quail, grouse, and woodcock, and maybe fetch ducks and even run a rabbit. The Vizsla is—or at least can be—such a dog.

The key to the development of any multipurpose dog is its training. Only by positive training in control and field work

German Wirehaired Pointer

HISTORY: Much speculation and assumption is involved in tracing the origins of most dog breeds, and the German Wirehair is no exception. It is known, however, that this breed's development began in Germany about 1870, when it was known as the Deutsche Drahthaar.

According to historical accounts, the early Wirehairs represented a combination of the Wirehaired Pointing Griffon, the Deutsche Stichelhaar, and the Pudel-Pointer (those dogs being three other wire-coated German pointing breeds), as well as the German Shorthaired Pointer. It is likely that the German Wirehair's makeup also includes the blood of a strain of terrier.

German Wirehaired Pointer

The German Wirehair was first brought to the U.S. in about 1920. It was known as Drahthaar until the American Kennel Club recognized it in 1959 (the Field Dog Stud Book recognized the breed some years earlier).

The first Wirehair to win an A.K.C.-licensed field trial was Haar Baron's Mike, who won the German Pointing Dog National in 1959. However, the individual Wirehair that probably had the most to do with publicizing the breed was Herr Schmardt v. Fox River. Owned by an Illinois couple, Mr. and Mrs. A.H. Gallagher, Schmardt was widely hunted in the Midwest, placed in many trials, and took part in numerous hunting-dog demonstrations. Mr. Gallagher was a prime mover in the German Drahthaar Pointer Club of America.

DESCRIPTION: The German Wirehaired Pointer resembles the German Shorthaired Pointer except for its coarse coat and whiskered face. Essentially a pointing dog in general type, the Wirehair is usually an aristocratic-looking animal of sturdy build, lively manner, and an intelligent, determined expression. That facial expression, on the other hand, can sometimes appear almost monkeylike.

The Wirehair's coat is straight, harsh, wiry, and rather flat-lying. Its color is best described as grizzle (gray), with sizable patches of liver or brown on the head and body. Rare individuals are self-colored (solid) brown.

The eyebrows are heavy, and there is a short beard and whiskers. The undercoat ranges from dense to quite thin, depending upon the season, and is sometimes absent. The tail is usually docked to one-third of its normal length.

The better Wirehairs are trim and agile, rather than blocky, though some individual specimens are heavy-boned and plodding.

SIZE: According to the American Kennel Club standard, the German Wirehair ranges in shoulder height from 22 to 26 inches. Weight averages 55 to 65 pounds.

HUNTING ABILITY: Like most of the other Continental pointing breeds, the German Wirehair is best described as a general-purpose hunting dog that points and retrieves. He is agile, has a fine nose, and he will work relatively close to the hunter, though he will move out there a fair distance if the situation calls for it. He is easily taught his manners on game and just as quickly picks up the knack of fetching shot birds, including waterfowl.

What gamebirds will the breed work best? That depends on the individual dog and on his training. But generally, the breed does best in relatively thick cover on tight-sitting birds. Because of the coat's color, however, the Wirehair is a bit hard to see in heavy cover.

In general, the Wirehair has a bit more range than the Shorthair and a good deal more than the Weimaraner and Brittany Spaniel. The Wirehair's gait is freer and more flowing than that of the Weimaraner and the Shorthair.

For water work and in rugged cover, the Wirehair's rough coat gives him an edge over the other German breeds. And he has the drive and stamina to hunt hard all day. The Wirehair's coat dries out very fast. On the other hand, that coat tends to pick up a great quantity of burrs and dirt.

DISPOSITION: The German Wirehair is intelligent, sensitive, and inherently clownish, having quite a sense of humor. He is quick to learn, has a retentive memory, and is eager to please.

Like most intelligent dogs, however, the Wirehair requires firm (but not harsh) and consistent discipline. He is easily bored and will become mischievous if left to his own devices.

The Wirehair tends to be aloof or suspicious with strangers. But to those humans he knows he is ingratiatingly affectionate. He makes a good house dog and family companion.

PART IX / First Aid

First Aid

Let's suppose that you and a companion are well out in the woods on a fishing, hunting, or camping trip and one of the following mishaps occurs:

Your friend is bitten by a snake that escapes before either of you can identify it. Could you tell from the bite itself whether or not the snake was a poisonous species? If it was, what would you do?

Your companion suffers a severe fall and begins to act strangely. You fear that he may be going into shock. How do you tell for sure? How do you treat it?

You've made an ambitious hike on snowshoes on a brilliantly sunny day after a heavy snowfall the night before. Your eyes begin to burn and smart, your forehead aches, you can't seem to stand the glare from the glistening snow — all symptoms of snow blindness. What do you do?

A toothache comes on suddenly and savagely. The nearest dentist is hours away by foot and car. Is there anything you can do to ease the pain?

The outdoor sports — as proved by studies made by American insurance companies — are among the safest of pastimes. But accidents do happen, and a knowledge of first-aid procedures is especially important to outdoorsmen, whose favorite haunts are seldom down the street from the doctor's office or within arm's reach of a telephone.

Most accidents or maladies suffered in the outdoors are minor. But if a serious injury should occur, these actions should be taken, in the order given:

1. Give urgently needed first aid immediately: stop severe bleeding, restore breathing, treat for poisoning, treat for shock. Keep the victim lying down.

2. Examine the victim as carefully — and calmly — as you can, and try to determine the extent of his injuries.

3. Send someone for help if possible. If not, try signaling with a rifle (three quick shots are a widely recognized distress signal) or by building a smoky fire.

4. Take necessary first-aid steps for secondary injuries, making patient as comfortable as possible and moving him only if absolutely necessary.

This chapter will give detailed step-by-step procedures for every first-aid situation the sportsman is likely to run into. It should be remembered, however, that these procedures, though vitally important, aren't the only form of first aid. The victim's mental distress also needs treatment. A reassuring word, a smile, your obvious willingness and ability to help — all will have an encouraging effect. The knowledgeable first-aider also knows what *not* to do and thereby avoids compounding the problem by making errors that could be serious.

The procedures and instructions that follow reflect recommendations of the American National Red Cross, American Medical Association, the U.S. Department of Agriculture, and respected physicians.

Bleeding

External Bleeding. If a large blood vessel is severed, death from loss of blood can result in 3 to 5 minutes. So it is vital to stop the bleeding at once. Always do so, if possible, by applying pressure directly over the wound.

Use a clean cloth — a handkerchief, an item of clothing, or whatever is near at hand. Use your bare hand if nothing else is available, and then, once the bleeding is under control, apply a cloth. Put on additional layers of cloth, and when the covering is substantial, bandage snugly with strips of cloth cut from a bedsheet, neckties, or similar materials. Don't remove the bandage. If it becomes saturated with blood, put on more layers of cloth, and perhaps tighten the dressing directly over the wound.

If you are sure that no bones are broken, try to raise the bleeding area higher than the rest of the body.

If extremely quick action is needed, or if the above method fails to stop the flow of blood, you may be able to diminish the flow by pressing your fingers or the heel of your hand at one of two pressure points. One of these is located on the inner half of the arm midway between elbow and armpit; pressure applied here will reduce bleeding in the lower area of the arm. Pressure on the other point, located just below the groin on the front, inner half of the thigh, will reduce bleeding on the extremity below that point.

To control heavy bleeding, apply pressure directly over wound, using clean cloth.

Another way to stop heavy bleeding is to apply pressure to one of two main pressure points: inner part of arm between elbow and armpit (*left*), and just below groin on inner part of thigh (*right*).

Internal Bleeding. Often caused by a severe fall or a violent blow, bleeding within the body can be difficult to diagnose, though it may be revealed by bleeding from the nose or mouth when no injury can be detected in those organs. Other symptoms may include restlessness, nausea, anxiety, a weak and rapid pulse, thirst, paleness, and general weakness.

The first treatment procedure is to use pillows, knapsacks, folded clothes, or something similar to raise the victim's head and shoulders if he is having difficulty breathing. Otherwise, place him flat on his back.

Keep him as immobile as possible, and try to have him control the movements caused by vomiting. Turn his head to the side for vomiting.

Do not give stimulants, even if the bleeding seems to stop.

If victim loses consciousness, turn him on his side, with head and chest lower than hips.

Medical care is a must. Get the victim to a doctor or hospital as soon as possible.

Nosebleed. Nosebleeds often occur "for no reason," while at other times they are caused by an injury. Most of them are more annoying than serious. It occasionally happens, though, that the bleeding is heavy and prolonged and this can be dangerous.

The person should remain quiet, preferably in a sitting position with his head thrown back or lying down with head and shoulders raised.

Pinch the victim's nostrils together, keeping the pressure on for 5 to 10 minutes. If bleeding doesn't stop, pack gauze lightly into the bleeding nostril and then pinch.

Sometimes the application of cold wet towels to the face will help.

Use of Tourniquet. According to The American National Red Cross, the use of a tourniquet to stop bleeding in an extremity is "justifiable only rarely." Because its use involves a high risk of losing a limb, a tourniquet should be applied only if the bleeding seems sure to cause death.

Use only a wide, strong piece of cloth—never a narrow strip of material such a rope or wire. Wrap the cloth around the upper part of the limb above the wound, and tie a simple overhand knot (half a square knot). Place a short stick on the knot, and tie another simple overhand knot (that is, complete the square knot) over the stick. Twist the stick just enough to stop the bleeding. Loosen the binding (untwist the stick) for a few seconds every 15 minutes.

Once the bleeding has been controlled, keep the victim quiet and warm. If he is conscious and can swallow easily, give him some water or maybe some weak tea—no alcoholic drinks. If he is not conscious, or if abdominal or other internal injuries are suspected, do not give him any fluid.

Artificial Respiration

Artificial respiration is the technique of causing air to flow into and out of the lungs of a person whose normal breathing has stopped. Causes of stoppage of normal breathing include inhalation of water, smoke, or gas, electric shock, choking, and drug overdose. In most instances, death will result within 6 minutes unless artificial respiration is administered.

The treatment may also be needed if breathing does not stop completely but becomes slow and shallow and the

APPLYING A TOURNIQUET

Wrap strong, wide cloth around limb above wound, and tie a simple overhand knot.

Place a short stick on the knot and tie another overhand knot over the stick, and twist stick to stem bleeding.

Bind stick with ends of tourniquet, but be sure to loosen it every 15 minutes.

victim's lips, tongue, and fingernails turn blue. If you're in doubt, give artificial respiration—it is seldom harmful and can save a life.

Before beginning any of the artificial respiration methods described below, check the victim's mouth and throat opening for obstructions; remove any foreign objects.

Mouth-to-Mouth. Place the victim on his back. Put one hand under the victim's neck. At the same time, place the other hand on his forehead and tilt the head back.

Using the hand that was under the neck, pull the victim's chin up, thereby insuring a free air passage. Take a deep breath, place your mouth over the victim's mouth, trying to make the seal as airtight as possible, and pinch the victim's nostrils closed. Blow into the victim's mouth until you see his chest rise.

Lift your head from the victim, and take another deep breath while his chest falls, causing him to exhale. Repeat the process. For the first few minutes, do so as rapidly as the victim's lungs are emptied. After that, do it about 12 times per minute.

If the victim is an infant or small child, use the same procedure, but place your mouth over both the mouth and nose, and force air into his lungs gently.

MOUTH-TO-MOUTH RESUSCITATION
FOR ADULTS

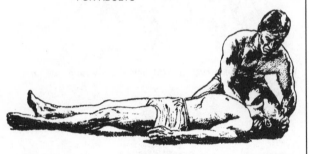

Lift victim's neck with one hand and tilt the head back by holding top of the head with other hand.

MOUTH-TO-MOUTH RESUSCITATION
FOR CHILD

Lift victim's neck with your right hand and with your left lift his lower jaw so that it juts out.

Pull victim's chin up with the hand that was lifting the neck. This insures a free air passage.

Place your mouth over the victim's *mouth and nose,* making a leakproof seal, and force air into his lungs gently until you see the chest rise and you feel the lungs expand.

Take a deep breath, place your mouth over victim's mouth and pinch his nostrils. Breathe into his lungs until you see his chest rise. Remove your mouth and let him exhale. Repeat this cycle as rapidly as victim's lungs empty themselves for first few minutes, then 15 times per minute.

Arm-Lift Method. Place victim on his back. If someone is available to assist you, have him push upward on the victim's chin so that the jaw juts outward.

Kneel at the victim's head, facing him. Grasp his wrists, cross them, and use the weight of the upper part of your body to press his wrists down on the lower chest.

Immediately pull his arms upward and outward as far as possible.

Repeat the procedure about 15 times per minute.

ARM-LIFT METHOD

With the victim on his back, put something under his shoulders to raise them and allow head to drop backwards. Kneel at victim's head and grasp his arms at the wrists, crossing and pressing his wrists against the lower chest.

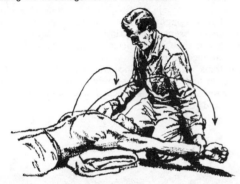

Immediately pull arms upward and outward as far as possible. Repeat this sequence 15 times a minute.

Heart Stoppage

If artificial respiration produces no response in an injured person, it may mean that his heart has stopped beating. You can make a fairly certain diagnosis by checking his pulse at the wrist and holding your ear to the victim's chest. If you feel no pulse and hear no heartbeat, you will have to use external heart massage in addition to artificial respiration. Take the following steps promptly:

Place the victim on his back, raise his legs so that blood drains toward the heart, and support the shoulders so that the neck is arched backward and the chin juts out.

Place the heel of one of your hands on the lower end of the breastbone (the large bone running down the center of the chest to which the ribs are attached), and place the other hand on top of the first one.

Using the weight of the upper part of your body, press down firmly with both hands, and then lift both hands to let the chest expand.

Repeat the press-lift procedure once every second or two.

Without an assistant, the artificial respiration and artificial circulation should be done at a 15:2 ratio. This consists of two very quick lung inflations after each 15 chest

Heart stoppage: employing the closed heart massage, using weight of upper part of rescuer's body to press down firmly.

compressions. Because of the interruptions for lung inflation, the single rescuer must perform each series of 15 chest compressions at a faster rate (80 compressions per minute) in order to achieve the actual desired compression rate of 60 per minute. The two full lung inflations must be delivered in rapid succession, within a period of 5 seconds, without allowing full lung exhalation between breaths.

Choking

More than one person has died from choking on a fish bone, an inadvertently swallowed hard object, a piece of food that went down the "wrong pipe," and the like. Anything that lodges in the throat or air passages must be removed as soon as possible. Here's how to do it:

If the victim is conscious, give him four back blows between the shoulder blades. If the victim is lying down — roll him on his side, facing you with his chest against your knee. If the victim is sitting or standing — you should be behind and to one side of him. If the victim is an infant — face him on your forearm, head down. Make sharp blows with the heel of your hand on the spine, between his shoulder blades.

If this doesn't remove the object, and the victim is standing or sitting, do this: 1) Stand behind the victim and wrap your arms around his waist. 2) Place the thumb side of your fist against the victim's abdomen, slightly above the navel and below the rib cage. 3) Grasp your fist with your other hand and press into the victim's abdomen with a quick upward thrust.

If the victim is in a lying position, do this: 1) Place him on his back and kneel close to his side. 2) Place your hands, one on top of the other, with the heel of the bottom hand in the middle of the abdomen, slightly above the navel and below the rib cage. 3) Rock forward so that your shoulders are directly over the victim's abdomen and press toward the victim's diaphragm with a quick forward thrust. 4) Don't press to either side.

If the victim is unconscious, tilt the head back and attempt to give the victim artificial respiration. If this fails, give the victim four back blows in rapid succession. If the object has still not been forced out of the air passages, then stand behind the victim, put both your fists into his abdomen, and give eight upward thrusts.

Finally, if none of these methods works, you should insert your index finger deep into the victim's throat, using a hooking action to try to dislodge the object.

STANDING BACK BLOWS

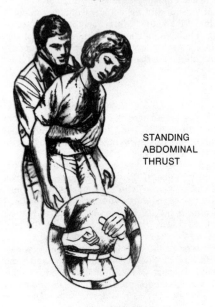

STANDING
ABDOMINAL
THRUST

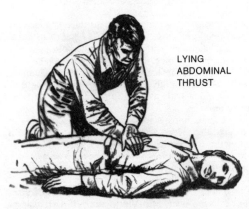

LYING
ABDOMINAL
THRUST

SMALL CHILD: Put one arm around the youngster's waist from behind, and lift him up so that his head and upper torso are leaning toward the ground. With your free hand, give him several sharp taps between the shoulder blades. When the object has been dislodged, clear his throat with your fingers, and pull the tongue forward.

INFANT: Hold him up by the ankles, head hanging straight down. Open his mouth, pull his tongue forward, and the object will likely fall out. If not, give him a tap or two on the back.

Shock

Medical (traumatic) shock is a depressed condition of many bodily functions and is usually caused by loss of blood following a serious injury (a burn, wound, fracture, exposure, and the like). However, some degree of shock can result from even minor injuries.

Prolonged shock can result in death even if the injury causing it would not be fatal otherwise. In every health emergency, the possibility of shock should be considered. Signs of shock include the following: vacant and lackluster eyes and dilated pupils, shallow or irregular breathing, weak or seemingly absent pulse, skin that is pale and moist and cooler than it should be, nausea, perspiration, restlessness, thirst, and unconsciousness.

Symptoms usually develop gradually and may not be apparent at first. Even if a severely injured person exhibits none of the signs, shock is a real danger, and the following steps should be taken:

HOW TO TREAT FOR SHOCK

Keep the victim lying down, preferably with his head lower than the rest of his body. *Exception*: If there is difficulty in breathing, the head and chest should be elevated.

Raise his legs 8 to 12 inches. *Exceptions*: Do not raise the legs if there is a head injury, if breathing difficulty is thereby increased, or if the patient complains of pain during the raising process. If you are in doubt about the correct position, keep the victim lying flat.

Keep the victim warm. If the weather is cold or damp, cover him and put a blanket underneath as well. Do not overheat; keep him just warm enough to prevent his shivering.

Fluids can have value in shock, but don't give the victim liquids unless medical help will be delayed at least an hour. If the victim is conscious and able to swallow, give him water that is neither hot nor cold—a few sips at first and then increasing the amount. If medical help will be considerably delayed, give the victim half-glass doses (at 15-minute intervals) of a solution made by adding 1 teaspoon of salt and ½ teaspoon of baking soda to 1 quart of water. Do not give any fluids if the victim is only partly conscious, if an abdominal injury is suspected, or if he is nauseated.

Fever

A rise in body temperature is a signal that something is amiss internally. There are many causes of fever, infection being the most common. In fact, fever is one of the body's defense mechanisms against infection. But if the fever reaches 104° or higher, it may become a danger in itself. Here's what to do:

Get the victim into bed, and take his temperature if possible.

Send for a doctor.

Sponge the victim's body with cool or luke-warm water, treating one part of the body at a time and keeping the other parts covered.

Apply an ice bag or cool cloths to his head.

If he is conscious and there is no evidence of abdominal injury, give him some cold water to drink.

Oral Poisoning

If the victim has ingested poisonous material and is unconscious or otherwise unable to tell you what it was, you may be able to ascertain the source by the odor on his breath, discoloration on his lips or mouth, or a telltale container nearby.

Speed is vital in treating the victim of poisoning. You must take the following steps quickly, before the body has a chance to absorb much of the poison:

If you know the antidote (antidotes are printed on containers of almost all potentially dangerous materials) and if it is at hand, give it at once.

If not, dilute the poison by giving the victim four or more glasses of milk or water.

Call a doctor or hospital if possible.

Induce vomiting by sticking your finger into the victim's throat or by making him drink a glass of warm water into which have been mixed two tablespoons of salt. *Exceptions*: Do not induce vomiting if the victim is unconscious, has pain or a burning sensation in mouth or throat, has swallowed a petroleum product (gasoline, kerosene, white gas, or the like) or any acid or any alkali (caustic soda, an ammonia solution, and so on).

When the vomiting begins, position the victim face down, with his head lower than his hips, to prevent the expelled material from getting into his lungs.

If you can't identify the poison, save some of the vomitus for subsequent examination by a physician or hospital laboratory.

Snakebite

It is doubtful whether any other first-aid situation is more feared and less understood than snakebite. And there is little agreement, even among leading authorities, about its treatment.

About 6,500 humans are bitten by poisonous snakes in the U.S. each year. Of those, only about 350 are hunters or fishermen. And the death rate is very low, an average of 15 persons annually in the entire country. Most of those bites occur south of an imaginary line drawn from North Carolina to southern California. More than half occur in Texas, North Carolina, Florida, Georgia, Louisiana, and Arkansas.

There are four kinds of poisonous snakes in the U.S. Three are of the pit-viper variety: rattlesnakes, copperheads, and cottonmouth moccasins. The fourth, the coral snake, is a member of the cobra family. The pit vipers are so named because they have a small deep depression between the eyes and the nostrils. The coral snake has broad red and black bands separated by narrow yellow bands, giving rise to the saying, "Red on yellow, kill a fellow."

The bite of a poisonous snake—except for the coral snake, which chews rather than bites—is in the form of fang punctures of the skin. If you are bitten by a snake that leaves two U-shaped rows of tooth marks on your skin, relax—it is almost certainly a nonpoisonous species. The bite of a nonpoisonous snake produces little pain or swelling.

Symptoms of the bite of a venomous snake include immediate pain, swelling and discoloration in the area of the wound, general weakness, nausea and vomiting, a weak and rapid pulse, dimming of vision, faintness, and eventually unconsciousness.

Medical authorities agree on one point: that the most effective treatment is to administer as quickly as possible enough Antivenin to overcome the poison. Most bites, however, occur in the field, often many miles from a road, so the victim cannot always get Antivenin quick enough. Survival in such cases depends upon the first-aid steps taken by the victim and his companions. And here is where the disagreement among medical authorities is most prevalent.

The best and most up-to-date tactics for treating snakebite seem to be those advocated by Dr. Clifford C. Snyder, chairman of the Division of Plastic Surgery at the University of Utah and chief of surgery at the Veterans Hospital in Salt Lake City. Dr. Snyder is rated among the world's foremost authorities on snakebite.

Here's what to do, according to Dr. Snyder, if a poisonous snake strikes:

Avoid exertion and excitement. Sit down, and try to calm yourself. Panic could bring on shock.

Kill the snake if you can. Take it with you when you leave, for identification later.

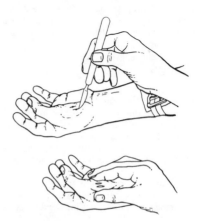

Snakebite treatment: Make a linear ½-inch incision through each fang mark; gently force venom from incisions, using finger pressure or a suction device.

Apply a constricting band—belt, tie, shirtsleeve, or hand-kerchief—between the bite and the heart. If the bite is on a leg or arm, put the constricting band 2 to 3 inches above the bite. But be sure it is above the swelling. Use no constricting band if the bite is on the face. *The constricting band should be loose enough so that you can insert a finger beneath it without force.* Any tighter, and it may cut off blood circulation. Such a loose band can be left in place for an hour without harm. Don't loosen it every few minutes, as many handbooks suggest (periodic loosening tends to actually "milk" venom from the bite into the body, according to Dr. Snyder's studies).

Sterilize the fang wounds with a sponge soaked in alcohol.

Using a scalpel, or a knife sterilized in a flame, make ½-inch linear incisions through each fang mark—the cuts should extend ¼ inch past each puncture. Deepen the cut through skin and fat, but do not cut into muscle, tendon, or nerve. *Do not use cross incisions through fang marks,* as suggested in some publications.

Squeeze venom gently from the incisions with the fingers. Do so for 30 to 60 minutes or for as long as it takes to get the victim to a doctor. Do not use oral suction.

If ice is handy, put some into a towel, shirt, or other such makeshift "bag," and apply it to the area of the bite—but for no longer than an hour. Keeping the wound cool will slow absorption. Do not *pack* the limb in ice or bind the ice tightly to the skin. Be sure to remove the ice gradually—sudden removal can result in rapid uptake of the venom.

In an emergency, Antivenin can be injected in the field, but the instructions printed on each package must be followed rigidly, and the required skin test for allergy (many persons are allergic to the horse-blood serum from which Antivenin is prepared) must have proven negative.

Get the victim to a doctor or a hospital as soon as possible but without exertion on his part.

Alcoholic beverages, Dr. Snyder points out, are worse than useless to the snakebite victim. They are likely to speed the uptake of the venom.

Sportsmen would do well to take along a snakebite kit on all trips into a terrain known to contain poisonous snakes. Such a kit should include the following items: 1) constricting band, 2) 2 surgical prep sponges presaturated with alcohol and protected in aluminum foil, 3) a disposable scalpel in foil, 4) one kit of Antivenin. The sponges and scalpel can be bought at a drug store.

Bee Stings

Stinging insects are seldom more than an annoyance, even if they hit the target on your hide. Some people, however, are highly allergic to the stings of certain insects. If you or a member of your party has had a severe reaction to a bee sting in the past and is again stung, take the following steps:

Use a tight constricting band above the sting if it is on an arm or leg. Loosen the band for a few seconds every 15 minutes.

Apply an icepack or cold cloths to the sting area.

Get the victim to a doctor as soon as possible.

For the average bee-sting victim, these procedures will suffice:

Remove the stinger with tweezers.

Make a paste of baking soda and cold cream (if it is available), and apply it to the sting area.

Apply cold cloths to help ease the pain.

If there is itching, use calamine lotion.

Spider and Scorpion Bites

Scorpions are most common in the southwestern U.S. and are found in such spots as cool and damp buildings, debris, and under loose banks. Most species of scorpions in the U.S. are nonpoisonous; few of their stings are dangerous.

The biting spiders in the U.S. include the black widow, the brown widow, and the tarantula. The brown widow—its abdomen has a dull-orange hourglass marking against a brown body—is harmless in almost all cases. The tarantula is a large (up to three inches long, not including the legs) and hairy spider, but despite its awesome appearance its bite is almost always harmless, though it may cause allergic reactions in sensitive persons. The black widow—the female's body is about ½ inch long, shiny black, usually with a red hourglass marking on the underside of the abdomen—has a poisonous bite, but its victims almost always recover.

The symptoms of these bites may include some swelling and redness, immediate pain that may—especially with a black-widow bite—become quite severe and spread throughout the body, much sweating, nausea, and difficulty in breathing and speaking.

First-aid procedures are as follows:

Keep the victim warm and calm, lying down.

Apply a wide constricting band above the bite, loosening it every 15 minutes.

Apply wrapped-up ice or cold compresses to the bite area.

Get medical help as quickly as possible.

Chigger and Tick Bites

The irritation produced by chiggers, which are the larval stage of a mite, results from fluid the tiny insects inject. Chiggers do not burrow under the skin, as is often suggested.

Since chiggers do not usually attach themselves to the skin until an hour or more after they reach the body, bathing promptly after exposure, using a brush and soapy water, may eliminate them. Once the bites have been inflicted,

REMOVING TICK
WITH TWEEZERS

application of ice water may help. The itching and discomfort can be relieved by applying calamine lotion or a paste made of baking soda and a little water.

Ticks—flat, usually brown, and about ¼ inch long—attach themselves to the skin by making a tiny puncture, and they feed by sucking blood. They can thereby transmit the germs of several diseases, including Rocky Mountain spotted fever.

If you have been in a tick-infested area, be sure to examine your clothes and body for the insects, paying particular attention to hairy areas. Removing ticks promptly is insurance against the transmission of any germs they may be carrying since that process seldom begins until 6 hours or so after the insect attaches itself and begins to feed.

Use tweezers to remove a tick, but don't yank—that may cause the tick's head or mouth parts to break off and remain in the flesh. Pull it gently, taking care not to crush the body, which may be full of germs. If it can't be pulled off gently, cover the entire tick with heavy oil, which closes off its breathing pores and may make it disengage itself. Another method, though not as effective, is to hold a lighted cigarette or hot needle to its posterior until it lets go. Scrub the area of the bite with soap and water.

Poison Ivy, Poison Oak, and Poison Sumac

There are virtually no areas in the U.S. in which at least one of these plants does not exist. Poison ivy is found throughout the country, with the possible exception of California and Nevada. Poison oak occurs in the southeastern states, and a western variety exists in the West Coast states. Poison sumac grows in most of the states in the eastern one-third of the country.

The symptoms of poisoning from one of these three plants may begin to appear as soon as a few hours after exposure or may hold off until several days later. They include redness of skin, itching, and the appearance of blisters. In later stages the involved area may spread considerably, large blisters may result, and marked swelling may occur. The victim may become feverish.

As soon as possible after exposure, wash the area with soap (preferably brown laundry soap) and hot water. But omit this step if large blisters have already begun to form.

Sponge the area with rubbing alcohol.

Apply calamine lotion, which should reduce itching and other discomfort. A suitable in-the-field substitute for calamine lotion is a paste made of melted soap and water; apply a thick coating to the affected area, let it dry, and leave it on overnight.

Thermal Burns

Burns are classified according to degree. In first-degree burns, the skin is reddened. In second-degree burns, blisters develop. Third-degree burns result in destruction of tissue and the cells that form new skin. Another important factor in determining the seriousness of any burn is the extent of the affected area.

The following first-aid procedures have the primary objectives of treating shock (a major hazard that can quickly cause death in severely burned persons), relieving pain, and preventing contamination.

Here is how to treat relatively minor first- and second-degree burns:

For first degree burns, medical treatment is usually not required. To relieve pain, apply cold water applications to the affected area or submerge the burned area in cold water. A dry dressing may be applied, if desired.

For second degree burns (minor), immerse the burned parts in cold water (not ice water) or apply freshly ironed or laundered cloths that have been wrung out in ice water until the pain subsides. Immediate cooling can reduce the burning effect of heat in the deeper layers of skin. Never add salt to ice water; it lowers the temperature and may produce further injury. Gently blot the area dry with sterile gauze, a clean cloth, a towel, or other household linen. Don't use absorbent cotton. Apply dry, sterile gauze or a clean cloth as a protective dressing. Don't break blisters or remove shreds of tissue, and don't use an antiseptic preparation, ointment, spray, or home remedy on a severe burn.

Because the degree of a burn is often difficult to determine at first, it pays—except with obviously minor burns—to seek medical help.

Here is how to treat extensive second-and third-degree burns:

If a doctor or hospital is within easy reach, cover the burn with a sterile (or at least clean) dressing, treat for shock (procedures for shock appear elsewhere in this section), and rush the victim to the doctor or a hospital.

If the burn occurs in a remote area, take the following steps:

Remove all clothing from the burn area, cutting around any cloth that may adhere to the flesh and leaving it there (trying to remove it may well worsen the wound).

Apply a sterile dry dressing to the entire burn area. Do not treat a serious burn with any substance; that is, don't apply ointment, antiseptic, oil, or anything similar. Cover the dressing with at least 6 more layers of dressing (or clean tightly woven cloth material). Try not to rupture blisters.

Bandage the dressings in place. Make the bandage snug enough to protect the burned area from possible contamination from the air but not so tight as to cut off circulation.

Treat for shock, if medical help will be delayed more than an hour. Give the victim the shock solution: 1 teaspoon of salt and 1 teaspoon of baking soda in 1 quart of water.

Arrange for medical help as quickly as possible, notifying authorities that plasma may be needed.

Don't try to change the dressing. That is a job for a doctor.

Sunburn Burns

In addition to skin redness, sunburn may result in swelling and blistering, tissue damage, fever, and headache.

The discomfort from mild cases of sunburn can be relieved by applying cold cream, salad oil, shortening, calamine lotion, or one of the aerosol sprays for that purpose now on the market. Do not apply butter or margarine.

Severe cases of sunburn should be treated as thermal burns, the treatment for which is given elsewhere in this chapter.

Chemical Burns

Chemical burns—from acid, alkali, lime, petroleum products, cleansing agents, and the like—are unusual in the outdoors but do happen occasionally.

CHEMICAL BURN
IN EYE

For such burns on exposed skin, the first step is to immediately flush the area with water, thereby lessening the pain and probably reducing the extent of the skin damage. Thereafter, treat as you would a thermal burn.

If a noxious chemical gets into an eye, flush the eye with water at once. Do so by having the victim lie down with his head tilted slightly to one side. Pour the water into the corner of the eye nearest the nose so that it flows across the entire eye and out the other corner and does not enter the unaffected eye.

Cover the eye with a sterile compress, bandage it into place, and get the victim to medical help as fast as possible.

Sunstroke

Sunstroke is extremely dangerous. Aged people are the most susceptible. The usual symptoms are headache, dry skin, and rapid pulse. Dizziness and nausea may occur, and in severe cases the victim may lapse into unconsciousness. Body temperature soars, sometimes as high as 109°.

Medical help, as soon as possible, is a must. Until it arrives, do the following:

Undress the victim, and sponge the body freely with cool water, or apply cold cloths, the objective being to reduce body temperature to a tolerable level of 103° or below. If you have no thermometer, check the victim's pulse; a pulse rate of 110 or below usually means a tolerable body temperature.

When the body temperature lowers to 103°, stop the sponging or cool-cloth treatment for about 10 minutes. If the temperature again starts to rise, resume the sponging.

If the victim is conscious and can swallow, give him as much as he can drink of a salt-water solution (1 teaspoon of salt to 1 quart of water).

Later, provide covering according to the victim's comfort.

Exposure

Fall from a boat into frigid water well out from shore, get "turned around" while tracking a deer in unfamiliar territory, or try an over-ambitious cross-country hike that sees bitter nightfall catch you while you're still far from camp, and you are a candidate for exposure.

Symptoms include numbness, difficulty of movement, and drowsiness that is hard to resist. The exposure victim eventually staggers, loses his vision, and falls unconscious.

The victim must be warmed as quickly as possible. Get him indoors or into a warm tent or other shelter.

If breathing has stopped, use artificial respiration.

Wrap him in blankets, or, if possible, put him into a tub of warm (78° to 82°) water—*not hot water.*

Once he responds, dry him completely if the water treatment was used, and give him hot drinks.

Frostbite

Frostbite is the freezing of an area of the body, usually the nose, ears, cheeks, fingers, or toes.

Just before the actual onset of frostbite, the skin may appear slightly flushed. Then, as frostbite develops, the skin becomes white or grayish-yellow. Blisters may develop later. In the early stages the victim may feel pain, which later subsides. The affected area feels intensely cold and numb, but the victim is often unaware of the problem until someone tells him or he notices the pale glossy skin. First-aid treatment is as follows:

Enclose the frostbitten area with warm hands or warm cloth, using firm pressure. Do not rub with the hands or with snow. If the affected area is on fingers or hands, have the victim put his hands into his armpits.

Cover the area with woolen cloth.

Get the victim indoors or into a warm shelter as soon as possible.

Immerse the frostbitten area in warm—not hot—water. If that is not possible, wrap the area in warm blankets. Do not use hot-water bottles or heat lamps, and do not place the affected area near fire or a hot stove.

When the frostbitten part has been warmed, encourage the victim to move it.

Give the victim something warm to drink.

If the victim must travel, apply a sterile dressing that widely overlaps the affected area, and be sure that enough clothing covers it to keep it warm.

Medical attention is usually necessary.

Snow Blindness

The symptoms of this winter malady include a burning or smarting sensation in the eyes, pain in the eyes or in the forehead, and extreme sensitivity to light. First-aid steps include the following:

Get the victim into a shelter or some kind, or at least out of the sun.

Apply cold compresses to the eyes.

Apply mild eye drops. Mineral oil is a suitable substitute.

Have the victim wear dark glasses.

Cuts, Abrasions, and Bruises

Minor mishaps frequently involve one of these three injuries. With abrasions (the rubbing or scraping off of skin) and small cuts, the emphasis should be on preventing infection.

Immediately clean the cut or abrasion and the surrounding area with soap and warm water. Don't breathe on the wound or let fingers or soiled cloth contact it.

If there is bleeding, put a sterile pad over the wound and hold it there firmly until the bleeding stops. Then apply an antiseptic, if available, and apply a fresh sterile pad, bandaging it in place loosely.

A bruise results when small blood vessels under the skin

are broken, causing discoloration of the skin and swelling, which is often painful.

First aid may be unnecessary if the bruise is minor. If it is more severe, apply an ice pack or cold cloths to reduce the swelling and relieve the pain. Bruises on an extremity can be made less painful if the limb is elevated.

Bone Dislocations

A dislocation results when the end of a bone is displaced from its normal position in the joint. The surrounding ligaments and other soft tissue always suffer some damage. Fingers, thumb, and shoulder are the areas most often affected.

Symptoms include severe pain, swelling, and loss of movement. Unless a dislodged bone is properly relocated and cared for, dislocations of the bone may occur repeatedly and eventually cause considerable disability.

Relocating a seriously dislodged bone should be done only by a doctor. The first-aider's primary concerns here are to prevent further injury and to see to the victim's comfort.

The dislocated part should be kept as immobile as possible. Apply cold compresses, and get the victim to a doctor.

DISLOCATED HIP

DISLOCATED FINGER

If an elbow or shoulder is dislocated, use a loose sling to keep the part immobile during transport. If the dislocation is in the hip, transport the victim on a wide board or on a stretcher that has been made rigid, and use blankets or clothing as a pad to support the affected-side leg in whatever position the victim finds most comfortable.

If the dislocation is in a finger and medical help is far away, you might try pulling—very cautiously—on the finger in an attempt to bring the bone back into place. If a gentle pull does not work, do not persist. And do not try this on a dislocated thumb—the problem is more complicated at this joint, and further injury may result.

Bone Fractures

There are two kinds of bone fractures (breaks). In a simple fracture the broken bone does not push through the skin. In an open fracture the skin is broken and a wound extends from the skin to the fracture area.

It is often difficult to tell whether or not a bone has been broken. If the first-aider was not there when the injury was suffered, he should ask the victim to tell him exactly what happened and then check the injured area for physical evidence.

Symptoms of a break include tenderness to the touch, difficulty or pain in moving the injured part, swelling, skin discoloration, and deformity.

If you're not sure, treat the injury as a break. Never try to reset a broken bone yourself. Your basic objectives are to prevent further injury, treat for shock if necessary, and make the patient as comfortable as possible until medical help arrives.

With any break, handle the victim gently. Careless handling will increase the pain and may also increase the severity of shock and cause jagged bone ends to damage muscle, nerves, blood vessels, and skin.

First-aid procedures for various kinds of breaks are as follows:

Arm or Leg. If medical help will arrive shortly, don't move either the broken limb or the victim.

If there is bleeding, cut away as much clothing as necessary, place a sterile pad or a piece of clean cloth over the wound, and apply firm pressure. Bandage the pad in place.

If the patient must be moved, position the limb as naturally and comfortably as possible, and put on two splints. Boards, poles, metal rods, or any other firm objects—even a thick layer of newspaper folded to the proper shape and firmness—will do. Splints must be long enough to extend beyond the

FRACTURED ARM

FRACTURED LEG

FRACTURED NECK OR BACK

joints above and below the break. Use soft material as padding between the limb and the splints. Fasten the splints in place with bandage material (or handkerchiefs, cloth strips, etc.) at a minimum of three places: adjacent to the break, near the joint above the break, and near the joint below the break.

Check the splints every 15 minutes or so. If swelling of the limb has caused tightening of the bandaging so that circulation is cut off, loosening the bindings accordingly.

Apply cold packs to the fracture.

Get victim to medical help.

Skull. Skull fracture symptoms include unconsciousness, mental confusion or dazedness, variation in size of eye pupils, and bleeding from mouth, ears, or nose.

Keep victim lying down. If his face has normal color or is flushed, prop up his head and shoulders. If his face is pale, try to position him so that his head is slightly lower than the rest of his body.

If there is an open scalp wound, apply a sterile gauze pad, and bandage it in place.

If the victim must be moved, transport him in a prone position.

Never leave the victim alone, even during transport. If he begins to choke on blood, lower his head and turn it to one side so that the blood can drain from mouth and throat.

FRACTURED SKULL

Neck and Back. If the victim can't readily open or close his fingers or grip anything firmly, his neck may be broken. If finger movement seems normal but he can't move feet or toes, the back may be broken. If he is unconscious and you suspect a spinal injury, treat as if the neck were fractured.

Do not let the victim move his head.

Cover him with blankets.

Watch his breathing closely. If breathing stops, begin mouth-to-mouth resuscitation, but do not move his head as you do so.

Medical help should be brought to the scene if at all possible. If a move is absolutely necessary, extreme caution is a must, for a slight twist or jerk can be fatal to the victim

of a broken neck or spine. Pad the head at the sides to prevent movement. Tie the victim's hands across his chest, and tie his head and body rigidly to the stretcher, which should itself be rigid. Put a pad under the neck.

Pelvis. The pelvis is a basin-shaped bone that connects spine and legs. It also encloses or protects many important organs; therefore a fracture of the pelvis is a serious injury that requires careful handling. Evidence of damage to organs or blood vessels includes difficulty in urinating or blood in the urine.

FRACTURED PELVIS

Treat for shock, which may be severe.

Bandage the knees together; bandage ankles together.

Keep victim lying down, either with legs flat on ground or with knees flexed up and pads positioned under the knees, whichever position is most comfortable for the patient.

If the victim complains of pain when his lower extremities are moved, apply splints to the extremity.

If victim must be moved, transport him in a prone position on a rigid stretcher.

Rib. Symptoms include pain in the break area and shallow breathing (deep breathing usually causes pain). A broken rib sometimes punctures a lung, causing the victim to cough up frothy bright-red blood.

If the broken rib has punctured the skin, infection must be guarded against. Apply a dressing that is airtight.

Keep victim lying down and calm.

If the skin is not punctured, apply one or more wide bandages around the chest, thereby restricting rib motion. One of the bandages should cross the area of the injury. The knot or knots should be on the side of the chest opposite the break. Put a folded cloth under the knots. If the bandages cause pain, remove them.

If the broken rib seems to be depressed—that is, pushed down into the chest cavity, do not apply bandages.

If victim must be moved, transport him in prone position.

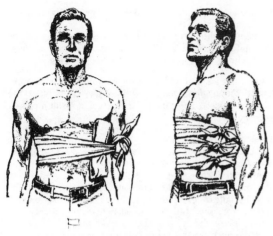

FRACTURED RIB

Position the middle of a wide strip of clean cloth under the chin, and tie the ends on top of the head, thereby supporting the jaw.

If the victim begins to vomit, remove the cloth bandage at once. Support the jaw with your hand. Replace the bandage when the vomiting stops.

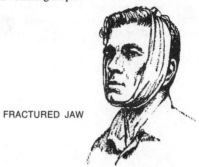

FRACTURED JAW

Nose. Most nose-break victims have a noticeable wound — at least a bruise. There is usually some swelling and discoloration, and sometimes the shape of the nose is altered. Broken nose bones must be treated properly, or permanent deformity and breathing difficulties may result.

If there is bleeding, hold the lower end of the nose between thumb and forefinger and press the sides of the nose against the septum (middle partition) for about five minutes. Avoid any side-to-side movement. Release pressure gradually. Apply cold cloths. Have the victim sit up, hold his head back, and breathe through his mouth.

If there is a wound, apply a sterile protective dressing, and tape it into place. Or bandage the dressing in place with strips of clean cloth tied around the head.

The nose-break victim should see a doctor as soon as possible.

Collarbone. Victim of this break will usually assume the following position: shoulder bent forward, elbow flexed, forearm across the chest and supported by the hand on the opposite side. There may be swelling, local tenderness, and possibly some deformity.

Use a sling — wide enough to extend from elbow to wrist — to support the arm on the injured side. Adjust the sling so that the hand is slightly above the level of the elbow.

FRACTURED NOSE

FRACTURED COLLARBONE

Jaw. In a fracture of the lower jaw, the upper and lower teeth often do not line up properly. There may be mild bleeding of the gum near the break, and jaw movement will cause pain. Speaking and swallowing are usually difficult.

Lift the lower jaw gently so that the lower and upper teeth meet.

Tie another bandage, not so wide, so that it encircles the injured-side arm and the chest, snugging the arm against the side of the body. Don't tie the bandage so tight that it interferes with circulation.

Try to keep the victim's shoulder's erect.

Elbow. One symptom is swelling above the elbow joint. Leave the arm in the position in which the victim holds it. Prevent the elbow joint from being moved.

If the arm is held straight, put on a single splint that extends from fingertips to armpit. Position the splint on the palm side of the arm. Tie it on securely, but do not wrap any of the bindings around the elbow area.

If the arm is bent, put it in a sling, and use an around-the-chest bandage to bind the arm to the side of the body.

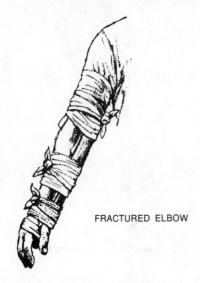

FRACTURED ELBOW

Wrist or Forearm. A break in one of the two bones in the forearm is quite common. The break is usually near the wrist. A break in one of the eight small wrist bones is sometimes thought to be only a sprain. With a break in either place, the fingers and thumb can be moved freely, though movement may cause some pain.

Put on a padded splint that extends from palm to elbow.

FRACTURED FOREARM OR WRIST

Put the arm in a sling arranged so that the fingers are about 4 inches higher than the elbow.

The fingers should remain uncovered so that they can be watched for swelling or discoloration. If either of those signs occurs, carefully loosen the splint, the sling, or both.

Finger. Put a splint on the finger, immobilizing it. Support the hand with a sling. Don't treat this injury casually: get the victim to a doctor. Permanent deformity can result if proper treatment isn't given.

Kneecap. Prompt and proper treatment of this injury is a must, because flexion of the knee can pull apart the pieces of a broken kneecap (patella).

Gently straighten the victim's leg.

Put on a splint on the underside of the leg. The splint should be inflexible, about 6 inches wide, and long enough to reach from the buttocks to just below the heel. Tie the splint in place firmly, but not so tight that circulation is impeded (check the ties every half-hour or so). Do not make any of the ties over the kneecap itself.

Transport victim in prone position.

FRACTURED KNEECAP

Foot or Toe. Remove the victim's shoe and sock quickly—swelling may be extremely rapid. Cut away the footwear if necessary.

Apply clean dressings padded with cotton. Or tie a small pillow, folded blanket, or something similar around foot and bottom of leg.

Caution victim against movement of foot, ankle, or toes.

FRACTURED FOOT OR TOE

Sprains

Sprains are injuries to the soft tissues that surround joints. Ligaments, tendons, and blood vessels are stretched and sometimes torn. Ankles, fingers, wrists, and knees are the areas most often affected.

Symptoms include pain when the area is moved, swelling, and tenderness to the touch. Sometimes a large area of skin becomes discolored because small blood vessels are ruptured.

It is often difficult to tell whether the injury is a sprain or a fracture. If in doubt, treat as a fracture. Otherwise, take the following steps:

Elevate the injured joint, using pillows or something similar. A sprained ankle should be raised about 12 inches higher than the torso. For a wrist or elbow sprain, put the arm into a sling.

Apply an ice pack or cold cloths to reduce swelling and pain. Continue the cold treatment for half an hour.

Always have a sprain X-rayed. There may indeed be a fracture or a bone chip.

If the victim of a sprained ankle is far from help and must walk, make the following preparations: 1) untie the shoelaces to allow for swelling, but do not take off the shoe; 2) place the middle of a long bandage (a folded triangular bandage is best) under the shoe just forward of the heel; 3) bring the ends of the bandage up and back, crossing them above (at the back of) the heel; 4) bring ends forward around ankle, and cross them over the instep; 5) bring ends downward toward the heel, and slip each end beneath the wrap that comes up from each side of the heel; 6) bring ends all the way around the ankle again, pull on them to produce the desired tension, and tie square knot in front.

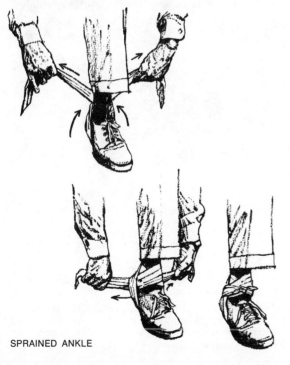

SPRAINED ANKLE

Puncture Wounds

A puncture wound results when a sharp object — knife, needle, branch end, jagged glass, or the like — penetrates the skin and the tissue underneath. The first-aider's primary objectives here, and in all other wounds, are to prevent infection and control bleeding.

Puncture wounds are often unusual in that they may be quite deep and the bleeding, because of the small opening in the skin, may be relatively light. The lighter the bleeding, generally, the lesser the chance that germs embedded by the penetrating object will be washed out. This means that the danger of infection is greater in puncture wounds than in other types.

The danger of tetanus (lockjaw) infection is also greater in puncture wounds.

First-aid procedures are as follows:

If the bleeding is limited, try to increase the flow by applying gentle pressure to the areas surrounding the wound. Do not squeeze hard, or you may cause further tissue damage.

Do not probe inside the wound. If a large splinter or a piece of glass or metal protrudes from it, try to remove it, *but do so with extreme caution.* If the sliver cannot be withdrawn with very gentle pulling pressure, leave it where it is, or you may cause further damage and severe bleeding.

Wash the wound with soap and water.

Apply a sterile pad, and bandage it in place.

Get the victim to a doctor for treatment, including a tetanus shot if necessary.

Gunshot Wounds

Tetanus is a special problem in gunshot wounds. First-aid steps are as follows:

Stop the bleeding (see "Bleeding," elsewhere in this section).

Apply a sterile pad, and bandage it in place.

If there is a fracture or a suspected fracture, immobilize the part (see "Bone Fractures" elsewhere in this section).

Treat for shock (see "Shock" elsewhere in this section).

Get the victim to a doctor quickly. A tetanus shot may be needed.

Fishhook Removal

A doctor's care — and a tetanus shot, if needed — are recommended for anyone who has had a fishhook embedded past the barb in the flesh. In many cases, however, medical help is not within easy reach. The severity of the injury and the size of the hook determine what action the first-aider should take.

If the hook has penetrated only up as far as the barb or slightly past it — and if it is not in a critical spot such as the eye — you should be able to pull or jerk it out. Then clean the wound, and treat it as you would any other superficial wound (see "Cuts, Abrasions, and Bruises," elsewhere in this section).

If the hook has penetrated well past the barb and is not in a critical area, there are two recommended methods of removal:

1) Force the hook in the direction in which it became embedded so that point and barb exit through the skin. Try

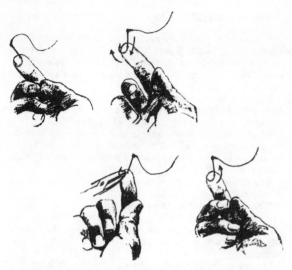

REMOVING A FISH HOOK

to make the angle of exit as shallow as possible. This can be quite painful, so the victim should anchor the affected part as solidly as possible before the process is begun. Using wire cutters or a similar tool, cut the hook in two at a point on the shank just before the bend. Remove the two pieces.

2) Have the victim anchor the affected part solidly. Take a 12 to 18-inch piece of strong string (30-pound-test fishing line is ideal), and run one end around the bend of the hook as if you were threading a needle. Bring the two ends together, and tie them in a sturdy knot. With thumb or forefinger, push down (toward the affected part) on the shank of the hook at the point where the bend begins. Maintaining that pressure, grasp the line firmly at the knotted end, and give a strong yank. The finger pressure on the shank should reduce flesh damage to a minimum as the barb comes out the same way it went in. Do not use this method if the hook is a large one.

If bleeding is minimal after either of these procedures, squeeze the wound gently to encourage blood flow, which has a cleansing effect. Put on a sterile dressing, and get medical help.

If the hook is a large one and is deeply embedded, or if it is in a critical area, do not try to remove it. Cover the wound, hook and all, with a sterile dressing, and get the victim to a doctor.

Eye Injuries, Foreign Body in Eye

For first-aid purposes, eye injuries fall into three categories: 1) injury to eyelids and soft tissue above the eye, 2) injury to the surface of the eyeball, 3) injury that extends into tissue beneath the eyeball surface.

In category 1, treatment involves putting on a sterile dressing and bandaging it in place. If the injury is in the form of a bruise (the familiar "black eye"), the immediate application of cold cloths or an ice pack should halt any bleeding

and prevent some swelling. Later, apply warm wet towels to reduce discoloration.

Category 2 injuries usually occur when a foreign body lodges on the surface of the eyeball. To remove the object, pull the upper eyelid down over the lower one, and hold it there for a moment, instructing the victim to look upward. Tears will flow naturally and may wash out the object.

If that doesn't work, put two fingers of your hand on the skin just below the victim's lower eyelid, and force the skin gently downward, thereby exposing the inner area of the lower lid. Inspect the area closely, and if the object is visible, lift it out carefully, using a corner of a clean handkerchief or a small wad of sterile cotton that has been moistened with water and wrapped around the end of a toothpick.

If the foreign object can't be seen, it can sometimes be flushed out. Boil some water, add table salt (¼ teaspoon to an average glassful), and let the salt water cool to about body temperature. With the victim lying down, tilt his head toward the injured side, hold his eyelids open with your fingers, and pour the liquid into the inner corner of his eye so that it runs across the eyeball and drains on the opposite side.

Category 3 eye injuries are extremely serious. Never attempt to remove an object that has penetrated the eyeball, no matter how shallow. Apply a sterile compress or clean cloth, cover it with a loose bandage, and get the victim to a doctor at once.

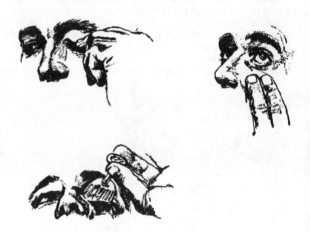

FOREIGN BODY IN THE EYE

Blisters and Boils

It is generally inadvisable to purposely break a blister. The fluid will be gradually absorbed, and the skin will soon return to normal.

However, if the blister is quite large or is on the heel, palm, or any other area where it is likely to be broken, take the following steps:

Using soap and water, clean the area around the blister—and the blister itself, gently.

Sterilize a needle over a flame, and use it to puncture the blister at its edge.

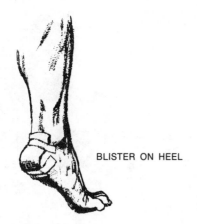

BLISTER ON HEEL

Gently press the edges of the blister so that the fluid flows out at the puncture point. Use a tissue or clean cloth to blot up the escaping fluid.

Put on a sterile gauze pad, and bandage it in place.

To treat an already-broken blister, wash the area well with soap and water, and apply a sterile gauze pad.

A boil—a round, reddened, and usually painful elevation in the skin—is mostly dead tissue and germ-laden pus. Actually, it is an attempt by the body to keep an infection localized.

Do not squeeze a boil, or you may spread the infection. If the boil is very painful or appears to be spreading, apply hot wet compresses. These may reduce the pain and cause the boil to come to a head more quickly.

When the boil comes to a head and discharges its contents, do not touch the escaping pus. Soak it up thoroughly with a gauze pad or clean cloth, thereby preventing infection of the surrounding skin. Cover the boil with a sterile dressing.

Infected Wounds

One of the primary objectives in any first-aid situation is the prevention of infection, but the first-aider is sometimes called on to treat a wound that has already become infected. Symptoms of infection include swelling, redness (including red streaks emanating out from the wound), throbbing pain, and a "hot" feeling in the infected area.

First-aid steps are as follows:

Keep the victim lying down and as comfortable and calm as possible.

Apply heat to the area with hot water bottles, or put warm, moist towels or cloths over the wound dressing. Change the wet packs often enough to keep them warm and cover them with a dry towel wrapped in plastic, aluminum foil, or waxed paper to hold in the warmth and to protect bedclothing.

Continue applying the warm packs for 30 minutes. Then remove them and cover the wound with a sterile dressing for another 30 minutes. Apply the warm packs again. Repeat the whole process until medical care can be obtained.

Heart Attack

Symptoms of heart failure include shortness of breath, pain in the chest or down the arms, the appearance of fainting, pale or flushed facial color, bluish color in the lips and around the fingernails, and considerable alarm by the victim about his condition.

If the victim has been under medical care for heart disease and can tell you the proper action to take, follow his directions, giving prescribed medicines if available.

Otherwise, take the following steps:

Have the patient lie down, but if the pain is too great in that position, let him assume whatever position is most comfortable. Generally, however, the prone position is best because it creates the least amount of strain on the body. If he has trouble breathing, elevate his head and shoulders with as many pillows as necessary.

Provide adequate ventilation, but keep the victim warm.

Give him coffee or tea if he can drink it comfortably.

A smile, encouraging words, and tactful suggestions will benefit the victim. Try not to show extreme concern, and avoid calling his difficulty a heart attack.

Unless absolutely necessary, do not transport the victim until medical help arrives on the scene.

Epilepsy

In a full-blown epileptic attack, the victim becomes pale, his eyes roll, and he falls down, usually with a hoarse cry. He may turn blue, bite his tongue, and froth at the mouth. Head, arms, and legs jerk violently, and he loses consciousness.

First-aid steps are as follows:

Do not try to restrain the victim's convulsions or thrashing; that phase of the attack will pass, usually within a few minutes.

Try to protect him against injury by moving away nearby objects.

To prevent him from biting his tongue, try to place an appropriate object (wad of cloth, piece of thick rubber, piece of a book cover) between upper and lower teeth in one side of the mouth. Be sure the object does not obstruct his breathing.

Give the victim no stimulants.

When the attack subsides, let the patient rest undisturbed.

Appendicitis

The principal symptom is pain in the lower right part of the abdomen and sometimes over the entire abdominal region. Nausea and vomiting may be present, as may a mild fever. Constipation often occurs and is sometimes thought to be the cause of the victim's discomfort. Do not give a laxative if appendicitis is suspected—it will increase the danger that the appendix will rupture.

Have the patient lie down, and keep him comfortable.

Do not give him any food or water.

An ice pack placed over the appendix area may relieve pain. Do not apply heat to the appendix area.

Get medical help as soon as possible.

Diarrhea

Diarrhea is a common malady among outdoorsmen. Its causes are often associated with change: during an extended hunting or fishing trip, for example, the sportsman's eating and drinking habits are often much different than what they are at home. Attacks of diarrhea usually subside once the body adapts to those changes.

Paregoric is helpful in combating diarrhea, as are many of the products designed for that purpose and sold in drugstores. If you or your companions are particularly subject to attacks of diarrhea, see a doctor and ask him to prescribe a drug, preferably in tablet form, that will combat the problem during trips afield.

Earache

An earache is usually a sign of an infection, so the sufferer should seek medical attention as soon as feasible.

The following first-aid procedures should give some relief:

Treat with either heat or cold. There is no way to predict which will work best, but try cold first, putting an ice pack or cold compress over the ear. If that doesn't work, try a hot-water bottle or hot compresses.

For further relief, put a few drops of warm mineral oil in the affected ear, if it is not ruptured.

Caution the sufferer against blowing his nose hard, which probably will increase the pain and may spread the infection.

Toothache

First-aid procedures are as follows:

Inspect the sufferer's mouth under the strongest light available.

If no cavity is visible, place an ice pack or cold compress against the jaw on the painful side. If that doesn't provide relief, try a hot-water bottle or hot compress.

If a cavity can be seen, use a piece of sterile cotton wrapped on the end of a toothpick to clean the cavity as thoroughly as possible.

Oil of cloves, if available, can give relief. Pack it gently into the cavity with a toothpick. Do not let the oil touch the tongue or the inside of the mouth — the stuff burns.

Transporting the Seriously Injured

The first-aider's principal objectives in transporting a seriously injured person are to avoid disturbing the victim unnecessarily and to prevent injured body areas from twisting, bending, or shaking.

Transportation is a vital factor, and it requires proper planning by the first-aider and proper preparation of the victim. The rescuers must make every effort to remain calm and mentally alert.

In some situations, however — such as an auto accident, fire, and the like — there is not time for planning or preparation; the victim must be moved from the danger area, or he may suffer further injury.

If such a victim must be pulled to safety, the pull should be along the length of his body (that is, head-first or feet-first), not sideways. The danger of compounding the injury during pulling is reduced if a blanket or something similar can be placed beneath him so that he can "ride" the blanket.

If a victim must be lifted to safety, the rescuers should try to protect all parts of his body from the tensions of lifting. The body should be supported at a minimum of three places along its length, not jackknifed (lifted by head and feet only). Keep the body as straight as possible.

PULLING VICTIM TO SAFETY

Once a victim is moved to safety, further transportation is inadvisable unless absolutely necessary. The first-aider should make every effort to get medical help to the scene. If the injury occurs deep in the backwoods, it may be possible to arrange for a doctor to come in via float plane or helicopter.

If there is no way to get medical help to the scene and the victim must be carried to a cabin, farmhouse, or road, a stretcher of some sort is a must. A well-padded folding-type cot will serve adequately. If no cot is available, a serviceable stretcher can be made by inserting two sturdy poles inside a buttoned coat or a couple of buttoned heavy-duty shirts, or by wrapping a blanket around two poles as shown in the accompanying sketch.

STRETCHER MADE OF POLES AND BLANKET

STRETCHER MADE OF POLES AND BUTTONED COAT

The victim must be properly prepared for a long carry. In addition to being given the first-aid treatments called for by his particular injury, he may need a period of rest before the ordeal of transportation. Broken bones and other injured areas should be made as immobile as possible. Loosen any tight clothing, and in general make the victim as comfortable as you can.

Care is the watchword when loading a victim onto a stretcher. It is best if at least three persons take part in the loading. The victim should be lying on his back with his feet tied together if feasible. Place the stretcher next to the victim.

The loaders should position themselves facing the victim's uninjured side, one loader at the head, another at the midsection, the third at the feet. Each loader should kneel on the knee nearest the victim's feet. Arms are positioned under the victim as follows: loader at head cradles the victim's head and shoulders with one arm and puts the other arm under the lower back; loader at midsection supports back and area just below the victim's buttocks; the third loader's arms supports the victim's thighs and calves.

One loader gives the command, "Lift," and all three together bring the victim up onto their knees, supporting him there without putting undue strain on the victim's body. One loader pulls the stretcher under the victim, and then all three, again on command, lower the victim down gently.

Provide enough blankets to keep the victim warm during the carry. Place padding wherever it's needed. (If victim's injury is to the back of the head, he should be positioned on his side.) Tie the victim to the stretcher firmly enough to prevent him from slipping or rolling but not so tightly as to interfere with blood circulation. Be sure that none of the bindings exert pressure on the injured area.

Ideally, there should be four stretcher-bearers, one at each end and one on each side. It's best to carry the victim so that he can see where he is going. In most cases, the head should be a bit lower than the rest of the body; however, the head should be elevated if there is a head injury or difficulty in breathing.

Woods trails can be treacherous, so stretcher-bearers should be especially alert for roots and other snags, rocks, slippery mud, and the like. If the carriers should lose their balance, the victim can incur further injury.

Bearers should watch the victim closely for signs of shock, discomfort, breathing difficulties, and other problems. Check the dressings periodically, and change or adjust them if necessary.

LOADING VICTIM ONTO STRETCHER

Loaders should be on victim's uninjured side, all kneeling on knee nearest victim's feet.

Loader in command moves stretcher under victim and he is lowered to stretcher.

At command "Lift," loaders raise victim gently to their knees.

Victim is covered and tied to stretcher. If possible, there should be a bearer at each end and at each side.

First-aid Kits

Improvisation is an ability that most outdoorsmen seem to develop naturally. But an improvised dressing for a wound, for example, is a poor second best to a prepackaged, sterile dressing. Any first-aider can function more effectively if he has the proper equipment.

A first-aid kit—whether it is bought in a drug store or medical-supply house or is put together by the individual—should meet the following requirements:

Its contents should be complete enough for the purposes for which it will be used.

The contents should be arranged so that any component desired can be located quickly and without removing the other components.

Each component should be wrapped so that any unused portion can be repacked and thereby prevented from leaking, becoming soiled, and so on.

How and where the kit will be used are the main factors to consider when assembling a first-aid kit. The three kits described below should fill the needs of most outdoor situations:

POCKET KIT: (Suitable for one-day, overnight, or short term backpacking trips in areas not far from medical help.)
1 × 1-inch packaged sterile bandages (2)
2 × 2-inch packaged sterile bandages (2)
2 × 2-inch packaged sterile gauze pads (2)
Roll of adhesive tape
Band-Aids (10)
Ammonia inhalant (1)
Tube of antiseptic cream
Small tin of aspirin (or 12 aspirins wrapped in foil)

ALL PURPOSE SPORTSMAN'S FIRST-AID KIT: (Suitable for general outings.)
4-inch Ace bandages (2)
2-inch Ace bandages (2)*

2 × 2-inch sterile gauze pads (1 pkg.)*
5 × 9-inch combine dressing (3)
Triangular bandage (1)
Sterile eye pads (2)
1/2-inch adhesive tape (5 yards)
Assorted Band-Aids (1 pkg.)*
Betadine liquid antiseptic
Yellow mercuric oxide ointment (eyes)*
Bacitracin (ointment)
Tylenol (aspirin substitute)
Dramamine (motion sickness)
PreSun (sun-screen lotion)
Snakebite kit*
Insect repellent
Single-edge razor blade
Tweezers (flat tip)
Small scissors
Eye patch
Needle
Matches in waterproof container
Needle-nose pliers with cutting edge
First-aid manual

Add these items if going into remote area for extended period:
Tylenol with codeine (pain killer)**
Antibiotic (Tetracycline)**
Lomotil, 2.5 mg. (cramps, diarrhea)**
Antihistamine tablets
Phillips Milk of Magnesia (antacid, laxative)

* Items, in lesser quantities, recommended for a small first-aid kit for day trips.

** Requires prescription.

PART X | *Outdoor Information Guide*

Fish and Game Departments and State Park Commissions

United States

ALABAMA

Division of Game and Fish
64 N. Union St.
Montgomery, AL 36104

Department of Conservation and Natural Resources
Division of Parks
64 N. Union St.
Montgomery, AL 36104

ALASKA

Department of the Fish and Game
Subport Bldg.
Juneau, AK 99801

ARIZONA

Game and Fish Department
2222 W. Greenway
Phoenix, AZ 85023

ARKANSAS

Game and Fish Commission
Game and Fish Bldg.
Little Rock, AR 72201

Department of Parks and Tourism
149 State Capitol
Little Rock, AR 72201

CALIFORNIA

Department of Fish and Game
1416 9th St.
Sacramento, CA 95814

Department of Parks and Recreation
1416 9th St.
Sacramento, CA 95814

COLORADO

Division of Wildlife
6060 Broadway
Denver, CO 80216

CONNECTICUT

Department of Environmental Protection
State Office Bldg.
Hartford, CT 06115

Department of Environmental Protection
165 Capitol Ave.
Hartford, CT 06115

DELAWARE

Division of Fish and Wildlife
"D" St.
Dover, DE 19901

Department of Natural Resources
Edward Tatnall Bldg.
Legislative Ave. and William Penn St.
Dover, DE 19901

FLORIDA

Game and Freshwater Fish Commission
620 So. Meridian
Tallahassee, FL 32304

Division of Recreation and Parks
Crown Bldg.
202 Blount St.
Tallahassee, FL 32304

GEORGIA

State Game and Fish Commission
Trinity-Washington Bldg.
270 Washington St. S.W.
Atlanta, GA 30334

Department of Natural Resources
270 Washington St. S.W.
Atlanta, GA 30334

HAWAII

Division of Fish and Game
1179 Punchbowl St.
Honolulu, HI 96813

IDAHO

Fish and Game Department
600 S. Walnut
Box 25
Boise, ID 83707

ILLINOIS

Department of Conservation
State Office Bldg.
Springfield, IL 62706

INDIANA

Division of Fish and Wildlife
State Office Bldg.
Indianapolis, IN 46204

Department of Natural Resources
608 State Office Bldg.
Indianapolis, IN 46204

IOWA

State Conservation Commission
State Office Bldg.
300 4th St.
Des Moines, IA 50319

KANSAS

Forestry, Fish and Game Commission
Box 1028
Pratt, KS 67124

State Park and Resources Authority
P.O. Box 997
503 Kansas Ave.
Topeka, KS 66601

KENTUCKY

Department of Fish and Wildlife Resources
Capitol Plaza Tower
Frankfort, KY 40601

Department of Parks
Capital Plaza Bldg., 10th Floor
Frankfort, KY 40601

LOUISIANA

Wildlife and Fisheries Commission
P.O. Box 44095
Capitol Station
Baton Rouge, LA 70804

State Parks and Recreation Commission
P.O. Drawer 1111
Old State Capitol Bldg.
Baton Rouge, LA 70821

MAINE

Department of Inland Fisheries and Wildlife
284 State St.
Augusta, ME 04333

Bureau of Parks and Recreation
State House
Augusta, ME 04333

MARYLAND

Fish and Wildlife Administration
Natural Resources Bldg.
Annapolis, MD 21401

Department of Natural Resources
Tawes State Office Bldg.
Annapolis, MD 21401

MASSACHUSETTS

Department of Fisheries and Wildlife
100 Cambridge St.
Boston, MA 02202

Department of Environmental Management
Division of Forests and Parks
100 Cambridge St.
Boston, MA 02202

MICHIGAN

Department of Natural Resources
Mason Bldg.
Lansing, MI 48926

MINNESOTA

Division of Game and Fish
Department of Natural Resources
300 Centennial Bldg.
658 Cedar St.
St. Paul, MN 55101

MISSISSIPPI

Game and Fish Commission
P.O. Box 451
Robert E. Lee Office Bldg.
239 N. Lamar St.
Jackson, MS 39205

Mississippi Parks Commission
717 Robert E. Lee Bldg.
Jackson, MS 39201

MISSOURI

Department of Conservation
Box 180
Jefferson City, MO 65101

Division of Parks and Recreation
P.O. Box 176
Jefferson City, MO 65101

MONTANA

Fish and Game Department
Helena, MT 59601

NEBRASKA

Game and Parks Commission
P.O. Box 30370
2200 N. 33rd St.
Lincoln, NB 68503

NEVADA

Department of Fish and Game
Box 10678
Reno, NV 89510

Division of State Parks
Capitol Complex
Nye Bldg.
201 S. Fall St.
Carson City, NV 89710

NEW HAMPSHIRE

Fish and Game Department
34 Bridge St.
Concord, NH 03301

Department of Resources and Economic Development
Division of Parks
P.O. Box 856
State House Annex
Concord, NH 03301

NEW JERSEY

Division of Fish, Game, and Shellfisheries
Box 1390
Trenton, NJ 08625

NEW MEXICO

Department of Game and Fish
State Capitol
Santa Fe, NM 87501

State Park and Recreation Commission
P.O. Box 1147
Santa Fe, NM 87503

NEW YORK

Division of Fish and Wildlife
Department of Environmental Conservation
50 Wolf Rd.
Albany, NY 12201

NORTH CAROLINA

Wildlife Resources Commission
325 N. Salisbury St.
Raleigh, NC 27611

NORTH DAKOTA

State Game and Fish Department
2121 Lovett Ave.
Bismarck, ND 58501

OHIO

Division of Wildlife
Department of Natural Resources
Fountain Square
Columbus, OH 43224

OKLAHOMA

Department of Wildlife Conservation
P.O. Box 53465
Oklahoma City, OK 73105

Tourism and Recreation Department
Division of Parks
500 Will Rogers Bldg.
Oklahoma City, OK 73105

OREGON

Fish and Wildlife Commission
P.O. Box 3503
Portland, OR 97208

State Parks Branch
Department of Transportation
Transportation Bldg.
Salem, OR 97310

PENNSYLVANIA

Fish Commission
P.O. Box 1673
Harrisburg, PA 17120

Game Commission
P.O. Box 1567
Harrisburg, PA 17120

Bureau of State Parks
Department of Environmental Resources
Room 203, Box 1467
Harrisburg, PA 17120

RHODE ISLAND

Department of Natural Resources
Division of Fish and Wildlife
83 Park St.
Providence, RI 02903

SOUTH CAROLINA

Wildlife Resources Department
Box 167
105 Main St.
Columbia, SC 29202

State Commission of Forestry
Box 21707
Columbia, SC 29221

SOUTH DAKOTA

Department of Game, Fish and Parks
State Office Bldg.
Pierre, SD 57501

TENNESSEE

Wildlife Resources Agency
Box 40747
Ellington Center
Nashville, TN 37220

Department of Conservation
Division of Parks and Recreation
2611 West End Ave.
Nashville, TN 37203

TEXAS

Parks and Wildlife Department
John H. Reagan Bldg.
Austin, TX 78701

UTAH

Division of Fish and Game
1596 W.N. Temple
Salt Lake City, UT 84116

Division of Parks and Recreation
1596 W.N. Temple
Salt Lake City, UT 84116

VERMONT

Fish and Game Department
151 Main St.
Montpelier, VT 05602

Department of Forests and Parks
Agency of Environmental Conservation
Montpelier, VT 05602

VIRGINIA

Commission of Game and Inland Fisheries
Box 11104
4010 W. Broad St.
Richmond, VA 23230

Department of Conservation and Economic Development
Division of Parks
1201 State Office Bldg.
Richmond, VA 23219

WASHINGTON

Department of Fisheries
115 General Administration Bldg.
Olympia, WA 98504

Department of Game
600 N. Capitol Way
Olympia, WA 98504

State Parks and Recreation Commission
7150 Cleanwater Lane
Olympia, WA 98504

WEST VIRGINIA

Department of Wildlife Resources
1800 Washington St. East
Charleston, WV 25305

WISCONSIN

Department of Natural Resources
Box 450
Madison, WI 53701

WYOMING

Game and Fish Commission
Box 1589
Cheyenne, WY 82001

Canada and Territorial Agencies

ALBERTA

Department of Recreation, Parks and Wildlife
Fish and Wildlife Division
10015–103 Ave.
Edmonton, Alberta
Canada T5J 0H1

BRITISH COLUMBIA

Ministry of Recreation and Conservation
Fish and Wildlife Branch
Parliament Bldgs.
Victoria, BC
Canada, V8V 1X4

MANITOBA

Department of Renewable Resources and Transportation
  Services
Fisheries and Wildlife Branch
Box 18
1495 St. James St.
Winnipeg, Manitoba
Canada R3H 0W9

NEW BRUNSWICK

Department of Natural Resources
Fish and Wildlife and Mineral Resources Branch
Centennial Bldg.
Fredericton, NB
Canada E3B 5H1

NEWFOUNDLAND

Department of Tourism
Wildlife Division
130 Water St.
St. Johns, Newfoundland
Canada A1C 1A8

NORTHWEST TERRITORIES

Department of Natural and Cultural Affairs
Fish and Wildlife Service
Yellowknife, NWT
Canada OXE 1H0

NOVA SCOTIA

Department of Lands and Forests
Wildlife Conservation Division
Dennis Bldg.
1740 Granville St.
P.O. Box 698
Halifax, NS
Canada B3J 2T9

ONTARIO

Ministry of Natural Resources
Division of Fish and Wildlife
Whitney Block Parliament Bldgs.
Toronto, Ontario
Canada M7A 1W3

PRINCE EDWARD ISLAND

Department of Fisheries
Box 2000
Provincial Administration Bldg.
Charlottetown, PEI
Canada C1A 7N8

QUEBEC

Department of Tourism
Fish and Game
150 boul. St.-Cyrille E.
Quebec, Quebec
Canada G1R 4Y3

SASKATCHEWAN

Department of Tourism and Renewable Resources
Fisheries and Wildlife Branch
1825 Lorne St.
Regina, Saskatchewan
Canada S4P 3N1

YUKON

Department of Tourism
Conservation and Information Services
Game Branch
Box 2703
Whitehorse, Yukon Territory
Canada Y1A 2C6

National Parks
and Forests

National Park Regional Offices

SOUTHEAST REGIONAL OFFICE

National Park Service
1895 Phoenix Blvd.
Atlanta, GA 30349

MIDWEST REGIONAL OFFICE

National Park Service
1709 Jackson St.
Omaha, NB 68102

SOUTHWEST REGIONAL OFFICE

National Park Service
Box 728
Old Santa Fe Trail
Santa Fe, NM 87501

WESTERN REGIONAL OFFICE

National Park Service
P.O. Box 36063
450 Golden Gate Ave.
San Francisco, CA 94102

NORTH-ATLANTIC REGIONAL OFFICE

National Park Service
15 State St.
Boston, MA 02109

NATIONAL CAPITOL REGIONAL OFFICE

National Park Service
1100 Ohio Drive, S.W.
Washington, D.C. 20242

MAIN OFFICE

National Park Service
Department of the Interior Bldg.
Washington, D.C. 20240

MID-ATLANTIC REGIONAL OFFICE

National Park Service
143 S. Third St.
Philadelphia, PA 19106

PACIFIC NORTHWEST REGIONAL OFFICE

National Park Service
Room 922, Fourth and Pike Bldg.
Seattle, WA 98101

National Forest Headquarters

The following headquarters offices will supply booklets covering recreational activities in their regions.

NORTHERN REGION

National Forest Headquarters
Federal Bldg.
Missoula, MT 59807

ROCKY MOUNTAIN REGION

National Forest Headquarters
11177 W. 8th Ave.
Box 25127
Lakewood, CO 80225

SOUTHWESTERN REGION

National Forest Headquarters
Federal Bldg.
517 Gold Ave. S.W.
Albuquerque, NM 87101

INTERMOUNTAIN REGION

National Forest Headquarters
Federal Office Bldg.
324 25th St.
Ogden, UT 84401

CALIFORNIA REGION

National Forest Headquarters
630 Sansome St.
San Francisco, CA 94111

PACIFIC NORTHWEST REGION

National Forest Headquarters
319 S.W. Pine St.
P.O. Box 3623
Portland, OR 97208

EASTERN REGION

National Forest Headquarters
Clark Bldg.
633 W. Wisconsin Ave.
Milwaukee, WI 53203

SOUTHERN REGION

National Forest Headquarters
Suite 800
1720 Peachtree Rd. N.W.
Atlanta, GA 30309

ALASKA REGION

National Forest Headquarters
Federal Office Bldg.
Box 1628
Juneau, AK 99801

Travel Information

Organizations listed below will supply free travel information on request. The highway commissions in every state and all the provinces of Canada will also send road maps. Information usually includes directory of accommodations, campgrounds, and points of interest.

United States

ALABAMA

Bureau of Publicity and Information
403 State Highway Bldg.
Montgomery, AL 36130

State Chamber of Commerce
Box 76
468 S. Perry St.
Montgomery, AL 36104

ALASKA

Division of Tourism
State of Alaska
Pouch E
Juneau, AK 99811

AMERICAN SAMOA

Director of the Office of Tourism
Government of American Samoa
P.O. Box 1147
Pago Pago, American Samoa 96799

ARIZONA

Arizona State Office of Tourism
1700 W. Washington
Phoenix, AZ 85007

ARKANSAS

Tourism Division
Department of Parks and Tourism
149 State Capitol Bldg.
Little Rock, AR 72201

Ozark Playground Association
Box 187
Joplin, MO 64801

CALIFORNIA

No state tourism office.
Write local chamber of commerce.

COLORADO

Travel Marketing Section
Division of Commerce and Development
1313 Sherman St. Room 500
Denver, CO 80203

CONNECTICUT

Tourism Division
Department of Commerce
210 Washington St.
Hartford, CT 06106

New England Vacation Center
1268 Avenue of the Americas
New York, NY 10020

DELAWARE

State Visitors Service
Division of Economic Development
630 State College Rd.
Dover, DE 19901

DISTRICT OF COLUMBIA

Washington Area Convention and
Visitors Association
1129 20th St., N.W.
Washington, D.C. 20036

FLORIDA

Division of Tourism
Florida Department of Commerce
107 West Gaines St.
Tallahassee, FL 32304

GEORGIA

Tourist Division
Bureau of Industry and Trade
P.O. Box 1776
Atlanta, GA 30301

GUAM

Guam Visitor's Bureau
P.O. Box 3520
Agana, Guam 96910

HAWAII

Hawaii Visitor's Bureau
P.O. Box 8527
Honolulu, HI 96815

50 Rockefeller Plaza
New York, NY 10020

410 N. Michigan Ave.
Chicago, IL 60611

209 Post St.
San Francisco, CA 94108

IDAHO

Division of Tourism and Industrial Development
State Capitol Building, Room 108
Boise, ID 83720

ILLINOIS

Illinois Adventure Center
Office of Tourism
160 N. LaSalle
Chicago, IL 60601

INDIANA

Tourist Development Division
Department of Commerce
State House, Room 336
Indianapolis, IN 46204

IOWA

Travel Development Division
Iowa Development Commission
250 Jewett Bldg.
Des Moines, IA 50309

KANSAS

Tourist Division
Department of Economic Development
503 Kansas Avenue
Topeka, KS 66603

KENTUCKY

Division of Advertising and Travel Promotion
Department of Public Information
Capitol Annex
Frankfort, KY 40601

LOUISIANA

Tourist Development Commission
P.O. Box 44291
Capitol Station
Baton Rouge, LA 70804

MAINE

Maine Publicity Bureau
1 Gateway Circle
Portland, OR 04102

MARYLAND

Division of Tourist Development
Department of Economic and Community Development
1748 Forest Drive
Annapolis, MD 21401

MASSACHUSETTS

Division of Tourism
Department of Commerce and Development
Leverett Saltonstall Bldg.
Government Center, 13th Floor
100 Cambridge St.
Boston, MA 02202

New England Vacation Center
1268 Avenue of the Americas
New York, NY 10020

MICHIGAN

Travel Bureau
Michigan Department of Commerce
P.O. Box 30226
Lansing, MI 48909

West Michigan Tourist Assn.
135 Fulton East
Grand Rapids, MI 49503

Southeast Michigan Travel and Tourist Assn.
American Center, Suite 350
Detroit, MI 48226

Michigan Travel Information Center
55 E. Monroe
Chicago, IL 60603

Michigan Travel Information Center
29 Public Square
Cleveland, OH 44113

Upper Peninsula Travel and Recreation
Box 400
Iron Mountain, MI 49801

MINNESOTA

Tourism Division
Minnesota Department of Economic Development
Hanover Building
480 Cedar Street
St. Paul, MN 55101

MISSISSIPPI

Travel, Tourism, and Public Affairs Department
Mississippi Agricultural and Industrial Board
P.O. Box 849
Jackson, MS 39205

MISSOURI

Division of Tourism
P.O. Box 1055
Jefferson City, MO 65101

MONTANA

Travel Promotion Unit
Department of Highways
Helena, MT 59601

NEBRASKA

Division of Travel and Tourism
Department of Economic Development
P.O. Box 94666
Lincoln, NB 68509

NEVADA

Travel-Tourism Division
Department of Economic Development
Capitol Complex
Carson City, NV 89710

NEW HAMPSHIRE

Office of Vacation Travel
Division of Economic Development
P.O. Box 856
Concord, NH 03301

New England Vacation Center
1268 Avenue of the Americas
New York, NY 10020

NEW JERSEY

Office of Tourism and Promotion
Department of Labor and Industry
P.O. Box 400
Trenton, NJ 08625

NEW MEXICO

Tourist Division
Department of Development
Bataan Memorial Bldg.
Sante Fe, NM 87503

NEW YORK

Travel Bureau
New York State Department of Commerce
99 Washington Ave.
Albany, NY 12245

Department of Environmental Conservation
50 Wolf Rd.
Albany, NY 12233

Office of Parks and Recreation
Empire State Plaza
Albany, NY 12238

NEW YORK CITY, N.Y.

Convention and Visitors Bureau
90 East 42nd St.
New York, NY 10017

NORTH CAROLINA

Travel and Tourism Division
Department of Commerce
430 N. Salisbury St.
Raleigh, NC 27611

NORTH DAKOTA

Travel Division
State Highway Department
Capitol Grounds
Bismarck, ND 58505

OHIO

Office of Travel and Tourism
Department of Economic and Community Development
P.O. Box 1001
Columbus, OH 43216

OKLAHOMA

Tourist Promotion Division
Tourism and Recreation Department
500 Will Rogers Bldg.
Oklahoma City, OK 73105

OREGON

Travel Information Section
101 Transportation Bldg.
Salem, OR 97310

PENNSYLVANIA

Bureau of Travel Development
Department of Commerce
431 South Office Bldg.
Harrisburg, PA 17102

PUERTO RICO

Commonwealth of Puerto Rico
Tourism Company
GPO Box BN
San Juan, PR 00936

RHODE ISLAND

Tourist Promotion Division
Department of Economic Development
1 Weybosset Hill
Providence, RI 02903

New England Vacation Center
1268 Avenue of the Americas
New York, NY 10020

SOUTH CAROLINA

Division of Tourism
Department of Parks, Recreation and Tourism
Room 83, Box 71
Columbia, SC 29202

SOUTH DAKOTA

Department of Economic and Tourism Development
217 Joe Foss Bldg.
Pierre, SD 57501

TENNESSEE

Department of Tourist Development
505 Fesslers Lane
Nashville, TN 37210

TEXAS

Tourist Development Agency
Box 12008
Capitol Station
Austin, TX 78711

UTAH

Utah Travel Council
Council Hall
Capitol Hill
Salt Lake City, UT 84114

VERMONT

Travel Division
Agency of Development and Community Affairs
61 Elm St.
Montpelier, VT 05602

New England Vacation Center
1268 Avenue of the Americas
New York, NY 10020

VIRGIN ISLANDS

Division of Tourism
P.O. Box 1692
St. Thomas, Virgin Islands 00801

VIRGINIA

State Travel Service
6 North Sixth St.
Richmond, VA 23219

11 Rockefeller Plaza
New York, NY 10020

WASHINGTON

Travel Development Division
Department of Commerce and Economic Development
General Administration Bldg.
Olympia, WA 98504

WEST VIRGINIA

Travel Development Division
West Virginia Department of Commerce
1900 Washington St., East
Charleston, WV 25305

WISCONSIN
Division of Tourism
Box 7606
Madison, WI 53707

WYOMING
Wyoming Travel Commission
I-25 at Etchepare Circle
Cheyenne, WY 82002

Canada

GENERAL
Canadian Government Office of Tourism
235 Queen St., 4th Floor East
Ottawa, Ontario
Canada KIA 0H6

ALBERTA
Travel Alberta
Box 2500
Edmonton, Alberta
Canada T5J 2Z4

BRITISH COLUMBIA
British Columbia Tourism
1117 Wharf St.
Victoria, British Columbia
Canada V8W 1T7

MANITOBA
Manitoba Department of Tourism
Tourish Branch
200 Vaughan St. #304
Winnipeg, Manitoba
Canada R3C 1T5

NEW BRUNSWICK
New Brunswick Department of Tourism
Box 12345
Fredericton, New Brunswick
Canada E3B 5C3

NEWFOUNDLAND – LABRADOR
Newfoundland Department of Tourism
Tourist Services Division
Box 2016
St. John's, Newfoundland
Canada A1C 5R8

NOVA SCOTIA
Nova Scotia Department of Tourism
Box 130
Halifax, Nova Scotia
Canada B3J 2M7

ONTARIO
Ontario Travel
Queen's Park
Toronto, Ontario
Canada M7A 2E5

PRINCE EDWARD ISLAND
P.E.I. Department of Tourism
Tourist Services
Box 940
Charlottetown, Prince Edward Island
Canada C1A 7M5

QUEBEC
Quebec Department of Tourism
Place de la Capitale
150 Saint Cyrille Blvd. East
Quebec, Quebec
Canada G1R 2B2

SASKATCHEWAN
Saskatchewan Department of Tourism
Extension Services
1825 Lorne St.
Regina, Saskatchewan
Canada S4P 3V7

NORTHWEST TERRITORIES
TravelArctic
Government, Northwest Territories
Yellowknife, Northwest Territories
Canada X1A 2L9

YUKON
Yukon Department of Tourism
Box 2703
Whitehorse, Yukon Territory
Canada Y1A 2C6

Mexico

Mexican National Tourism Council
405 Park Ave.
New York, New York 10022

Organizations for Outdoor Recreation

Sportsmen who seek help in any phase of their outdoor activities will find the following organizations can provide advice and information. The organizations are listed under their specialty.

Shooting

National Rifle Association of America
1600 Rhode Island Ave., N.W.
Washington, D.C. 20036

National Shooting Sports Foundation, Inc.
1075 Post Road
Riverside, CT. 06878

National Skeet Shooting Association
P.O. Box 28188
San Antonio, TX 78228

Amateur Trapshooting Association
P.O. Box 246
West National Road
Vandalia, OH 45377

National Bench Rest Shooters Association, Inc.
5735 Sherwood Forest Dr.
Akron, OH 44319

National Muzzle Loading Rifle Association
P.O. Box 67
Friendship, IN 47021

Hunting

Boone and Crockett Club
424 N. Washington St.
Alexandria, VA 22314

Ducks Unlimited
P.O. Box 66300
Chicago, IL 60666

Fishing

International Game Fish Association
(for spinfishing and saltwater fly records)
3000 East Las Olas Blvd.
Ft. Lauderdale, FL 33316

Izaak Walton League of America
1800 North Kent St.
Suite 806
Arlington, VA 22209

Sport Fishing Institute
Suite 801
608 13th St. N.W.
Washington, D.C. 20005

Trout Unlimited
4260 East Evans Ave.
Denver, CO 80222

American Littoral Society
Sandy Hook Marine Laboratory
Box 117
Highlands, NJ 07732

Camping and Hiking

American Camping Association
Bradford Woods
Martinsville, IN 46151

Appalachian Trail Conference
P.O. Box 236
Harpers Ferry, WV 25425

Family Camping Federation
c/o American Camping Association
Bradford Woods
Martinsville, IN 46151

National Campers and Hikers Association, Inc.
7172 Transit Road
Buffalo, NY 14221

National Recreation and Park Association
1601 Kent St.
Arlington, VA 22209

North American Family Campers Association
P.O. Box 552
Newburyport, MA 01951

Archery

American Indoor Archery Association
P.O. Box 174
Grayling, MI 49738

National Archery Association
1951 Geraldson Dr.
Lancaster, PA 17601

Pope and Young Club
Route 1, Box 147
Salmon, ID 83467

National Field Archery Association
Route 2
Box 514
Redlands, CA 92373

United States Bare Bow Association
P.O. Box 75
Feeding Hills, MA 01030

National Crossbow Association
Mrs. William Forbes, Secretary
3605 Hewn Lane
Linden Knoll, 721
Wilmington, DE

American Cross Bow Association
P.O. Box 72
Huntsville, AR 72740

Fred Bear Sports Club
Dept. TBS
Rural Route 4
Gainesville, FL 32601

Professional Bowhunters' Society
Box 13
New Concord, OH 43762

Boating

Outboard Boating Club of America
401 N. Michigan Ave.
Chicago, IL 60611

United States Canoe Association
4260 Evans Ave.
Denver, CO 80222

American Power Boat Association
22811 Greater Mack
St. Clair Shore, MI 48080

American White Water Affiliation
P.O. Box 1584
San Bruno, CA 94066

Index

Index